Contemporary Authors

Contemporary

Authors

A Bio-Bibliographical Guide to
Current Writers in Fiction, General Nonfiction,
Poetry, Journalism, Drama, Motion Pictures,
Television, and Other Fields

HAL MAY
Editor

DIANE L. DUPUIS
DEBRA G. JONES
LILLIAN S. SIMS
SUSAN M. TROSKY
Associate Editors

volume 109

GALE RESEARCH COMPANY • THE BOOK TOWER • DETROIT, MICHIGAN 48226

EDITORIAL STAFF

Christine Nasso, *General Editor, Contemporary Authors*

Hal May, *Editor, Original Volumes*

Diane L. Dupuis, Debra G. Jones, Lillian S. Sims,
and Susan M. Trosky, *Associate Editors*

Charity Anne Dorgan, Les Stone, Mary Sullivan,
and Marian Walters, *Senior Assistant Editors*

Nancy H. Evans, Susan D. Finley, Nancy S. Gearhart, Michael L. LaBlanc,
Louise Mooney, Nancy Pear, Duane P. Stewart, and Mary E. Teller, *Assistant Editors*

Arlene True and Benjamin True, *Sketchwriters*

Peter Benjaminson, Mary V. McLeod, Jean W. Ross, and Judith Spiegelman, *Interviewers*

Dean D. Dauphinais, Ellen Koral, Shirley Kuenz, Timothy P. Loszewski, Christine J. May,
Barbara Rutkowski, Norma Sawaya, Shirley Seip, and Aida Smith, *Editorial Assistants*

Frances C. Locher, *Consulting Editor*

Adele Sarkissian, *Contributing Editor*

Linda Metzger, *Index Coordinator*

Eunice Bergin, *Copy Editor*

Special recognition is given to the staff of
Young People's Literature Department, Gale Research Company

Frederick G. Ruffner, *Publisher*   James M. Ethridge, *Editorial Director*

Copyright © 1983 by
GALE RESEARCH COMPANY

Library of Congress Catalog Card Number 62-52046
ISBN 0-8103-1909-8
ISSN 0010-7468

Authors and Media People
Featured in This Volume

Martin Agronsky—American broadcast journalist; moderator of weekly NBC-TV program "Agronsky and Company"; well known for his political commentary and interviewing skills; recipient of numerous awards, including Peabody Award and Emmy Award. (Sketch includes interview.)

Nathan Asch—Polish-born American expatriate novelist who died in 1964; his novels, which are stylistically reminiscent of those of Ernest Hemingway, include *The Office, Love in Chartres,* and *The Valley.*

John Chancellor—Well-known American broadcast journalist; has served with NBC-TV for over thirty years as foreign correspondent, host of "Today" show, White House correspondent, and, from 1970 to 1982, anchor of "NBC Nightly News." (Sketch includes interview.)

Barbara P. Conklin—American romance writer; author of teenage romance novels, including the best-selling *P.S. I Love You,* and numerous stories published in *True Confessions* and *Modern Romances.*

Brian De Palma—American screenwriter, producer, and motion picture director; a controversial filmmaker, he has been criticized as a "derivative manipulator" and praised as an "artist"; his best-known films include "Greetings," "Carrie," "The Fury," and "Dressed to Kill."

Milos Forman—Czechoslovakian screenwriter and director of motion pictures, notably "Cerny Petr" ("Black Peter"), "One Flew Over the Cuckoo's Nest," "Hair," and "Ragtime"; has won many film awards, including an Academy Award in 1975 for best director.

Clark Gesner—American writer, composer, and lyricist; contributing writer and composer for "Sesame Street" and "Electric Company" television programs; composer and lyricist of popular musical "You're a Good Man, Charlie Brown."

Juergen Habermas—German philosopher; one of Germany's best-known social theorists; author of several works translated into English, including *Theory and Practice, Knowledge and Human Interests,* and *Toward a Rational Society.*

Lorraine Hansberry—American playwright who died in 1965; best known for award-winning play "A Raisin in the Sun," the first drama by a black woman to be produced on Broadway; awarded a New York Drama Critics Circle Award, this play was later adapted as a motion picture and produced as the popular Broadway musical "Raisin."

Moss Hart—American playwright, librettist, and director of stage productions who died in 1961; junior member of one of the most famous playwriting teams in the history of American theatre; with George S. Kaufman wrote many successful plays, notably "Once in a Lifetime," "You Can't Take It With You," and "I'd Rather Be Right."

William Hood—American intelligence official; associated with the Central Intelligence Agency for thirty years; author of well-received nonfiction book *Mole,* about a Russian spy's association with the CIA.

Bettina Huerlimann—German-born Swiss publisher and editor; with husband, Martin Huerlimann, directed Atlantis Verlag until 1967; author of many books, including the award-winning *William Tell and His Son.*

Lawrence Kasdan—American screenwriter and director of motion pictures; screenplays include "The Empire Strikes Back," "Raiders of the Lost Ark," and "Return of the Jedi." (Sketch includes interview.)

Jack Kemp—American politician; former professional football player, now congressman from New York; Kemp's economic theories were adopted into the Republican platform in the 1980 presidential race; Kemp is the author of two books.

Tracy Kidder—American journalist; awarded the Pulitzer Prize and the American Book Award in 1982 for *The Soul of a New Machine,* a national best-seller that recounts the development of a super minicomputer. (Sketch includes interview.)

Gary Kinder—American writer; author of critically acclaimed *Victim: The Other Side of Murder,* a book that relates the incidents of a multiple murder in Utah in 1974 and has been favorably compared to Truman Capote's *In Cold Blood.*

Oskar Kokoschka—Austrian artist and writer who died in 1980; considered to be one of the most enduring and versatile artists of twentieth-century Vienna; also playwright of such controversial dramas as "Murderer, Hope of Women" and "The Burning Bush."

Christopher Lehmann-Haupt—Well-known American book critic, currently senior daily book reviewer for the *New York Times.* (Sketch includes interview.)

Catherine Mackin—American broadcast journalist who died in 1982; Mackin made history in 1972 as the first woman floor reporter at a national political convention.

Abby Mann—American writer and director of motion pictures; author of Academy Award-winning motion picture "Judgment at Nuremburg" and other controversial works for the screen, notably "A Child Is Waiting," "Ship of Fools," and the television docudrama "King." (Sketch includes interview.)

Veljko Micunovic—Yugoslavian diplomat and government official who died in 1982; his memoirs, *Moscow Diary,* concern his experiences while serving as Yugoslavian ambassador to the Soviet Union from 1956 to 1958.

Roger Moore—British actor in motion pictures and television; well known for his role as adventurer Simon Templar in the television series "The Saint" and, more recently, as secret agent

James Bond in movies, including "Live and Let Die," "The Spy Who Loved Me," "For Your Eyes Only," and "Octopussy"; author of *Roger Moore's James Bond Diary*.

Leonard O. Mosley—British biographer; formerly a journalist, critic, and novelist, Mosley is best known for his biographies, including *Lindbergh: A Biography, Hirohito: Emperor of Japan, Marshall: Hero of Our Times,* and *Zanuck: The Rise and Fall of Hollywood's Last Tycoon.* (Sketch includes interview.)

Charles Osgood—American radio and television correspondent; host of "Newsbreak" and "The Osgood File" for CBS-Radio; author of two books, *Nothing Could Be Finer Than a Crisis That Is Minor in the Morning* and *There's Nothing That I Wouldn't Do If You Would Be My POSSLQ.* (Sketch includes interview.)

Frank Pakenham—British aristocrat, statesman, and crusader for a variety of moral causes; as the Seventh Earl of Longford, head of a household dubbed the "literary Longfords," a well-known family of writers that includes himself, his wife, Elizabeth, his son, Thomas, and his daughters, Judith Kazantis, Rachel Billington, and Antonia Fraser; author of books about social reform as well as biographies, notably the critically acclaimed *Pope John Paul II* and *Eamon de Valera.*

Thomas Pakenham—British historical writer; son of Frank Pakenham and member of family of authors known as the "literary Longfords"; author of highly praised works *The Year of Liberty* and *The Boer War.* (Sketch includes interview.)

Sam Peckinpah—American screenwriter and director of motion pictures and television productions; known for his "graphically violent, yet curiously romantic films," his screen credits include "The Wild Bunch," "Straw Dogs," "Junior Bonner," and "Bring Me the Head of Alfredo Garcia."

Karl Rahner—German Jesuit priest and preeminent Roman Catholic theologian, considered by some to be "the most brilliant Catholic theologian since Thomas Aquinas"; a prolific writer, his works include the twenty-volume *Theological Investigations.*

Ruth Rendell—Award-winning British novelist; author of well-received mysteries featuring Chief Inspector Wexford, notably *A Demon in My View, Lake of Darkness,* and *Master of the Moor.*

Willard H. Scott, Jr.—American broadcaster; humorous weather reporter on NBC-TV's "Today" show; author of his autobiography, *The Joy of Living.*

Leonard Shatzkin—American publishing executive; long considered an innovator in the field, Shatzkin has made many important contributions related to book production; author of *In Cold Type: Overcoming the Book Crisis.*

Colin Welland—British actor and writer for stage, television, and screen; best known for his award-winning screenplay, "Chariots of Fire." (Sketch includes interview.)

Preface

The over 1,500 entries in *Contemporary Authors,* Volume 109, bring to more than 74,000 the number of authors now represented in the *Contemporary Authors* series. *CA* includes nontechnical writers in all genres—fiction, nonfiction, poetry, drama, etc.—whose books are issued by commercial, risk publishers or by university presses. Authors of books published only by known vanity or author-subsidized firms are ordinarily not included. Since native language and nationality have no bearing on inclusion in *CA,* authors who write in languages other than English are included in *CA* if their works have been published in the United States or translated into English.

Although *CA* focuses primarily on authors of published books, the series also encompasses prominent persons in communications: newspaper and television reporters and correspondents, columnists, newspaper and magazine editors, photojournalists, syndicated cartoonists, screenwriters, television scriptwriters, and other media people.

Starting with Volume 104, the editors of *CA* began to broaden the series' scope to encompass authors deceased since 1900 whose works are still of interest to today's readers. (Previously, *CA* covered only living writers and authors deceased 1960 or later.) Since the great poets, novelists, short story writers, and playwrights of the early twentieth century are popular writers for study in today's high school and college curriculums, and since their writings continue to be analyzed by today's literary critics, these writers are in many ways as contemporary as the authors *CA* has featured up to this point.

Therefore, *CA* now contains information on important authors who lived and wrote between 1900 and 1959. Numerous authors from this period, most of whom will receive longer treatment later, are presently represented in *CA* with brief, one-paragraph entries. These brief entries are further explained in the section of the preface below headed "Brief Entries."

No charge or obligation is attached to a *CA* listing. Authors are included in the series solely on the basis of the above criteria and their interest to *CA* users.

Compilation Methods

The editors make every effort to secure information directly from the authors through questionnaires and personal correspondence. If authors of special interest to *CA* users are deceased or fail to reply to requests for information, material is gathered from other reliable sources. Biographical dictionaries are checked (a task made easier through the use of Gale's *Biography and Genealogy Master Index* and other volumes in the "Gale Biographical Index Series"), as are bibliographical sources, such as *Cumulative Book Index* and *The National Union Catalog.* Published interviews, feature stories, and book reviews are examined, and often material is supplied by the authors' publishers. All sketches, whether prepared from questionnaires or through extensive research, are sent to the authors for review prior to publication. Sketches on recently deceased authors are sent to family members, agents, etc., if possible, for a similar review.

Brief Entries

CA users have indicated that having some information, however brief, on authors not yet in the series would be preferable to waiting until full-length sketches can be prepared as outlined above under "Compilation Methods." Since Volume 104, therefore, *CA* has included one-paragraph entries on both early twentieth-century and current writers who presently do not have sketches in *CA.* These short listings, identified by the heading *BRIEF ENTRY,* highlight the author's career and writings and often provide a few sources where additional information can be found.

Brief entries are not intended to serve as sketches. Instead, they are designed to increase *CA*'s comprehensiveness and thus better serve *CA* users by providing pertinent information about a large number of authors, many of whom will be the subjects of full sketches in forthcoming volumes.

Informative Sidelights

Numerous *CA* sketches contain Sidelights, which provide personal dimensions to the listings, supply information about the critical reception the authors' works have received, or both. Some authors listed in Volume 109 worked closely with *CA*'s editors to develop lengthy, incisive Sidelights. Among these authors is award-winning journalist J.J. Maloney, an ex-convict who served twelve years in the Missouri State Penitentiary for armed robbery and murder. He writes: "I have had a unique opportunity—to go directly from prison to the newsroom of a legendary newspaper [the *Kansas City Star*]. Because of those unusual circumstances, my view of journalism will not be the normal one, in some ways. In many ways, however, I was able to overcome the initial liability of being an ex-convict and to subsequently function on my merits as a newspaper reporter. The editors of the *Kansas City Star* nominated me almost every year for the Pulitzer Prize, and by the time I left in 1978, I was considered one of the top reporters at the paper. . . . Now I'm trying a different route—journalism by way of book and magazine."

"I think of myself as a man of letters," remarks Frank Allen, an educator, author, and free-lance editor who has taught English at several eastern Pennsylvania colleges. As a teacher, he observes "that most American education does not entail the pursuit of truth or development of the mind but preparation for a vocation and inculcation of usable skills, that consumership has replaced citizenship in literature as well as society." Nevertheless, in his "somewhat old-fashioned role" as a man of letters, Allen would "like to make the past relevant to contemporary writing and to be worthy of it. Equally, I'd like to make writers today aware that there is a dynamic, accessible body of literature in the past. If the two, past and present, do not maintain a dialogue, I don't see how a nation's letters can help being peripheral and impermanent."

CA's editors compile equally incisive Sidelights when authors and media people of particular interest to *CA* readers do not supply Sidelights material, or when demand for information about the critical reception their works have received is especially high. Assistant editor Nancy Pear, for instance, relays the general critical perception that playwright Lorraine Hansberry, author of "A Raisin in the Sun," was not "a particularly political or 'black' writer, but rather . . . one who dealt more with human universals." In what critics have called "a true-life adventure" and "compelling entertainment," Tracy Kidder's award-winning best-seller, *The Soul of a New Machine,* uniquely advanced the popular discussion and understanding of computer technology. Kidder's Sidelights, prepared by assistant editor Mary E. Teller, survey the wide critical acclaim accorded this book and provide a crisp introduction to *CA*'s interview with the author. In her Sidelights for theologian Karl Rahner, senior assistant editor Charity Anne Dorgan begins with Martin E. Marty's succinct observation that "Compared to Karl Rahner, most other contemporary Christian theologians are scrub oak"; she goes on to explain why Rahner may be "the most influential teacher of the modern Catholic church." And Oskar Kokoschka's Sidelights, composed by senior assistant editor Les Stone, depict Kokoschka as "one of Europe's most talented, if eccentric, artists."

These sketches, as well as others compiled by *CA*'s editors, provide informative and enjoyable reading.

Writers of Special Interest

CA's editors make every effort to include a substantial number of entries in each volume on active authors and media people of special interest to *CA*'s readers. Since *CA* also includes sketches on noteworthy deceased writers, a significant amount of work on the part of *CA*'s editors goes into the compilation of full-length entries on important deceased authors. Some of the prominent writers, both living and deceased, whose sketches are contained in this volume are noted in the list headed "Authors and Media People Featured in This Volume" immediately preceding the preface.

Exclusive Interviews

CA provides exclusive, primary information on certain authors in the form of interviews. Prepared specifically for *CA,* the never-before-published conversations presented in the section of the sketch headed *CA INTERVIEW* give *CA* users the opportunity to learn the authors' thoughts, in depth, about their craft. Subjects chosen for interviews are, the editors feel, authors who hold special interest for *CA*'s readers.

Authors and journalists in this volume whose sketches include interviews are Martin Agronsky, John Chancellor, Lawrence Kasdan, Tracy Kidder, Christopher Lehmann-Haupt, Abby Mann, Leonard O. Mosley, Charles Osgood, Thomas Pakenham, and Colin Welland.

Obituary Notices Make *CA* Timely and Comprehensive

To be as timely and comprehensive as possible, *CA* publishes brief, one-paragraph obituary notices on deceased authors within the scope of the series. These notices provide date and place of birth and death, highlight the author's career and writings, and list other sources where additional biographical information and obituaries may be found. To distinguish them from full-length sketches, obituaries are identified with the heading *OBITUARY NOTICE*.

CA includes obituary notices for authors who already have full-length entries in earlier *CA* volumes—23 percent of the obituary notices in this volume are for such authors—as well as for authors who do not yet have sketches in the series. Deceased authors of special interest presently represented only by obituary notices are scheduled for full-length sketch treatment in forthcoming *CA* volumes.

Contemporary Authors New Revision Series

A major change in the preparation of *CA* revision volumes began with the first volume of the newly titled *Contemporary Authors New Revision Series*. No longer are all of the sketches in a given *CA* volume updated and published together as a revision volume. Instead, entries from a number of volumes are assessed, and only those sketches requiring *significant change* are revised and published in a *New Revision Series* volume. This enables us to provide *CA* users with updated information about active writers on a more timely basis and avoids printing entries in which there has been little or no change. As always, the most recent *CA* cumulative index continues to be the user's guide to the location of an individual author's revised listing.

CA Numbering System

Occasionally questions arise about the *CA* numbering system. Despite numbers like "97-100" and "109," however, the entire *CA* series consists of only 46 physical volumes with the publication of *CA* Volume 109 in December, 1983. The information below notes changes in the numbering system, as well as in cover design, to help *CA* users better understand the organization of the entire *CA* series.

CA **First Revisions**	• 1-4R through 41-44R (11 books) *Cover:* Brown with black and gold trim. There will be no further *First Revisions* because revised entries are now being handled exclusively through the more efficient *New Revision Series* mentioned below.
CA **Original Volumes**	• 45-48 through 97-100 (14 books) *Cover:* Brown with black and gold trim. • 101 through 109 (9 books) *Cover:* Blue and black with orange bands. The same as previous *CA* original volumes but with a new, simplified numbering system and new cover design.
CA **New Revision Series**	• *CANR*-1 through *CANR*-10 (10 books) *Cover:* Blue and black with green bands. Includes only sketches requiring extensive change; **sketches are taken from any previously published *CA* volume.**
CA **Permanent Series**	• *CAP*-1 and *CAP*-2 (2 books) *Cover:* Brown with red and gold trim. There will be no further *Permanent Series* volumes because revised entries are now being handled exclusively through the more efficient *New Revision Series* mentioned above.

Retaining *CA* Volumes

As new volumes in the series are published, users often ask which *CA* volumes, if any, can be discarded. The chart following the preface is designed to assist users in keeping their collections as complete as possible. All volumes in the left column of the chart should be retained to have the most complete, up-to-date coverage possible; volumes in the right column can be discarded if the appropriate replacements are held.

Cumulative Index Should Always Be Consulted

The key to locating an individual author's listing is the *CA* cumulative index bound into the back of alternate original volumes (and available separately as an offprint). Since the *CA* cumulative index provides access to *all* entries in the *CA* series, the latest cumulative index should always be consulted to find the specific volume containing an author's original or most recently revised sketch.

For the convenience of *CA* users, the *CA* cumulative index also includes references to all entries in three related Gale series—*Contemporary Literary Criticism* (CLC), which is devoted entirely to current criticism of the works of today's novelists, poets, playwrights, short story writers, filmmakers, scriptwriters, and other creative writers, *Something About the Author* (SATA), a series of heavily illustrated sketches on authors and illustrators of books for young people, and *Authors in the News* (AITN), a compilation of news stories and feature articles from American newspapers and magazines covering writers and other members of the communications media.

As always, suggestions from users about any aspect of *CA* will be welcomed.

IF YOU HAVE:	YOU MAY DISCARD:
1-4 First Revision (1967)	1 (1962) 2 (1963) 3 (1963) 4 (1963)
5-8 First Revision (1969)	5-6 (1963) 7-8 (1963)
Both 9-12 First Revision (1974) AND *Contemporary Authors Permanent Series,* Volume 1 (1975)	9-10 (1964) 11-12 (1965)
Both 13-16 First Revision (1975) AND *Contemporary Authors Permanent Series,* Volumes 1 and 2 (1975, 1978)	13-14 (1965) 15-16 (1966)
Both 17-20 First Revision (1976) AND *Contemporary Authors Permanent Series,* Volumes 1 and 2 (1975, 1978)	17-18 (1967) 19-20 (1968)
Both 21-24 First Revision (1977) AND *Contemporary Authors Permanent Series,* Volumes 1 and 2 (1975, 1978)	21-22 (1969) 23-24 (1970)
Both 25-28 First Revision (1977) AND *Contemporary Authors Permanent Series,* Volume 2 (1978)	25-28 (1971)
Both 29-32 First Revision (1978) AND *Contemporary Authors Permanent Series,* Volume 2 (1978)	29-32 (1972)
Both 33-36 First Revision (1978) AND *Contemporary Authors Permanent Series,* Volume 2 (1978)	33-36 (1973)
37-40 First Revision (1979)	37-40 (1973)
41-44 First Revision (1979)	41-44 (1974)
45-48 (1974) 49-52 (1975) 53-56 (1975) 57-60 (1976) ↓ ↓ 109 (1983)	NONE: These volumes will not be super-seded by corresponding revised vol-umes. Individual entries from these and all other volumes appearing in the left column of this chart will be revised and included in the *New Revision Series.*
Volumes in the *Contemporary Authors New Revision Series*	NONE: The *New Revision Series* does not replace any single volume of *CA*. All volumes appearing in the left column of this chart must be retained to have in-formation on all authors in the series.

Contemporary Authors

Indicates that a listing has been compiled from secondary sources believed to be reliable, but has not been personally verified for this edition by the author sketched.

ABEEL, Erica (Hennefeld) 1937-

BRIEF ENTRY: Born in 1937 in New York. American educator, journalist, and author. An associate professor of French and English at John Jay College of Criminal Justice of the City University of New York, Abeel formerly taught for five years at Barnard College. She is the author of "Hers," a column that appears in the *New York Times,* and a contributor of articles to a number of magazines, including *New York* and *Ladies' Home Journal.* In addition, Abeel has written two books: *Only When I Laugh* (Morrow, 1978) and *I'll Call You Tomorrow, and Other Lies Between Men and Women* (Morrow, 1981). In the *New York Times Book Review,* critic Jill Robinson called *Only When I Laugh* "funny and incisive," and she noted that it is "unpretentious, written with a glowing, earnest simplicity." *Address:* Department of French, John Jay College of Criminal Justice of the City University of New York, 445 West 56th St., New York, N.Y. 10019. *Biographical/critical sources: New York Times Book Review,* June 11, 1978.

* * *

ABRAMOV, Fyodor Aleksandrovich 1920-1983

OBITUARY NOTICE: Born February 29, 1920, in Verkola, Russia (now U.S.S.R.); died in 1983. Educator and author. Abramov is best known as the author of several novels, including *Brothers and Sisters* and *Round and About,* which were approved reading in the Soviet Union despite their often critical depictions of rural life. He taught at Leningrad University. Obituaries and other sources: *New York Times,* May 17, 1983; *Chicago Tribune,* May 18, 1983; *London Times,* May 20, 1983.

* * *

ABRAMSKY, Chimen 1916-

BRIEF ENTRY: Born September 12, 1916, in Minsk, Russia (now U.S.S.R.). British historian, educator, and author. Recipient of the Humanitarian Trust Award and senior fellow of St. Antony's College, Oxford, Abramsky has taught Hebrew and Jewish studies at the University of London since 1969. His writings include *Karl Marx and the British Labour Movement: Years of the First International* (St. Martin's, 1965), *Marx and the General Council of the IWMA* (1968), *Lenin and*

the Jews (1973), and *Essays in Honour of E. H. Carr* (Macmillan, 1975). *Address:* 5 Hillway St., London N.6, England; and Department of Hebrew and Jewish Studies, University College, University of London, Gower St., London WC1E 6BT, England. *Biographical/critical sources: Times Literary Supplement,* May 13, 1965; *Economist,* August 7, 1965; *Who's Who in World Jewry: A Biographical Dictionary of Outstanding Jews,* Pitman, 1972.

* * *

ACKART, Robert 1921-

PERSONAL: Born August 29, 1921, in Wilmington, Del.; son of Everett Gunner (an engineer) and Agnes (Jenks) Ackart. *Education:* Wesleyan University, Middletown, Conn., B.A. (summa cum laude), 1943; Harvard University, M.A., 1945; Yale University, M.F.A., 1952. *Politics:* Independent. *Residence:* Katonah, N.Y. 10536. *Agent:* McIntosh & Otis, Inc., 475 Fifth Ave., New York, N.Y. 10017.

CAREER: Tufts University, Medford, Mass., instructor in English literature, 1945-47; Swarthmore College, Swarthmore, Pa., instructor in English literature, 1947-49; Salzburg Festival, Salzburg, Austria, operatic stage director, 1952-55; Royal Opera, London, England, stage director, 1955-56; Chicago Lyric Opera, Chicago, Ill., stage director, 1956-58; Santa Fe Opera, Santa Fe, N.M., stage director, 1957; Honolulu Opera Festival, Honolulu, Hawaii, stage director, 1963-64; writer, 1965—. President of Katonah Village Improvement Society, 1969-72; member of board of trustees of Katonah Village Library, 1970-72.

WRITINGS: Cooking in a Casserole, Grosset, 1967; *The One-Hundred Menu Chicken Cookbook,* Grosset, 1971; *Fruits in Cooking,* Macmillan, 1973; *The One-Dish Cookbook,* Grosset, 1975; *A Celebration of Vegetables,* Atheneum, 1977; *The Cheese Cookbook,* Grosset, 1978; *Souffles, Mousses, Jellies, and Creams,* Atheneum, 1980; *A Celebration of Soups,* Doubleday, 1982; *The Frugal Fish,* Little, Brown, 1983.

WORK IN PROGRESS: Spirited Cooking, on using wines and spirits in cooking, publication by Atheneum expected in 1984.

AVOCATIONAL INTERESTS: Serious music, gardening, travel.

13

ACOMB, Frances (Dorothy) 1907-

BRIEF ENTRY: Born October 15, 1907, in Donora, Pa. American historian, educator, and author. Frances Acomb's teaching career began in 1929. She taught history at Duke University from 1945 to 1975 when she was named professor emerita. Her writings include *Anglophobia in France, 1763-1789: An Essay in the History of Constitutionalism and Nationalism* (Duke University Press, 1950), *Statistical Control in the Army Air Forces* (History Division, U.S. Air Force, 1952), and *Mallet Du Pan, 1749-1800: A Career in Political Journalism* (Duke University Press, 1973). *Address:* P.O. Box 6777, College Station, Durham, N.C. 27708. *Biographical/critical sources: American Historical Review,* October, 1950, October, 1974.

* * *

ADAMIC, Alojzij 1899(?)-1951
(Louis Adamic)

BRIEF ENTRY: Born March 23, 1899 (some sources say 1898) in Blato, Slovenia, Austria-Hungary (now Yugoslavia); came to the United States, 1913, naturalized citizen, 1918; died of alleged self-inflicted gunshot wound (although murder was suspected), September 4, 1951. American translator and author. Adamic's first major literary works were translations of South Slavic writings into English. The translator began his own writing career around 1925, contributing essays and stories, under the pseudonym Louis Adamic, to various Haldeman-Julius publications and to the *American Mercury.* The writer's subjective commentaries on American social phenomena became forerunners of the 1950's "New Journalism." In 1932 and 1933 Adamic visited his native Slovenia, producing the best-selling *The Native's Return: An American Immigrant Visits Yugoslavia and Discovers His Old Country* (1934) upon his return to the United States. The work established him as America's expert on Yugoslavia; it also prompted the author to explore, in subsequent writings, the problems of immigrants and their children. The author produced his first novel, *Grandsons: A Story of American Lives,* in 1935. Nearly a dozen books followed, including *From Many Lands* (1940), which earned the John Anisfield Award for its significant contribution to the study of race relations. *Address:* R.F.D. 1, Milford, N.J. *Biographical/critical sources: Current Biography,* Wilson, 1940, October, 1951; *The Oxford Companion to American Literature,* 4th edition, Oxford University Press, 1965; *Who Was Who in America,* Volume III: *1951-1960,* Marquis, 1966; *Dictionary of Literary Biography,* Volume 9: *American Novelists, 1910-1945,* Gale, 1981.

* * *

ADAMIC, Louis
See ADAMIC, Alojzij

* * *

ADAMS, Val 1917(?)-1983

OBITUARY NOTICE: Born c. 1917; died February 12, 1983, in Ridgewood, N.J., following surgery for lung cancer. Journalist. Adams ended twenty years of service with the *New York Times* in 1969, whereupon he became assistant radio and television news editor for the *New York Daily News.* Obituaries and other sources: *New York Times,* February 14, 1983.

ADDANKI, Sam 1932-

PERSONAL: Born March 7, 1932, in Lakkavaram, India; came to the United States in 1960, naturalized citizen, 1971; son of Veeraraghavaiah (a merchant) and Surbaraju Addanki; married Sathyayathi Rachuri, May 4, 1954; children: Rathna Rachuri, Usha/Kamisette, Sheila. *Education:* University of Madras, B.Sc., 1957; Ohio State University, M.Sc. and Ph.D., 1964; D.A.B.C.C., 1970. *Politics:* Democrat. *Religion:* Hindu. *Home:* 1739 Blue Ash Pl., Columbus, Ohio 43229. *Office:* Department of Pediatrics, Ohio State University, P.O. Box 29250, Columbus, Ohio 43229.

CAREER: Ohio State University, Columbus, assistant professor, 1966-70, associate professor of pediatrics, 1970—. President of Nu-Diet Enterprises, Inc., 1978—; general partner of Nu-Care Diabetes and Health Center; public speaker; guest on television programs. *Member:* American Society of Biological Chemists, American Association for Cancer Research, American Diabetes Association, American Federation of Clinical Research, American Institute of Chemists (fellow), American Board of Clinical Chemistry, National Speakers Association, Biochemical Society (England).

WRITINGS: Diabetes Breakthrough, Pinnacle Books, 1982; *Renewed Health for Diabetics,* Nu-Diet Enterprises, 1982.

WORK IN PROGRESS: Diet, Obesity, Sexuality: Diet for the Eighties, publication expected in 1984; *Sex and Diet,* publication expected in 1984.

SIDELIGHTS: Sam Addanki told *CA:* "During the past fifteen years I was obese and diabetic. I was abrasive and short with my family. My father died of diabetes. My wife was diagnosed diabetic. My marriage was breaking up because I was impotent for six years. At times I could not find any good reason to continue living. Then one day in 1972 my wife shouted: 'I can't take it any more, Sam! I am leaving!' I was crushed. We were separated for three months. That was the reason I undertook this research. I want to prevent this from happening to others.

"I took a journey that led me to this moment. Now I am proud to stand before others and say that I feel very strong. I have energy, and I have fun. Impotency is only a bad memory of the past. I know the answer. I would like to share with others what I have discovered. I want to be an evangelist."

* * *

AGNELLI, Susanna 1922-

PERSONAL: Born April 24, 1922, in Turin, Italy; daughter of Edoardo (an industrial manager) and Virginia Bourbon del Monte Agnelli; divorced; children: Ilaria, Samaritana, Cristiano, Delfina, Lupo, Priscilla. *Education:* Received general certificate of education from Classical High School. *Politics:* Republican. *Religion:* Roman Catholic. *Residence:* Santa Liberata, Grosseto, Italy. *Office:* Camera dei Deputati, Rome, Italy 00150.

CAREER: Volunteer nurse with Italian Red Cross, c. 1939-45; chairman of the board of Edoardo e Virginia Agnelli School for professional nurses, 1945-75; mayor of Monte Argentario, Italy, 1974—; Republican member of Italian Parliament, 1976-79. Elected member of European Parliament, 1979. *Member:* Soroptimist Club of Grosseto (Italy). *Awards, honors:* Scanno and Bancarella literary prizes, both 1975, both for *Vestivamo all marinara.*

WRITINGS: Vestivamo all marinara, Mondadori, 1975, translation by Agnelli published as *We Always Wore Sailor Suits,*

Viking, 1975; *Gente alla deriva* (title means "People Drifting"), Rizzoli, 1980; *Ricordati gualeguaychu* (title means "Remember Gualeguaychu"), Mondadori, 1982. Contributor of articles to magazines and newspapers.

SIDELIGHTS: Granddaughter of the founder of the FIAT automobile company, Susanna Agnelli became active in city politics to soothe her dissatisfaction with local government. In 1974 the people of Monte Argentario elected Agnelli mayor, at which time she found her stature as an influential, wealthy citizen both an enhancement and a hindrance to her career. "On the plus side," she told Alvin Shuster in a *New York Times* interview, "people think I am in a position where I might be able to get more things done. On the minus side, they look at you as a privileged person who is not going to understand their problems." With this in mind, Agnelli opens her office for two hours every day so that members of her constituency can bring their concerns to her. Typical problems, she said, include sewerage, water, and housing.

The politician is credited for her work in encouraging Italian women to take a more active role in public life. "People in Italy sort of think that I am going to be the real thing that is going to make women try harder to go into politics," she explained.

Though Agnelli's book does not chronicle her political career, it does provide a view of a childhood spent in the opulent atmosphere of Mussolini's Italy. *We Always Wore Sailor Suits* was written to illustrate Agnelli's life as a privileged citizen, not to reveal the scandal and gossip of fascist Italy. Covering her life until her marriage, the memoir includes a portrait of Agnelli's paternal grandfather, who attempted to gain custody of his grandchildren after their father died, and a loving tribute to her mother, who shared a special relationship with the famous writer Malaparte.

Well received by critics, *We Always Wore Sailor Suits* contains "vivid memories of a life worth retelling," commented a *Washington Post Book World* reviewer. According to Joan Dash in the *New York Times Book Review*, it is "an exquisite concoction," with flavor and texture. "Never is this book a glorification of being rich and powerful," observed N. G. Reed in the *Christian Science Monitor*, "nor an apology for mistakes which . . . [Agnelli] may have made. It is a vivid recording of war-ravaged Italy, seen by a young girl whose normal zest for life—punctuated with naughty humor and teenage romance—was interrupted by a universally unforeseeable, and impartially cruel, world event." Alistair Forbes, writing in the *Times Literary Supplement*, called Agnelli "a natural writer" who "handles her material with superb skill and selectivity."

Agnelli told *CA:* "I am interested in any question related to suffering human beings—wherever they are and whoever they are."

BIOGRAPHICAL/CRITICAL SOURCES: New York Times, August 27, 1975, October 10, 1975; *New York Times Book Review,* October 12, 1975, December 7, 1975; *Christian Science Monitor,* October 22, 1975; *Times Literary Supplement,* December 19, 1975, April 23, 1976; *Best Sellers,* January, 1976; *New Statesman,* February 27, 1976; *Observer,* February 29, 1976; *Guardian Weekly,* March 28, 1976; *Washington Post Book World,* November 28, 1976.

*   *   *

AGRONSKY, Martin (Zama) 1915-

PERSONAL: Born January 12, 1915, in Philadelphia, Pa.; son of Isador Nathan and Marcia (Dvorin) Agronsky; married Helen Smathers, September 1, 1943 (died February, 1969); children: Marcia, Jonathan, David, Julie. *Education:* Rutgers University, B.S., 1936, M.A., 1949. *Home:* 2605 Tilden Pl. N.W., Washington, D.C. 20008. *Office:* Broadcast House, Washington, D.C. 20005; and 3620 27th St., South Arlington, Va. 22206.

CAREER: Journalist and host of programs such as "Agronsky and Company," PBS. *Palestine Post,* Jerusalem, Palestine (now Israel), reporter, 1936-37; free-lance journalist, 1937-40; National Broadcasting Co., New York City, correspondent in Europe, 1940-43; war correspondent in Mediterranean and Pacific theaters, 1940-43; American Broadcasting Corp., correspondent in Washington, D.C., 1943-64; National Broadcasting Co., television and radio correspondent in Washington, D.C., for "Today Show"; Columbia Broadcasting System, New York City, correspondent in Washington, D.C., 1964, correspondent and bureau chief in Paris, France, 1964-69; television commentator in Washington, D.C., for *Washington Post-Newsweek* stations, 1969—. *Member:* Conglomeration of Radio-Television Correspondents Association (president, 1953), Omicron Delta Kappa. *Awards, honors:* Heywood Broun Award for radio reporting from American Newspaper Guild, 1948; Peabody Award for distinguished reporting, 1952; Alfred Dupont Award for distinguished reporting for television, 1962; National Headliners Award for television reporting, 1962; award from Venice Film Festival, 1963, for "Polaris Submarine—Journal of an Undersea Voyage"; Emmy Award from Academy of Television Arts and Sciences, 1966, for "CBS Special."

WRITINGS: (With others) *Let Us Begin: The First 100 Days of the Kennedy Administration,* Simon & Schuster, 1961. Contributor to periodicals.

SIDELIGHTS: Agronsky has enjoyed a lengthy career as one of television's most prominent political commentators. Visible on all of the major networks, he is renowned for his keen insight into political activities. Agronsky has also received praise for his skill as an interviewer. "He bores in with questions that often make guests squirm," wrote one reporter, "and his slow-paced manner of reporting is deceiving." The *Cleveland Plain Dealer* also noted that "Agronsky would have made a classic trial lawyer . . . if he had not chosen electronic journalism."

CA INTERVIEW

CA interviewed Martin Agronsky by telephone on June 9 and June 15, 1982, at his home in Washington, D.C.

CA: A great many of the articles you write concern international affairs. What is it about international affairs that appeals to you?

AGRONSKY: The state of the world interests me. I began writing just before World War II began, when there was an enormous interest in what would happen internationally. One of the first major pieces I had published, about racism in Italy, was for *Foreign Affairs Quarterly.* Those were the areas of my interest. There was nothing mysterious or complicated about it.

CA: Which of your numerous broadcasts do you think most memorable?

AGRONSKY: The one that I liked to do most was a series for NBC called "Look Here," with weekly interviews with national and international figures in their native habitat, including Leonard Bernstein in his apartment in New York City, Sam Sneed down at Boca Raton, Budd Schulberg on a boat in Florida, that kind of thing. It was a lot of fun doing that, and interesting. When you interview people in their own atmosphere, they're more relaxed and you get a more interesting show.

But the assignment that interested me and affected me more than any other was the Eichmann trial in 1961 in Jerusalem. We all knew what had happened, but to have it spelled out in that detail revealed an incredible capacity for man's inhumanity to man. It got to me. Then there was another dimension coming at it from being a Jew. You had to sit there and say to yourself each day, "There but for the grace of God." My good fortune was that my family came to the United States from Russia in 1905. Well, suppose they hadn't? That was an additional dimension that involved me subjectively.

CA: You received an Emmy Award for your interview with U.S. Supreme Court Justice Hugo Black in 1966. Were you satisfied with that show?

AGRONSKY: Very much so. It was reported as the first television interview with a justice from the Supreme Court, but that isn't so. I had done two interviews with Justice William O. Douglas before that. I did one on a barge on the Chesapeake and Ohio canal. That's where Douglas, a conservationist and an outdoorsman, wanted to be. That was his native habitat. He was, in the end, one of those who preserved that tow path and the canal itself.

CA: You also received an award at the Venice Film Festival in 1963 for your documentary on the Polaris submarine.

AGRONSKY: Yes, I spent a month underwater doing that. It was a little confining but it was amazing how quickly we all adjusted to it. It was really quite extraordinary. The crew dealt well with the diurnal cycle. When the sun rose, the lighting went to white. When the sun set, the lighting went to red. So you had a sensation of a change in time and a change in externals. Psychologically, it worked very effectively.

CA: While we're talking about awards you've won, we should mention the 1952 Peabody Award for your coverage of Senator Joseph McCarthy. Do you think there's a possibility that another McCarthy will arise in this country?

AGRONSKY: It's always possible.

CA: Are there any signs now that another McCarthy may be coming along?

AGRONSKY: No. McCarthy didn't just happen along, he exploited a situation. He found that accusing people of being pro-Communist got him a lot of publicity. Some other politician without principle, like McCarthy, might try to do that again, but I don't know if he'd succeed.

CA: Regarding your career, one of your most interesting actions was your switch from commercial to public television and back again. Which of the two do you prefer?

AGRONSKY: I think commercial television is superior to public television. This is as a result of my experiences with public

broadcasting. I don't mean to give you the impression that I don't think public television is a good idea. That isn't my point at all. My point is that public television isn't as effective as I had hoped it would be, and that, actually, with public television more than with commercial television, the important thing is money.

For example, take Channel Thirteen in New York. It's run by an extremely effective money raiser. And the station that can raise the money to underwrite programming is more influential in the network than the stations that can't, because the other stations can't afford to put the shows on.

When I did public broadcasting—for example, when I did a show called "Evening Edition," which preceded the MacNeil-Lehrer Report—we were always so broke, I had to raise money for the show outside the network, through unions and that sort of thing. I didn't particularly like having to be involved in the fund raising.

CA: What did the lack of funds prevent you from doing with the show?

AGRONSKY: If you wanted to do remotes, you couldn't afford them. If you wanted to take the show abroad, it was extremely difficult; you didn't have the money to do it. If you wanted to move the show around the country, just the mere cost of transportation made it prohibitive. The reason the MacNeil-Lehrer Report, which succeeded ours, worked well and still functions is that the guy who ran Channel Thirteen was so successful in getting them the underwriting which enabled them to do an effective job. Technically, and in terms of travel, they were able to do more. Here I was working with a producer, a secretary, and two researchers who also functioned as secretaries and assistant producers. That's all we had, and we were turning out a half-hour show every night and trying to get the people on the show who were the focal point of the news. It's very difficult when you don't have the staff. Now, of course, a big station, like those in New York, Boston, Los Angeles, or San Francisco, where they're able to raise that kind of money, is able to provide the funding to do a more elaborate and professional job than the stations that can't afford it, and the Washington station—where we produced the show—was just never very good at raising money. It depends on who runs the stations.

CA: Do you think public television has a future, considering the fact that federal budget reductions will probably force it to go commercial?

AGRONSKY: Well look here, put it this way: Public television is supposed to be noncommercial and without sponsorship. Right? But that isn't true. When an underwriter provides the money for certain programming, even though he doesn't say, "Use my gasoline" or whatever on the show, the fact that this program carries the logo, "This program underwritten by Mobil" or Exxon or whoever, amounts to institutional advertising. I think the underwriters seek credit for underwriting the program. And then you'll find that the underwriters do a lot of institutional advertising in newspapers, boasting of their underwriting of various programs. They may insist that this has no commercial applications, but I think it does. So in that sense, public television is already commercial.

CA: You've worked in Washington, D.C., for a long time. What's your opinion of the charge that Washington reporters

are quite often co-opted or used by official sources and don't
actually get to the bottom of things?

AGRONSKY: I think that criticism is valid as far as some
reporters are concerned, and totally invalid as far as others are
concerned. There are lazy reporters and bad reporters and reporters who—not in any wicked sense—are used. But I think
the majority of good reporters are not co-opted.

CA: Is the situation worse in Washington than in other places?

AGRONSKY: No. In fact, I think there's more awareness on
the part of Washington reporters that that's a danger.

*CA: You're particularly well known as an interviewer. What's
the secret of great interviewing?*

AGRONSKY: Do your homework. Know as much as you can
about the person. If there are contradictions in his position,
your homework should indicate the point of view the person
took at one point and then at a later point, allowing you to ask
him why he changed his mind. Homework is the key.

BIOGRAPHICAL/CRITICAL SOURCES: Newsweek, May 4,
1953; *Cleveland Plain-Dealer,* August 17, 1974; *Authors in
the News,* Volume 2, Gale, 1976.*

                                        —*Interview by Peter Benjaminson*

                    *   *   *

AIKEN, Maurice C.   1909(?)-1983

OBITUARY NOTICE: Born c. 1909 in Fairmont, Neb.; died
May 20, 1983, in Chicago, Ill. Journalist and editor. Aiken
worked for the *Daily Nebraskan, Nebraska Farmer,* and *Nebraska State Journal* while studying at the University of Nebraska. In 1935 he began a long association with various branches
of the Bell Telephone Company. He was news service manager
of Bell's Illinois company from 1964 until his retirement in
1973. Obituaries and other sources: *Chicago Tribune,* May 24,
1983.

                    *   *   *

AKARE, Thomas   1950-

PERSONAL: Born April 4, 1950, in Kisumu, Kenya; son of
Mzee Agustino Mulo Opondo and Juliana Anyango Oyoyo;
married Alima Ramadhani, 1966 (divorced); married Saada
Juma, 1973 (divorced); children: Juju Fauziya, Asha Athango,
Juma. *Education:* Attended high school in Nairobi, Kenya.
Religion: Christian. *Home address:* P.O. Box 77198, Nairobi,
Kenya.

CAREER: Nation Newspapers, Nairobi, Kenya, pasteup artist,
1971-72; Stellascope Ltd., Nairobi, pasteup artist, 1976-79;
writer, 1979—.

WRITINGS: The Slums (novel), Heinemann, 1981.

WORK IN PROGRESS—Novels: *The Curses of Doom,* for
Heinemann; *Sorry My Love,* for Heinemann; *Social Ills,* about
detention; *Twilight Woman,* about prostitution; *Town Talks.*

SIDELIGHTS: In Thomas Akare's first novel, *The Slums,* Nairobi's slums are seen through the eyes of protagonist Eddy
Chura, a twenty-five-year-old orphan who was "born once, to
suffer and then die" and who lives in abandoned cars, frequents
the area's drinking houses, and eventually commits a robbery
and turns himself in to the police, hoping to find shelter and
"a proper meal."

"This is a novel of despair," wrote Simon Gikandi in the
Nairobi Times. "Both the author and his hero have given up
hope of social regeneration and hang on the edge of the abyss
waiting for their turn to take the plunge. . . . The prose in *The
Slums* is rough . . . [but] it is partly Akare's roughshod style
that makes his image of the slums so salient." An *Africa Now*
critic opined: "This novel deserves a wide audience for treating
a little-explored facet of urban African life with accuracy and
sympathy. . . . This novel is tough and unsparing, and well
worth it."

Akare told *CA:* "Having read many of the books by our authors
here in Kenya, I found that the lot were only based on the Mau
Mau thème. I got bored with this and decided to try my hand
at writing about life in Nairobi. The slums are the worst part.
They are ignored by our politicians.

"My view on detention is that detaining anyone is always due
to fear. It is due to how afraid the detainer is because of his
own time for his own end. I don't see why a leader should be
afraid of having an opposer whose work is only to correct
where wrongs are. I can't see the reason for someone being
afraid of calling a spade a spade. It is unfortunate to us blacks
that our leaders are afraid of having opposers, and it is really
unfortunate that their advisers, the whites, don't advise them
to have opposition parties like they themselves are having in
their countries. These are all due to funny politics—the politics
of funny politicians who are only fooling the common man to
exploit him, the common man, for their own ends. It is due
to this that my view on politics is that it is a dirty game.

"As for prostitution, the cause of it also comes from politics.
Once the politicians have failed to regard poverty, prostitution
is there for women to try to make ends meet.

"As for my writing, I began when I felt bored with reading
the same theme by our authors here, which of course is nothing
but Mau Mau. And through writing I hope to achieve recognition of other authors. As for my habits when writing, they
are always the same. I am always myself when writing.

"The purpose for my writing is to record whatever happens
that should be recorded for history. That is the reason I wrote
the book *The Slums.*"

BIOGRAPHICAL/CRITICAL SOURCES: New Statesman, September 11, 1981; *Nairobi Times,* October 25, 1981; *Times
Educational Supplement,* February 26, 1982; *Africa Now,* April,
1982; *Daily Nation,* July 16, 1982; *Viva,* November, 1982.

                    *   *   *

ALBA, Richard D(enis)   1942-

PERSONAL: Born December 22, 1942, in New York, N.Y.;
son of Richard and Mary (O'Sullivan) Alba; married Gwen
Lova Moore (a college professor), January 15, 1977; children:
Michael. *Education:* Columbia University, A.B., 1963, Ph.D.,
1974. *Home:* 45 Union Ave., Delmar, N.Y. 12054. *Office:*
Department of Sociology, State University of New York at
Albany, Albany, N.Y. 12222.

CAREER: Worked for Service Bureau Corporation, 1965-66,
Bureau of Applied Social Research, 1967-68, and Columbia
University Computer Center, 1968-69; City University of New
York, New York, N.Y., assistant professor of sociology, 1974-
77; Cornell University, Ithaca, N.Y., assistant professor of
sociology, 1977-80; State University of New York at Albany,
associate professor of sociology, 1980—, director of Center
for Social and Demographic Analysis, 1981—. *Member:*

American Sociological Association, American Educational Research Association, Eastern Sociological Society.

WRITINGS: (With David Lavin and Richard Silberstein) *Right Versus Privilege,* Free Press, 1981; (contributor) Samuel Bacharach, editor, *Research in the Sociology of Organizations,* Volume I, Jai Press, 1982; *The Italian-Americans: The Twilight of Ethnicity,* Prentice-Hall, in press. Contributor to sociology journals and newspapers.

SIDELIGHTS: Alba told *CA:* "The basic question I have pursued in my work concerns the significance of group boundaries: Just how much do they separate us? I have grappled with this question in a variety of guises—in studies of intermarriage, organized crime, political elites, and higher education, as well as in mathematical studies of group structure.

"I have used the metaphor of 'twilight' to characterize what seems to be an unusual evolution among European ancestry groups in the United States: namely, that ethnic boundaries have largely faded for them and that their cultural and social distinctiveness is now only faintly visible. I am increasingly concerned with explaining how this process of integration has come about and have formulated the beginnings of an answer in my book on Italian-Americans."

* * *

ALDEN, Jack
See BARROWS, (Ruth) Marjorie

* * *

ALEKSIN, Anatolii Georgievich 1924-

PERSONAL: Born August 3, 1924, in Moscow, U.S.S.R. *Education:* Graduated from Moscow Institute for Oriental Studies, 1950.

CAREER: Author, playwright. Secretary of Soviet newspaper *Kepost' oborony* ("Fortress of Defense"), beginning 1941; speaker on "Litsa druzei," monthly television show on children's education; editorial board member of *Yunost'* and *Detskaya Literatura* (magazines). *Member:* Association of Activists of Literature and Art for Children in the Union of Soviet Societies of Friendship and Cultural Ties With Foreign Countries (vice-president), Union of Writers of the Russian Soviet Federated Socialist Republic (secretary of directorate for children and young adult literature). *Awards, honors:* Mildred Batchelder Award nomination, 1973, for *A Late-Born Child;* numerous awards in Soviet Union include the Lenin Komsomol prize (Young Communist League), RSFSR Government N.K. Krupskaya prize, order of the Labor Red Banner.

*WRITINGS—*In English translation: *Moi brat igraet na klarnete* (juvenile), 1968, translation by Fainna Glagoleva published as *My Brother Plays the Clarinet,* Progress Publishers (Moscow), 1972, also published as *My Brother Plays the Clarinet: Two Stories* (illustrated by Judith Gwyn Brown), Walck, 1975; *Ochen' strashnaia istoriia* (juvenile), 1969, translation by Bonnie Carey published as *Alik the Detective,* Morrow, 1977; *Pozdnii rebenok* (juvenile), translation by Maria Polushkin published as *A Late-Born Child* (illustrated by Charles Robinson), World, 1971.

Other writings: *Sasha i Shura* (juvenile; title means "Sasha and Shura"), Detgiz, 1956; *Neobychainye pokhozhdeniia Sevy Kotlova* (juvenile; title means "The Unusual Adventures of Seva Kotlov"), Molodaia gvardiia, 1958; *Pis'ma i tele-*

grammy: rasskazy, Pravda, 1966; (editor) *Al'bom mestorozhdenii nefti i gaza neftegazonosnykh basselnov territorii RSFSR, USSR i kazakhskoi SSR,* Nedra, 1967; *Pozavchera i poslezavtra* (title means "The Day Before Yesterday and the Day After Tomorrow"), Pravda, 1974; *Sobranie sochinenii* (selected works), Detlit, 1979.

Also author of *Tridtsat' odin den'* (title means "1931"), 1950; *V odonom pionerskom lagere* (title means "In a Pioneer Camp"), 1954; *Bud' dostoinym synom rodiny,* 1955; *Zapiski El'viry* (title means "Elvira's Notes"), 1956; *Dva pocherka,* 1957; *O druzhbe serdets* (title means "On the Friendship of Hearts"), 1958; *Shkola na novom puti* (title means "The School on the New Path"), 1959; *Pogovorim o sovesti,* 1961; *V strane vechnykh kanikul* (juvenile; title means "In the Land of Holidays"), 1967; *"Ty menia slyshish'?",* 1968; *Povesti,* 1969; (with Viktor Iezekiilevich Viktorov) *Vse nachalos' s telegrammy,* 1969.

Uznaete? Alik Detkin (collection), 1970; *Veselye povesti,* 1971; *Vstretimsia zavtra,* 1971; (with others) *Geologicheskie formatsii Zapadnogo Predkavkaz'ia,* 1973; *Povesti i rasskazy,* 1973; *IAblonia vo dvore,* 1974; *Zvonite i priezzhaite,* 1974; *Deistvuiushchie litsa i ispolniteli* (juvenile; title means "Characters and their Performers"), 1975; *Geologiia i razrabotka neftianykh mestorozhdenii vostoka Volg-Ural'skoi provintsii* (geology on Russian oil in the Volga-Ural region), 1975; *Molodaia gvardiia* (young adult; based on the novel by Alexander Fadeev; title means "Young Guard"), 1975; *Parus-77* (juvenile), 1977; *Tretii v piatom riadu* (title means "Third Seat in the Fifth Row"), 1977.

Kolya pishet Ole, Olya pishet Kole (title means "Kolya Writes to Olya, Olya Writes to Kolya"); *Govorit sed'moi etazh* (title means "This is the Seventh Floor Speaking"); *Pro nashu sem'yu* (title means "About Our Family"); *A tem vremenem gde-to . . .* (title means "At the Same Time Somewhere . . ."); *Bezumnaya Evdokiya* (title means "Crazy Yevdikiya"). Also author of plays, including "Obratnyi adres" ("Return Address"), "Zvonite i priezzhaite!" ("Call and Visit Us!"), "Moi brat igraet na klarnete" ("My Brother Plays the Clarinet"), "Desyatiklassniki" ("High School Seniors"), and "Molodaya gvardiya" ("Young Guard"), first produced at the Central Children's Theatre in Moscow, spring, 1974.

SIDELIGHTS: A spokesman for Aleksin told *CA:* "Anatolii Aleksin addresses his stories to children and young people, as well as to those that are responsible for educating them. The main theme of his work is the problem of training and educating a young person. Aleksin appears every month on television in his very popular program 'Litsa druzei,' which is devoted to the problems of educating the upcoming generation of children.

"In his works, Anatolii Aleksin primarily talks about how a young person enters the adult world. His works affirm that being an adult is not a concept of age. Rather, it is a moral concept. Adulthood is not determined by the date of birth indicated in a passport, but by a person's actions and deeds. The children and teenagers in his stories reveal their spiritual maturity and high concepts of duty through noble deeds that are imbued with true humanism."

* * *

ALESSANDRINI, Federico 1906(?)-1983

OBITUARY NOTICE: Born c. 1906 in Recanati, Italy; died May 2, 1983, in Rome, Italy. Educator and journalist. Alessandrini served the Vatican in both journalistic and administrative capacities, including director of the press office from

1970 to 1976. He was also on the staff of the Vatican's daily newspaper *L'Osservatore Romano* and was director of the Catholic daily *Il Quotidiano*. Obituaries and other sources: *Chicago Tribune,* May 5, 1983.

* * *

ALGER, Philip Langdon 1894-1979

OBITUARY NOTICE: Born January 27, 1894, in Washington, D.C.; died September 24, 1979, in Schenectady, N.Y. Engineer, educator, and author of works in his field, including *The Nature of Induction Machines* and *The Human Side of Engineering.* During his long association with General Electric Company, Alger pioneered the use of electric motors. He taught at Massachusetts Institute of Technology. Obituaries and other sources: *New York Times,* September 26, 1979; *Who Was Who in America, With World Notables,* Volume VII: *1977-1981,* Marquis, 1981.

* * *

AL-ISSA, Ihsan 1931-

PERSONAL: Born March 10, 1931, in Basrah, Iraq; son of Abdulla Issa Bin Ali (in business) and Badria Nasser Mulla Omar; married wife, Birgitta Helena, 1964; children: Moosif (son), Moosa (son). *Education:* Higher Teachers Training College, Baghdad, Iraq, B.A., 1953; attended Baghdad University; American University of Beirut, M.A., 1959; University of London, Ph.D., 1962. *Office:* Department of Psychology, University of Calgary, 2920 24th Ave. N.W., Calgary, Alberta, Canada T2N 1N4.

CAREER: High school teacher of English in Basrah, Iraq, 1953-56; Hollymoor Hospital, Birmingham, England, psychologist, 1961; Netherne Hospital, Surrey, England, psychologist, 1962-63; University of Baghdad, Baghdad, Iraq, lecturer in psychology, 1964-66; University of Calgary, Calgary, Alberta, assistant professor, 1966-71, associate professor, 1971-80, professor of psychology, 1980—. *Member:* American Psychological Association, British Psychological Society (fellow).

WRITINGS: (Contributor) Hans J. Eysenck, editor, *Experiments in Motivation,* Pergamon, 1964; (editor) *Cross-Cultural Studies of Behavior,* Holt, 1970; *The Psychopathology of Women,* Prentice-Hall, 1980; (editor) *Culture and Psychopathology,* University Park Press, 1982; (editor) *Gender and Psychopathology,* Academic Press, 1982. Contributor to psychology journals. Member of editorial board of *Canadian Journal of Behavioral Science.*

WORK IN PROGRESS: Abnormal Psychology: An Inderdisciplinary Approach.

SIDELIGHTS: Al-Issa told *CA:* "I am a native Iraqi. I was brought up in the semi-literate village of Abul-Khassib near Basrah in the south of Iraq. I belong to the first generation to attend modern schools, but my early 'scientific' curiosity was more stimulated by the books on language, literature, astrology, witchcraft, and sorcery that I found at home than by my schoolwork. After studying English at Baghdad University, I joined the Department of Psychology at the American University of Beirut, Lebanon. In the 1950's, this department was active in both animal and cross-cultural research. For my M.A. thesis, I carried out an experimental investigation applying concepts from various avoidance learning to accident-proneness. This work stimulated my interest in learning theory, and

I decided to join the Institute of Psychiatry at the University of London to work in the learning laboratories of Hans J. Eysenck, where I did a Ph.D. thesis on eyelid conditioning. Later I worked as a clinical psychologist in England and as a lecturer at Baghdad University. Since 1966, I have been teaching in the Department of Psychology at the University of Calgary.

"My interest in the area of sex differences in mental illness started during the cultural revolution of the 1960's. I was stimulated by the finding that there is an excess of mental illness among women. Such research reports fascinated me because of their similarity to those revealing an excess of the use of psychiatric facilities among other minority groups in the United States; for example, blacks and new immigrants. As an Asian immigrant myself, I am personally involved in research on minority groups, including women, which should not be surprising given my background."

* * *

ALLEN, Frank 1939-

PERSONAL: Born March 22, 1939, in Evanston, Ill.; son of William Gordon and Eathal (Wallace) Allen; divorced. *Education:* University of Maryland, B.A., 1961, Ph.D., 1969; New York University, M.A., 1963. *Home:* 7 East Butler Ave., Ambler, Pa. 19002.

CAREER: Wilkes College, Wilkes-Barre, Pa., assistant professor of English, 1969-72; free-lance editor, 1972-74; Moravian College, Bethlehem, Pa., adjunct professor of English, 1974-82; Allentown College of St. Francis de Sales, Allentown, Pa., member of access program, 1982-83; Northampton County Area Community College, Bethlehem, adjunct professor of English, 1982; free-lance editor, 1982—. Gives poetry readings and workshops; guest on radio programs. *Military service:* U.S. Army, 1961-67.

WRITINGS: A Critical Edition of Browning's "Bishop Blougram's Apology," University of Salzburg, 1976; *Magna Mater* (poetry chapbook), Cumberland Journal, 1981. Contributor of poems, articles, and reviews to literature journals and literary magazines, including *Victorian Poetry, Snowy Egret, Common Ground, Philadelphia Poets, Literature East and West,* and *Insight.* Co-editor of *Fusion,* 1976-78; literary editor of *New Valley Press,* 1981-82.

WORK IN PROGRESS: A literary journal; rewriting a comic novel, *The Tablets;* poetry and criticism.

SIDELIGHTS: Allen told *CA:* "I think of myself as a man of letters, that somewhat old-fashioned role that summons up an image of Dr. Arnold of Rugby, Sainte-Beuve, and Chesterton, a kind of twentieth-century scholar-gypsy. In the mid-1960's I was educated in a trance, assuming that Henry Vaughn's 'The World' was the most inspired poem ever written and that with enough degrees, I'd have a guaranteed job. I was half in love with being inside literature as a person rereads *The Big Sleep* for the sheer delight of escape. Since my degrees are from factory-type universities, the best that can be said is that my regard for fantasy, myth, and folklore was never finally violated. Of course, I fell into adjunct teaching and did much of it in small eastern Pennsylvania colleges.

"My shock of recognition was that most American education does not entail the pursuit of truth or development of the mind but preparation for a vocation and inculcation of usable skills; consumerism has replaced citizenship in literature as well as society. Undaunted, I tried most species of writing, from limericks to a novel. My most fruitful reading was after I finished acquiring degrees. Only then did I realize that the essence of writing is that which was or is being done on the discordant, painful cutting edge of life.

"On the one hand, I'd like to make the past relevant to contemporary writing and to be worthy of it. Equally, I'd like to make writers today aware that there is a dynamic, accessible body of literature in the past. If the two, past and present, do not maintain a dialogue, I don't see how a nation's letters can help being peripheral and impermanent. Of course, each claims the other is deficient. The 'street poet,' overwhelmed by the pressure of his pulse, tries to articulate experience through a complaisant fervor. The literary elitist escapes to overrefined exegesis and fixed authority. Originality vs. truth. Intensification vs. clarity. Like a man or woman alone, neither completes a culture. Poetry without criticism is obscure anarchy; criticism without poetry is exclusive and sterile. Hence, I'm not overly concerned with what forms this perception takes, only that there be commerce between them. I'd just as soon be evaluating John Lyly's *Euphues: The Anatomy of Wit* as Allen Ginsberg's 'A Supermarket in California.' The letters of Keats seem just as relevant to my life as the poetry of H. D. [Hilda Doolittle]. The old woman in 'Guests of the Nation' who says 'Nothing but sorrow and want can follow the people that disturb the hidden powers' seems to shed much light on *The Aeneid.* I see nothing arcane about this, but I've come to accept that the world does.

"I suppose I most come alive when I'm writing speculative criticism and poetry. When any group of poets gets together, the dirtiest word usually uttered (sometimes for good reason) is 'critic.' True criticism is accountability, commitment, an informed sensibility—ultimately, knowledge in the form of literary action. I care about literature, and I don't want to see it abused, in the same way, I hope, that Edmund Wilson, Guy Davenport and thousands of contemporary writers and readers care about literature. If I say I'd like to reset America's literary watch, I hope it doesn't sound portentous but that is my vision. Because I woke up in a world I can't understand, I try to interpret it.

"I've taught writing, made indexes, helped young poets, taken workshops, given readings, edited little magazines, done reviewing, bought poetry volumes, all in trying to keep literature plastic, diversified, whole—not sheltered or pure, but as vivid as W. C. Williams's 'rotting apple on a porch rail.'

"Critically, I'd like to be inside the work as a biologist will analyze the nucleus of a cell or an astronomer will chart the position of the earth within the Milky Way. I'd like to be able to place where any work falls on the historical spectrum of artists who have more in common with one another than to the computer programmer down the street. It's perhaps a dreamy, luxuriant thing to go to bed trying to maintain a precarious balance between imagination and reality or to decide if after all poetry is the supreme fiction, but, to me, it's unavoidably necessary. In the future I hope to be able to find literary forms that can focus energies of the past and the present and bring them to bear in a hard, bright point, much like a blowtorch joins oxygen and acetylene to cut through iron."

BIOGRAPHICAL/CRITICAL SOURCES: Bethlehem Globe Times, March 30, 1974, August 7, 1978, September 7, 1979; *Forbes,* August 7, 1978; *Easton Express,* September 3, 1982; *Philadelphia Inquirer,* September 11, 1982.

ALLEN, Ivan, Jr. 1911-

PERSONAL: Born March 15, 1911, in Atlanta, Ga.; son of Ivan (in business) and Irene (Beaumont) Allen; married Louise Richardson, January 1, 1936; children: Ivan III, Inman, Beaumont. *Education:* Georgia Institute of Technology, B.S., 1933. *Home:* 3700 Northside Dr., Atlanta, Ga. 30305. *Office:* 221 Ivy St., Atlanta, Ga. 30303.

CAREER: Ivan Allen Co., Atlanta, Ga., in sales, 1933-46; president, 1946-57, vice-chairman of board of directors, 1957-61, chairman of board of directors, 1969—; mayor of Atlanta, Ga., 1961-70. Member of board of directors of Cox Broadcasting Corp., Equitable Life Assurance Society, Atlanta Braves (professional baseball team), Southern Bell Telephone Co., Mead Corp., Rich's Inc., and Southern Airways. Served on Georgia governor's staff, 1936; Georgia State Hospital Authority, treasurer, 1936; State of Georgia executive department, secretary, 1945-46; Greater Atlanta Community Chest, chairman, 1949. Trustee of Spelman College, Agnes Scott College, and Georgia Foundation; chairman of Police Foundation. Scout, scoutmaster, area president, regional committeeman, and member of national executive board of Boy Scouts of America. *Military service:* Served in U.S. Army, Infantry; became major.

MEMBER: National Stationary and Office Equipment Association (district governor, 1938-40; president, 1955-56), Georgia Tech Alumni Association (president, 1953-54), Georgia Chamber of Commerce (president, 1956-57; director), Atlanta Chamber of Commerce (president, 1961; director), Sigma Alpha Epsilon, Rotary Club. *Awards, honors:* Armin Maier Award from Rotary Club, 1952; Silver Beaver, Silver Antelope, and Silver Buffalo awards from Boy Scouts of America. Honorary degrees from Morehouse College, Spelman College, Emory University, Davidson College, Clark College, Atlanta University, Morris Brown College, LaGrange College, and Juniata College.

WRITINGS: (With Paul Hemphill) *Mayor: Notes on the Sixties,* Simon & Schuster, 1971.

SIDELIGHTS: Allen became active in the Atlanta business community in 1933, when he joined his family's office supply firm. Over the course of the next few years, while he was compounding the success of the business and his own personal fortune, Allen began his involvement with public service; in 1936 he became treasurer of the Georgia State Hospital Authority and served on the governor's staff. Following service in the U.S. Army during World War II, he spent two years as executive secretary to liberal Georgia Governor Ellis Arnall.

Allen first entered the political arena in 1954, when he made a brief run for the governorship of Georgia. Before he withdrew his candidacy, Allen assumed the then-traditional white Southern view of segregation as a way of life. Allen aborted his campaign after it became apparent that he could not garner enough support for a victory and returned his attention to the family business.

Over the course of the next few years Allen and other business leaders in Atlanta abandoned segregationist views, deeming them divisive and counterproductive to economic growth and community development. Allen emerged as a leading figure in the transformation of Atlanta into one of the nation's most vital commercial centers and was elected president of the city's chamber of commerce in 1960.

Allen defeated arch-segregationist Lester Maddox in the 1961 Atlanta mayoral primary by assembling a moderate coalition of blacks, who comprised nearly one-third of the electorate, and progressive whites. Allen's support of racial integration was reflected in the primary results: he received nearly all of the black vote and posted a landslide victory over Maddox. He was unopposed in the general election.

There was some friction between the city administration and Atlanta's black community during Allen's first term, largely the result of Forward Atlanta, a municipal building program Allen felt was essential for the continued development of the city. Blacks there thought expenditures for a convention center and a downtown expressway were excessive, and they also opposed the leveling of a black neighborhood to provide a site for an $18 million sports stadium.

Despite opposition from reluctant city department heads Allen managed to influence the integration of many of Atlanta's public facilities. He appeared before the Senate Commerce Committee in July, 1963, to testify in support of the Kennedy Administration's bill calling for the desegregation of public schools, the only major Southern white politician to do so. "I am firmly convinced," Allen told the Senate committee, "that the Supreme Court insists that the same fundamental rights must be held by every American citizen."

During Allen's second term Atlanta was rocked by the wave of racial unrest that swept America in the mid- and late 1960's. He went into the riot-torn areas at the height of the September, 1966, disturbance and personally appealed for an end to the violence. A strong believer in non-violent solutions to problems, Allen denounced Stokely Carmichael and other black militants as he had white segregationists who advocated the use of force to terrorize society into social change.

The social and economic growth Atlanta experienced under Allen's leadership are recounted in his political autobiography, *Mayor: Notes on the Sixties.* Jonathan Yardley, reviewing in *New Republic,* felt that although the book "wants to present itself as a casebook in model city government, [it] speaks more to the past than to the future. Not that either Mr. Allen or his accomplishments should be underestimated." A *New York Times Book Review* critic praised the account as "clear and unpretentious."

BIOGRAPHICAL/CRITICAL SOURCES: New York Times Book Review, August 8, 1971; *New Republic,* August 21, 1971.

*   *   *

ALLEN, John Stuart 1907-1982

OBITUARY NOTICE: Born May 13, 1907, in Pendleton, Ind.; died in 1982. Astronomer, educator, administrator, and author. In 1957 Allen began a thirteen-year tenure as founding president of University of South Florida. Previously, he had taught at Colgate University and at University of Florida. Among his writings are *Astronomy: What Everyone Should Know* and *Atoms, Rocks, and Galaxies: A Survey in Physical Science.* Obituaries and other sources: *American Men and Women of Science: The Physical and Biological Sciences,* 12th edition, Bowker, 1971-73; *Who's Who in America,* 41st edition, Marquis, 1980; *New York Times,* December 28, 1982.

*   *   *

ALLEN, Mary (Charlotte Chocqueel) 1909-

PERSONAL: Born September 6, 1909, in London, England; daughter of Frank Walter and Alice Maude (Chocqueel) Tyler;

married John de Gruchy Allen, October 20, 1934; children: David John, Maureen Ruth Murphy. *Education:* Attended Polytechnic of Central London, 1926-33. *Religion:* Christian. *Home:* Melita, West Leigh, Ship St., East Grinstead, Sussex RH19 4DU, England.

CAREER: Premium pupil of Walter Stoneman (photographer), England, and managing director of J. Russell & Sons (photographers), London, England, 1926-28; Herbert Lambert (photographer), Bath and London, England, retoucher, 1928-30; owner of photographic studio in Bromley, Kent, England, 1930-34; portrait photographer, 1934—. Teacher of photography; lecturer throughout Great Britain, 1950—. *Member:* Royal Photographic Society (associate member, 1931), Institute of Corporated Photographers (associate member, 1956; president of Sussex Centre, 1968-70; secretary of Sussex area, 1976—).

WRITINGS: Portrait Photography: How and Why, Focal Press, 1973, 2nd edition, 1977. Contributor to photography magazines.

WORK IN PROGRESS: Two books on portrait techniques in photography, publication by Focal Press; *Practical Portrait Photography,* publication expected in 1983.

SIDELIGHTS: Mary Allen wrote: "A portrait, to me, is not only a picture of surface beauty, but a vital, living essence of the hidden beauty that is revealed through the expression, mainly of the mouth and eyes. This beauty can shine through physically ill-proportioned features if the techniques of lighting and camera angle are used to minimize negative traits and emphasize the positive.

"I am continuously seeking fresh approaches to penetrate individual personalities, using a study of psychology and physiognomy together with the thoughts of both sculptors and painter-artists to achieve my aim. Paracelsus wrote, 'The outward man is not the real man. The real man is the soul allied to the Divine Spirit!' What a challenge for a portraitist! Each human being is different and each has something no one else has! This is the basis for the techniques that were described in my first book and that will be continued in the next ones."

*   *   *

ALPERS, Edward Alter 1941-

PERSONAL: Born April 23, 1941, in Philadelphia, Pa.; son of Bernard J. (a physician) and Lillian (a physician; maiden name, Sher) Alpers; married Ann Dixon (a student counselor), June 14, 1963; children: Joel Dixon, Leila Sher. *Education:* Harvard University, A.B., 1963; University of London, Ph.D., 1966. *Office:* Department of History, University of California, 405 Hilgard Ave., Los Angeles, Calif. 90024.

CAREER: University of California, Los Angeles, assistant professor, 1966-74, associate professor, 1974-82, professor of history, 1982—. Lecturer at University of Dar es Salaam, 1966-68, research associate, 1972-73; research associate at African Study Center, Universidade Eduardo Mondlane, 1976—. *Member:* International Conference Group on Modern Portugal, African Studies Association, British Institute in East Africa, Tanzania Society, Pacific Coast Africanist Association. *Awards, honors:* Ford Foundation grant, 1972-73; Gulbenkian Foundation grant, 1975; senior fellow of National Endowment for the Humanities, 1978-79; Fulbright scholar at Somali National University, 1980.

WRITINGS: *The East African Slave Trade*, East African Publishing House, 1967; (contributor) *The Historical Study of African Religion*, Heinemann, 1982; *Ivory and Slaves in East Central Africa: Changing Patterns of International Trade to the Late Nineteenth Century*, University of California Press, 1975; (editor with Pierre-Michel Fontaine) *Walter Rodney, Revolutionary and Scholar: A Tribute*, Center for Afro-American Studies and African Studies Center, University of California, Los Angeles, 1982. Contributor to history journals.

WORK IN PROGRESS: *The Transition to Colonial Rule in Eastern Tanzania, Circa 1840-1884; A History of Nineteenth-Century Muqdisho, Somalia*.

BIOGRAPHICAL/CRITICAL SOURCES: *Times Literary Supplement*, October 17, 1975; *American Historical Review*, October, 1976.

* * *

ALTER, Stephen   1956-

PERSONAL: Born in 1956 in India; American citizen born abroad. *Education:* Attended Wesleyan University. *Residence:* Uttar Pradesh, India.

CAREER: Writer.

WRITINGS: *Neglected Lives* (novel), Farrar, Straus, 1978; *Silk and Steel* (novel), Farrar, Straus, 1980.

SIDELIGHTS: Both of Stephen Alter's novels are set in India, where the American author was born and raised, and both books illuminate the lives of India's mixed-race descendants of the British raj. These people are, according to *Time*, "strangers in their own skins, exiles in their own country . . . half-castes yearn[ing] for some homeland that does not exist."

Neglected Lives, for example, is the story of Lionel, a young Anglo-Indian man in contemporary India, exiled to an isolated hill station in Debrakot because he had an affair with a Hindu girl. Like others who share his heritage, the young man is a victim of racism, Peter S. Prescott observed in a review for *Newsweek*. But, he qualified, "Alter seems to intend us to think of Lionel as a survivor . . . [who] will endure by bringing an Anglo-Indian bride to the hill and thereby reaffirming the life of the community." A *Time* review called *Neglected Lives* "one of the most unusual replies" to the questions E. M. Forster raised about British colonialism in *A Passage to India*. And Holly Eley noted in the *Times Literary Supplement* that *Neglected Lives* "showed an understanding of present day India as impressive as Ruth Prawer Jhabala's: from the first assured pages one could feel the oppressive limitations of caste barriers and of the English Victorian tradition."

Alter's second novel, *Silk and Steel*, focuses on the early nineteenth-century expansion of British landholdings in India and, according to John Calvin Batchelor of the *Village Voice*, "can be regarded as Alter's attempt to investigate the subjugation, organization, and dislocation of the Indian subcontinent by the British Empire." Reviewing the book in the *Washington Post*, novelist Joan Aiken suggested that Alter "made a shrewd choice of historical period" for his second novel. Through Alter's historical perspective, Aiken contended, "the reader is made aware of the inexorable, insensitive advance of the British across the continent that will presently toss them out again; history motivates the hero, that is its function." Eley, however, was not enthusiastic about Alter's second book, writing that "although universal themes (alienation, social change) are considered in *Silk and Steel*, there is no sense of universal vision."

Commenting that "it is difficult to recommend such a disappointing book," the critic continued, "we should view *Silk and Steel* as both an experiment and a catharsis, an unfortunate but necessary stage in the career of a gifted writer."

BIOGRAPHICAL/CRITICAL SOURCES: *New Yorker*, September 4, 1978; *Newsweek*, October 2, 1978, May 26, 1980; *Time*, October 30, 1978; *Saturday Review*, June, 1980; *Washington Post*, July 8, 1980; *Times Literary Supplement*, July 25, 1980; *New York Times Book Review*, July 27, 1980; *Village Voice*, August 20, 1980; *Chicago Tribune Book World*, September 28, 1980; *Books of the Times*, October, 1980.*

* * *

AMES, Noel
      See BARROWS, (Ruth) Marjorie

* * *

AMTER, Joseph A.   ?-1982

OBITUARY NOTICE: Died in December, 1982. Author of *Vietnam Verdict: A Citizen's History*. (Date of death provided by Crossroad Publishing Co.)

* * *

ANDERSON, Robert A(ndrew)   1944-

PERSONAL: Born November 7, 1944, in Morristown, N.J.; son of Andrew (in business) and Anna (Witkas) Anderson; married Rose Marie Wright (a dance rehearsal director with Twyla Tharpe Dance Foundation), December 18, 1977. *Education:* Yale University, B.A., 1966; also attended University of Chicago, 1969, and Columbia University, 1971-74. *Residence:* Walton, N.Y. *Agent:* Joseph Spieler, 410 West 24th St., New York, N.Y. 10011.

CAREER: Writer, 1969—. Also worked as a teacher, editor, and waiter. *Military service:* U.S. Marine Corps, 1966-69; received Purple Heart. *Member:* Authors Guild, Marine Corps Association.

WRITINGS: *Cooks and Bakers* (novel), Avon, 1982. Senior editor of *Mystery Monthly;* contributing editor of *Juris Doctor*.

WORK IN PROGRESS: *Service for the Dead*, a novel.

* * *

ANDREE, Louise
      See COURY, Louise Andree

* * *

ANDREWS, Laura
      See COURY, Louise Andree

* * *

ANDRIOLA, Alfred J.   1912-1983

OBITUARY NOTICE: Born May 24, 1912, in New York, N.Y.; died of cancer, March 29, 1983, in New York, N.Y. Cartoonist best known as creator of the "Kerry Drake" comic strip. Andriola, who assisted Milton Caniff with producing the "Terry and the Pirates" strip, also created the "Charlie Chan" cartoon strip. With Mel Casson, he co-edited *Ever Since Adam and Eve*. Obituaries and other sources: *The World Encyclopedia of*

Comics, Chelsea House, 1976; *Who's Who in America*, 42nd edition, Marquis, 1982; *New York Times*, March 30, 1983; *Chicago Tribune*, April 1, 1983.

* * *

ANDRZEJEWSKI, Jerzy 1909-1983
(George Andrzeyevski)

OBITUARY NOTICE—See index for *CA* sketch: Born August 19, 1909, in Warsaw, Poland; died of a heart attack, April 19, 1983, in Warsaw, Poland. Novelist. A former member of the Polish Communist party, Andrzejewski broke with the organization in 1957 after party officials banned a new literary magazine. In 1976 he helped found the Workers' Defense Committee (KOR) to assist the families of jailed workers. KOR members later served as advisers in the formation of the Solidarity trade union. A major author, Andrzejewski was best known for his critically acclaimed 1948 novel *Ashes and Diamonds*, which director Andrzej Wajda later made into a film. The novelist also wrote *Ciemnosci kryja ziemie*, published in the United States as *The Inquisitors*, *Idzie, skaczac po gorach*, published as *A Sitter for a Satyr*, and *Apelacja*, published as *The Appeal*. Obituaries and other sources: *New York Times*, April 21, 1983, April 27, 1983; *London Times*, April 21, 1983; *Washington Post*, April 21, 1983; *Chicago Tribune*, April 22, 1983; *Time*, May 2, 1983; *Newsweek*, May 2, 1983.

* * *

ANDRZEYEVSKI, George
See ANDRZEJEWSKI, Jerzy

* * *

APPLE, Michael W(hitman) 1942-

PERSONAL: Born August 20, 1942, in Paterson, N.J.; son of Harry and Russak Apple; married Rima Dombrow (a historian), 1965; children: Paul, Peter. *Education:* Glassboro State College, B.A., 1967; Columbia University, M.A., 1968, Ed.D., 1970. *Home:* 2013 Madison St., Madison, Wis. 53711. *Office:* Department of Curriculum and Instruction, University of Wisconsin—Madison, 225 North Mills St., Madison, Wis. 53706.

CAREER: University of Wisconsin—Madison, assistant professor, 1970-73, associate professor, 1973-76, professor of curriculum and instruction and educational policy studies, 1976—, Romnes Professor, 1979-84. *Military service:* U.S. Army, 1961-65; became sergeant.

WRITINGS: (Editor) *Educational Evaluation*, McCutchan, 1974; (editor) *Schooling and the Rights of Children*, McCutchan, 1975; *Ideology and Curriculum*, Routledge & Kegan Paul, 1979; (editor) *Cultural and Economic Reproduction in Education*, Routledge & Kegan Paul, 1982; *Education and Power*, Routledge & Kegan Paul, 1982; (editor) *Ideology and Practice in Schooling*, Temple University Press, 1983.

WORK IN PROGRESS: Research on the relationships among class, gender, and race in education.

* * *

ARNOLD, Edwin L(ester Linden) 1857(?)-1935

BRIEF ENTRY: Born in May, 1857 (one source says 1856), in Swanscombe, England; died March 1, 1935. British cattle breeder, forester, and author. Arnold wrote several travel and nature books, but he was best known for his fantasy and science fiction novels. Arnold's deep interest in Eastern philosophy, which the author acquired from his father, is reflected in his tale of reincarnation, *The Wonderful Adventures of Phra the Phoenician* (1890). Arnold's science fiction novel *Lieutenant Gullivar Jones: His Vacation* (1905) is said to have inspired the later Martian writings of Edgar Rice Burroughs. He also wrote *The Constable of St. Nicholas* (1894), *The Story of Ulla and Other Tales* (1895), *Lepidus the Centurion: A Roman of To-day* (1902), and *The Soul of the Beast* (1960). *Address:* 30 London Rd., Reigate, Surrey, England. *Biographical/critical sources: Who Was Who Among English and European Authors, 1931-1949*, Gale, 1978.

* * *

ARNOLD, Emily 1939-
(Emily Arnold McCully)

PERSONAL: Born July 1, 1939, in Galesburg, Ill.; daughter of Wade E. (a writer) and Kathryn (a teacher; maiden name, Maher) Arnold; married George E. McCully (a historian), June 3, 1961 (divorced, 1975); children: Nathaniel, Thaddeus. *Education:* Brown University, B.A., 1961; Columbia University, M.A., 1964. *Residence:* Chatham, N.Y. *Agent:* Harriet Wasserman Agency.

CAREER: Worked in advertising and as a free-lance magazine artist; illustrator of children's books, 1966—; writer, 1975—. Teacher at workshops at Brown University, Boston University, St. Clements, Cummington Community of the Arts, and Rockland Center for the Arts. *Member:* Authors Guild, Writers Community, Cummington Community for the Arts, Phi Beta Kappa. *Awards, honors:* Gold medal from Philadelphia Art Directors, 1968; National Book Award, 1969, for *Journey From Peppermint Street*; *Hurray for Captain Jane!* was named a showcase title by the Children's Book Council, 1972; awards for graphic excellence from the Brooklyn Museum and the New York Public Library, 1976, for *MA nDA LA*.

WRITINGS: A Craving (novel), Avon, 1982; *Help! From Camp Whatsis* (juvenile novel), Western Publishing, 1983.

Illustrator; under name Emily Arnold McCully: George Panetta, *Sea Beach Express*, Harper, 1966; Emily Cheney Neville, *The Seventeenth Street Gang*, Harper, 1966; Marjorie W. Sharmat, *Rex*, Harper, 1967; Natalie S. Carlson, *Luigi of the Streets*, Harper, 1967; Liesel M. Skorpen, *That Mean Man*, Harper, 1968; Barbara Borack, *Gooney*, Harper, 1968; Meindert De Jong, *Journey From Peppermint Street*, Harper, 1968; Barbara K. Wheeler and Naki Tezel, *The Mouse and the Elephant*, Parents' Magazine Press, 1969; Jan Wahl, *The Fisherman*, Norton, 1969; Pierre Gripari, *Tales From the Rue Brocca*, translated by Doriane Grutman, Bobbs, 1969; Virginia O. Baron, editor, *Here I Am* (anthology of poems by young people), Dutton, 1969; Janet Louise Swoboda Lunn, *Twin Spell*, Harper, 1969.

Jane H. Yolen, *Hobo Toad and the Motorcycle Gang*, World, 1970; Jeanne B. Hardendorff, *Slip! Slop! Gobble!*, Lippincott, 1970; Ruth A. Sonneborn, *Friday Night Is Papa Night* (Junior Literary Guild selection), Viking, 1970; Mildred Kantrowitz, *Maxie*, Parents' Magazine Press, 1970; Phyllis M. Hoffman, *Steffie and Me*, Harper, 1970; Jeanne B. Hardendorf, *The Cat and the Parrot*, Lippincott, 1970; Miska Miles, *Gertrude's Pocket*, Little, Brown, 1970; Betsy Byars, *Go and Hush the Baby*, Viking, 1971; Alix Shulman, *Finders Keepers*, Bradbury Press, 1971; Arnold Adoff, *MA nDA LA*, Harper, 1971;

Sam Reavin, *Hurray for Captain Jane!*, Parents' Magazine Press, 1971; Helen E. Buckley, *Michael Is Brave*, Lothrop, 1971; Seymour Simon, *Finding Out With Your Senses*, McGraw, 1971; Louise McNamara, *Henry's Pennies*, F. Watts, 1972; Arthur Miller, *Jane's Blanket*, Viking, 1972; Lynn Schoettle, *Grandpa's Long Red Underwear*, Lothrop, Lee & Shepard, 1972; Lee Bennett Hopkins, *Girls Can, Too!*, F. Watts, 1972; Jane Langton, *The Boyhood of Grace Jones*, Harper, 1972; Adoff, *Black Is Brown Is Tan*, Harper, 1973; Constance C. Greene, *Isabelle the Itch*, Viking, 1973; Kantrowitz, *When Violet Died*, Parents' Magazine Press, 1973; Mary H. Lystad, *That New Boy*, Crown, 1973; Thomas Rockwell, *How to Eat Fried Worms*, F. Watts, 1973; Anne Norris Baldwin, *Jenny's Revenge*, Four Winds Press, 1974; Langton, *Her Majesty, Grace Jones*, Harper, 1974; Miles, *Tree House Town*, Little, Brown, 1974; Marjorie Weinman Sharmat, *I Want Mama*, Harper, 1974.

Susan Terris, *Amanda, the Panda and the Redhead*, Doubleday, 1975; Sylvia Plath, *The Bed Book*, Harper, 1976; Ianthe Thomas, *My Street's a Morning Cool Street*, Harper, 1976; Rita Golden Geiman, *Professor Coconut and the Thief*, Holt, 1977; Miranda Hapgood, *Martha's Mad Day*, Crown, 1977; Elizabeth Winthrop, *That's Mine*, Holiday House, 1977; Adolf, *Where Wild Willie*, Harper, 1978; Betty Baker, *No Help at All*, Greenwillow, 1978; B. Baker, *Partners*, Greenwillow, 1978; Russel Hoban, *The Twenty-Elephant Restaurant*, Atheneum, 1978; Glory St. John, *What I Did Last Summer*, Atheneum, 1978; Nancy Willard, *The Highest Hit*, Harcourt, 1978; C. C. Greene, *I and Sproggy*, Viking, 1978; Sarah Sargent, *Edward Troy and the Witch Cat*, Follett, 1978; Kathryn Lasky, *My Island Grandma*, F. Warne, 1979; Barbara Williams, *Whatever Happened to Beverly Bigler's Birthday?*, Harcourt, 1979; Clyde Robert Bulla, *Last Look*, Crowell, 1979; Mirra Ginsburg, *Ookie-Spooky*, Crown, 1979.

Edith Thacher Hurd, *The Black Dog Who Went Into the Woods*, Harper, 1980; Pat Rhoads Mauser, *How I Found Myself at the Fair*, Atheneum, 1980; Tobi Tobias, *How We Got Our First Cat*, F. Watts, 1980; Jane Breskin Zalben, *Oliver and Allison's Week*, Farrar, Straus, 1980; Vicki Kimmel Artis, *Pajama Walking*, Houghton, 1981; Alice Schertle, *The April Fool*, Lothrop, 1981.

(Contributor) William Abrahams, editor, *The O'Henry Collection: Best Short Stories*, Doubleday, 1976. Also contributor of short stories to *Massachusetts Review*, *Dark Horse*, and *Cricket*.

WORK IN PROGRESS: An adult novel, *To the Careless;* several picture books for children.

SIDELIGHTS: Using the name Emily Arnold, the author wrote her first novel, *A Craving*, the story of an alcoholic artist's struggles with her failing marriage, her alienated children, the loss of her job, and also with herself, whom she calls an "accomplice" in the destruction of her sanity and composure.

According to *Newsday*'s John Gabree, *A Craving* "is an honest, engaging and moving accomplishment." And *Saturday Review*, noting Arnold's "compelling, clear-headed eloquence," deemed the novel a "noteworthy debut." Calling *A Craving* a "treat," Don Strachan in the *Los Angeles Times* claimed Arnold "treats her subjects with intelligence and sensitivity."

Though long involved in the production of children's literature, Arnold did not begin writing for adults until she was thirty-five. Her first project, a short story titled "How's Your Vac-

uum Cleaner Working?," took more than two years to complete. She told *CA:* "Writing is a second career, begun rather late, although I wrote a great deal as a student. But my first story and then my first book had to wait until I had a story demanding to be told."

BIOGRAPHICAL/CRITICAL SOURCES: Newsday, May 16, 1982; *Los Angeles Times Book Review*, June 6, 1982; *Washington Post*, June 20, 1982; *Los Angeles Herald Examiner*, July 4, 1982.

*   *   *

ASCH, Nathan   1902-1964

PERSONAL: Born July 10, 1902, in Warsaw, Poland; came to the United States, 1915; died of lung cancer, December 23, 1964; son of Sholem (a novelist) and Mathilda (Spira) Asch; married wife, Liesl (divorced, 1930); married Caroline Tasker Miles, 1939; children: David. *Education:* Attended schools in Poland, Switzerland, France, and Brooklyn and attended Columbia and Syracuse universities. *Home:* 63 Woodside Ln., Mill Valley, Calif. *Agent:* Maxim Lieber, 489 5th Ave., New York, N.Y. 10017.

CAREER: Writer, 1925-64. Worked on Wall Street during the 1920's. Special assistant with Works Progress Administration (WPA), Washington, D.C., 1937-39. Instructor at writing workshops. *Military service:* U.S. Army Air Forces, 1942-45; received Air Medal and Bronze Star.

WRITINGS—Novels, except as noted: *The Office*, Harcourt, 1925; *Love in Chartres*, A. & C. Boni, 1927; *Pay Day*, Brewer & Warren, 1930; *The Valley*, Macmillan, 1935; *The Road: In Search of America* (nonfiction), Norton, 1937; "Inland, Western Sea" (short story; recorded July 18, 1959), Folkways Records, 1978.

Also author of screenplays for Paramount Pictures, RKO General, and Metro-Goldwyn-Mayer (MGM), all during the 1930's. Work anthologized in *The Best Stories of 1925*, edited by Edward O'Brien, Small, Maynard, 1926. Contributor of articles, stories, and reviews to periodicals, including *Transatlantic Review*, *Nation*, *New Republic*, *Dial*, *New Yorker*, *Virginia Quarterly*, *Commentary*, *Yale Review*, *Harper's Bazaar*, *Redbook*, and *Forum*.

SIDELIGHTS: The oldest child of famed Jewish novelist Sholem Asch, Nathan Asch became a noted author in his own right during the 1920's. Though he lived throughout Europe and the United States as a child, the second-generation novelist settled in Paris to concentrate on his craft, surrounding himself with such expatriate writers as Josephine Herbst, Malcolm Cowley, Ford Maddox Ford, who assisted in the publication of Asch's first novel, and Ernest Hemingway, of whom Asch's work is reminiscent. By 1935, a *Books* critic labeled Asch "a prose writer of unusual discernment and vigor," but today critics and scholars remember him as a novelist who demonstrated an uncanny awareness of humanity and places.

Stylistically, Asch is close to Hemingway and Sherwood Anderson, who undoubtedly influenced his first novel, *The Office*, as well as *Love in Chartres*. Considered to be an autobiographical love story of a Paris-based writer and his wife, whom he leaves for greater artistic freedom, *Love in Chartres*, a *New York Times* reviewer noted, was written by "a craftsman who must have learned much from Sherwood Anderson and 'Dark Laughter.'" Similarly, the work reminded critics of Hemingway. As Herbert Gorman suggested in the *New York Herald*

Tribune Books, "It is . . . in a certain honest integrity of purpose, in a refusal to compromise with the terms of life, in an absolute freedom from sentimentality and in a disciplined compression that he [Asch] allies himself with Hemingway."

The foremost quality of Asch's writing is the author's sympathy for the human condition, his sensitivity to individuals. Asch mastered human psychology early in his career—in fact, in his first endeavor. *The Office*, which describes the reactions of brokerage employees when the stock market suddenly fails, reveals Asch's acute eye for characterization. The work consists of fourteen sketches, including three stories ("Gertrude Donovan," "Marc Kranz," and "The Voice of the Office") previously published in the *Transatlantic Review*, and several background scenarios. "His selections are amazingly apposite," said a *New York Times* reviewer. *The Office*, he added, "is fluid and plastic and enormously fresh and stimulating. The effect amply justifies the form."

Taken together, a *Boston Transcript* critic reported, the sketches illustrate "human nature under the grinding wheels of economic disaster." "The pettiness and tawdriness, together with the large puzzling tragedy of most human lives,—these aspects of commercial and financial existence are vividly revealed," a writer put forth in the *Saturday Review of Literature*. It is *The Office*'s "insight into human nature," he decided, that "lifts it above the ruck."

Likewise, *The Valley*'s miscellaneous sketches of decay in rural New England present an accurate picture of the people there. Here Asch draws poor, rugged, grubby farmers, some of whom are suicidal, insane, or alcoholic, all of whom are dying with their surroundings. "They are people, or ghosts, or shadows of them in a doomed place," Slater Brown submitted in the *New Republic*. Writing in the *New York Times*, R. C. Feld concurred, explaining that Asch portrays these "lives as they impinge on the analytic and sympathetic consciousness of the outlander." According to R. M. Gray's *Atlantic Bookshelf* review, "both the people and the Valley are comprehensible because their creator has detected the hidden human springs of their surface aberrations and has managed to combine in his style a manly force with poetic sensitiveness and beauty."

Following *The Valley*, *Pay Day*, a novel suppressed because of its realism, juxtaposes the exploits of Jim, a young clerk who dreams of liquor, cigars, women, and a career as a traveling salesman, with the execution of Sacco and Vanzetti. Jim is "an excellent study of the type," a *Nation* reviewer said. And a *New Republic* critic commented that "the shallowness of the pimpled clerk who revels while the persecuted Italians are electrocuted, seems more terrible in contrast to their burning."

Abandoning fictional characters, Asch transmits the animation of actual individuals in *The Road*, which chronicles his travels through the United States, picturing the desolation and the misery the writer observed. "The book is honestly written," Robert Van Gelder submitted in the *New York Times*, "sincere in its portrayal of the disinherited."

Moreover, *The Road* illustrates Asch's sharp sense of place. His scenarios of America reveal what the *Saturday Review of Literature*'s John Chamberlain termed the writer's "happy knack of hitting off people, places, and institutions in a few pungent phrases." Though Otis Ferguson suspected in the *New Republic* that Asch realized half-way across America that the nation would "remain as near and everywhere and inscrutable as the heavens," he emphasized that the travelogue still provides "a one-man show of revealing pictures."

Of course, Asch exhibits this sense of place in his novels as well. Having been employed on Wall Street, he knew the nuances of that area, so the setting of *The Office* "is New York as people generally conceive New York," the *Boston Transcript* reviewer assessed. Asch once again captures New York City in *Pay Day*. The subway scenes, the speakeasy, the mob in Times Square, among other incidents, all communicate the atmosphere and manners of the metropolis. *Pay Day* "is very detailed," the *Saturday Review of Literature* purported, "very life-like, very sordid. The outstanding impression left by the book is that of sheer physical disgust."

For *The Valley*, the novelist became, in the words of another *Saturday Review* critic, "a sympathetic outsider taking notes" on rural New England. Unlike many writers, Asch approached this dying area with caring and insight. He, the critic noted, "has more than a trace of the high pity which so many of his contemporaries have abjured with suspiciously shrill laughter." "He has understood the nature of the problem," Brown maintained, "for here there is no individual tragedy; it is the tragedy of rural New England. The soil is spent, drained of its strength by men who drained their own strength and that of their wives with the same silent ferocity. And now they have before them a rash of sumac spreading through their pastures, and a waste land."

According to Malcolm Cowley, Asch left five other novels unpublished at the time of his death in 1964. The whereabouts of the manuscripts, however, are unknown.

AVOCATIONAL INTERESTS: Raising Siamese cats, making furniture.

BIOGRAPHICAL/CRITICAL SOURCES: New York Times, October 11, 1925, December 6, 1925, October 30, 1927, May 11, 1930, September 8, 1935, June 6, 1937; *Saturday Review of Literature*, October 17, 1925, September 14, 1935, June 2, 1937; *New York Tribune*, October 18, 1925; *New York World*, November 13, 1925, April 29, 1930; *Boston Transcript*, November 14, 1925, November 5, 1927, September 14, 1935, June 5, 1937; *Bookman*, December, 1925, April, 1930; *New Republic*, December 16, 1925, November 23, 1927, June 16, 1930, October 16, 1935, June 30, 1937; *Literary Review of the New York Evening Post*, December 19, 1925.

Literary Digest International Book Review, January, 1926; *New York Herald Tribune Books*, October 23, 1927; *Springfield Republican*, November 6, 1927, September 8, 1935, June 9, 1937; *New York Evening Post*, November 12, 1927, February 22, 1930; *Times Literary Supplement*, November 17, 1927; *Nation*, March 12, 1930, July 3, 1937; *Books*, April 13, 1930, September 8, 1935, May 30, 1937; *Atlantic Bookshelf*, October, 1935; *Current History*, October, 1935; *Christian Science Monitor*, October 2, 1935; *Time*, May 24, 1937; *Cleveland Open Shelf*, July, 1937; *Booklist*, July, 1937; *Dictionary of Literary Biography*, Volume 4: *American Writers in Paris, 1920-1939*, Gale, 1980.

OBITUARIES: New York Times, December 25, 1964.*

—*Sketch by Charity Anne Dorgan*

*   *   *

ASHLEY, Sally   1935-

PERSONAL: Born January 30, 1935, in Minneapolis, Minn.; daughter of James M. (a business executive) and Ruth (Sloan) Ashley; married David Dolgenos, December 12, 1956 (divorced, 1979); children: Peter, Margaret, Carolyn, Thomas.

Education: Sarah Lawrence College, B.A., 1974; Columbia University, M.A., 1976. *Home and office:* 110 Riverside Dr., New York, N.Y. 10024. *Agent:* Elise Goodman, Goodman Associates, 500 West End Ave., New York, N.Y. 10024.

CAREER: Oliver & Rozner, New York City, executive recruiter, 1976-79; Career Connection, New York City, president and career counselor, 1979—. *Member:* Authors League of America.

WRITINGS: Connecting: A Handbook for Housewives Returning to Paid Work, Avon, 1982.

WORK IN PROGRESS: A biography of a twentieth-century journalist.

* * *

ASKIN, I(da) Jayne 1940-

PERSONAL: Born April 25, 1940, in Memphis, Tenn.; daughter of William Alexander and Lois Beryl (Griffen) Patrick; married Charles Robert Askin (in sales), June 13, 1959; children: Shan Robert, Molly Lynn. *Education:* Attended Orange Coast College. *Home:* 2730 Albatross, Costa Mesa, Calif. 92626.

CAREER: Writer. Member of Orange County Grand Jury, 1982-83, and Costa Mesa Friends of the Library.

WRITINGS: (With Bob Oskam) *Search: A Handbook for Adoptees and Birthparents,* Harper, 1982.

WORK IN PROGRESS: Legacies: Things We Leave Our Children, a guide to legal, financial, historical, social, and personal legacies, completion expected in 1984; *Two or More on the Farm,* a children's book; *Two or More in the Zoo, Two or More in the Water, Two or More in the Sky,* and *Two or More in the Wild,* all juveniles.

SIDELIGHTS: Jayne Askin wrote: "From childhood, I have always turned to the library to answer a question or give me direction. I was shocked and amazed when, as an adult, I could find nothing to help me (as an adoptee) search for my birth parents.

"With the publication of my book, *Search,* I discovered a new dimension to my love of libraries, that of a contributor. I hope to continue writing on other subjects and expand my writing to include fiction, children's stories, and television scripts.

"I wrote the children's book series because I have always been fascinated with terminology and language. I believe young children should be provided with literature that is entertaining but adds to their knowledge. Children are fascinated with animals. What they eat, where they live, how their babies are cared for and raised. Some animal group terminology is commonplace: a gaggle of geese, a school of fish. Most is not: a trip of goats, a bale of turtles, a drift of hogs. A friend and I were talking about what we call a group of snakes. The conversation progressed to other animals and we became intrigued. After several visits to the library we decided to write (I would write, she would illustrate) a children's book on this subject."

* * *

ATKINSON, William Christopher 1902-

PERSONAL: Born August 9, 1902, in Belfast, Northern Ireland; son of Robert Joseph Atkinson; married Evelyn Lucy Wakefield, 1928; children: one son, three daughters. *Educa-*

tion: Attended University of Belfast and University of Madrid. *Home:* 39 Manse Rd., Bearsden, Glasgow, Scotland.

CAREER: Armstrong College, Newcastle upon Tyne, England, lecturer in Spanish, 1926-32; University of Glasgow, Glasgow, Scotland, Stevenson Professor of Hispanic Studies, 1932-72, director of Institute of Latin-American Studies, 1966-72; writer. Visiting British Council lecturer in Latin America, 1946, 1960, and 1971; honorary professor at National University of Colombia, 1946; visiting professor at University College of Rhodesia and Nyasaland, 1963. Chairman of first Scottish delegation to U.S.S.R., 1954.

MEMBER: Royal Institute of International Affairs (head of Spanish and Portuguese sections and Foreign Research and Press Service, 1939-43), Modern Humanities Research Association (honorary secretary), Hispanic Society of America. *Awards, honors:* Carnegie Foundation fellowship for the United States, 1955; Rockefeller Foundation fellowship for Latin America, 1957; Commander of Portugal's Order of Prince Henry the Navigator, 1972.

WRITINGS: (Editor) Miguel de Unamuno, *Recuerdos de Ninez y de Mocedad,* Longman's Spanish Texts, 1929; *Spain: A Brief History,* Methuen, 1934; (with A. E. Peers and W. J. Entwistle) *A Handbook to the Study and Teaching of Spanish,* Methuen, 1938; *British Contributions to Portuguese and Brazilian Studies,* Longmans, Green, 1945, revised edition, British Council, 1974; (translator) Luis Vaz de Camoens, *The Lusiads,* Penguin, 1952, new edition, 1973; (translator) Diego de Torres Villarroel, *The Remarkable Life of Don Diego* (autobiography), illustrations by Harold Bennett, Folio Society, 1958; *A History of Spain and Portugal,* Penguin, 1960, new edition, 1973; (translator) Juan Rodriguez Fresle, *The Conquest of Granada,* illustrations by Bennett, Folio Society, 1961; (translator) Francisco Nunez de Pineda y Bascunan, *The Happy Captive,* Folio Society, 1978. Also co-author of *Spain: A Companion to Spanish Studies,* 1929, 3rd edition, 1956. Contributor to *Encyclopaedia Britannica.* Contributor to scholarly journals.

* * *

AUCHMUTY, James Johnston 1909-1981

OBITUARY NOTICE—See index for *CA* sketch: Born November 29, 1909, in Portadown, Northern Ireland; died October 16, 1981. Educator, historian, and author. During his lengthy career as an educator, Auchmuty taught at a number of universities, including University of Dublin, University of New South Wales, and University of Newcastle. Among his writings are *The U.S. Government and Latin American Independence, 1810-1830, Sir Thomas Wyse, 1791-1862, The Teaching of History,* and *John Hunter.* Auchmuty also edited *The Voyage of Governor Phillip to Botany Bay,* which appeared in 1970. Obituaries and other sources: *The Writers Directory: 1982-1984,* Gale, 1981; *International Authors and Writers Who's Who and International Who's Who in Poetry,* 9th edition, Melrose, 1982; *Who's Who,* 134th edition, St. Martin's, 1982.

* * *

AUGE, Bud
See AUGE, Henry J., Jr.

* * *

AUGE, Henry J., Jr. 1930(?)-1983
(Bud Auge)

OBITUARY NOTICE: Born c. 1930; died February 8, 1983,

in Roseville, Minn. Songwriter best known for his numerous country-western tunes, including ''Honky-tonk Town,'' ''Simple Simon,'' and ''I Keep Meeting Girls Like You.'' Auge's songs were recorded by performers such as Mel Tillis and Porter Wagoner. Obituaries and other sources: *Chicago Tribune,* February 12, 1983.

* * *

AULICINO, Armand 1920(?)-1983

OBITUARY NOTICE: Born c. 1920; died of cancer, May 16, 1983, in Pelham, N.Y. Playwright and author of cookbooks. Aulicino's plays include ''The Shoemaker and the Peddler'' and ''The Judgment of St. Francis.'' Among his cookbooks is *The New French Cuisine.* Obituaries and other sources: *New York Times,* May 18, 1983.

* * *

AUNTIE DEB
See COURY, Louise Andree

* * *

AUNTIE LOUISE
See COURY, Louise Andree

* * *

AUSTEN, Michael (Edward) 1951-

PERSONAL: Born July 2, 1951, in Stratford-on-Avon, England; son of Stanley George (a teacher) and Ruth (Pearce) Austen. *Education:* University of Leeds, England, B.A., 1973; University College of North Wales, certificate in education, 1976. *Residence:* Norwich, England. *Agent:* c/o Jonathan Cape Ltd., 30 Bedford Sq., London WC1B 3EL, England.

CAREER: Voluntary Service Overseas, Senegal, West Africa, teacher, 1969-70; Oulujoki Oskakeyhtio, Leppiniemi, Finland, teacher, 1974-75; Instituto Britanico, Oporto, Portugal, teacher, 1976-78; Bell School of Languages, Norwich, England, teacher of English as a foreign language, 1978-80; part-time teacher and writer in Norwich, 1980-82; full-time writer, 1982—.

WRITINGS: Love-Act, Harmony, 1982.

WORK IN PROGRESS: ''I am presently working on two novels, neither of which uses the same style, subject matter, or theme.''

SIDELIGHTS: Austen's first novel, *Love-Act,* is the story of a London call girl who becomes so involved in the fantasy world of a client that she begins to lose her own identity. Christopher Shemering described it as a ''psychologically provocative'' tale in his *Washington Post Book World* review, writing that Austen's ''twisted Cinderella story, with its subtext of grand irony, is diverting—a fairy tale with a cruel but erotic kicker.'' It is ''an interesting story,'' David Montrose agreed

in the *Times Literary Supplement,* replete with successful plot twists and interesting characters. Austen's ''*Love-Act* represents a commendable debut.''

Austen told *CA:* ''Although *Love Act* is the first work I have had published, I have been writing intermittently since I was a teenager—poetry, short stories, and one other complete novel. I find writing to be a self-generative process and (in my case) almost impossible to perform without a large block of free time. Thus in 1980, when I wished to have at least a break from teaching, I decided to try writing a novel again, living off my savings, and was very lucky to choose Cape as the publishers to whom to send it. *Love Act* was an attempt to examine the relationship that readers and writers have towards fiction and the erotic nature of the 'thriller' form.''

BIOGRAPHICAL/CRITICAL SOURCES: Times Literary Supplement, May 21, 1982; *Washington Post Book World,* August 1, 1982.

* * *

AUSTIN, Mary (Hunter) 1868-1934
(Gordon Stairs)

BRIEF ENTRY: Born September 9, 1868, in Carlinville, Ill.; died August 14 (some sources say August 13), 1934. American author. During her lifetime Austin published thirty-one books as well as numerous short stories, poems, essays, and articles. She is best remembered for her collections of regional sketches of the Southwest, including *The Flock* (1906), *Lost Borders* (1909), *The Land of Journeys' Ending* (1924), and *The Land of Little Rain* (1903), which firmly established the author in the literary milieu of her day. Also a playwright and a novelist, Austin's panoply of works reflected her wide-ranging interests in mysticism, folklore, feminism, Indian rights, and conservation. She published an autobiography, the highly praised *Earth Horizon,* in 1932. *Biographical/critical sources: Who Was Who in America,* Volume I: *1897-1942,* Marquis, 1943; *American Authors and Books, 1640 to the Present Day,* 3rd revised edition, Crown, 1962; *The Oxford Companion to American Literature,* 4th edition, Oxford University Press, 1965; *Dictionary of Literary Biography,* Volume 9: *American Novelists, 1910-1945,* Gale, 1981.

* * *

AYEARST, Morley 1899-1983

OBITUARY NOTICE—See index for CA sketch: Born October 15, 1899, in Courtwright, Ontario, Canada; died April 12, 1983, in Southampton, N.Y. Educator and author. Ayearst began his career at New York University in 1930 as an instructor in government. In 1962 he was made full professor and chairman of the department of government and international affairs. He was the author of several books, including *The British West Indies: The Search for Self-Government* and *The Republic of Ireland: Its Government and Politics.* Obituaries and other sources: *New York Times,* April 15, 1983.

B

BAACK, Lawrence James 1943-

PERSONAL: Born May 13, 1943, in Berkeley, Calif.; son of Ernest C. (in business) and Frieda (Baggley) Baack; married Jane Ellyn Williams, September 12, 1964; children: two. *Education:* University of California, Berkeley, B.A., 1964; Stanford University, M.A., 1970, Ph.D., 1973. *Office:* Pacific Gas and Electric Co., 77 Beale St., San Francisco, Calif. 94106.

CAREER: University of Nebraska, Lincoln, assistant professor, 1973-79, associate professor of history, 1979-80, vice-chairman of department, 1977-80, coordinator of International Affairs Program, 1979; Pacific Gas & Electric Co., San Francisco, Calif., educational activities director, 1980-82, assistant to vice-president of corporate communications, 1982—. Member of board of directors, Bay Area Science Fair, 1980—; chairman, education committee, San Francisco Chamber of Commerce, 1982—; member of board of governors, Economic Literary Council of California; member, Commonwealth Club of California. *Military service:* U.S. Navy, 1964-69; became lieutenant. *Member:* American Historical Association, Phi Beta Kappa. *Awards, honors:* Research fellowship from Historische Kommission zu Berlin, 1971, 1972, and 1976; research fellowship from National Endowment for the Humanities and National Science Foundation, 1979.

WRITINGS: (Editor) *The Worlds of Brutus Hamilton*, Tafnews, 1975; *Agrarian Reform in Eighteenth-Century Denmark*, University of Nebraska Press, 1977; *Christian Bernstorff and Prussia: Diplomacy and Reform Conservatism, 1818-1832*, Rutgers University Press, 1980. Contributor of articles to history journals.

WORK IN PROGRESS: An article on Antarctic policy of the United States.

SIDELIGHTS: Baack's third book, *Christian Bernstorff and Prussia*, is a study of Bernstorff's reign as Prussian foreign minister for the fourteen years between 1818 and 1832. The book was highly regarded by *Times Literary Supplement* reviewer David Blackburn, who praised Baack for his clear and skillful arguments, concluding that "this is a well-written and excellently documented study which will surely enter all standard bibliographies of the period."

BIOGRAPHICAL/CRITICAL SOURCES: Times Literary Supplement, November 14, 1980.

BABA, Meher 1894-1969

PERSONAL: Birth-given name, Merwan S. Irani; born in 1894 in Poona, India; died January 31, 1969. *Education:* Attended Christian high school.

CAREER: Mystic and teacher, c. 1913-69.

WRITINGS: (With Malcolm Schloss) *Ways to Attain the Supreme Reality*, Sufism Reoriented, 1952, reprinted, 1972; *God Speaks: The Theme of Creation and Its Purpose*, Dodd, 1955, revised edition, 1973; *Life at Its Best*, edited by Ivy Oneita Duce, Sufism Reoriented, 1957; *Listen, Humanity*, edited by Don E. Stevens, Dodd, 1957; *The Wisdom of Meher Baba*, [Charleston, S.C.], 1957; *Beams From Meher Baba on the Spiritual Panorama*, Sufism Reoriented, 1958; *The Everything and the Nothing*, Meher Baba Information, 1963; *Discourses*, three volumes, Sufism Reoriented, 1967.

Sparks From the Truth: From the Dissertations of Meher Baba, edited by C. D. Deshmukh, Sheriar Press, 1971; *Darshan Hours*, edited by Eruch Jessawala and Rich Chapman, Meher Baba Information, 1973; *God to Man and Man to God: The Discourses of Meher Baba*, edited by Charles Purdom, Sheriar Press, 1975; *The Mastery of Consciousness: An Introduction and Guide to Practical Mysticism and Methods of Spiritual Development*, edited by Allan Y. Cohen, Harper, 1977; *Not We But One: Meher Baba on Life, Living and Love*, edited by William Le Page, Sheriar Press, 1977; *Meher Miniatures for Daily Living*, edited by William C. Bodman, Sufism Reoriented, 1978; *The Narrow Lane*, edited by Le Page, Sheriar Press, 1979; *Treasures From the Meher Baba Journals*, edited by Jane B. Haynes, Sheriar Press, 1980. Also author with Adah Shifrin of *Meher Baba Is Love*, illustrated by Patricia Sargent, Sheriar Press.

BIOGRAPHICAL/CRITICAL SOURCES: New Yorker, June 21, 1969; Tom Hopkinson and Dorothy Hopkinson, *Much Silence: Meher Baba, His Life and Work*, Dodd, 1974; Ivy Oneita Duce, *How a Master Works*, Sufism Reoriented, 1975.*

*   *   *

BACKHOUSE, Janet 1938-

PERSONAL: Born February 8, 1938, in Corsham, England;

daughter of Joseph Helme and Jessie (Chivers) Backhouse. *Education:* Attended Bedford College, London, 1956-59, and Institute of Historical Research, London, 1959-62. *Office:* Department of Manuscripts, British Library, Great Russell St., London WC1B 3DG, England.

CAREER: British Library, London, assistant keeper of manuscripts, 1962—. *Member:* British Archaeological Association, Henry Bradshaw Society, Plainsong and Medieval Music Society, Bibliographical Society, Society of Art Historians.

WRITINGS: John Scottowe's Alphabet Books, Oxford University Press, 1974; *The Madresfield Hours,* Oxford University Press, 1975; *The Illuminated Manuscript,* Phaidon, 1979; *The Lindisfarne Gospels,* Phaidon, 1981; (contributor) Helen Wallis, editor, *The Boke of Idrography Presented by Jean Rotz to Henry VIII,* Oxford University Press, 1981. Author of exhibition catalogs. Contributor of articles and reviews to library and museum journals and newspapers.

* * *

BAGLEY, Desmond 1923-1983

OBITUARY NOTICE—See index for *CA* sketch: Birth-given name, Simon Bagley; born October 29 (some sources say October 23), 1923, in Kendal, England; died April 12, 1983, in Southampton, England. Author of mystery novels. At the time of his death Bagley was one of the most highly paid mystery novelists in the world. His first novel, *The Golden Keel,* was published in 1963, and together his fourteen novels have sold more than twenty million copies. A *London Times* writer observed that Bagley's extensive travels in such places as Africa, the United States, Antarctica, and Australia are reflected in "the authenticity of setting for which his novels were . . . noted." Among his works are *High Citadel, Running Blind, The Freedom Trap,* and *Flyaway.* Obituaries and other sources: *London Times,* April 14, 1983; *Los Angeles Times,* April 15, 1983; *New York Times,* April 15, 1983; *Chicago Tribune,* April 16, 1983; *Washington Post,* April 16, 1983; *Publishers Weekly,* May 20, 1983.

* * *

BAILEY, Harold (Walter) 1899-

PERSONAL: Born December 16, 1899, in Devizes, England; son of Frederick C. and Emma J. (Reichart) Bailey. *Education:* Attended University of Western Australia and Oxford University; received M.A. and D.Phil. *Office:* Queen's College, Cambridge University, Cambridge, England.

CAREER: University of London, London School of Oriental and African Studies, London, England, lecturer in Iranian studies, 1929-36; Cambridge University, Cambridge, England, professor of Sanskrit, 1936-67, professor emeritus, 1967—. Honorary fellow of Queen's College, London School of Oriental and African Studies, 1963, and of St. Catherine's College, Oxford, 1976.

MEMBER: Society for Afghan Studies (president, 1972-79), Philological Society (president, 1948-52), Royal Asiatic Society (president, 1964-67), British Academy (fellow), Danish Academy (corresponding member), Norwegian Academy (corresponding member), Academy of History and Antiquities (Sweden; corresponding member), Institut de France, Australian Academy of the Humanities (fellow). *Awards, honors:* Knighted; D.Litt. from University of Western Australia, Aus-

tralian National University, and Oxford University; D.D. from Victoria University of Manchester, 1979.

WRITINGS: Codices Khotanenses, Levin & Munksgaard, 1938; *Zoroastrian Problems in the Ninth-Century Books,* Clarendon Press, 1943; (editor) *Indoscythian Studies: Khotanese Texts,* Cambridge University Press, Volume I, 1945, Volume II, 1953, Volume III, 1956, Volume IV, 1961, Volume V, 1963, Volume VI, 1967, revised edition (includes Volumes I-III in one volume), 1969; (editor) *Khotanese Buddhist Texts,* Cambridge University Press, 1951; *Corpus Inscriptionum Iranicarum: Saka Documents,* Volumes I-VI, Lund, Humphries, 1960-67; *Saka Documents: Text Volume,* Lund, Humphreys, 1968; (editor) *Dictionary of Khotan Saka,* Cambridge University Press, 1979. Contributor to learned journals.

* * *

BAIRD, John D. 1941-

PERSONAL: Born May 9, 1941, in Glasgow, Scotland; son of Gerald (a land agent) and Easter (Clifton) Baird; married Eileen Ann Coumont, May 31, 1975; children: Eleanor, Caroline. *Education:* University of St. Andrews, M.A., 1963; McMaster University, M.A., 1964; Princeton University, M.A., 1967, Ph.D., 1970. *Office:* Department of English, Victoria College, University of Toronto, Ontario, Canada M5S 1K7.

CAREER: University of Toronto, Toronto, Ontario, lecturer, 1967-68, assistant professor, 1968-73, associate professor, 1973-81, professor of English, 1981—. Visiting fellow, Princeton University, 1973-74 and 1976-77. *Member:* American Society for Eighteenth-Century Studies, American Philatelic Society, Association of Canadian University Teachers of English (secretary-treasurer, 1980-82). *Awards, honors:* Canada Council grants, 1971 and 1972, fellowships, 1973-74 and 1981-82; fellowship from American Council of Learned Societies.

WRITINGS: (Editor) *Editing Texts of the Romantic Period,* Hakkert, 1972; (editor with Charles Ryskamp) *The Poems of William Cowper,* Volume I: *1748-1782,* Oxford University Press, 1980. Contributor of articles to literature journals.

WORK IN PROGRESS: An edition of Cowper's poetry, for Oxford University Press; research into the English novel as social commentary.

SIDELIGHTS: Editors Baird and Ryskamp include Cowper's poems to 1782 in their first volume of *The Poems of William Cowper.* According to C. J. Rawson, who reviewed the book for the *Times Literary Supplement,* "this first volume of the *Poems,* together with a first volume of *Letters and Prose Writings,* recently edited by Charles Ryskamp and James King, . . . gives us the best materials we have ever had for studying the earlier career of an enormously interesting and attractive poet." The critic concluded, "it is a pleasure to welcome this first volume."

Baird told *CA:* "I have conducted a life-long campaign against the use of 'john' as a euphemism for toilet."

BIOGRAPHICAL/CRITICAL SOURCES: Times Literary Supplement, January 2, 1981.

* * *

BAKER, Frank S. 1899(?)-1983

OBITUARY NOTICE: Born c. 1899; died March 21, 1983, in Yonkers, N.Y. Journalist. Baker began working for the *Yon-*

kers Herald Statesman in 1937 and became vice-president and general manager before retiring in 1970. Obituaries and other sources: *New York Times*, March 24, 1983.

*   *   *

BAKER, Lynn S.   1948-

PERSONAL: Born September 14, 1948, in St. Paul, Minn.; daughter of Robert Eugene (an orthodontist) and Marilyn (Harris) Baker; married Jean-Yves Pitoun (a screenwriter), August 22, 1981. *Education:* Attended Mills College (Oakland, Calif.), 1966-68; University of Minnesota, Minneapolis, B.A., 1970; Mayo Medical School, M.D., 1977. *Residence:* Los Angeles, Calif.

CAREER: Psychiatrist and author. Actress, singer, and dancer in all media including stage (female lead in "Hair," produced in Los Angeles, Calif., 1969-70) and film ("Billy Jack," released by Warner Bros., 1971, and "The Trial of Billy Jack," Warner Bros., 1974); University of California, Los Angeles, resident in psychiatry at Neuropsychiatric Institute, 1979-82; psychiatrist in private practice, 1982—. St. Paul (Minn.) Public Schools, lecturer in humanities program, 1967—, mass media consultant, 1971-72; lecturer at University of California, Los Angeles. Medical consultant to MENTA, Inc., 1978-79; media consultant to Wadsworth Veterans Administration Hospital, Los Angeles, 1978-80. *Member:* American Federation of Television and Radio Artists, American Society of Composers, Authors, and Publishers, Screen Actors Guild, Mayo Alumnae Association.

WRITINGS: (With Charles G. Roland and Gerald S. Gilchrist; also illustrator) *You and Leukemia: A Day at a Time* (for young people), Mayo Comprehensive Cancer Center (Rochester, Minn.), 1976, revised edition, Saunders, 1978; "Common Scents" (full-length play), produced in Rochester, Minn., at Rochester Civic Theatre, February, 1977; (contributor) A. Cherkin, C. Finch, K. Kharasch, and others, editors, *Physiology and Cell Biology of Aging*, Raven Press, 1979; (with K. Oota, T. Makinodan, and M. Iriki) *Aging Phenomenae*, Plenum, 1980; *The Fertility Fallacy: Sexuality in the Post-Pill Age*, Saunders, 1981.

Composer and lyricist of songs: "A Rainbow Made of Children," Snake in the Sun Music, 1971; "When Will Billy Love Me," Snake in the Sun Music, 1971; "A Little Song," Loveday Productions, 1973; "Golden Lady," Sunshine Snake Music Corp., 1974.

Contributor to proceedings of the Mayo Clinic. Contributor of articles and book reviews to professional and popular periodicals, including *New England Journal of Medicine*, *Health Care Education*, and *Mademoiselle*.

WORK IN PROGRESS: Researching a novel about medical research; researching a nonfiction book on biopsychiatry "on the effectiveness and desirability of obtaining informed consent from patients prior to their taking psychoactive medications (preliminary research results challenge some legislative assumptions)."

SIDELIGHTS: In the late 1960's, while attending Mills College in Oakland, California, Lynn Baker auditioned for a part in the San Francisco cast of the rock opera "Hair." The producer was so impressed he gave her the lead female role in the Los Angeles production. In the early 1970's, Baker had roles in two movies, "Billy Jack" and "The Trial of Billy Jack," but began to lose interest in show business. "The acting got boring,"

she told Debra Stone of the *St. Paul Sunday Pioneer Press*. "I guess I wanted to do something that was more real than that, where you spend a whole lot of time and . . . energy and in the end . . . instead of applause you see someone getting better."

Baker pursued a medical degree at the Mayo Medical School, where she became interested in the weak efforts made to educate patients and their families about patients' conditions. "A particular concern of mine is for children, and most recently for children having leukemia. This is a situation to tax almost any method of instruction," Baker told *Health Care Education*. The very word *leukemia* initially causes both patients and their families to block out any efforts made to explain the disease, Baker discovered. She thought a book containing the information in an understandable, illustrated format would serve a special purpose because the book "can be consulted. For example, the patient may be told that he's soon to start a new medication. The new medication is covered in the book, and can be read about at that time."

In the planning stages of the book *You and Leukemia*, Baker envisioned it "as a loose-leaf binder kind of thing. We would insert pages . . . as the doctor prescribed them—so that the resulting book was a custom effort—for that particular patient." Eventually, Baker explained to *Health Care Education*, the loose-leaf approach was abandoned "because the patient may discover that you've left out something. That you have 'edited' his book. It gives rise to suspicions that you are concealing something."

Another of Baker's concerns resulted in the book *The Fertility Fallacy: Sexuality in the Post-Pill Age*. Elaine Kendall described in her review of the book in the *Los Angeles Times* that "the issue here is human fertility in an era when conception can be regulated biologically as well as behaviorally. . . . Entrenched attitudes about sex and reproduction, however, lag far behind these advances." Since "neither law nor nostalgia will whisk us back to a less complicated age[,] we have no choice but to create a revised and workable morality for the present and future." In Kendall's opinion, "Baker cannot offer that [morality], but she does interpret the available information so that we may begin to cope with the job on our own." Kendall pronounced *The Fertility Fallacy* "original, provocative and intellectually adventurous[;] the book exceeds expectations and explores some challenging and uncharted territory."

BIOGRAPHICAL/CRITICAL SOURCES: St. Paul Dispatch, January 12, 1970; *Minneapolis Tribune*, April 22, 1973, July 17, 1981; *Rochester* (Minn.) *Post-Bulletin*, January 4, 1977; *Health Care Education*, December, 1978; *St. Paul Sunday Pioneer Press*, July 12, 1981; *Los Angeles Times*, August 27, 1981.

*   *   *

BAKER, Robert Andrew   1910-

PERSONAL: Born December 22, 1910, in St. Louis, Mo.; son of William and Grace (Wolfenbarger) Baker; married Fredona C. McCaulley, June 5, 1939; children: Colleen Kay, Robert Andrew. *Education:* Baylor University, A.B., 1939; Southwestern Baptist Theological Seminary, Th.M., 1942, Th.D., 1944; Yale University, Ph.D., 1947. *Home:* 1801 West Boyce St., Fort Worth, Tex. 76115. *Office:* School of Theology, Southwestern Baptist Theological Seminary, P.O. Box 22006, Fort Worth, Tex. 76122.

CAREER: Operative of U.S. Secret Service, 1932-36. Ordained Baptist minister, 1939; pastor of Baptist churches in Texas, 1939-42; Southwestern Baptist Theological Seminary, Fort Worth, Tex., professor of church history, 1942-81. Pastor of Baptist churches in Mt. Calm, Tex., 1942-43, and Dallas, Tex., 1949-52. Guest member of faculty at Southern Seminary, Louisville, Ky., summers, 1949, 1975, and New Orleans Seminary, summer, 1961; Carver-Barnes Lecturer at Southeastern Baptist Theological Seminary, 1967. Chairman of Southern Baptist Historical Commission, 1968-71, 1972-76.

MEMBER: American Society for Church History, American Association of Theological Schools, Southern Baptist Historical Society, Texas Baptist Historical Society (president, 1977). *Awards, honors:* LL.D. from Baylor University, 1981; distinguished service award from Southern Baptist Historical Commission, 1982.

WRITINGS: J. B. Tidwell Plus God, Broadman, 1946, revised edition, 1949; *Relations Between Northern and Southern Baptists,* Seminary Hill Press, 1948, revised edition, edited by Edwin S. Gaustad, 1954, reprinted, Arno, 1980; *The Baptist March in History,* Convention Press, 1958; (editor with Davis Woolley) *Baptist Advance,* Broadman, 1958; *A Summary of Christian History,* Broadman, 1959.

(Contributor) H. C. Brown, editor, *Southwestern Sermons,* Broadman, 1960; (contributor) Brown and Charles P. Johnson, editors, *J. Howard Williams,* Naylor Press, 1963; (contributor) James Leo Garrett and Jeremiah Vardaman, editors, *The Teacher's Yoke: Studies in Memory of Henry Trantham,* Baylor University Press, 1964; *The First Southern Baptists,* Broadman, 1966; *The Story of the Sunday School Board,* Convention Press, 1966; (contributor) Brown, editor, *Chapel Messages,* Baker Book, 1966; *A Baptist Source Book,* Broadman, 1966; *The Thirteenth Check: The Jubilee History of the Annuity Board of the Southern Baptist Convention, 1918-1968,* Broadman, 1968.

The Blossoming Desert: A Concise History of Texas Baptists, Word, Inc., 1970; (with James Coggin) *J. D. Wadley: A Tree God Planted,* Evans (Fort Worth, Tex.), 1971; *The Southern Baptist Convention and Its People, 1607-1972,* Broadman, 1974; *Her Walls Before Thee Stand: Centennial Story, First Baptist Church, Texarkana, Texas,* Evans, 1977; (with Paul J. Craven) *Adventures in Faith: First Baptist Church, Charleston, South Carolina, 1682-1982,* Broadman, 1982; *Tell the Generations Following: History of the Southwestern Baptist Theological Seminary, 1908-1983,* Broadman, 1983.

Contributor to *Encyclopedia of Southern Baptists.* Contributor to scholarly journals and church magazines. Member of editorial board of *Encyclopedia of Southern Baptists.*

*   *   *

BAKER, Victor Richard 1945-

PERSONAL: Born February 19, 1945, in Waterbury, Conn.; son of Victor A. and Doris E. (Day) Baker; married Pauline Marie Heaton (an artist), June 10, 1967; children: Trent Heaton, Theodore William. *Education:* Rensselaer Polytechnic Institute, B.S., 1967; University of Colorado, Ph.D., 1971. *Home:* 6164 East Paseo Cimarron, Tucson, Ariz. 85715. *Office:* Department of Geosciences, University of Arizona, Tucson, Ariz. 85721.

CAREER: U.S. Geological Survey, Albany, N.Y., and Denver, Colo., geophysicist in hydrology, 1967-69; City of Boulder, Boulder, Colo., city geologist, 1969-71; University of

Texas, Austin, assistant professor, 1971-76, research scientist at Bureau of Economic Geology, 1973, associate professor of geological sciences, 1976-81; University of Arizona, Tucson, professor of geosciences, 1981—, and professor of planetary sciences, 1982—. Visiting fellow at Australian National University, 1979-80. *Military service:* U.S. Army Reserve, active duty, 1967-73; became captain. *Member:* International Association of Sedimentologists, Geological Society of America (fellow), American Geophysical Union, American Association for the Advancement of Science, American Quaternary Association, Society of Sigma Xi. *Awards, honors:* Fulbright-Hays Senior Research Scholar, 1979-80.

WRITINGS: Paleohydrology and Sedimentology of Lake Missoula: Flooding in Eastern Washington, Geological Society of America, 1973; *The Channeled Scabland,* National Aeronautics and Space Administration, 1978; *Surficial Geology Building With the Earth,* Wiley, 1981; (editor) *Catastrophic Flooding: The Origin of the Channeled Scabland,* Dowden, 1981; *The Channels of Mars,* University of Texas Press, 1982. Contributor of articles to professional journals, including *Nature, Science, Geology, Journal of Geology, Quaternary Research, Journal of Geophysical Research, American Journal of Science,* and *Journal of Sedimentary Petrology.*

WORK IN PROGRESS: Flood Geomorphology; research on the geology of planet Mars, the effects of floods on the landscape, natural hazards (floods, volcanism, landslides), and geological processes on planetary surfaces.

SIDELIGHTS: Baker's *The Channels of Mars* is an analysis of existing information about the history and nature of the surface of Mars. Using high-definition photographs transmitted by six American spacecraft dispatched to Mars between 1965 and 1980, Baker traced the development of major surface features of the planet. He also compares this development with developments on Earth and the Moon, noting that study of Mars is valuable for understanding planetary features of Earth as well.

"The authoritative nature of [*The Channels of Mars*] is beyond question," wrote Bernard Lovell in the *New York Review of Books.* And praising the "vast and impressive array" of "splendidly reproduced photographs" that are "the predominant interest" of the book, Lovell asserted that the reader "is left in astonishment at the special conditions that allowed life to develop on Earth and not on our neighboring planet."

Baker told *CA:* "From the scientific exploration of other planets we are learning revolutionary new concepts of earth history. The comparative study of geological processes on the inner planets of the solar system will transform the earth sciences in the next decade. Also, the very detailed study of stratigraphy in recent sediments is now allowing the assessment of process magnitudes and frequencies, as well as the evaluation of natural hazards."

BIOGRAPHICAL/CRITICAL SOURCES: New York Review of Books, June 10, 1982.

*   *   *

BALANCHINE, George 1904-1983

OBITUARY NOTICE: Birth-given name, Georgi Melitonovitch Balanchivadze; name changed, c. 1926; born January 9, 1904, in St. Petersburg, Russia (now Leningrad, U.S.S.R.); died of cardiac arrest following pneumonia, April 30, 1983, in New York, N.Y. Ballet dancer, choreographer, and author. Balanchine was probably the most influential figure in twentieth-century ballet. His first important works, including "Apollo" and "The Prodigal Son," were choreographed for Serge Diaghilev's Ballet Russe in the late 1920's, and, though brief, they adhered to the tradition of narrative dance. After Diaghilev's death, Balanchine worked with the Royal Danish Ballet and established Les Ballets. Performances by the latter company prompted ballet enthusiast Lincoln Kirstein to invite Balanchine to America, and together they established the School of American Ballet in 1934. For the next fourteen years Balanchine developed his neoclassical, or nonnarrative, style, in which technique and the physical expression of a given score constituted the sole significance of a work. Among his best-known pieces from this period are "Ballet Imperial," set to music by Tchaikovsky, and "Concerto Barocco," with music by J. S. Bach. He also collaborated with Igor Stravinsky, for whose music he provided some of his finest choreography. In 1948 he established, with Kirstein, the New York City Ballet, which became the prime vehicle for Balanchine's work. The company introduced many of his greatest pieces, including "Divertimento No. 15" and "Mozartiana." With this company, Balanchine also reworked classics such as "Don Quixote," in which he performed the title role, and helped develop or refine the talents of dancers such as Gelsey Kirkland, Suzanne Farrell, and Peter Martins. Along with choreographer Jerome Kern, Martin assumed leadership of the company in 1983 after Balanchine was hospitalized with neurological disorders. The famed choreographer, who declared, "I have no successor," died soon afterward. He wrote *Balanchine's Complete Stories of the Great Ballets.* Obituaries and other sources: *New York Times,* May 1, 1983; *Chicago Tribune,* May 1, 1983; *Los Angeles Times,* May 1, 1983; *Newsweek,* May 9, 1983; *Time,* May 9, 1983.

*   *   *

BALMONT, Konstantin (Dmitriyevich)   1867-1943

BRIEF ENTRY: Born July 15, 1867, in Vladimir Oblast, Russia (now U.S.S.R.); died in 1943 in Paris, France. Russian poet. Balmont was one of the symbolist movement's foremost practitioners in turn-of-the-century Russia. The son of a nobleman, Balmont broke from his aristocratic heritage at an early age. He was temporarily suspended from secondary school for promoting revolution. Later, while studying the French Revolution at the University of Moscow, he led student protests. At age twenty-two, suffering from emotional instability, Balmont hurled himself from a window in a futile attempt at suicide. In 1890 he published his first volume, *Sbornik stikhotvoreni* (title means "Collection of Verses"), and soon afterward began supporting the symbolists. Throughout the remainder of the decade, Balmont's verse evolved from the somber tone of both his first collection and *Pod severnym nebom* (title means "Under Northern Skies"; 1894) into the overtly symbolic and romantic poems of *V bezbrezhnosti* (title means "In the Infinite"; 1895) and *Tishina* (title means "Quietude"; 1898). He achieved further popularity in the early 1900's when he abandoned the melancholy quality of his earlier work to adopt a Nietzschean stance, notably in collections such as *Tolko lyubov* (title means "Love Alone"; 1903) and *Liturgiya krasoty* (title means "Liturgy of Beauty"; 1905). Following the publication of several poems espousing revolution, Balmont was obliged to leave Russia in 1905. He traveled throughout Europe and the Orient before returning home in 1913. Four years later he enthusiastically supported the Russian Revolution. His zeal was short-lived, however, and he eventually departed for Paris. There

Balmont spent the remainder of his life. *Biographical/critical sources: Columbia Dictionary of Modern Literature,* Columbia University Press, 1947; *The Reader's Encyclopedia,* 2nd edition, Crowell, 1965; *Everyman's Dictionary of European Writers,* Dutton, 1968; *The Penguin Companion to European Literature,* McGraw, 1969; *Cassell's Encyclopaedia of World Literature,* revised edition, Morrow, 1973; *Twentieth-Century Literary Criticism,* Volume 11, Gale, 1983.

*   *   *

BAMBER, Linda   1945-

PERSONAL: Born September 25, 1945, in Washington, D.C.; daughter of Alfred G. (a foreign service officer) and Edythe (Auster) Vigderman; married Frederick Bamber (a venture capitalist), August 20, 1967. *Education:* Vassar College, B.A., 1966; Columbia University, M.A., 1967; Tufts University, Ph.D., 1974. *Politics:* "Feminist." *Residence:* Lexington, Mass. *Office:* Department of English, Tufts University, Medford, Mass. 02155.

CAREER: Tufts University, Medford, Mass., assistant professor, 1975-80, associate professor of English, 1980—. *Member:* Modern Language Association of America. *Awards, honors:* Woodrow Wilson fellowship, 1966.

WRITINGS: Comic Men, Tragic Women: A Study of Gender and Genre in Shakespeare, Stanford University Press, 1982. Contributor of articles and reviews to magazines, including *Nation, Partisan Review, Working Papers, Ploughshares,* and *Victorian Studies.*

WORK IN PROGRESS: Research on fiction written by women.

*   *   *

BARABAS, Steven   1904-1983

OBITUARY NOTICE—See index for *CA* sketch: Born August 7, 1904, in Passaic, N.J.; died May 22, 1983, in Winfield, Ill. Theologian, educator, editor, and author. In 1949, after serving for a number of years as a pastor of a Presbyterian church in Ballston Spa, N.Y., Barabas became a professor of theology at Wheaton College in Illinois. He held that post for the next twenty-five years. Barabas was a writer and editor for Zondervan's *Pictorial Bible Dictionary* and the author of *So Great Salvation: The History and Message of the Keswick Convention.* He also edited the religious quarterly *Peniel.* Obituaries and other sources: *Chicago Tribune,* May 26, 1983.

*   *   *

BARANOV, Alexander A.   1931(?)-1983

OBITUARY NOTICE: Journalist. Baranov was chief foreign editor of the Soviet news agency Tass, with which he had been associated for thirty years. Obituaries and other sources: *Chicago Tribune,* May 13, 1983.

*   *   *

BAREHAM, Terence   1937-

PERSONAL: Born October 17, 1937, in Clacton-on-Sea, England; son of Thomas William (a civil engineer) and Margaret Hilda (a teacher; maiden name, Sutherwood) Bareham; married, 1958; children: Simon Alastair, Tristan, Gareth. *Education:* Lincoln College, Oxford, B.A. (with honors), 1962; New University of Ulster, D.Phil., 1977. *Office:* Department of English, New University of Ulster, Coleraine, Northern Ireland.

CAREER: University of Rhodesia (now Zimbabwe), Salisbury, lecturer in English, 1963-67; University of York, Heslington, England, lecturer in English, 1967-68; New University of Ulster, Coleraine, Northern Ireland, senior lecturer in English, 1968—. *Military service:* British Army, 1957-59; became second lieutenant. *Awards, honors:* Nuffield Foundation grants, 1975 and 1983.

WRITINGS: George Crabbe: A Critical Study, Vision Press, 1977; (with S. J. Gatrell) *A Bibliography of George Crabbe,* Dawson, 1978; (editor and contributor) *Anthony Trollope* (criticism), Vision Press, 1980; *Robert Bolt's "A Man for All Seasons"* (criticism), Longman, 1980; *T. S. Eliot's "Murder in the Cathedral"* (criticism), Longman, 1981; (editor) *The Barsetshire Novels of Trollope,* Macmillan, 1983.

WORK IN PROGRESS: A critical biography of Charles Lever; an edition of Thomas Hardy's *The Trumpet Major,* for Oxford University Press.

SIDELIGHTS: Bareham told *CA:* "I am especially interested in the teaching of dramatic literature by practical means and have pioneered special techniques for this while being notably supported by the Nuffield Foundation. I am essentially a practical person rather than a theoretician, and drama offers me the chance to combine creative with organizational concerns. As an amateur (I hope in the best sense of the word), my principal concern as a university teacher is to pass on to others my own love of literature as enjoyment quite as much as material for intellectual dissection. For this reason, I admire Trollope as an author genuinely appreciated by many non-academic readers, although I also feel strongly that his *quality* as a writer is undervalued by many of the so-called pundits."

*   *   *

BARON, J. W.
  See KRAUZER, Steven M(ark)

*   *   *

BARR, Anthony   1921-
  (Tony Barr)

PERSONAL: Original name, Morris Yaffe; name legally changed in 1948; born March 14, 1921, in St. Louis, Mo.; son of Isidore (a scrap dealer) and Pearl (Brown) Yaffe; married Barbara Barr (a school administrator), February 24, 1944; children: Suza, John Yaffe, David Yaffe. *Education:* Washington University, St. Louis, Mo., B.S., 1942. *Office:* Film Actors Workshop, 5004 Vineland, North Hollywood, Calif. 91601.

CAREER: Theatre Guild, New York City, actor and stage manager, 1944-46; Katherine Dunham Dancers, New York City and on tour in the United States and Mexico, stage manager, 1946-47; actor in Hollywood, Calif., 1947-52; CBS-TV, Hollywood, stage manager, 1952-54, associate director of "Climax," 1954-55, associate producer of "Climax," 1955-58, associate producer of "Playhouse 90," 1958-60; ABC-TV, Century City, Calif., director of "The Ben Alexander Show," 1961-62; Metro-Goldwyn-Mayer, Culver City, Calif., co-producer of film, "Dime With a Halo," 1962; ABC-TV, program executive, 1963-76, vice-president of current prime-time series, 1973-76; CBS-TV, vice-president of current dramatic program production, 1976—. Operator of Film Actors Workshop,

1960—. *Member:* Academy of Television Arts and Sciences (member of board of governors, 1976-78).

WRITINGS: (Under name Tony Barr) *Acting for the Camera,* Allyn & Bacon, 1981.

WORK IN PROGRESS: "Various screenplays."

SIDELIGHTS: As an actor in California, Barr appeared in sixteen feature films and several early television films. In the fifties, as a stage manager for Columbia Broadcasting System, he was associated with such popular series as "The Burns and Allen Show," "The Jack Benny Show," "The Alan Young Show," and "My Friend Irma."

He joined ABC-TV in 1963, and worked as a program executive for "Ben Casey," "Peyton Place," "Mod Squad," "The Courtship of Eddie's Father," and "Love, American Style." As vice-president of current prime-times series, he supervised all the creative elements of "Marcus Welby, M.D.," "The Rookies," "Baretta," and "The Six-Million-Dollar Man."

Barr emphasizes, however, that his real "labor of love" has been the Film Actors Workshop, an acting studio. His dedication to teaching young actors led him to realize that acting for films is completely different from acting on stage, and he has devoted the workshop entirely to adapting existing stage techniques and talents to fit the needs of the film actor.

Barr commented: "The idea for my book came because there were no books available that dealt specifically with acting for the camera. Virtually all existing books on acting were theater-oriented, and the camera makes significantly different demands.

"I also felt that most books on acting were far too theoretical and complicated—too abstract to be of real value to the struggling actor. I wanted to take the mystique away from the acting process, and give the actor some guidance in simple, direct, pragmatic terms—and to make him understand that simplicity is the key word in all acting, but especially in acting before the camera."

AVOCATIONAL INTERESTS: Golf, photography.

*   *   *

BARR, Tony
  See BARR, Anthony

*   *   *

BARRETT, Susan (Mary)   1938-

BRIEF ENTRY: Born in 1938 in Plymouth, England. British copywriter and author. Barrett has worked as an advertising copywriter for McCann-Erickson, Pritchard Wood & Partners, Greenlys, and Waddicor Clark Wilkinson. Her novels include *Louisa* (Delacorte, 1969), *Moses* (M. Joseph, 1970), *Noah's Ark* (M. Joseph, 1971), *Private View* (M. Joseph, 1972), *Rubbish* (M. Joseph, 1974), and *The Beacon* (Hamish Hamilton, 1981). *Biographical/critical sources: Observer,* April 18, 1971; *Times Literary Supplement,* November 3, 1972, May 22, 1981.

*   *   *

BARRIER, (John) Michael   1940-

PERSONAL: Born June 15, 1940, in Little Rock, Ark.; son of Jack A., Jr. (in business) and Flora (Canant) Barrier; married Phyllis Mathews (a nutritionist), November 6, 1970. *Educa-*

tion: Northwestern University, B.S., 1962; University of Chicago, J.D., 1965. *Religion:* Presbyterian. *Home:* 226 North St. Asaph St., Alexandria, Va. 22314.

CAREER: Arkansas Gazette, Little Rock, reporter and copy editor, 1966-68; State of Arkansas, Little Rock, assistant attorney general, 1968-70; *Arkansas Gazette,* columnist, 1970-74; Southern Newspaper Publishers Association, Atlanta, Ga., director of information, 1974-75; legislative assistant to U.S. Senator Dale Bumpers, 1975-78; free-lance writer and editor, 1978-81; legislative director for U.S. Representative Tom Tauke, 1981-82; *Nation's Business,* Washington, D.C., associate editor, 1982—. Consultant to Library of Congress and Smithsonian Institution.

WRITINGS: (Editor with Martin Williams) *A Smithsonian Book of Comic-Book Comics,* Abrams, 1982; *Carl Barks and the Art of the Comic Book,* M. Lilien, 1982. Editor of *Funnyworld,* 1966-80.

WORK IN PROGRESS: That's Not All, Folks, a book about Warner Brothers cartoons; a history of American animated cartoons for Oxford University Press.

* * *

BARRIS, Chuck 1929-

BRIEF ENTRY: Born June 2, 1929, in Philadelphia, Pa. American game show producer and author. Barris has been well known to American television watchers since the 1960's. He produced a string of game shows for American Broadcasting Companies, Incorporated (ABC-TV), including "The Dating Game" (1965-73), "The Newlywed Game" (1966-74), "Operation Entertainment" (1968-69), and "The New Treasure Hunt" (1974). Barris was also responsible for "The Gong Show," which was first broadcast in 1976. Barris wrote a novel, *You and Me, Babe* (Harper's Magazine Press, 1974). *Address:* Chuck Barris Productions, 6430 Sunset Blvd., Hollywood, Calif. 90028. *Biographical/critical sources: Dallas News,* April 12, 1974; *Best Sellers,* April 15, 1974; *Denver Post,* May 1, 1974; *Who's Who in America,* 42nd edition, Marquis, 1982.

* * *

BARRON, Gayle 1945-

PERSONAL: Born April 6, 1945, in Atlanta, Ga.; daughter of Franklin Thomas IV and Gloria (LaRoche) Stocks; married James Ben Barron III (a fitness consultant), August 30, 1969 (separated). *Education:* University of Georgia, A.B.J., 1967. *Religion:* Episcopal. *Home:* 12 Valley Forge Pl., Atlanta, Ga. 30318. *Agent:* Caroline Harkleroad, Oldfield Rd., Atlanta, Ga. 30318. *Office:* WAGA-TV, 1551 Briarcliff Rd. N.E., Atlanta, Ga. 30306.

CAREER: WAGA-TV, Atlanta, Ga., sportscaster, 1978-80, became field reporter for "Weekend Magazine." Conducts men's and women's running camps throughout the United States. Fitness consultant for Stouffer's Food Corp. tour for Lean Cuisine, General Foods Corp. "Chrystal Light" media, and for promotional tour for Evian French Water Co. Member of advisory staff of Converse Shoe Co. Member of board of trustees of Special Olympics Committee; member of editorial board of Employee Health and Fitness Council, Atlanta, Ga. *Member:* National Roadrunners Club of America, Georgia Fitness Council, Atlanta Lung Association (sports ambassador, 1978, 1979). *Awards, honors:* Named female athlete of the year by

the One Hundred Percent Wrong Club, amateur athlete of the year by the Athletic Hall of Fame, and outstanding athlete of the year by Atlanta Athletic Club, all 1979.

WRITINGS: (With Kim Chapin) *The Beauty of Running,* Harcourt, 1980; *Stretch and Strengthening Exercise* (sound recording), 1983.

SIDELIGHTS: Gayle Barron has run in a total of eighteen marathons. She completed seventeen of those in under three hours. She was the winner of the women's division of the 1978 Boston Marathon.

* * *

BARROWS, (Ruth) Marjorie 1892(?)-1983
(R. M. Barrows, Ruth Barrows; Jack Alden, Noel Ames, Ruth Dixon, Hugh Graham, pseudonyms)

OBITUARY NOTICE—See index for *CA* sketch: Born c. 1892 in Chicago, Ill.; died March 29, 1983, in Evanston, Ill. Editor and author. From 1922 to 1966 Barrows held various editorial posts with *Child Life,* Consolidated Books, *Children's Hour, Treasure Trails, Junior Treasure Chest of Family Weekly,* and *Highlights for Children.* She wrote numerous children's books under the names Marjorie Barrows, R. M. Barrows, and Ruth Barrows, as well as under several pseudonyms, including Jack Alden and Noel Ames. Among her writings are *Muggins, Fraidy Cat, Hoppity,* and *Little Red Balloon.* Obituaries and other sources: *American Authors and Books: 1640 to the Present Day,* 3rd revised edition, Crown, 1962; *Who's Who in America,* 42nd edition, Marquis, 1982; *Chicago Tribune,* April 2, 1983.

* * *

BARROWS, R. M.
See BARROWS, (Ruth) Marjorie

* * *

BARROWS, Ruth
See BARROWS, (Ruth) Marjorie

* * *

BARRY, Philip 1896-1949

BRIEF ENTRY: Born June 18, 1896, in Rochester, N.Y.; died of a heart attack, December 3, 1949, in New York, N.Y. American novelist and playwright. Barry rose to prominence in the early 1920's when his third play, "The Jilts," was produced on Broadway as *You and I* (1923). This production mirrored Barry's own predicament in its depiction of a young man's decision to forsake security for the stage. It was an immense success and proved the beginning of Barry's sixteen-year association with Broadway. In his canon of twenty-three plays, however, only a few works, notably *Holiday* (1929) and *The Philadelphia Story* (1939), have earned both popular and critical acclaim. Barry's best work is characterized by a sardonic portrayal of strife within sophisticated society. His forays into drama proved largely unsuccessful with most critics, though both *Hotel Universe* (1930) and *Here Come the Clowns* (1939) enjoyed runs of more than eighty performances on Broadway. Barry's only novel, *War in Heaven,* was published in 1938. *Biographical/critical sources: The Reader's Encyclopedia of American Literature,* Crowell, 1962; *The Oxford Companion to American Literature,* Oxford University Press, 1965; *Web-*

ster's New World Companion to English and American Literature, World Publishing, 1973; *Cassell's Encyclopaedia of World Literature*, revised edition, Morrow, 1973; *Twentieth-Century Literary Criticism*, Volume 11, Gale, 1983.

* * *

BASH, Deborah M. Blumenthal 1940-

PERSONAL: Born February 28, 1940, in Brooklyn, N.Y.; daughter of Isidor (in business) and Ann (Selevan) Blumenthal; married Marvin I. Bash (a rabbi), December 24, 1959; children: Robert, Gila, Alan, Jeremy. *Education:* Hunter College of the City University of New York, B.S.N., 1961; Catholic University of America, M.S.N., 1969; Georgetown University, C.N.M., 1977. *Religion:* Jewish. *Home:* 3000 First St. N., Arlington, Va. 22201. *Office:* Obstetrical-Gynecological Association of Northern Virginia, 5021 Seminary Rd., Alexandria, Va. 22311.

CAREER: Part-time nurse, 1961-74; George Mason University, Fairfax, Va., assistant professor of nursing, 1974-76; Georgetown University, Washington, D.C., instructor in nursing, 1978—, nurse midwife with the university's Community Health Plan, 1978—. Certified nurse midwife with Arlington Health Department, 1981-82. *Member:* American College of Nurse-Midwives, Alliance for Perinatal Research and Services (vice-president), Sigma Theta Tau.

WRITINGS: (With Winifred Gold) *The Nurse and the Childbearing Family*, Wiley, 1981; (with Rae Grad and others) *The Father Book: Pregnancy and Beyond*, Acropolis Books, 1981. Contributor of articles and reviews to magazines. Editor of *APRS Federal Monitor*.

* * *

BATCHELOR, John (Dennis) 1947-

PERSONAL: Born August 22, 1947, in London, England; married Julie Frances Elizabeth Clarke (a writer), August 3, 1973. *Home and office:* 52 Thorndon Court, Eagle Way, Warley, Brentwood, Essex, England.

CAREER: Writer. *Member:* Royal Geographical Society (fellow), Globetrotters Club (chairman, 1980—).

WRITINGS: (With wife, Julie Batchelor) *The Congo*, Silver Burdett, 1980; (with Julie Batchelor) *The Euphrates*, Silver Burdett, 1981. Contributor to *Geographical*.

WORK IN PROGRESS: A factual, humorous account of his travels around the world, including Africa, with wife, Julie Batchelor.

SIDELIGHTS: John Batchelor and his co-author/wife Julie have traveled to relatively unexplored places throughout the world. Please see Julie Batchelor's sketch in this volume for an account of these ventures.

* * *

BATCHELOR, Julie F(rances) E(lizabeth) 1947-

PERSONAL: Born January 30, 1947, in Manchester, England; daughter of Fred (a master grocer) and Dora (Millington) Clarke; married John Dennis Batchelor (a writer), August 3, 1973. *Education:* University of Leeds, B.A. (with honors), 1968; Homerton College, postgraduate certificate in education, 1969. *Home and office:* 52 Thorndon Court, Eagle Way, Warley, Brentwood, Essex, England.

CAREER: Teacher at primary and secondary schools in London, England, 1969-73; writer and broadcaster, 1973-78; Business Language School, London, administrator and director, 1979—. *Member:* Globetrotters Club.

WRITINGS: (With husband, John Batchelor) *The Congo*, Silver Burdett, 1980; (with John Batchelor) *The Euphrates*, Silver Burdett, 1981.

WORK IN PROGRESS: A factual, humorous account of her travels around the world, including Africa, with husband, John Batchelor.

SIDELIGHTS: Julie Batchelor told *CA:* "My husband and I enjoy visiting little-known parts of the world and meeting the people—and animals—who inhabit them. In 1974 we spent four-and-a-half months making the first descent of the Congo River by kayak. In 1976 we spent several months in Irian Jaya, the easternmost province of Indonesia and the western half of the island of New Guinea, traveling on foot among the cannibalistic, Stone-Age Yali people of the remote central highlands. In 1978 we spent three months in Gabon, West Africa, photographing forest elephants and the little-known gorilla of the western lowlands."

* * *

BATCHER, Elaine Kotler 1944-

PERSONAL: Born September 22, 1944, in Toronto, Ontario, Canada; daughter of Irving H. (a merchant) and Anne Celia (Merkur) Kotler; married Theodore Batcher (a lawyer), July 12, 1967; children: Russell Lorne, Gillian Eve. *Education:* University of Toronto, B.A., 1966, M.Ed., 1974, Ph.D., 1979. *Home:* 52 Leacock Cres., Don Mills, Ontario, Canada M3B 1P1.

CAREER: Teacher at public schools in Toronto, Ontario, 1967-73; part-time researcher for Ontario Ministry of Education, Toronto, and Federation of Women Teachers' Associations of Ontario, Toronto, 1973-79; independent consultant in education, 1979—. Lecturer at Ontario Institute for Studies in Education, 1979, 1982. *Member:* Canadian Society for the Study of Education, Canadian Association for the Study of Educational Administration, Canadian Educational Researchers Association, Federation of Women Teachers' Associations of Ontario.

WRITINGS: Emotion in the Classroom: A Study of Children's Experience, Praeger, 1979.

WORK IN PROGRESS: A fictionalized treatment of Toronto's garment industry, 1910-12; a study of teenagers' attitudes about school, family, and life, for a sequel to *Emotion in the Classroom;* short fiction and poetry.

SIDELIGHTS: Batcher told *CA:* "Children's experience of classroom life is not intellectual but emotional. In other words, while a teacher may believe herself to be dealing with a group, the individual child exists only within a dyadic relationship of self and teacher, and understands everything within the question 'what is this to me?,' which I theorize is the essence of emotion. I want to develop the theory of emotion a little farther in my study of teenagers, but more important, I want to look at so-called ordinary girls because I think we need to know more about everyday experience in all phases of life. Teens are usually examined within the question of delinquency, but typical existence interests me far more.

"My interest in Toronto garment workers was prompted by my chance discovery that there had once been a strike at the

T. Eaton Co., a major institution in this city. It didn't take long to discover who the workers were—recent immigrants—and what the issue was—unionization. It had all the earmarks of an interesting story, and when I found out that people who participated were still alive to talk about it, I went ahead and did the research. My book centers on aspects of immigration, women's rights, and trade unionization, all of which are on the curriculum of middle schools (grades seven through ten) here in Ontario.''

*   *   *

BAUMANN, Edward (Weston) 1925-

PERSONAL: Born December 31, 1925, in Kenosha, Wis.; son of Irvin John Edward and Mabel (Austerland) Baumann; married Caroline Skeels, September 13, 1959 (died, 1975); married Lenore Schend (a registered nurse), August 6, 1976; children: Corey (son), Amy. *Education:* University of Wisconsin—Madison, B.S., 1951. *Religion:* Lutheran. *Home:* 7115 Seventh Ave., Kenosha, Wis. 53140. *Office: Chicago Tribune,* 435 North Michigan Ave., Chicago, Ill. 60611.

CAREER: Waukegan News-Sun, Waukegan, Ill., reporter, 1951-56; *Chicago Daily News,* Chicago, Ill., reporter, 1956-59, editor, 1959-63; *Chicago American-Chicago Today,* Chicago, city editor, 1963-74; *Chicago Tribune,* Chicago, writer and author of column "Inc.," 1974—. Member of board of directors of Hall of Flame Firefighting Museum, 1965-70. *Military service:* U.S. Army Air Corps, 1944-46; served in New Guinea and the Philippines; received three battle stars. U.S. Naval Reserve, 1946-52. *Member:* Chicago Newspaper Reporters Association, Chicago Press Veterans Association (president, 1977, 1978), Chicago Press Club (president, 1974). *Awards, honors:* Page One Award from Chicago Newspaper Guild, 1953 and 1959, both for investigative reporting; named newsman of the year by Lake County Press Club, 1959, for expose of judicial corruption.

WRITINGS: (With John O'Brien) *Chicago Heist* (nonfiction), And Books, 1981; *Compendium of Crime,* Hallberg, Volume I, 1983, Volume II, in press. Contributor to detective magazines and *Ebony.*

WORK IN PROGRESS: Compendium of Crime, Volume III, publication by Hallberg expected in 1985; *Teresita,* "a true 'voice from the grave' murder mystery."

SIDELIGHTS: Baumann commented: "I write for my own enjoyment. I am particularly interested in crime stories. *Chicago Heist* is the true story of America's biggest cash theft, $4.3 million—and the men who did it. *Teresita* is the true story of the murder of Teresita Basa, a member of the Philippine aristocracy, and how the dead woman's voice, projected through a stranger's body, named the killer—who subsequently confessed! *Compendium of Crime* is a series of great crime stories that never made the headlines."

AVOCATIONAL INTERESTS: Travel (the South Pacific, England, Scotland, Austria, Hungary, Liechtenstein, the Netherlands, Germany, Spain, Portugal, Kenya, Peru, Ecuador, the Galapagos Islands).

*   *   *

BAUSCH, Robert (Charles) 1945-

PERSONAL: Born April 18, 1945, in Fort Benning, Ga.; son of Robert Carl (a businessman) and Helen (Simmons) Bausch;

married Geri Marrese (an accounting analyst), March 21, 1970; children: Sara Hadley, Julie Ann. *Education:* Attended University of Illinois, 1967-68, and Northern Virginia College, 1970-72; George Mason University, B.A., 1974, M.A., 1975. *Politics:* Liberal ("I mistrust most institutions"). *Religion:* Roman Catholic. *Residence:* Oakton, Va. *Agent:* Judith Weber, Nat Sobel Associates, 158 East 56th St., New York, N.Y. 10022. *Office:* Northern Virginia Community College, 15200 Smoketown Rd., Woodbridge, Va. 22191.

CAREER: Worked in a laundromat, as a cabdriver, and as a salesman of vacuum cleaners, encyclopedias, appliances, and cars; Fairfax County Public Library, Fairfax, Va., member of circulation department, 1973-74; Glebe Acres Prep School (private high school), Fairfax, teacher of English, French, and biology, 1974-76; Northern Virginia Community College, Annandale, Va., instructor in creative writing, 1975—. *Military service:* U.S. Air Force, 1965-69, instructor in survival tactics; stationed in Illinois; became sergeant.

WRITINGS: On the Way Home (novel), St. Martin's, 1982; *The Lives and Times of Riley Chance,* St. Martin's, in press.

SIDELIGHTS: On the Way Home examines the difficulties in adjustment the Sumner family experiences after first being told that their son Michael has been killed in action in Vietnam, and then finding out that he was actually taken prisoner and has managed to escape. Between these two events, however, Dale Sumner retires from the Chicago police force and moves with his wife to Florida in an attempt to start a new life away from reminders of Michael. Just as the Sumners have begun to accept Michael's death he returns.

The normally difficult period of readjustment to civilian life is compounded for the Sumners by the fact that Michael's new surroundings offer no positive link to his prewar existence. Withdrawn and uncommunicative, Michael angers his father, who is unable to understand why there is no hint of improvement in his son. He also suffers from a growing fear that his son might commit an insane act of violence, a fear that rises when one of Michael's female friends disappears.

Los Angeles Times book editor Art Seidenbaum observed: "The Bausch style is as clean and firm as a new butcher block. He does not decorate or overstate; even the mess in Michael's mind comes under the disciplined control of a storyteller who measured his sentences and trimmed his paragraphs for credibility." Ray Anello, reviewing *On the Way Home* in *Newsweek,* shared Seidenbaum's approval of the book, and noted: "It's not just the pain of a Vietnam vet that makes this story compelling. Robert Bausch uses Michael's homecoming to expose the discord and pain of family life as well." The story's larger, universal themes were also remarked upon by Phil DiFebo, reviewing in *Best Sellers,* who commended Bausch for having "written a novel that is suffused with that mournfulness attending the lives of those who see everywhere the reminders of some great loss. That his work speaks of Viet Nam and one of its victims seems to this reader to be posterior to the book's greater themes of human love and folly."

Bausch told *CA:* "I didn't think I'd ever write a novel. Now that I have I don't think I'll ever write anything else. I began writing when I was in the eighth grade, wrote steadily (and loved it best—I've not since felt as excited about writing as I did then) until my high school English teachers (who meant well, I'm sure) convinced me (by correcting my writing instead of responding to it) that I had nothing of any importance to say.

"I started writing again in the service—when I went to funerals three to five times a month (and more frequently as the war in Vietnam unraveled)—and have continued to write ever since.

"I am more a teacher than a writer, since I derive as much satisfaction out of a good job there, and since I devote more of my time to teaching than writing. Writing is totally separate and by itself and doesn't seem to be influenced by things—crises, horrors, games, shows, or picnics—in my life. When the writing is going easily it is not related to anything that I can figure out. The same applies for when it's not going at all.

"I don't believe the saying 'writers are born, not made.' I also don't believe in any spirit or muse or any other Romantic notion about what drives a writer to write. I could stop writing tomorrow, increase my tennis time, and live quite contentedly for the rest of my life. I *like* it, however, that everybody *thinks* a writer is driven to his work by some demon inside him. I'm not sure *why* I like that, but I'm glad I like it. It may keep me writing."

AVOCATIONAL INTERESTS: "My children, books, tennis, pipes and pipe tobaccos, the Washington Redskins, music, art, Pac Man, horse racing, gambling, swimming, baseball, basketball, chess, cooking, organic gardening, movies, eating heart-attack food, David Letterman."

BIOGRAPHICAL/CRITICAL SOURCES: Los Angeles Times, March 3, 1982; *Newsweek,* March 22, 1982; *Washington Post Book World,* March 26, 1982; *Best Sellers,* May, 1982.

*   *   *

BAXTER, Glen 1944-

PERSONAL: Born March 4, 1944, in Leeds, England; son of Charles (a welder) and Florence B. (Wood) Baxter; married Carole Suzanne Turner (a teacher), February 3, 1970; children: Zoe, Harry. *Education:* Leeds College of Art, earned diploma, 1965. *Politics:* "None." *Religion:* "None." *Residence:* London, England. *Agent:* Deborah Rogers, 49 Blenheim Crescent, London W11 2EF, England.

CAREER: Victoria & Albert Museum, London, England, teacher, 1968-74; writer and artist. Part-time lecturer at Royal College of Art in Canterbury, England, and in Norwich, England. Art exhibited in galleries in London, Amsterdam, and New York.

WRITINGS—And illustrator: The Works, Wyrd Press, 1977; *Atlas,* De Harmonie, 1979, Knopf, 1983; *The Impending Gleam,* J. Cape, 1981, Knopf, 1982; *Glen Baxter—His Life,* Thames & Hudson, 1983, Knopf, in press. Drawings have been published as postcards by Bug House Productions. Contributor to periodicals, including *London.*

WORK IN PROGRESS: A collection of writings and drawings, *Jodphurs in the Quantocks;* drawings and stories in collaboration with American poets Clark Coolidge and Larry Fagin.

SIDELIGHTS: The multi-talented Baxter is probably best known in America for his humorous illustrations, accompanied by appropriately absurd captions, collected in *The Impending Gleam* and *Atlas.* His drawings are characterized by a rough, sketchy style—at once reminiscent of the less reserved Edward Gorey and the less refined R. Crumb—whose subjects include hare-brained cowboys or outraged adolescents. The pictures bear captions which alternately highlight or contrast the bizarre activities of characters such as a grizzled old cowboy, inexplicably called Mrs. Botham, given to charging from behind a fellow westerner's chaps to fire at a threatening rattlesnake, or

Mr. Phelport, a placid fellow whose looks conceal the devilish intrigue he provokes by employing a set of pulleys to dangle a fish above the head of an increasingly suspicious lad. Among the other highlights of *The Impending Gleam* are grown men feuding over the use of whimples and cowboys debating the merits of abstract art.

In *Atlas,* Baxter adds appendages resembling squirrel's tails to his characters, most of whose absurdity is rendered through their accentuation of matters seemingly unrelated to their situations. Thus children resort to hilarious, though often violent, extremes to thwart the boring activities of stodgy adults, and explorers celebrate their discovery of a "legendary ball of soot." A reviewer for *New York Times Book Review* described Baxter's work as "deadpan drawings . . . at once beguiling and entertaining." And a critic in the *Times Literary Supplement* contended that Baxter "applies techniques of fusing the familiar with the absurd and the improbable, but also a memorably fresh eye and ear, to the task of giving new, surprising and hilarious life to verbal and visual cliches."

Baxter told *CA:* "My interest in the works of Ron Padgett, Larry Fagin, Bill Zavatsky, and Clark Coolidge first brought me to America, and especially to New York City. It was here that I gave my first public reading of my work at St. Mark's Church in 1974 and that the Gotham Book Mart Gallery first showed my drawings and watercolors, also in 1974.

"My inspiration for my work can be blamed partly on reading Roger Shattuck's *The Banquet Years* when I was at college. Much earlier influences were Ludwig Wittgenstein, Randolph Scott, and Gabby Hayes. My prose work simply allows me to create pictures without the use of drawn images."

BIOGRAPHICAL/CRITICAL SOURCES: Times Literary Supplement, November 6, 1981; *New York Times Book Review,* May 16, 1982; *Village Voice,* June 1, 1982; *Newsweek,* July 19, 1982; *Books & Bookmen,* October, 1982.

*   *   *

BAYLESS, John 1913(?)-1983

OBITUARY NOTICE: Born c. 1913 in Mulkeytown, Ill.; died March 19, 1983, in Chicago, Ill. Journalist who became features copy editor of the *Chicago Tribune* before ending his forty-five-year tenure in 1975. Obituaries and other sources: *Chicago Tribune,* March 21, 1983.

*   *   *

BEALE, Howard 1898-

PERSONAL: Born December 10, 1898, in Tamworth, Australia; son of Joseph (a clergyman) and Clara Elizabeth (Vickery) Beale; married Margery Ellen Wood, 1927; children: Julian. *Education:* Attended University of Sydney. *Home:* 4 Marathon Rd., Darling Point, New South Wales 2027, Australia.

CAREER: Called to the Bar, 1925; Australian Parliament, Canberra, Liberal member of Parliament for Parramatta, New South Wales, 1946-58, member of Commonwealth Parliamentary Public Works Committee, 1947-49, minister for information and transport and chairman of Australian Transport Advisory Council, both 1949-50, minister in charge of Australian Aluminum Production Commission and Australian Atomic Energy Commission, both 1950-58, minister for supply and defense production, 1956-58, member of Australian Defence Council,

Cabinet Defence Preparations Committee. and Cabinet Committee on Uranium and Atomic Energy, all 1950-58, acting minister for immigration, 1951-54, acting minister for national development, 1952-53, acting minister for air, 1952, acting minister for defense, 1957; ambassador to the United States, 1958-64; director and adviser to various Australian and U.S. industrial and financial corporations.

Australian delegate to International Bar Congress, 1948, and to Australia, New Zealand, and United States Council (ANZUS), 1958-59 and 1962. Leader of Australian delegation to Colombo Plan Conference, 1958; deputy leader of Australian delegation to the United Nations, 1959; leader of Australian delegation to Antarctic Conference, 1959; Australian delegate to Southeast Asia Treaty Organization Conference, 1959-60; alternate governor of International Monetary Fund, 1960, 1962, and 1964; leader of Australian delegation to World Food Congress, 1963; Australian state visitor to Chile and Mexico, 1963; Australian government representative at Independence of Zambia, 1964. Vice-president for Australia of Occidental Mining Corp.; past chairman of Pye Industries Ltd., Oil Basins Ltd., and Munduna Investments Ltd.; past vice-chairman of Weeks Natural Resources Ltd.; past president of Mineral Holdings Ltd.; past director of Australian Equitable Insurance Co. Ltd., Australian Selection Pty. Ltd., Engelhard Industries Ltd., and Seltrust Iron Ore Ltd.

Lecturer with Army Educational Department, 1940; Woodward Lecturer at Yale University, 1960. Regents' Visiting Professor at University of California, 1966, and at Marquette University, 1967-69. *Military service:* Royal Australian Navy, 1942-45. *Member:* Arts Council of Australia (president, 1964-68), Australasian Pioneers Club (president, 1964-66), Union Club. *Awards, honors:* Appointed King's Counsel, 1950, and Queen's Counsel; Knight Commander of Order of the British Empire; D.H.Lit. from University of Nebraska, 1962; LL.D. from Kent University and Marquette University, 1969.

WRITINGS: This Inch of Time: Memoirs of Politics and Diplomacy, Melbourne University Press, 1977. Contributor of articles and reviews to *Australian.*

AVOCATIONAL INTERESTS: Yachting, reading, music.

*   *   *

BEAMISH, Anthony Hamilton   ?-1983

OBITUARY NOTICE: Died May 2, 1983. Conservationist, broadcaster, filmmaker, and author. Beamish was especially interested in the wildlife of the Far East and filmed a series of documentaries on the subject. He also worked for the British Broadcasting Corporation and wrote *Aldabra Alone.* Obituaries and other sources: *London Times,* May 10, 1983.

*   *   *

BEAN, Henry (Schorr)   1945-

PERSONAL: Born August 3, 1945, in Philadelphia, Pa.; son of Donald (a lawyer) and Fahny (Schorr) Bean; married Nancy Eliason, January 3, 1968 (divorced February 14, 1970); married Leora Barish (a writer), March 23, 1980; children: Max. *Education:* Yale Univesity, B.A., 1967; Stanford University, M.A., 1973. *Politics:* "Left." *Religion:* Jewish. *Residence:* Venice, Calif. *Agent:* Molly Friedrich, 344 East 51st St., New York, N.Y. 10022.

CAREER: Monte Vista High School, Danville, Calif., teacher of English and journalism, 1969-71; writer, 1971—. *Member:*

Writers Guild of America, West. *Awards, honors:* First book of fiction award from PEN—Los Angeles, 1983, for *False Match.*

WRITINGS: False Match (novel), Simon & Schuster, 1982. Also author of screenplays, including "Desire" and "Labyrinth Nine," both with wife, Leora Barish, and "Who You Know."

WORK IN PROGRESS: A novel.

SIDELIGHTS: Harold Raab, the protagonist of Henry Bean's *False Match,* is "a dropout from the 1960's who can only connect with the world around him through the exercise of fantasy," explained Bruce Allen in the *Chicago Tribune Book World.* "Some readers may find 'False Match' excessively mannered," Allen continued, "[but] for me, its steely concentration and understated emotional force make it a thoroughly successful experiment."

BIOGRAPHICAL/CRITICAL SOURCES: Chicago Tribune Book World, February 13, 1983.

*   *   *

BEARDSLEY, John   1952-

PERSONAL: Born October 28, 1952, in New York, N.Y. *Education:* Harvard University, A.B., 1974. *Office:* Corcoran Gallery of Art, 17th St. at New York Ave., Washington, D.C. 20006.

CAREER: Hirshhorn Museum, Washington, D.C., member of curatorial staff, 1974-78; free-lance art critic and curator, 1978-80; National Endowment for the Arts, Washington, D.C., writer, 1980-81; Corcoran Gallery of Art, Washington, D.C., adjunct curator, 1981—.

WRITINGS: Probing the Earth: Contemporary Land Projects, Smithsonian Institution Press, 1977; *Art in Public Places,* Partners for Livable Places, 1981; (with Jane Livingston) *Black Folk Art in America: 1930-1980* (museum catalogue), Corcoran Gallery of Art and University Press of Mississippi, 1982.

WORK IN PROGRESS: A book on contemporary art in the landscape, which will include a survey of recent earthworks and environmental art, publication by Abbeville Press expected in 1984.

SIDELIGHTS: In his *Village Voice Literary Supplement* review of *Black Folk Art in America,* critic Jeff Weinstein noted that museum catalogues are becoming a valuable source of art information, offering "reproductions and art criticism unavailable elsewhere." "Such is the case with *Black Folk Art in America,*" Weinstein continued, noting also that while it is "at first merely a gorgeous selection of works by a few familiar and many just discovered artists, it becomes, as the text unfolds the pictures, a messenger bearing a new definition of contemporary folk art."

BIOGRAPHICAL/CRITICAL SOURCES: Village Voice Literary Supplement, May, 1982.

*   *   *

BEATTY, Warren
See BEATY, Warren

BEATY, Warren 1937(?)-
(Warren Beatty)

BRIEF ENTRY: Professionally known as Warren Beatty; born March 30, 1937 (some sources say 1938), in Richmond, Va. American actor, producer, director, and screenwriter. A highly successful actor, Warren Beatty first appeared on screen opposite Natalie Wood in the 1961 movie "Splendor in the Grass." He later starred in such movies as "Bonnie and Clyde" (1967), "McCabe and Mrs. Miller" (1971), "Shampoo" (1975), "Heaven Can Wait" (1978), and "Reds" (1981). Several of his screenwriting, acting, directing, and producing efforts earned Beatty Academy Award nominations, including best screenplay nominations for "Shampoo," "Heaven Can Wait," and "Reds"; best actor nominations for "Bonnie and Clyde" and "Reds"; and best director and best picture nominations for "Reds." "Reds," for which Beatty won an Academy Award as best director, is an epic movie about journalist John Reed. Vincent Canby of the *New York Times* called it "an extraordinary film, a big romantic adventure movie, the best since David Lean's 'Lawrence of Arabia,' as well as a commercial movie with a rare sense of history." *Address:* c/o Directors Guild of America, 7950 Sunset Blvd., Hollywood, Calif. 90046. *Biographical/critical sources: Current Biography,* Wilson, 1962; *Celebrity Register,* 3rd edition, Simon & Schuster, 1973; *New York Times,* December 4, 1981; *International Motion Picture Almanac,* Quigley, 1982; *Who's Who in America,* 42nd edition, Marquis, 1982.

* * *

BECKEY, Fred W(olfgang) 1923-

PERSONAL: Born January 14, 1923, in Zuelpich, Germany; naturalized U.S. citizen, 1925; son of Klaus (a physician) and Marta (an opera singer; maiden name, Thienhaus) Beckey. *Education:* University of Washington, B.B.A., 1949; graduate study at University of California, Los Angeles, 1952. *Home:* 258 Kathleen Dr., Pleasant Hill, Calif. 94523.

CAREER: Mountaineering specialist, 1941—. Climbing expeditions around the world have included expeditions in Nepal, China, Africa, Canada, and Alaska. *Member:* American Alpine Club, Sierra Club, Appalachian Mountains Club, Mountaineers, Wilderness Society.

WRITINGS: Climber's Guide to the Cascade and Olympic Mountains, American Alpine Club, 1949; *Challenge of the North Cascades,* Mountaineers, 1969; *Cascade Alpine Guide,* Mountaineers, Volume 1, 1973, Volume 2, 1975, Volume 3, 1980; *The Cascades,* Graphic Arts Center, 1982; *Mountains of North America,* Sierra Books, 1982. Also author (with Eric Bjornstad) of *Guide to Leavenworth Rock-Climbing,* 1965. Contributor to newspapers and magazines, including *Sports Illustrated, Mountains of the World, American Alpine Journal, Les Alpes, Die Alpen,* and *Backpacker.*

WORK IN PROGRESS: Alaskan Explorations.

SIDELIGHTS: Fred Beckey is a renowned mountaineer and the author of several books about mountains and mountain climbing. His 1982 book, *The Mountains of North America,* features color plates, photographs, and commentary about thirty-five North American peaks, including Long's Peak in Colorado, Mt. St. Elias and Mt. McKinley in Alaska, Mt. St. Helens and Mt. Rainier in Washington, and Clingman's Dome on the Tennessee-North Carolina border of the Great Smokey Mountains. According to *Los Angeles Times Book Review* critic David

Graber, Beckey's *The Mountains of North America* is "a thoroughly exciting and beautiful book," and "Beckey is a hell of a writer."

BIOGRAPHICAL/CRITICAL SOURCES: Los Angeles Times Book Review, November 14, 1982.

* * *

BECKMAN, Patti
See BOECKMAN, Patti

* * *

BEE, Clair (Francis) 1900-1983

OBITUARY NOTICE—See index for *CA* sketch: Born March 2, 1900 (some sources say 1896), in Grafton, W.Va.; died of cardiac arrest, May 20, 1983, in Cleveland, Ohio. Basketball coach and author. In 1931 Bee became the basketball coach for Long Island University, a post he held until 1952. He later served for two years as coach of the Baltimore Bullets and for thirteen years as athletic director of the New York Military Academy. In 1967 Bee was elected to the Basketball Hall of Fame. He was the author of numerous books, including the five-volume *Clair Bee Basketball Library* and *Basketball for Everyone.* He also wrote the Chip Hilton sports stories for boys, a series that was comprised of such titles as *Championship Ball, Ten Seconds to Play, Fourth Down Showdown,* and *Home Run Feud.* Obituaries and other sources: *New York Times,* May 21, 1983.

* * *

BEEBY, C(larence) E(dward) 1902-

PERSONAL: Born June 16, 1902, in Leeds, England; son of Anthony and Alice (Rhodes) Beeby; married Beatrice Eleanor Newnham (a psychologist), June 3, 1926; children: Helen (Mrs. Neil Leckie), Christopher David. *Education:* University of Canterbury, M.A., 1923; attended University of London; Victoria University of Manchester, Ph.D., 1926. *Politics:* Labour. *Home:* 73 Barnard St., Wellington 1, New Zealand.

CAREER: University of New Zealand, Christchurch, lecturer in philosophy and education, 1923-34; New Zealand Council for Educational Research, Wellington, director, 1934-38; Education Department, Wellington, New Zealand, assistant director of education, 1938-40, director of education for New Zealand, 1940-60; Ministry of Foreign Affairs, New Zealand, ambassador to France, 1960-63; Harvard University, Cambridge, Mass., research associate at Center for Studies in Education and Development, 1963-67; University of London, London, England, Commonwealth Visiting Professor of Education in Developing Countries, 1967-68; New Zealand Council for Educational Research, international educational consultant, 1969-83; writer, 1938—. Assistant director-general of UNESCO, 1948-49, permanent delegate from New Zealand, 1960-63, member of executive board, 1961-64, chairman, 1963, chairman of evaluation panel for world functional literacy projects; consultant to Ford Foundation, Government of Australia in Papua, New Guinea, International Institute for Educational Planning, United Nations Development Program in Libya and Malaysia, Indian Education Commission, and University of Papua New Guinea.

MEMBER: International P.E.N., New Zealand Association for Research in Education, National Academy of Education (United States; foreign associate), New Zealand Book Council. *Awards, honors:* Companion of Order of St. Michael and St. George, 1956; Order of St. Gregory, Grand Cross, 1964; LL.D. from University of Otago, 1969; Litt.D. from Victoria University of Wellington, 1970; Mackie Medal from Australasian Association for the Advancement of Science, 1971, for recent contributions to education; honorary fellow of New Zealand Educational Institute, 1971.

WRITINGS: The Intermediate Schools of New Zealand: A Survey, Whitcombe & Tombs, 1938; (with William Thomas and Matthew Henry Oram) *Entrance to the University,* New Zealand Council for Educational Research, 1939; *Report on Education in Western Samoa,* Government Printer (Wellington, New Zealand), 1954; (with George Currie) *Training for Technology in New Zealand,* University of New Zealand Press, 1956; *The Quality of Education in Developing Countries,* Harvard University Press, 1966; (editor) *Qualitative Aspects of Educational Planning,* International Institute for Educational Planning, 1969; (with W. J. Weedon and Gabriel Gris) *Report of the Advisory Committee on Education in Papua and New Guinea,* A.C.T. Ministry of External Territories, 1969; (contributor) G.Z.F. Bereday, editor, *Essays on World Education: The Crisis of Supply and Demand,* Oxford University Press, 1969; *Assessment of Indonesian Education: A Guide in Planning,* New Zealand Council for Educational Research, 1979; *The Biography of an Idea of Education,* New Zealand Council for Educational Research, in press. General editor of booklet series, International Institute of Educational Planning, 1965-71. Contributor to education journals.

SIDELIGHTS: C. E. Beeby told *CA:* "My interest in education in developing countries began in 1945, when I suddenly became responsible for educational policy in two countries, New Zealand and the Trusteeship Territory of Western Samoa, whose educational systems were at least eighty years apart in their levels of development. To my surprise, I found myself recommending for Western Samoa the introduction of highly formal teaching methods and materials, which, as director (secretary) of education in New Zealand, I had been trying to get rid of even in my own country. Even a hardened educational administrator cannot live with such apparent inconsistency without some basis of theory to explain it, and so I began to write about it to clarify my own thinking.

"Except for articles in journals, my theorizing did not appear in more permanent form until twenty years later, in *The Quality of Education in Developing Countries,* a small book, since translated into several languages and still used in many developing countries, particularly those with a British colonial background. In the meantime, I had led the New Zealand delegation to the founding conference of UNESCO in 1946, and had been invited by Julian Huxley, its director-general, to spend a term as assistant director-general to establish its educational program. From then on, I was caught in a web of programs that still fascinate me by their intricacy, and that call for ever more writing.

"At the age of eighty, I am trying to switch my writing from a professional to a rather more personal style. I haven't the slightest wish to write an autobiography—except that I have the perfect title for one, *Yours in All Senility*—but I am working on *The Biography of an Idea of Education.* It is the story of my own idea of education from earliest childhood to the present, as affected by my home background, schooling and professional training, and by my experience as teacher and research worker in several universities, head of a national educational system for twenty years, international civil servant, diplomat, consultant and educational busybody in a dozen developing countries, and an old man sitting at a typewriter. It is the Idea that will hold center-stage; I am only one of the supporting cast.

"I forget who it was who first said, 'I don't know what I think until I hear what I have said,' but it was little more than a clever quip. As one who has made much of his living by speaking, I have decreasing faith in the spoken word and find, more than ever before, that I don't know what I think until I see what I have written."

BIOGRAPHICAL/CRITICAL SOURCES: Times Literary Supplement, January 26, 1967; *New Zealand International Review,* July/August, 1979; *Australian Journal of Education,* October, 1979; *International Review of Education,* Volume XXVI, number 1, 1980.

*   *   *

BEGIN, Menachem   1913-

BRIEF ENTRY: Born August 16, 1913, in Brest-Litovsk, Poland (now Brest, U.S.S.R.). Israeli lawyer, statesman, and author. Begin's 1977 election as prime minister of Israel represented the culmination of a lifelong struggle for Jewish freedom. As a young man, Begin headed a Zionist youth movement in Poland. He weathered the early years of World War II and the Holocaust in a Siberian prison camp; he recorded that period in *White Nights: The Story of a Prisoner in Russia* (MacDonald, 1957). By 1942 Begin had made his way to Palestine, where he assumed control of the anti-British, anti-Arab terrorist organization Irgun Zva'i Leumi. Begin's account of those violent years appears in *The Revolt: Story of the Irgun* (Schuman, 1951) and *In the Underground: Writings and Documents* (Hadar, 1975-77). After the independent State of Israel became a legal reality, Begin became a member of the Knesset, or parliament. He continued the Israeli fight against communism and Arab encroachment with unabated militance for several years. By 1977, however, Israel's power and influence in the Middle East had been firmly established, and the small nation began to move toward peaceful working relations with her neighbors. In 1978 Prime Minister Begin's efforts in this direction were acknowledged by the rest of the world when he and Egyptian President Anwar Sadat shared the Nobel Peace Prize. *Address:* 1 Rosenbaum St., Tel Aviv, Israel. *Biographical/critical sources:* Eitan Haber, *Menahem Begin: The Legend and the Man,* Delacorte, 1978; Frank Gervasi, *The Life and Times of Menahem Begin: Rebel to Statesman,* Putnam, 1979; *New Statesman,* January 4, 1980.

*   *   *

BEGIN, Menahem
See BEGIN, Menachem

*   *   *

BELLVILLE, Cheryl Walsh   1944-

PERSONAL: Born August 27, 1944, in Deming, N.M.; daughter of William Vincent (a horseman) and Elsie (Lofback) Walsh; married Rod Bellville (a musician, writer, and photographer), July 28, 1972; children: Luke Kyper, Katherine Anne. *Education:* Attended South Dakota State University, 1965; University of Minnesota, B.F.A., 1970. *Politics:* Liberal. *Religion:* "Pantheist." *Residence:* Boyceville, Wis. *Office:* Cheryl Walsh Bellville Photography, 2823 Eighth St. S., Minneapolis, Minn. 55454.

CAREER: Cheryl Walsh Bellville Photography, Minneapolis, Minn., photographer, 1968—. Teacher of photography and art at schools for Native Americans in Minneapolis, 1969; public school teacher of photography for Minneapolis Urban Arts, 1970-71; photographs have been exhibited in Minnesota. *Member:* Friends of Planned Parenthood.

WRITINGS—Juvenile; all self-illustrated with photographs: *Round-Up,* Carolrhoda, 1982; (with husband, Rod Bellville) *Large Animal Veterinarians,* Carolrhoda, 1983; (with R. Bellville) *Stockyards,* Carolrhoda, 1983; *All Things Bright and Beautiful,* Winston Press, 1983; *Farming With Horses,* Carolrhoda, in press. Staff writer and editorial photographer for newspaper, *Hundred Flowers,* 1970-71.

WORK IN PROGRESS: A children's book on rodeo.

SIDELIGHTS: Cheryl Bellville wrote: "My primary motivation is the desire to communicate the impact of the natural world in an aesthetic/visual sense. I try to provide a bridge between the technical urban present and the fragile, traditional stewardship of the ecosystem. I consider man's (people's) inhumanity to their own kind more threatening than direct damage to our environment, because we are inextricably bound to our organic origin, whatever our philosophical divergence."

* * *

BELPRE, Pura   1899-1982

OBITUARY NOTICE—See index for CA sketch: Born February 2, 1899, in Cidra, Puerto Rico; died July 1, 1982. Librarian, puppeteer, and author of books for children. Belpre began her career as a children's librarian in 1921, when she became the first Hispanic librarian in the New York Public Library. During her years of service at various branches within the city, she was responsible for the expansion of Puerto Rican folklore programs, which included storytelling and puppet theatres. Her first book, *Perez and Martina: A Puerto Rican Folktale,* was published in 1932. It was followed by other folklore books, including *Juan Bobo and the Queen's Necklace, The Tiger and the Rabbit, and Other Tales,* and *The Rainbow Colored Horse.* Belpre resigned from the library in 1945 to travel and write but returned in 1961 after the death of her husband, Clarence Cameron White, a concert violinist and conductor. Following her retirement in 1968, she continued to work on a special services basis for the South Bronx Project and the Office of Special Services. In 1973 she received a citation from Brooklyn Art Books for Children for *Santiago.* In 1978 she was honored for her distinguished contribution to Spanish literature by the Bay Area Bilingual Education League and the University of San Francisco. Obituaries and other sources: *Authors of Books for Young People,* 2nd edition, Scarecrow, 1971; *Fourth Book of Junior Authors and Illustrators,* H. W. Wilson, 1978; *School Library Journal,* August, 1982.

* * *

BENEDICT, Burton   1923-

PERSONAL: Born May 20, 1923, in Baltimore, Md.; son of Burton Eli Oppenheim (a civil servant) and Helen (Dieches) Benedict; married Marion Steuber (a writer), September 23, 1950; children: Helen, Barbara. *Education:* Harvard University, A.B., 1949; University of London, Ph.D., 1954. *Office:* Department of Anthropology, University of California, Berkeley, Calif. 94720.

CAREER: University of London, London School of Economics and Political Science, London, England, assistant lecturer, 1958-

61, lecturer, 1961-64, senior lecturer in social anthropology, 1964-68; University of California, Berkeley, professor of anthropology, 1968—, dean of social sciences, 1971-74. Senior research fellow at Institute of Islamic Studies, McGill University, 1954-55. *Member:* American Anthropological Association (fellow), Royal Anthropological Institute of Great Britain and Ireland (fellow), Zoological Society (London, England; scientific fellow). *Awards, honors:* Grant from Colonial Social Science Research Council for Mauritius, 1955-57; grant from United Kingdom Department of Technological Cooperation for the Seychelles, 1960.

WRITINGS: Indians in a Plural Society, H.M.S.O., 1961; *Mauritius: The Problems of a Plural Society,* Pall Mall, 1965; *People of the Seychelles,* H.M.S.O., 1966; (editor and contributor) *Problems of Smaller Territories,* Athlone Press, 1967; (contributor) Leonard Plotinicov and Arthur Tuden, editors, *Essays in Comparative Social Stratification,* University of Pittsburgh Press, 1970; (with wife, Marion Benedict) *Men, Women, and Money in Seychelles,* University of California Press, 1982; *An Anthropology of World's Fairs,* Lowie Museum of Anthropology, University of California, Berkeley, 1983. Contributor to anthropology journals.

WORK IN PROGRESS: The Display of Dependent Peoples at World's Fairs; The Cultural Dimension of Zoos.

SIDELIGHTS: Benedict told *CA:* "I did two years of field work in Mauritius, where I lived in two Indian villages, and spent five months in Seychelles, where I lived in villages and the poor area of a town.

"I see world's fairs as giant secular rituals comparable to the potlatch. They are multi-ethnic happenings indicative of changes in the class structure and are full of wishful thinking."

* * *

BENEDICT, Marion   1923-

PERSONAL: Born October 19, 1923, in Chester, Pa.; daughter of Frederick Walter (an architect, engineer, and builder) and Helen (MacVean) Steuben; married Burton Benedict (a professor of anthropology), September 23, 1950; children: Helen, Barbara. *Education:* Attended Swarthmore College, 1941-44; University of California, Berkeley, A.B. (with honors), 1968, M.A., 1978. *Home:* 2805 Hilgard Ave., Berkeley, Calif. 94709.

CAREER: Secretary with Citizens Committee for United Nations Reform in New York, 1944-49; Inland Waterways Association, London, England, secretary, 1951. *Member:* League of Women Voters.

WRITINGS: (With husband, Burton Benedict) *Men, Women, and Money in Seychelles,* University of California Press, 1982. Contributor to newspapers.

WORK IN PROGRESS: A novel set in contemporary California.

SIDELIGHTS: Marion Benedict has lived in Mauritius and Seychelles.

* * *

BENJAMIN, Robert (Irving)   1949-

PERSONAL: Born November 8, 1949, in Cincinnati, Ohio; son of Irving Samuel (a businessman) and Betty (a fund raiser; maiden name, Eichenbaum) Benjamin; divorced. *Education:* University of Pennsylvania, B.A., 1971; graduate study at University of Texas at Austin, 1975. *Residence:* Columbia, Md. *Office: Baltimore Sun,* 501 North Calvert St., Baltimore, Md. 21203.

CAREER: Cincinnati Post, Cincinnati, Ohio, reporter, 1977-81; *Baltimore Sun,* Baltimore, Md., reporter, 1981—. *Member:* Authors Guild, Newspaper Guild, Education Writers Association. *Awards, honors:* Journalism awards from Education Writers Association, 1978, National School Boards Association, 1979, International Reading Association, 1979, and Cincinnati chapter of Sigma Delta Chi, 1980.

WRITINGS: Making Schools Work: A Reporter's Journey Through Some of America's Most Remarkable Classrooms, Continuum, 1981.

SIDELIGHTS: In *Making Schools Work* Benjamin focuses on a rare set of elementary schools that have succeeded despite their locations in low-income areas. While pointing in detail to several successful programs across the country, Benjamin reiterates the importance of able and caring teachers and administrators to all schools. He finds that methods of instruction, secondary in importance to capable teaching staffs, work best when they are highly structured, clear in the goals they set, and paced to the individual student. The book also profiles several teaching professionals who, in Benjamin's view, help make the difference.

Joseph Featherstone, in the *New York Times Book Review,* deemed *Making Schools Work* a "useful book," while Dan Morgan termed it a "painstakingly reported examination" in his *Washington Post Book World* review.

BIOGRAPHICAL/CRITICAL SOURCES: Washington Post Book World, April 19, 1981; *New York Times Book Review,* August 9, 1981.

*   *   *

BENOIST-MECHIN, Jacques   1901-1983

OBITUARY NOTICE—See index for *CA* sketch: Born July 1, 1901, in Paris, France; died after a long illness, February 24, 1983, in Paris, France. Historian, translator, and author. During World War II Benoist-Mechin was a key member of the Vichy government of Nazi-occupied France. After the war he was prosecuted by the French High Court, and on June 6, 1947, he was condemned to death for treason. His sentence was later commuted to life imprisonment, and on July 14, 1953, he was released from prison. Benoist-Mechin was the author of many books, including the three-volume *Soixante jours qui ebranlerent l'occident,* which was published in one volume as *Sixty Days That Shook the West: The Fall of France, 1940.* His *Alexandre le Grand; ou, Le Reve depasse* was published as *Alexander the Great: The Meeting of East and West,* and his *Eclaircissements sur "Mein Kampf" d'Adolf Hitler* appeared in 1939. Obituaries and other sources: *New York Times,* February 27, 1983; *Chicago Tribune,* February 28, 1983, March 1, 1983.

*   *   *

BERGER, Mark L(ewis)   1942-

BRIEF ENTRY: Born December 2, 1942, in Brooklyn, N.Y. American historian, educator, and author. Berger began teaching at Columbus College in 1969; in 1980 he was appointed professor of American history. He wrote *The Revolution in the New York Party Systems, 1840-1860* (Kennikat, 1973). *Ad-*

dress: Department of History, Columbus College, Columbus, Ga. 31907. *Biographical/critical sources: Annals of the American Academy of Political and Social Science,* January, 1974; *Journal of American History,* March, 1974; *American Historical Review,* April, 1974.

*   *   *

BERGER, Raymond M(ark)   1950-

PERSONAL: Born August 23, 1950, in Buffalo, N.Y.; son of David (a laborer) and Mila Berger. *Education:* State University of New York at Stony Brook, B.A. (summa cum laude), 1972; University of Wisconsin—Madison, M.S.S.W., 1973, Ph.D., 1976. *Office:* School of Social Work, University of Illinois, 1207 West Oregon St., Urbana, Ill. 61801.

CAREER: State University of New York at Stony Brook, member of organizing staff of University Volunteer Ambulance Corps and director of recruitment, training, and supervision of volunteers, 1971-72; Renaissance of Madison, Inc., Madison, Wis., director of venereal disease program, 1972-76; University of Wisconsin—Madison, lecturer in social work, 1976-77; Florida International University, Miami, assistant professor of social work, 1977-79; University of Illinois, Urbana-Champaign, assistant professor of social work, 1980—. Lecturer at University of Wisconsin—Madison, autumn, 1979. Psychotherapist with Outreach Counseling Service, Miami, 1978; consultant to Four Winds Nursing Manor, 1979-80; outpatient clinician at Champaign County Mental Health Center, 1980—.

MEMBER: National Association of Social Workers, Council on Social Work Education, Social Work Group for the Study of Behavioral Methods, Association of Social Work Educators Concerned With Lesbian and Gay Issues, Association of Gay Gerontologists. *Awards, honors:* Grant from National Institute of Mental Health, 1976-77; grant under Title IV A of Older Americans Act, 1978; grant from Florida International University, 1978; human rights award from Dade County Coalition for Human Rights, 1979; Evelyn C. Hooker Research Award from Gay Academic Union, 1982.

WRITINGS: (Contributor) S. D. Rose, editor, *A Casebook in Group Therapy,* Prentice-Hall, 1980; (contributor) Steven Schinke, editor, *Behavioral Methods in Social Welfare: Helping Children, Adults, and Families in Community Settings,* Aldine, 1981; *Gay and Gray: The Older Homosexual Male,* University of Illinois Press, 1982; (contributor) *Supplement to the Seventeenth Edition of the Encyclopedia of Social Work,* National Association of Social Workers, 1983. Contributor of numerous articles and reviews to journals in the behavioral sciences. Member of editorial board of *Social Work,* 1980—.

SIDELIGHTS: Berger told *CA:* "Because only a few members of my family survived the holocaust of the Second World War, I have always been intensely interested in understanding people who survive adversity. Older gay men and women are such a group. They are an inspiration for having survived so well despite enormous social odds, and they are a reservoir of history which must be tapped soon or lost forever.

"If I have learned anything in my career it is the importance of personal commitment. 'Anything worth doing is worth doing well.'"

BIOGRAPHICAL/CRITICAL SOURCES: Los Angeles Times, September 3, 1982.

BERNSTEIN, Mordechai 1893-1983

OBITUARY NOTICE: Born in 1893 in the Ukraine (now U.S.S.R.); died March 28, 1983, in Haifa, Israel. Playwright, publishing executive, and author of novels and short stories. Bernstein was general manager of Dvir publishers and presided over the Hebrew Book Publishers Association. Obituaries and other sources: *AB Bookman's Weekly,* April 18, 1983.

*   *   *

BERNSTEIN, Seymour

PERSONAL: Born in New Jersey; son of Max (in business) and Nellie (Haberman) Bernstein. *Education:* Studied music with Alexander Brailowsky, Jan Gorbaty, Hans Neumann, and Clifford Curzon; attended Weequahic Hight School and Conservatoire de Fontainebleau. *Home:* 10 West 76th St., New York, N.Y. 10023.

CAREER: Pianist and composer, 1969—. Performer in concert tours in the United States, Canada, Europe, Asia, the Far East, and South America and on television programs. Member of Alsop-Bernstein Trio and New York Philomusica Chamber Ensemble. Lecturer and teacher. *Military service:* U.S. Army, 1950-52. *Member:* American Society of Composers, Authors and Publishers (ASCAP), National Association of Music Teachers, National Federation of Music Clubs, Bohemian Club. *Awards, honors:* Griffith Artist Award from Griffith Music Foundation, 1945, for piano performance; Instrumental Award from New York Madrigal Society, 1948, for piano performance; Premiere Prix and Prix Jacques Durand from Fontainebleau, France, 1953, for piano performance; grants from U.S. Department of State for Southeast Asia, the Far East, and South America, 1955, 1960, 1961, and 1967; Martha Baird Rockefeller grants for study with Clifford Curzon and debuts in Europe, 1958, and England, 1959; grant from Beebe Foundation, 1960; award from National Federation of Music Clubs, 1961, for furthering American music abroad; performance awards from American Society of Composers, Authors and Publishers (ASCAP), 1979, for performances of *BIRDS,* Books 1 and 2, and *New Pictures at an Exhibition,* and 1980 and 1982, for performances of *Tocatta francaise.*

WRITINGS: With Your Own Two Hands: Self-Discovery Through Music, Schirmer Books, 1981.

Compositions: *The Interrupted Waltz,* Schroeder & Gunther, 1964; *The Sad Puppet* [and] *Korean Bluebird,* Seesaw Music, 1967; *Toccata francaise,* Carl Fischer, 1969; *Birds,* Schroeder & Gunther, Book 1, 1972, Book 2, 1973; *Concerto for Our Time,* Schroeder & Gunther, 1972; *New Pictures at an Exhibition,* Alexander Broude, 1977; *Insects,* Books 1 and 2, Alexander Broude, 1977; *Raccoons,* Alexander Broude, Book 1, 1977, Book 2, 1983; *The Earth Music Series,* Books 1 and 2, Alexander Broude, 1977, Books 3-5, G. Schirmer, 1983; *One World* (choral work), Alexander Broude, 1977.

Recordings: *Sixty Piano Works by American Composers* (includes own compositions), Desto Records, 1972; *Twenty-six Piano Works by American Composers* (includes own compositions), Desto Records, 1973; *Three Pieces for Eight* [and] *Fugue for Trumpet and Piano by Josef Alexander,* Serenus Record Editions, 1976.

Contributor to magazines and to newspapers, including *Newsweek, Music Journal,* and *Keynote.*

WORK IN PROGRESS: A book, *Surviving a Career in Music;* two recordings, *Sonata for Cello and Piano by Ian Hamilton*

and *Goethe Cycle for Soprano, Horn and Piano by Meyer Kupferman,* both to be released in 1983.

SIDELIGHTS: Seymour Bernstein commented on practicing in *With Your Own Two Hands:* "During the last few years, when I came to understand the real reasons for practicing, I began to hold seminars for teachers and pupils. At the opportune moment, I invariably asked, 'Why do you practice?' The most common responses were: 'I practice to perfect my technique so that I will be able to play more beautifully' or 'I want to make my New York debut and eventually go on tours.' More disturbing was the comment, 'I've never thought about it.' The most encouraging answer was simply: 'I practice because I love music.'

"Naturally, you want to perfect your technique; perhaps you will even make a successful debut one day and eventually go on concert tours. Certainly, it is hard to imagine your doing all this without loving your art. Yet, there is an ultimate goal that transcends all these possible accomplishments: *Productive practicing is a process that promotes self-integration.* It is the kind of practicing that puts you in touch with an all-pervasive order—an order that creates a total synthesis of your emotions, reason, sensory perceptions, and physical coordination. The result is an integration that builds your self-confidence and affirms the unification of you and your talent. You can begin by believing that such an integration is possible, and that through it you can achieve a wholeness that affects your behavior in everything you do. The benefits you can thus bring to the lives of others justify the process of practicing."

BIOGRAPHICAL/CRITICAL SOURCES: Seymour Bernstein, *With Your Own Hands: Self-Discovery Through Music,* Schirmer Books, 1981.

*   *   *

BIAGGINI, Adriana Ivancich 1930(?)-1983

OBITUARY NOTICE: Born c. 1930 in Venice, Italy; committed suicide by hanging, March, 1983, in Capalbio, Italy. Author of *The White Tower,* a book in which Biaggini detailed her relationship with Ernest Hemingway. She was said to have been the model for the character Renata in the noted author's novel *Across the River and Into the Trees.* Biaggini was also known for her prize-winning cover designs for such Hemingway novels as *The Old Man and the Sea.* Obituaries and other sources: *Chicago Tribune,* March 28, 1983; *Time,* April 4, 1983.

*   *   *

BIANCHI, Robert S(teven) 1943-

PERSONAL: Born November 30, 1943, in New York, N.Y.; son of Robert V. and Bessie Bianchi; divorced; children: one daughter. *Education:* New York University, Ph.D., 1976. *Residence:* Brooklyn, N.Y. *Office:* Department of Egyptian and Classical Art, Brooklyn Museum, Brooklyn, N.Y. 11238.

CAREER: Brooklyn Museum, Brooklyn, N.Y., associate curator of department of Egyptian and classical art, 1976—. Adjunct professor at New York University, 1979, and Columbia University, 1981. Archaeologist and epigrapher for Brooklyn Museum excavations at Precinct of Mut in Egypt. *Member:* Archaeological Institute of America (member of state executive committee), American Association of Museums, Corpus Antiquitatum Aegyptiacarum, Explorers Club, Egypt Exploration Society, Egyptological Seminar of New York (secretary-treasurer). *Awards, honors:* Fulbright fellow in West Berlin, Germany, 1977; Mellon Humanist at Howard University, 1980; Bourse Jacques Vandier from the Louvre in Paris, France, 1981.

WRITINGS: (With A. Mercatante) *Who's Who in Egyptian Mythology,* C. N. Potter, 1978; *Egyptian Treasures,* Abrams, 1979; *Ancient Egyptian Sculpture From the Brooklyn Museum,* Brooklyn Museum, 1979; *Treasures of the Nile,* Newsweek, 1980; *Museums of Egypt,* Newsweek, 1980. Contributor of about fifty articles and reviews to magazines.

WORK IN PROGRESS: A book on ancient Egyptian costume; a children's series on famous people from history; a feature film about Cleopatra the Great.

SIDELIGHTS: Bianchi told *CA:* "Writing is the process of translating a very vivid visual experience, such as discovering a find on a dig, into prose at a later date in such a way that the intensity of the experience can be conveyed to the reader. There is really no substitute for that firsthand visual experience."

*   *   *

BIANCO, Margery (Williams)   1881-1944

BRIEF ENTRY: Born July 22, 1881, in London, England; died September 4, 1944, in New York, N.Y. British novelist, translator, and author of books for children. Bianco's first published works were the adult novels *The Late Returning* (1902), *Spendthrift Summer* (1903), and *The Price of Youth* (1904), but she is best known for her children's books. Of her nearly twenty works of children's fiction published between 1922 and 1944, the most popular were the "toy" stories *The Velveteen Rabbit; or, How Toys Become Real* (1922) and *Poor Cecco: The Wonderful Story of a Wonderful Wooden Dog Who Was the Jolliest Toy in the House Until He Went Out to Explore the World* (1925), illustrated by William Nicolson and Arthur Rackham, respectively. Her story *Winterbound* (1936) was a runner-up for the 1937 Newbery Medal. *Biographical/critical sources:* Anne C. Moore and Bertha M. Miller, editors, *Writing and Criticism: A Book for Margery Bianco,* Horn Book, 1951; *The Who's Who of Children's Literature,* Schocken, 1968; *Authors of Books for Young People,* 2nd edition, Scarecrow, 1971; *Notable American Women, 1607-1950: A Biographical Dictionary,* Belknap Press, 1971; *The Lincoln Library of Language Arts,* 3rd edition, Frontier Press (Columbus, Ohio), 1978.

*   *   *

BIDAULT, Georges   1899-1983

OBITUARY NOTICE: Born October 5, 1899, in Moulins, France; died January 27, 1983, in Cambo-les-Bains, France. Government official and author. Bidault was a renowned resistance fighter against the Germans during World War II. Imprisoned briefly by the Nazis, he was released and eventually joined the French underground movement and presided over the National Council of Resistance. He later recorded his experiences in *Resistance,* an autobiography. Bidault also served France as prime minister and foreign minister. He was exiled in 1962 for opposing Charles de Gaulle, but he returned to his country in 1968 following a general amnesty. Obituaries and other sources: *Current Biography,* Wilson, 1945, March, 1983; *Who's Who in the World,* 14th edition, Marquis, 1974; *The International Who's Who,* 45th edition, Europa, 1981; *Who's Who,* 134th edition, St. Martin's, 1982; *New York Times,* January 28, 1983.

BIRENBAUM, Harvey   1936-

PERSONAL: Born July 8, 1936, in Philadelphia, Pa.; son of Samuel (a furrier) and Fanny (a furrier; maiden name, Tannenbaum) Birenbaum; married Elizabeth Mezey (a writer), 1962; children: Tanya Alisa, Joshua Daniel. *Education:* Antioch College, B.A., 1958; Yale University, Ph.D., 1963. *Residence:* San Jose, Calif. *Office:* Department of English, San Jose State University, San Jose, Calif. 95192.

CAREER: Queens College of the City University of New York, Flushing, N.Y., lecturer in English, 1964-65; San Jose State University, San Jose, Calif., assistant professor, 1965-69, associate professor, 1969-81, professor of English, 1981—. Visiting lecturer at University of East Anglia, 1972-73; member of faculty at Psychological Studies Institute, Palo Alto, Calif., 1981. *Member:* Philological Association of the Pacific Coast. *Awards, honors:* Woodrow Wilson fellow, 1958-62.

WRITINGS: (Contributor) Robert W. Corrigan, editor, *Tragedy: Vision and Form,* 2nd edition, Harper, 1981; *Tragedy and Innocence,* University Press of America, 1983. Contributor to magazines, including *Mosaic, Yale Review, San Jose Studies,* and *Pacific Coast Philology.*

WORK IN PROGRESS: The Art of Our Necessities: Myth and Consciousness in Shakespeare; Myth and Mind, an introduction to the psychology and philosophy of myth.

SIDELIGHTS: Birenbaum told *CA:* "My writing is a direct outgrowth of my teaching. Both have been driven by a need to unite two sides of my mental life: my love of traditional literature—as it has been developed through an academic sense of responsibility for knowledge; and my deep concern for the immediacy of personal experience—heightened by the apocalyptic rumblings of the 1960's. By attempting to justify each side in terms of the other, I have tried to help feel out where I think our culture needs to go: towards the development of a sense of mind that breaks down distinctions between the intellectual and the passionate, the personal and the objective, the rational and the mystical, the need for change and the constant roots of our humanity.

"On my specific writings: *Tragedy and Innocence* is an experimental coupling of two brief complementary treatises on the relation of life to literature—one exploring the tragic vision of life and the other (through the poetry of Blake), the ecstatic. *The Art of Our Necessities* studies a sequence of Shakespeare's major plays, emphasizing their nature as psychological experiences which reveal and explore the structure of consciousness. I emphasize the plays' relation to romance conventions and archetypal form, their nature as symbolic projections, and their expression of selfhood. *Myth and Mind* analyzes the nonlinear features of mythic imagery—in space, time, causation, identity, values, truthfulness, and mode of being—in order to suggest an overall conception of reality."

*   *   *

BISHOP, Eugene C.   1909-1983

OBITUARY NOTICE: Born in 1909 in Tigard, Ore.; died April 4, 1983, in Stanford, Calif. Journalist. Bishop helped develop Peninsula Newspapers, Incorporated, after World War II. He served in several capacities for the California Newspaper Publishers Association and was president of the *Palo Alto Times* and the *Redwood City Tribune* (now the *Peninsula Times Tri-*

bune). Obituaries and other sources: *New York Times*, April 7, 1983; *Chicago Tribune*, April 8, 1983.

* * *

BITTKER, Boris I(rving) 1916-

BRIEF ENTRY: Born November 28, 1916, in Rochester, N.Y. American lawyer, educator, and author. Bittker joined the law faculty of Yale University in 1946. He was named Southmayd Professor of Law in 1958 and Sterling Professor of Law in 1970. Bittker has been a Fulbright lecturer at University of Pavia and University of Siena, and he has taught at Stanford University, University of San Diego, Hastings College of the Law, and New York University. He was Charles Inglis Thomson Professor of Law at University of Colorado in 1966. Bittker's books include *Federal Income, Estate, and Gift Taxation* (Prentice-Hall, 1955), *Federal Income Taxation of Corporations and Shareholders* (Federal Tax Press, 1959), *Professional Responsibility and Federal Tax Practice* (New York University School of Commerce, 1965), and *The Case for Black Reparations* (Random House, 1973). *Address:* School of Law, Yale University, New Haven, Conn. 06520. *Biographical/critical sources: New York Review of Books*, April 5, 1973; *Yale Review*, October, 1973; *Directory of American Scholars*, Volume IV: *Philosophy, Religion, and Law*, 8th edition, 1982.

* * *

BLACK, Robert B(ruce) 1920-

PERSONAL: Born May 23, 1920, in Arlington, Mass.; son of S. Bruce and Adele B. Black; married Jeannetta Wilson, June 14, 1964; children: Brenda, Rebecca. *Education:* Harvard University, B.S., 1942, M.A., 1947, M.P.A., 1948, Ph.D., 1950. *Politics:* Democrat. *Religion:* Christian. *Home:* 6655 MacArthur Blvd., Bethesda, Md. 20816.

CAREER: U.S. Bureau of the Budget, Washington, D.C., fiscal analyst, 1949-52; programmer for U.S. foreign aid agencies, Washington, D.C., 1952-58; Agency for International Development, Washington, D.C., deputy director of mission to Tunisia, 1958-61, director of missions to Segegal, 1963-64, and Costa Rica, 1967-68; associated with U.S. War College, 1963-64; U.S. Department of State, Washington, D.C., foreign affairs officer, 1964-72; director of Office of Population and Civic Development, 1972-74; economic consultant, 1975—. *Military service:* U.S. Navy, 1942-46.

WRITINGS: (With John Esterline) *Inside Foreign Policy*, Mayfield, 1975. Contributor to journals.

* * *

BLACK, Theodore Michael 1919-

PERSONAL: Born October 3, 1919, in Brooklyn, N.Y.; son of Walter Joseph (a publisher) and Elsie (a philanthropist; maiden name, Jantzer) Black; married Barbara A. Somerville (an executive), November 10, 1956; children: Walter Joseph II, Theodore Michael; (stepchildren) Beverly A. Pavlak, Dorothy B. Scharkopf. *Education:* Princeton University, B.A. (summa cum laude), 1941. *Politics:* Republican. *Religion:* Roman Catholic. *Home:* 47 Cornwell's Beach Rd., Sands Point, N.Y. 11050. *Office:* Walter J. Black, Inc., 1075 Northern Blvd., Flower Hill, Roslyn, N.Y. 11576.

CAREER: Walter J. Black, Inc. (publisher), Roslyn, N.Y., 1945—, vice-president, 1952-58, president, 1958—, treasurer,

1958-80, chief executive officer, 1980—. General partner of Black's Readers Service Co., Roslyn, 1949—, president, 1958—; president of Classics Club, Detective Book Club, and Zane Grey Library. Member of Federal Advisory Panel on Financing Elementary and Secondary Education, 1979—; member of North Hempstead Board of Ethics; member of Better Business Bureau of Long Island; member of board of trustees of Roslyn Savings Bank, 1973—; member of executive committee of Princeton University Alumni Council, 1950-63. Executive director of Citizens for Nixon-Lodge, 1960; chairman of Citizens for Congressman S.B. Derounian, 1962-64, and Seldin for Congress, 1968; delegate to Republican National Convention, 1980. *Military service:* U.S. Army, Counterintelligence Corps, 1941-45; became captain; received Bronze Star with cluster, Belgian and French Fourrageres. U.S. Army Reserve, 1945-67; became lieutenant colonel.

MEMBER: Reserve Officers Association of the United States (Military Intelligence Reserve Society chapter), U.S. Armor Association, Association of the United States Army, American Legion, National Counterintelligence Corps Association, Direct Mail Merchandising Association, Association of Third Class Mail Users, United Service Organizations, Third Armored Division Association, Long Island Advertising Club, Long Island Association (member of board of directors), Nassau Heart Association, Phi Beta Kappa, Elks, Lions, Port Washington Republican Club, Congressional Club (chairman, 1980), Port Washington Yacht Club, Sands Point Golf Club, Capitol Hill Club, Publishers/Lunch Club.

AWARDS, HONORS: Medal from Sons of the American Revolution, 1941; honorary degrees include Litt.D. from Siena College, 1971, LL.D. from Adelphi University, 1974, and Fordham University, 1978, Ph.D. from Hofstra University, 1974, D.C.L. from Molloy College, 1975, and L.H.D. from C. W. Post College of Long Island University, 1976, and Pace University, 1978; distinguished service award from Nassau-Suffolk School Boards Association, 1973; award from Polytechnic Institute of New York, 1974; award from Long Island Association of Special Education Administrators, 1975; man of the year award from Long Island Advertising Club, 1975; humanitarian award from American Jewish Committee, 1976; John Jay Higher Education Public Policy Award, 1980; citizen of the year award from New York State Society of Professional Engineers, 1980; St. John Neumann Award, 1980.

WRITINGS: Know Your Stamps, Plymouth Press, 1934; *Democratic Party Publicity in the 1940 Campaign*, Plymouth Press, 1941; *How to Organize and Run a Citizen's Committee for Your Candidate*, Republican Citizens Committee, 1964; *Straight Talk About American Education*, Harcourt, 1982.

SIDELIGHTS: Black told *CA:* "Eleven years of service as a member of the New York State Board of Regents, the final five years as chancellor, convinced me that we are permitting too many extraneous considerations to detract from our primary goal: the attainment of excellence in education. *Straight Talk About American Education* tells how we can do our jobs as educators better and more effectively."

BIOGRAPHICAL/CRITICAL SOURCES: Washington Post Book World, January 9, 1983.

* * *

BLACKMAN, Audrey 1907-

PERSONAL: Born July 28, 1907, in London, England; daughter of Richard and Hilda (McDowell) Seligman; married Geoffrey Emett Blackman, October 8, 1931 (died August 2, 1980). *Education:* Attended Goldsmith's College, London, and University of Reading. *Politics:* Social Democrat. *Religion:* Church of England. *Home:* Wood Croft, Foxcombe Lane, Boars Hill, Oxford OX1 5DH, England.

CAREER: Painter and sculptor in ceramics and bronze. Work exhibited at home and abroad and in permanent collections at Fitzwilliam Museum, Cambridge, City of Stoke-on-Trent Museum, Paisley Museum, Cecil Higgins Museum, Bedford, Melbourne University, Magdalen College, Oxford, Czechoslovak Ceramics Museum, Bechyne, Oxfordshire County Museum, Crafts Study Centre, and Holbourne Museum, Bath. Founder of Federation of British Craft Societies, 1970. Member of Government Advisory Committee on the Crafts (now Crafts Council), 1971-73. *Member:* International Academy of Ceramics, Society of Designer-Craftsman (fellow; chairman, 1967-70), Craftsmen Potters Association, Brother Art Workers' Guild.

WRITINGS: Rolled Pottery Figures, Pitman, 1978.

*   *   *

BLAIR, Harry Wallace   1938-

PERSONAL: Born March 25, 1938, in Washington, D.C.; son of Newell and Greta (Flintermann) Blair; married Barbara A. Shailor (a professor), December 26, 1981; children: Emily. *Education:* Cornell University, A.B., 1960; Duke University, M.A., 1968, Ph.D., 1970. *Office:* Department of Political Science, Bucknell University, Lewisburg, Pa. 17837.

CAREER: Conducted field research in India, 1966-67; Colgate University, Hamilton, N.Y., instructor in political science, 1968-70; Bucknell University, Lewisburg, Pa., assistant professor, 1970-77, associate professor, 1977-83, professor of political science, 1983—, head of department, 1982—. Visiting fellow at Center for International Studies, Cornell University, 1972-73, visiting associate professor, 1979, 1980-81, research associate, 1979, research associate at South Asian Institute, Columbia University, 1974. Conducted field research in Bangladesh, 1973, 1980, and India, 1978-79, 1980. Social analyst for U.S. Agency for International Development, 1981-82. *Military service:* U.S. Army, 1961-63; became first lieutenant.

AWARDS, HONORS: Fellow of Social Science Research Council, 1972-73, grants, 1978, 1980; senior fellow at American Institute of Indian Studies, 1973-74; grant from American Council of Learned Societies, 1974; Fulbright fellow, 1978-79; grant from Smithsonian Institution, 1980.

WRITINGS: The Elusiveness of Equity: Institutional Approaches to Rural Development in Bangladesh, Rural Development Committee, Center for International Studies, Cornell University, 1974; *Voting, Caste, Community, Society: Explorations in Aggregate Data Analysis in India and Bangladesh,* Young Asia, 1979; (contributor) N. Gerald Barrier, editor, *The Census in British India: New Perspectives,* Manohar, 1981; *The Political Economy of Participation in Local Development Programs: Short-Term Impasse and Long-Term Change in South Asia and the United States From the 1950s to the 1970s,* Rural Development Committee, Center for International Studies, Cornell University, 1982; (contributor) Dale W. Adams and other editors, *Why Cheap Credit Undermines Rural Development,* World Bank, 1983; (contributor) Walter Hauser and James Manor, editors, *Social Change in Two Indian States: Bihar and Karnataka,* Oxford University Press, in press. Con-

tributor of articles and reviews to political science and sociology journals, and to newspapers.

WORK IN PROGRESS: Room for Maneuver in the Longer Term: Promoting Structural Change in Bangladesh.

*   *   *

BLAKE, Brian   1918-

PERSONAL: Born September 13, 1918, in Rochdale, England; son of Herbert (an engineer)and Elizabeth (a confectioner; maiden name, Kelly) Blake; married Joyce Smith (a lecturer), January, 1946. *Education:* Cambridge University, B.A., 1948, M.A., 1950. *Politics:* Socialist. *Home and office:* Silver Beck, Silverhowe, Grasmere, Cumbria LA22 9PX, England.

CAREER: Adult Education Settlement, Maryport, England, warden, 1948-52; free-lance consultant, 1952-59; British Broadcasting Corp., London, England, talks producer and broadcaster, 1959-66; industrial consultant in human and industrial relations with Associated Industrial Consultants, 1966-68; free-lance consultant, 1968-70; University of Lancaster, Bailrigg, England, lecturer in media services, 1970-82, director of media services, 1976-82; free-lance consultant, 1982—. *Military service:* British Army, Royal Artillery, 1939-46; served in India and Burma; became staff sergeant.

WRITINGS: The Solway Firth, R. Hale, 1955, 3rd edition, 1982; (with wife, Joyce Blake) *The Story of Carlisle,* Carlisle City Council, 1958; *People in the Electronic Age,* Open University Press, 1973. Contributor to magazines and newspapers.

WORK IN PROGRESS: A book on interviewing and being interviewed, publication expected in 1984.

AVOCATIONAL INTERESTS: Archaeology (including directing excavations), rock climbing, sailing, swimming, cats.

*   *   *

BLAKE, Eubie
See BLAKE, James Hubert

*   *   *

BLAKE, James Hubert   1883-1983
(Eubie Blake)

OBITUARY NOTICE: Born February 7, 1883, in Baltimore, Md.; died of pneumonia, February 12, 1983, in New York, N.Y. Performer and songwriter whose numerous compositions include "Memories of You" and "I'm Just Wild About Harry." Blake's musical roots were in the ragtime music of the early twentieth century. A contemporary of Scott Joplin, Blake wrote his first song, "Charleston Rag," in 1899. He later joined Noble Sissle in a partnership that culminated in the production of "Shuffle Along," the first black musical performed on Broadway. After World War II, during which Blake had entertained American troops in Europe, he retired to study composition. Twenty years later, with a renewed interest in ragtime underway across America, Blake was enticed by legendary producer John Hammond to perform on a series of recordings. The records revived Blake's career, and the songwriter resumed performing in America and Europe. Hailed as one of America's greatest musical talents, Blake appeared on television and in publications, where interest in his music was matched only by a fascination with his longevity. Throughout the last ten years of his life, Blake's birthdays were occasions for public celebrations. He was awarded the Medal of Freedom by President Ronald Reagan in 1981 and was the subject of a massive tribute at Kennedy Center in 1983. Blake, who smoked a pack of cigarets every day from age six and refused to drink water, claimed, "If I'd known I was going to live this long, I'd have taken better care of myself." He attributed his fortune to a natural penchant for ragtime's rhythm and declared: "I first heard it when I was about 11 or 12. It had no name. It just swung and made me feel good. It was my baby. Goodbye, Beethoven." He died after celebrating his one hundredth birthday. *Obituaries and other sources: Los Angeles Times,* February 13, 1983; *Washington Post,* February 13, 1983; *New York Times,* February 14, 1983; *Chicago Tribune,* February 14, 1983; *London Times,* February 14, 1983; *Time,* February 21, 1983; *New Yorker,* February 28, 1983.

* * *

BLAND, Larry I(rvin) 1940-

PERSONAL: Born August 20, 1940, in Indianapolis, Ind.; son of Harold I. (a railway postal clerk) and Emma C. (Watt) Bland; married Joellen R. Kuerst (a writer and theatre director); children: Neil, Ryan. *Education:* Purdue University, B.S., 1962; University of Wisconsin—Madison, Ph.D., 1972. *Home:* 502 Pickett St., Lexington, Va. 24450. *Office:* George C. Marshall Research Foundation, Drawer 1600, Lexington, Va. 24450.

CAREER: P. R. Mallory Capacitor Co., Indianapolis, Ind., resident engineer, 1962-67; Gaston College, Dallas, N.C., assistant professor of history, 1971-76; editor. *Member:* Organization of American Historians, Association for Documentary Editing, Society for Historians of American Foreign Relations, Rockbridge Historical Society. *Awards, honors:* College teaching fellowship from National Endowment for the Humanities, 1976-77.

WRITINGS: (Editor with Sharon R. Ritenour) *The Papers of George Catlett Marshall,* Volume 1: *The Soldierly Spirit, December 1880-June 1939,* Johns Hopkins University Press, 1982; (editor) *Proceedings of the Rockbridge Historical Society,* Rockbridge County, Va., Historical Society, Volume 8, 1979, Volume 9, 1982. Consulting editor of Historic Lexington Foundation. Contributor to journals.

WORK IN PROGRESS: Editing *The Papers of George Catlett Marshall,* Volume 2: *1939-1941,* publication expected in 1984.

SIDELIGHTS: The Papers of George Catlett Marshall, Volume 1, contains 506 articles of correspondence and assorted writings by the general and former chief of staff whose Marshall Plan helped restore the defeated nations of World War II. Gladwin Hill, writing in the *Los Angeles Times Book Review,* noted, "The accumulated Marshalliana speak not only of Marshall, but of the armed forces and the politics and personalities of his time." Hill also wrote, "Some may wonder if this is not a pursuit like saving tinfoil or collecting matchbooks. But any writer or investigator knows that in trying to reconstruct the past . . . almost any shred of evidence may fill a significant gap in a mosaic."

Hugh Brogan's lengthy review in the *Times Literary Supplement* focused on the merits of the editors' particular selections. "Larry I. Bland and Sharon R. Ritenour might have justified themselves by picking out of the Marshall archive those documents which throw light on American army life in the first forty years of our century, and only incidentally reveal Marshall," he wrote. "Very wisely they have rejected this course and instead produced what amounts to a documentary biog-

raphy." Brogan added, "All the items printed . . . throw light on Marshall's mind, or personality, or career." He praised the volume's publication as "an important, even a necessary, event."

BIOGRAPHICAL/CRITICAL SOURCES: Los Angeles Times Book Review, April 25, 1982; *Times Literary Supplement,* June 25, 1982.

* * *

BLUMBERG, Rena J(oy) 1934-

PERSONAL: Born October 31, 1934, in Cleveland, Ohio; daughter of Ezra Z. and Sylvia L. (Lamport) Shapiro; married Michael S. Blumberg, March 6, 1964; children: Catharyn Ashley, David Monte, Stuart Ethan. *Education:* Brandeis University, B.A. (cum laude), 1956. *Home:* 18910 South Woodland Rd., Shaker Heights, Ohio 44122. *Office:* 1250 Superior Ave., Cleveland, Ohio 44114.

CAREER: Brandeis University, Waltham, Mass., interviewer, 1956—, fellow, 1973—, member of board of trustee, 1978—, past chairman of council of Ohio Area Alumni Conference. Co-host of "Cleveland Connection," an interview program on WKYC-TV, 1976-77; director of community relations for WIXY-AM Radio, 1972-80, WDOK-FM Radio, 1972—, and WWWE-AM Radio, 1980—; radio interviewer; teacher; lecturer. Founder of WomenSpace; member of executive board of National U.S. Commission for Women; chairman of communications committee of Jewish Community Federation; media adviser to Junior League of Cleveland; media representative of Radio-TV Council and co-chairman of Media Marathon. Member of board of directors of Cleveland Committee for the Economic Growth of Israel, Federation for Community Planning, Greater Cleveland Growth Association, Jewish Community Federation, Medical Mutual, Ohio School of Broadcasting Technique, Playhouse Square Foundation, Housing Advocates, and WVIZ-TV; member of advisory board of Arthritis Foundation and Friends of Shaker Square. Past member of board of directors of Bureau of Jewish Education, Cleveland Restoration Society, College of Jewish Studies, Council of Human Relations, Jewish Community Center, and School on Magnolia; past co-chairman of Women's Division of Jewish Welfare Fund; vice-president of Cleveland Area Arts Council, 1974-76, and WVIZ-TV Women's Council, 1976. *Member:* American Cancer Society (member of board of directors), Cleveland City Club (member of board of directors; vice-president, 1976), Oakwood Club.

AWARDS, HONORS: Marvin and Milton Kane Young Leadership Award, 1968; public relations award from Council on Jewish Welfare Funds and Federations, 1971; Business Women Leader Award from Young Women's Christian Association, 1977; Twyla M. Conway Awards from Radio-Television Council of Greater Cleveland, 1978, 1979, 1981, and 1982, for public affairs programming; outstanding service award from WomanSpace Coalition, 1978; Abe Lincoln Award to Distinguished Broadcasters from Southern Baptist Radio and Television Commission, 1978; Ohio State Media Awards from American Cancer Society, 1979, 1980, 1981, and 1982, and Courage Award, 1982; award from Jewish Theological Seminary of American, 1979; special award from Radio-TV Council, 1980, for service to broadcasting and the community; Matrix Award from Women in Communications, 1981; Lighthouse Award from Public Relations Society of America, 1981; awards from U.S. Small Business Administration, 1982; Newsleader Award from United Press International, 1982, for best public service program; named "man of the year" by Organization for Rehabilitation Through Planning, 1982.

WRITINGS: Headstrong: A Story of Conquest and Celebrations . . . Living Through Chemotherapy, Crown, 1982.

SIDELIGHTS: In *Headstrong,* Blumberg relates her experiences during a course of chemotherapy she underwent following a mastectomy. She describes the physical changes that occurred during the treatment, answers questions others fear to ask of chemotherapy patients, and throughout the book, illustrates the "fighting mad" attitude that helped her through the physical and emotional ordeal.

Blumberg commented: "I am extremely interested in women's issues and in maintaining control over one's life."

* * *

BLUNT, Anthony (Frederick) 1907-1983

OBITUARY NOTICE: Born September 26, 1907, in Bournemouth, England; died of a heart attack, March 26, 1983, in London, England. Art historian, Soviet spy, educator, and author. Prior to 1979, Blunt was best known for his authoritative volumes on European art, including *Sicilian Baroque, The Art of William Blake,* and *Art and Architecture in France, 1500 to 1700.* In 1979, seven years after Blunt had resigned as art advisor to the queen of England, author Michael Straight exposed Blunt as a Soviet spy who had attempted to recruit Straight when the two men met at Cambridge University in the 1930's. It was then discovered that Blunt had already confessed his treason upon guarantee of immunity in 1964. Blunt disclosed that he had recruited agents for the Soviets and passed information while working for British intelligence during World War II. He was subsequently stripped of his knighthood. Obituaries and other sources: *International Authors and Writers Who's Who,* 8th edition, Melrose, 1977; *Who's Who in the World,* 4th edition, Marquis, 1978; *The Writers Directory: 1982-1984,* Gale, 1981; *The International Who's Who,* 46th edition, Europa, 1982; *Washington Post,* March 27, 1983; *Los Angeles Times,* March 27, 1983; *Chicago Tribune,* March 28, 1983; *London Times,* March 28, 1983; *Newsweek,* April 4, 1983; *Time,* April 4, 1983.

* * *

BLYTH, Estelle 1882(?)-1983

OBITUARY NOTICE: Born c. 1882; died March 8, 1983, in London, England. Secretary and author of religious works. Blyth was secretary to her father, Bishop George Popham Blyth, who was the first Anglican bishop in Jerusalem. Her writings include *The Children's History of the Crusades* and the autobiographical *When We Lived in Jerusalem.* Obituaries and other sources: *London Times,* March 24, 1983.

* * *

BOECKMAN, Patti
(Patti Beckman)

PERSONAL: Born in Chicago, Ill.; daughter of Levi Towle (an accountant) and Juanita (a nurse; maiden name, Vezie) Kennelly; married Charles Boeckman (a writer), July 25, 1965; children: Sharla Tricia. *Education:* Attended Del Mar Junior College, 1958-59; North Texas State University, B.A., 1962; Texas A & I University, M.A., 1972. *Religion:* Baptist. *Home and office:* 322 Del Mar Blvd., Corpus Christi, Tex. 78404.

CAREER: Secretary to county auditor of Nueces County, Tex., summers, 1958-62; teacher of English and Spanish at public secondary schools in Corpus Christi, 1962-65, 1966-74, and Victoria, Tex., 1965-66; photographer, 1974-76; writer, 1976—. Bass player with Dixieland band, 1970-76; sponsor of local jazz festival, 1973-74, 1976. Lecturer at writers' workshops; guest on "Today Show." *Member:* Romance Writers of America.

WRITINGS—Romance novels; under name Patti Beckman; published by Simon & Schuster: *Captive Heart,* 1980; *The Beachcomber,* 1980; *Louisiana Lady,* 1981; *Angry Lover,* 1981; *Love's Treacherous Journey,* 1981; *Spotlight to Fame,* 1982; *Bitter Victory,* 1982; *Daring Encounter,* 1982; *Mermaid's Touch,* 1982; *Please Let Me In,* 1982; *Tender Deception,* 1982; *Forbidden Affair,* 1983.

Contributor of several hundred articles to national magazines.

WORK IN PROGRESS: Romance novels.

SIDELIGHTS: Patti Boeckman told *CA:* "I am interested in people and human nature, both of which help me in my characterizations. I like research about what is going on today. I have traveled extensively in Mexico and speak Spanish. I enjoy people more than I enjoy things. My family and I enjoy trailering, and we have seen much of the United States."

She added: "Learn everything you can about everything you can. That's the best advice I can give anyone, whether an aspiring writer or not. You never know what God has in store for you. You might be surprised some day at the usefulness of little bits and pieces of information you have picked up. You never know how an experience may help you some time in the future.

"In my case, for example, I never expected to become a writer. But I married a successful writer, became one myself, and my flying experiences, incidents from my life, and all sorts of things I learned as I was growing up have shown up in the pages of my books.

"Writing takes practice, just like any other skill or art. No one would expect to become a championship skater or an accomplished pianist without a great deal of practice. The same is true of writing. To learn to write, you must spend time writing.

"I give my husband a great deal of the credit for my writing ability. Not only has he taught me how to write fiction, and I'm still learning, but he also has given me advice about how to avoid common pitfalls that writers often encounter."

Boeckman's books have been published in England, Japan, France, Brazil, Canada, Spain, Israel, and Switzerland.

AVOCATIONAL INTERESTS: Flying.

* * *

BOETIE, Dugmore 1920(?)-1966

OBITUARY NOTICE: Born c. 1920; died in November, 1966, in South Africa. Author of *Familiarity Is the Kingdom of the Lost: The Story of a Black Man in South Africa,* the partially autobiographical account of a crippled jailbird who fantasizes avenging his repeated incarcerations for drug peddling. Obituaries and other sources: *African Authors: A Companion to Black African Writing,* Volume I: *1300-1973,* Black Orpheus Press, 1973.

BOLTON, Muriel Roy   1909(?)-1983

OBITUARY NOTICE: Born c. 1909; died March 4, 1983, in Los Feliz, Calif. Author. Bolton wrote for films and television. He also contributed short stories to publications such as *Redbook* and *McCall's* and wrote a historical novel, *The Golden Porcupine*. She was probably best known as head writer and story consultant for the popular television series "The Millionaire," which depicted each week the actions of someone who received $1 million from an eccentric tycoon. Obituaries and other sources: *Los Angeles Times,* March 8, 1983.

* * *

BONN, Thomas L.   1939-

PERSONAL: Born January 14, 1939, in Scranton, Pa.; son of Fred T. (an optician) and Teresa (Reilly) Bonn; married Ellen Murphy (an editor), August 10, 1963; children: Frederic F., Amy E. *Education:* University of Notre Dame, A.B., 1960; New York University, M.A., 1961, graduate study, 1968-69; Syracuse University, M.S.L.S., 1969. *Home:* 527 Main St., Etna, N.Y. 13062. *Office:* Memorial Library, State University of New York College at Cortland, Cortland, N.Y. 13045.

CAREER: New American Library (publishers), New York City, educational field representative, 1962-64; Franklin Book Programs (sponsor of publishing programs in developing countries), New York City, textbook consultant and assistant director of training, 1964-66; Cornell University Press, Ithaca, N.Y., sales manager, 1966-67; William Cameron Forbes Cultural Center, the George Junior Republic, Freeville, N.Y., director, 1967-68; State University of New York College at Cortland, Cortland, electronic media center librarian and reference bibliographer for law, political science, physical education, and recreation, 1969-72, 1973—, member of library personnel committee (chairman, 1975 and 1980), long-range planning committee, educational policy committee, and budget committee. Acting executive director of South Central Research Library Council, 1972-73. Adjunct professor at Syracuse University, 1975-77. *Military service:* U.S. Army Reserve, 1960-67.

MEMBER: American Library Association, New York Library Association, College and Research Library Association, Social Responsibilities Round Table of the Finger Lakes, Dryden School Board Nominating Committee (chairman, 1974), Dryden Town Planning Board. *Awards, honors:* Research grant from State University of New York Research Foundation, 1970, for "The Evolution of Mass Market Paperback Books, 1939-49," 1977, for "Interviews on Mass Market Paperback Publishing," and 1981, for "Editorial Papers of Victor Weybright"; grants from Friends of Tompkins County Public Library, 1974 and 1978; chancellor's award from State University of New York, 1982, for excellence in librarianship.

WRITINGS: (Contributor) Dominic Salvatore, editor, *The Paperback Goes to School,* BIPAD, 1972; (contributor) Ed Schilders, editor, *Brooklyn Bridge,* Drukwerk, 1979; (contributor) Jean Peters, editor, *Collectible Books: Some New Paths,* Bowker, 1979; *Paperback Primer: A Guide for Collectors,* Pecan Valley Press, 1981; (contributor) William Crider, editor, *Mass Market American Paperbacks: 1973-1979,* G. K. Hall, 1982; *Under Cover: An Illustrated History of American Mass Market Paperbacks,* Penguin, 1982. Contributor of articles and book reviews to periodicals, including *Library Journal, Choice, Paperback Quarterly, Bookmark,* and *American Collector.*

WORK IN PROGRESS: American Publishing: A Research Guide, tentative title, highlighting the significant publications issued since 1945, reflecting on and explaining the changes that have occurred in the field over the past thirty-five years, publication by Greenwood Press expected in 1986; research on the editorial activities of Victor Weybright, intended for inclusion in a lengthy study of publishing.

SIDELIGHTS: Under Cover: An Illustrated History of American Mass Market Paperbacks traces the publication of softcover books from mid-nineteenth-century Europe to the founding of an American paperback publishing house in 1939, and the rise of numerous American competitors. Reproductions of paperback covers, many in color, illustrate the text.

Bonn told *CA:* "The book as a physical object has always fascinated me. My work as a student book clerk at the Notre Dame Bookstore gave me direct experience dealing not only with books but with people who read them. This experience coincided with the great expansion of trade paperback publishing in the late 1950's. All sorts of wonderful works of nonfiction were made available for the first time in affordable editions, thus making it possible for hundreds of students and faculty to assemble personal libraries devoted to one's intellectual interests.

"This was also a period of change in the cover designs of mass market paperbacks. New retail bookstore arrangements directly influenced the appearance of the 'drugstore' paperback. After completing a degree at New York University's Graduate Institute of Book Publishing and army service, my first job was with the paperback publisher New American Library. As their first college traveler, I learned about paperback publishing from the inside. While completing my third degree at Syracuse University, I began researching the non-illustrative design features of paperbacks. My work as a librarian in the State University of New York further encouraged research into the paperback industry. Subsequent grants have allowed me to interview dozens of people connected with the start of various successful softcover operations in the twentieth century. In turn, this has led to the publication of two books, *Paperback Primer* and *Under Cover.* The increased recognition given to mass market publishing as the major development in twentieth-century American book publishing, augmented by the advent of hundreds of collectors of old paperbacks, should keep both of these publications in print for a long time."

BIOGRAPHICAL/CRITICAL SOURCES: Chicago Tribune, June 6, 1982; *New York Times,* July 4, 1982; *Washington Post Book World,* July 11, 1982; *Los Angeles Herald Examiner,* September 5, 1982.

* * *

BONNAMY, Francis
See WALZ, Audrey Boyers

* * *

BOONE, Buford   1909(?)-1983

OBITUARY NOTICE: Born c. 1909; died of cancer, February 7, 1983, in Druid City, Ala. Journalist who received a Pulitzer Prize in 1957 for "courage and independence" in reporting on racism involving admission of the first black student to the University of Alabama. Boone was president and publisher of the *Tuscaloosa News* before retiring in 1968. He remained with that paper as board chairman until 1974. Obituaries and other sources: *New York Times*, February 9, 1983; *Chicago Tribune*, February 10, 1983; *Washington Post*, February 12, 1983.

*   *   *

BORRIE, Wilfred David   1913-

PERSONAL: Born September 2, 1913, in Waimate, New Zealand; son of Peter William (a farmer) and Isabella (Doig) Borrie; married Alice H. Miller (an educator), January 4, 1942; children: Catherine. *Education:* Otago University, B.A., 1935, M.A., 1937; graduate study at Cambridge University, 1939. *Home:* 29 Norman St., Deakin, Australian Capital Territory 2600, Australia. *Office:* Academy of the Social Sciences in Australia, National Library Building, Canberra 2600, Australia.

CAREER: University of Sydney, Sydney, Australia, research fellow in economics department, 1942-43, lecturer, 1944-46, senior lecturer and member of board of social studies, 1947-48; Australian National University, Canberra, senior research fellow, 1948-51, reader in charge of department, 1952-57, professor of demography, 1957-79, professor emeritus, 1979—, director of Research School of Social Sciences, 1968-73. Chairman of United Nations Population Commission, 1965-69. *Member:* Academy of the Social Sciences in Australia (executive director, 1979—), Social Science Research Council of Australia (chairman, 1962-64). *Awards, honors:* D.Litt., University of Tasmania, 1975; Commander of Order of the British Empire, 1979; D.Sc.Econ., University of Sydney, 1979; LL.D., Australian National University, 1982.

WRITINGS: (Co-author) *A White Australia: Australia's Population Problem*, Australasian Publishing Co., 1947; *Population Trends and Policies: A Study in Australian and World Demography*, Australasian Publishing Co., 1948; *Immigration: Australia's Problems and Prospects*, Angus & Robertson, 1949; (with D.R.G. Parker) *Italians and Germans in Australia: A Study of Assimilation*, F. W. Cheshire, 1954; (with M. Diegues, Jr., and others) *The Cultural Integration of Immigrants*, United Nations Educational, Scientific & Cultural Organization, 1959; (with Geraldine Spencer) *Australia's Population Structure and Growth*, Committee for Economic Development of Australia, 1964, 2nd edition, 1965; (with Spencer) *Statistical Appendix to Australia's Population Structure and Growth: The Projections by Single Years of Age and Single Year Intervals, 1964-1978*, Department of Demography, Australian National University, 1965; (editor with Morag Cameron) *Population Change: Asia and Oceania*, Department of Demography, Australian National University, 1969; *The Growth and Control of World Population*, Weidenfeld & Nicolson, 1970; *Population, Environment, and Society*, Auckland University Press, 1973; *Population and Australia: A Demographic Analysis and Projection*, two volumes, Australian Government Publishing Service, 1975; *Population and Australia: Recent Demographic Trends and Their Implications*, Australian Government Publishing Service, 1978; (editor and contributor) *Implications of Australian Population Trends*, Academy of the Social Sciences in Australia, 1982.

SIDELIGHTS: Borrie told CA: "As a social historian my interests were initially in imperial migration and overseas settlement from Europe to the New World; then followed investigations into other factors of population change (fertility and mortality) and studies of population theory and the causation of emerging trends of a 'small family' system. I was able to teach in these fields at Sydney University, and the establishment of a post in demography at the new Australian National

University, to which I was lucky enough to be appointed, gave me the chance to become a professional demographer. I was hooked on a research career, and to the best of my knowledge, my chair of demography was the first chair to go by that name in the world. (Others practicing demography were economists, historians, sociologists, and the like.) However, there are now numerous chairs of demography and six of these are held by graduates of our department at the Australian National University.''

*   *   *

BOULGER, James Denis   1931-1979

PERSONAL: Born June 9, 1931, in North Adams, Mass.; died in 1979; son of James Francis and Marguerite (O'Brien) Boulger; married Jean Marie Stumpf, July 13, 1957; children: Ellen, James, John, Geoffrey. *Education:* College of the Holy Cross, A.B., 1953; Yale University, M.A., 1954, Ph.D., 1957. *Residence:* Providence, R.I.

CAREER: Yale University, New Haven, Conn., instructor in English, 1957-61; Cambridge University, Cambridge, England, Morse junior faculty fellow at St. Catharine's College, 1961-62; Yale University, assistant professor of English, 1962-64; Brown University, Providence, R.I., associate professor, 1964-69, professor of English, 1969-79. *Awards, honors:* Bronson fellow, 1970-71; fellow of American Philosophical Society, 1971.

WRITINGS: Coleridge as Religious Thinker, Yale University Press, 1961; (editor) *Twentieth-Century Interpretations of the Rime of the Ancient Mariner: A Collection of Critical Essays*, Prentice-Hall, 1969; *The Calvinistic Temper in English Poetry*, Mouton, 1980. Contributor to literature journals.

[Date of death provided by wife, Jean S. Boulger]

*   *   *

BOULT, Adrian (Cedric)   1889-1983

OBITUARY NOTICE: Born April 8, 1889, in Chester, England; died February 23, 1983, near London, England. Conductor, educator, and author. Boult was renowned for his interpretations of contemporary British composers, including Ralph Vaughan Williams and Edward Elgar. After studying at the Leipzig Conservatory in 1912, Boult accepted a position with the Covent Garden Opera. He debuted there in 1918 and won acclaim for his renditions of Vaughan Williams's second symphony ("London") and the premiere of Gustav Holst's "The Planets." In the 1920's Boult also conducted the London and Liverpool philharmonics and taught at the Royal College of Music. In 1930 he became the initial director of the BBC Symphony Orchestra, which he used to present further works of Vaughan Williams and Elgar as well as stirring performances of Johannes Brahms's symphonies. For the next forty years Boult continued conducting both in England and abroad, appearing with musical ensembles such as the NBC Symphony, the New York Philharmonic, and the Boston Symphony Orchestra. He assumed the musical directorship of the London Philharmonic Orchestra and added to the reputations of both with numerous outstanding recordings of works by Vaughan Williams, Elgar, and Franz Schubert. In the 1970's Boult reduced his schedule because of back pains suffered from countless years at the conductor's podium. He continued to record, though, by sitting throughout the sessions. He finally retired from conducting in 1981. Boult wrote an autobiography, *My*

Own Trumpet, and two handbooks on conducting. In 1971 he was the subject of a documentary film, "The Point of the Stick." Obituaries and other sources: *Current Biography*, Wilson, 1946, April, 1983; *The Oxford Companion to Music*, 10th edition, Oxford University Press, 1974; *New York Times*, February 23, 1983; *Washington Post*, February 24, 1983; *London Times*, February 24, 1983; *Los Angeles Times*, February 24, 1983; *Newsweek*, March 7, 1983; *Time*, March 7, 1983.

* * *

BOWDER, Diana (Ruth)   1942-

PERSONAL: Born May 14, 1942, in Oxford, England; daughter of Donald Valentine (a modern languages teacher) and Anne (a botanic artist; maiden name, Slater) Gilbert; married John Bowder (in government service), August 6, 1966; children: Catharine, Marina. *Education:* Lady Margaret Hall, Oxford, B.A., 1965, M.A., 1969, Ph.D., 1977. *Religion:* Church of England. *Residence:* Oxford, England. *Office:* Lady Margaret Hall, Oxford, England.

CAREER: Reading University, Berkshire, England, part-time lecturer in classical studies, 1979-80; historian and writer, 1978—. Member of West Hanney Parish Council, West Hanney Parochial Church Council, and governing body of East Hanney Church of England Primary School, near Wantage, Oxford. *Member:* Society for the Promotion of Roman Studies, Royal Archaeological Institute.

WRITINGS: The Age of Constantine and Julian, Barnes & Noble, 1978; (editor and contributor) *Who Was Who in the Roman World: 753 B.C.-476 A.D.*, Cornell University Press, 1980; (editor) *Who Was Who in the Greek World: 776 B.C.-30 B.C.*, Cornell University Press, 1982.

WORK IN PROGRESS: Nine Hundred Years of Hanney, a revised edition of village history, completion expected in 1983; *Christian and Late Pagan Antiquities of Britain and Gaul*, completion expected in 1985.

SIDELIGHTS: Bowder's first book, *The Age of Constantine and Julian*, studies the spread of Christianity in the ancient world. The result of the author's investigation, Robert Browning observed in the *Times Literary Supplement*, is a "valuable contribution" to the literature documenting the progression of Christianity.

Likewise, according to D.J.R. Bruckner's *New York Times Book Review* critique, Bowder's *Who Was Who in the Roman World* and *Who Was Who in the Greek World* are "invaluable guides" that animate historical and legendary figures from ancient history, excluding gods and goddesses. The first volume, Bruckner noted, "gives you a real acquaintance with the Romans." Historically accurate, *Who Was Who in the Roman World* was composed "virtually without a stumble," the critic maintained. Robin Seager, writing in the *Times Literary Supplement*, noticed the dictionary's admirable balance of political, literary, and philosophical Romans and significant non-Romans. Biographies of the Church Fathers are also among the entries.

The later work on the Greeks contains biographical sketches of poets, such as Homer, Sappho, and Pindar, playwrights, notably Aeschylus and Euripides, and philosophers, including Heraclitus. At least one critic cited Bowder's imaginative use of illustrations as an innovation in biographical dictionaries; for example, aerial photographs of battle sites complement the entries on military figures, and pictures of Greek theatres cor-

respond to playwrights. "These two 'Who Was Who' volumes are reliable and useful companions, much more than simple reference books," wrote Bruckner. "They have a rich texture—woven of history, personality, art, sculpture, photographs, drawings and maps. Learning from them is a pleasure."

Bowder told *CA*: "I was converted to the late Roman Empire by seeing the Ravenna mosaics during a four-month stay there at the age of nineteen. I think it is important to visit for myself the places and monuments I write about whenever this is possible. And to this end I have traveled widely within the Roman Empire."

BIOGRAPHICAL/CRITICAL SOURCES: Observer, September 17, 1978; *Times Literary Supplement*, November 3, 1978, May 22, 1981; *New York Times Book Review*, January 16, 1983.

* * *

BOX, Sydney   1907-1983

OBITUARY NOTICE: Born April 29, 1907, in Beckenham, England; died May 25, 1983, in Perth, Australia. Producer, director, and author of plays and motion pictures. During World War II Box used his own production company to produce training films for British troops. With former wife Muriel Box he wrote numerous screenplays, including the 1946 Academy Award winner "The Seventh Veil" and "The Man Within." In 1958 Box ended his profitable partnership with Muriel to accept an executive position in British television. They divorced in 1969. Obituaries and other sources: *International Authors and Writers Who's Who*, 8th edition, Melrose, 1977; *Film Encyclopedia*, Crowell, 1979; *London Times*, May 26, 1983; *New York Times*, May 26, 1983; *Washington Post*, May 26, 1983; *Chicago Tribune*, May 27, 1983; *Los Angeles Times*, May 28, 1983.

* * *

BOYD, William C(louser)   1903-1983

OBITUARY NOTICE: Born March 4, 1903, in Dearborn, Mo.; died of cancer, February 19, 1983, in Falmouth, Mo. Biochemist, educator, and author. In 1945 Boyd discovered that blood types could be determined by testing their reactions to lectins. This discovery enabled other scientists to further pursue studies in antibodies and allowed Boyd to determine that blood types were unalterable. Later work in blood science enabled Boyd to conclude that there are thirteen human blood types. He wrote hundreds of papers on blood science, as well as an early anthropological textbook, *Genetics and the Races of Man*, which he and Isaac Asimov later revised for children as *Races and People*. Boyd taught at Boston University. Obituaries and other sources: *American Men and Women of Science: The Physical and Biological Sciences*, 14th edition, Bowker, 1979; *Who's Who in America*, 42nd edition, Marquis, 1982; *Washington Post*, February 22, 1983; *New York Times*, February 23, 1983; *Chicago Tribune*, February 23, 1983.

* * *

BRADFORD, Roy Hamilton   1920-

PERSONAL: Born July 7, 1920; son of Joseph Hamilton and Isabel Mary (McNamee) Bradford; married Hazel Elizabeth Lindsay, 1946; children: Conor, Tobias. *Education:* Trinity

College, Dublin, B.A. (with first class honors), 1942. *Home:* Ardkeen, Carnalea, County Down, Northern Ireland.

CAREER: Television producer and writer for British Broadcasting Corp. (BBC); producer and writer for Instructional Television (ITV); Parliament of Northern Ireland, Unionist member of Parliament for Victoria, 1965-73, assistant whip, 1966, parliamentary secretary of Ministry of Education, 1967-68, chief whip, 1969, minister of commerce, 1969-71, minister of development, 1971-72; Northern Ireland Assembly, Unionist member for East Belfast, 1973—, minister for the environment, 1973-74. Member of Privy Council of Northern Ireland, 1969. Chairman of Northern Ireland Council of the European Movement, 1977-82. Member of board of directors of Geoffrey Sharp Ltd., 1962—. *Military service:* British Army, Intelligence, 1943-47; served in France, Belgium, and Germany. *Member:* Ulster Club (Belfast).

WRITINGS: Excelsior (novel), Barker, 1960; *The Last Ditch* (political novel), Blackstaff Press, 1982.

*   *   *

BRADY, Kristin   1949-

PERSONAL: Born February 20, 1949, in Buffalo, N.Y.; daughter of Charles A. (a writer and professor) and Eileen (Larson) Brady; married Avrum Fenson (a lawyer), July 19, 1981. *Education:* Canisius College, B.A., 1970; University of Toronto, M.A., 1972, Ph.D., 1978. *Office:* Department of English, University of Western Ontario, London, Ontario, Canada N6A 3K7.

CAREER: De Paul University, Chicago, Ill., assistant professor of English, 1979-82; University of Western Ontario, London, Ontario, assistant professor of English, 1982—. *Member:* Modern Language Association of America, Victorian Studies Association of Ontario, Midwest Victorian Studies Association, Hawthorne Society.

WRITINGS: The Short Stories of Thomas Hardy (criticism), St. Martin's, 1982.

WORK IN PROGRESS: Work on Thomas Hardy and Nathaniel Hawthorne.

SIDELIGHTS: Brady's *The Short Stories of Thomas Hardy* traces the evolution of the noted writer's short-story writing from 1865 to 1900. "It has often been lamented of late that Hardy's short stories are neglected," wrote John Adlard in the *Times Literary Supplement.* "Now Kristin Brady, in a comprehensive study, has done her best to remedy this."

BIOGRAPHICAL/CRITICAL SOURCES: New York Review of Books, October 7, 1982; *Times Literary Supplement,* October 22, 1982; *Times Higher Education Supplement,* November 4, 1982.

*   *   *

BRAGG, Bill
See BRAGG, William Fredrick, Jr.

*   *   *

BRAGG, William Fredrick, Jr.   1922-
(Bill Bragg)

PERSONAL: Born May 15, 1922, in Casper, Wyo.; son of William Fredrick (a writer) and Mary (a journalist; maiden name, Coburn) Bragg; married Rita Dean Reesy (a registered nurse), September 8, 1950; children: Laura Dean (Mrs. Tom Gaddis), Robert Fredrick, Barbara Lee, Betty Ellen. *Education:* University of Wyoming, B.A., 1952, M.A., 1953, further graduate study, 1953. *Politics:* Republican. *Religion:* Methodist. *Home:* 2921 Hanway, Casper, Wyo. 82601. *Office:* Office of Public Information, Casper College, 125 College Dr., Casper, Wyo. 82601.

CAREER: Eastern Wyoming College, Torrington, instructor in social science, 1953-55; Wyoming Travel Commission, Cheyenne, assistant director, 1955-57; University of Wyoming, Laramie, alumni director, 1957-58; Jackson Hole Corp., Jackson Hole, Wyo., executive director, 1959-61; sold sporting firearms and fishing tackle, 1961-64; Wyoming State Republican Party, Casper, executive director, 1964-67; *In Wyoming,* Casper, publisher and co-owner, 1967-68; free-lance radio writer, 1967-75; Casper College, Casper, public information director and instructor in Wyoming history, 1975—. Film location manager, actor, narrator, and writer, 1957-80; writer and narrator of advertising films for Grunkco Films. Seasonal regional historian at Fort Laramie National Monument, 1953-54. Advertising director of Jackson Hole Fine Arts Foundation and Symphony, 1959-61. Jobber sales representative for Little America Refinery, 1967-68. Writer for and director of Republican election campaigns; past member of Wyoming House of Representatives. Past member of Fort Caspar Commission. *Military service:* U.S. Marine Corps, Infantry, 1942-46; served in the southwest Pacific; became sergeant.

MEMBER: Western Writers of America, National Dude Ranchers Association (executive director, 1958-60), Wyoming State Historical Society (past president of county chapter; state president, 1980), Wyoming Writers, Natrona County Historical Society (president), University of Wyoming Alumni Association, Casper College Faculty Association, Sigma Alpha Epsilon, Phi Alpha, Veterans of Foreign Wars, American Legion, Masons.

AWARDS, HONORS: Named honorary Colorado Mountain Man by governor of Wyoming, 1960; named honorary Wyoming fish and game warden by Wyoming Game and Fish Commission, 1960; Wyoming Historical Awards from Wyoming State Historical Society, 1973, for *Wyoming's Wealth: A History of Wyoming,* 1975, for *Wyoming: Rugged But Right,* 1976, for film "Wyoming: From the Beginning," 1976, for story "Red Revenge," and 1978, for radio series "Wyoming's Colorful Past"; special award from Western Writers of American, 1980, for radio series "Wyoming's Colorful Past"; grant from Wyoming Council of the Humanities, 1977.

WRITINGS—Under name Bill Bragg: *Wyoming's Wealth: A History of Wyoming,* Big Horn Books, 1975; *Wyoming: Rugged But Right,* Pruett, 1980; *The War Horses* (western novel), Tower Publications, 1980; *Enemy in Sight* (western novel), Tower Publications, 1980; *The Sand Bar,* BASO, 1981; *Wyoming: Wild and Wooly,* Pruett, 1983; *Some Bad Men and Worse Women,* Pruett, 1983.

Films: "Wyoming's Waterway," released by Vacationland Studio, in 1955; "Wyoming's Wealth," Vacationland Studio, 1956; "Trout for Tarpon," Vacationland Studio, 1957; "Wyoming Snapshoot," Paramount Pictures, 1963; "Welcome to Winter," Pallerson Films, 1967; "Wyoming: From the Beginning," Grunkco Films, 1976.

Writer for television series "Zoo Parade" (now "Wild Kingdom") and "High Road to Danger," and for radio serials based on Wyoming history. Contributor of hundreds of stories to magazines, including *Western* and *Far West,* and to newspapers.

WORK IN PROGRESS: Fort Caspar: The Forgotten Fort, publication expected in 1985; *Drumm's War; Red Sword; Deadline at No Water;* "Overkill" (screenplay); *A Cavalcade of Cowmen; Ye Gods! Wyoming!;* a history of Casper College.

SIDELIGHTS: Bragg commented: "I am not satisfied with authors who try to interpret the West, and Wyoming in particular. All of my work is aimed at telling the true story of my native state. My family is a pre-territorial family, and, as such, we have a deep and abiding love for Wyoming. I am not a great writer, but I keep on honing my words so that before I die I will have written some few really good words about the West."

* * *

BRANCATI, Vitaliano 1907-1954

BRIEF ENTRY: Born July 24, 1907, in Pachino, Syracuse Province, Sicily; died September 25, 1954, in Turin, Italy. Italian teacher, playwright, and novelist. Brancati is probably best known for his anti-Fascist novels, including *Singalore avventura di viaggio* (title means "Strange Travel Tale"; 1934) *Don Giovanni in Sicilia* (title means "Don Juan in Sicily"; 1941), and *Il bell' Antonio* (1949; translation published as *Antonio, the Great Lover,* 1952). Brancati's early works, including the plays *Fedor* (1928) and *Piave* (1932; first produced in 1932), reveal an enthusiasm for fascism. The counsel of anti-Fascist Giuseppe Borgese swayed the young writer to oppose the repressive party. *Antonio, the Great Lover,* Brancati's only work published in America, concerns a renowned lover's reluctant association with manipulative Fascists. The lover, Antonio, is used as an example of Fascist might before the impressionable citizenry, but when he is revealed to be an impotent fraud, the Fascists likewise are humiliated. Brancati was most recognized as a moralist, but the posthumous publication of *Paolo il caldo* (title means "Paolo the Hot"; 1955) indicated that he had been developing as a stylist as well. *Biographical/critical sources: Encyclopedia of World Literature in the Twentieth Century,* updated edition, Ungar, 1967; *The Penguin Companion to European Literature,* McGraw, 1969; *Cassell's Encyclopaedia of World Literature,* revised edition, Morrow, 1973; *World Authors, 1950-70,* H. W. Wilson, 1980; *Twentieth-Century Literary Criticism,* Volume 11, Gale, 1983.

* * *

BRANTLEY, Cynthia Louise 1943-

PERSONAL: Born March 13, 1943, in Port Arthur, Tex.; divorced. *Education:* University of Texas at Austin, B.A., 1965; University of California, Los Angeles, M.A., 1967, Ph.D., 1973. *Office:* Department of History, University of California, Davis, Calif. 95616.

CAREER: University of California, Davis, assistant professor, 1972-80, associate professor of history, 1980—. *Member:* American Historical Association, African Studies Association.

WRITINGS: The Giriama and Colonial Resistance in Kenya, 1800-1920, University of California Press, 1982.

WORK IN PROGRESS: Aging in Africa.

BRAUNBURG, Rudolf 1924-

PERSONAL: Born July 19, 1924, in Landsberg, Germany; son of Willy and Hedwig (Schulz) Braunburg; married Annemarie Pohl, September 20, 1969; children: Viola. *Education:* Attended high school in Lueneburg, Germany. *Home:* Felsenweg 15, D-5520, Broel, West Germany.

CAREER: Rudolf Steiner School, Hamburg, West Germany, teacher, 1949-55; German Air Lines Lufthansa, Frankfurt, West Germany, pilot and flight captain, 1955-79; writer, 1979—. *Military service:* German Luftwaffe, fighter pilot, 1943-44.

WRITINGS: Der verratene Himmel (novel), [West Germany], 1979, translation by J. Maxwell Brownjohn published as *Betrayed Skies,* Doubleday, 1979.

Novels in German: *Dem Himmel naeher als der Erde* (title means "Nearer to Sky Than to Earth"), Marion V. Schroeder, 1957; *Geh nicht nach Dalaba* (title means "Don't Go to Dalaba"), Marion V. Schroeder, 1961; *Zwischenlandung* (title means "Intermission-Stop"), Schneekluth-Verlag, 1971; *Kennwort Koenigsberg* (title means "Codeword Koenigsberg"), Schneekluth-Verlag, 1980; *Masurengold* (title means "The Gold of Masuren"), Schneekluth-Verlag, 1981; *Drachensturz* (title means "The Fall of the Dragon"), Schneekluth-Verlag, 1982; *Ein Leben auf Flugeln* (autobiography; title means "Life on Wings"), Kindler-Verlag, 1982; *Die schwarze Jagd* (title means "The Black Hunt"), Schneekluth-Verlag, 1983; *Jetliner,* Hoffmann & Campe, 1983.

WORK IN PROGRESS: The Wall, a novel about a youth in Nazi Germany; *Voices in the Sky,* a mystery-novel about an aircraft accident.

SIDELIGHTS: Braunburg told *CA:* "The time I have spent as an airline captain for more than twenty years is important to my career as a writer. I began writing as a schoolboy in Nazi Germany, when I couldn't agree with the official line of social and political communication. I considered my notices a protest against this. My style and ability then, however, were too simple and unskilled to have any effect. I was eighteen at the time.

"I write ten hours a day, without relaxing or taking time for vacations, etc. I work standing before my typewriter. As I have been sitting on the lefthand seat of a jetliner for more than twenty years, I am always happy when I can stand. I have written more than twenty-five novels and about twenty nonfiction books which have been translated into Dutch, English, French, Italian, Japanese, and Indonesian. I have also been writing some nonfiction scripts about flying for German television, including 'No Fear of Flying' (Westdeutscher Rundfunk).

"My advice to aspiring writers is: don't talk, just listen. Then, ten years later, try your first work. I have been strongly influenced by Ernest Hemingway, Hermann Hesse, and Henry Miller. I feel I can learn from other writers."

BIOGRAPHICAL/CRITICAL SOURCES: Library Journal, October, 1980.

* * *

BREASTED, James Henry, Jr. 1908-1983

OBITUARY NOTICE: Born in 1908 in Chicago, Ill.; died May 4, 1983, in Laconia, N.H. Art historian, curator, educator, and author. Breasted, who was one of the first people to enter the tomb of King Tut when it was opened in 1922, was a former director of the Los Angeles County Museum. He taught at several universities, including Colorado College. He wrote *Egyptian Servant Statues.* Obituaries and other sources: *New York Times,* May 6, 1983; *Chicago Tribune,* May 7, 1983.

* * *

BREGMAN, Jay 1940-

PERSONAL: Born February 7, 1940, in New York, N.Y.; son of Arthur (a clothing manufacturer) and Gertrude (a literary agent; maiden name, Dimmerman) Bregman; children: Alexandra, Rachel. *Education:* Hunter College of the City University of New York, A.B., 1968; Yale University, M.Phil., 1972, Ph.D., 1974. *Politics:* "Rational." *Religion:* "Mystical." *Office:* Department of History, University of Maine, Orono, Maine 04469.

CAREER: University of California, Los Angeles, assistant professor of history, 1972-73; University of California, Berkeley, assistant professor of history, 1973-75; University of Maine, Orono, associate professor of history, 1975—. Lecturer at Howard University, 1978-79. *Member:* International Society for Neoplatonic Studies, American Philosophical Association, American Academy of Religion, American Historical Association, Phi Beta Kappa. *Awards, honors:* Fellow of National Endowment for the Humanities.

WRITINGS: Synesius of Cyrene: Philosopher-Bishop, University of California Press, 1982. Contributor to academic journals.

WORK IN PROGRESS: The Religion of the Emperor Julian: The Reform of Hellenism in Late Antiquity.

SIDELIGHTS: Bregman wrote: "In an age when collective neuroses have been given the legitimacy of ideological and moral causes, it is most important to study the 'mentality' of the past in order to understand the ways in which ideas, often noble in intent, have become confused, corrupted, and ultimately little more than 'masks' for self-interested activity under the guise of virtue."

AVOCATIONAL INTERESTS: Travel (France, England, Greece, Italy), American music (including that of Charlie Parker, John Coltrane, Lester Young, Bud Powell, Charles Ives, Donald Stratton, and Lennie Tristano), basketball, football, baseball, tennis.

* * *

BRENNAN, Anne 1936-

PERSONAL: Born February 26, 1936, in New York, N.Y.; daughter of Michael J. (in small business) and Anne (Brennan) Brennan. *Education:* St. Joseph College, Brooklyn, N.Y., B.A., 1967; La Salle College, M.A., 1974; doctoral study at San Francisco Theological Seminary, 1979—. *Religion:* Roman Catholic. *Home and office:* Mid-Life Directions, 45 Poe Ave., Vailsburg, N.J. 07106.

CAREER: Entered order of Sisters of St. Joseph and became Roman Catholic nun, 1954; teacher at parochial schools in Brooklyn, N.Y., 1955-67; pastoral minister and religious educator at Roman Catholic parish in Melville, N.Y., 1967-81; Mid-Life Directions, Vailsburg, N.J., partner and counselor, 1981—. Member of adjunct faculty at Seton Hall University; member of C. G. Jung Institute. *Member:* Religious Education Association, Association for Psychological Types, Delta Epsilon Sigma.

WRITINGS: (With Janice Brewi) *Mid-Life: Psychological and Spiritual Perspectives,* Crossroads, 1982. Contributor to religious magazines.

WORK IN PROGRESS: Three books, all with Janice Brewi, *Mid-Life Spirituality: Praying and Playing,* publication expected in 1984, *Mid-Life Transition,* and *Jungian Typology and the Second Half of Life.*

SIDELIGHTS: Sister Anne Brennan wrote: "I am deeply concerned about the ongoing development of the personality and spiritual growth of the person throughout the 'mid-life crisis' transition and period. I give workshops, seminars, and courses that combine psychological and theological insights. My research and writing flow out of this same experience and concern.

"The lethargy, boredom, listlessness or the anger, regret and hopelessness of mid-life crisis are in fact angels of light. They force upon us the awareness that there is another side of the personality to be developed, a whole new inner world to be explored. As we recognize new meanings, values, and goals and as we face the adaptations and pressures which have dictated our life-long attitudes, we may discover our true selves, which long to be enfleshed and lived out in the second half of life. We are the first generations that, in large numbers, will create a new image of the whole aging process. We will be the ones to give hope that there is a whole new dynamism for the second half of life."

* * *

BRENNAN, Louis A(rthur) 1911-1983

OBITUARY NOTICE—See index for *CA* sketch: Born February 5, 1911, in Portsmouth, Ohio; died of arteriosclerosis, March 18, 1983, in Ossining, N.Y. Archaeologist, educator, and author. Brennan, the founder and director of Briarcliff College Museum and Laboratory for Archaeology, served as professor of field archaeology at Briarcliff College (now Pace University—Pleasantville/Briarcliff). He wrote several novels, including *Masque of Virtue, The Long Knife,* and *Death at Floodtide,* as well as a number of works on archaeology, including *No Stone Unturned: An Almanac of North American Prehistory* and *Beginners Guide to Archaeology.* For twenty years Brennan was the editor of the New York State Archaeological Association's *Bulletin.* Obituaries and other sources: *New York Times,* March 21, 1983.

* * *

BRIGHT, Pamela Mia 1914-

PERSONAL: Born in April, 1914, in Bristol, England; daughter of Trevor and Mia (Harper) Bright. *Education:* Studied nursing at Edinburgh Royal Infirmary, 1934-38. *Religion:* Church of England. *Home:* 8 Pelham Court, Fulham Rd., London S.W.3, England.

CAREER: London Hospital, London, England, nursing sister, 1945-48; Middlesex Hospital, London, nursing sister, 1948-50, night supervisor, 1960-64; Brompton Chest Hospital, London, night sister, 1953-54; associated with National Heart Hospital, London, 1969-71; Chelsea/Kensington/Westminster Group of Hospitals, London, infection control sister, 1972-76; writer. *Military service:* British Army, territorial nurse, 1938-45. *Awards, honors:* Award from Royal Literary Fund, 1981, for literary merit; award from Society of Authors Literary Trust, 1981, for biography of Richard Bright.

WRITINGS: *Life in Our Hands,* MacGibbon & Key, 1955; *Breakfast at Night,* MacGibbon & Key, 1957; *The Day's End,* MacGibbon & Key, 1960; *Poor Man's Riches,* Macdonald & Co., 1962; *The Nurse and Her World,* Gollancz, 1962; *Hospital at Night,* Macdonald & Co., 1970; *Dr. Richard Bright, 1789-1858,* Bodley Head, 1983.

WORK IN PROGRESS: ''A love story of 1777-78.''

SIDELIGHTS: Pamela Bright told *CA:* ''To escape the absorption of hospital work, I have traveled. I worked at an asthma clinic in Switzerland, spent two years administering first aid at an Israeli kibbutz, and worked for the United Nations.

''Family papers covering the years 1700-1880 prompted me to write the biography of Dr. Richard Bright, who discovered nephritis, the kidney disease which was later given the name Bright's disease. He was a genius and a man of remarkable talents and interests who was a forerunner of modern medicine and who emerged as the Victorian equivalent of the Renaissance man.''

* * *

BRISCOE, Mary Louise 1937-

PERSONAL: Born May 24, 1937, in Hutchinson, Kan.; daughter of Arthur D. and Charlotte B. Briscoe; children: Brenna. *Education:* Kansas State University, B.A., 1959; Bowling Green State University, M.A., 1961; University of Wisconsin—Madison, Ph.D., 1968. *Office:* Department of English, University of Pittsburgh, 526 Cathedral of Learning, Pittsburgh, Pa. 15260.

CAREER: Wisconsin State University—Whitewater (now University of Wisconsin—Whitewater), assistant professor, 1967-68, associate professor of English, 1968-71; University of Pittsburgh, Pittsburgh, Pa., associate professor, 1972-82, professor of English, 1983—, head of department, 1977—, coordinator of women's studies program, 1972-77. *Member:* Modern Language Association of America, National Women's Studies Association.

WRITINGS: (Editor with Elsie Adams) *Up Against the Wall, Mother: On Women's Liberation,* Glencoe, 1971; *First Person Female American,* Whitston Publishing, 1978; *American Autobiography, 1945-1980: A Bibliography,* University of Wisconsin Press, 1982.

WORK IN PROGRESS: *Criticism of American Autobiography: A Bibliography; A House in the Country,* tentative title for a book-length study of American autobiography since 1940; *Fictions in Autobiography: Myths of the Journey,* a collection of essays.

* * *

BRODSKY, Vera
See LAWRENCE, Vera Brodsky

* * *

BROGAN, Frankie Fonde 1922-

PERSONAL: Maiden name is pronounced *Fon*-dee; born December 17, 1922, in Knoxville, Tenn.; daughter of Charles Henry (an engineer) and Rhea (King) Fonde; married Robert Thomas Brogan (an advertising executive), January 8, 1944; children: Becki Brogan Bishop, Robert Thomas, Jr., Susan Brogan Klemmt, Katherine Brogan Enyart. *Education:* University of Tennessee, B.A., 1944. *Religion:* Episcopalian. *Home:* 1750 South Gessner, Houston, Tex. 77063.

CAREER: Town and Country Real Estate, Inc., Houston, Tex., real estate agent, 1969—.

WRITINGS: *The Snare of the Fowler* (nonfiction), Chosen Books, 1983 (published in England as *Snared,* Marshall Scott, 1984).

WORK IN PROGRESS: A sequel to *The Snare of the Fowler;* a novel.

SIDELIGHTS: Frankie Brogan told *CA:* ''A lifelong ambition to write was fulfilled when my book was published. It came at the three-score mark in my life, and was far from the fantasies I had envisioned. It is the painful story of our son's involvement with a cult and our whole family's reaction to it.

''In 1971, at a vulnerable and searching time in our son Bob's life, he entered the Children of God. The Christian churches he saw seemed to have no answers and the lure of the cult with its exciting concepts, rigid discipline, and pat solutions apparently did. His father and I were blissfully unaware of the cult scene and totally unprepared for what lay ahead. I take the reader with us through the anguish and pain of it, letting it all unfold as naturally as possible. Though a true story, it reads as a novel and I won't spoil the suspense by telling how it all evolves.

''The writing of *The Snare of the Fowler* was a mind-expanding experience for this novice. Like a child thrown into deep water and forced to swim for its life, I found the actual doing of it to be a wild mixture of abject terror, strange exhilaration, hard work, and delicious satisfaction. Pushed into a vulnerable kind of honesty, I discovered the need to be 'real'; to tell it like it was—warts and all—allowing the memory pictures to flow freely from mind to page. As I did, it became a catharsis for me, revealing and healing even unknown wounds.

''The whole thing was a powerful learning adventure. Perhaps writing always is, or should be. I do know it has created a strong desire in me to 'jump back in the water again!' I want to learn more!''

* * *

BRONFELD, Stewart 1929-

PERSONAL: Born November 1, 1929, in New York, N.Y.; son of Harry (a manufacturing jeweler) and Anne (Sherman) Bronfeld; married Beverly Hanson (an actress and singer), 1964. *Education:* Attended City College of New York (now City College of the City University of New York) and Fordham University. *Residence:* Westport, Conn.

CAREER: Television editor and columnist for *Show Business,* 1950; writer of ''Closeup,'' WNBC-TV, New York, 1956-57; writer of ''The Tex and Jinx Show,'' NBC (National Broadcasting Co.) Television Network, 1957-58, staff producer-writer, NBC Television Network, 1962-79; host-moderator of ''University Forum'' on Public Television, 1979. Adjunct faculty member of New School for Social Research, 1968-73; Visiting Lecturer at Yale University, spring, 1983. *Member:* Writers Guild of America, Broadcast Education Association. *Awards, honors:* Emmy Award nomination, 1957, as writer of ''The Tex and Jinx Show''; International Broadcasting awards from the Hollywood Radio and Television Society, 1967, for work as producer-writer of ''Thursday,'' and 1968, for work as producer of ''Historical Election.''

WRITINGS: Writing for Film and Television (Book-of-the-Month Club Quality Paperback Selection), Prentice-Hall, 1981; *Producing A Film*, Prentice-Hall, in press; *Careers In Television*, Prentice-Hall, in press. Also writer of scripts for motion picture featurettes released by Columbia Pictures and Universal Pictures. Contributor of articles to periodicals, including *New York Times Magazine, Variety,* and *Writer.*

WORK IN PROGRESS: The Inspiration of Fear, a book about life behind the scenes at NBC during the fierce network ratings war of the 1970's.

SIDELIGHTS: Bronfeld told *CA:* "I consider myself lucky to have spent so much of my career (so far) in television because, for good or bad or a mixture of both, television is undeniably one of the most pervasive influences in the lives of everyone. In a way, I grew up with television. At age nineteen, when I was the TV editor and columnist for *Show Business,* a theatrical trade weekly, I saw new TV stations start to go on the air, still not sure how to handle what was then a kind of radio with cameras. Then, in the late 1950's, as the writer of 'The Tex and Jinx Show,' a celebrity interview program telecast from Peacock Alley of the Waldorf-Astoria, I experienced the wonderfully scary excitement of live television (now almost extinct). And the day I left NBC, I saw my last production for the network routinely sent out from the RCA Building in New York City to the NBC Studios in Los Angeles by way of a satellite. But, despite its advances, television is still in the process of growing up—and of course, so am I.

"In my work and travels, I meet a lot of professional writers and also would-be writers, who would like to write for television, but who are somewhat uncertain about what they see as an explosion of new technologies whose import is not yet clear. I refer them—and writers everywhere—to something I not only feel philosophically, but also know professionally, with which I ended the first chapter of *Writing for Film and Television:* 'No matter how complex and sophisticated [television's] technology becomes, from earth stations to laser beam transmission, it will always depend on what the poet Rimbaud called the 'alchemy of the word.'"

BIOGRAPHICAL/CRITICAL SOURCES: Times Literary Supplement, May 8, 1981.

*   *   *

BROOKS, Albert
See EINSTEIN, Albert

*   *   *

BROOKS, Jerome E(dmund)   1895(?)-1983

OBITUARY NOTICE: Born c. 1895; died February 15, 1983, in New York, N.Y. Author of numerous books, including the four-volume *Tobacco: Its History Illustrated by the Books, Manuscripts, and Engravings in the Library of George Arents, Jr., etc.* and *The Mighty Leaf: Tobacco Through the Centuries.* Obituaries and other sources: *New York Times,* February 17, 1983; *AB Bookman's Weekly,* March 7, 1983.

*   *   *

BROWN, Cecil H(ooper)   1944-

PERSONAL: Born December 3, 1944, in Jackson, Tenn.; son of Cecil H. (a doctor) and Carolyn (Robbins)Brown; married Pamela Ward; children: Anne Theresa, Jason Stratford, Rufus

Stennis. *Education:* Attended University of Newcastle upon Tyne, 1964-65; Tulane University, B.A. (with honors), 1966, Ph.D., 1971. *Office:* Department of Anthropology, Northern Illinois University, DeKalb, Ill. 60115.

CAREER: Northern Illinois University, DeKalb, assistant professor, 1970-76, associate professor, 1976-82, professor of anthropology, 1982—, chairman of department, 1981—. Conducted field work in Mexico. *Member:* American Anthropological Association, Society for Ethnobiology. *Awards, honors:* Shell Oil Co. grant for Mexico, 1969-70; National Science Foundation grant, 1979-82.

WRITINGS: Wittgensteinian Linguistics, Mouton, 1974; (contributor) David Levinson and Martin Malone, editors, *Toward Explaining Human Culture,* Human Relations Area File Press, 1980; (contributor) Ronald Casson, editor, *Language, Culture, and Cognition: Anthropological Perspectives,* Macmillan, 1981; *Language and Living Things: Uniformities in Folk Classification and Naming,* Rutgers University Press, 1984. Contributor of more than forty articles and reviews to anthropology journals.

WORK IN PROGRESS: Researching topics in lexical universals, historical linguistics, and ethnobiology.

SIDELIGHTS: Brown told *CA:* "Beginning with ethnolinguistic field work among Huastec speakers in Northern Veracruz, Mexico, in the late 1960's, my research has led me to worldwide cross-language studies of human naming behavior which have revealed universal patterns. I strongly feel that the study of these regular lexical patterns can contribute significantly to the delineation of processes and mechanisms underlying not only the human language faculty, but also human culture-creating capacity."

*   *   *

BROWN, Raymond George   1924-

PERSONAL: Born in 1924 in Western Australia; married Joan Body (a special education teacher), 1951; children: Christine, Judith, Susan. *Education:* University of Melbourne, B.A., 1949, diploma in social studies, 1950; Bryn Mawr College, M.Soc.Sci., 1953; University of Birmingham, Ph.D., 1956. *Office:* School of Social Sciences, Flinders University of South Australia, Bedford Park, South Australia 5042.

CAREER: University of Birmingham, Birmingham, England, lecturer in social medicine, 1954-57; University of Melbourne, Parkville, Australia, lecturer in social studies, 1958; University of Adelaide, Adelaide, Australia, reader in charge of social studies, 1959-64; Flinders University of South Australia, Bedford Park, professor of social administration, 1965—. Foundation member of Australian Government National Commission on Social Welfare, South Australian Government Social Welfare Advisory Council, Advisory Committee of Australian Government National Population Enquiry, Council of Australian Institute of Urban Studies, and Governing Council of Flinders University; member of Convocation of Australian National University; past member of South Australian Government Committee of Enquiry into Health Services. *Member:* Fellow of Academy of Social Sciences in Australia. *Awards, honors:* Fulbright-Smith Mundt scholar, 1951-52; Woershoffer research scholar, 1952-53.

WRITINGS: (With Thomas McKeown) *Medical Evidence Related to English Population Changes* (monograph), University of Birmingham, 1955; (with H. M. Whyte) *Medicine and the*

Community, Australian National University Press, 1970; (with McKeown and R. G. Record) *An Interpretation of the Modern Rise of Population in Europe* (monograph), University of Birmingham, 1972; *Children in Australia*, Allen & Unwin, 1980. Contributor to scholarly journals.

WORK IN PROGRESS: Society and Social Welfare, "a study of the original and present influence of Australia's welfare state, an attempt to understand what were the influences which assisted the development of social programs, and what their present status is."

SIDELIGHTS: Brown told *CA:* "My chief concern for many years has been to try to understand what the scope and limits of social provision might be, what are its strengths and weaknesses, and what its contribution to individual and social development can and should be."

* * *

BROWN, Richard H(arvey) 1940-

PERSONAL: Born May 12, 1940, in New York, N.Y.; son of Samuel Robert and Sylvia Brown; married Nathalie Babel (a dealer in art and antiques), April 5, 1967; children: Ramiro. *Education:* University of Lausanne, Certificate, 1960; University of California, Berkeley, B.A., 1961; Columbia University, M.A., 1965; University of California, San Diego, Ph.D., 1973. *Politics:* Socialist. *Religion:* Jewish. *Residence:* Washington, D.C. *Office:* Department of Sociology, University of Maryland, College Park, Md. 20742.

CAREER: Community Development Foundation (consultants), New York City, regional director for Latin America, 1965-67; Hudson Institute, Harmon, N.Y., member of senior research staff, 1967; Human Resources Administration, Community Development Agency, New York City, assistant commissioner for planning and budgeting, 1968-69; Social Engineering Technology (consulting firm), Los Angeles, Calif., principal, 1969-74; University of Maryland, College Park, associate professor of sociology, 1975—. Founder and president of Washington Institute for Social Research, 1978—. Visiting instructor at New School for Social Research, autumn, 1968; lecturer at University of California, San Diego, 1971-72; guest professor at University of Ottawa, 1978-79. Consultant to various governmental, private sector, and international organizations.

MEMBER: International Society for the Comparative Study of Civilizations, International Sociological Association, American Sociological Association, American Political Science Association, American Academy of Political and Social Science, American Association of University Professors, American Society for Public Administration, Society for International Development, Modern Language Association of America, Democratic Socialists of America, Union for Democratic Communication. *Awards, honors:* Resident fellow of National Center for Alcohol Education, 1974-75; grant from National Institutes of Health, 1976; Legion of Honor award from Chapel of the Four Chaplains, Temple University, 1983.

WRITINGS: Problems and Prospects for Community Development in Brazil, Community Development Foundation Press, 1967; *A Poetic for Sociology: Toward a Logic of Discovery for the Human Sciences*, Cambridge University Press, 1977; (contributor) Jack D. Douglas and John M. Johnston, editors, *Existential Sociology*, Cambridge University Press, 1977; (with Stanford M. Lyman and others) *Structure, Consciousness and History*, Cambridge University Press, 1978; (contributor) George Coelho, editor, *Uprooting: Essays in the Social Psychology of*

Social Change, Plenum, 1980; (editor) *American Society: Essays on the Political Economy and Cultural Psychology of an Advanced Capitalist Democracy*, Ginn, 1981; *Utopia, Theory, and Practice: Essays on the Political Phenomenology of Language*, University of Chicago Press, in press; (with G. Coelho, Murali Nais, and Jacqueline Wasilewski) *Traditions and Transformations*, Humanities Press, in press. Contributor of more than forty articles and reviews to social science and humanities journals.

WORK IN PROGRESS: Homecoming: Reflections on Indian Sensibility and Culture, with Amrit Baruah, publication expected in 1984.

SIDELIGHTS: In the preface to *A Poetic for Sociology*, Brown wrote: "After receiving a statistical functionalist version of sociology at Berkeley and Columbia, I spent a number of years 'applying' this knowledge in programs of intentional social change—economic development planning in Latin America, antipoverty activities in New York City, stints with think-tanks and consulting firms. What struck me most in this work was the dissonance between social theory as I had learned it and political reality as I was experiencing it. . . .

"In the hands of conservatives the social systems models encouraged efforts to control society much in the manner that experiments are controlled. When liberals were in charge their reluctance to exercise such control insured that programs simply failed. In either case the intention of helping people was vitiated by the manipulativeness of the helping techniques; the increasing demand for experts to run larger and more complex organizations violated the increasing need for nonalienating forms of work and of governance.

"While I was out in the field there had emerged in America a 'new' sociology that promised to be true to the data as existentially enacted. . . . Yet the problems that interested me most were still the old-fashioned ones—class conflict, social mobility, and institutional change. I wanted a macrotheory of action but instead found microtheories of consciousness.

"In trying to bridge these two realms, I discovered that the conflicts between schools are not so much a war of armies as an anarchy in the streets. . . . Thus, no bridge could carry the weight I wanted to put on it unless its foundations were set in the deeper, epistemological substrata that underlies the conflicts between sociological schools. . . .

"I set out to find a conceptual vocabulary that could justify interpretive procedures as a rigorous way of knowing and under which, at the same time, the epistemology of positive sociology could be subsumed. Cognitive aesthetics, or what might be called a critical poetic, provided the beginnings of such a vocabulary."

Brown told *CA:* "*Utopia, Theory, and Practice* completes my plan of studies in philosophic sociology. It is at once a philosophical critique of social theory and a social theoretical critique of politics. Philosophy seeks to define our nature and destiny—what we are, what we can know, and what we should become. Social thought concerns the scarcities inherent in any social order, and the possibilities and constraints that these provide for human freedom. Politics is the creation of reality through conflictual action, the determining of who gets what. 'Utopias' are never far from 'reality,' however, because yesterday's utopias provide the warrant for present practices, and because today's fictions become tomorrow's factions.

"These three domains of human experience—the utopian 'ought,' the theoretical description of what 'is,' and the political practice seeking to bring the 'is' closer to the 'ought'—all are conducted through language, all are modes of persuasive discourse. By focusing on the shaping of experience through language, therefore, we become able to see that the dehumanizing segregations of modern life need not be absolute. Art and science are both communitarian, linguistic constructions. Moral discourse and objective descriptions both are products of situationally-constrained, socially-embedded, rhetorical performance. Knowledge of experts and the understandings of ordinary folks both are 'worlds' created through socially symbolic interaction. Such reformulations may encourage a less alienated, fragmented vision of our politics and our culture, and a more authentic understanding of ourselves.

"I have sought to infuse humane values into the social sciences by reformulating their epistemological foundations. At the same time, I am exploring ways to link humanistic theories of society with practical interventions. The Washington Institute for Social Research was formed in 1978 for this purpose. We sponsor public debates on current issues, prepare tapes of symposia for broadcast on national public radio, consult with governmental business and community service organizations, and conduct practically-directed social research on problems that invite theoretical reconceptualization and institutional redirection.

"The broad intellectual framework for these activities is a conception of the emerging world political economy and America's role in it. On the one hand, we are faced with potential apocalyptic catastrophes on a global scale—ecological disasters, nuclear wars, food/population imbalances, and the like. On the other hand, our collective means for addressing these difficulties are limited to nationalistic and technocratic interventions which, even if successful, would buy physical survival for some by sacrificing the human dignity of all.

"In addition, the United States is experiencing a special crisis. In our first century we had a frontier to conquer; in our second we made an industrial revolution and gained world economic and military domination. But with the rise of Soviet power, the emergence of Europe and Japan as competitors, and the diffusion of power through formerly placid Third World nations, the days of continuous easy growth for America are over. This has led to a decline of American power, deepening economic scarcity, and a crisis of legitimacy of our cultural values. Moreover, advanced capitalism itself has generated enormous economic concentrations, a hugely expanded role for the state, and the destruction of traditional communities and values, thereby further eroding our democratic institutions and commitments.

"I believe that the agenda of democratic socialism—though still halting and incomplete—can provide some solutions. To cite but one example, in former times it was thought that economic efficiency required the authoritarian control of workers. Indeed this was accepted even in so-called Marxist states. Such an assumption is no longer tenable. Experience with job enrichment, co-management, and worker's direct control of the means of production has been proven successful as a way not only to deepen democracy by extending it to the economic realm, but also to enhance productive efficiency and political legitimacy. This is only one illustration. Many other experiments in this spirit have already shown their practical effectiveness and moral worth in numerous countries and settings. But even if such democratic socialist ideas were purely 'utopian,' we should remember that mass material comfort also was utopian before the industrial revolution, and that political democracy was itself a utopian dream before its realization for many in our American Revolution."

BROWNE, William P(aul) 1945-

PERSONAL: Born May 15, 1945, in Cherokee, Iowa; son of William D. (an automobile salesman) and Inena Etta (a hair stylist; maiden name, Lopan) Browne; married Linda S. Thomas (a teacher), June 1, 1968. *Education:* Iowa State University, B.S., 1967, M.S., 1969; Washington University, St. Louis, Mo., Ph.D., 1971. *Home:* 8085 Essex Dr., Lake Isabella, Weidman, Mich. 48893. *Office:* Department of Political Science, Central Michigan University, Mount Pleasant, Mich. 48859.

CAREER: Central Michigan University, Mount Pleasant, assistant professor, 1971-74, associate professor, 1974-77, professor of political science, 1977—. Consultant to U.S. Department of Defense. *Member:* American Political Science Association, American Society of Public Administration, Policy Studies Organization, Midwest Political Science Association, Michigan Conference of Political Scientists (member of board of directors, 1981—), Weidman Lions Club (president, 1982). *Awards, honors:* Grants from Farm Foundation and Economics Research Service, 1976, 1979-80.

WRITINGS: (With C. W. Wiggins) *Local Government in Tenco* (monograph), Iowa State University Press, 1968; *Manpower in Michigan: A Study of Local Government Personnel* (monograph), Center for Study and Research in Local Government, 1973; (contributor) Joseph DeBolt, editor, *Critical Explorations in the Science Fiction of John Brunner*, Kennikat, 1975; (with Don Hadwiger) *The New Politics of Food*, Lexington Books, 1978; (editor with Hadwiger and Richard Fraenkel) *The Role of U.S. Agriculture in Foreign Policy*, Praeger, 1979.

Politics, Programs and Bureaucrats, Kennikat, 1980; (editor with Hadwiger) *Rural Policy Problems: Changing Dimensions*, Lexington Books, 1982; (contributor) David Brewster, Wayne Rasmussen, and Garth Youngberg, editors, *Farms in Transition: Interdisciplinary Perspectives on Farm Structure*, Iowa State University Press, 1982; (editor with Laura Katz Olson) *Public Policy and the Elderly: The Politics of Growing Old in America*, Greenwood Press, 1983.

Contributor of about twenty articles to scholarly journals. Member of editorial board of Policy Studies Organization, 1979-81.

WORK IN PROGRESS: Research on agribusiness in public policy and senior citizen legislation in state government.

SIDELIGHTS: Browne told *CA:* "I've always been struck by the observation that professors, in particular, are little involved in the areas of their individual interest. As a result, they too often seem shallow and aloof from real world problems. Life should be advancement of knowledge, the identification of problems, and the search for solutions.

"Because I feel so strongly, I've operated under the personal rule that research and writing are the most critical parts of my professional life. To do neither, seems to me, an affront to those who hope to learn something under my direction. As a political scientist, my greatest contribution seems to be possible in the areas of public policy analysis, for the bottom line for government is how well it meets its goals in meeting social needs.

"I guess that food policy will always be my favorite area of policy studies. I was born in farm country, raised among those who produce food, and appreciate the prominent part food plays in both national and international politics. We all gravitate to those things that are most familiar to us.''

*   *   *

BROZEN, Yale 1917-

PERSONAL: Born July 6, 1917, in Kansas City, Mo.; son of Oscar and Sarah (Sholtz) Brozen; married Lee Parsons, April 26, 1962; children: Yale II, Reed. *Education:* Massachusetts Institute of Technology, B.S., 1938; University of Chicago, Ph.D., 1941. *Office:* Graduate School of Business, University of Chicago, Chicago, Ill. 60637.

CAREER: University of Florida, Gainesville, assistant professor of social science, 1940-41; Illinois Institute of Technology, Chicago, assistant professor, 1941-44, associate professor of economics, 1944-46; University of Minnesota, Minneapolis, associate professor, 1946-47, visiting professor of economics, 1948; Northwestern University, Evanston, Ill., professor of economics, 1947-57, director of Research Transportation Center, 1957-59; University of Chicago, Chicago, professor of economics, 1957—, director of research management program at Graduate School of Business, 1959-67, director of applied economics program, 1960—. Visiting professor at Escola Sociologia, Sao Paulo, Brazil, 1954, Rikkyo University, 1964, University of Virginia, 1965, and Graduate Institute of International Studies, Geneva, Switzerland, 1969; adjunct scholar at American Enterprise Institute for Public Policy Research, 1972—. Director of economic training at American Telephone & Telegraph Co., 1951; member of board of directors of University National Bank, Carus Corp., and West Burton Place Corp.; consultant to U.S. Department of State, U.S. Department of Justice, and Loewi & Co. *Military service:* U.S. Army, Signal Corps, administrator of civilian training, 1942-43. *Member:* American Economic Association, Mont Pelerin Society, Phi Beta Kappa, Delta Sigma Pi, Quadrangle Club, Technology Club.

WRITINGS: Workbook for Economics, W. C. Brown, 1946; *Textbook for Economics,* Volume I, W. C. Brown, 1948; *Automation: The Impact of Technological Change,* American Enterprise Institute, 1963; (editor) *Advertising and Society,* New York University Press, 1974; *The Competitive Economy: Selected Readings,* General Learning Press, 1975; *Is the Government the Source of Monopoly? and Other Essays,* Cato Institute, 1980; *Concentration, Mergers, and Public Policy,* Macmillan, 1982; *Mergers in Perspective,* American Enterprise Institute for Public Policy Research, 1982.

WORK IN PROGRESS: Essays in Public Policy.

BIOGRAPHICAL/CRITICAL SOURCES: National Review, March 17, 1978, July 11, 1980.

*   *   *

BRUCK, Lilly 1918-

PERSONAL: Born May 13, 1918, in Vienna, Austria; came to the United States in 1941, naturalized citizen, 1943; daughter of Max (an executive) and Sophie M. Hahn; married Sandor Bruck, March 7, 1943 (deceased, 1982); children: Sandra Lee. *Education:* University of Vienna, Ph.D., 1938; postdoctoral study at Sorbonne, University of Paris, London School of Economics and Political Science, London, 1938-40, and Columbia University, 1942-43; New York University, M.S.W., 1967. *Politics:* Democrat. *Religion:* Jewish. *Home:* 55 Secor Rd.,

Scarsdale, N.Y. 10583. *Office:* In Touch Networks, Inc., 322 West 48th St., New York, N.Y. 10036.

CAREER: R. H. Macy, New York City, member of statistical department, 1941; worked for General Foods, New York City, 1942-43; worked for Statistics Scarsdale, Scarsdale, N.Y., 1945-67; New York City Department of Consumer Affairs, New York City, director of consumer education, 1969-78; In Touch Networks, Inc., New York City, broadcaster of interview program "Access," consumer advocate, and member of board of directors, 1978—. Consumer affairs commentator on "Let's Hear It," a weekly program on National Public Radio, 1979-81; associate of Knauer Associates (consultants), Washington, D.C. Project director for American Coalition of Citizens With Disabilities, 1977-78, and Office of Consumers Education, 1977-78, 1979-80; member of executive committee and advisory council of Westchester County Office for the Disabled; member of Mount Vernon Consumers Union; officer and member of board of trustees of White Plains Jewish Community Center. Westchester chairperson for Bonds for Israel, 1965-67. Associated with Girl Scouts and PTA.

MEMBER: Authors Guild, American Women in Radio and Television, Society of Consumer Affairs Professionals in Business, American Workers for the Blind, Hadassah (president of Scarsdale chapter). *Awards, honors:* Named woman of the year by Anti-Defamation League of B'nai B'rith, 1971; community service award from Girl Scout Council of Greater New York, 1974; Big Apple Radio Award from New York Market Radio Broadcasters Association, 1982, for series of public service broadcasts on the disabled.

WRITINGS: Consumer Rights for Disabled Citizens, New York City Department of Consumer Affairs, 1976; *ACCESS: The Guide to a Better Life for Disabled Americans,* Random House, 1978 (published as a "Talking Book" on audio cassettes by Library of Congress, Division for the Blind and Physically Handicapped, 1979); *Disability and Rehabilitation Handbook,* McGraw, 1978; (contributor) Kathy Matthews, editor, *Disabled People as Second-Class Citizens* (selected as a CU Book by Consumers Union), Springer Publishing, 1982. Author of "Consumerism," a column in *Mainstream,* 1980—. Contributor to *Funk & Wagnalls Bicentennial Encyclopedia.* Contributor to magazines.

WORK IN PROGRESS—Audio tape series: "The Assertive Jobseeker," for In Touch Networks, Inc.; "The Assertive Patient."

SIDELIGHTS: Lilly Bruck told *CA:* "As a consumer educator, I made the astounding discovery that nobody had considered disabled persons as consumers, even though they represent America's largest minority (thirty-six million people). Since 1976, I have dedicated my career to alerting disabled consumers to their rights and informing providers of goods and services about their responsibilities.

"My book, *ACCESS,* is a consumer activist book for disabled consumers, alerting them to their rights in the marketplace. It discusses all types of shopping, in person and by mail and phone, banking, insurance, travel, etc., encouraging customers with impairment to demand their equal access to premises, to information, and to communication. It was described as a primer in its field, and became a textbook for university courses in rehabilitation.

"After 1978 disabled Americans had a brief respite in the sun when Section 504 of the Rehabilitation Act of 1973 was implemented, assuring the disabled rights to equal access to all functions and programs receiving federal funding. Transportation, housing, employment, and affirmative action were taken seriously. But the current [Reagan] administration has reduced all hard-won rights to bare or non-existent minimums. Discontinuance of programs and supports causes suicides and neglect.

"However, the private sector has now become more receptive. Disabled Americans have become vocal, demanding equal access. Disabled people have entered the mainstream. Buildings are more accessible, air and ground transportation have opened, sign language and captioned television communicate with the deaf, and braille, large type, and audio communications serve the blind.

"Officially: two steps back; socially and commercially: two steps forward. More has to be done."

AVOCATIONAL INTERESTS: Photography, skiing, world travel.

BIOGRAPHICAL/CRITICAL SOURCES: New York Post, March 5, 1973; *White Plains Reporter Dispatch*, February 18, 1977; *Spotlight on Scarsdale*, July, 1981.

*　　*　　*

BRUNS, George   1914(?)-1983

OBITUARY NOTICE: Born c. 1914; died of a heart attack, May 23, 1983, in Portland, Ore. Musician, composer, and songwriter. Bruns wrote music for several Walt Disney productions, including "Son of Flubber," "The Absent-Minded Professor," and the television series "The Legend of Davy Crockett." He also wrote "The Ballad of Davy Crockett." Bruns played fifteen instruments. Obituaries and other sources: *Los Angeles Times*, May 26, 1983; *Chicago Tribune*, May 27, 1983.

*　　*　　*

BUCHAN, Norman Findlay   1922-

PERSONAL: Born October 27, 1922, in Helmsdale, Scotland; son of John Buchanan; married Janey Kent, 1945; children: one son. *Education:* Attended University of Glasgow. *Home:* 72 Peel St., Glasgow W.1, Scotland. *Office:* House of Commons, London S.W.1, England.

CAREER: Teacher of English and history; Parliament, London, England, Labour member of House of Commons for Renfrewshire West, 1964—, parliamentary under secretary at Scottish Office, 1967-70, opposition spokesman on agriculture, fisheries, and food, 1970-74 and 1981—, minister of state for ministry of Agriculture and Fisheries, 1974, shadow minister for agriculture, 1981. President of Rutherglen District Educational Institute of Scotland. *Military service:* British Army, Royal Tank Regiment, 1942-45; served in North Africa, Sicily, and Italy. *Member:* Scottish Association of Labour Teachers.

WRITINGS: (Editor) *One Hundred One Scottish Songs*, Scotia Books, 1962; (editor with Peter Hall) *The Scottish Folksinger*, Collins, 1973. Contributor to magazines and newspapers, including *New Statesman*.

BIOGRAPHICAL/CRITICAL SOURCES: Books and Bookmen, June, 1973.

*　　*　　*

BUCKMASTER, Henrietta
See STEPHENS, Henrietta Henkle

BUMP, Jerome   1943-

PERSONAL: Born June 13, 1943, in Brainerd, Minn.; son of Eli Clinton (a dental technician) and Marie Isabelle (O'Connor) Bump; married Barbara Rae Pence (a switchboard operator), September 12, 1964; children: Jennifer, Melissa. *Education:* Attended Amherst College, 1961-63; University of Minnesota, B.A. (summa cum laude), 1965; University of California, Berkeley, M.A., 1966, Ph.D., 1972. *Home:* 8910 Currywood, Austin, Tex. 78759. *Office:* Department of English, University of Texas, Austin, Tex. 78712.

CAREER: University of Texas, Austin, assistant professor, 1970-76, associate professor of English, 1976—. *Member:* Modern Language Association of America, National Council of Teachers of English, South Central Modern Language Association, Philological Association of the Pacific Coast, College Conference of Teachers of English of Texas. *Awards, honors:* Woodrow Wilson fellow, 1965-66; National Defense Education Act fellowships, 1967-70; fellow of National Endowment for the Humanities, 1974-75.

WRITINGS: Gerard Manley Hopkins, G. K. Hall, 1982. Contributor to magazines, including *Georgia Review, Southern Review, Texas Quarterly*, and *Thought*. Member of editorial board, *Texas Studies in Language and Literature*, 1978, and *Hopkins Quarterly*, 1981.

WORK IN PROGRESS: Toward a Theory of Creativity: Hopkins and His Contemporaries, publication expected in 1985.

SIDELIGHTS: Bump told *CA:* "I grew up close to nature in Minnesota, and when I discovered that very little had been written about the nature poetry of Gerard Manley Hopkins—the poet that Robert Lowell called 'probably the finest of English poets of nature'—Hopkins's nature poetry became the focus of my writing. Since then I have written about many aspects of his life and art and about other writers, including Lewis Carroll, Rupert Brooke, Walter De La Mare, Edward Fitzgerald, Francis Thompson, Christina Rossetti, Robert Pirsig, Walter Pater, Wallace Stevens, D. H. Lawrence, John Keats, and John Ruskin. I am now the annual reviewer of Hopkins scholarship for *Victorian Poetry* and review books on other authors for various magazines."

*　　*　　*

BURCH, George Bosworth   1902-1973

OBITUARY NOTICE: Born July 12, 1902, in Hartford, Conn.; died June 4, 1973. Educator and author. Burch, who taught philosophy at Tufts University, wrote *Early Medieval Philosophy*. Obituaries and other sources: *Who Was Who in America, With World Notables*, Volume VI: *1974-76*, Marquis, 1976.

*　　*　　*

BURD, Laurence Hull   1915-1983

OBITUARY NOTICE: Born in 1915 in Kansas City, Mo.; died of cardiopulmonary arrest, May 20, 1983, in Bethesda, Md. Journalist. Burd was White House correspondent for the *Chicago Tribune* from 1947 to 1963, whereupon he became news editor of the *Los Angeles Times*'s Washington, D.C., bureau. Obituaries and other sources: *Washington Post*, May 21, 1983; *Los Angeles Times*, May 21, 1983; *Chicago Tribune*, May 22, 1983; *New York Times*, May 22, 1983.

BURLINGHAM, Dorothy (Tiffany) 1891-1979

PERSONAL: Born in 1891 in New York, N.Y.; died November 19, 1979, in Hampstead, London, England; daughter of Louis Comfort Tiffany (an artist); married Robert Burlingham (a doctor), 1914; children: Michael, Katrina Valenstein, another son, another daughter. *Education:* Attended Columbia University. *Address:* 20 Maresfield Gdns., London N.W.3, England.

CAREER: Psychoanalyst and child psychologist. Founder, with Anna Freud, of the Organization of Hampstead Nurseries in London, England. Trustee of the Hampstead Child-Therapy Course and Clinic, beginning in 1952. *Member:* British Psycho-Analyst Society.

WRITINGS: (With Anna Freud) *Young Children in War-Time: A Year's Work in a Residential War Nursery,* Allen & Unwin, 1942; (with Freud) *War and Children,* Medical War Books, 1943, reprinted, edited by Philip R. Lehrman, Greenwood Press, 1973; (with Freud) *Infants Without Families: The Case For and Against Residential Nurseries,* Allen & Unwin, 1943; *Twins: A Study of Three Pairs of Identical Twins,* International Universities Press, 1952; (contributor) George Devereux, editor, *Psychoanalysis and the Occult,* International Universities Press, 1953; (with Freud) *The Writings of Anna Freud,* International Universities Press, 1966; (with Freud) *Heimatlose Kinder: Wissens auf der Kinderziehung,* S. Fischer, 1971; *Psychoanalytic Studies of the Sighted and the Blind,* International Universities Press, 1972; (with Freud) *Infants Without Families: Reports on the Hampstead Nurseries, 1939-1945,* International Universities Press, 1973.

SIDELIGHTS: Daughter of Louis Comfort Tiffany, the creator of "Tiffany Glass," and granddaughter of Charles Lewis Tiffany, the noted jewelry merchant, Dorothy Tiffany Burlingham was a child psychologist who achieved notability in her own right for her work regarding the effects of war on orphaned and displaced children.

A native New Yorker, Burlingham moved to Vienna in 1924 where she studied psychoanalysis and began a lifelong professional collaboration with Anna Freud, the daughter of Sigmund Freud. Burlingham and her four children lived with Anna Freud's family until 1938 when, forced to flee by the Nazis, both families moved to London. There, with financial support from the Foster Parents' Plan for War Children, a New York agency, Burlingham and Freud founded the Organization of Hampstead Nurseries—three houses that provided homes for children whose family lives had been disrupted by war.

The goal of the Hampstead Organization, outlined in the authors' foreword to *Infants Without Families,* was to "re-establish for the children what they have lost: the security of a stable home with its opportunities for individual development." The women hoped that by studying the "lack of continuous emotional contact between the infant and his parents with the consequent absence of the specific formative influence inherent in the family tie," they could make better recommendations for child care in residential settings and thus help to resolve the problem of homeless children.

BIOGRAPHICAL/CRITICAL SOURCES: Dorothy Burlingham and Anna Freud, *Infants Without Families: The Case For and Against Residential Nurseries,* Allen & Unwin, 1943.

OBITUARIES: New York Times, November 22, 1979.*

BURMAN, Jose Lionel 1917-

PERSONAL: Born April 10, 1917, in Jagersfontein, South Africa; son of Elias Lewis and Dora (Loewenberg) Burman; married Ruth Valerie Herbert (deceased); married Cecily Kathleen Cheetham Robertson, August 28, 1940; children: (first marriage) Carol Lesley Burman Katz. *Education:* University of South Africa, B.A., 1938, LL.B., 1940. *Religion:* Jewish. *Home address:* P.O. Box 3538, Cape Town, South Africa.

CAREER: Solicitor in Cape Town, South Africa, 1945-70; writer, 1970—. Lecturer at University of Cape Town. *Military service:* South African Army, 1940-45. *Member:* International P.E.N., Mountain Club of South Africa, South African Spelaeological Association (president, 1967-77), Institute of Directors, South African Camping Club (chairman, 1965-70), British Alpine Club, Historical Society of Cape Town (founder; chairman, 1972), Masons (past district senior grand warden). *Awards, honors:* Gold medal from South African Spelaeological Association, 1965; award from International Wine Organization, 1980, for *Wine of Constantia.*

*WRITINGS—*Published by Human & Rousseau, except as noted: *Safe to the Sea,* 1962; *Peninsula Profile,* Thomas Nelson, 1963; *So High the Road,* 1963; *The Garden Route,* 1964; *A Peak to Climb,* Struik, 1966; *Great Shipwrecks off the Coast of Southern Africa,* Struik, 1967; *Strange Shipwrecks of the Southern Seas,* Struik, 1968; *Cape of Good Intent,* 1969; *Who Really Discovered South Africa,* Struik, 1969.

Waters of the Western Cape, 1970; *Disaster Struck South Africa,* Struik, 1971; *Guide to the Garden Route,* 1972; *1652 and So Forth,* 1973; *The Saldanha Bay Story,* 1974; *Bay of Storms,* 1976; *False Bay Story,* 1977; *Wine of Constantia,* 1979; *Last Walks in the Cape Peninsula,* 2nd edition, 1980. Also author of *Cape Drives and Places of Interest, Coastal Holiday, Trails and Walks in the Southern Cape,* and *The Little Karoo.*

Contributor to *Standard Encyclopedia of South Africa.* Contributor to magazines.

WORK IN PROGRESS: A botanical flower guide to the southern cape of South Africa, with wife, Cecily Burman.

SIDELIGHTS: Jose Burman told *CA:* "My interests are basically outdoor activities, and my writings are mostly a combination of the history and geography of South Africa. My driving motive is to let others share in enjoying the wildness and beauty of my country."

* * *

BURNETT, Leon R. 1925(?)-1983

OBITUARY NOTICE: Born c. 1925, in Asheville, N.C.; died of cancer, April 26, 1983. Journalist. Burnett worked in various capacities, including positions as day editor and night editor for the *Washington Post.* He also covered several space flights from Houston, Texas. In later years, Burnett was a reporter and editor for United Press International (UPI). Obituaries and other sources: *Washington Post,* April 27, 1983.

* * *

BURNS, John McLauren 1932-

BRIEF ENTRY: Born June 6, 1932, in Rochester, N.Y. American zoologist, educator, and author. Burns taught biology at Wesleyan University from 1961 to 1969 and at Harvard University from 1972 to 1975. In 1978 he was appointed curator of entomology at the National Museum of Natural History. Burns wrote *Evolution in Skipper Butterflies of the Genus "Erynnis"* (University of California Press, 1964) and *Biograffiti: A Natural Selection* (Quadrangle, 1975). *Address:* Department of Entomology, National Museum of Natural History, Smithsonian Institution, Washington, D.C. 20560.

* * *

BURROUGHS, John 1837-1921

BRIEF ENTRY: Born April 3 (some sources say April 13), 1837, in Delaware County (near Roxbury), N.Y.; died March 29, 1921. American naturalist, poet, and author who became a nationally-known figure for his essays on nature. Burroughs developed a love of nature while growing up on his family's farm in the Catskill Mountains. In 1863 he began a twenty-one-year career in the federal banking system, eventually becoming a U.S. bank examiner. In 1874 Burroughs bought a small fruit farm on the Hudson River and spent the remainder of his life there, studying nature and writing. His early work, which was greatly influenced by Ralph Waldo Emerson and Walt Whitman (who became Burroughs's friend), stressed a more poetic approach to nature than his later, scientific observations about the natural world. Late in life Burroughs became disenchanted with science and developed the belief that only the poets and mystics could save society. He was the author of numerous books, including *Wake-Robin* (1871), *Birds and Poets* (1877), *Ways of Nature* (1908), *The Breath of Life* (1915), and *Accepting the Universe* (1920). *Residence:* West Park, N.Y. *Biographical/critical sources: The National Cyclopaedia of American Biography,* Volume 1, James T. White, 1892; *Who Was Who in America,* Volume 1: *1897-1942,* Marquis, 1943; *American Authors and Books, 1640 to the Present Day,* 3rd revised edition, Crown, 1962; *The Reader's Encyclopedia of American Literature,* Crowell, 1962; *The Oxford Companion to American Literature,* 4th edition, Oxford University Press, 1965.

* * *

BURTON, Ivor Flower 1923-

PERSONAL: Born March 2, 1923, in Derby, England; son of Frank (in telecommunications) and Alice (Thurgood) Burton; married Peggy Joan Clayden, July 14, 1944; children: Jill Burton Allen, Hannah Jane Burton Leader, Timothy James. *Education:* Queen's University, Belfast, Northern Ireland, B.A., 1949; University of London, Ph.D., 1960. *Politics:* Social Democrat. *Religion:* Atheist. *Home:* 21 Downs View Lodge, Oakhill Rd., Surbiton, Surrey KT6 6EG, England. *Office:* Bedford College, University of London, Regent's Park, London N.W.1 4NS, England.

CAREER: University of London, Bedford College, London, England, assistant lecturer, 1950-53, lecturer, 1953-64, senior lecturer, 1964-82, reader in social administration, 1982—, head of department of sociology, 1977—. Member of Council for National Academic Awards in the 1970's; member of Kingston and Esher Community Health Council. Justice of the peace, 1967—. *Military service:* Royal Air Force, pilot and warrant officer, 1942-46. *Member:* Royal Institute of Public Administration, Social Administration Association.

WRITINGS: The Captain General: The Career of John Churchill, First Duke of Marlborough, 1702-11, Constable, 1968; (with Gavin Drewry) *Legislation and Public Policy: Public*

Bills in the 1970-74 Parliament, Holmes & Meier, 1980. Contributor to government and administration journals.

WORK IN PROGRESS: Legislation and the Implementation of Public Policy, completion expected in 1986.

SIDELIGHTS: Burton told *CA:* "My interest in the role of the administration in policymaking has been explored in historical research (leading to the book on Marlborough), in the analysis of current legislation (the subject of the second work and of regular journal articles), in public service in education administration and elsewhere, as a justice of the peace, and of course as an academic (including a long spell as head of a large department—alas, likely to continue). I believe in the value of a variety of experience and that academics should try to practice what they preach (in my case administration and policymaking)."

* * *

BUSBY, Edith (A. Lake) ?-1964

OBITUARY NOTICE: Born in Terre Haute, Ind.; died November 16, 1964, in New York, N.Y. Librarian, educator, and author of children's books, including *Behind the Scenes at the Library* and *What Does a Librarian Do?* She worked at the Brooklyn Public Library and taught at Pratt Institute and Columbia University. Obituaries and other sources: *New York Times,* November 17, 1964; *Publishers Weekly,* November 23, 1964.

* * *

BUSCH, Hans (Peter) 1914-

PERSONAL: Born April 4, 1914, in Aachen, Germany (now West Germany); came to the United States in 1940, naturalized citizen, 1942; son of Fritz (an orchestra conductor) and Grete (a writer; maiden name, Boettcher); married Giuliana Conti, June 5, 1946 (marriage ended); married second wife, Carolyn Joy Lockwood (an opera production manager), August 29, 1963; children: (first marriage) John Anthony; (second marriage) Carroll Frederick. *Education:* Attended University of Geneva, 1933-34; attended Max Reinhardt Seminar in Vienna, Austria, 1935-36. *Home:* 1700 East Hunter Ave., Bloomington, Ind. 47401.

CAREER: Assistant to stage director Carl Ebert, 1933-39; assistant to Arturo Toscanini, 1937; stage director of operas in Turin, Buenos Aires, Montevideo, Basel, Berne, Brussels, and Stockholm, 1935-40; co-founder and stage director of New Opera Company, New York, N.Y., 1941; in charge of reconstruction and reorganization of La Scala Opera, 1945; stage director of operas in Florence, Amsterdam, and Copenhagen, 1945-46; Royal Opera, Stockholm, Sweden, stage director, 1946-49; Indiana University, Bloomington, associate professor, 1949-65, professor of music, 1966-80, professor emeritus, 1980—.

Member of faculty at Juilliard School, 1948-49, and Kathryn Long Studio of the Metropolitan Opera, 1950-53; guest director of Metropolitan Opera, 1951, and other opera companies in the United States and Canada, 1950-58; director of NBC-TV Opera Theatre, 1951-52, Boston South Shore Music Circus, 1952-55, and Santa Fe Opera, 1960-61; guest director of Frankfurt Opera, 1954, Covent Garden, 1959, and San Carlo Opera, 1969; stage director of Metropolitan Opera, 1956-60. *Military service:* U.S. Army, 1942-45; served in North Africa and Italy; became staff sergeant.

MEMBER: American Institute for Verdi Studies. *Awards, honors:* Ford Foundation fellow in Europe, 1953-54; Fulbright fellow in Germany, 1963, 1964, 1966, 1967; grants from German Academic Exchange, 1963, 1964, 1966, Indiana University, 1970, American Council of Learned Societies and American Philosophical Society, 1970—, and National Endowment for the Humanities, 1979—.

WRITINGS: Verdi's "Aida": The History of an Opera in Letters and Documents Collected and Translated by Hans Busch, University of Minnesota Press, 1978; *Giuseppe Verdi Briefe* (in German), Fischer Taschenbuch Verlag, 1979; (contributor) Thomas Noblitt, editor, *Music East and West,* Pendragon Press, 1981; *Giuseppe Verdi-Arrigo Boito Briefe* (title means "Giuseppe Verdi-Arrigo Boito Letters"), S. Fischer, 1984.

WORK IN PROGRESS: Verdi's "Otello": The History of an Opera in Letters and Documents Collected and Translated by Hans Busch; Verdi's "Falstaff": The History of an Opera in Letters and Documents Collected and Translated by Hans Busch.

SIDELIGHTS: Busch told *CA:* "I enjoyed a humanistic education in Dresden, Germany, where my father, Fritz Busch, was artistic director of a famous opera house. We left Germany in 1933 in protest of the Nazi regime.

"The highlights of my career as a stage director of opera must include my apprenticeship under my father and the director Carl Ebert at the Glyndebourne Festival in England from 1934 to 1939, my assistantship to Arturo Toscanini in Salzburg, Austria, in 1937, and—among the trials and errors of youth—some of my own first productions in Turin, Italy, Buenos Aires, Argentina, and in Basel and Berne, Switzerland. The stagings of Mozart's *Cosi fan tutte* at the Royal Opera in Stockholm, Sweden, and Verdi's *Macbeth* at the Forty-fourth Street Theatre in New York City, both with my father conducting, were among the most rewarding accomplishments of my young life.

"Volunteering for the U.S. Army, I served in North Africa and Italy from 1943 to 1945, and participated in the landings at Salerno. I later directed several operas in Florence with Tullio Serafin conducting, and I was in charge of the reconstruction of La Scala in Milan.

"It happened that *Falstaff* was the first production I directed after returning to the Royal Opera House in Stockholm. Birgit Nilsson, whom I was fortunate enough to discover, appeared in several of the operas that I staged in Stockholm, where an uncommonly friendly atmosphere prevailed. I next answered the call to collaborate in the ambitious project of establishing an opera department at Indiana University. I cherished the privilege of being entrusted with the training of young American singers and directors in an opera workshop which during some twenty-five years gave over one hundred fifty productions under my direction.

"During leaves of absence from Indiana University I found time to meet new challenges, which included opera productions in Europe, operas on NBC Television in New York City, forty musical comedies in 'theatre in the round' style, two summers at the Santa Fe Opera with Igor Stravinsky, and three seasons as a stage director of the Metropolitan Opera.

"As a teenager in Dresden, inspired by my father's celebrated Verdi Renaissance, I secretly read Franz Werfel's *Verdi Letters* while flunking mathematics. Years later I spent unforgettable hours talking with Werfel after the premiere of my production of *Macbeth* in New York City—the first American production of that opera in this century. Three decades after that I was shocked to learn how many Verdi letters had not been published, even in Italy. This led to my book on *Aida,* which filled an unforeseen gap in the Verdi literature.

"In order to devote the rest of my life to concentrated Verdi research for similar publications in which the composer is permitted to speak as his own interpreter, I chose early retirement from Indiana University in 1980. Since then I have completed one major book on Verdi's correspondence with Arrigo Boito and have nearly completed another on *Otello.* In addition, I have given a large number of lectures in this country and abroad."

*   *   *

BUSE, Rueben C. 1932-

PERSONAL: Born July 8, 1932, in Fergus Falls, Minn.; son of August and Emma Buse; divorced; children: Charles, Paul. *Education:* University of Minnesota, B.S., 1954, M.S., 1956; Pennsylvania State University, Ph.D., 1959. *Office:* Department of Agricultural Economics, University of Wisconsin—Madison, Madison, Wis. 53706.

CAREER: University of Wisconsin—Madison, assistant professor, 1959-63, associate professor, 1963-69, professor of agricultural economics, 1969—.

WRITINGS: The Conservation Research in Wisconsin, 1956-1959, University of Wisconsin Press, 1961; *Study Guide for Applied Micro-Economics,* Iowa State University Press, 1974; *A Bibliography on the Theory and Research on Household Expenditures,* Economic Research Service, U.S. Department of Agriculture, 1975; (with Daniel W. Bromley) *Applied Economics: Resource Allocation in Rural America,* Iowa State University Press, 1975; (with A. C. Johnson and M. B. Johnson) *Tyros Tryst With Econometrics,* Macmillan, in press.

*   *   *

BUSH, (John Nash) Douglas 1896-1983

OBITUARY NOTICE—See index for *CA* sketch: Born March 21, 1896, in Morrisburg, Ontario, Canada; died of pneumonia, March 2, 1983, in Boston, Mass. Educator and author. A professor of English literature at Harvard University for thirty-three years, Bush was an authority on John Milton. He was the author of *John Milton: A Sketch of His Life and Writing* and the editor of *The Portable Milton* and *Milton: Complete Poetical Works.* Among his other writings are *Mythology and the Romantic Tradition in English Poetry* and *Matthew Arnold.* Obituaries and other sources: *New York Times,* March 8, 1983; *AB Bookman's Weekly,* April 11, 1983.

*   *   *

BUSH, George Edward, Jr. 1938-

PERSONAL: Born December 8, 1938, in Brooklyn, N.Y.; son of George Edward (an accountant) and Mary Agnes (Conway) Bush. *Education:* St. John's University, Jamaica, N.Y., B.A., 1960, M.A., 1962, Ph.D., 1965. *Religion:* Roman Catholic. *Office:* Department of English, St. Francis College, 180 Remsen St., Brooklyn, N.Y. 11201.

CAREER: St. Francis College, Brooklyn, N.Y., assistant professor, 1965-72, associate professor, 1972-76, professor of English, 1976—, professor of ballet, 1973—. Ballet soloist with New Jersey Classical Ballet Company, 1972, and Igor Youskevitch Concert Dance Group, 1972; artistic director of

Forest Hills Ballet Centre, 1976—; music director at Roman Catholic church in Forest Hills. *Member:* Modern Language Association of America, National Council of Teachers of English. *Awards, honors:* Grant from American Philosophical Society, 1967-78.

WRITINGS: (Editor) *Shorter Imitations of Gulliver's Travels,* Scholars' Facsimiles & Reprints, 1974; (editor) *Critique of Gulliver's Travels and Allusions Thereunto: Facsimile Reproductions,* Scholars' Facsimiles & Reprints, 1976; (editor with Jeanne K. Welcher) *Gulliveriana,* Scholars' Facsimiles & Reprints, Volume I, 1976, Volume II, 1978, Volume III, 1979, Volume IV, 1980, Volume V, 1981, Volume VI, 1981.

WORK IN PROGRESS: "Working on an article which may develop into a full-length book on Samuel Johnson's attitudes towards religion in general and Catholicism in particular."

SIDELIGHTS: Bush told *CA:* "The work on *Gulliver's Travels* grew out of a college seminar entitled 'Eighteenth-Century Satire.' The students asked about the reaction to the original work when it was published, and when I investigated I found that there was a large body of unedited *Gulliveriana.*

"I studied ballet as a child and young adult, both in the United States and in Europe. I became a professional ballet dancer and was able to pursue a ballet career and attend college simultaneously but with great difficulty and very hard work.

"In addition to my college teaching, I am the artistic director of my own ballet school, Ballet Centre, in Forest Hills, New York. I have formed a small performing group with some of my advanced students. The group is called Ballet Centre Company, and we give lecture demonstrations and performances of classical ballet and modern dance locally."

*   *   *

BUSH, Larry
See BUSH, Lawrence Dana

*   *   *

BUSH, Lawrence Dana   1951-
(Larry Bush)

PERSONAL: Born December 18, 1951, in New York, N.Y.; son of Morris (a pharmacist) and Jacqueline (a teacher; maiden name, Sayet) Bush; married Susan Griss (a dancer and choreographer), June 10, 1979. *Education:* City College of the City University of New York, B.A., 1973. *Politics:* "Democratic left." *Religion:* "Secular Jew." *Home:* 291 Sterling Place, Brooklyn, N.Y. 11238. *Agent:* Bobbe Siegel, 41 West 83rd St., New York, N.Y. 10024.

CAREER: Poor People's Puppets, New York City, puppeteer, 1972-76; Independence High School, Newark, N.J., teacher of music, 1974-75; Print Center, Inc., Brooklyn, N.Y., typesetter, 1977-80; *Jewish Currents,* New York City, assistant editor, 1980—; lecturer and writer. Co-organizer of local Brooklyn community center, 1977-78. *Member:* National Writers Union, New Jewish Agenda (member of steering committee of Brooklyn chapter).

WRITINGS: Bessie (novel), Seaview/Putnam, 1983. Contributor, sometimes under name Larry Bush, to periodicals, including *Moment, Village Voice, In These Times,* and *Jewish Currents.*

WORK IN PROGRESS: "Writing a novel, set within the context of the anti-nuclear movement, about the interaction between political and family commitments—specifically, about the growth of understanding between a woman activist, age fifty-five, and her grown son."

SIDELIGHTS: Bush's novel, *Bessie,* is based on the life of his grandmother, whose experiences include several harrowing confrontations with treacherous guards in a Siberian prison camp, a subsequent escape to America, a return to Russia during that country's civil war, and years of radical activism in the United States. Neil Barsky wrote in *Jewish World:* "*Bessie* is much more than the saga of a hapless woman. It is a powerful story of a Jewish heroine who, through experiencing all of life's adversities, emerges confident and optimistic about the future of humankind. It is a book to read for its powerful imagery, its lifelike depiction of history, its warmth and—most of all—for *Bessie.*"

Bush told *CA:* "The creation of *Bessie* was for me an act of emigration from the 'youth nation' or 'Woodstock nation' of the 1960's to a historical community dating back generations. I was fascinated and strengthened by the parallels I saw between my grandmother's generation of radicals and my own: I could see her odyssey to America as an 'altered state of consciousness,' her *yiddishkeit* as my rock 'n' roll, her fraternal organizations as my communes, her blind faith in Soviet communism as my New Left messianism, her Sholom Aleichem as my John Lennon, and her survival as an idealist, intact at ninety, as a good omen for my survival as a searcher for values in an increasingly faceless world.

"I am concerned as a writer with people's efforts to make meaning of their experience, to endure the pain of deep feelings, to juggle self-awareness and social awareness, to break with numbness and two-dimensionality, to rebel. These concerns were the essential stuff of the '60's, which I took *so* seriously—or else I might have become a doctor or a lawyer (I was elected 'most intelligent boy' in high school and was an all-round whiz kid with triple-A ratings). So I took a risk, became a writer, neglected to build a more stable and lucrative career. I've lived for the ten years since my college graduation on very little income, never working a full-time job, never wearing a tie. My reward: time to think, feel, and write.

"Fortunately my wife is also a committed starving artist, as our children will be, until they rebel, make a lot of money, and become our patrons. Though I'm over thirty, off drugs and less giddy, I feel no less committed to living the 'examined life' and no less worried about the risk. I like how Abbie Hoffman put it in his *Soon to Be a Major Picture:* 'Jews, especially first-born male Jews, have to make a choice very quickly in life whether to go for the money or go for broke. Wise guys who go around saying things like "Workers of the world unite," or "Every guy wants to screw his mother," or "$E = mc^2$," obviously choose to go for broke. It's the greatest Jewish tradition.' It's also cause for a nervous breakdown.

"Ironically, I've so far been unable to write successfully in an autobiographical voice—to avoid first-person self-indulgence. As I mature in my craft, I hope to be able to do so, and to write about my own generation, draw upon my own experience. Ah, but what a pleasure to glimpse goals beyond that first looming monster: to be published!"

BIOGRAPHICAL/CRITICAL SOURCES: Village Voice, February 10, 1982; *Moment,* September, 1982; *Jewish World,* April 15-21, 1983; *Hadassah,* May, 1983; *Ms.,* July, 1983.

BUSS, Claude Albert 1903-

PERSONAL: Born November 29, 1903, in Sunbury, Pa.; son of W. Claude and Clara (Fetter) Buss; married Evelyn Lukens, January 20, 1928; children: Lynne. *Education:* Washington Missionary College, Takoma Park, Md., A.B., 1922; Susquehanna University, M.A., 1924; University of Pennsylvania, Ph.D., 1927; also attended Ecole Libre des Science Politiques, 1927-28, and L'Institut des Hautes Etudes Internationales. *Home:* 1234 Pitman Ave., Palo Alto, Calif. 94301.

CAREER: U.S. Department of State, Washington, D.C., attache for language study at U.S. Legation in China, 1929-31, vice-consul in Nanking, China, 1931-34; University of Southern California, Los Angeles, professor of international relations, 1934-41; Stanford University, Stanford, Calif., professor of history, 1946-69, professor emeritus, 1969—; Institute for Foreign Studies, Monterey, Calif., professor of history, 1968-75; U.S. Naval Post Graduate School, Monterey, professor of history, 1976—. Professor at San Jose State University, 1971-77; director of studies at National War College, 1949, member of civilian faculty, 1963-64. Executive assistant to U.S. High Commissioner to the Philippine Islands, 1941-44; chief of San Francisco Office of War Information, 1944-46; member of Brookings Institution Seminar on U.S. Foreign Policy, 1949; adviser to U.S. Department of State's Bureau of East Asia and Pacific Affairs, 1967-68; U.S. delegate to international conferences of Institute for Pacific Relations; executive consultant to U.S. Strategic Bombing Survey (Japan). *Awards, honors:* Carnegie fellow in Europe, 1927-28; LL.D. from University of Southern California, 1945; Fulbright scholar at University of the Philippines, 1957, 1959.

WRITINGS: War and Diplomacy in Eastern Asia, Macmillan, 1941; *The Far East,* Macmillan, 1955, reprinted as *Asia in the Modern World,* Macmillan, 1964; *The Arc of Crisis,* Doubleday, 1955; *The People's Republic of China,* Van Nostrand, 1962; *Contemporary Southeast Asia,* Van Nostrand, 1970; *The People's Republic of China and Richard Nixon,* Stanford Alumni Association, 1972, reprinted as *China: The People's Republic of China and Richard Nixon,* W. H. Freeman, 1974; *The United States and the Philippines: Background for Policy,* American Enterprise Institute for Public Policy Research, 1977; *Southeast Asia and the World Today,* Peter Smith, 1980.

WORK IN PROGRESS: The United States and the Pacific Basin, for Hoover Institution on War, Revolution, and Peace.

* * *

BUSSARD, Paul 1904-1983

OBITUARY NOTICE: Born November 22, 1904, in Essex, Iowa; died February 22, 1983, in St. Paul, Minn. Clergyman, publisher, and author. Bussard was a co-founder and publisher of *Catholic Digest* from 1936 to 1965. He wrote several religious volumes, including *If I Be Lifted Up* and *Staircase to a Star.* Obituaries and other sources: *Catholic Authors: Contemporary Biographical Sketches,* Volume I: *1930-1947,* St. Mary's Abbey, 1948; *Chicago Tribune,* February 26, 1983.

* * *

BUTLER, Colin Gasking 1913-

PERSONAL: Born October 26, 1913, in West Horsham, England; son of Walter Gasking and Phyllis (Pearce) Butler; married Jean March Innes (a biochemist), September, 1937; children: Jonathan, Gillian (Mrs. Robert John Dutton). *Education:*

Queens' College, Cambridge, B.A., 1935, Ph.D., 1938. *Religion:* Society of Friends (Quakers). *Home:* Silver Birches, Porthpean, St. Austell, Cornwall, England.

CAREER: Rothamsted Experimental Station, Harpenden, England, assistant entomologist in charge of bee section, 1939-43, head of bee department, 1943-72, head of combined entomology and bee department, 1972-76; writer, 1939—. *Member:* International Union for the Study of Social Insects (president, 1969-74), Royal Entomological Society (president, 1971-73), Royal Society (fellow), Institute of Biology (founding member; fellow), Cornwall Naturalists Trust (president). *Awards, honors:* Silver Medal from Royal Society of Arts, 1945, for lecture; Officer of Order of the British Empire, 1970.

WRITINGS: The Honey Bee: An Introduction to Her Sense Physiology and Behaviour, Oxford University Press, 1949; *The World of the Honey Bee,* Collins, 1954, revised edition, 1974; *Bumblebees,* Collins, 1959; (with R. M. Bere and P. B. Blamey) *The Nature of Cornwall,* Barracuda Books, 1982.

SIDELIGHTS: Butler told *CA:* "I have always been interested in natural history and nature photography since I can remember. I have been lucky enough to be able to earn my living doing entomological research, mostly on honeybees. I am very anxious to show others, particularly young people, how interesting natural history is and to encourage them to work for nature conservation before it is too late."

* * *

BUTLER, Rohan D'Olier 1917-

PERSONAL: Born January 21, 1917, in London, England; son of Harold Beresford and Olive Augusta Newnham (Waters) Butler; married Lucy Rosemary Byron, August 6, 1956. *Education:* Balliol College, Oxford, B.A. (with first class honors), 1938, M.A., 1942. *Home:* White Notley Hall, near Witham, Essex, England. *Office:* All Souls College, Oxford University, Oxford, England.

CAREER: Oxford University, Oxford, England, fellow of All Souls College, 1938—, senior research fellow, 1956—, subwarden, 1961-63. Historical adviser to England's secretary of state for foreign affairs, 1963-68, and foreign and commonwealth affairs, 1968—; member of advisory council on public records, 1982—. Member of court of University of Essex, 1971—; member of board of governors of Felsted School; trustee of Feldstead Almshouse; member of management committee of Institute of Historical Research, University of London. *Military service:* British Army, 1941-44. *Member:* Royal Historical Society (fellow), Beefsteak Club. *Awards, honors:* Leverhulme Fellow, 1955-57; companion of Order of St. Michael and St. George.

WRITINGS: The Roots of National Socialism, Faber, 1941; *Choiseul,* Clarendon Press, 1980. Contributor to "The New Cambridge Modern History" series, Cambridge University Press, 1957-70. "Documents on British Foreign Policy: 1919-1939," H.M.S.O., editor, 1945-65, senior editor, 1955-65.

* * *

BUTTIGEIG, Anton 1912-1983

OBITUARY NOTICE: Born February 19, 1912, in Qala, Gozo, Malta; died May 5, 1983. Public servant, journalist, and poet. Buttigeig served Malta as deputy prime minister and as minister of justice and parliamentary affairs. Prior to working in the

Maltese Government he worked as a reporter for *Times of Malta* and then as editor of *Voice of Malta*. Among his collections of poetry are *Mill-gallerija ta' zghoziti* (title means "From the Balcony of My Youth"), *Ejjew nidkju ftit* (title means "Let Us Laugh a Bit"), and, in English, *The Lamplighter*. Obituaries and other sources: *The International Year Book and Statesmen's Who's Who*, Kelley's Directories, 1979; *The International Who's Who*, 46th edition, Europa, 1982; *Who's Who in the World*, 6th edition, Marquis, 1982; *London Times*, May 6, 1983.

* * *

BYCK, Robert 1933-

PERSONAL: Born April 26, 1933, in Newark, N.J.; son of Louis (a physician) and Lucy (a teacher; maiden name, Landou) Byck; married Susan Wheeler, 1976; children: (previous marriage) Carl, Gillian, Lucas. *Education:* University of Pennsylvania, A.B., 1954, M.D., 1959. *Office:* Department of Pharmacology, School of Medicine, B-244, Yale University, 333 Cedar St., New Haven, Conn. 06510.

CAREER: University of California, San Francisco, rotating intern at university hospitals, 1959-60; National Institutes of Health, Bethesda, Md., research associate, 1960-62; University of California, Medical Center, San Francisco, visiting scientist and visiting assistant professor of pharmacology, 1963; Yeshiva University, Albert Einstein College of Medicine, Bronx, N.Y., assistant professor of pharmacology and rehabilitation medicine, 1964-69; Yale University, New Haven, Conn., resident in psychiatry and fellow in psychiatry, 1969-72, lecturer in pharmacology, 1969-75, associate professor of pharmacology in psychiatry, 1972-77, professor of psychiatry and pharmacology, 1977—, clinical fellow at Yale-New Haven Hospital, 1969-72, associate physician, 1972—, resident fellow of Pierson College, 1976-80. Assistant attending physician at Bronx Municipal Hospital Center, 1964-69; associate of Columbia University Seminar on Drugs and Society, 1977-82; member of Drug Abuse Review Committee of National Institute on Drug Abuse Research, 1977-80. *Military service:* U.S. Public Health Service, surgeon, 1960-62.

MEMBER: American Association for the Advancement of Science, American Society for Pharmacology and Experimental Therapeutics, American Society for Clinical Pharmacology and Therapeutics, American College of Neuropsychopharmacology, American Psychiatric Association. *Awards, honors:* Grant from National Institute of Mental Health, 1967-68; Burroughs-Wellcome Fund scholar in clinical pharmacology, 1972; M.A. from Yale University, 1978.

WRITINGS: (Co-author) "Drugs: Educational Resources" (tape cassette and filmstrip series), Educational Resources, 1970; (editor and author of introduction) *Cocaine Papers: Sigmund Freud*, Stonehill Publishing, 1975.

Contributor: Richard Goldsby, editor, *Biology*, Harper, 1975; Louis Goodman and Alfred Gilman, editors, *The Pharmacological Basis of Therapeutics*, 5th edition (Byck was not included in earlier editions), Macmillan, 1975; E. H. Ellinwood and M. M. Kilbey, editors, *Cocaine and Other Stimulants*, Plenum, 1977; R. C. Peterson and R. C. Stillman, editors, *Cocaine 1977* (monograph), National Institute on Drug Abuse Research, 1977; K. L. Melmon and H. F. Morelli, editors, *Clinical Pharmacology*, Macmillan, 1978; Peterson, editor, *The International Challenge of Drug Abuse* (monograph), National Institute on Drug Abuse Research, 1978; F. R. Jeri,

editor, *Cocaine 1980: Proceedings of the Inter-American Seminar on Coca and Cocaine*, Pacific Press, 1980; N. K. Mello, editor, *Advances in Substance Abuse*, JAI Press, 1982. Also contributor to *Pharmacology of Conditioning, Learning, and Retention*, edited by M. Mikhel'son and V. G. Longo, Pergamon.

Contributor to *Encyclopedia Americana*. Contributor of about seventy articles to medical journals and newspapers. Member of advisory board of *The Medical Letter on Drugs and Therapeutics*, 1975—.

WORK IN PROGRESS: Studying the biological basis of good feelings.

* * *

BYRD, Emmett
See HINDEN, Michael C(harles)

* * *

BYRD, John Crowe
See HINDEN, Michael C(harles)

* * *

BYTWERK, Randall Lee 1950-

PERSONAL: Surname is pronounced *Bite*-work; born April 13, 1950, in Grand Rapids, Mich.; son of Robert Louis (in business) and Ruth (Stromback) Bytwerk; married Sharon Van Haitsma (a free-lance interpreter for the deaf), May 27, 1978; children: David Paul. *Education:* Calvin College, B.A., 1971; Northwestern University, M.A., 1973, Ph.D., 1975. *Religion:* Presbyterian. *Home:* 705 West Elm, Carbondale, Ill. 62901. *Office:* Department of Speech Communication, Southern Illinois University, Carbondale, Ill. 62901.

CAREER: Southern Illinois University, Carbondale, assistant professor, 1975-80, associate professor of speech communication, 1980—. *Member:* International Society for the History of Rhetoric, Speech Communication Association, Rhetoric Society of America, Sierra Club (chairman of Shawnee group, 1976-80), Central States Speech Association.

WRITINGS: Julius Streicher: The Man Who Persuaded a Nation to Hate Jews, Stein & Day, 1983. Contributor to history, journalism, and speech journals.

WORK IN PROGRESS: Research on the organization of the German Nazi system of political meetings prior to 1933, on pre-1933 Nazi anti-Semitic propaganda, and on propaganda in East German newspapers.

SIDELIGHTS: "Most of my work has centered on German Nazi political propaganda," Bytwerk commented. "Part of the reason, I suppose, is that it is interesting to study people who are very nasty morally, but very good technically. That is part of the reason that Al Capone is so interesting—he was nasty, but a capable gangster. The Nazis were able to use most of the available means of persuasion, and very effectively, in a dreadful cause.

''My research has given me good reason to travel. I've worked at archives and libraries in London, Munich, Nuremberg, and Koblenz, as well as in the United States. I've been invited to teach for a term at the University of Mainz in Germany. The people there are particularly interested in my work on Nazi propaganda.

''My whole interest in propaganda goes back to high school. My father speaks some German, and he used to tease me in that language. In high school I studied German, and continued it in college. As a graduate student, I was the only incoming student who could handle German, so my adviser did his best to win me over to an interest in Nazi propaganda. He obviously succeeded.''

AVOCATIONAL INTERESTS: Backpacking, mountaineering.

C

CABRERA, James C. 1935-

PERSONAL: Born July 9, 1935, in White Plains, N.Y.; son of Joseph and Esther (Pellird) Cabrera; married Helen Napoli, August 25, 1956; children: Joseph, James C., Jr. *Education:* Rider College, B.S., 1958. *Politics:* Republican. *Religion:* Roman Catholic. *Home:* 4 Shorehame Club Rd., Old Greenwich, Conn. 06890. *Office:* Drake Beam Morin, Inc., 277 Park Ave., New York, N.Y. 10172.

CAREER: Electrolux Corp., Old Greenwich, Conn., assistant personnel manager, 1958-61; Chesebrough-Ponds, Greenwich, Conn., personnel director, 1961-63; Bishop Industries, Union, N.J., corporate personnel director, 1963-65; Drake Beam Morin, Inc., New York, N.Y., director, 1966-68, president, 1968—, and member of board of directors. Member of board of directors of Data Papers, Inc. *Member:* American Management Association.

WRITINGS: Parting Company: How to Survive the Loss of a Job and Find Another Successfully, Harcourt, 1982.

*   *   *

CADY, Arthur 1920-1983

OBITUARY NOTICE: Born in 1920 in Buffalo, N.Y.; died April 5, 1983, in Brewster, N.Y. Artist and author. Cady was best known for his depictions of rural and urban environments. He had held three one-man shows in New York City since 1978. He wrote *The Art Buff's Book: What Artists Do and How-They-Do-It* and created the film "El hombre de hoy" for the archdiocese of New York. Obituaries and other sources: *New York Times,* April 6, 1983.

*   *   *

CALHOUN, James Frank 1941-

PERSONAL: Born March 1, 1941, in Sherman, Tex.; son of Frank and Mary Elizabeth (Deaver) Calhoun; married Gwen Guillet, June 10, 1967 (divorced); married Judith Babb Chandler (an educator), July 28, 1979; children: Mary Martha, Carolyn Elizabeth, Margaret Abigail. *Education:* University of Florida, B.A., 1963; Southern Methodist University, B.D., 1966; University of Illinois, M.A., 1968, Ph.D., 1969. *Politics:* Democrat. *Home:* 155 Crossbow Pl., Winterville, Ga.

30683. *Office:* Department of Psychology, University of Georgia, Athens, Ga. 30602.

CAREER: Ordained Methodist minister, 1964; Methodist Hospital, Dallas, Tex., chaplain, 1964-66; University of Illinois, Champaign-Urbana, research associate with Community Mental Health Study, 1966-69; Adolf Mayer Zone Center, Decatur, Ill., psychologist with rehabilitation project, 1969-70; State University of New York at Stony Brook, assistant professor of psychology, 1970-77, director of Psychology Center, 1971-77; University of Georgia, Athens, associate professor of psychology, 1977—. *Member:* American Psychological Association, American Association for the Advancement of Science, Association for the Advancement of Behavior Therapy, Eastern Psychological Association, Southwestern Psychological Association, Rocky Mountain Psychological Association.

WRITINGS: Psychology of Adjustment and Human Relationships, Random House, 1978. Contributor to psychology journals.

WORK IN PROGRESS: Revising *Psychology of Adjustment and Human Relationships.*

*   *   *

CALLAN, Jamie 1954-

PERSONAL: Born January 26, 1954, in Long Island, N.Y.; daughter of John (a personnel administrator) and June (a secretary; maiden name, Dingwall) Callan; married Eugene Silver (an actor), June 20, 1981. *Education:* Norwalk Community College, A.A., 1973; Bard College, B.A., 1975; Goddard College, M.A., 1980. *Religion:* Presbyterian. *Residence:* New York, N.Y. *Address:* c/o New American Library, 1633 Broadway, New York, N.Y. 10019.

CAREER: Fishkill Correctional Facility, Fishkill, N.Y., teacher, 1974-75; Western Union International, New York City, editorial assistant and editor of *TelexTalk,* 1976-78; Mid-Orange Correctional Facility, Warwick, N.Y., teacher, 1980; Fiction Project, New York City, teacher of creative writing at New York Hospital/Cornell Medical Center's Psychiatric Unit, 1982—. Free-lance copywriter for Estee Lauder, 1981—. Teacher of young adult fiction course at New York University School of Continuing Education, 1983. *Awards, honors:* Creative Artists Public Service Award, 1980, for *Andrea Darcy;*

fellow at Millay Colony for the Arts, summer, 1981; Doubleday/Columbia Fellowship, 1982; fellow at Virginia Center for the Arts, winter, 1983.

WRITINGS: Over the Hill at Fourteen (young adult novel; Scholastic Book Club selection), New American Library, 1982; *The Young and the Soapy* (young adult novel), New American Library, in press. Contributor of articles, stories, and poems to magazines, including *Greenfield Review, Back Bay View, Wellspring,* and *Buckle.*

WORK IN PROGRESS: Andrea Darcy, a novel.

SIDELIGHTS: Callan told *CA:* "My career as an author of novels for young adults started by accident. My very first novel, *Andrea Darcy,* won an award in 1980, and because of this, several publishers, including New American Library, contacted me. While New American Library could not publish *Andrea Darcy,* they asked me if I would be interested in writing a book on assignment about a teenage fashion model. I did a great deal of soul-searching before I accepted, then decided that it is better to write, even if it's not on a truly heartfelt subject, than not to write at all.

"To my surprise, I began to enjoy writing *Over the Hill at Fourteen,* and when it was complete I was thrilled by the response. Scholastic Book Club bought it, and it was favorably reviewed in several publications. The most exciting result was getting fan mail. Teenagers from all over the country wrote to me, and my book seemed important and meaningful to them. That was when I decided to take the genre seriously. I no longer say 'Oh, I only write young adult novels.' I have just completed my second novel for young adults, *The Young and the Soapy.* It is about two sixteen-year-old girls addicted to soap operas. I hope this book will be as well received as the first."

* * *

CAMERON, Angus Fraser 1941-1983

OBITUARY NOTICE: Born February 11, 1941, in Truro, Nova Scotia, Canada; died May 27, 1983, in Toronto, Ontario, Canada. Educator, lexicographer, editor, and author. Educated at Mount Allison University and at Oxford University, which he attended as a Rhodes scholar, Cameron taught for two years at Mount Allison before joining the English faculty of University of Toronto in 1968. There he specialized in Old English language and literature and served for a time as director of the school's Centre for Medieval Studies. Cameron wrote *Saint Gildas and Scyld Scefing* and *Neuphilol Mitteil* in 1969, and since 1970 had served as editor of the *Dictionary of Old English,* a work sponsored by the Canada Council that was left incomplete at the time of his death. Cameron, who was one of the first editors to bring computers into the field of lexicography, used the technology to compile a *Microfiche Concordance* and *Old English Word Studies: A Preliminary Author and Word Index.* He was named a fellow of the Royal Society of Canada in 1982. Obituaries and other sources: *Directory of American Scholars,* Volume II: *English, Speech, and Drama,* 8th edition, Bowker, 1982; *London Times,* June 11, 1983.

* * *

CAMERON, Kim S(terling) 1946-

PERSONAL: Born September 30, 1946, in Payson, Utah; married, August 24, 1983; children: Austin Sterling, Brittany Ruth Renee, Cheyenne Cherie Marie, Asher Ephraim, Tiara Mary Monique, Carter Melinda Katrina. *Education:* Brigham Young University, B.S., 1970, M.S., 1971; Yale University, M.A., 1976, Ph.D., 1978. *Home:* 4350 Drew Circle, Boulder, Colo. 80303. *Office:* National Center for Higher Education Management Systems, 1540 30th St., Boulder, Colo. 80302.

CAREER: Ricks College, Rexburg, Idaho, instructor in sociology, 1971-74; Southern Connecticut State College, New Haven, visiting instructor in sociology, 1974-78; University of Wisconsin—Madison, assistant professor of business and industrial relations, 1978-81; University of Colorado, Boulder, adjunct associate professor of business administration, 1981—. Director of Organizational Studies Division at National Center for Higher Education Management Systems, 1981—; conducts research and training on the management of colleges and universities. *Member:* Academy of Management, Association for the Study of Higher Education, Phi Kappa Phi, Phi Delta Kappa. *Awards, honors:* Research grants from American Nurses' Association, 1980, and National Institute of Education, 1981, 1982, and 1983.

WRITINGS: (With David A. Whetten) *Management: A Practical Guide to Professional Skill Development,* Ginn, 1980, revised edition, 1981; (contributor) Dan Baugher, editor, *New Directions for Program Evaluation: Assessing Effectiveness,* Jossey-Bass, 1981; (with Robert H. Miles) *Coffin Nails and Corporate Strategies,* Prentice-Hall, 1982; (contributor) James L. Bess, editor, *Organization of Colleges and Universities: Insights From the Behavioral Sciences,* New York University Press, 1983; (with Whetten) *Organizational Effectiveness: A Comparison of Multiple Models,* Academic Press, 1983; (contributor) Barry M. Staw, editor, *Research in Organizational Behavior,* Jai Press, 1983; (with Whetten) *Developing Management Skills,* Scott, Foresman, in press; (with Robert E. Quinn) *Classics of Organizational Development,* Moore Publishing, in press. Contributor of articles and reviews to management and business journals.

WORK IN PROGRESS: Organizational Effectiveness in Colleges and Universities (tentative title), publication by Jossey-Bass expected in 1985.

SIDELIGHTS: Cameron told *CA:* "At one time I thought that the best way to help make individuals and organizations more effective was through face-to-face interaction. Much of my energy was spent with university students and managers in organizations trying to verbalize ideas and principles that would be helpful. A colleague convinced me, however, that writing could be at least as influential and certainly less constrained by location. My writing has since been focused on broadening the general pool of knowledge and understanding of individual and organizational effectiveness, and also on helping individuals and organizations to behave in ways that are more effective. Writing for scholarly audiences has been aimed at increasing knowledge and understanding, whereas writing for leaders and managers in organizations has been aimed at helping to enhance effective behaviors."

* * *

CAMPBELL, Enid (Mona) 1932-

PERSONAL: Born October 30, 1932, in Launceston, Australia; daughter of Neil Lachlan and Mona (Hutton) Campbell. *Education:* Attended University of Tasmania, 1950-55, and Duke University, 1956-59. *Home:* 72 Catherine Ave., Mount Waverley, Victoria, Australia. *Office:* Faculty of Law, Monash University, Clayton, Victoria 3168, Australia.

CAREER: University of Tasmania, Hobart, Australia, lecturer in political science, 1959; University of Sydney, Sydney, Australia, lecturer, 1960-62, senior lecturer, 1962-65, associate professor of law, 1965-67; Sir Isaac Isaacs Professor of Law at Monash University, Clayton, Australia. Member of Royal Commission on Australian Government Administration, 1974-76. *Member:* Australasian Law Schools Association, Society of Public Teachers of Law, Australian Political Studies Association, Australian Academy of Social Sciences (fellow). *Awards, honors:* Officer of the Order of the British Empire.

WRITINGS: Parliamentary Privilege in Australia, Melbourne University Press, 1966; (with Harry Whitmore) *Freedom in Australia,* Sydney University Press, 1967, 2nd edition, 1973; (with D. J. MacDougall) *Legal Research,* Law Book Co., 1967, 2nd edition (with E. J. Glasser and H. Lahore), 1979. Contributor to law journals.

*   *   *

CAMPBELL, Jeremy 1931-

PERSONAL: Born November 7, 1931, in Fareham, England; came to United States in 1965; son of Robert C. (a salesman) and Alfreda R. (Way) Campbell; married Edwina Dorothy Esme George, January 19, 1963. *Education:* Keble College, Oxford, B.A., 1955. *Home and office:* 4312 Fessenden St. N.W., Washington, D.C. 20016. *Agent:* Richard A. Balkin, The Balkin Agency, 880 West 181st St., New York, N.Y. 10033.

CAREER: Metal Box Co., London, England, management trainee, 1955-57; *London Evening Standard,* London, England, staff journalist, 1957, reporter, 1957-61, chief editorial writer, 1961-65, correspondent in Washington, D.C., 1965—.

WRITINGS: Grammatical Man: Information, Entropy, Language, and Life, Simon & Schuster, 1982.

WORK IN PROGRESS: A work of nonfiction, publication by Simon & Schuster expected in 1985.

SIDELIGHTS: Campbell's book, *Grammatical Man: Information, Entropy, Language, and Life,* is a survey of work being done in the developing field of information theory, a science which studies our use of words and other tools of communication in order to determine whether the rules of language are like laws of nature. The importance of this theory, Campbell explained, is that if the world acts according to the same principals as language, then by observing language, the actions of the universe may be predictable.

Washington Post writer Joseph McLellan acknowledged that information theory involves "complex and abstruse fields," but praised Campbell's work, calling *Grammatical Man* "a model of clarity," which "will introduce the nonspecialized reader easily and enjoyably to a strange and fascinating new world of ideas that is certain to have a major impact on the future of mankind." And Jack Miles wrote in the *Los Angeles Times Book Review* that *Grammatical Man* is "good science journalism . . . an independent, speculative attempt at scientific synthesis."

Campbell told *CA:* "I am fascinated by the streak of optimism that runs through many of the ideas developed by science in the past three decades. The ruling principle of a world 'running down' has given way to the more sanguine view that part of it at least is 'winding up.' We can no longer think of disorder as being the natural state of things, while order is somehow freakish and accidental. In linguistics and computer theory, physical chemistry and biology, a greater emphasis is being placed on processes that are self-organizing, and fundamentally constructive. The word 'entropy,' for example, used to denote only dissipation, the unraveling of structure with the passage of time. Today it is also associated with the notion of variety, of the potential for new structures, to arise. This is almost the reverse of the pessimistic interpretation of time as the enemy of order that prevailed in the Victorian period and afterward. I am always delighted when someone tells me, 'Your book cheered me up.'"

BIOGRAPHICAL/CRITICAL SOURCES: Washington Post, September 1, 1982; *Los Angeles Times Book Review,* September 26, 1982.

*   *   *

CAMPBELL, Joan 1929-

PERSONAL: Born June 22, 1929, in Berlin, Germany; daughter of Gustav (an economist, journalist, and author) and Antonie (a journalist and author; maiden name, Kassowitz) Stolper; married Dugal Campbell (a professor of psychology), June 12, 1954; children: Alister; Anna, Beverly, David (adopted). *Education:* Radcliffe College, B.A., 1950; Oxford University, M.A., 1952; Queen's University at Kingston, Ph.D., 1975. *Home:* 43 Cross St., Dundas, Ontario, Canada L9H 2R5.

CAREER: Oxford University Press, New York, N.Y., editorial assistant, 1952-54; McGraw-Hill (publishers), London, England, assistant editor, 1954-56; McCann-Erickson Advertising, London, executive assistant, 1956-57; Avondale College, Auckland, New Zealand, senior history mistress, 1959; University of Toronto, Toronto, Ontario, assistant professor of history, 1977—. Part-time instructor at Queen's University at Kingston, Kingston, Ontario, 1961-76; contributor to symposia at McMaster University and University of Toronto. Member of board of directors of Children's Aid Society, Kingston, 1965-72 (president, 1974-76). *Member:* American Historical Association, Canadian Historical Association, Kingston Choral Society (president, 1965), Dundas Heritage Association (vice-president, 1981—), Phi Beta Kappa.

WRITINGS: The German Werkbund: The Politics of Reform in the Applied Arts, Princeton University Press, 1978. Contributor of reviews to scholarly journals, including *Canadian Journal of History.*

WORK IN PROGRESS: Joy in Work, German Work, tentative title of a book on German ideas about work in the nineteenth and twentieth centuries.

SIDELIGHTS: The German Werkbund: The Politics of Reform in the Applied Arts traces the history of the German guild for arts, crafts, and industry—the Werkbund—from its inception in 1907 through 1934. Writing in the *Times Literary Supplement,* Reyner Banham called the book "an exhaustive new study" of the Werkbund, adding that "Campbell rightly keeps the crises and continuities of German public life at large well in view, and she seems to have made some real breakthroughs in our comprehension of the Weimar period as a result."

Campbell told *CA:* "German history is my main professional interest. I am currently teaching European socialism and a seminar on Weimar culture at the University of Toronto, as well as doing research on the history of work, attitudes toward work, and the changing work ethic in nineteenth- and twentieth-century Germany. Hard times in the university have made it impossible for me to obtain a tenured position in Canada despite my qualifications and experience—there simply are no openings in my field within range of where we live. Writing is hampered by the need to teach if and when I can and the lack of continuity and security of employment, but I hope to make progress on my next book with the help of research grants, starting with one I just received from the Historical Commission in Berlin, Germany.''

BIOGRAPHICAL/CRITICAL SOURCES: Times Literary Supplement, September 15, 1978.

* * *

CANFIELD, Jane White 1897-

PERSONAL: Born April 29, 1897, in Syracuse, N.Y.; daughter of Ernest Ingersol and Katharine Curtin (Sage) White; married Charles F. Fuller, September 9, 1922; children: Jane Sage Cowles, Isabel Fox, Blair. *Education:* Attended Art Students League, 1918-20, James Earle & Laura Gardin Fraser Studio, and Borglum School, 1920-22; also studied with A. Bourdelle in Paris. *Home:* Guard Hill Rd., Bedford, N.Y. 10506. *Agent:* (Artworks) Far Gallery, 20 East 80th St., New York, N.Y. 10021.

CAREER: Sculptor. Commissioned works include sculptures for Paul Mellon estate, Upperville, Va., 1940, Miss Porter's School, Farmington, Conn., 1960, Church of St. John of Lattington, Locust Valley, N.Y., 1963, and Memorial Sanctuary, Fishers Island, N.Y., 1969. Exhibited work in group shows, including World's Fair, N.Y., 1939, Architectural League, Knoedler Gallery, and American Academy. Work featured in one-man shows at American-British Art Gallery, New York City, 1951, County Art Gallery, Westbury, N.Y., 1960, Far Gallery, New York City, 1961, 1965, and 1974, and Country Art Gallery, Locust Valley, 1971. Work represented in permanent collections at Whitney Museum of American Art and Cornell University Museum of Art. Board chairman of Bedford-Rippowam School, 1933-38; board member of ARC Arts and Skills, Washington, D.C., 1942-45, Planned Parenthood, 1945-55, International Planned Parenthood, 1955-65, and Margaret Sanger Bureau, 1965—.

WRITINGS—For children: *The Frog Prince: A True Story,* illustrated by Winn Smith, Harper, 1970; *Swan Cove,* illustrated by Jo Polseno, Harper, 1978. Contributor to periodicals, including *Reader's Digest.**

* * *

CANNON, Cornelia (James) 1876-1969

OBITUARY NOTICE: Born November 17, 1876, in St. Paul, Minn.; died December 7, 1969, in Franklin, N.H. Author. Best known for her children's books about the Pueblo Indian tribe, including *The Pueblo Girl, Lazaro in the Pueblos,* and *The Fight for the Pueblo,* Cannon began her career writing articles on social and economic issues for such magazines as *Harper's, North American Review,* and *Atlantic Monthly.* An early, outspoken supporter of the birth control movement, she served with the Planned Parenthood League of Massachusetts and was president of the state's Mothers' Health Council. Cannon and her husband, Dr. Walter B. Cannon, were the first people to scale Mount Cannon, an eight-thousand-foot peak in Glacier National Park. The mountain peak was named in their honor. Obituaries and other sources: *Junior Book of Authors,* Wilson, 1934; *Twentieth Century Authors: A Biographical Dictionary of Modern Literature,* 1st supplement, H. W. Wilson, 1955; *Who's Who of American Women,* 2nd edition, Marquis,

1961; *American Authors and Books: 1640 to the Present Day,* 3rd revised edition, Crown, 1962; *New York Times,* December 10, 1969.

* * *

CARDEW, Michael (Ambrose) 1901-1983

OBITUARY NOTICE—See index for *CA* sketch: Born May 26, 1901, in London, England; died February 11, 1983, in Truro, Cornwall, England. Artist, educator, and author. In 1950 Cardew was invited by the government of Nigeria to serve as senior pottery officer in the Department of Commerce and Industry. During his fifteen-year stay there he developed a pottery training center in Abuja. Cardew lectured widely on pottery at a number of universities in the United States. He wrote *Pioneer Pottery* and contributed to art journals. Obituaries and other sources: *London Times,* February 16, 1983.

* * *

CARE, Felicity
See COURY, Louise Andree

* * *

CAREY, John A(ndrew) 1949-

PERSONAL: Born May 27, 1949, in Glendale, Calif.; son of John Nelson (an artist) and Dorothea (Bordwell) Carey; married Harriet Stolmeier (a physician), June 19, 1982. *Education:* Columbia University, B.A., 1971; Harvard University, A.M., 1972, Ph.D., 1979. *Home:* 151 Tremont St., No. 9C, Boston, Mass. 02111. *Office:* Pioneer Group, Inc., 60 State St., Boston, Mass. 02109.

CAREER: Harvard University, Cambridge, Mass., teaching fellow, 1973-77; Yankelovich, Skelly & White, Stamford, Conn., senior council representative, 1977-79; Pioneer Group, Inc. (investment company), Boston, Mass., senior analyst, 1979—. *Member:* Institute of Chartered Financial Analysts, Boston Security Analysts Society, Boston Athenaeum, Harvard Club of Boston, John Jay Fellows of Columbia College.

WRITINGS: Judicial Reform in France Before the Revolution of 1789 (nonfiction), Harvard University Press, 1981.

WORK IN PROGRESS: Research into American business history and early modern French history.

SIDELIGHTS: Carey's *Judicial Reform in France Before the Revolution of 1789* explores attempts to modify the French legal system by such personages as clergyman and author Abbe de Saint-Pierre, Chancellor Henri-Francois Daquesseau, and Foreign Minister Rene-Louis de Voyer d'Argenson. Writing in the *Times Literary Supplement,* critic J.M.J. Register commented, "some interesting considerations about the reform of the presidial courts emerge [from Carey's book]." Register, however, noted that more information about the "social and political fabric of the *ancien regime*" would have made the book less confusing.

Carey told *CA:* "My graduate training was as a historian. Although I have since become, for personal and practical reasons, a securities analyst, I maintain my interest in history and intend to make further professional contributions. I believe that a working life may embrace different activities. I hope that mine will."

BIOGRAPHICAL/CRITICAL SOURCES: Times Literary Supplement, July 30, 1982.

CARGILL, Jennifer S(ue) 1944-

PERSONAL: Born July 15, 1944, in Ruston, La.; daughter of Barnett Rabb and Claudie (Norris) Cargill. *Education:* Louisiana Polytechnic Institute, B.A., 1965; Louisiana State University, M.S., 1967; Miami University, Oxford, Ohio, M.Ed., 1975. *Home:* 209 South Main, Oxford, Ohio 45056. *Office: Technicalities,* 26l Circle Dr., Springfield, Ill. 62703.

CAREER: University of Houston, Houston, Tex., assistant acquisitions librarian, 1967-68, health sciences librarian, 1969-72; Miami University, Oxford, Ohio, science librarian, 1972-74, acquisitions librarian, 1974—. Acquisitions editor of Oryx Press, 1981—. *Member:* American Library Association (member of council, 1982—), American Society for Information Science, Reference and Subscription Books Review Committee (RSBRC; member of editorial board), OHIONET, Southern Ohio Chapter of American Society for Information Science (SOASIS), Ohio Valley Group of Technical Services Librarians, Beta Phi Mu, Phi Kappa Phi.

WRITINGS: (With Brian Alley) *Practical Approval Plan Management,* Oryx, 1979; (contributor) Nancy Jean Melin, editor, *The Serials Collection: Organization and Administration,* Pierian, 1982; (contributor) Diane Ellsworth, editor, *Union Lists: Issues and Answers,* Pierian, 1982; (with Alley) *Keeping Track of What You Spend,* Oryx, 1982. Contributor of articles and reviews to library journals. Associate editor of *IULC Technical Services Newsletter,* 1977-81; co-editor of *Technicalities,* 1981—.

WORK IN PROGRESS: Directory of Biographical Sources, publication by Oryx expected in 1985.

SIDELIGHTS: Cargill told *CA:* "My writing reflects a businesslike and practical approach to my profession. I am interested in relating solutions to common problems or in discussing issues as they arise."

*   *   *

CARGOE, Richard
See PAYNE, (Pierre Stephen) Robert

*   *   *

CARLSON, Harry Gilbert 1930-

PERSONAL: Born September 27, 1930, in New York, N.Y.; married Carolyn L. Peterson (an architect), March 22, 1957. *Education:* Brooklyn College (now of the City University of New York), B.A., 1952; Ohio State University, M.A., 1955, Ph.D., 1958. *Office:* Department of Theatre-Drama, Graduate Center, Queens College of the City University of New York, Flushing, N.Y. 11367.

CAREER: Southwest Missouri State College, Springfield, assistant professor of drama, 1957-59; Valparaiso University, Valparaiso, Ind., assistant professor of drama, 1959-61; Northern Illinois University, DeKalb, assistant professor of drama and speech, 1961-64; University of Georgia, Athens, associate professor of theatre and drama, 1964-66; Queens College of the City University of New York, Flushing, N.Y., associate professor, 1967-72, professor of theatre and drama, 1972—. Member of board of trustees of American Scandinavian Foundation. Chairman of theatre arts screening committee of Committee for International Exchange of Persons, 1971-72.

MEMBER: American Theatre Association, Society for the Advancement of Scandinavian Studies, Strindberg Society. *Awards, honors:* Guggenheim fellowship, 1966-67; grant from Research Foundation of City University of New York, 1970-71; translation award from Artur Lundkvist Foundation, 1976; travel grant from Swedish Government, 1976.

WRITINGS: (Editor and translator) Martin Lamm, *August Strindberg,* Blom, 1971; (co-editor and contributor) *Handbook of Contemporary Drama,* Crowell, 1971; (co-editor and contributor) *Encyclopedia of World Drama,* McGraw, 1972; *Strindberg and the Poetry of Myth,* University of California Press, 1982; (translator) *Strindberg: Five Plays,* University of California Press, 1983.

Translator of "The Father" (two-act play by August Strindberg), first produced in New York, N.Y., at Circle in the Square, 1981. Contributor to drama and Scandinavian studies journals.

WORK IN PROGRESS: A book on Strindberg's history plays; translating two contemporary Swedish plays and a contemporary Swedish opera.

SIDELIGHTS: Carlson's *Strindberg and the Poetry of Myth* explores the similarities between the Swedish playwright's naturalist works and the dream plays of his later years. Carlson concentrates on Strindberg's use of myths in plays such as "Master Olaf" and "The Ghost Sonata" to reveal the wide range of materials that seem to have inspired the bleak and frequently eerie works. Peter Engel, reviewing Carlson's book for the *New York Times Book Review,* declared, "While mythological allusions of diverse origin underlie all of Strindberg's work, Mr. Carlson astutely discerns a general progression over time." Engel also noted that Carlson "convincingly demonstrates the importance of mythology—not only in the late dream plays, where the mythical allusions are overt, but in the earlier plays, where the use of mythology is masked by realist technique."

BIOGRAPHICAL/CRITICAL SOURCES: New York Times Book Review, February 20, 1983.

*   *   *

CARLSON, Raymond 1906-1983

OBITUARY NOTICE: Born in 1906; died in 1983 in Scottsdale, Ariz. Editor. Carlson edited *Arizona Highways,* a travel and tourism magazine, from 1938 to 1971. Obituaries and other sources: *Journal of the West,* spring, 1980; *Time,* February 28, 1983.

*   *   *

CAROE, Olaf Kirkpatrick 1892-1982

PERSONAL: Born November 15, 1892, in London, England; died November 23, 1981, in Sussex, England; son of William Douglas and Grace Desborough (Rendall) Caroe; married Frances Marion Rawstorne, 1920 (died, 1969); children: two sons. *Education:* Magdalen College, Oxford, B.A., M.A., 1919.

CAREER: Indian Civil Service, worked in Punjab, 1919-23, began as officer of political department in Northwest Frontier Province, 1923, served as deputy commissioner there until 1932, chief secretary to government, 1933-34, deputy secretary of India's Foreign and Political Department in Delhi, 1934-37, political resident in Persian Gulf, resident in Waziristan, and agent to the governor-general in Baluchistan, 1937-38, revenue and judicial commissioner in Baluchistan, 1938-39, secretary of Department of External Affairs in Delhi, 1939-45, governor of North West Frontier Province, 1946-47; writer, 1947-81. Deputy chairman of Conservative Commonwealth Council, 1966-69, vice-president, 1969. Member of Chichester Diocesan Pastoral Reform Committee. *Military service:* British Army, Territorial Forces, Queen's Regiment, 1914-19; became captain. *Awards, honors:* Companion of Order of the Indian Empire, 1932, Knight Commander, 1944; Companion of Star of India, 1941, Knight Commander, 1945; D.Litt. from Oxford University, 1962; Lawrence of Arabia Memorial Medal from Royal Central Asian Society, 1973.

WRITINGS: Wells of Power: The Oilfields of South-Western Asia; A Regional and Global Study, Macmillan, 1951, reprinted, Da Capo Press, 1976; *Soviet Empire: The Turks of Central Asia and Stalinism,* Macmillan, 1953, 2nd edition, 1967; *The Pathans, 550 B.C.-A.D. 1957,* St. Martin's, 1958; (with Patrick Reid and Thomas Rapp) *From Nile to Indus: Economics and Security in the Middle East,* Conservative Political Centre (London, England), 1960; (translator with Evelyn Howell) Khatak Khvush-Hal Khan, *The Poems of Khushhal Khan Khatak,* University of Peshawar, 1963. Contributor to scholarly journals and newspapers.

OBITUARIES: London Times, November 25, 1981.*

*   *   *

CARR, Michael Harold 1935-

PERSONAL: Born May 26, 1935, in Leeds, England; came to United States, 1956; naturalized U.S. citizen, 1965; son of Harry (a draftsman) and Monica Mary (Burn) Carr; married Rachel F. Harvey, April 14, 1961; children: Ian M. *Education:* University College, London, B.S., 1956; Yale University, M.S., 1957, Ph.D., 1960. *Home:* 1389 Canada Rd., Woodside, Calif. 94062. *Office:* U.S. Geological Survey, Menlo Park, Calif. 94025.

CAREER: University of Western Ontario, London, Ontario, research associate, 1960-62; U.S. Geological Survey, Menlo Park, Calif., 1962—, member of Mariner Mars imaging team, 1969-73, leader of Viking Mars Orbiter imaging team, 1969-80, chief of astrogeologic studies, 1973-79, member of Voyager and Galileo imaging teams, 1978—. Member of National Academy of Science Committee on Planetary Exploration, 1979-81. *Member:* Geological Society of America, American Association for the Advancement of Science, American Geophysical Union. *Awards, honors:* Meritorious Service Award from U.S. Department of the Interior, 1979, for contributions to astrogeology; medal for exceptional scientific achievement from National Aeronautics and Space Administration for work on Viking Mars project.

WRITINGS: The Surface of Mars, Yale University Press, 1981; *Geology of the Terrestrial Planets,* National Aeronautics and Space Administration, 1983.

SIDELIGHTS: In the course of his work with the U.S. Geological Survey, Carr served on the imaging teams of a series of Mariner and Viking spacecraft which photographed the planetary surface of Mars. Many of these photographs are reproduced in Carr's book *The Surface of Mars,* in which he traces the nature and history of the major planetary surface features, comparing their development with developments on the surfaces of Earth and Earth's moon.

"The authoritative nature of [*The Surface of Mars*] is beyond question," Bernard Lovell claimed in the *New York Review of*

Books. Lovell continued: "The splendidly reproduced photographs of the surface of Mars are the predominant interest. . . . Again and again as the pages turn the reader must surely gasp with astonishment at the extraordinary feat of American scientists and engineers in procuring this detailed evidence of a distant and inhospitable land. At the end one is left in astonishment at the special conditions that allowed life to develop on Earth and not on our neighboring planet."

Carr told *CA:* "I feel fortunate to have been so deeply involved in our exploration of the solar system during the last ten years. Exploration is a singular event; you can only do it once. Those of us who were there when the first close-up pictures were returned from Mercury, Mars, Jupiter, and Saturn experienced a unique sense of awe and wonder, and I will always feel a special bond with those whom I shared those feelings with. For me, Mars is especially exciting. It is a strange planet with huge volcanoes, vast canyons, and enormous dry river beds, all preserved in almost pristine condition. We have been able to reconstruct in broad outline how the planet evolved and why it differs so from the Earth, but many questions remain. Unfortunately, funding for the U.S. planetary program has been severely cut back, so these questions are not likely to be answered soon. I hope they will be answered in my lifetime."

BIOGRAPHICAL/CRITICAL SOURCES: New York Review of Books, June 10, 1982.

*   *   *

CARROLL, Archie B(enjamin III) 1943-

PERSONAL: Born February 4, 1943, in Jacksonville, Fla.; son of Archie Benjamin, Jr., and Margaret (Ives) Carroll; married Priscilla Gossett, June 9, 1968; children: Bradley. *Education:* Florida State University, B.S., 1965, M.B.A., 1966, D.B.A., 1972. *Office:* Department of Management, College of Business Administration, University of Georgia, Athens, Ga. 30602.

CAREER: Athens College, Athens, Ala., assistant professor of business, 1966-69; Florida State University, Tallahassee, instructor in management, 1971-72; University of Georgia, Athens, assistant professor, 1972-75, associate professor, 1975-79, professor of management, 1979—. Academic coordinator of Southeast Regional Credit Union School, 1976-79; charter member of Business and Society Initiative Council, Cambridge, Mass., 1977—; management development instructor at University of Notre Dame, 1975-77, 1982, University of Santa Clara, 1975-76, Mills College, 1976-77, University of Delaware, 1975-82, University of Colorado, 1981, and San Jose State University, 1981, for U.S. Chamber of Commerce. *Member:* Academy of Management (chairperson of Social Issues in Management Division, 1976-77), American Institute for Decision Sciences, Southeast American Institute for Decision Sciences, Southern Management Association, Beta Gamma Sigma (president, 1981-82), Sigma Iota Epsilon.

WRITINGS: (With Hugh J. Watson) *An Introduction to Computers for Management,* revised edition, College of Business Administration, University of Georgia, 1973; (editor with Ted F. Anthony, and contributor) *Contemporary Perspectives in the Decision Sciences,* Southeast American Institute for Decision Sciences, 1975; (editor) *Managing Corporate Social Responsibility,* Little, Brown, 1977; (editor with Richard C. Huseman, and contributor) *Readings in Organizational Behavior: Dimensions of Management Actions,* Allyn & Bacon, 1979; (contributor) Rogene A. Buchholz, editor, *Public Policy and the Business Firm: Proceedings of a Conference,* Center for the

Study of American Business, 1980; (editor with Watson, H. R. Smith, and Asterios G. Kefalas) *Readings in Management: Making Organizations Perform* (supplementary readings for following text), Macmillan, 1980; (with Watson, Smith, and Kefalas) *Management: Making Organizations Perform* (textbook), Macmillan, 1980; (editor with Watson, and contributor) *Computers for Business: A Book of Readings* (supplementary readings for following text), Business Publications (Dallas, Tex.), 1980, revised edition, in press; (with Watson) *Computers for Business: A Managerial Emphasis* (textbook), revised edition, Business Publications, 1980; *Business and Society: Managing Corporate Social Performance*, Little, Brown, 1981; *Social Responsibility of Management* (monograph), Science Research Associates, in press.

Contributor to *Encyclopedia of Professional Management*. Contributor of more than fifty articles to management and computer journals. Member of editorial review board of *Journal of Management*, 1975-79, *Academy of Management Review*, 1977-81, and "Collegiate Forum," in *Wall Street Journal*, 1978.

WORK IN PROGRESS: Numerous articles.

SIDELIGHTS: Carroll told *CA:* "My work is focused primarily on the relationship between business and society and the social impacts organizations create as they function. My principal interests are in corporate social policy, business ethics, and managing organizations in a dynamic environment. I am also interested in the social consequences and societal implications of technology—for example, computers."

* * *

CARY, William L(ucius) 1910-1983

OBITUARY NOTICE: Born November 27, 1910, in Columbus, Ohio; died of cancer, February 7, 1983, in New York, N.Y. Attorney, educator, and author. Cary graduated from the Yale Law School in 1934, received an M.B.A. from the Harvard Business School in 1938, and, following short stints with the Securities and Exchange Commission and the Justice Department, served as a major in the U.S. Marines during World War II. Cary taught at Northwestern University for eight years before joining the faculty of Columbia University, where he was a full professor from 1955 to 1964 and Dwight Professor of Law from 1964 until his retirement in 1979. An expert in corporate and tax law, Cary was appointed chairman of the Securities and Exchange Commission in 1961 by President John F. Kennedy and served in that capacity until 1964. During his tenure, the watchdog body reorganized the American Stock Exchange, strengthened its own enforcement powers, and called for the elimination of "fixed commissions" for securities brokers. Cary wrote several books, including *Cases and Materials on Corporations, Effects of Taxation on Corporate Mergers,* and *Politics and the Regulatory Agencies.* Obituaries and other sources: *Time,* February 10, 1961, February 21, 1983; *Current Biography,* Wilson, 1964, April, 1983; *Newsweek,* November 30, 1970, February 21, 1983; *Directory of American Scholars,* Volume IV: *Philosophy, Religion, and Law,* 8th edition, Bowker, 1982; *New York Times,* February 9, 1983; *Washington Post,* February 12, 1983.

* * *

CASADA, James A(llen) 1942-

PERSONAL: Born January 28, 1942, in Sylva, N.C.; son of

Commodore and Anna Lou Casada; married wife, Ann; children: Natasha. *Education;* King College, Bristol, Tenn., B.A., 1964; Virginia Polytechnic Institute and State University, M.A., 1968; Vanderbilt University, Ph.D., 1972. *Home:* 1250 Yorkdale Dr., Rock Hill, S.C. 29730. *Office:* Department of History, 205B Kinard, Winthrop College, Rock Hill, S.C. 29733.

CAREER: Hargrave Military Academy, Chatham, Va., teacher and soccer coach, 1964-67; Winthrop College, Rock Hill, S.C., assistant professor, 1971-75, associate professor, 1975-78, professor of history, 1978—, varsity soccer coach, 1975—. Fellow of Institute for Advanced Studies in the Humanities, University of Edinburgh, 1977; regional supervisor of South Carolina high school soccer officials, 1979—. Member of South Carolina Committee for the Humanities.

MEMBER: National Intercollegiate Soccer Officials of America, Intercollegiate Soccer Association of America (member of Southern Region Rating Board), African Studies Association, Hakluyt Society, Royal Geographical Society (fellow), African Studies Association (England), Southern Conference on British Studies (member of executive committee, 1980—), Carolinas Symposium on British Studies (member of executive committee, 1978-80), Dorset Record Society, Phi Alpha Theta, Phi Kappa Phi, Omicron Delta Kappa. *Awards, honors:* Grants from American Philosophical Society, 1973, 1977, 1983, National Geographic Society, 1976, and Southern Regional Education Board, 1981; excellence in teaching awards from Phi Kappa Phi, 1976, 1977; named district soccer coach of the year by National Association of Intercollegiate Athletics, 1979, 1982.

WRITINGS: Dr. David Livingstone and Sir Henry Morton Stanley: An Annotated Bibliography, Garland Publishing, 1977; *Sir Harry H. Johnston: A Bio-Bibliographical Study,* Basler Afrika Bibliographien, 1977; (contributor) Helen Delpar, editor, *The Discoverers: An Encyclopedia of Exploration,* McGraw, 1980.

Editor: *African and Afro-American History: A Review of Recent Trends,* Conch, 1978; Rouleyn Gordon-Cumming, *The Lion Hunter in Africa,* two volumes, Books of Zimbabwe, 1980; Frederick C. Selous, *A Hunter's Wanderings in Africa,* Books of Zimbabwe, 1981; Arthur H. Neumann, *Elephant Hunting in East Equatorial Africa,* Books of Zimbabwe, 1982; C. H. Stigand, *Hunting the Elephant in Africa,* Books of Zimbabwe, 1983; W. Cornwallis Harris, *Portraits of Game and Wild Animals of Southern Africa,* Books of Zimbabwe, 1983; (editor) *The Letterbooks of John Fitzjames,* Dorset Record Society, 1983; J. G. Millais, *A Breath From the Veldt,* Africana Book Society, 1983; *Cecil Rhodes: A Bio-Bibliographical Study,* American Bibliographical Center-Clio Press, in press; (editor) *The Travel Diaries and Papers of Frederick C. Selous,* Van Riebeeck Society, in press.

General editor of "Themes in European Expansion: Exploration, Colonization, and the Impact of Empire," a series, Garland Publishing. Contributor to geography, history, and African studies journals.

WORK IN PROGRESS: Zaire: A Bibliography, publication by American Bibliographical Center-Clio Press expected in 1985; *Rwanada: A Historical Dictionary,* publication by Scarecrow expected in 1986; *Sir Richard F. Burton: A Bio-Bibliographical Study,* publication by Mansell expected in 1986; *A Biography of Frederick C. Selous* for A. A. Balkema; *A Bibliography of Exploration in Africa From Earliest Times to the Present;* editing reprints of books by William C. Oswell, F. Vaughan Kirby, and James Sutherland, all for Books of Zimbabwe.

SIDELIGHTS: Casada told *CA:* "My writing is, in a sense, a scholar's duty, but it is also a source of distinct pleasure. I feel it strengthens my teaching, and of course one always hopes that others will profit from one's endeavors. For me, research is a great joy, writing is agony, but to have written brings considerable satisfaction. My greatest concern is to bridge the very real gap between stiff academic presentations and material which can be enjoyed by the general public."

* * *

CAST, David (Jesse Dale) 1942-

PERSONAL: Born January 8, 1942, in London, England; son of Jesse Dale (a painter) and Vedwina (George) Cast; married Jacqueline Falkenheim (a professor), July 30, 1981. *Education:* Wadham College, Oxford, B.A. (with honors), 1965; Columbia University, M.A., 1967, Ph.D., 1970. *Home:* 353 North Bowman Ave., Merion, Pa. 19066. *Office:* Bryn Mawr College, 244 Thomas, Bryn Mawr, Pa. 19010.

CAREER: Yale University, New Haven, Conn., assistant professor, 1970-76, associate professor of art history, 1976-80; Bryn Mawr College, Bryn Mawr, Pa., associate professor of art history, 1981—. *Member:* American College Art Association, Renaissance Society of America, Museum of Modern Art. *Awards, honors:* Penrose Grants from American Philosophical Society, 1970 and 1980; Ingram-Merril Foundation Grant, 1980.

WRITINGS: The Calumny of Apelles: A Study in the Humanist Tradition, Yale University Press, 1980. Also author of scripts for Yale/Video television series, "The Story of Italy." Contributor of articles to professional journals.

WORK IN PROGRESS: Vasari on Influence and Imitation, a study on the portrayal of the artists and the self in Giorgio Vasari, publication by Princeton University Press expected in 1984; *The Idea of Classicism,* a study on classicism in architecture, completion expected in 1984.

SIDELIGHTS: The Calumny of Apelles: A Study in the Humanist Tradition traces the development of calumny as a theme in European art from the second century A.D. until the nineteenth century. In the second century Lucian described an allegorical picture of calumny which he attributed to the Greek master Apelles. By the fifteenth century Lucian's essay was well known in Italy and had been translated from the original Greek into both Italian and Latin. Though art historians are now aware that Apelles could not have produced the painting that Lucian described, artists for centuries tried to reproduce the "Calumny" from Lucian's description. Cast examined several of the artists' interpretations in *The Calumny of Apelles,* including paintings by Nicolo dell'Abate and Fedrigo Zuccari.

Francis Haskell commented in the *Times Literary Supplement:* "Close examination of the surviving compositions brings to light curious and significant differences between Lucian's account of the picture and the way it was sometimes interpreted by Renaissance artists." Haskell also noted that Cast "gives us some useful insights into Renaissance attitudes to Envy, Calumny and other vices which aroused special concern, and he allows us to follow the development, spread and eventual decline of paintings devoted to such themes."

Cast told *CA:* "I have long been interested in the positive and negative aspects of tradition. This interest reinforced my move to this country from England. I am interested in art as a part of social class."

BIOGRAPHICAL/CRITICAL SOURCES: Times Literary Supplement, January 15, 1982.

* * *

CASTLEMAN, Harry 1953-

PERSONAL: Born April 4, 1953, in Salem, Mass.; son of Lloyd (a manufacturer) and Fay (Gilberg) Castleman. *Education:* Northwestern University, B.A., 1974; Boston University, J.D. (cum laude), 1982. *Home:* 2125 River Blvd., Jacksonville, Fla. 32204. *Agent:* Richard Curtis Associates, Inc., 340 East 66th St., New York, N.Y. 10021. *Office:* Smith & Hulsey, 500 Barnett Bank Building, Jacksonville, Fla. 32202.

CAREER: Democratic National Committee, Washington, D.C., reporter and program producer in radio-television department, 1974-75; Sunshine Amendment/No Casinos, Inc., Tallahassee, Fla., media specialist, 1975-76; Democratic National Committee, regional media director in radio-television department, 1976-77; Sunshine Amendment/No Casinos, Inc., media specialist, 1978; Democratic Party of Florida, Tallahassee, press secretary, 1978-79; Smith & Hulsey (law firm), Tallahassee, attorney, 1982—. *Member:* American Bar Association, Florida Bar Association, Jacksonville Bar Association.

WRITINGS: (With Walter J. Podrazik) *All Together Now: The First Complete Beatles Discography,* Pierian, 1976; *The Beatles Again,* Pierian, 1977; (with Podrazik) *Watching TV: Four Decades of American Television,* McGraw, 1981; *Five Hundred Five TV/Radio Questions Your Friends Can't Answer,* Walker & Co., 1983; *Watching TV Schedule Book,* McGraw, 1983; *The End of the Beatles?,* Pierian, in press.

SIDELIGHTS: Castleman told *CA:* "I met Walter Podrazik at our college radio station, where we both worked, when I did a weekly Beatles hour in 1971. We exchanged Beatles information and built that up over the years. Thanks to some Northwestern University Democratic National Committee (DNC) connections, both Wally and I wound up at the DNC after graduation, doing (what else?) radio work. Just before graduation we had done an eighteen-hour Beatles documentary which was well received. People said our information might make a good book, so while in Washington, D.C., we worked for the DNC by day and wrote our first book by night.

"By the time President Carter was inaugurated and our jobs at the DNC ended, it was time for another book, and TV seemed a good choice. The Beatles books and the TV books are all consumer oriented. That is, they are written from the vantage point of a knowledgeable outsider, conveying information to others. Our books have few 'Inside Revelations.' Rather, they try to put interesting and perishable information together in one place, to be enjoyed and recalled."

* * *

CATLEDGE, Turner 1901-1983

OBITUARY NOTICE—See index for *CA* sketch: Born March 17, 1901, in Ackerman, Miss.; died after suffering a stroke, April 27, 1983, in New Orleans, La. Journalist and author. After working for a variety of daily newspapers, Catledge joined the *New York Times* as a reporter in 1929. He remained with the *Times* until 1970, except for a brief period in the early 1940's when he served as chief correspondent and editor of the *Chicago Sun.* In 1951 Catledge became managing editor of the *New York Times.* He went on to serve as that paper's executive editor, vice-president, and director. He was co-author of *The 168 Days,* a best-selling book about President Franklin D. Roosevelt's attempt to pack the Supreme Court. Catledge's autobiography, *My Life and the Times,* was published in 1971. Obituaries and other sources: *New York Times,* April 28, 1983; *Los Angeles Times,* April 28, 1983; *Washington Post,* April 28, 1983; *Chicago Tribune,* April 29, 1983; *London Times,* May 4, 1983; *Time,* May 9, 1983; *Newsweek,* May 9, 1983.

* * *

CATTON, William R(obert), Jr. 1926-

PERSONAL: Born January 15, 1926, in Minneapolis, Minn.; son of William Robert (a minister) and Helen (Willard) Catton; married Nancy Lewis, September 3, 1949; children: Stephen Lewis, Philip Ellery, Theodore Randolph, Jonathan Muir. *Education:* Attended Millikin University, 1946-47; Oberlin College, A.B., 1950; University of Washington, Seattle, M.A., 1952, Ph.D., 1954. *Home:* Southeast 500 Crestview, Pullman, Wash. 99163. *Office:* Department of Sociology, Washington State University, Pullman, Wash. 99164.

CAREER: RAND Corp., Santa Monica, Calif., system training specialist, 1955-56; University of North Carolina, Chapel Hill, assistant professor of sociology, 1956-57; University of Washington, Seattle, assistant professor, 1957-62, associate professor, 1962-66, professor of sociology, 1966-70; University of Canterbury, Christchurch, New Zealand, professor of sociology, 1970-72; Washington State University, Pullman, professor of sociology, 1973—. *Military service:* U.S. Naval Reserve, active duty, 1943-46; received Purple Heart. *Member:* American Association for the Advancement of Science, American Sociological Association, Sociological Association of Australia and New Zealand, Pacific Sociological Association.

WRITINGS: From Animistic to Naturalistic Sociology, McGraw, 1966; (with O. N. Larsen) *Conceptual Sociology,* Harper, 1966, 2nd edition, 1971; (with John C. Hendee, Larry D. Marlow, and C. Frank Brockman) *Wilderness Users in the Pacific Northwest: Their Characteristics, Values and Management Preferences,* Pacific Northwest Forest and Range Experiment Station, U.S. Department of Agriculture, 1968; (with Larsen, G. A. Lundberg, and C. C. Schrag) *Sociology,* 4th edition (Catton was not associated with earlier editions), Harper, 1968; *Overshoot: The Ecological Basis of Revolutionary Change,* University of Illinois Press, 1982.

Contributor: R.E.L. Faris, editor, *Handbook of Modern Sociology,* Rand McNally, 1964; Fred Massarik and Philburn Ratoosh, editors, *Mathematical Explorations in Behavioral Science,* Irwin, 1965; Alfred deGrazia, Rollo Handy, and others, editors, *The Behavioral Sciences: Essays in Honor of George A. Lundberg,* Behavioral Research Council, 1968; R. K. Baker and S. J. Ball, editors, *Mass Media and Violence: A Report to the National Commission on the Causes and Prevention of Violence,* U.S. Government Printing Office, 1969.

John Michael Barrington, editor, *Violence,* Department of Justice (Wellington, New Zealand), 1971; Gerald Thielbar and Saul Feldman, editors, *Issues in Social Inequality,* Little, Brown, 1972; C. F. Brockman and Lawrence C. Merriam, Jr., editors, *Recreational Use of Wild Lands,* 2nd edition, McGraw, 1973, 3rd edition, 1979; H.C.D. Somerset, editor, *Littledene: Patterns of Change,* New Zealand Council for Educational Research, 1974; C. P. Wolf, editor, *Social Impact Assessment: Test Edition,* American Association for the Advancement of Science, 1975; David C. Thorns, editor, *New Directions in*

Sociology, David & Charles, 1976; J. Milton Yinger and Stephen J. Cutler, editors, *Major Social Issues: A Multidisciplinary View,* Free Press, 1978; Timothy O'Riordan and Ralph C. D'Arge, editors, *Progress in Resource Management and Environmental Planning,* Volume I, Wiley, 1979.

Marvin E. Olsen and Michael Micklin, editors, *Handbook of Applied Sociology: Frontiers of Contemporary Research,* Praeger, 1981; Irwin Altman and Joachim F. Wohlwill, editors, *Behavior and the Natural Environment,* Plenum, 1983; Michael Tobias, editor, *Deep Ecology,* Avant Books, 1983. Contributor to *International Encyclopedia of the Social Sciences.* Contributor of about eighty articles to scholarly journals.

WORK IN PROGRESS: Contributing to *Sociological Human Ecology: Contemporary Issues and Applications,* edited by Michael Micklin and Harvey M. Choldin; research on the impacts of carrying capacity deficit on social and cultural phenomena, ranging from religion to social stratification, war, and violence.

SIDELIGHTS: Catton wrote: "Research in the 1960's on wild land recreation, which resulted in numerous published articles, aroused my interest in ecological processes. Three years residence in New Zealand broadened my perspective on world events and international relations. I became convinced that the industrial era in human history was less a culmination of perpetual technological progress than a reversion to dependence on fortuitously available natural resources (on a vaster scale, but in principle similar to the situation of prehistoric hunters and gatherers). My chief concerns now are societal adaptations to scarcity."

* * *

CHAMBERLAIN, Betty 1908-1983

OBITUARY NOTICE—See index for *CA* sketch: Born February 10, 1908, in East Orange, N.J.; died of a stroke, May 14, 1983, in Brattleboro, Vt. Founder and director of Art Information Center, editor, columnist, and author. In 1959 Chamberlain founded the Art Information Center in New York City. "I am a catalyst," she was quoted as saying in the *New York Times.* "I bring together artists and people who might be interested in their work, and then let the chips fall where they may." Prior to founding the art center, Chamberlain worked in various capacities for a number of libraries and art museums. From 1954 to 1956 she was managing editor of *Art News.* The most recent revision of her book *The Artist's Guide to the Art Market* appeared in 1983. Obituaries and other sources: *New York Times,* May 18, 1983.

* * *

CHAMBERS, Jane 1937-1983

OBITUARY NOTICE—See index for *CA* sketch: Born March 27, 1937, in Columbia, S.C.; died of a brain tumor, February 15, 1983, in Greenport, New York. Playwright and novelist. In addition to a novel entitled *Burning,* Chambers wrote several plays, including "Last Summer at Bluefish Cove," for which she won a DramaLogue Critics Circle Award. Among her other plays are "My Blue Heaven," "Kudzu," and "The Quintessential Image." In 1982 she received the annual award of the Fund for Human Dignity. Obituaries and other sources: *New York Times,* February 17, 1983; *AB Bookman's Weekly,* March 7, 1983.

CHANCELLOR, John (William) 1927-

PERSONAL: Born July 14, 1927, in Chicago, Ill.; son of Estil M. (in real estate and hotels) and Mollie (Barrett) Chancellor; married Constance Herbert in 1950 (divorced, 1956); married Barbara Upshaw (a graphic designer) in 1958; children: (first marriage) Mary; (second marriage) Laura Campbell, Barnaby John. *Education:* Attended University of Illinois at Navy Pier, Chicago, 1947-48. *Residence:* New York, N.Y. *Agent:* Esther Newberg, International Creative Management, 40 West 57th St., New York, N.Y. 10019. *Office:* NBC News, 30 Rockefeller Plaza, New York, N.Y. 10020.

CAREER: Chicago Times (now *Chicago Sun-Times*), Chicago, Ill., copyboy, reporter, feature writer, 1947-50; National Broadcasting Co. (NBC-TV), Midwest correspondent based in Chicago, 1950-58, correspondent in Vienna, London, Moscow, 1958-61, host of "Today" show, New York City, 1961-62, correspondent in Brussels, 1963-64, correspondent in Washington, D.C., 1964-65; Voice of America, Washington, D.C., director, 1965-67; NBC-TV, Washington, D.C., national affairs correspondent, 1967-70, anchor of "NBC Nightly News," New York City, 1970-82, commentator, 1982—. Writer and broadcaster for NBC-Radio's "The Chancellor Report," 1970-82. *Military service:* U.S. Army, 1945-47; served as a public relations specialist. *Member:* Council on Foreign Relations, Century Association, Federal City Club (Washington, D.C.). *Awards, honors:* Named broadcaster of the year by International Radio and Television Society, 1982.

WRITINGS: (Contributor) *Memo to JFK From NBC News,* Putnam, 1961; (with Walter R. Mears) *The News Business,* Harper, 1983.

SIDELIGHTS: In his lengthy career with the National Broadcasting Co. (NBC-TV), John Chancellor has served variously as foreign correspondent, host of the network's "Today" program, White House correspondent, and, from 1970 to 1982, anchor of "NBC Nightly News." In April of 1982 he stepped down from the anchor post to become a commentator. "I had money and I had fame," he explained to *Newsweek,* "but the last thing I wanted was to be a 65-year-old anchor man. So I decided it was time to take control of my life."

Chancellor "seems happier as a commentator than as a news reader," observed Thomas Griffith in *Time.* "Temperamentally, he has always been an explainer." As commentator, Chancellor strives to "open up the not-fully-made-up mind." "Commentary is different from opinion," he told Leslie Bennetts of the *Philadelphia Bulletin.* "You give the thought process you went through, rather than the conclusion, and let people draw their own judgment."

CA INTERVIEW

CA interviewed John Chancellor by phone on September 29, 1982, at his office in New York City.

CA: You went to NBC by way of the Chicago Times *[later merged with the* Chicago Sun-Times*], where you started as a copyboy and worked up to reporter and feature writer. Was it an early ambition of yours to become a newsman, or did it just happen?*

CHANCELLOR: My first job on a newspaper was when I was fourteen years old, running advertising copy for the *Chicago Daily News* for a couple of hours in the afternoons after school, and I was dazzled by it at that early age. Then when I was in the army, toward the end of World War II, I worked on the post newspaper and in public relations. When I came out and went back to school, I knew what I wanted to do and I tailored my education to it. (The only interruption was that I took about six months off and tried to write a novel. It was *terrible*.) I was a history major and a philosophy minor at the University of Illinois, with the clear idea that literature would probably not be my metier, but that journalism would. I took all the history courses that I could get, then left school without a degree and went to work for the *Chicago Times.* So the ambition was there from the beginning.

CA: What you seem to love above all is reporting the latest news from wherever it's being made—being on the spot. Did you feel confined during your years as anchorman for the "NBC Nightly News," even though you managed to get around more than many anchorpeople?

CHANCELLOR: I did feel confined. I anchored the "Nightly News" for twelve years. It is one of the few occupations in the United States in which your day is timed to the second. You have rigid scheduling obligations, the biggest one being that you must be in the studio when the program begins. I found that confining after a while. The other thing about being an anchorperson, although it's a good job and everybody wants to get it, is that it demands a very specialized kind of writing, and not everybody does it well. It is not what I would call truly creative writing. I tried to do all my own writing, though we had a writer in case I got behind or news broke late. What you have to do in that kind of job is make sense of the material you're introducing. That means either finding things the correspondent didn't put in the story that you think are relevant or important, or trying to set it up to give the audience a kind of perspective on what they're about to learn. It's complicated because it has to come out in fairly short bursts. I suppose I could win every contest in the world for saying something in twenty-five words or less. You don't get bored doing that kind of writing—it's demanding intellectually—but after twelve years I had a hunger to use language in a different way, which I'm now able to do on "Commentary."

CA: In that spot you also get to state your opinion on current issues regularly and forcefully. Are you getting a lot of mail in response?

CHANCELLOR: I did one "Commentary" piece out of Beirut on the Israeli bombing that produced more than a thousand letters for me alone. NBC got about six hundred. I think that was the most response they've ever had to a "Commentary" piece. The interesting breakdown was that the letters addressed to me personally were sixty-five percent in my favor, and the letters addressed to NBC were sixty-five percent against me. People write to networks to complain, generally, but they also generally write letters to commentators to complain, so I was stunned when I realized that I was winning the election by what Lyndon Johnson would have called a landslide.

CA: Do you respond to the mail?

CHANCELLOR: Sure. You have to. When you get a thousand letters, though, you rely on NBC and you send everybody a little card. We sifted through that particular mail trying to find letters from friends and found that there were a lot of people I knew who wrote, so I was quite busy answering my mail.

CA: Do you think anchorpeople have a better public image now than they did ten years or so ago?

CHANCELLOR: In 1972, we were heading into Watergate and we still had Vietnam. We had Huntley and Brinkley and Cronkite, and I think they were terribly respected people. The bad period for people in my business was a short bad period, between 1969 and 1971. Spiro Agnew made his attack on the newspeople in the fall of 1969. The Vietnam War was beginning to have its abrasive effect in this country. I became an anchorman in 1970, so I came in at a time when there was a certain amount of criticism. Then along about 1971 it started to go away. I never have found much hostility personally. The American people tend to be very, very courteous, even when they disagree with things you've said—at least they're courteous in person; sometimes the letters burn your fingers. I've always believed that if you have one of these jobs, if you're a broadcast journalist especially, you ought to be accountable to people. They ought to be able to come up and argue with you. There shouldn't be any kind of shield around you. I think most of us believe that. Still to this day people stop me on the street and want to talk about the news, and I think you have to give them a minute or so. That's part of the job.

There's no way I can judge what will happen in the future, but in the years that I've been associated with the ''Nightly News,'' and before that with ''The Huntley-Brinkley Report'' as a contributing editor, I've seen the program improve and the attitude of the public toward the program grow more positive almost every year, except for that little kick when Agnew tried to mobilize people against us, and there are a lot of interesting analyses of that. Even immediately after Agnew's attack, the response, in terms of mail, telegrams, and telephone calls to NBC, was 50 percent in favor of the networks and 50 percent against. All of us here felt that was pretty heartening, given the fact that the vice-president had said in a very carefully crafted speech that we were a lot of bums.

CA: Several years ago you said you opposed extending the nightly news coverage to an hour. You felt that television should give the news concisely and viewers should then turn to newspapers and magazines for more background. Most viewers don't seem to do that, unfortunately. Has your opinion changed?

CHANCELLOR: I've now come around. I think an hour *would* be very useful, partially for the reason you give; more and more people are becoming dependent on television as a primary source of information about their society and the world. This is very troubling to me, because even if we had a three-hour program I don't think we could give it all. No individual medium of information or news can do the whole job. That can only come out of a mix. You can't get all the news by reading the *New York Times* only, though there's no question they do a wonderful job. The Associated Press on its high-speed wire moves about four-hundred thousand words a day, which is about a thousand stories every twenty-four hours. Yet you can't get the whole picture by reading only the AP. I've always argued that Americans ought to share out their time and read magazines and books and newspapers, listen to the radio a little bit, and watch the television. That's what I do, and all the professionals I know do, people whose income depends on having some knowledge of current affairs.

CA: What newspapers and magazines do you rely on besides the New York Times?

CHANCELLOR: Here in the office it's a little more complicated because I have associates who clip things for me as well, so I could give you a very long list. But the basic newspapers are

the *New York Times*, the *Washington Post*, the *Wall Street Journal*, the *Christian Science Monitor*, and various others like the *Financial Times*. Of the magazines, I read *Time*, *Newsweek*, the *Economist*, *U.S. News & World Report*, *Congressional Quarterly;* and then magazines that represent points of view, like *Public Interest*, *National Review*, *New Republic*, and the *Nation*. We try to spread it out so that we get different attitudes. That's why the magazines are both interesting and valuable. The smaller they are, very often the more interesting they are.

CA: What criticism would you make of television news coverage?

CHANCELLOR: We first ought to make the distinction that I'm only commenting on network television. I don't watch a lot of local television, and much of the local television I watch I don't happen to care for. In terms of network television, I think one of the things it lacks is a more active memory; it forgets things. It has a tendency to focus on the news of the day without checking, say, what politicians are saying against what they said before. This may be getting a little better now, as it's getting better on the wire services because they're using computers as memories. But I think there's a kind of willingness to accept simply the news of that particular day without enough context in the presentation.

I don't think I want to criticize the fact that when there's a spectacular fire or something like that, television puts it on. We need to remember that television is a visual medium, and those stories never take very long. One problem with local television that I'm afraid may become a problem with network television is the idea that simply by putting a camera at the scene of a plane crash, for example, and turning it on and feeding the picture back in and out to the audience, you're engaged in journalism. That isn't journalism, it's electronics. Journalism is editing and sifting facts, using the journalist's professional skills in such a way as to make the news meaningful to the reader or the viewer. I worry a little bit about electronics overcoming us in that sense, because it's so beguiling. It's so nice to press a button and get a picture.

CA: Many people would go a step further with your point about television's showing the spectacular fire. The charge is often leveled that television actually makes *news by focusing on issues with the most visual impact and neglecting other issues. Do you think there's any justification for this criticism?*

CHANCELLOR: Again, I think you have to ask yourself about the capacity of the different media to accomplish certain tasks. For example, there's no way that the regular television newscasts could have carried the Pentagon Papers. These were documents. You needed the newspapers to carry them. You needed to spread them out, look at them, photostat them, read them three times. On the other hand, there was no way the *New York Times* or *Time* magazine could have shown the face of Richard Nixon as he approached resignation, and the body language he used. There's no way a print operation could have shown as fully as television what happened in the Palestinian camps in Beirut, or the bombing of Beirut, or the Tet offensive in Vietnam, or the look of the Falkland Islands. I'm not trying to duck the question, but I don't mind when television utilizes fully its visual capacity.

As to the criticism that our definition of news tends to be biased toward visual news, I think probably there's some truth to that, and again I go back to saying that no single medium can do the whole job. We are dealing in pictures, and we're dealing competitively in pictures, in images. The great change that's come over network television in the last fifteen or twenty years is the increased willingness on the part of the nightly news programs to handle such things as economic news. We bend over backward to show the unemployment situation by getting pictures of people standing in line to collect unemployment compensation. We develop graphics and charts which flow across the screen to give viewers all kinds of different economic information. I think there's been an enormous increase in the understanding of economic issues since 1973, when OPEC raised the price of oil. Think of the work of somebody like Irving R. Levine; he is dealing with information that nine years ago was arcane. We *are* willing to do news that you might call nonvisual news. Certainly economics, the dismal science, does not lend itself to visualization, but because we're trying to respond to the economic disasters of recent years, we have found ways to show it. I'm not without hope that television will continue in this direction and continue to expand. At the same time, I think there are things it does extremely well, and they are visual.

I don't know who decides what's news. In journalism, nobody has ever really agreed on what news *is* in the first place. So when people call us gatekeepers and agendamakers, as some of the scholars do, yes, I think that's probably true. For a particular audience on nightly news, we use the resources at hand to give a news report. And to some degree that does in fact set the agenda. But aside from having a ministry of information that gives an outline of the news each day for all the media to follow, I can't think of a way to organize news presentation for all the media.

CA: Some years ago you expressed an interest in teaching. Have you had an opportunity to do any teaching?

CHANCELLOR: No, but I've just finished a book called *The News Business* with Walter Mears, of the Associated Press. Roughly speaking, it's a writing guide for young journalists. It's not a grammar or an English text, but it talks about sourcing, the analysis of color, how to write leads. It even has a chapter on how to get jobs. We also use the device of telling how we handled certain specific stories that people will remember. Our target audience is young people who are in journalism or thinking of going into journalism.

Mears, who won a Pulitzer for national reporting, is an old friend of mine. We found that we wrote pretty much alike. A lot of the techniques we use are similar, such as reading the lead aloud. So we collaborated on this, and we hope it will be of some use. There wasn't such a book. That's the closest I've come to teaching per se, and I find that the job as a commentator here at NBC is as time consuming as the anchor job was, believe it or not, so I don't have any immediate plans for teaching. But down the line—probably.

CA: What about a memoir? Is that in the future?

CHANCELLOR: Sort of. But the one book I don't want to write is a book that says, here's the famous anchorman and how he got to be an anchorman. It has to be a little better than that. I could write that in one chapter, and I don't know how interesting it would be. I'm fiddling around with something about the changes I've seen in my professional life—when I started there was *no* television—and the places I've been. Yes, there are vague ideas in my head. I don't have a written outline, but I think such a book is down the line.

CA: What hobbies or pastimes do you enjoy away from work? Music must be one, since you've expressed a love for Mozart.

CHANCELLOR: Yes, and I enjoy Handel now, and Purcell. I am a Mozart freak. I suppose I have the normal range of hobbies. I play tennis and I take a lot of pictures. I use a bicycle for exercise, but one of my hobbies is walking. I did a Cotswold trip last year with a backpack. I like to be outdoors as much as I can. But I suppose I'd have to say now that writing is taking up a larger percentage of my non-NBC time than anything else. The work we did on this book was very rewarding for me. I got the rhythm started, and I think I'm probably going to continue writing.

BIOGRAPHICAL/CRITICAL SOURCES: Milwaukee Journal, April 28, 1974; *Denver Post,* April 27, 1975; *Philadelphia Bulletin,* May 11, 1975; *Authors in the News,* Volume 1, Gale, 1976; *Newsweek,* December 12, 1977; *Time,* July 13, 1981, May 24, 1982.

—*Interview by Jean W. Ross*

* * *

CHAPIN, Victor 1919(?)-1983

OBITUARY NOTICE: Born c. 1919; died of a heart attack, March 4 (some sources say March 6), 1983, in New York, N.Y. Actor, literary agent, and author. A former actor with a traveling repertory company, Chapin also appeared in Broadway productions of "The Hasty Heart" and "Ah, Wilderness!." He wrote three books, including the novel *The Company of Players* and a nonfiction account of his experiences as an attendant in a mental hospital, *The Hill.* He joined John Schaffner Associates literary agency in 1973, becoming a vice-president and partner in the firm in 1979. Obituaries and other sources: *New York Times,* March 12, 1983; *Publishers Weekly,* April 8, 1983.

* * *

CHAPMAN, (William) Donald 1923-

PERSONAL: Born November 25, 1923; son of William H. and Norah F.E. Chapman. *Education:* Received M.A. (first class honors) and degree in agriculture from Emmanuel College, Cambridge. *Home:* 60 Courtenay St., London S.E.11, England. *Office:* Priorslee Hall, Telford, Shropshire, England; and House of Lords, London S.W.1, England.

CAREER: Cambridge University, Cambridge, England, senior scholar at Emmanuel College, in agricultural economics research, 1943-46; secretary of British Labour Party, 1945-57; Parliament, London, England, Labour member of House of Commons for Birmingham (Northfield), 1951-70, chairman of select committee on procedure, 1966-70; Oxford University, Oxford, England, Gwilym Gibbon fellow at Nuffield College, 1971-73; became Lord Northfield, 1975; Parliament, member of House of Lords, 1975—. Visiting fellow at Centre for Contemporary European Studies, University of Sussex, 1973—. Member of Cambridge City Council, 1945-47; secretary of Trades Council, 1945-57; chairman of Her Majesty's Development Commission, 1974-86, and Telford Development Corp., 1975—; chairman of Inquiry Into Recent Trends in Acquisition and Occupancy of Agricultural Land, 1977-79; special adviser to European Economic Community Commission, 1978—. *Member:* Fabian Society (general secretary, 1948-53). *Awards, honors:* Created baron and life peer, 1975.

WRITINGS: *The Road to European Union: Proposals to the EEC Institutions and Governments,* Centre for Contemporary European Studies, University of Sussex, 1975. Also author of *The European Parliament: The Years Ahead,* 1973. Contributor to magazines.

* * *

CHARLOTTE, Susan 1954-

PERSONAL: Born July 21, 1954, in Brooklyn, N.Y.; daughter of Leo Wiener (a writer) and Lily (a secretary; maiden name, Greenblatt) Weiner. *Education:* State University of New York at Purchase, B.A., 1978; Columbia University, M.F.A., 1982. *Religion:* Jewish. *Home:* 160 West End Ave., Apt. 17G, New York, N.Y. 10024. *Agent:* Helen Harvey, 410 West 24th St., New York, N.Y. 10011. *Office:* The Writers Community, 120 East 89th St., New York, N.Y. 10023.

CAREER: Theatre for the Forgotten, Long Island, N.Y., program coordinator, 1977-78; Spofford Juvenile Center, The Bronx, N.Y., and Riker's Island Penitentiary, Riker's Island, N.Y., instructor of drama and poetry, 1977-78; Pratt Institute, Brooklyn, N.Y., job developer, 1978-79; free-lance writer for *Shop* magazine and other periodicals, 1981; Barbara Zimmerman Rights and Permissions, New York City, permission obtainer to reprint authors' works in anthologies, 1980-82; Network for Learning, New York City, instructor in playwriting, 1981; New York University, New York City, instructor in playwriting, 1982; Circle Repertory Company, New York City, literary assistant to B. Rodney Marriott, 1982; researcher, reader, and organizer of materials for a new play by writer Peter Stone, 1982—; conductor of advanced playwriting workshop, 1983—. Writers Community, New York City, executive director, 1983—. Arranger of a one-woman cabaret show featuring Ellen Gould. *Member:* Dramatists Guild, Editorial Freelancers Association. *Awards, honors:* Finalist in the Creative Artists Public Service Program awards for playwriting, and Joseph Kesselring award in playwriting from National Arts Club, both 1980, both for "Prism Blues."

WRITINGS—Plays: "Mythical Merry-Go-Round" (two-act), first produced in New York City at Theatre for the Forgotten, July, 1977; "Is It Raining or Just My Desire?" (two-act), first performed in reading in New York City at Gene Frankel Theatre, May, 1980; *Prism Blues* (two-act; first produced in New York City at Horace Mann Theatre, February 14, 1980), Proscenium Press, 1982; "Delicate Choices" (two-act), first produced in New York City at New York Theatre Ensemble, October 7, 1982; "Mothers and Daughters," first performed in reading in New York at Playwright's Forum, March, 1983.

Other: (With Robert McBride) "Loving" (teleplay), Earthrise and Warner Communications, 1982; (with George Butler, Charles Gaines, Brooke Hayward, and Richard Wesley) "Detroit City" (screenplay), King-Hitzig Productions and White Mountain Films, 1982.

SIDELIGHTS: Charlotte told CA: "'Mothers and Daughters,' a musical, consists of a series of vignettes revolving around the relationships between mothers and daughters. Each vignette focuses on a specific issue; in one, for example, a young black inmate asks her mother for bail, and in another, a writer in her early thirties is pregnant and conflicted about having the baby. Several of the vignettes revolve around white characters; several around black characters, and one or two are an integration of both black and white characters.

"I have spent many years teaching theatre in a variety of places ranging from universities to prisons. Though all of my classes have been challenging, perhaps the most growthful experience has been my work in prisons. I have taught young people, ages ten through fourteen at Spofford Juvenile Center, people in their late teens at Riker's Island, and adults at various other prisons. I have used theatre as a means of therapy and communication with people in prisons. I strongly believe in the craft of playwriting, but also feel that writing and other aspects of theatre can provide a catharsis of sorts for both the writer and the audience. I have thus encouraged the prisoners I've worked with to use the material of their lives to create plays. Most of my own plays are based strongly on my life, and have helped me to confront areas that I might not otherwise have been able to come to terms with.

"I'd like to say that whatever area a writer chooses to participate in, he/she should bring a certain integrity to that particular media. That is to say, one should not be limited by any form of writing, whether it is television, screenwriting or playwriting, but rather explore that form to the utmost point, in order to present a theme in a deeply compelling way. Though my own background is in theatre, I have recently expanded into other areas, such as film and television. I was reluctant at first to work outside of theatre. But I have found that each area of writing has helped me to grow in different ways. And that the most important thing that a writer can do is simple: Just keep writing and write with courage!"

* * *

CHARLTON, Jack
See CHARLTON, John

* * *

CHARLTON, John 1935-
(Jack Charlton)

PERSONAL: Born in 1935; married Patricia Kemp; children: John, Deborah, Peter.

CAREER: Leeds United Football Club, Leeds, England, football player, 1953-73; Middlesbrough Football Club, Middlesbrough, England, manager, 1973-77; manager of Sheffield Wednesday (football club), beginning 1977. Television football commentator; appeared in documentary television films on fishing. *Awards, honors:* Officer of Order of the British Empire; named manager of the year, 1974.

WRITINGS: (Under name Jack Charlton) *Jack Charlton's Coaching for Junior Players,* Hutchinson, 1978. Contributor to newspapers.

AVOCATIONAL INTERESTS: Shooting, fishing.

BIOGRAPHICAL/CRITICAL SOURCES: Norman Harris, *Charlton Brothers,* Stanley Paul, 1971.

* * *

CHATTERJE, Sarat Chandra 1876-1936(?)
(Saratchandra Chatterji)

BRIEF ENTRY: Born in 1876; died in 1936 (some sources say 1938). Bengali novelist known for his advocacy of minorities' rights in works such as his four-volume *Shrinkanta* (1917-33; translation of Volume I published as *Srikanta,* 1922) and *Grihadaha* (1920; translation published as *The Fire,* 1964). *Bio-*

graphical/critical sources: Humayun Kabir, editor, *Green and Gold: Stories and Poems From Bengal,* Asia Publishing House, 1957; *Cassell's Encyclopaedia of World Literature,* revised edition, Morrow, 1973; *Twentieth-Century Literary Criticism,* Volume 11, Gale, 1983.

*   *   *

CHATTERJI, Saratchandra
See CHATTERJE, Sarat Chandra

*   *   *

CHEETHAM, Erika 1939-

PERSONAL: Born July 7, 1939, in London, England; daughter of Eric Arthur (under secretary to the Admiralty and a company director) and Helen Lilian McMahon (Calan) Turner; married James Nicholas Milne Cheetham (a money broker), August 4, 1961 (divorced, 1981); children: Alexander Nicholas Milne. *Education:* St. Anne's College, Oxford, M.A. (with first class honors), 1961, Ph.D., 1962. *Politics:* "Humanist." *Residence:* Louveciennes, France. *Agent:* Phyllis Westberg, Harold Ober Associates, Inc., 40 East 49th St., New York, N.Y. 10017; Brian Stone, Hughes Massle Ltd., 31 Southampton Row, London WC1 SW3, England.

CAREER: Harcourt Tutors, London, England, owner, 1962-68; writer, 1968—. Past member of editorial staff of London's Daily Mail Newspaper Group. Member of British Museum, Warburg Institute, and London Library. *Member:* Guards and Cavalry Club, Liberal Club, Les Ambassadeurs, Press Club.

WRITINGS: (Editor, translator, and author of introduction), Michel de Notredame, *The Prophesies of Nostradamus,* Putnam, 1971, Neville Spearman, 1973, Transworld, 1974, revised edition, 1980; *The Man Who Saw Tomorrow,* Putnam, 1982; *Nostradamus, 1984 and Beyond,* Putnam, 1983.

Films: Two made-for-television films on Nostradamus, and an as yet-unproduced full-length black comedy for women, tentatively titled "Cheque Mate."

Contributor to periodicals, including *Vogue, Cosmopolitan, Nova, Reader's Digest,* and *Over 21.* Contributor to encyclopedias.

SIDELIGHTS: Cheetham told *CA:* "I was prompted to write a definitive book on Nostradamus because he wrote mainly in Ancien Provencal (he lived there). Ancien Provencal was the subject of my M.A. at Oxford. I came across Nostradamus's work by accident when researching another book in the Taylorian Library at Oxford. Two or three years after the birth of my son I decided to go back and research Nostradamus further.

"I am basically lazy, always meeting deadlines, however long, by hours, if not minutes, and my main source of relaxation is good detective fiction. I also collect boxes—mainly eighteenth-century porcelain boxes—and sixteenth-century books, particularly those relating to Nostradamus and Catherine de Medici. When you can get me out-of-doors, I love gardening. My great fault is that I find organizing easy, but I prefer someone else do the donkey work."

*   *   *

CHENEY, Glenn Alan 1951-

PERSONAL: Born September 6, 1951, in Melrose, Mass.; son of Theodore A. Rees (a professor and writer) and Dorothy (Bates) Cheney; married Solange Aurora Cavalcante (a secretary), May 24, 1978; children: Ian Alan. *Education:* Fairfield University, B.A., 1974, M.A., 1982. *Politics:* "Neither Democrat nor Republican." *Religion:* "Personal." *Home:* 30-14 21st St., Astoria, N.Y. 11102. *Office:* Grey & Davis Advertising, 777 Third Ave., New York, N.Y. 10017.

CAREER: American Heart Association, Norwalk, Conn., director of public information, 1980-82; free-lance writer and photographer, 1981—; Grey & Davis Advertising, New york, N.Y., account executive, 1983—. Executive editor and writer for Jay Nisberg & Associates; writer and researcher for Xerox Learning Systems. English teacher in Sao Paulo and Minas Gerais, Brazil, 1975, 1978-80; teacher of English as a foreign language for English Language Services at University of Bridgeport, 1977.

WRITINGS—For children: *El Salvador: Country in Crisis,* F. Watts, 1982; *Mahatma Gandhi,* F. Watts, 1983; *Television in American Society,* F. Watts, 1983; *Revolution in Central America,* F. Watts, 1983; *The Amazon,* F. Watts, in press.

WORK IN PROGRESS: A cookbook, publication expected in 1984; a novel about the frustrations inherent in U.S. society, publication expected in 1985.

SIDELIGHTS: "In 1974 I hitchhiked from Connecticut to Brazil," Cheney told *CA.* "This trip gave me a basic understanding of and deep sympathy with the situation of the people in Latin America, and led to my first book, *El Salvador: Country in Crisis.*

"In 1977 I traveled around northern Africa, crossing the Sahara and finally getting very sick in Ouagadougou, Upper Volta.

"In 1979 I went to Brazil and married a Brazilian girl I had met in Bridgeport, Connecticut, where I had been teaching English. We stayed in Brazil for two years, then returned to Bridgeport. Now we are planning to return to Brazil as soon as I publish a healthy novel. Then I will be a very free free-lancer, living on a farm in Brazil while having the income of books published in the United States—a nice plan.

"I suppose that is the primary motivation behind my writing: freedom. A long time ago I figured out that if I wrote for a living, I could live anywhere in the world. At the slightest whim or urge, I could get up and go live somewhere else. No boss, government, or social pressure could force me to do anything I couldn't run away from—another nice plan.

"Look at the fringe benefits: fame, respect, virtual immortality, and big bucks to boot. Can you beat that?

"Somebody beat it. I live in a tiny apartment in Queens. No one has heard of me. Respect is still a dream. The books I've put my name on have shelf lives of an estimated eighteen months. Last year I qualified for food stamps. So I took a job at a public relations agency. My boss, my government, and my peers have me pretty well squared away. But I still write. It doesn't do me any good, but it keeps life from being a complete waste of time. And you can't beat that."

AVOCATIONAL INTERESTS: Photography, travel.

*   *   *

CHERNER, Anne 1954-

PERSONAL: Born January 30, 1954, in Birmingham, Ala.; daughter of Marvin (a judge) and Leona (Roth) Cherner; married Stephen Compton Whitehouse (a landscape architect and urban designer), June 24, 1979. *Education:* Harvard University, B.A. (magna cum laude), 1976; Columbia University, M.F.A., 1979. *Home:* 301 West 108th St., New York, N.Y. 10025.

CAREER: Participant in New York Poets-in-the-Schools, 1978—. Member of New York Teachers and Writers Collaborative, 1979 —. *Member:* Poets and Writers, Associated Writing Programs, Phi Beta Kappa. *Awards, honors:* Poetry prize from *Mademoiselle*, 1976, for "For Claes Oldenburg of *Geometric Mouse,* Variation I, Scale A, 1971' "; Joan Grey Untermeyer Poetry Prize from Radcliffe College, 1976, for a group of poems; Hackney Literary Award from Alabama Arts Alliance, 1976, for poems, 1979, for story "Minnie Lee's Funeral"; prize from Academy of American Poets, 1977, for a group of poems; *Black Warrior Review* poetry prize, 1978, for a group of poems; Mary Roberts Rinehart fellowship, 1979.

WRITINGS: The Surveyor's Hand (poems), Compton, 1981. Work represented in *Contemporary Literature in Birmingham: An Anthology,* edited by Steven Ford Brown, Thunder City, 1983. Contributor to magazines, including *New England Review, Poetry Northwest, Ploughshares,* and *Black Warrior Review.*

SIDELIGHTS: In her essay "Regarding 'The Reappraisal,' " Anne Cherner shares the circumstances and feelings that accompanied the writing of her poem "The Reappraisal." The essay reveals a poet in the process of creating. Cherner wrote: "Small but intense sensations—the swish of a pencil across paper and the faint cloud of a smudge superimposed over neat, slanting script because the pencil is being moved by a down-curved left hand. An eraser also fades the blue lines ruled on the paper, and the washed-out red of the left hand margin is always more prominent than the right.

"I begin with the writing materials of every schoolchild because teaching gave them to me again, although, like everything adult, my current versions are more refined: perfectly round maroon draughting pencils that don't callous the fingers, their butter-soft leads sharpened to pin-sized points by a manual sharpener of a solid and weighty brass that, unlike the mechanical sharpeners that Nabokov's Pnin thought said 'Ti-con-der-oga, ti-con-der-oga,' don't greedily devour half the pencil in half-a-minute.

"When I am writing with these materials in the stillness of my living room, I am not thinking about teaching, but I suspect that the spectre of a little girl also inhabits the quiet, meditative atmosphere, for whom writing was also a diversion, albeit a less disciplined one. I sharpen my pencil, tap the sharpener against the carved wooden ashtray I use as a repository for the shavings, and inhale the cool cellar odors of graphite and wood.

"Sometimes I wonder what this ghost child would make of one of my writing assignments, but she is not in the classroom when I rivet the other pairs of eyes on me, and then on the blackboard. The children I have worked with in a fashionable corner of Manhattan, in the ghettoes of Harlem and the Bronx, suburban Westchester and Long Island, and a Brooklyn as far removed as twenty years do not bring me back to the Alabama schoolgirl of the early sixties. . . .' "

* * *

CHESTER, (Daniel) Norman 1907-

PERSONAL: Born in 1907. *Home:* 136 Woodstock Rd., Oxford, England.

CAREER: Oxford University, Oxford, England, official fellow of Nuffield College, 1945-54, warden of college, 1954-78, chairman of Oxford Centre for Management Studies, 1965-75. Alderman of Oxford City Council, 1965-74. *Member:* International Political Science Association (president, 1961-64), Royal Institute of Public Administration (vice-president), Political Studies Association (president). *Awards, honors:* Commander of Order of the British Empire.

WRITINGS: Public Control of Road Passenger Transport: A Study in Administration and Economics, Manchester University Press, 1936; *The Nationalised Industries: A Statutory Analysis,* Institute of Public Administration (London), 1948, revised edition published as *The Nationalised Industries: An Analysis of the Statutory Provisions,* Allen & Unwin, 1951; *Central and Local Government: Financial and Administrative Relations,* Macmillan, 1951; (editor) *The Lessons of the British War Economy,* Cambridge University Press, 1951, reprinted, Greenwood Press, 1972; (editor) F.M.G. Wilson, *The Organization of British Government, 1914-56,* Macmillan, 1957; (with Nona Bowring) *Questions in Parliament,* Clarendon Press, 1962; *The Nationalisation of British Industry, 1945-51,* H.M.S.O., 1975. Editor of *Public Administration,* 1943-66.

BIOGRAPHICAL/CRITICAL SOURCES: Times Literary Supplement, February 27, 1976.

* * *

CHIARENZA, Carl 1935-

PERSONAL: Surname is pronounced Kee-a-*ren*-za; born September 5, 1935, in Rochester, N.Y.; son of Charles (a cabinetmaker) and Mary Rose (a seamstress; maiden name, Russo) Chiarenza; married Heidi Faith Katz, August 13, 1978; children: Suzanne Mari, Jonah Katz. *Education:* Rochester Institute of Technology, B.F.A., 1957; Boston University, M.S., 1959, M.A., 1964; Harvard University, Ph.D., 1972. *Office:* Department of Art History, Boston University, 725 Commonwealth Ave., Boston, Mass. 02215.

CAREER: Boston University, Boston, Mass., lecturer, 1963-64, instructor, 1964-68, assistant professor, 1968-72, associate professor, 1973-80, professor of art history, 1980—, chairman of department, 1976-81. Guest curator at Boston's Institute for Contemporary Art, 1980-81; member of board of trustees of Visual Studies Workshop of State University of New York (adjunct visiting professor, 1972-73) and Photographic Resource Center; member of advisory council of International Center for Photography. Photographs exhibited in nearly one hundred fifty solo and group shows; represented in permanent collections of International Museum of Photography, Fogg Art Museum, Center for Creative Photography, and Minneapolis Institute of Art. *Military service:* U.S. Army, 1960-62.

MEMBER: Society for Photographic Education, American Association of University Professors, College Art Association of America, Association of Historians of American Art. *Awards, honors:* Danforth Foundation grants, 1966-67, 1967-68; Kress Foundation grant, 1970-71; fellow of Massachusetts Art and Humanities Foundation, 1975-76, and National Endowment for the Arts, 1977-78.

WRITINGS: Aaron Siskind: Pleasures and Terrors, New York Graphic Society/Little, Brown, 1982. Contributor of articles and reviews to magazines, including *Afterimage.* Past editor of *Contemporary Photographer.*

WORK IN PROGRESS: Pictures for exhibitions and publications; book reviews.

SIDELIGHTS: Chiarenza told *CA:* "I'm a switch-hitter. I have been making pictures and writing about pictures since high school. Because I seem to do both best when working in concentrated spurts on each, I sometimes feel torn between the two. I work intuitively and in what seems to me to be a constant state of agitation until things find their rightful place on a page or in a picture. Thus the subtitle 'Pleasures and Terrors,' while borrowed from a series of pictures by Siskind ('Pleasures and Terrors of Levitation'), applies to me as well as to him: it's about reaching for a sense of equilibrium, a place of understanding, for the individual as he or she moves through the world in a state of essential ignorance about the meaning of life.

"I wrote about Siskind's life and work for many reasons, but primarily because Siskind brought together a complex web of twentieth-century American issues. Born in 1903, the son of Jewish immigrants, he fought his way through significantly modern and American personal and societal problems. He produced a vast body of work which in its progression reflects the history of twentieth-century American art from figurative and social to abstract and personal. It seemed to me that his story and a critical analysis of his work had much to say about finding and expressing selfness to my own and to succeeding generations of Americans. I wrote, then, to learn about myself, and I hope that my readers read for the same reason.

"My own pictures are about my experience of this quest for self within a complex environment. It is difficult today to dwell for long on the notion of an external picturesque world. Much of what we see depends upon it first being pictured in the mind. Our landscape is indeed in the mind, but the mind now survives in an environment which is neither the natural one of the nineteenth century and earlier nor the urban one of the first half of the twentieth century. It is a more thoroughly technological landscape, yet it remains as mysterious and full of unknown forces as any landscape of the past.

"My photographs 'document' this contemporary landscape. For source material I use the discarded products of man's technological work. These tend to be inorganic and inhospitable, yet as they reenter the world as shapes and tones of a photograph, they become for me organic and inviting. References to traditional aesthetics in landscape appear in my work, but they are now pictured as abstract and imaginary structures—places which are as real as any field or stretch of mountain but which can exist only in one's private visual and mental ordering."

*   *   *

CHILDS, W(illiam) H(arold) J(oseph) 1905(?)-1983

OBITUARY NOTICE: Born c. 1905; died April 26, 1983, in Lundin Links, Fife, Scotland. Educator and author. Childs received a Ph.D. from the University of London in 1928 and spent several years doing research in spectroscopy at Heidelburg University, the Royal Institution, and the University of Michigan. During World War II he worked in the armaments research department of the British Ministry of Supply, where he developed an electrical device used to defuse magnetic mines. Childs joined the faculty of Heriot Watt University as a professor of physics in 1947 and was named dean of the school's faculty of science in 1966. He retired as professor emeritus in 1969. Childs wrote *Physical Constants*, an internationally used text. Obituaries and other sources: *London Times*, May 3, 1983.

CHILVER, Guy (Edward Farquhar) 1910-1982

PERSONAL: Born February 11, 1910; died September 7, 1982, in Canterbury, England; son of Arthur Farquhar and Florence (Ranking) Chilver; married Sylvia Chloe Littell, 1945 (marriage ended, 1972); married Marie Elizabeth Powell, 1973. *Education:* Trinity College, Oxford, M.A.; Merton College, Oxford, D.Phil. *Residence:* Oak Lodge, Boughton, near Faversham, Kent, England.

CAREER: Oxford University, Queen's College, Oxford, England, fellow in ancient history, 1934-63, fellow emeritus, 1964-82, dean of college, 1935-39, senior tutor, 1948-63, member of Hebdomadal Council, 1949-63; University of Kent at Canterbury, Canterbury, England, professor of classical studies, 1964-76, dean of humanities, 1964-76 (one source said 1964-74), deputy vice-chancellor, 1966-72. Visiting professor at University of Texas, 1963. Member of Ministry of Food, 1940-45; member of British food mission to Washington, D.C., 1943-45. Member of Society for Promotion of Roman Studies (vice-president, beginning in 1964) and British School at Rome. *Member:* Reform Club, Kent and Canterbury Club.

WRITINGS: Cisalpine Gaul: Social and Economic History From 49 B.C. to the Death of Trajan, Clarendon Press, 1941, reprinted, Arno, 1975; (translator from Italian; with first wife, Sylvia Chilver) Luigi Pareti and others, *The Ancient World, 1200 B.C. to A.D. 500,* Allen & Unwin, 1965; *A Historical Commentary on Tacitus' Histories I and II,* Clarendon Press, 1979. Contributor to scholarly journals. Co-editor of *Classical Quarterly.*

AVOCATIONAL INTERESTS: Bridge.

OBITUARIES: London Times, September 11, 1982.*

*   *   *

CHISHOLM, Anne

CAREER: Journalist. *Awards, honors:* Silver Pen Award from International P.E.N., 1979, for *Nancy Cunard.*

WRITINGS: Philosophers of the Earth: Conversations With Ecologists, Dutton, 1972; *Nancy Cunard: A Biography,* Knopf, 1979.

SIDELIGHTS: Chisholm's award-winning biography, *Nancy Cunard,* is the story of the wealthy "femme fatale," poet and avant-garde publisher who scandalized English society with her life-style and liberal causes during the 1920's. Chisholm portrays Cunard as a sad and lonely child driven in all her pursuits by her hostility for her mother. The biographer argues, Auberon Waugh noted in the *New York Times Book Review,* that Cunard's resentfulness accounted for all the traumas of her adult life—"her inability to sustain a relationship, her nymphomania, her adoption of the black cause, her left-wing politics and finally her dipsomania, drug history, insanity and lonely death in the public ward of a Paris hospital." Chisholm even "suggests that it was largely to annoy her mother that Nancy took up with the black American musician Henry Crowder in 1928," Waugh wrote. "One suspects that her earlier involvement with Louis Aragon, the French Communist, was similarly inspired."

Nevertheless, observed Katherine Winton Evans in the *Washington Post Book World,* Henry Crowder was "the most significant figure in [Cunard's] life. . . . Indeed, he sparked her interest in racial justice and inspired her one great work, the compilation of an anthology of black history, politics and culture called *Negro*." Waugh speculated that Cunard's marriage to Crowder also may have inspired the relationship between the characters Mrs. Beste-Chetwynde and Chokey in Evelyn Waugh's *Decline and Fall*. Cunard fired the imaginations of other novelists as well, serving as the model for Iris March in Michael Arlen's *The Green Hat* and Myra Viveash in Aldous Huxley's *Antic Hay*.

"Nancy Cunard is a sad example of a fine intelligence and artistic sensibility destroyed by a violent temper," Philippa Toomey observed in the *London Times*. "It might seem a sad and wasted life, but Anne Chisholm has set Nancy Cunard in her times with remarkable skill, making a most worthwhile book from a difficult subject." Evans agreed, writing that Cunard was "so complicated and bizarre it takes a first-rate, full biography like this to do her justice."

BIOGRAPHICAL/CRITICAL SOURCES: New York Times, May 26, 1979; *New York Times Book Review,* June 17, 1979; *Washington Post Book World,* July 15, 1979; *London Times,* April 10, 1980.*

*   *   *

CHOLDIN, Marianna Tax   1942-

PERSONAL: Born February 26, 1942, in Chicago, Ill.; daughter of Sol (a professor) and Gertrude (Katz) Tax; married Harvey M. Choldin (a professor); children: Mary, Kate. *Education:* University of Chicago, B.A., 1962, M.A., 1967, Ph.D., 1979. *Religion:* Jewish. *Home:* 1111 South Pine St., Champaign, Ill. 61820. *Office:* Slavic and East European Library, University of Illinois, Urbana, Ill. 61801.

CAREER: Michigan State University, East Lansing, Slavic bibliographer at library, 1967-69; University of Illinois, Urbana, Slavic bibliographer, 1969—, research director at Russian and East European Center, 1980—, assistant director for Slavic and East European Library, 1982—. *Member:* American Library Association, American Association for the Advancement of Slavic Studies (chairperson of bibliography and documentation committee, 1978—), Phi Beta Kappa, Nu Pi Sigma.

WRITINGS: Access to Information in the Eighties, Russica Publishers, 1982. Contributor to *Encyclopedia of Library and Information Science.* Contributor to library and Slavic studies journals.

WORK IN PROGRESS: A Fence Around the Empire: Russian Censorship of Western Ideas; editor, with Maurice Friedberg, of proceedings of conference on Soviet censorship held in 1983; a book on Soviet censorship of foreign publications.

SIDELIGHTS: Choldin told *CA:* "As a librarian I am interested in the flow of information between countries. As a Russian specialist I cannot help but be aware of serious obstructions to that flow, especially from other countries into the Soviet Union. Before the revolution, censorship was openly acknowledged in Russia, and I was able to find ample material describing the operation of the system controlling Western publications entering the empire. Now censorship is no longer acknowledged, and it is much more difficult to describe the system, which creates a great challenge for the writer. I am interested in finding the continuities between the Russian and Soviet systems, and in exploring the changes which have taken place. In general, I think it is very important that we strive to understand the nature of obstructions to the flow of information. Such obstructions do no one any good in the long run, and it

will be to the mutual benefit of the United States and the Soviet Union if we can find ways to remove the obstructions."

*   *   *

CHRISTENSEN, Anna
See MAYER, Deborah Anne

*   *   *

CHULAK, Armando   ?-1975

OBITUARY NOTICE: Playwright. Chulak, an Argentinian, collaborated with countryman Sergio de Cecco on "The Great Confession," a play about the breakdown of a marriage. Obituaries and other sources: *New York Times,* April 1, 1983.

*   *   *

CHUTE, Robert M.   1926-
(L. W. Pond)

PERSONAL: Born February 13, 1926, in Bridgton, Me. *Education:* University of Maine at Orono, B.A., 1950; Johns Hopkins University, D.Sc., 1953. *Home Address:* R.F.D.3, Box 269A, Freeport, Me. 04032. *Office:* Department of Biology, Bates College, Lewiston, Me. 04240.

CAREER: Middlebury College, Middlebury, Vt., instructor, 1953-58, assistant professor of biology, 1959-61; Lincoln University, Lincoln University, Pa., associate professor of biology and chairman of department, 1961-62; Bates College, Lewiston, Me., professor of biology and chairman of department, 1962-82, chairman of Division of Science, 1983—. Assistant professor at San Fernando State College, 1959-61. Plumbing inspector and code enforcement officer in Mt. Vernon, Me., 1976-79. *Military service:* U.S. Army Air Forces, 1944-46; became sergeant. *Member:* American Association for the Advancement of Science (honorary life member; past president), Maine State Biologists, Phi Beta Kappa, Sigma Xi.

WRITINGS: Environmental Insight, Harper, 1971; *Introductory Biology,* Harper, 1974; *Quiet Thunder* (poems), privately printed, 1975; *The Uncle George Poems,* Cider Press, 1977; *Voices Great and Small* (poems), Cider Press, 1977; *Thirteen Moons* (poems), Blackberry Press, 1978 (published in Canada as *Thirteen Moons/Treize Lunes* [French-English bilingual edition], Penumbra Press [Ontario], 1982). Contributor of articles to scientific journals; contributor of more than three hundred poems to little magazines. Editor of *Small Pond* under pseudonym L. W. Pond.

WORK IN PROGRESS: A long series of poems on the New Hebrides islands of Vanuatu, publication expected in 1984.

SIDELIGHTS: Chute told *CA:* "My work in biological sciences leads me to see what others might not see in nature, but I do not consider my poems 'nature poetry'—except that I see everything as natural in a deep sense. Some of my friends say I am a lyric poet, others say a religious poet. That's all up to the reader.

"My environmental views have not changed much since the publication of *Environmental Insight.* I see all as natural. I side with Garret Hardin on the need for self-imposed repression of human free action—but I am less optimistic now than in 1971."

CIOFFI, Lou(is James) 1926-

BRIEF ENTRY: Born April 30, 1926, in New York, N.Y. American broadcast journalist. In 1947 Cioffi began his career in broadcast journalism at Columbia Broadcasting System (CBS-News), where he worked as a copyboy, writer, and editor. From 1952 to 1961 he served as foreign correspondent for that network—first in Korea and later in Paris. In 1961 he joined American Broadcasting Companies (ABC-News), where he served as foreign correspondent in various European bureaus and in the Far East. In 1977 he became ABC's United Nations bureau chief. In 1970 and 1974 Cioffi received Overseas Press Club awards for radio and television coverage. He also received a National Headliners Club award in 1970. *Address:* c/o ABC Public Relations, 1330 Avenue of the Americas, New York, N.Y. 10019. *Biographical/critical sources: Who's Who in America,* 42nd edition, Marquis, 1982.

* * *

CITRINE, Walter McLennan 1887-1983

OBITUARY NOTICE: Born August 22, 1887, in Liverpool, England; died January 22, 1983, in Brixham, England. Labor leader and author. A leader in the British labor movement who strove to increase industrial productivity, Citrine began his career in the Electrical Trades Union in 1924 and ascended to the posts of general secretary of Britain's Trade Unions Congress from 1926 to 1946 and president of the International Federation of Trade Unions from 1928 to 1945. He was also director and vice-chairman of the *Daily Herald* from 1929 to 1946. Citrine wrote two books about trips he took to the Soviet Union, *I Search for Truth in Russia* and *In Russia Now,* and an autobiography, *Men and Work.* Obituaries and other sources: *Current Biography,* Wilson, 1941, April, 1983; *New Statesman,* March 5, 1955; *The International Year Book and Statesmen's Who's Who,* Kelly's Directories, 1980; *London Times,* January 26, 1983; *Newsweek,* February 7, 1983.

* * *

CLAPHAM, Arthur Roy 1904-

PERSONAL: Born May 24, 1904, in Norwich, England; son of George and Dora (Harvey) Clapham; married Brenda North Stoessiger (a statistician), March 27, 1933; children: Elizabeth Harvey (Mrs. Humphrey Rang), Jennifer Margaret (Mrs. David Newton), David Harvey. *Education:* Downing College, Cambridge, B.A., 1925, Ph.D., 1929, M.A., 1930. *Home:* Parrock, Arkholme, Carnforth, England.

CAREER: Rothamsted Agricultural Experimental Station, Harpenden, England, crop physiologist, 1928-30; Oxford University, Oxford, England, demonstrator in botany, 1930-44; University of Sheffield, Sheffield, England, professor of botany, 1944-69, professor emeritus, 1969—, pro-vice-chancellor of university, 1954-58. Member of Field Studies Council, 1943—; chairman of British National Committee for International Biological Programme, 1964—; member of board of trustees of British Museum of Natural History, 1965-75. *Member:* Royal Society (fellow), Linnean Society (president, 1967-70), British Ecological Society, Botanical Society of the British Isles, Society of Experimental Biologists, Nature Conservancy (chairman of science policy committee, 1963-70). *Awards, honors:* Commander of Order of the British Empire.

WRITINGS: (With W. O. James) *The Biology of Flowers,* Clarendon Press, 1935; (with T. G. Tutin and E. F. Warburg) *Flora of the British Isles,* Cambridge University Press, 1952, 2nd edition, 1962; (with Tutin and Warburg) *Excursion Flora of the British Isles,* Cambridge University Press, 1959, 2nd edition, 1968; (editor) *Flora of Derbyshire,* Derby Museum and Art Gallery, 1969; (author of text) *The Oxford Book of Trees,* illustrated by B. E. Nicholson, Oxford University Press, 1975; (editor) *Upper Teesdale: The Area and Its Natural History,* Collins & World, 1978; (editor) *The IBP Survey of Conservation Sites: An Experimental Study,* Cambridge University Press, 1980.

* * *

CLARK, Diana Cooper
See COOPER-CLARK, Diana

* * *

CLARK, Kenneth (Mackenzie) 1903-1983

OBITUARY NOTICE—See index for *CA* sketch: Born July 13, 1903, in London, England; died after a short illness, May 21, 1983, in Kent, England. Art historian, museum director, educator, and author. Clark is perhaps best remembered for "Civilisation," the highly successful thirteen-part television series that he wrote and narrated for the British Broadcasting Corporation (BBC-TV). The series, which contained Clark's personal commentary on thirteen hundred years of Western culture, was broadcast in the United States by the Public Broadcasting System (PBS-TV). Among the posts Clark held in his long and varied career as an art historian was that of director of the National Gallery in London. From 1934 to 1944 he held the prestigious post of surveyor to the king's pictures, and during the 1950's he was chairman of the Arts Council of Great Britain and the Independent Television Authority. He also served as Slade Professor of Fine Arts at Oxford University from 1946 to 1950 and from 1961 to 1962. Robert Hughes noted in *Time* that Clark's many books were characterized by his "lovely, supple prose style, short on ornament and full of sense." Among them are *Leonardo da Vinci: An Account of His Development as an Artist, The Nude: A Study in Ideal Pictures, The Drawings by Sandro Botticelli for Dante's "Divine Comedy,"* and *Introduction to Rembrandt.* Clark was knighted in 1938 and named a life peer in 1969. He wrote two autobiographical works, *Another Part of the Wood,* which was published in 1974, and *The Other Half,* which appeared in 1977. Obituaries and other sources: *New York Times,* May 22, 1983; *Los Angeles Times,* May 22, 1983; *London Times,* May 23, 1983; *Chicago Tribune,* May 23, 1983; *Newsweek,* May 30, 1983; *Time,* May 30, 1983, June 6, 1983.

* * *

CLARK, William Bedford 1947-

PERSONAL: Born January 23, 1947, in Oklahoma City, Okla.; son of William B. (a pipeliner) and Florine (Griggs) Clark; married Charlene Kerne (an energy information specialist), December 22, 1972; children: Mary Frances, Eleanor Kerne. *Education:* University of Oklahoma, B.A., 1969; Louisiana State University, M.A., 1971, Ph.D., 1973. *Home:* 1009 Winter, Bryan, Tex. 77801. *Office:* Department of English, Texas A&M University, College Station, Tex. 77843.

CAREER: North Carolina Agricultural and Technical State University, Greensboro, assistant professor of English, 1974-77; Texas A&M University, College Station, 1977—, began as assistant professor, became associate professor of English.

Member: Modern Language Association of America, Society for the Study of Southern Literature, Conference on Christianity and Literature, South Central Modern Language Association. *Awards, honors:* Grants from National Endowment for the Humanities, 1973-74, 1977, 1980.

WRITINGS: (Contributor) George Carter and Bruce Mouser, editors, *Identity and Awareness: Selected Proceedings of the First and Second Minorities Studies Conferences,* [La Crosse], 1975; (editor and author of introduction) *Critical Essays on Robert Penn Warren,* G. K. Hall, 1981. Contributor of about thirty articles and reviews to literature journals and literary magazines, including *Southern Review, Antioch Review, American Literature, Renascence, South Atlantic Quarterly,* and *Studies in American Humor.*

WORK IN PROGRESS: Continuing research on the career and writings of Robert Penn Warren, the literature of the American West, and American humor.

SIDELIGHTS: Clark told *CA:* "For me, literary criticism is not only the exploration of a text but a mode of self-exploration. I am often surprised by the degree to which my own writings represent an implicit autobiography."

*   *   *

CLYMER, Kenton James 1943-

BRIEF ENTRY: Born November 17, 1943, in Brooklyn, N.Y. American historian, educator, and author. Clymer has taught U.S. diplomatic history at University of Texas since 1974. He has also been a Fulbright Professor at Silliman University in the Philippines. He wrote *John Hay: The Gentleman as Diplomat* (University of Michigan Press, 1975). *Address:* 905 McKelligon Dr., El Paso, Tex. 79902; and Department of History, University of Texas, El Paso, Tex. 79902. *Biographical/critical sources: Times Literary Supplement,* January 14, 1977; *American Historical Review,* February, 1977.

*   *   *

COHEN, Margie K(anter) 1912-

PERSONAL: Born June 29, 1912, in Chicago, Ill.; daughter of Victor (a merchant) and Etta (Grant) Kanter; married Louis N. Cohen (in business), July 10, 1933; children: Jacqueline, Bobette Cohen Takiff, Pattee Cohen Schnitzer. *Education:* University of Illinois, B.A., 1933. *Religion:* Jewish. *Home:* 107 South Ave., Glencoe, Ill. 60022. *Office:* Margie K. Cohen Associates, 2332 North Clark, Chicago, Ill. 60614.

CAREER: Margie K. Cohen Associates, Chicago, Ill., real estate rehabilitator, 1967—.

WRITINGS: Old Houses Into New: Successful Real Estate Renovation for Profit, Prentice-Hall, 1982.

WORK IN PROGRESS: A comic play about tenants, completion expected in 1984.

SIDELIGHTS: In her book *Old Houses Into New* Cohen, who owns a number of Chicago apartment buildings, describes her experiences of purchasing and renovating buildings for profit. The book contains tips on mortgages, financing, property management, depreciation, and tax shelters.

Cohen told *CA:* "Real estate is a natural field for women and it's easier to do the work than it is to write about it. The hard part of working in real estate is getting started, and it takes time to build a team to work with, but it's fun and profitable."

COHEN, Norm(an) 1936-

PERSONAL: Born December 13, 1936, in New York, N.Y.; son of Moshe (a social worker) and Yetta (Pickman) Cohen; married Anne Billings, July 11, 1959 (divorced, 1983); children: Alexandra Elizabeth and Carson Benjamin (twins). *Education:* Reed College, A.B., 1958; attended University of California, Los Angeles, 1958-59; University of California, Berkeley, M.A., 1960, Ph.D., 1963. *Politics:* Democrat. *Religion:* Jewish. *Home:* 7833 Truxton Ave., Westchester, Calif. 90045. *Office:* Aerospace Corp., 2350 El Segundo Blvd., El Segundo, Calif. 90245.

CAREER: Associated with Aerospace Corp., El Segundo, Calif., 1963—, head of department of chemical kinetics, 1972—. Executive secretary of John Edwards Memorial Foundation. *Member:* American Chemical Society, American Physical Society, American Folklore Society, Society for Ethnomusicology, Society of Recorded Sound Archives, California Folklore Society, Sigma Xi. *Awards, honors:* Folklore prize from University of Chicago and Deems Taylor Award from American Society of Composers, Authors and Publishers, both 1982, for *Long Steel Rail;* nominated for Grammy Award from National Academy of Recording Arts and Sciences, 1983, for record album, *Minstrels and Tunesmiths: The Commercial Roots of Early Country Music.*

WRITINGS: (Contributor) W. A. Noyes, Jr., G. S. Hammond, and J. N. Pitts, Jr., editors, *Advances in Photochemistry,* Volume V, Wiley, 1968; (contributor) Bill C. Malone and Judith McCulloh, editors, *Stars of Country Music,* University of Illinois Press, 1975; *Long Steel Rail: The Railroad in American Folksong,* University of Illinois Press, 1981; (editor) *Ozark Folksongs,* revised and abridged edition (Cohen not associated with earlier editions), University of Illinois Press, 1982; (contributor) *Ethnic Recordings in America: A Neglected Heritage,* Library of Congress, 1982. Contributor to *History and Encyclopedia of Country, Western and Gospel Music.* Contributor to music and folklore journals. Editor of *John Edwards Memorial Foundation* (JEMF) *Quarterly,* 1965-80; assistant editor of *International Journal of Chemical Kinetics.*

SIDELIGHTS: Cohen told *CA:* "My interest in folk music began in my early teens and was confined to Jewish and Eastern European cultures. It wasn't until I left high school that I really became aware of traditional American music. Initially my attention was drawn to traditional southeastern folk music, but as I was exposed to other forms—hillbilly, blues, jazz, and even pop music—I was intrigued by the problems of how different musical genres influence one another and how they reflect American social history and culture.

"A central focus in my study of American railroad songs, which occupied the better part of a dozen years, was the role the railroads played in shaping America, what the public attitudes toward the railroads were at different epochs, and how those attitudes were reflected in American folk and popular songs."

AVOCATIONAL INTERESTS: Music, folklore, photography, art, mythology.

*   *   *

COHLER, Bertram J(oseph) 1938-

PERSONAL: Born December 3, 1938, in Chicago, Ill.; son of

Jonas Robert (a lawyer) and Betty (Cahn) Cohler; married Anne Meyers (a political scientist), June 11, 1962; children: Jonathan Richard, James Joseph. *Education:* University of Chicago, B.A., 1961; Harvard University, Ph.D., 1967, postdoctoral study, 1967-69; postdoctoral study at Institute for Psychoanalysis, Chicago, Ill., 1975—. *Home:* 5408 South Blackstone Ave., Chicago, Ill. 60615. *Office:* Committee on Human Development, University of Chicago, 5730 South Woodlawn Ave., Chicago, Ill. 60637.

CAREER: University of Chicago, Chicago, Ill., assistant professor, 1969-1975, associate professor, 1975-1980, professor of behavioral science, education, and psychiatry, 1980—, William Rainey Harper Professor of Social Sciences in the College, 1979—. Member of attending psychiatry staff at Michael Reese Hospital; consultant to Illinois State Psychiatric Institute. *Member:* American Psychological Association, American Sociological Association, American Orthopsychiatric Association (member of board of directors, 1981-84), Gerontological Society of America (fellow), Society for Research in Child Development, Society for Personality Assessment (fellow), Chicago Association for Psychoanalytic Psychology (president, 1982-83), Institute of Medicine of Chicago (fellow).

WRITINGS: (With Henry U. Grunebaum, Justin L. Weiss, and others) *Mentally Ill Mothers and Their Children,* University of Chicago Press, 1975, 2nd edition, 1982; (with Grunebaum) *Mothers, Grandmothers, and Daughters,* Wiley, 1981; (with Rebecca Cohen and Sidney Weissman) *Parenthood: A Psychodynamic Perspective,* Guilford Press, 1983; (with James Anthony) *The Invulnerable Child,* Guilford Press, 1983; (with K. Field and Glorye Wool) *Psychoanalysis and Education,* International Universities Press, in press.

Contributor: F. Walsh, editor, *Normal Family Processes,* Guilford Press, 1982; H. Barrison, editor, *Children of Depressed Parents: Risk, Identification and Intervention,* Grune, 1983; D. Offer and M. Sabshin, editors, *Normality,* Basic Books, in press. Contributor of more than seventy-five articles to psychology and sociology journals.

WORK IN PROGRESS: Research on studies of parent-child relations, family relations, and aging.

SIDELIGHTS: Cohler told *CA:* "Study of social life, and of the social context of lives, has been fascinating to me since I read about other cultures during sixth-grade social studies classes. More recently, I have begun to study lives in context, and to recognize that 'place' in the course of life vitally affects the ways in which persons understand the meaning of life. Reminiscence and nostalgia are also important, yet we know so little about such subjective aspects of lives. The use of psychoanalytic methods, based on the clinical interview, may help in this study. I am also impressed with the resilience which persons show, and which has been so seldom studied. Children, especially, seem resilient to psychological distress in the face of such serious problems as parental psychopathology, inherent limitations of coping abilities, and social disorganization (seen among children of poverty and in areas of conflict).

"*Mothers, Grandmothers, and Daughters* was inspired both by our clinical work with emotionally troubled women—mothers of young children—in which the mother's relationship with her own mother proved to be important as a major area of both concern and satisfaction—and from the larger observation that American families are more positively bonded and a greater source of strength for members than is often realized. Adults continue to care for each other, and to express genuine affection and concern even though, at times, family members may disagree with each other.

"There is little evidence to suggest the 'death of the family.' Indeed, at no time in history has the family been more effective in providing for emotional and material needs than in contemporary urban society. Family members maintain frequent contact with each other, and generally obtain pleasure from participation in family rituals and gatherings. At the same time, there are clearly some areas upon which family members agree to disagree. Much more study is required of ways in which families work to support their members. Particular study is needed of the manner in which families care for aged or ill members, a problem which will increase in an aging society."

AVOCATIONAL INTERESTS: Family activities, wilderness camping, sailing.

*   *   *

COLE, Lewis 1946-

PERSONAL: Born May 25, 1946, in New York, N.Y.; son of Bernard (a photographer) and Helen (a writer; maiden name, Bassine) Yglesiasi; married Andrea Triguba (divorced); married Cathy Wein (a psychologist), June 24, 1978. *Education:* Attended McGill University, 1963-64; Columbia University, B.A., 1968. *Politics:* "Radical." *Religion:* "None." *Home and office:* 785 West End Ave., New York, N.Y. 10025. *Agent:* Elaine Markson, 44 Greenwich Ave., New York, N.Y. 10012; and Ronda Gomez, Adams, Ray & Rosenberg, 9200 Sunset Blvd., Los Angeles, Calif.

CAREER: Students for a Democratic Society, New York City, political organizer, 1968-70; W. W. Norton, New York City, manuscript reader, 1970-72; State University of New York, Purchase, instructor in English, 1970-75; writer, 1976—. Worked with Health and Hospital Worker's Union Bread and Roses project, 1979—. *Member:* Authors Guild, Writers Guild of America, Professional Basketball Writers Association of America, National Writers Union (member of organizing committee). *Awards, honors:* Grant in creative prose from National Endowment for the Arts, 1983, for *Dream Team.*

WRITINGS: A Loose Game (nonfiction), Bobbs-Merrill, 1978; *Dream Team* (nonfiction), Morrow, 1982. Also co-author with Eve Merriam and Mickey Grant of musical revue "Take Care, Take Care!," first performed in 1979. Co-author with brother, Rafael Yglesias, of "as yet unproduced (but contracted)" screenplays, including "The Diary," "MVP," "American Dreams," "National Secret," "Wall Street," and "The Kill."

WORK IN PROGRESS: Houston Bazaar, a novel "about a New Yorker who moves to Houston, Texas," completion expected in late 1983.

SIDELIGHTS: Cole's *A Loose Game* and *Dream Team* both center on basketball. His *Dream Team* focuses on the National Basketball Association's New York Knickerbockers, world champions of the 1969-70 season. Cole recreates the highlights of that season, then tracks down the former players and records their comments.

Cole told *CA:* "My two books tried to deal with basketball as a unique American phenomenon and use the game and sport as a way of examining some particulars of American society from my social and political viewpoint. *Dream Team* met with widely varied reactions. Several reviewers reacted strongly to its political content. Others praised it highly. The *New York Times* selected it among its recommended reading list for summer, 1982, and it was selected to be part of the permanent collection of the White House library.''

BIOGRAPHICAL/CRITICAL SOURCES: Soho Weekly News, February 8, 1979; *Washington Post Book World,* December 23, 1981; *New York Times Book Review,* January 10, 1982; *United Mainliner,* March, 1982; *Chattanooga Times,* April 24, 1982; *Pittsburgh Press,* April 28, 1982.

* * *

COLEMAN, Patricia R(egister)   1936-

PERSONAL: Born November 1, 1936, in Orlando, Fla.; daughter of Oliver C. (an engineer) and Athena (an accountant; maiden name, Athanasaw) Register; married William V. Coleman (a writer and publisher); children: Lisa Coleman-Greaney, Sarah Angela. *Education:* University of Georgia, A.A., 1956; Florida State University, B.A., 1974. *Religion:* Roman Catholic. *Office:* Growth Associates, 22 Willow St., Mystic, Conn. 06355.

CAREER: St. Joseph's Church, Macon, Ga., director of religious education, 1970-72; Growth Associates (ministerial service), Mystic, Conn., co-founder and vice-president, 1972—, artistic director of publications, 1980—. Diocesan associate director of Department of Christian Formation, Savannah, Ga., 1971-74. Member of board of directors of Norwich Community Ministries, 1981—, and Martin House, Inc., 1982—.

WRITINGS—With husband, William V. Coleman: *Mine Is the Morning,* ten volumes, Twenty-Third Publications, 1973-75, revised and enlarged edition, 1978; *God Believes in Me,* five volumes, Ave Maria Press, 1974; *Daybreak,* ten volumes, Twenty-Third Publications, 1975-77; *Only Love Can Make It Easy* (marriage preparation manual), two volumes, Twenty-Third Publications, 1976, revised edition, 1982; *God's Own Child,* two volumes, Twenty-Third Publications, 1977, revised edition, 1983; *Parish Youth Ministry,* Twenty-Third Publications, 1977; *Make Friends With God,* Growth Associates, 1979; *What Is Youth Ministry?,* Growth Associates, 1979; *Sex Today,* Growth Associates, 1980; *The Youth Ministry Handbook,* Growth Associates, 1980; *No-Pain Learning,* Growth Associates, 1981; *You, Your Life, and Jesus,* Growth Associates, 1982; *The Mass Today,* Growth Associates, 1982; *The Mustard Seed People,* Growth Associates, 1983. Co-founder and editor of *Catholic Youth Ministry* and *Parish Communication;* co-founder of *Synthesis.*

WORK IN PROGRESS: Handbook for Young Catholics; The Mustard Seed Experience, on a simple lifestyle, publication expected in 1984.

SIDELIGHTS: Coleman told *CA:* ''I was an artist when I was drawn into religious education by the renewal of the Catholic church after Vatican Council II. My life work has been to struggle with my husband to develop a contemporary synthesis of religious ideas and contemporary faith for those participating in the diverse community we call 'church.'

''Years ago my husband and I decided that what kept most couples in tension with one another was the dissimilarities of their development. Husbands went one way, wives another. We decided that we would work together on the same projects so that this would not happen to us.

''We struggle with every new idea and wonder together what each new experience means to us. It is hard to define our working time and our family time. It has all merged together, as have we. Sometimes we marvel together at how close our thoughts and values have become. These have, in turn, influ-

enced our girls, who live in the midst of all our questioning and writing.

''I love being a woman, a wife, and a writer. The older I become, the more I see my many roles merging into one, to be a disciple of the Lord Jesus and to follow him wherever he leads Bill and me. I am confident that, short of death, he will never lead us anywhere except together.''

* * *

COLLIER, Johnnie Lucille
See COLLIER, Lucille Ann

* * *

COLLIER, Louise Wilbourn   1925-

PERSONAL: Born March 7, 1925, in Memphis, Tenn.; daughter of Frank Wallace (a cotton broker) and Louise (Robertson) Wilbourn; married John Stuart Collier (vice-president of an insurance agency), December 12, 1953; children: John Stuart, Jr., Louise (Mrs. James Howard Calandruccio), Katharine (Mrs. Archie Browne Creech), Margaret. *Education:* Attended Sweet Briar College, 1942-44; Southwestern University, B.A., 1946. *Religion:* Episcopalian. *Home:* 95 Grove Park Circle, Memphis, Tenn. 38117. *Agent:* Phyllis Tickle, 1407 Union St., Memphis, Tenn. 38104.

CAREER: Worked as staff assistant in continuing education at Southwestern University, 1953. Member of board of Pink Palace Museum, 1959-60; chairman of Yout Museum, 1960. *Member:* Memphis Garden Club, Memphis Symphony League, Junior League of Memphis (program chairman, 1963).

WRITINGS: Pilgrimage: A Tale of Old Natchez, St. Luke's Press, 1983.

SIDELIGHTS: Louise Collier's first book, *Pilgrimage: A Tale of Old Natchez,* is ''a fascinating new novel ... a very readable book, at times poignant, but uplifting,'' wrote book reviewer Mary George Beggs in the *Memphis Commercial Appeal.* Collier began writing her novel as a true history of the family of her great-great grandfather, John Walworth, and the family estate in Natchez, Mississippi. What she wrote instead is a fictionalized account, compiled from family documents, memories of stories Collier had heard as a child, and imagined details. As Collier told Beggs, ''I felt I had to make an interesting story. The truth is so complicated.''

Memphis Press-Scimitar book critic Edwin Howard found in *Pilgrimage* ''some of the finest writing I have encountered in years'' and a ''persuasive and moving theme'' that takes the novel beyond the restrictions of its genre. He saw the book as a testimony to the ''continuity and circularity of life,'' the power of a family to survive and thrive from generation to generation. ''Mrs. Collier handles the many characters and events of the Walworth saga masterfully,'' the critic concluded. ''The South has a brilliant new writer.''

Collier told *CA:* ''When my first draft of *Pilgrimage* brought such an enthusiastic response from my family and a few friends, I was encouraged to make it into a novel. I had always dreamed of writing a novel. Like Emily Dickinson, I wanted to write a 'letter to the world.' I think I also wanted to portray the South that I loved and was a part of. The South I read about or watched on film had always seemed so different from the one I knew. I don't pretend that this South of mine is typical or definitive, or that its characteristics are strictly geographical, only that it is real. My characters were my ancestors. They really led the sort of lives that the characters do in my story. They were human beings who had faith in something beyond themselves; they demanded a lot of themselves. Believing as they did in duty and honor and service, they achieved a quality of living and of being that is rarely seen in today's world. They were heroic in the highest sense of that word. It was my privilege to know some of these characters in person and the others through them. In *Pilgrimage* I have celebrated my heroes: I have sought to share my precious heritage with the world.''

BIOGRAPHICAL/CRITICAL SOURCES: Memphis Commercial Appeal, January 25, 1983; *Memphis Press-Scimitar*, March 12, 1983.

* * *

COLLIER, Lucille Ann   1919(?)-
(Johnnie Lucille Collier, Lucy Ann Collier; Ann Miller, a pseudonym)

BRIEF ENTRY: Born April 12, 1919 (some sources say 1923), in Chireno (some sources say Houston), Tex. American actress, dancer, singer, and author. Best known under the stage name Ann Miller, the performer began her film career in 1937 when she appeared in ''New Faces of 1937.'' That was followed by roles in dozens of films, including ''You Can't Take It With You'' (1938), ''Easter Parade'' (1948), and ''Kiss Me Kate'' (1956). Miller has also appeared in stage productions, most notably in a Broadway revival of ''Mame'' (1969) and in ''Sugar Babies'' (1979). Her autobiography, *Miller's High Life*, was published by Doubleday in 1972. *Address:* 618 North Alta Dr., Beverly Hills, Calif. 90210. *Biographical/critical sources: Saturday Review*, December 16, 1972; *New York Times Book Review*, March 25, 1973; *New York Times*, October 28, 1979; *Current Biography*, Wilson, 1980.

* * *

COLLIER, Lucy Ann
See COLLIER, Lucille Ann

* * *

COMITO, Terry Allen   1935-

PERSONAL: Born December 17, 1935, in Santa Ana, Calif.; son of William (a bookkeeper) and Barbara (Allen) Comito. *Education:* Stanford University, A.B., 1957, A.M., 1958; Harvard University, Ph.D., 1968. *Home:* 1789 Lanier Pl. N.W., Apt. 4, Washington, D.C. 20009. *Office:* Department of English, George Mason University, Fairfax, Va. 22030.

CAREER: Rutgers University, New Brunswick, N.J., assistant professor of English, 1963-71; Hunter College of the City University of New York, New York, N.Y., assistant professor of English, 1971-76; Stanford University, Stanford, Calif., visiting assistant professor of English, 1977-80; George Mason University, Fairfax, Va., associate professor of English, 1980—. *Member:* Modern Language Association of America, Renaissance Society of America, American Film Institute, Phi Beta Kappa.

WRITINGS: The Idea of the Garden in the Renaissance, Rutgers University Press, 1978.

Contributor: (Author of introduction) Henry James, *The Princess Casamassima*, Crowell, 1976; Elisabeth MacDougall, editor, *Fons Sapientiae: Renaissance Garden Fountains*, Dum-

barton Oaks, 1979; Victor Carrabino, editor, *The Power of Myth in Literature and Film*, University Presses of Florida, 1980.

Work represented in anthologies, including *Stanford Short Stories, 1957*, edited by Richard Scowcroft and Wallace Stegner, Stanford University Press, 1958. Contributor to *Spenser Encyclopedia*. Contributor of articles and reviews to magazines, including *Shakespeare Studies, Southern Review, Film Comment, Arion, Studies in Philology*, and *Journal of the History of Ideas*.

WORK IN PROGRESS: Space and Place in Renaissance Romance; editing *Anthology of British Literature* with Donald Howard, Patricia Spacks, Spenser Hall, and others; *Yvor Winters*, for Twayne.

* * *

COMMINS, William Dollard, Sr.   1899-1983

OBITUARY NOTICE: Born December 7, 1899, in St. Stephen, New Brunswick, Canada; died of pneumonia, February 11, 1983, in Washington, D.C. Educator and author. After receiving his Ph.D. from Stanford University, Commins joined the faculty of Catholic University, where he remained as professor of psychology until his retirement as emeritus professor in 1969. He was a fellow of the American Psychological Association and the author of a textbook, *Principles of Educational Psychology*. Obituaries and other sources: *American Men and Women of Science: The Social and Behavioral Sciences*, 12th edition, Bowker, 1973; *Washington Post*, February 14, 1983.

* * *

CONKLIN, Barbara P.   1927-

PERSONAL: Born March 29, 1927, in Berwick, Pa.; daughter of Carl Frederick (a chiropractor) and Prudence Elmira (Thomas) Seyfried; married Robert Samuel Conklin (a public relations manager), October 20, 1945; children: Constance Riese, Catherine Ames, Barbara Fafard, Robert C., John, Thomas. *Education:* Attended Orange Coast College, 1965-66. *Politics:* Democrat. *Religion:* Protestant. *Residence:* Costa Mesa, Calif. *Agent:* Writers House, Inc., 21 West 26th St., New York, N.Y. 10010.

CAREER: Huntington Beach Police Department, Huntington Beach, Calif., records supervisor, 1966-82. Writer, 1965—. Member of Friends of the Library, Costa Mesa, Santa Ana, and Fullerton, Calif. *Member:* PEN, Romance Writers of America.

WRITINGS—Published by Bantam; for young adults: *P.S. I Love You*, 1981; *The Summer Jenny Fell in Love*, 1982; *Falling in Love Again*, 1982; *Summer Dreams*, 1983; *Tell Me That You Love Me*, 1983.

Editor and author of society column and serialized children's story, ''The Adventures of Lulubelle,'' for *Levittown Times*, 1952-56. Contributor of about sixty romance stories to *True Confessions* and *Modern Romances*, 1965-79.

WORK IN PROGRESS: Two novels for Bantam, including the sequel to *Falling in Love Again*.

SIDELIGHTS: In the early 1960's, Barbara Conklin worked during the day and wrote at night, when her children were asleep. She wrote purely for her own enjoyment, and she stashed her stories under the mattress. "It's the place to put them . . . when you're unsure of yourself," Conklin recalled to Dennis McLellan in the *Los Angeles Times*. "Then no one can laugh, and you're not hurt."

In 1965 Conklin signed up for a creative writing class at a local college and discovered that her stories were not laughable at all. In fact, by the end of the course, she had sold one romance for four hundred dollars to *Modern Romances*. Her writing teacher showed her how to study the confession story and learn the formula—and armed with that knowledge Conklin went on to sell sixty romance stories to popular magazines within the next fourteen years. The demand for her work was actually so insistent that it kept the author from writing anything else.

Yet when confession magazine editors started asking Conklin to reduce the ages of her characters so that they would appeal more to teenagers, the author decided it was time to write a romantic novel for young people. "I developed an itch to write a novel," Conklin reminisced to a reporter for the *Orange Coast College Alumni News*. "Romance stories don't last. People read a magazine, then toss it in the trash. I wanted to write novels that would be read, then placed on a shelf and read again. I wanted something that would outlast me."

Conklin's first novel, *P.S. I Love You*, was published in 1981 and, within a month, climbed to the number one spot on the national juvenile best-sellers list. The country's largest publisher of soft-cover books, Bantam, had chosen Conklin's novel to be one of its first "Sweet Dreams" stories, a new line created to capitalize on the popularity of paperback teenage romances. Still, the author took a chance with her theme in *P.S. I Love You*—she explores the unorthodox subject of death as her heroine's boyfriend dies of cancer. "[Teen romance novels are] supposed to be little upbeat books," Conklin explained to McLellan. But the author would like to examine taboo subjects in her books, like alcoholism, drug abuse, and teenage pregnancy, for those are the problems of young people today.

The idea for *P.S. I Love You* grew from Conklin's own experiences as a young woman when, at fifteen, her first boyfriend was killed in World War II. Then the author's father had insisted that eventually she would be able to cherish the memories of her dead lover and somehow learn to carry on. "He was right," Conklin revealed. "A year later I met Bob [her husband of thirty-six years] and realized that life *does* go on. That's how I wanted Mariah to feel about her experience with Paul, too [in *P.S. I Love You*]."

Conklin's subsequent romances have met with similar success. "A lot of people will wonder how you can think like a 16-year-old in a 54-year-old body," she told McLellan. Yet "I just don't think I've ever gone past the age of 16," she confessed to *Orange Coast Daily Pilot*'s Jodi Cadenhead, "even though I have [ten] grandchildren. It's the first time for a kiss, the first time to fall in love, the first time for so many things."

BIOGRAPHICAL/CRITICAL SOURCES: Orange Coast Daily Pilot, September 6, 1981; *Los Angeles Times*, October 14, 1981; *News Times/Lincoln County Leader*, October 20, 1982; *Orange Coast College Alumni News*, October, 1981.

* * *

CONNOR, Ralph
See GORDON, Charles William

CONRAD, Robert Arnold
See MOSS, Hart

* * *

CONSTANT, Alberta Wilson 1908-1981

OBITUARY NOTICE—See index for *CA* sketch: Born September 16, 1908, in Dalhart, Tex.; died in 1981 in Independence, Mo. Author. Constant served as educational director of Phi Eta National Sorority from 1938 to 1950 and as poetry editor of *Veterans' Voices*—a writing project for hospitalized veterans—from 1958 to 1970. She wrote the narrative material for Jack Kilpatrick's symphony "Oklahoma," commissioned for that state's fiftieth anniversary celebration. Constant also wrote a number of children's books, including *Doesn't Anybody Care About Lou Emma Miller?*, *Miss Charity Comes to Stay*, *Paintbox on the Frontier: The Life and Times of George Caleb Bingham*, and *Willie and the Wildcat Well*. Obituaries and other sources: *Authors of Books for Young People*, 2nd edition supplement, Scarecrow, 1979; *Horn Book*, December, 1981.

* * *

COOMBS, Charles Anthony 1918-1981

PERSONAL: Born April 9, 1918, in Newton, Mass.; died September 20, 1981, in Green Village, N.J.; married Ilona Harman (one source said Karman), April 5, 1945; children: Claire. *Education:* Harvard University, A.B., 1940, M.P.A. and M.A., both 1942, Ph.D., 1953.

CAREER: Federal Reserve Bank of New York, foreign exchange banker, 1946-59, senior vice-president in charge of foreign function, 1959-75; financial consultant and writer, 1975-81. Special manager of open market committee of national Federal Reserve System, financial adviser to American Mission to Greece, 1947; member of President's Task Force Promoting Foreign Investment in the United States, 1963. Member of board of directors of Discount Corp. of New York, American International Group, American Express International Banking Corp., First Chicago International Banking Corp., and Lehman Multi-Currency Assets Fund, Inc. *Military service:* U.S. Army, counterintelligence agent, 1942-44; served in the Middle East. *Awards, honors:* Distinguished service award from U.S. Treasury Department, 1968; commendation from Italian Government, 1975.

WRITINGS: The Arena of International Finance, Wiley, 1976. Contributor to magazines, including *Monthly Review*.

OBITUARIES: New York Times, September 21, 1981.*

* * *

COOPER-CLARK, Diana 1945-

PERSONAL: Born July 24, 1945, in Kingston, Jamaica; daughter of Horace Errington and Aileen Isabel (Courtney) Cooper; married Trevor William Clark (a writer), June 23, 1979. *Education:* York University, B.A., 1969, M.A., 1971, B.F.A., 1975; University of Toronto, B.E.D., 1972. *Home:* 56 Thorncliffe Park Dr., No. 104, Toronto, Ontario, Canada M4H 1K7. *Agent:* Nancy Colbert, 303 Davenport Rd., Toronto, Ontario, Canada M5R 1K5. *Office:* Atkinson College, York University, 4700 Keele St., Toronto, Ontario, Canada.

CAREER: Centennial College, Toronto, Ontario, teacher of English, 1969-72; York University, Toronto, course director of English and humanities, 1970—. *Member:* William Morris

Society, Wagner Society, 1890's Society, Crime Writers Association of Canada, William Morris Society of Canada (founding member).

WRITINGS: Designs of Darkness (nonfiction), Bowling Green University, 1983. Contributor to magazines, including *Atlantic Monthly, London Magazine, Canadian Literature, Commonweal,* and *Armchair Detective.*

WORK IN PROGRESS: The Pilgrim Travellers: Interviews With Contemporary Novelists; a novel; "Wasps, Wings, and Santiago Blues," a play, and "Art Under Suspicion," a screenplay, both with Barbara Brown; short stories.

SIDELIGHTS: Cooper-Clark wrote: "Like Beckett, I want to make a stain upon the silence. In fiction or in scholarly works, I'm a mind in motion, observing myself. As a white Jamaican living in Canada, I am less a citizen of the world and more a disembodied soul. I travel, read, think, feel, write, and, most of all, I try to make it through a day.

"I came to Canada because my parents emigrated. I won't return to Jamaica because, like other emigrants, I am neither fish nor fowl. Toronto is my home now. In 1972 I returned to Jamaica for three months to teach illiterate students who wanted to learn. There was much opposition for the obvious reason that it didn't suit the minority elite. Most of the people on the island were illiterate at the time, and obligatory education did not come into being until 1975.

"*Designs of Darkness* is a book of interviews with contemporary crime novelists. They are Ruth Rendell, P. D. James, Peter Lovesey, Jean Stubbs, Howard Engel, Ross Macdonald, Margaret Millar, Julian Symons, Janwillem Van de Wetering, Anne Perry, Amanda Cross, Patricia Highsmith, and Dick Francis. The *Pilgrim Travellers* is also a book of interviews with major contemporary novelists. They are Isaac Bashevis Singer, Margaret Drabble, Carlos Fuentes, Julio Cortazar, Nadine Gordimer, Elie Wiesel, Colin Wilson, Mary Gordon, Robertson Davies, Toni Morrison, Erica Jong, and Vasily Aksyonov. I wanted to do these books because I wanted to personally and professionally give order to the Tower of Babel that is contemporary literature.

"I wrote *Designs of Darkness* because I initially was ignorant about detective literature and I disliked my subliminal prejudice against the genre. When I was no longer ignorant, I couldn't find material about the writers I admired. So I interviewed them and wrote a critical introduction. My scholarly works and my fiction fulfill the creative energies I can best respond to. As far as literature is concerned, I feel that my talents lie in prose. I love its scope, its visceral texture, its flexibility, its enigma, its beauty, its ugliness, and its passion. My personal and aesthetic viewpoint is Janus-faced, yet it is the same. Win or lose, I will always write."

* * *

COPE, Oliver   1902-

BRIEF ENTRY: Born August 15, 1902, in Germantown, Pa. American surgeon, educator, and author. Cope served his internship and residency at Massachusetts General Hospital, then worked on the hospital's surgical staff from 1934 to 1969. He was a professor of surgery at Harvard University until 1969; in that year he was named professor emeritus. He was also chief of staff of the Shriners Burn Institute in Boston from 1964 to 1969. Cope wrote *Medical Education Reconsidered* (Lippincott, 1966), *Man, Mind, and Medicine: The Doctor's*

Education (Lippincott, 1968), and *The Breast: Its Problems, Benign and Malignant, and How to Deal With Them* (G. K. Hall, 1978). *Address:* 30 Windingwood Lane, Lincoln, Mass. 01773; and Massachusetts General Hospital, P.O. Box 100, Boston, Mass. 02114. *Biographical/critical sources: New York Times,* August 9, 1968; *American Men and Women of Science: The Physical and Biological Sciences,* 14th edition, Bowker, 1979.

* * *

CORNWALL, J. Spencer   1888(?)-1983

OBITUARY NOTICE: Born c. 1888; died February 26, 1983, in Salt Lake City, Utah. Conductor and author. Cornwall, conductor of the Mormon Tabernacle Choir from 1935 through 1957, wrote three books: *Fundamentals of Conducting, A Century of Singing,* and *Stories of Our Hymns.* Obituaries and other sources: *Washington Post,* March 2, 1983.

* * *

CORTAZZO, Carman   1936-

PERSONAL: Born April 11, 1936, in Turtle Creek, Pa.; son of Barney (a projectionist) and Dorothy Cortazzo. *Education:* American Academy of Dramatic Arts, drama degree, 1958. *Politics:* "None." *Religion:* Catholic. *Residence:* Turtle Creek, Pa. *Agent:* Bertha Klausner, 71 Park Ave., New York, N.Y. 10016.

CAREER: Actor and writer. Worked as laborer in steel mills and in construction, as beautician, bartender, trucker, janitor, and in other occupations.

WRITINGS: Nowhere to Go but Home (novel), Pinnacle Books, 1982. Also author of "Across the Creek" (three-act play), first produced in Pittsburgh, Pa., at Carnegie-Mellon University, 1960.

WORK IN PROGRESS: Obtaining publishers for three novels—*A Long Way From Turtle Creek, The Spaghetti Dreamer,* a children's story, and *The Cracker*—and a collection of short stories, *A View From the Projectionist Booth;* a novel about bars, *All the King's Whores and All the King's Men.*

SIDELIGHTS: Cortazzo's *Nowhere to Go But Home* concerns a budding novelist's disappointing return to his home town during the 1950's. A reviewer in the *Los Angeles Times Book Review* wrote, "By following the rules—sticking to what he knows and letting small, significant events unfold his tale—[Cortazzo] captures the harshness and disappointment of small-town life."

Cortazzo told *CA:* "Everything I know about writing and acting I learned in my father's projection booth—he read me Hemingway, Jack London, Ring Lardner, and others before I could read and taught me how to watch movies from a screenwriter's viewpoint.

"I write only about the 'little people'—the working man. They are the 'big' people to me. I did a stint as a doorman in an after-hours bar so as to write a novel (from a bouncer's point of view) about the 'lounge' world."

BIOGRAPHICAL/CRITICAL SOURCES: Los Angeles Times Book Review, August 1, 1982.

COULTER, Stephen 1914-
(James Mayo)

BRIEF ENTRY: British journalist and author. Coulter, who was a parliamentary correspondent for Reuters News Agency during the 1930's, served as one of General Dwight Eisenhower's staff officers at Allied headquarters during World War II. In 1945 he became staff correspondent in Paris for Kemsley Newspapers and remained with that organization for twenty years. Though best known for his novels of crime and intrigue, Coulter also writes historical fiction, including *Damned Shall Be Desire: The Loves of Guy de Maupassant* (J. Cape, 1958) and *The Devil Inside: A Novel of Dostoevsky's Life* (Doubleday, 1960). Under the pseudonym James Mayo, Coulter created secret agent Charles Hood, who was modeled after Ian Fleming's James Bond. Hood's escapades are featured in such spy novels as *Let Sleeping Girls Lie* (Heinemann, 1965) and *Sergeant Death* (Morrow, 1968). Coulter's other books include *The Loved Enemy* (Deutsch, 1962) and *The Chateau* (Simon & Schuster, 1974). *Biographical/critical sources: Times Literary Supplement,* May 22, 1969, December 25, 1970; *New York Times Book Review,* June 1, 1969; *Listener,* November 19, 1970; *Observer,* November 29, 1970, October 23, 1977; *Who's Who in Spy Fiction,* Elm Tree Books, 1977.

*   *   *

COURTNEY, Winifred F(isk) 1918-

PERSONAL: Born April 29, 1918, in Flushing, N.Y.; daughter of Charles Fisk (in business) and Cara (a suffragette; maiden name, Lane) Fisk; married Denis Courtney (former director of the Society of Motion Picture and Television Engineers), June 20, 1942; children: Jennifer L. Courtney Justice, Stephen D. *Education:* Attended Radcliffe College, 1936-39; Barnard College, B.A., 1941; State University of New York College at New Paltz, M.S., 1959. *Politics:* Democrat. *Religion:* Society of Friends. *Home:* 197 Cleveland Dr., Croton-on-Hudson, N.Y. 10520.

CAREER: Free-lance editor, 1941-42; New Zealand Supply Mission, Washington, D.C., statistical clerk, 1942; Indian Supply Mission, New York City, statistical clerk, 1942; Standard Oil of New Jersey, New York City, statistical clerk, 1942-43; nursery school teacher in Flushing, N.Y., 1950-54; elementary school teacher in public schools, Peekskill, N.Y., 1956-59; free-lance editor, 1959-62; Reader's Digest, New York City, copy editor, 1962-66, chief copy editor in Special Books, 1965-66; R. R. Bowker Co., New York City, editor of *Reader's Adviser,* 1966-71; full-time writer, 1971—. Volunteer observer for American Committee on Africa and Women's International League for Peace and Freedom, U.S. Section, on issues of African freedom at United Nations during the 1950's. Served for two years on Croton Democratic Committee during the 1960's. Served on board of managers of Oakwood School, Poughkeepsie, N.Y., 1972-77. *Member:* Authors Guild, Charles Lamb Society, Keats-Shelley Association.

WRITINGS: (Editor) *The Reader's Adviser: A Guide to the Best in Literature,* 11th edition, revised and enlarged, Bowker, 1968, 2nd volume published as *The Reader's Adviser: A Layman's Guide,* 1969; *Young Charles Lamb, 1775-1802,* New York University Press, 1982. Contributor to reference work, *British Literary Magazines,* Greenwood Press, 1983. Also contributor of articles and reviews to periodicals, including *Charles Lamb Bulletin, British Literary Magazines, Friends Journal,* and *Africa South.*

WORK IN PROGRESS: A sequel to *Young Charles Lamb,* covering the years between 1803 and the year of his death, 1834.

SIDELIGHTS: In *Young Charles Lamb, 1775-1802,* Courtney explores the early years of the English essayist: his museful boyhood, his commitment to his mentally-ill sister, his circle of literary friends. "The style," Richard Holmes noted in the *London Times,* "is that of a scrapbook rather than a fully-fashioned biography: beautifully researched and assembled, but not altogether narrated . . . lacking in depth and continuity perhaps, yet pearled with oddities as Lamb would have approved." The critic concluded that Courtney's study was a welcome volume, since much had come to light about the man of letters since E. V. Lucas's standard work on Lamb was published over seventy years ago.

Courtney told *CA:* "I have always read compulsively and longed to do books of my own, so commenced my working career with free-lance copyediting for several New York publishers and a poetry column for the *Saturday Review.* Marriage and a move to Washington, with the need to earn money when my English husband was drafted for World War II, stopped this project. I took what was available—jobs as a statistical clerk—not my metier. Children followed, and a stay in Germany with my husband, now a U.S. citizen and civilian with the U.S. Occupation.

"When we came home with young children, my teaching helped with buying the house in Croton in 1955. But I was happier at editing. Free-lance copyediting led to various publishing jobs, from which I resigned in 1971 (the children being educated and soon settled) for full-time writing. My publishing experience was a help in shaping a book of my own, arising from an adolescent interest in Keats and from John Livingston Lowes's course in Romanticism at Radcliffe.

"For many years I had cherished a small shelf of books by and about the Romantics (now a library). I arrived at Lamb from reading about him in the painter B. R. Haydon's autobiography and was determined to produce a book manuscript before my husband retired (1979) and to establish a regular writing/research schedule at home and the New York Public Library.

"This was hard going for the neophyte, but I loved reducing research to a readable account of a writer I admired and enjoyed delving into his period and into contemporary forces which shaped him—living in another world, as it were. New York University Press encouraged me from an early stage. We were now going to England regularly both for my husband's work and to see our daughter, who worked for London publishers, so it was possible to do some research on the spot, with the invaluable aid of the Charles Lamb Society. I sold the book to Macmillan Press (in London) myself; New York University Press then imported copies with its own title page.

"Much rewriting went into *Young Charles Lamb,* with professional advice from an editor friend. Cutting the manuscript by one hundred pages at the end improved the text; my husband was always a most helpful ally. Good reviews from three English dailies and all the important weeklies are an encouragement to a second volume.

"Persistence, a willingness to listen to constructive criticism, a consuming interest in one's subject and in saying something new about it, and just plain luck are perhaps the keys to publication—also finding others working close to your subject and being alert to new developments concerning it. Three visits to the Wordsworth Summer Conference at Grasmere put me in touch with leading Romantic scholars and provided wonderful walks in the English Lake District. Earlier, of course, I had always done much writing in volunteer work and written two unpublishable book manuscripts.

"With a good husband I've always been a liberated woman—i.e., very, very occupied, though not always at what I wanted most to do. I loved raising children and found the necessity to earn vastly broadening. (I've never written mainly for money—other occupations proved more immediately profitable.) I regret little except my own failings. I continue to look mainly ahead."

AVOCATIONAL INTERESTS: Reading, gardening, walking, painting, choral singing, grandchildren, friendships, world peace, travel (including England, Scotland, Wales, Frances, Switzerland, Belgium,, Holland, Italy, Iran, India, Sri Lanka, Nepal, U.S.S.R., Caribbean, Canada, Mexico, Guatemala, Honduras, Costa Rica, Bermuda).

BIOGRAPHICAL/CRITICAL SOURCES: London Daily Telegraph, July 19, 1982; *London Financial Times,* August 14, 1982; *London Times,* August 29, 1982, September 23, 1982; *Observer,* August 29, 1982; *London Review of Books,* October 21-November 3, 1982; *Times Literary Supplement,* November 26, 1982; *Ossining Citizen Register,* December 26, 1982.

*   *   *

COURY, Louise Andree   1895(?)-1983
(Louise Andree; Laura Andrews, Auntie Deb, Auntie Louise, Felicity Care, Mary H. Mortimer, Philippa Strange, pseudonyms)

OBITUARY NOTICE: Born c. 1895 in Liverpool, England; died May 17, 1983, in London, England. Editor, illustrator, and author. Coury, a writer and illustrator of children's books, was a former editor of *Queen* magazine and the founder of the Men and Women of Today Society, a literary club that flourished in London during the 1930's. Obituaries and other sources: *London Times,* May 24, 1983.

*   *   *

COUTTS, Frederick Lee   1899-

PERSONAL: Born September 21, 1899; married Bessie Lee, 1925 (died, 1967); married Olive Gatrall, 1969; children: Margaret Coutts Rogers, Molly Coutts West, John, Elizabeth Coutts Lawson. *Home:* 3 Dubrae Close, St. Albans AL3 4JT, England.

CAREER: Salvation Army, London, England, 1920-52, literary secretary to general, 1952, training principal at International Training College, 1953-57, territorial commander for Eastern Australia, 1957-63, general, 1963-69; writer, 1969—. *Awards, honors:* Commander of Order of the British Empire; D.D. from University of Aberdeen, 1981.

WRITINGS: He Had No Revolver, and Other Stories, Bannisdale Press, 1944; *Well Played!,* Salvationist Publications and Supplies, 1953; *Portrait of a Salvationist,* Salvationist Publications and Supplies, 1955; *The Call to Holiness,* Salvationist Publications and Supplies, 1957, reprinted, Salvationist, 1977; *The Better Fight: The Salvation Army, 1914-1976,* Salvationist, 1973; *No Discharge in This War,* Salvationist, 1975; *No Continuing City,* Salvationist, 1976; *Christ Is the Answer,* Salvationist, 1977; *Bread for My Neighbour,* Hodder & Stoughton, 1978; *In Good Company,* Salvationist, 1980; *Essentials*

of Christian Experience, Salvationist, 1980. Also author of *The Timeless Prophets,* 1944; *The Battle and the Breeze,* 1945, *Jesus and Our Need,* 1956, and *More Than One Homeland,* 1982.

*   *   *

COWLES, John, Sr.   1898-1983

OBITUARY NOTICE: Born December 14, 1898, in Algona, Iowa; died February 25, 1983, in Minneapolis, Minn. Journalist and newspaper publisher. After graduating from Harvard University and serving with the U.S. Army during World War I, Cowles began his career as a reporter for a Des Moines, Iowa, newspaper. In 1928 he was elected vice-president of the Associated Press and went on to serve as a director of the news-gathering organization for many years. Cowles bought the *Minneapolis Star* in 1934 and within six years made the paper a success. He also purchased its two competitors, the *Journal* and the *Tribune.* The journalist widened his newspaper empire over the next decade, acquiring several other dailies in Minnesota, North Dakota, South Dakota, and Wisconsin. An editorially active publisher, Cowles often sent his editors pages with errors circled in red grease pencil. He was named honorary president of Sigma Delta Chi, the journalism society, in 1954 and was the recipient of numerous honorary degrees. Obituaries and other sources: *New Republic,* December 1, 1947; *Current Biography,* Wilson, 1954, April, 1983; *Time,* December 8, 1958, March 7, 1983; *Harper's,* June, 1963; *Chicago Tribune,* February 26, 1983; *Los Angeles Times,* February 26, 1983; *Washington Post,* February 26, 1983; *New York Times,* February 26, 1983; *Newsweek,* March 7, 1983.

*   *   *

CRABBE, Buster
See CRABBE, Clarence Linden

*   *   *

CRABBE, Clarence Linden   1908-1983
(Buster Crabbe)

*OBITUARY NOTICE—*See index for *CA* sketch: Born February 7, 1908, in Oakland, Calif.; died of a heart attack, April 23, 1983, in Scottsdale, Ariz. Swimming champion, film actor, and author. During his competitive swimming career, Crabbe broke five world records and captured thirty-five national and sixteen international titles. In the 1928 Olympics at Amsterdam, he placed third in the 1,500-meter freestyle swim, and in the 1932 Olympics at Los Angeles, he won a gold medal in the 400-meter freestyle swim. Three days after Crabbe won the Olympic gold medal, Paramount Pictures selected him to star in "King of the Jungle." He went on to appear in more than one hundred seventy-five movies, including "Tarzan the Fearless," "Buck Rogers," and "Caged Fury." In later years he lectured on fitness and weight control. He wrote *Energistics* and *Buster Crabbe's Arthritis Exercise Book.* Obituaries and other sources: *Los Angeles Times,* April 24, 1983; *Washington Post,* April 24, 1983; *New York Times,* April 25, 1983; *Chicago Tribune,* April 25, 1983; *Time,* May 2, 1983.

*   *   *

CRAFTS, Kathy   1952-

PERSONAL: Born October 12, 1952, in Rome, N.Y.; daughter of Cliff (a disc jockey) and Eileen (a voice-over announcer;

maiden name, Scanlon) Crafts; married Robin McCaffrey, February 14, 1974 (divorced August 29, 1974); married Jamie Flynn, October 12, 1976 (divorced May, 1980); married David P. Trimble (an antinuclear lobbyist), June 10, 1981; children: Mike, Dudley, Casey, Harvey. *Education:* Barnard College, B.A. (summa cum laude), 1974; Columbia University, M.B.A., 1981. *Politics:* Democrat. *Religion:* Baha'i. *Home:* 149 Franklin St., New York, N.Y. 10013. *Agent:* Paul R. Reynolds, Inc., 12 East 41st St., New York, N.Y. 10017. *Office:* Wyse Advertising, 505 Park Ave., New York, N.Y. 10017.

CAREER: LNLIX-Radio, West Islip, N.Y., disc jockey, 1974-75; associated with Paul Weiss, Rifkind, Wharton & Garrison (law firm), New York City, 1975-79; Ogilvy & Mather (advertising agency), New York City, account executive, 1980-82; Wyse Advertising, New York City, copywriter, 1982—. *Member:* Lower Manhattan Democrats, Tribeca Restoration Society (president, 1976-83).

WRITINGS: (With Brenda Hauther) *Surviving the Undergraduate Jungle: The Student's Guide to Good Grades,* Grove, 1977; *How to Beat the System,* Grove, 1981.

WORK IN PROGRESS: In the Event Of, a nonfiction work about global devastation; *The IGBT,* a science fiction novel.

SIDELIGHTS: Kathy Crafts and Brenda Hauther provide tips for getting an undergraduate education, complete with advice on how best to choose professors, write last-minute term papers, and even cheat, in their book *Surviving the Undergraduate Jungle: The Student's Guide to Good Grades.* "It is a bittersweet book that combines the authors' unrelenting cynicism about the system with some rather rueful amusement at the many ways it can be beaten," Merrill Sheils wrote in *Newsweek.* And Sheils added: "Many academics, parents and students will certainly resent the book's wheeler-dealer approach to college. But as Crafts and Hauther see it, clever students have been playing by pretty much these same cavalier rules for generations. So long as grades are crucial to a student's admission to graduate school and jobs, they see no reason why everyone shouldn't be coached on tried and true ways to get good ones."

Crafts told *CA:* "Right now, in addition to doing my own sort of writing, I write television commercials. It's a very different type of writing, writing to specs—working precisely and packing it all into thirty seconds—but it's a lot of fun. And you know ten times more people have already seen my commercials than will ever read my books. Sad but true. It makes you wish they ran credits with commercials."

BIOGRAPHICAL/CRITICAL SOURCES: Newsweek, January 17, 1977.

*   *   *

CRANE, Stephen (Townley)   1871-1900
(Johnston Smith)

BRIEF ENTRY: Born November 1, 1871, in Newark, N.J.; died of tuberculosis, June 5, 1900, in Badenweiler, Germany (now West Germany); buried in Hillside, N.J. American historian, journalist, poet, and author of short stories and novels. Crane is regarded by many critics as one of American literature's most fascinating figures. Renouncing the Methodist teachings of his clergyman father, Crane led a profligate and exhausting life. At twenty-one he obtained a position with the *New York Herald* and began stalking the beggars and whores

of the Bowery in search of stories. Crane vividly recreated the squalor of the Bowery and the plight of its denizens in his first novel, *Maggie: A Girl of the Streets* (written under pseudonym Johnston Smith; 1893), a work which failed to impress its few readers. He then focused his attention on rendering the confusion and horror of the Civil War in his novel *The Red Badge of Courage* (1895), a saga whose intense portrayal of emotional conflict and suffering established it in the pantheon of American classics. Two more novels, *George's Mother* (1897) and *The Third Violet* (1897), appeared while Crane was in Europe reporting on the Greco-Turkish War for the *New York Journal.* Crane's story "The Open Boat" (1898), which was based on the author's experiences while shipwrecked on an expedition to Cuba, is ranked with America's finest short works. Crane at last settled in England and began devoting his attention to horsemanship and sharpshooting, possibly to dispel rumors that he had become both an alcoholic and a drug addict. Within two years he fell seriously ill with tuberculosis. He died in the spring of 1900 while traveling through Germany's Black Forest in search of a cure. *Biographical/critical sources: Cassell's Encyclopaedia of World Literature,* revised edition, Morrow, 1973; *The McGraw-Hill Encyclopedia of World Biography,* McGraw, 1973; *Twentieth-Century Literary Criticism,* Volume 11, Gale, 1983.

*   *   *

CRAWFORD, Charles F.   ?-1983

OBITUARY NOTICE: Died March 4, 1983, in Harbor City, Calif. Journalist. Crawford was a reporter for the *Los Angeles Times* from 1942 to 1969. He covered the harbor areas of Los Angeles and Long Beach. Obituaries and other sources: *Los Angeles Times,* March 5, 1983.

*   *   *

CRAWLEY, C(harles) W(illiam)   1899-

PERSONAL: Born April 1, 1899, in London, England; son of Charles (a barrister) and Augusta (Butcher) Crawley; married Kathleen Elizabeth Leahy, July 2, 1930 (deceased, 1982); children: Mary, John, Thomas, Philip, William. *Education:* Trinity College, Cambridge, M.A., 1925. *Home:* 1 Madingley Rd., Cambridge, England.

CAREER: Cambridge University, Cambridge, England, fellow of Trinity Hall, 1924-66, emeritus fellow, 1966—, honorary fellow, 1971—, assistant tutor, 1929-40, acting senior tutor, 1940-45, senior tutor, 1945-58, vice-master, 1950-66, lecturer in history, 1931-66, past member of council of New Hall, chairman of trustees of Lucy Cavendish College, 1970-78. *Military service:* British Army, 1917-18. *Member:* Royal Historical Society (fellow), Athenaeum Club.

WRITINGS: The Question of Greek Independence: A Study of British Policy in the Near East, 1821-1833, Cambridge University Press, 1930, reprinted, Fertig, 1972; (editor) *New Cambridge Modern History,* Volume IX, *War and Peace in an Age of Upheaval, 1793-1830,* Cambridge University Press, 1965; *John Capodistrias: Some Unpublished Documents,* Balkan, 1970; *Trinity Hall: The History of a Cambridge College, 1350-1975,* Trinity Hall, Cambridge University, 1976. Contributor to history journals.

SIDELIGHTS: Crawley told *CA:* "Being, on my mother's side, of an Anglo-Irish family, and having had some cousins gunrunning for both sides (the Irish Volunteers of Redmond and

Carsons Ulster) in the summer of 1914, I wanted after 1918 to ask myself how this and other national conflicts came about. It was for that reason that I switched at Cambridge from Classics to history. The theme of modern Greece was suggested by one of my teachers.

"A problem which has much interested me is that of the difference between a spontaneous sense of *nationality*, based partly on 'race,' but more on language, religion, and dislike of partly alien rulers on one hand, and on the other hand a doctrine or secular creed of *nationalism*, usually becoming aggressive and sometimes fanatical. What I have taught or written has been largely to satisfy myself in pursuit of this problem, but I doubt whether it has achieved anything.

"The unpublished documents I chose for *John Capodistrias* were selected from his papers in Corfu and were thought sufficiently useful to specialists by the Greek Institute for Balkan Studies for them to publish without any payment by or to myself. They illustrate the way in which a man with an almost eighteenth century non-national diplomatic career, speaking and writing in French and Italian (and serving the czar of Russia until he seemed to be leaning too much to the Greek hopes of his Confoit countrymen), could become the first president of semi-independent Greece (pending the protecting powers of a king for an independent Greece). Hence the resentment of the Warriors of the War. At one time I thought of attempting a biography of him but had no opportunity to work in the Greek state archives."

*   *   *

CRIBB, Larry   1934-

PERSONAL: Born November 28, 1934, in Georgetown, S.C.; son of Rufus Jackson and Ruby (Harmon) Cribb; married Joyce Wolfe (a teacher), August 11, 1958; children: Sharon Ruth, Laura Elaine. *Education:* University of South Carolina, B.A., 1957. *Religion:* Methodist. *Home:* 1900 Elm Abode Ter., Columbia, S.C. 29210. *Office:* South Carolina Electric Cooperative Association, 808 Knox Abbott Dr., Cayce, S.C. 29033.

CAREER: Gallery Photo Studio, Columbia, S.C., owner, 1967-77; *Carolina Outdoors*, Columbia, editor and publisher, 1975-79; *Living in South Carolina*, Cayce, S.C., editor, 1979—. Editor of *St. Andrews News*, 1967-72. Lecturer in photography. Consultant to South Carolina Mental Health Commission. *Military service:* U.S. Navy, 1957-58; became lieutenant junior grade. *Member:* Outdoor Writers Association of America, National Press Club, National Electric Cooperative Editors Association, Southeastern Outdoor Press Association, South Carolina Press Association, South Carolina Press Photographers Association, Cooperative Editorial Association.

WRITINGS: How You Can Make Twenty-Five Thousand Dollars a Year With Your Camera (No Matter Where You Live), Writer's Digest, 1981. Author of a column for a weekly newspaper.

SIDELIGHTS: Cribb told *CA*: "I began a career in photojournalism at the age of fifteen, and have been working at it in one form or another since that time. I have found that all the positions I have held, including work in public relations, depended on having a good background in writing."

*   *   *

CRIGHTON, Richard E.   1921-

PERSONAL: Born August 19, 1921, in Twickenham, England;

son of Arthur Edward (an engineer) and Louisette (Lefebvre) Crighton; married Keitha Mary McDermott (an artist), December 5, 1953; children: Timothy, Andrew, Nicola. *Education:* Clare College, Cambridge, M.A., 1941. *Home:* 329 St. John St., Fredericton, New Brunswick, Canada E3B 4B5. *Agent:* Dominick Abel Literary Agency, Inc., 498 West End Ave., No. 12C, New York, N.Y. 10024. *Office:* Community Improvement Corporation, P.O. Box 428, Fredericton, New Brunswick, Canada E3B 5R4.

CAREER: Barrister-at-law in London, England, 1946-48; Fina Petroleum Ltd., London, assistant to general manager and fuel oil sales manager, 1948-50; Colgate-Palmolive Co., London, assistant to president and creator of Institutional Division, 1950-52; Imperial Oil Ltd., Toronto, Ontario, district manager in Sherbrooke, Ontario, 1952-53, and Hamilton, Ontario, 1953-54; Canadian Petrofina Ltd., Montreal, Quebec, division manager, 1954-56; BP Oil Ltd., Montreal, general sales manager and creator of Marketing Division, 1956-64; Collyer Advertising Ltd., Montreal, vice-president, group supervisor, director of research, and director of new business, 1964-66; McConnell Advertising Ltd., Montreal, vice-president and group supervisor, 1966-70; Bombardier Ltd., Valcourt [Canada], vice-president for marketing, 1970-76; Community Improvement Corp., Fredericton, New Brunswick, director of program coordination, 1976-81; New Brunswick Bicentennial Commission, Fredricton, program director, 1981—. *Military service:* Royal Naval Volunteer Reserve, Intelligence, 1942-46; served in Mediterranean theater; became lieutenant. *Member:* Authors Guild.

WRITINGS: The Million Dollar Lift (suspense novel), Avon, 1981; *Red for Terror* (suspense novel), Dodd, 1982.

WORK IN PROGRESS: A book on bureaucracy.

SIDELIGHTS: Crighton told *CA*: "*The Million Dollar Lift* is a thriller about the hijacking of a gondola ski lift in Lake Tahoe. During my equipment marketing days, when I was selling ski hill grooming vehicles, I got an intimate insight into the ski resort business. I used this knowledge to add to my book an authentic inside look at the workings of a major ski area.

"*Red for Terror* is a thriller which concerns an international hostage incident involving Italy's infamous Red Brigade terrorists. The plot follows the desperate efforts of police, politicians, and the hostages themselves to contrive an escape from the terrorists. Maurice Tugwell, of the University of New Brunswick Conflict Centre, supplied expert advice on the sinister mentality and the internal structure of Europe's most lethal terrorist organization."

Crighton added: "I planned to be an author ever since I was fifteen, but I didn't want to be a penniless one. So I got a few careers under my belt first. Now I prefer to be referred to as a novelist (rather than a writer). Too many people launching a writing career are overly concerned about language perfection. They get fascinated with their own ability to manipulate words. The real skills that an aspiring author must master are plot structure, pace, tension, and character portrayal. I see my role as that of an entertainer. A writer must have a clear picture of the reader in mind, and must present the tale in language that makes the reader comfortable.

"I get along just fine with my editors and accept gladly much of their advice. I have marketed a lot of products. I never knew one where the designer's original concept couldn't be improved by subjecting it to informed criticism."

CRISP, Quentin   1908(?)-

BRIEF ENTRY: Born c. 1908 in England. British artist, model, journalist, poet, and author. For much of his life Quentin Crisp, a well-known homosexual, has been "obsessed with projecting such a flamboyantly effeminate image that even other homosexuals [have] recoiled in rage," observed Alix Nelson in the *New York Times Book Review.* Crisp's autobiography, *The Naked Civil Servant* (J. Cape, 1968), served as the basis of an award-winning television documentary and brought the eccentric author to the attention of American audiences. *The Naked Civil Servant* is marked by Crisp's brilliant wit, Nelson noted, and its author is a "one-man Theater of the Absurd." In her review of Crisp's *How to Have a Life-style* (Cecil Woolf, 1975) for the *New York Times Book Review,* Doris Grumbach wrote: "[Crisp] is his own best advertisement, and his book is another witty, aphoristic, outrageous and often very acute description of Quentin Crisp." Other works by Crisp include *Love Made Easy* (Duckworth, 1977), *Chog: A Gothic Fable* (Methuen, 1980), and *How to Become a Virgin* (St. Martin's, 1982). *Biographical/critical sources: New York Times Book Review,* September 18, 1977, February 3, 1980; *Washington Post Book World,* February 17, 1980, February 14, 1982; *Time,* January 25, 1982.

*   *   *

CROCKETT, Christina
See GRAY, Linda Crockett

*   *   *

CROFTON, Denis Hayes   1908-

PERSONAL: Born December 14, 1908, in Hong Kong; son of Richard Hayes and Mabel Annie (Smith) Crofton; married Alison Carr McClure, October 18, 1933; children: Philip, Margaret (Mrs. Peter Lehman Bedford), Richard, Stephen. *Education:* Corpus Christi College, Oxford, B.A., 1931, M.A., 1961. *Home:* Tilebarn House, 147 Hadlow Rd., Tonbridge, Kent, England.

CAREER: Indian Civil Service, 1934-47, subdivisional officer in Giridih, 1934, and in Jamshedpur, 1935, under secretary of provincial government of Bihar, 1936-38, and of government of India, 1939-41, private secretary to Indian member of Eastern Group Supply Council, 1941-42, district officer in Shahabad, Bihar, 1944-47, secretary to the governor of Bihar, 1944-47; United Kingdom Civil Service, 1948-68, assistant secretary of Petroleum Division and chairman of oil committee of Organization for European Economic Cooperation in Paris, France, 1950-53, assistant secretary of Monopolies and Restrictive Practices Commission, 1953-56, assistant secretary of Electricity Division in Ministry of Power, 1956-61, and in Petroleum Division, 1961-62, accountant-general and under secretary for finance in Ministry of Power, 1962-68; Department of the Environment, London, England, member of Panel of Inspectors, 1969-79; writer, 1979—. *Member:* Royal Commonwealth Society. *Awards, honors:* Member of Order of the British Empire, 1943, Officer of Order of the British Empire, 1948.

WRITINGS: The Children of Edmondstown Park: Memoirs of an Irish Family, Volturna Press, 1981; (editor) Francis Maylett Smith, *The Surgery at Aberffrwd: Some Encounters of a Colliery Doctor Seventy Years Ago,* Volturna Press, 1982; (editor)

Francis Maylett Smith, *A G.P.'s Progress to the Black Country,* Volturna Press, in press.

SIDELIGHTS: Crofton told *CA:* "*The Children of Edmondstown Park* is the story of a Protestant family from Dublin—that of my great-grandfather William Armstrong Hayes and his wife Elizabeth Carlile, a Presbyterian from County Cavan, Northern Ireland, their predecessors, and successors. Having inherited and had access to an accumulation of letters, notebooks, diaries and reminiscences, as well as many Victorian and Edwardian photographs, I have tried to piece together a coherent family portrait of four generations from Georgian times to the end of the Second World War, touching upon individual enthusiasms, antipathies, romances, and occasional eccentricities. The book includes about sixty illustrations.

"*The Surgery at Aberffrwd* I have edited from the papers of my English uncle, Francis Maylett Smith (1877-1945). They contain the lively reminiscences of a young doctor in the South Wales coalfield in the years from 1908 to 1915, with a number of intimate portraits of members of the mining community. *A G.P.'s Progress to the Black Country* is likewise a memoir, which I have edited from my uncle's papers, about the rest of his medical life.

"In 1916 he bought an industrial practice in the Black Country near Birmingham, England, from which he retired in 1933. In the early days of the Second World War he volunteered for service and worked as an assistant to a doctor in Shropshire until his death from heart failure in January, 1945. These two books of Dr. Smith's reminiscences seemed to me to be of interest in shedding some light on general medical practice in the industrial parts of Britain in the first half of the present century before the National Health Service came into being in July, 1948."

*   *   *

CROUCH, Steve   1915-1983

OBITUARY NOTICE—See index for *CA* sketch: Born February 25, 1915, in Anson, Tex.; died of natural causes, May 1, 1983, in Carmel, Calif. Photographer and author. Crouch published several collections of photography, each accompanied by his own text. Among them are *Steinbeck Country,* which earned him a silver medal from the Commonwealth Club of California, *Desert Country,* and *Fog and Sun, Sea and Stone: The Monterey Coast.* In addition, he served as field instructor in photography at the University of California, Santa Cruz. Obituaries and other sources: *Chicago Tribune,* May 6, 1983.

*   *   *

CROWELL, Robert Leland   1909-

PERSONAL: Born May 11, 1909, in Montclair, N.J.; son of Thomas Irving (a publisher) and Minnie Helen (Leland) Crowell; married Ruth Brown Shurtleff, December 23, 1938 (divorced, 1966); married Muriel B. Hutchinson (a writer and artist), December 19, 1967; children: (first marriage) John Leland, Timothy Adams, Benjamin Shurtleff (deceased). *Education:* Yale University, A.B., 1931. *Politics:* Independent. *Religion:* Society of Friends (Quakers). *Home address:* P.O. Box 92, Newfane, Vt. 05345.

CAREER: Thomas Y. Crowell Co. (publisher), New York, N.Y., sales manager, 1933-37, president, 1937-72, treasurer, 1937-60, chairman of board of directors, 1960-68, principal executive officer, 1968-72, member of board of directors, 1972-

74; writer, 1974—. Member of board of directors of Franklin Publications, 1952-63, treasurer, 1958-63; member of board of directors of Dun-Donnelley Corp., 1972-74; member of board of governors of Yale University Press, 1952-67; past member of board of trustees of Brattleboro Museum and Art Center and Marlboro College. U.S. State Department lecturer in India, 1957; member of U.S. Information Agency advisory committee on books abroad, 1952-63.

MEMBER: American Civil Liberties Union (past member of board of directors), American Schools of Oriental Research (past member of board of directors), American Book Publishers Council (past member of board of directors), Archaeological Institute of America (past member of board of directors), Moore Free Library Association (member of board of trustees), Century Association. *Awards, honors:* Grant from U.S. State Department, 1957.

WRITINGS: The Lore and Legends of Flowers, Crowell, 1982.

WORK IN PROGRESS: "A book on the thirteenth century that embodies a new approach, which I call horizontal history."

SIDELIGHTS: Crowell told *CA:* "I am fascinated by facts (and 'false facts'). My aim is to write informatively, interestingly—and very concisely. I like foreign travel, dabbling in languages, and gardening. Therefore, much of the lore and information in my book came from Mexico and other countries, from research in a variety of languages (ancient and modern), and, of course, from my own flower gardens."

* * *

CUFF, Robert Dennis 1941-

BRIEF ENTRY: Born May 2, 1941, in Peterborough, Ontario, Canada. Canadian historian, educator, and author. Cuff, who received a Newcomen Award in 1970, has taught at Princeton University and University of Rochester. He joined the faculty of York University in 1969 and became a professor of modern American history in 1978. Cuff wrote *The War Industries Board: Business-Government Relations During World War I* (Johns Hopkins University Press, 1973) and co-authored *Canadian-American Relations in Wartime: From the Great War to the Cold War* (Hakkert, 1975) and *American Dollars, Canadian Prosperity: Canadian-American Economic Relations, 1945-1950* (Samuel-Stevens, 1978). He co-edited *War and Society in North America* (Thomas Nelson, 1971) and *Enterprise and National Development: Essays in Canadian Business and Economic History* (Hakkert, 1973). *Address:* Department of History, York University, 4700 Keele St., Downsview, Ontario, Canada M3J 1P3. *Biographical/critical sources: American Historical Review,* December, 1973, June, 1976, February, 1980.

* * *

CURRAN, Samuel (Crowe) 1912-

PERSONAL: Born May 23, 1912, in Ballymena, Northern Ireland; son of John Hamilton and Sarah Owen (Crowe) Curran; married Joan Elizabeth Strothers, November 7, 1940; children: Sheena, John, Charles, James. *Education:* University of Glasgow, M.A., 1933, B.Sc., 1934, Ph.D., 1937, D.Sc., 1950; St. John's College, Cambridge, Ph.D., 1939. *Religion:* Presbyterian. *Home:* 93 Kelvin Court, Glasgow G12 0AH, Scotland. *Office:* McCance Building, University of Strathclyde, Richmond St., Glasgow G1 1XQ, Scotland.

CAREER: Affiliated with Royal Aircraft Establishment in England, 1939-40, Ministry of Aircraft Production, 1940-42, and

Ministry of Supply, 1942-44; University of California, Berkeley, associated with Manhattan Project, 1944-45; University of Glasgow, Glasgow, Scotland, senior lecturer in natural philosophy, 1945-55; United Kingdom Atomic Energy Authority, board member of Atomic Weapons Research Establishment and Harwell, 1956-59; Atomic Weapons Research Establishment, Aldermaston, England, chief scientist, 1958-59; Royal College of Science and Technology, Glasgow, principal, 1959-64; University of Strathclyde, Glasgow, principal and vice-chancellor, 1964-80; Glasgow University, Glasgow, professor of energy studies, 1980—. Chief scientific adviser for civil defense to secretary of state for Scotland; chairman of Advisory Committee on Medical Research; member of Oil Development Council of Scotland; deputy chairman of Electricity Council and chairman of Electricity Supply Research Council. Freeman and deputy lieutenant of county, for city of Glasgow. Member of Council for Scientific and Industrial Research, 1962-65, Science Research Council, 1965-68, and Scottish Economic Planning Council, 1965-68; chairman of Advisory Board on Relations with Universities, of Ministry of Technology, 1966-71. Member of board of directors and chairman of Nuclear Structures Ltd. and Scottish Television Ltd. Consultant to Atomic Energy Authority.

MEMBER: Royal Society (fellow), Institute of Energy (fellow), Physical Society (fellow), Scottish Society for the Mentally Handicapped (president), Royal Society of Edinburgh (fellow), Saltire Society (honorary president), St. Andrew Society of Glasgow (president). *Awards, honors:* Commander of St. Olaf (Norway), 1966; named freeman of Motherwell and Wishaw, 1966; honorary degrees from University of Glasgow, 1968, University of Aberdeen, 1971, University of Lodz, 1973, University of Strathclyde, 1980, and Technical University of Nova Scotia, 1982; created Knight Bachelor, 1970; St. Mungo Prize from Council of City of Glasgow, 1976; commander of Order of the Polish People's Republic, 1976.

WRITINGS: (With J. D. Craggs) *Counting Tubes,* Academic Press, 1949; *Luminescence and the Scintillation Counter,* Academic Press, 1953; *Alpha, Beta, and Gamma Ray Spectroscopy,* Academic Press, 1964; *Energy Resources and the Environment,* Scottish Academic Press, 1976; (with son, J. S. Curran) *Energy and Human Needs,* Scottish Academic Press, 1979; *Fuelling the Future,* Scottish Review Press, 1982.

WORK IN PROGRESS: Technological Education in Scotland and *Science in the Twentieth Century,* publication expected in 1983.

SIDELIGHTS: Sir Samuel commented: "I have a great interest in university-level education, particularly in science and technology, in a wide variety of countries, including Poland, Nigeria, and Malaysia. I am always anxious to do all I can to convince scientists that they must speak and write well to convey their ideas effectively to the general public and to decision-makers. Much of our difficulty in modern society springs from a divorce of advanced science from the public scene. The gap has to be bridged."

* * *

CURREY, R(onald) F(airbridge) 1894-1983

*OBITUARY NOTICE—*See index for CA sketch: Born October 23, 1894, in London, England; died May 13, 1983, in South Africa. Educator and author. Currey was headmaster at a number of schools in Africa, including St. Andrews College in Grahamstown, South Africa, where he served from 1939 to

1955. In 1962 he joined the faculty of Rhodes University in Grahamstown, where he lectured in classics until 1968. His history of that university's first sixty-six years, *Rhodes University, 1904-1970,* was published in 1970. Obituaries and other sources: *London Times,* May 16, 1983.

*   *   *

CURTIS, Gerald   1904-1983

OBITUARY NOTICE: Born in 1904 in Ootacamund, India; died February 14, 1983. Civil servant, historian, and author. Curtis worked as a political agent for the Indian Civil Service in the warring Pakistani province of South Waziristan for several years, and while stationed there he wrote a monograph on the area's Mahsud leaders. After moving to England in 1947, he became active in the county government of Essex, serving as the high sheriff in 1973. As a member of the County Council's landscape, conservation, and planning committees from 1968 through 1977, Curtis worked to preserve the historical legacy of the area. He related the history of two Essex parishes in *The Story of the Sampfords.* Obituaries and other sources: *London Times,* March 11, 1983.

*   *   *

CURTIS, Philip (Delacourt)   1920-

PERSONAL: Born June 23, 1920, in Westcliff, England; son of Harold (a headmaster) and Pauline (a teacher; maiden name, Saundes) Curtis; married Elsa Schroer; children: John, Elizabeth. *Education:* Attended Eastbourne Training College for Teachers, 1948-49. *Home:* 224 Station Rd., Leigh-on-Sea, Essex SS9 3BS, England.

CAREER: Worked as teacher until 1968, deputy headmaster, 1968-81, and headmaster, 1981—. *Member:* Society of Authors.

WRITINGS—For children: *Mr. Browser and the Brain Sharpeners,* illustrated by Tony Ross, Andersen Press, 1979, published as *Invasion of the Brain Sharpeners,* Knopf, 1981; *Mr. Browser Meets the Burrowers,* illustrated by Ross, Andersen Press, 1980, published as *Invasion From Below the Earth,* Knopf, 1981; *Mr. Browser and the Comet Crisis,* Andersen Press, 1981; *The Revenge of the Brain Sharpeners,* Andersen Press, 1982.

Contributor of short stories, plays, and articles to British magazines.

WORK IN PROGRESS: Another "Brain Sharpener" book; a collection of stories for children.

SIDELIGHTS: Curtis wrote: "My books have arisen, I hope, from a desire, as a teacher, to represent a realistic view of school life, mixed with fantasy and influenced, perhaps, by admiration of various writers of humor. I have traveled in India and Pakistan (which provided background for *Revenge of the Brain Sharpeners*) and Europe."

BIOGRAPHICAL/CRITICAL SOURCES: Listener, November 8, 1979; *Observer,* March 1, 1981; *Times Educational Supplement,* May 22, 1981; *Times Literary Supplement,* November 20, 1981.

D

DANBY, John B(lench) 1905-1983

OBITUARY NOTICE: Born June 3, 1905, in North Riding, Yorkshire, England; died April 24, 1983, in Paterson, N.J. Editor. Before serving as managing editor of *Good Housekeeping* magazine from 1960 to 1972, Danby worked as news editor of the *Wilmington Evening Journal,* assistant national news editor of the *New York Herald Tribune,* editor of *Liberty* magazine, and executive editor of *Redbook.* A polio victim, Danby was chairman of the magazine committee of the President's Committee on Employment of the Physically Handicapped. Obituaries and other sources: *Who's Who in America,* 39th edition, Marquis, 1976; *New York Times,* April 26, 1983.

*   *   *

DANIELS, Draper 1913-1983

OBITUARY NOTICE—See index for *CA* sketch: Born August 12, 1913, in Morris, N.Y.; died May 7, 1983, in Naples, Fla. Advertising executive and author. Daniels began his career in advertising in 1935, when he joined Vick Chemical Company in New York City. He went on to serve with a number of other agencies, including Young and Rubicam in New York City and Leo Burnett Company in Chicago. In 1963 President John F. Kennedy named Daniels to the post of national export expansion coordinator for the Department of Commerce. In 1965 the advertising executive established Draper Daniels, Incorporated, where he served as chairman of the board and chief executive officer until his retirement. He was the author of *Giants, Pigmies, and Other Advertising People.* He also contributed numerous articles on advertising to various periodicals. Obituaries and other sources: *Chicago Tribune,* May 12, 1983.

*   *   *

D'ARCY, Jean (Marie) 1913-1983

OBITUARY NOTICE: Born June 10, 1913, in Versailles, France; died of a heart attack, January 19, 1983, in Paris, France. Communications executive and author. D'Arcy served as technical adviser to France's minister of information in 1948, directed programming for the nation's government-run television and radio network throughout the 1950's, and worked as the network's director of international relations for two years before moving to New York City to work as director of the United Nations radio and television service in 1961. He returned to France in 1971 and founded Multivision, a cable television company. D'Arcy wrote *The Right of Man to Communicate.* Obituaries and other sources: *Who's Who in the World,* 4th edition, Marquis, 1978; *New York Times,* February 27, 1983.

*   *   *

DAVEY, Frank 1907(?)-1983

OBITUARY NOTICE: Born c. 1907; died March 24, 1983. Physician, missionary, editor, and author. After receiving his medical training at Manchester University and training for the ministry at Hartley Victoria College, Day went to Nigeria, where from 1939 to 1959 he served as director of the Methodist Leprosy Settlement in Uzuakoli. He returned to England in 1959 and worked as medical secretary for the Methodist Missionary Society until 1968. Davey then became director of the Victoria Leprosy Hospital in Dichpalli, India, where he worked for five years before retiring from field work to edit *Leprosy Review.* He wrote *A Medical Te Deum,* a collection of prayers in the Ibo language. Davey also wrote *Leprosy in Theory and Practice* with R. G. Cochrane. Obituaries and other sources: *London Times,* March 31, 1983.

*   *   *

DAVIES, David Michael 1929-

BRIEF ENTRY: Born October 5, 1929, in Stroud, Gloucestershire, England. British human ecologist, anthropologist, educator, and author. Davies, who taught at Chulalongkorn University during the 1950's, has been a professor of anthropology at University of London's University College Hospital Medical School since 1963. His books include *The Rice Bowl of Asia* (R. Hale, 1967), *Journey Into the Stone Age* (R. Hale, 1969), *The Influence of Teeth, Diet, and Habits on the Human Face* (Heinemann, 1972), *A Dictionary of Anthropology* (F. Muller, 1972), *The Last of the Tasmanians* (F. Muller, 1973), and *The Centenarians of the Andes* (Barrie & Jenkins, 1975). *Biographical/critical sources: International Authors and Writers Who's Who,* 8th edition, Melrose, 1977.

*   *   *

DAVIS, Gilbert 1899-1983

OBITUARY NOTICE: Born May 9, 1899, in Johannesburg,

South Africa; died in 1983 in Montreux, Switzerland. Actor, journalist, and playwright. After graduating from Oxford University and serving with the British Army in France during World War I, Davis embarked on an acting career in 1921. He appeared in such plays as "The Lost Hat" and Luigi Pirandello's "Six Characters in Search of an Author" before leaving the theatre to work as a journalist. Davis wrote two plays, "Young Shoulders" and "Three's Company," during his eight-year absence from the stage, then returned to acting full time in 1931. He was a featured player in several West End productions and also appeared in a number of films. Obituaries and other sources: *Who Was Who in the Theatre, 1912-1976*, Gale, 1978; *London Times*, March 9, 1983.

*   *   *

DAY, Melvin Norman   1923-

PERSONAL: Born June 30, 1923, in Hamilton, New Zealand; son of Norman Darcy and Cora May (Melvin) Day; married Oroya McAuley (an art historian and part-time university lecturer), 1952. *Education:* University of New Zealand, B.A., 1960; Courtauld Institute of Art, London, B.A. (with honors), 1966; University of London, M.Phil., 1976. *Home:* 6 Pinelands Ave., Seatoun, Wellington 3, New Zealand. *Office:* Department of Internal Affairs, Wellington, New Zealand.

CAREER: Teacher at primary and secondary schools in New Zealand, 1945-63; lecturer in art history at London University Extension at Walthamstow School of Art, London, England, and Epsom School of Art, Surrey, England, 1964-68; National Art Gallery of New Zealand, Wellington, director, 1968-78; Department of Internal Affairs, Wellington, government art historian, 1978—. *Military service:* New Zealand Army, 1941-43. Royal New Zealand Air Force, 1944-45. *Member:* Royal Society of Arts (fellow), Association of Art Historians.

WRITINGS: Nicholas Chevalier: Artist, Milkwood Press, 1981. Contributor to art journals, newspapers, and catalogues for National Art Gallery of New Zealand.

WORK IN PROGRESS: Research on New Zealand painting in the nineteenth century and in the 1930's and 1940's.

SIDELIGHTS: Day told *CA:* "I have practiced as a painter for over thirty years and have exhibited work in a number of countries other than New Zealand."

BIOGRAPHICAL/CRITICAL SOURCES: Art International, Volume XIX, number 2, 1975; *Debrett's Handbook of Australia and New Zealand*, Debrett's Peerage, 1982.

*   *   *

DEAKIN, Rose   1937-

PERSONAL: Born November 4, 1937, in London, England; daughter of Lord Donaldson of Kingsbridge and Frances Annesley (a writer; maiden name, Lonsdale) Donaldson; married Nicholas Deakin (a professor), December 16, 1961; children: Fred, Camilla, Ellen. *Education:* Somerville College, Oxford, B.A., 1956-59; London School of Economics and Political Science, earned diploma, 1960; attended Open University, 1971-76. *Agent:* Abner Stein, 54 Lyndhurst Grove, Camberwell, London SE15 5AH, England.

CAREER: Worked for Family Service Units in London, England, 1959-64; associated with social medicine unit of Medical Research Council, 1969-71; worked for Institute of Com-

munity Studies, 1976-79; computer software consultant with Transam Microsystems Ltd., 1981—. Teacher.

WRITINGS: Microcomputing: Introducing the New Smaller Computers, Sphere Books, 1982, New American Library, 1983; *Database Primer*, Century Press, 1983; *Database II Explored*, New Century Press, 1983.

SIDELIGHTS: "I changed from social work to research because social work is too arduous with a small family. An interest in computers plus a shortage of work in my research field led to the change. This was achieved by buying my own microcomputer and working/studying at home for one year. The results of that year form the content of *Microcomputing*. Then I became a software consultant for the firm from whom the microcomputer was originally purchased. I am especially interested in customers and their problems, hence this is a natural profession from social work, where customers are also the main focus, though the problems are different. General illiteracy of the computer world gives a particular kind of advantage to the immigrant from the arts world. This more than compensates for a lack of scientific background. I was prompted to write by a desire to pass on knowledge, so painfully acquired, to the many who will be treading the same path."

*   *   *

DEAN, Karen Strickler   1923-

PERSONAL: Born November 24, 1923, in Los Angeles, Calif.; daughter of R. V. (a commercial artist and watercolor painter) and Laura (a teacher; maiden name, Ness) Strickler; married Ervin S. Dean, Jr. (an engineer), June 16, 1947; children: Pamela, Nathan C., Lucie Signa, Thomas S. *Education:* University of California, Los Angeles, B.A., 1946; San Jose State University, elementary teaching credential, 1973, specialist teaching credential, 1976, M.A., 1979. *Residence:* Palo Alto, Calif.

CAREER: Highland-Park News Herald, Los Angeles, Calif., reporter and society editor, 1943-45; Cutter Laboratories, Berkeley, Calif., advertising and publicity copywriter, 1946-47; University of California Press, Berkeley, publicity and book jacket copywriter, 1947-49; Palo Alto Unified Schools, Palo Alto, Calif., instructional aide, 1974-76, volunteer creative writing teacher, 1975; Morland School District, San Jose, Calif., teacher of learning-disabled children, 1976-77; New Haven Unified School District, Union City, Calif., teacher of learning-disabled children at Alvarado Middle School, 1977-82, school newspaper sponsor, 1979-81; writer, 1982—. Home teacher in Whisman School District, Mountain View, Calif., 1974-77. *Member:* Society of Children's Book Writers, California Writers. *Awards, honors:* Winner of numerous prizes in local writing competitions, including Christmas short story contest in *Peninsula Living*, 1973, for "How Silently, How Silently."

WRITINGS—For children: (Contributor) *Sullivan Reading Comprehension*, Books 5-20, Behavioral Research Labs, 1973; (contributor) Joanne Robinson Mitchell and Anne Libby Pyle, editors, *Prisms*, Heath, 1975; (contributor) *Independent Reading Skills Laboratory*, Educational Progress, 1976; *Maggie Adams, Dancer* (novel), Avon, 1980; *Mariana* (novel), Avon, 1981; *Between Dances: Maggie Adams' Eighteenth Summer* (novel), Avon, 1982.

WORK IN PROGRESS: Research for an adult historical novel; a young-adult novel with a ballet background; a children's novel for ages eight to twelve.

SIDELIGHTS: Dean's first novel, *Maggie Adams, Dancer*, details a year in the life of a fourteen year old who encounters problems and must ultimately choose between parental expectations, typical teenage distractions, and her chosen and demanding craft, ballet. Among the sidetracking possibilities for Maggie, who narrates her own story, are a boyfriend with little patience, a father who wants her to study something practical, and a dance teacher who is less than encouraging. The rigors of ballet are illustrated in many scenes: the competition for starring roles, the dominance of a "stage mother" in troupe politics, and the girlfriend who becomes anorexic in an effort to maintain the body type demanded by her art. All ends well for Maggie, though. She receives a full scholarship to the "City Ballet" and wins the approval of both her parents and her teacher.

A dual career naturally put constraints on Dean's role as author. In an *Argus* interview, Dean told Joette Dignan Weir that when she taught her writing time was limited to "about two hours, two or three times a week" and "about four hours on weekends." Summers, in Weir's words, had "become a writing marathon" for Dean. The double career, however, also had its benefits; Dean's students provided experiences that enriched her characterizations. Dean commented, "The characters in my next three books are not based on one recognizable person, but a composite. The multi-culture thing has always interested me." Dean's writing method begins, she told Weir, with "a detailed history of each character and a brief outline of my idea." This preparation allows her to work "completely off the outline."

In a *Peninsula Times Tribune* article by Angelika von der Assen, Dean called *Maggie Adams* "a realistic—unrealistic story. All the obstacles in a young dancer's way do exist—but successful girls like Maggie are hard to find." Critics, too, centered their praise on these realistic aspects of Maggie's life. Barbara Karlin related in her *Los Angeles Times* review of the book that "Dean has shown how tough, how demanding a life devoted to dance can be, and . . . [the book] points out the importance of family and friends." Similarly, Beverly Kobrin, in a *Palo Alto Weekly* critique, found that "Dean hasn't given us another Cinderella story. . . . She has written a realistic, insightful, and engaging story about an aspiring young dancer, her family and friends, and the disappointments and pleasures that accompany the growth of a performing artist."

AVOCATIONAL INTERESTS: Reading, Mexican-American culture, skiing, swimming, ballet (studied with Branislava and Irina Nijinska and San Francisco Ballet School).

BIOGRAPHICAL/CRITICAL SOURCES: Argus, June 8, 1980; *Peninsula Times Tribune*, July 11, 1980; *Los Angeles Times*, July 13, 1980; *Palo Alto Weekly*, December 4, 1980.

* * *

DEBEVEC HENNING, Sylvie Marie 1948-

PERSONAL: Born April 11, 1948; married E. M. Henning. *Education:* Case Western Reserve University, B.A. (summa cum laude), 1970, M.A., 1974, Ph.D., 1975. *Home:* 148 Penhurst St., Rochester, N.Y. 14619. *Office:* Department of Foreign Languages, Literature, and Linguistics, University of Rochester, Rochester, N.Y. 14627.

CAREER: Demonstration School of Foreign Languages, Cleveland, Ohio, instructor in French, summer, 1971; University of Wisconsin—Parkside, assistant professor of French, 1975-77; University of Rochester, Rochester, N.Y., assistant professor,

1977-83, associate professor of French, 1983—. *Member:* Midwest Modern Language Association, Phi Beta Kappa. *Awards, honors:* Rochester Mellon faculty fellowship, 1981.

WRITINGS: Genet's Ritual Play (monograph), Rodopi, 1981. Contributor of articles and reviews to language and literature journals.

WORK IN PROGRESS: A book on menippean satire in the works of Samuel Beckett; research on nineteenth- and twentieth-century French literature, on literary criticism, and on philosophy and literature.

* * *

DECOLTA, Ramon
See WHITFIELD, Raoul

* * *

de GOURMONT, Remy
See GOURMONT, Remy de

* * *

DEINDORFER, Robert Greene 1922-1983

OBITUARY NOTICE—See index for *CA* sketch: Born July 3, 1922, in Galena, Ill.; died of a heart attack, March 26, 1983, in New York, N.Y. Public relations executive, free-lance magazine writer, and author. From 1955 to 1970 Deindorfer was manager of the New York Stock Exchange's magazine, newspaper feature, and book department. He also served as public relations adviser to the City of New York. He was the author of several books, including *The Great Gridiron Plot, True Spy Stories, Life in Lower Slaughter*, and *The Incompleat Angler: Fishing Walten's Water*. Obituaries and other sources: *New York Times*, March 30, 1983.

* * *

de la GUARDIA, Ernesto, Jr. 1904-1983

OBITUARY NOTICE: Born May 30, 1904, in Panama City, Panama; died May 2, 1983, in Panama City, Panama. Diplomat, politician, editor, and author. A graduate of Dartmouth College, where he received an M.B.A. in 1925, de la Guardia was chief of the Panamanian diplomatic service from 1928 to 1931, first vice-president of Panama in 1945, and a leader of the National Patriotic Coalition before becoming his nation's chief executive. De la Guardia was president of Panama from 1956 to 1960, a period marked by turmoil in that country. In 1959 de la Guardia asked the Organization of American States to help him remove a group of Cuban militiamen who had attacked Panama's Atlantic coast. Riots against the American presence in the Canal Zone broke out later that same year after the United States protested the raising of Panamanian flags in the U.S.-controlled area. De la Guardia edited *El Mundo Grafico*, a weekly, in the 1940's and wrote several biographies and books on economic subjects. Obituaries and other sources: *Newsweek*, May 28, 1956; *New York Herald Tribune*, October 2, 1956, October 7, 1956; *Current Biography*, Wilson, 1957; *London Times*, May 4, 1983; *Washington Post*, May 4, 1983; *Chicago Tribune*, May 6, 1983; *Time*, May 16, 1983.

* * *

del CASTILLO, Michel 1933-

PERSONAL: Born August 3, 1933, in Madrid, Spain. *Edu-*

cation: Educated at Lycee Janson-de-Sailly and Sorbonne, University of Paris. *Address:* 95 rue de Longchamps, Paris XVIe, France.

CAREER: Writer, 1957—. *Awards, honors:* Theophraste Renaudot Prize, 1981, for *La Nuit du Decret.*

WRITINGS: Tanguy: Histoire d'un enfant d'aujourd'hui (novel), R. Julliard, 1957, translation by Peter Green published as *Child of Our Time,* Knopf, 1958; *La Guitare* (story) R. Julliard, 1957, translation by Humphrey Hare published as *The Guitar,* Hart-Davis, 1959; *Le Colleur d'affiches* (novel), R. Julliard, 1958, translation by Hare published as *The Billsticker,* Hart-Davis, 1959, published as *The Disinherited,* Knopf, 1960; *La Mort de Tristan* (novel), R. Julliard, 1959, translation by Hare published as *The Death of Tristan,* Hart-Davis, 1961.

Le Manege espagnol (novel), R. Julliard, 1960, translation by Peter Wiles published as *Through the Hoop,* Hart-Davis, 1962, Knopf, 1963; *Tara* (novel), R. Julliard, 1962, Presses de la Cite Presses Club, 1966; *Les Louves de l'Escurial* (novel), R. Laffont (Paris), 1964, Perrin, 1980; *Les Aveux interdits,* R. Julliard, 1965; *Gerardo Lain* (novel), C. Bourgeois, 1967, translation by George Robinson published as *The Seminarian,* Holt, 1970; (with Andre Fermigier, Jean Grenier, Paul Guinard, and others) *Picasso,* Hachette, 1967; *Attitudes espagnoles,* photographs by Richard de Combray, R. Julliard, 1969.

Les Ecrous de la haine, R. Julliard, 1970; *Le Vent de la nuit* (novel), R. Julliard, 1972; *Le Silence des pierres* (novel), R. Julliard, 1975; *Le Sortilege espagnol,* R. Julliard, 1977; *Les Cypres meurent en Italie* (novel), R. Julliard, 1979; *La Nuit du Decret* (novel), Seuil, 1981.

SIDELIGHTS: In his lightly fictionalized autobiography, *A Child of Our Time,* Michel del Castillo depicts his early life, which took a tragic turn when he and his mother, a pro-Republican, fled Spain after the Civil War and went to France to join Michel's father, who had left the family because he vehemently disagreed with his wife's outspoken politics. The man offered no shelter, however. Instead, he denounced them as communists. The two were arrested and interned in a concentration camp in the Midi, but they were eventually separated; the mother was returned to Spain, and Michel was moved from camp to camp in France and Germany, where he led a hellish existence, experiencing incessant hunger, labor far too arduous for an undernourished youth, the deaths of his friends, and the possibility of his own death at any moment. Although it looked as if this nightmare would end with the close of World War II, it did not. Del Castillo was sent to an orphanage in Spain where he and the other charges were frequently beaten and starved. They were also forced to attend Mass daily and participate in their keepers' religious rituals. Del Castillo found the orphanage more tolerable than the Nazi camps because his pain was inflicted by men claiming to represent God, but their hypocrisy sickened Michel. He escaped in 1949 and returned to Paris, where he received the education he dreamed of during his captivity.

Reviewing *A Child of Our Time* in *New Republic,* Daniel M. Friedenberg wrote: "We have had many studies of modern depravity. What makes this book different is its ring of truth. The child tells his tale; there is no falsetto voice of sentiment and no moralizing. It was not without reason that Jean Cocteau in a French review wrote that after reading the book he would never dare complain of anything again." Jerrold Lanes of *Saturday Review,* who called the book "simply heartbreaking," also admired del Castillo's tolerance: "He has no complaint,

although his life has been one of incessant suffering; no demands, although he has had nothing, and no expectations because he has seen everything. . . . The refusal of the author to express a condemnation he has every right to pronounce, and the extraordinary poignancy of his voice, make our failure still harder to bear. We cannot live down the impact of this innocence and simplicity; but can we live up to it, either?"

Quelled innocents also dominate del Castillo's subsequent works, such as *The Guitar,* about a disfigured dwarf who is despised by his townspeople; *The Disinherited,* about a young communist living in Madrid's slums during the Spanish Civil War; and *The Seminarian,* dealing with the poignant homosexual relationship between two young seminary students. In a *Saturday Review* critique of *The Disinherited,* Richard Wright noted: "Castillo writes with blazing fury about men thrown into conflict by forces in themselves they but dimly perceive. His is a new voice whose accent is on the wordless words of the heart."

BIOGRAPHICAL/CRITICAL SOURCES: New Republic, November 3, 1958; *Saturday Review,* December 20, 1958, April 16, 1960; *Commonweal,* March 1, 1963; *New York Times Book Review,* March 1, 1970; *Best Sellers,* March 15, 1970; *Times Literary Supplement,* December 18, 1981.*

*　　　*　　　*

De LISSER, Herbert George　1878-1944

BRIEF ENTRY: Born December 9, 1878, in Falmouth, Jamaica; died May 18, 1944, in Kingston, Jamaica. West Indian journalist and novelist. De Lisser is known for his novels that depict the Jamaican political arena, including the activities of nationalists and their opponents. His writings include *Jane's Career* (1914), *Susan Proudleigh* (1915), and *The White Witch of Rosehall* (1929). *Biographical/critical sources: Cassell's Encyclopaedia of World Literature,* revised edition, Morrow, 1973; *Twentieth-Century Literary Criticism,* Volume 11, Gale, 1983.

*　　　*　　　*

DEMANT, Vigo Auguste　1893-1983

OBITUARY NOTICE: Born November 8, 1893, in Newcastle Upon Tyne, England; died March 3, 1983. Clergyman, educator, and author. Demant, whose major theological interest was Christian sociology, served as vicar of St. John's, Surrey, from 1933 to 1942 and as canon of St. Paul's Cathedral, London, from 1942 to 1949. From 1941 until his retirement in 1971, Demant was canon of Christ Church and Regius Professor of Moral and Pastoral Theology at Oxford University. He contributed to the journal *Christendom* and wrote several books, including *God, Man, and Society, Christian Polity, Theology of Society,* and *Christian Sexual Ethics.* Obituaries and other sources: *The Author's and Writer's Who's Who,* 6th edition, Burke's Peerage, 1971; *International Authors and Writers Who's Who,* 7th edition, Melrose, 1976; *The International Who's Who,* 41st edition, Europa, 1977; *Who's Who in the World,* 4th edition, Marquis, 1978; *London Times,* March 7, 1983.

*　　　*　　　*

DEMAREST, Chris(topher) L(ynn)　1951-

PERSONAL: Born April 18, 1951, in Hartford, Conn.; son of Robert and Shirley Mavis (a librarian; maiden name, Johnston)

Demarest; married Larkin Dorsey Upson (a carpenter), February 2, 1982. *Education:* University of Massachusetts, B.F.A., 1976. *Home and office:* 10 Sanborn St., Winchester, Mass. 01890. *Agent:* Dilys Evans, 40 Park Ave., New York, N.Y. 10016.

CAREER: House painter in Seattle, Wash., 1976-77; artist, 1977—.

WRITINGS—Self-illustrated children's books: Benedict Finds a Home, Lothrop, 1982; *Clemens' Kingdom,* Lothrop, 1983.

Illustrator: Elizabeth Isele, *Pooks,* Lippincott, 1983; Betty Jo Stanovich, *Hedgehog and Friends,* Lothrop, 1983. Illustrator of greeting cards and newspaper columns.

*WORK IN PROGRESS—*Children's books: *The Keeper of the Stars,* self-illustrated, publication by Lothrop expected in 1985; illustrating *Hedgehog and Friends II,* by Betty Jo Stanovich, for Lothrop, and *Muriel,* by Sue Alexander, for Little, Brown.

SIDELIGHTS: Demarest commented: "Whether it is with a single cartoon or an entire book, I try to leave my readers with a warm smile and the feeling they've been included in the joke.

"Making the switch from my traditional training in fine arts to cartooning was an unconscious but necessary transition. As soon as I started taking myself too seriously as a painter (without realizing it), my personality became lost. That prompted the question: Is humor acceptable in fine arts?

"I wasn't equipped to answer that question as a student, but a year after completing college I began to find more affinity with the likes of George Booth and Robert Bleckman than with Velasquez or Raphael. I found more enjoyment in dashing off a drawing in minutes than in slaving for weeks over one painting, and even then questioning the result. It was my training in interpreting the human form with only lines that allowed a natural shift to the simple lines of cartooning.

"Now, when I look at the rash of new humor books on the market, next to the classic works of H. T. Webster and James Thurber, I realize it is obvious that the need for humor will never die. My ability to translate a funny idea visually is what makes my work so enjoyable.

"With my own children's books, my motive is pure entertainment. It is fun to tell a story which makes the reader laugh, without having to sneak in some sort of message designed to awaken the child philosophically."

AVOCATIONAL INTERESTS: Sailing.

* * *

DEMOS, Paul 1888-1983

OBITUARY NOTICE: Born in 1888 in Corinth, Greece; died March 12, 1983, in Chicago, Ill. Lawyer and editor. A graduate of the University of Chicago Law School, Demos was the first Greek-born American admitted to the State Bar of Illinois, and he later served as president of the Hellenic Lawyers Association. Demos attended the Versailles Peace Conference at the close of World War I and, for several years, acted as adviser to President Warren G. Harding on Greek matters. Demos published a Greek language newspaper, the *Greek Herald,* during the 1940's and 1950's. He retired from the Chicago law firm of Demos, Karafotias & Chrones in 1958. Obituaries and other sources: *Chicago Tribune,* March 15, 1983.

DEMPSEY, Jack
See DEMPSEY, William Harrison

* * *

DEMPSEY, William Harrison 1895-1983
(Jack Dempsey)

*OBITUARY NOTICE—*See index for *CA* sketch: Born June 24, 1895, in Manassa, Colo.; died May 31, 1983, in New York, N.Y. Heavyweight boxer, restaurateur, and author. From 1919 to 1926 Dempsey was heavyweight champion of the world, and experts usually rank him with Joe Louis as the two greatest pre-1950 fighters. Dempsey compiled a record featuring several quick knockouts before his title bout with Jess Willard. Dempsey was declared the new champion in the fourth round after breaking Willard's cheekbone and sending him reeling to the canvas several times. He defended the title for seven years against such heavyweights as Gene Tunney and Luis Firpo. Some consider the Firpo-Dempsey fight to be one of boxing's greatest moments: The two men battered each other to the floor twelve times, and Firpo threw a right that sent Dempsey flying completely out of the ring. Dempsey returned to the ring as the round ended, then rendered Firpo unconscious within the first minute of the second round. Dempsey's matches against Gene Tunney brought both boxers fame. In the "long count" bout Dempsey lingered over the fallen Tunney instead of heading to a neutral corner, an error that allowed Tunney extra seconds to regain his senses and cost Dempsey the fight. Dempsey retired in 1932 with a record of fifty-four victories—including forty-seven knockouts—in sixty-nine bouts. He then managed a restaurant in New York City. Dempsey wrote two autobiographies, *Round by Round* and *Dempsey, by the Man Himself,* as well as two volumes about boxing. Obituaries and other sources: *Los Angeles Times,* June 1, 1983; *Washington Post,* June 1, 1983; *London Times,* June 2, 1983; *Time,* June 13, 1983.

* * *

DENHAM, Reginald 1894-1983

*OBITUARY NOTICE—*See index for *CA* sketch: Born January 10, 1894, in London, England; died following a stroke, February 4, 1983, in Englewood, N.J. Theatrical director, playwright, and autobiographer. Before coming to the United States in 1940, Denham directed more than two hundred plays in London. He made his U.S. directorial debut in 1929 with the thriller "Rope's End." He went on to direct a number of Broadway plays, including "The Two Mrs. Carrolls," "Dial M for Murder," and "Ladies in Retirement," which he co-authored with Edward Percy. Among the plays Denham wrote in collaboration with his wife, Mary Orr, are *Wallflower, Be Your Age, The Wisdom of Eve,* and *Minor Murder.* The two also wrote a great many scripts for television plays. *Stars in My Hair,* Denham's autobiography, appeared in 1958. Obituaries and other sources: *New York Times,* February 7, 1983; *Newsweek,* February 21, 1983; *London Times,* March 7, 1983.

* * *

DENISON, (John) Michael (Terence Wellesley) 1915-

PERSONAL: Born November 1, 1915, in Doncaster, England; son of Gilbert Dixon (a paint manufacturer) and Marie Louise (Bain) Denison; married Dulcie Gray (an actress and writer),

April 29, 1939. *Education:* Magdalen College, Oxford, B.A., 1937. *Religion:* Church of England. *Home:* Shardeloes, Amersham, Buckinghamshire, England.

CAREER: Actor, 1938—. Director of New Shakespeare Company, 1971—; member of Arts Council drama panel, 1975-79. *Military service:* British Army, Intelligence Corps, 1940-46; became captain. *Member:* Royal Society of Arts (fellow), British Actors Equity Association (member of council, 1949-77; vice-president, 1952, 1961-63, 1973), Marylebone Cricket Club. *Awards, honors:* Queen's Jubilee Medal from Queen Elizabeth II, 1977.

WRITINGS: (With wife, Dulcie Gray) *The Actor and His World* (juvenile), Gollancz, 1964; *Overture and Beginners* (memoirs), Gollancz, 1973.

WORK IN PROGRESS: A second volume of memoirs, the sequel to *Overture and Beginners.*

SIDELIGHTS: Denison has appeared in forty-four London plays since 1938, co-starring in twenty-five of them with his wife, Dulcie Gray. They include "The Fourposter," "Candida," "Heartbreak House," "Where Angels Fear to Tread," "An Ideal Husband," "On Approval," "The Wild Duck," "Bedroom Farce," and "The School for Scandal." Denison's individual credits include the roles of Henry Higgins in "My Fair Lady," Captain Hook in "Peter Pan," Poohbah in "The Black Mikado," and Malvolio in "Twelfth Night." He appeared in the films "The Importance of Being Earnest," "My Brother Jonathan," and "The Glass Mountain." Denison's best-known television role was the title character in "Boyd, Q.C." He appeared in eighty episodes of the series between 1956 and 1964.

Denison told *CA:* "Since the deaths of Lewis Carson and Sybil Thorndike, my wife and I are Britain's senior *once-married* couple working together in the theatre."

*   *   *

DENNEHY, Raymond L(eo) 1934-

PERSONAL: Born August 31, 1934, in San Francisco, Calif.; son of Joseph Patrick and Mary Agnes (McGaffin) Dennehy; married Geraldine Patricia Kine (a stockbroker); children: Mark, Bridget, Andrew, Rosalind. *Education:* University of San Francisco, B.A., 1962; University of California, Berkeley, M.A., 1964; University of Toronto, Ph.D., 1973. *Home:* 64 Westpark Dr., Daly City, Calif. 94015. *Office:* Department of Philosophy, University of San Francisco, San Francisco, Calif. 94117.

CAREER: University of Santa Clara, Santa Clara, Calif., instructor, 1966-69, assistant professor of philosophy, 1969-72; West Valley Community College, Saratoga, Calif., lecturer in philosophy, 1972-74; University of San Francisco, San Francisco, Calif., lecturer, 1972-78, associate professor of philosophy, 1979—. *Military service:* U.S. Navy, radar operator, 1954-58; served in China and the Pacific theater. *Member:* American Catholic Philosophical Association (member of executive council, 1983—), American Maritain Association, Fellowship of Catholic Scholars, Alpha Sigma Nu.

WRITINGS: Reason and Dignity, University Press of America, 1981; *Christian Married Love,* Ignatius Press, 1981. Work anthologized in *Philosophy, Psychology, and Spirituality,* edited by J. Kidd, Golden Phoenix Press, 1983. Contributor to magazines and newspapers, including *Social Justice Review,*

Camillian, Thomist, New Scholasticism, Thought, and *Migrant Echo.*

WORK IN PROGRESS: What Is Man?, on the conception of human nature as the ideal of culture, and on the consequences of that idea, publication expected in 1984; research for a book on the ontological basis of certitude, or the question of knowledge of the real world and the warrant for true judgments about it.

SIDELIGHTS: Dennehy told *CA:* "*Reason and Dignity* is an amplification of a theme that has preoccupied me for the past decade and which dominates almost everything I write and teach and will write and teach: the crucial importance of a realistic philosophy for the survival and progress of Western culture. Specifically, *Reason and Dignity* expresses my conviction that human dignity, natural rights, and democratic society cannot be preserved without a philosophy that furnishes a rational and true-to-life account of human experience, a philosophy which represents the reflective and systematic complement to the spontaneous judgments of common sense. Only such a philosophy can rationally justify a conception of man which contains the ontological basis for his dignity and rights. It alone can, accordingly, rationally defend democratic society and, indeed, Western civilization.

"The reader of *Reason and Dignity* will detect an urgency, especially in the introductory pages but throughout the book as well. What generates the urgency is my perception of the mortal threat to these values posed by empiricist philosophy, the philosophy which reduces all knowledge to sensation. Presupposing a distorted conception of the nature and power of the human mind, this philosophy mutilates human experience and animalizes man in the process. So pervasive is its influence that social scientists, lawyers, physicians, natural scientists, and educators are hardly aware that their professional and intellectual judgments are more often than not its children. A chief sign of the influence of empiricist philosophy is the near universal assumption that the experimental sciences alone give us knowledge of reality."

Dennehy described *Christian Married Love* as a work dealing with "the family and the dignity of the relationship between men and women." He added: "Secularized culture—the culture of the modern world—is unique in that this is the first age in history to be anti-God. Consequently, we are today all but blinded to the truth that the love between man and woman and the procreative power of that love to bring new life into existence (which new life is an embodiment of that love and proof that the spouses become two in one flesh) is an analogy of God's relationship to his creatures. I am persuaded that the contraceptive society—in so far as it repudiates human creativity at its primordial source—will stifle human creativity absolutely: in art, science, politics, etc. This is a theme I shall return to in a future work. A glimmering of this project is to be seen in my article 'Sex, Survival, and Progress,' published in the *Linacre Quarterly.*"

*   *   *

DENNISON, Sam 1926-

PERSONAL: Born September 26, 1926, in Geary, Okla.; son of Frank Houston (an entrepreneur) and Ada Lee (a fashion designer; maiden name, Williams) Dennison; children: Paul Scott, David Houston, Lee Ann. *Education:* University of Oklahoma, B.M., 1950; University of Southern California, M.M., 1962; Drexel University, M.S.L.S., 1966. *Residence:*

Philadelphia, Pa. *Office:* Fleisher Collection, Free Library of Philadelphia, Philadelphia, Pa. 19103.

CAREER: Teacher and free-lance musician in the United States and abroad, 1952-60; Inter-American University, San German, P.R., professor of music, 1960-64; Free Library of Philadelphia, Philadelphia, Pa., music librarian, 1964-75, curator, 1975—. Music consultant and appraiser; lecturer; composer. *Military service:* U.S. Naval Reserve, active duty, 1944-46. *Member:* Sonneck Society, Musical Fund Society of Philadelphia, Sigma Alpha Iota.

WRITINGS: (Editor) *Catalog of Orchestral and Choral Compositions From the Library of the Musical Fund Society of Philadelphia,* Musical Fund Society of Philadelphia, 1974; (chief editor) *The Edwin A. Fleisher Collection of Orchestral Music in the Free Library of Philadelphia,* G. K. Hall, 1977; *Scandalize My Name: Black Imagery in American Popular Music,* Garland Publishing, 1982. Contributor to *Grove's Dictionary of Music and Musicians.* Co-editor of series of biographies of American composers, Scarecrow.

Musical compositions: "Thirteen Pieces for Helen," 1948; "Monologue of a Water Faucet," 1948; "Mother Wears Army Boots," 1949; "The Last Man on Earth," 1952; "Quodlibet," 1953; "The Days of the Week," 1953; "Folksong Medley," 1957; "Brass Sextet," 1963; "Jesus Christes Milde Moder," 1963; "The Faucon Hath Taken My Mate Away," 1963; "Suite for Flute," 1968; "Epithalamium," 1968; "Adagio for Horn and Orchestra," 1978; "Cirrus," 1980; "Lyric Piece and Rondo," 1982.

Also composer of film scores for "Good Speech for Gary," 1952, "Penn Relays," 1968, and "History of Delaware."

WORK IN PROGRESS: A book on orchestral librarianship, for Scarecrow; "Rappaccini's Daugher," a one-act opera.

SIDELIGHTS: Dennison commented that he wondered whether he spent years researching and writing *Scandalize My Name* because the Jim Crow laws in the Bible Belt where he grew up kept him from blacks and blacks from him. As he (and his black secretary) were cataloging "coon songs," he seemed to face the enormous task of finding out why songwriters would attack a race that already had troubles enough to deal with. As a professional musician, he had played some of this music and was disturbed by it, without fully realizing why.

BIOGRAPHICAL/CRITICAL SOURCES: Pan Pipes of Sigma Alpha Iota, winter, 1982.

*   *   *

De PALMA, Brian (Russell) 1940-

PERSONAL: Born September 11, 1940 (listed in some sources as 1944), in Newark, N.J.; son of Anthony Frederick (an orthopedic surgeon) and Vivenne (Muti) De Palma; married Nancy Allen (an actress), January 12, 1979. *Education:* Columbia University, B.A., 1962; Sarah Lawrence College, M.A., 1964. *Religion:* Presbyterian. *Home:* 25 Fifth Ave., New York, N.Y. 10003. *Office:* Fetch Productions, 1600 Broadway, New York, N.Y.

CAREER: Screenwriter, producer, and director of motion pictures. *Awards, honors:* Award from Rosenthal Foundation, 1963, for "Woton's Wake"; Silver Bear from Berlin Film Festival, 1969, for "Greetings"; Avoriaz Prize, 1977, for "Carrie"; and other film awards.

WRITINGS: (With Campbell Black) *Dressed to Kill* (novel; adapted from the screenplay by De Palma; also see below), Bantam, 1980.

Screenplays, except as noted; and director: "Murder a la Mod," Aries Documentaries, 1968; (co-author) "Greetings," Sigma III, 1968; (with Cynthia Munroe and Wilford Leach) "The Wedding Party," Powell Productions and Ondine Presentations, 1969; (with Charles Hirsch) "Hi, Mom," Sigma III, 1970; (with Louisa Rose) "Sisters," American International Pictures (AIP), 1973; "Phantom of the Paradise," Twentieth Century-Fox, 1974; "Dressed to Kill," Filmways, 1980; "Blow Out," Filmways, 1981. Also writer and director of short films, including "Woton's Wake," 1963, and documentaries, including "The Responsive Eye," 1966.

Author of screen story; also director: (With Paul Schrader; screenplay by Schrader) "Obsession," Columbia, 1976; (sole author of screen story; screenplay by Robert Harders, Gloria Norris, and others) "Home Movies," United Artists Classics, 1980.

WORK IN PROGRESS: Directing a remake of "Scarface."

SIDELIGHTS: De Palma is one of the most controversial filmmakers in a generation of American directors that includes George Lucas, Steven Spielberg, and Martin Scorsese. Hailed by *New Yorker*'s Pauline Kael as an "artist" and denounced by *Village Voice*'s Andrew Sarris as a "derivative manipulator," De Palma stands out as a self-described 'aberrant" in an industry that prizes commercialism over creativity. Critics vehemently disagree on the merits of his work, which features both slapstick and gore, and his style, which he defines as a developing command of "cinematic grammar." But most observers would probably concur that De Palma is unsurpassable in his ability to elicit specific responses from his audience. "He knows where to put the camera and how to make every move count," Kael declared, "and his timing is so great that when he wants you to feel something he gets you every time." *New York*'s David Denby agreed, noting that "you admire his sadistic virtuosity even as he's manipulating you unconscionably." He called De Palma's style "sensational."

To critics such as Sarris and *Time*'s Richard Corliss, however, De Palma's films are largely derived from the suspenseful works of Alfred Hitchcock. Corliss called De Palma a "scavenger" of Hitchcock's canon, and Sarris complained that De Palma "seems shameless in filching" from the vaunted British director. Sarris added that De Palma "still seems to be scrambling for a personal style that he can truly call his own."

De Palma responds to charges of mimicry by acknowledging Hitchcock's mastery of technique. "Hitchcock thought up practically every cinematic idea that has been used and probably ever will be used in [the thriller] form," he conceded. "But I'll take the grammar wherever I can get it." He also admits that "it's hard to resent all the comparisons—[Hitchcock] was, after all, the best director ever, the man who pioneered the grammar of the cinema—but one still gets tired of them."

As for accusations that he ransacks Hitchcock's stories, De Palma comments that the director "had some terrific ideas. It's a shame not to use them." But he maintains, "My films are very different from Hitchcock's, and I think anyone with a brain can see that." He also contends that critics are too quick to relate his work to Hitchcock's films and notes, "Every time someone sees running water, he starts yelling 'Hitchcock shower scene!'"

But Hitchcock isn't the only filmmaker who affected De Palma's work. Michelangelo Antonioni's ''Zabriskie Point'' inspired the apocalyptic climax of ''The Fury,'' and his ''Blow Up,'' in which a photographer uncovers a possible murder while developing his footage, is refrained in ''Blow Out,'' where a sound man accidently records an automobile accident that may have been intentional. Critics have also noted the influence of such varied talents as Sam Peckinpah, whose graphically violent, slow-motion shoot-outs revolutionized the western, and Luis Bunuel, the Spanish surrealist who alienated audiences in 1930 with ''L'Age d'Or'' much as De Palma outraged viewers fifty years later with ''Dressed to Kill.''

Perhaps the most profound initial influence on De Palma, however, was Jean-Luc Godard, the radical French filmmaker whose quick-cutting and improvisatory tone leant a you-are-there sense to the viewer. Both Godard's technique and his penchant for political commentary are evident in De Palma's early comedies, especially ''Greetings'' and ''Hi, Mom.'' ''Greetings'' concerns the actions of three friends—including a Peeping-Tom pornographer and a Kennedy assassination-conspiracy fanatic—when one of them prepares for induction into the army. Paul Schrader catalogued the film's subjects as ''the draft, computer dating, shoplifting, stag films, JFK's assassination, abstract sculpture, sex positions, Vietnam, high-culture movies, and peeping-toms.'' Schrader also noted similarities between the styles of Godard and De Palma. ''Like Godard,'' he wrote, ''De Palma has the courage not to move the camera to let a scene play out its inherent humor . . . [and] it exhibits an artificial and ambiguous frame of reference, teasing the viewer with wry camera movements.'' He called ''Greetings'' ''the funniest and most contemporary American comedy since 'Dr. Strangelove.'''

''Hi, Mom'' recalls ''Greetings'' in its frenetic pacing and its mocking of the bourgeois sensibility. It concerns the efforts of a novice filmmaker to secretly film his neighbors in sexual intercourse. When a failed seduction results in love between the director and one of his subjects, he becomes co-opted into the middle-class life. Eventually he takes a temporary position as a pseudo-policeman in a performance of ''Be Black, Baby!'' The play involves the humiliation and brutalization of its audience by "politically aware" actors. When the film's hero ends the performance by preventing the rape of one spectator, the other viewers immediately praise the production as a breakthrough in the theatre. ''Hi, Mom'' ends with the failed director's retaliation against middle-class life by destroying his apartment building.

New York Times's Roger Greenspun lauded ''Hi, Mom'' for its ''wit, its ironic good humor, its multilevel sophistications, and its technical ingenuity.'' John Simon, however, accused De Palma and his collaborators of ineptly repeating the themes of ''Greetings.'' He called the film ''an almost total waste of time'' and contended, ''The filmmakers have run out of ideas: they either try to milk the same situations . . . , or if they come up with something new . . . , they stretch it out as desperately as beggars their last crust of bread.''

But ''Hi, Mom'' managed to match the generally favorable critical and box-office reception of ''Greetings.'' The film industry in Hollywood was impressed with De Palma's low-budget works, and in 1971 Warner Brothers offered him the directorship of a promising comedy, ''Get to Know Your Rabbit.'' The film tells of a businessman who quits his profession to become a traveling magician. ''It's a movie in many ways close to Woody Allen in that it creates a feeling of an absurd,

mad and rather threatening universe,'' De Palma explained. ''But the humor isn't warm, it has a cruel twist that's part of me.''

Unfortunately for De Palma, both Warner Brothers and lead actor Tommy Smothers were dissatisfied with the film. De Palma noted that Smothers ''identified Warner Brothers with the commercial monolith . . . the magician was dropping out of.'' He added that Smothers ''refused to come back for retakes . . . , and as a result some scenes in the film are very bad and unfunny.'' Warner Brothers executives, after viewing De Palma's version, forwarded the film to a project coordinator for revision. ''Warners took the picture from the producers,'' De Palma later recalled, ''and gave it to . . . Peter Nelson who cut it, rearranged some scenes, directed a new sequence, and put in other scenes that I had decided to eliminate.'' Meanwhile, De Palma was unable to obtain further work. ''I walked around Hollywood like a corpse,'' he recalled in 1980, ''not realizing that I was dead, dead because I had a picture on the shelf.''

De Palma returned to New York City in 1972 and managed to secure enough funds to begin work on ''Sisters.'' The film is about Siamese twins, one of whom may be a homicidal schizophrenic. When a journalist gazes from her apartment and witnesses a murder in the twins' building, she tries to alert the police. They are unable to find any indications of foul play, though, and it is left to the reporter to solve the crime. She eventually tracks the neighboring twin to an eerie mental institution. There, she is captured by the doctor who performed the separation of the Siamese twins. He hypnotizes the reporter and subjects her to a frightening explanation of the twins' past. ''Sisters'' was deemed ''an intelligent horror film'' by Vincent Canby, and its modest critical success helped re-establish De Palma in the film industry.

''Sisters'' also provided De Palma with an opportunity to return to the theme of voyeurism he had unveiled in ''Greetings'' and ''Hi, Mom.'' ''Like most directors,'' he declared, ''I'm a voyeur at heart. I loved dragging the audience through the whole psychodrama of an insane situation. The audience *becomes* this girl, peering through a psychological hole.''

Some critics, however, protested that ''Sisters'' was derivative of Hitchcock's work, notably ''Rear Window'' and ''Psycho.'' Canby complained that the film's associations with ''Psycho'' ''tip one important plot sooner than is absolutely necessary.'' De Palma conceded that ''Sisters'' was influenced by both Hitchcock's work and Roman Polanski's ''Repulsion,'' but later noted that much of his own style, including the use of split screens and speeded film, was alien to Hitchcock's. ''People sometimes address . . . what is like Hitchcock in my movies as opposed to what is De Palma that isn't Hitchcock,'' he observed. ''I can rant and rave about other kinds of form like split screens or slow motion that Hitchcock never used, but that's not the point.''

De Palma's next film, ''The Phantom of the Paradise,'' recalls the often madcap humor of ''Greetings'' and ''Hi, Mom'' in its rock-music parodying of both ''The Phantom of the Opera'' and the Faust legend. *New Yorker*'s Pauline Kael was especially enthusiastic in considering the film ''a new Guignol,'' and she imagined De Palma ''cackling with happiness'' during a sequence featuring contorting dancers before an audience of dismembered viewers. Kael was also impressed with De Palma's apparent directorial zeal. She wrote: ''De Palma's timing is sometimes wantonly unpredictable and dampening, but mostly it has a lift to it. You practically get a kinetic charge from the breakneck wit he put into 'Phantom'; it isn't just that the picture has vitality but that one can feel the tremendous kick the director got out of making it." She added, however, that De Palma "can't do the routine scenes that establish character relations and give a movie 'heart,'" and contended that he "needs to let his own attitudes towards these scenes come out."

De Palma followed "The Phantom of the Paradise" with "Obsession," a thriller that triggered more comparisons to Hitchcock. Like Hitchcock's "Vertigo," "Obsession" details one man's efforts to redeem his past by fashioning the likeness—both in physique and behavior—of a former love in another woman. The main character, Michael Courtland, has spent years grieving for his wife, Elizabeth, who died in an automobile accident as police attempted to rescue her from kidnappers. Courtland eventually meets a student identical to his late wife. A bizarre courtship follows, during which Courtland convinces his fiancee to adopt his first wife's appearance. Then, under circumstances duplicating the first kidnapping, Courtland's second wife is abducted. The deranged Courtland seizes the opportunity to relive the previous incident without causing another death.

Time's Richard Schickel called "Obsession" an "exquisite entertainment that sends one back to Hitchcock . . . for comparison," and he praised De Palma's "triumph of style over substance." *Film*'s Barrie Pattison also called the film a "stylish and accomplished achievement." But both Penelope Gilliatt and John Simon, reiterating Kael's criticism of "The Phantom of the Paradise," complained of weak character development in "Obsession." "Toward the end," declared Simon, "the behavior of all the characters becomes even less explicable, and the last slender links to sanity, indeed humanity, are frenetically severed." Gilliatt charged that the film "is sometimes fogged enough to let a plot point rely on characters' witlessness, and such a reliance is not at all the same thing as dramatic irony."

By 1976, despite fair acclaim for "Greetings" and "Sisters," De Palma still found himself unwanted in the film industry. Unlike fellow directors George Lucas and Steven Spielberg, who received substantial studio support for their third films, De Palma was still trying to rustle funds after directing more films than both of his friends. "Frankly, by then I was more than ready for big-time success," he recalled in 1980. "All my best friends in the business . . . had already made it in a huge way, and there was I . . . still struggling."

But De Palma's career was about to take a positive turn. He discovered that a major studio was planning an adaptation of Stephen King's novel *Carrie,* and pursued the directorship. "When *Carrie* came along," he revealed in *Esquire*, "I pleaded . . . to be allowed to direct it." The studio granted De Palma's request. The result was a horrifying and often gory work that received both critical and popular acclaim.

In "Carrie," the title character is a high-school student living an extremely sheltered existence with her mother, a religious fanatic. The film begins with Carrie experiencing her first menstruation while showering after gym class. Ignorant of her predicament, Carrie appeals to her fellow students for help. But the other girls only taunt her and laugh. Later, while Carrie's classmates are being punished for their abusive behavior, they plot her further humiliation. Meanwhile, Carrie has been punished for menstruating by being locked in a closet by her mother. Upon release, Carrie momentarily unleashes her telekinetic powers, which include the ability to mentally control objects as diverse as bicycles and mirrors. These powers reach

full force in the film's bloody climax when Carrie, doused with pig's blood by cruel students, mentally seals the exits at the homecoming dance and begins willing objects to tear into and crush the other celebrants. When she returns home after destroying the high school, Carrie is stabbed in the back by her zealous mother. As she dies, Carrie uses her powers to pin her mother to the wall and sends the kitchenware into her. Carrie's home then collapses in flames.

"Carrie" was an immense success at box offices and with critics, many of whom considered it De Palma's finest work. Kael called it a "terrifying lyrical thriller." She added, "This is the first time a De Palma picture has had heart—which may explain why De Palma, despite his originality, has never made it into the big winners' circle before." *Time*'s Richard Schickel deemed De Palma's direction "an exercise in high style" and noted that "there is a pointed glee in De Palma's satirical vision of high school society, an oddly compelling power in his juxtaposition of the banal and the awesome moving unsuspected amidst it."

De Palma's following film, "The Fury," featured further terrors of telekinesis. The film centers on the efforts of a retired government agent, Peter Sanza, to locate his telekinetic son, Robin, who has been kidnapped by his father's ex-employer, Childress, in an attempt to create a human weapon. Peter is ultimately aided in his journey by a woman whose own telekinesis enables her to cause massive bleeding in others. When Peter finally arrives at Childress's hideaway, he is informed that his son is berserk and lurks within the house. Peter climbs upstairs and attempts to reason with Robin, who hovers in the air over his unsuspecting father. Finally, Robin swoops onto Peter and together they fall through the window. While holding on to the ledge with one hand, Peter tries to pull his son to safety. Robin, however, tries to claw his father's eyes out, and both men eventually fall from the roof. It is left to the telekinetic woman to assume Robin's place. But in a climax that some critics contended was one of the grisliest ever filmed, she rejects Childress's guidance and causes him to explode.

"The Fury" features some of De Palma's best known sequences. In one scene, Robin's memory of his kidnapping by pseudo-Arabs is triggered by a glimpse of Arabs enjoying a ride at an amusement park. Robin, whose telekinetic powers have increased as his judgment has diminished, uses his psychic force to loosen the Arabs' car on the ride and send them crashing into more Arabs dining in a restaurant overlooking the park. In a later scene, Robin forces his counselor/mistress to levitate and spin. As the woman's speed increases, blood begins to flow from her eyes and pores. Her head eventually tears away from her body.

Kael called "The Fury" an "inferno comedy." She deemed it "a far more hallucinatory film" than "Carrie" and declared, "You feel [De Palma] never has to make another horror film. To go on would mean trying to kill people in ever more photogenically horrific ways." *Village Voice*'s Andrew Sarris conceded that "the bloody, extra-sensory carnage seems a bit much" but added that he was "entertained." He noted: "De Palma develops his own gruesome variations on . . . stylistic flourishes, and overall there is more bloodshed here than in any movie since Sam Peckinpah's *The Wild Bunch*." Kael also compared "The Fury" to Peckinpah's classic western. She reserved much of her praise, though, for De Palma's directorial style. "What distinguishes De Palma's visual style is smoothness combined with a jazzy willingness to appear crazy or camp," she wrote. And in anticipating comparisons to Hitchcock's work, Kael added, "No Hitchcock thriller was ever so intense, went so far, or had so many 'classic' sequences."

After directing "Carrie" and "The Fury," De Palma was inundated with offers to make more thrillers and horror films. He had decided, however, to return to comedy. But the project he was involved with—actor Peter Boyle's script about 1940's Marines—failed to find funding. So De Palma wrote his own story, "Home Movies," about Denis Byrd, a college student who enrolls at Now College to become something more than "an extra in his own life." To get away from the film industry, and to provide experience for his students at Sarah Lawrence College, De Palma made "Home Movies" a class project. "I took my class and broke it up into producers and creators," he wrote in *Esquire*. "Meanwhile, other kids concentrated on raising the $350,000 we needed. . . . Those kids may have gotten the most valuable experience of all. In the end, if you can't hustle, you're not going to make it in this business."

During pre-production, the students' enthusiasm was further buoyed by the signing of actor Kirk Douglas, who had already worked with De Palma in "The Fury" and now offered his services in exchange for a percentage of the new film's earnings. In "Home Movies," he plays the pivotal role of the Maestro, Dennis Byrd's instructor in Star Therapy. The Maestro equips Dennis with a movie camera and encourages him to film his own life. But Dennis's life is so boring that he falls asleep while screening his footage. Later, he manages to film his father's liaison with a nurse. The film then becomes a comedy of errors and coincidences: Dennis's brother, James, is discovered by his fiancee—an ex-porno-performer played by De Palma's wife, Nancy Allen—in the act of simulating sexual techniques on one of his students while teaching Spartanetics; Allen's character suffers a breakdown after a brief tryst with Dennis and begins taking orders from a bawdy hand puppet. The end parodies the apocalyptic finales of "Carrie" and "The Fury," as Dennis plummets from a tree and becomes catatonic while trying to prevent James from shooting his fiancee, who flees him only to be struck by an ambulance.

"Home Movies" ultimately proved a disappointing project for De Palma. He told *Village Voice*'s J. Hoberman that it was "more work than I ever imagined," and he wrote in *Esquire* that "the film took twice as long to make as I usually spend on a feature, because every step of the way I had to stop and explain what was going on." The frustration continued after filming was completed, as De Palma vehemently disagreed with the distributor's handling of the film. And when it was finally released, briefly, in 1980, it received harsh reviews from Hoberman and *New Yorker*'s Roger Angell, who noted the absence of "a sharp script, first-class acting, and rigorous cutting and pacing." De Palma contended that critics were biased against the film. "It's about me, that's my family," he told Hoberman. "If Francois Truffaut had made the film he would have had no problems." He added that "in this business, good intentions aren't work a f———."

De Palma was more satisfied with the reception accorded his next film, "Dressed to Kill." Even before filming commenced, he found himself in the unfamiliar position of popularity with major studios. "It's the first thing I've written that everyone has responded positively to," he told *New York Times*'s Tom Buckley. "It's usually taken me years to get my pictures made, but several studios wanted to do this one and we began shooting six months after I finished the script."

Like the earlier "Sisters," "Dressed to Kill" involves the solving of a grisly murder. The victim is Kate Miller, a sexually

repressed housewife who fantasizes about rape while making love with her unfeeling husband. After Kate has confessed her desires to her psychiatrist, she indulges in an extra-marital encounter with a stranger she meets in a museum. As she leaves her lover's apartment, though, Kate discovers that he has been notified by the health department that he has a venereal disease. Stunned, Kate leaves the apartment but forgets her wedding ring. She remembers it while in the elevator and tries to return to the apartment. Then the doors open to reveal a razor wielding woman garbed in a garish blonde wig, sunglasses, and a trench coat. The woman viciously slashes Kate's throat and body, then phones the psychiatrist and confesses to the killing. The remainder of the film concerns the efforts of Kate's son, Peter, and Liz, a prostitute and prime suspect of the police, to capture the killer. Their pursuit culminates in a shocking revelation of madness and murder.

Although "Dressed to Kill" contains graphic violence, its sardonic tone links it to "Greetings" and even "Home Movies." Like "Greetings," "Dressed to Kill" exposes the fatuous nature of contemporary mores, including Kate's supposedly self-sustaining infidelity; and like "Home Movies," it exploits the irony of potentially terrifying situations, including a chase scene in which Liz attempts to escape the killer by enlisting the aid of several thugs, to a humorous resolution. "De Palma is definitely a new kind of movie amoralist," conceded *New York*'s David Denby. "He combines moods normally kept apart—frivolous joking and terror—and he's so single-minded in his pursuit of beautifully bloody thrills, and then in drawing the laughter out of them, that he can't be bothered with socially responsible statements or even with our feelings about his characters." He added that "De Palma releases terror in laughter: Even Hitchcock could not have been as entertaining as this." Kael agreed, declaring that De Palma was "probably the only American director who knows how to use jokiness to make horror more intense."

Kael and Denby were also among the critics impressed with De Palma's florid technique in "Dressed to Kill." Kael called his style "insidious, jewelled" and added, "The gliding . . . cinematography is intoxicating." Denby called De Palma "a sensational director" and noted that he "heads straight for what's gorgeously lurid, for what appeals to the senses as pure excitement." Even Hoberman, who admitted that he had "trashed" "Home Movies," found "Dressed to Kill" "voluptuously crafted, formally dazzling."

Other critics, notably Sarris and *Time*'s Richard Corliss, were outraged by De Palma's seemingly blatant use of both Hitchcock's style and subject matter. Sarris called "Dressed to Kill" "a shamefully straight steal from *Psycho*," Hitchcock's film of a schizophrenic murderer. Sarris also found De Palma's technique at odds with his humor. "There is no depth of feeling in De Palma's flourishes," he wrote, "because they do not mesh with De Palma's obtrusive facetiousness." He also implied that De Palma's "psychological range still does not extend much past high school." Corliss was even more vehement in his criticism of the film. He declared that De Palma's technical accomplishments "operate in a narrative void" and deemed the characters "animated mannequins." "De Palma's movies no longer explore . . . tensions," he wrote. "They have become exhibitions of a master puppeteer pulling high-tension strings."

De Palma, as always, openly acknowledged Hitchcock's influence. "I hope this is a Hitchcockian film," he told the *New York Times*. He also told Hoberman that his film was "not a slavish imitation'' and added: ''Hitchcock had some terrific ideas. It's a shame not to use them.''

De Palma followed ''Dressed to Kill'' with ''Blow Out,'' a tale of conspiracy and murder. The blowout of the title is recorded by Jack Terri, a sound technician capturing effects for a horror film. While in the woods, Terri watches a car careen towards a bridge. Then the blowout occurs, followed by the car's plunge from the bridge into the river. Terri is able to rescue one of the occupants, Sally Bedina, but the car's driver, presidential candidate McRyan, dies. Later, when replaying the tape, Terri discovers that the blowout was actually a gunshot. He also learns that the gun was fired to cause the accident and that Bedina's partner, Manny Carp, was on hand to photograph McRyan in a compromising position with her after the accident. Unfortunately, Terri cannot convince authorities that a cover-up conspiracy is taking place to conceal McRyan's association with Bedina. When he publicizes his possession of the tape, Terri becomes a target for the marksman who caused the accident. Like ''Carrie,'' ''The Fury,'' and ''Dressed to Kill,'' ''Blow Out'' features a harrowing climax, complete with fireworks, as Terri tries to prevent the assassin from killing Sally.

''Blow Out'' failed to match the wildly favorable praise of ''Dressed to Kill,'' but it elicited a more generally positive response from critics. *New York Times*'s Vincent Canby recommended the film on the basis of its technical virtuosity. ''Mr. De Palma has said . . . style is really content,'' Canby wrote. ''If that is the case, 'Blow Out' is exclusively concerned with the mechanics of movie making.'' He cautioned viewers that the narrative was frequently implausible, but added that viewers sharing De Palma's interest in style would find the film ''great if chilly fun.'' Kael and *Rolling Stone*'s Michael Sragow disagreed with Canby's interpretation of ''Blow Out,'' and were consequently more impressed with the work. ''*Blow Out* is thrillingly complicated,'' wrote Sragow, who was especially pleased with De Palma's ability to use the conspiracy and the political theme to make a comment on contemporary America. ''By using suspense technique at full tilt,'' Sragow declared, ''De Palma has managed to turn national torpor into an American moviemaking triumph.'' Kael deemed ''Blow Out'' ''a great movie,'' and she praised De Palma's triumph in finally uniting technique with content. ''When we see Jack surrounded by all the machinery that he tries to control things with, De Palma seems to be giving it a last . . . look,'' she noted. ''It's as if he'd finally understood what technique is for. This is the first film he has made about the things that really matter to him.''

De Palma remains unaffected by the success or failure of his work and cites the equally damaging potential of both notoriety and obscurity in an industry of ''shoddy behavior.'' ''In this business,'' he declared, ''success can be even more destructive than failure, because it can isolate you and leave you surrounded by film people talking about deals and budgets and percentage points, and soon you yourself begin to forget what you want to do.'' He added that his up-and-down career has enabled him to ''pick up some perspective.'' ''If a picture of mine came out today and died, I really don't think it would get to me,'' he declared, ''and neither would a monster success.''

BIOGRAPHICAL/CRITICAL SOURCES: New York Times, May 2, 1968, April 10, 1969, March 23, 1970, April 28, 1970, May 28, 1970, September 21, 1973, September 27, 1973, October 28, 1973, January 15, 1974, November 2, 1974, March 15, 1978, October 30, 1979, May 16, 1980, July 24, 1981; *Cinema*, Volume 5, number 2, 1969; *New Leader*, May 25, 1970, August 11, 1980; *New Yorker*, November 11, 1974, November 22, 1976, March 20, 1978, May 19, 1980, August 4, 1980, July 27, 1981; *Monthly Film Bulletin*, May, 1975; *New York*, August 16, 1976, July 28, 1980, August 4, 1980, August 3, 1981; *Time*, August 16, 1976, November 8, 1976, July 28, 1980; *Film*, December, 1976; *American Film*, July-August, 1977; *Village Voice*, March 20, 1978, July 23, 1980; *Films in Review*, August, 1978; *Newsweek*, August 4, 1980; *Esquire*, October, 1980; *Chicago Tribune*, July 24, 1981; *People*, August 17, 1981; *Rolling Stone*, September 3, 1981; *Contemporary Literary Criticism*, Volume 20, Gale, 1982.*

—*Sketch by Les Stone*

* * *

de SAINT-GALL, Auguste Amedee
See STRICH, Christian

* * *

DEVER, William Gwinn 1933-

BRIEF ENTRY: Born November 27, 1933, in Louisville, Ky. American archaeologist, educator, and author. Dever has been a professor of Near Eastern archaeology at University of Arizona since 1975. He has directed excavations in Israel and, from 1971 to 1975, served as director of W. F. Albright Institute for Archaeological Research in Jerusalem. His books include the two-volume *Gezer I-II* (Nelson Glueck School of Biblical Archaeology, Hebrew Union College, 1970-74), *Biblical Archaeology* (Keter Publishing House, 1973), and *A Manual of Field Excavation: Handbook for Field Archaeologists* (Hebrew Union College, 1978). *Address:* Department of Oriental Studies, University of Arizona, Tucson, Ariz. 85721.

* * *

DEVON, John Anthony
See PAYNE, (Pierre Stephen) Robert

* * *

de WAAL MALEFIJT, Annemarie 1914-1982

OBITUARY NOTICE—See index for *CA* sketch: Born May 23, 1914, in Amsterdam, Netherlands; died December 15, 1982, in Bronx, N.Y. Educator and author. At the time of her death, de Waal Malefijt was professor emeritus of anthropology at Hunter College of the City University of New York. She began her affiliation with that college in 1960 as an assistant professor. She was the author of *The Javanese of Surinam, Religion and Culture*, and *Images of Man*. Obituaries and other sources: *Chronicle of Higher Education*, January 5, 1983.

* * *

DEWHURST, Eileen (Mary) 1929-

PERSONAL: Born May 27, 1929, in Liverpool, England; daughter of Henry Dewhurst (an electrical engineer) and Edith (Adams) Shea. *Education:* Attended Huyton College, 1938-47; St. Anne's College, Oxford, B.A., 1951, M.A., 1958. *Religion:* Church of England. *Home:* 4 The Garth, Waterford Rd., Oxton, Birkenhead, Merseyside, England. *Agent:* Sheila Watson, Bolt & Watson Ltd., 26 Charing Cross Rd., London

WC2H 0DG, England; and George Borchardt, Inc., 136 East 57th St., New York, N.Y. 10022.

CAREER: University of London, London, England, assistant secretary in School of Slavonic and East European Studies, 1953-54; University of Liverpool, Liverpool, England, personal assistant to assistant registrar, 1954-57; Liverpool Chamber of Commerce, Liverpool, committee secretary, 1957-63; free-lance journalist, 1964—. Former director of electrical engineering firm. Volunteer guide to Lady Lever Art Collection, Port Sunlight, Merseyside, England, 1976—. *Member:* Crime Writers Association, Oxford Society.

WRITINGS—Crime novels: *Death Came Smiling,* R. Hale (London), 1975; *After the Ball,* Macmillan (London), 1976; *Curtain Fall* (U.S. Detective Book Club Inner Circle selection), Macmillan (London), 1977, Doubleday, 1982; *Drink This* (U.S. Detective Book Club Inner Circle selection), Collins Crime Club (London), 1980, Doubleday, 1981; *Trio in Three Flats,* Doubleday, 1981; *Whoever I Am,* Collins Crime Club, 1982, Doubleday, 1983; *The House That Jack Built,* Collins Crime Club, 1983. Contributor to column, "Christian Viewpoint," in the *Birkenhead News,* 1978-81; contributor to *Liverpool Daily Post,* 1965-70.

WORK IN PROGRESS: "A murder mystery set in the New Forest, Hampshire, England, in which my detective-inspector Neil Carter, single in three previous books, gets married and spends an unusual working honeymoon."

SIDELIGHTS: Dewhurst told *CA:* "As a crime writer I have of course portrayed a variety of violent deaths and as a writer of modern fiction have written of sexual encounters outside marriage, but believe it is my Christian view of the world which has contained them in an overall structure which tends toward the triumph of good. Perhaps in fact, I feel at home in the crime genre because its basic theme is the disclosing and routing of the bad!

"Despite writing crime novels exclusively (apart from journalistic articles and a few plays which have been produced by amateur companies in England), my chief concern is human relationships and everyday life—out of which the frightening, the suspenseful, the mysterious can arise with peculiar shock.

"My main interests apart from writing are the fine arts (particularly pictures and furniture) and animals. I am also very fond of classical music. I am a compulsive crossword puzzle solver (on a good day I can complete the *London Times* crossword in fifteen minutes) and good at Scrabble, but have no brain for those strategies required in chess, bridge, etc. Since childhood I have visited France regularly, sometimes for months at a time, and love the French language."

BIOGRAPHICAL/CRITICAL SOURCES: Washington Post Book World, June 21, 1981.

* * *

DeWIT, Dorothy May Knowles 1916-1980

OBITUARY NOTICE: Born May 24, 1916, in Youngstown, Ohio; died June 19, 1980. Librarian and author. DeWit, who received her M.S.L.S. from Case Western Reserve University, was head of children's services at the Maple Heights (Ohio) Regional Library from 1966 until her death. She was a member of the Newbery, Caldecott, and Wilder awards committees, and she wrote a book about storytelling in classroom settings, *Children's Faces Looking Up,* in 1979. DeWit also edited *The Talking Stone: An Anthology of Native American Tales and*

Legends. Obituaries and other sources: *School Library Journal,* August, 1980; *Horn Book,* October, 1980; *Who's Who in Library and Information Services,* American Library Association, 1982.

* * *

de WOFLE, Ivor
See HASTINGS, Hubert de Cronin

* * *

de WOLFE, Ivy
See HASTINGS, Hubert de Cronin

* * *

DIAMOND, John 1907-

PERSONAL: Born in 1907 in Leeds, England; son of Solomon and Henrietta (Beckerman) Diamond; children: Derek, Martin, Ruth, Joan. *Education:* Attended grammar school in Leeds, England. *Home:* Aynhoe, Doggetts Wood Lane, Chalfont-St.-Giles, Buckinghamshire, England. *Office:* House of Lords, London S.W.1, England.

CAREER: Chartered accountant, 1931; owner of John Diamond & Co. (chartered accountants), 1931-64; Parliament, London, England, Labour member of House of Commons for Blackley division of Manchester, 1945-51; chairman and managing director of Capital and Provincial News Theatres Ltd., 1951-57; Parliament, Labour member of House of Commons for Gloucester, 1957-70, member of House of Lords, 1970—, chief secretary to Treasury, 1964-70, member of Cabinet, 1968-70, deputy chairman of committees, 1974, member of Privy Council. Chairman of finance and general purposes committee of General Nursing Council, 1947-53; chairman of Royal Commission on the Distribution of Income and Wealth, 1974-79, and Industry and Parliament Trust, 1976-82. Member of board of directors of Sadler's Wells Trust, 1957-64; honorary treasurer of Labour Committee for Europe, 1961-64, and the European Movement; member of board of trustees of Social Democratic Party, 1981-82, leader of party in House of Lords, 1982—. *Member:* Institute of Chartered Accountants (fellow), Fabian Society (honorary treasurer). *Awards, honors:* Created baron, 1970; LL.D. from Leeds University, 1978.

WRITINGS: Public Expenditure in Practice, Allen & Unwin, 1975. Contributor to *Socialism: The British Way,* 1948, and magazines.

* * *

DiBONA, Joseph E. 1927-

BRIEF ENTRY: Born July 18, 1927, in New York, N.Y. American educator and author. DiBona taught at Brooklyn College of the City University of New York from 1965 to 1967 when he began teaching comparative education and South Asian language and area studies at Duke University. He was a Fulbright fellow in India in 1970. DiBona's writings include *Change and Conflict in the Indian University* (Program in Comparative Studies on Southern Asia, Duke University, 1969) and *Language Change and Modernization: The Development of Hindi-English, English-Hindi Glossary of Technical Terms in the Field of Education* (Gujarat Vidyapith, 1970). He edited *The Context of Education in Indian Development* (Duke University Press, 1974). *Address:* Department of Education, Duke University, Durham, N.C. 27706. *Biographical/critical sources: Leaders in Education,* 5th edition, Bowker, 1974.

* * *

DICKINSON, Richard D(onald) N(ye, Jr.) 1929-

BRIEF ENTRY: Born August 1, 1929, in Monson, Mass. American minister, educator, and author. Dickinson is an ordained minister of the United Church of Christ. He has worked in Southern Asia, the Netherlands, and Switzerland. In 1968 Dickinson became professor of Christian social ethics at Christian Theological Seminary and six years later was named dean and vice-president of the seminary. His books include *The Christian College and National Development* (Christian Literature Society, 1967), *Directory of Information for Christian Colleges in India* (Christian Literature Society, 1967), *Line and Plummet: The Churches and Development* (World Council of Churches, 1968), *The Christian College in Developing India: A Sociological Inquiry* (Oxford University Press, 1971), and *To Set at Liberty the Oppressed: Towards an Understanding of Christian Responsibilities of Development/Liberation* (Commission on the Churches' Participation in Development, World Council of Churches, 1975). *Address:* 5173 North Kenwood Ave., Indianapolis, Ind. 46208; and Christian Theological Seminary, 1000 West 42nd St., Indianapolis, Ind. 46208. *Biographical/critical sources: Times Literary Supplement,* April 7, 1972; *Directory of American Scholars,* Volume IV: *Philosophy, Religion, and Law,* 7th edition, Bowker, 1978.

* * *

DICKMEYER, Lowell A. 1939-

PERSONAL: Born May 14, 1939, in Fort Wayne, Ind.; son of Alfred W. (a railway clerk) and Clara A. (Van Horn) Dickmeyer; married Rita R. Schaus (a secretary), August 7, 1965; children: Todd, Tammy, Troy. *Education:* Concordia Teacher's College, Seward, Neb., B.S., 1962; Ball State University, M.A., 1965. *Politics:* "Non-partisan." *Religion:* Christian. *Home and office:* 4611 Alta Canyada, La Canada, Calif. 91011.

CAREER: Classroom teacher and learning disabilities specialist at public schools in Valley Oaks, Calif., 1967-72; Moorpark College, Moorpark, Calif., instructor in physical education, varsity coach, and assistant director of student activities, 1972-78, director of youth sports camps, 1975-81; public relations specialist, lecturer, and writer, 1981—. Part-time teacher in English and social studies for Glendale, Calif., Unified School District. Assistant tennis professional at Sunset Hills Country Club, 1972; teaching supervisor at California Lutheran College, 1973-75; national director of Cultural Exchange, 1978; conducted international youth cultural exchanges, 1975-81. *Member:* Society of Children's Book Writers, Southern California Council on Literature for Children.

WRITINGS: Coaching Very Young Soccer Players, Visual Media Publishing, 1976.

Juveniles; published by Lerner, except as noted: *Soccer Is for Me,* 1978; *Baseball Is for Me,* 1978; *Skateboarding Is for Me,* 1979; *Football Is for Me,* 1979; *Basketball Is for Me,* 1979; *Track Is for Me,* 1980; *Swimming Is for Me,* 1980; (with Lin Rolens) *Ice Skating Is for Me,* 1980; *Hockey Is for Me,* 1980; (with Annette Jo Chappell) *Tennis Is for Me,* 1980; *Winning and Losing,* F. Watts, 1983; *Teamwork,* F. Watts, 1983.

Author of "Soccer for Young People" (filmstrip series), released by Lyceum Productions. Contributor to magazines, including *Young Athlete* and *Soccer America.*

WORK IN PROGRESS—Juvenile fiction: "Soccer Adventure Series," six volumes, publication by Dillon expected in 1983; four easy-read sports books for F. Watts expected in 1984.

SIDELIGHTS: Dickmeyer told *CA:* "For the past seven years I have taken youth groups to various foreign countries on 'Youth Sports Cultural Exchanges.' They are structured to be educational experiences using sports as the medium for activity. I am also involved in sports psychology, studying the nature of sports for young people. Using some of my knowledge and experience, I am producing 'values' books for F. Watts.

"I actually didn't begin writing until 1976. It all began when I was asked to coach a youth soccer team. Not seeing any books on soccer for very young kids, I thought it would be nice to do an easy-reading book for kids ages seven to nine. I sent the story and photos to Lerner. They thought the concept was good and asked me if I was interested in doing a whole series of children's sports books. I signed a contract for twelve books.

"It took a couple of years to do these books. This led me to thinking about other sports books. I decided to do stories about my sports trips to foreign countries with young soccer players. I fictionalized the events and sent the manuscripts to Dillon Press. Thus I am currently working on a six-book 'Soccer Adventure Series.' I am also interested in sports psychology. This led to my series proposal to F. Watts suggesting books dealing with sports values. These books tell children how to gain more enjoyment out of their sports activities. I have future plans to do high-interest, easy-reading books about careers and countries, and stories about special events and special places in America.

"My advice to aspiring writers is to study the current market carefully. Canvass the publishers to find out what they are looking for. Be observant as to the things that are going on in society. Publishers want to keep up with what is going to be potentially 'hot.'"

BIOGRAPHICAL/CRITICAL SOURCES: News-Chronicle (Thousand Oaks, Calif.), October 26, 1977.

* * *

DICKSON, K. A.
See DICKSON, Kwesi A(botsia)

* * *

DICKSON, Kwesi A(botsia) 1929-
(K. A. Dickson)

BRIEF ENTRY: Born July 7, 1929, in Saltpond, Ghana. Ghanaian clergyman, educator, and author. Dickson is a professor of religion at University of Ghana. He wrote *Religions of the World* (Ghana Publishing, 1970) and *The Story of the Early Church as Found in the Acts of the Apostles* (Darton, Longman & Todd, 1976). Dickson edited *Akan Religion and the Christian Faith: A Comparative Study of the Impact of the Two Religions* (Ghana Universities Press, 1965) and co-edited *Biblical Revelation and African Beliefs* (Orbis, 1969). *Address:* Department for the Study of Religions, University of Ghana, P.O. Box 66, Legon, Ghana. *Biographical/critical sources: Times Literary Supplement,* October 2, 1969.

* * *

DIGGS, Elizabeth 1939-

PERSONAL: Born August 6, 1939, in Tulsa, Okla.; daughter

of James B. (a lawyer) and Virginia (Francis) Diggs; children: Jennifer Evans Mackenzie. *Education:* Brown University, B.A., 1961; Columbia University, M.A., 1963, Ph.D., 1980. *Home:* 219 Mulberry St., New York, N.Y. 10012. *Agent:* George Lane, William Morris Agency, 1350 Avenue of the Americas, New York, N.Y. 10019.

CAREER: Queens College of the City University of New York, Flushing, N.Y., lecturer in English, 1970-71; Jersey City State College, Jersey City, N.J., assistant professor of English, 1971-76; Ensemble Studio Theatre, New York, N.Y., member of staff, 1980—.

WRITINGS—Plays: "Close Ties" (two-act), first produced in New Haven, Conn., at Long Wharf Theatre, February, 1981; "Dumping Ground" (one-act), first produced in New York City at Ensemble Studio Theatre, June, 1981. Also author of "Scapegoat" (one-act), "Daddy's Girl" (one-act), and "Goodbye Freddy" (two-act), as yet unpublished and unproduced. Author of a television script for NBC-TV's "St. Elsewhere" series.

WORK IN PROGRESS: A full-length drama, tentatively titled "B.J.'s War," set on a ranch in Oklahoma.

SIDELIGHTS: Diggs's play "Close Ties" reveals the emotions of family members who are confronted by the growing senility of a grandparent when they meet for a summer weekend at a Berkshire retreat. In a *Los Angeles Times* interview with Lawrence Christon, Diggs said she wrote the play "because there was something I wanted to get out that was true, a family portrait. I think I got out the essential, incredibly strong feelings of growing up together. It's a loving family—it's what families aspire to be."

Several reviews of the play's productions in Connecticut, Chicago, and Los Angeles, noted Diggs's gift for characterization. Matthew D. Arkin, in the *Middletown Press*, concluded, "Diggs has taken the time to show the inner workings of her people; this commands respect. Without resorting to any showy tricks or flagrant and glaring techniques of characterization, she slowly, and with craft, illustrates all the individuals so that they become as personal and well-known to us as the family next door becomes after a lifetime. . . . This play cannot be recommended highly enough." Tom Killen echoed this reaction in the *Darien News*, where he declared, "Diggs takes time to develop her characters, and the result is an unflinchingly honest play, devoid of a single false moment or grandiose embellishment. . . . It's an awesome achievement."

Other reviewers compared "Close Ties" favorably with other family plays or those touching on the topic of aging. Richard Christiansen of the *Chicago Tribune* stated, "unlike other works concerned with this same topic—'On Golden Pond' comes immediately to mind—Diggs's play doesn't let the sentiment become too sticky. . . . This play and production are very well done." "Family drama is the heart of American theater . . . but by now so much cheap traffic has clogged the arteries that a family play must be special to be of value," claimed *Chicago Sun-Times* critic David Elliot. "Elizabeth Diggs's 'Close Ties,'" he continued, "is special." Roger Montgomery of the New London *Day* noted that "unlike many such contemporary plays, . . . the social concern in 'Close Ties' does not overwhelm the dramatic and linguistic craft of the author. . . . The drama builds well and works. In short, this is a fine new play and Elizabeth Diggs can write."

Another play, "Dumping Ground," addresses the environmental concerns of two average citizens who blockade a chem-

ical company's dumping site. According to Mel Gussow, who reviewed the play in the *New York Times*, "by the end of the drama, the two begin to share more than their outrage, but Miss Diggs' handling of the romance is as subtle as her attempt to understand how the average man can become enraged at oppressive institutions." Gussow was impressed with Diggs's "talent for portraying recognizable people in emotionally charged situations." A *Los Angeles Times* article concurred, claiming that in "Dumping Ground," "Diggs displays her own unique skill at ferreting out humanity under difficult circumstances." In the *Los Angeles Herald-Examiner,* Eric Lerner observed that "within a single act, playwright Diggs has created a whole lifetime of character." He termed the play "a perfect balance of good comedy and poignant revelation."

Diggs told *CA:* "Thornton Wilder once said that a dramatist is one for whom it is sufficient to show 'what is' without commenting on it. This is true for me. My desire is to listen to my characters with enough attention so that what they say and do is authentic—so that I do not betray them.

"I love both essential aspects of writing for the theatre—the isolation of writing, and the joyous collaborative chaos of production. A play exists in its true form only while it is being performed, and each performance is different—it can never be fixed. That is both its mystery and truth."

BIOGRAPHICAL/CRITICAL SOURCES: Day, February 17, 1981; *Middletown Press,* February 20, 1981; *Darien News,* March 5, 1981; *New York Times,* June 10, 1981; *Los Angeles Times,* December 19, 1981, March 22, 1982; *Los Angeles Herald-Examiner,* January 7, 1982; *Chicago Sun-Times,* January 29, 1982; *Chicago Tribune,* February 1, 1982.

*   *   *

DILLE, Robert Crabtree   1924(?)-1983

OBITUARY NOTICE: Born c. 1924 in Chicago, Ill.; died March 31, 1983, in Chicago, Ill. Communications executive and author. Dille worked as membership director of the National Safety Council and as director of sales and marketing for Encyclopaedia Britannica before joining National Newspaper Syndicate, a distributor of comics, features, and columns, in 1952. He served as the firm's president from 1957 to 1973 and was chairman of its board of directors from 1973 to 1976. Dille wrote *The Collected Works of Buck Rogers in the Twenty-fifth Century.* Obituaries and other sources: *Who's Who in America,* 40th edition, 1978; *International Year Book and Statesmen's Who's Who,* Thomas Skinner Directories, 1982; *Chicago Tribune,* April 2, 1983.

*   *   *

DINMAN, Bertram David   1925-

BRIEF ENTRY: Born August 9, 1925, in Philadelphia, Pa. American physician, company vice-president, and author. Dinman was a professor of medicine at Ohio State University and a professor of environmental and industrial health at University of Michigan. In 1973 he became corporate medical director of Aluminum Company of America; in 1978 he became the firm's vice-president for health and safety. Dinman wrote *The Nature of Occupational Cancer: A Critical Review of Present Problems* (C. C Thomas, 1974). He and Rolf Hartung edited *Environmental Mercury Contamination* (Ann Arbor Science Publishers, 1972). *Address:* Aluminum Company of America, 1501 Alcoa Blvd., Pittsburgh, Pa. 15219. *Biographical/critical* sources: *American Men and Women of Science: The Physical and Biological Sciences*, 14th edition, Bowker, 1979.

*   *   *

DIX, Albert V.   1901(?)-1983

OBITUARY NOTICE: Born c. 1901; died March 4, 1983, in Honolulu, Hawaii. Newspaper publisher. While an undergraduate at Ohio State University, Dix collaborated with humorist James Thurber on scripts for the Scarlet Mask theatre club. Following his graduation, Dix worked as an advertising salesman before becoming publisher of the *Ravenna Evening Record* in 1926 and the *Martins Ferry Daily Times* in 1929. After acquiring the *Bellaire Evening Leader* the next year, he formed the *Martins Ferry Times-Leader* and served as its president until his death. Dix Newspapers, of which Albert Dix was chairman, also published the *St. Clairsville Gazette-Chronicle*. Obituaries and other sources: *Chicago Tribune*, March 8, 1983.

*   *   *

DIXON, Roger Edmund   1935-1983

OBITUARY NOTICE: Born in 1935; died April 18, 1983, in London, England. Educator and author. A graduate of Cambridge University, Dixon joined the faculty of London's Polytechnic of the South Bank in 1964 and taught architectural history there, becoming a reader in the subject shortly before his death. He wrote a widely used textbook, *Victorian Architecture*, with Stefan Muthesius in 1978. Obituaries and other sources: *London Times*, April 20, 1983.

*   *   *

DIXON, Ruth
See BARROWS, (Ruth) Marjorie

*   *   *

DOBSON, Theodore E(lliott)   1946-

PERSONAL: Born December 4, 1946, in Chicago, Ill.; son of Theodore Arthur (an artist) and Ruth Virginia (Hacker) Dobson. *Education:* St. Mary of the Lake Seminary, M.Div., 1972. *Home:* 1792 Kline Way, Lakewood, Colo. 80226. *Office:* Spiritual Renewal Services, 1204 Wadsworth Blvd., Denver, Colo. 80215.

CAREER: Ordained Roman Catholic priest, 1972; associate pastor of Roman Catholic parishes in Chicago, Ill., 1972-78; free-lance lecturer and retreat master, 1978-81; Roman Catholic Archdiocese of Denver, Denver, Colo., director of Spiritual Renewal Services, 1981—. *Member:* Association of Christian Therapists.

WRITINGS: Inner Healing: God's Great Assurance, Paulist Press, 1978; (contributor) Robert Heyer, editor, *Healing Family Hurts*, Paulist Press, 1980; *How to Pray for Spiritual Growth*, Paulist Press, 1981.

WORK IN PROGRESS: Say But the Word: How the Lord's Supper Can Transform Your Life, "a book on the healing power of the Eucharist," publication expected in 1984.

SIDELIGHTS: Dobson commented: "Spiritual Renewal Services is an agency promoting Charismatic Renewal, parish renewal, and spiritual healing. I write on topics which I believe will help people to grow spiritually in their love of God and which help them to become more whole psychologically. I

believe psychology and spirituality are connected. If human beings do not learn how to connect with the spiritual world through God, they find it much more difficult to become whole or happy; thus they create sickness, relationship difficulties, and social evils within themselves and around themselves. I travel throughout North America giving workshops and retreats to deal with this topic.

"*Say But the Word* is a practical book that will help people understand the rite of the Lord's Supper as a means of personal growth and healing. It will also help people understand various parts of the rite, why they are there, and how we can enter them to find wholeness in God."

*   *   *

DODGE, Mary (Elizabeth) Mapes   1831(?)-1905

BRIEF ENTRY: Born January 26, 1831 (some sources say 1838), in New York, N.Y.; died August 21, 1905, in Onteora Park, N.Y. American magazine editor and author of books for children. Dodge was associate editor of Harriet Beecher Stowe's *Hearth and Home* before founding *St. Nicholas* magazine, which she edited from 1873 until her death in 1905. Dodge's two most successful books for children appeared in 1865. The first, *Irvington Stories*, is a collection of eight tales based on Mapes family legends and American colonial history. Its reception prompted Dodge's publisher to request a second manuscript. *Hans Brinker; or, The Silver Skates: A Story of Life in Holland*, the famous work which followed, was inspired in part by John Motley's *Story of the Dutch Republic* and by stories told to Dodge by her Dutch immigrant neighbors. The book was translated into several languages and won the French Academy's Montyon Prize in 1869. Other juvenile works by Dodge include *Donald and Dorothy* (1883), *The Land of Pluck: Stories and Sketches for Young Folk* (1894), *The Golden Gate* (1903), and *Po-no-kah: An Indian Tale of Long Ago* (1903). *Biographical/critical sources:* Alice B. Howard, *Mary Mapes Dodge of "St. Nicholas,"* Messner, 1943; Miriam E. Mason, *Mary Mapes Dodge, Jolly Girl*, Bobbs-Merrill, 1949; *Authors of Books for Young People*, 2nd edition, Scarecrow, 1971; *The Lincoln Library of Language Arts*, 3rd edition, Frontier Press (Columbus, Ohio), 1978; *Webster's American Biographies*, Merriam, 1979.

*   *   *

DOLLEY, Michael   1925-1983

OBITUARY NOTICE: Birth-given name, Reginald Hugh Dolley; born July 6, 1925, in Oxford, England; died March 29, 1983, in Cork, Ireland. Educator, historian, and author. An expert in Anglo-Saxon and Irish coinage, Dolley worked as assistant keeper in the Department of Coins and Metals at the British Museum from 1951 to 1963. He then joined the faculty of Queen's University of Belfast, where he began as lecturer in medieval history and was awarded a personal chair in 1975. Dolley edited the *British Numismatics Journal* for fifteen years and wrote several books on currency and medieval history, including *Anglo-Saxon Coins*, *Medieval Anglo-Irish Coins*, and *Anglo-Norman Ireland*. He was elected a member of the Royal Irish Academy in 1964 and received medals from the numismatic societies of several nations as well as honorary degrees from the University of London and the National University of Ireland. Obituaries and other sources: *Who's Who in the World*, 4th edition, Marquis, 1978; *Who's Who*, 134th edition, St. Martin's, 1982; *London Times*, April 4, 1983.

DOMB, Cyril 1920-

PERSONAL: Born in 1920; married Shirley Esther Galinsky. *Education:* Received Ph.D. *Office:* Department of Physics, Bar-Ilan University, Ramat Gan, Israel.

CAREER: Clarendon Laboratory, Oxford, England, Imperial Chemical Industries fellow, 1949-52; Cambridge University, Cambridge, England, lecturer in mathematics, 1952-54; University of London, King's College, London, England, professor of theoretical physics, 1954-81; Bar-Ilan University, Ramat Gan, Israel, professor of physics, 1981—.

WRITINGS: (Editor) *Clerk Maxwell and Modern Science,* Athlone Press, 1963; (editor) *Memories of Kopul Rosen,* Carmel College, 1970; (editor with M. S. Green) *Phase Transitions and Critical Phenomena,* Academic Press, Volumes I-II, 1972, Volume III, 1974, Volumes V-VI, 1976; (editor with A. Carmell) *Challenge: Torah Views on Science and Its Problems,* Feldheim, 1976, 2nd edition, 1978; (editor) *Maaser Kesafim,* Feldheim, 1980.

* * *

DOMBROWSKI, James A. 1897-1983

OBITUARY NOTICE: Born in 1897 in Tampa, Fla.; died May 2, 1983, in New Orleans, La. Civil rights activist and author. In 1932 Dombrowski founded the Highlander Folk School, a training ground for labor organizers and civil rights activists. He joined the staff of the Southern Conference for Human Welfare in 1938 and became executive director of that body's educational fund in 1948, retiring from the position in 1966. As head of the fund, which worked for the desegregation of schools and colleges, Dombrowski was bitterly opposed by segregationists, and in the early 1960's he was accused under Louisiana law of "failure to register as a member of a Communist front organization." The Supreme Court ruled in 1965 that Louisiana authorities were using unconstitutional laws to harass civil rights activists and thereby prevented the state from trying Dombrowski on the charge. He wrote *The Early Days of Christian Socialism in America* in 1936. Obituaries and other sources: *New York Times,* May 4, 1983.

* * *

DONALDSON, Sam(uel Andrew) 1934-

BRIEF ENTRY: Born March 11, 1934, in El Paso, Tex. American broadcast journalist. Sam Donaldson, who began his career in broadcast journalism in 1959, joined the American Broadcasting Companies (ABC-TV) in 1967. He has served for many years in Washington, D.C., first as Capitol Hill correspondent and later as White House correspondent. *Address:* 11404 Fairfax Dr., Great Falls, Va. 22066; and 1124 Connecticut Ave. N.W., Washington, D.C. 20016. *Biographical/critical sources: Who's Who in America,* 42nd edition, Marquis, 1982; *Time,* April 11, 1983.

* * *

DORPALEN, Andreas 1911-1982

OBITUARY NOTICE—See index for *CA* sketch: Born May 2, 1911, in Berlin, Germany; died December 18, 1982, in Columbus, Ohio. Educator and author. At the time of his death Dorpalen was professor emeritus of twentieth-century German history at Ohio State University. He had previously taught at Kenyon College and at St. Lawrence University before moving

to Ohio State University in 1958. He was the author of several books, including *Heinrich von Treitschke, Hindenburg and the Weimar Republic,* and *Europe in the Twentieth Century.* He also contributed to historical journals. Obituaries and other sources: *Chronicle of Higher Education,* January 12, 1983.

* * *

DOTY, Richard (George) 1942-

PERSONAL: Born January 11, 1942, in Portland, Ore.; son of George B. and Angeline C. (Portland) Doty. *Education:* Portland State University, B.A., 1964; University of Southern California, Ph.D., 1968. *Home:* 160 Cabrini Blvd., New York, N.Y. 10033. *Office:* American Numismatic Society, Broadway at 156th St., New York, N.Y. 10032.

CAREER: Central College, Pella, Iowa, assistant professor of Latin American history and studies, 1967-70; York College of the City University of New York, New York City, assistant professor of Latin American and world history, 1970-71; University of Guam, Agana, assistant professor of American and Latin American history, 1971-73; American Numismatic Society, New York City, assistant curator of modern coins, 1974-76, associate curator of modern coins, 1976-81, curator of modern coins and paper money, 1981—. *Member:* International Bank Note Society, American Numismatic Association, British Numismatic Society, Scottish Numismatic Society. *Awards, honors:* Fulbright fellowship to University of Madrid, fellowships from Mexican Government and University of New Mexico, and teaching assistantship from University of Oregon, all 1964; NDEA fellowship from University of Southern California, 1964-67; teaching fellowship from United States Government, 1967; Del Amo Foundation fellowship for research in Spain, 1969.

WRITINGS: (Contributor) *Community Sensitizing Handbook,* Midwest Research Institute, 1973; *Coins of the World,* Bantam, 1976; *Paper Money of the World,* Bantam, 1977; *Money of the World,* Grosset, 1978; *The Macmillan Encyclopedic Dictionary of Numismatics,* Macmillan, 1982. Associate editor of *Studies in Early American Coinage,* 1976. Contributor of book reviews to *Revista Interamericana.* Contributor to periodicals, including *Coinage, Museum Notes,* and *Guam Recorder.*

WORK IN PROGRESS: Translating Andres Molina Enriquez's *Los Grandes problemas nacionales;* a financial history of North Carolina under the Confederacy; work on the impact of the industrial revolution on coining technology, with particular emphasis on England; work on proclamation coinage of Bolivia and Peru; more articles and a book.

SIDELIGHTS: Doty's *Coins of the World* and *Paper Money of the World* were described by Russ Mackendrick in the *New York Times* as "about the best value in numismatic literature that we have seen for some time." Mackendrick added that *Coins of the World* "is aimed at the collector of modest means, and takes up, in large part, coins that he is most likely to encounter." He also wrote, "Author Doty imparts the flavor of different types of coinage throughout the world, starting with the Lydians of Asia Minor in the 7th century B.C."

In *The Macmillan Encyclopedic Dictionary of Numismatics,* Doty defines more than four hundred numismatic terms, "topics chosen on the basis of their importance to numismatics as a whole and to its sub-disciplines," the author described in *Coin World.* The book covers numismatics from ancient times to the present, exploring coins, currency, medals, tokens, and decorations, offering numerous illustrations. Aimed at the hobbyist as well as the expert, the updated dictionary of terms "has class, yet is definitely for the mass," judged a *Coin World* writer. "Not since Albert R. Frey's 1917 *Dictionary of Numismatic Names* has a work of its nature and scope been attempted in the field."

Doty told *CA:* "The study of coins has been the primary determinant in my professional life. It got me into history, from which I eventually emerged with a doctorate. It eventually landed me in New York. The writing came about by accident, but I saw it initially as a chance to share my enthusiasm for the story of coinage with others, and so it has remained. There is something tactile about an old coin for me: in an almost literal fashion, it puts me into a direct, intimate contact with the past. If I have done my job well, I will communicate this feeling to my readers."

BIOGRAPHICAL/CRITICAL SOURCES: New York Times, June 11, 1978, June 20, 1982; *Coin World,* June 9, 1982, June 16, 1982.

* * *

DOUGLAS, Charles H(erbert) 1926-

BRIEF ENTRY: Born December 2, 1926, in Loughman, Fla. American educator, university research administrator, and author. Douglas taught music at public, parochial, and private schools and at Converse College. In 1961 he began teaching at University of Georgia, where he was later named assistant vice-president for research and director of general research. Douglas's books include *Basic Music Theory* (General Words and Music Co., 1970) and *Playing Social and Recreational Instruments* (Prentice-Hall, 1972). *Address:* Office of the Vice-President for Research, University of Georgia, Athens, Ga. 30602.

* * *

DOVE, Rita 1952-

PERSONAL: Born August 28, 1952, in Akron, Ohio; daughter of Ray (a chemist) and Elvira (Hord) Dove; married Fred Viebahn (a writer), children: Aviva Chantal Tamu Dove-Viebahn. *Education:* Miami University, Oxford, Ohio, B.A. (summa cum laude), 1973; attended University of Iowa, M.F.A., 1977. *Office:* Department of English, Arizona State University, Tempe, Ariz. 85287.

CAREER: Arizona State University, Tempe, assistant professor of creative writing, 1981— . Writer-in-residence at Tuskegee Institute, 1982. *Member:* Academy of American Poets, Poetry Society of American, Poets and Writers, Phi Beta Kappa, Phi Kappa Phi. *Awards, honors:* Fulbright fellowship, 1974-75; grants from National Endowment for the Arts, 1978, and Ohio Arts Council, 1979; International Working Period for Authors fellowship for West Germany, 1980; Portia Pittman fellowship at Tuskegee Institute from National Endowment for the Humanities, 1982; John Simon Guggenheim Fellowship, 1983.

WRITINGS: Ten Poems (chapbook), Penumbra Press, 1977; *The Only Dark Spot in the Sky* (poetry chapbook), Porch Publications, 1980; *The Yellow House on the Corner* (poems), Carnegie-Mellon University Press, 1980; *Mandolin* (poetry chapbook), Ohio Review, 1982; *Museum* (poems), Carnegie-Mellon University Press, 1983. Work represented in anthologies. Contributor of poems and stories to magazines, including *Agni Review, Anteus, Georgia Review, Nation,* and *Poetry.*

WORK IN PROGRESS: Thomas and Beulah, poems; "Lake Erie Skyline," a long narrative poem.

SIDELIGHTS: Dove told *CA:* "Poetry, for me, must explore the felicities of language; the events of the poem should never be more important than how that event is recreated. This is why the stock question, 'What is your poetry about?,' seems fruitless. In recent work I have been trying to combine historical occurrences with the epiphanal quality of the lyric poem. I find travel to be a good way to gain different perspectives and to avoid becoming complacent."

AVOCATIONAL INTERESTS: Travel (Israel, southern Europe, West Germany).

* * *

DOYLE, Denis P. 1940-

PERSONAL: Born April 22, 1940, in Chicago, Ill.; son of Phil A. and Alyce D. Doyle; married Gloria Revilla; children: Alicia, Christopher. *Education:* University of California, Berkeley, A.B., 1962, M.A., 1964. *Home:* 110 Summerfield Rd., Chevy Chase, Md. 20815. *Office:* American Enterprise Institute for Public Policy Research, 1150 17th St. N.W., Washington, D.C. 20036.

CAREER: Sequoia Institute, Sacramento, Calif., president, 1968-72; U.S. Office of Economic Opportunity, Washington, D.C., director of Voucher Project, 1972-73; National Institute of Education, Washington, D.C., assistant director of education finance, 1973-79; Brookings Institution, Washington, D.C., federal executive fellow, 1979-80; American Enterprise Institute for Public Policy Research, Washington, D.C., director of education policy studies, 1981— . Member of board of directors of Sequoia Institute and Institute for Finance and Governance, at Stanford University; consultant to Ford Foundation. *Member:* American Educational Research Association.

WRITINGS: Debating National Education Policy: The Question of Standards, American Enterprise Institute for Public Policy Research, 1981.

Contributor: Paul A. Olsen and others, editors, *Education for 1984,* University of Nebraska Press, 1971; Joel Bergsman and Howard L. Wiener, editors, *Urban Problems Public Policy Choice,* Praeger, 1975; Lawrence Chickering, editor, *Parents, Teachers, and Children: Prospects for Choice in American Education,* Institute for Contemporary Studies (San Francisco, Calif.), 1977; Susan Abramowitz, editor, *The Private High School Today: A Survey of Private School Heads,* U.S. Government Printing Office, 1981; Edward McGlynn Gaffney, editor, *Private Schools and the Public Good: Alternatives for the Eighties,* University of Notre Dame Press, 1981; Jack A. Meyer, editor, *Meeting Human Needs: Toward a New Public Philosophy,* American Enterprise Institute for Public Policy Research, 1982. Contributor to *Standard Education Almanac* and *International Encyclopedia of Education.* Contributor of nearly fifty articles to education journals, popular magazines, and newspapers, including *California Journal* and *New Republic.*

WORK IN PROGRESS: The Brain Race, for Empire Press.

SIDELIGHTS: Doyle told *CA:* "At an early age my father told me, 'If you can't put it in writing, you don't know what you're thinking.' The comment has never left me. My field is public policy analysis, and because I am convinced that much public policy is only weakly supported by evidence, my role is constructive critic. I write, then, to test my own ideas and to reach opinion makers, those who eventually establish public policy.

I balance my work between professional journals and mass publications to keep my research and analytic skills sharpened as I satisfy the stylistic demands of different publications.''

* * *

DOYLE, Frank D.   1909(?)-1983

OBITUARY NOTICE: Born c. 1909 in Manhattan, N.Y.; died of cancer, February 15, 1983, in Brooklyn, N.Y. Public relations executive and journalist. Doyle was a reporter and editor for the *New York Daily Mirror* for sixteen years before serving as press secretary for the New York City Police, Fire, and Sanitation departments between 1945 and 1978. He established the Police Department's first public relations bureau and directed City Hall press relations during the administration of Mayor Robert F. Wagner. Obituaries and other sources: *Organizational Dynamics,* winter, 1982; *New York Times,* February 17, 1983.

* * *

DR. ALPHABET
See MORICE, Dave

* * *

DRAGO, Edmund Leon   1942-

PERSONAL: Born October 16, 1942, in Chicago, Ill.; son of Rosario C. (a physician) and Marguerite (Burke) Drago; married Cheryle Choi (a technical writer), December 20, 1970. *Education:* University of Santa Clara, B.A., 1964; University of California, Berkeley, M.A., 1966, Ph.D., 1975. *Home:* 958 Cottingham Dr., Mount Pleasant, S.C. 29464. *Office:* Department of History, College of Charleston, Charleston, S.C. 29401.

CAREER: Associated with department of history, College of Charleston, Charleston, S.C. *Military service:* U.S. Army, Adjutant General's Corps, 1969-71; served in Vietnam; became captain. *Member:* American Historical Association, Organization of American Historians, Association for the Study of Afro-American Life and History, Southern Historical Association. *Awards, honors:* National Endowment for the Humanities fellowship, 1981.

WRITINGS: Black Politicians and Reconstruction in Georgia: A Splendid Failure, Louisiana State University Press, 1982.

WORK IN PROGRESS: A history of Avery Normal Institute, Charleston, S.C., 1865-1954; a history of the Middleton family of South Carolina.

SIDELIGHTS: Drago told *CA:* ''Hopefully, my book on Georgia will inspire other historians to examine more closely the relation between religion and black politics. Most academics, secular in their orientation, fail to grasp the meaning of religion to most Americans.

''Members of the Middleton family of South Carolina signed both the Declaration of Independence and the ordinances of secession. I think their history will tell us a good deal about both slavery and why the Southern elite went to war.''

* * *

DRAKE, Elizabeth   1948-

PERSONAL: Born March 8, 1948, in New York, N.Y.; daughter of Gregory (a certified public accountant) and Miriam (a high school teacher; maiden name, Lieberman) Drake; divorced; children: Severia Anya, Anton Josef. *Education:* Attended University of Wisconsin (now University of Wisconsin—Madison), 1964-65, and New York University, 1965-66; University of Hartford, B.A., 1972, M.Ed., 1975; Central Connecticut State University, Teachers Certificate and Counselors Certificate, 1980. *Home:* 18 Lancaster Rd., West Hartford, Conn. 06119. *Agent:* Marilyn Marlow, Curtis Brown Ltd., 575 Madison Ave., New York, N.Y. 10022. *Office:* West Hartford Board of Education, 211 Steele Rd., West Hartford, Conn. 06107.

CAREER: Poor People's Federation, Hartford, Conn., paraprofessional social worker, 1968-71; Criminal and Social Justice Coordinating Committee, Hartford, legal researcher, 1971-72; Board of Education, West Hartford, Conn., junior high school guidance counselor, 1976-78, teacher of English as a second language, 1979-82, community facilitator, 1982—. Member of Whiting Lane Neighborhood Advisory Council, 1982-83. *Member:* Connecticut Writers League.

WRITINGS: The Last Score (young adult novel), Four Winds Press, 1981. Contributor to newspapers. Fiction editor of Connecticut Writers League magazine.

WORK IN PROGRESS: A murder mystery for young adults; a science fiction novel for young adults.

SIDELIGHTS: Drake told *CA:* ''Although I wrote through elementary school, high school, and college, I stopped writing for about ten years after I got married. When my daughter was seven years old she was an excellent reader, but she did not have the concentration span necessary to read the books at her interest and reading level. I wrote her a novel for her eighth birthday (it was never published), and once I started writing again I could not stop.

''I was working as a guidance counselor in a local junior high school at that time and was touched by the strength and courage exhibited by many students who had horrendous family situations. I feel that adolescents are often in a frustrating bind. In some ways they are adults, in some ways they are almost adults, and in some ways they are children. When they are exposed to bad home situations they may be forced to act as adults, mentally, but most of the options open to adults are closed to them. I wanted to write about young people in these situations and emphasize their strength as well as their vulnerability. I hope I have accomplished that in *The Last Score.*''

* * *

DREWRY, John E(ldridge)   1902-1983

OBITUARY NOTICE: Born June 4, 1902, in Griffin, Ga.; died February 11, 1983, in Athens, Ga. Educator, journalist, and author. Drewry, dean of the University of Georgia's Henry W. Grady School of Journalism from 1940 to 1969, created the George Foster Peabody Radio and Television Awards administered by the school. He was associate editor of the *Georgia Alumni Record* from 1925 to 1939 and wrote several books on communications topics, including *Contemporary American Magazines, Dimensional Journalism,* and *Onward and Upward With Communications.* Drewry received a Gold Key Award from the Columbia Scholastic Press Association in 1954. Obituaries and other sources: *International Authors and Writers Who's Who,* 8th edition, Melrose, 1977; *Who Was Who in Journalism, 1925-1928,* Gale, 1978; *The Writers Directory:*

1982-1984, Gale, 1981; *Who's Who in America,* 42nd edition, Marquis, 1982; *Chicago Tribune,* February 15, 1983.

* * *

DRINKWATER, John 1882-1937

BRIEF ENTRY: Born June 1, 1882, in Leytonstone, Essex, England; died March 25, 1937, in London, England. British actor, director, dramatist, poet, and biographer. In 1913 Drinkwater became the general manager of the Birmingham Repertory Theatre in Birmingham, England. There he directed more than sixty productions, performed in about forty roles, and wrote several verse plays in the hope of reviving poetic drama in England. Drinkwater wrote his first historical drama, *Abraham Lincoln,* in 1918. Its success prompted the playwright to use historical subjects for several of his subsequent plays, including *Oliver Cromwell* (1921; first produced in 1921), *Mary Stuart* (1921; first produced in 1921), and *Robert E. Lee* (1923; first produced in 1923). Drinkwater also wrote the powerful antiwar play *X = o: A Night of the Trojan War* (1917; first produced in 1917), in addition to more than twenty volumes of poetry, several biographies, a novel, and an autobiography. *Biographical/critical sources: Twentieth-Century Authors: A Biographical Dictionary of Modern Literature,* H. W. Wilson, 1942, 1st supplement, 1955; *The Oxford Companion to English Literature,* 4th editon, Oxford University Press, 1967; *A Concise Encyclopedia of the Theatre,* Osprey, 1974; *Dictionary of Literary Biography,* Volume 10: *Modern British Dramatists, 1940-45,* Gale, 1982.

* * *

DROWN, Merle 1943-

PERSONAL: Born January 14, 1943, in York, Maine; son of Merle F. and Hazel (Gallagher) Drown. *Education:* Macalester College, B.A., 1965; attended University of Washington, Seattle, 1965-66; Goddard College, M.F.A., 1978. *Home:* 60 West Parish Rd., Concord, N.H. 03301. *Agent:* Gerard McCauley Agency, Inc., Box AE, Katonah, N.Y. 10536.

CAREER: Writer.

WRITINGS: Plowing Up a Snake (novel), Dial, 1982; *The Two-Sided House* (novel), Dial, in press.

SIDELIGHTS: Merle Drown told *CA:* "My first novel is about an actual murder in a small town, a murder that remained unsolved, although many apparently knew the murderers' identities. What stimulated me to write about this event was that for twenty years I had been hearing people talking about it, making stories about it. They were groping to find the truth, not of the murder, but of the human spirit.

"It is when characters come alive that fiction can reveal the truth of ideals and ideas. For me that means finding an occurrence, whether it is a personal experience or an anecdote or a news item, that can provide the situation for my characters to become themselves and to live out their lives, separate from me. It is what I believe is creativity."

In a *San Francisco Chronicle* review of *Plowing Up a Snake,* Bruce Colman wrote: "First-time novelist Merle Drown is so good with characters, weather and landscape that we can practically walk the streets of Enoch, New Hampshire, where this story takes place. . . . [It] is compelling reading, the kind of fiction you can stay up with half the night."

BIOGRAPHICAL/CRITICAL SOURCES: San Francisco Chronicle, September 8, 1982.

du CANN, Charles Garfield Lott 1889(?)-1983

OBITUARY NOTICE: Born c. 1889; died February 24, 1983. Journalist, lawyer, and author. Before entering the practice of criminal law in 1919, du Cann was a teacher and a member of the editorial staff of the *London Evening News.* During a fifty-year period he wrote seventeen books, including *Treason Trials, Antiques for Amateurs,* and *The Love Lives of Charles Dickens.* Obituaries and other sources: *The Author's and Writer's Who's Who,* 6th edition, Burke's Peerage, 1971; *Who Was Who Among English and European Authors, 1931-1949,* Gale, 1978; *London Times,* March 12, 1983.

* * *

DUGUID, Charles 1884-

PERSONAL: Born April 6, 1884, in Saltcoats, Scotland; son of Charles and Jane Duguid; married Irene Young, October, 1912 (died, 1927); married Phyllis Evelyn Lade (an educator), December 18, 1930; children: (first marriage) Charles; (second marriage) Andrew, Rosemary (Mrs. R. M. Douglas). *Education:* Univerity of Glasgow, M.A., 1905, M.B., Ch.B., 1907. *Religion:* Presbyterian. *Home:* 33 Dequetteville Ter., Kenttown, South Australia 5067.

CAREER: University of Glasgow, Glasgow, Scotland, surgeon assistant to Sir William MacEwen, 1909-11; general practice of surgery, 1912-55; moderator of Presbyterian Church of Australia, 1935-36. Founder of Ernabella Mission to Pitjantjatjara Tribe in the Musgrave Ranges of Australia, 1935-36; member of South Australia Government Aborigines Protection Board, 1940-47; president of Aborigines Advancement League of South Australia, 1951-61. *Military service:* Australian Imperial Forces, Army Medical Corps; became captain. *Member:* Royal Australasian College of Surgeons (fellow), Royal College of Surgeons of Glasgow (fellow). *Awards, honors:* Officer of Order of the British Empire; Annisfield-Wolf Award in Race Relations from Cleveland Foundation, 1974, for *Doctor and the Aborigines.*

WRITINGS: The Desert Trail, Department of Repatriation, 1919; *MacEwen of Glasgow: A Recollection of the Chief,* Oliver & Boyd, 1957; *No Dying Race,* Rigby, 1963; *Doctor and the Aborigines* (autobiography), Rigby, 1972, published as *Doctor Goes Walkabout,* 1977.

BIOGRAPHICA/CRITICAL SOURCES: Adelaide Advertiser, February 12, 1981.

* * *

DUJARDIN, Edouard (Emile Louis) 1861-1949

BRIEF ENTRY: Born November 10, 1861, in St. Gervais, France; died in 1949. French poet, playwright, and novelist. Dujardin is credited with introducing the stream of consciousness technique into fiction with his novel *Les Lauriers sont coupes* (1888). He also founded two publications, *Revue wagnerienne* and *Revue independante.* His collections of poetry include *Poesies* (1913) and *Mari Magno* (1922). Dujardin's plays were collected in the two-volume *Theatre* (1920-24). *Biographical/critical sources: The Reader's Encyclopedia,* 2nd edition, Crowell, 1965; *The Oxford Companion to French Literature,* corrected edition, Clarendon Press, 1966; *The New Century Handbook of English Literature,* revised edition, Appleton, 1967; *Longman Companion to Twentieth Century Lit-*

erature, Longman, 1970; *Twentieth-Century Literary Criticism,* Volume 11, Gale, 1983.

* * *

DUNN, Jean 1921-

PERSONAL: Born March 9, 1921, in Arkansas. *Home:* 116 Sunset Dr., Vacaville, Calif. 95688.

WRITINGS: (Editor) *Seeds of Consciousness: The Wisdom of Sri Nisargadatta Maharaj,* Grove, 1982. Contributor to philosophy and theology journals.

WORK IN PROGRESS: Editing *Prior to Consciousness.*

SIDELIGHTS: Jean Dunn commented: "My two books are the teachings of a great sage, and at their completion I have no further interest in publishing anything. Sri Nisargadatta Maharaj was my guru, and I promised him that I would complete the books."

* * *

DUNNIGAN, Alice Allison 1906-1983

OBITUARY NOTICE: Born April 27, 1906, in Russellville, Ky.; died of ischemic bowel disease, May 6, 1983, in Washington, D.C. Journalist and author. After teaching school and working as a writer for several Kentucky newspapers, Dunnigan moved to Washington, D.C., where, from 1947 to 1961, she served as chief of the Washington bureau of the Associated Negro Press. Dunnigan was named education consultant to the President's Committee on Equal Employment Opportunity in 1961 and was an associate editor with the President's Commission on Youth Opportunity from 1967 to 1970. The recipient of numerous journalism awards, the newswoman was the first black elected to the Women's National Press Club. Dunnigan wrote an autobiography, *A Black Woman's Experience: From Schoolhouse to White House,* and a history of black Kentuckians. Obituaries and other sources: *Foremost Women in Communications,* Bowker, 1970; *Who's Who of American Women,* Marquis, 1972; *The International Year Book and Statesmen's Who's Who,* Thomas Skinner Directories, 1982; *Washington Post,* May 8, 1983; *New York Times,* May 9, 1983.

* * *

DUNSTON, Arthur John 1922-

PERSONAL: Born January 17, 1922, in Reading, England; son of Frederick Arthur and Lillian Grace (Avery) Dunston; married Lynette Meryl McAuley (a dental surgeon), December, 1961; children: Colin, Cynthia (Mrs. Rob Smithson). *Education:* University of Reading, B.A., 1947; St. John's College,

Cambridge, B.A., 1949, M.A., 1951. *Home:* 24A Rednal St., Mona Vale, New South Wales 2103, Australia. *Office:* Deputy Vice-Chancellor's Office, University of Sydney, Sydney, New South Wales 2006, Australia.

CAREER: University of London, London, England, assistant lecturer in Latin, 1949-51; University of Reading, Reading, England, lecturer in Latin, 1951-53; University of Sydney, Sydney, Australia, professor of Latin, 1953—, dean of faculty of arts, 1956-61, deputy vice-chancellor, 1968 and 1981—. Member of board of trustees of Sydney Grammar School; past president of Library Council of New South Wales. *Military service:* British Army, Royal Warwickshire Regiment, 1941-44; became lieutenant. *Member:* Bibliographical Society of Australia and New Zealand (vice-president), Australian Society for Classical Studies (past president), Classical Association of New South Wales (past president). *Awards, honors:* Cavaliere nell'Ordine al Merito della Repubblica Italiana, 1968.

WRITINGS: Studies in Domizio Calderini, Antenore, 1968; *Four Centres of Classical Learning in Renaissance Italy,* University of Sydney Press, 1972. Contributor to learned journals.

WORK IN PROGRESS: An edition of the commentary of Calderini on the *Punica* by Silius Halicus.

SIDELIGHTS: Dunston told *CA:* "I became interested in the Renaissance humanists (i.e., classical scholars) while at Cambridge, on realizing that the extent of their contribution to scholarship had not been matched by the comparatively scanty attention paid to them by their modern counterparts."

* * *

DUSTER, Alfreda Barnett 1904-1983

OBITUARY NOTICE: Born September 3, 1904, in Chicago, Ill.; died April 2, 1983, in Chicago, Ill. Sociologist, civic leader, and editor. Duster, daughter of Ferdinand Barnett, founder of the first black newspaper in Chicago, was coordinator of delinquency prevention for the Illinois Youth Commission from 1947 to 1965 and chairman of Chicago's Woodlawn Model Cities Council in the early 1970's. She edited *Crusade for Justice,* an autobiography of her mother, journalist Ida B. Wells, in 1970. For the next decade, she gave lectures on her mother's contributions to furthering black rights. Duster received an honorary doctorate from Chicago State University. Obituaries and other sources: *Living Black American Authors: A Biographical Directory,* Bowker, 1973; *Who's Who Among Black Americans,* 2nd edition, Who's Who Among Black Americans, 1977; *Who's Who of American Women,* 10th edition, Marquis, 1977; *Chicago Tribune,* April 5, 1983.

E

EARL OF ARRAN
   See GORE, Arthur Kattendyke S(trange) D(avid)
   A(rchibald)

*   *   *

EASTERLIN, Richard A(inley) 1926-

PERSONAL: Born January 12, 1926, in Ridgefield Park, N.J.; son of John Daniel and Helen Maud (Booth) Easterlin; married Jacqueline Miller, September 11, 1949; children: John Daniel, Nancy Lincoln, Susan Provost, Andrew M. *Education:* Stevens Institute of Technology, M.E. (with distinction), 1945; University of Pennsylvania, A.M., 1949, Ph.D., 1953. *Home:* 246 Chester Rd., Devon, Pa. 19333. *Office:* Department of Economics, University of Pennsylvania, Philadelphia, Pa. 19104.

CAREER: University of Pennsylvania, Philadelphia, assistant professor, 1953-56, associate professor, 1956-60, professor of economics, 1960—, chairman of department, 1958-62, 1965, and 1968, associate dean for budget and planning of the faculty of arts and sciences, 1974-77. Visiting professor of economics at Stanford University, 1960-61; visiting centennial professor at Texas A & M University, 1976. Research associate at University of Pennsylvania, 1953-55, and National Bureau of Economic Research, 1955-56, member of research staff, 1956-66. United Nations expert at Economic Commission for Asia and the Far East Conference on Asian Population, 1963. Member of National Science Foundation Economics Advisory Panel, 1963-65, executive committee of Conference on Research in Income and Wealth, 1963-66, Social Science Research Council (SSRC) Committee on Economic Growth, 1964-68, SSRC Committee on Population, Manpower, and Economic Change, 1965-68, National Institute of Child Health and Human Development (NICHHD) Advisory Panel on Antecedents, Processes, and Consequences of Population Structure, Distribution, and Change, 1968-70, and NICHHD Behaviorial Sciences Research Contract Advisory Committee (chairman, 1973-76). Convenor of Section on Innovation and Diffusion of Technology, Third International Economic History Congress, Munich, 1965. Organizer of Section on Relations Between Population Pressure and Economic and Demographic Change, General Assembly of International Union for the Scientific Study of Population, London, 1969.

MEMBER: International Union for the Scientific Study of Population, Population Association of America (member of board of directors, 1964-65, 1969-72; second vice-president, 1973-74; president, 1977) American Economic Association, Mathematical Social Sciences Board (representative for history, 1976—), Economic History Association (member of Council on Research in Economic History; vice-president, 1971-72). *Awards, honors:* Social Science Research Council predoctoral research training fellowship, 1951-52; Israel Summer Fellowship, 1959; faculty research fellowship from Ford Foundation, 1965-66; University of Michigan Sesquicentennial Award, 1967; fellowship from Center for Advanced Study in the Behavioral Sciences, 1970-71.

WRITINGS: Population, Labor Force, and Long Swings in Economic Growth: The American Experience, National Bureau of Economic Research, 1968; (editor with Lance E. Davis and William N. Parker) *American Economic Growth: An Economist's History of the United States,* Harper, 1972; *The Economics and Sociology of Fertility: A Synthesis,* two volumes, University of Pennsylvania Press, 1973; *Birth and Fortune: The Impact of Numbers on Personal Welfare,* Basic Books, 1980; (editor) *Population and Economic Change in Developing Countries,* University of Chicago Press, 1980.

Contributor: Seymour E. Harris, editor, *American Economic History,* McGraw, 1961; Mark Perlman, editor, *Human Resources in the Urban Economy,* Johns Hopkins University Press, 1963; C. Arnold Anderson and Mary Jean Bowman, editors, *Education and Economic Growth,* Aldine, 1965; Robert Aaron Gordon and Margaret S. Gordon, editors, *Prosperity and Unemployment,* Wiley, 1966; Victor R. Fuchs, editor, *Production and Productivity in the Service Industries,* Columbia University Press, 1969; S. J. Behrman and others, editors, *Fertility and Family Planning: A World View,* University of Michigan Press, 1969.

Neil W. Chamberlain, editor, *Contemporary Economic Issues,* revised edition, Irwin, 1972; E. R. Meiss and R. H. Reed, editors, *Research Reports,* Volume II: *Economic Aspects of Population Change,* U.S. Government Printing Office, 1973; Meyer H. Fishbein, editor, *The National Archives and Statistical Research,* Ohio University Press, 1973; A. Weintraub, E. Schwartz, and J. R. Aronson, *The Economic Growth Controversy,* International Arts and Sciences Press, 1973; Eleanor B. Sheldon, editor, *Family Economic Behavior: Problems and Prospects,* Lippincott, 1973; Paul A. David and Melvin W. Reder, editors, *Nations and Households in Economic Growth: Essays in Honor of Moses Abramovitz,* Academic Press, 1974; David C. Klingaman and Richard K. Vedder, editors, *Essays in Nineteenth Century Economic History,* Ohio University Press, 1975; (with Gretchen A. Condran) Hamish Richards, editor, *Population, Factor Movements, and Economic Development: Studies Presented to Brinley Thomas,* University of Wales Press, 1976; Glenn Porter, editor, *Regional Economic History: The Mid-Atlantic Area Since 1700,* Eleutherian Mills-Hagley Foundation, 1976; Sidney Weintraub, editor, *Some Trends in Modern Economic Thought,* University of Pennsylvania Press, 1977; Robert E. Gallman, editor, *Recent Developments in the Study of Business and Economic History: Essays in Honor of Herman E. Krooss,* Jai Press, 1977; Tamara Hareven and Maris Vinovskis, editors, *Family and Population in Nineteenth-Century America,* Princeton University Press, 1978.

Also contributor to encyclopedias and professional journals, including *Dictionary of American Economic History, International Encyclopedia of the Social Sciences, The Annals, Journal of American History, Prospectives, Journal of Economic History,* and *American Economic Review.*

Editorial consultant for *Demography,* 1965-67; member of editorial board of *Journal of Economic History,* 1965-70; member of board of editors of *American Economic Review,* 1965-67, and *Journal of Economic Literature,* 1968-70.

SIDELIGHTS: In *Birth and Fortune: The Impact of Numbers on Personal Welfare,* Easterlin introduces his theory about the fluctuations in birth rates common to an industrial society. According to a *New York Times* review by Christopher Lehmann-Haupt, Easterlin differs from "demographers of the past who thought the populations of industrial societies either grew or declined in a steady pattern." Easterlin's hypothesis, Lehmann-Haupt continued, is that "people actually decide how many children to have according to how well off they see themselves economically." Consequently, the economic boom after World War II precipitated a baby boom, and conversely, the less prosperous economy of the 1960's and 1970's was followed by a decline in the birth rate.

Easterlin's theory is significant for two reasons, Lehmann-Haupt wrote. "For one thing, it means, according to Professor Easterlin, that the 'Stagflation' our economy is currently mired in can be largely explained by the post war baby boom and will presently abate. . . . For another thing, Professor Easterlin's thesis means that the end of the traditional nuclear family may not be as imminent as it seemed. The accelerated rise in the divorce rate and the increasingly rapid entry of women into the work force may simply be symptoms of the baby boom's coming of age." "What's useful about this line of thought," E. J. Dionne observed in a *New York Times Book Review* article, "is that it shows how quick we are to draw sweeping conclusions about the decay of traditional values or the liberation of women without considering narrower causes of these events, such as population trends." "Mr. Easterlin," Dionne continued, "is willing to accept other than demographic explanations of things. He's written a book designed to provoke, and provoke it does."

BIOGRAPHICAL/CRITICAL SOURCES: New York Times, October 20, 1980; *New York Times Book Review,* November 9, 1980.

EDDISON, E(ric) R(ucker)   1882-1945

BRIEF ENTRY: Born November 24, 1882, in Adel, Yorkshire, England; died August 18, 1945. British civil servant and author. Eddison's masterpiece is the fantasy novel *The Worm Ouroboros* (1922). This epic adventure, which plunges the reader into a medieval world full of magic and wizardry, has remained popular with fantasy lovers to the present day. Eddison also wrote a romantic Viking saga, *Styrbiorn the Strong* (1926), and three sequels to *Ouroboros, Mistress of Mistresses: A Vision of Zimiamvia* (1935), *A Fish Dinner in Memison* (1941), and *The Menzentian Gate* (1958). *Biographical/critical sources: Who's Who in Horror and Fantasy Fiction,* Elm Tree Books, 1977; *The Encyclopedia of Science Fiction: An Illustrated A to Z,* Grenada, 1979.

*   *   *

EDGERTON, Joseph S.   1900(?)-1983

OBITUARY NOTICE: Born c. 1900 in Denver, Colo.; died April 22, 1983. Military officer and journalist. Edgerton worked as a reporter, assistant city editor, and aviation editor with the *Washington Evening Star* between 1920 and 1941, then entered the Army Air Forces (now U.S. Air Force), where he served in a public relations capacity during World War II. Prior to retiring from active duty in 1959, Colonel Edgerton was branch chief of the War Department's public relations bureau and worked in the Defense Department's security review division. He was military governor of the Aviation Writers Association. Obituaries and other sources: *Washington Post,* April 24, 1983.

*   *   *

EDWARDS, Alexander
See FLEISCHER, Leonore

*   *   *

EDWARDS, Harry   1942-

BRIEF ENTRY: Born November 22, 1942, in St. Louis, Mo. American sociologist, educator, and author. Edwards was at the center of controversy at the 1968 Olympics in Mexico City when he organized and led other black athletes in a boycott of the games, an action which resulted in his becoming the subject of an intensive FBI investigation. His autobiography, *The Struggle That Must Be* (Macmillan, 1981), graphically recounts his childhood in an East St. Louis, Illinois, ghetto and traces his life through the civil rights days and the struggles of militant black activists in the 1960's to his highly publicized fight for tenure at the University of California, Berkeley. Edwards, who is credited with developing the academic field of sports sociology, contends that sports have long been used to suppress black youth by diverting their attention from pursuits more meaningful to the status of black Americans. Edwards's critical views of sports, politics, capitalism, and American society in general are expressed in his books *The Revolt of the Black Athlete* (Free Press, 1969), *Black Students* (Free Press, 1970), *Sociology of Sport* (Dorsey, 1973), and *Playing to Win: A Short Guide to Sensible Black Sports Participation* (Institute for the Study of Social Change, University of California, Berkeley, 1982). *Biographical/critical sources: Civil Rights: A Current Guide to the People, Organizations, and Events,* Bowker, 1974; *New York Times Magazine,* May 12, 1978; *New York Times Book Review,* December 21, 1980; *Los Angeles Times,* December 23, 1980; *New York Times,* January 10, 1981.

EDWARDS, Peter (William) 1934-

PERSONAL: Born February 4, 1934, in London, England; married wife, Gunvor (an artist); children: six. *Education:* Attended Regent Street Polytechnic School of Art. *Residence:* London, England.

CAREER: Full-time illustrator of books for children.

WRITINGS—For young children; published by Macmillan (London): *Simply Salt,* 1978; *Simply Sell,* 1978; *Simply Size,* 1978; *Simply Song,* 1978; *Simply Soup,* 1978; *Simply Stones,* 1978.

Illustrator; school texts: Patrick W. Cordin, *Number in Mathematics,* Books 3-5, Macmillan, 1970; John O. Herrington, *A New Secondary School English,* Book 1: *Laying the Foundations,* Heinemann Educational, 1971; Thomas C. Jupp and John Milne, *Guided Paragraph Writing,* Heinemann Educational, 1972; Neil Dalgleish, *Living in a Changing World* (secondary social studies text), Thomas Nelson, Volume 1, 1973, Volume 2, 1974; Michael Coles and Basil Lord, *Access to English* (exercises for nonEnglish-speaking students), Oxford University Press, Part 1: *Starting Out,* 1974, teacher's edition, 1975, Part 2: *Getting On,* 1975, teacher's edition, 1976; Christopher Pearson, *Getting Down to Business in English,* Heinemann Educational, Book 1, 1974, Book 2, 1976; *Oxford Comprehensive Mathematics: A Secondary Course for Mixed Abilities,* Books 1 and 3, Oxford University Press, 1975; Leslie A. Hill, *An Elementary Refresher Course,* 2nd edition (Edwards was not associated with earlier edition), Oxford University Press, 1976.

Illustrator; for children: Roger Pilkington, *The Eisenbart Mystery,* St. Martin's, 1963; Kenneth Rudge, *Man Builds Houses,* Hamish Hamilton, 1963; Carl Memling, *Seals for Sale,* Abelard, 1964; (illustrator with wife, Gunvor Edwards) Wilbert Awdry, *Duke, the Lost Engine,* Kaye & Ward, 1970; Edward Ramsbottom, *Boxes, Bags, and Bottles,* Macmillan, 1971; John O. Clark, *Chemistry,* Hamlyn Publishing, 1971; Monica Dickens, *The Great Escape,* Kaye & Ward, 1971; Ramsbottom, *In Fashion,* Macmillan, 1971; Ramsbottom, *On the Move,* Macmillan, 1971; Augstine Oppong-Affi, *Powers of Darkness,* Heinemann Educational, 1971; James V. Clinton, *The Rescue of Charlie Kalu,* Heinemann Educational, 1971; Laurence Meynell, *Troy Trotter and the Kitten,* Kaye & Ward, 1971; Michael Holt and Ronald Ridout, *The Big Book of Puzzles,* Longman Young Books, 1972; Compton Mackenzie, *The Dining-Room Battle,* Kaye & Ward, 1972; Elizabeth Berridge, *That Surprising Summer,* Kaye & Ward, 1972; (illustrated with G. Edwards) Awdry, *Tramway Engines,* Kaye & Ward, 1972; Holt and Ridout, *The Second Big Book of Puzzles,* Longman Young Books, 1973; Albert James, *Wheels,* Macdonald & Co., 1973; Aidan Chambers, *Great Ghosts of the World,* Pan Books, 1974; John Milne, *The Black Cat,* Heinemann Educational, 1975; John Denton, *The Colour Factory,* Puffin, 1976; Dorothy Edwards, *A Look, See, and Touch Book,* Methuen, 1976; D. Edwards, *A Walk Your Fingers Story,* Methuen, 1976; Sybil Marshall, *Nicholas and Finnegan,* Puffin, 1977; Harold Shampan, *Tony and the Magic Watering-Can,* Hutchinson, 1978; Holt, *Puma Puzzles,* Puffin, 1980.

* * *

EHMANN, James 1948-

PERSONAL: Born August 6, 1948, in Long Island, N.Y.; son of John Lloyd (a merchant) and Mary Ruth (Morgan) Ehmann. *Education:* Allegheny College, B.A., 1970. *Home:* 218 Jasper St., Syracuse, N.Y. 13203. *Agent:* Betty Marks, 176 East 77th St., New York, N.Y. 10021. *Office:* Syracuse Post-Standard, P.O. Box 4818, Clinton Sq., Syracuse, N.Y. 13221.

CAREER: Adult Education Center, Cleveland, Ohio, teacher, 1971-73; Morgan's Chimney Sweeping, Oneonta, N.Y., chimney sweep, 1973-75; Adult Education Center, Cleveland, teacher, 1975-76; *Wheeling News-Register,* Wheeling, W.Va., reporter, 1976; *Syracuse Post-Standard,* Syracuse, N.Y., reporter, 1977-80; *New York Times,* New York, N.Y., central New York contributor, 1978-81; *Syracuse Post-Standard,* reporter, 1982—.

WRITINGS: *Chattey's Island* (nonfiction), Ticknor & Fields, 1982. Author of "Ehmann's People," a daily column in *Syracuse Post-Standard.*

WORK IN PROGRESS: To Whom It May Concern, nonfiction dealing with "creative expression evidenced in the art of Siri, an elephant"; *Onondaga,* nonfiction on "the struggle of native people to survive."

SIDELIGHTS: Ehmann wrote: "The partial phases of a solar eclipse are typically visible from much of the planet's surface. The viewing is exclusive only because special filters are required for looking at the crescent sun, and the experience, at best, is mildly curious. Mostly it is boring, very boring.

"The sight of the same eclipse, if observed from within the tiny, limited path of the moon's shadow as it races over the face of the earth, is another thing entirely. Viewed safely with the naked eye, a total eclipse of the sun—with starlight surrounding the living corona and the pastel hues of sunrise and sunset holding calm along the horizon—is exquisite and awesome and a thing of wonder, profound on the scale of religious vision.

"Much of what happens every day in the world around us is like that, to one degree or another. The difference between the mundane and the extraordinary is often no more than a difference in perspective, so the journalist's job is to discover and achieve the thoughtful, creative perspective. Every good writer I ever met was a vantage hunter.

"*Chattey's Island* is a real-life adventure, the tale of a man who conceived a patently sensible plan to solve dozens of America's most pressing economic and environmental dilemmas; and of how our institutions—government, media, and so on—respond to so magnificent a scheme. On another level the book presents a classic story, epic in scope, of the human spirit and the American dream.

"The ramifications of the plan take some explaining, but the proposal itself is simple enough. Nigel Chattey wants to create an enormous industrial super-port on a man-made island about twenty miles off the coast of New York and to connect the facility to its optimal hinterland by modernizing America's first great public works project—the venerable Erie Canal."

* * *

EICHMAN, Mark 1949-

PERSONAL: Born October 2, 1949, in Cedar Rapids, Iowa; son of David William (in business) and Iris Ann (Halverson) Eichman. *Education:* California Lutheran College, B.A., 1971; University of Arizona, M.A., 1976. *Residence:* Pontiac, Mich. *Agent:* Audrey Wood, International Creative Management, 40 West 57th St., New York, N.Y. 10019.

CAREER: Florida State University, Tallahassee, teaching assistant, 1977-78; writer, 1978—. Actor in summer stock, and with Children's Theatre Troupe in California and Arizona. *Military service:* U.S. Army, 1971-73. *Member:* American Film Institute, Dramatists Guild. *Awards, honors:* Playwriting award from Western States Art Foundations, 1976, for "As to the Meaning of Words"; California Lutheran College alumni achievement award, 1980.

WRITINGS—Plays: "The Pawn" (one-act), first produced at the University of Arizona, 1975; *American Gothic* (one-act; first produced at the University of Arizona, 1977), Dramatic Publishing Co., 1977; "As to the Meaning of Words," first produced by Hartman Theatre Co., Stamford, Conn., 1977; "Sharing" (juvenile), first produced at the Looking Glass Theatre, Providence, R.I., 1982.

WORK IN PROGRESS: "Kaliope," a full-length drama; "Simple Persuasion," a romantic comedy.

SIDELIGHTS: Ranging from serious drama to black comedy and including productions for children, Eichman's works, according to the playwright, are simply "plays about people and the situations they find themselves in." In "American Gothic," for example, a magazine writer travels to Iowa to interview a family chosen on the basis of statistical information as the most typical family in the United States. What the writer finds, and what Eichman intends to point out, however, is the inanity in proposing that there is, indeed, a typical American style of life.

Eichman fictionalized an actual court case in "As to the Meaning of Words." In this full-length drama, abortion is the main issue and the primary questions are "When does a fetus become 'viable'?" and "When does 'termination of pregnancy' become manslaughter?" Based on the trial of Kenneth Edelin, the doctor convicted in 1975 of manslaughter after performing an abortion on a seventeen-year-old Boston girl, "As to the Meaning of Words" demonstrates that the physician's trial was little more than a debate in semantics.

Eichman, commenting on writing, told *CA:* "It's not all that it's cracked up to be. The hours are long. The pay is laughable. But when you can push that aside, writing is as great a journey as any. You come to know a strange assortment of characters. And you experience truths about yourself. When you succeed, there's nothing like it. And when you fail, it's only a temporary setback."

BIOGRAPHICAL/CRITICAL SOURCES: *New York Times,* April 16, 1977, April 11, 1981, June 3, 1981; *Boston Globe,* April 17, 1977; *Time,* April 18, 1977.

* * *

EINSTEIN, Albert 1947-
(Albert Brooks)

BRIEF ENTRY: Born July 22, 1947. American comedian, motion picture actor and director, and screenwriter, who has used the name Albert Brooks since high school. Brooks, who may be best known to American television audiences of his numerous appearances on the "Tonight" show, has written many short films for the program "Saturday Night Live." "Regarded as sort of a godfather to the 'Saturday Night Live' school of comedy," Brooks declined an offer to act as permanent host of the popular program, deciding instead to pursue a career in feature filmmaking. His first such effort was the critically acclaimed "Real Life," which he co-authored, starred in, and

directed. The movie is a satire of the *cinema verite* approach that characterizes many television documentaries, particularly "An American Family," the 1973 Public Broadcasting System (PBS-TV) series on the Louds. Brooks later co-authored the screenplay for the 1981 movie "Modern Romance," which he starred in and directed as well. In his *Chicago Tribune* review of "Modern Romance," Gene Siskel called Brooks "a superb writer with a marvelous ear for the slogan-filled way a lot of people talk," adding that he "excels at skewering trendy modern man." *Biographical/critical sources: New York Times,* March 2, 1979, March 13, 1981; *Chicago Tribune,* July 23, 1979, April 3, 1981; *Washington Post,* April 3, 1981.

* * *

EINSTEIN, Elizabeth (Ann) 1939-

PERSONAL: Born October 7, 1939, in Loyal, Wis.; daughter of Andrew (a farmer) and Betty Mae (a bookkeeper; maiden name, Lee) Weyer; married Billy Ralston Matteson (divorced); married Walter O. Einstein (a college professor), February 14, 1969; children: (first marriage) Christopher Alan, Jeffrey Scott (adopted sons); (second marriage) Beverly V. Einstein Grulke, Brenda Lorraine Einstein Wilcox, Kurt W. (stepchildren). *Education:* Onondaga Community College, A.A. (with highest honors), 1974; Syracuse University, B.A., 1977. *Religion:* Christian. *Home and office address:* P.O. Box 6760, Ithaca, N.Y. 14850. *Agent:* Francis Greenburger, Sanford J. Greenburger Associates, Inc., 825 Third Ave., New York, N.Y. 10022.

CAREER: Robert Fulton Printing Co., Sacramento, Calif., office manager, 1967-70; State University of New York College of Environmental Science and Forestry, Syracuse, intern feature writer, 1976, staff writer, 1977, editorial assistant, 1977-78; free-lance writer, 1978—. Lecturer and community educator on stepfamilies. *Member:* Stepfamily Association of America (member of national board of directors), National Mental Health Association, Alpha Sigma Lambda, Phi Kappa Phi. *Awards, honors:* National media awards from American Psychological Association, 1978, for newspaper series on behavior modification techniques, and 1980, for *The Stepfamily.*

WRITINGS: *The Stepfamily: Living, Loving, and Learning,* Macmillan, 1982. Author of "Cook of the Week," a column in *Chittenango-Bridgeport Times,* 1976-78. Correspondent for *Human Behavior,* 1978-79. Contributor to magazines and newspapers, including *Empire, Air Progress, Parents, Marriage and Family,* and *National Observer.* Contributing editor of *Outlook,* 1975, associate editor, 1976; founding editor of *Stepfamily Bulletin,* 1980-82.

WORK IN PROGRESS: "Stepfamily Living," a nationally syndicated column; SOS ("Strengthening Our Stepfamilies"), a "multimedia kit for teaching stepparenting skills," publication by Educational Media Corp. expected in 1985; *Changes and Challenges: College and the Older Student,* completion expected in 1985.

SIDELIGHTS: Einstein told *CA:* "Both my first book and my work in progress are an integration of personal experience with journalistic research with others in similar situations, and with the professionals working with them. Empathy can provide both pitfalls and possibilities for the writer. It provides insights and personal anecdotes, but it also makes hooking into selective perception easier.

"The same is true for stepfamilies. When they have the information most of us lack about how living in a stepfamily is different, they can accept those differences and make them work for them. The inherent pitfalls in stepfamily living become possibilities after this acceptance occurs. But like writing, becoming a stepfamily is a process, and it takes time—a lot of time—to get it right.

"Many times I think I write for selfish reasons. Writing about universal experiences that have personally touched my life forces me to work things through, and sometimes that means in deep ways that I never dreamed of. Completing *The Stepfamily*, for instance, meant going back to the drawing board after a very perceptive author rejected the manuscript 'because my subjectiveness caused my writing to be unclear.' Rewriting the manuscript until I got it right meant yielding my biases and dumping my selective perception from the interviews until I got it right.

"It is the same way with my work in progress about college and older students. I am being forced to explore the intense changes that occurred as I experienced my education as an adult. While all the changes were not mine by choice, they have touched my life in a profound way, and researching and writing them through is changing me still. First comes confusion—in the research, the organization, and the writing. But that leads to curiosity, and that cannot help but create growth—in my writing and in me as a person."

BIOGRAPHICAL/CRITICAL SOURCES: *Los Angeles Times*, June 10, 1982; *Washington Post*, August 3, 1982; *Baltimore Sun*, September 9, 1982; *Philadelphia Inquirer*, September 26, 1982; *Buffalo Evening News*, January 6, 1983; *New York Times*, January 10, 1983; *U.S. News and World Report*, January 17, 1983.

*   *   *

EKIRCH, A(rthur) Roger 1950-

PERSONAL: Surname is pronounced *Ee*-kirch; born February 6, 1950, in Washington, D.C.; son of Arthur A., Jr. and Dorothy (Gustafson) Ekirch. *Education:* Dartmouth College, A.B., 1972; Johns Hopkins University, M.A., 1974, Ph.D., 1978. *Religion:* Lutheran. *Home:* 302 West Eheart St., Blacksburg, Va. 24060. *Office:* Department of History, Virginia Polytechnic Institute and State University, Blacksburg, Va. 24061.

CAREER: Virginia Polytechnic Institute and State University, Blacksburg, instructor, 1977-78, assistant professor, 1978-82, associate professor of history, 1982—. Mellon research fellow at Cambridge University and fellow commoner of Peterhouse, 1981-82. *Member:* American Historical Association, Organization of American Historians, American Society for Legal History, Associates of the Institute of Early American History and Culture. *Awards, honors:* Fellowship from National Endowment for the Humanities, 1982-83.

WRITINGS: *"Poor Carolina": Politics and Society in Colonial North Carolina, 1729-1776*, University of North Carolina Press, 1981. Contributor to history journals.

WORK IN PROGRESS: *Bound for America: Convict Labor, Great Britain, and the Colonies, 1718-1776.*

*   *   *

ELBORN, Geoffrey 1950-

PERSONAL: Born February 27, 1950, in Edinburgh, Scotland; son of Arthur John (an architect) and Janet (a teacher; maiden name, Milne) Elborn. *Education:* University of Leeds, B.A. (with honors), 1979. *Home:* 14 Grimthorpe House, Percival

St., London EC1, England. *Agent:* Richard Scott Simon, 32 College Cross, London N1 1PR, England.

CAREER: Edinburgh City Libraries, Edinburgh, Scotland, assistant librarian, 1968-75; City of London School for Girls, London, England, music teacher, 1980-81; writer, 1981—. *Member:* Society of Authors, London.

WRITINGS: *Poems*, Castlelaw Press, 1971; (editor) *Hand and Eye* (poetry anthology), Tragara Press, 1977; *Edith Sitwell: A Biography*, Doubleday, 1981; *Princess Alexandra: A Biography*, Sheldon Press, 1982; *John Piper: A Festschrift for His Eightieth Birthday*, Stourton Press; *Mr. Toad and His Friends*, Fairfax Press, 1983. Contributor of reviews to *Books and Bookmen, London Times, Women and Home, Aquarius, Literary Review,* and *Scotsman.*

SIDELIGHTS: Elborn's biography of poet, novelist, and critic Edith Sitwell was authorized by her brother and fellow writer, Sacheverell, the surviving member of the famous English literary family. A friend of Sir Sacheverell's since he first wrote to him as a teenager, Elborn was given sole access to a wealth of Edith Sitwell's correspondence, which was scattered through several attics. The cataloging and arranging of these letters prior to the writing of the biography took several months, with Elborn spending much of his vacation time at the Sitwell home in Northamptonshire to accomplish the task.

"What emerges from the resulting book," declared a *Sunday Telegraph* review, "is a portrait of Edith as a warm and funny, albeit difficult, human being." The article went on to note that "it is the private, previously unpublished material, denied to previous biographers that makes the difference." Some critics elected to compare and contrast Elborn's book with Victoria Glendinning's *Edith Sitwell: A Unicorn Among Lions.* Christopher Hawtree, writing in the *Spectator,* held that although Elborn's "approach is less scholarly than Mrs. Glendinning's, his more exuberant manner provides a better read." Nigel Nicolson observed "more reflection in Glendinning's book, more anecdote in Elborn's" in his *Washington Post Book World* critique. Like Hawtree, he conceded that Elborn's work was "richer in humor," but concluded, "Marginally, I award the prize to Glendinning, because there is more thought in it and a finer style." Alan Pryce-Jones of the *New York Review of Books* judged that while *Edith Sitwell: A Biography* "has not the confidence of Ms. Glendinning's manner," the book "is perfectly competent."

In the *New York Times Book Review,* critic Michael Holroyd termed Elborn's *Edith Sitwell* "a straightforward account of her life and career, rather pedestrian in structure and admiring in tone." The *Sunday Telegraph,* on the other hand, found the book "so far from being sycophantic . . . that it tackles areas of Edith's life previously untouched by biography, for example her growing dependence on, and abuse of, alcohol in the late 1950s."

Elborn told *CA:* "I am interested in trying to focus attention on many writers and creative artists who have something valid for our time, but who may be neglected because they are not regarded as 'commercial.' The whole popular culture nauseates me, for it suppresses by its force much that is good outside it. Individuality in everything creative is more important than easy acceptance of fashionable movements, followed by so many sheep. I prefer to write of the unfashionable."

BIOGRAPHICAL/CRITICAL SOURCES: *Times Literary Supplement*, November 18, 1977; *Washington Post Book World*, June 7, 1981; *New York Times Book Review*, June 14, 1981;

Sunday Telegraph, October 25, 1981; *New York Review of Books,* December 17, 1981; *Spectator,* January 2, 1982.

*   *   *

ELFENBEIN, Julien 1897-1983

OBITUARY NOTICE—See index for *CA* sketch: Born August 12, 1897, in Chicago, Ill.; died April 28, 1983, in Port Chester, N.Y. Artist, educator, editor, journalist, and author. Elfenbein began his career as a police reporter and columnist for Scripps-Howard newspapers in Texas. He later worked as an artist for the *New York Times* and in various capacities at a number of advertising agencies. In 1930 he began a long affiliation with Haire Publishing Company, where he served as editor, editorial director, and publication manager. In addition, Elfenbein lectured in journalism at City College (now City College of the City University of New York) and at New York University. He was the author of several books, including *Business Journalism: Its Function and Future* and *Businesspaper Publishing Practice.* He also edited *Manual of Editorial, Production, and Publishing Procedure* and *Handbook of Business Form Letters.* Obituaries and other sources: *New York Times,* April 30, 1983.

*   *   *

ELKIN, H. V.
See HINKLE, Vernon

*   *   *

ELLICOTT, V. L.
See ELLICOTT, Valcoulon MeMoyne

*   *   *

ELLICOTT, Valcoulon MeMoyne 1893-1983
(V. L. Ellicott)

OBITUARY NOTICE: Born in 1893 in Baltimore, Md.; died of a stroke, February 10, 1983, in Cockeysville, Md. Physician and author. Ellicott, best known for his contributions to the care and rehabilitation of the chronically ill, was health officer of Montgomery County, Maryland, from 1932 to 1954 and chief of the Bureau of Medical Services and Hospitals in the Maryland Health Department from 1954 to 1963. He wrote *Genetic Babies* in 1976. Obituaries and other sources: *Washington Post,* February 12, 1983.

*   *   *

ELLIOTT, Bob 1923-
(Robert B. Elliott)

BRIEF ENTRY: Born March 26, 1923, in Boston, Mass. American radio announcer, comedian, and author. Best known as one of the stars of the popular Bob and Ray comedy duo, Elliott teamed up with partner Ray Goulding in 1946, when both men were employed by WHDH-Radio in Boston. Elliott, then a disc jockey, and Goulding, then a newscaster, began engaging in on-the-air repartee that revealed the good-natured humor of the two broadcasters. The pair were soon offered their own radio show, "Matinee With Bob and Ray," the first of numerous programs and series on which they appeared. Their satirical versions of well-known radio commericals became especially popular with listeners. Elliott and Goulding, who won two Peabody Broadcasting Awards from the University of Georgia, began making television appearances in the 1950's.

They also performed on Broadway in "The Two and Only" (1970) and in the motion picture "Cold Turkey" (1971). Elliott and Goulding wrote *Bob and Ray's Story of Linda Lovely and the Fleebus* (Dodd, 1960) and *Write If You Get Work: The Best of Bob and Ray* (Random House, 1975). *Biographical/critical sources: Current Biography,* Wilson, 1957; *New Yorker,* September 24, 1973; *Village Voice,* September 15, 1975, January 26, 1976; *Time,* November 24, 1975; *Atlantic Monthly,* December, 1975.

*   *   *

ELLIOTT, Robert B.
See ELLIOTT, Bob

*   *   *

ELLIS, (Henry) Havelock 1859-1939

BRIEF ENTRY: Born February 2, 1859, in Croydon, Surrey, England; died July 8, 1939, in Hintlesham, England. British physician, anthropologist, novelist, and author of numerous theoretical works on human sexuality. Ellis is best known as the author of the pioneering, seven-volume tome, *The Psychology of Sex* (1897-1928), in which he avoided the titillating and addressed sexuality in a clinical and highly scholarly manner. Ellis became interested in psychology and sexuality while practicing medicine and participating in the editing of *Westminster Review* in the late 1880's. He then began delving into the anthropological and biological aspects of sexuality and publishing his observations in works such as *The New Spirit* (1890) and *Man and Woman* (1894). Though Ellis's work is now prized for the author's scholarly approach, it was considered quite controversial in post-Victorian England. Ellis's publisher was charged with obscenity after *The Psychology of Sex* began appearing in 1897, and Ellis was forced to publish his work abroad. He continued producing work at a prolific rate, however, and made few concessions to either the curious layman or the disapproving moralist. Among Ellis's numerous twentieth-century volumes are *The World of Dreams* (1911), *The Task of Social Hygiene* (1912), and *The Art of Life* (1929). Ellis's only novel was published in 1922, and his autobiography appeared in the year of his death, 1939. *Biographical/critical sources: Longman Companion to Twentieth Century Literature,* Longman, 1970; *Cassell's Encyclopaedia of World Literature,* revised edition, Morrow, 1973; Phyllis Grosskurth, *Havelock Ellis: A Biography,* Knopf, 1980; *Twentieth-Century Literary Criticism,* Volume 11, Gale, 1983.

*   *   *

ELLISON, Lucile Watkins 1907(?)-1979

PERSONAL: Born c. 1907 in Pennington, Ala.; died of cancer, December 20, 1979, in Washington, D.C.; married George Ellison, 1935. *Education:* Received degree from Mississippi State College for Women (now Mississippi State University for Women). *Residence:* Washington, D.C.

CAREER: Worked as a reporter and teacher in Meridian, Mass.; served National Education Association as member of field services staff and as assistant secretary of National Committee for the Defense of Democracy Through Education, c. 1937-61, executive secretary of citizenship committee, 1961-70.

WRITINGS: Butter on Both Sides (juvenile stories), illustrations by Judith Gwyn Brown, Scribner, 1979.

SIDELIGHTS: Lucile Ellison began writing stories for children in 1974, after learning that she was terminally ill with cancer. She regarded her writing as therapy, a chance to relive her childhood in Alabama. As she told the *Washington Post,* she chose to write about her own childhood for other children because "I realized that I had a year to live. And I realized that things had happened to me that will never happen again." The first of her books, *Butter on Both Sides,* was followed by four more volumes of stories, left unpublished at the time of her death.

OBITUARIES: Washington Post, December 22, 1979.

* * *

ELLSWORTH, Scott 1954-

PERSONAL: Born March 17, 1954, in Tulsa, Okla.; son of Elmer William and Helen (Solberg) Ellsworth. *Education:* Reed College, B.A., 1976; Duke University, M.A., 1977, Ph.D., 1982. *Home:* 2819 38th St. N.W., Washington, D.C. 20007.

CAREER: Free-lance writer, 1979—. Consultant to government.

WRITINGS: Death in a Promised Land: The Tulsa Race Riot of 1921, Louisiana State University Press, 1982. Author of radio documentaries.

WORK IN PROGRESS: Journalism, film treatments, and fiction and nonfiction works.

BIOGRAPHICAL/CRITICAL SOURCES: Tulsa World, March 7, 1982; *Dallas Morning News,* April 18, 1982.

* * *

EMERSON, Connie 1930-

PERSONAL: Born February 19, 1930, in Valley City, N.D.; daughter of George H. (a jeweler) and Edith (in jewelry business; maiden name, Odne) Toring; married Ralph H. Emerson (in business), January 25, 1953; children: Ralph H. III, George Toring. *Education:* Stanford University, A.B., 1951; University of Nevada, M.A., 1977. *Home and office:* 1740 Fairfield Ave., Reno, Nev. 89509. *Agent:* Jacques de Spoelberch, Shagbark Rd., Wilson Point, South Norwalk, Conn. 06854.

CAREER: Squire, Contra Costa County, Calif., reporter, 1969-71; Truckee Meadows Community College, Reno, Nev., part-time instructor in nonfiction writing, 1977-78; Dunn, Draper, Gustin, Curtis, Reno, publicist, 1981—. Also worked as clerk, secretary, and craftsperson.

WRITINGS: Write on Target, Writer's Digest, 1981; *How to Make Money Writing Fillers,* Writer's Digest, 1983. Contributor of more than two hundred fifty articles to magazines. Contributing editor of *Sky.*

WORK IN PROGRESS: A travel book; a book on making money.

SIDELIGHTS: Connie Emerson told *CA:* "My writing was definitely a delayed vocation. I didn't get started until I was certain that my children wouldn't turn out to be juvenile delinquents because of neglect. My first query resulted in an assignment, and I've been selling my work regularly ever since—for nine years. My passion is travel, and I can communicate well in Spanish and Norwegian. I'm also quite successful at entering skill contests. For instance, I won the grand prize in the 1981 Oyster Cook-Offs.

"Contesting was a change-of-pace activity I became involved in while writing my first book. Just as my love of travel provided the inspiration for my first articles, each new challenge I've encountered in the course of my late-blooming career has led me on to new adventures."

* * *

ENGEMAN, Thomas S(ledge) 1944-

PERSONAL: Born September 7, 1944, in Washington, D.C.; son of George Hyde and Ida (Sledge) Engeman. *Education:* Cornell University, A.B. (cum laude), 1967; Claremont Graduate School, M.A., 1970, Ph.D. (with distinction), 1973. *Home:* 1445 North State Parkway, Chicago, Ill. 60610. *Office:* Department of Political Science, Loyola University, 820 North Michigan Ave., Chicago, Ill. 60611.

CAREER: Scripps College, Claremont, Calif., instructor in philosophy, 1969-71; Claremont Men's College (now Claremont McKenna College), Claremont, lecturer in political science, 1971, research associate, 1972-75; Loyola University, Chicago, Ill., assistant professor, 1975-82, associate professor of political science, 1982—. *Member:* American Political Science Association, Midwest Political Science Association, Illinois Political Science Association (president and member of executive committee, 1982-83), Phi Eta Sigma. *Awards, honors:* Woodrow Wilson fellowship, 1970; National Endowment for the Humanities summer research fellow, 1983.

WRITINGS: (With Edward J. Erler and Thomas Hofeller) *The Federalist Concordance,* Wesleyan University Press, 1980; (contributor) Ralph Rossum and G. L. McDowell, editors, *The American Founding: Politics, Statesmanship, and the Constitution,* Kennikat, 1981; (with G.C.S. Benson) *Amoral America: Sources of Morality in a Liberal Society,* Carolina Academic Press, 1982; (contributor) Paul Peterson, editor, *Readings in American Democracy,* 2nd edition, Kendall/Hunt, 1983; (contributor) Peter Schramm and Thomas Silver, editors, *Essays in Honor of Harry V. Jaffa,* Carolina Academic Press, 1983. Contributor of about fifteen articles and reviews to political science and education journals and newspapers.

WORK IN PROGRESS: A long monograph on the political thought of William Dean Howells, publication expected in 1984; editing *Readings in American Political Thought,* with Jean Yarbrough.

* * *

ENQUIST, Per Olov 1934-

BRIEF ENTRY: Born September 23, 1934, in Hjoggbole, Sweden. Swedish author. Enquist's award-winning books include *The Legionnaires: A Documentary Novel* (Delacorte, 1973) and a play, *The Night of the Tribades* (Dramatists Play Service, 1978). *Biographical/critical sources: Times Literary Supplement,* June 2, 1972, September 6, 1974; *New York Times Book Review,* January 6, 1974; *Washington Post Book World,* January 20, 1974; *New Republic,* February 2, 1974; *Observer,* September 15, 1974.

* * *

EPSTEIN, Benjamin Robert 1912-1983

OBITUARY NOTICE—See index for *CA* sketch: Born June 11, 1912, in New York, N.Y.; died of cancer, May 2, 1983, in New York, N.Y. Former national director of the Anti-Defamation League of B'nai B'rith, educator, and author. Epstein began his career as an instructor in German at the University of Pennsylvania. In 1939 he became a staff member with the Anti-Defamation League (ADL). He went on to serve as the ADL's eastern regional director and later as that organization's national director. In 1960 he met with Pope John XXIII to discuss Catholic-Jewish relations, and he later met twice with Pope Paul VI. Epstein co-authored several books, including *Some of My Best Friends . . . , The Radical Right: Report on the John Birch Society and Its Allies,* and *The New Anti-Semitism.* Obituaries and other sources: *New York Times,* May 4, 1983; *Los Angeles Times,* May 6, 1983.

* * *

ERDAHL, Lowell O. 1931-

PERSONAL: Born February 27, 1931, in Minnesota; son of Christian A. (a farmer) and Ingeborg (Fosness) Erdahl; married Carol Syvertsen (a librarian), January 15, 1955; children: Rebecca, Paul, Elizabeth. *Education:* Received B.A. from St. Olaf College, B.D. from Luther Theological Seminary, and S.T.M. from Union Theological Seminary. *Home:* 1773 Eldridge Ave. W., Roseville, Minn. 55113. *Office:* University Lutheran Church of Hope, 601 13th Ave. S.E., Minneapolis, Minn. 55414.

CAREER: Ordained Lutheran minister; pastor of Lutheran church in Farmington, Minn., 1958-68; Luther Theological Seminary, St. Paul, Minn., assistant professor, 1968-73; University Lutheran Church of Hope, Minneapolis, Minn., senior pastor, 1973—.

WRITINGS: Unwitting Witnesses, Augsburg, 1974; *Preaching for the People,* Abingdon, 1975; (with wife, Carol Erdahl) *Be Good to Each Other,* Hawthorn, 1976; *The Lonely House,* Abingdon, 1977; *Authentic Living,* Abingdon, 1979. Also author of monograph *Better Preaching,* Concordia, and Bible study guides *Royalty Redeemed* and *Forgiveness,* Augsburg. Contributor to *Word and World.*

WORK IN PROGRESS: Research on the church's role in peace and disarmament.

* * *

ERICHSEN-NELSON, Jean 1934-

PERSONAL: Born January 19, 1934, in Sacred Heart, Minn.; daughter of Carl Henry (in dairy and real estate business) and Phyllis (Mausolf) Nelson; married Heino R. Erichsen (an administrative director), December 29, 1962; children: Joerg, Arthur, Kirk; Tatiana and Rosana (adopted twins). *Education:* Metropolitan Community College, Minneapolis, Minn., A.A., 1976; Metropolitan State University, St. Paul, Minn., B.A., 1978; St. Mary's College, Winona, Minn., M.A., 1980. *Home:* 1106 Radam Circle, Austin, Tex. 78745.

CAREER: International Adoption Consultant, Minneapolis, Minn., consultant, 1973—. Program director and social worker at Los Ninos International Adoption Center, Austin, Tex., and Minneapolis, 1980—.

WRITINGS: International Children, Trend Publications, 1980; *Gamines: How to Adopt From Latin America,* Dillon, 1981; *The Adoption Kit: U.S. Adoptions,* Los Ninos International, 1982; *Copito the Christmas Chihuahua* (juvenile), May Davenport Books, 1982; *How to Adopt From Asia, Europe, and the South Pacific,* Los Ninos International, 1983.

SIDELIGHTS: Jean Erichsen-Nelson told *CA:* "My writing career began in 1973, after my husband and I returned from a trip to Colombia, South America, to adopt infant twins. I was driven by the memory of the abandoned children to write instructions for prospective adoptive parents. These 'fact sheets' gradually expanded into booklets and finally into the first comprehensive guide ever written on Latin American adoptions.

"In the meantime, our Hispanic children were growing up with little knowledge of their cultural heritage. As a result, I researched cultures and customs in order to write children's educational materials, which include the Eastern Hemisphere as well.

"My book on adoption in the Eastern Hemisphere is nearly finished. It follows the same organization as *Gamines;* the first half contains adoption stories written by a psychologist who is also an adoptive mother, and the second half lists foreign adoption sources, their requirements and procedures, and summarizes the adoption laws of each country."

BIOGRAPHICAL/CRITICAL SOURCES: Beaumont Enterprise, August 8, 1982; *Los Angeles Times,* September 24, 1982; *Daily Texan,* October 12, 1982; *Austin American Statesman,* October 29, 1982.

* * *

ERICKSON, Robert 1917-

BRIEF ENTRY: Born March 7, 1917, in Marquette, Mich. American composer, educator, and author. Erickson composes music for stringed instruments, clarinet, flute, trombone, piano, and orchestra. He also composes electronic music, including "Birdland" (1967) and "Ricercar" (1967), and has invented and constructed instruments that will produce the musical sounds his experimental compositions require. In 1967 Erickson became a professor of composition at University of California, San Diego. He has also taught at College of St. Catherine and San Francisco Conservatory of Music. Erickson's books include *The Structure of Music: A Listener's Guide; A Study of Music in Terms of Melody and Counterpoint* (Noonday, 1955) and *Sound Structure in Music* (University of California Press, 1975). *Address:* Department of Music, University of California, San Diego, La Jolla, Calif. 92037. *Biographical/critical sources: Dictionary of Contemporary Music,* Dutton, 1974; *Times Literary Supplement,* May 28, 1976.

* * *

ERNST, Joseph Albert 1931-

BRIEF ENTRY: Born August 19, 1931, in Brooklyn, N.Y. American historian, educator, and author. Ernst has taught at University of Wisconsin, San Fernando Valley State College, and University of California, Los Angeles. He has been a professor of U.S. history at York University since 1971. He wrote *Money and Politics in America, 1755-1775: A Study in the Currency Act of 1764 and the Political Economy of Revolution* (University of North Carolina Press, 1973) and co-authored *The Movable Airport: The Politics of Government Planning* (Hakkert, 1973). He edited *The Forming of a Nation, 1607-1781* (Random House, 1970) and co-edited *Essays on the National Past,* Volume I: *1607-1865* (Random House, 1970). *Address:* Department of History, York University, Toronto, Ontario, Canada M3J 1P3.

ERNST, Sheila 1941-

PERSONAL: Born July 25, 1941, in Oxford, England; daughter of Menachem Mendel (a psychiatrist) and Shifra (a child psychiatrist; maiden name, Natanson) Ernst; married Robert M. Young, July 18, 1963 (divorced December, 1979); children: Sarah, Emma, Rosie Ernst Trustram. *Education:* Newnham College, Cambridge, B.A., 1962; Homerton College, Certificate in Education, 1963; Southwest London College, Diploma in Counseling, 1979. *Politics:* "Socialist-Feminist." *Religion:* Jewish. *Home:* 8 Tufwell Park Rd., London N.7, England. *Office:* Women's Therapy Centre, 6 Manor Gardens, London N.7, England.

CAREER: Primary school teacher in Cambridge, England, 1963-65; social worker in Cambridge, 1965-68; teacher at school in London, England, 1972-77; psychotherapist in London, 1977—.

WRITINGS: (With Lucy Goodison) *In Our Own Hands,* J. P. Tarcher, 1982.

WORK IN PROGRESS: Research on feminist therapy.

SIDELIGHTS: Sheila Ernst wrote: "My interest is in exploring new approaches to psychotherapy in the light of the women's movement and a feminist understanding of women's social, political, and psychological experience. This began with self-help therapy (the subject of my book), and I have now become immersed in psychoanalytic approaches."

* * *

ERWIN, John D(raper) 1883-1983

OBITUARY NOTICE: Born November 14, 1883, in Meador, Ky.; died of heart failure, February 26, 1983, in Washington, D.C. Diplomat and journalist. Erwin worked as a reporter for the *Chattanooga News* from 1908 to 1913. As Washington correspondent for the *New York Evening World* and *Nashville Tennessean* during the 1920's, the journalist helped uncover details of the Teapot Dome oil scandal. Erwin left newspaper work in 1937 after being appointed minister to Honduras by President Franklin D. Roosevelt. Erwin served as U.S. ambassador to the Central American nation from 1937 to 1943 and again from 1951 to 1953. He retired from the State Department in 1956. Obituaries and other sources: *Who Was Who in America, With World Notables,* Volume VII: *1977-1981,* Marquis, 1981; *New York Times,* March 3, 1983; *Chicago Tribune,* March 3, 1983; *Washington Post,* March 4, 1983.

* * *

EULO, Ken 1939-

BRIEF ENTRY: Born November 17, 1939, in Newark, N.J. American director, playwright, poet, and novelist. Eulo has been associated with Actors Studio Playwriting Workshop and O'Neill Playwrights. He received a grant from the Howard P. Foster Memorial Fund in 1972. Eulo's plays include "48 Spring Street," "Bang?," "Final Exams," "Two If by Sea," and "Black Jesus." He also wrote the mystery novels *The Brownstone* (Pocket Books, 1980), *The Bloodstone* (Pocket Books, 1981), and *The Deathstone* (Pocket Books, 1982). *Address:* 6251 West Washington, Las Vegas, Nev. 89107.

* * *

EVANS, Harold 1911-1983

OBITUARY NOTICE: Born April 29, 1911; died April 21, 1983, in Hove, England. Public relations adviser, journalist, and author. Evans began his career as a newsman during the 1930's. He later became chief information officer at the British Ministry of Information's London Colonial Office and served as chief public relations adviser to Prime Minister Harold Macmillan from 1957 to 1964. A popular figure with the American press during his tenure, Evans was the first British press secretary to permit televised coverage of high-level talks. From 1966 through 1976 Evans was public relations adviser to the board of directors of Vickers Limited. He edited an anthology, *Men in the Tropics,* in 1949 and wrote *Vickers: Against the Odds, 1956-77* and *Downing Street Diary.* Obituaries and other sources: *International Year Book and Statesmen's Who's Who,* Thomas Skinner Directories, 1982; *Who's Who,* 134th edition, St. Martin's, 1982; *London Times,* April 23, 1983.

* * *

EVANS, Richard Evan 1898-1983

OBITUARY NOTICE: Born May 30, 1898, in North Wales; died May 17, 1983, in Aberystwyth, Wales. Educator, researcher, and editor. A graduate of both University College of Wales and Cambridge University, Evans specialized in the field of animal nutrition. He was university lecturer in the subject at Cambridge University for twenty-five years, retiring in 1969, and served as an editor of the *Journal of Agricultural Science.* Obituaries and other sources: *London Times,* May 24, 1983.

* * *

EWERS, Hanns Heinz 1871-1943

BRIEF ENTRY: Born in 1871 in Duesseldorf, Germany (now West Germany); died in 1943 in Berlin, Germany. German author of short stories and novels dealing with aberrant behavior and the occult. *Das Grauen* (1908) and *Nachtmahr* (1922) are among Ewers's short story collections. His novels include *Alraune* (1911; translation published in 1929) and *Vampir* (1921; translation published as *Vampire,* 1934). Ewers also wrote a biography of Edgar Allen Poe in 1916. *Biographical/critical sources: The Oxford Companion to German Literature,* Clarendon Press, 1976; *Twentieth-Century Literary Criticism,* Volume 11, Gale, 1983.

* * *

EZZELL, Marilyn 1937-

PERSONAL: Surname is accented on second syllable; born March 11, 1937, in Teaneck, N.J.; daughter of Paul Herbert and Thelma (a secretary; maiden name, Hoagland) Ezzell. *Education:* St. Luke's Hospital, New York, N.Y., R.N., 1958; attended Columbia University, 1964-65. *Religion:* Christian. *Residence:* New York, N.Y.

CAREER: Englewood Hospital, Englewood, N.J., nurse, 1958-59; nurse in doctor's office in Teaneck, N.J., 1959-61; Holy Name Hospital, Teaneck, teacher of nursing, 1966; Columbia University, New York, N.Y., typist and secretary, 1968-81.

WRITINGS—For young people: The Mystery at Hollowhearth House, Pinnacle Books, 1982; *The Secret of Clovercrest Castle,* Pinnacle Books, 1982; *The Clue in Witchwhistle Well,* Pinnacle Books, 1982; *The Riddle of Raggedrock Ridge,* Pinnacle Books, 1982; *The Phantom of Featherford Falls,* Pinnacle Books, 1983.

WORK IN PROGRESS: The Password to Diamonddwarf Dale, The Search for the Snowship Songs, and *The Mystery of Beggarbay Bluff.*

AVOCATIONAL INTERESTS: Classical music (especially *lieder* of Franz Schubert), walking, swimming, reading, games, cats.

F

FABRE, Genevieve E. 1936-

PERSONAL: Born February 15, 1936, in Paris, France; daughter of Robert and Madeleine (Chassaing) Moreau; married Michel J. Fabre (a professor), July 13, 1960; children: Pierre, Jean-Marc. *Education:* Sorbonne, University of Paris, B.A., M.A., Doctorat de troisieme cycle, 1969, Doctorat d'etat, 1979. *Home:* 12, Square Montsouris, 75014 Paris, France. *Office:* University Paris VII, 10 rue Charles V, 75014 Paris, France.

CAREER: Assistant lecturer and lecturer in French at University of Wisconsin, 1959-60; Pine Manor College, Chestnut Hill, Mass., lecturer in French, 1962-63; Tufts University, Medford, Mass., lecturer in French, 1963-64; University of Paris VII, Paris, France, assistant professor, 1969, associate professor, 1970-78, professor of American studies, 1978—.

WRITINGS: (Contributor) Bernard J. Poli, *Francis Scott Fitzgerald,* A. Colin (Paris), 1969; (with Rachel Ertel and Elise Marienstras) *En Marge: Les minorites aux Etats-Unis,* F. Maspero, 1971; (editor with William French, Ameritjit Singh, and husband, Michel J. Fabre, and contributor) *Afro-American Poetry and Drama, 1760-1975: A Guide to Information Sources,* Gale, 1979; *Theatre noir: USA,* CNRS, 1982; *Drumbeats, Masks, and Plays: Afro American Theatre,* Harvard University Press, 1983. Also contributor to books about Stephen Crane, Joyce Carol Oates, Soyinka, and other authors. Contributor to American studies magazines and to French, German, and American journals, including *American Quarterly, Black World,* and *Commonwealth Literature.*

WORK IN PROGRESS: Research on masks in American theatre, on the oral history of the Louisiana Cajun community, and on Teatro Campesino.

*   *   *

FAGUE, William Robert 1927-
(William Robert Faith)

PERSONAL: Born September 25, 1927, in Utica, N.Y.; son of Lloyd Fague. *Education:* Wesleyan University, Middletown, Conn., B.A., 1949; McGill University, M.A., 1950; University of Southern California, Ph.D., 1976. *Religion:* Episcopalian. *Home:* 4244 National Ave., Burbank, Calif. 91505. *Agent:* Robert Lescher, Lescher Agency, 155 East 71st St., New York, N.Y. 10021. *Office:* School of Journalism, University of Southern California, Los Angeles, Calif. 90089.

CAREER: Associated with National Broadcasting Co., 1959-65; Hope Enterprises, North Hollywood, Calif., director of public relations, 1965-73; University of Southern California, Los Angeles, associate professor of journalism, 1979—, chairman of public relations sequence, 1979—. Public relations adviser to Cancer Prevention Society; consultant to Bob Hope Museum Projects. *Military service:* U.S. Army, 1946-48. *Member:* Public Relations Society of America, Association for Education in Journalism.

WRITINGS—Under pseudonym William Robert Faith: *Thru These Eyes* (poems), Wesleyan University Press, 1948; *Bob Hope and the Popular Oracle Tradition in American Humor,* University of Southern California Press, 1976; *Bob Hope: A Life in Comedy* (biography), Putnam, 1982. Contributor to periodicals.

WORK IN PROGRESS: A biography of Beatrice Lillie; a public relations textbook; a bibliography of humor.

*   *   *

FAIRLIE, Gerard 1899-1983

OBITUARY NOTICE: Born November 1, 1899, in London, England; died in 1983. Soldier, journalist, screenwriter, and author of mystery novels. After attending Sandhurst and serving with the Scots Guards from 1917 to 1924, Fairlie embarked on a productive writing career, working first as sports correspondent for the *London Times, Bystander,* and *Britannia.* He also wrote more than thirty crime novels, as well as plays and screenplays. The last seven "Bulldog Drummond" books were written by Fairlie after the death of his friend and series originator, H. C. McNeile. Fairlie's fictional titles include *Scissors Cut Paper, Calling Bulldog Drummond,* and *No Sleep for Macall.* He wrote an autobiography, *With Prejudice,* in 1952. Obituaries and other sources: *The Author's and Writer's Who's Who,* 6th edition, Burke's Peerage, 1971; *Encyclopedia of Mystery and Detection,* McGraw, 1976; *Who Was Who Among English and European Authors, 1931-1949,* Gale, 1978; *Twentieth-Century Crime and Mystery Writers,* St. Martin's, 1980; *London Times,* April 19, 1983.

FAITH, William Robert
See FAGUE, William Robert

* * *

FALCON, Walter Phillip 1936-

BRIEF ENTRY: Born September 28, 1936, in Cedar Rapids, Iowa. American economist, educator, and author. After teaching at Harvard University for about ten years, Falcon became a professor of economics at Stanford University and director of its Food Research Institute. In 1976 he was named Helen C. Farnsworth Professor of International Agricultural Policy. He has also worked as consultant to the governments of the United States, Pakistan, and Indonesia. Falcon's publications include *Growth and Development in Pakistan, 1955-1969* (Center for International Affairs, Harvard University, 1970) and *Development Policy II: The Pakistan Experience* (Harvard University Press, 1971). *Address:* 415 Gerona Rd., Stanford, Calif. 94305; and Food Research Institute, Stanford University, Stanford, Calif. 94305.

* * *

FALK, Minna Regina 1900-1983

OBITUARY NOTICE: Born August 2, 1900, in New York, N.Y.; died May 1, 1983, in New York, N.Y. Educator and author. The first woman to become a full professor of history at New York University, Falk joined the faculty in 1926 and taught central European and German history until her retirement in 1967. Among Falk's writings is *The History of Germany: From the Reformation to the Present Day.* Obituaries and other sources: *Directory of American Scholars,* Volume I: *History,* 7th edition, Bowker, 1978; *New York Times,* May 5, 1983.

* * *

FANTE, John (Thomas) 1911-1983

OBITUARY NOTICE—See index for *CA* sketch: Born April 8, 1911, in Denver, Colo.; died of complications from diabetes, May 8, 1983, in Woodland Hills, Calif. Screenwriter, novelist, and author of short stories. Fante was best known for his series of novels about Arturo Bandini, a fictional young poet coming of age in Los Angeles during the 1930's. The first of these, *Wait Until Spring, Bandini,* was followed by *Ask the Dust, Full of Life,* and *Brotherhood of the Grape.* Fante also contributed to the screenplays for "Walk on the Wild Side" and "Jeanne Eagles" and published a collection of short stories titled *Dago Red.* Obituaries and other sources: *Los Angeles Times,* May 12, 1983; *Washington Post,* May 13, 1983; *New York Times,* May 13, 1983; *Chicago Tribune,* May 14, 1983; *Newsweek,* May 23, 1983.

* * *

FARAMELLI, Norman Joseph 1932-

BRIEF ENTRY: Born August 26, 1932, in Wilkes-Barre, Pa. American clergyman, church official, and author. Faramelli has been an ordained Episcopal priest since 1960. In 1967 he became co-director of Boston Industrial Mission, and four years later he was appointed president of the Center for the Study of Development and Social Change. Faramelli wrote *Technethics: Christian Mission in an Age of Technology* (Friendship, 1971). *Address:* 29 Harris St., Waltham, Mass. 02154; and 56 Boylston St., Cambridge, Mass. 02138. *Biographical/critical sources: Spectator,* September, 1971.

FARGUE, Leon-Paul 1876(?)-1947

BRIEF ENTRY: Born March 4, 1876 (some sources say 1878), in Paris, France; died November 25, 1947, in Paris, France. French journalist and poet. Fargue's work is usually associated with Paris, a city the poet commemorated in numerous poems throughout the early twentieth century. He began writing at an early age, founding the publication *Le Centaur* at age twelve and publishing the long poem "Tancrede" in *Pan* at age eighteen. In the late 1890's Fargue befriended Stephane Mallarme who, in turn, introduced Fargue to Paul Verlaine, Pierre Renoir, and Claude Debussy. At that time, the prestigious review *Mercure de France* devoted almost an entire issue to Fargue's work. Fargue began prowling all over Paris, from the cafes of Saint-Germain to the seedy bars of Montmartre, befriending more artists, including Pablo Picasso, Maurice Ravel, Igor Stravinsky, and Paul Cezanne. He developed a reputation as an idle denizen of Parisian society—a persona he cultivated—even as he had begun concentrating on his poetry. His first collection, *Poemes* (1912), attracted little notice outside the poet's circle of acquaintances. The collection, however, was republished in 1918 to great acclaim. During the 1920's Fargue worked with Paul Valery on publishing a review, *Commerce,* and completed two more collections, *Espaces* (1929) and *Sous la lampe* (1929). In the 1930's, despite his success as a poet, Fargue abandoned verse for the more lucrative journalism. He wrote columns and articles on Parisian nightlife and spoke of his experiences on radio. Following a stroke in 1944, Fargue became paralyzed. He was unproductive during his remaining years. *Biographical/critical sources: Everyman's Dictionary of Literary Biography, English and American,* revised edition, Dutton, 1960; *The Penguin Companion to European Literature,* McGraw, 1969; *World Authors, 1950-75,* H. W. Wilson, 1975; *Twentieth-Century Literary Criticism,* Volume 11, Gale, 1983.

* * *

FARMER, William R(euben) 1921-

BRIEF ENTRY: Born February 1, 1921, in Needles, Calif. American clergyman, educator, and author. Farmer has been a United Methodist minister since 1952. He has taught at Emory University, DePauw University, and Drew University, and in 1964 he became a professor of theology at Southern Methodist University. Farmer wrote *Maccabees, Zealots, and Josephus: An Inquiry Into Jewish Nationalism in the Greco-Roman Period* (Columbia University Press, 1956), *The Synoptic Problem: A Critical Analysis* (Macmillan, 1964), and *The Last Twelve Verses of Mark* (Cambridge University Press, 1974). He co-edited *Christian History and Interpretation: Studies Presented to John Knox* (Cambridge University Press, 1967) and *The Great Roman-Jewish War: A.D.66-70 (De bello Judaico); The William Whiston Translation* (Peter Smith, 1970). *Address:* 3324 Southwestern Blvd., Dallas, Tex. 75225; and Department of New Testament, Perkins School of Theology, Southern Methodist University, Dallas, Tex. 75275.

* * *

FARRELL, Francis (Thomas) 1912-1983
(Frank Farrell)

OBITUARY NOTICE: Born October 9, 1912, in New York, N.Y.; died in his sleep, February 17, 1983, in New York,

N.Y. Public relations executive and journalist. Farrell was a columnist and features editor for the *World-Telegram,* the *World-Telegram Sun,* and the *World Journal Tribune* until 1967 when the latter folded. He then went into public relations, serving as president of PR Associates at the time of his death. A Marine Corps captain in World War II, Farrell helped to uncover a Nazi spy network operating in the Far East and was instrumental in securing the arrest of some twenty Nazis in Shanghai in 1946. He received many awards for his war efforts, including the Silver Star. Obituaries and other sources: *Who's Who in Finance and Industry,* 18th edition, Marquis, 1974; *New York Times,* February 22, 1983.

* * *

FARRELL, Frank
   See FARRELL, Francis (Thomas)

* * *

FARRER, (Bryan) David   1906-1983

OBITUARY NOTICE—See index for *CA* sketch: Born June 30, 1906, in Betchworth, England; died in 1983 in London, England. Publisher, editor, and author. Although trained as a lawyer, Farrer left that profession after just a few years. He later joined Secker & Warburg, a British publishing firm, where he served for many years as literary director. He was the author of *A Career for the Gentleman, The Sky's the Limit, G for God Almighty,* and *The Warburgs.* Obituaries and other sources: *London Times,* March 3, 1983; *AB Bookman's Weekly,* April 11, 1983.

* * *

FARRINGTON, S(elwyn) Kip, Jr.   1904-1983

OBITUARY NOTICE—See index for *CA* sketch: Born May 7, 1904, in Orange, N.J.; died February 7, 1983, in Southampton, N.Y. Stockbroker, sportsman, and author. When he was sixteen years old, Farrington joined his family's brokerage firm. He was made a partner at age twenty-one, but he left the firm a few years later to devote himself to deep-sea fishing. From 1937 to 1972 he served as saltwater-fishing editor of *Field and Stream* magazine. He also wrote a number of books on fishing and other sports, including *Atlantic Game Fishing, Fishing With Hemingway and Glassell,* and *Skates, Sticks, and Men: The Story of Amateur Hockey in the United States.* Another of Farrington's abiding interests was railroading. He wrote many books on the subject, including *Railroading Around the World, The Santa Fe's Big Three: The Life Story of a Trio of the World's Greatest Locomotives,* and *Railroading Coast to Coast.* Obituaries and other sources: *New York Times,* February 8, 1983; *Time,* February 21, 1983.

* * *

FARSTAD, Arthur L(eonard)   1935-

PERSONAL: Born March 7, 1935, in Yonkers, N.Y.; son of Marcus August (a carpenter) and Olga (Oedegaard) Farstad. *Education:* National Art Academy, Diploma, 1956; Emmaus Bible School, Diploma, 1960; Washington Bible College, B.A., 1963; Dallas Theological Seminary, Th.M., 1967, Th.D., 1972. *Politics:* Republican. *Religion:* Brethren Assemblies. *Home and office:* 6218 Prospect Ave., Dallas, Tex. 75214.

CAREER: Free-lance illustrator in Washington, D.C., 1956-57; free-lance writer, 1972-74; Dallas Theological Seminary,

Dallas, Tex., assistant professor of New Testament language and literature, 1975-78; Thomas Nelson, Inc. (publisher), Nashville, Tenn., New Testament editor, 1975—.

WRITINGS: (New Testament editor) *New King James New Testament,* Thomas Nelson, 1979; (executive editor) *Holy Bible: New King James Version,* Thomas Nelson, 1982; (editor with Zane C. Hodges) *The Greek New Testament According to the Majority Text,* Thomas Nelson, 1982.

WORK IN PROGRESS: A biography of J. N. Darby.

SIDELIGHTS: Farstad told *CA:* "I feel that a great deal of the best in American art, literature, music, and mores is a by-product (sometimes a very direct one) of our great biblical heritage. This is seen to a lesser degree in Europe where the great cathedrals—alas, so often now empty—sought to teach the Bible in stone and stained glass. Having been raised in the East, by European parents, I am more objective about the Southwest, where I now live, and I see how frontier religion helped to produce the friendliness, co-operation, and high standard of life that we associate especially with Texas.

"My love for Israel is a direct outcome of years of Bible study.

"I am interested in John Darby because he was a linguist, Bible translator, hymn writer, and the theologian most influential in the revival of the so-called dispensational interpretation of the Scriptures (later made very popular by the Scofield Bible, Moody Bible Institute, etc.). A person of Darby's stature in any other group but the Brethren would have had several full-length biographies and probably a school, church, and seminary named after him, but the extreme conservatism of most of Darby's followers has precluded this. It is high time someone writes an objective, yet friendly biography about this great man of God."

BIOGRAPHICAL/CRITICAL SOURCES: Interest, October, 1979.

* * *

FAULKNER, Alex   1905(?)-1983

OBITUARY NOTICE: Born c. 1905; died March 12, 1983, in London, England. Journalist. Faulkner joined the staff of the *London Daily Telegraph* in 1929. He became the paper's chief correspondent in the United States in 1939, serving in that position until his retirement in 1974. In 1962 he became a Commander of the Order of the British Empire. Obituaries and other sources: *New York Times,* March 14, 1983.

* * *

FAURE, William C(aldwell), Jr.   1949-

PERSONAL: Born July 17, 1949, in Pretoria, South Africa; son of William (a business executive) and Toni (a champion swimmer) Faure. *Education:* Graduated from International London Film School (first class honors), 1972. *Office:* 25a Seventh Ave., Melville, Johannesburg, South Africa.

CAREER: Film editor with South African Broadcast Corp. (SABC), 1973-74, became director and producer, 1974, then senior director and producer; director for William C. Faure Productions Ltd., Johannesburg, South Africa. Director and producer of independent feature films "A Place in the Sun" and "Ricochet." Lecturer on the subject of violence in film and television. *Awards, honors:* South African Academy of Science and Arts award for "outstanding contribution to television,'' 1980; Artes award for television production of Oscar Wilde's ''Salome,'' 1980; winner of six ''Tonight'' television critics' awards, 1976-80.

WRITINGS: Images of Violence, Studio Vista, 1973. Contributor of series of articles on producing television dramas and documentaries to South African newspaper *Citizen,* 1980, and of articles on violence and the media to South African newspaper *Star,* 1981.

* * *

FAUSET, Jessie Redmon 1884(?)-1961

PERSONAL: Born April 27, 1884 (some sources say 1882 or 1886), in Snow Hill, N.J.; died April 30, 1961, in Philadelphia, Pa.; daughter of Redmon (a minister) and Annie (Seamon) Fauset; married Herbert Harris, 1929. *Education:* Cornell University, B.A., 1905; University of Pennsylvania, M.A.; attended Sorbonne, University of Paris.

CAREER: Teacher of French at high schools in Washington, D.C., and New York, N.Y.; literary editor of *The Crisis,* New York City, 1919-26, and *Brownie's Book,* 1920-21; novelist, critic, and poet. *Member:* Phi Beta Kappa.

WRITINGS: There Is Confusion (novel), Boni & Liveright, 1924, AMS Press, 1974; *Plum Bun* (novel), Mathews & Marrot (London), 1928, Frederick A. Stokes, 1929; *The Chinaberry Tree* (novel), Frederick A. Stokes, 1931, AMS Press, 1969; *Comedy, American Style* (novel), Frederick A. Stokes, 1933, AMS Press, 1969. Contributor of poems, short stories, and essays to periodicals, including *The Crisis* and *Brownie's Book.*

SIDELIGHTS: The first black female to be graduated from Cornell University, Fauset taught French at an all-black high school in Washington, D.C., until 1919 when sociologist W.E.B. DuBois asked her to move to New York City to work for *The Crisis* magazine, of which he was editor. As literary editor, Fauset published the works of many Harlem Renaissance writers, such as Countee Cullen, Langston Hughes, and Jean Toomer, as well as her own writings. Fauset also edited and was the primary writer for *Brownie's Book,* a magazine for black children.

Fauset wrote poetry, essays, short stories, and novels, most of which portrayed black life in a prejudice-wrought world. Her last novel, *Comedy, American Style,* is considered her most direct statement about the various effects of racial discrimination. The main character, Olivia Carey, is a woman who, because of the prejudice she encounters, hates being black and vainly desires to be white. Her passionate and futile desires threaten to destroy her, while at the same time her husband and son are proud of their heritage and exemplify the richness of black culture.

Fauset's novels received largely mixed reviews, some critics feeling the author unrealistically characterized her subjects. In *Black Writers of the Thirties,* for example, James O. Young commented: ''The black middle class was not an invalid subject for fiction, but Miss Fauset's idealized treatment of it had little redeeming value. . . . [Instead] of presenting a serious, realistic interpretation of middle-class black life, as she professed to do, Miss Fauset concocted a highly idealized romance. Her characters are not real human beings, they are idealizations of what the Negro middle class conceived itself to be.'' And Gerald Sykes, reviewing *The Chinaberry Tree,* wrote in *Nation:* ''[It] attempts to idealize [the] polite colored world in terms of the white standards that it has adopted. . . . When

she parades the possessions of her upper classes and when she puts her lovers through their Fauntleroy courtesies, she is not only stressing the white standards that they have adopted; she is definitely minimizing the colored blood in them. This is a decided weakness, for it steals truth and life from the book. Is not the most precious part of a Negro work of art that which is specifically Negroid, which none but a Negro could contribute?'' Despite her ''artistic errors,'' however, Sykes found ''Fauset has a rare understanding of people and their motives. . . . Inspired by the religious motive which so many Negro writers seem to feel, she has simply been trying to justify her world to the world at large. Her mistake has consisted in trying to do this in terms of the white standard.''

On the other hand, in a review of Fauset's *Comedy, American Style,* Hugh M. Gloster hailed Fauset's ''description of the lives and difficulties of Philadelphia's colored elite'' as ''one of the major achievements of American Negro fiction.'' And Joseph J. Feeney defended Fauset's portrayal of blacks, claiming in his *CLA Journal* article that critics ''who speak of her middle-class respectability and her 'genteel lace-curtain romances' miss the dark world of prejudice, sadness, and frustration just below the surface of her novels. There are two worlds in Jessie Fauset: the first is sunlit, a place of pride, talent, family love, and contentment; the other world is shadowed by prejudice, lost opportunities, a forced choice between color and country.'' Feeney continued: ''Miss Fauset, through structure and content has offered a far more complex and harrowing portrait of American black life than the critics have recognized. She is far more than a conventional writer of middle-class romances, and her reputation must be revised accordingly. . . . She was not a major writer. But she cannot be dismissed as 'vapidly genteel' or 'sophomoric.' In the construction of her novels and in her vision of the Negro world, she displayed a sensibility which comprehended tragedy, sardonic comedy, disillusioned hopes, slavery, prejudice, confusion, and bitterness against America.''

BIOGRAPHICAL/CRITICAL SOURCES—Books: Hugh M. Gloster, *Negro Voices in American Fiction,* University of North Carolina Press, 1948; Robert Bone, *The Negro Novel in America,* Yale University Press, 1965; James O. Young, *Black Writers of the Thirties,* Louisiana State University Press, 1973.

Periodicals: *New Republic,* July 9, 1924, April 10, 1929; *Saturday Review of Literature,* April 6, 1929; *Nation,* July 27, 1932; *New York Times Book Review,* November 19, 1933; *Ebony,* February, 1949, August, 1966; *CLA Journal,* December, 1974, June, 1979.*

* * *

FEINBERG, Gloria (Granditer) 1923-

BRIEF ENTRY: December 18, 1923, in New York, N.Y. American psychologist and author. Feinberg has worked as a psychologist for Grasslands Hospital in Valhalla, New York, American and Foreign Market Research, and BFC Psychological Associates. In 1965 she became associated with BFS Appraisals. Feinberg co-authored *Leavetaking: When and How to Say Goodbye* (Simon & Schuster, 1978). *Address:* 34 Brook Lane, Peekskill, N.Y. 10566; and 666 Fifth Ave., New York, N.Y. 10019.

* * *

FENELON, Kevin G(erard) 1898-1983

OBITUARY NOTICE—See index for *CA* sketch: Born December 6, 1898, in London, England; died March 12, 1983. Educator, economist, and author. Beginning in 1951 Fenelon served as statistical adviser to a number of governments, including those of Iraq, Kuwait, Jordan, and Bahrain. He previously lectured in economics at the University of Edinburgh and served as director of the department of industrial administration at Victoria University of Manchester. From 1958 to 1961 Fenelon was a professor of statistics and economics at the American University of Beirut. Among his many writings are *The Economics of Road Transport, Management and Labour, Planning Local Prosperity, Iraq's National Income and Expenditure,* and *The United Arab Emirates.* Obituaries and other sources: *London Times,* March 29, 1983.

*   *   *

FIELD, Elinor Whitney 1889-1980

OBITUARY NOTICE: Born in 1889; died November 24, 1980. Editor and author. A longtime vice-president and member of the board of directors of Horn Book, Incorporated, Field was an assistant editor of *Horn Book* magazine from 1924 to 1939 and an associate editor of the publication from 1939 to 1957. With Bertha E. Mahony, *Horn Book*'s founder, Field issued several volumes, among them *Realms of Gold in Children's Books* and *Illustrators of Children's Books: 1774 to 1945.* Field also wrote books for children, including *Tod of the Fens,* a Newbery Honor Book of 1929. Obituaries and other sources: *Horn Book,* June, 1981.

*   *   *

FIELD, Rachel (Lyman) 1894-1942

BRIEF ENTRY: Born September 19, 1894, in New York, N.Y.; died March 15, 1942, in Beverly Hills, Calif. American editor, novelist, playwright, poet, illustrator, and children's author. Field attended Radcliffe College from 1914 to 1918 and worked in the editorial department of the Players-Lasky film company in Hollywood before pursuing a diverse free-lance writing career. Her best-known children's work, *Hitty: Her First Hundred Years* (1930), chronicles in a first person narrative one hundred years in the life of the wooden doll Mehitable. The Newbery Medal that Field received for *Hitty* in 1930 was the first ever awarded to a woman author. In addition to twelve other juvenile novels, Field wrote children's plays, including the collection *Patchwork Plays* (1930), poetry, and adult fiction. Her greatest success, the novel *All This and Heaven Too* (1938), was based on the life of her great-aunt, a participant in the controversial de Praslin murder case. A best-seller, the novel was adapted into a motion picture starring Bette Davis and Charles Boyer in 1940. Field's poetry collections include *The Pointed People: Verses and Silhouettes* (1924) and *Fear Is the Thorn* (1936). *Biographical/critical sources: New York Times,* March 16, 1942; Elizabeth R. Montgomery, *Story Behind Modern Books,* Dodd, 1949; *The Oxford Companion to American Literature,* 4th edition, Oxford University Press, 1965; *Longman Companion to Twentieth Century Literature,* Longman, 1970; *The Lincoln Library of Language Arts,* 3rd edition, Frontier Press (Columbus, Ohio), 1978.

*   *   *

FIELDING, Temple (Hornaday) 1913-1983

OBITUARY NOTICE—See index for *CA* sketch: Born October 8, 1913, in New York, N.Y.; died of a heart attack, May 18, 1983, in Palma, Majorca; buried in town cemetery, Pollensa,

Majorca. Author of travel books. *Fielding's Travel Guide to Europe,* which was later called *Fielding's Europe,* was published annually for more than thirty years. Since the first edition appeared in 1948, more than 3 million copies of Fielding's guidebooks on low-cost travel have been sold. Obituaries and other sources: *New York Times,* May 19, 1983; *Washington Post,* May 20, 1983; *Chicago Tribune,* May 20, 1983; *Time,* May 30, 1983; *Newsweek,* May 30, 1983; *Publishers Weekly,* June 3, 1983.

*   *   *

FIERRO, Robert Daniel 1945-

PERSONAL: Born February 11, 1945, in New York, N.Y.; son of Fierro Salvatore and Lucy (Lattarulo) Fierro; married Alice Loughlin, September 3, 1966; children: Andrea, Philip. *Education:* Fordham University, B.A., 1966. *Home and office address:* P.O. Box 361, Whitestone, N.Y. 11357. *Agent:* Writer's House, Inc., 21 West 26th St., New York, N.Y. 10010.

CAREER: Worked in editorial and promotion departments of Prentice-Hall, Inc., Pan American Airways, and United Way of America, 1966-72; Trendsetter Group Ltd., New York City, president, 1972-76; *Identity,* New York City, editor and publisher, 1976-77; McGraw-Hill Book Co., New York City, associate editor, 1977-79; Old Empire Thoroughbreds Ltd., Whitestone, N.Y., president, 1980—. *Member:* American Horse Council, New York Thoroughbred Breeders.

WRITINGS: Tax Shelters in Plain English, McGraw, 1978; *The New American Entrepreneur: How to Get Off the Fast Track Into a Business of Your Own,* Morrow, 1982. Contributor to magazines, including *Travel and Leisure, Money, Venture,* and *Thoroughbred Record.*

SIDELIGHTS: Fierro told *CA:* "I am known as a writer on finance, business, travel, and thoroughbred horses. This may sound like an odd mixture, but all those subjects touch each other and intertwine. I find the subject of money inherently hilarious (because we take it so seriously), and try to get a better perspective by traveling and watching the ponies go 'round. My book on tax shelters is probably considered to be my claim to fame.

"Tax shelters are an integral but misunderstood element of the American economy. They also provide a jaundiced writer an opportunity to poke around and have some fun. If you wish to start your own business, the best advice is to stick with something you love—and know—and add your own unique fillip to the industry. I have always liked horses, mainly because they don't talk back and invariably do their job as best they can. So far they're doing a fair enough job for me to keep me happy."

*   *   *

FIGLER, Howard Elliot 1939-

BRIEF ENTRY: Born May 2, 1939, in Brooklyn, N.Y. American psychologist and author. Figler was a counseling psychologist at University of Tennessee from 1969 to 1970. He then became director of the counseling center at Dickinson College. Figler wrote *Outreach in Counseling: Applying the Growth and Prevention Model in Schools and Colleges* (Intext Educational Publishers, 1973), *PATH: A Career Workbook for Liberal Arts Students* (Carroll Press, 1975), and *The Complete Job-Search Handbook: All the Skills You Need to Get Any Job and Have a Good Time Doing It* (Holt, 1979). *Address:* Counseling Center, Dickinson College, Carlisle, Pa. 17013.

*   *   *

FISCH, Martin L.   1924-

PERSONAL: Born October 12, 1924, in Brooklyn, N.Y.; son of Isidore (an immigration officer) and Augusta (Reicher) Fisch; married Betty Ruth Currinder (an antique dealer and appraiser), May 24, 1946; children: Ronni Lynne Fisch Sergeant, Richard David. *Education:* New York University, B.A., 1947, Ph.D., 1964; postdoctoral study at Harvard University, 1980. *Home address:* Laurelwood Dr., Mountain Lakes, N.J. 07046. *Agent:* Richard Boehm Agency, 737 Park Ave., New York, N.Y. 10021.

CAREER: Long Island College Hospital, Brooklyn, N.Y., clinical psychologist, 1951-64, chief of psychological services, 1964—, assistant director for administration, 1967—, vice-president, 1976—. Private practice in psychodiagnostics and psychotherapy, 1964—. Executive director of Lamm Institute, 1974—. Lecturer at University of Kentucky, 1953-54; lecturer at State University of New York Downstate Medical Center, 1959-62, now associate clinical professor. Member of New York State Commission for the International Year of the Disabled, 1981-82; director of interagency council of mental retardation agencies in New York City; consultant to U.S. Peace Corps and Division of Children's Services of New Jersey. *Military service:* U.S. Army, Medical Corps, 1943-46. *Member:* American Psychological Association, American Association for Mental Deficiency, American Management Association, American College of Hospital Administrators.

WRITINGS: (Contributor) Nolan D. C. Lewis and Carney Landis, editors, *Studies in Topectomy*, Grune, 1956; *Learning Disabilities Explained*, Doubleday, 1982. Contributor to psychology journals.

WORK IN PROGRESS: Research on computer applications in medicine and on computer-assisted learning in the areas of learning disabilities and communication disorders.

SIDELIGHTS: Fisch told *CA:* "*Learning Disabilities Explained* was written to fill the need for a clearly written, comprehensive compendium for both professional and lay readers. I believe that we are entering an exciting period of cognitive habilitation and rehabilitation programs using new computer graphics and voice synthesis technology. The relatively low cost of microcomputers and the motivational potential of educational games will lead to their widespread acceptance and use in the nation's classrooms.

"I continue to maintain a limited private practice in order to provide a much needed service while maintaining my professional and clinical skills. From 1965 to 1969 I trained Peace Corps volunteers for health-related programs in Latin America, and I traveled extensively in Mexico, Paraguay, Argentina, and Puerto Rico. I enjoy foreign travel and cultural exchange."

AVOCATIONAL INTERESTS: Skiing, swimming, gardening, woodworking, photography.

BIOGRAPHICAL/CRITICAL SOURCES: Washington Post Book World, January 9, 1983.

*   *   *

FISCHER, Roger Adrian   1939-

BRIEF ENTRY: Born May 8, 1939, in Minneapolis, Minn.

American historian, educator, and author. Fischer has been a member of the history faculty of University of Minnesota since 1972. He has also taught at University of Southwestern Louisiana, Southern University, Sam Houston State College, and Southwest Missouri State College. Fischer wrote *The Segregation Struggle in Louisiana* (University of Illinois Press, 1974). *Address:* Department of History, University of Minnesota, Duluth, Minn. 55812. *Biographical/critical sources: American Historical Review*, February, 1978.

*   *   *

FISHER, Robert (Tempest)   1943-

PERSONAL: Born August 2, 1943, in Perivale, England; son of John Tempest (a civil servant) and Doris (an antique dealer; maiden name, Hiscock) Fisher; married Celia Margaret Fulton (an editor), April 13, 1969; children: Jacob Alexander, Thomas Gabriel. *Education:* Goldsmiths College, London, B.A. (with honors), 1976. *Home:* 7 Maze Rd., Kew, Surrey TW9 3DA, England.

CAREER: Teacher at primary schools in London, England, 1964-66 and 1969-72, and Addis Ababa, Ethiopia, 1966-69; Beacon Hill School (primary school), Hong Kong, deputy principal, 1972-74; St. Mary's Primary School, Twickenham, England, deputy headmaster, 1974-82; Archdeacon Cambridge School, Twickenham, head teacher, 1983—. *Member:* Folklore Society.

WRITINGS: Together Today (for teachers), Evans Brothers, 1981; (editor) *Amazing Monsters: Verses to Chill and Thrill* (poems for children), Faber, 1982; *Together With Infants* (for teachers), Evans Brothers, 1982; (editor) *Ghosts Galore* (poems for children), Faber, 1983. Contributor to education journals.

WORK IN PROGRESS: Your Gifted Child, a guide for parents on ways to educate young children; books for children and teachers.

SIDELIGHTS: Fisher told *CA:* "I have taught in the United Kingdom, Ethiopia, and Hong Kong, at all age levels from preschool to adult. I write books for teachers to foster a creative and integrative approach to education. In my poetry books for children, my aim is to freshen and stimulate the imagination, whether the child is eight or eighty. The distinction between child and adult is often a false one. Poetry is one aspect of creative education which can reach both the mind of the child and the child within the adult."

*   *   *

FitzGERALD, Garret   1926-

PERSONAL: Born February 9, 1926, in Dublin, Ireland; son of Desmond (a statesman) and Mabel (McConnell) FitzGerald; married Joan O'Farrell, October 10, 1947; children: John, Mary (Mrs. Vincent Deane), Mark. *Education:* Received B.A., Ph.D., and B.L. from National University of Ireland, University College, Dublin. *Religion:* Roman Catholic. *Home:* 30 Palmerston Rd., Dublin 6, Ireland. *Office:* Office of the Prime Minister, Government Buildings, Upper Merrion St., Dublin 2, Ireland.

CAREER: Research and schedules manager for Aer Lingus (Irish Airlines), 1947-58; National University of Ireland, University College, Dublin, lecturer in political economy, 1959-73; Dail Eireann (Irish Parliament), Dublin, Fine Gael member of Parliament for Dublin Southeast, 1969—, member of Committee on Public Accounts, 1969-73, minister for foreign affairs, 1973-77, leader of Fine Gael party, 1977—, prime minister of Ireland, 1981—. Member of Irish Senate, 1965-69, member of Electoral Law Commission. Member of international executive committee of European Movement, vice-president and president of its Irish Council. Past member of Workmen's Compensation Commission, Committee on Industrial Organization, and General Purposes Committee of National Industrial Economic Council; past managing director of *Economist* Intelligence Unit of Ireland; chairman of ESB General Employees Arbitration Tribunal, 1961-63, Hosiery Adaptation Council, 1964-66, and Woollen and Worsted Adaptation Council, 1964-67; member of Garda Siochana Representative Body, 1963-73. Member of governing body of National University of Ireland, University College, Dublin, and member of senate of the university; member of board of governors of Atlantic Institute of International Relations.

MEMBER: Statistical and Social Enquiry Society of Ireland (member of council, 1956—), Irish Management Institute (member of council, 1959-64; executive member), Institute of Transport (associate member), Irish Federation of University Teachers (member of council, 1966-69), Electoral Reform Society (vice-president, 1968-81; president, 1981—), Institute of Public Administration (member of executive committee and council, 1961—), Academic Staff Association of University College, Dublin. *Awards, honors:* LL.D. from New York University and from St. Louis University.

WRITINGS: Planning in Ireland, Institute of Public Administration (Dublin, Ireland), 1968; *Towards a New Ireland,* C. Knight, 1972. Also author of *State-Sponsored Bodies,* 1959, and *Unequal Partners,* 1979. Irish correspondent for British Broadcasting Corp. (BBC), *Financial Times,* and *Economist;* economic correspondent for *Irish Times.*

* * *

FitzGERALD, Kathleen Whalen 1938-

PERSONAL: Born October 14, 1938, in Cleveland, Ohio; daughter of Thomas J. (an attorney) and Catherine H. (a dental hygienist; maiden name, Plunkett) Whalen; married Thomas FitzGerald (a consultant), September 12, 1973; children: Garrett Plunkett, Meghan O'Neill. *Education:* Siena Heights College, B.A., 1962; DePaul University, M.A., 1969; Northwestern University, Ph.D., 1979. *Politics:* Democrat. *Religion:* Roman Catholic. *Home:* 160 Wildwood, Lake Forest, Ill. 60045. *Agent:* Jane Rotrosen Agency, 226 East 32nd St., New York, N.Y. 10016.

CAREER: Archdiocese of Chicago, Chicago, Ill., teacher, 1958-69; Commission on Catholic Community Action, Cleveland, Ohio, associate director, 1969-71; Department of Health, Education, and Welfare, Chicago, equal opportunity specialist, 1971-74.

WRITINGS: Brass: Jane Byrne and the Pursuit of Power, Contemporary Books, 1981; *The Good Sisters* (novel), Contemporary Books, 1981.

WORK IN PROGRESS: The Black Swan, a novel about three generations of an Irish-American family, covering 1880 to 1975.

SIDELIGHTS: FitzGerald's book *Brass: Jane Byrne and the Pursuit of Power* records the life of former Chicago mayor Jane Byrne from childhood to her election to office in 1979. Gerard Einhaus commented in *New Review* that "short of a book by an immediate family member, a more intimate biography of the outspoken, often controversial mayor of Chi-

cago could not have been written." But Len O'Connor objected in the *Chicago Times Book World* that *Brass* "provides an almost tedious amount of detail of her Irish-Catholic upbringing," but falls short in explaining Byrne's political successes, including her unexpected victory in 1979.

BIOGRAPHICAL/CRITICAL SOURCES: Chicago Times Book World, May 10, 1981, October 25, 1981; *National Review,* October 30, 1981.

* * *

FitzGIBBON, (Robert Louis) Constantine (Lee-Dillon) 1919-1983

OBITUARY NOTICE—See index for *CA* sketch: Born June 8, 1919, in Lenox, Mass.; died March 23, 1983, in Dublin, Ireland. Translator, biographer, and author of fiction and nonfiction. FitzGibbon was best known as the biographer of Irish politician Eamon de Valera and Welsh poet Dylan Thomas. In addition to writing *The Life of Dylan Thomas,* FitzGibbon edited *Selected Letters of Dylan Thomas.* His most popular novel, *When the Kissing Had to Stop,* first appeared in 1960 and was reissued in 1973. *Through the Minefield,* his autobiography, was published in 1967. According to a writer for the *London Times, Drink,* which appeared in 1979, was FitzGibbon's "candid admission of his lifelong alcoholism." FitzGibbon also wrote numerous works of nonfiction and translated the writings of a great many other authors. Obituaries and other sources: *New York Times,* March 25, 1983; *London Times,* March 25, 1983; *Washington Post,* March 25, 1983; *Chicago Tribune,* March 26, 1983; *AB Bookman's Weekly,* April 11, 1983.

* * *

FLECKER, (Herman) James Elroy 1884-1915

BRIEF ENTRY: Born November 5, 1884, in London, England; died of tuberculosis, January 3, 1915, in Switzerland. British playwright, novelist, and poet. After studying Eastern languages at Cambridge University, Flecker entered the Consular Service and officiated in Constantinople (now Istanbul), Turkey, and Beirut, Lebanon, before severe tuberculosis cut short his career. A lyric poet, Flecker's attraction to Eastern culture was reflected in much of his writing. The author's Eastern drama *Hassan* (1922; first produced in 1923), combining prose, poetry, dance, music, and spectacle, was hailed as a masterpiece by both critics and the public. Flecker's other writings include the novel *The King Alsander* (1914), *Collected Poems* (1916), *Collected Prose* (1920), and a second play, *Don Juan* (1925; first produced in 1926). *Biographical/critical sources: The Oxford Companion to English Literature,* 4th edition, Oxford University Press, 1967; *Longman Companion to Twentieth Century Literature,* Longman, 1970; *Cassell's Encyclopaedia of World Literature,* revised edition, Morrow, 1973; *Dictionary of Literary Biography,* Volume 10: *Modern British Dramatists, 1940-1945,* Gale, 1982.

* * *

FLEISCHER, Leonore (Alexander Edwards)

BRIEF ENTRY: American journalist, editor, and author. Fleischer has worked as an advertising copywriter for *Publishers Weekly,* as an editor for Ballantine Books, and as a columnist for the *Washington Post* and *New York* magazine. She is also the author of more than thirty-five paperback novelizations of motion pictures, including *Funny Lady* (Bantam, 1975), *The Lords of Flatbush* (Bantam, 1977), and the best-selling *Ice Castles* (Fawcett, 1979). Fleischer's adaptation of the film "A Star Is Born," which was published by Warner Books in 1976, appeared under the pseudonym Alexander Edwards. Fleischer has also written several short biographies of well-known entertainers and a book about Jewish cookery entitled *The Chicken Soup Book* (Taplinger, 1977). *Address:* 258 Riverside Dr., No. 1C, New York, N.Y. 10025. *Biographical/critical sources: Publishers Weekly,* February 8, 1980.

* * *

FLEISCHER, Max   1889-1972

OBITUARY NOTICE: Born July 17, 1889 (some sources say 1883, 1885, or 1888), in Vienna, Austria; died September 11, 1972. Inventor and cartoonist. Considered a pioneer of film animation, Fleischer invented more than twenty motion picture production devices, including the Rotoscope, a machine used for drawing animals in motion. Fleischer created the "Out of the Inkwell" cartoon series in 1917 and later produced full-length animated feature films, including "Koko the Clown," "Betty Boop," "Popeye the Sailor," "Superman," "Gulliver's Travels," and "Mr. Bugs Goes to Town." In 1942 "Out of the Inkwell" productions was sold to Paramount Pictures, and Fleischer joined that company as production chief of cartooning, serving in that capacity until his retirement in the 1960's. Obituaries and other sources: *New York Times,* September 12, 1972; *Newsweek,* September 25, 1972; *Time,* September 25, 1972.

* * *

FLETCHER, Basil Alais   1900-1983

OBITUARY NOTICE—See index for *CA* sketch: Born April 10, 1900, in London, England; died February 19, 1983. Educator and author. In his lengthy career in education, Fletcher held a variety of posts in England, Africa, and Canada. From 1961 to 1967 he served as director of the Institute of Education at the University of Leeds. He was the author of many works on the philosophy and development of education, including *Education and Crisis: Educational Issues of Today, A Philosophy for the Teacher: A Study of the Child and Human Knowledge, Universities in the Modern World,* and *Outward Bound: Students of Outward Bound Schools in Great Britain: A Follow-Up Study.* Obituaries and other sources: *London Times,* March 7, 1983.

* * *

FLETCHER, J(oseph) S(mith)   1863-1935
(Son of the Soil)

BRIEF ENTRY: Born February 7, 1863, in Halifax, Yorkshire, England; died January 30, 1935, in Dorking, Surrey, England. British editor, columnist, and author. Fletcher, who was an extremely popular and prolific detective novelist during the 1920's and 1930's, wrote books that ranged from classical tales of detection to thrillers. His most critically acclaimed books are *The Middle Temple Murder* (1918) and *The Charing Cross Mystery* (1923). Each became popular on both sides of the Atlantic. Fletcher's stories have been collected in *The Adventures of Archer Dawe, Sleuth-Hound* (1909), *The Ravenswood Mystery and Other Stories* (1929), and *Find the Woman* (1933). He also wrote articles about country life, using the pseudonym

Son of the Soil. *Address:* Falklands, Dorking, Surrey, England. *Biographical/critical sources: Encyclopedia of Mystery and Detection,* McGraw, 1976.

* * *

FLETCHER, Richard E.   1917(?)-1983
(Rick Fletcher)

OBITUARY NOTICE: Born c. 1917; died of cancer, March 16, 1983, in Woodstock, Ill. Artist and cartoonist. Formerly a staff artist with the *Chicago Tribune,* Fletcher drew the "Dick Tracy" cartoon strip after the retirement of Chester Gould, the strip's creator, in 1977. He had assisted Gould with the detective cartoon since 1961. Obituaries and other sources: *Chicago Tribune,* March 18, 1983; *Los Angeles Times,* March 19, 1983; *Washington Post,* March 19, 1983.

* * *

FLETCHER, Rick
See FLETCHER, Richard E.

* * *

FLOWER, (Walter) Newman   1879-1964

OBITUARY NOTICE: Born July 8, 1879, in Fontmell Magna, Dorset, England; died March 12, 1964. Publisher, editor, and author. Flower purchased the publishing house Cassell & Company Limited in 1927, twenty-one years after joining the firm. Among the books he published while directing Cassell was Winston Churchill's *The Second World War;* Churchill had insisted that anything he wrote about the war be issued by Flower's company. Flower, who was knighted in 1938, wrote a number of books, including *Through My Garden Gate* and *Just As It Happened* and the biographies *George Frederic Handel, Franz Schubert,* and *Sir Arthur Sullivan: His Life and Letters.* He also edited Arnold Bennett's *Journal.* Obituaries and other sources: *New York Times,* March 13, 1964; *Illustrated London News,* March 21, 1964; *Publishers Weekly,* March 23, 1964; *Who Was Who,* Volume VI: *1961-1970,* A. & C. Black, 1972.

* * *

FOILES, Keith Andrew   1926-1983

OBITUARY NOTICE: Born March 14, 1926, in Genoa, Ill.; died suddenly, March 5, 1983, in New York. Educator, publishing executive, and editor. Foiles was a teacher of English in high schools before beginning his career in publishing with Harcourt Brace Jovanovich in 1957. He became an executive editor and was later made general sales manager. In 1976 he was named director of the college department. At the time of his death Foiles was serving as a senior vice-president of the company and director of the school department. Obituaries and other sources: *Who's Who in America,* 42nd edition, Marquis, 1982; *Publishers Weekly,* March 25, 1983.

* * *

FOLEY, June   1944-

PERSONAL: Born June 6, 1944, in Trenton, N.J.; daughter of William Patrick and June (Gadsby) Foley; married Michael Lindenman, June 13, 1970 (divorced, 1976); children: Max. *Education:* Attended New York University, 1969-70; Montclair State College, B.A., 1974, Teacher's Certificate in Social

Studies, 1976. *Agent:* Marilyn Marlow, Curtis Brown Ltd., 575 Madison Ave., New York, N.Y. 10022. *Office:* World Almanac, 200 Park Ave., New York, N.Y. 10166.

CAREER: World Almanac, New York, N.Y., assistant editor, 1978—.

WRITINGS: It's No Crush, I'm in Love! (young adult novel), Delacorte, 1982; *Love by Any Other Name* (young adult novel), Delacorte, 1983; *How Do I Love You?* (young adult novel), Delacorte, in press.

WORK IN PROGRESS: A young adult novel, publication by Delacorte expected in 1985.

SIDELIGHTS: Foley told *CA:* "I write about adolescence because I think it's the most awkward, exciting, and poignant time of life. It's like being pregnant for years and years—and the person you're going to give birth to is yourself. Adolescents are like everybody else, only more so; their feelings are more intense, they're more alive. Adolescents still have dreams, and they also have energy and time so that some of those dreams may indeed be fulfilled. I write about adolescents because I can give them a happy ending—which is only the beginning."

BIOGRAPHICAL/CRITICAL SOURCES: Trentonian, October 20, 1982.

* * *

FOLKARD, Charles James   1878-1963

OBITUARY NOTICE: Born April 6, 1878, in Lewisham, London, England; died in 1963. Illustrator and author. Folkard drew England's first newspaper cartoon strip, "Teddy Tail," which featured the escapades of a mouse. "Teddy Tail" later was expanded for a series of books published by A. & C. Black and was the basis of a play. Folkard illustrated many children's books, including *Mother Goose Nursery Rhymes, Grimm's Fairy Tales, The Swiss Family Robinson,* and *Pinocchio.* Obituaries and other sources: *Illustrators of Children's Books: 1744-1945,* Horn Book, 1947; *The Who's Who of Children's Literature,* Schoken, 1968; *Contemporary Illustrators of Children's Books,* Gale, 1978.

* * *

FORCHE, Carolyn (Louise)   1950-

BRIEF ENTRY: Born April 28, 1950, in Detroit, Mich. American educator, journalist, and poet. Forche's first book, *Gathering the Tribes* (Yale University Press, 1976), earned her a Yale Series of Younger Poets Award in 1976. An educator as well as a poet, Forche has held teaching posts at several universities, including San Diego State University, University of Arkansas, and University of Virginia. From 1978 to 1980 she worked as a journalist in El Salvador, where she reported on human rights violations for Amnesty International. Forche's *The Country Between Us* (Harper, 1982), which was the Lamont Selection of the Academy of American Poets, contains a number of poems that draw on her experiences in El Salvador. In the introduction to a *Rolling Stone* interview with Forche, Jonathan Cott wrote: "Perhaps no one better exemplifies the power and excellence of contemporary poetry than Carolyn Forche, who is not only one of the most affecting younger poets in America, but also one of the best poets writing anywhere in the world today." *Address:* Department of English, Wilson Hall, University of Virginia, Charlottesville, Va. 22901. *Biographical/critical sources: Who's Who of American Women,*

11th edition, Marquis, 1979; *Dictionary of Literary Biography,* Volume 5: *American Poets Since World War II,* Gale, 1980; *Nation,* May 8, 1982; *Los Angeles Times,* August 29, 1982; *Rolling Stone,* April 14, 1983.

* * *

FORD, Nancy K(effer)   1906-1961

OBITUARY NOTICE: Born April 1, 1906, in Camp Hill, Pa.; died in May, 1961. Editor and author. Ford was a reporter for the *Harrisburg Evening News* (Pennsylvania) before beginning her editorial career with *Jack and Jill* magazine. She was a senior editor for the magazine at the time of her death. In addition to the stories, poems, and plays she wrote for children's publications, Ford wrote several books of fairy tales, among them *Baba Yaga's Secret, Baba Yaga and the Enchanted Rings,* and *Baba Yaga and the Prince.* Obituaries and other sources: *Who Was Who in America, With World Notables,* Volume IV: *1961-1968,* Marquis, 1968.

* * *

FORMAN, Milos   1932-

PERSONAL: Born February 18, 1932, in Caslav, Czechoslovakia; came to United States, 1968; son of Rudolf (a teacher) and Anna (Svabova) Forman; married Jana Brejchova (an actress; marriage ended); married Vera Kresadlova (a singer), 1964; children: Petr, Matej. *Education:* Prague Film Faculty, diploma, 1954. *Agent:* Robert Lantz, Ltd., 144 East 55th St., New York, N.Y. 10022.

CAREER: Screenwriter and director of motion pictures, including "One Flew Over the Cuckoo's Nest," 1975, "Hair," 1979, and "Ragtime," 1982. Production assistant for Barrandov Studios in Czechoslovakia, 1962-63. Member of Sebor-Bor Film Producing Group, c. 1963. Honorary chairman of Columbia University Department of Film, 1978. *Awards, honors:* Prize from Czechoslovakian film critics, 1963, first prize from Locarno International Film Festival's young critics, 1964, first prize in twentieth anniversary celebration for liberation of Czechoslovakia, 1965, and young critics prize from film competition in Oberhausen, 1965, all for "Cerny Petr"; CIDALC Prize from Venice Film Festival, 1965, Grand International Prize from French Film Academy, 1966, and Trilobite from Union of Czechoslovakian Film and Television Artists, 1966, all for "Lasky jedne plavovlasky"; Academy Award for best director from Academy of Motion Picture Arts and Sciences, 1975, for "One Flew Over the Cuckoo's Nest"; and other film awards.

WRITINGS: (With Nancy Hardin) *Taking Off* (adapted from the screenplay directed by Forman and co-authored by Forman, John Guare, Jean-Claude Carriere, and John Klein; released by Universal, 1971), New American Library, 1971; (with Antonin J. Liehm) *The Milos Forman Stories,* International Arts and Sciences Press, 1975.

Screenplays; and director: (With Ivan Passer) "Konkurs" (contains two medium-length films whose titles mean "Audition" and "If It Wasn't for Music"; released in the U.S. as "Audition"), Filmstudio Barrandov, 1963; (with Jaroslav Papousek) "Cerny Petr" (released in the U.S. as "Black Peter," Altura Films, 1971; released in England as "Peter and Pavla"), Srebo, 1964; (with Passer and Papousek) "Lasky jedne plavovlasky" (released in the U.S. as "Loves of a Blonde," Prominent Films, 1966), Sebor-Bor/Filmstudio Barrandov, 1965;

(with Passer and Papousek) "Hori, ma panenko" (released in the U.S. as "Fireman's Ball," Cinema V, 1968; released in England as "Like a House on Fire"), Filmstudio Barrandov/ Carlo Ponti, 1967; (contributor) "Visions of Eight" (contains "Decathlon" by Forman), Cinema V, 1973.

Also author of screenplays produced in Czechoslovakia whose titles mean "Leave It to Me," 1955, and "Puppies," 1957.

WORK IN PROGRESS: Directing the motion picture "Amadeus."

SIDELIGHTS: During the mid-1960's, when three of his most acclaimed works were shown in the West, Forman gained recognition as one of Eastern Europe's finest, and most sardonic, filmmakers. "Black Peter" earned international honors for its humorous depiction of a dispirited floorwalker who arbitrarily reports the numerous shoplifters. Like Peter, Andula, the protagonist of "Loves of a Blonde," is disillusioned and haphazard in her pursuit of pleasure. Andula falls in love with a young pianist and pursues him to Prague, where she creates a crisis when confronting his parents with an account of her tryst with their son. Bosley Crowther, writing in the *New York Times,* called "Loves of a Blonde" "delightful and unusual— comic and sad and comprehending in a curiously inarticulate way." He added that "it is human, true but understated— inconclusive, indeed, as is life—and it leaves one amused and wistful over the romantic hopes of its little blonde."

"The Firemen's Ball," Forman's other success from the mid-1960's, concerns a ceremony conceived to honor a retiring fire chief. Recognition comes slowly to the chief, however, for the ball is disrupted by a beauty contest, a marching band, and a raffle. Even a fire disrupts the proceedings, and while the owner of the burning home sits and watches, thoughtful neighbors turn his chair away to lessen the shock, then move the fellow closer to the fire to warm him. Among the other outrageous acts during the banquet are a copulating couple writhing beneath the table from which the raffle is conducted, and a reveller aghast with shame as other celebrants catch him attempting to return his headcheese prize. *New York Times*'s Renata Adler described "The Firemen's Ball" as "a hilarious shaggy dog story, with the pessimism of the exquisite logic that leads nowhere." She also noted, "That a director who sees things so bitterly and clearly can be this funny . . . may mean that we are in for a comic renaissance after all."

Forman's career was briefly disrupted in 1967 when Czechoslovakia was invaded by Soviet troops. He had already been forced to publicly apologize to forty thousand firemen who walked off their jobs after the release of "The Firemen's Ball." He assured the workers that the film was actually a political allegory, and they returned to their stations. But the Communist rule seemed to signal an end to allegoric work, so Forman, who had been observing the student protests in Paris when the Soviets entered his country, remained abroad. He landed in Hollywood in 1967 with plans to adapt Franz Kafka's *Amerika.* Unable to recruit producers, though, he opted for a work that would present actor Jimmy Durante as a wealthy bear hunter roaming the Slavic woodlands. That project also failed to interest appropriate producers.

In 1968 Forman was enlisted by Paramount Pictures to direct one of his own works. With several other writers, including playwright John Guare, Forman fashioned "Taking Off," which matched the acclaim of his Slavic works. The film depicts the increasingly permissive American society of the late 1960's as personified by staid businessman Larry Tyne and his family.

When Tyne's daughter, Jeannie, becomes involved in a Greenwich Village theatre production and decides to stay in the Village, Larry and his wife try to become better acquainted with their daughter's environment in an attempt to woo her return. Their adventures take them to a meeting of the Society for Parents of Fugitive Children, where they learn how to smoke marijuana, and into the Village, where they are appalled by the habitants' casual attitude towards sex and drugs. *New York Times*'s critic Vincent Canby hailed "Taking Off" as a "charming" work. He wrote, "Forman's America is made up of neighborhood bars to which lonely ladies come accompanied by their Siamese cats; of the sort of mother who, when told her daughter has shoplifted a portable Japanese TV set, asks whether it's a Sony." Focusing on the serious aspects of the film, Sandra Hochman claimed that "Taking Off" verges on being "a very good, very bizarre vision of what 20th-century New York American rock-youth is like." She added that "the film itself is both fierce and gentle, filled with the ambiguities of an urban culture that has lost its identity as a place where people want to live."

Despite the acclaim accorded "Taking Off," Forman was unable to obtain funding for another project. In 1972 he filmed decathlon competitors at the Olympics for inclusion in the omnibus production, "Visions of Eight," but that proved to be his sole production throughout the next two years. In 1975, however, he regained his prominence in the film world with the direction of "One Flew Over the Cuckoo's Nest." Working from Bo Goldman's adaptation of Ken Kesey's novel, Forman fashioned a compelling portrait of the individual against the system. The film earned a host of awards, including Academy Awards for Jack Nicholson for his performance as R. P. McMurphy, an anti-social, but engaging, patient in a mental hospital; and Louise Fletcher as Nurse Ratched, the domineering nurse whose confrontations with McMurphy lead to violence and, eventually, death. Goldman's screenplay was also cited by the academy as the best adapted work, and Forman was acknowledged as the year's best director.

Since "Taking Off," Forman has refrained from directing his own scripts. After working with Goldman on "Cuckoo's Nest," he linked with playwright Michael Weller for both "Hair" and "Ragtime." In filming "Hair," Forman concentrated on the mood of rebellion and affection that fostered the youth movement typified by the popular musical of the late 1960's. "It is no accident that Forman took on the direction of 'Hair,'" declared *New Yorker*'s Penelope Gilliatt. "The score, with— to his ears—its newness and its eloquence about his adopted country, must have sung strongly to him. So, clearly, did moments of ease and fun that he catches on to in the book and lyrics."

"Ragtime" fared less successfully with critics. *New Yorker*'s Pauline Kael, for instance, contended that Forman was the wrong director to re-create the turbulent events of E. L. Doctorow's popular novel of the early 1900's. "Forman simply didn't have the storehouse of associations to make a 'Ragtime,'" she claimed. "It's limp—it always seems to be aiming about halfway to Doctorow's effects." *Newsweek*'s Jack Kroll echoed Kael's comments, declaring that "all the book's wit is gone." He called the film "a high-class . . . , carefully mounted but oddly tamed and domesticated 'Ragtime.'"

BIOGRAPHICAL/CRITICAL SOURCES: New York Times, October 23, 1966, September 30, 1968, March 23, 1971, April 18, 1971, May 14, 1971, November 11, 1971, November 23,

1971; *Life,* January 20, 1967; *New Yorker,* April 16, 1979, November 23, 1981; *Newsweek,* November 23, 1981.*

—*Sketch by Les Stone*

* * *

FORMBY, William A(rthur)   1943-

PERSONAL: Born May 31, 1943, in Mobile, Ala.; son of Robert E. (a plant manager) and Anntoinette (Allen) Terry; married Patricia Allen (a medical receptionist), February 7, 1967; children: Tonya Lynn, Shannon Dale. *Education:* University of Alabama, B.S., 1973, M.S., 1974, Ph.D., 1981. *Religion:* Methodist. *Home:* 17517 Northwood Lake, Northport, Ala. 35476. *Office:* Department of Criminal Justice, University of Alabama, P.O. Box 6365, University, Ala. 35486.

CAREER: Tuscaloosa Police Department, Tuscaloosa, Ala., patrolman, 1968-73; East Carolina University, Greenville, N.C., assistant professor of social work, 1974-76, member of executive committee of the department of social work and correctional services, 1974-76, member of personnel action committee, 1975-76, co-director of reorganization study of the university police department, 1976; University of Alabama, University, lecturer, 1977-80, assistant professor of criminal justice, 1980—. Conference coordinator of the advanced law enforcement training project, Jefferson State Junior College, Birmingham, Ala., 1974. Consultant to Jefferson State Junior College, 1974, Charlotte, N.C., Police Department, 1975, Greenville Police Department, 1975, North Carolina Department of Justice, 1976, Birmingham Police Department, 1976-80, Tuscaloosa Police Department, 1980—. Instructor of Birmingham Police Department's Community Service Officer Training Program, 1978. *Military service:* U.S. Marine Corps, 1961-65; became corporal.

MEMBER: International Society of Crime Prevention Practitioners, Southern Association of Criminal Justice Educators, North Carolina Criminal Justice Educators Association, Alabama Criminal Justice Educators Association, Academy of Criminal Justice Sciences, Kappa Delta Pi. *Awards, honors:* Named outstanding law enforcement officer in the State of Alabama for 1972; received merit service award from Tuscaloosa Police Department, 1973.

WRITINGS: (Contributor) Eugene Anderson and Louis Nelson, editors, *Helping Others,* East Tennessee State University Press, 1979; (contributor) Michael T. Farmer, editor, *Differential Police Response Strategies,* Police Executive Research Forum, 1981; (with John C. Watkins and Vergil L. Williams) *Introduction to Criminal Justice,* Delmar, 1982; (with Williams) *Law Enforcement in the United States,* Brooks/Cole, in press. Contributor of articles to periodicals, including *Social Perspectives, Police Chief, Journal of Humanics, Journal of Police Science and Administration, Criminal Justice Review, Educational Forum, Victimology, American Journal of Small Business,* and *Journal of Criminal Justice.*

WORK IN PROGRESS: Campus Victimization; Issues in Crime Control, with Virgil L. Williams.

SIDELIGHTS: Formby told *CA:* "As a writer, primarily of textbooks and research reports, I simply wish to convey an idea or raise a question that may someday lead someone to an answer to one of our many societal problems. Writing is the sharing of ideas and perceptions of the world around us. It is regretful that everyone will not be able to share his world with everyone else."

FORTES, Meyer   1906-1983

OBITUARY NOTICE: Born April 25, 1906, in Britstown, Cape Province, South Africa; died January 27, 1983, in Cambridge, England. Educator, anthropologist, and author. Fortes is remembered primarily for his studies of the Tallensi of Northern Ghana during the 1930's and for his pioneering work in the theory of social anthropology. With his first wife, Sonia, Fortes studied the domestic economy of the Tallensi. After her death he married American psychoanalyst Doris Mayer, with whom he observed the effects of social change on mental disorders among the Tallensi. Fortes also explored religious systems in Africa. Among the anthropologist's writings are *The Dynamics of Clanship Among the Tallensi, The Web of Kinship Among the Tallensi,* and *Oedipus and Job in West African Religion.* Obituaries and other sources: *Who's Who,* 134th edition, St. Martin's, 1982; *London Times,* January 29, 1983.

* * *

FOSTER, (Reginald) Francis   1896-1975

PERSONAL: Born April 13, 1896, in Sussex, England; died March 28, 1975; son of B. H. Foster; married Joan Elizabeth Bibby, 1951; children: three sons, three daughters. *Education:* Educated privately.

CAREER: Entered Third Order of Friars Minor, 1927, ordained priest of Syro-Chaldean Church, 1933. Journalist, 1924; Elkin Mathews & Marrot Ltd. (publisher), London, England, chief literary adviser, 1925-27; superior of Order of the Divine Mission, 1934-40; writer, 1940-75. *Military service:* British Army, Artists' Rifles and East Lancashire Regiment, 1915-17; served in France; became lieutenant. Indian Army, 1918-23; served in Palestine and Egypt; became major. British Army, Queen's Royal Regiment, 1941-45.

WRITINGS: The Lift Murder, Jarrolds, 1924; *The Missing Gates* (novel), Jarrolds, 1924, abridged edition, Mellifont Press, 1938; *How to Write and Sell Short Stories,* Allen & Unwin, 1926; *Anthony Ravenhill, Crime Merchant,* Jarrolds, 1926; *Confession,* Nash & Grayson, 1927; *The Music Gallery Murder,* T. F. Unwin, 1927, abridged edition, Mellifont Press, 1939; *The Captive King,* 1927; *The Trail of the Thugs,* 1927; *The Moat House Mystery,* Nash & Grayson, 1928; *The Secret Places, Being a Chronicle of Vagabondage,* Mathews & Marrot, 1929.

The Dark Night, Nash & Grayson, 1930; *Joyous Pilgrimage, Being the Chronicle of a Strange Journey* (stories), Mathews & Marrot, 1930; *The Mystery at Chillery,* Fiction League, 1931 (published in England as *Something Wrong at Chillery,* Nash & Grayson, 1931); *Murder From Beyond,* Macauley Co., 1931; (with Jess Mary Mardon Foster) *The Wayside Book: A Book for Ramblers, Campers, and All Wayfarers,* C. A. Pearson, 1932; (author of foreword and commentary) *Famous Short Stories Analysed,* Fleet Publications, 1932, reprinted, Folcroft, 1974; *The Chillery Court Mystery,* Mellifont Press, 1936; *Separate Star: An Autobiography,* Gollancz, 1938; *Longshanks and I,* Hodder & Stoughton, 1939.

Dover Front, Secker & Warburg, 1941; *Modern Punctuation Handbook,* Fleet Publications, 1947; *The Ancient Way,* 1949; *The Island,* 1949.

Desert Journey, 1965; (contributor) *Promise of Greatness,* 1968; *The Perennial Religion,* Regency Press, 1969.

The Unknown God, 1973. Contributor of stories and articles to magazines in England, India, and South Africa.*

FOSTER, Malcolm (Burton) 1931-

PERSONAL: Born February 24, 1931, in Montreal, Quebec, Canada; son of Orval Allison and Olive Eva (Burton) Foster; married Carol Bertha Royce, July 2, 1954; children: John David, Laura, Victoria Elizabeth, Cynthia Ann. *Education:* Attended Humberside Collegiate Institute, 1950; Syracuse University, B.A., 1955; University of Minnesota, M.A., 1958. *Home:* 2466 Benny Crescent, Apt. 612, Montreal, Quebec, Canada H4B 2P9. *Office:* Department of English, Concordia University, Loyola Campus, Montreal, Quebec, Canada H4B 1R6.

CAREER: Teacher at high school in West Lorne, Ontario, 1956; Michigan College of Mining and Technology (now Michigan Technological University), Houghton, Mich., lecturer in English, 1958-60; University of Cincinnati, Cincinnati, Ohio, lecturer in English, 1960-63; Concordia University, Montreal, Quebec, lecturer, 1963-65, assistant professor, 1965-68, associate professor, 1968-76, professor of English, 1976—. *Member:* Association of Canadian University Teachers of English, Canadian Association of American Studies, Canadian Authors Association (president, 1974-76). *Awards, honors:* Indiana University Short Story Prize, 1962; McGraw-Hill novel fellowship, 1962; Canada Council grants, 1964, 1965, 1967-68, and 1976-77; British Council travel grant, 1964; Houghton Mifflin literary fellowship, 1967-68.

WRITINGS: The Prince With a Hundred Dragons (juvenile), illustrations by Barbara Remington, Doubleday, 1963; *Alan Paton: A Critical Study,* Cole, 1965; *Joyce Cary: A Biography,* Houghton, 1968. Also author of *The Anderson Affair: A Personal Study,* 1979; *The Bird Whose Feathers Were Stolen,* 1979; *The Italian White Horse,* 1979.

Assistant art editor of *Liberty,* 1955. Contributor of articles to newspapers and professional journals, including *Journal of Canadian Studies, Modern Fiction Studies,* and *Journal of International Fiction,* and of reviews to the *Montreal Gazette.*

SIDELIGHTS: Malcolm Foster, a specialist in twentieth-century literature, drew critical attention with his book *Joyce Cary.* It was the first definitive biography of Cary, the creator of such novels as *The Horse's Mouth* and *Mister Johnson.* A prolific yet relatively obscure novelist, Cary achieved recognition late in life, following a series of what modern analysts might call identity crises. In a *Christian Science Monitor* review, Robert W. Haney described the difficulty of Foster's task in chronicling Cary's development as a serious novelist. The reviewer assessed Cary as "a complicated person: debonairly formal, yet puckish; rigid in his habits, yet gay and dynamic in spirit. His fiction may easily be read as a divertissement, but it expresses a serious purpose."

Other reviewers called Joyce Cary a difficult subject. Scholars have long puzzled over the relationship between his varied life experiences and his novels. He was never popular in the literary circles of his time, and critics have trouble placing him in a specific literary tradition. The challenge lies in understanding a man whose fiction might be considered ahead of its time. In many critics' opinion, Foster fails to meet the challenge. A reviewer for *Time* commented: "Cary was a writer of imagination whose life had only oblique relation to his works. The admirable research by Malcolm Foster . . . consequently does not illuminate many hidden corners. But by telling what Cary was he helps define the flights of imagination the author had to make when he created his gallery of characters."

Foster's shortcomings seem to lie in what one critic calls the author's "laundry list approach." Reviewers complain that instead of plumbing the depths of Cary's intricate philosophy, Foster is content merely to reconstruct the particulars of the novelist's life. G. Davenport of *National Review* offered this tongue-in-cheek comment on Foster's zealous approach to detail: "Glory Be. Mr. Foster was given access to Cary's papers and has used them with admirable skill. His research is impeccable; he even checked a drawer knob tightened by Cary in the apartment of his American publisher . . . to discover that ten years later it was still tight." In a more serious vein, Jeffrey Meyers, writing in *Commonweal,* echoed the prevailing criticism: "Though Mr. Foster has rendered a complete and accurate account of the facts, his book suffers from painful repetition, lack of selectivity and proportion, glutinous style and an emphasis on the obvious."

Some reviewers also found fault with Foster's attempts to insert literary analysis into this biography. Meyers noted: "Perhaps the primary weakness of the book is the superficiality of the literary criticism, which is mainly an exposition of the plot and general theme of the novels and fails to do justice to the moral complexity of Cary's fiction." Charles G. Hoffman added his opinion in a *South Atlantic Quarterly* review: "These chapters seem an afterthought rather than an integral part of the book."

Although disappointed with Foster's biographical style, critics agree he has done the literary world a service by providing such a complete picture of Cary's life. In *Saturday Review,* Granville Hicks softened the criticism by stating: "Although there is more detail than is strictly necessary, it is good to have so full an account set down while so many who knew Cary are still alive." For his part, Haney maintained that "Foster offers us a vivid and sympathetic full-length portrait" of Cary.

BIOGRAPHICAL/CRITICAL SOURCES: Washington Post Book World, October 20, 1968; *Life,* October 25, 1968; *Atlantic,* November, 1968; *Esquire,* November, 1968; *Saturday Review,* November 30, 1968; *Best Sellers,* December 1, 1968; *Time,* January 10, 1969; *National Review,* January 28, 1969; *Commonweal,* June 13, 1969; *South Atlantic Quarterly,* summer, 1969; *Christian Science Monitor,* August 28, 1969; *Observer,* December 14, 1969; *London Magazine,* January, 1970.*

*   *   *

FOUREST, Henri-Pierre 1911-

BRIEF ENTRY: Born December 22, 1911, in Paris, France. French museum curator, ceramist, and author. During World War II Fourest was an assistant in the department of paintings at the Louvre. In 1945 he was named curator of France's National Museum of Ceramics, and in 1973 he became conservator in chief. He has been named chevalier of the French Legion of Honor and officer of Ordre National du Merite. English translations of Fourest's books include *French Ceramics* (Kodansha, 1979) and *Delftware: Faience Production at Delft* (Rizzoli International, 1980). Other books by Fourest include *L'Oeuvre des faienciers francais du seizieme a la fin du dix-huitieme siecle* (Hachette, 1966) and *La Ceramique francaise: Faience et porcelaine* (Publications Filmees d'art et d'histoire, 1970). *Address:* 12 rue de Liege, Paris 975, France; and Musee Nationale de Ceramique, Sevres 92, France. *Biographical/critical sources: The International Who's Who,* Europa, 1976; *New York Times,* December 12, 1980.

FOWLER, (Edward) Michael (Coulson) 1929-

PERSONAL: Born December 19, 1929, in Marton, New Zealand; son of William Coulson and Faith Agnes (Netherclift) Fowler; married Barbara Hamilton Hall, June 27, 1953; children: Antony Coulson, Mark Coulson, Anna Hamilton. *Education:* University of Auckland, Dip.Arch., 1952, M.Arch., 1972. *Politics:* National party. *Religion:* Church of England. *Home:* 31 Hobson Cres., Thorndon, Wellington 1, New Zealand. *Office:* Office of the Mayor, Town Hall, Wellington 1, New Zealand.

CAREER: Ove Arup & Partners, London, England, architect, 1954-56; private practice of architecture in Wellington, New Zealand, 1957-59; Calder Fowler Styles & Tuner (architects), Wellington, partner, 1960—. City of Wellington, member of city council, 1968-74, mayor, 1974-83. Chairman of New Zealand Municipal Cooperative Insurance Co., 1981-83. *Member:* New Zealand Institute of Architects (fellow), Royal Institute of British Architects (associate). *Awards, honors:* Created Knight Bachelor, 1981.

WRITINGS: Wellington Sketches, Folios I and II, Whitcoulls, 1971, 2nd edition, 1974; *Country Houses of New Zealand,* A. H. & A. W. Reed, 1972, 2nd edition, 1977; (with Pauline Clayton) *Eating Houses in Wellington,* Anchor Communications, 1980; *The Architecture and Planning of Moscow,* Novosti Publications, 1980; *Wellington-Wellington,* Mallinson-Rendel, 1981; (with Clayton) *Eating Houses in Canterbury,* Anchor Communications, 1982; *New Zealand House,* Landsdowne Press, 1983; *Wellington Celebration,* Brick Row, 1983.

Author of "Capital View," a regular column in *Sunday News,* 1977-83. Contributor to magazines and newspapers, including *NZIA Journal, Town & Country, Dominion,* and *Evening Post.*

WORK IN PROGRESS: The Parian Episode, a contemporary adventure novel set on the Greek island of Paros; *The Acquisition and Maintenance of Property.*

AVOCATIONAL INTERESTS: Sketching, reading, history, politics.

* * *

FOX, Annette Baker 1912-

BRIEF ENTRY: Born March 2, 1912, in Buffalo, N.Y. American political scientist, educator, and author. Fox has taught at Bryn Mawr College, Hunter College of the City University of New York, Sarah Lawrence College, and Barnard College, where she currently is a lecturer in international relations. She is also a research associate at Columbia University and has served as the school's director of Canadian studies since 1976. Fox wrote *Freedom and Welfare in the Caribbean: A Colonial Dilemma* (Harcourt, 1949), *The Power of Small States: Diplomacy in World War II* (University of Chicago Press, 1959), *NATO and the Range of American Choice* (Columbia University Press, 1967), and *The Politics of Attraction: Four Middle Powers and the United States* (Columbia University Press, 1977). She also co-edited *Canada and the United States: Transnational and Transgovernmental Relations* (World Peace Foundation and University of Wisconsin-Madison, 1976). *Address:* Institute of War and Peace Studies, Columbia University, New York, N.Y. 10027; and Department of Political Science, Barnard College, Morningside Heights, New York, N.Y. 10027. *Biographical/critical sources: American Historical Review,* December, 1977.

FOX, Frank W(ayne) 1940-

PERSONAL: Born October 7, 1940, in Salt Lake City, Utah; son of Arley Wayne (a printer) and Mary Fae (Openshaw) Fox; married Elaine Tebbs, September 9, 1969; children: David Ryan, Michael Jordan. *Education:* University of Utah, B.A. (cum laude), 1966, M.A., 1969; Stanford University, Ph.D., 1973. *Politics:* Independent. *Religion:* Church of Jesus Christ of Latter-day Saints (Mormons). *Home:* 3259 Mohawk Lane, Provo, Utah 84604. *Office:* Department of History, Brigham Young University, Provo, Utah 84602.

CAREER: Utah State Road Commission, Salt Lake City, supervisor of highways and highway construction, 1958-60; Church of Jesus Christ of Latter-day Saints, Salt Lake City, missionary in Brazil, 1960-63; Highway Supply Corp., Centerville, Utah, supervisor of highways and highway construction, 1964-69; Brigham Young University, Provo, Utah, instructor, 1971-73, assistant professor, 1973-78, associate professor, 1978-83, professor of American cultural history and American studies, 1983—. Guest lecturer at J. Reuben Clark Law School, 1976.

MEMBER: Organization of American Historians, Institute of Early American History and Culture, American Studies Association, Phi Kappa Phi. *Awards, honors:* Named teacher of the year by Phi Alpha Theta, 1975; general publication prize from Association for Mormon Letters, 1980, for *J. Reuben Clark: The Public Years.*

WRITINGS: Madison Avenue Goes to War: The Strange Military Career of American Advertising, 1941-1945 (monograph), C. E. Merrill, 1974; *J. Reuben Clark: The Public Years,* Brigham Young University Press, 1980; *American Heritage: An Interdisciplinary Approach to the American Experience,* Burgess, in press. Contributor of articles and reviews to scholarly journals and popular magazines, including *Utah Holiday, Utah Heritage,* and *Ensign.*

WORK IN PROGRESS: The Last Frontier: San Francisco and the American Experience; Western Gate: An Anthology of Writings on San Francisco, completion expected in 1984.

SIDELIGHTS: Fox wrote: "Since long before Homer, historians have been called upon to provide the vital core of their respective cultures. In the twentieth century, however, historians have become progressively more concerned with professionalization of their craft, which seems to mean addressing themselves to ever more esoteric questions. History, as the people know and experience it, is thus left to popular writers, many of whom lack professional standards of research and analysis. I see my work as an attempt to bridge that gap.

"Madison Avenue [the subject of Fox's 1974 monograph] has always played an ambiguous role in American life. On the one hand it has ever been devoted to the simple selling of goods and services. On the other hand it has made constant forays into the world of ideas, attempting to shape the consciousness and value structure of the American public. When the Second World War broke out, admen asked for a chance to put their idea-making power to use in a constructive way, promising to become the voice of democracy to the world. This odd experiment affords us a rare glimpse into the workings not only of advertising but of the American mind itself, as it attempted to comprehend the war and its meaning in terms of its own consumption mentality."

Fox also commented on the topic of his work in progress: "Why does everything happen first in San Francisco? I believe that the San Francisco Bay Area affords us a particularly good view of the forces that power modern America. In a dynamic, pluralistic society, San Francisco is driven with a circuit-breaking dynamism, and it carries pluralism to the point of logical absurdity. To a materialistic society it has contributed a gold rush, a silver bonanza, and repeated bouts of frenzied speculation. In our technological quest it has given us everything from the cable car to nuclear warheads and 'Silicon Valley.' Amid increasing fears about the environment, San Francisco has supplied the stage for every conceivable drama of man and nature, from save-the-redwoods to rescue-the-bay. It has rewarded our search for alternative lifestyles with a kaleidoscope of new ones—and just enough self-doubt to make judgments among them hazardous. It is the city that brings together Paris and Peking and renders both of them relevant to the American experience. With its beauty, bounty, whimsy, and grandeur, it is the last West of our literary imagination—and perhaps it is the ultimate one.''

BIOGRAPHICAL/CRITICAL SOURCES: Journal of American History, December, 1981.

* * *

FOX, Matthew (Timothy) 1940-

BRIEF ENTRY: Born December 21, 1940, in Madison, Wis. American theologian, educator, clergyman, and author. Fox has been an ordained Roman Catholic priest of the Dominican order since 1967. He was a member of the faculties of Aquinas Institute of Theology, Emmanuel College, Boston, Loyola University of Chicago, and Barat College. Fox then became a professor of religion at Mundelein College. He wrote *Religion USA: An Inquiry Into Religion and Culture by Way of "Time" Magazine* (Listening Press, 1971), *On Becoming a Musical, Mystical Bear: Spirituality American Style* (Harper, 1972), *Whee! We, Wee, All the Way Home: A Guide to the New Sensual Spirituality* (Consortium, 1976), and *A Spirituality Named Compassion and the Healing of the Global Village: Humpty Dumpty and Us* (Winston Press, 1979). Fox edited *Western Spirituality: Historical Roots, Ecumenical Routes* (Fides/Claretian, 1979). *Address:* Department of Religion, Mundelein College, 6363 North Sheridan Rd., Chicago, Ill. 60660.

* * *

FOXLEY-NORRIS, Christopher Neil 1917-

PERSONAL: Born March 16, 1917, in Birkenhead, England; son of John Perceval and Dorothy Kathleen Foxley-Norris; married Joan Lovell Hughes, November 10, 1948. *Education:* Trinity College, Oxford, M.A., 1938; studied law at Middle Temple, 1938-39. *Politics:* Conservative. *Religion:* Church of England. *Home:* Tumble Wood, Northend Common, Henley, Oxfordshire, England. *Agent:* John Farquharson Ltd., 15 Red Lion Sq., London WC1R 4QW, England. *Office:* Cheshire Foundation, 26-29 Maunsel St., London S.W.1, England.

CAREER: Royal Air Force, career officer, 1936-74, director of organizational and administrative plans at Air Ministry, 1962-63, assistant chief of defense staff, 1963, air officer commanding 224 Group of Far East Air Force, 1964-67, director-general of Royal Air Force organization at Air Ministry, 1967-68, commander in chief in Germany and commander of North Atlantic Treaty Organization's Second Tactical Air Force, 1968-70, chief of personnel and logistics at Ministry of Defence, 1971-74, retiring as air chief marshal; Cheshire Foundation, London, England, chairman, 1974—. Chairman of General Portfolio Life Insurance Co., 1975—, Freedom Organization

for the Right to Enjoy Smoking Tobacco, 1978—, and Gardening for the Disabled; director of General Portfolio Investments and Royal Air Force Disabled Holiday Trust.

MEMBER: Royal Society of Arts (fellow), British Institute of Management (fellow), Institute for the Study of Conflict (member of council), Royal United Service Institute (vice-president), Battle of Britain Fighter Association (chairman, 1976—). *Awards, honors*—Military: Officer of Order of the British Empire, 1956; Distinguished Service Order, 1965; Knight Grand Cross of Order of the Bath, 1972. Other: Honorary fellow of Trinity College, Oxford, 1972.

WRITINGS: A Lighter Shade of Blue, Ian Allan, 1978; (editor) *The Royal Air Force at War,* Ian Allan, 1983. Contributor to military journals.

SIDELIGHTS: Foxley-Norris wrote: ''Most of my life is now dedicated to the care of the handicapped. The Cheshire Foundation operates nearly two hundred homes in thirty-eight countries around the world. I am also still deeply involved in defense and international matters.''

* * *

FOXX, Rosalind
See HAYDON, June

* * *

FRAENKEL, Osmond K. 1888-1983

OBITUARY NOTICE—See index for *CA* sketch: Born October 17, 1888, in New York, N.Y.; died of a heart attack, May 16, 1983, in New York, N.Y. Lawyer well known for his work in defense of civil liberties and author. Fraenkel defended two of the ''Scottsboro boys''—nine black youths who were accused of raping two white women in Alabama in 1935. He appeared before the Supreme Court numerous times and served as consultant in several notable Supreme Court cases, including the court's rulings on the internment of Japanese-Americans during World War II and the publication of the Pentagon Papers. Some of Fraenkel's more celebrated clients were educator and philosopher Bertrand Russell, labor leader Harry Bridges, and David Miller, the first of the Vietnam War protesters to burn his draft card. From 1954 to 1977 Fraenkel served as chief counsel for the American Civil Liberties Union (ACLU). He was the author of several books, including *The Sacco-Vanzetti Case, Our Civil Liberties, The Supreme Court and Civil Liberties,* and *The Rights We Have.* Obituaries and other sources: *New York Times,* May 17, 1983; *Chicago Tribune,* May 19, 1983; *Los Angeles Times,* May 19, 1983.

* * *

FRALEY, Oscar (B.) 1914-

BRIEF ENTRY: Born August 2, 1914, in Philadelphia, Pa. American author. Fraley was a golf writer as early as 1939. He has worked for United Press International and *Golf,* and he has covered and played in tournaments all over the world. Fraley wrote *The All-Star Athletes Cook Book* (Centaur House, 1965) with David Huntley, *The Million Dollar Gate* (Macmillan, 1966) with Jack ''Doc'' Kearns, *The Untouchables* (Bailey Brothers & Swinfen, 1967), *''I Can Help Your Game''* (Fawcett, 1971) with Lee Trevino, *Vizzini: The Secret Lives of America's Most Successful Undercover Agent* (Arbor House, 1972) with Sal Vizzini, and *Hoffa: The Real Story* (Stein & Day, 1975) with James R. Hoffa.

FRANCISCO, Charles 1930-

PERSONAL: Born October 23, 1930, in East St. Louis, Ill.; son of Roy (a painter) and Nellie (Williams) Francisco; married Patricia Warner, December 19, 1955 (divorced, 1966); married Suzanne McDonald (an accounting executive), November 7, 1974; children: Norma, Bill (stepson). *Education:* Received B.A. from University of Illinois. *Agent:* Julia Coopersmith Literary Agency, 10 West 15th St., New York, N.Y. 10011.

CAREER: Actor in New York City, 1952-54, Chicago, Ill., 1955-62, and Hollywood, Calif., 1962-67; WPAT-Radio, New York City, news director, 1967-76. *Military service:* U.S. Army, combat correspondent, 1950-52; served in Korea; became staff sergeant; received Bronze Star and five battle stars. *Member:* American Irish Historical Society, American Federation of Television and Radio Artists, Actors Equity Association, Screen Actors Guild, Authors Guild. *Awards, honors:* Special commendation from U.S. Secretary of the Army for a guest column, "A G.I.'s View of the War."

WRITINGS: The Radio City Music Hall: An Affectionate History of the World's Greatest Theatre, Dutton, 1979; *You Must Remember This: The Filming of "Casablanca,"* Prentice-Hall, 1980. Began as assistant sports editor of *Champaign-Urbana Evening Courier,* became sportswriter; drama critic for *Fanfare.*

SIDELIGHTS: Francisco told *CA:* "The threatened razing of the Radio City Music Hall, my interest in preserving it as a theatrical landmark, and a long-time friendship with one of the Rockettes prompted me to rush work on my first published book.

"Although all branches of my family have been in America for more than one hundred fifty years and despite the Latin-sounding name, my ethnic background is proudly Irish. I have made annual trips to Ireland for many years, have a working knowledge of the Gaelic language, and harbor a dream of eventually owning a 'writer's hideout' on that island."

BIOGRAPHICAL/CRITICAL SOURCES: Los Angeles Times Book Review, June 17, 1979.

*　*　*　*

FRANK, Gerold 1907-

BRIEF ENTRY: Born August 2, 1907, in Cleveland, Ohio. American author. Frank was a newspaper reporter from 1933 to 1950, senior editor of *Coronet* from 1952 to 1958, and a screenwriter for Warner Brothers in 1960. He won a Christopher Award for *I'll Cry Tomorrow* (Fell, 1954) and Edgar Allan Poe Awards from Mystery Writers of America for *The Deed* (Simon & Schuster, 1963) and *The Boston Strangler* (New American Library, 1966). Frank also wrote *Zsa Zsa Gabor: My Story* (World Publishing, 1960), *An American Death: The True Story of the Assassination of Dr. Martin Luther King, Jr. and the Greatest Manhunt of Our Time* (Doubleday, 1972), and *Judy* (Harper, 1975). *Address:* 930 Fifth Ave., New York, N.Y. 10021; and c/o William Morris Agency, 1350 Avenue of the Americas, New York, N.Y. 10019. *Biographical/critical sources: Saturday Review,* April 8, 1972, June 28, 1975; *Time,* April 10, 1972, June 16, 1975; *Newsweek,* April 10, 1972, June 9, 1975; *New York Times,* April 11, 1972, June 30, 1975; *Esquire,* October, 1975; *Who's Who in America,* 42nd edition, Marquis, 1982.

FRASER, Bruce (Donald) 1910-

PERSONAL: Born November 18, 1910, in Quetta, India (now Pakistan); son of Theodore (a major-general in the armed forces) and Constance Ruth (Stevenson) Fraser; married Audrey Croslegh, 1939 (died, 1982); children: Jonathan (deceased), Caroline Fraser Harrison (deceased). *Education:* Trinity College, Cambridge, B.A. (with first class honors), 1932, M.A., 1964. *Home:* Jonathan, St. Dogmael's, Cardigan Dyfed SA43 3LF, Wales.

CAREER: United Kingdom Civil Service, London, England, assistant principal in Scottish Office, 1933-36, private secretary to financial secretary at treasury, 1937-41, private secretary to permanent secretary, 1941-45, assistant secretary, 1945-51, under secretary, 1951-56, third secretary, 1956-60; Ministry of Aviation, London, deputy secretary, 1960; Ministry of Health, London, permanent secretary, 1960-64; Department of Education and Science, London, joint permanent under secretary of state, 1964-65; Ministry of Land and Natural Resources, London, permanent secretary, 1965-66; Exchequer and Audit Department, London, comptroller and auditor general, 1966-71. *Member:* Athenaeum Club. *Awards, honors:* Commander of Order of the Bath, 1956, Knight Commander, 1961.

WRITINGS: (Editor of revision) Ernest Gowers, *The Complete Plain Words,* H.M.S.O., 1973.

SIDELIGHTS: Fraser told *CA:* "*The Complete Plain Words,* by Ernest Gowers, is a wise and witty guide to the use of decent English in everyday writing, particularly in administration and business. It is widely regarded as the best book of its kind ever written (in Britain, at any rate), and its sales worldwide (including in the United States) have been enormous. But it was beginning to get out of date here and there. I did the revised edition because I was commissioned by the government to do so."

*　*　*　*

FRAZER, Mark Petrovich
See MACLEAN, Donald Duart

*　*　*　*

FRAZIER, Cliff(ord) 1934-

BRIEF ENTRY: Born August 27, 1934, in Detroit, Mich. American actor, director, producer, and author. Frazier, who founded theatres in the Detroit area in the early 1960's, has been executive director of the Community Film Workshop Council since 1968 and administrator of Third World Cinema Productions since 1972. He served as executive producer of such films as "No Place to Go," "A Day for Shooting," and "Jive." Frazier has also acted in stage plays and appeared on television programs, including "N.Y.P.D." and "The Negro Experimental Theatre." He has received Emmy Awards and an award from the Martin Luther King Film Festival. He co-authored *Discovery in Drama* (Paulist/Newman, 1969). *Address:* 62 West 45th St., New York, N.Y. 10036. *Biographical/critical sources: Directory of Blacks in the Performing Arts,* Scarecrow, 1978; *International Motion Picture Almanac,* Quigley, 1979.

FREEMAN, Douglas Southall   1886-1953

BRIEF ENTRY: Born May 16, 1886, in Lynchburg, Va.; died June 13, 1953, in Richmond, Va. American journalist, educator, editor, and historian. Freeman is best known as the author of *R. E. Lee* (1934-35), a four-volume biography of the Confederate general, for which he received his first Pulitzer Prize. Freeman commenced the biography while simultaneously editing the *Richmond News Leader,* where he worked from 1911 to 1949. After completing the biography, Freeman taught at Columbia University and wrote another multi-volume work, *Lee's Lieutenants* (1942-44). In 1945 he began a seven-volume biography of George Washington; Freeman died eight years later with only one volume incomplete. Freeman's widely-praised *George Washington* (1948-57) was awarded a Pulitzer Prize in 1958. *Biographical/critical sources: Cyclopedia of World Authors,* Harper, 1958; *The Reader's Encyclopedia of American Literature,* Crowell, 1962; *The Oxford Companion to American Literature,* 4th edition, Oxford University Press, 1965; *The McGraw-Hill Encyclopedia of World Biography,* McGraw, 1973; *Twentieth-Century Literary Criticism,* Volume 11, Gale, 1983.

*   *   *

FREEMAN, Margaret B.   1899-1980

PERSONAL: Born in 1899 in West Orange, N.J.; died May 24, 1980, in New York, N.Y. *Education:* Received B.A. from Wellesley College; M.A. from Columbia University; graduate study at Sorbonne, University of Paris. *Residence:* New York, N.Y.

CAREER: Worked as a research assistant at Newark Museum, 1924-25; instructor at Dana Hall School, 1925-27; secretary of Wellesley College of Art Museum, 1927-28; Cloisters Museum of the Metropolitan Museum of Art, New York, N.Y., lecturer in Egyptian and medieval art, 1928-40, assistant curator, 1940-43, associate curator, 1943-55, curator, 1955-65, curator emeritus, 1965-80. *Member:* Mediaeval Academy of America, American Association of Museum Curators, Medieval Club of New York, Museum Council of New York, International Center for Romanesque Art, Phi Beta Kappa. *Awards, honors:* Phi Beta Kappa Award.

WRITINGS: Herbs for the Mediaeval Household: For Cooking, Healing, and Diverse Uses, Metropolitan Museum of Art, 1943; (adapter) *The Story of the Three Kings: Melchior, Balthasar, and Jaspar,* Metropolitan Museum of Art, 1955; *Les Belles Heures du Duc de Berry,* Thames & Hudson, c. 1959; *The St. Martin Embroideries,* Metropolitan Museum of Art, 1968; *The Unicorn Tapestries,* Metropolitan Museum of Art, 1976. Contributor to *Metropolitan Museum of Art Bulletin.*

SIDELIGHTS: During her fifty-two year association with the Cloisters Museum, Margaret Freeman introduced theatre and musical programs and developed the center's medieval gardens. She also wrote several books about medieval topics, including her last book, *The Unicorn Tapestries.*

The Unicorn Tapestries explains the history and symbolism of seven medieval tapestries hanging on permanent display at the Cloisters Museum. *New York Times* writer Anatole Broyard praised Freeman's book about the tapestries, observing that she "has done full justice to what is undoubtedly one of the finest flowerings of medieval art." "Miss Freeman's reconstruction of the history of the Unicorn Tapestries is a masterpiece of learned detection," Broyard concluded, and *Time* agreed that

Freeman "has written a scholarly and enthralling analysis of the tapestries, including an explanation of the weaving techniques that were used to produce one of the glories of Western art."

BIOGRAPHICAL/CRITICAL SOURCES: New York Times, November 4, 1976; *Time,* December 13, 1976; *Nation,* December 18, 1976.

OBITUARIES: New York Times, May 28, 1980.*

*   *   *

FREEMAN, Max Herbert   1907-

BRIEF ENTRY: Born October 12, 1907, in Poland. Accountant, educator, and author. Freeman, who has maintained a private practice as an accountant since 1924, taught business in high schools until 1943. He was a professor of business and dean of graduate studies at Montclair State College from 1954 to 1975 and was also president of Sherwood School of Business. Freeman's books include *Bookkeeping and Accounting Simplified: Advanced Course* (McGraw, 1958), *Accounting Ten/ Twelve* (McGraw, 1968), *Mathematics in Marketing* (McGraw, 1970), *Merchandising Mathematics* (McGraw, 1973), *Sun-n-Ski: An Accounting Simulation* (McGraw, 1977), and *Money Management: Guide to Saving, Spending, and Investing* (Bobbs-Merrill, 1980). *Address:* 113 Buckingham Rd., Upper Montclair, N.J. 07043.

*   *   *

FRENTZEN, Jeffrey   1956-
(J. Ketchum, Buck Sanders, Lauren Scott)

PERSONAL: Born September 7, 1956, in Oakland, Calif.; son of Joseph A. and Marilyn (an artist; maiden name, Kennedy) Frentzen; married Suzanne Fields (a graphic designer), February, 1982; children: Derek James. *Education:* Attended Diablo Valley College, 1974-77, and University of California, Berkeley, 1977-78. *Politics:* "Neo-apathetic." *Religion:* "Atheistic tendencies." *Home and office:* 2180 Payne Rd., Medford, Ore. 97501.

CAREER: Cinefantastique, Oak Park, Ill., San Francisco correspondent, 1975-78, managing editor, 1978-79; WGBH-TV, Boston, Mass., assistant to producer of "Reel Image," 1980; KQED-TV, San Francisco, Calif., assistant film editor, 1981; Dark Fenster of Oregon, Visalia, Calif., and Jacksonville, Ore., armadillo breeder, 1981. Co-founder of Moonstone Press, Medford, Ore. Film historian for "Creature Features" on KTVU-TV; writer and assistant film editor of "Doubtful Thomas," broadcast by KQED-TV; production assistant for "American Short Story," Public Broadcasting System (PBS). *Member:* Writers Guild of America West.

WRITINGS: Please Stand By (nonfiction), Moonstone Press, 1982, 2nd edition, in press.

Under pseudonym Buck Sanders: *Star of Egypt,* Warner Books, 1981; *The Bayou Brigade,* Warner Books, 1982.

Under pseudonym Lauren Scott: *Suburban Roulette,* Grove, 1981.

Also author of fiction under pseudonym J. Ketchum.

Also author of screenplays "Catharsis" and "United," a short feature.

Contributor to magazines and newspapers, including *Yankee*, *Parents' Magazine*, *Pine Grove Press*, *Exit*, *Jump River Review*, and *Cinefan Journal*.

WORK IN PROGRESS: Summer With Frost, a suspense novel; *Shockers*, a history and review of horror films, with David Schow; a book of interviews with film directors of the 1970's and 1980's.

SIDELIGHTS: Frentzen told *CA:* "Moonstone Press will be my (and David Schow's) outlet for serious, marginally commercial nonfiction. We will write, edit, and publish our work and distribute it ourselves. Our aim is to open the horizons for public acceptance of good, interesting, nonfiction material. For example, our initial production, *Please Stand By*, is an enlightening history of the 'Outer Limits' television series. It is hardly blockbuster stuff. But it is aimed at an audience small in number, specialized, OUT THERE, which big conglomerate publishers would never try or know how to reach."

*   *   *

FREY, Andrew   1905(?)-1983

OBITUARY NOTICE: Born c. 1905 in Hungary; died March 16, 1983, in New York, N.Y. Journalist. Frey came to the United States in 1949. He left Hungary after its Communist takeover and became a United Nations correspondent for Swiss, West German, French, and Italian publications. He was associated with Voice of America during the 1950's and contributed to Hungarian periodicals until shortly before his death. Obituaries and other sources: *New York Times*, March 22, 1983.

*   *   *

FRIEDMAN, Arnold D'Arcy   1900-1981

OBITUARY NOTICE: Born July 24, 1900, in Plumerville, Ark.; died July 29, 1981, in East Hampton, N.Y. Publisher. Friedman was chairman and co-founder of the business and trade newspaper publishing company Lebhar-Friedman, which was formed in 1925 with the magazine *Chain Store Age Executive*, a publication directed at retailers. Other magazines and newspapers issued by the firm include *Drug Store News*, *National Home Center News*, and *Nation's Restaurant News*. By the time of Friedman's death, Lebhar-Friedman had expanded to include the publication of business guides, a Japanese periodical, and books. Obituaries and other sources: *New York Times*, July 31, 1981; *Chain Store Age Executive*, September, 1981; *Who's Who in America*, 42nd edition, Marquis, 1982.

*   *   *

FRIEDMAN, Susan Stanford   1943-

PERSONAL: Born May 3, 1943, in Bluefield, W.Va.; daughter of Ralph B. (in business) and Anne (Thompson) Stanford; married Edward Friedman (a professor), 1969; children: Ruth Jennifer, JoAnna Stanford. *Education:* Swarthmore College, B.A., 1965; University of Wisconsin—Madison, Ph.D., 1973. *Politics:* "Feminist." *Religion:* None. *Home:* 2326 Rugby Row, Madison, Wis. 53705. *Office:* Department of English, University of Wisconsin—Madison, Helen C. White Hall, Madison, Wis. 53706.

CAREER: Brooklyn College of the City University of New York, Brooklyn, N.Y., assistant professor of literature, 1973-76; University of Wisconsin—Madison, assistant professor,

1976-81, associate professor of English and women's studies, 1981—. Public speaker on feminist issues. *Member:* Modern Language Association of America, National Women's Studies Association, Women's Caucus of the Modern Languages, National Organization for Women.

AWARDS, HONORS: Florence Howe Award from Women's Caucus of Modern Language Association, 1978, for article "Psyche Reborn: Tradition, Re-Vision, and the Goddess as Mother-Symbol in H.D.'s Poetry"; American Council of Learned Societies grant, 1978; National Endowment for the Humanities fellow, 1981-82; *Psyche Reborn* was named one of the best academic books of the year by *Choice*, 1981; Fund for Psychoanalytic Research grant, 1983.

WRITINGS: (With Linda Gams, Nancy Gottlieb, and Cindy Nesselson) *A Woman's Guide to Therapy*, Prentice-Hall, 1978; *Psyche Reborn: The Emergence of H.D.*, Indiana University Press, 1981. Contributor to literature and women's studies journals.

WORK IN PROGRESS: Sages of the Self: A Study of H.D.'s Prose, publication by Cambridge University Press expected in 1985; *Portrait of an Analysis With Freud: The H.D.-Bryher Letters, 1933-1934*, completion expected in 1984.

SIDELIGHTS: Susan Friedman commented: "Personal and professional associations intersect with my own desire for the words that can capture a reality, an idea. Writing, as a focus of my intellectual life, is an end in itself, as it must be to sustain the exhausting labor of birthing a book, whose significance to me is necessarily greater than it can be to anyone else. But my writing is also caught up in the moment of history to which I was born. I owe the dimensions of my work and its plea for audience most fundamentally to feminism. The urgency I feel to write, read, and teach is tied to my sense of my work as a small portion of a larger task: the re-vision and transformation of culture."

*   *   *

FRIEDMAN, Thomas L(oren)   1953-

PERSONAL: Born July 20, 1953, in Minneapolis, Minn.; son of Harold Abraham and Margaret (a real estate broker; maiden name, Philips) Friedman; married Ann Bucksbaum (a copy editor), November 23, 1978. *Education:* Brandeis University, B.A. (summa cum laude), 1975; St. Antony's College, Oxford, M.Phil., 1978. *Address:* P.O. Box 113-6964, Beirut, Lebanon. *Office:* New York Times, 229 West 43rd St., New York, N.Y. 10036.

CAREER/WRITINGS: Correspondent in London, England, and Beirut, Lebanon, for United Press International, 1978-81; *New York Times*, New York, N.Y., foreign correspondent, 1981—. Phi Beta Kappa. *Awards, honors:* Award from Overseas Press Club, 1980, for best business reporting from abroad; George Polk Award, 1982, and Pulitzer Prize and Livingston Award, both 1983, all for coverage of war in Lebanon.

SIDELIGHTS: Friedman told *CA:* "My major area of vocational interest is the Middle East, a subject I have devoted both my academic training and professional journalism career to pursuing.

"Whenever I complete my tour in the Middle East I hope to write a book on Arab politics and how the Arab rulers actually rule. It is a subject which Middle East experts have largely ignored, but which I think is essential to the understanding of modern Arab politics."

BIOGRAPHICAL/CRITICAL SOURCES: New York Times, February 27, 1983, April 19, 1983; *Detroit News*, April 19, 1983.

* * *

FRIEDRICH, Anton
See STRICH, Christian

* * *

FROMKIN, David 1932-

PERSONAL: Born August 27, 1932, in Milwaukee, Wis.; son of Morris (an attorney) and Selma (Strelsin) Fromkin. *Education:* University of Chicago, B.A., 1950, J.D., 1953; Institute of Advanced Legal Studies, London, postgraduate diploma in law, 1958. *Politics:* Democrat. *Religion:* Jewish. *Agent:* Dorothy Olding, Harold Ober Associates, Inc., 40 East 49th St., New York, N.Y. 10017. *Office:* 950 Third Ave., New York, N.Y. 10022.

CAREER: Admitted to the Bar of Illinois, 1953, New York, 1959, and U.S. Supreme Court, 1963; associated with Simpson, Thacher & Bartlett (law firm), New York City, 1958-60; attorney, New York City, 1960—. Consultant to Vice-president Hubert H. Humphrey, 1965; coordinator for foreign policy for presidential primary campaign of Senator Hubert H. Humphrey, 1972. *Military service:* U.S. Army, 1954-57; became first lieutenant. *Member:* International Institute for Strategic Studies, American Society of International Law, American Bar Association, Council on Foreign Relations.

WRITINGS: The Question of Government: An Inquiry Into the Breakdown of Modern Political Systems, Scribner, 1975; *The Independence of Nations*, Praeger, 1981. Contributor of articles to *Foreign Affairs*.

SIDELIGHTS: In his first book, *The Question of Government: An Inquiry Into the Breakdown of Modern Political Systems*, Fromkin analyzes the institution and nature of U.S. government, arguing that the political structures have not adapted to societal changes wrought by the Industrial Revolution. He urges the development of "a truly modern government," capable of the coordination and planning necessary for social cohesion otherwise unachieved in a highly industrialized state. *The Question of Government* is "a provocative, original study," Carey McWilliams noted in *Nation*, and one "that deserves more attention than it is likely to receive."

BIOGRAPHICAL/CRITICAL SOURCES: Nation, August 30, 1975.

* * *

FRY, Dennis Butler 1907-

PERSONAL: Born November 3, 1907, in Stockbridge, England; son of Fred C.B. (a master grocer) and Jane Anne (Butler) Fry; married Chrystabel Smith; children: Josephine Fry Dent, Nicholas, Anthea Fry Higham. *Education:* University of London, B.A., 1929, Ph.D., 1948. *Home:* 18 Lauriston Rd., London SW19 4TQ, England.

CAREER: University of London, London, England, assistant lecturer, 1934-37, lecturer and superintendent of Phonetics Laboratory, 1937-49, reader, 1949-58, professor of experimental phonetics, 1958-75, professor emeritus, 1975—, head of department of phonetics, 1949-71; writer, 1975—. Member of board of governors of Sadler's Wells Foundation; founder and trustee of Institute for Cultural Research. *Military service:* Royal Air Force, squadron leader, 1940-45. *Member:* Permanent International Council for Phonetic Sciences (president), Acoustical Society of America (fellow), College of Speech Therapists (honorary fellow).

WRITINGS: (With Edith Whetnall) *The Deaf Child*, Heinemann, 1963; (with Whetnall) *Learning to Hear*, Heinemann, 1970; (editor) *Acoustic Phonetics*, Cambridge University Press, 1976; *Homo Loquens*, Cambridge University Press, 1977; *The Physics of Speech*, Cambridge University Press, 1979; (editor) *The Nature of Religious Man*, Octagon, 1982. Editor of *Language and Speech*, 1958-78.

SIDELIGHTS: Fry told *CA:* "*Homo Loquens* is an account written for the layman of all the processes involved in language, speech, and hearing; it is the fruit of a lifetime of teaching and research in this field, including work on behalf of the deaf child. My major interests have been the perception and reception of speech sounds and their physical analysis.

"I am a founder member and trustee of the Institute for Cultural Research, a registered educational charity devoted to the encouragement of cross-cultural and interdisciplinary studies in a wide variety of fields. *The Nature of Religious Man* is an account of a symposium organized by the Institute."

* * *

FUKUDA, Haruko 1946-

PERSONAL: Born July 21, 1946, in Tokyo, Japan; daughter of Masaru and Yoko Fukuda; married James Inglis Dunnett (an architect). *Education:* Cambridge University, B.A. (with honors), 1968, M.A., 1971. *Home:* 3 Ensor Mews, London S.W.7, England. *Office:* Winchester House, 100 Old Broad St., London EC2N 1DH, England.

CAREER: Research officer with Trade Policy Research Centre, 1968-70; research officer with Overseas Development Institute, 1970-71; International Bank for Reconstruction and Development, Washington, D.C., research officer in economics department, 1971-72; economist with Vickers da Costa & Co. Ltd., 1972-74; James Capel & Co., London, England, partner, 1974—.

WRITINGS: Europe's Free Trade Area Experiment, Pergamon, 1970; *Britain in Europe: The Impact on the Third World*, Macmillan, 1973; *Japan and World Trade: The Years Ahead*, Saxon House, 1974.

BIOGRAPHICAL/CRITICAL SOURCES: Times Literary Supplement, February 15, 1974.

* * *

FULFORD, Roger (Thomas Baldwin) 1902-1983

OBITUARY NOTICE—See index for *CA* sketch: Born November 24, 1902, in Flaxley, Gloucestershire, England; died May 18, 1983, near Carnforth, Lancashire, England. Historian, educator, and author. During the 1930's Fulford served on the editorial staff of the *London Times*. Although he left the *Times* in 1939, he continued to contribute articles to that newspaper for many years. He was a lecturer in English at King's College, London, from 1937 to 1948. A prolific writer, Fulford produced a number of books on the history of the monarchy, including *George the Fourth, Queen Victoria, The Prince Consort*, and *The Trial of Queen Caroline*. With Lytton Strachey, he edited the eight-volume work *The Greville Memoirs*. He also edited *Your Dear Letter: Private Correspondence of Queen Victoria and the Crown Princess of Prussia, 1865-1871* and *Darling Child: Private Correspondence of Queen Victoria and the Crown Prince of Prussia, 1871-1878.* Obituaries and other sources: *London Times,* May 19, 1983.

* * *

FULLER, R(ichard) Buckminster 1895-1983

OBITUARY NOTICE—See index for *CA* sketch: Born July 12, 1895, in Milton, Mass.; died of a heart attack, July 1, 1983, in Los Angeles, Calif. Mathematician, geometrician, cartographer, engineer, architect-designer, environmentalist, world planner, educator, and author best known as the inventor of the geodesic dome. Fuller's youthful restlessness and excesses led to his expulsion from Harvard University and resulted in his taking a job in a factory, where he first became interested in design and construction methods. He formed a construction firm with his father-in-law, but after the death of his first child Fuller began to drink heavily, and, when the business failed, contemplated suicide. At this point Fuller came to a realization of his own worth and decided to devote all his creative energies to benefit humankind. He spent the next year absorbed in his ideas, speaking to no one; not even his wife. At the end of that period Fuller began to implement the principle he had become aware of—namely, that design was more essential than matter. He offered all patent rights to his revolutionary Dymaxion House to the American Institute of Architects in 1929, but they refused the gift, condemning all such prefabricated designs. Fuller's three-wheeled Dymaxion automobile performed well but was doomed by negative publicity resulting from a fatal accident involving one of the vehicles. He first attracted the serious attention of the scientific world in 1943 with his Dymaxion Airocean World Map, which displayed the Earth on a flat surface without distortion. His most successful invention, however, was the geodesic dome, a hemispherical structure composed of flat, triangular panels. The domes are inexpensive and lightweight yet strong, space-efficient buildings which captured the interest of the scientific community as well as the public when first shown in 1947. Through the 1960's and 1970's Fuller stressed the importance of planning to deal with growing world population (which he felt was not beyond manageable limits) and the necessity of mankind's co-operation with the environment. *Nine Chains to the Moon, What I Am Trying to Do,* and *Intuition* are among Fuller's numerous books. Obituaries and other sources: *Who's Who in America,* 42nd edition, Marquis, 1982; *New York Times,* July 3, 1983; *Washington Post,* July 3, 1983.

* * *

FULLINWIDER, S. P(endleton) 1933-

BRIEF ENTRY: Born October 17, 1933, in Washington, D.C. American historian, educator, and author. Fullinwider, who began teaching American history at Arizona State University in 1968, was a Rockefeller Foundation fellow in 1975. He wrote *The Mind and Mood of Black America: Twentieth-Century Thought* (Dorsey, 1969) and *Technicians of the Finite: The Rise and Decline of the Schizophrenic in American Thought, 1840-1960* (Greenwood Press, 1981). *Address:* Department of History, Arizona State University, Tempe, Ariz. 85281.

* * *

FUNK, Rainer 1943-

PERSONAL: Born February 18, 1943, in Creglingen, Germany; son of Alfons and Maria (Burger) Funk; married Renate Oetker, June 15, 1979; children: Martin Jan. *Education:* University of Tuebingen, Diplomtheologie, 1968, D.Th., 1977; Stuttgarter Akademie fuer Tiefenpsychologie und Analytische Psychotherapie, Psychotherapeut, 1982. *Home:* Hennentalweg 5, D 7400 Tuebingen, West Germany.

CAREER: Personal assistant to Erich Fromm in Locarno, Switzerland, 1974-75; psychoanalyst in Tuebingen, West Germany, 1979—.

WRITINGS: Froemmiegkeit zwischen Haben und Sein (title means "Spirituality Between Having and Being"), Benziger Verlag, 1977; *Mut zum Menschen,* Deutsche Verlags-Anstalt, 1978, translation published as *Erich Fromm: The Courage to Be Human,* Continuum, 1982; (editor) Fromm, *Gesamtausgabe un Zehn Baenden* (title means "Collected Works in Ten Volumes"), Deutsche Verlags-Anstalt, 1980-81; *Erich Fromm Bildmonographie* (biography), Rowohlt, 1983.

WORK IN PROGRESS: An edition of unpublished writings by Erich Fromm on psychoanalysis and humanism.

SIDELIGHTS: Funk has been the literary executor of the estate of Erich Fromm since Fromm's death in 1980. He is compiling an archive in Tuebingen which will include the psychoanalyst's library, correspondence, and manuscripts, as well as a collection of literature written about Fromm.

Rainer Funk told *CA:* "The main purpose of my editing and of the archive is to further scientific scholarship. My personal interests are the relationship of psychoanalysis and ethics as well as the psychoanalytic research of religion."

* * *

FURNISS, Tim 1948-

PERSONAL: Born April 14, 1948, in Epsom, England; son of John (in business) and Marnie (Battersby) Furniss; married Susan Jacob (a trampoline instructor), January 6, 1979; children: Tom. *Education:* Attended private school in Guildford, England. *Politics:* Conservative. *Religion:* Roman Catholic. *Home and office:* 23 Downs Way, Epsom, Surrey KT18 5LU, England.

CAREER: Publisher's assistant, 1966-68; public relations assistant, 1968-70; public relations manager, 1970-73; advertising manager for Air Products, 1973-82; free-lance writer, broadcaster, and public relations consultant, 1982—. *Member:* British Interplanetary Society, Institute of Public Relations.

WRITINGS: A Trip to the Moon, Pitman, 1973; *A Sourcebook of Rockets, Spacecraft, and Spacemen,* Ward, Lock, 1973; *UFOs,* World, 1978; *Space Today,* Kaye & Ward, 1979; *The Story of the Space Shuttle,* Hodder & Stoughton, 1979, 3rd edition, in press; *Space Satellites,* Hodder & Stoughton, 1980; *The Sun,* F. Watts, 1980; *Man in Space,* Batsford, 1981; *Space Stoway,* Kaye & Ward, 1982; *Jane's Manned Spaceflight Log,* Jane's Yearbooks, 1983; *Space Exploitation,* Batsford, in press; *Shuttle to Mars* (juvenile novel), Kaye & Ward, in press. Contributor to magazines.

SIDELIGHTS: Tim Furniss told *CA:* "I have been interested in space since Gagarin's adventure in 1961. It has been my ambition to write and broadcast on space ever since I was fourteen, when in 1962 John Glenn's flight inspired me. From then on I collected news cuttings, magazine articles, pictures, and books on space. I was quite simply a 'space nut.' The sixties, culminating with Apollo on the moon, was a most exciting period for me, and then as I was beginning to write about space professionally (two small books and some local radio), interest in the seventies dwindled to such an extent that I spent a very frustrating time waiting for the shuttle to arrive. Then pow! Everything started to happen. From 1979 onwards I wrote more books and did national radio and television, including a regular 'space spot' on national radio for kids.

"In the early seventies I went to the Cape to see *Apollo XIII* and *XV* launched and met a number of the astronauts, including some that landed on the moon. I even got to wear a moon suit. I hope to return very soon to cover a shuttle launch in a more professional capacity. I fully intend to fly on a shuttle one day.

"I have a long way to go yet to achieve my ultimate objective, but sometimes do allow myself a smile of pride at what my perseverance, determination, enthusiasm, and luck have earned me since those days when I used to sit during school breaks trying to pick up a news station on the radio during a launch. I well remember listening in awe to Gordon Cooper's launch on my faithful blue transistor radio in 1963. I remember quite clearly thinking to myself then how good it would be to write and broadcast about space when I grew up."

*   *   *

FURSE, John 1932-

PERSONAL: Born January 30, 1932, in London, England; son of Richard (a civil servant) and E. W. (Bonney) Furse; married Pamela Goodwin (a genealogist), January 29, 1955 (divorced); married Soo Hudson (an artist), December 22, 1977; children: Miranda Furse-Nield Dumper, James, Jessica, Josef. *Education:* Willesden School of Art, National Diploma in Design, 1953; University of London, diploma in art history, 1966; University of Sussex, M.A., 1977, D.Phil., 1983. *Politics:* Socialist. *Religion:* None. *Home:* 4 Beechwood Ter., Plymouth PL4 6PP, England. *Agent:* Michael Bakewell & Associates, 118 Tottenham Court Rd., London W1P 9HL, England. *Office:* Humanities Unit, Plymouth Polytechnic, Plymouth, England.

CAREER: Workers Educational Association, London, England, lecturer in drawing and painting, 1953-74; lecturer at Plymouth Polytechnic, 1975—. Visiting lecturer at colleges of art and higher education, including Barnet College, London, 1966-74; part-time tutor at Open University, 1972-84. Member of Arts for Labour. *Member:* International Association of Artists, Association of Art Historians.

WRITINGS: Inside Whitechapel, Whitechapel Art Gallery, 1972; (editor with Alison Smithson) *Team X at Royaumont,* Architectural Design, 1975; *Michelangelo,* Hamlyn, 1975; *Rene Halket,* South West Arts, 1981.

Contributor: B. S. Johnson, editor, *The Evacuees,* Gollancz, 1969; Johnson, editor, *You Always Remember the First Time,* Quartet, 1975; Muriel Emanuel, editor, *Contemporary Architects,* Macmillan, 1980; Justin Wintle, editor, *Makers of Modern Culture,* Routledge & Kegan Paul, 1981; Wintle, editor, *Makers of Nineteenth-Century Culture,* Routledge & Kegan Paul, 1982. Contributor to *Academic America Encyclopedia* and *Theatre Grotesque.*

WORK IN PROGRESS: "Scenes From the Life of James Ensor," a marionette play, production by Theatre Grotesque expected in 1984; research into mass housing for working-class black people in London's East End.

SIDELIGHTS: Furse wrote: "Urban discontent distresses and appalls me. I am currently living at my twenty-ninth 'permanent address,' so I am also preoccupied by the notion of the exile in his own country. In an increasingly divided nation, it is essential that those in a position to do so comment on the injustice of a situation through their writings. The working-class black is as much an exile in London's East End as was the Jewish immigrant before him."

*   *   *

FURTH, Alex
See SASULY, Richard

G

GAINER, Bernard 1944-

BRIEF ENTRY: Born March 6, 1944, in New York, N.Y. American historian, educator, and author. Educated in the United States and England, Gainer has taught British and European history at the University of Kansas since 1970. He has also taught in England. He wrote *The Alien Invasion: The Origins of the Aliens Act of 1905* (Heinemann, 1972). *Address:* Department of History, University of Kansas, Lawrence, Kan. 66044. *Biographical/critical sources: New Statesman,* October 6, 1972; *Times Literary Supplement,* December 15, 1972; *Commentary,* April, 1973; *American Historical Review,* December, 1973; *Directory of American Scholars,* Volume I: *History,* 7th edition, Bowker, 1978.

*   *   *

GALL, Auguste Amedee de Saint
See STRICH, Christian

*   *   *

GALLIX, Francois 1939-

PERSONAL: Born March 1, 1939, in Paris, France; son of Pierre Vincent (an insurance executive) and Andree (a secretary; maiden name, Mouchard) Gallix; married Carolyn Wanless, March 2, 1963 (divorced December 19, 1967); children: Andrew, Sophie. *Education:* Faculte de Droit de Paris, licence, 1962; Sorbonne, University of Paris, licence, 1969, maitrise, 1970. *Home:* 9 rue de Douai, 75009 Paris, France. *Agent:* David Higham, 5 Lower John St., London W1R 4HA, England. *Office:* Sorbonne 1, rue Victor Cousin, 75230 Paris, France.

CAREER: Teacher of English in secondary schools, 1964-72; Karaouigine University, Fes, Morocco, teacher of English, 1965 and 1967; Sorbonne, University of Paris, Paris, France, assistant lecturer in English, 1972—. *Member:* Association of International American Universities, Society of Agreges. *Awards, honors:* Fulbright Awards, 1978 and 1982.

WRITINGS: (Editor and author of introduction) *T. H. White: Letters to a Friend,* Putnam, 1982, revised edition, Sutton, 1983. Contributor of articles to periodicals, including *Mosaic, Cerli, Etudes Anglaises,* and *Stoic.*

WORK IN PROGRESS: Researching two articles, one on the influence of the Stowe school on White's *Mistress Masham's Repose,* the other on the friendship between T. H. White and David Garnett; translating some of White's works into French, including *The Goshawk.*

SIDELIGHTS: T. H. White, the renowned author of *The Once and Future King* and many other highly respected works, maintained a nearly life-long correspondence with his teacher and friend, L. J. Potts. Many of White's letters to Potts, as well as some to Potts's wife, are reproduced by Gallix in *Letters to a Friend.* The letters include criticism of Potts's poetry, insights into his own work, and reflections of White's personal life.

Gallix told *CA:* "During my research on T. H. White, I met several of his friends, including Mary Potts, who asked me to edit White's letters to herself and her husband, who was White's tutor at Queen's College, Cambridge. I recorded most of my interviews on cassettes. I went to see White's biographer, Sylvia Townsend Warner, several times in Dorset and we exchanged many letters. I also visited the author David Garnett and we corresponded about White's works and his own. I am now extremely interested in the novels of Sylvia Townsend Warner and David Garnett.

"I also interviewed the author Sir John Verney, the actor Michael Trubshawe, and many of White's friends in England and on the Channel island of Alderney, where White lived from 1946 until his death in 1964. I have a lot of White's unpublished material and letters, and have collected most of his first editions, as well as those of David Garnett and Sylvia Townsend Warner.

"Twice, in June, 1978, and in July, 1982, I went to Austin, Texas, on Fulbright Awards and was able to work on the White collection at the Humanities Research Center."

BIOGRAPHICAL/CRITICAL SOURCES: New York Times, September 10, 1982.

*   *   *

GALLWITZ, Klaus 1930-

BRIEF ENTRY: Born September 14, 1930, in Dresden, Germany (now East Germany). German art historian, art gallery director, and author. Gallwitz managed art galleries in Karlsruhe, West Germany, until 1967, and then served as director of the Staatliche Kunsthalle in Baden-Baden, West Germany, until 1974. At that time he was named director of the Staedelsches Kunstinstitut in Frankfurt am Main, West Germany. Gallwitz has written dozens of books; English translations of his works include *Picasso at Ninety* (Putnam, 1971) and *Botero* (Rizzoli International, 1976). *Address:* 1 Holbeinstrasse, Frankfurt am Main 70, West Germany; and 2 Duererstrasse, Frankfurt am Main 70, West Germany. *Biographical/critical sources: New York Times Book Review,*December 5, 1971; *Washington Post Book World,* December 12, 1971; *Observer,* December 12, 1971; *Newsweek,* December 13, 1971.

*   *   *

GANNON, Thomas M(ichael) 1936-

PERSONAL: Born October 19, 1936, in Chicago, Ill.; son of Thomas M. (a district sales manager) and Bernice D. (Pouk) Gannon. *Education:* Loyola University of Chicago, B.A., 1959, Ph.L. and M.A., both 1961; Jesuit School of Theology, Chicago, Ill., S.T.L., 1968; University of Chicago, Ph.D., 1972. *Office:* Department of Sociology, Loyola University, 6525 North Sheridan Rd., Chicago, Ill. 60626.

CAREER: Entered Societas Jesu (Society of Jesus; Jesuits; S.J.), 1954, ordained Roman Catholic priest, 1967; St. Ignatius High School, Cleveland, Ohio, instructor, 1961-64; Loyola University, Chicago, Ill., lecturer, 1966-68, assistant professor, 1971-73, associate professor, 1974-77, professor of sociology, 1978—, chairman of department, 1972-82. Professor of sociology and director of Woodstock Theological Center at Georgetown University, 1983—; director of professional and graduate studies for Chicago Province of Society of Jesus, 1970-80. Consultant to New York City Youth Board, Federal Poverty Program, and Chicago Commission on Youth Welfare.

MEMBER: International Conference for the Sociology of Religion, International Sociological Association (U.S. secretary, 1971—), Religious Research Association (president, 1970-73), Association for the Sociology of Religion (president, 1977-78), American Sociological Association, Society for the Scientific Study of Religion. *Awards, honors:* Fellow of Japan Society for the Promotion of Science, 1981; fellow of St. Edmunds House, Cambridge University, 1982; named faculty member of the year by Loyola University of Chicago, 1983.

WRITINGS: (Contributor) George A. Lane, editor, *Christian Spirituality,* Argus Communications, 1968; (with George W. Traub) *The Desert and the City: An Interpretation of the History of Christian Spirituality,* Macmillan, 1969; *General Survey of the Society of Jesus: North America,* five volumes, Argus Communications, 1970-71; (editor) *Military Ethics and Civilian Control,* Sage Publications, 1976. Contributor of more than fifty articles to sociology journals.

WORK IN PROGRESS: Research on religious and social change, and on the culture of unbelief.

SIDELIGHTS: Gannon told *CA:* "People today, everywhere on the globe, are involved as never before in a quest for meaning in their lives and for their identity in a rapidly-changing world. In reality, human beings have always sought such knowledge, but rarely with such urgency or with so tormenting a sense of loss. At the same time, people also search—often secretly and unconsciously—for the identity of God and God's meaning in their lives. Here too, men and women struggle with a numbing sense of lost awareness. I believe that these two identities—human beings' and God's—are found together or

not at all: that only in knowing God can people come to know themselves, and in knowing themselves they know God.

"Most of what I have written is an attempt to explore how people have pursued this double quest. I use an approach that emphasizes social-cultural analysis, though at times my methods are more theological. Regardless of approach, it has been to better comprehend this quest that I undertook a study of the history of Christian spirituality and, later, edited a collection of essays on military ethics. It is this same concern that, ultimately, underlies my other writings as well, coupled with an abiding passion for promoting justice and moral solidarity."

*   *   *

GARDNER, Frank Matthias 1908-1980

OBITUARY NOTICE: Born January 13, 1908; died July 24, 1980. Librarian and author. Gardner was a librarian in England from 1938 to 1972 and served on numerous library advisory panels. Among his books are *Sequels, Letters to a Younger Librarian, Reading Round the World,* and *Public Library Legislation: A Comparative Study.* Obituaries and other sources: *The Writers Directory: 1980-82,* St. Martin's, 1979; *Who Was Who,* Volume VII: *1971-1980,* A. & C. Black, 1981.

*   *   *

GARRETT, Albert Charles 1915-1983

OBITUARY NOTICE: Born May 14, 1915, in Kingsclere, England; died suddenly, February 1, 1983, in London, England. Artist, educator, and author. Although primarily known for his art work, which has been exhibited in London and Paris, Garrett was also familiar in England for his research on the link between road safety and car colors, the results of which were published in *Automobile Engineer.* A senior lecturer at Polytechnic of North London School of Architecture until 1980, Garrett wrote several volumes about wood engraving, including *A History of the British Wood Engraving, British Wood Engraving of the Twentieth Century,* and *Wood Engraving and Drawings of Iain Macnab.* Obituaries and other sources: *Who's Who in the World,* 4th edition, Marquis, 1978; *London Times,* February 9, 1983.

*   *   *

GARVEY, Robert 1908-1983

OBITUARY NOTICE—See index for *CA* sketch: Birth-given name, Robert Cohn; born November 13, 1908, in New York, N.Y.; died of a heart attack, February 16, 1983, in New York, N.Y. Editor and author. From 1956 to 1971 Garvey worked as a manager in sales and promotion in the book department of the Union of American Hebrew Congregations. He later served as executive secretary for the Association of Jewish Book Publishers. He was the author of several books for children, including *Good Shabbos, Everybody, The Wonderful World of Jewish Holidays, What Feast and Other Tales,* and *Let's Learn About Jewish Holidays: Discover, Explore, and Play.* Obituaries and other sources: *New York Times,* February 18, 1983.

*   *   *

GASTON, Georg M(eri-) A(kri) 1938-

PERSONAL: Born October 22, 1938, in Kiev, Russia (now Ukrainian S.S.R.); came to the United States in 1950, naturalized citizen, 1955; son of Y. Tischenkov (a civil engineer) and Angelina Meri-Akri; married Karen L. Carmean (a professor of English), 1968. *Education:* Texas A & M University, B.A., 1962; Auburn University, M.A., 1963, Ph.D., 1974; also attended Tulane University, Texas Christian University, North Texas State University, and University of Illinois. *Home:* 405 Stadium Dr., Boone, N.C. 28607. *Office:* Department of English, Appalachian State University, Boone, N.C. 28608.

CAREER: Texas A & I University, Kingsville, instructor in English, 1964-66; North Texas State University, Denton, instructor in English, 1966-71; Auburn University, Auburn, Ala., instructor in English, 1973-74; Appalachian State University, Boone, N.C., associate professor of English, 1974—, chairman of Intercultural Film Festival. *Member:* Phi Kappa Phi. *Awards, honors:* Grant from National Endowment for the Humanities, 1978.

WRITINGS: Karel Reisz, Twayne, 1980; *Jack Clayton: A Guide to References and Resources,* G. K. Hall, 1981; *The Pursuit of Salvation: A Critical Guide to the Novels of Graham Greene,* Whitston Publishing, 1983. Contributor to magazines and newspapers, including *Observer, Renascence, Studies in Contemporary Satire,* and *Southern Humanities Review.* Contributing editor of *Washington Book Review.*

WORK IN PROGRESS: Robert Shaw: A Creative Life, a biography.

SIDELIGHTS: Gaston told *CA:* "There is nothing like writing at length about a major author to bring about not only a thorough understanding of his ultimate intent but also a discovery of why one was drawn to him in the first place. Before I wrote my book on Graham Greene, I could recognize many of the unique virtues of his works, but I couldn't be sure of why he seemed to speak with such directness to me. Writing good criticism demands an immense amount of studied objectivity. Without intellectual integrity, the critic is just a hack. Still, the best criticism is also highly personal. There has never been a more opinionated critic than Dr. Johnson. But because Dr. Johnson was profoundly learned, and because he was also passionate in his views, people listened eagerly, willing to be swayed by a forceful mind.

"This is the kind of response every critic must hope for. If he doesn't quite manage that, however, there might still be the reward of appreciating the attraction of one's subject to the point where criticism meets with self-revelation. Criticism, then, can be a subjectively creative act while it pursues the strict truth of the subject. The key factor is passionate involvement."

*   *   *

GATES, Henry Louis, Jr. 1950-

PERSONAL: Born September 16, 1950, in Keyser, W.Va.; son of Henry Louis and Pauline Augusta (Coleman) Gates; married Sharon Adams (a potter), 1979; children: Maude, Elizabeth. *Education:* Yale University, B.A. (summa cum laude), 1973; Clare College, Cambridge, M.A., 1974, Ph.D., 1979. *Home:* 3041 Yale Station, New Haven, Conn. 06520. *Agent:* Carl Brandt, Brandt & Brandt Literary Agents, Inc., 1501 Broadway, New York, N.Y. 10036. *Office:* 3388 Yale Station, New Haven, Conn. 06520.

CAREER: Anglican Mission Hospital, Kilimatinde, Tanzania, general anesthetist, 1970-71; John D. Rockefeller Gubernatorial Campaign, Charleston, W.Va., director of student af-

fairs, 1971, director of research, 1972; *Time,* London Bureau, London, England, staff correspondent, 1973-75; American Cyanamid Co., Wayne, N.J., public relations representative, 1975; Yale University, New Haven, Conn., lecturer, 1976-79, assistant professor of English and director of undergraduate Afro-American studies, both 1979—. Created television series "The Image of the Black in the Western Imagination" for Public Broadcasting Service, 1982. Consultant to Menil Foundation. *Member:* Afro-American Academy, African Literature Association, Modern Language Association of America, Union of African Writers, College Language Association, Phi Beta Kappa.

AWARDS, HONORS: Carnegie Foundation fellowship for Africa, 1970-71; Phelps fellowship from Yale University, 1970-71; Mellon fellowship from Yale University, 1973-75, and 1983—; grants from National Endowment for the Humanities, 1980—, 1981-82; A. Whitney Griswold fellowship from Yale University, 1980—, Rockefeller Foundation fellowship, 1981—; MacArthur Prize fellowship from MacArthur Foundation, 1981-86; award from Whitney Humanities Center, 1982-84; Afro-American teaching prize, 1983.

WRITINGS: (Editor and contributor) *Black Is the Color of the Cosmos: Charles T. Davis's Essays on Black Literature and Culture, 1942-1981,* Garland Publishing, 1983; (editor with Davis) *The Slave's Narrative: Texts and Contexts,* Oxford University Press, 1983; (editor) *In the House of Oshugbo: A Collection of Essays on Wole Soyinka,* Oxford University Press, 1983; (editor) *The Fiction of the New Negro,* Garland Publishing, 1983; (author of introduction and notes) Harriet E. Wilson, *Our Nig: or, Sketches From the Life of a Free Black,* Random House, 1983; (editor) *Critical Essays on Jean Toomer,* G. K. Hall, in press; *An Annotated Bibliography of the Works of Wole Soyinka,* Greenwood Press, in press; (editor) *Frederick Douglass, the Author,* Howard University Press, in press; *The Signifying Monkey,* University of Chicago Press, in press; (editor) *Black Literature and Literary Theory,* Methuen, in press; *Figures in Black: Words, Signs, and the Racial Self,* University of Chicago Press, in press.

Contributor: Herbert Sacks, editor, *The Book of Hurdles,* Atheneum, 1978; Robert Stepto and Dexter Fisher, editors, *Afro-American Literature: The Reconstruction of Instruction,* Modern Language Association of America, 1979; William H. Robinson, editor, *Critical Essays on Phyllis Wheatley,* G. K. Hall, 1982; Kimberly W. Benston, editor, *On Ralph Ellison,* University Press of Mississippi, in press.

Contributor of articles and reviews to periodicals and journals, including *Critical Inquiry, Black World, Black American Literature Forum, Yale Review, Black World, Antioch Review,* and *New York Times Book Review.* Member of board of editors of *American Quarterly, Black American Literature, Forum, Studies in American Fiction,* and *Proteus.*

WORK IN PROGRESS: Co-editing *The Black Periodical Fiction Project, 1821-1919.*

BIOGRAPHICAL/CRITICAL SOURCES: Washington Post Book World, July 3, 1983.

*   *   *

GERLACH, Larry R(euben) 1941-

BRIEF ENTRY: Born November 9, 1941, in Lincoln, Neb. American historian, educator, and author. In 1968 Gerlach began teaching at University of Utah, where he later became a professor of American history. Gerlach received the William A. Whitehead Award from the New Jersey Historical Society in 1973 and an award of merit from the American Association for State and Local History in 1977. He wrote *Prologue to Independence: New Jersey in the Coming of the American Revolution* (Rutgers University Press, 1976), *Connecticut Congressman: Samuel Huntington, 1731-1796* (American Revolution Bicentennial Commission of Connecticut, 1976), and *The Men in Blue: Conversations With Umpires* (Viking, 1980). Gerlach edited *The American Revolution: New York as a Case Study* (Wadsworth, 1972) and *New Jersey in the American Revolution, 1763-1783: A Documentary History* (New Jersey Historical Commission, 1975). *Address:* Department of History, University of Utah, Salt Lake City, Utah 84112. *Biographical/critical sources: Washington Post Book World,* July 20, 1980; *New Yorker,* August 4, 1980; *Time,* August 4, 1980.

* * *

GESNER, Clark 1938-
(John Gordon)

PERSONAL: Born March 27, 1938, in Augusta, Me. *Education:* Princeton University, B.A., 1960. *Home:* 87 Remsen St., Brooklyn, N.Y. 11201. *Agent:* Gilbert Parker, Curtis Brown Ltd., 575 Madison Ave., New York, N.Y. 10022.

CAREER: Writer for television and free-lance composer, filmmaker, and director. Columbia Broadcasting System, Inc., New York, N.Y., staff writer and composer for "Captain Kangaroo" and "Mister Mayor," 1963-66; contributing writer and composer for "Sesame Street" and "Electric Company" for Public Broadcasting Service, 1968—. *Military service:* U.S. Army Special Services, 1961-63. *Member:* American Society of Composers, Artists, and Performers. *Awards, honors:* Recipient of New York Park Association award for song, "Ode to a Park."

WRITINGS: (Composer and lyricist; book written under pseudonym John Gordon) *You're a Good Man, Charlie Brown* (musical play based on comic strip "Peanuts" by Charles M. Schulz; first produced off Broadway at Theatre 80 St. Marks, March 7, 1967; produced on Broadway at John Golden Theatre, June 1, 1971), Random House, 1967; *Finnerty Flynn and the Singing City* (juvenile; illustrated by Ferd A. Sondern), Lancelot Press, 1969; (under pseudonym John Gordon) *Stuff, Etc.: A Collection,* Lippincott, 1970; (composer and lyricist; book written with Nagle Jackson) "The Utter Glory of Morrissey Hall" (musical comedy; first produced in Santa Barbara, Calif., at Pacific Conservatory of the Performing Arts, summer, 1976; produced on Broadway at Mark Hellinger Theatre, May 13, 1979).

Composer of numerous songs, including "Fourteen Hours and Thirty-Seven Minutes," "A Funny Way to Spend the Day," "The Peanut Butter Affair," "Ode to a Park," and "Societus Magnificat." Also composer for shows, including Julius Monk reviews, "Baker's Dozen," and "Bits and Pieces."

SIDELIGHTS: "Who can pooh-pooh the eclipse of Pooh? By who? By you! But what did you do? Why, read Charlie Brown instead." That was the comment made by William McNeill in his *Washington Post* review of Clark Gesner's musical, "You're a Good Man, Charlie Brown." In his review, McNeill addressed the "Peanuts" phenomenon in general, comparing its appeal to that held by an earlier generation for Winnie the Pooh. McNeill queried: "What does [the enthusiasm for 'Peanuts'] signify? A coming of age of American culture? . . . Or is it the new psychological perspective—the knee-high view—

that recognizes big sister as a tyrant, and the ability to catch a baseball as the pinnacle of manly success?" For thousands of theatergoers, the answer to McNeill's query was a resounding "Yes!" The off-Broadway production of "Charlie Brown" lasted through what reviewer Mel Gussow called a "surprising" 1,597 performances and reopened on Broadway in 1971 after a worldwide tour.

According to McNeill, the popularity of Gesner's creation had little to do with the quality of the play itself. He observed: "Deprived of music and spectacle, most musical comedies are poor things; the same, alas, is true here. There is no plot, no overall structure; no movement of pace or tone that runs through the whole in any pattern I could perceive. It is, in short, a comic strip in two acts." Mel Gussow, following the Broadway reopening, avoided a similar technical critique of the play; instead, he explored the psychology behind the show's lasting appeal. "Gesner," stated Gussow, "loved 'Peanuts' as much as we all did and had no intention of tampering with the purity of the merchandise. . . . The original 'Charlie Brown' was innocence observed and preserved."

Gesner's second venture as a playwright did not meet with similar success. "The Utter Glory of Morrissey Hall" opened and closed on the same evening. Set in an English finishing school for girls, the play follows the misadventures of the students as they plot to undermine the sanity of their headmistress, Miss Faysle, played by Celeste Holm. Reviewer Brendan Gill of *New Yorker* said of the play: "It was relentlessly arch and silly, and not a single word uttered or sung in the course of it failed to ring false. . . ." *New York Times* critic Richard Eder had this comment: "It takes off at times in a chain of delightful absurdities; the chain breaks frequently, leaving a great many limp and uncertain intervals. . . . Yet, there is a playfulness to it that is most appealing, and a momentum that takes us over some considerable empty spaces and encourages us to wait for something better to show up; and sooner or later it does. . . . 'Morrissey Hall' is untidy, uneven, and often a mess; yet, despite the crucial failure in the casting of its central role, it has a charm and sprightliness that are never quite extinguished."

BIOGRAPHICAL/CRITICAL SOURCES: Washington Post Book World, June 2, 1968; *New York Times,* June 2, 1971, May 14, 1979; *New Yorker,* May 21, 1979.*

* * *

GEVIRTZ, Stanley 1929-

BRIEF ENTRY: Born January 27, 1929, in Brooklyn, N.Y. American historian, educator, and author. Gevirtz taught history at University of Chicago for sixteen years before becoming professor of Bible and ancient Near Eastern civilization at Hebrew Union College in 1972. He wrote *Patterns in the Early Poetry of Israel* (University of Chicago Press, 1963). *Address:* Hebrew Union College-Jewish Institute of Religion, 3077 University Mall, Los Angeles, Calif. 90007.

* * *

GIBBONS, Faye 1938-

PERSONAL: Born January 31, 1938, in Carter's Quarter, Ga.; daughter of George Manley (a welder and mechanic) and Alice Lenell (a mill worker; maiden name, Searcy) Junkins; married Benjamin Turner Gibbons III (a mathematician and computer analyst), August 29, 1964; children: Benjamin Turner IV, David.

Education: Attended Oglethorpe University, 1960, and Emory University, 1961; Berry College, B.A. 1961; graduate study at Auburn University, 1965. *Religion:* Methodist. *Home and office address:* Route 3, Box 356, Deatsville, Ala. 36022.

CAREER: Teacher at North Whitfield High School, Dalton, Ga., 1961-63, at Waterman State Elementary School, Marietta, Ga., 1963-64, at Beauregard High School, Lee County, Ala., 1964-66, and at Lincoln Elementary School, Huntsville, Ala., 1966-69. *Member:* Alabama Library Association, Montgomery Creative Writers.

WRITINGS: Some Glad Morning (novel for young adults), Morrow, 1982. Contributor of articles to newspapers and magazines, including *Old House Journal.*

WORK IN PROGRESS: A book, set in Georgia during the 1950's, about a twelve-year-old boy.

SIDELIGHTS: Faye Gibbons's novel for young adults, *Some Glad Morning,* tells the story of Maude, a ten-year-old girl whose mother packs the family up to Georgia's mountains in response to her alcoholic husband. Though the novel illustrates Maude's process of self-discovery, it also explores the position of women in rural families. Maude's mother, for example, is seen as a proud and independent person while Ma Fields, her grandmother, is a strong but soft matriarch. For her part, Maude, who aspires for more than the factory-worker status of her mother, hopes to become a teacher. Gibbons, said Lou Willet Stanek in the *New York Times Book Review,* is "especially adept in portraying minor adult characters who love and hurt and have flaws just like ours."

Some Glad Morning, the critic continued, "is a charming story that captures the ambience of the Georgia mountain culture." "That's part of Faye Gibbons' skill, the ability to set down life as it was for many people in Georgia and the rest of the South in the late 1940s without glossing over it or making it unbearably sad," Celestine Sibley maintained in the *Atlanta Constitution.* "You feel that it is as true as life, which is a mixed bag at best." The novel "is a welcome addition to the literature about a tenacious and strong-willed people of the back woods. We hope that this will be followed by others," remarked Marilou Sorensen in the *Deseret News.*

Gibbons told *CA:* "The most important motivating force in my career is the way I grew up. I was born to very intelligent, but uneducated, mountain parents. Our family was always poor, and we moved constantly—sometimes living in the mountains, but more often living in various north Georgia mill towns. Only after I was grown, educated, and a mother did I realize how many positive values had come out of my childhood.

"I began writing when my first son was born. During eight years of teaching, I had dreamed of being a writer but never had time to devote to it. Suddenly, as a mother to one of the world's least troublesome babies and housekeeper for a small, sparsely furnished house, I had plenty of time.

"I hope to tell stories about young people and older people who have problems like all of us and learn to solve them. I want young people and adults to read my books and feel better about who they are.

"Many writers have influenced me, either directly or indirectly. I could not list them all because they go back to my earliest childhood and extend to the present day. At the top of any list would have to be Marjorie Kinnan Rawlings, Laura Ingalls Wilder, C. S. Lewis, and Katherine Paterson.

"I think the very best books being written today are those classified as children's books. Perhaps it is because children expect more than adults. Children want characters who learn from mistakes, plots which make sense, and values which are lasting. Fortunately, a good children's book is for everybody.

"I feel strongly about the importance of the family, caring for our environment, and upgrading educational standards. I share an enthusiasm for hiking with my husband and sons. Our favorite hiking area is the Appalachian Trail."

BIOGRAPHICAL/CRITICAL SOURCES: Atlanta Constitution, May 11, 1982; *New York Times Book Review,* September 19, 1982; *Deseret News* (Salt Lake City, Utah), September 25, 1982.

*   *   *

GIBBONS, John William   1907-1983

OBITUARY NOTICE: Born March 16, 1907, in Salt Lake City, Utah; died of cancer, April 19, 1983, in Washington, D.C. Public relations executive, editor, and journalist. Gibbons worked as a reporter and editor for newspapers in Idaho, Indiana, and Oregon before joining the Automotive Safety Foundation (now a part of the Highway Users Federation) in 1942. He served for the next thirty years as a government consultant and public relations director. A board member of the National Safety Council, Gibbons was a public information secretary for the 1946 White House Safety Conference. In 1958 he edited a traffic safety edition of the *Annals of the American Academy of Political and Social Science.* Obituaries and other sources: *Who's Who in Public Relations (International),* 4th edition, PR Publishing, 1972; *Washington Post,* April 21, 1983.

*   *   *

GIBNEY, Harriet
See HARVEY, Harriet

*   *   *

GIBSON, Ronald George   1909-

PERSONAL: Born November 9, 1909, in Southampton, England; son of George Edward and Gladys Muriel (Prince) Gibson; married Dorothy Elisabeth Alberta Rainey, June 9, 1934; children: Janet Elisabeth Ann (Mrs. John Mansfield Paulet King), Alison Sara (Mrs. Michael Anthony Philip Shaw Downham). *Education:* St. John's College, Cambridge, B.A., 1932, M.A., 1946; St. Bartholomew's Hospital, London, L.R.C.P., 1937. *Religion:* Church of England. *Home:* 21 St. Thomas St., Winchester, Hampshire SO23 9HJ, England. *Agent:* John Austin, Passatempo, Welcomes Rd., Kenley, Surrey CR2 5HB, England.

CAREER: General medical practitioner in Winchester, England, 1938-77; writer, 1977—. James Mackenzie Lecturer, 1968; medical officer at Winchester College and St. Swithun's School; member of court at University of Southampton, 1980—. Chairman of council of Department of Health and Social Security's standing medical advisory committee, 1972-76; vice-chairman of Central Health Services Council, 1972-76; member of Home Office Advisory Council on Misuse of Drugs, 1970-77, Personal Social Services Council, 1972-78, and General Medical Council; chairman of British Library's medical research information panel, 1978-81. Member of southern advisory council of British Broadcasting Crop. *Military service:*

British Army, Royal Army Medical Corps, 1940-46; became lieutenant colonel.

MEMBER: British Medical Association (chairman of council, 1966-71), Royal College of Surgeons (fellow; member of council, 1962-67), Royal College of General Practitioners, Worshipful Society of Apothecaries of London (master, 1981-82), Athenaeum Club, Marylebone Cricket Club. *Awards, honors:* Butterworth Gold Medal, 1956, for article ''Care of the Elderly in General Practice''; Officer of Order of the British Empire, 1961, Commander, 1970; LL.D. from University of Wales, 1965; foundation fellow at Royal College of General Practitioners, 1969; created Knight Bachelor, 1974; D.M. from University of Southampton, 1980.

WRITINGS: The Family Doctor: His Life and History, Allen & Unwin, 1981. Contributor to medical journals and newspapers.

SIDELIGHTS: Gibson's particular concerns are problems of adolescence and history of the general practice of medicine.

* * *

GIDDINGS, John Calvin 1930-

PERSONAL: Born September 26, 1930, in American Fork, Utah; son of Luther W. and Berniece (Crandall) Giddings; children: Steven B., Michael C. *Education:* Brigham Young University, B.S., 1952; University of Utah, Ph.D., 1954. *Home:* 3978 Emigration Canyon, Salt Lake City, Utah 84105. *Office:* Department of Chemistry, University of Utah, Salt Lake City, Utah 84112.

CAREER: University of Utah, Salt Lake City, assistant professor, 1957-59, associate professor, 1959-62, research professor, 1962-66, professor of chemistry, 1966—. Nebraska Lecturer and Venable Lecturer at University of North Carolina, both 1969; Foster Lecturer at State University of New York at Buffalo, 1971; Dow-Bucknell Lecturer, 1978; Phillips Lecturer at University of Pittsburgh, 1980. Member of advisory board of Negative Population Growth, Inc.; member of chemistry research evaluation panel of Air Force Office of Scientific Research, 1964-69. *Member:* American Whitewater Affiliation (president, 1972-77).

AWARDS, HONORS: Chromatography and electrophoresis award, 1967, Utah Award, 1970, and award in analytical chemistry, 1980, all from American Chemical Society; award from ROMCOE, 1973, for environmental achievement in education; Fulbright grant for Lima, Peru, 1974; Tswett Medal in Chromatography, 1978; Stephen Dal Nogare Chromatography Award, 1979; chromatography award from Russian Scientific Council, 1980.

WRITINGS: Dynamics of Chromatography, Dekker, 1965; (editor with M. B. Monroe) *Our Chemical Environment,* Canfield Press, 1972; *Chemistry, Man, and Environmental Change,* Canfield Press, 1973.

Co-editor of ''Advances in Chromatography'' series, Dekker, 1965—. Contributor of more than two hundred articles to scientific journals. Executive editor of *Separation Science and Technology,* 1966—; honorary editor of *Pakistan Journal of Sciences and Mathematics;* member of editorial review board of *Journal of Liquid Chromatography.*

SIDELIGHTS: Giddings reported that his main area of research is chromatography, ''where I have been especially active in relating chromatographic separability to the underlying molec-

ular processes. I have also worked on general separation theory and methods, new separation methodology, macromolecular separations, development of techniques for diffusion coefficient measurements, theory of diffusion, chemical kinetics, and snow and avalanche physics. I invented the field-flow fractionation method for chemical separations and am active in research and education dealing with the chemistry of environmental and population problems.''

In 1975 Giddings organized the expedition that achieved the first successful exploration and descent of the upper canyons of the Apurimac River in Peru, the source of the Amazon River.

AVOCATIONAL INTERESTS: Conservation, river running, ski mountaineering, skiing, hiking.

* * *

GIFFORD, Francis Newton
See GIFFORD, Frank

* * *

GIFFORD, Frank 1930-
(Francis Newton Gifford)

BRIEF ENTRY: Born August 16, 1930, in Santa Monica (one source says Bakersfield), Calif. American sportscaster and author. Gifford, a running back for the New York Giants professional football team from 1952 to 1965, set numerous records for touchdowns and pass receptions. Following his retirement from football, Gifford began working as a sportscaster for Columbia Broadcasting System (CBS-TV) and became color commentator for the network's ''NFL Monday Night Football'' program. The former athlete also appeared in the motion pictures ''Up Periscope!'' and ''Paper Lion.'' Gifford was named most valuable player in the National Football League in 1956, and he received an Emmy Award as television's outstanding sports personality of 1977. His books include *Frank Gifford's Football Guide Book: Basic Plays and Playing Techniques for Boys* (McGraw, 1965), *Frank Gifford's NFL-AFL Football Guide* (New American Library, 1968), *Pro Football Guide for 1970* (New American Library, 1970), and *Gifford on Courage* (M. Evans, 1976). *Address:* 355 Taconic Rd., Greenwich, Conn. 06830; and c/o American Broadcasting Companies, Inc., 1330 Avenue of the Americas, New York, N.Y. 10019. *Biographical/critical sources: Current Biography,* Wilson, 1964; *Who's Who in Football,* Arlington House, 1974; *New York Times Book Review,* December 5, 1976; *Who's Who in America,* 42nd edition, Marquis, 1982.

* * *

GILBERT, Rod(rigue Gabriel) 1941-

BRIEF ENTRY: Born July 1, 1941, in Montreal, Quebec, Canada; came to United States, 1962, naturalized citizen, 1969. American professional hockey player and author. Gilbert joined the New York Rangers hockey team in 1962. Since then he has played in more than one thousand games and has set nearly two dozen team records. In 1977 Gilbert established the Rod Gilbert Foundation and became a marketing communications executive at Madison Square Garden. He wrote *Goal!: My Life on Ice* (Hawthorn, 1968) and *Playing Hockey the Professional Way* (Harper, 1972). *Address:* Madison Square Garden, 4 Pennsylvania Plaza, New York, N.Y. 10001. *Biographical/critical sources: Current Biography,* Wilson, 1969; *New York*

Times Book Review, December 3, 1972; *Washington Post Book World,* December 3, 1972; *New York Times,* March 6, 1977.

* * *

GILCHRIST, Andrew (Graham) 1910-

PERSONAL: Born April 19, 1910, in Scotland; son of James Graham (a farmer) and Jane Ann (Hepburn) Gilchrist; married Freda Grace Slack, 1946; children: Christopher, Jeremy, Janet Gilchrist Rayner. *Education:* Attended Oxford University. *Home:* Arthur's Crag, Hazelbank, by Lanark, Scotland.

CAREER: British Foreign Service, London, England, served in Bangkok, Thailand, 1933-36 and 1938-42, in Paris, France, 1936-37, in Marseilles, France, 1937-38, in Rabat, Morocco, 1942-43, at Foreign Office in London, 1946-51, served as consul-general in Stuttgart, West Germany, 1951-54, counselor on staff of commissioner-general for Southeast Asia in Singapore, 1954-56, ambassador to Iceland, 1956-59, consul-general in Chicago, Ill., 1960-63, ambassador to Indonesia, 1963-66, and to Ireland, 1967-70; writer, 1970—. Chairman of Scottish Highlands and Islands Development Board, 1965-71; past member of Scottish Economic Council. *Military service:* British Army, 1943-46. *Awards, honors*—Military: Mentioned in dispatches. Other: Knight Commander of St. Michael and St. George.

WRITINGS: Bangkok Top Secret, Hutchinson, 1970; *Cod Wars and How to Lose Them,* Edinburgh University Press, 1978.

WORK IN PROGRESS: An autobiography; a novel set in the Scottish Highlands.

SIDELIGHTS: Andrew Gilchrist told *CA:* "Back in 1960, the *Chicago Tribune* asked me to review one or two books. I obliged and threw in a few poems for free. This is what really got me hooked on writing, an enjoyable though not (for me) a lucrative pursuit. I still review books, and I still have hopes that my Highland novel (whose hero is a young American who falls heir to a huge estate in Scotland) will prove a best-seller and so enable me to visit my old friends in the Midwest and other distant places.

"*Bangkok Top Secret* was a success but not quite sufficiently so to justify a reprint. It is about secret military operations and intelligence contacts behind the Japanese lines in Southeast Asia from 1944 to 1946, all entirely authentic.

"*Cod Wars and How to Lose Them* is an account of the 'cod wars' between Britain and Iceland, in which the Icelanders were victorious and drove British fishermen out of their waters, despite the attempted interference of the Royal Navy. The political background is fully set out (after all, I was the British ambassador at the time), and the errors of the British are in no way minimized. To explain the strange events, there is a light-hearted survey of Icelandic history and social customs, together with a chapter on the best salmon fishing in the world. The book sold very well in Iceland, but not so well at home."

* * *

GIMMESTAD, Victor E(dward) 1912-1982

OBITUARY NOTICE—See index for *CA* sketch: Born August 13, 1912, in Galesville, Wis.; died December 26, 1982, in Bloomington, Ind. Educator and author. Gimmestad, a professor emeritus of English at Illinois State University, was the author of *John Trumbull,* which was published in 1974. Obit-

uaries and other sources: *Chronicle of Higher Education,* January 19, 1983.

* * *

GIUNTI, Renato 1905-1983

OBITUARY NOTICE: Born in May, 1905; died April 5, 1983, in Florence, Italy. Publisher. Giunti was president of Italy's Giunti publishing group, which includes Marzocco, Barbera, Martello, and Nardini. Obituaries and other sources: *Publishers Weekly,* April 29, 1983.

* * *

GLADWIN, William Zachary
See ZOLLINGER, Gulielma

* * *

GLASS, Albert J(ulius) 1908-1983

OBITUARY NOTICE: Born June 16, 1908, in Baltimore, Md.; died following a heart attack, March 17, 1983, in Bethesda, Md. Psychiatrist and author. Specializing in the treatment of battle fatigue, Glass was commissioned in the Army Medical Corps in 1941 and served in North Africa and Europe. He was later chief of psychiatry at Brooke Army Hospital in Texas and at the Presidio in San Francisco, California. Glass, who also served in Korea during the police action there, wrote *The Official History of Military Psychiatry of World War II* and *The Official History of Military Psychiatry in the Korean War.* Obituaries and other sources: *Who's Who in the South and Southwest,* 14th edition, Marquis, 1975; *Washington Post,* March 21, 1983.

* * *

GODWIN, Harry 1901-

PERSONAL: Born in 1901; married Margaret Elizabeth Daniels; children: David. *Education:* Earned Sc.D. *Home:* 30 Barton Rd., Cambridge, England.

CAREER: Cambridge University, Cambridge, England, fellow of Clare College, 1925—, lecturer, 1934-48, reader, 1948-60, professor of botany, 1960-68, professor emeritus, 1968—, director of subdepartment of quaternary research, 1948-66. *Member:* British Ecological Society (president, 1943), Royal Society (fellow).

WRITINGS: The History of the British Flora: A Factual Basis for Phytogeography, Cambridge University Press, 1956; *Finland: Its Ancient Past and Uncertain Future,* Cambridge University Press, 1978. Also author of *Plant Biology,* 1930, and *Archives of the Peat Bogs,* 1981.

* * *

GOELZ, Paul Cornelius 1914-

PERSONAL: Born October 7, 1914, in Bartelso, Ill.; son of Peter Paul and Clara (Bross) Goelz. *Education:* University of Dayton, B.B.A., 1943, M.A., 1946; Northwestern University, M.B.A., 1951, Ph.D., 1954. *Home:* 1 Camino Santa Maria, San Antonio, Tex. 78284. *Office:* School of Business and Administration, St. Mary's University, San Antonio, Tex. 78284.

CAREER: St. Mary's University, San Antonio, Tex., instructor, 1946-52, assistant professor, 1953-59, associate professor,

1960-63, professor, 1964—, M. S. Pryor Professor of Free Enterprise, 1977—, chairman of department of marketing management, 1946-62, chairman of Bureau of Economic Research, 1957-60, dean of School of Business and Administration, 1962-77. Member of board of directors of American Assembly of Collegiate Schools of Business; consultant to American businesses and the federal government.

MEMBER: Academy of Management, National Association of Business Economists, American Institute of Industrial Engineers, American Marketing Association, Association of Private Enterprise Education (president-elect, 1981-82), Southwestern Business Administration Association (president, 1968-69; member of executive committee). *Awards, honors:* Award for excellence in private enterprise education from Freedoms Foundation at Valley Forge, 1978; Liberty Bell Award from San Antonio Young Lawyers Association, 1982.

WRITINGS: (With co-author) *Principles of Retailing*, Pitman, 1955; *An Economic Philosophy for a Free People*, St. Mary's University Press, 1980; *Economic Freedom in the Eighties*, St. Mary's University Press, 1981. Editor of *Entrepreneurial Commentary*.

WORK IN PROGRESS: *The Economic System of Free Enterprise: Its Judeo-Christian Values and Philosophical Concepts.*

SIDELIGHTS: Goelz told *CA:* "It is my belief that the hunger, employment, and upward mobility problems of nations across the world can be effectively approached through educational programs focusing on resource development, creation of small businesses, and management technology on behalf of economic growth. I am dedicated to advancing, through research and writing, liberty, self-determination, democracy, and a greater scope for individual expression, creativity, productivity, and social participation."

* * *

GOGARTY, Oliver St. John 1878-1957

BRIEF ENTRY: Born August 17, 1878, in Dublin, Ireland; died September 22, 1957, in New York, N.Y. Irish physician, politician, poet, and novelist. An outspoken opponent of the politics of Eamon de Valera, leader of the Sinn Fein nationalist movement, Gogarty and his family were forced to leave Ireland and take refuge in England in 1921. He returned to Ireland the following year and began a fourteen-year term as senator of the Irish Free State. Gogarty was acquainted with many writers of the Irish Literary Renaissance, including James Joyce, who based the character Buck Mulligan in *Ulysses* on him. Gogarty also kept company with William Butler Yeats, Francis Hackett, George Moore, and George William "AE" Russell, who once dubbed the author "the wildest wit in Ireland." Gogarty issued several books of poetry, including *An Offering of Swans* (1924), *Others to Adorn* (1938), and *Elbow Room* (1939), but is best remembered for his memoir *As I Was Going Down Sackville Street* (1937) and his autobiographical novel *Tumbling in the Hay* (1939). *Biographical/critical sources:* Oliver St. John Gogarty, *As I Was Going Down Sackville Street*, Reynal & Hitchcock, 1937; *Twentieth-Century Authors: A Biographical Dictionary of Modern Literature*, H. W. Wilson, 1942, 1st supplement, 1955; Ulick O'Connor, *The Times I've Seen: Oliver Gogarty*, Obolensky, 1963; James F. Carens, *Surpassing Wit: Oliver St. John Gogarty, His Poetry and Prose*, Columbia University Press, 1979; *Twentieth-Century Literary Criticism*, Volume 11, Gale, 1983.

GOLD, Aaron 1937-1983

OBITUARY NOTICE—See index for *CA* sketch: Born August 4, 1937, in Chicago, Ill.; died of complications resulting from leukemia, May 23, 1983, in Chicago, Ill. Columnist. Gold is remembered as a gossip columnist who considered how what he wrote affected those about whom he wrote. His co-columnist Michael Sneed believed that "it was never his instinct to hurt, only to be accurate. He was a really, really caring man." Before becoming a columnist, Gold held various positions at WBBM-TV, a CBS affiliate, from 1956 to 1964. In 1964 he founded a public relations firm, Gold/Wilson Associates, which he operated until 1973. At that time, he joined the *Chicago Tribune*'s staff as a celebrity and entertainment columnist, contributing the "Tower Ticker" column from 1973 to 1981. He later wrote the "Inc." column with Sneed. In addition to his writing duties, Gold appeared on WGN-TV and "PM Magazine." He was named humanitarian of the year by the Easter Seal Society of Metropolitan Chicago in 1981. Obituaries and other sources: *Chicago Tribune*, May 25, 1983; *Newsweek*, June 6, 1983.

* * *

GOLDEN, James L. 1919-

BRIEF ENTRY: Born December 17, 1919, in Indian Head, Md. American educator and author. Golden taught speech at University of Maryland, University of Richmond, Pasadena College, Muskingum College, and Illinois State University before becoming a professor at Ohio State University in 1966. He co-authored *The Rhetoric of Western Thought* (Kendall/Hunt, 1976). Golden also co-edited *The Rhetoric of Blair, Campbell, and Whately* (Holt, 1968) and *The Rhetoric of Black Americans* (C. E. Merrill, 1971). *Address:* Department of Speech Communication, Ohio State University, 154 North Oval Dr., Columbus, Ohio 43210.

* * *

GOLDENBERG, Robert 1942-

PERSONAL: Born October 21, 1942, in Brooklyn, N.Y.; son of Bernard (a teacher) and Irene (a teacher; maiden name, Shapiro) Goldenberg; married Judith Plaskow, June 22, 1969; children: Alexander. *Education:* Cornell University, B.A., 1963; Jewish Theological Seminary of America, M.H.L., 1966; Brown University, Ph.D., 1974. *Home:* 64-53 Bell Blvd., Bayside, N.Y. 11364. *Office:* Program in Judaic Studies, State University of New York at Stony Brook, Stony Brook, N.Y. 11794.

CAREER: Sir George Williams University, Montreal, Quebec, assistant professor of religion, 1971-74; New York University, New York, N.Y., assistant professor of history and literature of religion, 1974-76; Wichita State University, Wichita, Kan., assistant professor of religion, 1976-79; State University of New York at Stony Brook, associate professor of Judaic studies, 1979—, director of undergraduate Judaic studies program, 1980-82, director of Stony Brook Center for Religious Studies, 1982—. *Member:* Society of Biblical Literature, Association for Jewish Studies (member of board of directors, 1980—), Society for Values in Higher Education. *Awards, honors:* Grant from Memorial Foundation for Jewish Culture, 1980-81.

WRITINGS: (Contributor) Jacob Neusner, editor, *The Formation of the Babylonian Talmud*, E. J. Brill, 1970; *The Sabbath-Law of Rabbi Meir*, Scholars Press (Missoula, Mont.), 1978; (contributor) Robert Polzin and Eugene Rothman, editors, *The*

Biblical Mosaic, Scholars Press, 1982. Contributor of articles and reviews to theology journals and popular magazines. Member of editorial board of *Association for Jewish Studies Journal,* 1982—.

WORK IN PROGRESS: Contributing to *Approaches to Ancient Judaism,* Volume V, edited by W. S. Green, for Scholars Press (Chico, Calif.); *Rabbinic Re-Interpretations of Prophetic Teaching; The Sabbath in Ancient Judaism.*

SIDELIGHTS: Goldenberg told *CA:* "I am interested in the ancient rabbinic reconstruction of Judaism after the disaster of the destruction of the Jerusalem Temple and its parallel to the contemporary situation."

*   *   *

GOLDMAN, Bo   1932-

BRIEF ENTRY: Born September 10, 1932, in New York, N.Y. American playwright and author of screenplays. Goldman and Laurence Hauber won an Academy Award in 1975 for their adaptation of Ken Kesey's novel *One Flew Over the Cuckoo's Nest.* Goldman won his second Academy Award in 1980 for best original screenplay for the film "Melvin and Howard." He also co-authored the screenplay for "The Rose" (1979), which featured Bette Midler in the lead role. Goldman's 1982 screenplay for "Shoot the Moon," a movie about the breakup of a marriage, earned the writer this praise from *Time's* Richard Schickel: "As he proved in *Melvin and Howard,* Bo Goldman is a very good writer, a man whose world appears to be filled with mild eccentrics and funny overheard remarks that he gets down just right in his mental notebook." *Address:* c/o William Morris Agency, 151 El Camino, Beverly Hills, Calif. 90212. *Biographical/critical sources: Chicago Tribune,* February 13, 1981; *Washington Post,* February 13, 1981, July 11, 1982; *New York Times,* January 22, 1982; *Time,* February 1, 1982.

*   *   *

GOLDSMITH, Emanuel S(idney)   1935-

BRIEF ENTRY: Born August 15, 1935, in New York, N.Y. American rabbi, educator, and author. Goldsmith, who has been a rabbi since 1960, served as executive vice-president of the Jewish Reconstructionist Federation from 1965 to 1967. He has also taught Hebrew and Judaic studies at University of Connecticut since 1975 and has been a member of the faculty of Brandeis University and Clark University. Goldsmith wrote *Architects of Yiddishism at the Beginning of the Twentieth Century: A Study in Jewish Cultural History* (Fairleigh Dickinson University Press, 1976). *Address:* 10 Willowbrook Rd., Storrs, Conn.; and Department of Romance and Classical Languages, University of Connecticut, Storrs, Conn. 06268. *Biographical/critical sources: Directory of American Scholars,* Volume III: *Foreign Languages, Linguistics, and Philology,* 7th edition, Bowker, 1978.

*   *   *

GOLDSMITH, Joel S.   1892(?)-1964

OBITUARY NOTICE: Born c. 1892 in New York; died June 17, 1964, in London, England. Lecturer and author. Many considered Goldsmith to be a modern-day mystic. Among his books are *The Art of Meditation, The Art of Spiritual Healing, The Thunder of Silence, A Parenthesis in Eternity,* and *Man Was Not Born to Cry.* Obituaries and other sources: *New York Times,* June 18, 1964; *Publishers Weekly,* July 6, 1964; Lor-

raine Sinkler, *Spiritual Journey of Joel S. Goldsmith, Modern Mystic,* Harper, 1973.

*   *   *

GOLDSTEIN, Marc   1948-

PERSONAL: Born March 22, 1948, in New York, N.Y.; son of Leon (a high school chemistry teacher) and Helen (a photographer; maiden name, Kassel) Goldstein; married Jody Allyson Newman (an artist), September 20, 1975; children: Brandon. *Education:* Brooklyn College of the City University of New York, B.S. (cum laude), 1968; State University of New York Downstate Medical Center, M.D. (summa cum laude), 1972. *Home:* 500 East 63rd St., New York, N.Y. 10021. *Agent:* John Brockman Associates, Inc., 2307 Broadway, New York, N.Y. 10024.

CAREER: Columbia-Presbyterian Medical Center, New York, N.Y., surgical intern, 1972-73, surgical resident, 1973-74; State University of New York Downstate Medical Center, Brooklyn, resident, 1977-79, chief resident, 1979-80, assistant instructor, 1977-80, assistant professor of urology, 1980-82; Cornell University Medical Center, assistant professor of urological surgery, 1982—. Assistant attending surgeon at State University Hospital and Kings County Hospital Center, 1980-82; fellow-in-residence at Rockefeller University's Population Council, 1980-82, staff scientist, 1982—, research associate and associate physician at Rockefeller University Hospital, 1980—; director of Male Reproduction and Urologic Microsurgery Unit of New York Hospital-Cornell Medical Center, Population Council, and Rockefeller University, 1982—. Associate member of British Mountaineering Council, 1974-75; member of Mongejura-West Face expedition, Romsdal, Norway, 1975. *Military service:* U.S. Air Force, Medical Corps, 1974-77; became major. U.S. Air Force Reserve, 1977—.

MEMBER: International Microsurgical Society, American Fertility Society, American Society of Andrology, Alpha Omega Alpha (vice-president of Eta chapter, 1972), Amateur Athletic Union, New York Road Runners Club. *Awards, honors:* Ferdinand C. Valentine fellow of New York Academy of Medicine, 1980-82; scholar of American Urological Association, 1980-82; Ferdinand C. Valentine urology prize from New York Academy of Medicine and New York section of American Urological Association, 1981, for essay, "Microsurgical Orthotopic Testicular Transplantation in Isogenic Rats."

WRITINGS: (With Michael Feldberg) *The Vasectomy Book: A Complete Guide to Decision Making,* J. P. Tarcher, 1982; (contributor) Dorothy Krieger and C. W. Bardin, editors, *Current Endocrinologic Therapy,* B. D. Decker, 1983; (contributor) *Recent Advances in Male Reproduction,* Plenum, 1983. Contributor to medical journals.

SIDELIGHTS: Goldstein graduated from the School of Aerospace Medicine and flew more than eighty missions as an Air Force flight surgeon. He operated a medical facility in Norway, 120 miles north of the Arctic Circle. Then he established a vasectomy clinic at a Royal Air Force base, where he performed four hundred vasectomies. He is best known in the scientific and medical world for developing microsurgical techniques for the transplantation of testes in rats and the reversal of vasectomies in humans.

AVOCATIONAL INTERESTS: Marathon running, mountaineering.

BIOGRAPHICAL/CRITICAL SOURCES: *Stars and Stripes*, December 6, 1975; *Los Angeles Times Book Review*, October 10, 1982.

* * *

GONZALEZ, Edward 1933-

BRIEF ENTRY: Born February 25, 1933, in Los Angeles, Calif. American political scientist, educator, and author. Gonzalez was a member of the faculty of Wellesley College from 1964 to 1966. He then began teaching political science at University of California, Los Angeles. Gonzalez is also a consultant to RAND Corporation. He wrote *Cuba Under Castro: The Limits of Charisma* (Houghton, 1974) and *Post-Revolutionary Cuba in a Changing World* (RAND Corp., 1975). *Address:* 2049 Sichel, Los Angeles, Calif. 90031; and Department of Political Science, University of California, 405 Hilgard Ave., Los Angeles, Calif. 90024.

* * *

GONZALEZ-WIPPLER, Migene 1936-

PERSONAL: Given name is pronounced Mee-*geen;* born August 4, 1936, in Arecibo, P.R.; daughter of Rene (an importer) and Lila (Quinones) Gonzalez; married Keith Wippler (a military artist), December 9, 1960 (divorced, 1968); children: John, Joseph. *Education:* University of Puerto Rico, B.A., 1959; Columbia University, M.A., 1961. *Religion:* Roman Catholic. *Residence:* Forest Hills, N.Y. *Office:* c/o Prentice-Hall, 301 Sylvan Ave., Englewood Cliffs, N.J. 07632.

CAREER: American Institute of Physics, New York City, science editor, 1962-64; John Wiley & Sons, Inc., New York City, science editor, 1964-66; Academic Press, Inc., New York City, science editor, 1966-67; American Museum of Natural History, New York City, science editor, 1967-68; United Nations Industrial Development Organization, Vienna, Austria, associate English editor, 1969-71; International Telephone & Telegraph, Vienna, English correspondent, 1971-73; full-time writer, 1973—.

WRITINGS: *Santeria: African Magic in Latin America*, Crown, 1973; *A Kabbalah for the Modern World*, Crown, 1974, revised edition, Llewellyn, 1983; *The Complete Book of Spells, Magic, and Ceremonies*, Crown, 1978; *The Santeria Experience*, Prentice-Hall, 1982; *The Force*, Prentice-Hall, in press. Author of "The Santeria Experience," a column in *Latin New York*. Contributor to *Forum* and *Viva*.

WORK IN PROGRESS: "Santo," a screenplay about Santeria; "The Goya Portrait," a screenplay; "The Ritual," a screenplay.

SIDELIGHTS: Migene Gonzalez-Wippler told *CA:* "I was raised in Puerto Rico and all through my childhood and adolescence I saw people practicing magic alongside religion without any open conflicts of beliefs or ideologies. I therefore learned at an early age that there is a subtle link between magic and religion that at times is so tenuous that it can hardly be defined.

"I think that magic is the means by which man attempts to identify with God and tap God's powers for his own benefit. It is in fact as if man were saying, 'I *am* God, and I can do God-like things.' In religion, man asks God to do things for man. In magic he believes he's God and tries to do things for himself. In either case man is attempting to improve his life, to fill it with divine powers in order to survive the ordeals of an increasingly hostile environment.

"I see religion as man's initial contact with God, magic as the point where the initial contact has taken place and given way to identification with the Godhead. This theme and my childhood experiences in magic and religion are explored in depth in *The Santeria Experience*."

AVOCATIONAL INTERESTS: Travel (especially Europe), books.

BIOGRAPHICAL/CRITICAL SOURCES: *Viva*, March, 1975; *Latin New York*, June, 1982; *Us*, January, 1983.

* * *

GOODMAN, Arnold Abraham 1913-

PERSONAL: Born August 21, 1913. *Education:* Received M.H. from University of London and LL.M. from Downing College, Cambridge. *Office:* Goodman Derrick & Co., 9/11 Fulwood Pl., Gray's Inn, London WC1V 6HQ, England.

CAREER: Senior partner of Goodman Derrick & Co. (solicitors), London, England. Member of Industrial Reorganization Committee, 1969-71; past chairman of Committee of Inquiry on Charity Law. Dimbleby Memorial Lecturer, 1974. Chairman of Arts Council of Great Britain, 1965-72; deputy chairman of British Council, 1976—. Chairman of British Lion Films (Holdings), 1965-72, Housing Corp. and National Building Agency, 1973-77, Theatres' Trust, and Theatre Investment Fund; past member of South Bank Theatre Board; member of board of directors of Royal Opera House, 1972—; president of Theatre Advisory Council, 1972—; member of board of governors of Royal Shakespeare Theatre, 1972—; chairman of English National Opera, 1977—. President of National Book League, 1972—. Fellow of University College, London; master of University College, Oxford, 1976—. *Member:* Newspaper Publishers Association (chairman, 1970-75), Association for Business Sponsorship of the Arts (chairman). *Awards, honors:* Companion of Honour; created Baron of Westminster, 1965.

WRITINGS: *Not for the Record: Selected Speeches and Writings*, preface by Lord Annan, Deutsch, 1972, Norton, 1973.

* * *

GOODPASTER, Andrew J(ackson) 1915-

PERSONAL: Born February 12, 1915, in Granite City, Ill.; son of Andrew Jackson and Teresa (Mrovka) Goodpaster; married Dorothy Anderson, August 28, 1939; children: Susan Goodpaster Sullivan, Anne Goodpaster Wilson. *Education:* U.S. Military Academy, B.S., 1939; Princeton University, M.A. and M.S.E., 1949, Ph.D., 1950. *Home:* 409 North Fairfax St., Alexandria, Va. 22314.

CAREER: U.S. Army, career officer, 1939-81, 11th Engineers, Panama Canal Zone, 1939-42, 390th Engineers, Louisiana, 1942-43, 48th Engineers Combat Battalion, Italy, 1943-44, U.S. War Department, staff officer in Operations Division, 1944-47, Princeton University, Princeton, N.J., 1947-50, special assistant to chief of staff of Supreme Headquarters Allied Powers Europe (SHAPE), 1950-54, district engineer in San Francisco, Calif., 1954, defense liaison officer and staff secretary to president of the United States, 1954-61, assistant divisional commander of Third Infantry Division, 1961, commanding general of Eighth Infantry Division in Europe, 1961-62, special assistant for policy to chairman of Joint Chiefs of Staff in Washington, D.C., 1962-64, assistant to chairman, 1964-66, director of Joint Chiefs of Staff, 1966-67, director of special studies in Office of the Chief of Staff of the U.S. Army in Washington, D.C., 1967, commandant of National War College in Washington, D.C., and U.S. Army member of military staff committee of the United Nations, both 1967-68, member of U.S. delegation for negotiations with Vietnam in Paris, France, 1968, deputy commander of U.S. Military Command in Vietnam, 1968-69, Supreme Allied Commander (for Europe) of Supreme Headquarters Allied Powers Europe in Belgium, and commander-in-chief of U.S. European Command, both 1969-74, superintendent of U.S. Military Academy, 1977-81. Fellow of Woodrow Wilson International Center, 1975-76; professor at The Citadel, Charleston, S.C., 1976-77.

WRITINGS: For the Common Defense, Heath, 1977; (with Samuel Huntington) *Civil-Military Relations,* American Enterprise Institute, 1977.

SIDELIGHTS: Goodpaster told *CA:* "I retired from the Army in 1981. I now participate in studies, seminars, and organizations concerned with defense, national security policy, and governmental operations and organization. In my writings, I seek to formulate and present my views, based on my analysis and experience in these areas. My emphasis is on the importance of clear, realistic objectives for the nation's security, and on the need for clear, realistic strategy to link objectives and actions."

* * *

GOODWIN, Robert L. 1928(?)-1983

OBITUARY NOTICE: Born c. 1928; died of cancer, February 13, 1983, in San Diego, Calif. Dramatist. Goodwin was one of the first blacks to write for national television. He sold two scripts to a "Bonanza" producer in 1965, when producers were hesitant to promote programs that would star blacks and appeal to black audiences. He subsequently wrote scripts for such programs as "The Big Valley," "Julia," "All in the Family," "Dan August," and "Kaz." Goodwin also created a television special, "The Upper Chamber." Obituaries and other sources: *Los Angeles Times,* February 17, 1983; *New York Times,* February 18, 1983; *Washington Post,* February 20, 1983.

* * *

GORDON, Charles William 1860-1937
(Ralph Connor)

BRIEF ENTRY: Born September 13, 1860, in Indian Lands, Ontario, Canada; died October 31, 1937. Canadian educator, Presbyterian minister and missionary, and author. Gordon's novels, most written under the pseudonym Ralph Connor, reveal the author's admiration for the people of Canada's untamed wilderness. Many of the books are set in Gordon's native Glengarry County and describe a Scottish community working together to serve God. *Black Rock: A Tale of the Selkirks* (1898), *Glengarry School Days: A Story of Early Days in Glengarry* (1902), and *The Doctor: A Tale of the Rockies* (1906) immortalized in fiction events that have become a part of Canada's history and a source of national pride. Gordon also drew upon his personal experiences and background for his books. For example, *The Man From Glengarry: A Tale of the Ottawa* (1901) is a tribute to the stern morality of Gordon's Scottish forebears, *Christian Hope* (1912) reveals his strong personal religious convictions, and *The Sky Pilot in No Man's Land* (1919) is based upon his exploits in France during World War I. *Biographical/critical sources:* Charles W. Gordon,

Postscript to Adventure: The Autobiography of Ralph Connor—Charles W. Gordon, edited by J. King Gordon, Farrar & Rinehart, 1938; *The Oxford Companion to Canadian History and Literature,* Oxford University Press, 1967; *Twentieth-Century Children's Writers,* St. Martin's, 1978.

* * *

GORDON, John
See GESNER, Clark

* * *

GORDON, Strathearn 1902-1983

OBITUARY NOTICE: Born September 3, 1902; died April 2, 1983. Librarian and author. Gordon's desire for a military career was quelled when he contracted polio and was crippled while serving with the Highland Light Infantry in India. Following his convalescence, he took a job as a cashier at a bank in Monte Carlo. In 1930 he became a clerk in the British House of Commons, serving from 1950 to 1967 as librarian of the House. He wrote *Our Parliament.* Obituaries and other sources: *Who's Who,* 134th edition, St. Martin's, 1982; *London Times,* April 9, 1983.

* * *

GORE, Arthur Kattendyke S(trange) D(avid) A(rchibald) 1910-1983
(Earl of Arran)

OBITUARY NOTICE: Born July 5, 1910, in Sawbridgeworth, England; died in his sleep, February 23, 1983, in Hemel Hempstead, Hertfordshire, England. Columnist. Gore, who was known to his friends as Boofy, was primarily known for his often caustic columns in the *Daily Mail, Evening News, Observer,* and *Punch,* which expressed his views on, among other subjects, foreign presidents and countries he did not like. Because of his frequently abusive tone, Gore received many threats of lawsuits. Gore, the eighth Earl of Arran, was instrumental in the passage of the Sexual Offences Act, which legalized private homosexual acts, and the Badgers Protection Bill, which limited the killing of badgers. He suffered a stroke in 1978, citing his daily consumption of half a bottle of champagne before noon as the probable cause. Obituaries and other sources: *Who's Who in the World,* 3rd edition, Marquis, 1976; *London Times,* February 24, 1983; *New York Times,* February 23, 1983; *Publishers Weekly,* March 7, 1983; *Newsweek,* March 7, 1983.

* * *

GOSDIN, Rex 1938(?)-1983

OBITUARY NOTICE: Born c. 1938; died following a heart attack, May 23, 1983, in Jonesboro, Ga. Country music singer and songwriter. In the 1960's Gosdin and his brother Vern formed the singing team known as the Gosdin Brothers. Among the songs Rex Gosdin composed are "Someday Our Day Will Come" and "Just Give Me What You Think Is Fair." Obituaries and other sources: *Washington Post,* May 26, 1983.

* * *

GOURMONT, Remy de 1858-1915

BRIEF ENTRY: Born April 4, 1858, in Bazoches-en-Houlme, France; died following a cerebral hemorrhage, September 27

(one source says September 28), 1915, in Paris, France. French critic, poet, dramatist, and novelist. Gourmont held his only regular job, as an assistant librarian at the Bibliotheque Nationale in France, from 1883 until 1891, when he was fired for writing an "unpatriotic" article. During that same year he helped establish *Mercure de France,* a publication largely devoted to works by authors of the symbolist school. Gourmont contributed to the periodical from its inception until his death. Stricken with lupus while in his thirties, the author was severely disfigured and thereafter remained a recluse. Gourmont was attracted to numerous fields of study and constantly explored new vistas; thus his writings are varied and include critical works such as *Le Latin mystique* (1892) and *Promenades litteraires* (seven volumes, 1904-1927), collections of poems, including *Les Divertissements* (1912), and novels, among them *Lilith* (1892), *Les Chevaux de Diomede* (1897; translated as *The Horses of Diomedes,* 1923), and *Un Coeur virginal* (1907; translated as *A Virgin Heart,* 1921). At the time of his death the author was writing an article protesting the German bombing of Rheims Cathedral. *Biographical/critical sources: Twentieth-Century Authors: A Biographical Dictionary of Modern Literature,* H. W. Wilson, 1942; *Cyclopedia of World Authors,* Harper, 1958; *The McGraw-Hill Encyclopedia of World Biography,* McGraw, 1973; *Twentieth-Century Literary Criticism,* Volume 11, Gale, 1983.

*　　*　　*

GOVENAR, Alan B(ruce)　1952-

PERSONAL: Born August 5, 1952, in Boston, Mass.; son of Joseph and Charlotte (Cohen) Govenar; married Jody Weber (an artist), August 21, 1977; children: Breea. *Education:* Ohio State University, B.A., 1974; University of Texas, M.A., 1975, Ph.D., 1983. *Home and office:* 2307 Norwood Dr., Dallas, Tex. 75228.

CAREER: Columbus College of Art and Design, Columbus, Ohio, instructor in sociology and literary studies, 1976-80; El Centro College, Dallas, Tex., instructor in sociology and literary studies, 1982—; producer of projects in motion pictures, including "Stoney Knows How," and video, and radio for exhibitions and festivals; photographer and writer. *Member:* American Folklore Society, American Culture Association, Texas Folklore Society. *Awards, honors:* Recipient of ten research grants; honorable mention from Jacobsen's Short Story Prize, 1974, for "Pigeon-Toed Marine"; numerous awards for film "Stoney Knows How."

WRITINGS: Ohio Folk Traditions: A New Generation, Public Library of Columbus, Ohio/Lancaster [Ohio] Public Library, 1981; (with Leonard St. Clair) *Stoney Knows How: Life as a Tattoo Artist,* University Press of Kentucky, 1981.

WORK IN PROGRESS: Three novels, including *Done Up* and *Running Changes;* a photo-journalistic book on tattooing; a documentary motion picture, "Wear Your Dreams"; producing a thirteen-part radio series on traditional music; organizing the Dallas Folk Art Festival.

SIDELIGHTS: Govenar told *CA:* "For me writing is an intense but quiet activity. I prefer to work at home near a window in the early morning silence. At its best, my writing confronts ethical issues important to the world in which I live. I consider as many points of view as possible, and then interpret my findings with both gravity and humor."

BIOGRAPHICAL/CRITICAL SOURCES: New York Times, November 11, 1981; *Village Voice Literary Supplement,* March, 1982; *Dallas Times Herald,* March 26, 1982.

GRACIA, Jorge J(esus) E(miliano)　1942-

PERSONAL: Born July 18, 1942, in Camaguey, Cuba; naturalized Canadian citizen, 1971; permanent U.S. resident, 1975; son of Ignacio Jesus Loreto (a pharmacist and landowner) and Leonila (a poet; maiden name, Otero) Gracia; married Norma Elida Silva (a treasurer); children: Leticia Isabel, Clarisa Raquel. *Education:* Wheaton College, Wheaton, Ill., B.A., 1965; University of Chicago, M.A., 1966; Pontifical Institute of Mediaeval Studies, M.S.L., 1970; University of Toronto, Ph.D., 1971. *Home:* 420 Berryman Dr., Amherst, N.Y. 14226. *Office:* Department of Philosophy, Baldy Hall, State University of New York at Buffalo, Buffalo, N.Y. 14260.

CAREER: State University of New York at Buffalo, assistant professor, 1971-76, associate professor, 1976-80, professor of philosophy and chairman of department, both 1980—. Visiting professor at University of Puerto Rico, 1972-73. *Member:* Societe internationale pour l'etude de la philosophie medievale, American Philosophical Association, Metaphysical Society of America, Mediaeval Academy of America, Society for Medieval and Renaissance Philosophy. *Awards, honors:* Grant from National Endowment for the Humanitites, 1981-82.

WRITINGS: Man and His Conduct, University of Puerto Rico Press, 1980; *Suarez on Individuation,* Marquette University Press, 1982; *Introduction to the Problem of Individuation in the Early Middle Ages,* Philosophia Verlag, 1983; *Philosophical Analysis in Latin America,* Reidel, in press.

Not in English: *El hombre y los valores en la filosofia latinoamericana del siglo veintavo* (title means "Man and Values in Twentieth-Century Latin American Philosophy"), Fondo de Cultura Economica, 1975, 2nd edition, 1981; *Com usar be de beure e menjar* (title means "How to Drink and Eat Well"), Curial, 1977; *Filosofia e indentidad cultural* (title means "Philosophy and Cultural Identity"), Monte Avila, 1983; *Ensayos filosoficas de Risieri Frondizi,* Fondo de Cultura Economica, in press.

Contributor of about fifty articles to periodicals including *Review of Metaphysics, Journal of the History of Philosophy,* and *New Scholasticism.*

WORK IN PROGRESS: The Metaphysics of Evil in Scholasticism, publication expected in 1984; *The Metaphysics of the Good in Scholasticism,* 1985; *Instances and Instantiables,* 1983.

SIDELIGHTS: Jorge Gracia told *CA:* "My research and writing has centered on three subject areas: the Middle Ages, Latin America, and metaphysics. I was trained as a medievalist in Toronto and therefore a great part of my work is concerned with the history of medieval thought. Most of this is technical and deals with such questions as the views of individuality developed during the period. In my book on the problem of individuation I argue, for example, that the basic problems related to individuality, its causes and its nature, are raised for the first time in an explicit way in the early middle ages. The book on Francis Suarez, which contains a translation of his treatise on this topic as well as an extensive glossary of technical terms, argues that Suarez's views on individuality are the most sophisticated and developed to come out of the middle ages and that Suarez provides one of the most clear and systematic treatments of the topic to date.

"More recently I have been working on the theories of good and evil in late scholasticism and particularly on the views of

Suarez. In my book on evil I present the key texts on this topic by Suarez, and I argue that he gives a credible defense of the traditional scholastic interpretation of evil as privation by introducing the conception of evil as a kind of disagreeability. Likewise, I find much merit in the view of good as a kind of agreeability, which I explore in my other book in preparation. But I also argue that neither theory goes far enough, since neither of them develops sufficiently the relational character of value.

"After coming to Buffalo and visiting Puerto Rico for a year, I became interested in the thought and philosophy of Latin America both because I was asked to teach a course on the subject and because I have never forgotten my background. Given the scarcity of sources available I decided, with the help of my good friend, the late Risieri Frondizi, to put together a collection of readings from Latin American philosophers centered around the themes of man and values. These themes are the areas where Latin American philosophy has made its most important contributions in the first half of this century. This anthology-study was published in Spanish, but an English version is in preparation. *Man and His Conduct,* on the other hand, is in fact a *Festschrift* in Frondizi's honor. It contains twenty-six essays written especially for the volume by noted American, European, and Latin American philosophers. In addition it contains a complete bibliography of Frondizi's works and a brief biography.

"Another area of my research has been concerned with the impact that philosophical analysis, as practiced in the Anglo-American tradition, has had on Latin America. I have also been working on the crisis of philosophical identity which Latin America is undergoing. One of the most discussed issues in Latin America for the past thirty years has been the question of whether there is such a thing as a Latin American philosophy that may be idiosyncratically unique and authentic. In my forthcoming book on the subject, I point out that the source of the question is a misunderstanding about the very nature of philosophy and philosophical method and that once a proper understanding of these is achieved, the problem dissolves.

"Finally, in the area of metaphysics, my main concern has been with the so-called problem of universals and individuals—the ontological categorization of two of our most basic notions. In the book on instances and instantiables I present my view that individuality has to do primarily with non-instantiability, while universality has to do with instantiability. I argue, moreover, that much of the concern with individuals and universals in the course of the history of philosophy is a result of a lack of understanding this fact as well as a lack of understanding and distinguishing the various issues involved in the notions of individuality and universality. These are the faults that flaw the work of most philosophers concerned with these issues, from Plato to Strawson."

* * *

GRAHAM, Hugh
  See BARROWS, (Ruth) Marjorie

* * *

GRAHAM, Jory 1925-1983

OBITUARY NOTICE—See index for *CA* sketch: Born February 7, 1925, in Chicago, Ill.; died of cancer, May 11, 1983, in Chicago, Ill. Columnist and author. From 1977 until her death, Graham wrote a syndicated column on coping with cancer. She

suffered from the disease for eight years and was best known for encouraging others who were so afflicted. Shortly before she died, Graham told her readers: "Long ago I promised that I would let you know when I came to my time of dying. The time has come and you and I need to begin the painful, yet necessary process of learning to say goodbye." Graham had been a journalist since 1959, associated with such periodicals as *Time,* the *Chicago Daily News, Chicagoan, Movie Guide,* and *Dental Progress.* She wrote "Jory Graham's City," a column for the *Chicago Sun-Times,* from 1969 to 1974. Graham was a visiting professor at the Southern Illinois University School of Medicine and the co-founder of the Alliance for Cancer Patients and Their Families. In 1980 she received the Alamo Award. She wrote *In the Company of Others: Understanding the Human Needs of Cancer Patients, Chicago: An Extraordinary Guide, Instant Chicago: How to Cope,* and *Katie's Zoo,* among others. Obituaries and other sources: *New York Times,* May 13, 1983; *Chicago Tribune,* May 13, 1983; *Time,* May 23, 1983.

* * *

GRAHAM, (Roger) Neill 1941-

PERSONAL: Born February 21, 1941, in Augusta, Ga.; son of Roger Neill (a sales representative) and Charlie Mae (a teacher; maiden name, Scattergood) Graham. *Education:* Attended Augusta College, 1959-61; Valdosta State College, B.S., 1963; University of North Carolina, Ph.D., 1971. *Home:* 913 Papaya St., Augusta, Ga. 30904.

CAREER: Concord College, Athens, W.Va., assistant professor, 1968-76, associate professor of physics, 1976-78; freelance writer, 1978—. *Member:* Association for Computing Machinery, American Association of Physics Teachers, Sigma Xi.

WRITINGS: (Editor with Bryce S. Dewitt) *The Many Worlds Interpretation of Quantum Mechanics,* Princeton University Press, 1973; *The Mind Tool,* West Publishing, 1976, 3rd edition, 1983; *Microprocessor Programming for Computer Hobbyists,* TAB Books, 1977; *Artificial Intelligence,* TAB Books, 1979; *Introduction to Computer Science,* West Publishing, 1979, 2nd edition, 1982; *Introduction to PASCAL,* West Publishing, 1980, 2nd edition, 1983; *Computers and Computing,* West Publishing, 1982; *Programming the IBM Personal Computer: BASIC,* Holt, 1982.

WORK IN PROGRESS: College textbooks on computers and computing; books for persons using microcomputers, especially the IBM Personal Computer.

SIDELIGHTS: Graham commented: "As a youngster, I was interested in science and science fiction. My interest in science led to my studies of mathematics, physics, and computer science. My interest in science fiction led me first to the science fiction of Isaac Asimov, then to his science popularizations, which I greatly admired and which inspired me to write about science. When the opportunity to write about computer science arose, I grasped it eagerly and soon put aside my teaching and other scientific endeavors to devote my full time to writing."

* * *

GRANDA, Chabuca
  See LARCO, Isabel Granda

GRAVERSEN, Pat 1935-
(Tricia Graves)

PERSONAL: Born February 28, 1935, in Wheeling, W.Va.; daughter of Vernon James and Avis (Pethtel) Spears; married Paul Graversen (a truck driver), February 3, 1969; children: Jon Paul, Sonja Marie, Paul Erik, Angela Noel. *Education:* Attended Elliott School of Business. *Home and office:* 124 Downing St., Lakewood, N.J. 08701. *Agent:* Dominick Abel Literary Agency, Inc., 498 West End Ave., No. 12C, New York, N.Y. 10024.

CAREER: Legal secretary in Phoenix, Ariz., San Francisco, Calif., New Orleans, La., New York, N.Y., and other cities, 1953-69; writer, 1975—. *Member:* Authors Guild, Authors League of America, Science Fiction Writers of America, New Jersey Association of Women Business Owners.

WRITINGS: Invisible Fire (occult novel), Fawcett, 1981; *The Fagin* (occult novel), A & W Publishers, 1982; (under pseudonym Tricia Graves) *Heart on Trial* (romance novel), New American Library, 1983.

WORK IN PROGRESS: A Race for Love, a romance novel under pseudonym Tricia Graves; *In the Name of Love,* a family saga; *My Soul to Keep,* an occult novel.

SIDELIGHTS: Graversen told *CA:* "I cannot say what prompted me to choose writing as a career, but I doubt that I had a choice. I have always wanted to write. I was born and raised in the beautiful, wild, mystical hills of West Virginia. My grandmother frightened me with visions of the end of the world before I was old enough to write my name. She was a healer and a mystic, and the occult lore of the mountains was an integral part of my early childhood. In my occult novels, I like to write about ordinary people who have extraordinary things happen to them. I think this gives my novels a sense of reality that isn't found in many occult novels. And it is this reality that scares people—they feel, 'Maybe this could happen to me.'

"I enjoyed writing my first romance novel because I am a romantic at heart, in spite of my liberated ways, and I intend to write several more romances. I'm now outlining a family saga, which will cover three generations in the life of a Scandinavian-American family. My Danish husband and I lived in Denmark for two years and one of our four children was born there. I have a great interest in Scandinavian history and culture, and I think this background knowledge will add a great deal of authenticity to *In the Name of Love.*

"I like to write about things that interest me personally, or things that are important in my life. For instance, in *Invisible Fire* I delved (though not too deeply) into psychotronic power; in *The Fagin,* I wrote about a six year old boy abducted from a playground. *My Soul to Keep* centers on abortion and reincarnation. *In the Name of Love* will deal in depth with hemophilia and its effects on the parents of a small child who is stricken with the disease. I am either fascinated or angered by all of these things and therefore feel a great deal of satisfaction in being able to bring them to the attention of the readers of my books."

* * *

GRAVES, Edgar B(aldwin) 1898-1983

OBITUARY NOTICE: Born September 30, 1898, in Philadelphia, Pa.; died March 24, 1983, in Clinton, N.Y. Educator and author. From 1927 until 1969 Graves was a professor of history at Hamilton College. He edited *A Bibliography of English History to 1485.* Obituaries and other sources: *Who's Who in America,* 39th edition, Marquis, 1976; *New York Times,* March 31, 1983.

* * *

GRAVES, Tricia
See GRAVERSEN, Pat

* * *

GRAY, Gordon 1909-1982

OBITUARY NOTICE: Born May 30, 1909, in Baltimore, Md.; died of cancer, November 25, 1982, in Washington, D.C. Lawyer, government official, broadcasting executive, and publisher. Gray left his private law practice to pursue newspaper publishing prior to World War II, becoming the president and publisher of the *Winston-Salem Journal* and the *Twin City Sentinel.* In 1939 he was elected to the North Carolina Senate and was reelected in 1941, but enlisted as a private in the Army in 1942. In 1947 President Truman appointed Gray assistant secretary of the Army, and two years later he became secretary of the Army. In 1950 Gray acted as Truman's special assistant. Under the Eisenhower administration Gray was Assistant Secretary of Defense, director of the Office of Defense Mobilization, and special assistant to the President for National Security Affairs. Eisenhower honored Gray with the Medal of Freedom. Gray was chairman of the board of Piedmont Publishing Company from 1961 to 1969 and of the Triangle Broadcasting Company from 1969 to 1975. At his death Gray was chairman of Summit Communications, Inc. Obituaries and other sources: *Current Biography,* Wilson, 1949, February, 1983; *Who's Who in America,* 41st edition, Marquis, 1980; *New York Times,* November 28, 1982.

* * *

GRAY, Linda Crockett 1943-
(Christina Crockett)

PERSONAL: Born July 20, 1943, in Hamilton, Ontario, Canada; daughter of E.C.D. and Christina M. Crockett; married Daniel S. Gray (a historian), November 27, 1968; children: Jaisen, Jaimee, Juli. *Education:* Florida State University, B.A., 1964, M.A., 1968. *Residence:* Tampa, Fla. *Agent:* Martha Millard, Martha Millard Literary Agency, 357 West 19th St., New York, N.Y. 10011.

CAREER: Junior high school English teacher in Florida, 1964-70; U.S. Army Warrant Officer Career College, Fort Rucker, Ala., instructor in English, 1971-80.

WRITINGS: Fortune's Fugitive (historical romance), Playboy Press, 1979; *Satyr* (occult novel), Playboy Press, 1981; *Siren* (occult novel), Playboy Press, 1982; (under pseudonym Christina Crockett) *Passion's Key* (contemporary romance), Harlequin, 1983.

SIDELIGHTS: Gray told *CA:* "My interest in history led to my first book, a historical romance. A background in Latin and classical literature contributed to the occult books. I have also done research on rape, incest, and sexual crimes and criminals linked with occult themes.

"I turned to writing novels while my children were young and needed to have me at home to care for and teach them. I tried contemporary romance as a relief from the grim aspects of the occult novels—to strike some type of balance.''

BIOGRAPHICAL/CRITICAL SOURCES: *Twilight Zone*, November, 1982.

*   *   *

GREENE, Leonard M(ichael)   1918-

PERSONAL: Born June 8, 1918, in New York, N.Y.; son of Max (a chemist) and Lyn (a poet and artist; maiden name, Furman) Greene; married Beverly Kaufman, June 27, 1943 (divorced, 1957); married Phyllis Saks, June 8, 1958 (died, 1965); married Joyce Teck (an interior designer), January 2, 1967; children: Randall, Bonnie (Mrs. John LeVar), Laurie (Mrs. Norman Baldwin), Douglas, Charles, Donald, Stephen, Terry, Jeffrey Meller, Gary Meller, William Meller, Amy Meller (Mrs. Thomas Gerbe). *Education:* City College (now of the City University of New York), B.S., 1937, M.S., 1939; attended New York University, 1940. *Home:* 275 North Bedford Rd., Chappaqua, N.Y. 10514. *Office:* Institute for Socioeconomic Studies, New King St., White Plains, N.Y. 10602.

CAREER: Rubber and Asbestos Corp., Bloomfield, N.J., research chemist, 1938-41; Grumman Aircraft Corp., Bethpage, N.Y., aerodynamicist, 1941-45; Safe Flight Instrument Corp., White Plains, N.Y., president, 1946—; Institute for Socioeconomic Studies, White Plains, president, 1974—. Director of Urban League of Westchester; director of Blythedale Children's Hospital, 1965-73. Member of Community Service Society of New York (member of income maintenance committee). *Member:* National Business Aircraft Association, National Aviation Society of Experimental Test Pilots, U.S. Chamber of Commerce, American Institute of Aeronautics and Astronautics, Flight Safety Foundation, Society of Experimental Test Pilots, Institute of the Aeronautical Sciences, New York Yacht Club, Edgartown Yacht Club.

AWARDS, HONORS: Air Safety awards from Flight Safety Foundation, 1949 and 1981; Pilot Safety award from Business Aircraft Association, 1961; President's Employer Merit Award from President's Committee on Employment of the Handicapped, 1966; Albert Gallatin Award from Zurich-American Insurance Companies, 1974, for business leadership in the social sphere in the northeastern states; distinguished service award from Human Rights Commission of White Plains, 1976; honorary doctorate from Pace University, 1977; Outstanding Employer Award from New York State Interagency Task Force for the Employment of the Handicapped, 1977; named prime contractor of the year by U.S. Small Business Administration, 1982; quality excellence award from U.S. Department of Defense, 1982.

WRITINGS: *A Plan for a National Demogrant Financed by a Value-Added Tax*, Institute for Socioeconomic Studies, 1976; *Free Enterprise Without Poverty*, Norton, 1981. Author of ''Comments,'' a column in the *Socioeconomic Newsletter*. Contributor to *New York Times* and *Christian Science Monitor*.

WORK IN PROGRESS: *The Incentive Society*, completion expected in 1984.

SIDELIGHTS: In his book *Free Enterprise Without Poverty* Greene proposes a graduated income supplement as a work incentive program to replace welfare benefits. According to *Los Angeles Times Book Review* writer John Patrick Driscoll, the idea ''closely parallels Friedman's negative income tax in the '60s and Nixon's Family Assistance Plan of the '70s. . . .

Nonetheless it does represent a choice.'' *Free Enterprise*, Driscoll continued, ''presents straightforward analysis and a solid solution for a complex problem—an impressive book.''

Greene told *CA:* ''Given that our free economy has produced the wealthiest society in the history of the world, my concern has been that a significant portion of that society has been left out. My study of poverty over the years has convinced me that much of it is caused by the government and the manner in which we have attempted to help the poor. *Free Enterprise Without Poverty* is an examination of how welfare programs actually harm the poor by robbing them of the incentive to improve their lives. Since assistance is granted on the basis of need, welfare recipients know that if productive work is tried, government aid will be abruptly cut off—often leaving the poor worker with less than he got from welfare.

''The solution I outline in *Free Enterprise Without Poverty* is the Graduated Income Supplement. This is a universal tax credit that would be given in cash to those with little or no income. Assistance would thereby be gradual and everyone would always be better off by working. It would provide for the basic needs of those unable to work, but would always give incentive for self-help.

''The lack of incentive in our society is a problem not only in human terms. The economy as a whole suffers each time a potentially productive worker is kept off payrolls by work disincentives built into welfare programs. This is a major cause of our lack of productivity and resulting inflation.

''My aim in the writing I have done and continue to do is to contribute to the understanding of these problems. Everyone seems to agree that there is a 'welfare mess' and that the economy is out of control, but our attention has been diverted from the fact that we have almost abandoned the principles that have made our country great. America works because its people have the incentive to do so. It is time we extended this opportunity to the poor who have been barred from participating for so long.''

BIOGRAPHICAL/CRITICAL SOURCES: *New York Times*, April 23, 1978; *Los Angeles Times Book Review*, September 6, 1981.

*   *   *

GREENFEDER, Paul   1925(?)-1983

OBITUARY NOTICE: Born c. 1925; died of heart disease, May 13, 1983, in Staten Island, N.Y. Librarian and editor. Greenfeder served for more than twenty years as chief of the *New York Times* reference library, considered to be the largest newspaper reference library in the United States. He also edited two books, *The Kennedy Years* and *The Road to the White House: The Story of the Election of 1964*. Obituaries and other sources: *New York Times*, May 16, 1983.

*   *   *

GREENFIELD, Harry I.   1922-

BRIEF ENTRY: American economist, educator, and author. Greenfield became a professor of economics at Queens College of the City University of New York in 1963. He wrote *Manpower and the Growth of Producer Services* (Columbia University Press, 1966), *Allied Health Manpower: Trends and Prospects* (Columbia University Press, 1969), *Hospital Efficiency and Public Policy* (Praeger, 1973), and *Accountability in Health Facilities* (Praeger, 1975). He edited *Theory for*

Economic Efficiency: Essays in Honor of Abba P. Lerner (M.I.T. Press, 1979). *Address:* Department of Economics, Queens College of the City University of New York, 65-30 Kissena Blvd., Flushing, N.Y. 11367.

* * *

GREENHOOD, (Clarence) David 1895-1983
(Mark Sawyer)

OBITUARY NOTICE—See index for *CA* sketch: Born August 12, 1895, in Buffalo, N.Y.; died March 26, 1983, in Santa Fe, N.M. Editor, publisher, and author. Greenhood began his career in 1922 as a writer for the *San Francisco Argonaut.* Several years later he founded Holiday House, a publishing firm for children's books, with his wife, Helen Gentry, Vernon Ives, and Theodore Johnson. He wrote *The Chronology of Books and Print* with Gentry, but was the sole author of several other works, including *Down to Earth: Mapping for Everybody* (later retitled *Mapping*), *The Writer on His Own,* and *The Hill.* He also wrote children's poems under the pseudonym Mark Sawyer. Obituaries and other sources: *Publishers Weekly,* May 20, 1983.

* * *

GREGG, William H. 1904(?)-1983

OBITUARY NOTICE: Born c. 1904; died May 20, 1983, in Miami, Fla. Publisher. In publishing for nearly fifty years, Gregg was associated with Oxford University Press from 1944 to 1972, when he retired. Obituaries and other sources: *Publishers Weekly,* July 1, 1983.

* * *

GREY, Beryl (Elizabeth) 1927-

PERSONAL: Born June 11, 1927, in London, England; daughter of Arthur Ernest and Annie Elizabeth (Marshall) Groom; married Sven Gustav Svenson (a physician), July 15, 1950; children: Ingvar Neil. *Education:* Attended private school in London, England. *Politics:* Conservative. *Religion:* Church of England. *Home and office:* Fernhill, Priory Rd., Forest Row, East Sussex, England. *Agent:* David Higham Associates Ltd., 5-8 Lower John St., Golden Sq., London W1R 4HA, England.

CAREER: Sadler's Wells Ballet (now Royal Ballet), London, England, prima ballerina, 1941-57; ballerina, 1957-66, performed with Bolshoi Ballet, 1958-59, London's Festival Ballet, 1958-64, and Peking and Shanghai ballet companies, 1964; director-general of arts educational schools for Teacher Training College, 1966-68; London's Festival Ballet, London, artistic director, 1968-79. Writer, 1958—. Performer in the film "The Black Swan," 1952. Director-general of Arts Educational Trust, 1966-68; vice-president of Royal Academy of Dancing; vice-patron of London's Festival Ballet; member of board of governors of London City Ballet Company; president of Dance Council for Wales, 1982; member of board of governors of Adeline Genee Theatre, 1983. *Member:* Imperial Society of Teachers of Dancing (member of council). *Awards, honors:* Commander of Order of the British Empire, 1971; D.Mus. from University of Leicester; D.Litt. from University of London.

WRITINGS: Red Curtain Up!, Secker & Warburg, 1958; *Through the Bamboo Curtain,* photographs by husband, Sven Svenson, Collins, 1965; (editor) *My Favourite Ballet Stories,* Lutterworth, 1981.

SIDELIGHTS: Beryl Grey told *CA:* "*Red Curtain Up!* covers my four-and-a-half weeks performing as the first Western ballerina and guest artist in Russia during 1957 and 1958, the greatest experience in my dancing career. *Through the Bamboo Curtain* traces a four-and-a-half week period in China in 1964 when I was the first Western ballerina to dance with the Peking Ballet and the Shanghai Ballet. It gives the impression of certain areas in China as seen through the eyes of a visiting Westerner.''

* * *

GRIDLEY, Roy E. 1935-

BRIEF ENTRY: Born March 24, 1935, in Ellsworth, Kan. American educator and author. Gridley began teaching at University of Kansas in 1964, becoming a professor of English in 1973. He wrote *Browning* (Routledge & Kegan Paul, 1972) and *The Brownings and France* (Athlone Press, 1982). *Address:* Department of English, University of Kansas, Lawrence, Kan. 66044. *Biographical/critical sources: Times Literary Supplement,* November 24, 1972.

* * *

GRIFFITH, Paul 1921-1983

OBITUARY NOTICE—See index for *CA* sketch: Born December 11, 1921, in Huntington, Pa.; died of a heart attack, April 23, 1983, in Lawrenceville, N.J. Novelist and editor. During the 1940's Griffith worked as a researcher and writer for *Life* magazine and as an instructor at the Writers' Workshop of the State University of Iowa. In 1950 he joined the staff of *Presbyterian Life* as an art editor, leaving in 1963 to become a photo editor with the Religious News Service. He was also the executive director of Fellowship in Prayer. His novels include *The Mare's Nest* and *My Stillness.* Obituaries and other sources: *New York Times,* April 27, 1983.

* * *

GRIFFITH, Samuel Blair II 1906-1983

OBITUARY NOTICE: Born May 31, 1906, in Lewistown, Pa.; died of respiratory arrest, March 27, 1983, in Newport, R.I. Military officer and author. Brigadier General Griffith fought in the Pacific in World War II and was heavily decorated for his service. An expert on Chinese military affairs, he served in China before and after the war, retiring from the Marines in 1956; he received a doctorate in Chinese military history from Oxford University in 1961. Griffith translated Mao Tse-tung's *On Guerilla War* and Sun Tzu's *The Art of War* and wrote *The Chinese People's Liberation Army, The Battle for Guadalcanal,* and *In Defense of the Public Liberty.* He frequently contributed to such periodicals as *Saturday Evening Post, New Yorker,* and *Town and Country.* Obituaries and other sources: *Who's Who in America,* 40th edition, Marquis, 1978; *New York Times,* April 7, 1983; *Washington Post,* April 7, 1983; *Newsweek,* April 18, 1983.

* * *

GRIMSHAW, James A(lbert), Jr. 1940-

PERSONAL: Born December 10, 1940, in Kingsville, Tex.; son of James A. and Maureen (Haley) Grimshaw; married Darlene Hargett, June 10, 1961; children: Courtney Anne, James A. IV. *Education:* Texas Tech University, B.A., 1962, M.A., 1968; Louisiana State University, Ph.D., 1972. *Home:*

6916 Cherrywood Dr., Colorado Springs, Colo. 80918. *Office:* Department of English, U.S. Air Force Academy, Colorado Springs, Colo. 80840.

CAREER: U.S. Air Force, career officer, 1963-83, associated with personnel services in Waco, Tex., Tan Son Nhut Air Force Base, South Vietnam, and Sacramento, Calif., 1963-68, U.S. Air Force Academy, Colorado Springs, Colo., instructor, 1968-69, assistant professor, 1972-74, associate professor, 1974-79, professor of English, 1980-83, retiring as lieutenant colonel; East Texas State University, Commerce, professor of literature and languages and department head, 1983—. Visiting lecturer at University of Colorado, 1972-73; Flannery O'Connor Visiting Professor of English at Georgia College, 1977; visiting fellow in bibliography at Beinecke Rare Book and Manuscript Library, Yale University, 1979-80; reader in English for Educational Testing Service, 1979—.

MEMBER: Association of Teachers of Technical Writing, Modern Language Association of America, National Council of Teachers of English, Society for the Study of Southern Literature, Rocky Mountain American Studies Association, Bibliographical Society of the University of Virginia. *Awards, honors*—Military: Bronze Star.

WRITINGS: (General editor) *The United States Air Force Academy's First Twenty-Five Years: Some Perceptions,* Dean of Faculty, U.S. Air Force Academy, 1979; (editor) *Cleanth Brooks at the United States Air Force Academy,* Department of English, U.S. Air Force Academy, 1980; *The Flannery O'Connor Companion,* Greenwood Press, 1981; *Robert Penn Warren: A Descriptive Bibliography, 1922-1979,* University Press of Virginia, 1982; (contributor) Donald Ahern and Robert Shenk, editors, *Literature in the Education of the Military Professional,* Department of English, U.S. Air Force Academy, 1983; (editor) *Robert Penn Warren's "Brother to Dragons": A Discussion,* Louisiana State University Press, 1983; (contributor) Matthew J. Bruccoli and C. E. Frazer Clark, editors, *The Concise First Printings of American Authors,* Gale, 1983.

Contributor to *Annual Bibliography of English Language and Literature,* 1974-82. Contributor of articles, poems, and reviews to magazines, including *Southern Review, Daedalus, Southern Literary Journal, Kentucky Review, Shakespeare Quarterly,* and *Explicator.* Founder and editor of *Icarus: A Magazine of Creativity,* 1969-82.

WORK IN PROGRESS: Persuasive Technical Writing, with William E. McCarron, publication by Prentice-Hall expected in 1985; biographical sketches of Flannery O'Connor and Robert Penn Warren, to be included in *Encyclopedia USA,* edited by Archie P. McDonald, publication by Academic International Press expected in 1985; poems.

SIDELIGHTS: Grimshaw told *CA:* "I write because I want to, I need to, I like to. Writing is a way of thinking, a way of clarifying and refining my ideas. As a teacher of writing, I cannot imagine not being actively involved in the writing process.

"My books and articles grow out of my interests and of perceived needs. For example, *The Flannery O'Connor Companion* is a basic introduction to her fiction. I designed it for seniors in high school and freshmen in college. No such introduction was available. Unfortunately, a few reviewers misread my purpose and the intended audience. The Warren bibliography again filled a void. I started out to write a critical study on Robert Penn Warren, and I soon discovered no adequate compilation of the material necessary for proper preparation of such

a study. Thirteen years later, I feel ready to begin that critical study. The interim product, however, is my descriptive bibliography. Warren remains, for me, one of the most versatile and interesting authors writing today.

"In my involvement with writing, I've discovered that almost all writing is persuasive. The word 'persuasion' has been avoided in technical writing until recently. Bill McCarron and I show how persuasion plays an integral role in technical communication. The market is just about ready to accept our approach.

"Finally, writing is about life. It is making ideas available to others. I have two more reference books, two articles, a novel, a short story, and some poems in progress now. My wife laughingly says, 'When St. Peter calls, you'll reply, "Just six months more. I still have some projects to finish."' That's the way I'd want it."

*   *   *

GROSECLOSE, Elgin E.   1899-1983

OBITUARY NOTICE—See index for *CA* sketch: Born November 25, 1899, in Waukomis, Okla.; died after a stroke, April 4, 1983, in Washington, D.C. Economic and investment consultant and author. During his long career Groseclose was affiliated with the U.S. Commerce Department, Guaranty Trust Company, *Fortune* magazine, the Federal Communications Commission (FCC), and the U.S. Treasury Department. He taught at the University of Oklahoma and served as an adviser to the Iranian Government. In 1943 he was appointed treasurer-general by the Iranian Parliament. He founded the financial and investment consulting firm of Groseclose, Williams & Associates in 1959. Later he organized and served as the executive director of the Institute for Monetary Research. Groseclose performed refugee work in the Soviet Caucasus during the 1920's, which served as the basis of his novel *Ararat,* winner of the 1939 National Book Award and the Foundation for Literature Award. Groseclose was the president of the Washington Bible Society and of Welfare of the Blind, Inc., which he established in 1956. His books include *Comanche Country, Money: The Human Conflict, The Persian Journey of the Reverend Ashley Wishard and His Servant Fathi,* and *The Scimitar of Saladin.* Obituaries and other sources: *New York Times,* April 7, 1983; *Washington Post,* April 8, 1983.

*   *   *

GROSVENOR, Donna K(erkam)   1938-

PERSONAL: Born July 16, 1938, in Washington, D.C.; daughter of John Freeman and Eleanor (Beck) Kerkam; married Gilbert Melville Grosvenor (a writer), June 16, 1961; children: Gilbert Hovey, Alexandra Rowland. *Education:* Sweet Briar College, B.A., 1960. *Home:* 1259 Crest Lane, McLean, Va. 22101.

CAREER: Photojournalist and author of children's books. *National Geographic* and *National Geographic Scholastic Bulletin,* Washington, D.C., photojournalist in Egypt, East Africa, Ceylon, Monaco, Indonesia, and Washington, D.C., 1961—. Member of board of Child Health Center of Children's Hospital, 1965—; member of executive committee of Project Hope, 1967-68; member of board of Friends of the National Zoo, 1968—; member of governing board of National Cathedral School, 1972—. *Member:* Society of Woman Geographers, Junior League of Washington, D.C. (secretary, 1966-67), Sulgrave Club (Washington, D.C.).

WRITINGS—All for young people: *Pandas* (self-illustrated with photographs), National Geographic Society, 1973; *The Wild Ponies of Assateague Island* (illustrated with photographs by James L. Stanfield), National Geographic Society, 1975; *The Blue Whale* (illustrated by Larry Foster), National Geographic Society, 1977; *Zoo Babies* (self-illustrated with photographs), National Geographic Society, 1978.

Illustrator: Linda Bridge, *Cats: Little Tigers in Your House* (illustrated with photographs), National Geographic Society, 1974.

* * *

GRUENTHER, Alfred M(aximilian) 1899-1983

OBITUARY NOTICE: Born March 3, 1899, in Platte Center, Neb.; died of pneumonia, May 30, 1983, in Washington, D.C. Military officer, educator, bridge expert, and author. Nicknamed ''the Brain'' by colleagues, Gruenther was respected worldwide for his extraordinary analytical and strategic skills as a staff officer and soldier-diplomat. Gruenther's career of nearly forty years in the U.S. Army reached a pinnacle in 1951, when he was named chief of staff at North Atlantic Treaty Organization (NATO) headquarters and became, at fifty-three years of age, the youngest four-star general in Army history. Two years later he was promoted to commander of Supreme Headquarters Allied Powers, Europe (SHAPE). This triumph capped years of varied service. Gruenther's military posts prior to World War II included eight years of instructing in mathematics, electricity, and chemistry at West Point, the U.S. Military Academy. For part of World War II he served as deputy chief of staff of Allied Force Headquarters in London under General Dwight Eisenhower. Gruenther later served General Mark Clark as chief of staff of the Fifth Army and Fifteenth Army in the Mediterranean theater and was responsible for planning the invasions of North Africa, Salerno, and Sicily. Following his 1956 retirement as commander of SHAPE, he became president of the American Red Cross. He was also known internationally as a bridge player, tournament director, and referee. He wrote *The Referee's Analysis of the Decisive Hands of the Lenz-Culbertson Match* and *Duplicate Contract Complete*. Obituaries and other sources: *Who's Who in Government*, Marquis, 1972; *New York Times*, May 31, 1983; *Washington Post*, May 31, 1983; *Chicago Tribune*, June 1, 1983; *Los Angeles Times*, June 1, 1983; *London Times*, June 1, 1983; *Newsweek*, June 13, 1983; *Time*, June 13, 1983.

* * *

GRUNDY, Joan 1920-

PERSONAL: Born August 17, 1920, in Ulverston, England; daughter of Alfred (an insurance agent) and Margaret Jane (a school teacher; maiden name, Ireland) Grundy. *Education:* Bedford College, London, B.A. (with honors), 1943, M.A., 1947. *Home:* Rose Cottage, Lamb Park, Rosside, Ulverston, Cumbria LA12 7NR, England.

CAREER: University of Edinburgh, Edinburgh, Scotland, assistant lecturer in English, 1947-50; University of Liverpool, Liverpool, England, lecturer in English, 1950-65; University of London, Royal Holloway College, Egham, England, reader, 1965-79, professor of English literature, 1979-80, emeritus professor, 1980—. Member of board of trustees of Dove College, 1980—. *Member:* Thomas Hardy Society, Association of University Teachers.

WRITINGS: The Poems of Henry Constable, Liverpool University Press, 1960; *The Spensarian Poets*, Edward Arnold, 1969; *Hardy and the Sister Arts*, Macmillan, 1979. Contributor to *Encyclopaedia Britannica*. Also contributor of articles and reviews to periodicals, including *Review of English Studies*, *Modern Language Review*, *English*, *Essays in Criticism*, *Notes and Queries*, and *Shakespeare Survey*.

WORK IN PROGRESS: Research for a book on Wordsworth; a book, *Voices on the Green*, based on the author's childhood.

SIDELIGHTS: Joan Grundy's *Hardy and the Sister Arts* shows a synthesis of art forms in the works of Thomas Hardy. Portraying the famous writer as an impressionist, the author relates Hardy's knowledge of painting, drama, opera, and other art forms to his literary endeavors. Grundy ''offers a commentary on one aspect of Hardy's art which will enhance and enrich a 'normal' reading of the texts,'' David Lodge remarked in the *Tablet*. ''This is a cultured, articulate and pleasingly unpretentious book, based on deep familiarity with Hardy and impressively wide knowledge of the 'sister arts.' ''

Grundy told *CA:* ''After over thirty years of university teaching I am now in my third year of retirement, but my interest in literature has not diminished. The purpose of criticism, as I see it, is not to judge and censure but to deepen understanding and thereby increase the reader's enjoyment of the work criticized.

''I am passionately attached to the Lake District, where I was born and have now returned. I am also attached to animal rights and to other humanitarian causes.''

AVOCATIONAL INTERESTS: Music, cinema, the relationships between the arts and between different literatures.

BIOGRAPHICAL/CRITICAL SOURCES: Choice, September, 1970, November, 1979; *Tablet*, June 9, 1979; *Times Literary Supplement*, February 1, 1980.

* * *

GUARDIA, Ernesto de la, Jr.
See de la GUARDIA, Ernesto, Jr.

* * *

GUINEE, Kathleen K. 1902(?)-1982

OBITUARY NOTICE: Born c. 1902 in Burgess, Ontario, Canada; died of cancer, December 25, 1982, in New York, N.Y. Nurse, educator, and author. Guinee was professor emeritus of nursing at Hunter College, teaching there from 1950 until her retirement in 1972. She wrote several books on nursing, including *The Professional Nurse: Orientation, Roles, and Responsibilities*. Obituaries and other sources: *New York Times*, December 27, 1982; *Chronicle of Higher Education*, January 5, 1983.

* * *

GULA, Richard M(ichael) 1947-

PERSONAL: Born April 11, 1947, in Sharpsville, Pa.; son of Mike (a steelworker) and Theresa (Conti) Gula. *Education:* St. Mary's Seminary College, B.A., 1969; St. Mary's School of Theology, S.T.M., 1973, S.T.L., 1982; University of Toronto, Ph.D., 1978. *Home:* 320 Middlefield Rd., Menlo Park, Calif. 94025. *Office:* Department of Moral Theology, St. Patrick's Seminary, 320 Middlefield Rd., Menlo Park, Calif. 94025.

CAREER: Ordained Roman Catholic priest, 1973; entered Society of St. Sulpice (Sulpicians; S.S.), 1976; St. Patrick's Seminary, Menlo Park, Calif., associated with department of moral theology, 1978—. *Member:* American Society of Christian Ethics, College Theology Society, Society for Health and Human Values, Catholic Theological Society of America.

WRITINGS: What Are They Saying About Moral Norms?, Paulist Press, 1982; *To Walk Together Again: The Sacrament of Reconciliation,* Paulist Press, in press; (contributor) Clarence Rowe and Richard Sipe, editors, *Sanity, Sex, and Pastoral Care,* St. John's University Press, in press; (contributor) James Morgan, editor, *Christian Initiation Resources,* Sadlier, in press. Contributor to theology journals.

WORK IN PROGRESS: An essay, "Spiritual Direction in the RCIA," for *Christian Initiation Resources.*

SIDELIGHTS: Gula told *CA:* "My writing thus far has been oriented to pastoral use. I have tried to bring the concerns and discussions of contemporary theologians to a wider audience in order to provide resources for clergy and adult education. My work on moral norms has integrated into a survey the work of several leading moral theologians who have contributed to the discussion of moral norms. It shows the inseparable connection of our understanding of moral norms with other serious moral concerns, such as the range of interest of moral theology, the use of Scripture and natural law in moral theology, the relation of moral norms to magisterial teaching, and the use of moral norms in pastoral guidance.

"My work on the sacrament of reconciliation provides a resource book for adult and clergy education on this sacrament. It integrates the themes of systematic, liturgical, historical, moral, and spiritual theology which pertain to the implementation of the new rite of penance. The book is written for inquiring adults who wish to have adult conversations on the meaning and place of reconciliation in one's spiritual life. I hope these books, as well as the essays I have written in journals and other books, will serve the purpose of informing interested adults about the developments that are occurring in contemporary theology."

*   *   *

GUTIERREZ, Donald   1932-

PERSONAL: Born March 10, 1932, in Alameda, Calif.; son of J. Salvador and Alice (Ruiz y Chamorro) Gutierrez; married Marlene Zander (an artist), 1957; children: Hector, Trajan. *Education:* University of California, Berkeley, B.A., 1956, M.L.S., 1958; University of California, Los Angeles, M.A., 1966, Ph.D., 1969. *Home:* 2404 Swarthmore Dr., Silver City, N.M. 88061. *Office:* Department of English, Western New Mexico University, Silver City, N.M. 88061.

CAREER: Metropolitan Museum of Art, New York City, librarian, 1958-60; Tamiment Institute Library (now New York University Social Sciences Library), New York City, librarian, 1960-61; Grosset & Dunlap (publisher), New York City, editorial assistant and research librarian, 1961-63; University of Notre Dame, Notre Dame, Ind., assistant professor of English, 1968-75; Western New Mexico University, Silver City, assistant professor, 1975-80, associate professor of English, 1980—. Member of Silver City Peace Study Group, 1982-83. *Member:* D. H. Lawrence Society of America (member of executive committee, 1982), Rocky Mountain Modern Language Association.

WRITINGS: Lapsing Out: Embodiments of Death and Rebirth in the Last Works of D. H. Lawrence, Fairleigh Dickinson University Press, 1980; *The Maze in the Mind and the World: Labyrinths in Modern Literature,* Whitston Publishing, in press. Contributor of about forty articles and reviews to literature journals and literary magazines, including *Studies in Short Fiction, D. H. Lawrence Review, Mosaic, Literary Review, Texas Quarterly,* and *Malahat Review.*

WORK IN PROGRESS: Paradise Regained: Subject-Object Relations in William Wordsworth and D. H. Lawrence; a book "on the idea of the self in twentieth-century fiction," completion expected in 1985; research on D. H. Lawrence, Kenneth Rexroth, Richard Eberhart, James Joyce, Dostoevski, Celine, Diane Johnson, and Ralph Ellison.

SIDELIGHTS: Gutierrez told *CA:* "I believe that literary criticism and scholarship are basically modes for the exploration of ideas. This attitude, of course, forces one to consider the possibility that in criticizing a work of literature one is reading in one's own ideas or conceptions of life. But this is not necessarily a bad thing. Although critics are sometimes seen as parasites (or worse) by artists (except when the criticism pleases the artist!), critics can do and have done valuable work in bringing a wider audience to important new art and artists, in using the works of significant artists to develop a community of thought and values, or, most important, in representing and interpreting works of literature and art as examples of humane values in an era like ours that threatens to dehumanize and even destroy all societies and all life. Thus, I see the role of the academic and nonacademic critic and scholar as extremely valuable in keeping the spark of civilized life—and the drive of life itself—going through making as many people as possible aware of and dedicated to what it means to be alive in the most perilous age in human history.

"I also like the idea of literary scholars bridging the gulf between academic and popular interests in art, something easy to forget about in the routines and demands of academe. I like to write about authors who, though important, have either been ignored or underrated, or to focus on valuable but neglected areas of their work (such as the verse of D. H. Lawrence, for which I have collected a casebook of critical essays, or the poetry of Kenneth Rexroth and Richard Eberhart, whose works are still seriously unappreciated, though both men are major American poets). I believe in literary criticism and scholarship with a lively, tendentious (though not propagandistic) edge, and believe as well in directing literary criticism in ways that dramatize and preserve such values as autonomy, uniqueness, and human development for as many people as possible, as well as in decentering political and economic institutions and power.

"This last belief in part explains why my fifth and present book is concerned with the concept of the self in the modern novel. The self (and the family) is the concept and entity most threatened by the big social and political power structures of the twentieth century, whether the Soviet Union's political or America's commercial totalitarianism. Thus anything that can be done to exemplify and preserve great or memorable images of the tragic or threatened or noble self in modern literature seems to me much worth undertaking. In this study of the self, I start, after an introduction concerned with the philosophical problems of the concept of the self, with analyses of works by Dostoevski, go on to Hardy, Lawrence, and James, deal with Celine and Ralph Ellison, and will possibly conclude with one or two impressive contemporary women, novelists like Diane Johnson and Shirley Hazzard.

"Any artist worth his or her salt is virtually a philosophical anarchist, and that, I think, is true of literary critics and scholars too."

* * *

GWIN, Lucy 1943-

PERSONAL: Born January 5, 1943, in Beech Grove, Ind.; daughter of Robert Willard Gwin (a gambler and promoter) and Verna Bodine Gilcher (a teacher and artist); married Robert Keller, July, 1960 (divorced); married Philip Douglas, August, 1964 (deceased); married John Francis Foley (an auto worker), April, 1983; children: Tracy Keller Cremer, Christine Keller. *Education:* Attended public schools. *Politics:* "Leftie." *Religion:* Zen Buddhist. *Home:* 61 Brighton St., Rochester, N.Y. 14607. *Agent:* Rhoda Schlamm, 59-55 47th Ave., Woodside, N.Y. 10137.

CAREER: Worked as a busgirl, receptionist, envelope stuffer, legal secretary, advertising copywriter, creative supervisor and vice-president for Tatham-Laird & Kudner Advertising, Chicago, Ill., restaurant owner, seaman, ditchdigger, laborer, and truck driver, all beginning in 1958; writer, 1980-81; housecleaner, junior college instructor, and free-lance journalist, 1981—. Member of Rochester Area Unemployment Council; volunteer worker. *Member:* National Organization for Women, Lonely at the Top Club.

WRITINGS: Going Overboard, Viking Press, 1982. Contributor to periodicals, including *New Women's Times* and *Rochester Patriot.*

WORK IN PROGRESS: Bones, a novel; a history of the current unemployment situation (1981—), tentatively titled *Not Working,* completion expected "when the movement subsides."

SIDELIGHTS: In *Going Overboard,* Lucy Gwin tells the story of her year in an oil boom town, Morgan City, Louisiana. Hoping to live, work, and compete in this offshore oil frontier, "the author realizes she is confronting a far more difficult barrier—the frontier of sex roles," Grace Lichtenstein noted in the *Washington Post Book World.* The more competent Gwin becomes at her rig deckhand duties, the less acceptable she is to the all-male society of "rigrats." The author is compelled, before the year is over, to file charges of sexual harassment against her fellow workers.

Los Angeles Times reviewer Carolyn See called *Going Overboard* a "swell book" and found Gwin's writing style "straight-arrow." Yet the critic could not accept the author's total and repeated incredulity at her mistreatment by the oil workers; "they knew when you carried your typewriter on board that you didn't have their best interest at heart," See reproved. "You sneered at them, Lucy, even as you recorded their language and their personalities with a genius-ear. . . . The reader watches with helpless sadness the situation worsen between smart, obnoxious Lucy and those dumb, obnoxious guys." Lichtenstein, however, had no sympathy whatsoever for the coastal brotherhood and its "Testosterone Culture." "There is not a single hero in the book," the critic asserted, "but there certainly is a heroine. Lucy Gwin, as sassy and sure-handed at the typewriter as she is on deck, offers us a self-portrait of one helluva gutsy pioneer woman on a dangerous final frontier. 'Going Overboard,' in less capable hands, could have been a feminist tract. Instead, it is an unforgettable Southern horror story that calls to mind James Dickey's 'Deliverance,' and it's just as scary."

Gwin told *CA:* "Look, I don't think I'm going to be a regular writer, ever. Locking myself in a room for protracted periods just doesn't appeal. I wrote the first draft of *Overboard* in three weeks, spent two- and three-week slices of time rewriting it, can only write when I'm obsessed, angry, and amused. My metabolism can't take too much of that. I like to be smack in the middle of things, half-crazy, all-new things. When I center myself again afterward, sometimes writing is part of that centering. Oh, what bullshit: writers writing about themselves, particularly their motivations. Nabokov, you'll notice, never even attempted it.

"Just about the only good thing that came out of my getting *Overboard* published was a letter I got from a reader, a carpenter in Columbia, South Carolina. He got it the way I wrote it, the way I meant it. A miracle. My husband hasn't read it at all, and that's just as well."

BIOGRAPHICAL/CRITICAL SOURCES: Washington Post Book World, June 21, 1982; *Los Angeles Times,* July 6, 1982.

H

HAAFTEN, Julia Van
  See VAN HAAFTEN, Julia

*   *   *

HABERMAS, Juergen   1929-

PERSONAL: Born June 18, 1929, in Duesseldorf, Germany (now West Germany); son of Ernst and Grete (Koettgen) Habermas; married Ute Wesselhoeft (a teacher) in 1955; children: Tilmann, Rebekka, Judith. *Education:* Attended University of Goettingen and University of Zurich; University of Bonn, Ph.D., 1954. *Home:* Ringstrasse 8, 8130 Starnberg, West Germany. *Office:* Leopoldstrasse 24, 8000 Munich, West Germany.

CAREER: Habilitated at University of Marburg, Marburg, West Germany, 1961; University of Heidelberg, Heidelberg, West Germany, professor of philosophy, 1961-64; University of Frankfort on the Main, Frankfort on the Main, West Germany, professor of philosophy, 1964-71, adjunct professor, 1974—. Max-Planck-Institut zur Erforschung der Lebensbedingungen der Wissenschaftlichtechnischen Welt, Starnberg, West Germany, director, 1971-81; Max-Planck-Institut fur Sozialwissenschaften, Wissenschaftl Mitshid, Starnberg, director, 1981—. *Awards, honors:* Hegel-Preis for outstanding contribution to the advancement of human sciences from city of Stuttgart, West Germany, 1973; Sigmund-Freud-Preis for contribution to German scholarly prose from German Academy for Language and Poetry, 1976; Adoruo-Preis from city of Frankfort on the Main, 1980.

WRITINGS—All nonfiction; in English translation: *Theorie und Praxis: Sozialphilosophische Studien,* Luchterhand, 1963, revised edition, Suhrkamp, 1971, translation by John Viertel published as *Theory and Practice,* Beacon Press, 1973; *Erkenntnis und Interesse,* Suhrkamp, 1968, translation by Jeremy J. Shapiro published as *Knowledge and Human Interests,* Beacon Press, 1971; *Toward a Rational Society: Student Protest, Science, and Politics* (contains three essays from *Protestbewegung und Hochschulreform* [also see below] and three essays from *Technik und Wissenschaft als "Ideologie"* [also see below]), translation by Shapiro, Beacon Press, 1971; *Legitimationsprobleme im Spaetkapitalismus,* Suhrkamp, 1973, translation by Thomas McCarthy published as *Legitimation Crisis,* Beacon Press, 1975; *Communication and the Evolution*

of Society, introduction and translation by McCarthy, Beacon Press, 1979.

In German: *Student und Politik: Eine soziologische Untersuchung zum politischen Bewusstsein Frankfurter Studenten,* edited by Frank Benseler, Luchterhand, 1961; *Strukturwandel der Oeffentlichkeit,* Luchterhand, 1962; *Zur Logik der Sozialwissenschaften,* J.C.B. Mohr, 1967, enlarged edition, Suhrkamp, 1970; *Technik und Wissenschaft als "Ideologie"* (essays), Suhrkamp, 1968; *Protestbewegung und Hochschulreform* (essays), Suhrkamp, 1969; (contributor) Guenter Rohrmoser, editor, *Das Elend der kritischen Theorie,* Rombach, 1970; (with Niklas Lumann) *Theorie der Gessellschaft oder Sozialtechnologie,* Suhrkamp, 1971; *Philosophisch-politische Profile,* Suhrkamp, 1971; *Zur Rekonstruktion des historischen Materialismus,* Suhrkamp, 1976; *Politik, Kunst, Religion: Essays ueber zeitgenoess,* Redam, 1978; (contributor) *Das Erbe Hegels,* Suhrkamp, 1979.

Editor: *Antworten auf Herbert Marcuse* (essays), Suhrkamp, 1968; Friedrich Wilhelm Nietzsche, *Erkenntnistheoretische Schriften,* Suhrkamp, 1968; *Kultur and Kritik: Verstreute Aufsaetze* (addresses, essays, and lectures), Suhrkamp, 1973; (with Rainer Doebert and Gertrud Nunner-Winkler) *Entwicklung des Ichs* (articles), Kiepenheur & Witsch, 1977; *Stichworte zur geistigen Situation der Zeit* (addresses, essays, lectures), Suhrkamp, 1979.

SIDELIGHTS: One of Germany's best-known contemporary social theorists, "Habermas owes his great eminence to his efforts to reestablish German philosophy's lost connection to social practice and to put it on a durable . . . basis," wrote Michael Rosen in the *Times Literary Supplement.* And, said *Christian Century*'s Philip G. Altbach, "his writings have had a major impact on German liberal and radical thought and on the development of the student movement [of the 1960's] as well."

An advocate of Immanuel Kant's thesis that knowledge cannot be explicated with total objectivity because of the subjective conditions under which it is studied, Habermas rejects the positivist theory that all learning can be objectively verified by the empirical sciences; he asserts, reported Donald Capps in *Christian Century,* "that a radical critique of knowledge is possible only as social theory." During the early stages of the student movement," observed Bertram Schefold in *Cambridge*

Review, "his arguments against positivism provided an ideological weapon in the struggle for a democratic university reform."

According to Altbach, Habermas is concerned that higher education has become the servant of industrial capitalism and no longer contributes effectively to the growth of science. "Habermas feels," contended Altbach, "that the only way to deal with this situation is to democratize the university so that its own participants—notably the students and junior faculty—can bring pressure to bear against this technological role and can press for the involvement of the universities in criticism of the society."

Theory and Practice, Habermas's first major work, explains how theory is related to action and how the subject was approached in the past. His *Knowledge and Human Interests,* which Capps described as "an illumination . . . of the philosophical poverty of contemporary scientific theory," serves as an introduction to Habermas's subsequent work *Toward a Rational Society,* an account of the author's ideas about social change. Several critics praised the book's usefulness in helping readers to understand the role of higher education in society. Altbach agreed that the book "is a stimulating and important work," but pointed out that Habermas's "use of sociological and philosophical jargon sometimes makes this volume almost incomprehensible." Nevertheless, summarized James J. Conlin in *Best Sellers,* "it is a work to reread with profit for, although it lacks over-all unity and misses its aim of a sketch of society, this small book contains thought-provoking ideas about society and man's condition in it."

BIOGRAPHICAL/CRITICAL SOURCES: Best Sellers, November 15, 1970; *Christian Century,* November 25, 1970, September 29, 1971; *Cambridge Review,* May 7, 1971; *America,* October 16, 1971; *Contemporary Sociology,* July, 1974; Thomas A. McCarthy, *The Critical Theory of Juergen Habermas,* MIT Press, 1978; *Times Literary Supplement,* November 28, 1980; *Contemporary Issues Criticism,* volume 1, Gale, 1982.

*　　*　　*

HABERMAS, Jurgen
See HABERMAS, Juergen

*　　*　　*

HAGERTY, Sheward   1930-1983

OBITUARY NOTICE: Born in 1930; died of a heart attack, February 27, 1983, in Wilton, Conn. Editor. Hagerty joined the staff of *Newsweek* magazine in 1956, and from 1962 he served as chief of *Newsweek*'s London bureau. In 1970 he became features editor for the *New York Daily News,* returning to *Newsweek* in 1977. At his death he was a senior editor, in charge of the medicine, sports, newsmakers, periscope, letters, update, and transition sections of the magazine. Obituaries and other sources: *Chicago Tribune,* March 1, 1983; *New York Times,* March 1, 1983; *Washington Post,* March 2, 1983; *Newsweek,* March 14, 1983.

*　　*　　*

HAGGARD, Raymond (Gordon Rider)   1921-

BRIEF ENTRY: Born March 14, 1921, in Wolverhampton, Staffordshire, England. British town planning consultant and author. Trained in civil engineering, Haggard has been a town

planning consultant since 1945. He is also the author of a suspense novel, *Miss Ivory White* (Collins, 1970). *Address:* 6 Stanley Park Rd., Wallington, Surrey, England. *Biographical/critical sources: Spectator,* June 6, 1970; *Observer,* June 7, 1970; *Times Literary Supplement,* June 11, 1970.

*　　*　　*

HAGLUND, Elaine J(ean)   1937-

PERSONAL: Born April 1, 1937, in Los Angeles, Calif.; daughter of Vernon U. (a draftsman) and Lucile (Russell) Haglund. *Education:* University of California, Los Angeles, B.A., 1958; Michigan State University, M.A., 1969, Ph.D., 1972. *Home:* 1111 South Coast Dr., No. J-101, Costa Mesa, Calif. 92626. *Office:* Department of Educational Psychology, California State University, 1250 Bellflower Blvd., Long Beach, Calif. 90840.

CAREER: Elementary school teacher in Berkeley, Calif., 1958-60, Germany, 1960-66, Japan, 1966-68, Palos Verdes, Calif., 1968-69; California State University, Long Beach, assistant professor, 1972-76, associate professor, 1976-81, professor of educational psychology, 1981—, director of Educational Psychology Clinic, 1975—, academic supervisor of study abroad programs, 1981. Fulbright-Hays lecturer at University of Calabar, 1978-80. Visiting professor at Hangzou University, People's Republic of China, 1982-83. *Member:* World Council for Curriculum and Instruction, American Psychological Association, American Personnel and Guidance Association, American Anthropological Association, American Educational Research Association, Association for Supervision and Curriculum Development, Council for Exceptional Children, Phi Delta Kappa.

WRITINGS: A Resource Guide for Mainstreaming, C. C Thomas, 1980; (with Marcia Harris) *On This Day: A Collection of Everyday Learning Events and Activities for the Media Center, Library, and Classroom,* Libraries Unlimited, 1983. Contributor to education journals.

WORK IN PROGRESS: Research on higher education in the People's Republic of China, cross-cultural child development and institutionalized schooling, moral education in Nigeria, writing as a process of counseling, brain activity related to teaching and learning processes, international human resource development, developing support for international students, and the merits of studying abroad.

SIDELIGHTS: Elaine J. Haglund told *CA:* "I am interested not only in how people learn (retrieve information), but also how people process information and express themselves. Why is it that people who appear to be effective writers do not choose to write or even to correspond in letters? Perhaps the act itself—that of putting pen to paper—is not the medium for some people to express their ideas. I would like to explore simple ways that would encourage students to convey their thoughts and feelings, such as talking into a tape recorder or a voice-sensitive computer and then having the ideas transferred to paper by a typewriter or a printer. I am particularly impressed with the success that teachers are currently having through their training in The Writing Project—the nationwide institutes that are exploring numerous ways to motivate students to write."

*　　*　　*

HAIMSON, Leopold H.   1917-

BRIEF ENTRY: Born April 28, 1917, in Brussels, Belgium.

American historian, educator, and author. Haimson has taught at Harvard University and University of Chicago, and he has conducted research at the American Museum of Natural History and Princeton University. A professor of Russian history at Columbia University since 1966, Haimson wrote *The Russian Marxists and the Origins of Bolshevism* (Harvard University Press, 1955). He also edited *The Mensheviks: From the Revolution of 1917 to the Second World War* (University of Chicago Press, 1974) and *The Politics of Rural Russia, 1905-1914* (Indiana University Press, 1979). *Address:* Department of History, Columbia University, Broadway and West 116th, New York, N.Y. 10027. *Biographical/critical sources: American Historical Review,* October, 1976, April, 1980; *Virginia Quarterly Review,* winter, 1980.

* * *

HAINWORTH, Henry Charles 1914-

PERSONAL: Born September 12, 1914, in Tampico, Mexico; son of Charles Samuel and Emily (Laycock) Hainworth; married Mary Ady; children: Victoria, Daphne. *Education:* Attended Cambridge University. *Office:* c/o Barclay's Bank Ltd., 50 Jewry St., Winchester, Hampshire, England.

CAREER: United Kingdom Consular Service, London, England, served in Tokyo, Japan, 1939-42, affiliated with Ministry of Information in New Delhi, India, 1942-46, served in Tokyo, 1946-51, at Foreign Office in London, 1951-53, in Bucharest, Romania, 1953-55, at Political Office of Middle East Forces in Nicosia, Cyprus, 1956, and at Foreign Office, 1957; head of atomic energy and disarmament department at Foreign Office, 1958-61, counselor of United Kingdom delegation to the Brussels Conference, 1961-63, minister and consul-general in Vienna, Austria, 1963-68, ambassador to Indonesia, 1968-70, ambassador and permanent United Kingdom delegate to Disarmament Conference, 1970-74. *Awards, honors:* Companion of Order of St. Michael and St. George.

WRITINGS: A Collector's Dictionary, Routledge & Kegan Paul, 1981.

* * *

HALEY, Michael 1952-

PERSONAL: Born May 21, 1952, in Dodge City, Kan.; son of Kenneth Lee (a farmer) and Verla (a secretary; maiden name, Carlin) Haley. *Education:* Attended Dodge City Community Junior College, 1970-71, and Emporia State College, 1971-73; Kansas State University, B.A., 1974. *Home:* 95 Christopher St., New York, N.Y. 10014. *Agent:* John Boswell, 45 East 51st St., New York, N.Y. 10022.

CAREER: Continental Theatre Company (touring repertory company), Wichita, Kan., actor, 1974-76; writer.

WRITINGS: The Alfred Hitchcock Album, Prentice-Hall, 1981. Contributing editor of *Delta Airlines.*

WORK IN PROGRESS: "Lost Wax," a play.

* * *

HALL, Noel (Frederick) 1902-1983

OBITUARY NOTICE: Born December 23, 1902; died March 28, 1983, in Crete, Greece. Economist, educator, and author. He taught political economics at the University of London from 1927 to 1938. During World War II he served variously as

Britain's joint director of the Ministry of Economic Warfare, minister in charge of the War Trade Department in Washington, D.C., and development adviser in West Africa. In 1946 he became principal of the Administrative Staff College at Henley, an institution formed to educate business executives in management skills. Hall left his position there in 1961 for the post of principal of Brasenose College, Oxford, retiring in 1973. Knighted in 1957, he held the directorship at many companies, advised the British Government on the establishment of business schools, and was a member of the University of Lancaster Council. Among Hall's writings are *The Making of Higher Executives* and *The Modern Challenge.* Obituaries and other sources: *Who's Who,* 126th edition, St. Martin's, 1974; *The International Who's Who,* 44th edition, Europa, 1980; *London Times,* April 2, 1983.

* * *

HALL, Robert Burnett, Jr. 1923-

BRIEF ENTRY: Born December 4, 1923, in Ann Arbor, Mich. American geographer, educator, and author. Hall began teaching at University of Rochester in 1952 and has been a professor of history and geography there since 1965. He has also served as director of both the university's East Asia and South Asia centers, and he has been a Fulbright lecturer in Japan. Hall wrote *Japan* (Doubleday, 1956) and *Japan: Industrial Power of Asia* (Van Nostrand, 1963). *Address:* East Asia Language and Area Center, University of Rochester, Rochester, N.Y. 14627.

* * *

HALL, Rodney 1935-

PERSONAL: Born November 18, 1935, in Solihull, Warwickshire, England; married Maureen Elizabeth MacPhail; children: Imogen, Delia, Cressida. *Education:* University of Queensland, B.A., 1971. *Address:* c/o University of Queensland Press, St. Lucia, Queensland, Australia.

CAREER: Free-lance scriptwriter and actor, 1957-67; American Broadcasting Commission, Brisbane, Australia, film critic, 1966-67; *Australian* (daily newspaper), Sydney, Australia, poetry editor, 1967—. Tutor at New England University School of Music, Armidale, South Wales, summers, 1967 and 1971. Australian Department of Foreign Affairs, lecturer in India, 1970, and in Malaysia, 1972. Youth officer for Australian Council for the Arts, 1971-73. *Awards, honors:* Fellow of Australian National University, 1968, Commonwealth Literary Fund, 1970, and Literature Board, 1973.

WRITINGS: Penniless Till Doomsday (poems), Outposts Publications, 1962; (with David Malouf, Don Maynard, and Judith Green) *Four Poets* (poems), F. W. Cheshire (Melbourne, Australia), 1962; *Forty Beads on a Hangman's Rope: Fragments of Memory* (poems), Wattle Grove Press (Newnham, Tasmania), 1963; (with Shirley Andrews) *Social Services and the Aborigines,* Federal Council for Aboriginal Advancement, 1963; *Eyewitness* (poems), South Head Press (Sydney, Australia), 1967; *The Autobiography of a Gorgon and Other Poems,* F. W. Cheshire, 1968; *The Law of Karma: A Progression of Poems,* Australian National University Press, 1968; *Focus on Andrew Sibley,* University of Queensland Press, 1968; (editor with Thomas W. Shapcott) *New Impulses in Australian Poetry,* University of Queensland Press, 1968.

Heaven, in a Way (poems), University of Queensland Press, 1970; (compiler) *Australian Poetry 1970,* Angus & Robertson,

1970; *The Ship on the Coin: A Fable of the Bourgeoisie* (novel), University of Queensland Press, 1972; *A Soapbox Omnibus* (poems), University of Queensland Press, 1973; (editor) Jack Murray and others, *Poems From Prison,* University of Queensland Press, 1973; *A Place Among People,* University of Queensland Press, 1975; *Selected Poems,* University of Queensland Press, 1975; (compiler) *Australians Aware: Poems and Paintings,* Ure Smith (Sydney), 1975; *Black Bagatelles* (poems), University of Queensland Press, 1978; *J. S. Manifold: An Introduction to the Man and His Work,* University of Queensland Press, 1978; (author of introduction) Michael Dransfield, *Voyage Into Solitude,* University of Queensland Press, 1979; *Just Relations* (novel), Viking, 1983.

Recording: *Rodney Hall Reads "Romulus and Remus,"* University of Queensland Press, 1979.

SIDELIGHTS: Hall has written several volumes of poems in a style he calls a "progression." These poems, though they may stand complete and independent of one another, are closely related, therefore taking on the flavor of a single, long poem. A *Times Literary Supplement* critic wrote of the poet: "Rodney Hall has been an important influence . . . in the change which has come over Australian poetry since the 1950s."

BIOGRAPHICAL/CRITICAL SOURCES: Times Literary Supplement, May 8, 1969, April 9, 1976; *Washington Post Book World,* February 13, 1983; *New York Times Book Review,* March 13, 1983.*

*   *   *

HALLAHAN, William H(enry)

BRIEF ENTRY: Author. Hallahan has written several suspense novels, including *The Dead of Winter* (Bobbs-Merrill, 1972), *The Ross Forgery* (Bobbs-Merrill, 1973), *Catch Me: Kill Me* (Bobbs-Merrill, 1977), and *The Trade* (Morrow, 1981). *Biographical/critical sources: New York Times Book Review,* March 27, 1977; *New York Times,* January 21, 1981.

*   *   *

HALSTEAD, William Perdue   1906-1982

OBITUARY NOTICE: Born February 10, 1906, in Terre Haute, Ind.; died December 31, 1982, in California. Educator and author. Halstead was emeritus professor of speech at the University of Michigan, having begun his association with the university in 1935. Among his writings are *Stage Management for the Amateur Theatre* and *Shakespeare as Spoken.* Obituaries and other sources: *Chronicle of Higher Education,* January 12, 1983.

*   *   *

HALVERSON, Richard P(aul)   1941-

PERSONAL: Born October 17, 1941, in Salt Lake City, Utah; son of Lionel John (a millwright) and Anne (Linton) Halverson; married Kathleen Ballstaedt, July 7, 1965; children: Kirsten, Bradley, Taylor, Ryan, Tanner, Kimberly, Blake. *Education:* University of Utah, B.S. (magna cum laude), 1966; Harvard University, M.B.A. (with distinction), 1968. *Politics:* Republican. *Religion:* Church of Jesus Christ of Latter-day Saints (Mormons). *Home:* 7401 Pinehurst Court, Pine Springs, Minn. 55109. *Office:* First Trust Company of St. Paul, First Bank Building, St. Paul, Minn. 55101.

CAREER: Waddell & Reed, Inc. (mutual fund management complex), Kansas City, Mo., securities analyst, 1968-73, port-

folio manager, 1973-75, vice-president, 1975-77; First Trust Company of St. Paul, St. Paul, Minn., senior vice-president, 1977-80, executive vice-president, 1980—. Chartered financial analyst. Church of Jesus Christ of Latter-day Saints, missionary, 1961-63, bishop, 1970-77, high counselor, 1978-80, and counselor Stake Presidency, 1980—. Member of executive board of Indianhead Council of Boy Scouts of America. *Member:* Financial Analysts Federation, Twin Cities Society. *Awards, honors:* A. Van Biema Award from National Commercial Financial Conference, 1965, for essay "A Study and Approach to International Factoring."

WRITINGS: Financial Freedom: Your New Guide to Economic Security and Success, Harbor Publishing, 1982; (contributor) *The Handbook of Real Estate,* McGraw, 1983. Author of "Money Management," a column in *Smart Money,* 1983.

WORK IN PROGRESS: A book, *Modern Wealth Accumulation,* which explains new financial products of the 1980's.

SIDELIGHTS: Richard Halverson told *CA:* "Through my career, I have gained insight into the world of billion-dollar finance. Through my volunteer financial counseling, I have gained insight into the world of day-to-day personal finance. The merging of these experiences is the motivation for my writing.

"*Financial Freedom* is intended for anyone who has at times felt trapped by his personal finances and seeks to free himself. *Modern Wealth Accumulation* offers the general reader a straightforward explanation and comparison of today's modern financial products, ranging from money market deposit accounts to universal life insurance. The reader will learn how to use this new financial technology to increase his own wealth."

*   *   *

HAMBURG, David A(llen)   1925-

BRIEF ENTRY: Born in 1925 in Evanston, Ind. American psychiatrist, educator, and author. Hamburg, who has maintained a private practice of psychiatry since 1950, was a fellow at the Center for Advanced Study in the Behavioral Sciences from 1957 to 1958 and was chief of the National Institute of Mental Health's adult psychiatry branch from 1958 to 1961. He also taught at Stanford University, where he was named Reed-Hodgson Professor of Human Biology in 1972. Hamburg has served as president of the National Academy of Sciences Institute of Medicine and as director of Harvard University's Division of Health Policy Research and Education. He has received awards from the American College of Physicians and the American Psychiatric Association. Hamburg edited *Psychiatry as a Behavioral Science* (Prentice-Hall, 1970) and co-edited *Coping and Adaptation* (Basic Books, 1974), *New Psychiatric Frontiers* (Basic Books, 1975), *Neuroregulators and Psychiatric Disorders* (Oxford University Press, 1977), *The Great Apes* (Benjamin-Cummings, 1979), and *Biobehavioral Aspects of Aggression* (Alan R. Liss, 1981). *Address:* Center for Health Policy, Kennedy School of Government, Harvard University, 79 Boylston St., Cambridge, Mass. 02138.

*   *   *

HAMER, Mick   1946-

PERSONAL: Surname is pronounced *Hay*-mer; born July 30, 1946, in Gravesend, England; son of Brent (a transport manager) and May (Reader) Hamer; married Joanna Gordon Clark, October 13, 1973 (divorced, 1983). *Education:* North West Kent College of Technology, Higher National Certificate in

Chemistry, 1966. *Politics:* Labour. *Religion:* None. *Home:* 35 Arundel Gardens, Flat 1, London W11 2LW, England. *Office: New Scientist,* 1-19 New Oxford St., London W.E.1, England.

CAREER: Burroughs, Wellcome, Dartford, England, industrial chemist, 1964-66; Standard Telephones and Cables, Footscray, England, industrial chemist, 1966-67; free-lance musician, 1968-75; Friends of the Earth, London, England, member of transport staff, 1975-77; Transport Two Thousand Ltd. (lobbying group), London, director, 1977-79; free-lance journalist, 1980—. Associated with *New Scientist,* London, 1980—. Member of transport studies group at University College, London, 1981-83. *Member:* National Union of Journalists.

WRITINGS: Wheels Within Wheels, Friends of the Earth, 1974; *Getting Nowhere Fast,* Friends of the Earth, 1976; (with Stephen Potter) *Vital Travel Statistics,* Transport 2000/Open University Press, 1979; (contributor) David Blake and Paul Ormerod, editors, *The Economics of Prosperity,* Grant McIntyre, 1981; (contributor) Rosemary Delbridge and Martin Smith, editors, *Consuming Secrets,* Burnett Books, 1982; *Transport* (juvenile), F. Watts, 1982. Radio and television writer. Jazz critic for *Listener.* Contributor to magazines and newspapers, including *New Statesman, City Limits,* and *Labour Weekly.* News editor, *Vole,* 1981.

WORK IN PROGRESS: A chapter to be included in a book on the environment, edited by Des Wilson, for Heinemann; research on energy used by transport at University College, London.

SIDELIGHTS: Hamer told *CA:* "I am mainly a news journalist, specializing in writing about transport. My books tend to be sidelines. I also write about jazz and play the piano myself, although I rarely play in public these days. I hope to get round to writing my novel some day, but then, what writer doesn't?"

*   *   *

HAMEY, J(ohn) A(nthony)   1956-

PERSONAL: Born February 17, 1956, in Hitchin, England; son of Leonard Arnold (a civil engineer) and Joyce Margaret (Richardson) Hamey. *Education:* Emmanuel College, Cambridge, B.A., 1977, M.A., 1981; attended City University, London, England, 1977-78, and Inns of Court School of Law, 1978-79. *Home:* 29 Trinity Court, Gray's Inn Rd., London WC1X 8JX, England.

CAREER: Called to the Bar at Inner Temple; private practice of law, 1980—.

WRITINGS: (With father, L. A. Hamey) *The Roman Engineers* (juvenile), Cambridge University Press, 1981, Lerner, 1982. Contributor to *Scottish Home and Country.*

SIDELIGHTS: J. A. Hamey told *CA:* "Some knowledge of classical civilization is essential to a sound education. No opportunity should be missed to foster this through topics attractive to children. *The Roman Engineers* tries to give a brief account of the Romans' achievements in civil engineering, with special chapters on aqueducts, bridges, and roads. I was told by the Cambridge University Press that it hoped to include a title on Roman engineering as part of its series 'The Cambridge Introduction to the History of Mankind': This is an extensive series of books which tries to cover specific aspects of the history of civilization from the earliest times, with such titles as *The First Ships Round the World* (written by a master mariner) and *Building the Mediaeval Cathedrals.* There are also several more general books on Roman or Greek civilization,

for example, which serve to put the topic books like mine into context.

"Law keeps me too busy to plan further books on classical civilization at present, but I should very much like to do so if the opportunity arises."

*   *   *

HAMEY, L(eonard) A(rnold)   1918-

PERSONAL: Born May 20, 1918, in Sheffield, England; son of John George (a clerk) and Emily (a teacher; maiden name, White) Hamey; married Joyce Margaret Richardson, March 28, 1945; children: John Anthony. *Education:* Attended secondary school in Sheffield, England. *Home:* 10 Station Rd., Whittlesford, Cambridge CB2 4NL, England.

CAREER: Chartered civil engineer; L. & N.E. Railway, Sheffield, Leeds, and London, England, civil engineering assistant, 1937-47; British Railways, London, New Works assistant for Eastern Region, 1947-65, civil engineer for Scottish Region in Glasgow, 1965-74; British Railways Board London, planning and development engineer, 1974-78. *Member:* Institution of Civil Engineers (fellow).

WRITINGS: (With son, J. A. Hamey) *The Roman Engineers* (juvenile), Cambridge University Press, 1981, Lerner, 1982.

WORK IN PROGRESS: Further work on Roman engineering, possibly for adult readers; short stories.

SIDELIGHTS: Hamey told *CA:* "The combination of myself, a civil engineer, and my son, a classicist, backed by the resources and skill of the Cambridge University Press, seemed ideal for producing a junior-school book on a subject which could not fail to arouse interest in young readers. It is my opinion that the inborn interest of children in constructional engineering is not cultivated. General structural principles can be absorbed at a very early age, and this gives an established base for later detailed studies. Primary school is not too early for creating the basic understanding.

"So far as Roman engineering is concerned, it was apparent that there existed, on the one hand, a wealth of specialized, scholarly material on it and, on the other, a limited number of books presenting selected aspects for general reading. Our aim with *The Roman Engineers* was to sketch the contemporary background to Roman constructional activities, to indicate problems faced and solutions evolved by Roman engineers and, above all, to lead young readers towards appreciating how local conditions, a limited choice of materials, and purely manual techniques were exploited to create a constructional discipline which served the Romans well for one thousand years."

*   *   *

HAMILTON, (Arthur Douglas) Bruce   1900-1974

OBITUARY NOTICE: Born July 3, 1900, in London, England; died March 24, 1974. Educator and author. Hamilton was senior history master at Harrison College in Barbados from 1938 until 1950, when he became principal of the Barbados Evening Institute and Technical Institute. He served as chairman of the Barbados Public Service Commission from 1957 to 1964. Numbered among Hamilton's writings are the novels *To Be Hanged, Middle Class Murder,* and *So Sad, So Fresh,* the biography *The Light Went Out: The Life of Patrick Hamilton,* and the play "The Home Front." Obituaries and other sources: *The Author's and Writer's Who's Who,* 6th edition,

Burke's Peerage, 1971; *Who Was Who*, Volume VII, *1971-1980*, A. & C. Black, 1981.

* * *

HAMILTON, (Charles) Denis 1918-

PERSONAL: Born December 6, 1918, in South Shields, England; son of Charles and Helena (Trafford) Hamilton; married Olive Wanless, December 9, 1939; children: Michael Denis, Charles Nigel, Adrian Donald, John Andrew. *Education:* Attended high school in Middlesbrough, England. *Home and office:* 25 Roebuck House, Stag Pl., Palace St., London SW1E 5BA, England.

CAREER: International Thomson Organization (formerly Kemsley Newspapers), London, England, editorial assistant to Viscount Kemsley, 1946-50, editorial director, 1950-67, director, 1950—. Editor of Sunday edition of *London Times,* 1961-67, editor in chief of Times Newspapers Ltd., 1967-82, chief executive, 1967-70, chairman, 1971-82; director of Reuters Ltd., 1967-77, chairman, 1977—; member of board of directors of Independent Broadcasting Authority, 1982—. Past director of North Eastern Evening Gazette Ltd. and Newcastle Chronicle and Journal Ltd. Chairman of National Council for the Training of Journalists, 1957; chairman of British committee of International Press Institute; member of board of trustees of British Museum and British Library; chairman of British Museum Publications Ltd. *Military service:* British Army, 1939-46; became lieutenant colonel; received Distinguished Service Order and Territorial Decoration.

MEMBER: Newspaper Publishers Association (member of council), Press Council. *Awards, honors:* D.Litt. from University of Southampton, 1975, and City University, London, England, 1977; knighted, 1976; Grande Officiale of Italian Order of Merit, 1976; D.C.L. from University of Newcastle upon Tyne, 1979.

WRITINGS: (Editor) *Kemsley Manual of Journalism,* Cassell, 1950; *Who Is to Own the British Press?,* Birkbeck College, University of London, 1977.

WORK IN PROGRESS: History of the British Press, 1946-1982.

* * *

HAMILTON, Walter 1908-

PERSONAL: Born February 10, 1908, in London, England; son of Walter George and Caroline Mary Hamilton; married Elizabeth Jane Burrows, March 31, 1951; children: Robert, Charles, Simon, Caroline. *Education:* Trinity College, Cambridge, B.A., 1929. *Religion:* Anglican. *Home:* 6 Hedgerley Close, Cambridge CB3 0EW, England.

CAREER: Cambridge University, Cambridge, England, fellow of Trinity College, 1931-35; assistant master at private boys' secondary school in Windsor, England, 1933-37, master, 1937-46; Cambridge University, fellow of Trinity College and lecturer in classics, 1946-50; headmaster of private boys' secondary schools in London, England, 1950-57, and Rugby, England, 1957-66; Cambridge University, master of Magdalene College, 1967-78, honorary fellow of Trinity College, 1978—. Chairman of governing body of Shrewsbury School, 1968-81; fellow of Eton College, 1972-81; chairman of Headmasters Conference, 1955, 1956, 1965, 1966. *Member:* Royal Literary Society (fellow), Association of Independent Boys'

Schools (chairman, 1969-74). *Awards, honors:* D.Litt. from University of Durham, 1958.

WRITINGS—Translator: Plato's Symposium, Penguin, 1951; *Plato's Gorgias,* Penguin, 1960; *Plato's Phaedrus* [and] *The Seventh and Eighth Letters,* Penguin, 1973. Editor of *Classical Quarterly,* 1946-47.

WORK IN PROGRESS: Roman History of Ammianus Marcellinus, with A. F. Wallace-Hadrill, publication expected in 1984.

* * *

HAMPDEN, John 1898-

PERSONAL: Born February 6, 1898, in Folkestone, England; son of Francis John Hampden; married Doreen Springall; married second wife, Rosalind Vallance (an author and playwright); children: (first marriage) one son, one daughter; (second marriage) one daughter. *Education:* Received M.A. from Exeter College, Oxford. *Home:* Robin House, 55 St. Mary's Terrace, Hastings, Sussex, England.

CAREER: Royal Grammar School, Guildford, England, English master, 1922-29; Queen's College, London, 1929-32, began as lecturer, became professor of English literature; Thomas Nelson & Sons (publisher), London, general editor, 1932-37; associated with National Book Council, 1938-39, and Ministry of Information, 1940-41; British Council, London, editor of *British Book News,* 1942-46, head of literature group of departments, 1947-59, department controller of Arts and Sciences Division, 1950-59, books and periodicals adviser, 1959-63. Member of council, National Book League, 1946-63; member of board of directors, British National Bibliography, 1950-63. *Member:* Society of Authors, Society of Bookmen (honorary life member), P.E.N.

WRITINGS: Over the Garden Wall (one-act play based on Charles Dickens's *Nicholas Nickleby*), Gowans & Gray, 1927; *The King Decides* (one-act play), Samuel French, 1938; (with Esther S. Harley) *Books From Papyrus to Paperback* (juvenile), Methuen, 1964; *A Picture History of India* (juvenile; illustrated by Clarke Hutton), Oxford University Press, 1965.

Editor: Francis Beaumont and John Fletcher, *The Knight of the Burning Pestle,* Blackie & Son, 1925; Henry Fielding, *Tom Thumb the Great,* Wells, Gardner, 1925; Oliver Goldsmith, *She Stoops to Conquer,* Dent, 1927; Sheila Kaye Smith, *Mrs. Adia, With The Mockbeggar* (one-act plays), Thomas Nelson, 1929; Alfred Tennyson, *Idylls of the King,* Thomas Nelson, 1929; Edward A. Freeman, *The Men From the North* (adapted from *Old English History for Children*), Thomas Nelson, 1930; Sir Thomas Malory, *Knights of the Roundtable,* Thomas Nelson, 1930; Herman Melville, *Island Days* (adapted from *Typee*), Thomas Nelson, 1930; Sir Walter Scott, *The Queen's Escape* (adapted from *The Abbot*), Thomas Nelson, 1930; *Everyman, The Interlude of Youth, The World and the Child,* Thomas Nelson, 1931; Basil Blackwell and others, *The Book World,* Thomas Nelson, 1935; Richard Brinsley Sheridan, *The Plays of R. B. Sheridan,* Thomas Nelson, 1937; *The Drama Highway,* Dent, 1938; Christopher Marlowe, *Three Plays* (contains "Tamburlaine the Great," "Doctor Faustus," and "Edward the Second"), Thomas Nelson, 1940; Anthony Trollope, *Novels and Stories,* Pilot Press, 1946.

Trollope, *The Parson's Daughter, and Other Stories* (illustrated by John Hassall), Folio, 1949; Robert Louis Stevenson, *The Stevenson Companion,* McBride, 1950; Trollope, *Mary Gresley, and Other Stories* (illustrated by Joan Hassall), Folio,

1951; Jean Froissart, *The Days of Chivalry: Stories From Froissart's Chronicles*, Edmund Ward, 1952; *The Book World Today: A New Survey of the Making and Distribution of Books in Britain*, Allen & Unwin, 1957, reprinted, Books for Libraries, 1970; (with wife, Rosalind Vallance), Charles Lamb, *Essays* (illustrated by Frank Martin), Folio, 1963; John Galsworthy, *Loyalties: A Drama in Three Acts*, Duckworth, 1963; Galsworthy, *Escape: An Episodic Play*, Duckworth, 1964; (with Vallance), William Hazlitt the Elder, *Essays* (illustrated by Martin), Folio, 1964; Galsworthy, *Justice: A Tragedy in Four Acts*, Duckworth, 1964; Galsworthy, *Strife: A Drama in Three Acts*, Duckworth, 1964; Joseph Addison and others, *Sir Roger de Coverly* (illustrated by Richard S. Smith), Folio, 1967; Richard Hakluyt, *The Tudor Venturers*, Folio, 1970.

Editor and compiler: *Nine Modern Plays*, Thomas Nelson, 1926, published as *Nine Selected Plays*, 1952; *Eight Modern Plays for Juniors*, Thomas Nelson, 1927, published as *Eight Modern Plays*, 1931; *Eighteenth-Century Plays*, Dutton, 1928, reprinted, 1972; *Ten Modern Plays*, Thomas Nelson, 1928; *Ballads and Ballad-Plays*, Thomas Nelson, 1931; *Four Modern Plays*, Thomas Nelson, 1931; *Red Indians: Stories and Histories*, Thomas Nelson, 1931; *Six Modern Plays and Two Old Plays for Little Players*, Thomas Nelson, 1931; *Ten Modern Stories*, Thomas Nelson, 1931, Folcroft, 1976; *Four New Plays for Women and Girls*, Thomas Nelson, 1932; *Selected English Stories*, two volumes, Macmillan (London), 1932; *Seven Modern Plays for Younger Players*, Thomas Nelson, 1932; *Three Modern Plays and a Mime*, Thomas Nelson, 1932; *Sea Stories*, Thomas Nelson, 1933; *Fifteen Modern Plays*, Thomas Nelson, 1934; *Plays Without Fees*, Thomas Nelson, 1935; *Christmas Plays*, Thomas Nelson, 1937; *Twelve Modern Plays*, Duckworth, 1938; *Twenty One-Act Plays*, Dent, 1938, revised edition published as *Twenty-Four One-Act Plays*, 1954; *Ghost Stories*, Dent, 1939, reprinted, 1960; *Great English Short Stories: Defoe to Dickens*, two volumes, Penguin, 1940; *An Eighteenth-Century Journal, Being a Record of the Years 1774-1776*, Macmillan (London), 1940; *Plays for Boys and Girls*, Dent, 1940; *Great Poems, From Shakespeare to Manley Hopkins*, Pan Books, 1949, revised edition, London University Press, 1958.

Sea-Dogs and Pilgrim Fathers: Stories of Elizabethan and Stuart Voyages (juvenile; illustrated by C. Walter Hodges), Edmund Ward, 1953, new edition published as *New Worlds Ahead: Firsthand Accounts of English Voyages*, Farrar, Straus, 1968; *Crusader King: The Adventures of Richard the Lionheart on Crusade, Taken From a Chronicle of the Time*, Edmund Ward, 1956; *Sir William and the Wolf, and Other Stories From the Days of Chivalry* (illustrated by Eric Fraser), Dutton, 1960; *House of Cats, and Other Stories* (juvenile; illustrated by E. Arno), Farrar, Straus, 1967; *The Black Monkey, and Other Unfamiliar Tales From The Arabian Nights* (juvenile; illustrated by Sevin Unel), Deutsch, 1968, published as *Endless Treasure: Unfamiliar Tales From The Arabian Nights* (illustrated by Kurt Werth), World Publishing, 1970; *The Gypsy Fiddle, and Other Tales Told by the Gypsies* (juvenile; illustrated by Robin Jacques), World Publishing, 1969 (published in England as *The Yellow Dragon, and Other Gypsy Folk Tales*, illustrated by Gareth Floyd, Deutsch, 1969); *Francis Drake, Privateer: Contemporary Narratives and Documents*, University of Alabama Press, 1972; *Seventy-One Parrots: Folk Tales of Ancient Egypt and Mongolia* (illustrated by Matthew Meadows), Deutsch, 1972; *The Spanish Armada, July 1588* (illustrated by George Tuckwell), Lutterworth Press, 1972; *The Don-*

key and the Hobgoblin: Folk Tales From Nine Countries* (illustrated by Floyd), Deutsch, 1974.

Also editor of several of Shakespeare's plays, including *Julius Caesar*, 1926; *The Tempest*, 1926; *Henry IV, Part II*, 1928; *King John*, 1928; *Hamlet*, 1930. Contributor to literary journals and British Broadcasting Corp. (BBC) programs.

WORK IN PROGRESS: Beggars Opera, and Other Eighteenth-Century Plays.

SIDELIGHTS: John Hampden is best known as an editor and compiler of anthologies of plays, poems, folktales, and historical writings for adults and children. As general editor for Thomas Nelson & Sons he edited the "Little Theatre" and "Teaching of English" series; he also wrote notes and introductions to accompany the works of such writers as Shakespeare, Trollope, Sheridan, Galsworthy, and Goldsmith. Francis Drake and Sir Walter Raleigh are among the explorers and historians whose writings are included in Hampden's historical anthologies.

Of the histories edited and adapted by Hampden, one reviewer wrote in *Books and Bookmen*: "The effect is to give a startling sense of reality and immediacy to a theme whose interest might perhaps have worn thin if it were less skillfully handled." *New Worlds Ahead*, an anthology of records kept by English seamen headed for the new world, is an example of Hampden's ability to adapt the writings of the past to a modern audience.

Hampden has also edited folktales for children, including Gypsy tales and tales from the Middle East. *Sir William the Wolf, The Knight of the Burning Pestle, The Knights of the Roundtable*, and *Idylls of the King* are among the medieval tales Hampden has edited which the *London Times* praised as being "enthralling, even to the reader well-versed in the originals."

In addition to being the editor and compiler of anthologies, Hampden is the author of plays, books concerning the history and practice of publishing, and histories for young readers.

BIOGRAPHICAL/CRITICAL SOURCES: Times Literary Supplement, May 20, 1960; *Books and Bookmen*, November, 1968.

*   *   *

HANAGAN, Michael Patrick   1947-

PERSONAL: Born April 10, 1947, in St. Louis, Mo.; son of Francis Patrick (a lawyer) and Berenice (a lawyer; maiden name, Henke) Hanagan; married Miriam Cohen (a professor of history), September 6, 1974; children: Nora Ann. *Education:* University of Illinois, B.A., 1969, University of Michigan, M.A., 1973, Ph.D., 1976. *Home:* 507 West 113th St., No. 63, New York, N.Y. 10027. *Office:* Department of History, Columbia University, New York, N.Y. 10025.

CAREER: Wayne State University, Detroit, Mich., instructor in history, 1977; Vanderbilt University, Nashville, Tenn., assistant professor of history, 1978-82; Columbia University, New York, N.Y., assistant professor of history, 1982—. *Member:* American Historical Association, Economic History Association, Social Science History Association, Society for French Historical Studies, Population Association of America. *Awards, honors:* Fellow of Social Science Research Council, 1978-79, and American Council of Learned Societies, 1982-83.

WRITINGS: The Logic of Solidarity: Artisans and Industrial Workers in Three French Towns, 1871-1914, University of Illinois Press, 1982. Contributor to history journals.

WORK IN PROGRESS: A study "of the forces that influence the formation of a working class and how these demographic and economic forces affected working-class political consciousness in nineteenth-century France."

* * *

HANNAY, Allen 1946-

PERSONAL: Born November 27, 1946, in Austin, Tex.; son of Allen Burroughs, Jr. (a lawyer) and Alice (Cowgill) Hannay; married Sarah McGreevey (a writer), July 8, 1979; children: Ian Macdonald. Education: University of Texas at Austin, B.A., 1969; University of New Hampshire, M.A., 1976; University of Iowa, M.F.A., 1979. Home: 120A Trail Driver, Austin, Tex. 78737. Agent: Gail Hochman, Paul Reynolds, Inc., 12 East 41st St., New York, N.Y. 10017.

CAREER: University of Arkansas, Fayetteville, teaching assistant, 1977; University of Texas at Austin, Austin, lecturer in English, 1980——. Military service: U.S. Marine Corps, 1969-74; became captain. Awards, honors: Dobie-Paisano fellowship, 1980; National Endowment for the Arts fellowship, 1983-84.

WRITINGS: Love and Other Natural Disasters (novel), Atlantic/Little, Brown, 1982.

WORK IN PROGRESS: The Hair on Her Chest, publication expected in 1984.

SIDELIGHTS: Love and Other Natural Disasters, Hannay's first novel, is a romantic comedy about a nineteen-year-old Texas schoolboy, Bubber Drum, and his love affair with Rose, a thirty-five-year-old divorcee and the mother of one of his classmates. Rose tries her best to ignore Bubber's advances, but eventually falls as madly in love with him as he is with her. Disaster awaits them in the form of an unplanned pregnancy, however, and Bubber and Rose are forced to make some important decisions about the future.

Writing in the Los Angeles Times, critic Tom Clark commented that Love and Other Natural Disasters "has an engaging readability." And Chicago Tribune reviewer Peter Gorner called it "a delightful romp, a spring tonic, a perfect beach companion." "Quite subtly, amid rollicking scenes of mischief masked by his deceptively folksy style, Hannay deals with most of the relevant themes you find in more pretentious works. . . . I loved his laughing little book. May he write another soon," Gorner remarked.

BIOGRAPHICAL/CRITICAL SOURCES: Chicago Tribune, May 19, 1982; Los Angeles Times, June 3, 1982.

* * *

HANSBERRY, Lorraine (Vivian) 1930-1965

PERSONAL: Born May 19, 1930, in Chicago, Ill.; died of cancer, January 12, 1965, in New York, N.Y.; buried in Beth-El Cemetery, Croton-on-Hudson, N.Y.; daughter of Carl Augustus (a realtor and banker) and Nannie (Perry) Hansberry; married Robert B. Nemiroff (a music publisher and songwriter), June 20, 1953 (divorced March, 1964). Education: Attended University of Wisconsin, Art Institute of Chicago, Roosevelt College, New School for Social Research, and studied in Guadalajara, Mexico, 1948-50. Residence: New York, N.Y. Agent: c/o Vivian Productions, 137 West 52nd St., New York, N.Y. 10019.

CAREER: Playwright. Worked variously as clerk in a department store, tag girl in a fur shop, aide to a theatrical producer, and as waitress, hostess, and cashier in a restaurant in Greenwich Village run by the family of Robert Nemiroff; worked on monthly magazine, Freedom, for two years. Member: Dramatists Guild, Ira Aldrich Society, Institute for Advanced Study in the Theatre Arts. Awards, honors: New York Drama Critics Circle Award for best American play, 1959, for "A Raisin in the Sun"; Cannes Film Festival special award and Screen Writers Guild nomination, both 1961, both for screenplay "A Raisin in the Sun."

WRITINGS: (Author of text) The Movement: Documentary of a Struggle for Equality (collection of photographs), Simon & Schuster, 1964, published in England as A Matter of Colour: Documentary of the Struggle for Racial Equality in the U.S.A., introduction by Ronald Segal, Penguin, 1965; (contributor) Horst Frenz, editor, American Playwrights on Drama, Hill & Wang, 1965; To Be Young, Gifted and Black: Lorraine Hansberry in Her Own Words, self-illustrated, adapted by Robert Nemiroff, introduction by James Baldwin, Prentice-Hall, 1969, acting edition published as To Be Young, Gifted and Black: A Portrait of Lorraine Hansberry in Her Own Words, Samuel French, 1971. Contributor to Black Titan: W.E.B. Du Bois.

Plays: A Raisin in the Sun: A Drama in Three Acts (first produced in New York City at Ethel Barrymore Theatre, March 11, 1959), Random House, 1959 (also see below); "A Raisin in the Sun" (screenplay), released by Columbia, 1960; The Sign in Sidney Brustein's Window: A Drama in Three Acts (first produced in New York City at Longacre Theatre, October 15, 1964), Random House, 1965 (also see below); Les Blancs (two-act; first produced in New York City at Longacre Theatre, November 15, 1970), Hart Stenographic Bureau, 1966, later published as Lorraine Hansberry's "Les Blancs": A Drama in Two Acts, adapted by Nemiroff, Samuel French, 1972 (also see below); "A Raisin in the Sun," "The Sign in Sidney Brustein's Window," [and] "The 101 Final Performances of 'Sidney Brustein': Portrait of a Play and Its Author," by Robert Nemiroff, New American Library, 1966; Les Blancs: The Collected Last Plays of Lorraine Hansberry (contains "The Drinking Gourd" [three-act television drama], "What Use Are Flowers?" [one-act fable], and "Les Blancs"), edited by Nemiroff, introduction by Julius Lester, Random House, 1972.

Recordings: "A Raisin in the Sun," three cassettes, Caedmon, 1972; "Lorraine Hansberry Speaks Out: Art and the Black Revolution," Caedmon, 1972.

Work represented in anthologies, including Three Negro Plays, Penguin, 1969. Contributor to periodicals, including Negro Digest, Freedomways, Village Voice, and Theatre Arts.

SIDELIGHTS: Lorraine Hansberry was born into a middle-class black family on Chicago's south side in 1930. She recalled that her childhood was basically a happy one; "the insulation of life within the Southside ghetto, of what must have easily been half a million people, protected me from some of the harsher and more bestial aspects of white-supremacist culture," the playwright stated in Portraits in Color. At the age of seven or eight, Hansberry and her upwardly-mobile family deliberately attempted to move into a restricted white neighborhood. Her father fought the civil-rights case all the way to the U.S. Supreme Court, eventually winning his claim to a home within the restricted area. "The Hansberrys determination to continue to live in this home in spite of intimidation and threats from their angry, rock-throwing white neighbors is a study in courage and strength," Porter Kirkwood assessed in Freedomways.

"Lorraine's character and personality were forged in this atmosphere of resistence to injustice." "Both of my parents were strong-minded, civic-minded, exceptionally race-minded people who made enormous sacrifices in behalf of the struggle for civil rights throughout their lifetimes," Hansberry remembered.

While in high school, Hansberry first became interested in the theatre. "Mine was the same old story—" she recollected, "sort of hanging around little acting groups, and developing the feeling that the theatre embraces everything I liked all at one time." When Lorraine attended the University of Wisconsin she became further acquainted with great theatre, including the works of August Strindberg, Henrik Ibsen, and Sean O'Casey. She was particularly taken with the Irish dramatist's ability to express in his plays the complex and transcendant nature of man, to achieve "the emotional transformation of people on stage." After studying painting in Chicago and abroad, Hansberry eschewed her artistic plans and moved to New York City in 1950 to begin her career as a writer.

Politically active in New York, Hansberry wrote for Paul Robeson's *Freedom* magazine and participated in various liberal crusades. During one protest concerning practices of discrimination at New York University, Lorraine met Robert Nemiroff, himself a writer and pursuer of liberal politics. Although Nemiroff was white, a romance developed between the two, and in 1953 they married.

Nemiroff encouraged Hansberry in her writing efforts, going so far as to salvage her discarded pages from the wastebasket. One night in 1957, while the couple was entertaining a group of friends, they read a scene from Hansberry's play in progress, "A Raisin in the Sun." The impact left by the reading prompted Hansberry, Nemiroff, and friends to push for the completion, financing, and production of the drama within the next several months.

Enjoying solid success at tryout performances on the road, "A Raisin in the Sun" made its New York debut March 11, 1959, at the Ethel Barrymore Theatre. It was the first play written by a black woman to be produced on Broadway; it was the first to be directed by a black director in more than fifty years. When "A Raisin in the Sun" won the New York Drama Critics Circle Award, Hansberry became the youngest writer and the first black artist ever to receive the honor, competing that year with such theatre luminaries as Tennessee Williams, Eugene O'Neill, and Archibald MacLeish. In June, 1959, Hansberry was named the "most promising playwright" of the season by *Variety*'s poll of New York drama critics.

"A Raisin in the Sun" tells the story of a black family attempting to escape the poverty of the Chicago projects by buying a house in the suburbs with the money left from the insurance policy of their dead father. Conflict erupts when the son, Walter Lee, fights to use the money instead to buy his own business—a life's ambition. Yet when a white representative from the neighborhood that the family plans to integrate attempts to thwart their move, the young man submerges his materialistic aspirations—for a time, at least—and rallies to support the family's dream. Still Hansberry wonders, as expressed in the lines of poet Langston Hughes from which she takes her title, what will become of Walter Lee's frustrated desires: "What happens to a dream deferred? / Does it dry up like a raisin in the sun? / Or fester like a sore—and then run?"

Because the play explored a universal theme—the search for freedom and a better life—the majority of its audience loved

it. According to Gerald Weales in *Commentary,* it reflected neither the traditional Negro show, folksy and exotic, or the reactionary protest play, with black characters spouting about the injustices of white oppression. Rather, "A Raisin in the Sun" was a play about a family that just happened to be Negro. "The thing I tried to show," Hansberry told Ted Poston in the *New York Post,* "was the many gradations in even one Negro family, the clash of the old and the new."

New York Times critic Brooks Atkinson admired "A Raisin in the Sun" because it explored serious problems without becoming academic or ponderous. "[Hansberry] has told the inner as well as outer truth about a Negro family in Chicago," the critic observed. "The play has vigor as well as veracity and is likely to destroy the complacency of anyone who sees it." Weales labeled "Raisin" "a good play" whose "basic strength lies in the character and the problem of Walter Lee, which transcends his being a Negro. If the play were only the Negro-white conflict that crops up when the family's proposed move is about to take place, it would be editorial, momentarily effective, and nothing more. Walter Lee's difficulty, however, is that he has accepted the American myth of success at its face value, that he is trapped, as Willy Loman was trapped, by a false dream. In planting so indigenous an American image at the center of her play, Miss Hansberry has come as close as possible to what she intended—a play about Negroes which is not simply a Negro play." The reviewer also found the play "genuinely funny and touching," with the dialogue between family members believable.

"A Raisin in the Sun" ran for 530 performances. Shortly thereafter a film version of the drama was released; Hansberry won a special award at the Cannes Film Festival and was nominated for an award from the Screen Writers Guild for her screenplay. She then began working on a second play about a Jewish intellectual who vacillates between social commitment and paralyzing disillusionment. Entitled "The Sign in Sidney Brustein's Window," the play ran on Broadway for 101 performances despite mixed reviews and poor sales. "Its tenure on Broadway parallels the playwright's own failing health," Kirkwood noted. The play closed on January 12, 1965, the day Hansberry died of cancer at the age of thirty-five.

Although Hansberry and her husband divorced in 1964, Nemiroff remained dedicated to the playwright and her work. Appointed her literary executor, he collected his ex-wife's writings and words after her death and presented them in the autobiographical *To Be Young, Gifted and Black.* He also edited and published her three unfinished plays, which were subsequently produced: "Les Blancs," a psychological and social drama of a European-educated African who returns home to join the fight against Colonialism; "The Drinking Gourd," a drama on slavery and emancipation expressed through the story of a black woman; "What Use Are Flowers?," a fable about an aging hermit who, in a ravaged world, tries to impart to children his remembrances of the past civilization he had once renounced. "It's true that there's a great deal of pain for me in this," Nemiroff told Arlynn Nellhaus of the *Denver Post* about his custodianship, "but there's also a great deal of satisfaction. There is first-class writing and the joy of seeing [Lorraine's] ideas become a contemporary force again . . . [is] rewarding. . . . She was proud of black culture, the black experience and struggle. . . . But she was also in love with all cultures, and she related to the struggles of other people. . . . She was tremendously affected by the struggle of ordinary people—the heroism of ordinary people and the ability of people to laugh and transcend."

To Be Young, Gifted and Black was made into a play that ran Off-Broadway in 1969, keeping the memory of Hansberry and critical examination of her small body of work alive. Martin Gottfried, in *Women's Wear Daily*, hypothesized that "Miss Hansberry's tragically brief playwrighting career charted the postwar steps in the racial movement, from working within the system ('A Raisin in the Sun') to a burgeoning distrust of white liberals ('The Sign in Sidney Brustein's Window') to the association with Africa in 'Les Blancs' that would evolve, after her death, from the ashes of passive resistance into the energy and danger of militant activism." Writing in *Beautiful, Also, Are the Souls of My Black Sisters*, Jeanne L. Noble examined the author in a similar sociological light, wondering where, in today's political continuum, Hansberry would stand in comparison with the new breed of black writers. Yet she concluded: "Certainly for [Hansberry's] works to leave a continuing legacy—though she died at age 35, just before the fiercest testing period of the black revolution—is itself monumental. And we will always ponder these among her last words: 'I think when I get my health back I shall go into the South to find out what kind of revolutionary I am.'"

But most critics did not perceive of Hansberry as a particularly political or "black" writer, but rather as one who dealt more with human universals. Gerald Weales speculated in *Commonweal* that "it is impossible to guess how she might have grown as a writer, but her two [finished] plays indicate that she had wit and intelligence, a strong sense of social and political possibility and a respect for the contradictions in all men; that she could create a milieu (the family in *Raisin*, the Greenwich Village circle in *Sign*) with both bite and affection; that she was a playwright—like Odets, like Miller—with easily definable flaws but an inescapable talent that one cannot help admiring." And *Life* magazine's Cyclops concluded that Hansberry's gentle and intelligent sensibilities could best be read in these lines from "The Sign in Sidney Brustein's Window," when Sidney describes himself: "A fool who believes that death is a waste and love is sweet and that the earth turns and men change every day and that rivers run and that people wanna be better than they are and that flowers smell good and that I hurt terribly today, and that hurt is desperation and desperation is energy and energy can *move* things."

MEDIA ADAPTATIONS: A film version of "A Raisin in the Sun," starring Sidney Poitier and Claudia McNeil, was released by Columbia in 1961; *To Be Young, Gifted and Black* was adapted into a play, first produced Off-Broadway at Cherry Lane Theatre, January 2, 1969; a musical version of "The Sign in Sidney Brustein's Window" was first produced on Broadway at Longacre Theatre, January 26, 1972; a musical version of "A Raisin in the Sun," entitled "Raisin," was first produced on Broadway at Forty-Sixth Street Theatre, October 18, 1973.

AVOCATIONAL INTERESTS: Ping-pong, skiing, walking in the woods, reading biographies, conversation.

BIOGRAPHICAL/CRITICAL SOURCES—Books: Gwendolyn Cherry and others, *Portraits in Color*, Pageant Press, 1962; C.W.E. Bigsby, *Confrontation and Commitment: A Study of Contemporary American Drama*, MacGibbon & Kee, 1967; Bigsby, editor, *The Black American Writer*, Volume 2, Penguin, 1969; *Authors in the News*, Volume 2, Gale, 1976; Jeanne L. Noble, *Beautiful, Also, Are the Souls of My Black Sisters: A History of the Black Women in America*, Prentice-Hall, 1978; Catherine Scheader, *They Found a Way: Lorraine Hansberry*, Children's Press, 1978; *Contemporary Literary Criticism*, Volume 17, Gale, 1981.

Periodicals: *New York Times*, March 8, 1959, March 12, 1959, April 9, 1959; *New York Post*, March 22, 1959; *New Yorker*, May 9, 1959; *Commentary*, June, 1959; *Freedomways*, winter, 1963, summer, 1965, fourth quarter, 1978; *Commonweal*, September 5, 1969, January 22, 1971; *Esquire*, November, 1969; *Women's Wear Daily*, November 16, 1970; *Life*, January 14, 1972; *Denver Post*, March 14, 1976.

OBITUARIES: New York Times, January 13, 1965; *Time*, January 22, 1965; *Antiquarian Bookman*, January 25, 1965; *Newsweek*, January 25, 1965; *Publishers Weekly*, February 8, 1965; *Current Biography*, February, 1965; *Books Abroad*, spring, 1966.*

—*Sketch by Nancy Pear*

*   *   *

HARDING, Harry (Jr.) 1946-

PERSONAL: Born December 21, 1946, in Boston, Mass.; son of Harry (an executive) and Vernette (Vickers) Harding; married Roca Lau, July 5, 1971; children: James V.L. *Education:* Princeton University, A.B. (summa cum laude), 1967; Stanford University, M.A., 1969, Ph.D., 1974. *Residence:* Washington, D.C. *Office:* Brookings Institution, 1775 Massachusetts Ave. N.W., Washington, D.C. 20036.

CAREER: Swarthmore College, Swarthmore, Pa., instructor in political science, 1970-71; Stanford University, Stanford, Calif., acting assistant professor, 1971-73, assistant professor, 1973-79, associate professor of political science, 1979-83, vice-chairman of international relations program, 1982-83; Brookings Institution, Washington, D.C., senior fellow, 1983—. Visiting assistant professor at University of California, Berkeley, spring, 1977. Chairman of peninsula section of World Affairs Council of Northern California, 1978-79, member of board of trustees, 1978—; coordinator of East Asia program at Woodrow Wilson International Center for Scholars, 1979-80; member of Social Science Research Council-American Council of Learned Societies Joint Committee on Contemporary China, 1979-81; member of United States-People's Republic of China Joint Commission on Scientific and Technological Cooperation, 1981—; member of Committee on Advanced Study in China, Committee on Scholarly Communication With the People's Republic of China, 1982—, and National Committee on United States-China Relations; testified before U.S. Congress; consultant to Rand Corp.

MEMBER: American Political Science Association, Association of Asian Studies, Asia Society (associate of China Council), Council of Foreign Relations, Phi Beta Kappa. *Awards, honors:* Woodrow Wilson fellowship, 1967-68; national fellow at Hoover Institution on War, Revolution and Peace, 1977-78.

WRITINGS: China: The Uncertain Future, Foreign Policy Association, 1974; *China and the United States: Normalization and Beyond*, China Council, Asia Society and Foreign Policy Association, 1979; *Organizing China: The Problem of Bureaucracy, 1949-1976*, Stanford University Press, 1981.

Contributor: Thomas W. Robinson, editor, *The Cultural Revolution in China*, University of California Press, 1971; William W. Whitson, editor, *The Military and Political Power in China in the 1970's*, Praeger, 1972; Frank B. Horton and others, editors, *Comparative Defense Policy*, Johns Hopkins Press, 1974; Tsai Wei-ping, editor, *Proceedings of the Fifth Sino-American Conference on Mainland China*, Institute of International Relations (Taipei, Taiwan), 1976; Melvin Gurtov and Byong-Moo Hwang, editors, *China Under Threat: The Politics of Strategy and Diplomacy,* Johns Hopkins University Press, 1980; Thomas Fingar and others, editors, *China's Quest for Independence: Policy Evolution in the 1970's,* Westview, 1980; William Theodore de Bary and others, editors, *China's Future and Its Implications for U.S.-China Relations,* Woodrow Wilson International Center for Scholars, 1980; Franklin D. Margiotta, editor, *Evolving Strategic Realities: Implications for U.S. Policymakers,* National Defense University Press, 1980; Leo A. Orleans, editor, *Science in Contemporary China,* Stanford University Press, 1980; Richard H. Solomon, editor, *The China Factor,* Prentice-Hall, 1981. Contributor of articles and reviews to professional journals and newspapers.

WORK IN PROGRESS: Editing a book on contemporary Chinese foreign policy, publication by Yale University Press expected in 1983; a chapter on the role of the People's Liberation Army in Chinese politics, to be included in a book on the pursuit of political interest in China, edited by Victor Falkenheim; a section on Japanese, Korean, Southeast Asian, and European attitudes about American policy toward China, to be included in a book on U.S.-China relations, sponsored by the Atlantic Council of the United States; a chapter on the Cultural Revolution, to be included in *Cambridge History of China,* edited by John K. Fairbank and Roderick MacFarquhar, for Cambridge University Press.

SIDELIGHTS: Harding told *CA:* "I cannot imagine a more important topic than the fate of one quarter of humankind, nor a more interesting one than the evolution of modern China. In my own writings, I have tried not only to advance our scholarly understanding of Chinese politics and foreign relations, but also to communicate those findings to a broader audience. American attitudes toward China have, over the last century, oscillated wildly between the extremes of idealization and hostility. The challenge for China specialists interested in public affairs is to help dampen these oscillations, and to produce a more objective and balanced understanding of China and the Chinese."

*   *   *

HARLOW, Neal 1908-

PERSONAL: Born June 11, 1908, in Columbus, Ind.; son of Robert William (a minister) and Ora May (Rotan) Harlow; married Marian Gardner, September 12, 1936; children: Diane Harlow Killou, Nora. *Education:* University of California, Los Angeles, Ed.B., 1932; University of California, Berkeley, Certificate in Librarianship, 1933, M.A., 1949. *Home and office address:* P.O. Box 26101, Los Angeles, Calif. 90026.

CAREER: University of California, Berkeley, junior librarian at Bancroft Library, 1934-38; California State Library, Sacramento, senior librarian in California Section, 1938-45; University of California, Los Angeles, head of department of special collections and assistant librarian, 1945-51; University of British Columbia, Vancouver, university librarian, 1951-61; Rutgers University, New Brunswick, N.J., professor of library science and dean of Graduate School of Library Service, 1961-69; writer and consultant, 1969—. Chairman of board of managers of Pacific Northwest Bibliographic Center, 1954-57; member of drafting committee of Commission for a National Plan for Library Education, 1959-63; member of biomedical communications study section of National Institutes of Health, 1966-70; member of board of directors of U.S. Book Exchange, 1966-70. Member of scientific information committee of National Research Council of Canada, 1958-61; member of

library survey committee of National Conference of Canadian Universities and Colleges, 1959-61; member of British Columbia Board of Examiners of Professional Librarians, 1959-61. Member of Leon and Thea Koerner Foundation, 1956-61; member of board of directors of Vancouver's Community Arts Council, 1956-61.

MEMBER: American Library Association (member of council, 1952-63; member of executive board, 1959-63), Association of College and Research Libraries (member of board of directors, 1959-64; president, 1963-64), American Association of University Professors, Canadian Library Association (member of council, 1953-56; president, 1960-61), New Jersey Library Association (member of executive board, 1961-69), Rounce and Coffin Club, Zamorano Club. *Awards, honors:* L.H.D. from Moravian College, 1967.

WRITINGS: The Maps of San Francisco Bay From the Spanish Discovery to the American Occupation, Book Club of California, 1950; *Maps and Surveys of the Pueblo Lands of Los Angeles,* Dawson's Book Shop, 1976; (editor) E.O.C. Ord, *The City of the Angels and the City of the Saints,* Huntington Library, 1978; *California Conquered: War and Peace on the Pacific, 1846-1850,* University of California Press, 1982. Contributor to library and history journals. Editor of *California Library Bulletin,* 1957-59.

WORK IN PROGRESS: A book on maps of the pueblo lands of San Diego, for Dawson's Book Shop.

SIDELIGHTS: Harlow wrote: "A historian does not make up his characters and action, but recreates them from whatever believable sources are available and from his own insights into human character and motivation. History is no less remarkable than fiction, and it can be more poignant and appealing to readers because these people, engaged in these activities and consequences, actually lived. The historical writer's vocation is to view significant portions of life through the eyes and sensibilities of participants, to reveal the humanness of the people in their history without invention or exaggeration. This is no job for a tyro, and it might be argued that the later one comes to history the better. Experience, sympathy, and integrity, immersion in chosen fields of inquiry, and the ability through temperament and style to involve the reader in a course of thought and action are capital literary ingredients if one can muster them."

*   *   *

HARMAN, Claire
See SCHMIDT, Claire Harman

*   *   *

HARRIGAN, Kathryn Rudie 1951-

PERSONAL: Born March 15, 1951, in Minneapolis, Minn.; daughter of Norbert J. and Florence G. (Gelking) Rudie; married Richard Scott Harrigan (deceased). *Education:* Macalester College, B.A., 1973; University of Texas, M.B.A., 1976; Harvard University, D.B.A., 1979. *Residence:* New York, N.Y. *Office:* Graduate School of Business, 716 Uris Hall, Columbia University, New York, N.Y. 10027.

CAREER: Minneapolis Institute of Art, Children's Theatre Company, Minneapolis, Minn., apprentice, 1966-67; North Hennipen Young People's Theatre, Minneapolis, business manager, 1967-69; artistic director and designer of stage productions throughout the Midwest, 1973-75; Babson College,

Babson Park, Mass., assistant professor of business and management, 1976-79; University of Texas, Dallas, assistant professor of business administration, 1979-81; Columbia University, New York, N.Y., assistant professor, 1981-83, associate professor of business, 1983—. *Member:* Institute of Management Science, National Academy of Management, Southwest Academy of Management, Beta Gamma Sigma (Alpha chapter). *Awards, honors:* General Electric Award for Outstanding Research in Strategic Management from National Academy of Management, 1979, for *Strategies for Declining Businesses.*

WRITINGS: Strategies for Declining Businesses, Heath, 1980; (contributor) C. Roland Christensen, editor, *Teaching by the Case Method,* Division of Research, Business School, Harvard University, 1981; (contributor) J. Ronald Fox, editor, *Managing Business-Government Relations,* Irwin, 1982; (contributor) M. E. Porter, editor, *Cases in Competitive Strategy,* Free Press, 1982; *Strategies for Vertical Integration,* Heath, 1983; (contributor) Robert Lamb, editor, *Advances in Strategic Management,* Volume I, Jai Press, 1983; (contributor) Lamb, editor, *Latest Advances in Strategic Management,* Prentice-Hall, 1983. Contributor of articles and reviews to business journals. Member of editorial board of *Academy of Management Journal,* 1981—, *Journal of Business Strategy,* 1982, and *Strategic Management Journal,* 1983—.

WORK IN PROGRESS: Strategies for Joint Ventures, completion expected in 1984.

SIDELIGHTS: Harrigan told *CA:* "I first became involved in theatre when I met the members of a touring company of the Tyrone Guthrie Theatre backstage at my high school. It seemed to be a good occupation for a female during the 1960's (merit overcomes gender, like in athletics) and seemed more interesting than secretarial work. The vast interest in theatre in the Minneapolis-St. Paul community enabled me to earn enough cash to finance my education. (I also sorted mail with the Minneapolis Postal Service to finance my schooling.)

"I changed from theatre to management because I was interested in the chief executive function. As a director, designer, and producer, I was responsible for the same duties as the president of a small business. It became attractive to take an M.B.A. to manage other types of businesses.

"My limited acting experiences helped me to procure a teaching position to finance my doctorate. I continue to enjoy my classroom experiences, although my primary activities are research and consulting.

"*Strategies for Declining Businesses* addresses the problem of declining demand—how to rationalize industry capacity without inciting competitive bloodshed. Since this study of decline and exit barriers, many subsequent doctoral dissertations have been written on the problems of divestiture, and management consulting firms have added these concepts to the range of services they offer. Because I am a scholar, I can examine the patterns of strategic behavior in many industries and generalize concerning the efficacy of various generic strategies firms might undertake. Most corporations cannot afford the time needed to make such empirical studies. The insights I can offer prove beneficial."

*   *   *

HARRIS, Bill 1933-

PERSONAL: Born November 25, 1933, in Scranton, Pa.; son of William G. (a grocer) and Marjorie (Pierce) Harris; divorced;

children: Michael, Ellen, Scott, Matthew. *Education:* Attended high school in North Bellmore, N.Y. *Politics:* Democrat. *Religion:* Episcopalian. *Home:* 318 East 30th St., New York, N.Y. 10016. *Office: New York Times,* 229 West 43rd St., New York, N.Y. 10036.

CAREER: Crowell-Collier Publishing Co., New York City, in charge of sales promotion and public relations activities of magazines sold through schools, 1954-58; Dell Publishing Co., Inc., New York City, in charge of sales promotion and public relations for comic books, 1958-61; Western Publishing Co., Inc., New York City, editor of comic books, 1961-64; *New York Times,* New York City, in sales promotion, 1965-66; King Features Syndicate, New York City, creator and editor of Comic Book Division, 1966-69; *New York Times,* assistant to promotion manager, 1969—. Licensed tour director in New York City, 1969—; director and partner of tour agency ViewPoint International, 1981—.

WRITINGS: New York, Mayflower, 1979; *United States of America,* Mayflower, 1979; *Israel: The Promised Land,* Mayflower, 1980; *Florida,* Mayflower, 1980; *Hawaii,* Mayflower, 1980; *Philadelphia,* Mayflower, 1980; *Texas,* Mayflower, 1981; *New England,* Mayflower, 1981; *Boston,* Mayflower, 1981; *Chicago,* Mayflower, 1981; *Yellowstone and the Grand Tetons,* Mayflower, 1981; *The Plaza Hotel,* Poplar Books, 1982; *Washington, D.C.,* Abrams, 1982; *New York: City of Many Dreams,* Crown, 1983; *New York at Night,* Stewart, Tabori & Chang, 1983; *Colorado,* Crescent, 1983; *The Landscape of America,* Crescent, 1983.

Writer for comic books, including *Phantom.* Contributor to magazines, including *Print* and *Golden.* Editor of newsletters of Trans-National Research Company and Association of Major Symphony Orchestras.

WORK IN PROGRESS: A screenplay, "New York Renaissance," Renaissance Co., 1984.

SIDELIGHTS: Harris told *CA:* "Though I'm willing to admit there are other cities in the world, and even to write about them, I have to confess to a love affair with New York City that is almost unnatural. One of the most exciting days of my life was spent doing research for *New York at Night* when I watched a production at Radio City Music Hall from backstage and then spent the night aboard a tugboat in New York Harbor. I could live a happy life in Chicago, I think, and Venice is tempting. But there is only one New York, and it keeps getting better. The books I do are essentially picture books, the kind publishers call 'gift books' and their customers call 'coffee table books.' I'm a weekend writer. My nine-to-five life is spent in the service of the *New York Times.* The rest of the time, the *Times* serves me with what must be the most complete research facility in the world."

*   *   *

HARRIS, Frank 1856(?)-1931

BRIEF ENTRY: Birth-given name, James Thomas Harris; born February 14, 1856 (some sources say 1854 or 1855), in Galway, Ireland (Harris alternately claimed to have been born in Ireland and in Tenby, Wales); naturalized U.S. citizen; died August 26, 1931, in Nice, France. American journalist, editor, playwright, literary scholar, and author. Few verifiable facts are known about Harris, who was considered by his contemporaries to be a pathological liar. It is known that Harris came to the United States when he was a teenager and that he worked in a variety of jobs in New York, Illinois, Kansas, and Texas, where he claims to have been employed as a cowboy. At some point in the 1890's Harris returned to England and became editor of the *Evening News,* where he is credited with inventing yellow journalism. When Harris later became editor of *Saturday Review,* he performed a stylistic turnabout by hiring such writers as George Bernard Shaw, H. G. Wells, and Max Beerbohm, thereby creating a staff that provided the best literary coverage of its day. Harris was unable to find an American or British publisher for his erotic autobiography, *My Life and Loves* (three volumes; 1923-27), so he had the book published in Germany. The chronicle, which is considered to be largely fictional, caused a scandal upon its publication. In addition to his other writings, Harris was the author of the literary studies *The Man Shakespeare* (1911) and *The Women of Shakespeare* (1911) and a play, *Shakespeare and His Love* (1910). *Biographical/critical sources: Twentieth-Century Authors: A Biographical Dictionary of Modern Literature,* H. W. Wilson, 1942; *Who Was Who in America,* Volume 1: *1897-1942,* Marquis, 1943; *Longman Companion to Twentieth Century Literature,* 2nd edition, Longman, 1970; Philippa Pullar, *Frank Harris,* Simon & Schuster, 1976.

* * *

HARRIS, Kenneth   1904-1983

OBITUARY NOTICE: Born in 1904; died after a long illness, May 13, 1983, in Norfolk, Va. Artist and author. Harris was widely known for his drawings and watercolors of the countryside. He wrote *How to Make a Living as a Painter.* Obituaries and other sources: *Chicago Tribune,* May 17, 1983.

* * *

HARRIS, Marcia Lee   1951-

PERSONAL: Born October 30, 1951, in Los Angeles, Calif.; daughter of Marvin C. (a bookkeeper) and Arline R. (a teacher; maiden name, Robinson) Sokol; married Stephen Harris (a teacher); children: David. *Education:* California State University, Long Beach, B.A., 1973. *Home:* 4570 Gundry Ave., Long Beach, Calif. 90807.

CAREER: Jewish Community Center, Long Beach, Calif., camp counselor, 1968-71; Camp Coleman, Cleveland, Ga., creative arts specialist, 1971-72; media specialist at public schools in Long Beach, 1972-73; elementary school teacher in Los Alamitos, Calif., 1973-74; ABC Unified School District, Long Beach, teacher of gifted education, 1974—. *Member:* National Education Association, California Teachers Association, Mortar Board.

WRITINGS: (With Elaine J. Haglund) *On This Day: A Collection of Everyday Learning Events and Activities for the Media Center, Library, and Classroom,* Libraries Unlimited, 1983.

WORK IN PROGRESS: Educational games and filmstrips; a classroom management system.

SIDELIGHTS: Harris told *CA:* "As a fifth grader, I complained about each school day being routine. The teachers were not interested in the areas I enjoyed. We studied the same heroes year after year. I disliked finishing things early and having to sit and wait or do additional work. Whenever I asked how something got started I was told to look it up. Usually I couldn't find the information in available sources. It bothered me that school did not allow for my interests or provide a chance for me to shine. All these things frustrated me.

"My mother asked me how I would do things differently than the teachers, so I began collecting a file box of events and activities. From then on I was known as a trivia buff and collector. I turned in my ideas for an alternative teaching style as a college project, and they evolved into a book which I wrote with Elaine Haglund. I have been using the concept outlined in the book with my classes (both gifted and traditional) for the past ten years.

"I feel elementary education should expose students to a variety of people and things. My book was designed as a resource for people of all ages and walks of life and can be used in many ways. Hopefully, students will find their niche when they are exposed to many areas and are allowed to think, speculate, and create.

"My contract system was created to encourage students of varying abilities and grade levels to pursue their interests and to provide them with the chance to excel. The book offers an alternative to assigning additional work.

"The goal of gifted education (or any other type) should be to create happy, well-adjusted, well-rounded, and productive members of society. It is my hope that the individuals who use my book may one day be such members."

* * *

HARRIS, Thomas J.   1892(?)-1983

OBITUARY NOTICE: Born c. 1892; died February 26, 1983, in Glenview, Ill. Advertising executive and editor. Beginning in the 1920's, Harris worked for several advertising agencies, including the Thomas J. Harris Advertising Agency, Harris & Bond Agency, and Harris, Wilson & Walt Agency. During that time he edited and published *Scan,* an advertising periodical. Obituaries and other sources: *Chicago Tribune,* March 2, 1983.

* * *

HARRISON, Michelle Jessica   1942-

PERSONAL: Born November 27, 1942, in New York, N.Y.; daughter of David (a writer) and Emily (a lawyer; maiden name, Arnow) Alman; children: Heather Alecia. *Education:* Washington Square College, B.A., 1963; New York Medical College, M.D., 1967. *Office:* 763 Massachusetts Ave., Cambridge, Mass. 02139.

CAREER: Monmouth Medical Center, Long Branch, N.J., intern, 1967-68; Hillside Hospital, Glen Oaks, N.Y., resident in psychiatry, 1968-69; Sheppard Pratt Hospital, Towson, Md., resident in psychiatry, 1969-70; Raritan Valley Hospital, Greenbrook, N.J., staff physician, 1970-72; Beaufort Jasper Comprehensive Health, Inc., Beaufort, S.C., staff physician, 1972-75, director of health care services, 1974-75; Somerset Family Practice, Somerville, N.J., preceptor, 1975-78; Beth Israel Hospital, Boston, Mass., Harvard Medical School clinical fellow and resident in obstetrics and gynecology, 1978-79; Premenstrual Syndrome Program, Reading, Mass., staff physician, 1981-82; private practice in Cambridge, Mass., specializing in premenstrual syndrome, 1982—. Diplomate of American Board of Family Practice, 1975-82; clinical assistant professor in department of family medicine at Rutgers Medical School, College of Medicine and Dentistry, 1976-78. Chairman of Low County Family Planning Advisory Council, 1974-75; chairman of board of directors of Beaufort Day Care Center, 1974-75. *Member:* American Academy of Family Physicians (fellow), American Medical Women's Association (president of junior chapter, 1967-68), National Women's Health Network, American Public Health Association.

WRITINGS: A Woman in Residence: A Physician's Account of Her Training in Obstetrics and Gynecology, Random House, 1982; *Self-Help for Premenstrual Syndrome,* Matrix Press, 1982; (author of preface) Suzanne Morgan, *Coping With a Hysterectomy,* Dial, 1982.

WORK IN PROGRESS: Researching premenstrual syndrome, the meaning of the menstrual cycle in women's lives, and women's health care.

SIDELIGHTS: In 1978 Michelle Harrison, a successful practicing physician and professor of family medicine at Rutgers Medical School, assumed residency at Beth Israel Hospital in Boston for additional training in obstetrics and gynecology. Involved in the home-birth movement, the physician sought "to improve her skills in the area of medicine she felt most drawn to," Michele Slung noted in the *Washington Post Book World.* Yet after seven months in the four-year program, Harrison dropped out, frustrated and bitter. "There were just too many unnecessary and dehumanizing procedures that she found herself party to," Slung observed, "too many compromises with methods she didn't respect and far too many women patients who weren't being told what was going to happen to them." "Physicians are trained and conditioned to see patients as objects to be assembled and reassembled," Harrison contended.

Driving back and forth from work during her residency, Harrison spoke daily into a tape recorder, relating her reactions and observations in a verbal diary that eventually became *A Woman in Residence: A Physician's Account of Her Training in Obstetrics and Gynecology.* Besides presenting scathing indictments of the predominantly male medical profession's treatment of women, its interventionist approach to childbirth, and the appalling lack of time allotted to individual patient care, the author describes her difficulties as "a single mother trying to cope simultaneously with the needs of a young child and the requirements of a profession," Anna Fels wrote in *Nation.* "It is a painful story—single-parenthood and medicine could not, in the end, be combined—and [Harrison] tells it well. . . . The book has an immediacy and straightforwardness that make you believe the saga of medical abuse and callousness that she unfolds." "Harrison's sharp detailing of unnecessary procedures and surgeries too often imposed on female patients makes this worthwhile reading for every woman of childbearing age," C. Bertsh assessed in the *Los Angeles Times Book Review.*

Harrison told *CA:* "I am both a writer and a physician, with a strong commitment to continuing to do both. Sometimes my writing is part of my 'medical' life, and other times it is more distant. I feel strongly alive when I am gripped with that passion to put into words what streams through my mind. Everything else seems to stop.

"My present strong interest is in premenstrual syndrome. In *Self-Help for Premenstrual Syndrome* I write: 'I have conflicting feelings about PMS. The feminist in me wishes that our biology were irrelevant. The doctor in me sees the need for recognizing and treating premenstrual symptoms. The woman in me recognizes the power of the biological forces within me, and wishes I lived in a society in which my menstrual cycle were seen as an asset, not a liability. The writer in me keeps hoping that if I can get it all down on paper, it will be easier to understand, and in any case, I will not be alone in my dilemma or my conflict.'"

BIOGRAPHICAL/CRITICAL SOURCES: Washington Post Book World, May 23, 1982; *Time,* June 14, 1982; *Nation,* October 9, 1982; *Los Angeles Times Book Review,* October 31, 1982.

* * *

HARRISON, Richard John 1920-

PERSONAL: Born October 8, 1920, in London, England; son of Geoffrey Arthur and Theodora Beatrice Mary (West) Harrison; married Joanna Gillies, December 22, 1943 (marriage ended); married Barbara Jean Fuller, March 30, 1967; children: Evelina (Mrs. David Gold), Gavin, Nigel. *Education:* Attended Gonville and Caius College, Cambridge, 1939-41; St. Bartholomew's Hospital Medical School, London, B.A., 1942, M.B., B.Chir., 1944, L.R.C.P., M.R.C.S., 1944, M.A., 1948, D.Sc., 1949, M.D., 1954. *Home:* The Beeches, 8 Woodlands Rd., Great Shelford, Cambridgeshire, England. *Office:* School of Anatomy, Cambridge University, Downing St., Cambridge, England.

CAREER: St. Bartholomew's Hospital, house surgeon, 1944, demonstrator in anatomy at hospital medical college, 1944-45; Glasgow University, Glasgow, Scotland, lecturer in anatomy, 1946-47; senior lecturer and reader in anatomy at Charing Cross Hospital Medical School, 1947-51; University of London, London Hospital Medical College, London, England, reader in charge of anatomy department, 1951-54, professor of anatomy, 1954-68; Royal Institution, London, Fullerian Professor of Physiology, 1961-67; Cambridge University, Cambridge, England, fellow of Downing College and professor of anatomy, 1968-82, emeritus professor, 1982—. Chairman of Ministry of Agriculture's Farm Animal Welfare Advisory Committee, 1974-79, and of Farm Animal Welfare Council, 1979—. Member of board of trustees of British Museum (Natural History), 1978—.

MEMBER: European Association for Aquatic Mammals (president, 1974-76), Anatomical Society of Great Britain and Ireland (secretary, 1956-64; president, 1977-79), Zoological Society of London (member of council, 1974-78, 1980-83), Royal Society of London (fellow, 1973; member of council, 1981-82). *Awards, honors:* Symington Prize from Queen's University, Belfast, 1951, for research publications on human and comparative anatomy.

WRITINGS: (With E. J. Field) *Anatomical Terms,* Heffer, 1947, 3rd edition, 1968; *The Child Unborn,* Routledge & Kegan Paul, 1951; *Man: The Peculiar Animal,* Pelican, 1958; (with Frank Goldby) *Recent Advances in Anatomy,* Churchill, 1961; (contributor) S. Zuckerman, editor, *The Ovary,* Academic Press, Volume I, 1962, 2nd edition, 1977; (with Judith E. King) *Marine Mammals,* Hutchinson, 1965, 2nd edition, 1980; *Reproduction and Man,* Oliver & Boyd, 1967; (with William Montagna) *Man,* Appleton-Century Crofts, 1969, 2nd edition, Prentice-Hall, 1973; (contributor) G. J. Romanes, editor, *Cunningham's Textbook of Anatomy,* 11th edition, Oxford University Press, 1971, 12th edition, 1981; (editor and contributor) *Anatomy of Marine Animals,* Academic Press, Volume I, 1972, Volume II, 1974, Volume III, 1977; (with S. H. Ridgeway) *Deep Diving in Mammals,* Meadowfield Press, 1976; (contributor) Everhard Johannes Slijper, editor, *Whales,* 2nd edition, Hutchinson, 1979; (editor with Ridgeway) *Handbook of Marine Mammals,* two volumes, Academic Press, 1981; (editor with R. L. Holmes) *Progress in Anatomy,* Cambridge University Press, Volume I, 1981, (with V. Navaratnam) Volume II, 1982, Volume III, 1983. Also contributor to *Eden and*

Holland's Manual of Obstetrics, edited by A. Brews, 10th edition, 1953, 12th edition, 1963.

WORK IN PROGRESS: Editing and contributing to next volumes of *Handbook of Marine Mammals;* editing and contributing to *Research on Dolphins,* for Oxford University Press.

SIDELIGHTS: Harrison told *CA:* "My father had a weakness for constructing garden pools out of reinforced concrete in which he kept fish. His goal was to maintain a seawater pool for marine fish. After winning a scholarship, I had a year to spare before going to Cambridge, and it was arranged that I should go as a student naturalist to the Marine Biological Station at Plymouth to learn about keeping marine animals. World War II put an end to all this. I became medically qualified and was directed to train as an anatomist and surgeon for the Army.

"After the war my professor persuaded me to become a human anatomist and to join him in his research on human and animal reproduction. I began to do research on the ovary, and when I found out that the phenomenon of delayed implantation probably occurred in seals, I wanted to study their ovaries. I organized various expeditions around the British coasts and with the help of students and fishermen began to collect material for my studies, which soon included porpoises and dolphins.

"So here I was back with the sea and marine creatures, and it was not long before I became more ambitious and started to try to keep seals and cetaceans in pools in the garden and in the laboratory. They were marvelous animals, great swimmers and divers, so I soon had to write books about them and my research on them. I still enjoy doing so. I was much encouraged by the great expert on dolphins, F. C. Fraser of the British Museum of Natural History, and by L. H. Matthews of the London Zoo, with whom I published several papers on seals. Matthews describes some of our experiences in his book *The Seals and the Scientists.*

"The highlight of my professional travels was to be invited by the Chinese Academia Sinica to advise them about what might be done to save the very rare white dolphin. My wife and I visited China for six weeks in 1981 to observe the two species of dolphin that inhabit the Yangtse river. We did indeed see both species, and the experience satisfied a childhood dream to sail down the Yangtse. It was an experience that I shall never forget."

BIOGRAPHICAL/CRITICAL SOURCES: Leonard Harrison Matthews, *The Seals and the Scientists,* P. Owen, 1979.

*   *   *

HARROUN, Catherine   1907-

PERSONAL: Surname is accented on last syllable; born September 21, 1907, in St. Joseph, Mo.; daughter of William (a farm owner) and Eva (Kirkpatrick) Harroun. *Education:* Stanford University, B.A., 1929. *Politics:* Democrat. *Home:* 932 Vallejo St., San Francisco, Calif. 94133. *Agent:* Frederick Hill, 2237 Union, San Francisco, Calif. 94123.

CAREER: Wells Fargo Bank, San Francisco, Calif., advertising copywriter and director of history museum, both 1930-48; free-lance writer, photographer, and researcher, 1948-65; University of California, Berkeley, part-time interviewer and editor in Regional Oral History Office at Bancroft Library, 1965—. *Member:* California Historical Society, Book Club of California, Gleeson Library Associates, Friends of the Bancroft Library. *Awards, honors:* Award of merit from California His-

torical Society and silver medal from Commonwealth Club of California, both 1982, for *Winemaking in California.*

WRITINGS: (Editor with Ruth Teiser, and contributor) *Printing as a Performing Art,* Book Club of California, 1970; (editor with Teiser, and contributor) Arpad Haraszthy, *Winemaking in California,* Book Club of California, 1978; (with Teiser) *Winemaking in California,* McGraw, 1982; (contributor) Doris Muscatine, Maynard A. Amerine, and Bob Thompson, editors, *Book of California Wine,* University of California Press, in press. Contributor to magazines, including *Wine World, Wines and Vines,* and *Travel.*

WORK IN PROGRESS: A biography of painter Lawton Kennedy, with Ruth Teiser, publication by Book Club of California expected in 1985; a book on the history of winemaking in Monterey County, California, with Teiser.

*   *   *

HART, Jeffrey Allen   1947-

PERSONAL: Born December 29, 1947, in New Kensington, Pa.; son of Edwin (a retail merchant) and Enez (a retail merchant; maiden name, Blumm) Hart; married Joan Goldhammer, June 9, 1968. *Education:* Swarthmore College, B.A., 1969; University of California, Berkeley, M.A., 1970, Ph.D., 1975. *Home:* 4822 East Ridgewood Dr., Bloomington, Ind. 47401. *Office:* Department of Political Science, Indiana University, Bloomington, Ind. 47405.

CAREER: Princeton University, Princeton, N.J., lecturer, 1973-75, assistant professor of political science, 1975-79; President's Commission for a National Agenda for the Eighties, Washington, D.C., member of professional staff, 1980; Indiana University, Bloomington, associate professor of political science, 1981—. Visiting fellow at Lehrman Institute, 1980, and Harvard University's Center for International Affairs, 1982-83. *Member:* International Studies Association, American Political Science Association, Social Science History Association. *Awards, honors:* Paul Henri Spaak fellowship from Frank Boas Foundation, 1982-83.

WRITINGS: The Anglo-Icelandic Cod War of 1972-1973, Institute of International Studies, University of California, Berkeley, 1976; (with Paul Bunge) *The United States and the World Community in the Eighties,* Prentice-Hall, 1982; *The New International Economic Order,* Macmillan, 1983.

WORK IN PROGRESS: A book on competition among the largest industrial countries in three industries, steel, automobiles, and semiconductors, publication expected in 1985.

SIDELIGHTS: Hart wrote: "I got started in international politics when I joined my high school debating club and was given the assignment of arguing about the desirability of banning nuclear weapons.

"My graduate studies at the University of California, Berkeley, got me interested in the law of the sea and the potential for international conflict over scarce resources. I specialized increasingly in questions dealing with the interaction between international politics and economics. As a staff member of the President's Commission for a National Agenda for the Eighties, I wrote on the challenges to U.S. foreign policy proposed by changes in the world economy: increased interdependence, the rise of OPEC and the newly industrialized countries, and the increasing competitiveness of Japan and Europe. *The New International Economic Order* focuses on the negotiations between rich and poor countries that took place between 1974 and 1977 on the rules governing the international economic system. Now I am turning from North-South relations to North-North because I see this as a major area of conflict for the next decade.''

* * *

HART, John 1942-

PERSONAL: Born October 3, 1942, in London, England; adopted son of George Edward (a stoker) and Hilda Lindley (Edwards) Hart. *Education:* London School of Economics and Political Science, London, Diploma in Social Administration, 1965; University of Bristol, Certificate in Applied Social Studies, 1966; University of Bradford, M.A., 1972. *Politics:* "Left wing." *Religion:* None. *Home:* 441 Greystones Rd., Sheffield, South Yorkshire, England. *Office:* Department of Applied Social Studies, Sheffield City Polytechnic, Pond St., Sheffield S1 1WB, England.

CAREER: South-West London Probation and After-Care Service, London, England, probation officer, 1966-69; University of Leeds, St. James Hospital, Leeds, England, psychiatric social worker, 1969-72; University of Edinburgh, Edinburgh, Scotland, student counselor, 1972-73; Guy's Hospital, London, social worker, 1973; Social Services Department, Barnsley, England, training officer, 1974-75; University of Sheffield, Sheffield, England, part-time lecturer in social work and student supervisor, 1975-77; Sheffield City Polytechnic, Sheffield, principal lecturer in social work, 1977—. Part-time lecturer in social policy and social work at Manchester Polytechnic and Huddersfield Polytechnic, 1973-74; visiting member of faculty at University of Sydney, 1983. Guest of television programs, including "Gay Life" and "Exchange Flags." *Member:* Association of Psychiatric Social Workers (associate member). *Awards, honors:* Award from Education Television Association, 1977, for video production "Admission."

WRITINGS: (Contributor) Noel Timms, editor, *Recording in Social Work*, Routledge & Kegan Paul, 1972; (contributor) Timms, editor, *The Receiving End*, Routledge & Kegan Paul, 1973; *Social Work and Sexual Conduct*, Routledge & Kegan Paul, 1979; (contributor) Roy Bailey and Mike Brake, editors, *Radical Social Work and Practice*, Edward Arnold, 1980; (with Diane Richardson) *The Theory and Practice of Homosexuality*, Routledge & Kegan Paul, 1981; *Same Sex—Different Meanings*, Penguin, 1983. Contributor to social work journals.

WORK IN PROGRESS: A videobook series on the major personal problems brought to paraprofessionals and self-help groups; an article on theories of sexual identity development for *Journal of Homosexuality*.

SIDELIGHTS: Hart wrote: "My career in one of the caring professions progressed satisfactorily over a period of ten years. I worked for a number of agencies, then moved into teaching, where I began to specialize in the area of sexuality, especially sexual difference. After writing three books on the subject, I attempted to return to the practice of social work, only to find that my reputation had gone before me. It seemed that I was no longer able to work in government agencies.

"It appeared that I was judged an unsuitable person to hold a responsible public position. I had announced publicly that I believe one's private sexuality is a 'political' matter. I had appeared on television and radio programs, and had discussed sexuality as an openly gay person. Of course people of diverse sexual orientations *do* work in responsible positions, but people who keep silent about their own sexual politics can deal with similar subjects and not be questioned.

"After a decade I now wonder if my work has been worth the costs. This is one reason I'm delighted that I was asked to teach in Australia for three months. No doubt sexuality will make some appearance in my teaching a course on how to translate academic theory into clinical practice. However, in the future I plan to edit a series of books based on my experience with the less 'spectacular' problems which bring clients to the helping professions."

* * *

HART, Judith 1924-

PERSONAL: Born in September, 1924, in Burnley, Lancashire, England; daughter of Harry Ridehalgh; married Anthony Bernard Hart (a research scientist); children: Richard, Stephen. *Education:* Attended London School of Economics and Political Science, London. *Office:* House of Commons, London SW1A 0AA, England.

CAREER: Parliament, London, England, Labour member of House of Commons for Lanark Division of Lanarkshire, Scotland, 1959—, joint Parliamentary undersecretary of state for Scotland, 1964-66, minister of state for commonwealth affairs, 1966-67, minister of social security, 1967-68, paymaster-general, 1968-69, minister of overseas development, 1969-70, 1974-75, 1977-79, shadow minister of overseas development, 1970-74, 1979-80. Member of Privy Council. Member of national executive committee of Labour party, chairman of industrial policy committee, 1973-77, chairman of Labour party, 1981-82.

WRITINGS: Aid and Liberation, Gollancz, 1973.

* * *

HART, Milton R. 1896(?)-1983

OBITUARY NOTICE: Born c. 1896; died March 24, 1983, in Chicago, Ill. Newspaper editor. Hart served as day telegraph editor for *Chicago Today* and as a staff member of its predecessors for thirty-five years. He also worked as an editor for the *Milwaukee Journal*. Obituaries and other sources: *Chicago Tribune*, March 27, 1983.

* * *

HART, Moss 1904-1961
(Robert Arnold Conrad)

PERSONAL: Born October 24, 1904, in New York, N.Y.; died December 20, 1961, in Palm Springs, Calif.; son of Barnett (a cigar maker) and Lillian (Solomon) Hart; married Kitty Carlisle (an actress), August 10, 1946; children: Christopher, Cathy Carlisle. *Education:* Attended Columbia University. *Residence:* New York, N.Y., and New Hope, Pa.

CAREER: Playwright, librettist, and director of stage productions. Worked for A. L. Newberger Furs, Inc., New York City, c. 1918-21; traveled throughout the United States as secretary to Augustus Pitou, Jr. (theatrical manager), c. 1921-23; social director and entertainer at resort camps in Catskill Mountains, summers, c. 1923-29; director of "Little Theatre" in New York and New Jersey, winters, c. 1923-29; worked as an actor, including role of Smithers in "The Emperor Jones," Mayfair Theatre, New York City, 1926; director of stage productions, including "Once in a Lifetime," 1931, "Lady in the

Dark," 1941, 1943, "Junior Miss," 1941, "The Secret Room," 1942, 1945, "Winged Victory," 1943, "Dear Ruth," 1944, "Christopher Blake," 1946, "Light Up the Sky," 1948, (and producer) "Miss Liberty," 1949, "The Climate of Eden," 1952, "Anniversary Waltz," 1954, "My Fair Lady," 1956, 1958, (and producer) "Camelot," 1960.

AWARDS, HONORS: Roi Cooper McGrue Prize, 1930, for "Once in a Life Time"; Pulitzer Prize in drama, 1936, for "You Can't Take It With You"; Academy Award nominations for best screenplay from Academy of Motion Picture Arts and Sciences, 1935, for "Broadway Melody of 1936," and 1947, for "Gentleman's Agreement"; Writers Guild nominations, 1952, for "Hans Christian Andersen," and 1954, for "A Star Is Born"; New York Drama Critics Award for best director, 1955, and Antoinette F. Perry Award for best director, 1956, both for "My Fair Lady"; elected to the Theatre Hall of Fame, 1972.

WRITINGS—Plays: *Lady in the Dark* (musical comedy; lyrics by Ira Gershwin and music by Kurt Weill; first produced on Broadway at Alvin Theatre, January 23, 1941), Random House, 1941; *Winged Victory: The Air Force Play* (first produced on Broadway at Forty-fourth Street Theatre, November 20, 1943), Random House, 1943; *Christopher Blake* (drama; first produced on Broadway at Music Box Theatre, December, 1946), Random House, 1947; *Light Up the Sky: A Play* (first produced on Broadway at Royal Theatre, 1949), Random House, 1949; *The Climate of Eden: A Play* (two-act drama; adapted from the novel *Shadows Move Among Them* by Edgar Mittelholzer; first produced on Broadway at Martin Beck Theatre, November 13, 1952), Random House, 1953.

With George S. Kaufman: *Once in a Lifetime: A Comedy* (three-act; first produced on Broadway at Music Box Theatre, September 24, 1930; revival produced on Broadway at Circle in the Square Theatre, c. June 16, 1978), Farrar & Rinehart, 1930, published as *Once in a Lifetime: A Comedy in Three Acts,* Samuel French, 1933, reprinted, 1978; *Merrily We Roll Along* (three-act; first produced on Broadway at Music Box Theatre, September 29, 1934), Random House, 1934; *You Can't Take It With You: A Play* (three-act comedy; first produced on Broadway at Booth Theatre, December 14, 1936; revival produced on Broadway at Lyceum Theatre, November 23, 1965), Farrar & Rinehart, 1937, Samuel French, 1964; *The Fabulous Invalid: A Play in Two Acts* (first produced on Broadway at Broadhurst Theatre, October 8, 1938), Random House, 1938; *The Man Who Came to Dinner* (three-act comedy; first produced on Broadway at Music Box Theatre, October 16, 1939), Random House, 1939, acting edition, Dramatists Play Service, 1967; *The American Way* (two-act spectacle; first produced in New York at Center Theatre, January 21, 1939), Random House, 1939; *George Washington Slept Here: A Comedy in Three Acts* (first produced on Broadway at Lyceum Theatre, October 18, 1940), Random House, 1940, acting edition, Dramatists Play Service, 1941.

Unpublished plays: (Under pseudonym Robert Arnold Conrad) "The Hold-up Man" (also titled "The Beloved Bandit"), first produced in Chicago, Ill., at National Theatre, December, 1923; (with Dorothy Heyward) "Jonica," first produced in 1930; "Garrick Gaieties," first produced on Broadway at Guild Theatre, June 4, 1930; "The Show Is On," first produced on Broadway at Winter Garden Theatre, December 25, 1936; "Sing Out the News," first produced on Broadway at Music Box Theatre, September 24, 1938; "Inside U.S.A.," first produced on Broadway at Century Theatre, April 30, 1948. Also author

of "The Lunchtime Follies" and co-author of "Seven Lively Arts."

Screenplays: "Flesh," Metro-Goldwyn-Mayer (MGM), 1932; "Once in a Lifetime" (adapted from the play with the same title; also see above), Universal, 1932; "The Masquerader," United Artists, 1933; "Broadway Melody of 1936," MGM, 1935; "Frankie and Johnnie," RKO, 1935; "George Washington Slept Here" (adapted from the play with the same title; also see above), Warner Bros., 1942; "Winged Victory" (adapted from the play with the same title; also see above), Twentieth Century-Fox, 1944; "Lady in the Dark" (adapted from the play with the same title; also see above), Paramount, 1944; "Gentleman's Agreement," Twentieth Century-Fox, 1947; "The Decision of Christopher Blake" (adapted from the play *Christopher Blake*; also see above), Warner Bros., 1948; "Hans Christian Andersen" (adapted from a story by Myles Connolly), RKO, 1952; "A Star Is Born" (adapted from the screenplay by Dorthy Parker, Alan Campbell, and Robert Carson and from the story by William A. Wellman and Robert Carson), Warner Bros., 1954; "Prince of Players," Twentieth Century-Fox, 1955.

Librettos and musical revues: (With Irving Berlin) "Face the Music," first produced on Broadway at New Amsterdam Theatre, February, 1932; (with Berlin) "As Thousands Cheer," first produced in 1933; (with Johann Strauss, Sr., and Johann Strauss, Jr.) "The Great Waltz," 1934; (with Cole Porter) "Jubilee," 1935; (with George S. Kaufman) *I'd Rather Be Right* (two-act; music and lyrics by Richard Rodgers and Lorenz Hart; first produced on Broadway at Alvin Theatre, November 2, 1937), Random House, 1937.

Other: *Six Plays by George S. Kaufman and Moss Hart* (omnibus volume; includes "George Washington Slept Here"), Random House, 1942, new edition (with introduction by Brooks Atkinson), 1958; (author of foreword) *The Cole Porter Song Book: The Complete Words and Music of Cole Porter's Best-Loved Songs,* illustrations by Robert J. Lee, Simon & Schuster, 1959; *Act One: An Autobiography,* Random House, 1959.

Work represented in many anthologies, including *Six Modern American Plays,* edited by Allan G. Halline, Modern Library, 1966, and *Three Comedies of Family Life,* edited by Joseph E. Mersand.

SIDELIGHTS: Moss Hart's first play, "The Hold-up Man," lost his producer $45,000 and cost Hart his job. The producer of the play, Augustus Pitou, Jr., for whom Hart worked as an office boy, fired the writer after the play received dismal notices during its five-week Chicago premiere run. Undaunted by this initial disaster, Hart continued to write plays, all unsuccessful or unproduced until 1929 when he wrote the script for his first comedy, "Once in a Lifetime." Broadway producer Sam H. Harris recognized the merits of the work and agreed to produce it on the condition that Hart rewrite it with the assistance of established playwright George S. Kaufman.

Thus began one of the most famous playwriting teams in the history of the American theatre. Brooks Atkinson described the Hart-Kaufman partnership in *Broadway:* "In 1930, when he was forty-one years of age, Kaufman collaborated with an unknown man of twenty-six who turned out to be the most generally congenial of all the writers he worked with. . . . It is impossible to separate the individual contributions each writer made to the final script [of 'Once in a Lifetime']. By age and experience, Kaufman was no doubt the dominant figure in the final preparation of the script. But Hart's style resembled Kaufman's; the play represented each of them fairly."

"Once in a Lifetime" was an immediate success on Broadway. Opening at the Music Box Theatre on September 24, 1930, it was performed 305 times in two years, "a healthy record in the days before theatres were air-conditioned and before New York in the summer was acclaimed as a festival," Howard Taubman opined in the *New York Times.*

Following success with success, Hart and Kaufman wrote "Merrily We Roll Along" in 1934 and "You Can't Take It With You," a Pulitzer Prize-winning farce about an eccentric family, in 1937. "You Can't Take It With You" surpassed the "healthy record" established by "Once in a Lifetime," running for 837 performances. "I'd Rather Be Right," also written in 1937, was among the most popular of the Hart-Kaufman plays. It satirized New Deal politics and featured the legendary actor George M. Cohan in the role of President Franklin D. Roosevelt.

"Once in a Lifetime," "You Can't Take It With You," and many other Hart-Kaufman plays have withstood the test of time, remaining popular through several revivals. In 1962 Taubman wrote that "Once in a Lifetime" "earn[s] the laughs it continues to command." And in 1978 T. E. Kalem commented in *Time* that "Once in a Lifetime" is "a roller coaster of merriment, with hairpin turns of plot, zany swoops of emotion and a breakneck tempo." According to Taubman, "You Can't Take It With You" is the "dottiest, most enduring of the Moss Hart-George S. Kaufman collaborations." "It is still a wonderfully funny farce," Taubman wrote, "see for yourself . . . and laugh as happily as we did almost three decades ago."

According to comments by Atkinson in *Broadway,* Kaufman and Hart also "wrote a few plays that lacked distinction, like *The Fabulous Invalid,* a mechanically contrived affirmation of faith in the theater [and] *The American Way,* a well-meant though commonplace uplift drama about America at the time when another war seemed imminent." Atkinson was even more disparaging when he called "George Washington Slept Here" a "piece of hackwork."

Disappointed by the failure of "George Washington Slept Here" and fearing that he'd be remembered only as half of a writing team, Hart split from Kaufman in 1940. Hart continued to write and in 1941 brought out "Lady in the Dark," a musical comedy about a woman undergoing psychoanalysis. The play included conventional dramatic scenes that alternated with what *Nation* critic Joseph Wood Krutch characterized as "fantastic musical interludes representing her [the heroine's] dreams." Juxtaposed drama and fantasy were employed again in Hart's next play, "Christopher Blake," the story of a twelve-year-old boy traumatized by his parents' divorce. "The eight scenes [of 'Christopher Blake'] alternate between the courthouse itself and the inside of the boy's head, where elaborate phantasies act themselves out," Krutch explained. "Obviously, therefore, it suggests Mr. Hart's extravaganza 'Lady in the Dark,' but it is actually a much more sinister phenomenon." Whereas Krutch found "Lady in the Dark" to be "curiously evocative" and praised Hart for achieving "that mysterious thing called style," the critic assessed that "Christopher Blake" "can readily be shaken down to as neat a little collection of moral and dramatic cliches as was ever assembled."

After his break with Kaufman, Hart also became active as a director. In 1956 he won a Tony Award for his direction of Learner and Loewe's "My Fair Lady." It was his finest stage direction, Atkinson noted. As the critic explained: "Hart's instinct for the stage, casting, and performing—and his respect for Shaw, whom he venerated and hoped to emulate—made

the difference between a splendid musical play and a classic." The play ran on Broadway for several years and went to London in 1958 with Julie Andrews and Rex Harrison in the lead roles. Drew Middleton wrote in the *New York Times* that the premiere was a "dazzling success. Three hours of melody and laughter swept away inhibitions raised by Britons' gloomy forebodings that the show couldn't be as good as the Yanks said it was."

Atkinson eulogized Hart in *Broadway,* writing that "both Kaufman and Hart gave Broadway not only wit and skill but also integrity. . . . Broadway was the center of their lives; they loved its absurdities and ludicrous presentations as well as its professionalism. They presided over an era and pioneered the withering, iconoclastic play that made routine comedy obsolete."

MEDIA ADAPTATIONS: Robert Riskin adapted "You Can't Take It With You" into a film, produced by Columbia, 1938; the Epstein brothers adapted "The Man Who Came to Dinner" into a film produced by Warner Bros., 1942; Dore Schary created a screenplay from *Act One,* produced by Warner Bros., 1965, starring Jason Robards; L. Rosenthal and James Lipton wrote "Sherry!," a musical comedy based on "The Man Who Came to Dinner," first produced on Broadway at Alvin Theatre, March, 1967.

BIOGRAPHICAL/CRITICAL SOURCES—Books: Glenn Hughes, *A History of the American Theatre: 1700-1950,* Samuel French, 1951; David Ewen, *Complete Book of the American Musical Theatre,* Holt, 1958; Moss Hart, *Act One: An Autobiography,* Random House, 1959; Jean Gould, *Modern American Playwrights,* Dodd, 1966; Brooks Atkinson, *Broadway,* Macmillan, 1970; Ted Sennett, *Lunatics and Lovers,* Arlington, 1973.

Periodicals: *Commonweal,* October 25, 1935, December 25, 1936, October 21, 1938, February 7, 1941, December 10, 1943, December 20, 1946, December 3, 1948; *New Republic,* December 30, 1936, October 26, 1938, February 10, 1941, December 6, 1943, December 16, 1946; *Nation,* October 22, 1938, February 8, 1941, December 21, 1946, December 11, 1948; *New York Times,* March 8, 1952, November 7, 1952, November 16, 1952, November 26, 1952, November 21, 1953, January 12, 1954, April 8, 1954, October 12, 1954, March 16, 1956, March 25, 1956, April 29, 1956, June 3, 1956, March 9, 1958, May 1, 1958, October 10, 1960, December 5, 1960, December 11, 1960, October 30, 1962, December 27, 1963, January 29, 1964, May 21, 1964, November 24, 1965, December 5, 1965, March 29, 1967, April 9, 1967, June 14, 1968, June 16, 1978; *Life,* August 24, 1959; *McCall's,* September, 1959; *Vogue,* September 15, 1959; *Time,* September 21, 1959, July 17, 1978; *Cosmopolitan,* November, 1960; *Esquire,* January, 1962; *Saturday Review,* January 20, 1962.

OBITUARIES: New York Times, December 21, 1961, December 23, 1961; *Time,* December 29, 1961; *Illustrated London News,* December 30, 1961; *Newsweek,* January 1, 1962; *Publishers Weekly,* January 8, 1962; *Current Biography,* February, 1962.*

—*Sketch by Susan D. Finley*

*   *   *

HARTSOE, Colleen Ivey   1925-

PERSONAL: Born May 19, 1925, in Carlsbad, N.M.; daughter of Francis L. (a railroad telegrapher) and Evelyn (a teacher; maiden name, Miller) Ivey; married Charles W. Hartsoe (a corporate financial executive), December 27, 1951; children: Eileen, Karen, Charles. *Education:* Attended Del Mar College, 1941-43; University of Texas, B.S., 1944; University of Maryland, M.Ed., 1948. *Religion:* Episcopalian. *Home:* 925 Croyden St., High Point, N.C. 27260.

CAREER: Elementary school teacher in Corpus Christi, Tex., Montgomery County, Md., and Forsyth County, N.C., 1944-51; author.

WRITINGS: Dear Daughter: Letters From Eve and Other Women of the Bible, Morehouse, 1981.

SIDELIGHTS: Colleen Hartsoe wrote: "My special interest is the church. I want it to speak in relevant terms, yet without giving the impression of being without standards. I am also a feminist, but one who has only a limited understanding of what working women are coping with. I wrote my one book because I needed it in a study I was leading, and it didn't exist. If I write again it'll be for the same reason."

* * *

HARVEY, Earle Sherburn 1906-

PERSONAL: Born February 21, 1906, in Marshfield, Wis.; son of Jesse H. (a baker) and Nellie Bell (Bartle) Harvey; married Adelaide T. Karp, October 11, 1933 (died October 1, 1982); children: Paul E., James H. *Education:* Attended high school in Marshfield, Wis. *Politics:* Independent. *Religion:* Roman Catholic. *Home:* 3342 Pembrook Dr., Sarasota, Fla. 33579. *Office address* (summers): P.O. Box 56, Wallace, Mich. 49893.

CAREER: Milwaukee Sentinel, Milwaukee, Wis., staff artist, 1931-38; associated with *Waukegan Post,* Waukegan, Ill., 1939-41; *Chicago American,* Chicago, Ill., staff artist, 1941-48, assistant editorial art director, 1948-58, editorial art director, 1958-60; *Chicago Today,* Chicago, editorial art director, 1960-71. *Member:* Association of American Editorial Cartoonists, Chicago Press Veterans. *Awards, honors:* Award from *Cartoons Magazine,* 1926.

WRITINGS: Funny Laws (cartoons), New American Library, 1982. Author of "Wisconsin Oddities," a cartoon feature in *Milwaukee Sentinel,* 1933-36, "Chicago Firsts," in *Chicago American,* 1955-60, and "Speaking of the Law," syndicated by Associated Court and Commercial Newspapers News Service, 1963—.

SIDELIGHTS: Earle Harvey told *CA:* "Even before finishing grade school I had completed three cartoon and illustration correspondence courses. I didn't finish high school in Marshfield because I couldn't pass up an offer to join the *Milwaukee Herald,* a German language daily paper published in Milwaukee. The editor was surprised to find me so young, but we got along beautifully and with his coaching I was soon doing editorial cartoons in German. Many of the cartoons were reprinted in papers in Germany.

"In 1926 I won the annual, worldwide *Cartoons Magazine* contest. It opened a few doors for me. I joined a studio and went into commercial art. After a few years, illustrating advertising matter, drawing radios, furniture, etc., became boring to me. One day Frank Marasco called and asked if I would like to join his staff on the editorial art department of the *Milwaukee Sentinel.* That was 1931 and I was to spend the rest of my art career on newspapers.

"After a year or so I developed a cartoon panel called 'Wisconsin Historic Oddities.' It was an instant success—letters

poured in, and school kids all over Wisconsin were making scrap books. In 1936 I transferred to the *Wisconsin News,* serving there until the paper had labor troubles and folded in 1938.

"Hearing that a new daily newspaper was going to start publishing in Waukegan, Illinois, I went there and got a job with the *Waukegan Post.* Tough luck followed again: the *Post* folded in 1941. A few weeks later, however, I accepted a job with the *Chicago American.* I was assigned to making daily war maps during World War II, but told the editor that I would like to get back to cartooning. One day editor Ted Doyle called me into his office and asked if I would like to do a series on Chicago 'firsts.' I jumped at the opportunity. Again it was a success and school kids were pasting them in scrap books. I really enjoyed working on this feature. I was named editorial art director in 1958 and continued in that position when the paper's name changed to *Chicago Today.* I retired in 1971.

"While my son Jim was an editor for the *Chicago Daily Law Bulletin* he was in charge of national news and front page layout. One day in 1963 he mentioned to me that he wished he had better art to liven up a dull page of type. I suggested a cartoon, 'Speaking of the Law.' During all my years on the newspapers my one hobby was collecting stories and clips regarding odd laws. I had a box full of them. The first cartoon Jim ran was a hit. Lawyers and judges called asking for more. It became a regular feature. Other law papers asked to run them and soon the cartoon was syndicated to all Associated Court and Commercial Newspapers. *Funny Laws* is a collection of these cartoons. Jim and I hope it becomes one of a series of paperbacks."

AVOCATIONAL INTERESTS: Travel, baseball, photography, painting.

* * *

HARVEY, Harriet 1924-
(Harriet Gibney)

PERSONAL: Born April 23, 1924, in Lake Forest, Ill.; daughter of William Dow (in business) and Lucy (in business; maiden name, Smith) Harvey; married second husband, William S. Coffin, Jr. (a minister), August 23, 1969 (divorced December 16, 1982); children: (first marriage) Philip Alexander Gibney, Margot Madeleine Gibney. *Education:* Vassar College, B.A., 1945. *Politics:* Democrat. *Office:* PTV Production, Inc., 40 Harbor Oak Dr., Tiburon, Calif. 94920.

CAREER: Served with American Red Cross as overseas club worker in the Philippines and Japan, 1945-46; United Press (now United Press International), Tokyo, Japan, reporter, 1946; Public Information Office of the Supreme Commander of Allied Forces, Tokyo, reporter, 1947-48; *Hong Kong Telegraph,* Hong Kong, editor of women's page and feature writer, 1948-49; WJZ-TV, New York City, director and presenter of interview program "It's a Wonderful World," 1950; American Geographical Society, New York City, assistant to director, 1951-53; Redpath Agency, New York City, lecturer on Japan, China, and the Philippines, 1951-53; Ford Foundation, New York City, investigator in Public Affairs Section, 1956-57; Harvard University, Cambridge, Mass., assistant director of public relations for fund drive "A Program for Harvard College," 1957-58; Massachusetts Institute of Technology, Cambridge, staff writer for Physical Science Study Committee, 1958-60; Children's Hospital Medical Center, Boston, Mass., director of public relations, 1960-63, director of health education department and editorial director of ''Publications for Parents,'' 1963-69; Yale University, New Haven, Conn., instructor in psychology, 1970, visiting lecturer in English, 1970-76; Institute for Advanced Pastoral Studies, Bloomfield Hills, Mich., co-director of educational project, 1976-77; PTV Production, Inc., Tiburon, Calif., producer, writer, and member of board of trustees, 1977—. Broadcaster for Armed Forces Network, Tokyo. Fellow at Yale University, 1971. Member of board of directors of Yale University Women's Organization, 1971-76, Cornerstone, New Haven, 1971-74, Foundation for the Realization of Humankind, 1974-76, and Farallone's Institute, 1976-79. *Member:* Media Alliance, Authors Guild.

WRITINGS—Under name Harriet Harvey: *Stories Parents Seldom Hear: College Students Write About Their Lives and Families,* Delacorte, 1983.

Editor; under name Harriet Gibney: *Communications and Creative Endeavor,* Basic Books, 1960; *The Family and the Doctor,* U.S. Public Health Service, 1964; Margret Rey and H. A. Rey, *Curious George Goes to the Hospital* (juvenile), Houghton, 1965; *How to Prevent Childhood Poisoning: A New Approach,* Children's Hospital Medical Center (Boston, Mass.), 1966; *The Accident Handbook: A New Approach to Family Safety,* Children's Hospital Medical Center, 1966; *What to Do When ''There's Nothing to Do,''* Delacorte, 1968; *Pregnancy and the Newborn Child,* Delacorte, 1969; *Your Child and Ileal Conduit Surgery,* Thomas Nelson, 1970; George E. Gardner, *The Emerging Personality,* Delacorte, 1970; *Keeping Your Child Healthy Overseas,* Delacorte, 1975; *Child Health Encyclopedia,* Delacorte, 1975.

Scripts; under name Harriet Gibney: ''The Explorers: A Story of Discovery at the Frontiers of Physics,'' a live program produced in New York, N.Y., at Harvard Club, April, 1957; ''A New Picture of the Universe,'' released by Massachusetts Institute of Technology in 1958; ''The Development of Feelings in Children,'' released by *Parents' Magazine* in 1973.

Contributor to magazines and newspapers, including *New Yorker, Vogue, Parents' Magazine,* and *New York Times.*

WORK IN PROGRESS: A documentary film about Japanese business in America, ''The Human Side of Productivity,'' for PBS-TV.

SIDELIGHTS: Harriet Harvey wrote: ''I started my career as a foreign correspondent in Japan, China, and Hong Kong. I returned to the United States in the earliest days of television, hosted an interview program, and lectured along the East Coast.

''In 1952, I became intrigued by the problem of making the accelerated increase in knowledge available to laymen. I devoted the next sixteen years to this endeavor, translating scientific discoveries and other scholarly material into popular forms. I have been doing this ever since in writing or in film.

''As director of the health education department of Children's Hospital Medical Center in Boston, I directed a unique publishing program, 'Publications for Parents,' which produced popular books, filmstrips, and pamphlets on any subject parents or children wanted to know about. We used doctors, other child care experts, and parents themselves as authors and advisers.

''During this period, I also acted as a principal adviser for animated films produced by John and Faith Hubley. 'Cockaboody,' a film about childhood fantasy, was nominated for an Oscar. 'The Carousel' is an interpretation of Erik H. Erikson's *Eight Stages of Life.*

''In 1977, I joined PTV Production, Inc., a nonprofit corporation producing films for public broadcasting. These include a five-part documentary series, 'Work: As If People Mattered,' about new work humanization projects in major U.S. corporations.''

AVOCATIONAL INTERESTS: Flying (with private pilot's license), sailing, tennis, skiing, wilderness trips.

* * *

HARVIE-WATT, George Steven 1903-

PERSONAL: Born August 23, 1903, in Bathgate, Scotland; son of James McDougal and Jessie (Harvie) Watt; married Jane Elizabeth Taylor, 1932; children: James, Euan, Rachel. *Education:* University of Glasgow, M.A., 1924; further study in law at University of Edinburgh. *Home:* Sea Tangle, Elie, Fife, Scotland.

CAREER: Called to the Bar at Inner Temple, 1930, appointed King's Counsel, 1945; Parliament, London, England, Conservative member for Keighley, 1931-35, and Richmond, 1936-59, private secretary to secretary of Board of Trade, 1937, assistant government whip, 1938-40, private secretary to Prime Minister Winston Churchill, 1941-45, member of United Kingdom delegation to Commonwealth Parliamentary Association Conferences in Ottawa, Ontario, and Washington, D.C., 1949, and Australia and New Zealand, 1950; Consolidated Gold Fields Ltd., chairman, 1960-69, president, 1969-73. Chairman of Monotype Corp., 1953-73; chairman of Gold Fields Mining and Industrial Ltd. until 1970, honorary president, 1970-79; president of Printers Pension Corp., 1956-57; member of board of directors of Eagle Star Insurance Co., Midland Bank, Standard Bank, Clydesdale Bank, and North British Steel Corp.; past member of board of directors of Great Western Railway Co. Aide-de-camp to King George VI, 1948-52, and Queen Elizabeth II, 1952-58; member of Queen's Body Guard for Scotland, Royal Company of Archers. Member of Kensington Borough Council, 1934-45; member of Greater London Council, 1966; justice of the peace of the County of London, 1944-56. *Military service:* British Army, Royal Engineers, 1935-41, 1948-50; became brigadier general; received Territorial Decoration.

MEMBER: Royal Society of Arts (fellow), Highland Society (honorary vice-president), Pratt's Club, Caledonian Club. *Awards, honors:* Created baronet of Bathgate, 1945; gold medal from Institution of Mining and Metallurgy, 1969, for services to mining; honorary freeman of the City of London, 1976.

WRITINGS: Most of My Life (autobiography), Springwood Books, 1980.

* * *

HASEGAWA, Tsuyoshi 1941-

PERSONAL: Born February 23, 1941, in Tokyo, Japan; came to the United States in 1964, naturalized citizen, 1976; son of Chosei (a publisher) and Chiyo (Amemiya) Hasegawa; married, 1968 (marriage ended); children: Kim Marie, Stephen Shinobu. *Education:* University of Tokyo, B.A., 1964; University of Washington, Seattle, M.A., 1967, Ph.D., 1969. *Office:* Department of History, State University of New York College at Oswego, Oswego, N.Y. 13126.

CAREER: State University of New York College at Oswego, assistant professor, 1969-72, associate professor of history,

1972—. *Member:* American Historical Association, American Association for the Advancement of Slavic Studies, Japanese Association for Russian Studies. *Awards, honors:* Fulbright fellow and International Research and Exchange Board fellow in the Soviet Union, both 1976-77; fellow of National Endowment for the Humanities, 1981.

WRITINGS: (Translator with William L. MacDonald) Iulian Konstantinovich Shchutskii, *Researches on I Ching,* Princeton University Press, 1979; *The February Revolution: Petrograd, 1917,* University of Washington Press, 1981. Contributor to Slavic studies journals.

WORK IN PROGRESS: Crime and Revolution: Petrograd, 1917; Japanese-Soviet Relations and International Security.

SIDELIGHTS: Hasegawa commented: "I am sure that I made some errors in *The February Revolution,* and neither money nor fame will result from this scholarly monograph, but I am proud of it, because I can honestly say that I have done my very best to make it a good book. I have written a good book while getting stuck in an intellectual desert—an accomplishment quite comparable to that of a Soviet political prisoner managing to write a book in a Gulag in Siberia. In fact, looking back, it is a miracle that I managed it at all, rather than committing suicide."

*   *   *

HASLUCK, Paul (Meernaa Caedwalla)   1905-

PERSONAL: Born April 1, 1905, in Fremantle, Australia; son of E.M.C. Hasluck; married Alexandra Margaret Darker Martin, 1932; children: Nicholas, Rollo. *Education:* Received M.A. from University of Western Australia. *Home:* 2 Adams Rd., Dalkeith, Western Australia 6009.

CAREER: Member of literary staff of *West Australian,* 1922-38; University of Western Australia, Perth, lecturer in history, 1939-40; affiliated with Australian Department of External Affairs beginning in 1941, Australian delegate to executive committee of United Nations Preparatory Commission, 1945, director of Post-Hostilities Division, 1945; counselor in charge of Australian mission to the United Nations and delegate to United Nations General Assembly in New York, N.Y., 1946, acting representative to Security Council, Atomic Energy Commission, and Conventional Arms Commission, 1946-47; University of Western Australia, reader in history, 1948; Australian Parliament, Liberal member of Parliament for Curtin, 1949-69, minister for territories, 1951-63, minister for defense, 1963-64, minister for external affairs, 1964-69; Government of Australia, governor-general of Australia, 1969-74. Chairman of Ministerial Councils of Southeast Asia Treaty Organization and ANZUS (Australia, New Zealand, and the United States; ANZUS Pact Nations), 1966; chairman of Economic Commission for Asia and the Far East, and Asian and Pacific Council, both 1968; leader of delegations to Economic Commission for Asia and the Far East, Asian and Pacific Council, Southeast Asia Treaty Organization, and Five-Power Defense Meeting, 1964-68. Member of Privy Council.

MEMBER: Australian Academy of Social Science (fellow), Australian Academy of the Humanitites (fellow), Royal Australian Historical Society (fellow), Knights of St. John (fellow). *Awards, honors:* Knight of Order of the Garter; Knight Grand Cross of St. Michael and St. George; Knight Grand Cross of Royal Victorian Order.

WRITINGS: Into the Desert (poems), Freshwater Bay Press, 1939; *Black Australians: A Survey of Native Policy in Western*

Australia, 1829-1897, Melbourne University Press, 1942; *Workshop of Security,* F. W. Cheshire, 1948; *The Government and the People,* Australian War Memorial, Volume I: *1939-41,* 1951, Volume II: *1942-45,* 1970; *Native Welfare in Australia,* P. Brokensha, 1953; *Collected Verse,* Hawthorn Press, 1969; *An Open Go,* Hawthorn Press, 1971; *The Poet in Australia,* Hawthorn Press, 1975; *A Time for Building: Australian Administration in Papua-New Guinea, 1951-1963,* Melbourne University Press, 1976; *Mucking About: An Autobiography,* Melbourne University Press, 1977; *The Office of the Governor-General,* Melbourne University Press, 1979; *Sir Robert Menzies,* Melbourne University Press, 1980; *Diplomatic Witness: Australian Foreign Affairs,* Melbourne University Press, 1980; (contributor) Ronald M. Berndt and Catherine H. Berndt, editors, *Aborigines of the West,* revised edition, University of West Australia Press, 1980. Also author of *Our Southern Half-Castes,* 1938.

*   *   *

HASTINGS, Hubert de Cronin   1902-
(Ivor de Wofle, Ivy de Wolfe)

PERSONAL: Born July 18, 1902, in London, England; son of Percy and Julie Lilian (Bass) Hastings; married Hazel Rickman Garrard, July 23, 1927; children: one son, one daughter. *Education:* Attended University of London. *Politics:* Tory. *Religion:* Church of England. *Home:* Bedham Manor, Fittleworth, Sussex, England. *Office:* 9-13 Queen Anne's Gate, Westminster, London S.W.1, England.

CAREER: Architectural Review, London, England, served as editor, chairman, and managing director, 1923-72. Also served as editor of *Architects' Journal,* beginning in 1932, and as chairman of Architectural Press. *Awards, honors:* Royal Gold Medal from Royal Institute of British Architects, 1971.

WRITINGS: The Alternative Society: Software for the 1980s, David & Charles, 1979. Also author of *The Consumer Society,* 1982.

Also author of books *Characteurs, The Italian Townscape,* and *Civilia* under pseudonyms Ivor de Wofle and Ivy de Wolfe.

*   *   *

HATCH, Mary Cottam   1912-1970

OBITUARY NOTICE: Born in 1912 in Salt Lake City, Utah; died June 3, 1970, in White Plains, N.Y. Librarian and author. A graduate in library sciences, Hatch joined the New York Public Library system in 1941, where she headed several branches and edited "Branch Library Book News" for five years. Specializing in books for young people, Hatch also wrote stories for children. These include *Thirteen Danish Tales, More Danish Tales,* and *Rosamunda.* Obituaries and other sources: Miriam B. Huber, *Story and Verse for Children,* Macmillan, 1965; *Who's Who in Library Service,* 4th edition, Shoe String, 1966; *Anthology of Children's Literature,* 4th edition, Houghton, 1970; *A Biographical Directory of Librarians in the United States and Canada,* 5th edition, American Library Association, 1970; *New York Times,* June 6, 1970.

*   *   *

HATCH, Nathan O(rr)   1946-

BRIEF ENTRY: Born May 17, 1946, in Chicago, Ill. American historian, educator, and author. Hatch, who has been a research fellow at Johns Hopkins University and at the Charles Warren Center for Studies in American History at Harvard University, began teaching American history at University of Notre Dame in 1975. His publications include *The Sacred Cause of Liberty: Republican Thought and the Millennium in Revolutionary New England* (Yale University Press, 1977), *The Gospel in America: Themes in the Story of America's Evangelicals* (Zondervan, 1979), and *The Bible in America: Essays in Cultural History* (Oxford University Press, 1982). *Address:* Department of History, University of Notre Dame, Notre Dame, Ind. 46556. *Biographical/critical sources: American Historical Review*, October, 1978.

* * *

HATLEN, Burton (Norval) 1936-

PERSONAL: Born April 9, 1936, in Santa Barbara, Calif.; son of Julius H. (a farmer) and Lillie (Torvend) Hatlen; married wife, Barbara, September 20, 1961 (divorced January 31, 1983); children: Julia, Inger. *Education:* University of California, Berkeley, B.A., 1958; Columbia University, M.A., 1959; Harvard University, M.A., 1961; University of California, Davis, Ph.D., 1971. *Politics:* "Democratic Socialist." *Religion:* "Cheerful Agnostic." *Office:* Department of English, University of Maine, Orono, Me. 04473.

CAREER: King College, Bristol, Tenn., acting assistant professor of English, 1961-62; University of Cincinnati, Cincinnati, Ohio, instructor in English, 1962-65; University of Maine, Orono, assistant professor, 1967-73, associate professor of English, 1973—. *Member:* Modern Language Association of America, National Council of Teachers of English, Maine Writers and Publishers Alliance.

WRITINGS: (Editor) *George Oppen: Man and Poet*, University of Maine Press, 1982. Contributor of poetry to journals, including *Beloit Poetry Journal, Occident, Tar River Poetry, Penumbra, Kennebec, Black Fly Review*, and *Contraband*.

WORK IN PROGRESS: A biography of Charles Olson, publication by Twayne expected in 1984.

SIDELIGHTS: George Oppen: Man and Poet is an anthology of twenty-eight articles intended to better acquaint readers with this lesser-known American poet. Contributors include Eric Homberger, John Peck, Rachel Du Plessis, and the poet's wife, Mary, who contributed a memoir of her life with Oppen.

Hatlen told *CA:* "I would like to believe that the writing of poetry and the writing of criticism are not antithetical acts: that criticism is, in fact, a form of homage. Anyway, for me, the creation and the critical feed into each other."

BIOGRAPHICAL/CRITICAL SOURCES: Washington Post Book World, February 7, 1982; *Times Literary Supplement*, July 30, 1982.

* * *

HAULE, James M(ark) 1945-

PERSONAL: Born November 26, 1945, in Detroit, Mich.; son of Robert P. and Eileen M. Haule; married Margaret Ann Cyzeska (an elementary school teacher), November 29, 1968; children: Patricia, Katherine. *Education:* University of Michigan, B.A., 1968; Wayne State University, M.A., 1970, Ph.D., 1974. *Home:* 1505 Hawk, McAllen, Tex. 78501. *Office:* Department of English, Pan American University, Edinburg, Tex. 78539.

CAREER: Wayne State University, Detroit, Mich., instructor, 1974-75, assistant professor of English, 1975; Detroit College of Business, Dearborn, Mich., faculty coordinator, 1975-76; Detroit College of Business, Flint, Mich., associate professor of English and associate academic dean, 1976-78; Pan American University, Edinburg, Tex., associate professor of English, 1978—, assistant dean, 1978-80, director of Humanities Community Services, 1980—. Member of James Joyce Foundation. *Member:* Modern Language Association of America, American Association of University Professors, Conference of College Teachers of English, Virginia Woolf Society, South Central Modern Language Association.

WRITINGS: (Contributor) Patricia De La Fuente, Jan Seale, and Donald Fritz, editors, *James Dickey: Splintered Sunlight*, Pan American University, 1979; (with P. H. Smith, Jr.) *A Concordance to "The Waves" by Virginia Woolf*, Oxford Microform Publications, 1981; (with Smith) *A Concordance to "Between the Acts" by Virginia Woolf*, Oxford Microform Publications, 1982; (with Smith) *A Concordance to "To the Lighthouse" by Virginia Woolf*, Oxford Microform Publications, 1983; (with Smith) *A Concordance to "The Years" by Virginia Woolf*, Oxford Microform Publications, in press. General editor of "Living Authors Series," Pan American University, 1979—. Contributor of articles and reviews to literature journals, including *James Joyce Quarterly, Contemporary Literature*, and *Literature and Psychology*.

WORK IN PROGRESS: Five additional concordances to novels by Virginia Woolf; a book of poems.

SIDELIGHTS: Haule commented in *Contemporary Literature* on the practice of studying an author's letters, diaries, and discarded drafts: "The value of searching through the clutter of creative effort lies not in the secrets revealed about the life of the author, but rather in what we learn about the process of creation, the nature of style and, ultimately, what the search tells us about ourselves."

BIOGRAPHICAL/CRITICAL SOURCES: Contemporary Literature, winter, 1982.

* * *

HAUPT, Christopher (Charles Herbert) Lehmann
See LEHMANN-HAUPT, Christopher (Charles Herbert)

* * *

HAUSER, Robert Mason 1942-

PERSONAL: Born September 3, 1942, in Chicago, Ill.; son of Julius (a chemist) and Sylvia Ann (a social worker; maiden name, Gross) Hauser; married Taissa Louise Silvers, May 24, 1964; children: Joshua Matthew, Seth Morris. *Education:* University of Chicago, B.A., 1963; University of Michigan, M.A., 1966, Ph.D., 1968. *Home:* 592 Park Lane, Madison, Wis. 53711. *Office:* Department of Sociology, University of Wisconsin—Madison, Madison, Wis. 53706.

CAREER: Johns Hopkins University, Operations Research Office, Baltimore, Md. (now Research Analysis Corp., McLean, Va.), research assistant, summers, 1959-62; Jack Meltzer Associates (urban renewal and city planning consultants), Chicago, Ill., research assistant, 1962-63; Brown University, Providence, R.I., assistant professor of sociology, 1967-69; University of Wisconsin—Madison, assistant professor, 1969-71, associate professor, 1971-73, professor of sociology, 1973—,

Samuel A. Stouffer Professor of Sociology, 1981—, member of Center for Demography and Human Ecology, 1969—, member of Econometrics and Mathematical Economics Center and Social Systems Research Institute, both 1970-71, research associate at Institute for Research on Poverty, 1972—. Fellow at Center for Advanced Studies in the Behavioral Sciences, Palo Alto, Calif., 1977-78. Visiting professor at Institute for Advanced Study, Vienna, Austria, 1980; lecturer at colleges and universities. Research associate at American College Testing Program's Research Institute, 1971-73; member of advisory committee of University of Chicago's Educational Finance and Productivity Center, 1977-78; member of Social Science Research Council committees. Guest on WHA-Radio.

MEMBER: International Sociological Association (member of board of directors of research committee on social stratification), Sociological Research Association, American Association for the Advancement of Science (fellow), American Statistical Association (fellow; president of Madison chapter, 1973-75), American Sociological Association, Population Association of America, American Educational Research Association, Society for the Study of Social Biology, American Association of University Professors, Social Science History Association, Phi Kappa Phi.

WRITINGS: Socioeconomic Background and Educational Performance (monograph), American Sociological Association, 1971; (with William H. Sewell) *Education, Occupation, and Earnings: Achievement in the Early Career*, Academic Press, 1975; (editor with Sewell and David L. Featherman, and contributor) *Schooling and Achievement in American Society*, Academic Press, 1976; (with Featherman) *The Process of Stratification: Trends and Analysis*, Academic Press, 1977; (with Featherman) *Opportunity and Change*, Academic Press, 1978; (editor with David Mechanic, Archibald O. Haller, and Taissa S. Hauser, and contributor) *Social Structure and Behavior: Essays in Honor of William H. Sewell*, Academic Press, 1982.

Contributor: Edward O. Laumann, editor, *Social Stratification: Research and Theory for the 1970's*, Bobbs-Merrill, 1970; Herbert L. Costner, editor, *Sociology Methodology 1971*, Jossey-Bass, 1971; Arthur S. Goldberger and Otis D. Duncan, editors, *Structural Equation Models in the Social Sciences*, Seminar Press, 1973; Louis C. Solmon and Paul J. Taubman, editors, *Does College Matter?: Some Evidence on the Impacts of Higher Education*, Academic Press, 1973; Margaret S. Archer, editor, *Current Research in Sociology*, Mouton, 1974; Kenneth C. Land and Seymour Spilerman, editors, *Social Indicator Models*, Russell Sage Foundation, 1975; Taubman, editor, *Kinometrics: The Determinants of Educational Attainment, Mental Ability, and Occupational Success Within and Between Families*, North-Holland Publishing, 1977; Goldberger and Dennis J. Aigner, editors, *Latent Variables in Socioeconomic Models*, North-Holland Publishing, 1977; Wlodzimierz Wesolowski, Kazimierz M. Slomczynski, and Bogdan W. Mach, editors, *Social Mobility in Comparative Perspective*, Polish Academy of Sciences Press, 1978; Karl Taeuber, James A. Sweet, and Larry L. Bumpass, editors, *Social Demography: Research and Prospects*, Academic Press, 1978; Alan C. Kerckhoff, editor, *Research in Sociology of Education and Socialization: A Research Annual*, Volume I, Jai Press, 1980; Peter V. Marsden, editor, *Linear Models in Social Research*, Sage Publications, 1981.

Contributor of more than sixty articles and reviews to sociology, history, and education journals. Associate editor of *American Sociologist*, 1970-73, *American Journal of Sociology*, 1971-74, *Journal of Human Resources*, 1972-77, *Social Science Research*, 1972—, *Sociological Methods and Research*, 1972—, *American Sociological Review*, 1975-77, *Journal of the American Statistical Association*, 1977-79, and *Sociology of Education*, 1978—; member of editorial board of "Arnold and Caroline Rose Monograph Series," American Sociological Association, 1982—.

WORK IN PROGRESS: Contributing to *Social Stratification in Japan and the United States*, edited by Donald J. Treiman and Ken'ichi Tominaga; comparative studies of social mobility in industrial societies; longitudinal studies of sibling resemblance in social and economic achievement.

SIDELIGHTS: Hauser told *CA:* "I am a sociologist and statistician, not a writer. Neither discipline is noted for excellence in writing. All the same, I think that writing is an important part of the craft of social research. If I cannot explain what I have done, then I have not really done it, or have not done it well. I write papers, not books. My 'books' are at best collections of papers. The scientific paper is a literary form with several variations; my favorite is the *reductio ad absurdum*. Of course, a scientific paper must be worth writing; it must have some new theory, concept, method, or fact to report. Given that, most of my satisfaction comes from writing. I write to teach myself and others, to involve others in the process of my thoughts and activities. I like scientific writing that mirrors the process of discovery. My greatest dissatisfactions do not come from direct criticism or devaluation of my work, but from patent failures to understand it. Even though I want to be understood, I write for a select audience. I have written more than one paper with just one potential reader in mind. More often, I write for perhaps a dozen of my scientific colleagues.

"Someday, I hope to understand what I do well enough to write for a popular audience. I cringe at the thought of what journalists have attributed to me, yet I think it is no mean challenge to explain what I do so any intelligent person will understand it."

* * *

HAVER, Ronald D. 1939-

PERSONAL: Born January 14, 1939, in Oakland, Calif.; son of Raymond Haver and Ann (a bus driver; maiden name, Spikula) Calistro. *Education:* Educated in California. *Home:* 744 South Ridgeley Dr., Los Angeles, Calif. 90036. *Agent:* Robert Cornfield, 145 West 79th St., New York, N.Y. 10024. *Office:* Los Angeles County Museum of Art, 5905 Wilshire Blvd., Los Angeles, Calif. 90036.

CAREER: American Film Institute, Los Angeles, Calif., oral historian and staff member, 1969-71; Los Angeles County Museum of Art, head of film department, 1972—; writer. *Military service:* U.S. Army, 1960-62. *Member:* American Federation of Television and Radio Artists, Filmex Society. *Awards, honors:* National Film Book Award from National Film Society, 1981, for *David O. Selznick's Hollywood*.

WRITINGS: David O. Selznick's Hollywood, Knopf, 1980. Contributor to periodicals, including *American Film, Connoisseur*, and *Los Angeles*.

WORK IN PROGRESS: Little White Lies; researching motion pictures, including "A Star Is Born," 1954 version, and "Fantasia," the 1981 re-orchestration.

SIDELIGHTS: Haver's *David O. Selznick's Hollywood* was inspired by more than one hundred viewings of "Gone With the Wind," which Selznick produced in 1939. In 1954, Haver began compiling data on Selznick and "Gone With the Wind." In 1969, he began serious research into not only the making of the movie, but also on the thirty-year producing career of Selznick and the concurrent development of Hollywood as the center of American film production. After ten years of research, interviewing, and writing, the result was *David O. Selznick's Hollywood*, which the *New York Times* called "the last word and picture in Hollywood books" while *Newsweek* referred to it as "this year's knock-you-dead super collosal movie book." Stanley Kauffman in the *New Republic* said that "in its look, its care and its fascinating detail, this is the best book about the old Hollywood since Kevin Brownlow's 'The Parades Gone By.'"

It is a book which, according to the *Village Voice*'s Carrie Rickey, "is so unwieldly that you have to go into traction in order to read it." Rickey added, "To its credit, the book epitomizes Selznick production values—nothing but the best paper, color, and printing—and is crammed with photographs and fanzine memorabilia as informational as it is engaging." Rickey also noted that Haver is "no slouch when it comes to research, and the book's 411 pages are congested with production and technical details that are of great interest to industry junkies." A reviewer for *Saturday Review* also noted a similarity between Haver's book and Selznick's films, writing that Selznick "was one of a kind and deserves to be remembered in this splendid way."

Haver told *CA:* "I wrote *David O Selznick's Hollywood* because I felt that the function of the producer had not been fairly or intelligently treated in film literature. It was my hope to show the interaction of the various crafts that go into the creation of a film and to illustrate these areas so that the reader would have a fuller understanding of the technical aspects of filmmaking. I have also long been fascinated with the history and personalities of Hollywood, along with the corporate and business aspects of the American film and how all these elements effect the production and marketing of motion pictures."

BIOGRAPHICAL/CRITICAL SOURCES: Los Angeles Times Book Review, November 30, 1980; *Saturday Review*, December, 1980; *Village Voice*, December 3, 1980, January 7, 1981; *Chicago Tribune Book World*, December 7, 1980; *New York Times*, December 15, 1980; *New Republic*, December 20, 1980; *New York Times Book Review*, December 21, 1980; *Times Literary Supplement*, January 2, 1981; *London Times*, January 27, 1981; *Los Angeles Herald-Examiner*, February 19, 1981; *Washington Post*, March 22, 1981.

*   *   *

HAVREVOLD, Finn   1905-

PERSONAL: Born August 11, 1905, in Oslo, Norway; son of Lauritz Paulsen and Marta Malene (Nielsen) Havrevold; married Gunvor Oewre, March 14, 1939; children: Tone (daughter), Anne. *Education:* Norges Tekniske Hoeyskole, Certified Architect, 1929. *Home:* 64C Thomas Heftyes Gate, Oslo 2, Norway.

CAREER: Author, illustrator, and drama critic. *Dagbladet*, Oslo, Norway, radio critic, 1951-74; *Urd*, Oslo, drama critic, 1956-57. Has also worked as a commercial artist. *Member:* Den Norske Forfatterforening, Kunstnerforbundet, Norske Dramatikeres Forbund, P.E.N., Ungdomslitteraturens Forfat-

terlag. *Awards, honors:* Recipient of Damm prize, 1955 and 1957 for *Marens lille ugle;* Damm-Allers Film Prize, 1960; Prix Italia, 1970; Nordic Radio Prize, 1970.

WRITINGS—In English translation; for children: *Sommereventyret*, Damm, 1952, translation by Patricia Crampton published as *Summer Adventure*, illustrated by Emanuella Wallenta, Abelard, 1961; *Marens lille ugle* (self-illustrated), Damm, 1957, translation by Inge Smith published as *Maren's Little Owl*, Abelard, 1960. Also author of *Han var min venn*, 1960, translation by Cathy Babcock Curry published as *Undertow*, illustrated by Curry, Atheneum, 1968.

Other writings for children: *Droemmeveggen*, Damm, 1953; *Grunnbrott*, Damm, 1960; *Jeg flykter i natt*, Aschehoug, 1963; *Putsja*, Aschehoug, 1967; *Lommekniven*, Aschehoug, 1969. Also author of *Den ensomme kirger*, 1955, and *Viggo*, 1957.

Novels: *Til de dristige*, Aschehoug, 1946; *Walter den fredsommelige*, Aschehoug, 1947; *Skredet*, Aschehoug, 1949; *Den ytterste dag*, Gyldendal, 1963; *De gjenstridige*, Aschehoug, 1965; *Blaa rytter*, Aschehoug, 1968; *Pilen i lyset*, Aschehoug, 1971; *Under samme tak*, Aschehoug, 1972; *De naadeloese*, Aschehoug, 1975.

Plays: *Jubileum: En komedie*, Aschehoug, 1951; *Tomannsboligen*, Aschehoug, 1959; *Gruppen*, Pax forlag, 1966. Also author of *Uretten*, 1955, *Sommerhuset*, 1957, *Stakkars Anton*, 1961, and *Regissoeren*, 1964.

Other writings: *Det raker ikke Andersen* (short stories), Aschehoug, 1939, reprinted, 1970; *Helge Krog* (biography), Aschehoug, 1959; *Tapere* (short stories), Aschehoug, 1974; *Refleksjoner*, Aschehoug, 1975; *Vennskap*, Aschehoug, 1976; *I fjor sommer: beretning om en barndom*, Aschehoug, 1977; *Vinter i Vallegaten: beretning om venner*, Aschehoug, 1978; *Fars hus: beretninger om ensomhet*, Aschehoug, 1979.

Also author of numerous radio plays, including: "Sensommer," 1960; "Wilhelm og Alice," 1960; "Eskapade," 1960; "Katastrofe," 1960; "Arabesk," 1961; "I Kveldingen," 1961; "Svalene flyr lavt," 1961; "Hjemturen," 1961; "Brev til Tome," 1962; "Dikterjubileum," 1963; "Helens dagbok," 1964; *Duellen*, Aschehoug, 1965; *Helenes hjerte* (contains "Wilhelm og Alice," "Arabesk," "Svalene flyr lavt," and "Helenes hjerte"), Aschehoug, 1966; "Landskapet," 1967; *Situasjon*, 1967; "Leke blindebukk," 1968; *En benk i parken* (contains "Situasjon," "Landskapet," "En benk i parken," and "Credo"), Aschehoug, 1971; *Avreisen* (contains "Avreisen," "Broedre," "Gisselet," and "I Kveldingen"), Aschehoug, 1973; "Revolusjonsetyde," 1974.

Also author of television play, "En Smule Kjaerlighet," 1961, and two screenplays, "Drapen," 1960, and "Farlig Kurs," 1964.

*   *   *

HAWES, John T.   1906(?)-1983

OBITUARY NOTICE: Born c. 1906; died after a long illness, February 17, 1983, in New York, N.Y. Publishing director. Hawes served as director of the college textbook department for J. B. Lippincott from 1946 to 1952 and at Alfred A. Knopf from 1952 to 1958. He took up the same position at Thomas Y. Crowell, where he became vice-president. Obituaries and other sources: *Publishers Weekly*, March 11, 1983.

HAYDON, June 1932-
(Rosalind Foxx, Taria Hayford, Sara Logan, joint pseudonyms)

PERSONAL: Born July 9, 1932, in Roanoke, Va.; daughter of Baxter W. (a soldier) and Margaret (a teacher; maiden name, DeBusk) Logan; married William M. Haydon (an engineer), June 11, 1955; children: Margaret Clare, Jennifer, Mary. *Education:* Radford College, B.S., 1954. *Politics:* Democrat. *Religion:* Anglican. *Home and office:* 1028 Greenland Ave., South Charleston, W.Va. 25309. *Agent:* Steven Axelrod, Sterling Lord Agency, Inc., 660 Madison Ave., New York, N.Y. 10021.

CAREER: Public school teacher in Virginia, 1954-55, and West Virginia, 1960-80; writer. *Member:* American Association of University Women, Romance Writers of America, Daughters of the American Revolution, South Charleston Women's Club, St. Alban's Writers Club.

WRITINGS—Historical romances: (With Judy Simpson under joint pseudonym Rosalind Foxx) *Winds of Fury, Winds of Fire,* Dell, 1981; (with Simpson under Foxx pseudonym) *Reluctant Ward,* Fawcett, 1982; (under Foxx pseudonym) *Flame Against the Wind,* Dell, 1983.

Contemporary romances: (With Pat Rutherford under joint pseudonym Taria Hayford) *Trail of Love,* Serenade, 1981; (with Simpson under joint pseudonym Sara Logan) *Game of Hearts,* Silhouette, 1982.

WORK IN PROGRESS: Surrender to the Wind and *Passion of Eagles,* both historical romances under pseudonym Rosalind Foxx.

SIDELIGHTS: Haydon told *CA:* "I became a full-time writer in 1979 when my first novel was published. I have recently bought a word processor. It has changed my writing habits and I'm sure it will improve and expedite my writing. In Scotland, I searched out places mentioned in *Winds of Fury, Winds of Fire* and researched four other books. I think the romance market is a good place to serve apprenticeship because the stringent guidelines help the discipline of writing. They are light and enjoyable but *not easy* to write. The books are about young women searching for love. The historical novels are set during a war or some kind of external conflict so that the heroine is fighting the hero but also fighting the English, or whomever!

"My favorite novelist is Norah Lofts, whose books are generally pessimistic but whose style is carefully crafted. Her settings are so vivid one can actually see the Middle Ages or whatever period she is writing about.

"I hope to be able to move out of genre fiction someday and try a mid-line book, but at present I am happy where I am. Writing is a maddening career, but I can't think of doing anything else. It is essential for potential writers to read everything. Since I have become a professional writer my reading is almost entirely in the line of research—historical or trying to keep up with the current market. I write every day."

AVOCATIONAL INTERESTS: Travel (Scotland, England, Germany), bridge, cooking, cultivating roses, genealogy.

*   *   *

HAYFORD, Taria
See HAYDON, June

HAYWARD, John F(orrest) 1916-1983

OBITUARY NOTICE—See index for *CA* sketch: Born February 10, 1916, in Hounslow, England; died February 25, 1983, in London, England. Art historian and author. Hayward is best remembered as an art historian who studied arms, armor, and metalwork. Prior to embarking on his art career, Hayward worked with the Special Operations Executive, equipping British agents with false documents and kits during World War II. His art career followed in 1945 when he became a staff member of the Austrian Monuments and Fine Arts Office. Later he served in the metalwork and woodwork departments of the Victoria and Albert Museum and became the associate director of Sotheby Parke Bernet. In the 1950's Hayward made important contributions to the study of seventeenth- and eighteenth-century English firearms, then undertook wider studies of gold plate, silver plate, bronze, jewelry, and furniture. His books include *Huguenot Silver in England: 1688-1727, The Art of the Gunmaker,* and *Virtuoso Goldsmiths and the Triumph of Mannerism: 1540-1620.* Obituaries and other sources: *London Times,* March 2, 1983; *AB Bookman's Weekly,* April 11, 1983.

*   *   *

HEBBLETHWAITE, Brian Leslie 1939-

PERSONAL: Born January 3, 1939, in Bristol, England; son of Cyril H. and Sarah Anne (Nash) Hebblethwaite. *Education:* Magdalen College, Oxford, B.A., 1961, M.A., 1967; Magdalene College, Cambridge, B.A., 1964; M.A., 1968. *Politics:* Social Democrat. *Religion:* Church of England. *Home and office:* Queens' College, Cambridge University, Cambridge, England.

CAREER: Ordained priest of Church of England, 1966; Church of England, Bury, England, curate, 1965-68; Cambridge University, Cambridge, England, fellow and dean of chapel at Queens' College, 1969—, assistant lecturer in divinity, 1972-77, lecturer in divinity, 1977—. *Member:* Aristotelian Society, Societas Ethica, Society for the Study of Theology, Royal Institute of Philosophy.

WRITINGS: Evil, Suffering, and Religion, Sheldon Press, 1976; *The Problems of Theology,* Cambridge University Press, 1980; (editor with John Hick) *Christianity and Other Religions,* Collins, 1980; *Christian Ethics in the Modern Age,* Westminster, 1982; (editor with Stewart Sutherland) *The Philosophical Frontiers of Christian Theology,* Cambridge University Press, 1982; *The Christian Hope: An Introduction to Eschatology,* Marshall, Morgan & Scott, 1983. Ethics editor for *Theologische Realenzyklopaedie,* 1980—.

SIDELIGHTS: Hebblethwaite wrote: "I am interested in the critical study of Christian theology, in the context of the comparative study of religion, and in its relation to modern philosophy and science. The ethical implications of Christian theology are also my concern."

Sarah Coakley, in a *Times Literary Supplement* review, described Hebblethwaite's *The Problem of Theology* as "an introductory methodological work [which] provides an admirably lucid discussion of the place of theology in the university, and at the same time (though this is not a stated intention) reads something like a defense of the present Cambridge tripos in theology and religious studies." The book opens with Hebblethwaite's definition of his discipline as "rational thought about God" and goes on to indicate how such fields as comparative religion, philosophy, sociology, and anthropology relate to modern theological study. The remaining text is devoted to a discussion of varying points of view on general theological topics, such as revelation and ethics, and concludes with Hebblethwaite's arguments for specific Christian doctrines (Trinity, incarnation) which he believes can be proved; as Coakley observed, the author "recommends the 'cumulative case' method whereby a range of arguments, none of them individually conclusive, can none the less convince cumulatively."

Coakley questioned Hebblethwaite's emphasis on rationality and his belief that theology does not function to strengthen, defend, or even define religion. She wrote, "The wholly admirable insistence that theological debate be clear and rational is one thing, but the tendency to restrict the *inputs,* or raw material, on which that debate is based to the rationally comprehensible is quite another." Ralph Hjelm, in an *Interpretation* article, commented on the book's discussion of the relationship between other fields of study and theology: "Those looking for orientation will find Hebblethwaite's quick and clear surveys to be helpful." Considering the work in its entirety, however, Hjelm noted, "Critical readers will be unconvinced that this book has even named, let alone analyzed, *the problems* of theology or that Hebblethwaite has considered the problems *of theology.* He has, in fact, dealt mostly with the ways in which certain issues and options have been understood from outside theology as he defines it."

Writing in *Theologia Evangelica,* Brian Gaybba deemed Hebblethwaite's work "an introduction to theology I recommend to all who want to be forced to think again about what theology really is." James Barr echoed Gaybba's opinion in his *New Blackfriars* review, claiming, "this book gives a good impression of the manifold relations within which theology now operates, and should be widely used."

AVOCATIONAL INTERESTS: Music (especially opera), literature, fell-walking, travel.

BIOGRAPHICAL/CRITICAL SOURCES: Times Literary Supplement, October 31, 1980; *Theologia Evangelica,* September, 1981; *Interpretation,* January, 1982; *New Blackfriars,* February, 1982.

*   *   *

HECHLER, Ken 1914-

PERSONAL: Born September 20, 1914, in Roslyn, N.Y.; son of Charles Henry (an estate superintendent) and Catherine Elizabeth (Hauhart) Hechler. *Education:* Swarthmore College, A.B., 1935; Columbia University, A.M., 1936, Ph.D., 1940. *Politics:* Democrat. *Religion:* Episcopalian. *Home:* 917 Fifth Ave., Huntington, W.Va. 25701. *Agent:* Julian Bach, 747 Third Ave., New York, N.Y. 10017.

CAREER: U.S. Office for Emergency Management, Washington, D.C., personnel officer, 1941-42; U.S. Bureau of the Budget, Washington, D.C., administrative analyst in Division of Administrative Management, 1942 and 1946-47; Princeton University, Princeton, N.J., assistant professor of politics, 1947-49; special assistant and research director of speech-writing team for President Harry S. Truman, 1949-53; research director for presidential candidate Adlai E. Stevenson, 1956; Marshall College (now Marshall University), Huntington, W.Va., associate professor of political science, 1957; legislative assistant to Senator John A. Carroll of Colorado, 1957; U.S. House of

Representatives, Washington, D.C., representative from West Virginia, 1959-77; science consultant for House of Representatives committee on science and technology, 1978-80; University of Charleston, Charleston, W.Va., adjunct professor of political science, 1981; Marshall University, adjunct professor of political science, 1982-83. Worked with numerous charities, including National Foundation March of Dimes, 1976, Arthritis Foundation, National Cystic Fibrosis Research Foundation, and United Way. Lecturer and consultant. *Military service:* U.S. Army, 1942-46; became colonel; received Bronze Star. *Member:* American Political Science Association (associate director, 1953-55). *Awards, honors:* Named West Virginia's Son of the Year by West Virginia State Society, 1969; named West Virginia's Speaker of the Year by West Virginia University, 1970.

WRITINGS: Insurgency: Personalities and Politics of the Taft Era, Columbia University Press, 1940, reprinted, Russell & Russell, 1964; *The Bridge at Remagen* (nonfiction), Ballantine, 1957; *West Virginia Memories of President Kennedy,* privately printed, 1964; *Toward the Endless Frontier: A History of the House Committee on Science and Technology,* U.S. Government Printing Office, 1980; *The Endless Space Frontier,* American Astronautical Society, 1982; *Working With Truman: A Personal Memoir of the White House Years,* Putnam, 1982. Columnist for *Princeton Times, Gulf Times,* and *Parkersburg News,* 1973-76. Contributor to newspapers, including *Washington Post, Baltimore Sun, Charleston Gazette,* and *Huntington Herald-Dispatch.*

WORK IN PROGRESS: Biographies of Confederate General Albert Gallatin Jenkins and grandfather, Union Corporal George Hechler, latter work tentatively entitled *Soldier of the Union;* an account of Lieutenant Karl H. Timmermann's successful crossing of the Remagen Bridge during World War II, tentatively entitled *Hero of Remagen;* an autobiographical memoir focusing on Hechler's experiences in the U.S. House of Representatives, tentatively entitled *Maverick Congressman.*

SIDELIGHTS: Hechler's life has long been linked with American politics. Following World War II he was appointed to the five-man team that interrogated captured Nazis such as Hermann Goering, Admiral Doenitz, and Joachim von Ribbentrop. During President Truman's tenure, Hechler advised the president on local issues during tours into American communities. He then traveled with Adlai E. Stevenson during his unsuccessful campaign for the presidency. In 1959, Hechler began his eighteen years of service in the House of Representatives, where he became chairman of a sub-committee on advanced research and development of fossil fuels for the committee on science and technology. He was the principal author of safety legislation in the Federal Coal Mine Health and Safety Act in 1969. He also helped regulate strip mines and combated exploitation of the mail service by raising rates on third-class mail.

Hechler documented his years with Truman in *Working With Truman.* The volume relates numerous little-known incidents involving the former president. A reviewer in the *New York Times Book Review* called the book "warm and welcome" and noted, "the 33rd President who emerges from Mr. Hechler's pages is a loving husband and father, a man loyal to old friends even when it led to political embarrassment, an ardent history buff, a relaxed friend when vacationing with his staff."

Hechler told *CA:* "My mother, once a schoolteacher, stressed the value of good books by reading aloud every evening from biographies like *The Americanization of Edward Bok.* At both

Roslyn High School and Swarthmore College I earned quite a bit on the side by handling all the publicity for sports, concerts, and other events.

"At Columbia University I cultivated friendships with several political intimates of President Franklin D. Roosevelt, including Raymond Moley, James A. Farley, and New York Supreme Court Justice Samuel I. Rosenman. The first two men inspired me to pursue a writing career in the political field, but my relationship with Judge Rosenman was much closer and rewarding, especially since he was loyal to President Roosevelt from start to finish and also worked as special counsel to President Harry S. Truman. I assisted Judge Rosenman in the compilation of the thirteen-volume publication entitled *The Public Papers and Addresses of Franklin D. Roosevelt,* and also on a book of his reminiscences entitled *Working With Roosevelt.* Judge Rosenman instilled in me a burning desire to search out the truth wherever it might lead, plus a respect for clear, rather than flamboyant, expression. He also insisted that there was no subject, no matter how complicated, that could not be reduced to simple and direct exposition.

"After training as an infantry private and tank commander in the army, a very lucky break changed my life in 1943. I was assigned to write and produce what proved to be a smash success musical performed by Officer Candidate School graduates, entitled 'Praise the Lord and Pass Me My Commission.' This show, plus an autobiography required of all OCS graduates, caused the school commandant, Brigadier General S. G. Henry, to write to army headquarters in Washington a strong recommendation including these sentences: 'It is my sincere belief that this officer is one of the most outstanding young men ever to graduate from this school. . . . It is also my opinion that this outstanding officer can serve the war effort in a more advantageous manner than by assignment as a platoon commander in a tank company.' The letter resulted in my transfer to a new combat historians' unit which was headed in the European theater of operations by the brilliant military writer, S.L.A. Marshall. This gave me the opportunity to be on the spot to collect the interviews which developed into the book *The Bridge at Remagen.*

"My association with President Truman grew out of the work I had done for Judge Rosenman plus acquaintance with two other White House officials, Clark M. Clifford, whose nephew was a student of mine at Princeton University, and George M. Elsey, who later became national president of the American Red Cross. Elsey was a Princeton University graduate who visited my class to lecture on Truman's 1948 whistle-stop campaign, and he also shared my interest in war history. The research and writing I did during the 1949-53 period while working and traveling with President Truman formed the basis for the 1982 book *Working With Truman.*

"President Truman used to always tell us that the rich and the powerful have their own lobbyists and pressure groups, and it was his job to stand up and fight for the great, unrepresented mass of average people at the grass roots. This came to be the theme of my service for nine terms in the U.S. House of Representatives, to which I was elected in 1958 after only one year of residence in West Virginia as a political science professor at Marshall College. I intend to elaborate on this theme in a forthcoming book on some of my experiences in Congress and in West Virginian politics.

"My other projects include an account of the life and struggles of Karl H. Timmermann, the first officer to cross the Remagen Bridge, which the Americans captured in a surprise crossing

on March 7, 1945, thus shortening the war in Europe and saving thousands of American lives. This book will examine the fascinating life of a young man, born in Germany, brought up in West Point, Nebraska, and impelled to perform a great feat of military courage because his father was a World War I army deserter."

MEDIA ADAPTATIONS: The Bridge at Remagen was produced as a motion picture of the same title by United Artists, 1969.

BIOGRAPHICAL/CRITICAL SOURCES: Wichita Eagle, September 18, 1938; *New York Times,* October 26, 1939, January 29, 1941, January 31, 1941, April 17, 1941, November 6, 1958, August 8, 1975; *Saturday Evening Post,* May 8, 1948; *Time,* November 15, 1948; *New Republic,* September 29, 1958, October 9, 1976; *Washington Post,* May 22, 1960, October 1, 1961, July 25, 1966, December 1, 1975; *Detroit Free Press,* August 24, 1969; *Louisville Courier-Journal,* January 4, 1970; Brit Hume, *Death and the Mines,* Grossman, 1971; Joseph E. Finley, *The Corrupt Kingdom,* Simon & Schuster, 1972; Trevor Armbrister, *Act of Vengeance,* Dutton, 1975; *Nation,* March 20, 1976; *New York Times Book Review,* January 9, 1983; *Kansas City Times,* January 11, 1983; *Rocky Mountain News,* March 8, 1983; *St. Louis Post-Dispatch,* April 3, 1983.

* * *

HECKLER, Jonellen (Beth) 1943-

PERSONAL: Born October 28, 1943, in Pittsburgh, Pa.; daughter of John Edward (a mechanical engineer) and Florence (an artist; maiden name, Milliken) Munn; married Louis Roy Heckler (a management consultant), August 17, 1968; children: Steven Louis. *Education:* University of Pittsburgh, B.A., 1965. *Home and office:* 5562 Pernod Dr. S.W., Fort Myers, Fla. 33907. *Agent:* Elizabeth Trupin, JET Literary Associations, Inc., 124 East 84th St., Suite 4A, New York, N.Y. 10028.

CAREER: United Fund of Allegheny County, Pittsburgh, Pa., secretary to public relations director, 1965-67; United Fund of Broward County, Fort Lauderdale, Fla., director of public relations, 1967-68; North Carolina Heart Association, Chapel Hill, N.C., program planner, 1968-69; free-lance copywriter, Charlotte, N.C., 1969-70; Charlene Hillman Public Relations Associates, Indianapolis, Ind., copywriter, 1970-72; free-lance writer, 1972—. *Member:* Authors Guild.

WRITINGS: Safekeeping (novel; Literary Guild selection), Putnam, 1983.

Song lyrics; published by GlorySound, except as noted: "Christmas Stars," Shawnee Press, 1979; "Finding My Place In Your World, Lord," 1979; "Listen With Your Eyes," 1979; "Thine Is the Kingdom," Harold Flammer, 1979; "Strangers in Bethlehem," 1979; "He Is Here," 1979; "The Flowers of My World," 1979; "As Long as There Is Music," Shawnee Press, 1979; (with Loonis McGlohon) "In a Quiet Place," 1979; "The World Is Full of Hello's," Shawnee Press, 1980; "Prayer for Peace," 1980; "I Will Build an Ark," 1980; "Christ Child, Shepherd of Man," 1982.

Contributor of poems and stories to *Ladies' Home Journal.*

WORK IN PROGRESS: Another novel.

SIDELIGHTS: Jonellen Heckler told *CA:* "It has been my desire to reflect in my writing a very positive attitude about this wonderful life. I'm not trying to ignore its flaws and troubles, but I want to keep illuminating its joys. My novel, *Safekeeping,* was intended as a tribute to human love. For counterbalance I set it against one of the most tragic and perplexing eras in America history, the Vietnam war. It was my intent to record, in my own way, the confusion Americans felt about it. *Safekeeping* is the story of a prisoner of war's wife and child.''

* * *

HEINRICH, Bernd 1940-

PERSONAL: Born April 19, 1940, in Bad Polzin, Germany; came to United States, 1950; naturalized U.S. citizen, 1958; son of Gerd Hermann and Hildegard Maria (Bury) Heinrich; married wife, Margaret, 1968; children: one. *Education:* University of Maine, B.A., 1964, M.S., 1966; University of California, Los Angeles, Ph.D., 1970. *Office:* Department of Zoology, University of Vermont, Burlington, Vt. 05405.

CAREER: Biologist. University of California, Berkeley, assistant professor, 1971-78, professor of entomology, 1978-80; University of Vermont, Burlington, professor of zoology, 1980—. *Member:* American Association for the Advancement of Science (fellow), American Society of Zoologists, Ecological Society of America, American Institute of Biological Sciences. *Awards, honors:* National Science Foundation grant, 1971—; American Book Award nomination, 1980, for *Bumblebee Economics.*

WRITINGS: Bumblebee Economics, Harvard University Press, 1979; (editor) *Insect Thermoregulation,* Wiley, 1981; *In a Patch of Fireweed,* Harvard University Press, in press. Contributor of more than eighty articles to journals in his field.

SIDELIGHTS: Bernd Heinrich's book *Bumblebee Economics,* nominated for the American Book Award in science, has been praised as ''a fine, captivating exposition for scientist and nonscientist alike.'' The book stands out among the small number of books devoted entirely to bumblebee life and social economy, according to *New York Times Book Review* critic Caryl P. Haskins, who remarked, ''It is a merit of this remarkable new book that it treats the subject of bumblebee life, at both individual and social levels, in an unusual and particularly modern way.''

Energy economics is a major factor in Heinrich's discussion: ''At the colony level, the pollen and sugar [obtained by bumblebees from flowers during foraging] are the resources used to produce the machinery—combs and new workers—that will in turn use similar resources to produce drones and new queens, the factory's product,'' Heinrich wrote. ''In this context,'' Haskins remarked, ''bumblebee colonies can be regarded as complex, well-ordered mechanisms for maximizing output as defined by the number of young reproductives produced at the close of colony life.''

Another major factor in Heinrich's study is thermoregulation, the manner in which bumblebees generate and distribute heat as specific parts of their bodies require it, then dispel it without wasting it. In *Bumblebee Economics* Heinrich demonstrates that bumblebees are not cold-blooded animals, as is commonly thought. The bees' adaptation to cooler climates makes them unusual: ''Typically, bumblebees work longer and colder hours than honeybees, foraging at chilly dawn and into deepening twilight, while temperatures and failing light keep honeybees at home or quickly immobilize those enterprising individuals that may venture out,'' Haskins noted. Heinrich discusses how the bumblebees maintain body temperatures well above those of the environment as well as other insights on the way the bees regulate their body temperatures for greatest efficiency.

Thermoregulation is a subject in which ''Professor Heinrich contributes much original scholarship . . . ,'' observed Haskins, ''and his treatment of this subject is fascinating.''

Natural History reviewer H. E. Evans applauded the energy Heinrich brought to his study: ''The author is not satisfied with generalities, but consistently provides an abundance of facts and figures derived from careful measurements and various forms of 'electronic eavesdropping.' Yet none of this intrudes upon a style that is invariably lively and lucid.'' Evans was impressed with *Bumblebee Economics:* ''It is not true that science strips away the beauty of nature; it illumines it and deepens its impact.''

BIOGRAPHICAL/CRITICAL SOURCES: New York Times Book Review, September 2, 1979, June 7, 1981; *Natural History,* November, 1979; *Booklist,* December 15, 1979.

* * *

HELFEN, Otto J. Maenchen
See MAENCHEN, Otto John

* * *

HENDERSON, Harry B(rinton), Jr. 1914-

BRIEF ENTRY: Born September 9, 1914, in Kittanning, Pa. American editor and author. Henderson worked as a newspaper reporter in Pennsylvania until 1940. Then he began writing for such magazines as *Cosmopolitan, Redbook, Reader's Digest,* and *Harper's.* He was editor in chief of both *Medical Tribune* and *Hospital Tribune* from 1971 to 1979. Henderson's books include *War in Our Time: A Comprehensive and Analytical History in Pictures and Text of the First Eleven Years of World War II, Beginning With the Invasion of Manchuria by the Japanese* (Doubleday, 1942), *Six Black Masters of American Art* (Zenith Books, 1972), and *History of America's Black Artists* (1978). *Address:* 18 Franklin Ave., Croton-on-Hudson, N.Y. 10520; and *Medical Tribune,* 257 Park Ave. S., New York, N.Y. 10010.

* * *

HENLEY, Virginia 1935-

PERSONAL: Born December 5, 1935, in Bolton, Lancashire, England; daughter of Thomas (a steelworker) and Lillian (Bleakley) Syddall; married Arthur Howard Henley (an architect), July 7, 1956; children: Sean, Adam. *Education:* Attended University of Toronto, 1966-67. *Religion:* Anglican. *Home:* 53 Chancellor Dr., Scarborough, Ontario, Canada M1G 2W4.

CAREER: Steel Co. of Canada, Hamilton, Ontario, executive secretary, 1953-56; Labatts Brewery, London, Ontario, assistant buyer, 1956-61.

WRITINGS: The Irish Gypsy (historical romance), Avon, 1982; *The Conquest* (historical romance), Avon, 1983.

WORK IN PROGRESS: A Skulk of Foxes, a historical romance dealing with the Scottish borders, publication by Avon expected in 1984.

SIDELIGHTS: Virginia Henley commented: ''After my mother died of cancer in 1976, I desperately needed an outlet. She had been deeply interested in the occult and was a voracious reader. The books I gave her had to become lighter in subject matter, and we both started to enjoy historical romances. I decided I could write them as well as read them.

"Women need a romantic escape from everyday realities. I don't want women to read me to raise their consciousness! I want them to derive pure pleasure and escape. A romantic novel is a small luxury, like chocolates or perfume, with which a woman can indulge herself. If just one woman can put her feet up after she puts the kids to bed and lose herself in a book I have written, I will be satisfied. All of us at times meet situations we think we cannot face, but somehow we manage to cope, as my heroines do. I hope that between the first and last pages of any of my novels my heroine grows as a woman and as a human being, but that is all I require of her."

* * *

HENNING, Sylvie Marie Debevec
See DEBEVEC HENNING, Sylvie Marie

* * *

HENRY, Jules 1904-1969

OBITUARY NOTICE: Born November 29, 1904, in New York, N.Y.; died of a heart attack, September 23, 1969; buried at Oak Grove Cemetery, St. Louis, Mo. Anthropologist, educator, and author. A member of the faculty of Washington University from 1947 until his death, Henry researched such subjects as the American family and the Indian tribes of Mexico, Brazil, and Argentina. He wrote *Jungle People, Pathways to Madness,* and the high-praised study of American culture, *Culture Against Man.* Obituaries and other sources: *New York Times,* September 26, 1969; *Who Was Who in America, With World Notables,* Volume V: *1969-1973,* Marquis, 1973.

* * *

HENRY, Peter 1926-

PERSONAL: Born in 1926; married, 1952 (divorced, 1970); children: Claire, Ann, Alexis, Elizabeth. *Office:* Department of Slavonic Languages and Literatures, University of Glasgow, Glasgow G12 8QQ, Scotland.

CAREER: Senior master at secondary school in Cambridge, England, 1952; Joint Services School of Linguists, Coulsdon, England, instructor in Russian, 1952-54; senior German master at grammar school, 1954-57; University of Liverpool, Liverpool, England, lecturer in Russian, 1957-63; University of Hull, Hull, England, senior lecturer in Russian studies in charge of department, 1963-74; University of Glasgow, Glasgow, Scotland, professor of Slavonic languages and literatures, 1975—. *Military service:* British Army, Royal Tank Regiment, 1943-47. *Member:* British Universities Association of Slavists, Association of Scottish Slavists.

WRITINGS: (Editor and author of introduction and notes) Ivan Alekseevich Bunin, *Rasskazy: Selected Stories,* Bradda Books, 1962; (editor and author of introduction and notes) Aleksandr Sergeevich Pushkin, *TSgany: The Gipsies,* Bradda Books, 1962; *Manual of Modern Russian Prose Composition: Modern Russian Usage,* University of London Press, 1963, 2nd edition, 1971; *Modern Russian Prose Composition,* four volumes, University of London Press, 1963-64, 2nd edition, 1973; (author of introduction and notes) Konstantin Georgievich Paustovskii, *Selected Stories,* Pergamon, 1967; (editor) *Anthology of Soviet Satire,* Collett's, 1972; (editor) *Classics of Soviet Satire,* Collett's, 1972; (editor) *Modern Soviet Satire,* Collett's, 1974. Also editor of *Chaika* by Anton Pavlovich Chekhov, 1965.

Work represented in anthologies, including *The Penguin Book of Russian Short Stories.* Founder of *Journal of Scottish Slavonic Studies.*

WORK IN PROGRESS: Vsevolod Garshin; a textbook and reader on the Russian language; a television dramatization of *The Red Flower* by Garshin; translating stories by Garshin.

* * *

HEPPNER, Sam(uel) 1913-1983

OBITUARY NOTICE—See index for *CA* sketch: Born December 29, 1913, in London, England; died June 2, 1983. Composer, lyricist, broadcaster, and author. Heppner was best known for his work as a theatre publicist, though he was also a broadcaster featured on "Woman's Hour" and "Housewives' Choice." He wrote the lyrics for "Gay Rosalinda," an adaptation of Strauss's "Die Fledermaus," and he composed "Shadow Waltz" as the theme song of the television series "The Techman Biography." Heppner was associated with various organizations, namely, Oxfam, Amnesty International, Botleys Park Hospital, and the Council for Music in Hospitals. His writings include *Background to Music* and *Cockie,* a biography of showman Charles B. Cochran. Obituaries and other sources: *London Times,* June 4, 1983.

* * *

HERGE
See REMI, Georges

* * *

HERGESHEIMER, Joseph 1880-1954

BRIEF ENTRY: Born February 15, 1880, in Philadelphia, Pa.; died of complications from diabetes and arteriosclerosis, April 25, 1954; buried in Oakland Cemetery, West Chester, Pa. American author. Hergesheimer is best remembered for his historical and romance novels, which embrace such qualities as beauty, elegance, and honesty. Numbered among his books are *The Lay Anthony: A Romance* (1914), *The Three Black Pennys* (1917), *Java Head* (1919), *Cytherea* (1922), *The Presbyterian Child* (1923), and *From an Old House* (1925). *Residence:* Stone Harbor, N.J. *Biographical/critical sources: Twentieth-Century Authors: A Biographical Dictionary of Modern Literature,* H. W. Wilson, 1942, 1st supplement, 1955; *Dictionary of Literary Biography,* Volume 9: *American Novelists, 1910-1945,* Gale, 1981; *Twentieth-Century Literary Criticism,* Volume 11, Gale, 1983.

* * *

HERMAN, Melvin 1922(?)-1983

OBITUARY NOTICE: Born c. 1922; died of a heart attack, February 22, 1983, in New Rochelle, N.Y. Educator, social welfare leader, and author. Herman founded and directed Columbia University's Community Services Program, a project where graduate students train in the community, improving the conditions of the impoverished and displaced. The educator also served with the United States Department of Health and Human Services, acting as regional director of program coordination and review from 1972. He co-authored *Youth-Work Programs: Problems of Planning and Operation* and *Decision-Making in Poverty Programs: Case Studies From Youth-Work Agencies,* and co-edited *Work, Youth, and Unemployment.*

Obituaries and other sources: *New York Times*, February 25, 1983.

* * *

HERNDON, Venable 1927-

PERSONAL: Born October 19, 1927, in Philadelphia, Pa. *Education:* Princeton University, B.A., 1950; Harvard University, M.A., 1951. *Home:* 238 West 22nd St., New York, N.Y. 10011.

CAREER: Screenwriter, playwright, and writer. *Awards, honors:* Stanley Drama Award from Wagner College, 1967.

WRITINGS: (With Arthur Penn) *Alice's Restaurant* (screenplay for United Artists, based on Arlo Guthrie's song "The Alice's Restaurant Massacree"), Doubleday, 1970; *James Dean: A Short Life* (biography), Doubleday, 1974.

Plays: "Jesus Guerra Guerra" (two-act); "Independence Night" (two-act), first produced Off-Off Broadway at The Loft; "Bag of Flies," first produced Off-Off Broadway at The Cubiculo; "Tom Thumb"; *Until the Monkey Comes* (first produced Off-Broadway at Martinique Theatre), New American Plays.

Also author of screenplays, "Location," "Until the Monkey Comes," "Uncle Sam's Wild West Show," and "Jimmy Shine."

Contributor of articles to periodicals, including *Ms*. Co-founder of *Chelsea Review* (literary quarterly).

BIOGRAPHICAL/CRITICAL SOURCES: New York Times Book Review, September 22, 1974; *Best Sellers*, October 1, 1974.

* * *

HERON, Patrick 1920-

PERSONAL: Born January 30, 1920, in Leeds, England; son of Thomas Milner and Eulalie Mabel Heron; married Delia Reiss, April 17, 1945 (died May 3, 1979); children: Katharine, Susanna (Mrs. David Ward). *Education:* Attended Slade School, 1937-39. *Politics:* Labour. *Religion:* Church of England. *Home:* Eagle's Nest, Zennor, near St. Ives, Cornwall, England.

CAREER: Painter, with one-man shows in London, New York City, Canada, Australia, and major cities in Europe and South America; work represented in collections, including Tate Gallery, British Museum, Victoria and Albert Museum, National Portrait Gallery, Brooklyn Museum, Montreal Museum of Art, and Toronto Art Gallery. Member of board of trustees of Tate Gallery, 1980—. *Awards, honors:* Main prize from John Moore's Liverpool Exhibition, 1959; silver medal from Sao Paulo Bienal, Sao Paulo, Brazil, 1965; Commander of Order of the British Empire, 1977; D.Litt. from University of Exeter, 1982.

WRITINGS: Vlaminck, Lindsay Drummond, 1947; *The Changing Forms of Art*, Routledge & Kegan Paul, 1955, Noonday, 1958; *Ivon Hitchens: Penguin Modern Painters*, Penguin, 1955; *Braque*, Faber, 1958; *Bonnard in 1966*, Victor Waddington Gallery, 1966; *Colour and Abstraction in the Drawings of Bonnard*, American Federation of Arts, 1972; *The Shapes of Colour* (screen prints with text), Waddington Graphics, 1978; *Paintings by Patrick Heron, 1965-1977*, University of Texas Press, 1978; *The Colour of Colour: The E. William Doty Lectures in Fine Arts*, University of Texas Press, 1978. Art critic for *New English Weekly*, 1945-47, and *New Statesman*, 1947-50; London correspondent for *Arts*, 1955-58. Contributor to magazines, including *Studio International*, and newspapers.

HERRINGTON, Stuart A. 1941-

PERSONAL: Born December 11, 1941, in Hartford, Conn.; son of Lee Roy (a professional photographer) and Pluma (Garneau) Herrington; married Thuan Thi, April 5, 1975; children: Anne Juliet, Kim, Lynn, Thomas Lee. *Education:* Duquesne University, B.A. (cum laude), 1964; received M.A. from and pursued doctoral studies at University of Florida. *Home:* 531 Bellaire Dr., Venice, Fla. 33595.

CAREER: U.S. Army, career officer in Military Intelligence, 1967—, stationed in Europe, present rank, lieutenant colonel. *Member:* Association of the U.S. Army, American Defense Preparedness Association. *Awards, honors*—Military: Bronze Star; Air Medal; Vietnamese Honor Medal, first class; Vietnamese Cross of Gallantry; Leo Codd Memorial Trophy from American Defense Preparedness Association, 1979; Commandant's Trophy from Air Command and Staff College, 1980.

WRITINGS: Silence Was a Weapon: The Vietnam War in the Villages; a Personal Perspective, Presidio Press, 1982.

WORK IN PROGRESS: A book on the years of the cease-fire in South Vietnam, 1973-75, an eye-witness account of the fall of Saigon, including Herrington's trips to Hanoi as part of the negotiations delegation that worked with the Communists on the missing-in-action question.

SIDELIGHTS: Herrington told *CA:* "Armed with the advantage of perspective that comes from the opportunity to live in Europe and Asia for seven years (afforded by military service), I am a convinced believer in our political and social system and the values it represents. If the vast majority of our American people could see what I have seen and experience what I have, we would not be plagued in the United States with compulsive, corrosive, divisive fault-finding that seems to characterize this generation. Churchill had it right when he said, 'Democracy is the worst form of government except every other form that has been tried.'"

* * *

HERRMANN, R(obert) L(awrence) 1928-

PERSONAL: Born July 17, 1928, in New York, N.Y.; son of Philip Charles (in business) and Florence (Benn) Herrmann; married Elizabeth Ann Cook (a writer), August 12, 1950; children; Stephen, Karen, Holly, Anders. *Education:* Purdue University, B.S., 1951; Michigan State University, Ph.D., 1956; postdoctoral study at Massachusetts Institute of Technology, 1956-59. *Politics:* Independent Democrat. *Religion:* Evangelical Christian. *Home:* 12 Spillers Lane, Ipswich, Mass. 01938. *Office address:* Box J, Ipswich, Mass. 01938.

CAREER: Boston University, Boston, Mass., assistant professor, 1959-65, associate professor of biochemistry, 1965-76; Oral Roberts University, Tulsa, Okla., professor of biochemistry and chairman of department, 1976-81, associate dean, 1978-79; Gordon College, Wenham, Mass., lecturer in chemistry and premedical program adviser, 1981—, adjunct professor of chemistry, 1983. Staley Lecturer at Gordon College, 1974. Science editor of Christian University Press. Member of board of trustees of Barrington College. *Military service:* U.S. Navy 1946-48, 1951-52. *Member:* American Scientific Affiliation (fellow; executive director, 1981—), Christian Medical Society (chairman of medical ethics committee), American Society of Biological Chemists, American Association for the Advancement of Science (fellow), Gerontological Society (fellow), Sigma Xi (president of Boston University chapter, 1968).

WRITINGS: (Contributor) Carl F.H. Henry, editor, *Horizons of Science,* Harper, 1978; (contributor) Craig Ellison, editor, *Modifying Man,* University Press of America, 1978; (editor) *Making Whole Persons,* American Scientific Affiliation, 1980; (editor with David F. Allen and Lewis Penhall Bird) *Whole Person Medicine: An International Symposium,* Inter-Varsity Press, 1980.

WORK IN PROGRESS: Wholistic Science, on science as an integrated activity, publication expected in 1985; research on ethical issues in recombinant DNA technology.

SIDELIGHTS: Herrmann commented: "As executive director of the American Scientific Affiliation, I am responsible for promoting the integration of the Christian faith with the professional lives of twenty-five hundred academic and industrial scientists, engineers, and health professionals. I am organizing the Conference on Science and Faith to be held in Oxford, England, in 1985.

"The biomedical model has been overemphasized in medicine, to the exclusion of moral and spiritual dimensions not well articulated by science. Similarly, as research with recombinant DNA continues, the likelihood exists that we will begin to see ourselves as a kind of 'manufactured product' expected to meet certain physical and intellectual standards, again to the exclusion of the moral, ethical, and spiritual."

* * *

HERTZ, Aleksander   1895-1983

OBITUARY NOTICE: Born August 3, 1895, in Warsaw, Poland; died after a long illness, May 16, 1983, in New York, N.Y. Sociologist, editor, and author. A sociologist in his native Poland, Hertz immigrated to the United States in 1940. During his lifetime he produced a number of sociology books and articles. Among his best-known works are *Jews in Polish Culture, The Confessions of an Old Man,* and the 1939 study *Problems of Sociology of the Theater.* He also edited *Poland Fights,* a periodical of the Polish Labor Group in New York City. Obituaries and other sources: *Who's Who in Polish America,* 3rd edition, Harbinger House, 1943, reprinted, Arno, 1970; *New York Times,* May 18, 1983.

* * *

HETHERINGTON, (Hector) Alastair   1919-

PERSONAL: Born October 31, 1919, in Llanishen, Glamorganshire, Wales; son of Hector Hetherington; married Helen Miranda Oliver (a teacher), 1957 (divorced, 1978); married Sheila Cameron, 1979; children: (first marriage) Thomas, Alexander, Lucy, Mary. *Education:* Attended Corpus Christi College, Oxford. *Home:* High Corrie, Isle of Arran KA27 8JB, Scotland.

CAREER: Herald, Glasgow, Scotland, member of editorial staff, 1946-50; affiliated with *Guardian* in London and Manchester, England, beginning in 1950, foreign editor, 1953-56, editor, 1956-75, editor of Guardian Newspapers Ltd., 1967-75; affiliated with British Broadcasting Corp. in Scotland, controller, 1976-78; free-lance journalist and broadcaster, 1978—. Member of Royal Commission on the Police, 1960-62. Member of board of trustees of Scott Trust, 1970—.

WRITINGS: Press, Police, and Public Interest, B. Rose, 1974; *Guardian Years,* Chatto & Windus, 1981. Also author of *Patterns of the Hebrides,* 1981.

* * *

HICKMAN, Charles   1905-1983

OBITUARY NOTICE: Born January 18, 1905, at Snaresbrook, Essex, England; died in 1983. Actor, director, and playwright. An actor during his first twenty years in the theatre, Hickman took up directing in 1939. Among his most successful London productions were "Annie Get Your Gun" and "Bonaventure." In 1935 he wrote the three-act comedy "Half-Holiday." Obituaries and other sources: *Encyclopaedia of the Musical Theatre,* Dodd, 1976; *Who's Who in the Theatre: A Biographical Record of the Contemporary Stage,* 17th edition, Gale, 1981; *London Times,* April 13, 1983.

* * *

HICKS, Robert E(lden)   1920-

BRIEF ENTRY: Born June 8, 1920, in Hidalgo, Ky. American economist, educator, and author. Hicks spent twenty years in the U.S. Air Force, then began teaching at Florida Technological University. He was named professor of economics in 1968 and was appointed director of the university's Center for Economic Education in 1977. He co-edited *Economics: Myth, Method, or Madness?* (McCutchan, 1971). *Address:* Department of Economics, Florida Technological University, Box 25000, Orlando, Fla. 32816.

* * *

HILBORN, Ann   1942-

PERSONAL: Born September 23, 1942, in Baytown, Tex.; daughter of Wilburn C. and Lorraine (Whitworth) Simpson; married Charles R. Cauthen, November, 1962 (divorced); married Robert J. Hilborn (a contractor), July 4, 1968; children: Scott, Kelly. *Education:* University of Houston, B.A., 1965. *Home:* 9655 Val Verde, Houston, Tex. 77063. *Agent:* Charles Neighbors, Inc., 240 Waverly Pl., New York, N.Y. 10014. *Office:* Houston Independent School District, 7504 Bissonet, Houston, Tex. 77074.

CAREER: Bratten Homes, Houston, Tex., administrative assistant, 1965-66; Fred Astaire Dance Studios, Houston, dance teacher, 1966-68; Northeast Houston Independent School District, teacher, 1966-70; Houston Independent School District, teacher of English, 1970—.

WRITINGS: Personal Justice (novel), Avon, 1982.

WORK IN PROGRESS: When Eagles Cry, a novel, publication expected in 1984.

SIDELIGHTS: "I grew up in Baytown in the fifties," Ann Hilborn told *CA,* "in what now appears to have been a time without many complex issues to face. My childhood was fortunate, for my parents were solid people, loving and caring—the kind of parents one would expect from the fifties.

"When I was still in college, life began to take a decidedly more complex direction. My father died in 1962, and I married my high school sweetheart that same year. We were divorced a little over a year later. After graduation, I moved to Houston to take up a career in teaching, in a poor little district that was literally begging for teachers. I married again in 1968.

"Most of my endeavors have involved teaching, but occasionally I've taken other jobs, having decided years ago that I needed and wanted a number of varied work experiences. I taught ballroom dancing; I sold real estate for a year, then worked for a home builder, a developer, and an attorney; I spent some time as housewife/mother/civic and garden clubber. Of all those, teaching is my clear preference. It's fun, entertaining, challenging, and rewarding in every way a job should be—except, of course, financially.

"I've been teaching English off and on for the past twelve years at a senior high school in southwest Houston. My students are eleventh and twelfth graders, the most entertaining, outrageous, energetic, charming, enthusiastic group of people you'll ever meet. Obviously I like going to work each morning (although I wish it could be an hour or two later) because I expect to laugh a lot each day and I'm rarely disappointed. I do indeed love my job and, in that, I consider myself very fortunate.

"I began writing fiction in my early thirties, not believing that I had any exceptional ability, but wanting to try something new. I tried short story writing with no success, but something kept me going. In 1975, at the University of Houston, I began to get the idea that perhaps I did have some kind of writing talent.

"Today, I'd have to call myself a liberated woman. I no longer live with my husband, although we're still married and still very good friends. We share our children equally, neither of us claiming exclusive custody, and both of us sharing expenses relating to them. I feel good about my teaching profession, and I feel good about my potential as a writer. I work hard at both jobs, I enjoy my children more than ever before, my social life has never been better, and I'm exploring new possibilities all the time. For the first time in my life, I feel absolutely free of restraints, either those self-imposed or those imposed by others. For me, at least, it's the only way to live, and I'm convinced that I'm about to experience the very best years of my life—an exciting prospect. I have a feeling that whoever said that 'life begins at forty' must have known what he was talking about."

AVOCATIONAL INTERESTS: "I like to read because I have so little time for it. I also like water sports, lying on the beach, and eating seafood. I enjoy snow skiing, dancing, and Bloody Marys. I hate exercise, but do it three days a week anyway. I love Simon and Garfunkel and Tom Selleck (doesn't everyone?)."

BIOGRAPHICAL/CRITICAL SOURCES: Los Angeles Times Book Review, November 21, 1982.

* * *

HILDEBRAND, Joel H(enry)   1881-1983

OBITUARY NOTICE—See index for *CA* sketch: Born November 16, 1881, in Camden, N.J.; died of a stroke, April 30, 1983, in Kensington, Calif. Chemist and author. Hildebrand served as a faculty member of the University of California at Berkeley for seventy years. Beginning in 1913, he taught an estimated forty thousand students, continuing his teaching and researching duties after his official retirement in 1952. Hildebrand is best remembered for his studies of solution theory, since his research on the dissolution of helium resulted in ways to protect divers from caisson disease, commonly known as "the bends." In addition to his teaching and researching responsibilities, Hildebrand served as the president of the American Chemical Society and the Sierra Club and as the manager

of the 1936 U.S. Olympic ski team. He received many honors for his work, including the American Chemical Society's Priestly Medal. In 1929 he was elected to the National Academy of Science, and his work with the Army Chemical Corps in France during World War II earned the scientist the Distinguished Service Medal. The University of California at Berkeley named the chemistry building and a chair in the chemistry department after Hildebrand and established the Hildebrand Memorial Fund at the time of his death. He wrote more than three hundred scientific papers and books on camping, education, and chemistry. His best-known work is the textbook *Principles of Chemistry*. Obituaries and other sources: *New York Times*, May 3, 1983; *Chicago Tribune*, May 4, 1983; *Washington Post*, May 5, 1983; *Los Angeles Times*, May 6, 1983; *Time*, May 16, 1983; *Newsweek*, May 16, 1983.

* * *

HILL, Walter   1942-

BRIEF ENTRY: Born January 10, 1942, in Long Beach, Calif. American film director and screenwriter. Hill was a construction and oilfield worker before he turned to directing motion pictures and writing screenplays for action films. In 1972 he wrote scripts for the movies "Hickey and Boggs" (United Artists) and "The Getaway" (Metro-Goldwyn-Mayer); the following year he wrote "The Thief Who Came to Dinner" and "The Macintosh Man," both for Warner Brothers. He also coauthored screenplays for such films as "Hard Times" (Columbia, 1975), "The Drowning Pool" (Warner Brothers, 1975), and "Southern Comfort" (Twentieth Century-Fox, 1981). In addition to his screenwriting efforts, Hill has directed several films, including "The Driver" (Twentieth Century-Fox, 1978), "The Warriors" (Paramount, 1979), and "Forty-eight Hours" (Paramount, 1982). *Address:* c/o International Creative Management, 8899 Beverly Blvd., Los Angeles, Calif. 90048. *Biographical/critical sources: New York Times*, July 28, 1978, March 4,, 1979; *Saturday Review*, October, 1980; *Chicago Tribune*, October 16, 1981; *International Motion Picture Almanac*, Quigley, 1982.

* * *

HILLABY, John (D.)   1917-

BRIEF ENTRY: Born July 24, 1917, in Pontefract, England. British naturalist, journalist, and author. Hillaby, who has been a broadcaster since 1944, has also been zoological correspondent for the *Manchester Guardian*, European science writer for the *New York Times*, and biological consultant for *New Scientist*. In 1971 he was Woodward Lecturer at Yale University. Hillaby's walking tours through Canada, Africa, and Western Europe have inspired many of his books, including *Holiday Parade for Your Pleasure* (Hague & Gill, c. 1946), *Within the Streams* (Harvey & Blythe, 1949), *Journey to the Jade Sea* (Constable, 1964), *Journey Through Britain* (Constable, 1968), *Journey Through Europe* (Constable, 1972), and *Journey Through Love* (Constable, 1976). *Address:* 85 Cholmley Gardens, London N.W.6, England. *Biographical/critical sources: Washington Post Book World*, May 11, 1969, October 15, 1972; *Christian Science Monitor*, July 10, 1969, January 20, 1977; *Observer*, June 25, 1972, May 20, 1973, October 10, 1976; *Times Literary Supplement*, August 25, 1972, November 26, 1976; Garry Hogg, *They Did It the Hard Way*, Pantheon, 1973; *Who's Who*, 134th edition, St. Martin's, 1982.

HINDE, Robert Aubrey 1923-

PERSONAL: Born October 26, 1923, in Norwich, England; son of Earnest Bertram (a physician) and Isabella (a nurse; maiden name, Taylor) Hinde; married Hester Coutts (divorced, 1971); married Joan Gladys Stevenson; children: two sons, four daughters. *Education:* University of London, B.Sc., 1948; St. John's College, Cambridge, B.A., 1948, M.A., 1950, Sc.D., 1958; Balliol College, Oxford, D.Phil., 1950. *Home address:* Park Lane, Madingley, Cambridgeshire, England.

CAREER: Cambridge University, Cambridge, England, curator at Ornithological Field Station, 1950-65, research fellow at St. John's College, 1951-54, steward, 1956-58, tutor, 1958-63, fellow, 1958—, Royal Society Research Professor, 1963—. Honorary director of Medical Research Council Unit on Development and Integration of Behaviour, 1970—. *Military service:* Royal Air Force, Coastal Command, 1941-45. *Member:* British Psychological Society (honorary fellow), Royal Society (fellow), American Academy of Arts and Sciences (honorary foreign member), American Ornithologists Union (honorary fellow), National Academy of Sciences (honorary foreign associate member).

WRITINGS: Animal Behaviour: A Synthesis of Ethology and Comparative Psychology, McGraw, 1966, 2nd edition, 1970; *Social Behaviour and Its Development in Subhuman Primates,* University of Oregon Press, 1972; *Biological Bases of Human Social Behaviour,* McGraw, 1974; *Towards Understanding Relationships,* Academic Press, 1979; *Ethology,* Fontana, 1982.

Editor: *Advances in the Study of Behaviour,* Academic Press, Volume I (with D. S. Lehrman and E. Shaw), 1965, Volume II (with Lehrman and Shaw), 1969, Volume III (with Lehrman and Shaw), 1970, Volume IV (with Lehrman and Shaw), 1972, Volume V (with Lehrman, Shaw, and J. S. Rosenblatt), 1974, Volume VI (with Shaw, Rosenblatt, and C. Beer), 1976, Volume VII (with Shaw, Rosenblatt, and Beer), 1976, Volume VIII (with Rosenblatt, Beer, and M. C. Busnel), 1978, Volume IX (with Rosenblatt, Beer, and Busnel), 1979, Volume X (with Rosenblatt, Beer, and Busnel), 1979, Volume XI (with Rosenblatt, Beer, and Busnel), 1980; *Bird Vocalizations,* Cambridge University Press, 1969; (with Gabriel Horn) *Short-Term Changes in Neural Activity and Behaviour,* Cambridge University Press, 1970; *Non-Verbal Communication,* Cambridge University Press, 1972; (with wife, J. S. Hinde) *Constraints on Learning,* Academic Press, 1973; (with P.P.G. Bateson) *Growing Points in Ethology,* Cambridge University Press, 1976; *Primate Social Relationships,* Blackwell Scientific Publications, 1983; (with G. Prins and others) *Defended to Death,* Penguin, 1983.

Contributor to scientific journals.

SIDELIGHTS: Hinde told *CA:* "Having worked for some years on the effects of separation between mother and infant, using rhesus monkeys as experimental subjects, I have now focused on the nature of inter-individual relationships. My present research concerns the family and school relationships of preschool age children and their role in the development of personality."

*   *   *

HINDEN, Michael C(harles) 1941-
(Emmett Byrd, John Crowe Byrd)

PERSONAL: Born June 5, 1941, in New York, N.Y.; son of Samuel R. and Ada (Trachtenberg) Hinden; married Betsy Draine (a university associate professor), November 28, 1981. *Education:* Sorbonne, University of Paris, Degre Superieur (with high honors), 1962; Ohio University, B.A. (summa cum laude), 1963; Brown University, Ph.D., 1971. *Home:* 1446 Rutledge St., Madison, Wis. 53703. *Office:* Department of English, University of Wisconsin—Madison, 600 North Park St., Madison, Wis. 53706.

CAREER: Brown University, Providence, R.I., instructor in English, 1968-69; University of Wisconsin—Madison, instructor, 1969-70, assistant professor, 1970-74, associate professor of English, 1974—, chairman of integrated liberal studies program, 1980—. Senior Fulbright lecturer at University of Bucharest, 1975-76. Frequent guest on radio programs. Honorary charter member of Alexander Meiklejohn Foundation. *Member:* Modern Language Association of America, Canadian Association for American Studies, Eugene O'Neill Society (chairman of publications committee, 1980-81; chairman of board of directors, 1982—), Phi Beta Kappa, Phi Eta Sigma, Phi Kappa Phi.

WRITINGS: (Under pseudonym Emmett Byrd) *Byrd Thou Never Wert: The Collected Poems and Post Cards of Emmett Byrd* (humor), Ten Speed Press, 1980; (contributor) Joseph J. Waldmeir, editor, *Critical Essays on John Barth,* G. K. Hall, 1980; (contributor) Stephen H. Dill, editor, *Integrated Studies: Challenges to the College Curriculum,* University Press of America, 1982. Contributor of scholarly articles to critical theatre and arts journals and literary satire (under pseudonyms Emmett Byrd and John Crowe Byrd) to *Satire Newsletter, Pucred, Scholia Satyrica,* and *Northeast.*

WORK IN PROGRESS: The Pulse of Tragedy.

SIDELIGHTS: Hinden told *CA:* "The Greeks, of course, understood the profound relationship between tragedy and comedy, as symbolized by their intertwined theatrical masks of the upturned and downturned smile. I've been writing humor ever since I was a teenager, and now find it a necessary balance to my fascination with, and scholarly work on, tragedy. Yeats, I think, best expressed the connection: 'Tragedy must always be a drowning and breaking of the dykes that separate man and man, and . . . it is upon these dykes that comedy keeps house.'"

*   *   *

HINDLEY, Geoffrey 1935-

PERSONAL: Born in 1935 in Birmingham, England; married Diana Balden (a writer); children: one daughter. *Education:* Received M.A. from University College, Oxford.

CAREER: Lecturer in social history at Kingston College of Art. Member of tutorial panel of Open University.

WRITINGS; (Editor) *The Thames and Hudson Encyclopaedia of the Arts,* Thames & Hudson, 1966; *Castles of Europe,* Hamlyn, 1968; *The Medieval Establishment, 1200-1500,* Putnam, 1970; *Musical Instruments,* illustrations by Ron Geary, Hamlyn, 1971; *A History of Roads,* P. Davies, 1971, Citadel, 1972; *Medieval Warfare,* Wayland, 1971, Putnam, 1972; (editor) *Larousse Encyclopedia of Music,* World, 1971; *The Roof of the World,* Aldus Books, 1971; (with wife, Diana Hindley) *Advertising in Victorian England, 1837-1901,* Wayland, 1972; *Great Castles and Palaces,* Golden Press, 1973; *The Book of Houses,* Triune Books, 1973, Spring Books, 1974; (with Robin Clarke) *The Challenge of the Primitives,* McGraw, 1975; *Saladin,* Barnes & Noble, 1976; *Working With Light-Sensitive Ma-*

terials, Van Nostrand, 1978; *England in the Age of Caxton*, St. Martin's, 1979; (with Elizabeth Floyd) *Makers of History*, Aldus Books, 1980; *World Art Treasures*, Octopus Books, 1980; *Secret Agents*, illustrations by Paul Wright, Angus & Robinson, 1981.

SIDELIGHTS: The majority of Hindley's books are histories of various subjects, including European castles and houses, primitive societies, advertising, medieval warfare, music, secret agents, and other figures.

BIOGRAPHICAL/CRITICAL SOURCES: Times Literary Supplement, November 12, 1976, November 21, 1980.*

* * *

HINES, Earl Kenneth   1905-1983
(Fatha Hines)

OBITUARY NOTICE: Born December 28, 1905, in Duquesne, Pa.; died of a heart attack, April 22, 1983, in Oakland, Calif. Jazz pianist and author. Named "Fatha" by a Chicago disc jockey in the 1930's because he was "the father of modern piano," Hines redefined jazz piano, establishing it as a solo instrument with his inventive, style-setting performances. Working with several big bands in the 1920's, the pianist started his own band in 1928 at Chicago's Grand Terrace Ballroom, where he performed for more than a decade and was often heard in nationwide radio broadcasts. He later relocated to San Francisco. In his role as bandleader, Hines furthered the careers of such jazz artists as Charlie Parker, Dizzy Gillespie, and Sarah Vaughan; his 1920's jazz recordings with Louis Armstrong are still considered masterpieces. He wrote an autobiography with Stanley Dance, *The World of Earl Hines*, and a number of jazz works, including "Rosetta," "Piano Man," and "57 Varieties." Obituaries and other sources: *Current Biography*, Wilson, 1967; *Biographical Dictionary of American Music*, Parker Publishing, 1973; *Encyclopedia of Jazz in the Seventies*, Horizon Press, 1976; *Chicago Tribune*, April 24, 1983; *New York Times*, April 24, 1983; *Washington Post*, April 24, 1983; *Newsweek*, May 2, 1983; *Time*, May 2, 1983.

* * *

HINES, Fatha
See HINES, Earl Kenneth

* * *

HINKLE, Vernon   1935-
(H. V. Elkin)

PERSONAL: Born June 23, 1935, in Amsterdam, N.Y.; son of Vernon M. (a carpenter) and Lovina (Lawrence) Hinkle; married Sally Applegate, June 3, 1956 (divorced, 1975); married Mary Sanders Shartle (a writer), September 8, 1978; children: Lawrence. *Education:* Ithaca College, B.A., 1956; Yale University, M.F.A., 1961. *Home:* 470 West 24th St., New York, N.Y. 10011.

CAREER: Polka Dot Playhouse, Bridgeport, Conn., director, 1958; Bradford College, Bradford, Mass., instructor, 1961-66, chairman of drama department, 1966-71; J. C. Penney Co., New York, N.Y., writer of internal communications, 1971-75, benefits communicator in personnel, 1975-77; freelance corporate writer, 1977—. *Member:* Dramatists Guild. *Awards, honors:* Playwriting award from Ithaca College, 1953, for "Before Gabriel Blew"; faculty grant from Bradford College, 1966; named O'Neill Playwright, 1969.

WRITINGS—Novels; under pseudonym H. V. Elkin, except as noted: *Eagle Man*, Tower, 1978; (under name Vernon Hinkle) *Music to Murder By*, Tower, 1978; *Playground*, Tower, 1979; *Yellowstone*, Tower, 1980; *Mustang*, Tower, 1980; *Tiger's Chance*, Tower, 1980.

Plays; under name Vernon Hinkle: "Before Gabriel Blew" (one-act), first produced in Ithaca, N.Y., at Ithaca College, May 7, 1954; (music by Sally Applegate) "Musicians of Bremen" (one-act), first produced in Bradford, Mass., at Bradford College, December 11, 1963; "Character in a Play" (one-act), first produced Off-Broadway at La Mama Experimental Theatre Club, August, 1965; "The Concept" (two-act), first produced in Waterford, Conn., at O'Neill Theatre Center, July 9, 1969, rewritten as "Showcase," as yet unproduced; "Edna" (one-act), first produced in Salina, Kan., at Kansas Wesleyan University, October 17, 1973; "If I'm Dead, Start Without Me" (two-act), first produced in Bridgeport, Conn., at Polka Dot Playhouse, September 10, 1982.

WORK IN PROGRESS: A play titled "A Month in Maine," completion expected in 1983.

SIDELIGHTS: Hinkle told *CA:* "Play became private fantasies on the farm where I was brought up, isolated from friends my own age. Sometimes, in later years, it became difficult to collaborate on a fantasy, as in theatre work. After some unhappy experiences trying, I started my first novel and enjoyed the privacy and control. Finally restless, I emerged from the novelist's cocoon with a new readiness to collaborate in theatre, even with some entrepreneuring spirit—a necessary quality for most playwrights who want to work in, not out of, the theatre.

"If my work is any one thing besides eclectic, it is mystery, in the sense that each piece (novel or play) is a puzzle or a quest for unknown answers. In this respect, I regard most fiction as mystery."

* * *

HIRSH, James E(ric)   1946-

PERSONAL: Born July 12, 1946, in Brooklyn, N.Y.; son of Raymond M. and Claire (Depken) Hirsh; married Kathleen Kenny, August 23, 1969; children: Matthew, Elizabeth. *Education:* Cornell University, B.A., 1968; University of Washington, Ph.D., 1978. *Office:* Department of English, University of Hawaii, Honolulu, Hawaii 96822.

CAREER: University of Washington, Seattle, instructor, 1979-80; University of Hawaii, Honolulu, assistant professor of English, 1980—. *Member:* Modern Language Association of America, Shakespeare Association of America.

WRITINGS: The Structure of Shakespearean Scenes, Yale University Press, 1981. Contributor to periodicals, including *Modern Language Quarterly*.

WORK IN PROGRESS: Further research on Shakespearean drama.

SIDELIGHTS: Hirsh told *CA:* "In writing *The Structure of Shakespearean Scenes*, I was responding to the need for a comprehensive study of Shakespeare's essential artistic unit, the scene. The scene's structural flexibility—whether used for revealing the private thoughts of a single character or for depicting a public event involving a crowd of characters and whether comprising one incident or several—is the basis of the dramatic unity of Shakespeare's plays, a unity achieved through multiplicity."

In his review of *The Structure of Shakespearean Scenes* for the *Times Literary Supplement*, John Stachniewski commended Hirsh for having erected, on a "solidly constructed argumentative platform," a "systematic classification of scenes which yields illuminating discussion of uses to which particular scene types are put." He also praised Hirsh's "liberal and authentic" insights and added, "To focus on the structure of scenes is to reduce the gap between criticism of the plays and their theatrical impact while demystifying the actual processes of creation."

BIOGRAPHICAL/CRITICAL SOURCES: Times Literary Supplement, August 20, 1982.

* * *

HISCOCK, Eric 1899-
(Whitefriar)

PERSONAL: Surname is pronounced Hiscoe; born September 10, 1899, in Oxford, England; son of Frank (a butler) and Annie (Wilson) Hiscock; married Romilly Cavan (an author and playwright), February 10, 1940 (deceased). *Education:* Educated in England. *Politics:* Liberal. *Religion:* Church of England. *Home:* 26 Chesterfield House, London W.1, England. *Agent:* Desmond Elliott, 38 Bury Street, London W.1, England.

CAREER: Formerly associated with Bodleian Library; bookseller for W. H. Smith; worked in England as journalist, 1930; associated with *Bookseller*, 1954-79; worked as trade columnist, 1954-79. *Military service:* Royal Fusiliers, 1914-18. *Member:* Society of Bookmen.

WRITINGS: Last Boat to Folly Bridge (correspondence and reminiscences), Cassell, 1970; *The Bells of Hell Go Ting-a-Ling-a-Ling: An Autobiographical Fragment Without Maps*, Arlington Books, 1976; *A Far and Distant Prospect* (autobiography), Arlington Books, 1983.

Author of "Personally Speaking," a weekly column in *Trade Weekly*, under pseudonym Whitefriar for more than thirty years; associated with *Evening Standard* and *Bookseller*.

WORK IN PROGRESS: To Mary With Love, a novel, publication by Arlington Books expected in 1984.

SIDELIGHTS: Hiscock's wartime memoir, *The Bells of Hell Go Ting-a-Ling-a-Ling*, is a personal account of his experiences as a fifteen-year-old soldier fighting in the trenches of France during World War I. It is the story of the horrors Hiscock witnessed, like the screaming man without a jaw or the disembodied leg propping up a dugout, but as Matthew Coady wrote in the *New Statesman*, it is also a "personal, moving, [and] often funny account of a boy soldier's war." "If this is a story of blood and barbed wire, it is also a valentine thrown to the past," Coady continued. "If it remembers and mourns lost comrades it also conjures up a young manhood in a long-vanished provincial England. It evokes a world of teas at the Cadena with pig-tailed flappers, kisses in a hollow willow tree by the Cherwell and friendships that soothed the fears engendered where the rats stood a better chance than the human beings."

Spectator reviewer Benny Green joined Coady in his praise of *The Bells of Hell*, describing it as a "wonderfully vivid and moving evocation of trench life," and Hiscock as "ribald, scathing, sensitive, funny and very intelligent." *The Bells of Hell*, Green concluded, "will, I am sure, join that group of books by the Western Front survivors which posterity will study in its attempt to understand." Writing in *Books and Bookmen*,

Tom Pocock similarly determined that as "one of the last that can be written from personal knowledge about that war, this book deserves an honourable place in its literature."

Hiscock told *CA*: "I have been a publisher's talent scout, publisher's reader, and, since 1960, an acknowledged leading columnist and book-tipster to bookshop and publishing professions. I have now retired from such activities to concentrate on my own books."

BIOGRAPHICAL/CRITICAL SOURCES: Books and Bookmen, December, 1976, January, 1978; *New Statesman*, December 17, 1976; *Spectator*, December 18, 1976.

* * *

HODGELL, P(atricia) C(hristine) 1951-

PERSONAL: Born March 16, 1951, in Des Moines, Iowa; daughter of Robert Overman (an artist) and Lois (an artist and teacher; maiden name, Partridge) Hodgell. *Education:* Eckerd College, B.A., 1973; University of Minnesota, M.A., 1976, doctoral study, 1976—. *Home:* 1237 Liberty St., Oshkosh, Wis. 54901. *Agent:* Adele Leone Agency, 52 Riverside Dr., No. 6-A, New York, N.Y. 10024. *Office:* Department of English, University of Wisconsin—Oshkosh, Oshkosh, Wis. 54901.

CAREER: University of Wisconsin—Oshkosh, lecturer in English, 1981—. *Member:* Science Fiction Writers of America.

WRITINGS: God Stalk (fantasy novel), Atheneum, 1982.

Work represented in anthologies, including *Clarion Science Fiction*, edited by Kate Wilhelm, Berkley Publishing, 1977; *Berkley Showcase II*, edited by Victoria Schochet and John Silbersack, Berkley Publishing, 1980; *Elsewhere III*, Ace Books, 1983. Contributor to magazines, including *Empire* and *Riverside Quarterly*.

WORK IN PROGRESS: Blood Rite, a fantasy novel, publication by Atheneum expected in 1985.

SIDELIGHTS: Patricia Hodgell commented: "For as long as I can remember I've been making up stories to tell myself. Some children have imaginary friends. I had a host of them, but in a world all their own, which I visited only by invitation and rarely in my own person. All of this was largely to compensate for a lonely childhood, growing up in an old house with a grandmother after the divorce of my parents. It was (and still is) a wonderful old place, though, full of one hundred years of family history and haunted by the possessions, if not the ghosts, of four generations. The house and the stories each provided worlds in which I felt safe and happy, in contrast to the threatening 'real' world outside.

"I was also an avid reader, especially of fantasy and science fiction, by such writers as Andre Norton and Edgar Rice Burroughs. This fiction shaped my daydreams and stirred my ambition someday to become a writer myself. But I was afraid to commit myself.

"Years went by. Through grade school, high school, and even college, I spent nearly half my waking time on a secondary level in an imaginary world whose very existence was a secret to all but a few close friends. Despite all this mental activity, however, very little got written down. I was still afraid. Of what? Failure, I suppose, of being just one more would-be, talentless writer. But all this time the pressure was growing and so was the discipline. College taught me that. I had always been a wild fantasizer, groping for control over my material but easily distracted and hardly able to sit still long enough to write a page. Now the studies of literature and foreign languages taught me to concentrate and organize. Ready at last, after college I retreated to my old home with a typewriter and a ream of paper, determined to find out if my wildest daydream—that of becoming a real writer—could be made to come true.

"It would be nice to say that, after the long suppression of the writing impulse, the dam burst—but it didn't. Due to lack of practice, I simply didn't know how to put a story down on paper. However, I began to learn. By the next summer, I had several stories finished and an invitation to attend the Clarion Writers Workshop. There, for the first time, I found a whole community of people like me—storytellers, wordsmiths, an entire family I never knew I had. Even more wonderful, here suddenly were professionals like Harlan Ellison and Kate Wilhelm telling me that I could indeed write. I could hardly believe my luck.

"Then graduate school started and all writing stopped. Try as I would, I couldn't be both creative and academic at the same time, so again the fantasies had to be bottled up, although I still lived them as intensely as ever. That lasted until I received my M.A. in English literature and had safely passed the doctoral qualifying examination. Then I took another year's leave, went home, and started writing again. The result was *God Stalk*, a curious blend of Charles Dickens, Fritz Leiber, and *Marvel Comics*. To my great surprise, it was sold.

"Now I'm about to start work on the sequel, with plans maturing for at least three additional novels in the series. Actually, I seem to be working on what some people call a hypernovel, a continuous narrative cut into novel-sized lengths with the trimmings made into short stories. All those years of daydreaming seem to have generated a lot of material. I may spend the rest of my life writing it all down, sometimes with delight but just as often with exasperation at my stylistic shortcomings. At present my writing isn't as good as I hope someday it will be, but that's all right. I may be a chronic dreamer, but I'm also stubborn, and I can learn."

* * *

HODGES, Gil(bert Ray)   1924-1972

OBITUARY NOTICE: Born April 4, 1924, in Princeton, Ind.; died April 2, 1972. Baseball player and manager and author. Throughout the 1950's Hodges was one of baseball's finest hitting first basemen. He played for several pennant-winning teams with the Brooklyn Dodgers, where he was one of the players most admired by the often finicky Brooklyn fans. Among his best years were 1953 and 1954, in which he hit thirty-one and forty-two home runs, respectively. In 1958, when the Dodgers moved to Los Angeles, Hodges's career began to decline, reaching its nadir in 1960 when he collected only thirty-nine hits. He finished his career back in New York, spending two seasons with the New York Mets. Hodges then signed in 1963 as manager of the Washington Senators. In five seasons, he never won more than seventy-six games. In 1968 Hodges returned to New York as manager of the Mets. The following year, 1969, Hodges and the Mets, redubbed the "Amazing Mets," captured the National League pennant after a harrowing race with the Chicago Cubs. In the World Series that year, Hodges's Mets faced the overpowering Baltimore Orioles, who had compiled a record of 109 victories and only 53 defeats. After bowing in the first game, though, the Mets swept the Orioles in four straight games and captured their first World Series championship. Hodges followed the triumphant

1969 season with two consecutive years of 83 victories. Yogi Berra, who succeeded Hodges, led the Mets back to the World Series in 1973, where they lost to the Oakland Athletics in seven games. In 1969 Hodges wrote his autobiography, *The Game of Baseball*. Obituaries and other sources: *Current Biography,* Wilson, 1962, April, 1972; *New York Times,* April 3, 1972; *Who Was Who in America, With World Notables,* Volume V: *1969-1973,* Marquis, 1973.

* * *

HOFFA, James R(iddle)   1913-1975(?)

OBITUARY NOTICE: Born February 14, 1913, in Brazil, Ind.; reported missing, July 30, 1975; legally declared dead, December 8, 1982. Union leader and author. Hoffa, who was president of the Teamsters union from 1957 to 1971, first became involved in the labor movement at age seventeen when he organized a strike of Kroger warehousemen. After leading Kroger employees into the American Federation of Labor, Hoffa devoted full attention to union organizing. During the 1930's he was the target of numerous assaults from henchmen hired by employers to discourage union activity. In 1937 Hoffa, working with Farrell Dobbs, began recruiting truck drivers for the Central States Drivers Council. He quickly rose within the union echelon, becoming chairman in 1940 and vice-president the following year. In 1946 he became president of a Teamsters local in Detroit. Working under then union president Dave Beck, Hoffa helped restructure the previously autonomous locals to consolidate power within the central organization. In 1957 both Hoffa and Beck were accused of misusing union funds. Beck was found guilty, but Hoffa was acquitted and soon assumed control of the Teamsters. He became the target of a relentless investigation by Attorney General Robert Kennedy, who accused Hoffa of ties with organized crime. Though eventually convicted of jury tampering, fraud, and conspiracy to abuse union funds, Hoffa continued to serve as president of the Teamsters following his imprisonment in 1967. In 1971, after repeated denials of parole—presumably because of his refusal to resign his position—Hoffa stepped down from his post, whereupon the remainder of his sentence was commuted by President Richard Nixon. In 1975, after attempting to reintegrate himself into union activities, Hoffa disappeared. Rumors circulated that Hoffa had been murdered, but no compelling evidence was discovered. Hoffa wrote an autobiography titled *Hoffa: The Real Story*. Obituaries and other sources: *Current Biography,* Wilson, 1972, March, 1983; *Time,* August 11, 1975; *Newsweek,* August 18, 1975, August 30, 1976; *Biography News,* Gale, September, 1975.

* * *

HOFFER, Eric   1902-1983

OBITUARY NOTICE—See index for *CA* sketch: Born July 25, 1902, in New York, N.Y.; died of natural causes, May 21, 1983, in San Francisco, Calif. Hoffer, a longshoreman-turned-philosopher, described himself as "a tourist in life." He had no formal education and was partially blind—owing to a fall he took at age five—until he was fifteen. He then became a voracious reader. For twenty-three years of his adult life he worked as a migrant farmer and miner and as a stevedore until his mandatory retirement in 1967. He began to write philosophical books and commentaries while a laborer, which made him a media personality. He appeared on television programs, lectured at the University of California at Berkeley as a "conversationalist at large," and wrote columns that were syndicated in 200 newspapers. After a chat with Lyndon Johnson he was appointed to the president's commission on violence and protest in the 1960's. In 1970 he abandoned all such activities "to crawl back into my hole, where I started." Hoffer received the Presidential Medal of Freedom early in 1983. His writings include *True Believer,* a study of fanaticism; *Truth Imagined; In Our Time;* and *Before the Sabbath.* Obituaries and other sources: *New York Times,* May 22, 1983; *Washington Post,* May 22, 1983; *Chicago Tribune,* May 23, 1983; *Newsweek,* May 30, 1983; *Time,* May 30, 1983; *Publishers Weekly,* June 3, 1983.

* * *

HOLDGATE, Martin Wyatt 1931-

PERSONAL: Born January 14, 1931, in Horsham, England; son of Francis Wyatt and Lois Marjorie (Bebbington) Holdgate; married Elizabeth Mary Dickason, April 2, 1963; children: David; Robert Weil (stepson). *Education:* Queens' College, Cambridge, Ph.D., 1955, M.A., 1956. *Religion:* Church of England. *Home:* 35 Wingate Way, Trumpington, Cambridge CB2 2HD, England. *Office:* Department of the Environment, 2 Marsham St., London SW1P 3EB, England.

CAREER: Gough Island Scientific Survey, senior scientist, 1955-56; Victoria University of Manchester, Manchester, England, lecturer in zoology, 1956-57; zoology teacher at secondary schools in Durham, England, 1957-60; Scott Polar Research Institute, Cambridge, England, assistant director of research, 1960-63; senior biologist for British Antarctic Survey, 1963-66; Nature Conservancy, London, England, deputy director of research, 1966-70; Department of the Environment, London, director of Central Unit on Environmental Pollution, 1970-74; director of Institute of Terrestrial Ecology for Natural Environment Research Council, 1974-76; director general for Departments of Environment and Transport, 1976—. Deputy secretary of Department of Transport; vice-president of Young Explorers Trust. Leader of Royal Society expedition to Southern Chile, 1958-59; member of working group on biology of Scientific Committee on Antarctic Research, 1964-68. *Member:* Institute of Biology (fellow), Royal Geographical Society (fellow), Zoological Society (fellow), British School Exploring Society (chairman, 1967-78).

WRITINGS: Mountains in the Sea: The Story of the Gough Island Expedition, Macmillan, 1958; (editor with R. Carrick and J. Prevost) *Antarctic Biology,* Hermann, 1964; (editor) *Antarctic Ecology,* Academic Press, 1970; (with N. Wale) *Man and Nature in the Tristan da Cunha Islands,* International Union for the Conservation of Nature and Natural Resources, 1976; *A Perspective of Environmental Pollution,* Cambridge University Press, 1979; (editor with M. Kassas and G.F. White) *The World Environment: 1972-1982,* Tycooly International, 1982. Contributor to scientific journals.

WORK IN PROGRESS: A popular book on environmental pollution.

SIDELIGHTS: Martin Wyatt Holdgate told *CA:* "My writing is an important secondary activity to my work as an environmental scientist in government service. I also do a considerable amount of advisory scientific work for the United Nations environment program."

* * *

HOLLAND, Joyce
See MORICE, Dave

HOLLAND, Philip Welsby 1917-

PERSONAL: Born in 1917 in Middlewich, England; son of John (a solicitor) and Lilian (Walmesley) Holland; married Josephine Alma Hudson, 1943; children: Peter. *Education:* Educated in England. *Office:* House of Commons, London S.W.1, England.

CAREER: Parliament, London, England, Conservative member of Parliament for Acton, 1959-64, parliamentary private secretary to minister of pensions and national insurance, 1961-62, and to chief secretary of treasury, 1962-64; Ultra Electronics Group of Companies, Acton, personnel manager, 1964-66; Parliament, Conservative member for Carlton, 1966—, opposition spokesman on industrial relations and joint secretary of Conservative Parliamentary Labour Committee, 1967-70, vice-chairman of Conservative Parliamentary Committee on Employment and Productivity, 1970, parliamentary private secretary to minister for aerospace, 1970-72. Manufacturers' agent, 1949-60; industrial relations adviser to Standard Telephones and Cables Co., 1969-81. Member of council of Royal Borough of Kensington, 1955-59. *Military service:* Royal Air Force, 1936-46. *Awards, honors:* Free Enterprise Award from Aims of Industry, 1981, for anti-bureaucratic campaign.

WRITINGS: (With Michael Fallon) *The Quango Explosion: Public Bodies and Ministerial Patronage,* Conservative Political Centre, 1978; *Quango, Quango, Quango: Full Dossier on Patronage in Britain,* Adam Smith Institute, 1979; *Costing the Quango,* Adam Smith Institute, 1979; *The Quango Death List,* Adam Smith Institute, 1980; *The Governance of Quangos,* Adam Smith Institute, 1981; *Quelling the Quango,* Conservative Political Centre, 1982.

* * *

HOLLEY, Frederick S. 1924-

PERSONAL: Born February 1, 1924, in Peterborough, N.H.; son of Allan John (an Anglican minister) and Susan (Sherman) Holley; married Florence Harten (a realtor), September 11, 1959; children: Frederick S., Jr., Mary Susan, Mark Allan John, James Leo. *Education:* Washington and Lee University, B.A., 1948; attended Columbia University, 1950-51. *Politics:* Democrat. *Religion:* Episcopalian. *Home:* 3310 Law Behm Ter., Fullerton, Calif. 92635. *Office:* Los Angeles Times, Times Mirror Sq., Los Angeles, Calif. 90053.

CAREER: Virginian-Pilot, Norfolk, Va., police reporter, 1948-50, assistant Sunday editor, 1951-57, assistant chief of copy desk, 1957-63; *Los Angeles Times,* Los Angeles, Calif., copy editor, 1963-65, chief of foreign copy desk, 1965-69, copy editor, 1969-79, editor of stylebook, 1979-81, style usage consultant, 1981—. *Military service:* U.S. Army, 1943-45, served in infantry; received Purple Heart with cluster. *Member:* American Newspaper Guild (president of Southern District Council, 1958-62).

WRITINGS: Los Angeles Times Stylebook: A Manual for Writers, Editors, Journalists, and Students; An Authoritative and Practical Guide to Style and Usage, New American Library, 1981.

WORK IN PROGRESS: Research on the origins and current usage of the English language.

SIDELIGHTS: Holley commented: "I am now grateful for having been forced to study Latin. I am hopeful, too, as we all should be, even when there doesn't seem to be much hope."

* * *

HOLMAN, Portia Grenfell 1903-1983

OBITUARY NOTICE: Born November 20, 1903; died of a brain hemorrhage, May 16, 1983, in London, England. Psychiatrist and author. Specializing in disturbed children, Holman began her career as consultant psychiatrist to the Twickenham Child Guidance Clinic in 1944. The next year she joined West Middlesex Hospital as a consultant. She then was appointed to the staff of Elizabeth Garrett Anderson Hospital, where she remained until her 1969 retirement. Founder and first chairman of the Association of Workers for Maladjusted Children, Holman was awarded the Burlingham Prize in 1952. She wrote *Bedwetting* and *Psychology and Psychological Medicine for Nurses* and co-authored *Sebastion's: A Hospital School Experiment in Therapeutic Education,* which presented her teaching methods for disturbed children. Obituaries and other sources: *Who's Who,* 133rd edition, St. Martin's, 1981; *London Times,* May 28, 1983.

* * *

HOLMES, Frank Wakefield 1924-

PERSONAL: Born in 1924; married Nola Ruth Ross (a teacher); children: Ross, David. *Home:* 61 Cheviot Rd., Lowry Bay, Eastbourne, New Zealand.

CAREER: Economist with Department of the Prime Minister beginning in 1949; economist with Department of External Affairs, ending 1952; Victoria University of Wellington, Wellington, New Zealand, lecturer, 1952-54, senior lecturer, 1954-59, Macarthy Professor of Economics and head of department, 1959-67, professor of money and finance, 1970-77, dean of faculty of commerce, 1961-63; chairman of New Zealand Planning Council, 1977—. Manager of economics for Tasman Pulp & Paper Co. Ltd., 1967-70. Adviser to Royal Commission on Monetary, Banking, and Credit Systems, 1955; chairman of Monetary and Economic Council, 1961-64, 1969-72; member of New Zealand Council for Educational Research, 1965-76, chairman, 1970-74; chairman of executive committee of Educational Development Conference, 1973-74; chairman of Task Force on Economic and Social Planning, 1976. Justice of the peace, 1960—. Consultant to Bank of New Zealand. *Member:* Economic Society of Australia and New Zealand (president of central council, 1967-68), Australia and New Zealand Association for the Advancement of Science (president of educational section, 1979; past president of economic section), New Zealand Association of Economists (president, 1961-63).

WRITINGS: Money, Finance, and the Economy: An Introduction to the New Zealand Financial System, Heinemann, 1972.

* * *

HOLMES, John W(endell) 1910-

BRIEF ENTRY: Born June 18, 1910, in London, Ontario, Canada. Canadian diplomat, educator, and author. Holmes served the Canadian Department of External Affairs in London, England, and Moscow, U.S.S.R., during the 1940's. He was director general of the Canadian Institute of International Affairs from 1960 until 1973, when he was named research director of the institute. Holmes has taught at York University,

University of Toronto, and University of Leeds. He wrote *The Better Part of Valour: Essays on Canadian Diplomacy* (McClelland & Stewart, 1970), *Canada: A Middle-Aged Power* (McClelland & Stewart, 1976), and *The Shaping of Peace: Canada and the Search for World Order, 1943-1957* (University of Toronto Press, 1979). *Address:* 36 Castle Frank Rd., Toronto 5, Ontario, Canada M4W 2Z6; and 15 King's College Circle, Toronto, Ontario, Canada M5S 2V9. *Biographical/critical sources: The Canadian Who's Who,* Volume 14, University of Toronto Press, 1979; *Times Literary Supplement,* February 15, 1980.

* * *

HOLMES, Joseph R. 1928(?)-1983

OBITUARY NOTICE: Born c. 1928, in Scranton, Pa.; died of cancer, May 27, 1983, in Washington, D.C. Press agent, White House aide, journalist, and editor. Known for his expertise in media relations, Holmes first served President Ronald Reagan when the politician was governor of California, becoming his press aide during the 1980 presidential campaign. After Reagan's victory, the journalist was named presidential spokesman on the West Coast. Also coordinator of audio-visual operations in the White House, Holmes was in charge of a project to compile a videotape history of the Reagan presidency. Before joining the politician's staff in 1971, the journalist had worked as a press agent in Hollywood, operated a television advertising business, and founded and edited the *San Diego Dispatch.* Obituaries and other sources: *Washington Post,* May 28, 1983; *Chicago Tribune,* May 29, 1983.

* * *

HOLTZ, Barry W(illiam) 1947-

PERSONAL: Born March 26, 1947, in Boston, Mass.; son of Melvin (an accountant) and Meryl (Schlosberg) Holtz. *Education:* Tufts University, A.B. (cum laude), 1968; Brandeis University, M.A., 1971, Ph.D., 1973. *Home:* 711 West End Ave., New York, N.Y. 10025. *Office:* Melton Research Center for Jewish Education, Jewish Theological Seminary of America, 3080 Broadway, New York, N.Y. 10027.

CAREER: Teacher at Hebrew schools in Sharon, Mass., 1966-67, Brookline, Mass., 1967-71, Lexington, Mass., 1972-74, and Merion, Pa., 1974-77; Jerusalem Institute, Jerusalem, Israel, teacher, 1977-78; Jewish Theological Seminary of America, New York City, chairman of publications of Melton Research Center for Jewish Education, 1978-80, visiting assistant professor of Jewish education at seminary, 1979—, co-director of research center, 1980—. Guest lecturer at McGill University, 1976, and Pennsylvania State University, 1977; teacher of adult Hebrew education in Lexington, Mass., 1972-73, Newton, Mass., 1973, Philadelphia, Pa., 1975-76, New York City, 1978—, and at National Havurah Institute, 1981-82; teacher at World Union of Jewish Students, Arad, Israel, 1977-78. Member of board of directors of Heschel Day School, 1980—. *Member:* National Council of Teachers of English, National Association for Core Curriculum.

WRITINGS: (With Arthur Green) *Your Word Is Fire: The Hasidic Masters on Contemplative Prayer,* Paulist/Newman, 1977; *Back to the Sources: Reading the Classic Jewish Texts,* Summit Books, in press.

Editor: *Holidays/Mitzvot/Prayer for the Alef Level,* six volumes, Melton Research Center for Jewish Education, Jewish

Theological Seminary of America, 1979; *Holidays/Mitzvot/ Prayer for the Gimmel Level,* seven volumes, Melton Research Center for Jewish Education, Jewish Theological Seminary of America, 1979; *Genesis: A New Teachers Guide,* Melton Research Center for Jewish Education, Jewish Theological Seminary of America, 1979; *Genesis: A New Student Workbook,* Melton Research Center for Jewish Education, Jewish Theological Seminary of America, 1980; *Holidays/Mitzvot/Prayer for the Bet Level,* five volumes, Melton Research Center for Jewish Education, Jewish Theological Seminary of America, 1981-82.

Work represented in anthologies, including: *The New Jews,* Random House, 1971; *Voices From the Ark,* Avon, 1979; *Gates to the New City,* Avon, 1983. Contributor to *Jewish Almanac.* Contributor of articles and poems to magazines, including *Response, English Journal, Teachers College Record, Midstream,* and *Present Tense,* and to newspapers.

SIDELIGHTS: Holtz told *CA:* "My own writing has been primarily oriented toward exploring in what way the great Jewish texts can speak to people living today. The works that have in general been my concern are those of the so-called 'aggadic' tradition within Judaism—the legendary, interpretive, imaginative literature. Although I find in the 'halakhic' (legal) tradition sources of great richness, I have always been drawn to biblical narrative, and Midrash, Kabbalah, and Hasidism are the materials that communicate most directly to me. In my work in Jewish education I have also been concerned with similar questions: how can we mediate the texts of the past to the contemporary world, and how can we discover and transmit the spiritual wisdom embodied in the literary artifacts of an ancient and vibrant tradition?"

BIOGRAPHICAL/CRITICAL SOURCES: Jewish Spectator, autumn, 1978; *Genesis II,* March, 1979; *Sh'ma,* May 25, 1979; *Judaism,* autumn, 1979.

* * *

HOM, Ken 1949-

PERSONAL: Born May 3, 1949, in Tucson, Ariz.; son of J. Thomas and Fong (Ying) Hom. *Education:* Attended Roosevelt University, 1968-69, University of California, Berkeley, 1971-74, and University of Aix-Marseille, 1973-74. *Residence:* Berkeley, Calif. *Agent:* Martha Sternberg, 1263 12th Ave., San Francisco, Calif. 94122. *Office address:* P.O. Box 4303, Berkeley, Calif. 94704.

CAREER: Free-lance photographer in France, 1971-74; KQED-TV (public television), San Francisco, Calif., production assistant and free-lance producer, 1975-76; Ken Hom Cooking School, Berkeley, Calif., founder and owner, 1976-79; California Culinary Academy, San Francisco, member of faculty, 1979—. Guest on radio and television programs; gives cooking demonstrations. *Awards, honors:* Nominated for Emmy Award from Academy of Television Arts and Sciences, 1976, for film "The Long March"; second place award from Tastemaker, 1982, for *Chinese Technique.*

WRITINGS: Chinese Technique (cookbook), Simon & Schuster, 1981.

WORK IN PROGRESS: East Meets West: A Unique Blending of Western and Eastern Cuisines (tentative title), publication by Simon & Schuster expected in 1984.

BIOGRAPHICAL/CRITICAL SOURCES: Bon Appetit, April, 1980; *New York Times,* February 4, 1981; *Chicago Sun-Times,*

December 3, 1981; *Washington Post Book World,* December 13, 1981; *Cuisine,* February, 1982; *Seattle Post-Intelligencer,* March 24, 1982; *South China Morning Post,* April 25, 1982; *Newsweek,* June 7, 1982; *House and Garden,* July, 1982.

* * *

HOOD, William (Joseph) 1920-

PERSONAL: Born April 19, 1920, in Waterville, Me.; son of Walter J. (a musician) and Berthina (Hutchins) Hood; married Cordelia Dodson, 1951 (divorced, 1975); married Mary Carr Thomas (an editor), June, 1976. *Education:* Attended University of Southern Maine, 1939-40, and George Washington University, 1950. *Home:* 44 Galvin St., Portland, Me. 04105. *Agent:* Harold Ober Associates, Inc., 40 East 49th St., New York, N.Y. 10017. *Office:* 158 East 82nd St., New York, N.Y. 10028.

CAREER: Portland Press Herald, Portland, Me., reporter, 1939-40; Central Intelligence Agency (CIA), Washington, D.C., senior official in operational component stationed in Austria, Germany, Switzerland, France, and England, 1945-75; writer, 1975—. *Military service:* U.S. Army, 1941-45, served in Armored Force and with Office of Strategic Services (OSS) as special agent; became master sergeant. *Member:* Special Forces Club (London), The Players (New York), Waistcoat Club (Switzerland), The Beefsteak (Vienna).

WRITINGS: Mole (nonfiction), Norton, 1982. Contributor of reviews and articles to newspapers and magazines, including *Midstream, Portland Sunday Telegram,* and *Foreign Intelligence Literary Scene.*

WORK IN PROGRESS: Spy Wednesday, an adventure novel, completion expected in 1983; researching a nonfiction book on spying.

SIDELIGHTS: Hood describes a Russian spy's association with the Central Intelligence Agency in the book *Mole.* Pyotr Popov, a major in the Soviet military intelligence wing (GRU), agreed to spy for the United States in 1952. Working from Vienna and Berlin under the guise of a loyal GRU officer, Popov provided the names of Russian operatives in Europe and the United States and details of his country's military command to CIA "handlers" for the next six years. Major Popov was exposed in 1958, arrested by the Soviets, and later shot for treason.

Hood, who worked within the CIA and its World War II predecessor, the OSS, for nearly thirty-five years, was operations chief of the agency station in Vienna when Popov decided to switch sides, and he helped establish the agent in the American intelligence network. In *Mole,* his agency-approved memoir which illustrates Popov's day-to-day relationship with the organization and concludes with speculation on how the agent might have been discovered, Hood uses pseudonyms to protect himself and other CIA officials involved in the case.

In a *Washington Post Book World* review, Robert G. Kaiser found Hood's version of the Popov story "a good yarn, ably recounted" and deemed *Mole* "a wonderful book for the beach and a must for the aficionado." Phillip Taubman concurred, declaring in the *New York Times Book Review* that Hood "is surprisingly skilled at telling the story. The book moves along crisply and builds to a dramatic conclusion with the kind of mounting tension one would expect to find in the best novels about espionage." Walter Laqueur of the *Times Literary Supplement* proclaimed Hood's *Mole* "an authentic story told in convincing detail."

Hood told *CA:* "There has been so much outright nonsense written about espionage that I thought it past time for someone to give a more realistic picture of what is involved in handling an important spy. The Popov story is an interesting one—he had been given the best the U.S.S.R. had to offer, but rejected the system and, on his own, decided to fight against it. Along with telling a true spy story, I hoped to give Popov a small footnote in history."

BIOGRAPHICAL/CRITICAL SOURCES: New York Times Book Review, May 23, 1982; *Business Week,* July 5, 1982; *Washington Post Book World,* July 27, 1982; *Christian Science Monitor,* July 28, 1982; *Virginia Quarterly Review,* autumn, 1982; *Times Literary Supplement,* February 11, 1983.

* * *

HOPES, David Brendan 1953-

PERSONAL: Born September 1, 1953, in Akron, Ohio; son of Eugene David (an accountant) and Marion (Summers) Hopes. *Education:* Hiram College, B.A., 1972; attended Johns Hopkins University, 1972-73; Syracuse University, M.A., 1976, Ph.D., 1980. *Politics:* Democrat. *Religion:* Anglo-Catholic. *Home address:* P.O. Box 55, Hiram, Ohio 44234. *Agent:* Susan Cohen, Richard Curtis Associates, Inc., 156 East 52nd St., New York, N.Y. 10022. *Office:* Department of English, Hiram College, Hiram, Ohio 44234.

CAREER: City of Akron, Ohio, naturalist in department of parks and recreation, 1970-72; Koinonia Foundation, Baltimore, Md., resident naturalist, 1973; Syracuse University, Syracuse, N.Y., instructor in English, 1979-81; Hiram College, Hiram, Ohio, visiting assistant professor of English, 1982—. *Member:* National Audubon Society, Modern Language Association of America, Poets and Writers, National Gay Task Force, Foster Parents Society, Sierra Club, Phi Beta Kappa. *Awards, honors:* Juniper Prize from University of Massachusetts Press, 1981, for *The Glacier's Daughters;* Creative Artists Public Service grant, 1981; Saxifrage Prize from University of North Carolina, 1982, for *The Glacier's Daughters.*

WRITINGS: Shadow Mass (poems), Hiram Press, 1972; *The Basswood Tree* (poems), Climate Books, 1979; *The Glacier's Daughters* (poems), University of Massachusetts Press, 1981.

Work represented in anthologies, including *Seventy-Three Ohio Poets* and *On Turtle's Back.* Contributor of more than two hundred poems, stories, reviews, and articles to magazines, including *New Yorker, Audubon, Kansas Quarterly, Salmagundi,* and *Poetry Northwest.* Associate editor of *Porto de Contacto,* 1976-77, and *Hiram Poetry Review.*

WORK IN PROGRESS: The Age of Silver, a novel; *The Stone Thrower,* poems; *Those Women,* a novel.

SIDELIGHTS: Hopes wrote: "I am accustomed to beginning my frequent poetry performances with the statement that my work arises from the tension implicit in being at once a voluptuary and a religious fanatic. Reviews of and commentaries on my work have tended to define me as a poet of nature and a poet of Christianity, both accusations of which I initially found surprising, but to which I am becoming reconciled.

"My refusal to acknowledge a division between the 'traditional' and the 'contemporary' strikes some reviewers as effete and others as medicinal.

"Readers of my short fiction and novels have observed that they see two nearly opposite writers, a Dionysian poet and an Apollonian fiction writer, an extreme romantic and a limpid classicist. I have no explanation for this.

"Voice is foremost in my craft, in both fiction and poetry, and it is no accident that I am a singer and actor as well as a writer and academic. In my reviews of the work of other writers, I have praised what I hope to achieve in my own work: spiritual ambition, music, accessibility. My work possesses both the defects and the merits of these qualities. To some ears my desire to take heaven by storm sounds like mere chest-thumping; to some my musicality seems derivative or overdone; some fear that my anxiety for accessibility leads me close to the line where the poetic sensibility dissolves altogether, and only the subject matter remains."

* * *

HOPKIN, Alannah 1949-

PERSONAL: Born September 6, 1949, in Singapore; daughter of Denis Arthur Buxton (an anesthesiologist) and Angela Mary (Foley) Hopkin. *Education:* Queen Mary College, London, B.A. (with honors), 1974; University of Essex, M.A., 1976. *Religion:* Roman Catholic. *Residence:* Kinsale, Ireland. *Agent:* Literistic Ltd., 32 West 40th St., Apt. 5F, New York, N.Y. 10018.

CAREER: Free-lance journalist in London, England, 1976-82; writer, 1982—. *Member:* International P.E.N.., National Union of Journalists.

WRITINGS: A Joke Goes a Long Way in the Country (novel), Hamish Hamilton, 1982, Atheneum, 1983; *The Story of Morty Og* (novel), Hamish Hamilton, 1983. Contributor of articles and reviews to magazines and newspapers, including *Time Out.*

WORK IN PROGRESS: Contemporary short stories; poems.

SIDELIGHTS: Alannah Hopkin told *CA:* "I earned my living by writing for six years before I started work on my first novel. I worked on it for a year on weekends and wrote features and book reviews during the week. I wanted to write a novel which would be an honest exploration of certain aspects of contemporary life and which would also entertain people. I want my writing to make people question their fixed opinions about both life and literature.

"When I worked full-time on my second novel, I supplemented my income only by reviewing books. It's a very different way to work, and I'm very grateful to my publishers for enabling me to do it.

"I take writing very seriouly as a craft and learn something new with everything I write. The second novel is very different from the first. It has a strong narrative line based on a true story which took place in the middle of the eighteenth century, and it is set mainly in Ireland.

"I am also working on a collection of short stories which will probably become my third book. Some of these have been published in magazines in London and Dublin. Most of my stories tend to look at the current state of sexual behavior of men and women, so some of them are funny.

"In London I am thought of as an Irish writer. In Ireland (where I now live), a lot of people assume that I'm English. I have dual nationality, and as a writer I am both English and Irish. I am an Irish citizen. I was educated mainly in England. I am at home in both places sometimes. This somewhat ambivalent situation is one of many things explored in *A Joke Goes a Long Way in The Country.*"

AVOCATIONAL INTERESTS: "I live alone, and most of my close friends are writers of one sort or another. I live beside the sea. When I am not reading or writing, I go sailing or horseback riding or take long walks. I also like sitting in bars and talking to people and playing poker, and I enjoy baroque music and the opera."

BIOGRAPHICAL/CRITICAL SOURCES: New Statesman, July 16, 1982.

* * *

HOPKINS, Clark   1895-1976
(Roy Lee)

OBITUARY NOTICE: Born September 16, 1895, in New York, N.Y.; died May 21, 1976, in Ann Arbor, Mich. Archaeologist, educator, authority on ancient Greece, and author. Hopkins's expeditions in Mesopotamia during the mid-1960's led to greater insight into Greek culture in the third century, B.C. While teaching at Yale University and the University of Michigan, Hopkins wrote of ancient culture in works such as *The Early History of Central Greece* and *The Discovery of Dura-Europos.* He also hosted a series of University of Michigan-produced television programs on ancient Greece. Under the pseudonym Roy Lee, Hopkins wrote children's books. Obituaries and other sources: *Authors of Books for Young People,* 2nd edition, Scarecrow, 1971; *Directory of American Scholars,* Volume III: *Foreign Languages, Linguistics, and Philology,* 6th edition, Bowker, 1974; *The National Cyclopaedia of American Biography,* Volume 59, James T. White, 1980.

* * *

HOPKINS, Milton   1906-1983

OBITUARY NOTICE: Born September 12, 1906, in Glen Cove, N.Y.; died of a heart attack, March 25, 1983, in Long Island, N.Y. Educator and editor. From 1936 to 1945 Hopkins taught botany at the University of Oklahoma, where he became department chairman. He then joined Holt, Rinehart & Winston as editor in chief of college textbooks and science consultant, remaining there until his retirement in 1967. Obituaries and other sources: *American Men and Women of Science: The Physical and Biological Sciences,* 12th edition, Bowker, 1971-73; *New York Times,* March 28, 1983.

* * *

HORGAN, Edward R.   1934-

PERSONAL: Born March 23, 1934, in Fitchburg, Mass.; son of Bernard A. (a teacher) and Margaret (a teacher; maiden name, Feeherry) Horgan; married Margaret McKenna (a secretary), May 4, 1957; children: Richard, Laura, Mark, Lorraine. *Education:* Attended Fitchburg State College, 1953-54; Boston University, B.S., 1956; graduate study at Simmons College, 1966-67; Worcester State College, M.Ed., 1977. *Home:* 33 Hale St., Leominster, Mass. 01453.

CAREER: Worcester Telegram, Worcester, Mass., reporter, 1956-58; WEIM-Radio, Fitchburg, Mass., news director 1958-66; *Fitchburg Sentinel,* Fitchburg, reporter, 1967-71; English teacher and librarian in secondary schools in Massachusetts, 1971—. *Member:* National Historic Communal Societies Association, National Education Association, Massachusetts Teachers Association. *Awards, honors:* Freedom Foundation Award, 1966, for radio documentary.

WRITINGS: The Shaker Holy Land: A Community Portrait, Harvard Common, 1982. Contributor of an article to *Yankee.*

WORK IN PROGRESS: Researching Shaker topics, Concordia, and a Massachusetts murder case.

SIDELIGHTS: In *The Shaker Holy Land* Horgan recorded the history of a Protestant religious group, founded in England and imported to America in 1774, that required celibacy of all its members and whose name, Shakers, derived from the practice of violent shaking during religious ceremonies. Horgan recounts the persecution of the early Shakers, describes their still-famous techniques for furniture making, and portrays some of the individuals who were involved with this religious sect. His study focuses on the Shaker communities in Harvard and Shirley, Massachusetts, two establishments that maintained followings into the early 1900's.

Horgan presented his subject "through some affectingly human detail," observed John Demos in the *New York Times Book Review.* "Through it all," the critic continued, "he allows us to see and hear the Shakers on their own terms." And in her *Los Angeles Times* review of *The Shaker Holy Land,* Ruth C. Ikerman praised the maps, which Horgan drew himself, and the "Guide to Shaker Museums, Collections and Libraries," claiming that both sections "will be of value to modern tourists seeking religious nostalgia."

Horgan told *CA:* "My early career was confined to reporting and column writing for hometown newspapers where three of my colleagues, Bob Cormier, Jim Mills, and Noah Gordon, were budding novelists. My writing style and interests so far tend to be journalistic rather than literary, but I would eventually like to write historical fiction."

BIOGRAPHICAL/CRITICAL SOURCES: Worcester Sunday Telegram, April 25, 1982; *Los Angeles Times,* June 17, 1982; *New York Times Book Review,* August 15, 1982.

* * *

HORNBRUCH, Frederick William, Jr.   1913-

PERSONAL: Born July 14, 1913, in Roselle, N.J.; son of Frederick William and Elsa (Becker) Hornbruch; married Helen Novak, April 10, 1936; children: Frederick William III, Harlan Richard. *Education:* Stevens Institute of Technology, M.E., 1934. *Politics:* Republican. *Religion:* Presbyterian. *Home and office address:* Route 2, Three Lakes Rd., Barrington Hills, Ill. 60010.

CAREER: Weston Electric Instrument Corp., Newark, N.J., engineer, 1934-40; Falstrom Co., Passaic, N.J. engineer, 1940-41; Bendix Aviation Corp., Philadelphia, Pa., industrial engineer, 1941-43; Columbia Machine Works, Brooklyn, N.Y., production manager, 1943-44; Rath & Strong, Inc., Boston, Mass., chief engineer, 1944-57; Landers, Frary & Clark, Inc., New Britain, Conn., vice-president, 1957-59; Atlas Corp., New York City, vice-president and director, 1959-64; Calumet & Hecla, Inc., Chicago, Ill., vice-president, 1964-68; Aero-Chatillon Corp., Inc., New York City, vice-president, 1968-69; Macrodyne-Chatillon Corp., New York City, vice-president for administration, 1969; organizer of consulting business, Barrington Hills, Ill., 1970—; director of Macrodyne Industries, Inc., 1974-78. President and director of Titeflex, Inc., and chairman of board of directors of Mertronics Corp., 1960-64; president and director of International Air, Inc., 1962. *Member:* American Society of Mechanical Engineers (chairman of Management Division, 1957, and organization committee, 1966), Tau Beta Pi, Pi Delta Epsilon, Phi Sigma Kappa, Barrington Hills Country Club.

WRITINGS: (With Robert T. Bruce) *Practical Planning and Scheduling,* National Foremen's Institute, 1950; (contributor) *Handbook of Business Administration,* McGraw, 1967; (contributor) *Handbook of Modern Manufacturing Management,* McGraw, 1970; *Raising Productivity: Ten Case Histories and Their Lessons,* McGraw, 1977.

SIDELIGHTS: Frederick Hornbruch told *CA:* "Time is universal; what we do with it makes the difference."

* * *

HORNE, A(lexander) D(ouglas) 1932-

PERSONAL: Born November 9, 1932, in Warsaw, Poland; son of Marcel A. (in reinsurance) and Lydia (a bookkeeper; maiden name, Bryl) Horne; married Ann Elizabeth Hurd (a teacher), August 27, 1960; children: Julia, Owen, Elizabeth, Jennifer, Gary, Ellen, Brian. *Education:* Williams College, A.B., 1954. *Home:* 7214 Rebecca Dr., Alexandria, Va. 22307. *Office:* Washington Post, 1150 15th St. NW, Washington, D.C. 20071.

CAREER: Berkshire Eagle, Pittsfield, Mass., editor/reporter, 1955-56; *Washington Post,* Washington, D.C., 1958—, began as assistant city editor, became assistant foreign-news editor, 1982—. *Military service:* U.S. Army, 1956-58.

WRITINGS: (Editor) *The Wounded Generation: America After Vietnam,* Prentice-Hall, 1981. Author of weekly newspaper column, "The Magazine Rack," 1962-66.

SIDELIGHTS: The Wounded Generation: America After Vietnam grew out of a 1980 symposium that sought to establish a dialogue between Vietnam veterans and former war resisters in an attempt to form a basis for healing the split that developed during the 1960's and, in large measure, continued through the succeeding decade. Edited transcripts of the symposium constitute the central portion of the book and give voice to feelings of frustration and bitterness experienced by veterans, many of whom feel they unfairly bore the brunt of public displeasure with the war.

The Wounded Generation's opening section contains graphic descriptions of the Vietnam experience, including excerpts from books and articles written by three symposium participants, James Fallows, Philip Caputo, and James Webb. The book concludes with a collection of short essays that explore the meaning of the war and its aftermath on the American psyche. Richard Dudman, writing in the *Washington Post Book World,* remarked: "The result is engrossing, and may even succeed in pointing the way toward how to live with the memory of a rotten decade."

BIOGRAPHICAL/CRITICAL SOURCES: Washington Post Book World, November 29, 1981; *Village Voice,* April 6, 1982.

* * *

HORNE, Howard
See PAYNE, (Pierre Stephen) Robert

* * *

HOROWITZ, Joseph 1948-

PERSONAL: Born February 12, 1948, in New York, N.Y.; son of Jacob (a doctor) and Leah (a psychiatric social worker;

maiden name, Lurie) Horowitz. *Education:* Swarthmore College, B.A., 1970; University of California, Berkeley, M.J., 1975. *Home:* 309 West 104th St., No. 5D, New York, N.Y. 10025. *Agent:* Robert Cornfield Literary Agency, 145 West 79th St., New York, N.Y. 10024.

CAREER: New York Times, New York City, music critic, 1976-80; Kaufmann Concert Hall of 92nd St., New York City, program editor and chief annotator, 1981—. Chief program annotator for Los Angeles Chamber Orchestra, 1982—.

WRITINGS: Conversations With Arrau, Knopf, 1982. Contributor to periodicals, including *High Fidelity, Musical America,* and *New York Times Magazine.*

WORK IN PROGRESS: Understanding Toscanini: A Reappraisal of His New World Celebrity, publication by Knopf expected in 1985.

SIDELIGHTS: Conversations With Arrau is a retrospective look at the life and career of Chilean musician Claudio Arrau. It includes interviews with Arrau and his associates, among them Daniel Barenboim, Garrick Ohlsson, and Sir Colin Davis. Music critic Joseph McLellan reviewed the book in the *Washington Post,* noting that Arrau "is informative and readable on his performing preferences, techniques and quirks, his attitudes toward various composers and colleagues, his drives and superstitions, even the often harrowing details of his biography and his psyche." "In its balance of substance and readability," McLellan added, "'Conversations With Arrau' is very nearly a model of what this sort of book ought to be."

BIOGRAPHICAL/CRITICAL SOURCES: Washington Post, October 23, 1982; *New York Times Book Review,* March 20, 1983.

* * *

HORTON, Susan R. 1941-

PERSONAL: Born November 16, 1941, in Defiance, Ohio; daughter of R. L. (a machinist) and Mildred (Noneman) Seibenick; married William Richard Horton, May 30, 1965 (divorced, 1968); children: John J. *Education:* Defiance College, B.A., 1964; Brandeis University, M.A., 1969, Ph.D., 1973. *Office:* Department of English, University of Massachusetts, Harbor Campus, Boston, Mass. 02125.

CAREER: English teacher at private school in El Paso, Tex., 1964-65; University of Massachusetts, Boston, assistant professor, 1973-79, associate professor, 1979-82, professor of English, 1982—. Visiting professor at University of Hawaii, 1981-82. *Member:* Modern Language Association of America, Dickens Society, National Council of Teachers of English.

WRITINGS: Interpreting Interpreting, Johns Hopkins University Press, 1979; *The Reader in the Dickens World: Style and Response,* Macmillan, 1981; *Thinking Through Writing,* Johns Hopkins University Press, 1982. Contributor of articles and reviews to literature journals.

WORK IN PROGRESS: Creating the Self, Creating the Other, a study of travelers to India, Egypt, the Argentine, and other parts of the British Empire from 1880 to 1910.

SIDELIGHTS: Horton told *CA:* "We have come to see, in recent literary theory, that writers have always created their readers, in the most central sense of that word. I have always liked the way Dickens creates his audience: as people who have a deep sense of the injustices of the world and the complexities involved in trying to correct them, and who at the same time can laugh at human fallibility. That is what I wrote about first. That led me to a more extensive and theoretical analysis of Dickens, seeing him as a test case in how writers create readers and readers create, in their turn, the books they read. That led to *Interpreting Interpreting*. From there it was a short step to a writing book directed at students, a book that guides them to a realization that in and through writing they create both a self and an audience. This was *Thinking Through Writing*. My next project also follows logically. In it, I want to watch how people at the end of the nineteenth century traveled to far places in part to define themselves: to see how they were different from the 'other' they encountered in those foreign parts.''

BIOGRAPHICAL/CRITICAL SOURCES: Times Literary Supplement, February 6, 1981.

* * *

HOUGHTON, Walter Edwards 1904-1983

OBITUARY NOTICE—See index for CA sketch: Born September 21, 1904, in Stamford, Conn.; died of viral pneumonia, April 11, 1983, in Newton, Mass. Scholar, editor, and author. Houghton had been affiliated with Wellesley College since 1942, serving as the Sophie C. Hart Professor of English from 1957 until his retirement in 1969. He founded and edited *The Wellesley Index to Victorian Periodicals, 1824-1900*. His books include *The Victorian Frame of Mind, 1830-1870*, which won the Christian Gauss Prize, *The Art of Newman's "Apologia,"* *The Poetry of Clough: An Essay in Revaluation*, and *Victorian Poetry and Poetics*. Obituaries and other sources: *New York Times*, April 14, 1983; *London Times*, May 28, 1983.

* * *

HOUNSOME, Terry 1944-

PERSONAL: Born April 29, 1944, in Abingdon, England; son of Alfred Miles (a manager) and Frances (Pearman) Hounsome; married Christine Mary Parry, March 18, 1967; children: Claire Marie, Steven, Jonathan. *Education:* Attended secondary school in Southampton, England. *Home:* 13 Stanton Rd., Southampton, Hampshire, England.

CAREER: Writer.

WRITINGS: Rock Master, privately printed, 1978; *Rock Record*, privately printed, 1979; *New Rock Record*, Facts on File, 1981.

WORK IN PROGRESS: Revising *Rock Record*.

SIDELIGHTS: Hounsome told CA: ''I have collected pop, rock, and jazz records for more than twenty years. My books are an extension of my hobby.'' *Avocational interests:* Sports, films.

* * *

HOUSE, Victor 1893-1983

OBITUARY NOTICE: Born in 1893 in Austria; died March 3, 1983, in San Juan, Puerto Rico. Attorney and author. A former assistant United States attorney for the Southern District of New York and special assistant to the Manhattan district attorney, House practiced law with New York firms for many years. The attorney's memoirs, *Such Sometimes Is the Law*, recalls his most outstanding cases. In 1960 House was appointed regional counsel of the Federal Housing and Home Finance Agency in Puerto Rico. Obituaries and other sources: *New York Times*, March 10, 1983.

HOUTON, Kathleen
See KILGORE, Kathleen

* * *

HOWARD, Anthony (Michell) 1934-

PERSONAL: Born February 12, 1934, in London, England; son of William Guy and Janet (Rymer) Howard; married Carol Anne Gaynor, May 26, 1965. *Education:* Received degree (with honors) from Christ Church, Oxford. *Home:* 17 Addison Ave., London W.11, England. *Agent:* A. D. Peters & Co. Ltd., 10 Buckingham St., London WC2N 6BU, England. *Office:* 8 St. Andrew's Hill, London E.C.4, England.

CAREER: Guardian, Manchester, England, on editorial staff, 1959-61; *New Statesman*, London, England, political correspondent, 1961-64; *Sunday Times*, London, Whitehall correspondent, 1965; *Observer*, London, correspondent from Washington, D.C., 1966-69; *New Statesman*, assistant editor, 1970-72, editor, 1972-78; *Listener*, London, editor, 1979-81; *Observer*, deputy editor, 1981—.

WRITINGS: (With Richard West) *The Road to Number 10*, Macmillan, 1965 (published in England as *The Making of the Prime Minister*, J. Cape, 1965); (editor) Richard H. C. Crossman, *Diaries of a Cabinet Minister: Selections, 1964-70*, Hamish Hamilton, Volume I: *Minister of Housing, 1964-66*, 1975, Volume II: *Lord President of the Council, 1966-68*, 1976, Volume III: *Secretary of State for Social Services, 1968-70*, 1977, condensed edition in one volume, 1979.

* * *

HOWARD, Frederick James 1904-

PERSONAL: Born in 1904 in Australia; married Margaret Gipps. *Home:* 11 Brook St., Hawthorn, Victoria 3122, Australia.

CAREER: Stead's Review, Australia, editor, 1929-31; *Herald*, Melbourne, Australia, staff journalist, 1931-70, chief leader writer, 1948-70. Chairman of Australian television series ''Meet the Press,'' 1958-70. *Military service:* Australian Army, 1939-44; became lieutenant colonel; mentioned in dispatches. *Member:* Australian Institute of International Affairs (honorary life member; past member of council chairman of Victoria branch, 1957-59), Naval and Military Club.

WRITINGS: The Emigrant (novel), Longmans, Green, 1928; *Return Ticket* (novel), Longmans, Green, 1930; *Leave Us the Glory* (novel), M. Joseph, 1946; *The Negroes Begin at Calais* (novel), Heinemann, 1938; *No Music for Generals* (novel), Wingate, 1951; *Charles Kingsford Smith* (biography), Oxford University Press, 1966; *Kent Hughes: A Biography of Colonel the Honourable Sir Wilfrid Kent Hughes*, Macmillan, 1972; *The Moleskin Gentry: In Which Close Relations of Major John Bowler, of the 80th Regiment of Foot, Recall the Life and Times of the Family When Its Fortunes Became Linked With Those of the Colony of New South Wales*, Hawthorn Press, 1978. Also author of *Active Service* (nonfiction), 1941. Contributor to magazines and newspapers.

WORK IN PROGRESS: Research on political and military leadership during World War II.

SIDELIGHTS: Howard has traveled in Japan, South Korea, Southeast Asia, Israel, England, the Soviet Union, and the United States.

HOWARD, Leon 1903-1982

PERSONAL: Born November 8, 1903, in Talladega, Ala.; died December 21, 1982, in Albuquerque, N.M.; son of Percy L. and Georgia (Heacock) Howard; married Henrietta Starr March 6, 1931; children: Mary Morris, Charles Malone, Kathleen. *Education:* Birmingham-Southern College, A.B., 1923; University of Chicago, M.A., 1926; Johns Hopkins University, Ph.D., 1929. *Home:* 1200 Calle del Sol N.E., Albuquerque, N.M. 87106.

CAREER: Johns Hopkins University, Baltimore, Md., instructor in English, 1927-30; Pomona College, Claremont, Calif., instructor, 1930-32, assistant professor of English, 1932-37; Northwestern University, Evanston, Ill., associate professor, 1938-43, professor of English, 1943-50; University of California, Los Angeles, professor of English, 1950-71, professor emeritus, 1971-82. Visiting professor at Tokyo University, 1951 and 1954, Centre Universitaire Mediterranean, 1957, and University of New Mexico, 1971-82. *Member:* Modern Language Association of America, American Studies Association, American Academy of Arts and Sciences (fellow). *Awards, honors:* Fellow at Huntington Library, 1937-38; Guggenheim fellowship, 1944-45; L.H.D. from University of Chicago, 1961; senior fellow at Newberry Library, 1966; Ph.D. from University of Abo, 1968.

WRITINGS: The Connecticut Wits, University of Chicago Press, 1943, reissued, 1968; *Herman Melville: A Biography,* University of California Press, 1951; *Victorian Knight-Errant: A Study of the Early Literary Career of James Russell Lowell,* University of California Press, 1952; (editor with Carl Bode and Louis B. Wright) *American Heritage: An Anthology and Interpretive Survey of Our Literature,* Heath, 1955, published as *American Literature: An Anthology With Critical Introduction,* Washington Square Press, 1966; (editor) James Fenimore Cooper, *The Pioneers,* Holt, 1959; *Literature and the American Tradition,* Doubleday, 1960, revised edition, Gordian, 1972; (editor) Jonathan Edwards, *The Mind,* University of California Press, 1963; *The Logic of Hamlet's Soliloquies,* Lone Pine, 1964; *Mysteries and Manuscripts,* self-published, 1976.

OBITUARIES: Chronicle of Higher Education, January 12, 1983.*

*   *   *

HOWARD, Moses L(eon) 1928-
(Musa Nagenda)

PERSONAL: Born January 4, 1928, in Copiah County, Miss.; son of Willie (a plumber's helper) and Mizuri Bradley (a domestic worker; maiden name, Williams) Howard; married Alice Perry, 1949 (divorced, 1961); married Letha M. Bishop (a teacher of home economics), July 23, 1962 (divorced, 1983); children: Bonnie, Rodney, Constella, Hodari, Ngoma, Bilori, Morningside, Ruganzu. *Education:* Alcorn A & M College, B.S., 1952; Case Western Reserve University, M.S., 1956; further graduate study at University of Alaska, 1960, New York University, and Columbia University. *Politics:* None. *Religion:* "Humanist." *Home:* 622 South 35th St., Tacoma, Wash. 98408.

CAREER: Republic Steel Corp., Cleveland, Ohio, steelworker, 1950-54; Utica Junior College, Utica, Miss., instructor in biology and chemistry, 1956-61; African Ministry of Education,

Kampala, Uganda, head of science department at National Teachers' College, 1961-71; teacher in public schools in Seattle, Wash., 1972—. Curriculum adviser for UNESCO, 1971—. *Awards, honors:* Named outstanding educator of the year in Washington State, 1981.

WRITINGS: (Under pseudonym Musa Nagenda) *Dogs of Fear* (novel), Heinemann, 1971, Holt, 1972; (under pseudonym Musa Nagenda) *Ostrich Egg-shell Canteen* (novel), Heinemann, 1973, published under name Moses L. Howard as *Ostrich Chase,* Holt, 1974; *The Human Mandolin* (fiction), Holt, 1974.

Also author of two plays, "Hold Back Your Foot" and "Where Is Everybody?," as yet unpublished and unproduced. Contributor of stories and poems to periodicals, including *Sounder.*

WORK IN PROGRESS: Instant Culture, "an attempt to write about the things we do unawares in fresh language"; *Natural Solutions,* "essays on the effect nature has on people suffering from stress, insecurity, and the inability to adjust to urban technology"; a biography.

*   *   *

HOWARD, Oliver Otis 1830-1909

BRIEF ENTRY: Born November 8, 1830, in Leeds, Me.; died October 26, 1909, in Burlington, Vt. American soldier and author. Howard fought against the Indians following his graduation from the United States Military Academy at West Point in 1854, and during the early months of the Civil War he commanded the Third Maine Regiment as a Union colonel. Later, despite the loss of his right arm during the battle of Fair Oaks, Howard took part in many of the war's major confrontations, including Gettysburg and the capture of Atlanta. In 1864 he was promoted to the rank of brigadier general in command of the Army of the Tennessee; in July of that year he led the Fourth Corps of General William T. Sherman's army on its famous march through Georgia. After the war Howard was appointed commissioner of the Freedmen's Bureau by President Andrew Johnson. Sympathetic to the interests of both former slaves and former landowners, Howard sought an orderly, fair transition away from the slavery system. He returned to active military duty during the Indian wars and in 1877 defeated the Nez Perce Indians led by Chief Joseph. In addition to writing *The Autobiography of Oliver Otis Howard* (1907), the soldier wrote *Isabella of Castile* (1894), *Fighting for Humanity* (1898), *Donald's School Days* (1899), and *Famous Indian Chiefs I Have Known* (1908). *Biographical/critical sources: The National Cyclopaedia of American Biography,* Volume 4, James T. White, 1891; *Who Was Who in America,* Volume 1, *1897-1942,* Marquis, 1943; *The McGraw-Hill Encyclopedia of World Biography,* McGraw, 1973.

*   *   *

HOWE, Florence 1929-

BRIEF ENTRY: Born March 17, 1929, in Brooklyn, N.Y. American educator, publisher, and author. Howe, who is a professor of humanities at State University of New York College at Old Westbury as well as president of Feminist Press and editor of *Women's Studies Newsletter,* has been praised for her interdisciplinary approach to teaching and writing about women. Her dedication to women's studies has been reflected in her numerous speaking engagements throughout the United States and abroad. Howe has also participated in civil rights activities in the South and in the anti-war movement that accompanied U.S. involvement in Vietnam. She co-edited *Women Working: An Anthology of Stories and Poems* (Feminist Press, 1979), *Las Mujeres: Conversations From a Hispanic Community* (Webster, 1980), *The Sex-Role Cycle: Socialization From Infancy to Old Age* (Webster, 1980), *Women Have Always Worked: An Historical Overview* (Webster, 1980), and *Women's "True" Profession: Voices From the History of Teaching* (Webster, 1981). *Address:* Feminist Press, P.O. Box 334, Old Westbury, N.Y. 11568; and Department of American Studies, State University of New York College at Old Westbury, Box 210, Old Westbury, N.Y. 11568. *Biographical/ critical sources: Washington Post Book World,* June 17, 1973; *Western Humanities Review,* winter, 1974; *Christian Science Monitor,* September 29, 1975; *Virginia Quarterly Review,* spring, 1976.

* * *

HOWE, Tina

PERSONAL: Daughter of Quincy (a broadcaster and writer) and Mary (an artist; maiden name, Post) Howe; married Norman Levy; children: Eben, Dara. *Education:* Sarah Lawrence College, B.A., 1959; graduate study at Columbia University and Chicago Teachers College. *Residence:* New York, N.Y. *Agent:* Flora Roberts, 157 West 57th St., New York, N.Y. 10019.

CAREER: Author.

WRITINGS—Published plays: "Birth and After Birth" in *The New Women's Theatre,* Vintage Books, 1977; *Museum* (first produced in Los Angeles at Los Angeles Actors Theatre, 1976), Samuel French, 1979; *The Art of Dining* (first produced in New York at New York Shakespeare Festival, 1979), Samuel French, 1980.

Unpublished plays: "The Nest," first produced Off-Broadway, 1970; "Appearances," 1982; "Painting Churches," first produced in New York at South Street Theatre, February, 1983.

WORK IN PROGRESS: A screenplay, "A Man's Place"; a play, "Realities," to accompany "Appearances."

SIDELIGHTS: Howe has received praise in *New Yorker* for much of her work. "Museum," which featured several characters wandering about a museum while commenting on art, was praised by *New Yorker*'s Edith Oliver as "an enchanting show." She wrote: "The play is itself a collage of words and characters and action. . . . It has plenty of wit and humor, and no idea appears to be emphasized over any other."

Oliver was also impressed with Howe's "The Art of Dining." She called the play, which concerns the struggles of a young couple to operate a restaurant in New Jersey, a "delightful little comedy." The play resembles "Museum" in its vast array of characters and comedic incidents. Oliver was entertained especially by a "sensationally awkward, nearsighted . . . young writer . . . , who, dining with her middleaged publisher, manages to spill a full plate of soup into her lap and on being furnished with a second plate drowns her lipstick in it."

Howe told *CA:* "I find enormous pleasure in making playwriting as difficult as possible. I go out of my way to look for unlikely settings and situations; art museums, restaurants, fitting rooms, places that are basically predictable and uneventful. Nothing is more theatrical than putting the unexpected on stage. Because the theatre is a palace of dreams, the more original the spectacle, the better. I'm hopelessly drawn to digging out the flamboyant in everyday life."

BIOGRAPHICAL/CRITICAL SOURCES: New York Times, April 10, 1970, February 28, 1978, December 7, 1979, February 18, 1983; *New Yorker,* March 6, 1978, December 17, 1979, May 24, 1982.

* * *

HOWELL, David Arthur Russell 1936-

PERSONAL: Born January 18, 1936; son of A. H. E. (a military officer) and Beryl Howell; married Davina Wallace, 1967; children: one son, two daughters. *Education:* King's College, Cambridge, B.A. (with first-class honors), 1959. *Office:* House of Commons, London S.W.1, England.

CAREER: Served in Economic Section of Her Majesty's Treasury, 1959-60; *Daily Telegraph,* London, England, leader-writer and special correspondent, 1960-64; Conservative Political Centre, London, director, 1964-66; British Parliament, London, Conservative member representing Guildford, Surrey, 1966—. Parliamentary secretary of Civil Service Department and lord commissioner of Her Majesty's Treasury, 1970-72; parliamentary undersecretary of Department of Employment, 1971-72, and for Northern Ireland, 1972; minister of state for Northern Ireland, 1972-74, and of Department of Energy, 1974; secretary of state of Department of Energy, 1979-81, and for Transport, 1981—. Trustee of Federal Trust for Education and Research, London. Chairman of Bow Group, 1961-62. Honorary joint secretary of British Council of the European Movement, 1969-70. *Member:* Bucks Club.

WRITINGS: (Editor with Timothy Raison) *Principles in Practice: A Series of Bow Group Essays for the 1960's,* Conservative Political Centre, 1961; *The Conservative Opportunity,* edited by Lord Blake and John Patten, foreword by Lord Hailsham of St. Marylebone, Macmillan, 1965; *Freedom and Capital: Prospects for the Property-Owning Democracy,* Blackwell, 1981. Author of numerous articles and pamphlets. Editor of *Crossbow,* 1962-64.

AVOCATIONAL INTERESTS: Traveling, reading.

* * *

HUBBARD, Don 1926-

PERSONAL: Born January 15, 1926, in Bronx, N.Y.; son of Ernest Fortescue (a magazine editor) and Lillian (Beck) Hubbard; married Patricia Rosenburg (divorced); married Darlene Huber (a yacht broker), December 13, 1957; children: Cameron Hubbard McNall, Leslie Carol, Christopher Eric, Lauren Ivy. *Education:* Attended Brown University, 1944; George Washington University, B.A., 1959; attended Naval War College, 1966. *Home address:* P.O. Box 550, Coronado, Calif. 92118.

CAREER: U.S. Navy, naval aviator, 1943-47, involved in training command, 1943-47, served with heavy patrol squadron in Portlyautey, Morocco, 1947-50, instructor stationed in Pensacola, Fla., 1950-52, served with heavy attack squadron in San Diego, Calif., 1953-56, stationed with Squadron Sixty-two in Jacksonville, Fla., 1959-60, air officer with admiral's staff, Guantanamo Bay, Cuba, 1960-62, assigned to Defense Intelligence Agency, Washington, D.C., 1963-65, affiliated with Naval War College, Newport, R.I., 1965-66, member of General Westmorland's staff, Saigon, Vietnam, 1966-67, retiring as commander; Ocean Ventures, Inc. (small craft sales), San Diego, Calif., founder, owner, and president, 1969-77; marine artist and writer, 1977—. Registered yacht broker in California; underwater instructor associated with National Association of Underwater Instructors and Professional Association of Diving Instructors, 1969-72.

MEMBER: International Ships-in-Bottles Association (president of North American Division, 1982-83), Writers Guild, American Society of Marine Artists, San Diego Watercolor Society (member of board of directors, 1981-82). *Awards, honors*—Military: Air Medal; Joint Services Commendation Medal.

WRITINGS: Ships-in-Bottles, McGraw, 1971; *The Complete Book of Inflatable Boats,* Western Marine, 1980. Contributor to *Oceans.* Editor of *Bottle Shipwright.*

WORK IN PROGRESS: Rotten John, a book of satirical cartoons; *The Littlest Surfer,* a children's book; *The How-to Book of Nautical Decorative Techniques; Advanced Techniques in Ship-in-Bottle Building.*

SIDELIGHTS: Don Hubbard told *CA:* "Thanks to my naval service and subsequent activities, I am fortunate to have led a widely varied and interesting life. Because I was constantly shifting jobs in the service, and later in civilian life, I have never confined myself to one rigid field of endeavor and have allowed myself to follow any leads which I find attractive.

"The book on bottled ships was created because a friend asked me to build one. The little available literature was most basic and, at best, outdated.

"The basic material for the book on inflatable boats was written originally to help train my employees in my inflatable boat business. The boats were quite a new concept in this country at the time, and very few people knew a lot about them. I had used them extensively in my work as a scuba diving instructor and for diving tours, so when I began to sell them I was able to convince my customers of their worth. The effectiveness of my effort required that I pass along the knowledge to others."

*   *   *

HUBBARD, Paul H.   1900(?)-1983

OBITUARY NOTICE: Born c. 1900 in Mt. Pulaski, Ill.; died March 7, 1983, in La Grange, Ill. Journalist and editor. Hubbard began his journalism career as a police, city hall, and court reporter for the *Illinois State Journal.* He later served as the paper's city editor until 1929, when he joined the *Chicago Tribune* as a copy editor. Following his appointment as neighborhood news editor of the *Tribune* in 1940, Hubbard oversaw the publication of zoned neighborhood newspaper sections, with responsiblity for expanding their scope and features. The newsman, who retired from that position in 1965, is remembered for helping aspiring high school journalists enter the profession. Obituaries and other sources: *Chicago Tribune,* March 10, 1983.

*   *   *

HUDSON, Robert Vernon   1932-

PERSONAL: Born August 29, 1932, in Indianapolis, Ind.; son of Harlan King (in business) and Dorothy (a librarian; in business; maiden name, Davis) Hudson; married Marsha Van Syoc, August 16, 1963 (divorced March 10, 1977); children: Drew Robert, Robert Harlan. *Education:* Indiana University, B.S., 1954; University of Oregon, M.S., 1966; University of Minnesota, Ph.D., 1970. *Residence:* East Lansing, Mich. 48823. *Office:* School of Journalism, Michigan State University, East Lansing, Mich. 48824.

CAREER: Rochester News-Sentinel, Rochester, Ind., city editor, 1954; United Press International, Indianapolis, Ind., staff correspondent, 1954-56; *Chicago Daily News,* Chicago, Ill., reporter, 1956-57; Fairchild Publications, Chicago, reporter, 1957; free-lance writer, 1958; Public Relations Board, Chicago, service executive, 1958-59; Northwestern University, Evanston, Ill., publications assistant at Traffic Institute and Transportation Center, 1960-61, manager of university news bureau, 1961-63, acting director of information services, 1963; Arizona State University, Tempe, assistant director of News Bureau, 1963-65; Michigan State University, East Lansing, assistant professor, 1968-73, associate professor, 1973-80, professor of journalism, 1980—, assistant chairman of School of Journalism, 1972-74, acting assistant dean of College of Communication Arts and Sciences, 1974. Staff writer for *Traffic Digest and Review,* 1960-61; producer, writer, and anchor for "Dateline," on KTVK-TV and KAET-TV, 1964-65; professor and department head at California Polytechnic State University, 1975-76. *Military service:* U.S. Naval Reserve, 1949-59. *Member:* Association for Education in Journalism, Kappa Tau Alpha.

WRITINGS: (Contributor) Michael W. Singletary, editor, *Readings in Radio and Television News,* 1976; (contributor) Donovan H. Bond and W. Reynolds McLeod, editors, *Newsletters to Newspapers: Eighteenth-Century Journalism,* West Virginia University Press, 1977; *The Writing Game: A Biography of Will Irwin,* Iowa State University Press, 1982. Contributor to encyclopedias. Contributor to magazines and newspapers, including *Journalism Quarterly, Journalism History, Journalism Educator, Lakeland Boating, Ensign, Grassroots Editor, American Mercury,* and *Writer's Digest.* Corresponding editor of *Journalism History.*

WORK IN PROGRESS: A history of mass media, for Garland Publishing.

SIDELIGHTS: Hudson told *CA:* "*The Writing Game* is the result of sixteen years of research and writing. I traveled widely, and traced Will Irwin's character and career from his childhood in upper New York State to Leadville, Colorado, to his professional success as a free-lance writer of fact and fiction and drama in New York City and Europe. I used hundreds of primary sources, including the newspapers, magazines, and books in which he was published, as well as unpublished diaries and letters. I interviewed many of his relatives and associates, who remembered him vividly. Then I put his life in the context of his changing times (spanning two world wars, the Roaring Twenties, the Depression, and so on). Intrinsic in his story is a picture of the profession—or 'game'—of free-lance writing. That, and his close friendship with Herbert Hoover, are two of the most interesting aspects of Irwin's life."

*   *   *

HUERLIMANN, Bettina   1909-

PERSONAL: Born June 19, 1909, in Weimar, Germany (now East Germany); daughter of Gustav (a publisher) and Irmgard (a publisher; maiden name, Funcke) Kiepenheuer; married Martin Huerlimann (an author and publisher), February, 1933; children: Barbara (deceased), Regine, Christoph, Ulrich. *Education:* Attended Academy of Graphic Arts and Book Printing, Leipzig, Germany. *Address:* Witellikerstrasse 9, 8702 Zollikon, Zurich, Switzerland.

CAREER: Typographer with Monotype Corporation, England; free-lance publisher and writer; Atlantis Verlag (publishing firm), Zurich, Switzerland, publisher and editor, 1933—. Member of International Board on Books for Young People, 1950—. *Awards, honors:* Silver medal from BIB, 1967, and Mildred L. Batchelder Award nomination, 1969, both for *William Tell and His Son.*

WRITINGS: (Compiler) *Eia Popeia* (juvenile verse; title means "Hushaby Baby"), illustrations by Fritz Kredel, Atlantis Verlag, c. 1935, (author of introduction) *Kinderbilder in funf Jahrhunderten europaischer Malerei,* Atlantis Verlag, 1949, translation published as *Children's Portraits: The World of the Child in European Painting,* Thames & Hudson, 1950; *Europaische Kinderbuecher in drei Jahrhunderten,* Atlantis Verlag, 1959, translation by Brian W. Alderson published as *Three Centuries of Children's Books in Europe,* Oxford University Press, 1967, World Publishing, 1968; *Klein und Gross,* Atlantis Verlag, 1965; *Die Welt im Bilderbuch: Moderne Kinderbilderbuecher aus 24 Laendern,* Atlantis Verlag, 1965, translation by Alderson published as *Picture-book World: Modern Picture-books for Children From Twenty-four Countries,* Oxford University Press, 1968, World Publishing, 1969; *Der Knabe des Tell* (juvenile), illustrations by Paul Nussbaumer, Atlantis Verlag, 1965, translation by Elizabeth D. Crawford published as *William Tell and His Son,* Harcourt, 1967; *Barry: Ein Bilderbuch* (juvenile), illustrations by Nussbaumer, Atlantis Verlag, 1967, translation by Crawford published as *Barry: The Story of a Brave St. Bernard,* Harcourt, 1968.

(Adaptor) Chiyoko Nakatani, *Fumio und die Delphine* (title means "Fumio and the Dolphins"), Atlantis Verlag, 1970; *Sieben Hauser: Aufzeichnungen einer Buecherfrau,* Artemis Verlag, 1976, translation by Anthea Bell published as *Seven Houses: My Life With Books* (autobiography), Bodley Head, 1976, Crowell, 1977; *Zwischenfall in Lerida, und andere Texte,* Atlantis Verlag, 1979. Contributor of articles to periodicals, including *Graphis* and *Horn Book.*

SIDELIGHTS: The daughter of a bookseller and publisher, Bettina Huerlimann developed an early love of literature and a keen fascination with the writers her father brought home to discuss manuscripts; they included Bertolt Brecht, Ernst Toller, and Heinrich Mann. Bettina read virtually everything she could lay her hands on, encouraged by her parents to develop a broad range of political and social thought.

After graduating from high school, Huerlimann applied to the Academy of Art in Leipzig, but was denied entrance. She wrote in her autobiography, *Seven Houses:* "This was to have a decisive influence on my life, since I then turned to typography and printing in order to get into publishing on the production side, a job covering activities that had fascinated me in my childhood and youth and led to my early attempts at designing jackets, illustrations, and text pages. The making of books was in my blood." At nineteen the aspiring artist and publisher enrolled at the Academy of Graphic Arts and Book Printing where she was educated in painting and drawing, composing, printing, and bookbinding.

Desiring employment in her field, Huerlimann sought a position with *Atlantis,* an arts and travel magazine of which she was a devotee. She was directed to the periodical's publisher and editor, Martin Huerlimann. "I had already heard a lot about this man," she recalled in *Seven Houses.* "He was said to have seen half the world, and I felt that in many ways he was an adventurous figure. . . . So there I was, presenting myself to Martin Huerlimann in a rather awe-inspiring room containing some exotic sculpture. The globetrotter-cum-journalist had a pale, scholarly face, and wore rimless glasses which

added to the scholarly effect. He stood there looking rather lost. I told him what I knew and what my interests were; no doubt I was very hesitant and awkward, what with my unassuming looks, which were out of place here." Martin Huerlimann suggested Bettina travel the world and study further, then return later for a possible job in production.

Bettina Huerlimann left Germany in 1930 for England where she studied art and literature at the University of Bristol while working at a printing company. There she learned various styles of typesetting and perfected her own techniques. She returned to Germany in 1931 and secured a position as a trainee at Atlantis Verlag, Martin Huerlimann's publishing firm in Berlin. A diligent employee, Bettina became the director's assistant, and in 1933 married Martin Huerlimann. "Of course," she wrote, "one does not become the wife of such a man as quickly as it sounds written down like that. I only gradually came to realize that he was more to me than someone I respected and admired." Although Hitler had just come into power and the Reichstag had crumbled, the newlyweds were confident. "There were two of us," Huerlimann noted. "We were strong as lions and had publishing ideas enough to keep three firms occupied, and from now on we shared our joys and sorrows. We were to have plenty of both."

From 1933 until 1939 Atlantis Verlag published a variety of books, many of them on photography and art. In 1939, with the threat of war increasing, the Huerlimanns moved the company and their family to safety in Zurich, Switzerland. Although she related in her autobiography that she felt lost in the new country, Huerlimann eventually adapted and returned to her work with zeal. She also developed an interest in children's literature. "I was turning to the children's literature of the world at this time, and trying to trace the events that had occurred in the countries around us, so as to explain the shattered picture of the world to the young," she explained in *Seven Houses.* Appalled by the lack of quality in the books they reviewed, the Huerlimanns began publishing for children, their first effort being *Eia Popeia,* a compilation of German verses and songs. Numerous publications for children followed.

In 1967 the Huerlimanns sold Atlantis Verlag, but Bettina continued her involvement in children's literature, collecting and studying juvenile books on her trips to countries including Japan, the United States, Brazil, and China, and lecturing on the subject of books for children. Her collection of books includes many rare volumes, such as a first edition of the Grimm brothers' fairytales. In her autobiography she commented: "I see collecting old children's books and illustrations chiefly as a bridge to the past. Such bridges are often thoughtlessly broken down nowadays by people's lack of interest in past history, but they are preserved in such collections, whether private, public, or both. . . . In any case, books accumulated with loving care are good friends who will always be there when we need them, though they may show us their backs in daily life."

BIOGRAPHICAL/CRITICAL SOURCES: Times Literary Supplement, May 25, 1967, June 6, 1968; *New Statesman,* May 26, 1967; *Library Journal,* May 15, 1969; *Observer,* December 7, 1969; Bettina Huerlimann, *Seven Houses: My Life With Books,* Crowell, 1977.*

*   *   *

HUFBAUER, Karl (George) 1937-

PERSONAL: Born July 7, 1937, in San Diego, Calif.; son of

Clyde (an architect) and Arabelle (McKee) Hufbauer; married Sarah Grant Brannon (a violin teacher), August 6, 1960; children: Sarah Beth, Benjamin Grant, Ruth Arabelle. *Education:* Stanford University, B.S., 1959; Oxford University, Diploma in History and Philosophy of Science, 1961; University of California, Berkeley, Ph.D., 1970. *Home:* 20241 Bayview, Santa Ana, Calif. 92707. *Office:* Department of History, University of California, Irvine, Calif. 92717.

CAREER: University of California, Irvine, assistant professor, 1966-73, associate professor of history, 1973—. *Member:* American Association for the Advancement of Science, History of Science Society, Social Studies of Science Society, Sierra Club.

WRITINGS: The Formation of the German Chemical Community, 1720-1795, University of California Press, 1982. Contributor to history and social science journals.

WORK IN PROGRESS: The Stellar-Energy Problem, 1903-1939, about the discovery, by astronomers and physicists, of the energy-generating processes that power most stars, completion expected in 1987.

SIDELIGHTS: Hufbauer commented: "Studying under Hans Rosenberg, reading Thomas Kuhn, and participating in Berkeley's tumultuous student movement made me into a social historian of science. A fascination with origins led me to devote many years to examining the formation of the German chemical community during the eighteenth century as a means of understanding the subsequent prominence of German chemists in shaping modern scientific instruction and science-based technology. Having studied the first stage of discipline building and some of its effects on scientific work, I am now investigating interdisciplinary science. I believe that an extended case study of the research leading to one of this century's most striking interdisciplinary breakthroughs—Hans Bethe's solution of the stellar-energy problem—will illuminate the conditions favoring fruitful interaction across disciplinary boundaries.

"As a youth, several first ascents in the High Sierra and discoveries of Indian artifacts in Baja California gave me a taste for exploration. Strange as it may seem to one who has only read history, my research in libraries and archives suits this taste. So does my favorite recreational activity—diving along the California coast. I have come to regard the kelp forests on the lee side of Catalina Island as one of the world's least known natural wonders and rock scallops as one of the sea's most beautiful shells and greatest delicacies.

"In my more sedentary moments, I enjoy reading science fiction. My favorite author is Ursula Leguin."

*   *   *

HUGHES, Erica   1931-

PERSONAL: Born February 21, 1931, in London, England; daughter of Frederick Noel (a journalist) and Nancie (a dancer; maiden name, Hill) Brace; married Peter Hughes (an actor), August 14, 1958; children: Simon Peter, Bettany Mary. *Education:* Attended Royal Academy of Music, 1950-53. *Religion:* Church of England. *Home:* 21 Madeley Rd., Ealing, London W.5, England.

CAREER: Professional actress, 1954-65; writer.

WRITINGS: (With Peter Watkins) *Here's the Church,* Julia MacRae Books, 1980; (with Watkins) *Here's the Year* (juve-

nile), illustrated by Gill Tomblin, Julia MacRae Books, 1982; (with Watkins) *A Book of Prayer,* Julia MacRae Books, 1982.

*   *   *

HULL, Jesse Redding
See HULL, Jessie Redding

*   *   *

HULL, Jessie Redding   1932-
(Jesse Redding Hull)

PERSONAL: Born July 27, 1932, in Urbana, Ohio; daughter of William (an accountant) and Ethel (a florist; maiden name, Botkin) Redding; married Robert C. Hull (a writer), June 27, 1959; children: Robert W., Lisa K. *Education:* Ohio Wesleyan University, B.A., 1954; University of Missouri, A.M., 1956; also attended Cleveland State University, 1975-76. *Home and office:* 606 Crestview Dr., Bay Village, Ohio 44140.

CAREER: Speech therapist at public schools in Affton, Mo., 1956-59; Bob Hull Books, Bay Village, Ohio, business manager, 1980—. Volunteer language development teacher, 1967-73. Hostess at Rose Hill Museum, 1976—. *Member:* Bay Village Historical Society.

WRITINGS: Take Care of Millie (novel), New Readers Press, 1980; *The Other Side of Yellow* (novel), New Readers Press, 1980; *Marathon Madness* (juvenile), Bowmar/Noble, 1980; *Operation Airdrop* (juvenile), Bowmar/Noble, 1980; *The Ghost Car of Apple Valley* (juvenile), Bowmar/Noble, 1980; *The Bicycle Rip-Off* (juvenile), Bowmar/Noble, 1980; *Danger at the Racetrack* (juvenile), Bowmar/Noble, 1980; (under name Jesse Redding Hull) *Stanley's Secret Trip* (juvenile), Crestwood, 1981. Contributor of poems, articles, and stories to magazines.

WORK IN PROGRESS: A suspense novel, completion expected in 1984; two juvenile animal books, *Trouble With Four Legs* and *Just Plain Dog;* research for a juvenile book on Mary Katherine Goddard, printer of the Declaration of Independence.

SIDELIGHTS: Hull told *CA:* "Since childhood, writing has been as vital to me as eating and breathing. However, I did not try to make a living from this sacred aspect of my life until earning money was a necessity. Normal doors to employment slammed before me; and in desperation, I tried the longshot—writing. Publishers do not discriminate against a person because of too many college degrees, age, or sex. If a writer produces what the publisher believes his clients will buy, that writer steps through the door to become a part of the writing life.

"The books for New Readers Press were the most difficult to write, not because they were marketed for adults with low reading skills, but because they were problem situations. I suffered with my characters as I role-played my way through the stories. The problems of my characters became my problems, and I was emotionally drained at the conclusion of each book. Critics were kind, and I am proud of the books; however, I have much to learn about creating problem situation fiction. I tend to wrap up situations with neat little endings that aren't likely in real life.

"My other published books were easy to write, because they involved escapism in the form of unlikely escapades that allow our imaginations to deliver us from the real world for a brief adventure—usually fast-paced and humorous. These books were pure joy to write.

"My juvenile writing is moving in the direction of stories with historical background. Young people are often turned off by history because their exposure involves dry descriptions of events, without thorough characterizations of the exciting people involved in history. With my present research on Mary Katherine Goddard, I hope to convince a publisher that I can enliven history for children as John Jakes did for adults.''

AVOCATIONAL INTERESTS: Tent camping, caring for her two dogs and three cats.

* * *

HUME, Fergus(on Wright) 1859-1932

BRIEF ENTRY: Born July 8, 1859, in England; died July 13, 1932, in Southend, Essex, England. British barrister and novelist. Hume, who was educated in New Zealand, lived in Australia for three years before returning to England after the publication of his first and most notable work, *The Mystery of a Hansom Cab* (1886). This novel, one of the best-selling crime fiction books of its time, introduced the Victorian plot complexities that marked most of Hume's fiction. The author subsequently produced nearly one hundred fifty similarly structured crime novels, most set in London and many featuring the detective character Octavius Fanks. Hume, however, never again achieved the popular success of *The Mystery of a Hansom Cab.* His later works include *A Midnight Mystery* (1894), *The Rainbow Feather* (1898), *The Coin of Edward VII* (1903), *High Water Mark* (1910), and *The Unexpected* (1921). *Biographical/critical sources: Twentieth-Century Writing: A Reader's Guide to Contemporary Literature,* Transatlantic, 1969; *A Dictionary of Literature in the English Language: From Chaucer to 1940,* Pergamon, 1970; *Longman Companion to Twentieth Century Literature,* Longman, 1970; *Encyclopedia of Mystery and Detection,* McGraw, 1976; *Who's Who in Horror and Fantasy Literature,* Elm Tree Books, 1977.

* * *

HUMPHREYS, (Travers) Christmas 1901-1983

OBITUARY NOTICE—See index for *CA* sketch: Born February 15, 1901, in London, England; died of a heart attack, April 13, 1983, in London, England. Jurist, scholar, and author. Humphreys was a noted criminal lawyer and judge. He served as prosecutor at over two hundred fifty murder trials as well as at the Tokyo war crimes trials. He is best remembered for prosecuting Timothy Evans and Ruth Ellis. Evans, who was hanged for murdering his daughter, was posthumously pardoned, and Ruth Ellis—hanged for murdering her lover—was the last woman to be executed in England. When Humphreys later took the bench, he became known as the "gentle judge"; he believed in lenient sentencing and he never passed down the death sentence. Throughout his legal career, he served in various capacities, including junior treasury counsel at the Central Criminal Court, senior crown prosecutor, bencher of Inner Temple, Queen's Counsel, commissioner of Old Bailey, and additional judge. In 1924 Humphreys founded the London Buddhist Lodge, later known as the Buddhist Society. President of the Shakespearean Authorship Society, he believed that the Earl of Oxford wrote the plays credited to Shakespeare. Humphreys wrote many books in various genres, including *Seven Murders, Karma and Rebirth, Shadows and Other Poems,* and *The Search Within.* Obituaries and other sources: Christmas Humphreys, *Both Sides of the Circle* (memoirs), Allen & Unwin, 1978; *London Times,* April 15, 1983; *Washington Post,* April 18, 1983.

HUNGERFORD, Cy(rus Cotton) 1889(?)-1983

OBITUARY NOTICE: Born c. 1889 in Manilla, Ind.; died May 25, 1983, in Wexford, Pa. Cartoonist. Best known for his editorial cartoons, Hungerford sold his first drawings to the *Parkersburg Sentinel* at the age of thirteen. He went on to work for other newspapers in West Virginia and Pittsburgh, most notably the *Pittsburgh Post-Gazette* from 1927 to 1977. Between 1915 and 1925 the artist drew "Snoodles," a daily syndicated comic strip, yet his most popular creation was "Pa Pitt," a pudgy figure in colonial dress that represented the city of Pittsburgh. During World War II Hungerford's defense posters were exhibited throughout the country. Obituaries and other sources: *The World Encyclopedia of Cartoons,* Chelsea House, 1980; *Who's Who in American Art,* Bowker, 1980; *Chicago Tribune,* May 28, 1983; *New York Times,* May 28, 1983.

* * *

HUNSBERGER, Edith Mae 1927-
(Eydie Mae)

PERSONAL: Born July 1, 1927, in Evansville, Ind.; daughter of Travis and Rose (Schlegel) Miller; married Arnold Hunsberger, November 30, 1946; children: Robert Earl, Carol Jean Hunsberger Fitzpatrick. *Education:* Attended Methodist Hospital School of Nursing, 1945-46; Hahnemann Memorial Institute of Health Sciences, earned certificate, 1981, earned license, 1982. *Home address:* P.O. Box 44, Dulzura, Calif. 92017.

CAREER: Nutritionist and writer. *Awards, honors:* Humanitarian award from International Association of Cancer Victims and Friends, c. 1977; Dr. Hahnemann Humanitarian Award from Maryland State Homeopathic Society, 1977; award from American Nutrition Society, 1978; D.Sc. and Public Health from Hahnemann Memorial Institute of Health Sciences, 1981.

WRITINGS—Under name Eydie Mae: (With Chris Loeffler) *How I Conquered Cancer Naturally,* Production House, 1975, revised edition, Avery Books, 1983; *Eydie Mae's Natural Recipes,* Production House, 1978.

WORK IN PROGRESS: A children's series on health and nutrition, Avery Books, 1983.

SIDELIGHTS: Edith Hunsberger told *CA:* "In 1973 I was dying. I decided to try nutritional therapy, as I had nothing to lose. Today I enjoy good health and a happy life. I wrote my book hoping that, in some way, I could help someone else. The recipe book was an obligation. My present work is to expand and share new knowledge with others in need.

"Nutritional therapy consists of cleaning the toxins from the body, starting with a few days of juice fasting and using colonics and enemas. From there we used a therapeutic program of 'live foods' or raw, uncooked foods, omitting all sugar, oil, food supplements, refined foods, and animal products, including dairy items. My husband and I have worked with a scientist, Dr. Arthur Robinson, in our nutritional research. We found that food supplements caused cancer cells to grow. Later we learned that yeast and other leavening agents would also provide a good growing field for cancer because of the formation of carbon dioxide in the body. Cancer grows readily in a field of sugar, high protein, and carbon dioxide. This program does *not* cure cancer, but because of the immune factor it seems to *hold* most cancers plus many other diseases. We have watched cardiac problems, arthritis, diabetes, hypoglycemia, and high blood pressure respond.

"After my body responded and started to rebuild good health I changed to what I call phase II, or the maintenance program, which includes *some* cooked vegetables and grain."

*   *   *

HUNT, (Henry Cecil) John 1910-

PERSONAL: Born June 22, 1910, in India; son of C. E. (a career officer) and Ethel Helen (Crookshank) Hunt; married Joy Mowbray Green, 1936; children: Sally Hunt Crouch, Susan Hunt Leyden, Prudence Hunt Tarsnane, Jennifer Hunt Wright. *Education:* Attended Marlborough College; graduated from Royal Military College, Sandhurst. *Home:* Highway Cottage, Aston, Henley-on-Thames, England.

CAREER: British Army, career officer, 1930-56, member of King's Royal Rifle Corps, 1930-34, seconded to Indian Police, 1934-35 and 1937-40, commander of 11th Indian Infantry Brigade, 1944-46, general staff officer with Joint Planning Staffs of Middle East Land Forces, 1946-48, colonel (for training) of Allied Land Forces in Central European Command, France, 1949-52, member of general staff of First Corps, 1952, assistant commandant at Staff College, Camberley, 1953-55, commander of 168th Infantry Brigade of Territorial Army, 1955-56, retiring as colonel; director of Duke of Edinburgh's Award Scheme, 1956-66, became Baron of Llanfair Waterdine, 1966. Mountaineer and explorer; expeditions include James Weller's Karakorum expedition, 1935, expeditions to southeast Himalayas, 1937 and 1940, to Caucasus, 1958, and to northeast Greenland, 1960, British-Soviet expedition to Pamiers, 1962, and Canadian Central expedition in St. Elias Mountains, 1967.

Rector of Aberdeen University, 1963-66. Head of Relief Advisory Mission to Nigeria and personal representative of British prime minister in Nigeria, both 1968-70. Member of Youth Service Development Council, 1961-62, and of Royal Commission on the Press, 1974-77. Chairman of Committee of Enquiry on Young Immigrants, 1961-62, of Mount Everest Foundation, 1957-67, of parole board for England and Wales, 1968-74, of advisory committee on police forces in Northern Ireland, and of Intermediate Treatment Fund, 1980—. President of British Mountaineering Council, 1965-68, of Council for Volunteers Overseas, 1968-74, of National Ski Federation of Great Britain, 1969-72, of Rainier Foundation, 1972—, and of National Association of Probation Officers, 1974-80. *Member:* Alpine Club (president, 1956-58), Royal Geographical Society (president, 1977—).

AWARDS, HONORS: Companion of Distinguished Service Order, 1944; Commander of Order of the British Empire, 1945; Knight of Order of the Garter, 1953; Order (first class) of Strong Right Arms of the Gurkhas from King Tribhuvana Bir Bikram of Nepal, 1953; honorary member of Royal Institution of Chartered Surveyors, 1953; Cullum Medal from American Geographical Society, 1954; Hubbard Medal from National Geographic Society, 1954; Badge of Soviet Mountaineer (first class), 1954; Indian Police Medal; Indian Everest Medal; Founder's Medal from Royal Geographical Society; D.C.L. from universities of Durham and Leeds and from City University; LL.D. from universities of London and Aberdeen.

WRITINGS: (With Edmund Hillary) *The Ascent of Everest,* foreword by Philip Mountbatten, Hodder & Stoughton, 1953, published as *The Conquest of Everest,* Dutton, 1954; *Our Everest Adventures: A Pictoral History From Kathmandu to the Summit,* Dutton, 1954; (author of foreword and translator with Wilfrid Noyce) *Starlight and Storm: The Ascent of Six Great*

North Faces of the Alps, Dent, 1956; (with Christopher Brasher) *The Red Snows: An Account of the British Caucasus Expedition, 1958,* Hutchinson, 1960; (editor) *My Favourite Mountaineering Stories,* illustrations by Douglas Philips, Lutterworth, 1978; *Life Is Meeting,* Hodder & Stoughton, 1978.

SIDELIGHTS: John Hunt climbed nearly sixty Alpine peaks and participated in three Himalayan expeditions before serving as the leader of the team that conquered Mount Everest in 1953. "The last main outpost of the world unknown to man," Mount Everest stands 29,002 feet and defeated ten expeditions between 1921 and 1952. Fifteen mountaineers died attempting to reach its peak, and two, George Mallory and Andrew Irvine, disappeared somewhere near the pinnacle in 1924.

Sponsored by the Alpine Club, the Royal Geographical Society, and *London Times,* Hunt's expedition braved ice, snow, storms, dwindling supplies, and deadly altitudes to scale Everest in time for Queen Elizabeth II's coronation. Involving 15 climbers, 362 porters, 36 Sherpa guides, and 7½ tons of equipment, the British expedition lasted eighty days from beginning to end, with the base camp established on April 12, 1953. "For a rough idea of what it is like," Bruce Bliven offered as an analogy in the *New Republic,* "you might imagine starting on foot from Detroit, Michigan, to climb the outside of the Empire State Building, carrying with you everything you will need for the entire trip—including the return, on foot, to Detroit. Once arrived at the base of the building, you will mount the outside, establishing window-sill camps at the seventeenth, forty-third, seventy-ninth and ninety-fourth floors, using materials which you have of course carried with you from Detroit."

After three attempts to climb the final slopes, two members of Hunt's expedition, Tenzig Norkay and Edmund Hillary, chosen because of their demonstrated abilities, inched their way to the top of Mount Everest at 11:30 A.M. on May 29, 1953. The Sherpa, Norkay, who attempted the climb more times than any other mountaineer, buried food at the site as an offering to the gods and marked the site with the flags of Britain, India, Nepal, and the United Nations while Hillary placed a small crucifix nearby. "In the terms of physical effort and endurance," remarked Philip Mountbatten, Duke of Edinburgh, about the feat, "it will live in history as a shining example to all mankind."

The reasons Hunt's expeditions succeeded when so many others failed include thorough preparation, good weather conditions, the application of science and of the experiences of earlier attempts, and, of course, talented mountaineers. Moreover, the teamwork of Hunt's party contributed greatly in overtaking the mountain. "It is this, above all else," noted James Ramsey Ullman in the *New York Times Book Review,* "that seems the important and significant thing about the climbing of Everest: that it was a common victory in a common cause." Though Norkay and Hillary enjoyed the thrill of and the popularity from standing atop the "Goddess Mother of the World," the other mountaineers, especially Hunt, should be glorified as well, Ferdinand C. Lane suggested in the *Saturday Review.* "To exalt the men who made the final dash is unfair to the other members of the party," he maintained. "For each had contributed his share, particulary Sir John himself, . . . whose careful planning and supervision of all details was a masterpiece of efficiency."

Several writers, including a *New York Times* reporter, attributed the expedition's success to Hunt's leadership. According to the *Observer,* "Hunt knows that a climbing party is held together not by military discipline but by friendship and common enthusiasm; and mountains to him have always been far more than a technical or a physical challenge . . . his accounts of running downhill on skis with Athens spread out below . . . reveal a man with a feeling for the poetry as well as the problems of mountains.''

The Conquest of Everest, written within a month of the climb, chronicles the journey to the top ot Mount Everest, with Hillary providing an account of the final stages. ''In the story it has to tell it is unsurpassed—and unsurpassable,'' observed Ullman, who noted the authors' objective and detailed presentations. Covering everything from the initial planning stages to the selection of mountaineers and their training to the assembling of equipment, *The Conquest of Everest,* in Ullman's words, ''is a complete job. An utterly honest, modest and, of course, authoritative job.'' ''Over the years many books have been written about Everest,'' he continued. ''But here at last is *the* book—the book of triumph and fulfillment.''

Concurring, an *Atlantic* critic doubted ''that the literature of mountaineering contains a more explicit and lucid account of the ascent of a great peak'' than *The Conquest of Everest.* Likewise, Harry C. James, writing in the *Christian Science Monitor,* commented that the book ''is an eloquent, swift-moving, factual account. . . . In a world torn by personal ambition and nationalism, it is good to turn . . . to the final sentence in this account of one of the most imaginative undertakings of our time: 'There is no height, no depth, that the spirit of man, guided by a higher Spirit, cannot attain.'''

Unlike other critics, a *New Yorker* reviewer noticed something more in *The Conquest of Everest* than man overcoming a mountain. ''Nothing,'' he insisted, ''emerges more clearly from the book's quietly chilling pages than the subduing fact that the world's highest mountain has not been, and probably never will be, conquered. It has merely, at last, been climbed.''

BIOGRAPHICAL/CRITICAL SOURCES—Books: Yves Malartic, *Tenzig of Everest,* Crown, 1954; Hannah Bellis, *Twentieth-Century Cavalcade,* Hutchinson, 1956; Ronald William Clark, *Six Great Mountaineers,* Hamilton, 1956; Richard Stanton Lambert, *World's Most Daring Explorers,* Sterling, 1956; Norman George Wymer, *Sir John Hunt,* Oxford University Press, 1956.

Periodicals: *Observer,* January 14, 1953, December 17, 1978; *New York Times,* June 2, 1953; *Washington Post,* June 3, 1953; *New York Herald Tribune,* June 8, 1953, January 24, 1954; *Life,* June 29, 1953; *Christian Science Monitor,* July 2, 1953, January 21, 1954, August 26, 1954; *Spectator,* November 20, 1953; *New Statesman and Nation,* November 21, 1953; *Saturday Review,* January 23, 1954; *Springfield Republican,* January 24, 1954; *Chicago Tribune,* January 24, 1954; *New York Times Book Review,* January 24, 1954; *Time,* January 25, 1954; *New Yorker,* January 30, 1954; *San Francisco Chronicle,* January 31, 1954; *New Republic,* February 1, 1954; *Atlantic,* March, 1954; *Catholic World,* April, 1954; *Guardian Weekly,* September 10, 1978.

—*Sketch by Charity Anne Dorgan*

* * *

HUNT, Nan
See RAY, N(ancy) L(ouise)

* * *

HUNT, Patricia Joan   1922(?)-1983

OBITUARY NOTICE—See index for *CA* sketch: Born c. 1922

in Sefton Park, England; died of leukemia, February 28, 1983, in New York, N.Y. Editor and author. Hunt began her career as a reporter for *Life* in 1950, becoming the magazine's nature editor in 1954. Upon *Life*'s demise in 1972, she joined the staff of Time-Life as a picture editor. There she was associated with books on the American wilderness and the Old West until 1977. Hunt also wrote for Xerox Educational Publications. Her books include *Koalas, Tigers,* and *Snowy Owls.* Obituaries and other sources: *New York Times,* March 3, 1983; *Publishers Weekly,* April 1, 1983.

* * *

HUNTER, Henry MacGregor   1929-
(Mac Hunter)

BRIEF ENTRY: Born June 16, 1929, in Santa Monica, Calif. American professional golfer and author. During the 1940's Hunter won several amateur golf tournaments, including the National Junior Championship and California Amateur competitions. He became a professional golfer in 1952. Hunter wrote *Golf for Beginners* (Grosset, 1973). *Address:* 1250 Capri Dr., Pacific Palisades, Calif. 91403.

* * *

HUNTER, Mac
See HUNTER, Henry MacGregor

* * *

HURLEY, Kathy   1947-

PERSONAL: Born April 1, 1947, in Plainfield, N.J.; daughter of James F. and Gertrude F. Hurley. *Education:* Arizona State University, B.A. (summa cum laude), 1969; Illinois State University, M.A. (summa cum laude), 1971. *Politics:* Democrat. *Religion:* ''Christian mystic.'' *Home:* Manhattan Plaza, 484 West 43rd St., No. 22P, New York, N.Y. 10036. *Agent:* Gloria Safier, Inc., 667 Madison Ave., New York, N.Y. 10021. *Office:* Atheneum Publishers, 597 Fifth Ave., New York, N.Y. 10017.

CAREER: Worked as actress with touring dinner theatre company, 1971-72, actress with regional repertory company and social service assistant, 1972-74, and office temporary, 1974, 1979-80; Atheneum Publishers, New York, N.Y., assistant to editors, 1980—. Member of musical workshop program of Broadcast Music, Inc., 1981—. *Member:* American Federation of Television and Radio Artists, Authors League of America, Dramatists Guild, Actors' Equity Association. *Awards, honors:* First place in Scottsdale Theatre Playwrighting Contest, 1966, for ''For an Eggshell''; playwrighting award from National Society of Arts and Letters, 1972, for ''The Alchemist's Book''; Heckshire Grant for Children's Theatre, 1978; playwright-in-residency grant from National Endowment for the Arts for the Fourth Annual Metropolitan Short Play Festival, 1979.

WRITINGS—Plays: ''For an Eggshell'' (one-act), first produced in Scottsdale, Ariz., at Scottsdale Stagebrush Theatre, 1966; *The Alchemist's Book* (children's play; first produced in New York City at Henry Street Settlement, 1974), Samuel French, 1976; ''The Black Princess'' (children's play), first produced in New York City at Double Image Theatre, 1975; ''Beauty Like the Night'' (two-act), first produced Off-Broadway at the Octagon/Burt Wheeler Theatre, 1975; ''Duet at a Bus Stop'' (one-act), first produced at Double Image Theatre, 1976;

"The Forgotten Treasure" (children's play), first produced in New York City by Children's Humanities Theatre, 1978; "The Fading of Miss Dru" (one-act), first produced at Double Image Theatre, 1979; "Yes, But What Do You Do for a Living?" (one-act), first produced in New York City at Actor's Alliance, 1980; "From Our Point of View" (children's review), first produced at Double Image Theatre, 1982; "A Poet Against the World" (two-act), first produced at Actor's Alliance, 1982; "Bonny Jean" (two-act), first produced in New York City at Broadcast Music, Inc., workshop, 1983.

WORK IN PROGRESS: A children's play; the libretto of a musical scheduled for first performance in August, 1983.

SIDELIGHTS: Hurley told *CA:* "I've recently had the opportunity to work for a prominent New York publisher and to 'see things from the other side of the transom,' as it were. What I've learned has often been a revelation to me, and I'd like to share some of the findings with student writers and other fellow strugglers.

"First the good news. Most of 'them' (editors, publishers, readers, etc.) are really on your side. I know it's hard to believe that. You can just see them whipping out those rejections with a malevolent flourish and a cry of 'take that, peasant.' But they actually do get their 'kicks' finding the gem in the slush pile. In fact, that's what keeps many of them in the not-so-well-paying world of publishing. (I myself wept for joy—literally—at unearthing my first 'discovery.' And what a true pleasure it was sharing the unknown writer's work with higher-ups who, luckily, loved it as much as I did!)

"Now for the bad news. Perhaps the most stunning realization I came to was how appallingly similar and senseless are the mistakes made by even talented writers. (I cringe to think of my own—like some of the covering letters I'd sent—letters that can only be described as arrogant and slightly loony attempts at salesmanship. I'm sure many of them are now immortalized in countless editorial 'fun files'—those private files kept solely for the amusement of the staff.)

"Most of those mistakes seem to stem from the want of a professional attitude. You would be amazed at the number of people submitting for publication who treat the process as if it were some kind of raffle; as if the editors put all the manuscripts in a barrel, gave it a spin, reached in, and pulled out the winning 'best-seller.' To give you a concrete example of this attitude, I recently had a phone call from a dear lady who wanted to know if we would publish her children's book. Her friends had all told her she had a 'gift.' However, on further questioning, it came out that not only had she never written a children's book before, she had never even read one. A doctor, an accountant, or a lawyer wouldn't dream of offering their professional services without knowing their subjects inside out, and yet writers will regularly submit works for professional publication that they wouldn't dare hand in to their high school English teachers.

"But even the ones who do take the time to observe the niceties of spelling, punctuation, grammar, and typing (yes, handwritten manuscripts are regularly sent back unread) still sometimes fail to 'do the homework.' It doesn't take all that long to find out what a particular publisher or theatre is looking for. Just go to a public library and check out their books, or read a few old newspaper reviews of past productions. And still many writers waste time, postage, and stomach lining sending scripts for huge extravaganzas to tiny-staged theatres, steaming sex novels to children's book publishers, nonfiction to poetry quarterlies, etc.

"A little extra reading time on the writer's part can teach him not only what type of work the publisher is interested in, but what particular writing style, subject matter, point of view, philosophy, and prejudices the organization may hold dear. Knowing this can put you at a definite advantage. I read of one feature writer who goes at the magazines she buys with magic markers—one for subject, one for style, etc.—recording in an easily visible form the chief characteristics of the stories each periodical prints. I wouldn't recommend this with books from the library, but the approach not only betters your chance of success, but exhibits exactly what I mean by a professional attitude. This writer has taken the time and effort needed to research, not only her writing subject, but also the language of the publication she wants to reach. Writing is communication, after all, and before you can communicate, you must speak the language.

"And so, based on the things I've learned from my own writing experiences, as well as what I've learned on the 'inside' of the publishing game, I'd offer this advice to the student writer: First, love writing (or at least, like Dorothy Parker, love 'having written') as much as you love the idea of being a writer. Russian director Constantine Stanislavski told his actors to worship 'the art in themselves' rather than 'themselves in the art.' It's good advice for all of us.

"Second, pick a form and subject you really enjoy. Trying to guess what someone else will like or what will sell is always tricky business, and boredom and contempt for a project have a sneaky way of showing through in your writing. Besides, it may be some time before you have any reward for your efforts other than the pleasure you got from the writing itself.

"Third, keep your approach to submitting writings simple, straight-forward, and professional. If you don't know what a publisher or theatre wants, write for their guidelines. Most would be more than happy to tell you. Don't, however, play the helpless little waif and whine, 'I've never really written before, and gosh, if you could just take the time from your busy schedule. . . .' Publishers are not schools. If you want to learn the basics, or if you want information on starting a career in literature, take a course in creative writing (I recommend the continuing education program of your university) or buy a self-help book. Equally offensive is the 'Here's-your-next-masterpiece' approach. Long, hard-sell covering letters usually don't get read (if you're lucky). Save your efforts for the work itself (unless, of course, you have your heart set on landing in the 'fun file'). After all, a piece must be able to stand on its own.

"And finally, take that little bit of extra time and effort to do the homework. If no one seems to notice your masterpiece, if the audiences are 'staying away in droves,' maybe it's not the world. Maybe it is your masterpiece. If you can face the possibility of its being less than perfect, without giving up completely, if you can look for the mistakes, and what's more, set about correcting them, then you're acting like a pro, and success for you is a lot closer."

*   *   *

HURLIMANN, Bettina
See HUERLIMANN, Bettina

*   *   *

HUSEMAN, Richard C. 1939-

BRIEF ENTRY: Born February 16, 1939, in Lafayette, Ind.

American communication specialist, educator, editor, and author of books in his field. Huseman joined the faculty of University of Georgia in 1964 and became a professor of management in 1974. He directed the Bicentennial Youth Debates in Washington, D.C., from 1974 to 1976, and he has also served as chairman of the National Debate Tournament Committee. Huseman was named associate editor of the *Journal of Business Communication* in 1975. His publications include *Readings in Interpersonal and Organizational Communication* (Holbrook, 1969), *Communication in Conflict: A Communication Training Handbook for Law Enforcement Officers* (Georgia Center for Continuing Education, 1972), *Interpersonal Communication in Organizations: A Perceptual Approach* (Holbrook, 1976), *Readings in Organizational Behavior: Dimensions of Management Actions* (Allyn & Bacon, 1979), *Business Communication: Strategies and Skills* (Dryden, 1981), and *Readings in Business Communication: Strategies and Skills* (Dryden, 1981). *Address:* Department of Management, University of Georgia, Athens, Ga. 30602.

*   *   *

HUTCHINSON, Joseph (Burtt) 1902-

PERSONAL: Born March 21, 1902, in Burton Latimer, Northants, England; son of Edmund and Lydia Mary (Davy) Hutchinson; married Martha Leonora Johnson, July 9, 1930; children: Helga Leonora, Dennis Proctor. *Education:* St. John's College, Cambridge, B.A., 1923, M.A., 1931, Sc.D., 1941. *Home:* Huntingfield, Huntingdon Rd., Cambridge CB3 0LH, England. *Office:* St. John's College, Cambridge University, Cambridge, England.

CAREER: Geneticist with Empire Cotton Growing Corp., 1926-33; Institute of Plant Industry, Indore, India, geneticist and botanist, 1933-37; Empire Cotton Growing Corp., geneticist, 1937-57, chief geneticist, 1944-49, director of Cotton Research Station in Namulonge, Uganda, 1949-57; Cambridge University, Cambridge, England, Drapers Professor of Agriculture, 1957-69, professor emeritus, 1969——. Chairman of council of Makerere College, Uganda, 1953-57. Royal Society Leverhulme Visiting Professor at Indian Agricultural Research Institute, Delhi, 1960-70. Fellow of St. John's College, Cambridge, and of Linnean Society; foreign fellow of Indian Natural Science Academy, 1974. *Member:* Royal Society (fellow), British Association for the Advancement of Science (president, 1965-66), Nature Conservancy. *Awards, honors:* Royal Medal from Royal Society, 1967; honorary fellow of Makerere College; D.Sc. from universities of Nottingham and East Anglia; Companion of the Order of St. Michael and St. George.

WRITINGS—Published by Cambridge University Press, except as noted: (With R. A. Silow and S. G. Stephens) *The Evolution of Gossypium and the Differentiation of the Cultivated Cottons*, Empire Cotton Growing Corp., 1947; *Application of Genetics to Cotton Improvement*, 1959; (editor) *Essays on Crop Plant Evolution*, 1965; (editor) *Population and Food Supply: Essays on Human Need and Agricultural Prospects*, 1969; *Farming and Food Supply: Interdependence of Countryside and Town*, 1972; (editor) *Evolutionary Studies in World Crops: Diversity and Change in the Indian Subcontinent*, 1974; *The Challenge of the Third World*, 1975; (contributor) J. G. Clark and E. M. Jope, editors, *Early History of Agriculture: Symposium*, Oxford University Press, 1977.

Also author of *The Genetics of Gossypium*. Contributor to journals, including *Journal of Genetics, Tropical Agriculture*,

Journal of Textile Institute, Annals of Botany, and *Memoirs of the Cotton Research Station, Trinidad*.

AVOCATIONAL INTERESTS: Gardening.*

*   *   *

HUTTON, Richard 1949-

PERSONAL: Born October 26, 1949, in New York, N.Y.; son of Hubert Ernest (in business) and Irene (Spiegelberg) Hutton; married M. Susan Allison (an editor), March 1, 1980. *Education:* Attended University of North Carolina at Chapel Hill, 1967-69; University of California, Berkeley, B.A., 1971. *Home and office:* 34 Morton Pl., Chappaqua, N.Y. 10514. *Agent:* Barbara Lowenstein, 250 West 57th St., New York, N.Y. 10019.

CAREER: Rehabilitation/World (magazine), New York, N.Y., editor in chief, 1974-75; science writer.

WRITINGS—Nonfiction: *Bio-Revolution: DNA and the Ethics of Man-Made Life*, New American Library, 1978; (with David Sheinkin and Michael Schachter) *The Food Connection: How the Things You Eat Affect the Way You Feel, and What You Can Do About It*, introduction by Carlton Fredericks, Bobbs-Merrill, 1979, published as *Food, Mind, and Mood*, Warner Books, 1980; (with Frank Kendig) *Life-Spans; or, How Long Things Last*, Holt, 1980; *The Cosmic Chase*, New American Library, 1981; (with Zsolt Harsanyi) *Genetic Prophecy: Beyond the Double Helix*, Rawson, Wade, 1981. Contributor of articles to magazines, including *Omni, Cosmopolitan*, and *New York Times Magazine*.

WORK IN PROGRESS: "The Brain," an eight-part television series to be broadcast on Public Broadcasting Service (PBS-TV) in 1984.

SIDELIGHTS: Hutton, a free-lance writer, has written books on a variety of scientific topics, including DNA research, the longevity of a wide range of animate and inanimate objects, and the history of man's attempt to develop space colonies. In collaboration with geneticist Zsolt Harsanyi, Hutton also wrote *Genetic Prophecy: Beyond the Double Helix*, an account of recent breakthroughs in genetic research that enable medical scientists to predict with increasing accuracy the probability that a given individual will contract a particular disease.

For example, geneticists can administer laboratory tests to determine whether a person carries in his body any of the ten HLA antigens that have been linked with an increased susceptibility for disease. Science writer Robin Marantz Henig observed in *Washington Post Book World* that Hutton and Harsanyi report in *Genetic Prophecy* that "persons with type A blood and the HLA antigens B5 and Cw4 run a risk of bladder cancer 15 times [greater than] that of the general population. . . . And those who inherit different HLA antigens from each parent seem to live significantly longer than do those with matched pairs." More than eighty diseases have already been linked with HLA antigens from the ninety or so known to exist in the human gene pool.

The presence of the genetic marker GPT similarly indicates an increased risk for breast tumors in women. In the past, female relatives of breast cancer victims were often encouraged to submit to yearly mammograms and, in some cases, to mastectomies. Now these women can be tested for the GPT marker. If it is not present, their risk is no greater than that of the general population, and they can dispense with the X-rays that are themselves believed to increase a woman's cancer risk and with the disfiguring surgery. Conversely, 50 percent of those who do carry the marker will develop breast cancer before they turn fifty.

Hutton and Harsanyi acknowledge the potential for misuse of genetic prediction, noting that employers, insurers, and government agencies may discriminate against those who carry adverse markers. According to Henig, the authors believe "the possibility for abuse probably does not warrant the throttling of new knowledge. . . . The best protection we have against abuse . . . is an informed public ready to participate in meaningful debate about how guidelines and safeguards can best be applied."

BIOGRAPHICAL/CRITICAL SOURCES: *New York Times Book Review*, June 22, 1980; *New York Times*, September 1, 1981; *Washington Post Book World*, October 11, 1981.

* * *

HYDE, Douglas (Arnold) 1911-

BRIEF ENTRY: Born April 8, 1911, in Worthing, Sussex, England. British political activist, editor, and author. Hyde was a child preacher and theology student until he became preoccupied with the ills of society. He joined the Communist party before he was eighteen years old and for nearly twenty years expounded the Communist cause as a strike organizer, party administrator, and journalist. After being assigned by the party to the *Daily Worker* as a reporter and news editor, Hyde launched a campaign to expose organizations he thought to be Fascist, including the Roman Catholic church. He was sued for libel by the Catholic *Weekly Review* after he ran a series of articles claiming collusion between the publication and Fascist groups. While preparing his trial defense, Hyde began reading the works of classical and contemporary Catholic scholars in an attempt to better understand his opposition. Coupled

with his increasing discontent with the realities of twentieth-century society, this exposure to Catholic theology so altered his thinking that Hyde resigned from the Communist party and embraced Roman Catholicism. He began working for the *Catholic Herald* with the same zeal that he had once displayed at the *Daily Worker*. Hyde's books include *I Believed* (Putnam, 1950), *The Peaceful Assault: The Pattern of Subversion* (Bodley Head, 1963), *Dedication and Leadership: Learning From the Communists* (Sands, 1966), *God's Bandit: The Story of Don Orione, "Father of the Poor"* (Sons of Divine Providence, 1966), *The Roots of Guerrilla Warfare* (Dufour, 1968), and *Communism Today* (Gill & Macmillan, 1972). *Biographical/critical sources:* Bruno Schafer, editor, *They Heard His Voice*, McMullen, 1952.

* * *

HYTIER, Jean (Pierre) 1899-1983

OBITUARY NOTICE: Born January 4, 1899, in Paris, France; died of lymphoma, March 11, 1983, in New York, N.Y. Educator, editor, and author. Before coming to the United States, Hytier served as director of letters for the French National Ministry of Education from 1945 to 1947. An expert in French literature, he taught at several universities, including the University of California, Davis, and the University of Massachusetts. The educator also taught at Columbia University for nineteen years, becoming professor emeritus in 1967. Hytier's works include a biography of Andre Gide and books on French poetry and literature. He also edited *Oeuvres de Paul Valery* and the works of Pascal. Obituaries and other sources: *Directory of American Scholars*, Volume III: *Foreign Languages, Linguistics, and Philology*, 7th edition, Bowker, 1978; *New York Times*, March 13, 1983; *AB Bookman's Weekly*, April 11, 1983.

I

IDELSOHN, Abraham Zevi   1882-1938

BRIEF ENTRY: Born July 14 (some sources say July 13), 1882, in Pfilsburg, Latvia (now U.S.S.R.); died of complications following a paralytic stroke, July 14 (some sources say August 14), 1938, in Johannesburg, South Africa. Musicologist and author best known as the founder of serious modern scholarship of Jewish music. Idelsohn studied music in Germany before going, in 1905, to Jerusalem, where he founded the Institute for Jewish Music and the Jewish Music School. He came to the United States in 1922, and in 1924 took a post as a lecturer at Hebrew Union College in Cincinnati, Ohio. In 1934 Idelsohn suffered a paralytic stroke from which he never fully recovered. His writings, which were published in English, German, and Hebrew, include *History of Jewish Music* (1924), *The Ceremonies of Judaism* (1929), *Diwan of Hebrew and Arabic Poetry of the Yemenite Jews* (1930), and what is considered by scholars to be his greatest work, the ten-volume *Thesaurus of Hebrew-Oriental Melodies* (1914-32). *Biographical/critical sources: Ohio Authors and Their Books: Biographical Data and Selective Biographies for Ohio Authors, Native and Resident, 1796-1950,* World Publishing, 1962; *The Oxford Companion to Music,* 10th edition, Oxford University Press, 1974; *Baker's Biographical Dictionary of Musicians,* 6th edition, Schirmer Books, 1978.

*   *   *

IGLEHART, Alfreda P(aulette)   1950-

PERSONAL: Born May 9, 1950, in Waco, Tex.; daughter of Henry Dirks (a fish market owner and operator) and Willie (a fish market owner and operator; maiden name, Long) Iglehart; divorced. *Education:* St. Mary's University, San Antonio, Tex., B.A., 1971; Our Lady of the Lake University, M.S.W., 1974; University of Michigan, M.A., 1975, Ph.D., 1978. *Home:* 227 Crest Ave., Ann Arbor, Mich. 48103. *Office:* School of Social Work, University of Michigan, Ann Arbor, Mich. 48109.

CAREER: University of Michigan, Ann Arbor, assistant professor of social work, 1979—.

WRITINGS: *Married Women and Work,* Lexington Books, 1979; (with Josefina Figueira-McDonough, Rosemary Sarri, and Terry Williams) *Women in Prison in Michigan, 1968-1978,* University of Michigan, Institute for Social Research, 1981. Contributor to journals in the social sciences.

WORK IN PROGRESS: *The Truth About Child Abuse,* completion expected in 1984; *Social Work: The Sell-Out Profession?,* completion expected in 1985.

SIDELIGHTS: Inglehart told *CA:* "Many people criticize social science writing as being mundane, wordy, too theoretical, without practical application, and directed toward an academic audience. As a social scientist, I have tried to focus on topics that appeal to a wider audience. I have also attempted to stay away from social science jargon and buzz words. When I report on my research projects and critique the latest theoretical developments in the areas of interest to me, I want the general population, program planners, policy makers, and social work practitioners to be my consumers. Knowledge in a vacuum is of limited or no use to those people who, on a daily basis, have to struggle with the delivery of human services to individuals in a crisis.

"My study on women and their work looked at the attitudes of gainfully employed wives and the attitudes of housewives regarding their work. While so much has been written about working wives, little has been reported on housewives. So I took an issue of importance to thousands of women who have made the traditional choice of remaining in the home. I also advocated that professionals stop trying to rescue these women from the home by finding them jobs. I was dealing with a real world issue in a very down-to-earth manner.

"The prison work attempts to explain the dramatic increase in the Michigan female prison population. Are women committing more serious crimes? Are they becoming more male-like as the women's liberation movement gains hold? No, women are not becoming like the more assaultive male criminal. The majority of women are in prison because of property crimes. As more women face economic hardships, the courts are becoming more punitive. Here again, the real world application of the study emerges as the Michigan Department of Corrections uses this monograph to plan prison policies that address the unique needs of the female prisoner.

"In conclusion, the primary goal of my writing is to stimulate thinking, policies, programs, and action so that society in general and the profession of social work in particular can become more responsive to the needs of all Americans."

ILLYES, Gyula 1902-1983

OBITUARY NOTICE: Born November 2, 1902, in Racegres, Hungary; died April 14, 1983, in Budapest, Hungary. Public servant, playwright, poet, critic, and author of fiction. Illyes, who was highly critical of the Communist government that controlled Hungary after 1948, had favored land reforms proposed by the Soviets before World War II. In his 1936 novel *Pusztak nepe* (translation published as *People From the Puszta*), the Hungarian dissident denounced the living conditions of Hungarian peasants. Illyes took refuge in the underground during the Nazi occupation of his homeland. He then served as a member of the Hungarian Parliament until the Communist takeover in 1948. He avoided persecution by agreeing to produce only non-political works. Though Illyes appeared to comply, many of his writings contained subversive criticisms of the Communist regime. During the uprising of 1956 he published the inflammatory poem *Egy mondat a zsarnioksagrol* (translation published as *One Sentence on Tyranny*), which indicted the leadership of Matyas Rakosi. In spite of this criticism of Communist rule, Illyes's stature was such that authorities were unable to reprimand him for fear of sparking further conflict. Illyes ceased writing in the late 1950's to protest the imprisonment of other writers, and he remained silent until their release in 1960. Illyes was admired in Hungary for both his courage and his conviction under oppressive rule. In addition to his politically-oriented works, Illyes's writings include a retelling of several Hungarian folktales, published in England as *Once Upon a Time*, and several collections of poetry whose English titles include *You Cannot Escape* and *The Wonder Castle*. Obituaries and other sources: *Cassell's Encyclopaedia of World Literature*, revised edition, Morrow, 1973; *World Authors: 1950-1970*, H. W. Wilson, 1975; *International Who's Who in Poetry*, 5th edition, Melrose Press, 1977; *New York Times*, April 17, 1983; *London Times*, April 18, 1983; *Washington Post*, April 18, 1983.

* * *

INDELMAN, Elchanan Chonon 1908(?)-1983

OBITUARY NOTICE: Born May 22, 1908 (some sources say 1910 or 1913), in Zuromin, Poland; died of a stroke, April 21, 1983, in New York, N.Y. Educator, editor, and poet. Indelman was professor of Hebrew language and literature at Yeshiva University and Herzliah Hebrew Teachers Institute. Editor of two Hebrew publications, *Lamishpaha* and the children's magazine *Olam Hadash*, the scholar also wrote plays, essays, fiction, and several volumes of poetry in Hebrew and Yiddish, including *Shir Li* and *B'hatzrot Yalduti*. Obituaries and other sources: *Who's Who in World Jewry: A Biographical Dictionary of Outstanding Jews*, Olive Press, 1978; *Who's Who in American Jewry*, Standard Who's Who, 1980, *New York Times*, April 28, 1983.

* * *

INGRAHAM, Mark H(oyt) 1896-1982

OBITUARY NOTICE—See index for *CA* sketch: Born March 19, 1896, in Brooklyn, N.Y.; died November 14, 1982, in Madison, Wis. Educator and author. Ingraham had long been associated with the University of Wisconsin—Madison. He began there as an instructor in 1919 and retired in 1966 as dean of the College of Letters and Sciences and as emeritus professor of mathematics. His works include the biography *Charles Sumner Slichter: The Golden Vector*. Obituaries and other sources: *Chronicle of Higher Education*, January 5, 1983.

ISAKSSON, Ulla (Margareta Lundberg) 1916-

BRIEF ENTRY: Born June 12, 1916, in Stockholm, Sweden. Swedish screenwriter, novelist, and poet. Isaksson wrote the screenplay for "The Virgin Spring" (1959), the Oscar-winning film directed by Ingmar Bergman. She has written at least one dozen novels, including *The Blessed Ones* (Luce, 1970), which appeared in English translation. *Biographical/critical sources: New York Times Book Review*, December 20, 1970.

* * *

ISRAEL, Jonathan I. 1946-

PERSONAL: Born January 22, 1946, in London, England; son of David S. (a businessman) and Miriam (Pitel) Israel; married Jenny T. Winckel (a secretary), January 19, 1975; children: Daniel L. *Education:* Queens' College, Cambridge, B.A. (first class honors), 1967; graduate study at St. Antony's College, Oxford, 1967 and 1970, and Colegio de Mexico, 1968-69. *Religion:* Jewish. *Home:* 48 Parkside Dr., Edgware, Middlesex, England. *Office:* University College, London, Gower St., London W.C.1, England.

CAREER: University of Newcastle upon Tyne, Newcastle upon Tyne, England, research fellow, 1970-72; University of Hull, Hull, England, lecturer, 1972-73; University of London, University College, London, England, lecturer, 1974—, reader in history, 1982—. *Member:* Jewish Historical Society of England (honorary secretary, 1974-79), Nederlands Historisch Genootschap (Utrecht).

WRITINGS: Race, Class, and Politics in Colonial Mexico: 1610-1670, Oxford University Press, 1975; *The Dutch Republic and the Hispanic World: 1606-1661*, Oxford University Press, 1982. Contributor of articles to Dutch, German, Spanish, and British historical journals and of reviews to *Times Literary Supplement*.

WORK IN PROGRESS: Oxford History of the Dutch Republic, completion expected in 1990.

SIDELIGHTS: The Dutch Republic and the Hispanic World: 1606-1661 is about economic and political events that resulted in new Dutch-Spanish relations at the end of the Eighty Years War. Israel's thesis relies on an "analysis of political events in the light of economic trends and vice versa," C. H. Wilson explained in the *Times Literary Supplement*. Wilson continued: "No one will doubt that his achievement is of remarkable quality. His range and mastery of primary sources, in Spanish, Dutch, French, German, Italian and English alone establishes his claim to be an international historian of high order." "This is a brave history," Wilson wrote, and "Dr. Israel is to be congratulated on a work of research as elegant as it is arduous."

Israel told *CA:* "I believe that we are now at a new stage in the writing of history which will transcend the old, habitual separation of political from socioeconomic history. Increasingly, it is being realized that what is now most needed in the domain of history writing is to bring out the interactions between fields which, hitherto, have been deliberately and artificially kept apart. Before long, the work of the 'Braudelians' is going to seem thoroughly old-fashioned."

BIOGRAPHICAL/CRITICAL SOURCES: Times Literary Supplement, October 15, 1982.

ISRAEL, Martin 1927-

PERSONAL: Born April 30, 1927, in Johannesburg, South Africa; son of Elie Benjamin (an eye surgeon) and Minnie (Israel) Israel. *Education:* University of the Witwatersrand, M.B., Ch.B., 1949. *Home and office:* 26 Tregunter Rd., London SW10 9LS, England. *Agent:* Edward England, 12 Highlands Close, Crowborough, Sussex, England.

CAREER: Ordained Anglican priest, 1975. Royal College of Surgeons, London, England, lecturer, 1957-69, senior lecturer in pathology, 1969—. Priest in charge of Holy Trinity and All Saints Church, London. *Military service:* British Army, Royal Army Medical Corps, pathologist, 1955-57.

WRITINGS: (With J. B. Walter) *General Pathology,* Churchill-Livingstone, 1963, 5th edition, 1979; (contributor) Arnold Toynbee, editor, *Life After Death,* Weidenfield & Nicolson, 1976; *Smouldering Fire: The Work of the Holy Spirit,* Crossroad, 1981; *The Pain That Heals: The Place of Suffering in the Growth of the Person,* Crossroad, 1981; *Living Alone: The Inward Journey to Fellowship,* Crossroad, 1982; *The Spirit of Counsel,* Crossroad, 1983. Contributor to magazines.

SIDELIGHTS: "My movement towards ordination later in life was the natural consummation of my work in the areas of counseling and healing, which I had been practicing since 1963 as a sideline. The two vocations complement one another: pathology provides the rigorous intellectual discipline necessary to balance the more mystical side of religion and psychical research. My work in pathology goes on unimpeded, to the benefit of those around me and to God's glory. The message of my books is that man is a spiritual being and is fulfilled only in the worship of God, in whose image he was created."

IVORY, James (Francis) 1928-

BRIEF ENTRY: Born June 7, 1928, in Berkeley, Calif. American director of motion pictures and screenwriter. Ivory is best known as director of several motion pictures written with novelist R. Prawer Jhabvala and produced by Ismail Merchant. The three-way partnership began in 1969 when Ivory arrived in India to film a documentary commissioned by the Asia Society. He completed two such works before collaborating with Jhabvala on "Shakespeare Wallah" (1965), a tongue-in-cheek depiction of hollow conventions and values in an English theatre troupe traveling through India. The film proved a surprising critical success, but Ivory and Jhabvala were unable to match its acclaim with either of two successive collaborations. In 1971 Ivory returned to the United States to direct "Savages," an often sardonic allegory of evolving civilization as represented in a tribal environment. Ivory has subsequently devoted his talents to additional Indian subjects, including the film "Hullabaloo Over Georgie and Bonnie's Pictures" (1978), and American stories such as "The Wild Party" (1975), a film reportedly based on the Fatty Arbuckle scandal, and "Roseland" (1977), a three-part movie set in an old ballroom. In 1979 Ivory directed an adaptation of Henry James's novel *The Europeans.* Ivory also edited *Autobiography of a Princess: Also Being the Adventures of an American Film Director in the Land of the Maharajas* (Harper, 1975). *Address:* 400 East 52nd St., New York, N.Y. 10022. *Biographical/critical sources: A Biographical Dictionary of Film,* Morrow, 1976; *World Literature Today,* winter, 1977.

J

JACKSON, David Cooper 1931-

PERSONAL: Born in 1931; married Roma Pendergast. *Education:* Brasenose College, Oxford, B.A., 1953, B.C.L., 1954. *Office:* Faculty of Law, University of Southampton, Southampton, Hampshire, England.

CAREER: Called to the Bar, Inner Temple, London, England, and Victoria, Australia; barrister at law in London, 1958-62; University of Singapore, Singapore, senior lecturer in law, 1963-64; Monash University, Clayton, Australia, senior lecturer, 1964-65, Sir John Latham Professor of Law, 1965-70; University of Southampton, Southampton, England, professor of law, 1971—. Justice of the peace, 1980—. Consultant to United Nations Conference on Trade and Development. *Military service:* British Army, 1957-59.

WRITINGS: *Principles of Property Law,* Law Book Co., 1967; *Conflicts Process,* Oceana, 1975; *Enforcement of Maritime Claims,* Lloyds of London Press, 1982. Contributor to law journals.

WORK IN PROGRESS: A book on property law; research on maritime law, particularly ship financing.

*   *   *

JACKSON, Jesse 1908-1983

OBITUARY NOTICE—See index for *CA* sketch: Born January 1, 1908, in Columbus, Ohio; died April 14, 1983, in Boone, N.C. Author. Jackson was a noted black author of children's books. His first novel, *Call Me Charlie,* is his best-known work. First published in 1945, the novel chronicles a black boy's experiences in an all-white school. Jackson's other books include *Make a Joyful Noise Unto the Lord!: The Life of Mahalia Jackson* and *Black in America: A Fight for Freedom,* both of which won Carter G. Woodson awards. He also wrote *The Sickest Don't Always Die the Quickest* and *Room for Randy.* Obituaries and other sources: *Publishers Weekly,* June 3, 1983.

*   *   *

JACKSON, R(ichard) Eugene 1941-

PERSONAL: Born February 25, 1941, in Helena, Ark.; son of Howard L. (a steamfitter) and Edna (Warren) Jackson; children: Brandon D. *Education:* Memphis State University, B.S., 1963; Kent State University, M.A., 1964; Southern Illinois University, Ph.D., 1971. *Home:* 1901 Oakleaf Ct., Mobile, Ala. 36609. *Office:* Drama Department, University of South Alabama, Mobile, Ala. 36688.

CAREER: Teacher of English, speech, and drama at high school in Antwerp, Ohio, 1964-65; Wisconsin State University—Eau Claire (now University of Wisconsin—Eau Claire), instructor in drama, 1967-68; San Francisco State University, San Francisco, Calif., assistant professor of drama, 1968-70; University of South Alabama, Mobile, assistant professor, 1971-75, associate professor, 1975-78, professor of drama, 1980—, chairman of department of dramatic arts, 1978—. Director of numerous local and university theatre productions, including "The Imaginary Invalid," "Promises, Promises," and "Cat on a Hot Tin Roof."

MEMBER: American Theatre Association, Southeastern Theatre Conference (chairman of children's theatre division, 1979-80), Alabama Theatre League, Dramatists Guild, Mobile Jaycees, Phi Kappa Phi. *Awards, honors:* Winner of several local and university playwriting contests; "No Way" selected first alternate in O'Neill Playwriting Contest, 1973; winner of Pioneer Drama Service national playwriting contest, 1979, for "Brer Rabbit's Big Secret," and 1980, for "Snowhite and the Space Gwarfs."

WRITINGS—For children and teenagers, except as noted; published plays: *Ferdinand and the Dirty Knight* (two-act comedy; first produced by Kent State University in Kent, Ohio, at University Theatre, June, 1964), Pioneer Drama Service, 1968; *Little Red Riding Wolf* (three-act; first produced by Pixie Players in Mobile, Ala., at Pixie Playhouse), I. E. Clark, 1973; *Who Can Fix the Dragon's Wagon* (two-act; first produced by University of Wisconsin—Eau Claire at University Theatre, November, 1967), I. E. Clark, 1974; *Triple Play* (one-act), Dramatic Publishing, 1974; *The Creepy Castle Hassle* (three-act; first produced by Little Theatre Company in Mobile at Pixie Playhouse), Performance Publishing, 1975; *The Crazy Paper Caper* (three-act; first produced in Mobile at Pillans School Theatre), Performance Publishing, 1976; "Snowballs and Grapevines" (one-act; first produced by University of South Alabama in Mobile at Bethel Theatre, 1973), published in *Dekalb Literary Arts Journal,* summer, 1976; *The Wonderful Wizard of Oz* (three-act; first produced by Pixie Players in Mobile at Pixie Playhouse, 1975), I. E. Clark, 1976; (and lyricist) *The Sleeping Beauty* (two-act musical; first produced by Children's Musical Theatre in Mobile, 1975), Pioneer Drama Service, 1976; *Rumpelstiltskin Is My Name* (two-act), I. E. Clark, 1977; (with Susan Snider Osterberg) *Bumper Snickers* (two-act), I. E. Clark, 1978; (and lyricist) *Brer Rabbit's Big Secret* (two-act musical; first produced by Children's Musical Theatre in Mobile, October 1, 1978), Pioneer Drama Service, 1979.

Superkid (three-act), I. E. Clark, 1980; *A Golden Fleecing* (three-act; first produced by Alabama State Parks System in Gulf Shores, Ala., at State Park Theatre, June 1, 1980), Pioneer Drama Service, 1980; (and lyricist) *Snowhite and the Space Gwarfs* (two-act musical; first produced by Children's Musical Theatre in Mobile, October 1, 1980), Pioneer Drama Service, 1980; *Rag Dolls* (two-act), I. E. Clark, 1981; (and lyricist) *Lindy* (three-act musical), Performance Publishing, 1981; *The Adventures of Peter Cottontail* (two-act; first produced by Children's Musical Theatre in Mobile, summer, 1979), Pioneer Drama Service, 1981; (and lyricist) *The Hatfields and the McFangs* (two-act; first produced by Children's Musical Theatre in Mobile, October 1, 1981), Performance Publishing, 1982; *Unidentified Flying Reject* (three-act), I. E. Clark, 1982; *Coffee Pott and the Wolf Man* (three-act), I. E. Clark, 1982; *Animal Krackers* (two-act; first produced by Children's Musical Theatre in Mobile, October 1, 1981), Pioneer Drama Service, 1983.

Unpublished plays: "Carbolic Acid Is Not as Sweet as White Ribbons" (two-act; for adults), first produced in Memphis at Memphis Little Theatre, August, 1963; "A Thousand and One Spells to Cast" (two-act), first produced by Kent State University in Kent, Ohio, at University Theatre, June, 1964; "Sticks and Stones" (two-act), first produced at Memphis Little Theatre, August, 1964; "Mother Goose Follies" (two-act), first produced by Southern Illinois University in Carbondale, September, 1971. Also author of "Felicia and the Magic Pinks" (two-act), first produced by Pixie Players in Mobile at Pixie Playhouse.

Author of several as yet unpublished and unproduced plays. Also author of lyrics for numerous musical plays produced by Children's Musical Theatre. Contributor of articles to *Children's Theatre Review*.

WORK IN PROGRESS: "Super Snooper," a musical play for teens, *The Dog Ate My Homework,* a novel for teens, and "The Hunting of the Snark," a musical play for children, completion of all expected in 1983.

SIDELIGHTS: Jackson told *CA:* "I have a special interest in writing, whether plays or stories, for young folks. Other than teaching, a vocation I love, writing is simply an undeniable passion."

*　　*　　*

JACKSON, Robert Louis 1923-

PERSONAL: Born November 10, 1923, in New York, N.Y.; son of Eugene (a modern languages teacher) and Ella (an art teacher and painter; maiden name, Fred) Jackson; married Elizabeth Gillette (a painter), July 28, 1951; children: Emily Robin, Kathy Ellen. *Education:* Cornell University, B.A., 1944; Columbia University, M.A., 1949, certificate of the Russian Institute, 1949; University of California, Berkeley, Ph.D., 1956. *Office:* Box 3, Hall of Graduate Studies, Yale University, New Haven, Conn. 06520.

CAREER: Yale University, New Haven, Conn., assistant professor, 1959-62, associate professor, 1962-67, professor of Russian literature, 1967—. *Member:* International Dostoevsky Society (president), International Chekhov Society (president), North American Dostoevsky Society (president, 1970—), Modern Language Association of America, American Association of Teachers of Slavic and East European Languages, American Association for the Advancement of Slavic Studies, Vyacheslav I. Ivanov Convivium (president). *Awards, honors:* Grant from Inter-University Committee for Moscow, U.S.S.R., 1967; Guggenheim fellowship, 1967-68; National Endowment for the Humanities fellowship, 1974-75.

WRITINGS: Dostoevsky's Underground Man in Russian Literature, Mouton, 1958, 2nd edition, Greenwood Press, 1981; *Dostoevsky's Quest for Form: A Study of His Philosophy of Art,* Yale University Press, 1966, 2nd edition, Physsardt, 1974; (editor and author of introduction) *Chekhov: A Collection of Critical Essays,* Prentice-Hall, 1967; (editor and author of introduction) *Crime and Punishment: A Collection of Critical Essays,* Prentice-Hall, 1974; *The Art of Dostoevsky: Deliriums and Nocturnes,* Princeton University Press, 1981; (editor and author of introduction) *Dostoevsky II: A Collection of Critical Essays,* Prentice-Hall, in press.

WORK IN PROGRESS: Configurations: Comparative Essays on Dostoevsky and Russian and European Writers, publication expected in 1984.

BIOGRAPHICAL/CRITICAL SOURCES: Russian Review, July, 1967; *Times Literary Supplement,* June 4, 1982.

*　　*　　*

JACOBSON, Bernard Isaac 1936-

PERSONAL: Born March 2, 1936, in London, England; son of Cecil and Paula Jacobson; married Bonnie Brodsky (an editor), August 11, 1968 (divorced, 1982); married Laura Belcove (a physician), January 3, 1983; children: (first marriage) Katharine Elizabeth, Samuel Alexander. *Education:* Corpus Christi College, Oxford, B.A., 1960. *Politics:* Social Democrat. *Religion:* None. *Home:* 31 Cranbourne Rd., London N.10, England. *Agent:* Jacqueline Korn, David Higham Associates Ltd., 5-8 Lower John St., Golden Sq., London W1R 4HA, England. *Office:* Boosey & Hawkes Ltd., 295 Regent St., London W1R 8JH, England.

CAREER: Philips Phonographic Industries (now Phonogram), Baarn, Netherlands, writer for record album covers, 1960-62; EMI International, London, England, classical promotion officer, 1962-64; free-lance writer and broadcaster in New York, 1964-67; *Chicago Daily News,* Chicago, Ill., music critic, 1967-73; Southern Arts Association, Winchester, England, director, 1973-76; free-lance writer and lecturer in Wymondham, Norfolk, England, 1976-79; Boosey & Hawkes Ltd. (music publisher), London, deputy director of publications, 1979-81; director of promotion, 1982—. Visiting professor at Roosevelt University, 1972. Member of music panel of Illinois Arts Council, 1969-73. Television and radio broadcaster in the United States and England. *Awards, honors:* M.A. from Oxford University, 1962.

WRITINGS: (Contributor) Alan Walker, editor, *Frederic Chopin,* Barrie & Rockliff, 1964, Taplinger, 1966; (editor with David Dougas, and contributor) *The Arts in America,* Standing Conference of Regional Art Associations, 1976; *The Music of Johannes Brahms,* Fairleigh Dickinson University Press, 1977; (editor) *Conductors on Conducting,* Columbia Publishing, 1979;

(editor) *Singers on Singing*, Volume I, Columbia Publishing, 1983.

Recordings: (Narrator) Arnold Schoenberg, *Ode to Napoleon* (first performed in United States, 1967; performed in London, 1980), released by Nonesuch Records, 1967.

Music correspondent for *London Times, Manchester Guardian, Opera, Music and Musicians, Opera News,* and *Records and Recording;* Chicago correspondent for *Musical Times* and *American Choral Review.* Contributor to *Encyclopaedia Britannica, New Grove Dictionary of Music and Musicians,* and *Dictionary of Twentieth-Century Music.* Contributor to music journals. Contributing editor of *High Fidelity* and *Musical America,* both 1965-68, and *Stereo Review,* 1970-73.

WORK IN PROGRESS: Andrzej Panufnik.

SIDELIGHTS: Jacobson's *Conductors on Conducting* is a collection of interviews in which conductors speak on composers with whom they identify. The book, noted Joseph McLellan in his *Washington Post Book World* review, "gives a lucid picture of what is happening in the mind behind the baton as well as the special qualities of various composers."

Jacobson told *CA:* "The idea of *Conductors on Conducting* arose out of conversations with my publisher Bernard Rabb, who runs Columbia Publishing Company and who is an exceptionally imaginative and creative man as well as being the most meticulous and sympathetic editor a writer could wish for. I had long wanted to produce a manual of performing style, essentially a practical book for musicians. The idea of casting it in the form of interviews gave it, we felt, an interest for listeners, too. *Singers on Singing* is next in what could be a long series; I was late with it (a phrase that may ring bells with other writers), but I hope eventually to repay Bernard for all his patience.

"Working now for a music publisher is something I enjoy greatly because it's constructive, and it was the constructive side of criticism that I always found most satisfying. I feel that critics should not see themselves as on the 'other side' from composers and performers, but as fellow servants of the same art and the same public in the pursuit of improving standards and increasing enjoyment. (Pleasure, incidentally, is a key factor for me in the approach to any art: This ought to be a truism, but, intellectual fashions being what they are today, I don't think it is.) I combine my publishing activity with a good deal of general writing (but not criticism because of the potential conflict of interest) and with lecturing, teaching, and broadcasting, all of which I love and learn much from."

BIOGRAPHICAL/CRITICAL SOURCES: Washington Post Book World, December 13, 1979.

*   *   *

JACOBSON, Gary Charles 1944-

PERSONAL: Born July 7, 1944, in Santa Ana, Calif.; son of Charles William and Ruth Hope (Brown) Jacobson; married Martha Ellen Blake (a research technician), June 2, 1979. *Education:* Stanford University, A.B. (with honors), 1966; Yale University, M.Phil., 1969, Ph.D., 1972. *Residence:* San Diego, Calif. *Office:* Department of Political Science, Q-060, University of California, San Diego, La Jolla, Calif. 92093.

CAREER: University of California, Riverside, lecturer in political science, 1968; Trinity College, Hartford, Conn., instructor in political science, 1970-72; Yale University, New Haven,

Conn., visiting assistant professor of political science, 1973; Trinity College, assistant professor, 1972-76, associate professor of political science, 1976-79; University of California, San Diego, La Jolla, associate professor of political science, 1979—. Member of campaign finance study group at Institute of Politics, John F. Kennedy School of Government, Harvard University, 1977—; member of Committee on Congressional Election Research of National Election Studies, 1978—.

MEMBER: American Political Science Association, Public Choice Society, Midwest Political Science Association, Western Political Science Association, Southern Political Science Association. *Awards, honors:* National Science Foundation grant, 1980-82; Gladys M. Kammerer Award from American Political Science Association, 1980, for *Money in Congressional Elections.*

WRITINGS: Money in Congressional Elections, Yale University Press, 1980; (with William Crotty) *American Parties in Decline,* Little, Brown, 1980; (with Samuel Kernell) *Strategy and Choice in Congressional Elections,* Yale University Press, 1981; *The Politics of Congressional Elections,* Little, Brown, 1983.

Contributor: Herbert C. Alexander, editor, *Political Finance,* Sage Publications, 1979; *An Analysis of the Impact of the Federal Election Campaign Act, 1972-1978,* U.S. Government Printing Office, 1979; Crotty, editor, *Paths to Political Reform,* Lexington Books, 1980; Louis Maisel and Joseph Cooper, editors, *Congressional Elections,* Sage Publications, 1981; Dennis Hale, editor, *The United States Congress: Proceedings of the Thomas P. O'Neill, Jr., Symposium on the U.S. Congress, January 30-31, 1981,* Boston College, 1982; Raymond E. Wolfinger, editor, *Readings on Congress,* 2nd edition, Prentice-Hall, 1983; Michael J. Malbin, editor, *Parties, Interest Groups and Money in the 1980 Elections,* American Enterprise Institute for Public Policy Research, 1983. Contributor to political science journals.

WORK IN PROGRESS: Continuing research on congressional elections and campaign finance.

BIOGRAPHICAL/CRITICAL SOURCES: New York Times Book Review, April 13, 1980; *Washington Post Book World,* June 22, 1980; *Annals of the American Academy of Political and Social Science,* September, 1980, July, 1981; *Encounter,* December, 1980; *Political Science Quarterly,* winter, 1980-81.

*   *   *

JAMES, Bill
See JAMES, George W(illiam)

*   *   *

JAMES, Dorothy Buckton 1937-

BRIEF ENTRY: American political scientist, educator, and author. James became a professor of political science at Virginia Polytechnic Institute and State University in 1974. She has also taught at Hunter College and Herbert H. Lehman College, both of the City University of New York. Her books include *The Contemporary Presidency* (Pegasus, 1969), *Outside Looking In: Critiques of American Policies and Institutions, Left and Right* (Harper, 1972), *Poverty, Politics, and Change* (Prentice-Hall, 1972), *The Political Science of Poverty and Welfare* (Policy Studies, 1974), and *Analyzing Poverty Policy* (Lexington Books, 1975). *Address:* Department of Political Science, Virginia Polytechnic Institute and State University, Blacksburg, Va. 24061.

*   *   *

JAMES, George W(illiam)   1949-
(Bill James)

PERSONAL: Born October 5, 1949, in Holton, Kan.; son of George L. and Mildred (Burks) James; married Susan McCarthy (an artist), November 3, 1978. *Education:* University of Kansas, B.A., 1971, B.S., 1975. *Politics:* None. *Religion:* None. *Home address:* P.O. Box 171, Winchester, Kan. 66097. *Agent:* Liz Darhansoff, 1220 Park Ave., New York, N.Y. 10022. *Office address:* P.O. Box 2150, Lawrence, Kan. 66044.

CAREER: High school English teacher in small towns in Kansas, 1973-75; Pinkerton's, Lawrence, Kan., night watchman, 1974-77; Stokely Van Camp, Lawrence, boiler attendant, 1977-79. *Military service:* U.S. Army, 1971-73. *Member:* Society for American Baseball Research.

WRITINGS—Under name Bill James; "The Baseball Abstract" series; privately printed, except as noted: *The Baseball Abstract: 1977*, 1977; *. . . 1978*, 1978; *. . . 1979*, 1979; *. . . 1980*, 1980; *. . . 1981*, 1981; *The Bill James Baseball Abstract: 1982*, Ballantine, 1982; *The Bill James Baseball Abstract: 1983*, Ballantine, 1983.

Editor of *Baseball Analyst;* contributing editor of *Inside Sports*.

SIDELIGHTS: James wrote: "My profession is analyzing the game of baseball and writing about the results. When I began writing in 1975, I wrote about baseball because it was the only thing that I knew anything about. I began doing studies of certain small issues within the game so that I would have something to say that hadn't been said before, and I gradually moved more or less exclusively toward that type of work.

"Sabermetrics is the development and adaptation of statistics toward answering questions. To say where it is useful to the fan . . . well, baseball has so many records of so many things that when you begin to apply the records to the questions there isn't anywhere that they don't reach. Evaluating strategy and evaluating players are the obvious things, but baseball has an immense dogma, known lovingly as 'the book,' which covers things that people say about games, things that people say about pennant races, about ball parks, about positions, about front offices, about skill, about trades. What do you see when you hold all of these things up to the light? That's sabermetrics— figuring out ways to hold them up to the light."

BIOGRAPHICAL/CRITICAL SOURCES: Sports Illustrated, May 25, 1981; *Washington Post Book World*, May 23, 1982; *New York Times Book Review*, May 23, 1982, June 6, 1982; *Los Angeles Times Book Review*, September 19, 1982.

*   *   *

JAMES, Robert A.   1946-1983

OBITUARY NOTICE: Born in 1946; drowned March 20, 1983, off the west coast of England. Yachtsman and author. An expert seaman married to Naomi James, the first woman mariner to single-handedly circumnavigate the globe, Robert James wrote a textbook on long-distance sailing. Obituaries and other sources: *Chicago Tribune*, March 22, 1983.

JAMES, William   1842-1910

BRIEF ENTRY: Born January 11, 1842, in New York, N.Y.; died August 26, 1910, in Chocorua, N.H. American educator, philosopher, psychologist, and author. The son of theologian Henry James and elder brother of novelist Henry James, Jr., William James taught physiology, psychology, and philosophy at Harvard University for thirty-five years. He also modified the movement in philosophy known as pragmatism, which maintains that "the true . . . is only the expedient in our way of thinking." For example, if one's belief in God results in peace and happiness, then God is true; one accepts the belief that works best. James also helped formulate the James-Lange theory of emotion, which poses that emotional control is achieved through the control of physical responses because "we feel sorry because we cry, angry because we strike, afraid because we tremble." The philosopher's postulations influenced numerous writers of his day, including his brother Henry, Bertrand Russell, and Oliver Wendell Holmes. Among James's books are *The Principles of Psychology* (1890), *The Will to Believe, and Other Essays in Popular Philosophy* (1897), *The Varieties of Religious Experience: A Study in Human Nature* (1902), and *Memories and Studies* (1911). *Residence:* Chocorua, N.H. *Biographical/critical sources:* Ralph Barton Perry, *The Thought and Character of William James*, Little, Brown, 1935; *The Oxford Companion to American Literature*, 4th edition, Oxford University Press, 1965; *The McGraw-Hill Encyclopedia of World Biography*, McGraw, 1973; Patrick Kiaran Dooley, *Pragmatism as Humanism: The Philosophy of William James*, Nelson-Hall, 1975; *Twentieth-Century Literary Criticism*, Volume 11, Gale, 1983.

*   *   *

JARRIEL, Thomas Edwin   1934-
(Tom Jarriel)

BRIEF ENTRY: Born December 29, 1934, in La Grange, Ga. American journalist. Jarriel joined the American Broadcasting Companies (ABC-TV) in 1965, serving first as news correspondent and later as White House correspondent. Since 1975 he has served as anchor of the Sunday edition of "ABC Weekend News." In 1961 Jarriel won the National Press Photographers Association Columbia Journalism first-place award for his newsfilm of hurricane *Carla*. *Address:* 1124 Connecticut Ave. N.W., Washington, D.C. 20036. *Biographical/critical sources: Who's Who in America*, 40th edition, Marquis, 1978.

*   *   *

JARRIEL, Tom
See JARRIEL, Thomas Edwin

*   *   *

JAY, Peter   1937-

PERSONAL: Born February 7, 1937, in London, England; son of Douglas Patrick Thomas and Margaret Christian (Garnett) Jay; married Margaret Ann Callaghan (a television journalist), 1961; children: Tamsin, Alice, Patrick. *Education:* Christ Church, Oxford, M.A. (first class honors), 1960. *Home:* 39 Castlebar Rd., London W5 2DJ, England. *Office:* Breakfast Television Centre, Hawley Cres., London NW1 8EF, England.

CAREER: Her Majesty's Treasury, London, England, assistant principal, 1961-64, principal, 1964-67; *London Times*, London, economics editor, 1967-77, associate editor of *Times Busi-*

ness News, 1969-77; Independent Television (ITV), London, presenter of "Weekend World," 1972-77, and "The Jay Interview," 1975-77; British ambassador to the United States, 1977-79; chairman of TV-AM Ltd. Director of *Economist* Intelligence Unit and New National Theater, Washington, D.C.; chairman of National Council of Voluntary Organisations. *Military service:* Royal Naval Volunteer Reserve, 1956-57; became sub-lieutenant. *Member:* Royal Naval Sailing Association, Garrick Club, Royal Cork Yacht Club. *Awards, honors:* Harold Wincott Award for financial and economic journalism, 1973; named Political Broadcaster of the Year, 1973; named Male Personality of the Year by Royal TV Society, 1974; Shell International TV Award, 1974; D.H. from Ohio State University, 1978; D. Litt. from Wake Forest University, 1979.

WRITINGS: (Editor) *The Budget: A Collection of Documents,* Jackdaw Publications, 1972; (contributor) W. P. Bundy, editor, *America and the World, 1979,* Pergamon, 1981. Also contributor to *Foreign Affairs,* 1980. Author of a weekly column in *London Times,* 1981. Contributor to *Economist.*

WORK IN PROGRESS: The Crisis of the Political Economy in the West.

AVOCATIONAL INTERESTS: Sailing.

* * *

JEEF, Kalle
   See TSHIAMALA, Kabasele

* * *

JEFFREYS, Harold   1891-

PERSONAL: Born April 22, 1891, in Fatfield, England; son of Robert Hal and Elizabeth Mary Jeffreys; married Bertha Swirles (a lecturer and researcher), September 6, 1940. *Education:* University of Durham, B.Sc., 1910, D.Sc., 1917; St. John's College, Cambridge, B.A. (with honors), 1913, M.A., 1917. *Politics:* Liberal. *Home:* 160 Huntingdon Rd., Cambridge CB3 0LB, England.

CAREER: Cambridge University, Cambridge, England, fellow of St. John's College, 1914—, lecturer in mathematics, 1922-31, reader in geophysics, 1931-46, Plumian Professor of Astronomy, 1946-58. Professional assistant at Meteorological Office, 1917-22. British delegate to International Union of Geodesy and Geophysics ten times from 1922 to 1963; honorary director of International Seismological Summary, 1946-57; past member of National Committee for Geodesy and Geophysics and its seismology subcommittee; member of National Council for Astronomy and member of board of visitors at Royal Greenwich Observatory, 1955-57.

MEMBER: International Seismological Association (vice-president, 1933-36, 1951-54), International Association for Seismology and Physics of the Earth's Interior (president, 1960), Royal Society (fellow), Royal Astronomical Society (president, 1955-57), Royal Meteorological Society, Geological Society, National Academy of Sciences (United States; foreign associate), American Geological Society (foreign associate), American Geophysical Union (foreign associate), Accademia dei Lincei (Italy; foreign member), Academy of Science (Sweden; foreign member), Academy of Arts and Sciences (Massachusetts; foreign member), Royal Society of New Zealand (fellow), Academie Royale Scientifique Belgique (foreign member), Royal Society of London, Cambridge Philosophical

Society, London Mathematical Society, New York Academy of Sciences (foreign member).

AWARDS, HONORS: Buchan Prize from Royal Meteorological Society, 1929; gold medal from Royal Astronomical Society, 1937; Murchison Medal from Geological Society, 1939; Victoria Medal from Royal Geographical Society, 1942; Royal Medal from Royal Society, 1948; Ch. Lagrange prize from Brussels Academy, 1948; Bowie Medal from American Geophysical Union, 1952; created Knight Bachelor, 1953; honorary degrees from University of Liverpool, 1953, Trinity College, Dublin, 1956, University of Durham, 1960, Southern Methodist University, 1967, and University of Uppsala, 1977; Copley Medal from Royal Society, 1960; shared Vetlesen Prize for Geophysics from Columbia University, 1962; H. W. Wood Award from Carnegie Institution, 1963; Guy Medal in Gold from Royal Statistical Society, 1963; Wollaston Medal from Geological Society, 1964; medal from Seismological Society of America, 1979.

WRITINGS: The Earth: Its Origin, History, and Physical Constitution, Cambridge University Press, 1924, 6th edition, 1961; *Operational Methods in Mathematical Physics,* Cambridge University Press, 1927, 2nd edition, 1931; *The Future of the Earth,* Norton, 1929; *Scientific Inference,* Cambridge University Press, 1931, 3rd edition, 1973; *Cartesian Tensors,* Cambridge University Press, 1931, reprint, 1979; *Earthquakes and Mountains,* Methuen, 1935, 2nd edition, 1950; *Theory of Probability,* Oxford University Press, 1939, 3rd edition, 1961; (with Keith Edward Bullen) *Seismological Tables,* International Seismological Association, 1940, revised edition, 1958; (with wife, Bertha Jeffreys) *Methods of Mathematical Physics,* Cambridge University Press, 1946, 3rd edition, 1956; *Asymptotic Approximations,* Oxford University Press, 1962; (with B. Jeffreys) *Collected Papers on Geophysics and Other Sciences,* Gordon & Breach, Volume I: *Theoretical and Observational Seismology,* 1971, Volume II: *Observational Seismology,* 1975, Volume III: *Gravity,* 1975, Volume IV: *Dissipation of Energy and Thermal History,* 1975, Volume V: *Astronomy and Geophysics,* 1976, Volume VI: *Mathematics, Probability, and Miscellaneous Other Sciences,* 1977.

WORK IN PROGRESS: Research on earthquake travel times and tidal friction.

SIDELIGHTS: Harold Jeffreys wrote: "My interest in astronomy was acquired early through the works of Sir Robert Ball and G. F. Chambers. I was a keen naturalist from the age of nine. My undergraduate work was in mathematics, physics, chemistry, and geology. After taking my degree at Cambridge, I began research in dynamical astronomy. I discussed my work with Professor H. F. Newall, with Eddington, and, less often, with Larmor. I met E. P. Farrow, a plant physiologist, who introduced me to Karl Pearson's *Grammar of Science,* in my opinion the best general account of scientific method, first published in 1892. Pearson's treatment of scientific method as successive approximation to probability distributions can be regarded as leading to my work on probability. It was also owing to Farrow that I did some ecological work near my home in County Durham.

"My main interest became geophysics, and here the work of Sir George Darwin was my inspiration; although he was alive when I reached Cambridge, I did not meet him. With R. Stoneley I was active in promoting geophysics in the Royal Astronomical Society, and its *Geophysical Supplement* has now become the *Geophysical Journal.* Until the Second World War, my colleagues in the department at Cambridge were Sir Gerald

Lenox-Conyngham, E. C. Bullard (later Sir Edward), and B. C. Browne. An important step was the production in 1940 with K. E. Bullen of *Seismological Tables,* the travel times of earthquake waves. These are still a standard at the International Seismological Centre and are used as the basis for further work.

"For many years, I was regarded as a heretic by statisticians, but in 1963 the Royal Statistical Society gave me its Guy Medal. And a volume of essays on Bayesian analysis in econometrics and statistics was published in my honor by North-Holland Publishing in 1980.

"I was an opponent of Wegener's theory of continental drift and remain unconvinced by later work on plate tectonics. My arguments about this are contained in *The Earth* and in my collected papers."

* * *

JENKINS, Nancy (Harmon) 1937-
(Leonie St. John, a joint pseudonym)

PERSONAL: Born August 22, 1937, in Maine; daughter of Gilbert Gardner (a lawyer) and Dorothy (a teacher; maiden name, Thorndike) Harmon; married Loren Jenkins (a journalist), June, 1964; children: Sara, Nicholas. *Education:* Wellesely College, B.A., 1959; graduate work at American University of Beirut, 1971-73. *Home:* C.S. 125 Teverina, 52044 Cortona, Arezzo, Italy. *Agent:* Wallace & Sheil Agency, Inc., 177 East 70th St., New York, N.Y. 10021.

CAREER: Writer.

WRITINGS: (With W. S. Bayer, under joint pseudonym Leonie St. John) *Love With A Harvard Accent,* Ace, 1962; *The Boat Beneath the Pyramid* (nonfiction), Holt, 1980.

WORK IN PROGRESS: A nonfiction book about growth and change over several generations in a small New England town; a novel about nineteenth-century immigration to Palestine; a combination cookbook and discussion of Italian food and wine.

SIDELIGHTS: The Boat Beneath the Pyramid recounts the discovery and excavation of a 4,500-year-old ship discovered beneath the Great Pyramid of Egypt. Part of the tomb of King Cheops, the vessel consisted of 651 sections that were successfully reassembled and restored in the sixteen years following their discovery. Jenkins includes photographs of the ship's renovation and explains Egyptian religious and funerary beliefs that may account for the inclusion of the vessel in the tomb. Writing in the *Times Literary Supplement,* book reviewer Kenneth Kitchen observed that *The Boat Beneath the Pyramid* is "a reliable, readable popular account of one of the oldest and finest wooden ships in the world."

Jenkins told *CA:* "Although I am currently spending school terms in the United States (because of my children's educational needs), I consider a small village in Tuscany to be my permanent home. I have lived and worked and traveled in many parts of Europe, Asia, and the Middle East, writing about subjects as varied as the Arab trade with China during the Sung Dynasty and the planned villages of Egyptian architect Hassan Fathy, but Italian history and contemporary culture are the subjects I prefer."

BIOGRAPHICAL/CRITICAL SOURCES: Times Literary Supplement, October 31, 1980.

JESSUP, Michael H(yle) 1937-

BRIEF ENTRY: Born October 25, 1937, in Washington, D.C. American historian, social scientist, educator, and author. Jessup became a professor of education at Towson State University in 1972. He also teaches evening courses at Johns Hopkins University. Jessup co-authored *Discipline: Positive Attitudes for Learning* (Prentice-Hall, 1971). *Address:* Department of Secondary Education, Towson State University, Baltimore, Md. 21204.

* * *

JEZER, Marty 1940-

PERSONAL: Surname is pronounced *Jay-*zer; born November 21, 1940, in Bronx, N.Y.; son of Meyer (a lawyer) and Blanche (Litzky) Jezer; children: Kathryn Ruth. *Education:* Lafayette College, A.B., 1961; graduate study at Boston University, 1961-62. *Politics:* "Citizens' party." *Religion:* Jewish. *Home and office address:* R.D. 3, Box 160, Brattleboro, Vt. 05301.

CAREER: Gimbel's Department Store, New York City, advertising copywriter, 1963-65; Crowell-Collier Educational Corp., New York City, staff writer and editor of *Merit Student Encyclopedia,* 1964-67; farmer, 1968—. Solar technician with Solar Applications Co., 1979-82. Draft resistance organizer, 1967-69.

WRITINGS: (Editor of revision) *The Food Garden,* Signet, 1971; *Power for the People: Active Nonviolence in the United States,* Peace Press, 1977; *The Dark Ages: Life in the United States, 1945-1960,* South End Press, 1982.

Contributor: David Manning White and Robert Abel, editors, *The Funnies: An American Idiom,* Free Press, 1963; Alice Lynd, editor, *We Won't Go,* Beacon Press, 1968; Mitchell Goodman, editor, *Movement for a New America,* Knopf, 1970; Herbert H. Blumberg and A. Paul Hare, editors, *Nonviolent Direct Action,* Corpus, 1970; Richard Wizansky, editor, *Home Comfort: Life on the Total Loss Farm,* Saturday Review Press, 1974; Sally Freeman, editor, *The Green World,* Putnam, 1975; Jon Snodgrass, editor, *Men Against Sexism,* Times Change Press, 1977.

Contributor to magazines and newspapers, including *Progressive, New Republic, Saturday Review, Crawdaddy, Mother Earth News, In These Times, Music Journal,* and *Radical America.* Founder and editor of *Win,* 1966-74, member of editorial board, 1966—; contributing editor of *Liberation,* 1967-68.

WORK IN PROGRESS: A critical history of radical activism in the United States from 1960 to 1980; research on stuttering, based on his own experience as a stutterer; political essays on current events.

SIDELIGHTS: Jezer wrote: "I am a democratic socialist and a political activist; most of my writing is inspired by a commitment to progressive change. There's little money in that, so I do free-lance indexing and work on solar installations. As a writer, I prefer to concentrate on serious subjects and, if necessary, earn my living doing useful, healthy outdoor work (which has its own creative rewards). But I am not amiss to turning a buck with my pen."

* * *

JOHNSON, Dorris 1914-

PERSONAL: Born December 27, 1914, in Mississippi; daughter of James T. (a physician) and Lillian Belle (Darby) Bowdon; married Nunnally Johnson (a journalist and writer), February 4, 1940 (died March 25, 1977); children: Christie, Roxanna Lonergan, Scott. *Education:* Attended Southwestern College (now Southwestern at Memphis) and Louisiana State University. *Residence:* Beverly Hills, Calif. *Agent:* International Creative Management, 40 West 57th St., New York, N.Y. 10019.

CAREER: Twentieth Century-Fox, Westwood, Calif., 1938-45, actress in films, including "Young Mr. Lincoln," 1939, "Drums Along the Mohawk," 1939, "Grapes of Wrath," 1940, and "The Moon is Down," 1943.

WRITINGS: (Editor with Ellen Leventhal) *The Letters of Nunnally Johnson,* foreword by Alistair Cooke, Knopf, 1981.

SIDELIGHTS: In *The Letters of Nunnally Johnson,* Dorris Johnson and Ellen Leventhal present a selection of letters written by the successful film writer and journalist between 1944 and 1976. Nunnally Johnson wrote nearly seventy screenplays during his career, including "The Grapes of Wrath," and was "one of the handful of educated WASP's on whom Darryl Zanuck counted to write, produce, and direct the more sophisticated items in his vast annual output of motion pictures," John Houseman noted in the *New York Times Book Review.* "Now we learn he was a wonderful letter writer," stated Walter Clemons in *Newsweek.*

In the *New York Times,* John Leonard described Johnson's correspondence: "These are letters of surpassing charm, generous and whimsical, full of gossip and news of children, written to friends like Sullivan, Harold Ross, George S. Kaufman, James Thurber, Lauren Bacall, Helen Hayes and Groucho Marx; and written as well to strangers who wanted information—for books and magazine articles—about those friends. There isn't much here about money or betrayal or politics or literature, and no self-pity and no arrogance. We aren't talking here about a Scott Fitzgerald or a Dalton Trumbo. Nunnally Johnson was comfortable with himself." Yet Houseman regretted this lack of "personal and emotional reactions" in Johnson's letters, missing the more intense Johnson he had come to know in *Flashback,* Nora Johnson's account of her relationship with her screenwriter father. "This selection of letters seems to have been made with the limited but deliberate intention of presenting [Johnson] to the world mainly as a humorous and sophisticated commentator on the Hollywood scene," Houseman observed.

Critics agreed, however, that Nunnally Johnson was a "gifted, much-loved and loving man" and that *The Letters of Nunnally Johnson* is worthwhile reading. "Civilized fun" is what Leonard called the book. Daniel Fuchs of the *Chicago Tribune Book World* pronounced Johnson's stylish letters "a civilized man's way of speaking his mind without pestering or bludgeoning . . . wonderful." And Clemons found *Letters* "the most entertaining book" he had read about life in Hollywood in years. "This is a lovely book," he asserted. "A book twice this long would be welcome."

BIOGRAPHICAL/CRITICAL SOURCES: Chicago Tribune Book World, November 8, 1981; *New York Times Book Review,* November 22, 1981; *New York Times,* November 23, 1981; *Newsweek,* December 28, 1981.

*   *   *

JOHNSON, Richard D(avid) 1927-

PERSONAL: Born June 10, 1927, in Cleveland, Ohio; son of

Robert E. (in drafting) and Emma (Lindhorst) Johnson; married Harriett Herzog (a chemist), September 8, 1956; children: Ruth Ellen, Royce Emanuel. *Education:* Yale University, B.A., 1949; University of Chicago, M.A. in international relations, 1950, M.A. in library science, 1957. *Politics:* Republican. *Religion:* Presbyterian. *Home:* 2 Walling Blvd., Oneonta, N.Y. 13820. *Office:* James M. Milne Library, State University of New York College at Oneonta, Oneonta, N.Y. 13820.

CAREER: National Opinion Research Center, Chicago, Ill., librarian, 1956-57; Stanford University, Stanford, Calif., social science librarian, 1957-59, cataloger, 1959-62, head of Acquisitions Division, 1962-64, chief of undergraduate project, 1964-67, administrative assistant to the director of libraries, 1960-61, chief technical services librarian, 1967-68; Claremont Colleges, Claremont, Calif., director of libraries, 1968-73; State University of New York College at Oneonta, director of libraries, 1973—. Member of board of trustees of Four County Library System, Binghamton, N.Y., 1978—, vice-president, 1981—. *Military service:* U.S. Army, 1952-54; received Bronze Star.

MEMBER: American Library Association, Society for Scholarly Publishing, New York Library Association (second vice-president, 1982; president of Academic and Special Libraries Section, 1982), California Library Association (president, 1972). *Awards, honors:* H. W. Wilson Library Periodicals award from American Library Association, 1968, for editorship of *California Librarian;* fellowship from Council on Library Resources, 1972.

WRITINGS: (Editor) *Libraries for Teaching: Libraries for Research,* American Library Association, 1977; (editor with Robert D. Stueart) *New Horizons for Academic Libraries,* K. G. Saur, 1979. Editor of *California Librarian,* 1966-68, and *College and Research Libraries,* 1974-80; interim managing editor of *Journal of Library Automation,* 1980; acting editor of *Choice,* 1982.

WORK IN PROGRESS: An article to be published in *Advances in Librarianship.*

AVOCATIONAL INTERESTS: American musical theatre.

*   *   *

JOHNSON, Una E.

BRIEF ENTRY: Born in Dayton, Ohio. American museum curator and author. Johnson was a member of the staff of the Brooklyn Museum for more than twenty years. She was curator of prints and drawings from 1941 to 1969, and she was named curator emerita in 1969. Johnson spent the next two years at Storm King Art Center as curator of its collection. Her many books on art include *Twentieth Century Drawings* (Shorewood Publishers, 1964), *Paul Cadmus: Prints and Drawings, 1922-1967* (Brooklyn Museum, 1968), *Adja Yunkers: Prints, 1927-1967* (Brooklyn Museum, 1969), *Karl Schrag: A Catalogue Raisonne of the Graphic Works, 1939-1970* (School of Art, Syracuse University, 1971), and *American Prints and Printmakers: A Chronicle of Over Four Hundred Artists and Their Prints From 1900 to the Present* (Doubleday, 1980). *Address:* 341 West 24th St., New York, N.Y. 10011. *Biographical/critical sources: Who's Who in American Art,* Bowker, 1978; *New York Times Book Review,* December 14, 1980.

*   *   *

JOHNSTON, Mary 1870-1936

BRIEF ENTRY: Born November 21, 1870, in Buchanan, Va.;

died of cancer, May 9, 1936, near Warm Springs, Va. American author of historical novels. Influenced by the writings of Sir Walter Scott and Charlotte Yonge, Johnston produced her first historical novel, *Prisoners of Hope,* in 1898. Next came *To Have and to Hold* (1900), which tells the story of the women of Jamestown colony. Like several of the author's works, the novel was first serialized in a popular magazine; later, it was adapted into both a motion picture and a stage play. Twenty-one additional historical novels followed, which explored such diverse subjects as Henry VII's England, twelfth-century feudal France, and Christopher Columbus's voyage in 1492 to the New World. Johnston's two Civil War tales, *The Long Roll* (1911) and *Cease Firing* (1912), are ranked among the author's greatest achievements. *Biographical/critical sources: Who Was Who in America,* Volume I: *1897-1942,* Marquis, 1943; *The Oxford Companion to American Literature,* 4th edition, Oxford University Press, 1965; *Longman Companion to Twentieth Century Literature,* Longman, 1977; *Dictionary of Literary Biography,* Volume 9: *American Novelists, 1910-1945,* Gale, 1982.

*   *   *

JONES, Adam Mars
See MARS-JONES, Adam

*   *   *

JONES, Betty Millsaps   1940-

PERSONAL: Born June 23, 1940, in Chattanooga, Tenn.; daughter of Willard Newton (a teacher) and Lucille (a teacher; maiden name, Springfield) Millsaps; married William B. Jones (a college teacher), August 17, 1963; children: Bruce, Brad. *Education:* Vanderbilt University, B.A., 1962, M.A.T., 1963, M.A., 1965. *Religion:* Methodist. *Home:* 120 Convention Dr., Virginia Beach, Va. 23462. *Office:* Norfolk Collegiate School, 7336 Granby St., Norfolk, Va. 23505.

CAREER: English teacher at public schools in Nashville, Tenn., 1963-64; teacher of English and mathematics at private school in Charlotteville, Va., 1964-69; teacher of English and history at private school in Gainesville, Fla., 1970-75; Norfolk Collegiate School, Norfolk, Va., counselor and teacher, 1975—. *Member:* Authors Guild, Romance Writers of America, Society of Children's Book Writers, Delta Kappa Gamma.

WRITINGS—Juveniles: *Nancy Lieberman: Basketball's Magic Lady,* Harvey House, 1980; *Wonder Women of Sports,* Random House, 1981; *King Solomon's Mines* (adaptation), Random House, 1982.

Contributor of articles and reviews to *Highlights, Jack and Jill, Women's Sports, Scholastic Scope, Young Athlete,* and *Home Life.*

WORK IN PROGRESS: A book on women's basketball, publication expected in 1984; a historical novel, publication expected in 1985; research for a juvenile biography of Henry Knox, publication expected in 1985.

SIDELIGHTS: Betty Jones told *CA:* "At present I combine my writing with teaching, counseling, and motherhood. The keys to becoming a writer are belief in one's abilities, dedication, persistence, and a willingness to do market research.

"My first published work was a story in *Jack and Jill.* Approximately one thousand words long, it was written as a class assignment in a noncredit writing course taught by a local

writer. This instructor had much impact upon my writing career because she stressed that 'writers' must not only 'write': they must *submit* what they write to publishers.

"Two of my books and many of my magazine articles have dealt with sports. Although I did not play sports when I was in school, I have always been a sports fan. My father, who played professional baseball in the 1930's, was a tremendous influence upon me, and his intense interest in athletics was passed on to me. My first book, *Nancy Lieberman: Basketball's Magic Lady,* was contracted after I had written several articles about her. As the 1976 Olympian and as the 1979 and 1980 Wade Trophy winner, she led her Old Dominion University teammates (the Lady Monarchs) to two national championships. Since my husband is a professor at Old Dominion, I was able to follow her career closely.

"*King Solomon's Mines* is an adaptation of the nineteenth-century novel by H. Rider Haggard. Set in Africa, the book is an adventure story of a search for a fabulous treasure. The searchers must overcome the cruelties of nature as well as those of man before achieving their goal.

"A serious illness has limited my writing in recent months. However, I am now able to resume my writing and hope to complete a biography of Henry Knox within the next twelve months. I am also working on a historical novel but am finding the writing very, very 'slow going.' I greatly admire the historical novels of Roberta Gellis. Her erudition and craftsmanship are a powerful combination for which I have great respect."

*   *   *

JONES, C(lifton) Clyde   1922-

PERSONAL: Born December 21, 1922, in Huntington, W.Va.; son of Clifton Clark and Goldie (Williams) Jones; married Margaret Scheldrup, June 14, 1948; children: Karen (Mrs. E. P. Prevette), Kristin (Mrs. Eric W. Schoeff), Clifton. *Education:* Marshall University, B.A. (magna cum laude), 1944; Northwestern University, M.A., 1950, Ph.D., 1954. *Politics:* Republican. *Religion:* Presbyterian. *Home:* 2015 Rockhill Circle, Manhattan, Kan. 66502. *Office:* Department of Management, Kansas State University, Calvin Hall, Manhattan, Kan. 66506.

CAREER: Northwestern University, Evanston, Ill., instructor in business history, 1951-53; Georgia State College, Atlanta, assistant professor of economics, 1953-55; University of Illinois, Urbana, assistant professor, 1955-58, associate professor of economics, 1958-60; Kansas State University, Manhattan, professor of business administration, 1960—, head of department, 1960-62, dean of College of Commerce, 1962-67, vice-president for university development, 1966-70. Consultant with Development Planning and Research Associates. President of Manhattan Chamber of Commerce, 1965-66. Member of board of directors of Overland Enterprises and Manhattan Federal Savings and Loan Association. *Military service:* U.S. Naval Reserve, served on active duty, 1943-46; became lieutenant junior grade. *Member:* Agricultural History Society (president, 1967), Business History Conference, Manhattan Rotary (president, 1975-76).

WRITINGS: (With Donald L. Kemmerer) *American Economic History,* McGraw, 1959; *Caring for the Aged: An Appraisal of Nursing Homes and Their Alternatives,* Nelson-Hall, 1982. Editor of *Agricultural History,* 1958-60.

WORK IN PROGRESS: Research on nursing home management and economics.

SIDELIGHTS: Jones told *CA:* "My newly developed interests in gerontology and nursing homes resulted directly from the need to place my eighty-two-year-old mother in a nursing home in the fall of 1977. Suddenly, my wife and I discovered that we knew very little about nursing homes. We also realized that there were few, if any, alternatives available to us. The following year I took a leave of absence from teaching to see what I could learn.

"The study leave resulted in a publication directed primarily at families similar to our own—middle-aged children with frail, elderly parents desperately seeking information about elderly care institutions and services. My purposes in writing *Caring for the Aged* also included a wish that local community leaders would become better informed and would facilitate the creation of a *local* planning and coordination mechanism for the delivery of services to the elderly.

"From my studies, I have a more realistic view of the operation of nursing homes and the vital role they play in the continuum of care for the frail elderly. In spite of their image problems, nursing homes are the only answer for a large number of dependent persons—a number that is increasing at a very rapid rate. Thus, we as a civilization must work to improve, not displace, nursing homes.

"In reviewing the many proposals for improvement, I came across a reference to the hospice movement. This novel idea of caring for the terminally ill has enormous potential for those who work in the nursing home industry. Hospice is a philosophy of compassionate caring; if adopted by nursing homes, it could transform them into a vastly improved environment for the elderly.

"My present hope is that we can bring nursing homes into the mainstream of society and integrate them into a total system of care where they will provide quality services at affordable costs to those who have no options. At the same time, we must provide viable options to those who need them."

* * *

JONES, Jack 1913-
(Jack Reynolds)

BRIEF ENTRY: Born June 19, 1913, in Buntingford, England. British consultant and author. Jones has been employed by the United Nations as a vehicle management consultant. His books include *A Woman of Bangkok* (Ballantine, 1956) and *Daughters of an Ancient Race* (Heinemann, 1974). His writings have also appeared in popular magazines, including *New Yorker, Look,* and *Investor.*

* * *

JONES, Jack
See JONES, James Larkin

* * *

JONES, James Larkin 1913-
(Jack Jones)

PERSONAL: Born March 29, 1913, in Liverpool, England; son of George and Anne (Diplock) Jones; married Evelyn Mary Taylor (a factory worker and voluntary social worker); children: Jack, Michael. *Education:* Attended technical school and labor college. *Home:* 74 Ruskin Park House, Champion Hill, London SE5 8TH, England.

CAREER: Apprentice engineer and dock worker, 1927-39; Transport and General Workers Union, London, England, secretary of Coventry district, 1939-55, and Midlands region, 1955-63, assistant executive secretary, 1963-69, general secretary, 1969-78; vice-president of Age Concern, 1978—. Member of Liverpool City Council, 1936-39; city magistrate in Coventry, 1950-63. Member of general council of Trades Union Congress, 1968-78, past chairman of international and industrial committees, chairman of Midlands advisory committee, 1948-63. Member of Midland Regional Board for Industry, 1942-46, 1954-63; chairman of Birmingham Productivity Committee, 1957-63; member of national executive committee of Labour Party, 1964-67, chairman of special committee on industrial democracy, 1967; member of Lord Bullock Committee on Industrial Democracy, 1978; member of National Committee for Commonwealth Immigrants, 1965-69; deputy chairman of National Ports Council, 1967-79; fellow of Chartered Institute of Transport. *Awards, honors:* Member of Order of the British Empire, 1950; Companion of Honour, 1978; D.Litt. from University of Warwick, 1979; fellow of London School of Economics and Political Science, London.

WRITINGS—Under name Jack Jones: (With Charles Levinson) *Industry's Democratic Revolution,* Allen & Unwin, 1974; *The Human Face of Labour,* BBC Publications, 1977; *Bevin: Revolutionary by Consent,* Department of Employment Gazette, 1981; (with Max Morris) *A-Z Trade Unionism and Industrial Relations,* Heinemann, 1982. Contributor to magazines and newspapers.

WORK IN PROGRESS: "Twentieth Century Remembered," for British Broadcasting Corp. (BBC).

SIDELIGHTS: Jones told *CA:* "My main interest has been strengthening trade unionism and improving industrial relations. The work in each case has reflected some of my own experiences. For example, my writing on Ernest Bevin (former British Minister of Labour and Foreign Secretary) arose from my own knowledge of him. *The Human Face of Labour* gave my personal views on industrial democracy and the contemporary outlook of trade unionism in Britain. The *A-Z of Trade Unionism and Industrial Relations* is intended to provide shop stewards and trade union officials with a comprehensive guide in trade union practice and policy and on industrial legislation."

* * *

JONES, Linda Phillips
See PHILLIPS-JONES, Linda

* * *

JONES, Peggy 1947-
(Sidetracked Home Executives, a joint pseudonym)

PERSONAL: Born October 23, 1947, in Vancouver, Wash.; daughter of William L. (a truck driver) and Dolores R. (McLaughlin) Young; married Danny L. Jones; children: Christopher, Jeffrey, Allyson. *Education:* Attended Clark College and Southern Oregon State College. *Home:* 7102 Northwest Overlook Dr., Vancouver, Wash. 98665. *Agent:* John Boswell Associates, 41 East 51st St., New York, N.Y. 10022. *Office:* 7409 Northeast Hazeldell Ave., Vancouver, Wash. 98665.

CAREER: Homemaker and writer.

WRITINGS—With Pam Young, under joint pseudonym Sidetracked Home Executives: *Sidetracked Home Executives: From*

Pigpen to Paradise, Warner Books, 1981; *Sidetracked Sisters Catch-Up in the Kitchen,* Warner Books, 1983; *What Miss Cratzberry Never Taught Us,* Warner Books, in press.

SIDELIGHTS: Peggy Jones and Pam Young told *CA:* "In June, 1977, Peggy and Pam hit bottom. They were failing at their chosen profession—homemaking. They were always locked out, left behind, or overdrawn, and their homes were in total chaos and filled with endless clutter. They developed a three-by-five card file system that changed everything. The first book was one positive result of becoming organized."

*   *   *

JOOSSE, Barbara M(onnot) 1949-

PERSONAL: Born February 18, 1949, in Grafton, Wis.; daughter of Robert E. (a banker) and M. Eileen Monnot; married Peter C. Joosse (a psychiatrist), August 30, 1969; children: Maaike Sari, Anneke Els, Robert Collin. *Education:* Attended University of Wisconsin—Stevens Point, 1966; University of Wisconsin—Madison, B.A., 1970; graduate study at University of Wisconsin—Milwaukee, 1977-80. *Politics:* "Sometimes." *Religion:* "Rarely." *Home and office:* 2953 Kettle Moraine Dr., Hartford, Wis. 35027.

CAREER: Associated with Stephan & Brady, Madison, Wis., 1970-71; Waldbillig & Besteman, Madison, copywriter, 1971-74. *Member:* Society of Children's Book Writers.

*WRITINGS—*For children: *The Thinking Place,* Knopf, 1982; *Spiders in the Fruit Cellar,* Knopf, 1983; *Fourth of July,* Knopf, 1983.

WORK IN PROGRESS: Two children's books; short stories.

SIDELIGHTS: Barbara Joosse told *CA:* "I have always liked to write. Upon the birth of my second daughter (and with it, full-time housewife status), it became important for me to have another niche. I wanted to take writing as seriously as I took mothering, so I enrolled in the master's degree program in creative writing at the University of Wisconsin—Milwaukee.

"Early in the program, I discovered writing for children to be the most natural and exciting form for me. Writing for children combines the word power and rhythms of poetry, another form of writing I have loved. It demands absolute honesty in dialogue and characterization. There is plenty of psychology, fantasy, and drama. You have the opportunity to work with another medium (illustration), and your words will be read and, hopefully, cherished by small people. Words have added impact and incorporation when they are read repeatedly and by someone who loves you.

"My own daughters are frequently a source of inspiration for my stories. Both girls are also apt critics, quick to point out when a story gets boring or when they don't like an ending."

*   *   *

JOSEPH, Marie

PERSONAL: Born in Blackburn, Lancashire, England; married Frank Joseph (a chartered engineer), December, 1942; children: Marilyn Joseph Hampton, Kathryn Joseph Stevenson. *Education:* Attended girls' high school in Blackburn, Lancashire, England. *Religion:* Protestant. *Home:* Studio, Green Lane, Stanmore, Middlesex, England. *Agent:* Mary Irvine, 4 Coombe Gardens, Wimbledon, London, England.

CAREER: Civil servant. Post Office Telephones, Blackburn, England, clerical officer, 1938-44. *Member:* Romantic Novelists Association, Society of Women Writers and Journalists, Byron Ladies' Club.

*WRITINGS—*Romantic novels, except as noted: *One Step at a Time* (autobiography), St. Martin's, 1977; *Maggie Craig,* St. Martin's, 1980; *A Leaf in the Wind,* St. Martin's, 1981; *Emma Sparrow,* St. Martin's, 1982; *The Listening Silence,* St. Martin's, 1983. Contributor of stories to magazines.

WORK IN PROGRESS: A novel reaching from northern England to Washington, D.C., publication by Hutchinson expected in 1984.

SIDELIGHTS: Marie Joseph told *CA:* "My novels are all set in the north of England, in periods ranging from the turn of the century to the present day. I try to show the social history of the time, for instance the poverty of workers in Lancashire cotton mills, as opposed to the comparative affluence of the mill owners.

"I set my novels in the north of England because I was born there and have an in-depth knowledge of the area. My own mother, who died giving birth to me, was a weaver in a cotton mill, as were her four sisters, so my background is authentic. I lived as a child in the kind of house described in *Maggie Craig,* and the tight-knit community of near poverty and strict Methodism was my own. I was brought up by my maternal grandmother until the age of seven, and when she died, I lived with an uncle who was a magistrate, a teetotaler, a Trades Union secretary, and a Methodist, as well as being an idealistic socialist of the old school! So, it is obvious why my novels all have a strong leaning towards the conditions of the time.

"Although I have lived in the south of England for almost thirty years, I am still a Lancashire woman at heart and can never forget the hardships of those days. I grew up during the Thirties Depression and vividly remember the way women coped to bring up families on very little money. I remember too their sense of humor and their courage, and these qualities I hope to show in my novels.

"I am bringing Washington, D.C., into my current novel because my elder daughter is living there with her husband and five daughters at the present time. They live in an embassy house and are very happy in the United States. My husband and I have just returned from a visit where I had the details of my last chapter checked over by a Washingtonian!"

*   *   *

JOUVET, Jean
See STRICH, Christian

*   *   *

JUCOVY, Milton Edward 1918-

PERSONAL: Born June 2, 1918, in New York, N.Y.; son of Abraham (a physician) and Sophie (Cion) Jucovy; married Shirley Lieman (a nurse), April 23, 1944; children: Peter, Jon, Seth. *Education:* New York University, B.S., 1938, M.D., 1942. *Politics:* "Progressive-Left-wing Democrat." *Religion:* "Secular Jewish." *Home and office:* 32 Old Farm Rd., Great Neck, N.Y. 11020.

CAREER: Montefiore Hospital, Bronx, N.Y., intern, 1942-43, resident in neurology, 1945; Pilgrim State Hospital, West Brentwood, N.Y., psychiatrist, 1946-48; private practice of medicine, specializing in psychiatry and psychoanalysis, 1948—. Member of faculty at State University of New York Downstate

Medical Center, 1954-59, and New York Psychoanalytic Institute, 1963—, vice-president of institute, 1970-71. Visiting staff psychiatrist at Long Island Jewish-Hillside Medical Center, 1968—. *Military service:* U.S. Army Air Forces, Medical Corps, 1943-46; became captain. *Member:* International Psychoanalytic Association, American Psychoanalytic Association, American Psychiatric Association (life fellow), New York Psychoanalytic Society (president, 1981—). *Awards, honors:* Grant from Fund for Psychoanalytic Research, 1978-79.

WRITINGS: (Editor with Samuel Atkin) *Style, Character, and Language,* Jason Aronson, 1977; (editor with Martin Bergmann) *Generations of the Holocaust,* Basic Books, 1982. Contributor to psychoanalysis journals. Member of editorial board of *Annual Survey of Psychoanalysis,* 1961—.

WORK IN PROGRESS: Research on origins and roots of anti-Semitism; psychoanalytic research on the Holocaust.

SIDELIGHTS: Jucovy commented: "My decision to study medicine was largely determined by identification with my father, and the study and practice of psychoanalysis was a natural outcome of my awareness of my father's interest in his patients as human beings with emotions and conflicts. My psychoanalytic interest in the effects of the Holocaust on survivors and their children is based on a strong sense of Jewish identity, as well as hatred for tyranny and oppression."

BIOGRAPHICAL/CRITICAL SOURCES: Los Angeles Times Book Review, September 19, 1982.

*   *   *

JUERGENS, George Ivar   1932-

PERSONAL: Born March 20, 1932, in Brooklyn, N.Y.; son of Georg Oedegaard (a painter) and Magnhild (Julin) Juergens; married Jenifer Jane Beattie (a medical assistant), March 21, 1959; children: Steven Erik, Paul Andreas. *Education:* Columbia University, B.A., 1953, Ph.D., 1965; Oriel College, Oxford, B.A. and M.A., both 1956. *Home:* 2111 Meadowbluff Court, Bloomington, Ind. 47401. *Office:* Department of History, Indiana University, Bloomington, Ind. 47401.

CAREER: University of Maryland, Overseas Branch, London, England, lecturer in history, politics, and economics, 1958-59; Dartmouth College, Hanover, N.H., instructor in American history, 1962-65; Amherst College, Amherst, Mass., assistant professor of American studies, 1965-67; Indiana University, Bloomington, associate professor, 1967-80, professor of American history, 1980—. Consultant to National Endowment for the Humanities. *Military service:* U.S. Army, 1956-58.

MEMBER: Organization of American Historians, Phi Beta Kappa. *Awards, honors:* Senior fellow of National Endowment for the Humanities, 1971-72; Ford Foundation fellow, 1977; Brown Derby Award from Indiana University School of Journalism, 1977, for distinguished teaching; Rockefeller Foundation fellow, 1981-82; award from Amoco Foundation, 1982, for distinguished teaching.

WRITINGS: Joseph Pulitzer and the New York World, Princeton University Press, 1966; *News From the White House: The Presidential-Press Relationship in the Progressive Era,* University of Chicago Press, 1981. Contributor to history journals and *Business Horizons.* Associate editor of *Journal of American History,* 1968-69.

WORK IN PROGRESS: News From the White House: The New Deal Era, completion expected in 1984.

SIDELIGHTS: Juergens told *CA:* "I started out writing about the press in part because I am a newspaper junkie, fascinated by all facets of journalism, and in part because it struck me (and still does) as an area offering all sorts of possibilities for a historian because it is important and so far relatively neglected by practitioners of my craft. But as time has gone by another reason has become important and added a certain commitment to my work. It occurs to me that, of all the Constitutional guarantees we have, those in the First Amendment may be the most essential. It also strikes me that they are always more or less under attack, and particularly so in recent years. Perhaps a historian can make a contribution to defending those guarantees by recounting as accurately as possible the role of a free press in American development."

K

KABASELE, Joseph
See TSHIAMALA, Kabasele

*   *   *

KAHL, Joseph A(lan)   1923-

BRIEF ENTRY: Born July 26, 1923, in Chicago, Ill. American sociologist, educator, and author. Kahl became a professor of sociology at Cornell University in 1969. Before that, he taught at Harvard University, University of North Carolina, Mexico City College, and Washington University in St. Louis, Missouri. Kahl has lectured in Brazil and England and worked as a sociologist for UNESCO. He wrote *The American Class Structure* (Holt, 1957), *The Measurement of Modernism: A Study of Values in Brazil and Mexico* (University of Texas Press, 1968), and *Modernization, Exploitation, and Dependency in Latin America: Germani, Gonzalez Casanova, and Cardoso* (Transaction Books, 1976). Kahl also edited *Comparative Perspectives on Stratification: Mexico, Great Britain, Japan* (Little, Brown, 1968). *Address:* 105 Miller St., Ithaca, N.Y. 14850; and Department of Sociology, Cornell University, Ithaca, N.Y. 14850.

*   *   *

KAHN, Grace Leboy   1891-1983

OBITUARY NOTICE: Born September 22, 1891, in Brooklyn, N.Y.; died of a stroke, May, 1983, in Los Angeles, Calif. Composer and lyricist. Married to noted composer Gus Kahn, Grace Kahn collaborated with her husband on such songs as "I Wish I Had a Girl" and "Dream a Little Longer." In 1952 a film portraying the songwriting couple, "I'll See You in My Dreams," was released. Grace also wrote the lyrics for "You're My Love," the theme song of the popular Ed Sullivan television show. Obituaries and other sources: *The ASCAP Biographical Dictionary of Composers, Authors, and Publishers*, 3rd edition, American Society of Composers, Authors, and Publishers, 1966; *Los Angeles Times*, May 30, 1983.

*   *   *

KAHN, James   1947-

PERSONAL: Born December 30, 1947, in Chicago, Ill.; son of Alfred J. (a physician) and Judith (an artist; maiden name, Pesmen) Kahn; married Jill Alden Littlewood (an illustrator), August 30, 1975. *Education:* University of Chicago, B.A., 1970, M.D., 1974. *Agent:* Jane Jordan Browne, Multimedia Product Development, Inc., 410 South Michigan Ave., Room 828, Chicago, Ill. 60605.

CAREER: University of Wisconsin, Madison, intern, 1974-75; Los Angeles County Hospital, Los Angeles, Calif., emergency medicine resident, 1976-77; University of California, Los Angeles, emergency medicine resident, 1978-79; Rancho Encino Hospital, Los Angeles, emergency room physician, 1978—. *Member:* American College of Emergency Physicians.

WRITINGS: (With Jerome McGann) *Nerves in Patterns* (poems), X Press, 1978; *Diagnosis: Murder* (murder mystery), Carlyle, 1978; *World Enough and Time* (science fiction), Ballantine, 1980; *Time's Dark Laughter* (science fiction), Ballantine, 1982; *Poltergeist* (fiction), Warner Books, 1982; *Revenge of the Jedi* (novelization of the film), Ballantine, 1983. Contributor of stories to magazines, including *Playboy*.

WORK IN PROGRESS: *Timefall*, completing the trilogy begun with *World Enough and Time* and *Time's Dark Laughter*.

SIDELIGHTS: Kahn wrote: "I'm basically a storyteller. I stretch for metaphors at times, but only if they make good stories themselves. The way the story is told is the art, the craft, the game of it—what makes the writing (and reading) fun.

"I would like to be a man of letters, involved in all literary forms—the novel, short story, essay, screenplay, and poetry."

*   *   *

KAHN, Michael D.   1936-

PERSONAL: Born March 11, 1936, in Israel; son of Lester (an executive) and Helen (Baum) Kahn; married Ruth Jacobson (a special educator), March 29, 1958; children: Kim Lee, Tamara Regina, Benjamin Alexander. *Education:* City College (now of the City University of New York), B.A., 1960; New School for Social Research, M.A., 1965; University of North Carolina, Ph.D., 1970. *Politics:* Democrat. *Religion:* Jewish. *Home:* 54 Mount Brook Rd., West Hartford, Conn. 06117. *Office:* Department of Psychology, University of Hartford, 200 Bloomfield Ave., West Hartford, Conn. 06032.

CAREER: University of Hartford, West Hartford, Conn., assistant professor, 1970-78, associate professor of psychology,

1979—. Associate clinical professor at University of Connecticut, Farmington, 1974—. Private practice of psychology in Hartford, 1971—. Member of board of directors of Family Study Center of Connecticut, 1975—, president, 1982—; vice-president of Capital Region Mental Health Center, 1979-81, president, 1982—; consultant to Hartley Salmon Child Guidance Clinic and Veterans Administration Hospital, Newington, Conn. *Member:* American Psychological Association, American Orthopsychiatric Association (fellow), American Family Therapy Association (charter member), Connecticut Psychological Association.

WRITINGS: (With Stephen P. Bank) *The Sibling Bond*, Basic Books, 1982. Advisory editor of *Family Process;* member of editorial board of *International Journal of Family Therapy.*

WORK IN PROGRESS: A book on "the interface of the psychodynamic theory of individual therapy with the systems process theory of family therapy."

SIDELIGHTS: Kahn wrote: "I am an only child. The subject of siblings has always fascinated me, and the interaction of my own children gave me living evidence that brothers and sisters could be caring and loving to one another.

"I've learned, through my book, to love writing. I urge others to attempt the same painful and joyous exploration."

AVOCATIONAL INTERESTS: Sailing, travel, playing alto and tenor saxophone in jazz groups, research on the effects of immigration to a new culture on one's own identity.

* * *

KAHRL, William L. 1946-

PERSONAL: Born May 30, 1946, in Mt. Vernon, Ohio; son of F. William (a corporate controller) and Muriel (a professor of mathematics; maiden name, Barker) Kahrl; married Kathleen Mazzocco (a horse breeder), April 20, 1967; children: Christopher Geoffrey Barker, Benjamin Michael Eli, Justin Bartholomew Avelino. *Education:* Yale University, B.A., 1968, graduate study, 1968-69; attended CORO Foundation of San Francisco, 1970-71. *Home:* 4920 North Avenue, Carmichael, Calif. 95608. *Agent:* Amanda Urban, International Creative Management, 40 West 57th St., New York, N.Y. 10019.

CAREER: New Haven Department of Police Services, New Haven, Conn., special assistant, 1969; California Tomorrow (conservation group), San Francisco, Calif., staff director, 1971-72; Speaker of the California Assembly, Sacramento, Calif., senior consultant and chief of legislative program, 1973-76; Governor Edmund G. Brown, Jr., Sacramento, director of research, 1976-79; consultant to the Kingdom of Saudi Arabia, U.S. Geological Survey, U.S. Census Bureau, Graduate School of U.S. Department of Agriculture, National Geographic Society, Pacific Basin Institute, California Research, Inc., *The California Journal*, Los Angeles Bicentennial Commission, American Bibliographic Center/Clio Press, California Resources Agency, and Educational Exchange Foundation of New York, 1979—. Member of California Policy Seminar, University of California, and San Francisco Review of Books. Member of advisory council of California Water Resources Center and board of directors of League to Save Lake Tahoe, 1971-74.

MEMBER: California Historical Society (member of publication committee), Association of Yale Alumni (Sacramento representative, 1978-81), CORO Alumni Association (Sacramento co-chairman), Yale Alumni of Sacramento (president,

1974-78). *Awards, honors:* Research fellowships from Stern Foundation, 1966, and Smithsonian Institution, 1967; Lewis-Farmington Fellowship and Theodore J. Cuyler Fellowship, both from Yale Graduate School, both 1968-69; Irvine Fellowship from Irvine Foundation, 1970-71; fellowship from National Endowment for the Humanities, 1976; fellowship in environmental affairs from Rockefeller Foundation, 1978-79; awards of excellence from American Institute of Graphic Arts, Printing Industries of America, and Bookbuilders West, all 1980, all for *The California Water Atlas;* the *New York Times* listed *Water and Power* as one of the best books of 1982; nomination for Pulitzer Prize, 1983, for *Water and Power.*

WRITINGS: (Contributor) Alfred E. Heller, editor, *The California Tomorrow Plan*, William Kaufmann, 1972; (editor) *The California Water Atlas*, William Kaufmann, 1st edition, 1979, 2nd edition, 1980; (editor with Frank Gibney) *The Whole Pacific Catalog*, Access Press, 1981; *Water and Power: The Conflict Over Los Angeles' Water Supply in the Owens Valley*, University of California Press, 1982; *Paradise Reclaimed: The Army Corps of Engineers in California's Central Valley*, U.S. Government Printing Office, 1984. Contributor to periodicals, including the *Los Angeles Times, World's Fair Magazine*, and *California Historical Quarterly.* Associate editor of *World's Fair Magazine*, 1981—.

SIDELIGHTS: In the *Washington Post Book World*, Philip L. Fradkin observed that in writing about the subject of water one must make the topic somehow "exceptional" because it is "so ordinary." Several critics have noted that William Kahrl does exactly that in *Water and Power: The Conflict Over Los Angeles' Water Supply in the Owens Valley;* the author tells the dramatic story of Los Angeles' continuing water wars with exhaustive research and meticulous detachment. "*Water and Power* is not only the most detailed book on the subject," Benjamin Stein commented in the *New York Times Book Review*, "but the first one to attempt to be balanced and fair, and more important, to succeed. . . . Mr. Kahrl's realism and willingness to confront ultimate issues are rare and delightful."

The tale of how Los Angeles drained the lush Owens Valley dry is so complex and sensational that it has inspired countless novels and motion pictures (including "Chinatown"). Kahrl's historical narrative is filled with death, disgrace, debacle, and incarceration; Kahrl both "reports and appraises the portentious doings of the players in the historic cast," Richard G. Lillard wrote in the *Los Angeles Times Book Review.* Drawing his research from three quarters of a century of public documents, the author "sees the internal rhyming scheme of soil surveys and land records and committee reports," John Gregory Dunne remarked in the *New York Review of Books*, "finding in the impenetrable diction of officialdom the broken meters that conceal collusion and fraud."

Lillard concluded that *Water and Power* is the "most inclusive, impartial account yet published" on the Los Angeles water wars. Stein strongly agreed, stating that Kahrl "has written a brilliant book, by far the best I've ever read about the key element in the development of the American Southwest, water." "In laying out the fascinating story of water and power in Los Angeles and California," the *New York Times Book Review* critic added, "Mr. Kahrl has offered not only a lesson in how a city grew and what water means in the American West. He has also given a class on how to write history clearly, convincingly, with an eye on the bigger picture and, most of all, with common sense."

BIOGRAPHICAL/CRITICAL SOURCES: Los Angeles Times Book Review, May 23, 1982; *New York Times Book Review*, July 11, 1982; *Washington Post Book World*, August 22, 1982; *New York Review of Books*, October 21, 1982.

* * *

KALB, Bernard 1932-

BRIEF ENTRY: American journalist and author. Beginning in the mid-1950's, Kalb served for about fifteen years in Southeast Asia as a news correspondent, first for the *New York Times* and later for the Columbia Broadcasting System (CBS-TV). Currently a diplomatic correspondent for the National Broadcasting Company (NBC-TV), Kalb is the author, with his brother, Marvin Kalb, of *Kissinger* (Little, Brown, 1974) and a novel entitled *The Last Ambassador* (Little, Brown, 1981). *Biographical/critical sources:* Newsweek, August 19, 1974; *New York Times Book Review*, August 25, 1974, October 18, 1981; *Saturday Review/World*, October 5, 1974; *Washington Post Book World*, September 6, 1981.

* * *

KALEDIN, Eugenia 1929-

PERSONAL: Born September 11, 1929, in Philadelphia, Pa.; daughter of Samuel B. (in business) and Catherine (Greenwood) Oster; married Arthur D. Kaledin (a professor of history), January 24, 1954; children: Nicholas, Jonathan, Elizabeth. *Education:* Harvard University, A.B. (magna cum laude), 1951, A.M., 1953; attended Boston Psychoanalytic Institute, 1975-76, 1978; Boston University, Ph.D., 1977. *Politics:* Democrat. *Home:* 5 Watson Rd., Lexington, Mass. 02173. *Office:* Alliance of Independent Scholars, 6 Ash St., Cambridge, Mass. 02138.

CAREER: University of Maryland, Overseas Program, Bayreuth, West Germany, instructor in English, 1954-55; Harvard University extension program, Cambridge, Mass., instructor in composition, 1956-64; Northeastern University, Burlington, Mass., lecturer in American literature, 1964-80; Alliance of Independent Scholars, Cambridge, founding member and director of colloquia, 1979—. Member of faculty at Goddard College, 1978-82, and Massachusetts Institute of Technology, 1982—. Volunteer psychotherapist at Emerson Hospital, 1979-82. *Member:* American Studies Association (member of national executive board, 1973-76, and New England executive board, 1977-80), Phi Beta Kappa. *Awards, honors:* Fulbright fellow at Sorbonne, University of Paris, 1952; research fellow at Wellesley College, 1975.

WRITINGS: (Contributor) P. C. Harrell and M. S. Smith, editors, *Victorian Boston Today*, Victorian Society, 1975; *The Education of Mrs. Henry Adams*, Temple University Press, 1982; *Mothers and Thinkers: Women in the 1950s*, G. K. Hall, in press. Contributor to magazines, including *Women's Studies*, *Nation*, and *Radcliffe Quarterly*.

SIDELIGHTS: Kaledin told *CA:* "Teaching very bright adult women who had never been encouraged to use their minds made me aware of how much intellectual waste there still is in this society. I am trying to understand the traditions that shape the way women see themselves. I believe strongly that women still need constant encouragement to fulfill *all* their potentialities.

"At the moment, I am also tremendously interested in what is happening to people with Ph.D.'s who cannot find academic jobs. Our Alliance of Independent Scholars has grown from a handful of women seeking some sort of support to more than seventy members (we do not discriminate against men)."

When asked about her book entitled *The Education of Mrs. Henry Adams*, Kaledin commented: "I became interested in Clover Adams because Henry James thought she epitomized the American woman—the kind of free thinking spirit he often made into a literary heroine. Clover was connected with a tradition of independent reformers different from the domesticity of the other Adams women; she was not just a society hostess. The world she lived in, however, did little to encourage her intellect or develop her talent at photography."

BIOGRAPHICAL/CRITICAL SOURCES: Lexington Minute Man, August 5, 1982.

* * *

KALLIR, Jane K(atherine) 1954-

PERSONAL: Born July 30, 1954, in New York, N.Y.; daughter of John Otto (an advertising executive) and Joyce (a school principal; maiden name, Ruben) Kallir. *Education:* Brown University, B.A., 1976. *Office:* Galerie St. Etienne, 24 West 57th St., New York, N.Y. 10019.

CAREER: Galerie St. Etienne, New York, N.Y., co-director, 1979—. *Member:* Art Dealers Association of America. *Awards, honors:* Award from Art Library Society of New York, 1982, for *The Folk Art Tradition*.

WRITINGS: Gustav Klimt/Egon Schiele, Crown, 1980; *Austria's Expressionism*, Rizzoli International, 1981; *The Folk Art Tradition*, Viking, 1981; *Grandma Moses*, C. N. Potter, 1982.

WORK IN PROGRESS: Lovis Corinth, publication expected in 1984; *Eugene Mihaesco*, completion expected in 1986; *The Other Twentieth Century*, 1986.

SIDELIGHTS: Kallir told *CA:* "My writing career began as an adjunct to my work in gallery management—books complemented exhibitions as a way of making art accessible to the public. Inevitably, however, certain themes began to recur in my writing. In particular, I am interested in the discrepancies that exist between artists' perceptions of art, public taste, and the critical judgments of the art historians. Folk art—literally the art of the people—has always held a special appeal for me because it has generally existed beyond the confines of the European academic tradition. Grandma Moses, especially, personifies the conflict between folk and 'high' culture, between popular and elitist taste. *The Other Twentieth Century*, a project still very much in its infancy, explores another aspect of this conflict: the existence of a dual cultural system in this century, in which the art people buy to hang in their homes often differs from that endorsed by museums and art writers."

* * *

KAMIL, Alan C(urtis) 1941-

BRIEF ENTRY: Born November 20, 1941, in Bronx, N.Y. American psychologist, educator, and author. Kamil began teaching animal behavior and behavioral ecology at University of Massachusetts in 1967. He also taught psychology at University of California, Berkeley. Kamil wrote *Mastering Psychology: A Guide to Brown-Herrnstein's Psychology* (Little, Brown, 1975). He also co-edited *Patterns of Psychology: Issues and Prospects* (Little, Brown, 1973) and *Foraging Behavior: Ecological, Ethological, and Psychological Ap-*

proaches (STPM Press, 1981). *Address:* Department of Psychology, University of Massachusetts, Amherst, Mass. 01002.

* * *

KAPLAN, Flora S(tewart)

PERSONAL: Born in New York, N.Y. *Education:* Hunter College (now of the City University of New York), B.A. (cum laude), 1951; Columbia University, M.A., 1958; Graduate Center of the City University of New York, Ph.D., 1976. *Home address:* Gansett Lane, Amagansett, N.Y. 11930. *Agent:* Glenn Cowley Literary Management, 60 West 10th St., New York, N.Y. 10011. *Office:* Graduate School of Arts and Science, New York University, 19 University Pl., New York, N.Y. 10003.

CAREER: Brooklyn Museum, Brooklyn, N.Y., assistant in department of primitive art and New World cultures, 1951-54, acting curator, 1954-57; with Stewart associates in New York City and free-lance writer, 1957-70; Herbert H. Lehman College of the City University of New York, Bronx, N.Y., adjunct lecturer, 1970-73, lecturer in anthropology, 1973-74; New York University, New York City, adjunct assistant professor, 1976-77, assistant professor of anthropology and museum studies, 1977—, also director of certificate program in museum studies and associate of Center for Latin American and Caribbean studies, member of advisory board of Institute of Afro-American Affairs, 1982—. Project director at Statue of Liberty National Monument; research associate at Museum of the American Indian, 1979—; organizer of symposia. Guest on radio and television programs; photographer, with exhibitions of her work. Member of board of trustees of Anthropology Museum of the People of New York, 1978—(vice-president, 1980-82), and Aunt Len's Doll and Toy Museum, 1979; member of International Committee for Museums international committee for museology, 1981—; member of Citizens Union committee on New York City's cultural concerns, 1981—; consultant to Garibaldi Museum, Illinois Archaeological Foundation, and WGBH-TV.

MEMBER: International Council of Museums, American Anthropological Association (fellow), American Ethnological Society, American Folklore Society, American Association of Museums, Association for Political and Legal Anthropology, Society for American Archaeology, Society for the Anthropology of Visual Communication, Council for Museum Anthropology, Latin American Anthropology Group, New York Academy of Sciences (fellow), Phi Beta Kappa.

AWARDS, HONORS: Travel grants from Consulate General of Mexico, 1971, 1977, Graduate Center of the City University of New York, 1973, and New York University and Romanian Socialist Council for Education and Culture, 1979; grants from Mellon Foundation, 1978, National Endowment for the Humanities and National Endowment for the Arts, 1979, U.S.-Romania Cultural Exchange Program and New York City Humanities Council, 1980, New York Urban Coalition, J. M. Kaplan Fund, Inner City Broadcasting, Freedom National Bank, Engelhard Minerals and Chemicals Corp., American Broadcasting Co., and New York Community Trust, all 1981, and National Park Service, 1982.

WRITINGS: Una tradicion alfarera: Conocimiento y estilo (title means "A Pottery Tradition: Cognition and Style"), Instituto Nacional Indigenista, 1980; (contributor) Henry Kellerman, editor, *Group Cohesion: Theoretical and Clinical*

Perspectives, Grune, 1981; (editor and contributor) *The Royal Court of Benin: Images of Power,* New York University Press, 1981; (contributor) Mary Douglas, editor, *The Anthropology of Drinking,* Cambridge University Press, 1982; (contributor) James L. Connelly, Virginia Jackson, and others, editors, *Art Reference Book of the World,* Greenwood Press, 1983. Contributor to *Funk & Wagnalls New Encyclopedia* and *Encyclopedia Americana.* Contributor of articles and reviews to anthropology and museum journals. Contributing editor of *Museological Working Papers* of International Committee for Museums, 1981—; film editor of *Anthropology of Work Newsletter,* 1981—; chairperson of board of editors of *Centerpoint,* 1979—.

WORK IN PROGRESS: Earth Flowers: Mexican Folk Pottery, publication by Fondo de Cultura Economica (Mexico) expected in 1985; "The Dacians: Ancient Treasures From the National Museums of Romania," a museum exhibition and catalog.

SIDELIGHTS: Kaplan told *CA:* "My interest in Romania is an outgrowth of an exhibition being planned at New York University. This would be the first showing of national treasures, documenting the complex history and rise of Western civilization in one of the richest archaeological areas of Europe. I plan a catalog with essays by leading Romanian and American scholars, and full color photographs and illustrations of rare finds, never exhibited in the United States. I also have a continuing interest in Romanian folk art, which is part of a long and indigenous tradition. This parallels the research and writing I have done on the folk art of Mexico. Both countries have traditions in ceramics, textiles, wood, costumes, masks, and other media of unusual cultural richness and prehistoric roots. That my mother's family is from Romania gives these interests special meaning.

"In my writing I am especially interested in exploring the interpretation of material culture and symbolism through the study of cultures in Africa, Mexico, and the New World, including urban North America.

"I am attracted by nonverbal systems of communication because they are powerful in affecting what people think and do. They include what we call 'art' in our society as well as what constitutes artifacts, tools, and ceremonial ritual objects, their iconography and symbolism. I include also exhibitions, graffiti, and ethnographic film as systems which convey visual imagery having important ideas and feelings that communicate to people. The general methodological framework which I use is 'structural,' similar to but different from that proposed by Levi-Strauss and Piaget. If I were asked to express the single theme of my work it would be 'human creativity.'"

BIOGRAPHICAL/CRITICAL SOURCES: Anthropological Papers of the Museum of Anthropology, University of Michigan, Number 45, 1972; Richard L. Anderson, *Art in Primitive Societies,* Prentice-Hall, 1979; *American Anthropologist,* March, 1980; Willett Kempton, *The Folk Classification of Ceramics,* Academic Press, 1981.

* * *

KAPOOR, Sukhbir Singh 1935-

PERSONAL: Born November 21, 1935, in Amritsar, India; son of Kulwant Singh (a company director) and Lakhinder (Kaur) Kapoor; married Mohinder Kaur (a bank officer), September 21, 1958; children: Preetbir Singh (son), Ramanbir Singh (son). *Education:* Agra University, M.Com., 1957; University of Glasgow, D.Ed., 1966; City of London Polytechnic, M.A.,

1982; Panjab University, Ph.D., 1983. *Religion:* Sikh. *Home:* Bir Villa, 26 St. Thomas Dr., Pinner, Greater London HA5 4SX, England. *Office:* School of Accounting and Finance, City of London Polytechnic, 84 Moorgate, London E.C.2M., England.

CAREER: University of Delhi, Delhi, India, lecturer in accounting, 1957-65, senior lecturer in accounting, 1969-70; Glasgow College of Technology, Glasgow, Scotland, lecturer in accounting, 1971-77; City of London Polytechnic, London, England, senior lecturer in accounting, 1977—. *Member:* Institute of Cost and Management Accounting (London), British Institute of Management.

WRITINGS: Lectures on Business Organisation, Aryan, 1964; *Elements of Book-Keeping and Accountancy,* two volumes, Aryan, 1965; *Dynamic Approach to Economics,* Holmes & McDougal, 1976; *Sikhs and Sikhism,* Wayland, 1982. Contributor to accounting journals and *Sikh Courier.*

WORK IN PROGRESS: Research on Guru Gobind Singh's concept of an ideal man.

* * *

KASDAN, Lawrence 1949-

PERSONAL: Born January 14, 1949, in Miami Beach, Fla.; son of Clarence Norman (a retail manager) and Sylvia (an employment counselor; maiden name, Landau) Kasdan; married Meg Goldman, November 28, 1971; children: two sons. *Education:* University of Michigan, B.A., 1970, M.A., 1972. *Agent:* Peter Benedek, Weissman, Wolff, Bergman, Coleman, Schulman, 9601 Wilshire Blvd., Beverly Hills, Calif. 90210.

CAREER: Screenwriter and director of motion pictures. W. B. Doner & Co., Detroit, Mich., advertising copywriter, 1972-75; Doyle, Dane, Bernbach (advertisers), Los Angeles, Calif., 1975-77. *Member:* Writers Guild of America, West; Directors Guild of America, West.

WRITINGS—Screenplays: (With Leigh Brackett) "The Empire Strikes Back," Twentieth Century-Fox, 1980; "Raiders of the Lost Ark," Paramount, 1981; (and director) "Body Heat," Ladd/Warner Bros., 1981; "Continental Divide," Universal, 1981; "Return of the Jedi," Twentieth Century-Fox, 1983; (and director) "The Big Chill," Columbia, 1983. Also author of unproduced screenplay, "The Bodyguard."

SIDELIGHTS: Kasdan achieved his initial fame in Hollywood as one of the film industry's most versatile and effective screenwriters. His first produced work, "The Empire Strikes Back," was a sequel to George Lucas's immensely popular "Star Wars." In the second installment, characters Luke Skywalker and Han Solo continue in their efforts against the Empire and its leader, Darth Vadar. Also featured in the sequel are the popular robots, C3PO and R2D2, Princess Leia, and a new character, Lando Calrissian. The enormous success of "The Empire Strikes Back" resulted in the continuation of Kasdan's association with Lucas.

Kasdan's next screenplay, "Raiders of the Lost Ark," was produced by Lucas and directed by the extremely successful Steven Spielberg, and it too earned vast profits and accolades. Harkening back to the serials of the 1930's, "Raiders of the Lost Ark" chronicles the adventures of Indiana Jones, a professor/archaeologist/explorer who finds himself opposing Nazis in his efforts to obtain the Ark of the Covenant for the United States before it can be used by Germany in its attempt at world domination. The film is full of exciting chases and stunts, including the introductory sequence, in which Jones dodges

poisonous darts, a hurtling boulder, and rampaging natives in an unsuccessful attempt to obtain a valuable artifact. Critics were extremely enthused by "Raiders of the Lost Ark," including *Time*'s Richard Schickel, who called it "the best two hours of pure entertainment anyone is going to find in the summer of '81." And *Newsweek*'s David Ansen deemed it "the movie Hollywood was born to make, and was born making."

Kasdan's notoriety increased that summer with the release of "Body Heat," an erotic thriller which, like "Raiders of the Lost Ark," seemed inspired by its 1930's and '40's counterparts. In the film, lawyer Ned Racine is led into murder and fraud by the enticing wife of a land magnate. After killing the husband, however, Ned's plans fall apart, and he soon begins to suspect that he is as much victim as perpetrator. *Time*'s Richard Corliss praised "Body Heat" as a work with "more narrative drive, character congestion and sense of place than any original screenplay since *Chinatown.*" Corliss also hailed Kasdan's direction, noting, "There is intricacy in the movements of his prowling camera, in the pairing of shots and situations from different parts of the film, in the gradual muting of the film's colors from flaming orange to blacks and whites as the lovers' passion turns to calculation." Gene Siskel, writing in the *Chicago Tribune,* was similarly impressed; he called "Body Heat" "a very strong adult melodrama."

"Continental Divide," a comedy-of-the-sexes that strengthened Kasdan's reputation as an extremely versatile writer, was also released in 1981. The film centers on Ernie Souchak, a Chicago columnist whose muckraking has angered a corrupt alderman. After a beating by the alderman's thugs, Souchak is sent on a rest-and-recuperation assignment in the Rocky Mountains, where he is to report on a naturalist documenting the habits of bald eagles. A tug-of-war ensues between the aggressive Souchak and his nature-loving host, and the result is both hilarious and romantic. Siskel called "Continental Divide" "a very sweet, nice and funny little movie that is certain to be a crowd-pleaser." Corliss also praised the film, declaring that Kasdan's "script, and the movie, improve as they progress, and the ending is especially satisfying."

CA INTERVIEW

CA interviewed Lawrence Kasdan by phone on September 14. 1982, at his production offices in Studio City, Calitornia.

CA: You've spoken of the fifteen years of "being preoccupied with making movies and going to movies every day" before selling your first script. How far back did you know you wanted to make movies?

KASDAN: When I was young, I thought I wanted to be a movie star. I got over that. I *think* I got over that. Then while I was in college, around 1966, I realized I wanted to direct films.

CA: Had movies been an important part of your growing up?

KASDAN: Yes, a very important part. I had happy times in movie theatres.

CA: Did you have early favorites?

KASDAN: I did, but just about everything meant something to me. "The Great Escape" was an important movie to me, and "The Magnificent Seven"; and a lot of the old movies had stars that interested me—Cary Grant, Burt Lancaster, the Marx Brothers, and others.

CA: At the University of Michigan, where you won undergraduate writing awards every year to keep yourself in college, and then through five years of working in advertising, you kept writing screenplays and trying to get them sold. Were you ever tempted to give up?

KASDAN: You're always tempted to give up, but I had no alternative plan. Directing movies was all I wanted to do; I couldn't imagine being happy doing anything else. So all I could do was keep trying.

CA: Was the advertising work helpful to you in writing?

KASDAN: Not so much in writing as in life. It was a kind of graduate course in life after the womblike atmosphere of college. It was an immersion in the world of business, the politics of an office and co-workers, what kinds of things people were doing and why they were doing them. It was very useful in that way, and that's been reflected in everything I've written since.

CA: According to most accounts, the break came with the story idea for "Continental Divide," put together in two lunch hours. Did that make for abrupt changes in your life?

KASDAN: Actually, the real break came with a script called "The Bodyguard," which hasn't even been made. It was submitted to sixty-seven people over a two-year period. Finally it sold for a small amount of money but enough to let me leave advertising, at least temporarily. The day that it sold, I quit my job. I had written two more screenplays in the interim while I was trying to sell that script. One of them was "Continental Divide"; I was just finishing it when I sold "The Bodyguard." "Continental Divide" was a much more appealing prospect commercially to the studios, and suddenly everybody wanted to buy it. So it was a big break in terms of the amount of money I was able to get for it and therefore be out of advertising for good.

CA: It's hard to imagine how you could have worked in advertising full time and written those screenplays as well. You must have been at it seven days a week.

KASDAN: I would come home from work and play with my kid and have dinner, and when my son had gone to bed I'd start writing again. I wasn't always completely diligent, but I had a lot of guilt when I wasn't working. So I was either working all the time or feeling guilty about not working.

CA: "Raiders of the Lost Ark" and "The Empire Strikes Back" both rely a great deal on special visual effects. Did that make the screenplays particularly tough to write? Is it necessary to understand the technical aspects of production to write adequate screenplays for such movies?

KASDAN: I did know some of the technical aspects of filmmaking. "Raiders" is really just a story, and when you're writing a story, you don't have to worry about how they're going to do everything. You know it can be done. I was writing it for George Lucas, and he had plenty of experience in realizing fantastic things.

CA: What production experience had you had at that point?

KASDAN: Just that I'd been studying film informally on my own for years and years, so there was a good bit I knew. If you see thousands of movies and read everything you can get your hands on, you learn quite a lot about how movies are made.

CA: Then you didn't feel handicapped by having majored in English instead of film studies in college?

KASDAN: No, because I think that what success I've had in screenwriting, and what eventually got me a chance to direct, was based on the fact that my background was in drama. I started writing theatre in college. I studied playwriting with Kenneth Rowe, who was Arthur Miller's teacher at the University of Michigan. That's the reason I went to Michigan, aside from the Hopwood Contest. That solid background in dramatic structure has served me well in writing screenplays. And I think that's why my screenplays became much valued after a while. That background exposed me to an enormous amount of literature and theatre. The only way you can learn how to write is to read and write—read people who are good writers and try it yourself, and do it again and again and again. It was the writing that got me into a position where I could direct. Once you go to direct a movie, the technical aspects are not all that difficult. You can learn them rather quickly; everybody is there to help you. Of course you have to know what you want, what to ask people for, but directing really has a lot more to do with what kind of person you are than with your technical background.

CA: Reviewing "Body Heat" for the New York Times *(October 25, 1981), Vincent Canby wrote of you as director, "With one giant leap Mr. Kasdan has made the big time." Were there any problems for you as a first-time director?*

KASDAN: I kept anticipating that there would be problems, but they didn't develop. It was a real pleasure. I felt I was doing what I was supposed to do, and I just took to it. I liked it a lot. I was stimulated and pleased by the whole process. It's grueling work, but it was pleasant for me to be doing it. I can't think of any particular problems. It has a lot to do with people management.

CA: You've given actor William Hurt credit for being a great help to you in making "Body Heat." How so?

KASDAN: The thing about Bill is that he demands enormous seriousness about whatever work he's undertaking. A movie set can easily degenerate into a kind of noisy chaos. Bill, in order to do his work well, demanded that I demand of everyone else a really serious approach to the work we were about. That was an additional little edge I had. I could easily have been so concerned by the massive logistical problems of making a movie that I'd let slip the fact that you have to constantly assert the seriousness of the undertaking and demand from everyone a kind of concentration that makes a good movie.

CA: Reviews are sometimes almost incredibly mixed, as they were with "Body Heat." How much attention do you pay to reviews and to more serious movie criticism?

KASDAN: I think film criticism in this country is in a pitiful state. I don't know if it was ever any better. The only unfortunate thing is that some people pay attention to the critics. The mass audience doesn't really care; a movie lives or dies entirely on word of mouth: that means how well did the audience like it, what did they say to their friends about it? It has nothing to do with quality, really. A very bad movie can have wonderful word of mouth if it satisfies an audience in whatever way they were hoping it would, or in some unexpected way. So you have very successful films that are good and very successful films that are bad. Film criticism generally in this country is consumer work that tells you whether you should or shouldn't spend your $4.00. It's a yes-or-no vote. It's all black and white, and it's an absurd way to approach any art—and I consider movies an art.

The good literary criticism that's been written over hundreds of years has been exploratory. Positions are taken, but there's some kind of exploration of why, what's in the work, why might it be that way, how might it be better. Film criticism in this country is just "This is terrible" and "This is great." There's overstatement in both directions at all times. I was the beneficiary of a lot of positive overstatement and a little bit of negative overstatement. Both were wrong.

CA: Are there any film critics here whose writing you respect?

KASDAN: There are a few, whose names I won't mention, but they approach a movie in an open-minded way. They say, here's what I thought about it, this is what's interesting about it, this is what it does for me. They don't presume to speak for everyone who might see the movie. Those who do are the worst critics; they're the ones who adopt this mythical *we* and try to impress their perceptions upon an audience. Half of their sentences read like "Therefore *we* don't accept this character" or "*We* feel let down."

CA: You spoke earlier of the importance of the literary background to your work. Are there specific writers who influenced you?

KASDAN: I was very much struck by the work of Joseph Conrad when I was in school, and E. M. Forster and F. Scott Fitzgerald. I think every young American writer is struck by Hemingway. This doesn't mean that there are direct reflections in my work; these are the people that hit me in a strong way. Nabokov drove me crazy when I discovered him, and I also read a great deal of D. H. Lawrence. I was reading and seeing O'Neill and Shakespeare and George S. Kaufman. So who knows? Rock 'n' roll influenced me a lot, and great baseball players. If you grow up in the United States you're bombarded with images. If you then study literature and science and politics, and you're in college during the '60's, how can you say what influenced you the most?

CA: Do you have any theories about why the "Star Wars" kind of movies are so popular now?

KASDAN: I think television has made people lazy. Television is all about instant understanding of conflicts; before the first commercial you have to know who the good guys are and who the bad guys are—and why. Life is not like that. Life has complexity and ambiguity. Some of these movies—some in a delightful way—play into the desire for a simple and immediate understanding of the story line. More than this, people like simply to be delighted by an effect, a cut, or a sound. Those things are very easy. The pictures that require people to work their way through them are more difficult, and they're going to be less popular. Television has created a country that is not patient with art. And the people making films now are coming from a generation raised on television; we're feeling the sad

effects of that. The background of literature and drama, or any other discipline, is pretty much gone. We have people who decide when they're eight that they are going to make movies, and their entire lives are focused on that. They aren't going to come up with the most complex art.

CA: Diane Jacobs has written a book called Hollywood Renaissance, *in which she analyzes the work of John Cassavetes, Robert Altman, Francis Coppola, Martin Scorsese, and Paul Mazursky as exemplary of a new wave of independent talent in movies. I suspect from what you've just said that you don't see any kind of renaissance in progress?*

KASDAN: None, none at all. The economic changes in Hollywood have had the most destructive effect. They're making fewer and fewer movies. There were always a lot of bad movies, but they used to make so *many* movies that there were always a lot of good ones too. Now every movie is such a big roll of the dice, the people giving out the money are looking for ways to guarantee their investment. So they're always trying to second-guess the audience out there—what is it, how old are they, what are they willing to accept? That's what has ruined Hollywood now. I don't see any renaissance at all; I think it's a terribly bleak time, especially right now with the overall economic situation.

The people who distribute films have a stranglehold on the business, because no one else can do that job. Distributing film is terrible, grinding, uninteresting work. It has been historically linked with the people who produce films, though there's no real reason for it to be. As long as the people who run the distribution companies are also making the creative decisions, there will be no renaissance.

CA: Do you have favorite screenwriters and directors among your contemporaries?

KASDAN: I very much admire the work of Robert Towne, Bo Goldman, Alvin Sargent, and John Sayles. These are good screenwriters. And I think there are a lot of good directors working today; I can't even name them all. You know, directors get too much publicity, period. One of the things that's gone wrong in Hollywood is that they want to make directors famous, and the more famous they become, the more powerful they become. A director is not necessarily any better at picking material or realizing it than anyone else. But directors get more and more powerful and you have these *auteurs* springing up right and left. Their work tends to decline after they make their first big splash. The immediate pressure on them to succeed is enormous, and there are unrealistic expectations about what they should be able to do. What we've had in the last five years, I would say, is forty new directors that really emerge with one or two or three films. They're all interesting, and if they were just let be to do their work instead of made into media heroes, it would be great.

CA: You've managed somehow to control your life, to enjoy your home and family, instead of being taken over by Hollywood. Has that been difficult?

KASDAN: Not really. In a way I think you're always in danger of being seduced. The rewards of Hollywood are like the Seven Deadly Sins; they're right out front about what they're offering you. But if you can get past even your simplest base instincts, you'll be all right, because any second look at Hollywood is revolting. It's not that hard to resist; it's obviously such a bad set of values being promulgated.

CA: After "Return of the Jedi," what plans do you have? Any long-range goals you'd like to talk about?

KASDAN: I'm working on a picture right now that's a kind of ensemble comedy, a sort of mosaic. It's a comedy of values, about people around my age and where they're at in the world right now, how it conflicts with where they thought they'd be, what kind of values they're holding on to, the kind of pressures the world puts on them. I have no long-range goals other than to keep doing what I'm doing. It took me a long time to get to do it. The fact that not only do I know what I want to do but that I'm actually allowed to do it seems to me the greatest gift. I just want to continue to write and direct movies.

BIOGRAPHICAL/CRITICAL SOURCES: Chicago Tribune, May 18, 1980, May 25, 1980, June 12, 1981, August 28, 1981, September 18, 1981; *Newsweek,* May 19, 1980, June 15, 1981, August 31, 1981, October 5, 1981; *Time,* May 19, 1980, June 15, 1981, August 24, 1981, September 14, 1981; *New York Times,* June 12, 1981, August 28, 1981, September 18, 1981, November 1, 1981; *Washington Post,* August 30, 1981, September 18, 1981; *Detroit News,* September 20, 1981; *London Times,* January 16, 1982.

—Interview by Jean W. Ross

* * *

KASTAN, David Scott 1946-

PERSONAL: Born January 4, 1946, in Kew Gardens, N.Y.; son of Peter and Audrey Kastan; married Susan Clise. *Education:* Princeton University, A.B., 1967; University of Chicago, M.A., 1968, Ph.D., 1973. *Residence:* Hanover, N.H. *Office:* Department of English, Dartmouth College, Hanover, N.H. 03755.

CAREER: Dartmouth College, Hanover, N.H., instructor, 1973-75, assistant professor, 1975-80, associate professor of English, 1980—. Visiting professor at University of London, 1980-81 and 1983-84. *Member:* Modern Language Association of America, Shakespeare Association of America, Renaissance Society of America.

WRITINGS: Shakespeare and the Shapes of Time, Macmillan, 1982. Contributor of articles and reviews to language and literature journals, including *Daedalus.*

WORK IN PROGRESS: A book on Shakespeare's *The Tempest,* publication by Barnes & Noble expected in 1984; *From Icon to Image* (tentative title), on the Renaissance idea of the imagination, completion expected in 1985.

* * *

KATHMAN, Michael D(ennis) 1943-

PERSONAL: Born December 12, 1943, in Quincy, Ill.; son of William J. and Betty (Costigan) Kathman; married Jane McGurn (an assistant professor of economics and business administration), 1971; children: Kevin, Cara. *Education:* St. Procopius College, B.A., 1966; University of Michigan, A.M.L.S., 1967, A.M., 1969. *Home:* 414 Eighth Ave. N., Cold Spring, Minn. 56320. *Office:* Alcuin Library, St. John's University, Collegeville, Minn. 56321.

CAREER: Worked as reference and periodicals librarian at Monroe Community College, Monroe, Mich.; Wayne County Community College, Detroit, Mich., assistant director of learning research, 1970-72; St. John's University, Collegeville, Minn., director of public services, 1972-74, library director,

1973-80, colloquium instructor, 1974-80, director of joint libraries and media at College of St. Benedict / St. John's University, 1980—. Scholar-in-residence at Chicago Public Library, 1976-77; member of Cold Spring Planning Commission, 1977-80, and Cold Spring City Council, 1978—. *Member:* American Library Association, Minnesota Library Association (vice-president/president-elect, 1982).

WRITINGS: Options for the Eighties, Jai Press, 1982. Contributor to library journals and *St. John's.*

WORK IN PROGRESS: "Research on motivating library student workers."

SIDELIGHTS: Kathman told *CA:* "At first I found it difficult, as a practicing librarian, to do research and writing. After more than fifteen years in the profession I now make the time to write because I find it is both helpful in my day-to-day responsibilities and it is rejuvenating."

* * *

KAUFMAN, Debra Renee 1941-

PERSONAL: Born April 2, 1941, in Cleveland, Ohio; daughter of Max and Ida (a bookkeeper; maiden name, Hoffman) Horwitz; married Michael William Kaufman (a professor and dean), August 25, 1963; children: Alana Rebecca, Marc David. *Education:* University of Michigan, B.A. (with distinction), 1963, M.A., 1966; Cornell University, Ph.D., 1975. *Home:* 143 Ridge Ave., Newton Centre, Mass. 02159. *Office:* Department of Sociology and Anthropology, Northeastern University, Boston, Mass. 02115.

CAREER: State University of New York at Albany, lecturer at Allen Collegiate Center, 1974-75, assistant professor of sociology, 1975-76; Northeastern University, Boston, Mass., assistant professor, 1976-81, associate professor of sociology and anthropology, 1981—, director of women's studies program, 1981-83. Member of national advisory committee of Health Policy Task Force on Women and Mental Health, 1976-77; member of advisory board of Fenway Area Women's Consortium, 1978—; public speaker; guest on television programs.

MEMBER: American Sociological Association, Institute on the Family and Bureaucratic Society, Sociologists for Women in Society (national finance chairperson, 1978-79; member of national advisory board, 1979—), Eastern Sociological Association, Massachusetts Sociological Association (chairperson of academic grievance committee, 1980-81).

WRITINGS: (With Barbara Richardson) *Achievement and Women: Challenging the Assumptions,* Free Press, 1982; (contributor) J. Freeman, editor, *Women: A Feminist Perspective,* Mayfield, 1983; (contributor) C. M. Brody, editor, *Women Working With Women: New Theory and Process of Feminist Therapy,* Springer Publishing, 1983; (contributor) Richardson and Jeana Wirtenberg, editors, *Methodological Issues in Sex Roles and Social Change Research,* Praeger, 1983. Contributor of articles and reviews to academic journals.

WORK IN PROGRESS: Woman's Worth: How Valuable Is She?; Coming Home, a book about women who have returned to orthodox Judaism; an article for *Signs* rebutting "some of the work presently being done that emphasizes the differences between the sexes. Most of my work has emphasized that sex/gender role differences are maximized because of the social conditioning and social context rather than bio-psychological sources."

SIDELIGHTS: Debra Kaufman told *CA:* "I suspect that most of us who are working in the area of women's studies find our work quite exciting. It is truly exciting to be in the forefront of an emerging discipline—to be able to help generate and recreate through your professional expertise your personal roots and identity. In writing *Achievement and Women* I was able to understand the feminist thinkers of the nineteenth century and develop a whole new appreciation for their understanding about political, social, economic, and yes, even personal issues. They were neither passive nor accepting of the cultural constructs that defined them and actively worked to recreate images and new realities. They turned to one another for help, forged friendship networks, and labored in both the public and private spheres demanding that the value of their labors be recognized in both. Indeed their stories are not for women only. Twentieth century feminists have used some of those tactics and redeveloped some of those arguments (still quite relevant even one hundreds years later) as they push for domestic reform through the displaced homemakers bill in Congress and the building of feminist social networks.

"My current research interest on women's return to orthodox Judaism ties into some of the issues related to domestic reform. I believe their return is a blatant critique of current sex roles and family life. They are in many senses like some of the domestic reformers of the nineteenth century who wished to restore the value of domestic labor. I hope to elaborate on this in my forthcoming work. For now I can only say that this is the most exciting research I have done until now. As I speak to these women all over the country I am constantly in awe of them—noting how they bridge what appears to be a huge gap between a feminist orientation and the upgrading of that which is female. This is a feisty (and often formerly feminist) lot of women!"

* * *

KAUFMAN, Martin 1940-

PERSONAL: Born December 6, 1940, in Boston, Mass.; son of Irving (a meatmarket proprietor) and Rose (Langbort) Kaufman; married Henrietta Flax, December 22, 1968; children: Edward Brian, Richard Lee, Linda Gail. *Education:* Boston University, A.B., 1962; University of Pittsburgh, M.A., 1963; Tulane University, Ph.D., 1969. *Home:* 666 Western Ave., Westfield, Mass. 01085. *Office:* Department of History, Westfield State College, Westfield, Mass. 01085.

CAREER: High school history teacher in Winter Haven, Fla., 1964-65; Worcester State College, Worcester, Mass., instructor in history, 1968-69; Westfield State College, Westfield, Mass., assistant professor, 1969-72, associate professor, 1973-76, professor of history, 1977—, director of Institute for Massachusetts Studies, 1981—. Chairman of Westfield Area Interfaith Council, 1978—. *Military service:* U.S. Army Reserve, 1964-70. *Member:* Organization of American Historians, American Association for the History of Medicine.

WRITINGS: Homeopathy in America: The Rise and Fall of a Medical Heresy, Johns Hopkins University Press, 1971; *American Medical Education: The Formative Years, 1765-1910,* Greenwood Press, 1976; *University of Vermont College of Medicine,* University Press of New England, 1979; (editor in chief) *Dictionary of American Medical Biography,* Greenwood Press, 1983. Editorial director of *Historical Journal of Massachusetts,* 1972—.

WORK IN PROGRESS: American Medicine: Past, Present, Future, completion expected in 1987.

SIDELIGHTS: Kaufman told *CA:* "I am far from a brilliant historian and writer; I am a hard worker who does diligent research, tries to ask the right questions, analyzes material, and tries to develop a coherent synthesis. I try to write for the intelligent layman rather than for scholars, and I am most proud of the fact that I have had articles published in *Sports Illustrated, American History Illustrated,* and *Yankee.* Indeed, in one week, millions of people read my article in *Sports Illustrated,* as compared to the thousand who perhaps have read any of my books over a fifteen year period.

"In any discussion of my life and work, there must be mention of the impact of the birth of Richard Lee Kaufman, my son. Ricky is multiply-handicapped, being unable to either walk or talk, and the care he required, combined with his severe behavior problem, resulted in a great turmoil within the house and conflict within the family. From 1976, when we realized that Ricky had a serious problem, to 1981, when he was admitted into the Berkshire Children's Community in Great Barrington, Massachusetts, it was difficult to work, knowing how difficult it was at home. My wife had it much worse, however, since she was at home with the problem twenty-four hours a day, while I could escape by teaching, or by doing research and writing. Yet, many of my accomplishments during these years were achieved under duress.

"Now, with Ricky at a fine residential school, the home life has improved, but I will never be able to resume a normal scholarly life, as we try to visit Ricky at least weekly, and there are always problems related to his needs. Yet, life must go on. I am a better person for having been blessed with Ricky, although at times I was certain that it was more of a punishment than a 'blessing.'"

BIOGRAPHICAL/CRITICAL SOURCES: American Historical Review, autumn, 1973, June, 1977, April, 1980.

* * *

KAZIMIROFF, Theodore L. 1941-

PERSONAL: Born July 18, 1941, in New York, N.Y.; son of Theodore (a dentist) and Emelia (an attorney; maiden name, Pintauro) Kazimiroff; married Marietta Donato (a teacher), July 1, 1972; children: Theodore L., Jr., Michael D. *Education:* Attended Hunter College, 1963-65, Columbia University, 1966, and Brooklyn College of the City University of New York, 1980. *Home:* One Bayside Ave., Roxbury, Rockaway Point, N.Y. 11697.

CAREER: Teacher of the emotionally handicapped in New York, N.Y. *Military service:* U.S. Army, 1959-62. *Member:* United Federation of Teachers, Veterans of Foreign Wars, American Legion. *Awards, honors: The Last Algonquin* was named best book of 1982 by the American Library Association and the School Library Association.

WRITINGS: The Last Algonquin, Walker, 1982. Contributor of articles to magazines, including *Long Island Fisherman,* and to local newspapers.

WORK IN PROGRESS: Stranger in the Mist, a novel using an American Indian theme to convey a contemporary ghost story, publication expected in 1983; an elementary school level science textbook; a collection of Native American stories, myths, and legends for young people.

SIDELIGHTS: The story Kazimiroff tells in *The Last Algonquin* was passed on to him by his father. It is the life story of Two Trees, an old Indian the elder Kazimiroff befriended as a boy.

Two Trees, who claimed to be the only survivor of the Algonquin Indian tribe, told Kazimiroff's father his life story so that when he died, the history of his people would not die with him, but could be passed on. What Two Trees related were details of a journey he took as a youth, traveling across Manhattan and Staten Islands, through New Jersey and parts of Pennsylvania, and the return trek along the Hudson River. Two Trees's memories, the friendship of the man and the boy, and the telling of the tale, all are described by Kazimiroff in his book. "It is a beautiful and affecting story—a quest, a mythical adventure and journey that takes its hero both into himself and into the heartland of 19th-century America," Christopher Lehmann-Haupt described in his *New York Times* review of *The Last Algonquin,* adding, "it makes one visualize a time before the city became all garbage and concrete, when bears roamed the Bronx and trout could be caught in the Bronx River."

Kazimiroff told *CA:* "I am an amateur historian and archaeologist. My collection of Indian artifacts, colonial era and revolutionary war material includes about one million specimens. It is thought to be the largest of its type in private ownership. *All* of it was excavated by my father and me in New York City. My father, Dr. Theodore Kazimiroff, was, until his death in 1980, the official historian of Bronx County.

"The above-mentioned collection is used for study and research into the early lives of Native Americans and colonists. I make it available to interested and qualified groups or individuals."

BIOGRAPHICAL/CRITICAL SOURCES: Washington, D.C., Federal Times, April 19, 1982; *Bay City Times,* June 6, 1982; *Ypsilanti Press,* June 13, 1982; *Milwaukee Sentinel,* June 18, 1982; *El Paso Times,* July 4, 1982; *Richmond News Leader,* July 7, 1982; *Riverdale Press,* July 8, 1982; *New York Times,* July 30, 1982; *Winston-Salem Journal,* August 1, 1982; *Peninsula Times,* August 14, 1982; *Chapel Hill News,* August 22, 1982; *Bronx Press Review,* October 28, 1982.

*   *   *

KEATS, Ezra Jack   1916-1983

OBITUARY NOTICE—See index for *CA* sketch: Born March 11, 1916, in Brooklyn, N.Y.; died of a heart attack, May 6, 1983, in New York, N.Y. Illustrator and author. Keats was the author and illustrator of twenty-two well-received books for children. *The Snowy Day,* his most famous work, received the 1963 Caldecott Medal and was adapted into an award-winning film. *Goggles* was named a Caldecott Honor Book in 1970, and *Hi, Cat* won the Horn Book Award that same year. The film adaptation of *Apt. 3* received the Gold Venus Medallion, and, following the Japanese publication of *Skates,* a Tokyo roller-skating rink was built in Keats's honor. He illustrated eleven books in addition to his own, and he designed the sets and costumes for a musical adaptation of his story *The Trip.* He also designed Christmas cards for UNICEF. His books—some of which have been translated into sixteen languages—include *Whistle for Willie, A Letter to Amy, Pet Show,* and *Kitten for a Day.* Obituaries and other sources: *New York Times,* May 7, 1983; *Publishers Weekly,* May 20, 1983.

*   *   *

KEENE, James A(llen)   1932-

PERSONAL: Born October 27, 1932, in Detroit, Mich.; son of Samuel B. (a lawyer) and Bernice F. (Frazer) Keene; married

Mary Bloom (in energy management), August 12, 1956; children: Karen Keene Gamow, Judi Ann. *Education:* Eastman School of Music, B.M., 1954; Wayne State University, M.M.Ed., 1959; University of Michigan, Ph.D., 1969. *Home:* 1303 West Adams St., Macomb, Ill. 61455. *Office:* Department of Music, Western Illinois University, Browne Hall, Macomb, Ill. 61455.

CAREER: Montana State University, Bozeman, instructor in music, 1959-62; University of Vermont, Burlington, assistant professor of music, 1963-67; Mansfield State College, Mansfield, Pa., associate professor, 1967-69, professor of music 1969-80, chairman of department, 1975-80; Western Illinois University, Macomb, professor of music and chairman of department, 1980—.

WRITINGS: History of Music Education in the United States, University Press of New England, 1982. Contributor to music journals, including *American Music Teacher, Instrumentalist,* and *Journal of Research in Music Education.*

WORK IN PROGRESS: "A programmed text in music appreciation."

SIDELIGHTS: Keene told *CA:* "I was prompted to write my book because no one had written a history of music education in this country since the 1920's. It was a long subject and getting bigger all the time with the increasing interest of doctoral students from America's colleges and universities. The book took a long time to write and could have been written six more times from six different points of view.

"I was taken with the cyclic nature of educational methodology. In each period the educational status quo was criticized and reform was called for. In time, that very reform became suspect and we returned again to a previous philosophy. Yet in every period groups of talented young people grew up to take their places as intelligent, social, political, and business leaders as well as creative artists. They looked back and identified individual teachers who cared and made a difference."

*   *   *

KEESE, Parton   1926-

PERSONAL: Surname is pronounced Keeze; born April 2, 1926, in Brooklyn, N.Y.; son of Parton (an artist) and Grace (in business; maiden name, Crane) Keese; married Jane Wright, September 1, 1949 (divorced January, 1972); married Karen Eberhardt (a writer and photographer), May 29, 1977; children: Peter, Eugenie, John, William, Meredith. *Education:* Dartmouth College, B.A., 1950; University of Denver, M.A., 1951. *Politics:* Independent. *Religion:* "Eclectic." *Home:* 9899 Barnett Valley Rd., Sebastopol, Calif. 95472.

CAREER: Teacher of English and French at private school in Cambridge, Mass., 1951-54; *Worcester Gazette,* Worcester, Mass., copy editor and author of column "Off the Beaten Path," 1954-62; *New York World-Telegram & Sun,* New York City, copy editor, 1962-65; *New York Times,* New York City, sports writer, 1966-82; free-lance writer, 1982—. *Military service:* U.S. Army, 1944-46; became technical sergeant; received Combat Infantryman's Badge. *Member:* Fellowship of Reconciliation, Sierra Club. *Awards, honors:* Page One Award from Newspaper Guild of New York, 1977, for sports column in *New York Times.*

WRITINGS: The Measure of Greatness: An Inquiry Into the Unique Traits and Talents That Set Certain Athletes Apart

From the Rest of the Field, Prentice-Hall, 1980. Contributor to *Sports Illustrated* and *New York Times Magazine*.

WORK IN PROGRESS: Living in the Future Tents, publication expected in 1984; a novel; a screenplay.

SIDELIGHTS: Keese reported: "After sixteen years at the *Times*, and nearly thirty years as a journalist, I retired at age fifty-six to write books, travel, and follow temptation. There will be no restrictions, only attractions."

* * *

KEIDEL, Eudene 1921-

PERSONAL: Born February 9, 1921, in Flanagan, Ill.; daughter of Edward E. and Ida (Augsburger) King; married Levi O. Keidel (a journalist), September 24, 1948; children: Paul, Priscilla Keidel Miller, Perry, Ruth. *Education:* Mennonite Hospital School of Nursing, R.N., 1948; Fort Wayne Bible College, B.S., 1975. *Religion:* Mennonite. *Home:* 1104 West Wildwood Ave., Fort Wayne, Ind. 46807.

CAREER: General Conference of the Mennonite Church, Commission on Overseas Mission, Newton, Kan., missionary nurse in Africa, 1951-82.

WRITINGS: African Fables That Teach About God (for young people), Herald Press, Book I, 1977, Book II, 1980. Contributor to church magazines.

WORK IN PROGRESS: Research on stories in Tshiluba (the vernacular language of south central Zaire) for another book of African fables.

SIDELIGHTS: Keidel told *CA:* "When we discovered the popularity of fables in our public speaking engagements, my husband encouraged me to put together a collection in book form. I worked with Zairian church leaders—speaking in their language —for many years, and this was a rich resource.

"As a small child, whenever anyone asked what I wanted to be when I grew up, I'd reply, 'I'm going to be a missionary.' Our church supported missionaries in Africa, so it was only natural for me to want to go there as a missionary.

"We (my husband and I) worked in south central Zaire (formerly the Belgian Congo) all our years in Africa. Most of the time I worked at a rural dispensary fifty to one hundred miles from the nearest doctor. I learned to do many things there that I could not have done in the United States—like delivering babies and diagnosing and treating illnesses. Most of the time I was on call twenty-four hours a day, seven days a week. But it was rewarding work. I've also done village work, teaching the Bible and helping to establish churches.

"During our last term in Zaire, from 1977 to 1982, I didn't work in medicine, but rather with my husband in village church work. Because of very bad roads, our main means of travel was a Honda motorcycle. We often went out for weekend retreats in villages up to fifty miles away. One of our most interesting trips was made part way by road and part way in a dugout canoe—cycle and all—for a weekend retreat. We never lacked for excitement and plenty to do."

AVOCATIONAL INTERESTS: Travel (Africa and Europe).

* * *

KELLEY, Edith Summers 1884-1956

BRIEF ENTRY: Born April 28, 1884, in Ontario, Canada; died

June 9, 1956, in Los Gatos, Calif. American author. Although Kelley's two major works, the novels *Weeds* (1923) and *The Devil's Hand* (1974), brought the author scant recognition at the time they were published, their revival in the Southern Illinois University Press "Lost Fiction" series has augmented her literary reputation. Both novels reflect Kelley's real-life farm experiences and mirror the realistic/naturalistic literary styles of her acquaintances Sinclair Lewis and Upton Sinclair. Struggling to support her family, the author also wrote "frothy and inconsequential" stories for pulp magazines. *Biographical/critical sources: American Women Writers: A Critical Reference Guide From Colonial Times to the Present*, Ungar, 1979-80; *Dictionary of American Biography, Supplement Six: 1956-1960*, Scribner, 1980; *Dictionary of Literary Biography*, Volume 9: *American Novelists, 1910-1945*, Gale, 1981.

* * *

KELLY, John Maurice 1931-

PERSONAL: Born August 31, 1931, in Dublin, Ireland; son of Joseph and May (Boyle) Kelly; married Delphine Dudley (a solicitor), July 29, 1961; children: Nicholas, David, Alexia, Julia, Bernard. *Education:* National University of Ireland, University College, Dublin, M.A., 1953; University of Heidelberg, Dr.Jur., 1956; Oxford University, B.Litt., 1960, M.A., 1961, D.C.L., 1981; King's Inns, Senior Counsel, 1977. *Office:* Dail Eireann, Dublin 2, Ireland.

CAREER: Private practice of law in Dublin and Eastern Circuit, Ireland, 1957-62; Oxford University, Oxford, England, fellow of Trinity College, 1961-65; University College of the National University of Ireland, Dublin, professor of jurisprudence, 1965—, dean of faculty of law, 1967-70. Member of Irish Senate, 1969-73, and Dail Eireann (Irish Parliament) for Dublin South-Central, Dublin South County, and Dublin South, 1973—, parliamentary secretary to the prime minister and minister for defense, 1973-75, parliamentary secretary to the prime minister and minister for foreign affairs, 1975-77, attorney general, 1977, minister for industry, commerce, and tourism, 1981, minister for foreign affairs, 1981, minister for trade, commerce, and tourism, 1981—.

WRITINGS: Princeps IUDEX, Boehlau (Weimar), 1957; *Fundamental Rights in the Irish Law and Constitution*, Figgis (Dublin), 1961, 2nd edition, 1967; *Roman Litigation*, Oxford University Press, 1966; *Studies in the Civil Judicature of the Roman Republic*, Oxford University Press, 1976; *The Irish Constitution*, Jurist (Dublin), 1980.

WORK IN PROGRESS: The second edition of *The Irish Constitution*.

* * *

KELLY, Thomas 1929-

PERSONAL: Born August 27, 1929, in Dunmore, Pa. *Education:* Pennsylvania State University, B.A., 1958; University of Illinois, A.M., 1959, Ph.D., 1964. *Office:* Department of History, University of Minnesota, Minneapolis, Minn. 55455.

CAREER: University of Kansas, Lawrence, visiting instructor in history, 1963-64; University of Kentucky, Lexington, assistant professor of history, 1964-66; University of Alberta, Edmonton, assistant professor of history, 1966-68; University of Minnesota, Minneapolis, assistant professor, 1968-73, associate professor, 1973-78, professor of ancient Greek history, 1978—. *Military service:* U.S. Air Force, 1948-52. *Member:*

Archaeological Institute of America, Association of Ancient Historians. *Awards, honors:* Fulbright fellow in Greece, 1962-63.

WRITINGS: A History of Argos to 500 B.C., University of Minnesota Press, 1977. Contributor to history, archaeology, and philology journals.

BIOGRAPHICAL/CRITICAL SOURCES: New York Times, July 15, 1970; *American Historical Review,* February, 1978.

* * *

KEMP, Jack (French) 1935-

PERSONAL: Born July 13, 1935, in Los Angeles, Calif.; son of Paul R. (an owner of a trucking firm) and Frances (Pope) Kemp; married Joanne Main, July 19, 1958; children: Jeffrey, Jennifer, Judith, James. *Education:* Occidental College, B.A., 1957; graduate study at Long Beach State University and California Western University. *Politics:* Republican. *Religion:* Presbyterian. *Home:* 3542 South Creed Rd., Hamburg, N.Y. 14075. *Office:* 2235 Rayburn House Office Building, Washington, D.C. 20515.

CAREER: Associated with Detroit Lions and Pittsburgh Steelers (both National Football League [NFL] teams), 1957; member of "taxi squad" of New York Giants (NFL team), 1958, affiliated with Calgary Stampeders (Canadian Football League team), 1958, and with San Francisco 49ers (NFL team), 1959; San Diego Chargers (American Football League [AFL] team), San Diego, Calif., quarterback, 1961-62; Buffalo Bills (AFL team), Buffalo, N.Y., quarterback, 1962-68; Marine Midland Bank of Buffalo, Buffalo, public relations officer, 1969-70; U.S. House of Representatives, congressman from thirty-eighth New York district, 1971—, serving on Appropriations Committee and Defense Subcommittee. Special assistant to the governor of California, 1967; special assistant to the chairman of Republican National Committee, 1969. Member of President's Council on Physical Fitness and Sports. Author; television and radio commentator. *Military service:* U.S. Army, 1958. U.S. Army Reserve, 1958-62.

MEMBER: National Football League Players Association (member of executive committee), National Association of Broadcasters, Engineers, and Technicians, American Football League Players Association (president, 1965-70), Sierra Club, Buffalo Area Chamber of Commerce. *Awards, honors:* American Football League Player of the Year, 1965; All-American Football League quarterback; National Football Foundation and Hall of Fame Award; New York State Junior Chamber of Commerce Distinguished Service Award.

WRITINGS: (With Les Aspin) *How Much Defense Spending Is Enough?,* American Enterprise Institute for Public Policy Research, 1976; *An American Renaissance: A Strategy for the 1980's,* Harper, 1979.

SIDELIGHTS: After eleven years as a professional football quarterback, Kemp retired from the game when he suffered a knee injury in 1968. He ran for U.S. Congress in 1970 and was narrowly elected on this initial attempt. He has garnered outstanding majorities in subsequent elections and ran unopposed by the Democratic party in 1978. As early as 1974, after he had been influenced by the economic and social theories of Walter Laffer, Jude Wanniski, and Irving Kristol, *Time* chose Kemp as one of "Two Hundred Faces for the Future." Kemp had initiated a great deal of legislation in his first term and expressed a willingness to attack problems, which he called "opportunities."

A burgeoning public interest in Kemp's Laffer-influenced economic theory became evident in 1978 when he addressed seven state Republican (GOP) conventions and two national GOP meetings and campaigned aggressively for several other congressmen. At this time, *Newsweek* reported that his impact rested largely on the fact that he was "preaching big tax cuts to a tax-weary public." Kemp used this time in the public light to communicate the possibilities of what columnist George Will later called "activist conservatism."

In 1979, Kemp detailed his policy in *An American Renaissance: A Strategy for the 1980's,* which Paul A. Gigot of the *National Review* termed "the *Manifesto* to complement Wanniski's *Das Kapital.*" The work contained sections on national defense, inflation, and energy policy, but was primarily a treatise on Kemp's Laffer-influenced theory of economics. Together with William V. Roth, he proposed the Kemp-Roth 30 percent tax cut as a primary incentive to economic growth in an economy he felt had contracted because of overtaxation. Gigot noted that Kemp's proposal differed from classical Republican economic thought because it provided for "a tax cut without ties to specific reductions in government spending." His continuance of "safety net" programs for those unable to take advantage of the tax cut's resultant economic growth (particularly the elderly) was thought to anticipate and answer attacks from liberal opponents. Gigot concluded that Kemp's book offered "an innovative program, shrewdly articulated."

Robert Lekachman, in a *New Republic* article, viewed *An American Renaissance* differently. He found inconsistencies in its alignment of ideologies and criticized Kemp's tendency to ignore obstacles to the predicted expansion under his program. Although he considered the book "pleasantly written in a tone of agreeable idealism and malice toward none," he viewed it in total as "rather more interesting as a campaign document."

Kemp's important policy-making role in GOP politics became widely evident at the Republican National Convention held in Detroit in 1980. He was considered a possible vice-presidential candidate for a time, but more importantly, his Kemp-Roth tax-cut package and another proposal for the establishment of "urban enterprise zones" were fitted into the Republican platform and embraced by presidential candidate Ronald Reagan. One of Kemp's supporters told *Newsweek* that "Kemp could be what John F. Kennedy was to the 1956 Democratic convention—the guy who turns heads and will be heard from again."

BIOGRAPHICAL/CRITICAL SOURCES: Time, July 15, 1974; *Newsweek,* February 20, 1978, May 26, 1980, July 28, 1980; *New Republic,* August 4, 1979; *National Review,* September 14, 1979, January 25, 1980.*

* * *

KENDALL, Maurice (George) 1907-1983

OBITUARY NOTICE: Born September 6, 1907; died March 29, 1983. Mathematician, statistician, and author. Kendall first became interested in statistical research while working in the British Civil Service during the 1930's. During World War II he served as statistician for the British Chamber of Shipping, all the while working on statistics textbooks, including *An Introduction to the Theory of Statistics* and *The Advanced Theory of Statistics,* which are still considered leading works in the field. In 1949 Kendall joined the London School of Economics and Political Science statistics department, remaining for twelve years. He then became director and chairman of

SCICON, a computer consulting company. After assuming directorship of the World Fertility Survey in 1972, Kendall was awarded the United Nations Peace Medal for his studies of world population. His other notable books include *Dictionary of Statistical Terms* and *Bibliography of Statistical Literature*. Obituaries and other sources: *Who's Who*, 133rd edition, Marquis, 1981; *International Authors and Writers Who's Who [and] International Who's Who in Poetry*, 9th edition, Melrose, 1982; *The International Who's Who*, 46th edition, Europa, 1982; *London Times*, March 31, 1983.

* * *

KENNEDY, Marilyn Moats 1943-

PERSONAL: Born April 15, 1943, in Kansas City, Kan.; daughter of Orin L. (a lawyer) and Georgia (a secretary; maiden name, Jeffries) Moats; married Daniel Joseph Kennedy, Jr. (a banker), June 3, 1967; children: Anne Evelyn. *Education:* Attended Baker University, 1961-62; Northwestern University, B.S.J., 1965, M.S.J., 1966. *Politics:* Republican. *Religion:* Presbyterian. *Home and office:* 2762 Eastwood St., Evanston, Ill. 60201. *Agent:* Jane Jordan Browne Multimedia Product Development, Inc., 410 South Michigan Ave., Room 828, Chicago, Ill. 60605.

CAREER: DePaul University, Chicago, Ill., assistant professor of journalism and director of student publications, 1966-77, assistant dean of students, 1969-76, associate dean of students, 1976-77; Career Strategies (consultants), founder, 1975, managing partner and consultant in career planning and management, 1977—. *Member:* Women in Management (president of North Shore chapter, 1978-79; national secretary, 1981; national first vice-president, 1982), Chicago Headline Club (president, 1976-77), Chicago Women in Communications (president, 1980).

WRITINGS: Office Politics: Seizing Power, Wielding Clout, Follett, 1980; *Career Knockouts: How to Battle Back*, Follett, 1980; *Salary Strategies: Everything You Need to Know to Get the Salary You Want*, Rawson, Wade, 1982; *Building and Holding a Power Base*, Macmillan, in press. Also author of "Job Strategies," a monthly column for *Glamour*. Contributor of articles to periodicals, including *Mademoiselle, Graduating Engineer, Self*, and *Savvy*.

WORK IN PROGRESS: A novel about murder and office politics, completion expected in 1984.

SIDELIGHTS: While researching material for *Office Politics: Seizing Power, Wielding Clout*, Kennedy interviewed 1,000 people who had been fired from their jobs, discovering that only twenty-five percent were dismissed for incompetence, whereas conflicts with employers and co-workers accounted for most other firings. Her advice for preventing such conflict situations includes tips on developing skills in office politics and practicing "personal distancing" from the workplace in order to be better able to assess the situation from an objective stance. "She talks concretely—and not for women only—about how to assess what's going on within the organization, how to develop informal information networks, and cope with unforeseen change," Susan McHenry wrote in *Ms*.

Kennedy told *CA:* "I have been intensely interested in office politics for years. My consulting fits very nicely with writing because I usually consult with companies about employee-related problems and/or employees having work-related problems. This provides an unending source of ideas, information, and problems to write about. I have always been strongly re-search oriented and find focus group research especially valuable in trying to find out people's work-related attitudes.

"I think I'd find it very difficult to write as much as I do about careers and job-related problems if I weren't 'on the stump' so much. What audiences ask about is exactly what career articles will deal with six to eighteen months from now. By hearing the questions people ask and watching their work-related concerns change, I have an enormous advantage in timing my writing to appear when a trend is on the up side. Individual career counseling also helps direct my research.

"Office political problems are especially difficult to write about unless one is constantly in contact with people who have problems. If you would try to make up a problem you thought most people had, you'd find out most didn't. This is one kind of writing in which imagination doesn't enter into writing until the problem has been verified."

BIOGRAPHICAL/CRITICAL SOURCES: Ms., November, 1980.

* * *

KERESTESI, Michael 1929-

PERSONAL: Born January 24, 1929, in Rotko, Hungary. *Education:* Received M.A. from Eastern Michigan University; received M.A.L.S. and Ph.D. from University of Michigan. *Office:* Department of Library Science, Wayne State University, 315 Kresge, Detroit, Mich. 48202.

CAREER: University of Michigan, Ann Arbor, head of acquisitions department at Law Library, 1962-67; Tusculum College, Greeneville, Tenn., associate professor of history, 1967-69; University of Michigan, lecturer in library science, 1969-73; Wayne State University, Detroit, Mich., associate professor of library science, 1973—. *Member:* Association for the Bibliography of History (president, 1982-83), American Library Association, Association of American Internationalists, Association of College and Research Libraries, Association of American Library and Information Education, Beta Phi Mu.

WRITINGS: UNESCO's Contribution to Library Education and Training, University Microfilms, 1977; (with Gary Cocozzoli) *German-American History and Life*, Gale, 1980; (contributor) Cerise Oberman and Katina Strauch, editors, *Theories of Bibliographic Education*, Bowker, 1982. Contributor to library journals.

WORK IN PROGRESS: Guide to Holocaust and Genocide Research; Mass Culture in Hungary: Profile of a Maverick Soviet Satellite, completion expected in 1985.

* * *

KERIN, Roger A(nthony) 1947-

PERSONAL: Born April 19, 1947, in Duluth, Minn.; son of Joseph and Mary (Mekota) Kerin; married Shirley Goldman, June 22, 1979; children: Suzanne. *Education:* University of Minnesota, Duluth, B.A., 1969; University of Minnesota, Minneapolis, M.B.A., 1970, Ph.D., 1973. *Office:* Edwin L. Cox School of Business, Southern Methodist University, Dallas, Tex. 75275.

CAREER: Southern Methodist University, Dallas, Tex., assistant professor, 1973-76, associate professor, 1977-80, professor of marketing and director of research, 1980—. Visiting professor of marketing at University of Texas at Austin, 1976-77. *Member:* American Marketing Association, American Psychological Association, American Institute for Decision Sciences.

WRITINGS: Strategic Marketing Problems: Cases and Comments, Allyn & Bacon, 1978, 2nd edition, 1981; *Perspectives on Strategic Marketing Management,* Allyn & Bacon, 1980, 2nd edition, 1983. Contributor to marketing journals.

WORK IN PROGRESS: Research on strategic issues in retailing, improving data collection procedures in marketing research, and the impact of product and process innovation on marketing performance.

* * *

KESHET, Harry F(inkelstein) 1940-

PERSONAL: Original name, Harry Finkelstein; name legally changed in 1978; born August 6, 1940, in Philadelphia, Pa.; son of Samuel (in business) and Reba (Ladin) Finkelstein; married Jamie Kelem Keshet (a psychotherapist), April 25, 1976; children: Matthew, Ezra, Daniel. *Education:* Temple University, B.S., 1962, M.A., 1964; University of Michigan, Ph.D., 1974. *Home:* 124 Cabot St., Newton, Mass. 02158. *Office:* Riverside Family Counseling, 259 Walnut St., Newton, Mass. 02160.

CAREER: University of Massachusetts—Boston, instructor in psychology and sociology, 1972-75; Divorce Resource Center, Cambridge, Mass., clinical director, 1976-79; Riverside Family Counseling, Newton, Mass., director and psychologist, 1979—. *Member:* American Psychological Association, National Association of Social Workers.

WRITINGS: (With Kristine M. Rosenthal) *Fathers Without Partners: A Study of Fathers and the Family After Marital Separation,* Rowman & Littlefield, 1980. Contributor to magazines and newspapers.

WORK IN PROGRESS: Research on remarriage and step-families, and on fathering, marriage, and the family.

SIDELIGHTS: Keshet told *CA:* "A major difficulty in child development is the little time spent with fathers. Children of divorced parents frequently lose even this limited connection with their fathers. The need to encourage men to more involvement with their children, both within the nuclear family and after divorce, was the motivation for my book *Fathers Without Partners.* The divorced father can gain insights into his role as father and into the emotional, social, and personal problems of parenting. He can also gain knowledge of the great variety of post-divorce fathering roles available."

* * *

KESSLER, Francis P(aschal) 1944-
(Frank Kessler)

PERSONAL: Born December 15, 1944, in St. Louis, Mo.; son of Joseph J. (a physician) and Margaret (Burns) Kessler; married Mary Virginia Meeks (a guidance counselor), December 11, 1971; children: Julia, Gloria, Paul, Thomas. *Education:* St. Louis University, B.A., 1966, M.A., 1967; University of Notre Dame, Ph.D., 1971. *Religion:* Roman Catholic. *Residence:* St. Joseph, Mo. *Office:* Department of Political Science, Missouri Western State College, A-212-E, St. Joseph, Mo. 64507.

CAREER: Missouri Western State College, St. Joseph, assistant professor, 1971-75, associate professor, 1975-79, profes-

sor of political science, 1979—. Lecturer at U.S. and Canadian colleges and universities; guest on television and radio programs. *Member:* American Political Science Association, Presidency Research Group (member of national steering committee, 1982—), Danforth Foundation Associates, Center for the Study of the Presidency, Southern Political Science Association, Missouri Political Science Association (member of council, 1982-84). *Awards, honors:* Scholar-diplomat at U.S. Department of State's National Conference on Foreign Policy, 1975; grant from National Endowment for the Humanities, 1976; outstanding educator award from Metropolitan Jaycees, 1978; associate of Danforth Foundation, 1979-85.

WRITINGS: (Contributor) Edward N. Kearney, editor, *Dimensions of the Modern Presidency,* Forum Press, 1981; *Dilemmas of Presidential Leadership: Of Caretakers and Kings,* Prentice-Hall, 1982; (contributor) William C. Spraegens, editor, *Popular Images of the American Presidents,* Greenwood Press, 1982. Contributor of articles and reviews, sometimes under the name Frank Kessler, to political science and history journals and popular magazines.

WORK IN PROGRESS: Making a Mesh of Things: American Government Politics, publication expected in 1985.

* * *

KESSLER, Frank
See KESSLER, Francis P(aschal)

* * *

KESSNER, Lawrence 1957-

PERSONAL: Born November 28, 1957, in Lancaster, Pa.; son of Paul (a business executive) and Miriam (a business executive; maiden name, Lewitz) Kessner; married Audrey Bernstein (an attorney), August 7, 1982. *Education:* Johns Hopkins University, B.A., 1979. *Home:* 4000 North Charles St., Baltimore, Md. 21218. *Office:* Baltimore Sunpapers, 501 North Calvert St., Baltimore, Md. 21203.

CAREER: Baltimore Evening Sun, Baltimore, Md., reporter, 1979—. Member of advisory board of University of Maryland's Center for Public Policy conference on nuclear deterrence, 1983. *Member:* American Newspaper Guild, Alpha Tau Omega. *Awards, honors:* Gavel Award for excellence in law-related reporting from Maryland Bar Association, 1980, for "Killers at the Wheel," a series of articles.

WRITINGS: The Spy Next Door (novel), Crown, 1981.

SIDELIGHTS: Lawrence Kessner told *CA:* "My book came about as the result of an article I wrote in the *New York Times.* The article was a recollection of my high school years in Hartsdale, New York, as the classmate of Peter Hermann, who later turned out to be a second-generation Soviet spy. An editor at Arlington House, which is now a division of Crown Publishing, saw the article, contacted me, and within a few weeks I was offered a contract and an advance to write a book. I was twenty-two at the time and thrilled to have the opportunity to have a book published just a year after graduating from college."

* * *

KETCHUM, J.
See FRENTZEN, Jeffrey

KIDDER, Tracy 1945-

PERSONAL: Born November 12, 1945, in New York, N.Y.; son of Henry Maynard (a lawyer) and Reine (a high school teacher; maiden name, Tracy) Kidder; married Frances T. Toland, January 2, 1971. *Education:* Harvard University, A.B., 1967; University of Iowa, M.F.A., 1974. *Agent:* Georges Borchardt, Inc., 136 East 57th St., New York, N.Y. 10022.

CAREER: Writer, 1974—. *Military service:* U.S. Army, served in intelligence in Vietnam; became lieutenant. *Awards, honors:* Atlantic First Award from *Atlantic Monthly* for short story, "The Death of Major Great"; Sidney Hillman Foundation Prize, 1978, for article, "Soldiers of Misfortune"; Pulitzer Prize and American Book Award, both 1982, for *The Soul of a New Machine.*

WRITINGS: The Road to Yuba City: A Journey Into the Juan Corona Murders (nonfiction), Doubleday, 1974; *The Soul of a New Machine* (nonfiction), Little, Brown, 1981. Contributing editor, *Atlantic Monthly,* 1982—. Contributor to newspapers and magazines, including *New York Times Book Review, Science '83,* and *Country Journal.*

SIDELIGHTS: Tracy Kidder's *The Soul of a New Machine* garnered him two prestigious literary awards in 1982 and proved, by its critical reception, that technical subjects can be comprehensible and intriguing to laymen when they are skillfully presented.

The book details the eighteen-month-long struggle of engineers at Data General Corporation to create a competitive super-mini computer. Kidder, a newcomer to this highly technical world, spent months in a basement laboratory at the corporation's Massachusetts headquarters observing teams of young engineers at work: the hardware specialists, or "Hardy Boys," who put the computer's circuitry together, and the "Microkids," who developed the code that fused the hardware and software of the system. In the story of the assembly, the setbacks, and the perfection of the thirty-two "bit" prototype computer, the Eagle, Kidder exposes the inner workings of a highly competitive industry, illustrates both concentrated teamwork and moments of virtuosity on the part of the project's brilliant engineers, and produces what reviewer Edward R. Weidlein, in the *Washington Post Book World,* judged "a true-life adventure" and "compelling entertainment."

Critics agreed that Kidder's masterful handling of the complex subject matter in *The Soul of a New Machine* was one of the book's strongest features. "Even someone like this reviewer," wrote Christopher Lehmann-Haupt of the *New York Times,* "who barely understood the difference between computer hardware and software when he began 'The Soul of a New Machine,' was able to follow every step of the debugging mystery, even though it involves binary arithmetic, Boolean algebra, and a grasp of the difference between a System Cache and an Instruction Processor." Weidlein concurred, observing that Kidder "offers a fast, painless, enjoyable means to an initial understanding of computers, allowing us to understand the complexity of machines we could only marvel at before."

Kidder's portraits of the Eagle's engineers were applauded by reviewers as well. Samuel C. Florman claimed that in Kidder's narrative, the young men "are portrayed as eccentric knights errant, clad in blue jeans and open collars, seeking with awesome intensity the grail of technological achievement." A *New Yorker* review echoed Florman, declaring that Kidder "gives a full sense of the mind and motivation, the creative genius of the computer engineer." The *Saturday Review* claimed that

The Soul of a New Machine "tells a human story of tremendous effort."

Critics also lauded *The Soul of a New Machine* for its departure from the standard journalistic approach to nonfiction. Samuel C. Florman, for instance, found that "Kidder has endowed the tale with such pace, texture and poetic implication that he has elevated it to a high level of narrative art." Jeremy Bernstein, in the *New York Review of Books,* declared, "I strongly recommend Tracy Kidder's book. I do not know anything quite like it. It tells a story far removed from our daily experience, and while it may seem implausible, it has the ring of truth."

CA INTERVIEW

CA interviewed Tracy Kidder by phone July 2, 1982, at his home in Williamsburg, Massachusetts.

CA: The Soul of a New Machine has been praised on several counts, not least among them your being able to render technical information intelligible to a general reader. How did you feel starting out on the book with no technological background of your own?

KIDDER: I was used to that. I had done some articles for the *Atlantic Monthly* on technical subjects that I previously knew nothing about. If you're a journalist who doesn't cover a single beat, it's a familiar feeling to know nothing about what's going on. So, it wasn't all that unusual. It is a rather painful feeling not to know what the people around you are talking about. But that's also an impetus to figure it out. This topic was a little more forbidding than some things, that's true.

CA: The engineers involved in the building of the computer Eagle were working under tremendous physical and psychological stress, as you described in the book, yet they took the time to explain things to you. Did your presence ever create any problems?

KIDDER: Not that I know of; I don't think so. I tried to keep out of the way when I could. I think if I had created any important problems the engineers would have thrown me out. The company did throw me out for a while, but that's a different story.

CA: You described some extremely interesting people, such as twenty-two-year-old Neal Firth, who could write three hundred lines of computer programming code in his mind but couldn't remember his phone number.

KIDDER: Yes. They were a pretty varied bunch of people.

CA: Did you hear from any of the Eagle team after the book was published? Were they pleased with the book?

KIDDER: Yes. I've spoken to a number of them, and I think they were pleased. Some probably more than others, but I don't know of anyone who's angry.

CA: Have you had a lot of mail in response to The Soul of a New Machine?

KIDDER: Yes. I certainly have. The response to the book has made it very hard to get back to work, but I'm finally doing it. For a while it was rough.

CA: Do you try to answer all your mail?

KIDDER: Yes. I answer everything. But it's not that bad. It's just something one does. At one point it did get pretty hot and heavy; I had a friend who came down and I dictated letters to him. In fact, that's what I've been doing today, answering mail. But I don't let it get in the way anymore. I just do it, take three hours or five hours or whatever it takes at one time during the month to do it and then just let it sit for the rest of the time.

CA: Columbia Pictures bought the movie option. Are there definite plans for a movie?

KIDDER: I don't really know what the story is. There was a screenwriter who was working on it, but I think he may have dropped out; I don't know why or anything like that. I'm interested in it. I think it's sort of fun, and a nice idea, but I have nothing to do with it myself, either with the negotiations over the option or creating the screenplay. And I think that's the way it should be; it really is not a world that I understand. It's interesting, but I'm not terribly anxious to take it on to that point. I've got other things to do, and I'm not worrying about that at all.

CA: You said in an article in People *magazine (January 4, 1982) that, unlike many observers, you don't believe in a computer revolution.*

KIDDER: Well, mostly I should say I get a little annoyed at the "Gee Whiz" stuff you hear and read about computers sometimes. They've been made into something so different, it seems to me, from what they are or can be imagined to be. And *revolution* is a funny word: every time anything changes, every time there's anything new, there's somebody around who's willing to call it a revolution. *Revolution* implies a great social and political upheaval, and I think that in those terms the computer is a conservative instrument. That's not my idea, by the way. But like most new things, it's used by the people who are in power to *increase* their power. I'm not denouncing it on those grounds necessarily, but that's a fact. That's more or less what I was trying to say. Also, if you read about what computers do, it's really quite astonishing; they do seem so trivial. But I've been dealing with some scientists lately, and there is no question but that computers are vitally important in most sorts of scientific research these days—for good or ill, I don't know.

CA: Have you gotten one yourself?

KIDDER: No. I don't need one. I have an electric typewriter. I have my own way of doing things, and I'm a little superstitious, perhaps, a little bit set in my ways. I see no reason to change. In the kind of writing I do, I don't think it would be of any help at all. If I were a daily reporter, I'd feel very differently about it; if speed were of the essence, you know. Sometimes my deadlines *seem* excruciating, but when I'm doing articles I usually have a month or more, so I really don't need one of those things.

CA: You spent three years at the University of Iowa Writers' Workshop before your first book, The Road to Yuba City, *was published in 1974. Would you comment on what the Writers' Workshop meant to you as a young, beginning writer?*

KIDDER: The best thing about that place is that it's a nice refuge, a place where you can go. At that time I was broke and just trying to write, and I wasn't having any success. I got

a little fellowship there and it was wonderful for me. First of all, being there made me realize that there were an awful lot of other people in the world who were trying to do what I was attempting to do. It was good in that way. Humiliating, so to speak. I made a lot of friends there. Iowa gave me some feeling of legitimacy. At least I was earning a little money and I could call myself a writer. And Iowa City is one of the most interesting towns I've ever known.

CA: When had you first started to write seriously?

KIDDER: I started writing short stories in college, and I think that's when I fastened on the idea of being a writer. Then I went in the army and went to Vietnam, and when I got back there wasn't anything else I thought I really wanted to do except be a writer, so I gave it a shot.

CA: Edwin McDowell reported in the New York Times Book Review *(November 29, 1981) that you felt* The Road to Yuba City *hadn't sold particularly well because you weren't able to do the kind of personality study of Juan Corona, who was convicted of mass murder, that Capote and Mailer had done with their criminal subjects. Was that what you set out to do originally?*

KIDDER: No. I didn't know what I was doing. That was the first real piece of journalism I ever did; it started with an article I did for the *Atlantic Monthly.* I don't remember saying that to Edwin McDowell, but if he says I did, then I'm sure I did. But that seems a little strange, because I don't know what makes one book sell and another not. True, one of the big things missing in *The Road to Yuba City* was the real personality of the accused murderer. But I think it was a sufficiently interesting book; it just didn't get reviewed very widely. There are probably a lot of things wrong with it. It's way behind me now and it's very hard for me to talk about it. I tend to try to kill things off to get on with the next thing.

CA: From the topics that you've undertaken to write about—computers, solar energy devices, the Kennedy assassination, the problems of Vietnam veterans, and so on—I assume that you enjoy doing research.

KIDDER: Yes, I do once I get lost in it. I've gotten a little tired of traveling, to tell you the truth. I like to write. I particularly like to write after I've done a first draft—I don't much like doing that. It's an awfully nice profession because I'm able to meet a lot of different and interesting people and get into a lot of fascinating subjects.

CA: Most of your major articles have been published in the Atlantic Monthly, *where you are now a contributing editor. How did your association with the magazine come about?*

KIDDER: I met Dan Wakefield, another contributing editor at *Atlantic Monthly,* in Iowa, and he wrote to Bob Manning, who was then chief editor, and got me some credentials to cover the Juan Corona case. That's how it happened, and it's been my professional home ever since.

CA: You've cited George Orwell, A. J. Liebling, and John McPhee as journalistic models. Are there fiction writers whom you especially like?

KIDDER: Yes. Incidentally, I don't mean by conjuring up those three names to compare myself to them. They're just wonderful. I also read a lot of fiction. Among the contemporary writers of fiction, I like Updike and Cheever, Peter Matthiessen, and a fellow named Stuart Dybek, who I think is one of the best short-story writers around. And I like a lot of others, too.

CA: Would you like to write more fiction?

KIDDER: Yes, sure. I do dabble at it. But I'm mostly a journalist now. Someday I'd like to write more fiction, but not for a while, probably.

BIOGRAPHICAL/CRITICAL SOURCES: New York Times, August 11, 1981; *New York Times Book Review,* August 23, 1981, November 29, 1981; *Washington Post Book World,* September 9, 1981; *New York Review of Books,* October 8, 1981; *New Yorker,* October 19, 1981; *Saturday Review,* December, 1981.

—*Interview by Jean W. Ross*

*   *   *

KIDWELL, Catherine (Arthelia)   1921-

PERSONAL: Born January 14, 1921, in Lowry City, Mo.; daughter of Thomas A., Sr. (in sales) and Lela (a dental receptionist; maiden name, Riddle) Witty; married Don Basil Kidwell, June 30, 1946 (divorced February, 1976); children: Christopher Alan, Iva Jane Kidwell Washburn. *Education:* New York School of Interior Design, Certificate, 1958; University of Nebraska, B.F.A., 1974, M.F.A., 1977; University of London, Certificates, 1976, 1977. *Politics:* "Democrat or Independent." *Religion:* Unitarian-Universalist. *Home and office:* 643 South 11th, No. 1, Lincoln, Neb. 68508. *Agent:* Susan F. Schulman, 165 West End Ave., New York, N.Y. 10023.

CAREER: Secretary in Wichita, Kan., 1938-42; medical secretary in Lincoln, Neb., 1942-43; Elastic Stop Nut Corp., Lincoln, executive secretary, 1943-45; U.S. Veterans Administration, Lincoln, secretary to contact officer, 1945-47; Kidwell Electric Co., Inc., Lincoln, office manager and bookkeeper, 1948-58; Catherine Kidwell Interiors, Lincoln, interior designer, 1958-67; J. L. Brandeis (department store), Lincoln, interior designer, 1967-69; Southeast Community College, Lincoln, instructor in fiction writing, 1976—. Member of local symphony guild. *Member:* LaSertoma. *Awards, honors:* First prize for fiction from *Prairie Schooner,* 1977, for excerpts from novel, *The Woman I Am.*

WRITINGS: The Woman I Am (novel), Dell, 1979; *Dear Stranger* (novel; Literary Guild selection), W. H. Allen, 1982, Warner Books, 1983. Contributor of articles and poems to magazines, including *Broomstick* and *Nebraska Counselor.*

SIDELIGHTS: "My novels reflect my renaissance in middle age," Catherine Kidwell wrote. "I started college as a freshman along with my daughter. I began to live again, this time unfolding the real me instead of the character I had created to suit everyone else. One of the crucial precipitators of this rebirth was the novel I began in fiction writing classes, which ultimately became a master's thesis.

"As a child, I yearned to be an 'author,' but I left writing behind with high school. My marriage was the prime consideration of my life, both before and after the wedding. I raised two children and simultaneously worked in my husband's electrical contracting business (my existence was never acknowledged on company records). My aesthetic sensibility led to

attempts to find a career as an interior designer, but the limitations on the time and money I devoted to it made me a failure until a spur-of-the-moment decision led me to apply for and obtain a job as a department store designer. This was the first breakthrough that led to a return to college for an art degree and the eventual shift to English—to literature and writing.

"I never did get back to interior design. I still do oil painting, an unexpected side benefit from the art and design studies. I have had some shows. I don't paint as well as I write, but it is another creative outlet. I love to listen to music. All the arts are of tremendous importance to me: they make the difference between living and just existing.

"I left my husband in 1975, after twenty-nine years. The happiness I have found in single life makes me wonder if marriage should never have been my choice. I have been so thrilled to discover that it's not too late. I'm so much better equipped to enjoy the single life now than I was in my twenties.

"I have been abroad four times since 1976. Three trips involved college credit (summers in London and Paris, and an art tour on the continent); the fourth was a Smithsonian Institution trip to the U.S.S.R. I love big cities and still am a hopeless romantic about story-book places.

"I teach fiction writing to adults at our local community college. I think writing technique can be taught and can be very helpful to the aspiring writer who can add this asset to his/her talent and hard work. I enjoy contacts with other writers. We are people who see life a little differently, recognizing the dramatic possibilities in our own crises even as we experience them.

"My goal, always, is to produce quality writing. Being a 'good' writer means more to me than money or fame, although I would have no objection to having it all."

BIOGRAPHICAL/CRITICAL SOURCES: Lincoln Journal and Star, August 19, 1979; *Daily Nebraskan,* September 11, 1979; *Omaha World-Herald,* December 9, 1979; *Red Oak Express,* March 31, 1980; *Wichita Eagle-Beacon,* August 7, 1980, September 5, 1982; *Santa Ana Register,* December 28, 1982.

*   *   *

KILGORE, Kathleen   1946-
(Kathleen Houton)

PERSONAL: Born July 11, 1946, in Washington, D.C.; daughter of Lowell Berry (a chemist) and Helen (a teacher; maiden name, Ford) Kilgore; married Daniel J. Houton (a contract administrator), October 7, 1969; children: Hong phung Duong (adopted), Mariah Gifford. *Education:* Oberlin College, A.B., 1968; Fletcher School of Law and Diplomacy, A.B., 1968. *Politics:* Liberal Democrat. *Religion:* Unitarian-Universalist. *Home:* 63 Temple St., Dorchester, Mass. 02126. *Agent:* Llewellyn Howland III, 100 Rockwood St., Jamaica Plain, Mass. 02130.

CAREER: Harbridge House (business consultants), Boston, Mass., editor, 1969-70; *Metro: Boston* (magazine), Boston, contributing editor, 1970-71; *Boston,* Boston, contributing editor, 1972-75; free-lance writer, 1975-78; Word Guild, Cambridge, Mass., subcontractor, 1978-80. Clerk of corporation for Children's Centers, Inc., 1975—. Trustee of First Parish Unitarian Church, 1978-82; member of board of directors of Benevolent Fraternity of Unitarian Churches, 1979—; secretary of advisory committee of Unitarian-Universalist Legal Ministry in Dorchester, 1982—. *Member:* Irish National Caucus, Massachusetts Bay District Unitarian-Universalist Association (secretary, 1981—), Lower Mills Civil Association, Dorchester Residents for Racial Harmony, Friendly Sons of St. Patrick of Boston.

WRITINGS: The Wolfman of Beacon Hill (young adult), Little, Brown, 1982; *The Sorcerer's Apprentice* (young adult), Houghton, in press. Contributor of more than one hundred articles and stories, some written under the name Kathleen Houton, to magazines and newspapers, including *Yankee, Phoenix, New Englander,* and *Boston Herald-American.*

WORK IN PROGRESS: A novel set in Northern Ireland and Boston, completion expected in 1985; a novel about a Vietnamese-American girl's attempt to find her real father, completion expected in 1986.

SIDELIGHTS: Kathleen Kilgore wrote: "I grew up in Chevy Chase, Maryland, and spent some of my childhood in Geneva, Switzerland, where my father was a delegate to the General Agreements on Tariff and Trade, and where I served as his translator. I had intended to pursue a career in the U.S. Foreign Service but became involved in Boston politics instead when my husband ran for Congress as a peace candidate in 1970. We now live in Dorchester, a working-class neighborhood that seems much farther from Chevy Chase than any foreign service post. I came as an upper middle class WASP into a tight ethnic neighborhood and a large Irish-American family thirteen years ago, and I am still in the process of adjustment.

"My husband's family comes from a fishing village in a remote part of County Donegal, and my husband and I have made extended trips there, including time in occupied Derry and the border areas. We are involved in supporting groups that favor the reunification of Ireland. We see many parallels to the racial situation here in Boston and have organized meetings, committees, marches, and benefit parties around this issue over the past several years.

"Dorchester is an area of racial and ethnic conflict, as the older Irish American community has seen an influx of blacks, South Americans, Haitians, Cape Verdeans, Vietnamese, Laotians, and Cambodians. Two of my short stories, 'The Confrontation' and 'The Night Watch,' dealt directly with this theme, but it has also influenced my work indirectly. My daughter began school in Roxbury at the height of the busing crisis. Then, in 1981, we added to our family's diversity by becoming parents of a fifteen-year-old Vietnamese refugee.

"My first two novels are for young adults, and while I find this an interesting genre, I would like to reach a wider audience. I often find myself torn, in time and energy, between commitments to working on community problems and my profession as a writer. Sometimes the two coincide, and publicizing issues in nonfiction articles generates action. At other times, my community work provides the material for the beginning of a piece of fiction. It is difficult to balance the two."

* * *

KIM, David U(ngchon) 1932-

PERSONAL: Original name, Ung Chon Kim; name legally changed in 1975; born May 29, 1932, in Chunchon, Korea; came to the United States in 1965, naturalized citizen, 1975; son of Jong Shik and Jang Soon (Song) Kim; married Helen Kyongsook Yun, May 10, 1969; children: Douglas. *Education:* Kyung Hee University, B.A., 1962; Villanova University, M.S.L.S., 1967; Indiana University, Ph.D., 1980. *Home:* 1

Berryfrost Lane, The Woodlands, Tex. 77380. *Office:* University Library, Sam Houston State University, Huntsville, Tex. 77341.

CAREER: Indiana State University, Terre Haute, acquisitions librarian, 1969-78; University of Lowell, Lowell, Mass., head of technical services and collection development at university library, 1978-81; Sam Houston State Universtiy, Huntsville, Tex., assistant professor and director of library technical and automated services, 1981—. *Member:* American Library Association, Association of College and Research Libraries, Library and Information Technology Association.

WRITINGS: Policies of Publishers, Scarecrow, 1976, 3rd edition, 1982. Contributor to library journals.

WORK IN PROGRESS: Policies of Book Wholesalers.

SIDELIGHTS: Kim told *CA:* "*Policies of Publishers* was intended to help librarians find information concerning publishers from whom they often order. The information contained in the book enables librarians to prepare appropriate library orders, which in turn benefit publishers. In building library collections, however, I do not recommend direct orders from all publishers. Librarians should know the policies of individual publishers and use direct orders selectively. Publications of other publishers may be purchased more conveniently from dependable library book wholesalers. *Policies of Book Wholesalers,* when published, will complement *Policies of Publishers.*"

BIOGRAPHICAL/CRITICAL SOURCES: Reference Quarterly, summer, 1976; *Journal of Academic Librarianship,* July, 1976; *Special Libraries,* April, 1983.

* * *

KIMMEL, Stanley (Preston) 1894(?)-1982

OBITUARY NOTICE: Born c. 1894; died July 28, 1982, in Sarasota, Fla. Historian and author. Kimmel wrote several books during his lifetime, including *Mr. Lincoln's Washington* and *The Mad Booths of Maryland.* (Date of death provided by author Irving Dillard.)

* * *

KIMMEL, William (Breyfogel) 1908-1982

OBITUARY NOTICE: Born October 23, 1908, in Dayton, Ohio; died December 12, 1982, in New York, N.Y. Musicologist, educator, and author. At Hunter College of the City University of New York, Kimmel developed and taught more than forty-five music courses during his thirty-one-year tenure from 1948 to 1979. Specializing in music history and aesthetics, he also taught at the City University Graduate Center. He wrote *Polychoral Music and the Venetian School* and co-edited *Dimensions of Faith: Contemporary Prophetic Protestant Theology.* Obituaries and other sources: *Directory of American Scholars,* Volume I: *History,* 8th edition, Bowker, 1982; *New York Times,* December 15, 1982.

* * *

KINDER, Gary 1946-

PERSONAL: Born September 5, 1946, in Gainesville, Fla.; son of Irving William (an accountant) and Peggy (Grimm) Kinder; married Alison Evans (an interior designer), November 26, 1977. *Education:* University of Florida, B.S., 1968, J.D., 1971. *Home and office address:* Box 423, Sun Valley, Idaho

83353. *Agent:* Arthur Pine Associates, 1780 Broadway, New York, N.Y. 10019.

CAREER: University of Florida College of Law, Gainesville, instructor in legal writing and research, 1971; Sun Valley Resort, Sun Valley, Idaho, bellman, 1972-74; free-lance legal researcher, advertising copywriter, and teacher at writer's workshops, 1974—. Assistant part-time prosecutor of Blaine County, Hailey, Idaho, 1972-74.

WRITINGS: Victim: The Other Side of Murder (nonfiction), Delacorte, 1982.

SIDELIGHTS: Gary Kinder's first book, *Victim: The Other Side of Murder,* relates the incidents of a multiple murder that occurred in Utah in 1974. Three Air Force enlisted men commandeered and robbed a stereo store, taking two employees (Stan Walker and Michelle Ansley), one of the employee's fathers (Orren Walker), a sixteen-year-old customer (Cortney Naisbitt), and Naisbitt's mother, Carol, as hostages. After raping Ansley, the servicemen forced their prisoners, except Orren Walker, to drink Drano, an idea inspired by a Clint Eastwood movie, and then shot each of them in the head. The elder Walker was choked, and a pen was driven through his ear. Only he and Cortney Naisbitt, who was comatose for weeks, survived.

In effect, *Victim* is about Cortney Naisbitt and his recovery, though some of the shortcomings of the legal system are embodied in this work. As Kinder, an attorney, points out, the servicemen, all convicted of murder charges, may have their death sentences commuted, thus establishing their eligibility for parole. One is already at the sixth of the nine levels of appeal.

Critically, Kinder's book has been compared to the 1965 classic *In Cold Blood.* "'Victim' is, in many ways," noted William Smart in the *Washington Post Book World,* "a mirror of Truman Capote's 'In Cold Blood' in its intensity and the feeling of 'being there'—in the basement during the murders, in the hospital, in the morgue. But there is an important difference. In Kinder's book that focus is on the victims, not the murderers." Gene Lyons, writing in *Newsweek,* agreed. "'Victim,'" he stated, "is Truman Capote's 'In Cold Blood' turned inside out, the story of a ghastly 1974 mass murder from the point of view of the innocent, rather than the killers."

Continuing his praise for the book, Lyons indicated that *Victim* is "an absorbing, cleanly written story of love and survival that ennobles the family's awful ordeal. Though 'Victim' is Kinder's first book[,] . . . his ability to make complex medical and legal matters clear and dramatic is matched by his good judgment in allowing his subjects their own voices." "In 'Victim,'" Smart explained, "it is not the prose that rivets our attention: It is the story itself, and it is to Kinder's credit that he puts the story first. His writing style is clear and straightforward, and he pulls his readers into the story with a crisp, stark narrative and the actual words of the members of the Naisbitt family."

Kinder told *CA:* "Hemingway once said, and I am paraphrasing, 'If you know something about a story and you leave it out, you strengthen your story.' The process at work here is subconscious, and I don't know *how* it works. I only know *that* it works. It is the principle on which I structured the story in *Victim,* much as Hemingway produced the slim volume *The Old Man and the Sea* rather than a village epic. My purpose in *Victim* was not to tell the story of the Hi-Fi Murders; that sort of thing had been done many times before. I wanted to use the murders only as a vehicle to tell a much larger story—that of the victims' experience. And more than telling that experience, I wanted to convey it to the reader, to make it seem as if it had actually happened to the reader or someone close to him. The only way I could do that was to narrow the focus. So I cut out everything that was typical of a true-crime story: the community reaction to the murders, the police investigation after the arrest, most of the trial, and of course any emphasis on the perpetrators (though the primary one is profiled). What remains is a story of people, one that evokes a range of emotions."

BIOGRAPHICAL/CRITICAL SOURCES: Newsweek, September 13, 1982; *Washington Post Book World,* October 16, 1982.

*   *   *

KINDRED, Alton R(ichard) 1922-

PERSONAL: Born January 8, 1922, in Clermont, Fla.; son of Carl Landow (an accountant) and Eva (a teacher; maiden name, Isaac) Kindred; married Lucia C. Morris, August 23, 1942 (died, 1976); married Carolyn Estes (a patient representative), December 23, 1976; children: Marsha Kindred Polk, Alton Richard, Jr., John M. *Education:* Florida Southern College, B.S.E., 1943, M.A., 1949; Nova University, Ed.D., 1978. *Religion:* United Methodist. *Home:* 3503 20th Ave. Dr. W., Bradenton, Fla. 33505. *Office:* Department of Data Processing, Manatee Junior College, 5840 26th St. W., Bradenton, Fla. 33507.

CAREER: Florida Southern College, Lakeland, bursar, 1946-62; Manatee Junior College, Bradenton, Fla., chairman of data processing, 1962-82, director of institutional research, 1971-82, professor of computer science, 1983—. *Military service:* U.S. Marine Corps Reserve, 1943-46, 1950; became captain. *Member:* Data Processing Management Association (president, 1962-64), Association for Computing Machinery, Association for Educational Data Systems, Florida Association of Community Colleges (vice-president, 1981), Florida Association for Educational Data Systems (president, 1971-72).

WRITINGS: Data Systems and Management, Prentice-Hall, 1973, 3rd edition, in press; *Introduction to Computers,* Prentice-Hall, 1976, 2nd edition, 1982.

WORK IN PROGRESS: Structured Assembly Language for IBM Computers; Human Relations, with Burnette R. Tinsley.

AVOCATIONAL INTERESTS: Travel (Europe, Africa, China and the Orient, Central America, Iceland and Greenland, the Faroe Islands).

*   *   *

KING, Martha L. 1918-

BRIEF ENTRY: Born March 16, 1918, in Crooksville, Ohio. American educator and author. King was an elementary school teacher until 1959. In that year she became a professor of reading and language arts at Ohio State University. King coedited *Critical Reading* (Lippincott, 1967), *The Language Arts in the Elementary School: A Forum for Focus* (National Council of Teachers of English, 1973), and *Language, Children, and Society: The Effect of Social Factors on Children Learning to Communicate* (Pergamon, 1979). *Address:* Department of Early Childhood Education, Ohio State University, 1945 North High St., Columbus, Ohio 43210.

KING, Tony 1947-

PERSONAL: Born March 9, 1947, in Hull, England; son of James William Henry (a ship's carpenter) and Vera (Cooney) King; married Sylvia Davies (a medical secretary), April 9, 1983. *Education:* Hull College of Art, Diploma in Graphic Design, 1966. *Home and office:* Hines, 33 Gosmore Rd., Clehonger, Herefordshire, England.

CAREER: Graphic designer and illustrator at Wolff-Olins, London, England, 1966-70; free-lance graphic designer and illustrator, 1970—.

WRITINGS—Children's books: *Pea,* G. Whizzard, 1972; *The Moving Alphabet Book* (self-illustrated), Heinemann, 1982; *The Moving Animal Book* (self-illustrated), Heinemann, 1983.

Illustrator: Claire Rasner, *The Body Book,* G. Whizzard, 1978; G. Tarrant, *Butterflies,* Heinemann, 1982; Tarrant, *Frogs,* Heinemann, 1982.

WORK IN PROGRESS—Children's books: *Petrified Polar Bears; Where's Me Boots?,* for Heinemann; *The Moving Colour Book; Rabbits,* for Heinemann; *Bees,* for Heinemann.

SIDELIGHTS: Tony King told *CA:* "I have always liked drawing animals, watching films about them on television, and reading about them. My books were a heaven-sent opportunity to indulge my interests and create something interesting at the same time.

"I was looking for a way to do an alphabet book that hadn't been thought of before. I tried a few approaches and eventually came up with the wheel and window solution. There are eight pictures on the wheel—as you turn it a different picture comes up in the window on the page. *The Moving Alphabet Book* was successful so I was asked to think of some other books using the moving idea, hence the animal and color books."

The *New York Times Book Review* deemed *The Moving Alphabet Book* "intriguing fun" and noted "Tony King's illustrations are clear and appealing."

BIOGRAPHICAL/CRITICAL SOURCES: New York Times Book Review, September 26, 1982.

*   *   *

KINTER, Judith 1928-

PERSONAL: Born February 16, 1928, in Boston, Mass.; daughter of Ralph Andrew (an electrical engineer) and Alice (Tower) Potter; married Richard S. Kinter (a social worker), December 27, 1962; children: Laura Jane, Michael, Carol. *Education:* Attended Middlebury College, 1945-48; University of Utah, B.A., 1949, Elementary Teaching Certificate, 1960. *Home:* 6847 Sutter Ave., Carmichael, Calif. 95608.

CAREER: KDYL-TV, Salt Lake City, Utah, member of staff and part-time television writer, 1949-50; teacher in Salt Lake City, 1961; KSCI-TV, secretary, 1955-72; associated with Channel Eighteen in Los Angeles, Calif., 1972-73; free-lance typist, 1978—; free-lance writer.

WRITINGS: Cross Country Caper (for teens), Crestwood, 1981.

Author of "The Shot" (one-act adaptation of work by Pushkin), first broadcast by KDYL-TV, 1949. Author of column, "Discoveries in a Fig Grove." Contributor of about fifty stories and poems to church magazines and *My Weekly Reader.*

WORK IN PROGRESS: Robin Hood of San Francisco, a children's book.

SIDELIGHTS: Kinter told *CA:* "Everything I write is to share my awareness of life, my appreciation of what have been significant discoveries, to me, for all are variations of the theme that life is basically love and joy, available to everyone. *Cross Country Caper* is about a runner who succeeds when his heart catches up with the rest of him. *Robin Hood of San Francisco* is about a young idealist beggar who helps his friend adjust to the real world but can't do it himself. 'Discoveries in a Fig Grove' is a column of direct observations in living joyfully to share with anyone who may want to share them."

*   *   *

KIRP, David L(eslie) 1944-

PERSONAL: Born April 15, 1944, in New York, N.Y.; son of Murray and Ruth (Hamburger) Kirp. *Education:* Amherst College, B.A. (cum laude), 1965; Harvard University, LL.B. (cum laude), 1968. *Home:* 1058 Greenwich St., San Francisco, Calif. 94133. *Office:* Graduate School of Public Policy, University of California, 2607 Hearst Ave., Berkeley, Calif. 94720.

CAREER: Harvard University, Cambridge, Mass., instructor, 1968-69, assistant professor of education and director of Center for Law and Education, 1969-71, lecturer in education and social policy, 1969-71; University of California, Berkeley, acting associate professor, 1971-74, associate professor, 1974-78, professor of public policy, 1978—, lecturer in law, 1971—; *Sacramento Bee,* Sacramento, Calif., associate editor, 1983—. Distinguished lecturer at University of the Pacific, 1976; lecturer at colleges and universities in the United States and the Netherlands. National fellow at University of Chicago's Educational Finance and Productivity Center, 1979; senior research fellow and coordinator of law program at Stanford University's Institute for Research on Educational Finance and Governance, 1979—. Member of board of trustees of Amherst College, 1971-74; member of national advisory board of Vanderbilt University's Center for the Study of Families and Children, 1975-79; member of advisory board of Oakland Children's Advocacy Center, 1977—. Member of National Institute of Education's law and government study group, 1971—, Carnegie Council on Policy Studies in Higher Education's technical advisory committee, 1978, and American Academy of Arts and Sciences panel on ethnicity and schooling, 1978; consultant to Stanford Research Institute, Organization for Economic Cooperation and Development, and UNESCO.

MEMBER: Association for Public Policy Analysis and Management (chairman of panel on law and policy, 1980-81), Phi Beta Kappa. *Awards, honors:* Spencer fellow of National Academy of Education, 1976; Ford Foundation travel fellow, 1977; fellow of Van Leer Jerusalem Foundation, 1977.

WRITINGS: (With Mark Yudof) *Educational Policy and the Law,* McCutchan, 1974, 2nd edition (with Yudof, Tyll van Geel, and Betsy Levin), 1982; *Doing Good by Doing Little: Race and Schooling in Britain,* University of California Press, 1979; *Just Schools: The Idea of Racial Equality in American Education,* University of California Press, 1982.

Contributor: *Equal Educational Opportunity,* Harvard University Press, 1969; R. Grinnel and C. Clarke, editors, *Readings in Urban Education,* Simon & Schuster, 1971; Lowell Wingo, editor, *Metropolitanization and Public Service,* Johns Hopkins University Press, 1972; Allan Sindler, editor, *Policy and Politics in America,* Little, Brown, 1973; *The Rights of Children,* Harvard University Press, 1974; Nicholas Hobbs, editor, *Classification of Children,* Volume II, Jossey-Bass, 1975; *Contin-*

uing Challenge: The Past and the Future of Brown versus Board of Education, Notre Dame Center for Civil Rights, 1975; Sindler, editor, *America in the Seventies: Problems, Policies, and Politics*, Little, Brown, 1977; Howard Kalodner and James Fishman, editors, *Limits of Justice: The Courts' Role in School Desegregation*, Ballinger, 1978; Stephen Goldstein, editor, *Law and Equality in Education*, Van Leer Jerusalem Foundation, 1980; Louis Rubin, editor, *Critical Issues in Educational Policy*, Allyn & Bacon, 1980; Adam Yarmolinsky, Lance Liebman, and Corinne Schelling, editors, *Race and Schooling in the City*, Harvard University Press, 1981.

Reporter for *Time*, 1964. Correspondent for *Times Educational Supplement*, 1977—. Author of column in *Christian Science Monitor*, 1971-75. Contributor of more than fifty articles and reviews to education and law journals, magazines, including *Change* and *Urban Review*, and newspapers. Member of advisory board of *Social Policy*, 1974—.

WORK IN PROGRESS: Gender Justice, with Mark Yudof and Marlene Franks; editing *School Days, Rule Days: Regulating American Education*, publication expected in 1984.

BIOGRAPHICAL/CRITICAL SOURCES: Christian Science Monitor, June 21, 1974, September 15, 1980.

* * *

KIRSCH, Charlotte 1942-

PERSONAL: Born November 17, 1942, in Rockland, Maine; daughter of Max (an automobile dealer) and Ida (Shapiro) Gopan; married twice (divorced); children: Scott Andrew Cohen, Melissa Beth Cohen. *Education:* Attended Boston University, 1978; Antioch University, Cambridge, Mass., M.Ed., 1980. *Politics:* Independent. *Religion:* Jewish. *Residence:* West Newton, Mass. *Agent:* Peter Ginsberg, Curtis Brown Ltd., 575 Madison Ave., New York, N.Y. 10022. *Office:* Employee Communications Services, Inc., 12 Michigan Dr., Natick, Mass. 01760.

CAREER: WGUY-Radio, Bangor, Maine, copywriter, 1961-62; WBOS-Radio, Boston, Mass., traffic director, 1962-63; Aetna Life & Casualty Co., Boston, life insurance broker, 1975-81; Employee Communications Services, Inc., Natick, Mass., copy director, senior writer, and producer of audiovisual presentations, 1981—. Director of Boston Family Institute's national study of the bereaved. Poster conceptualizer for Studio One, Philadelphia, Pa., 1972-74. *Member:* International Association of Business Communicators, Hadassah (past president).

WRITINGS: A Survivor's Manual, Doubleday, 1981, reprinted as *Facing the Future*, Penguin, 1983. Author of insurance brochures.

WORK IN PROGRESS: Getting Rich With Gold Stocks, completion expected in 1983; *Maxwell and Rufus*, a children's book, completion expected in 1983; *Maxwell and Rufus Meet Dr. Peepers*, completion expected in 1983; *Whisper in His Ear*, a book exploring sexual fantasies; research on the effect of the women's movement on widowhood; research for a full-length children's film.

SIDELIGHTS: Kirsch told *CA:* "While I was working as a life insurance broker, I counseled newly-bereaved beneficiaries on the safe investment of their life insurance proceeds. It became clear to me that they were not in the right frame of mind to make investment decisions that could have a serious effect on the rest of their lives. Furthermore, at that time, there were no

publications dealing with the psychological connection of death and money. I approached a major life insurance company and was awarded a grant to study the effect of inheritance on mourning. While I was writing my book, I left the life insurance industry. I found much more satisfaction with writing, and decided to pursue it as my life's career.

"Since completion of my first book I have become the senior writer with a large employee benefits communications consulting company. This gives me the opportunity to explain employee benefits clearly and concisely, deleting all the legal mumbo-jumbo, so that employees can use their benefits effectively.

"My own children, who are teenagers, are a major force in my writing. I have been divorced from their father for many years and have raised them single-handedly. I often test my ideas and manuscripts on them. Not only do I value their input, but if they can understand my copy, then so can the average reader, who is my audience.

"When I studied for my master's degree in education, I became interested in audiovisual work, so it is not a mystery that I favor scriptwriting as the most challenging part of my job as a communicator. Someday I plan to write a feature-length film for television or the movies. Undoubtedly it will focus on widowhood, and undoubtedly my heroine will have financial troubles."

AVOCATIONAL INTERESTS: Writing children's stories, hiking (including the Alps, the White Mountains, and the Cape Cod dunes).

BIOGRAPHICAL/CRITICAL SOURCES: Money, May, 1981; *Houston Working Woman's Journal*, May, 1981.

* * *

KIRSCHEN, Leonard 1908-1983

OBITUARY NOTICE: Born in 1908 in Romania; died April 30, 1983. Journalist. Kirschen began his journalism career working for British national newspapers in Hungary and Turkey. Appointed Associated Press correspondent in Bucharest, Romania, after World War II, the journalist reported on the activities of the Soviet occupation forces and their eventual takeover of the country. In 1950 Kirschen was arrested, tortured, and sentenced to twenty-five years imprisonment by Communist authorities. Pressure from Western nations brought about his release in 1960, and he returned to work for the Associated Press in London. Kirschen recalled his decade of suffering and imprisonment in *Prisoner of Red Justice*, published in 1963. Obituaries and other sources: *London Times*, May 4, 1983.

* * *

KIS, Danilo 1935-

BRIEF ENTRY: Born February 22, 1935, in Subotica, Yugoslavia. Yugoslav author. Kis is best known for the antiwar sentiments that characterize much of his fiction, including two books published in English translation, *Garden, Ashes* (Harcourt, 1975) and *A Tomb for Boris Davidovich* (Harcourt, 1978). His *Pescanik* (title means "Sand-Glass") was named the best Yugoslav novel of 1972. *Biographical/critical sources: Christian Science Monitor*, September 22, 1975, October 23, 1978; *New Statesman*, December 19, 1975; *World Literature Today*, summer, 1977, winter, 1977, autumn, 1979.

KJELGAARD, James Arthur   1910-1959
(Jim Kjelgaard)

BRIEF ENTRY: Born December 6, 1910, in New York, N.Y.; died July 12, 1959, in Milwaukee, Wis. American author. Before becoming a full-time writer at age twenty-eight, Kjelgaard held a variety of jobs, including trapper and surveyor's assistant. His books for children are marked by their narrative simplicity, their diverse locales, and their preponderance of animal heroes. *Big Red* (1945), Kjelgaard's most notable work, is one in a series of three books about Irish Setters. He also wrote two books featuring a character based on his forest ranger brother, *A Nose for Trouble* (1949) and *Trailing Trouble* (1952). Kjelgaard won a Spur Award from the Western Writers of America in 1957 for *Wolf Brother. Biographical/critical sources: Publishers Weekly*, August 10, 1959; *Wilson Library Bulletin*, September, 1959; *Authors of Books for Young People*, 2nd edition, Scarecrow, 1971; *Twentieth-Century Children's Writers*, St. Martin's, 1978; *Science Fiction and Fantasy Literature*, Volume II: *Contemporary Science Fiction Authors II*, Gale, 1979.

* * *

KJELGAARD, Jim
See KJELGAARD, James Arthur

* * *

KLEE, James B(utt)   1916-

PERSONAL: Born August 5, 1916, in New York, N.Y.; son of Charles H. (a bank officer) and Anna Marie (Butt) Klee; married Martha Belle Ferar, December 21, 1941 (died October 1, 1946); married Lucille J. Hollies (a professor of education), September 20, 1959; children: Margaret Ann, Kathren Elizabeth. *Education:* University of Michigan, B.S., 1938, M.A., 1941, Ph.D., 1943. *Politics:* Independent Democrat. *Home:* 24 Forest Dr., Carrollton, Ga. 30117. *Office:* Department of Psychology, West Georgia College, Carrollton, Ga. 30118.

CAREER: Wesleyan University, Middletown, Conn., assistant professor of psychology and research associate, 1944-46; Carnegie Institute of Technology (now Carnegie-Mellon University), Pittsburgh, Pa., assistant professor of psychology, 1946-49; University of Arizona, Tucson, assistant professor of psychology, 1949-50; University of Nebraska, Lincoln, visiting professor of psychology, 1950-51; Brandeis University, Waltham, Mass., assistant professor, 1951-58, associate professor of psychology, 1958-71; West Georgia College, Carrollton, professor of psychology, 1969—. Fulbright lecturer at University of Allahabad, 1963-64. *Member:* American Psychological Association, Association for Humanistic Psychology, Transpersonal Psychology Association, Sigma Xi, Phi Kappa Phi.

WRITINGS: The Relation of Frustration and Motivation in the Production of Abnormal Fixation in the Rat (monograph), American Psychological Association, 1944; *Problems of Selective Behavior* (monograph), University of Nebraska, 1951; *Points of Departure: Aspects of the Tao*, And Books, 1982. Contributor of about thirty-five articles to learned journals in the United States, Japan, and India.

WORK IN PROGRESS: Research on psychology and religion, psychology and history, and creativity as an aspect of time.

AVOCATIONAL INTERESTS: Travel (Japan, China, Southeast Asia, including Burma, Thailand, Vietnam, Hong Kong, Malaysia, and Singapore), Oriental religions, driving, train travel, sailing small boats.

* * *

KLINE, Nathan S(chellenberg)   1916-1983

OBITUARY NOTICE—See index for *CA* sketch: Born March 22, 1916, in Philadelphia, Pa.; died during heart surgery, February 11, 1983, in New York, N.Y. Psychiatrist and author. Kline developed drug therapy to allow mentally ill patients to live outside of institutions, introducing the use of such drugs as the antidepressants lithium and iproniazid and the tranquilizer resperine. He became the director of research at Rockford State Hospital in 1952 and served as the research director of Haiti's Center of Psychiatry and Neurology, an organization he helped to establish. Kline acted as a consultant to the World Health Organization. He received Albert Lasker Medical Research awards in 1957 and 1964, but an associate credited himself with the research in question and successfully contested the second award. Kline's writings include *Synopsis of Eugen Bleuler's Dementia Praecox; or, The Group of Schizophrenias, Drugs: To Use, Not Abuse—You and Your Health*, and *From Sad to Glad: Kline on Depression.* Obituaries and other sources: *Current Biography*, Wilson, 1965, May, 1983; *Time*, February 28, 1983; *Newsweek*, February 28, 1983.

* * *

KNIES, Elizabeth   1941-

PERSONAL: Born March 31, 1941, in Harrisburg, Pa.; daughter of Russel K. (a police officer) and Mary (Burgan) Knies. *Education:* Allegheny College, B.A., 1963; graduate study at University of New Hampshire, 1983—. *Home:* 423 Court St., Apt. 3, Portsmouth, N.H. 03801.

CAREER: Strawbery Banke, Inc. (historical museum), Portsmouth, N.H., publicist, 1974-77; Strawbery Banke Chamber Music Festival, Portsmouth, administrator, 1977-79; free-lance writer and editor, 1979—. Poetry residencies in AIS programs, 1974-83.

WRITINGS: Streets After Rain (poems), Alice James Books, 1980. Work represented in anthologies, including *Threesome Poems*, Alice James Books, 1976. Film and drama critic.

WORK IN PROGRESS: A book of poems.

SIDELIGHTS: Elizabeth Knies told *CA:* "My most important literary affiliation has been with the Alice James Poetry Cooperative in Cambridge, Massachusetts, publishers of Alice James Books. The press is largely, though not exclusively, run by women. It was formed in 1974 and continues to operate successfully on the principles of shared work and cooperative decision making. Alice James Books publishes between two and four books of poetry each year and keeps its titles in print.

"As for writing itself, who knows anymore what is meaningful or what will last? With so many poets and so little poetry, the situation is certainly confusing. Yet what is the use of being disturbed about it? Better to concentrate on the process, which is the same as it always was—a private, even hermetic, endeavor. In the end I think the value of writing, for a poet at least, is not so much communication with the public as it is communication with the source of inspiration. Not that it isn't wonderful to have a reader, and that does happen from time to time."

KNIGHT, Charles   1910-

PERSONAL: Born August 26, 1910, in England; son of Herbert (a manager) Knight; married Rosina Brooks, May 22, 1934; children: Alan, Brian. *Education:* Attended schools in Watford, England. *Politics:* "Liberal (with a small 'l')." *Religion:* Church of England. *Home:* 87 High Rd., Leavesden Green, Watford, England.

CAREER: Book publisher, 1931-64; George Allen & Unwin Ltd. (publisher), London, England, director, 1964-76, managing director, 1970-76, vice-chairman, 1973-76; writer, 1976—. Member of board of directors of Blackie & Sons Ltd., Sir Joseph Caliston, George Allen & Unwin (India) Ltd., and Taylor Maynard Properties. *Military service:* Royal Air Force, 1940-45.

WRITINGS: (With Margaret Brooks) *Complete Guide to British Butterflies,* J. Cape, 1982. Contributor to journals.

WORK IN PROGRESS: Research on insect anatomy, physiology, and behavior.

SIDELIGHTS: Knight commented: "I want to bring a wider and more comprehensive understanding of all forms of animal life to the problem of conservation, without concentrating on just the members of a fortunate few species."

BIOGRAPHICAL/CRITICAL SOURCES: Times Literary Supplement, July 2, 1982.

*   *   *

KOEHLER, Lyle P(eter)   1944-

PERSONAL: Surname pronounced *Kay*-ler; born March 6, 1944, in Sparta, Wis.; son of Lyle Daniel (a lumberjack and farmer) and Irene (a factory worker; maiden name, Endres) Koehler. *Education:* Wisconsin State University—LaCrosse, B.A., 1966; University of Cincinnati, M.A., 1968. *Politics:* Independent. *Home:* 1736 Madison Rd., Cincinnati, Ohio 45206. *Office:* University of Cincinnati, Clifton Ave., Cincinnati, Ohio 45221.

CAREER: Worked as a lumberjack and as a strawberry and bean picker in Wisconsin, 1958-62; Ring & Brewer's Clothiers, Dallas, Tex., stock clerk, 1962-63; City of LaCrosse, Wis., city recreation director, 1963; Wisconsin State University—LaCrosse, instructor in Western civilization, 1966-67; University of Cincinnati, Cincinnati, Ohio, academic tutor in history and black studies, 1971-78, assistant director of campus-wide tutoring, 1978-79, director of tutorial and referral services, 1979—, instructor in history of education, 1974, instructor in psychology, 1977, research consultant to president of university, 1979-80, lecturer in American history and Western civilization, 1980—. Elected Democratic Party precinct executive from Hamilton County, Ohio, 1974. Arts Consortium, Cincinnati, Ohio, consultant, 1981—.

MEMBER: Organization of American Historians, National Association of Interdisciplinary Ethnic Studies, Society of American Legal History, Humanists Club (vice-president, 1965-66), Wisconsin Historical Society, Monroe County Historical Society, University of Cincinnati Association of Mid-Level Administrators. *Awards, honors:* Eugene B. Murphy fellowship, 1965; National Defense Education Act fellowship, 1967-71; Mott Foundation award to prepare history of Westwood, Ohio, 1979; Pulitzer Prize finalist for *A Search for Power,* 1981.

WRITINGS: History of Cataract, Wisconsin, Wisconsin State University, 1967; *From Frontier Settlement to Self-Conscious American Community: A History of One Rural Village (Sparta, Wisconsin) in the Nineteenth Century,* Unigraphics, 1977; *Feminism, Education, and Social Change: A Case Study of the Public School System in Cincinnati, Ohio, 1830-1880,* HEW (Department of Health, Education, and Welfare) Educational Resources Information Center, 1980; *A Search for Power: The "Weaker Sex" in Seventeenth-Century New England,* University of Illinois Press, 1980; *A History of Westwood in Ohio: Community, Continuity, Change,* Westwood Civic Association, 1981; *A Chronological History of Cincinnati's Black Peoples, 1787-1982,* Arts Consortium, in press. Contributor of articles to professional journals.

WORK IN PROGRESS: "An irreverent view of New England Puritans titled *Drunkards, Sex Maniacs, and Other Reprobates: A History of Joy in Old New England*"; a textbook history of America's ethnic peoples (including a considerable focus on women); and a comparison of violence in three colonial cultures (Puritan, Hispanic, and Dutch).

SIDELIGHTS: Koehler told *CA:* "*A Search for Power* attempts to do many things. First, it attempts to disprove the idea of a colonial paradise for women in New England, in line with the work done by Lois Green Carr, Linda Kerber, Carole Shammas, Carol Berkin, and Mary Beth Norton in other regions and for other times. Secondly, it asserts that women's options varied by locale, being more open in non-Puritan Rhode Island, New Hampshire, and Maine, and most restricted in Massachusetts and Connecticut. Thirdly, it maintains that society liberalized a bit at late century in the most restrictive locale, Massachusetts. Fourthly, it provides a psychological context for understanding men's and women's actions/reactions in early New England, including some analysis of the hysterical fit, witchcraft, suicide, religious heresy, infanticide, and deviant behavior. In effect, the work describes how women found individual ways to influence events in their lives and assert a sense of their own impact on others within the context of their culture.

"I wrote *A Search for Power,* beginning in 1971, after I had gone through a period of some anguish and culture shock in attempting to move from a rural to an urban environment. My own personal struggle contributed to my perceptions of the varied situations and needs of society's 'others'—be they women, blacks, Appalachians, Indians, or any of the many ethnic groups. I also believe, based on my research as well as my own experience, that, when faced with extremely disconcerting situations, people act; they find ways to cope. Nothing I found in the old New England records suggested otherwise.

"Although *A Search for Power* was nearly completed by the time Martin Seligman's *Helplessness: On Depression, Development, and Death* was widely available, I found his work very helpful in clarifying the psychological basis I had discovered operable in Puritan New England. Seligman unknowingly supplied the title for my book. Seligman reviewed a number of human and animal studies to come to the conclusion that most, if not all, creatures need a sense of control over their own lives and environments and, if deprived of the same, will fall into clinical depression and even die. His research implied that people, including New England Puritans, would, when frustrated and feeling that they had little control over their lives, attempt to exert such control in a variety of ways, including through social institutions, ideology, physical force, and imaginative (albeit often idiosyncratic) actions. Their psychological survival—their search for power—requires no less.

"Thus, the first third of my book sets the stage by describing how New England Puritans found themselves in a particularly 'powerless' state vis-a-vis the English authorities, the awesome wilderness, their all-powerful God, and their child-rearing patterns and how they compensated by holding women in an increasingly subordinate state. Women, then, in turn, devised strategies to enable them to exercise more control over their own lives and the lives of others by covert manipulation, hysteria, witchcraft, and overt/covert rebellion. Women as actors is the theme of this section of the book. A third section describes the changes occurring at late century.''

*   *   *

KOESTLER, Arthur   1905-1983

OBITUARY NOTICE—See index for *CA* sketch: Born September 5, 1905, in Budapest, Hungary; died of a drug overdose, c. March 3, 1983, in London, England. Journalist and author. A famed political writer who based his works on his personal experiences, Koestler was a member of the German Communist party from 1931 to 1938. While reporting on the Spanish Civil War for London and Budapest newspapers, he was arrested by Franco forces and sentenced to death. He was later released, however, following British intervention and worldwide protest against his imprisonment. At the start of World War II he was arrested by the Vichy Government and interned until 1940. His account of that experience is contained in the autobiographical work *Scum of the Earth.* After the war, he became a British subject and devoted himself to writing antitotalitarian literature. He explained his disillusionment with the Communist party in *The God That Failed,* a collection of writings by several ex-communists. His best known work, the highly acclaimed novel *Darkness at Noon,* was described in the *Washington Post* as "one of the most eloquent and widely read indictments of communism of the age." Koestler abandoned his political writings in the 1950's, saying "The bitter passion has burned itself out . . . Cassandra has gone hoarse and is due for a vocational change." He then turned to such other subjects as philosophy, parapsychology, and science. Works from this period include *The Act of Creation, The Thirteenth Tribe,* and *The Roots of Coincidence.* Koestler, who suffered from leukemia and Parkinson's Disease, was a fervent believer in euthanasia. He was vice-president of EXIT, a voluntary euthanasia society, and he wrote the introduction to *Guide to Self-Deliverance,* a primer on how to commit suicide. On March 3, 1983, Koestler was found dead in his London apartment in an apparent suicide pact with his third wife, Cynthia Jeffries. Obituaries and other sources: *Current Biography,* Wilson, 1962, April, 1983; *New York Times,* March 4, 1983; *Washington Post,* March 4, 1983; *Chicago Tribune,* March 4, 1983, March 6, 1983; *London Times,* March 4, 1983; *Newsweek,* March 14, 1983; *Time,* March 14, 1983; *Publishers Weekly,* March 18, 1983.

*   *   *

KOHN, Clyde F(rederick)   1911-

BRIEF ENTRY: Born April 10, 1911, in Mohawk, Mich. American geographer, educator, and author. Kohn was a professor of geography at University of Iowa from 1958 to 1980. Before that, he taught at Mississippi State College for Women, Harvard University, and Northwestern University. Kohn's publications include *Urban Responses to Agricultural Change: A Collection of Papers* (1961), *The World Today: Its Patterns and Cultures* (McGraw, 1963), *United States Studies* (Scott,

Foresman, 1970), *Regional Studies* (Scott, Foresman, 1970), *Metropolitan Studies* (Scott, Foresman, 1970), and *Family Studies* (Scott, Foresman, 1970). *Address:* 201 North First Ave., Apt. 109, Iowa City, Iowa 52240; and 934 Highwood Dr., Iowa City, Iowa 52240.

*   *   *

KOJIMA, Naomi   1950-

PERSONAL: Born June 4, 1950, in Tokyo, Japan; daughter of Genichi (a company president) and Masako (Miyashita) Maruyama; married Seiichiro Kojima (in business), August 25, 1977. *Education:* Southwestern at Memphis, B.A., 1973. *Home and office:* 4-18-8 Minami Aoyama, No. 402, Minatoku, Tokyo 107, Japan. *Agent:* Writers House, Inc., 21 West 26th St., New York, N.Y. 10010.

CAREER: Nishimachi International School, Tokyo, Japan, art teacher, 1973-77. Team hostess for Japan, Lake Placid Olympic Organizing Committee, 1980. *Awards, honors:* Certificate of excellence from American Institute of Graphic Artists' Book Show, 1981, for *The Flying Grandmother.*

WRITINGS—Self-illustrated children's books: *Mr. and Mrs. Thief,* Crowell, 1980; *The Flying Grandmother,* Crowell, 1981.

*   *   *

KOKOSCHKA, Oskar   1886-1980

PERSONAL: Born March 1, 1886, in Poechlarn, Austria; died February 22, 1980, in Montreux, Switzerland; married Olda Palkovsky. *Education:* Attended Vienna School of Arts and Crafts during early 1900's. *Home:* 1844 Villeneuve, Vaud, Switzerland. *Office:* c/o Galerie St. Etienne, 46 West 57th St., New York, N.Y.

CAREER: Painter, playwright, and set designer. Dresden Academy of Art, Dresden, Germany (now East Germany), professor of art, 1919-24; International Summer Academy of Fine Arts, Salzburg, Austria, founder and teacher of art during 1950's. First one-man exhibition of paintings held in Berlin, Germany, 1910. Works represented in permanent collections of museums throughout North America and Europe. Set designer for stage productions, including Mozart's opera "Die Zauberflote" (title means "The Magic Flute") in Salzburg, 1955. *Military service:* Served in Austrian Cavalry during World War I. *Awards, honors:* Order of Merit of Federal Republic of Germany, 1956; Rome Prize and Erasmus Prize, both 1960; named honorary academician of Royal Academy, 1970; and other awards.

WRITINGS—In English translation: *Spur im Treibsand* (short stories), Atlantis Verlag, 1956, translation from the German by Eithne Wilkins and Ernst Kaiser published as *A Sea Ringed With Visions,* Horizon Press, 1962; *Londoner Ansichten, englische Landschaften,* Bruckmann, 1972, translation by Christine Cope published as *London Views, British Landscapes,* Thames & Hudson, 1972, Praeger, 1973; *Mein Leben,* Bruckmann, 1972, translation by David Britt published as *My Life,* Macmillan, 1974.

In German: *Die traumenden Knaben und andere Dichtungen* (title means "The Dream Boys and Other Poems"), 1908, reprinted, Verlag Galerie Welz, 1959; *Vier dramen* (plays; contains "Morder, Hoffnung der Frauen" [title means "Murderer, Hope of Women"], first produced in 1907, "Orpheus und Eurydike," first produced in 1910, and "Der brennende

Dornbusch'' [title means "The Burning Bush"], first produced in 1911), P. Cassirer, 1919; *Die Wahrheit ist unteilbar* (lectures and essays), Jahrhunderts, 1966; *Oskar Kokoschka, vom Erlebnis im Leben: Schriften u. Bilder* (includes lectures and essays), Verlag Galerie Welz, 1976.

Unpublished plays: "Sphinx and Strohmann" (title means "Sphinx and Strawman"), first produced in 1907, revised version produced as "Hiob" (title means "Job"), 1917; "Der gefesselte Kolumbus" (title means "Columbus in Chains"; adapted from the poem by Kokoschka, "Der 'weisse Tiertoeter" [title means "The White Animal Killer"]), first produced in 1921.

Also author of *Schfriften, 1907-1955* (correspondence), 1956. Work represented in anthologies, including *An Anthology of German Expressionist Drama,* edited by Walter H. Sokel, 1963. Paintings and illustrations represented in numerous volumes. Contributor to periodicals, including *Der Sturm.*

SIDELIGHTS: Kokoschka is considered one of the most enduring and versatile artists to emerge from twentieth-century Vienna. He became interested in art in his teens upon attending an exhibition of African art. Adopting the primitive style, Kokoschka began producing sketches and drawings of a surprising quality, and though he aspired to chemistry, he followed the recommendations of his instructors and applied to the Vienna School of Arts and Crafts, to which he was accepted in 1904. Kokoschka then began focusing all his attention on his work, creating fans, small cards, and several drawings derived from the decorative panels of noted *art nouveau* practicioner Gustav Klimt. Within a few years, Kokoschka was also writing. His poem "The Dreaming Boys," published in 1908, was hailed by other artists for its naive, dream-like evocation of sexuality and violence and for its colorful illustrations. At the same time, however, several of his panels, including a hallucinatory self-portrait, were met with outrage and condemnation by the Viennese, and the academy, bowing to public pressure, dismissed Kokoschka.

The following year, production of two of Kokoschka's plays provoked outraged audiences to violence. During a performance of "Murderer, Hope of Women," in which a dying man repays the women who revive him by viciously killing the lot, police were even forced to quell the angry mob. Kokoschka then withdrew from the limelight to refine his technique as a portraiture. He devoted most of 1908 and 1909 to this genre, concentrating on friends such as Peter Altenberg and Auguste Forel to produce a series of peculiarly autobiographical works in which he projected his own anxieties and emotions onto his subjects.

In 1910 Kokoschka began dividing his time between Vienna, where his plays and paintings continued to be presented despite public outcry, and Berlin, where he befriended several Expressionists. Their artistic goal—the evocation of the psychological and the emotional—readily appealed to Kokoschka, who had already evinced a predilection for inner turmoil. He quickly began fusing the stark and horrific elements of Expressionism with his own crudely subjective style to produce acclaimed works such as "Two Nudes" and "The Tempest." The latter work, with its blurred, almost frenzied depiction of embracing lovers in a maelstrom, exemplifies both Expressionism's concern with the emotional and Kokoschka's unique ability to portray furious activity, and the painting is usually ranked among his finest creations.

Upon returning to Vienna in 1912, Kokoschka immediately fell in love with Alma Mahler, widow of the late composer and conductor, Gustav Mahler. They commenced a maddeningly passionate affair in which Kokoschka's obsessive jealousy and Alma's strange devotion to her late husband threatened both their love and their sanity. Alma, who insisted on traveling with a death mask of her late husband, tortured Kokoschka by constantly evoking memories of Gustav and by flirting with other men. The desperately possessive Kokoschka eventually absconded with Alma's birth certificate and began posting notices proclaiming their wedding day, whereupon Alma fled Vienna—with Kokoschka in tow! Their retreat was abbreviated, however, by the assassination of Archduke Ferdinand which signaled the beginning of World War I.

Kokoschka enlisted in the Austrian Cavalry soon after war broke out. In 1915, while on patrol, he sustained a head injury which resulted in his discharge two years later. Disillusioned by the catastrophe of world war, the deaths of several painters, and the recent marriage of Alma Mahler to prominent architect Walter Gropius, Kokoschka abandoned Vienna for Dresden. There, despite the presence of several other Expressionists, he remained despondent. He resumed painting and began teaching at the Dresden Academy of Art, but found that neither activity could dull his passion for Alma. Kokoschka then decided to fashion an artificial Alma. He commissioned a dollmaker and began producing detailed sketches for the lifesize toy. Upon completion, the doll, in which Kokoschka had invested much time and more than one thousand drawings, was remarkably lifelike, even featuring genitalia.

While teaching in Dresden, Kokoschka began frequenting that city's picture gallery, devoting special attention to Dutch paintings and Japanese prints. The works sparked his interest in composition which, in turn, revived his own work. He began producing Biblical scenes, landscapes, and self-portraits, all featuring bright colors slapped across the canvas in huge swaths. In 1924, Kokoschka abruptly left Dresden to commence traveling across Europe. He began studying the works of French Impressionists, whose paintings exhibited an objective depiction alien to his expressionism. Kokoschka's work soon featured this objective quality as he continued traveling through Switzerland, France, Spain, and Portugal. His landscapes from this period, full of brilliant colors and sharply executed lines, are usually considered his zenith.

By 1930 Kokoschka was being recognized as one of Europe's most talented, if eccentric, artists. He returned to Vienna, where his interest in the political climate prompted him to invest his paintings with social criticism. The assassination of Chancellor Dollfuss, however, quickly revived memories of World War I, and the fearful Kokoschka fled to Prague. There he produced several masterworks, which added to his stature, and resumed his production of political art. Kokoschka's criticism of Nazi Germany was repaid in 1937 when his works were featured in Munich as part of an exhibition entitled "Degenerate Art." Soon all of continental Europe seemed unsafe to Kokoschka, and he moved to London. He stayed in London throughout World War II, during which time he created several political works, most of which were deemed inferior to either his Expressionist works or the great landscapes of the 1920's and 1930's.

Following World War II, Kokoschka lived in Switzerland, then returned to London, and finally settled in Switzerland. He continued painting landscapes and expanded into set design and murals. In 1950 he completed one of his most impressive works, "The Saga of Prometheus," which covered the ceiling of a wealthy Londoner's home. Kokoschka's production diminished severely during the 1960's, and he shifted attention to the writing of his memoirs. *My Life*, published in America in 1974 when Kokoschka was already an octogenarian, recounts his experiences with other artists, including Schiele and Arnold Schoenberg, as well as his years with Alma Mahler, with whom he corresponded again in 1949, and his own opinions of his constantly evolving art. He died in 1980 at age ninety-three.

BIOGRAPHICAL/CRITICAL SOURCES—Books: Edith Hoffmann, *Kokoschka: Life and Work*, Faber & Faber, 1947, Boston Book and Art Shop, 1949; James S. Plaut, editor, *Kokoschka*, Chanticleer Press, 1948; Bernard Myers, *50 Great Artists*, Bantam, 1953; Bernard Samuel Myers, *German Expressionists*, Praeger, 1957; Bernhard Bultmann, *Oskar Kokoschka*, Abrams, 1961; Anthony Bosman, *Oskar Kokoschka*, Barnes & Noble, 1964; Joseph Paul Hodin, *Oskar Kokoschka: The Artist and His Time*, Cory, Adams & Mackay, 1966; Fritz Schmalenbach, *Oskar Kokoschka*, New York Graphic Society, 1967; Jan Tomes, *Kokoschka: The Artist in Prague*, Hamlyn, 1968; Giuseppe Gatt, *Kokoschka*, Hamlyn, 1971; Oskar Kokoschka, *My Life*, Macmillan, 1974; Alessandra Comini, *The Fantastic Art of Vienna*, Ballantine, 1978.

Periodicals: *Time*, July 12, 1948, August 3, 1953, May 5, 1958, March 14, 1969; *Art News*, October, 1948, February, 1974, March, 1979; *Newsweek*, October 18, 1948, October 10, 1955, October 8, 1962, November 7, 1966; *Studio*, August, 1958, February, 1962, October, 1962; *Arts*, September, 1959; *London News*, March 12, 1966; *Kenyon Review*, January, 1966; *Art & Artists*, February, 1976; *American Artist*, April, 1976; *New York Times*, February 23, 1980.*

—*Sketch by Les Stone*

*   *   *

KOLLER, Charles W.   1896(?)-1983

OBITUARY NOTICE—See index for *CA* sketch: Born c. 1896 in Texas; died May 19, 1983, in Melrose Park, Ill. Clergyman and author. Koller served as president of the Northern Baptist Theological Seminary from 1938 to 1962. He is known for espousing preaching techniques that facilitate speaking without notes. He taught others how to draw attention to the Bible in their sermons. His books include *Expository Preaching Without Notes Plus Sermons Preached Without Notes* and *Sermon Starters*. Obituaries and other sources: *Chicago Tribune*, May 22, 1983.

*   *   *

KONER, Marvin   1921(?)-1983

OBITUARY NOTICE: Born c. 1921; died March 27, 1983, in New York, N.Y. Photographer and photojournalist. Koner's early work appeared in such popular magazines as *Life*, *Collier's*, and *Esquire*. He later employed his photographic skills in the corporate and industrial sectors. Koner was a former vice-president of the American Society of Magazine Photographers. Obituaries and other sources: *New York Times*, March 29, 1983.

*   *   *

KONRAD, James
See MACLEAN, Charles

KRAMER, Hilton   1928-

BRIEF ENTRY: Born March 25, 1928, in Gloucester, Mass. American art critic and author. Prior to becoming the editor of *New Criterion*, a monthly review, in 1982, Kramer worked as an editor or art critic for various periodicals. As an interpreter of contemporary art, Kramer has been praised for his enthusiasm, seriousness, and knowledge. He has contributed analyses of art to the *New York Times*, where he served as chief art editor from 1965 to 1982, and made contributions to *Arts Magazine*, *Nation*, *New Leader*, *Book World*, *Commentary*, and *Harper's Bazaar*. Additionally, Kramer wrote the text material for the exhibition catalogues of Ben Benn and Julio Gonzalez, among others. He edited *Perspectives on the Arts* (Art Digest, 1961) and wrote *The Age of the Avant-Garde: An Art Chronicle of 1956-1972* (Farrar, Straus, 1973). *Address:* New Criterion, P.O. Box 5194, FDR Station, New York, N.Y. *Biographical/critical sources:* *Washington Post Book World*, January 6, 1974; *New York Times Book Review*, January 6, 1974; *Newsweek*, June 17, 1974.

*   *   *

KRAUZER, Steven M(ark)   1948-
(J. W. Baron; Owen Rountree, a joint pseudonym)

PERSONAL: Born June 9, 1948, in Jersey City, N.J.; son of Earl (in business) and Bernice (a high school principal) Krauzer. *Education:* Yale University, B.A., 1970; University of New Hampshire, M.A., 1974. *Residence:* Missoula, Mont. *Agent:* Ginger Barber, Virginia Barber Literary Agency, Inc., 353 West 21st St., New York, N.Y. 10011.

CAREER: Writer. *Member:* Authors Guild, Mystery Writers of America, Poets and Writers, Western Writers of America.

WRITINGS—Editor with William Kittredge: *Great Action Stories*, New American Library, 1977; *The Great American Detective*, New American Library, 1978; *Stories Into Film*, Harper, 1978.

"Cord" series of western novels; with Kittredge under joint pseudonym Owen Rountree; published by Ballantine: *Cord*, 1982; . . . *The Nevada War*, 1982; . . . *The Black Hills Duel*, 1983; . . . *Gunman Winter*, 1983.

Under pseudonym J. W. Baron: *Blaze* (western novel), Pinnacle Books, 1983.

Work represented in anthologies, including *That Awesome Space*, edited by E. Richard Hart, Westwater, 1982. Contributor of articles, stories, and reviews to magazines, including *Triquarterly*, *Far West*, *Cavalier*, *Armchair Detective*, and *Rocky Mountain*. Guest editor with Kittredge of *Triquarterly*, number 48, 1980.

WORK IN PROGRESS: Another "Cord" novel for Ballantine; adventure novels for "Dennison's War" series, written under an undetermined pseudonym, for Bantam; *The Diggers*, also under an undetermined pseudonym, "a historical action/adventure/romance set against a background of the Australian gold rush of 1851 to 1854; it is part of a ten-book series called 'The Making of Australia,' written by ten different writers for a package marketed by Richard Gallen," publication expected in 1984.

*   *   *

KRISE, Raymond (Owens, Jr.)   1949-

PERSONAL: Surname rhymes with "nice"; born April 17,

1949, in Syracuse, N.Y. *Education:* Union College, Schenectady, N.Y., B.A., 1971. *Politics:* Conservative. *Religion:* Episcopalian. *Residence:* Boston, Mass. *Agent:* Charles J. Speleotis, Guterman, Horvitz, Rubin & Rudman, 3 Center Plaza, Boston, Mass. 02108.

CAREER: Writer, 1971—. *Member:* Greater Boston Track Club (historian, 1979—; communications director, 1981—), Neighborhood Association of the Back Bay (member of board of directors, 1982—).

WRITINGS: (With Bill Squires) *Improving Your Running,* Stephen Greene, 1982; (with Squires) *Fast Tracks: The History of Distance Running,* Stephen Greene, 1982; (with Squires) *Improving Women's Running,* Stephen Greene, 1983.

WORK IN PROGRESS: Pleasure People, a novel about prostitutes, completion expected in 1984; research on religion, psychology, parapsychology, and politics.

SIDELIGHTS: Krise told *CA:* "I decided to be a writer instead of a minister because I felt I could reach a far larger audience as a writer. My goal is to make the reader feel braver, smarter, happier, and more cooperative than he or she was before reading my work.

"I want to be a poet and novelist. I do not want to be judged by the running books I have written, although they are worthwhile works. I wrote them strictly for the money and the exposure. I do not think highly of sportswriting or of sportswriters. My goals are far beyond those normally associated with sportswriting. The power of the spirit is far more important and beautiful to me than is the power of the statistic.

"I prepared for my career by becoming one of the best, if not in fact the best, academic ghostwriters in the world. Bluntly, I wrote masters theses and doctoral dissertations for people who were too stupid to be able to write them for themselves. I did this for eleven years and produced ten doctoral dissertations and more than forty (stopped counting) master's theses. I have never set foot in a graduate school. The topics on which I wrote these papers included military science, literature, education, politics, history, business, psychology, philosophy, religion, sociology, anthropology, medicine, art, ecology, and law—in short, every subject covered in academe with the exception of some of the hard sciences. My clients came from every state in the United States, from Canada, Mexico, Brazil, Sweden, France, Iran, Israel, Indonesia, Turkey, Greece, Zimbabwe, and perhaps from elsewhere. Although it was repugnant work, this apprenticeship gave me a range of expertise, research skills, and literary voices that, I daresay, is second to none in history. I am firmly established in my craft and may now devote my time to honing my art.

"I believe writing is the loneliest of the performing arts. I've no time for writers who demand the reader make a strong effort to understand their work. Until or unless the writer has established his or her literary credentials beyond challenge, such demands on the reader are arrogant. Those who say 'I may not be popular, but I make great art' are also saying 'Gee, I don't know how to write, and I don't really care to learn.' We live in an era where incompetence is rife. Far too many authors today are miserable, terrible writers—functional illiterates. I intend nothing less than to reinvigorate English literature, elevate it to a new status of both respectability and *fun.*

"I am a relatively young man who, having no effective parents, essentially raised himself. I have seen both sides of 'the tracks,' as my forthcoming novel, *Pleasure People,* details. My pur-

pose in this life is to exalt the powers of the mind and spirit, to awaken literature from its sycophantic, academic doze.''

BIOGRAPHICAL/CRITICAL SOURCES: Runner's World, March, 1983; *Runner,* May, 1983.

*   *   *

KRUG, Mark M.   1915-

BRIEF ENTRY: Born June 13, 1915, in Vienna, Austria; came to United States, 1940, naturalized citizen, 1946. American historian, educator, and author. Krug has taught at University of Chicago since 1961; he was named professor of education in history in 1964 and director of the Weekend University in 1979. Krug is also educational director of the Council for the Study of Mankind. He wrote *Lyman Trumbull, Conservative Radical* (A. S. Barnes, 1965), *History and the Social Sciences: New Approaches to the Teaching of Social Studies* (Blaisdell, 1967), and *The Melting of the Ethnics: Education of the Immigrants, 1880-1914* (Phi Delta Kappa Educational Foundation, 1976). Krug edited *What Will Be Taught: The Next Decade* (F. E. Peacock, 1972). *Address:* 355 West Irving Park Rd., Chicago, Ill. 60613; and Judd Hall, University of Chicago, Chicago, Ill. 60637.

*   *   *

KRUMM, John McGill   1913-

PERSONAL: Born March 15, 1913, in South Bend, Ind.; son of William Frederick and Harriet Vincent (McGill) Krumm. *Education:* Pasadena Junior College, A.A., 1933; University of California, Los Angeles, B.A., 1935; Virginia Theological Seminary, B.D. (cum laude), 1938; Yale University, Ph.D., 1943. *Politics:* Democrat. *Home:* 13 rue Sarrette, 75014 Paris, France. *Office:* 23 avenue George V, 75008 Paris, France.

CAREER: Ordained Episcopal priest, 1938; vicar of Episcopal churches in Hawthorne, Calif., Lynwood, Calif., and Compton, Calif., 1938-41; assistant minister of Episcopal church in New Haven, Conn., 1941-43; rector of Episcopal church in San Mateo, Calif., 1943-48; dean of Episcopal cathedral in Los Angeles, Calif., 1948-52; Columbia University, New York City, chaplain, 1952-65; rector of Episcopal church in New York City, 1965-71; Episcopal bishop of southern Ohio, 1971-80; bishop in charge of Episcopal churches in Europe, Paris, France, 1980—. Chairman of executive committee of Forward Movement Publications. Instructor at University of Southern California, 1949-51, and Union Theological Seminary, New York City, 1967-69; member of board of trustees of Mount Holyoke College, 1962-72.

WRITINGS: Why I Am an Episcopalian, Thomas Nelson, 1957; *Modern Heresies,* Seabury, 1961; *The Art of Being a Sinner,* Seabury, 1967; *Why Choose the Episcopal Church,* Seabury, 1974; (with Marian Kelleran) *Denver Crossroads,* Forward Movement Publications, 1979.

*   *   *

KUHN, Maggie
See KUHN, Margaret E.

*   *   *

KUHN, Margaret E.   1905-
(Maggie Kuhn)

BRIEF ENTRY: Born August 3, 1905, in Buffalo, N.Y. American social activist and author. A self-proclaimed radical, Kuhn became concerned about women's rights while working for the Young Women's Christian Association during the 1920's and 1930's. Her subsequent twenty-five-year career as a writer, editor, and program coordinator for the United Presbyterian Church of the United States of America broadened her interests to include race relations, housing, the aged, and medical care. Following her mandatory retirement at age sixty-five, Kuhn helped to establish the Gray Panthers, an activist movement for the elderly. She has also been associated with Hospice, Incorporated, the National Organization of Women, and the public television series "Over Easy." She makes numerous public appearances on behalf of social reform as well. In 1978 Kuhn was named humanist of the year by the American Humanist Association. She wrote *You Can't Be Human Alone: Handbook on Group Procedures for the Local Church* (National council of Churches of Christ in the U.S.A., 1956), *Get Out There and Do Something About Injustice* (Friendship, 1972), and *Maggie Kuhn on Aging: A Dialogue* (Westminster, 1977). *Address:* 6342 Green St., Philadelphia, Pa. 19144; and Gray Panthers, 2700 Chestnut St., Philadelphia, Pa. 19104. *Biographical/critical sources: Current Biography*, Wilson, 1978.

*   *   *

KUMAR, Krishna 1942-

PERSONAL: Born March 14, 1942, in Meerut, India; came to United States, 1969, naturalized citizen, 1983; son of Mohan Murari (a professor) and Rameshwari Devi; married Parizad Tahbazzadeh, May 15, 1977; children: Sonia, Sanaz. *Education:* Agra University, India, M.A. (economics), 1960; Michigan State University, M.A. (sociology), 1970, Ph.D., 1972. *Home:* 2499 Kapiolani Blvd., Apt. 1103, Honolulu, Hawaii 96826. *Office:* East-West Center, 1777 East-West Rd., Honolulu, Hawaii 96848.

CAREER: Gandhi Peace Foundation, New Delhi, India, research assistant, 1963-65, research officer, 1965-67, assistant director of research, 1967-69; Michigan State University, East Lansing, instructor, 1971-72, assistant professor of sociology, 1972-74; East-West Center, Honolulu, Hawaii, research associate, 1974—. Affiliated with the department of sociology at University of Hawaii, 1977—. Lecturer at universities and institutes, including Dacca University (Bangladesh), University of Jakarta (Indonesia), University of Malaya (Malaysia), Korea University, University of the Philippines, Institute of Southeast Asian Studies (Singapore), Thammasat University, and Asian and Pacific Development Institute (Thailand). Secretary of the committee of the Members of Parliament for Nuclear Non-Proliferation, 1967-69. *Member:* International Studies Association, Academy of International Business, American Sociological Association. *Awards, honors:* Gandhi Peace Foundation fellowship, 1960-62; Ford Foundation fellowship, 1969-70.

WRITINGS: Intercultural Transactions for the Future, East-West Center Books, 1975; (contributor) Lyle Webster, editor, *Integrated Communication*, East-West Center Books, 1975; *The Social and Cultural Impact of Transnational Enterprises*, Sydney University Press, 1979; (contributor) Anant K. Negandhi, editor, *Functioning of Multinational Corporations in the Global Context*, Pergamon, 1980; (contributor) *Intercultural Communication: A Reader*, Wadsworth, 1981; (contributor) Verner C. Bickley and P. J. Philip, editors, *Cultural Relations in the Global Community*, Abhinav, 1981; (with Mike Hammlett, Dough Pas Portes, and A. Singh) *Ethics and Politics of International Research*, University of Hawaii Press, 1983.

Editor: *Democracy and Nonviolence: A Study of Their Relationships*, Gandhi Peace Foundation, 1968; (with William Barclay and Ruth P. Simms) *Racial Conflict, Discrimination, and Power: Historical and Comparative Studies*, AMS Press, 1976; (and contributor) *Bonds Without Bondage: Explorations in Transnational Cultural Interactions*, University Press of Hawaii, 1979; (and contributor) *Transnational Enterprises: Their Impact on Third World Societies and Cultures*, Westview, 1980; (with Maxwell G. McLeod, and contributor) *Multinationals From Developing Countries*, Lexington Books, 1981.

Contributor to journals, including *International Journal of Comparative Sociology, International Studies Quarterly, American Sociological Review, Journal of Political and Military Sociology, Social Welfare, Indian Journal of Extension Education, Southeast Asian Journal of Social Science, Asian Finance*, and *Journal of International Business Studies*.

WORK IN PROGRESS: Completing studies, including "Role Parity in International Collaborative Research," "The Center and Peripheries in Social Sciences: The Communication Behavior of the Social Scientists From Industrialized and Developing Countries," and "The Impact of Foreign Education on Academic Styles and Behavior"; a book, *Monitoring and Evaluation of Development Projects in Developing Nations*.

SIDELIGHTS: An economist and sociologist born and raised in India, Kumar has spent more than twenty years pursuing his interests in development, comparative sociology, cross-national scientific and educational networks, and multinational corporations. During his early life, the economist was actively involved in the Gandhian movement.

His earlier writings focused on the sociology of development, and he was especially interested in the role of values in economic development. This interest led Kumar to study multinational corporations, which in his view profoundly affect the cultures, life-styles, and behavior patterns of people in some developing countries.

One book, *Transnational Enterprises: Their Impact on Third World Societies and Cultures*, considers the impact of transnational corporations (TNCs) on the processes of social change. A *Contemporary Sociology* reviewer pointed out that one of the book's best features is its organization of the impact of TNCs into three topical groups—social classes and inequality, knowledge systems, and consumption patterns and values— and that this structure is important insofar as it provides a framework for further research.

A more recent book, *Multinationals From Developing Countries*, deals with the growth of multinational corporations in many developing countries, such as India, Korea, Taiwan, Hong Kong, and Mexico. Though Kumar has published several papers on multinationals, his latest book, *Ethics and Politics of International Research*, critically examines the effects of international research on developing countries and suggests an alternate paradigm.

Kumar has consulted with several national and international organizations, including the United Nations Center on Transnational Corporations and the International Fund for Agricultural Development.

BIOGRAPHICAL/CRITICAL SOURCES: Contemporary Sociology, May, 1979, September, 1981.

KUTNER, Luis 1908-

PERSONAL: Born June 9, 1908, in Chicago, Ill. *Education:* University of Chicago, J.D., 1927. *Office:* 105 West Adams St., Chicago, Ill. 60603.

CAREER: Admitted to Bar of Illinois State, 1930; practicing attorney in Chicago, Ill., beginning 1930. Other positions include: Chairman, Commission of International Due Process in Law; chairman, Committee for World Habeas Corpus, World Peace Through Law Center; visiting associate professor of law, Yale University; special assistant attorney general for State of Illinois; special U.S. master in chancery; special U.S. commissioner; consul for Ecuador; consul general for Guatemala; legal counselor to Dalai Lama and Tibet; economic consultant to Venezuela, Haiti, and Ghana.

WRITINGS: (With Laurin Healy) *The Admiral* (biography of Admiral George Dewey), Ziff-Davis, 1944; *Flights and Cascades* (poems), A. Kroch, 1948; *Moon Splashed* (poems), A. Kroch, 1948; *Red Wine and Shadows* (poems), A. Kroch, 1948; *The International Court of Habeas Corpus and the United Nations Writ of Habeas Corpus*, World Freedom Press, 1957; *World Habeas Corpus*, Oceana, 1962; *I, the Lawyer* (young adult), Dodd, 1966; *Legal Aspects of Charitable Trusts and Foundations: A Guide for Philanthropoids*, Commerce Clearing House, 1970; (editor) *The Human Right to Individual Freedom: A Symposium on World Habeas Corpus*, University of Miami Press, 1970; *The Intelligent Woman's Guide to Future Security*, Dodd, 1970, also published as *How to Be a Wise Widow*, Dodd, 1970; *Due Process of Rebellion*, Bardian, 1974; *The Trialle of William Shakespeare* (three-act play), Bardian, 1974. Also co-author with W. T. Brannon of *Live in Twelve Minutes* (novel), 1953.

Author of television scripts, "Opportunities, U.S.A." and "Mad-Grams"; author of scenarios, "The Merchants of Venus" and "Aristotle Jones." Contributor to law journals, including *University of Detroit Law Journal* and *Tennessee Law Review*.

WORK IN PROGRESS: "The Crown of Thorns," a play.

SIDELIGHTS: Kutner described himself to *CA* as a "worldwide advocate for human rights." Among his most notorious cases is his current effort to procure the release of Raoul Wallenberg, a Swedish diplomat who aided in the escape of thousands of Jews from Europe during the Nazi reign and was ultimately imprisoned by the Soviets. Kutner insists that "the world must assume responsibility for each individual's freedom."

BIOGRAPHICAL/CRITICAL SOURCES: Life, April 28, 1958, September 3, 1969.

*   *   *

KUTTNA, Mari 1934-1983

OBITUARY NOTICE: Born February 4, 1934, in Budapest, Hungary; died March 27, 1983, in Southampton, England. Translator and film critic. Kuttna began her career as a freelance film critic, contributing to periodicals like *Sight and Sound* and *Montage*, and as a regular columnist for *The Lady*. Her film expertise led her to serve on the juries of international film festivals for many years, as a judge for the British Film Institute award, as a program director for the Melbourne Film Festival, and as secretary of the British section of the Federation International de la Presse Cinematographique. She was also a skilled translator of plays. Obituaries and other sources: *London Times,* April 2, 1983.

*   *   *

KUYKENDALL, Eleanor 1938-

BRIEF ENTRY: Born June 2, 1938, in Akron, Ohio. American philosopher, educator, and author. Kuykendall taught at Brooklyn College of the City University of New York until 1967, when she began teaching philosophy at State University of New York College at New Paltz. She edited *Philosophy in the Age of Crisis* (Harper, 1970). *Address:* Department of Philosophy, State University of New York College at New Paltz, New Paltz, N.Y. 12561. *Biographical/critical sources: Who's Who of American Women,* 8th edition, Marquis, 1974.

*   *   *

KYDD, Sam(uel) 1917-1982

PERSONAL: Born in 1917 in Belfast, Northern Ireland; died March 26, 1982, in London, England; married wife, Pinky; children: Jonathan. *Education:* Attended secondary school in Dunstable, England.

CAREER: Film actor, 1945-82, including roles in "The Captive Heart," "Treasure Island," "Trent's Last Case," "I'm All Right Jack," and "Too Late the Hero." *Military service:* British Army, 1939-40, prisoner of war, 1940-c. 1943.

WRITINGS: For You the War Is Over (memoirs), Bachman & Turner, 1973, 2nd edition, 1974.

OBITUARIES: London Times, April 6, 1982.*

L

LABUS, Marta Haake 1943-
(Claire McCormick)

PERSONAL: Born September 13, 1943, in Huntington, W.Va.; daughter of Donald Robert (a mining engineer) and Constance (a teacher of French; maiden name, Hay) Haake; married Otto Philleo Labus (a plastics manufacturer), May 10, 1982. *Education:* Ohio University, B.A. (summa cum laude), 1965; University of Illinois, M.A., 1966, Ph.D., 1971. *Residence:* Scottsdale, Ariz. *Agent:* Fox Chase Agency, Inc., 419 East 57th St., New York, N.Y. 10022.

CAREER: Westminster College, New Wilmington, Pa., assistant professor of English, 1971-78; part-time and short-term employment for state governmental agency, 1978-81; writer, 1981—. *Member:* Modern Language Association of America, Mystery Writers of America, Women in Communications, McCormick Ranch Women's Association Career Group, Phi Beta Kappa, Phi Kappa Phi. *Awards, honors:* Woodrow Wilson fellowship, 1965; University of Illinois dissertation fellowship, 1969; National Endowment for the Humanities fellowships, 1974, 1976-77.

WRITINGS—Mystery novels; under pseudonym Claire McCormick: *Resume for Murder,* Walker & Co., 1982; *The Club Paradis Murders,* Walker & Co., 1983.

Work represented in anthologies, including *I, That Am Ever Stranger: Poems on Woman's Experience,* Dawn Valley, 1974. Contributor to *Arizona.*

WORK IN PROGRESS: A third comedy-mystery, *Murder in Cowboy Bronze.*

SIDELIGHTS: "As a child," Marta Labus commented, "I always preferred fantasy to reality, and spent much time writing plays and acting in them, composing song lyrics, and even attempting serious poetry. In high school I wrote radio scripts for the local Junior Theater of the Air; one of them was subsequently published in *National Scholastic.* When I got to college, I stopped writing altogether. The worst grade I received in my major—English—was awarded me by my creative writing instructor, who liked *nothing* I produced for his class. As a result, I convinced myself that I ought to be a literary scholar instead of a writer, and went on to graduate school. As a frustrated writer, I made a pretty good teacher of literature—and a rotten scholar.

"In the years after graduate school, I wrote nothing except a few unmemorable poems. Five years ago, however, a series of personal disasters, and a chance meeting with a writer who offered me his attention and moral support, left me determined to do what I had always really wanted to do—write a novel. Two years later I began one.

"Writing my first novel was certainly the hardest thing I have ever done, and the most satisfying. After finishing my second book, I remain unconvinced that writing ever gets any easier; but, barring acts of God or Alzheimer's Disease, I hope to keep up the struggle until I'm ninety. Right now I am a mystery writer, working in a genre eminently suitable to the 1980's, with their apparently insoluble social and economic problems; for the mystery novel provides its readers with unfailingly solvable dilemmas and offers a cosmos in which ratiocination conquers all. While I shall probably always write mysteries, in the future I hope to attempt other sorts of fiction as well, while maintaining an abiding concern with style. In an age that threatens to become post-literate, I believe that all writers should be concerned with preserving their own sensitivity to language.

"To keep my own ear keen, I habitually read French fiction as well as English. As a Southwesterner, I also intend to learn Spanish thoroughly and well. My travels in France, French Polynesia, and Mexico have already provided me with actual and potential mystery novel characters and settings."

*   *   *

LaCAPRA, Dominick 1939-

PERSONAL: Born July 13, 1939, in New York, N.Y.; son of Joseph and Mildred (Sciascia) LaCapra; married Anne-Marie Hlasny, 1965 (divorced, 1970); children: Veronique. *Education:* Cornell University, B.A., 1961; Harvard University, Ph.D., 1969. *Home:* 119 Terrace Place, Ithaca, N.Y. 14850. *Office:* Department of History, Cornell University, Ithaca, N.Y. 14850.

CAREER: Cornell University, Ithaca, N.Y., assistant professor, 1969-74, associate professor, 1974-79, professor of history, 1979—. *Member:* International Association of Philosophy and Literature, American Historical Association. *Awards, honors:* Fulbright fellowship, 1961; Woodrow Wilson fellowship, 1962, Harvard University fellowship, 1963 and 1964; Foreign Area Studies fellowship, 1965 and 1966; National Endowment for the Humanities senior fellowship, 1976; Cornell Society for the Humanities senior fellowship, 1979.

WRITINGS—All published by Cornell University Press: *Emile Durkheim: Sociologist and Philosopher*, 1972; *A Preface to Sartre*, 1978; (co-editor with Steven L. Kaplan) *Modern European Intellectual History*, 1982; *"Madame Bovary" on Trial*, 1982; *Rethinking Intellectual History: Texts, Contexts, Language*, 1983. Contributor to journals, including *American Historical Review, Journal of Modern History, Diacritics, Philosophical Review*, and *Modern Language Notes*.

WORK IN PROGRESS: A study of nineteenth- and twentieth-century historical writing.

SIDELIGHTS: LaCapra's *Emile Durkheim* has been praised in the *New York Times Book Review* as a "serious, intelligent and important study" of one of sociology's foremost pioneers. Durkheim, whose *Suicide* and *The Elementary Forms of the Religious Life* helped define and explain the behavior of nineteenth-century humanity, is represented in LaCapra's work as both an innovator within budding sociology and as a perceptive analyst of his contemporary society. Philip Rosenberg, writing in the *New York Times Book Review*, declared that "Durkheim, as LaCapra interprets him, emerges as a social critic who recognized that it is not merely the case that our social system is subject to pathological distortions." LaCapra traces Durkheim's contention that the disorder within society has reached crisis proportions, but reproaches Durkheim for his refusal to acknowledge Karl Marx's observations on social conflict. He nonetheless contends that Durkheim's work provided the foundation for twentieth-century sociology.

In *A Preface to Sartre*, LaCapra makes selective use of Jacques Derrida's method of deconstruction to establish a historical and social context for Sartre's writings. He argues that Sartre, though more renowned for his link to Hegel and Heidegger, actually combined the work of these German philosophers with that of Descartes. "The basic continuity," writes LaCapra, "is that of a philosophy centred on man who, in his intentional consciousness and free praxis, creates meaning and value in the world." The book promotes further analysis of Sartre's philosophy through deconstruction, but suggests that definitive explication of the existentialist's work is not immediately forthcoming. Betty Abel, assessing *A Preface to Sartre* in *Contemporary Review*, called it "provocative, admirably conceived and lucidly written."

In *"Madame Bovary" on Trial*, LaCapra focuses on contrasting interpretations of Flaubert's novel during judicial debate of the work in the French courts in 1857. Upon establishing the misinterpretation of the novel by its opponents, who deemed the book detrimental to Christian values, and its defenders, who argued that *Madame Bovary* was extremely conventional in its depiction of contemporary morality, LaCapra then contends that the novel's most subversive function is in its unique—for its time—undermining of the relationship between the work and its readers. LaCapra establishes the narrative foundation of *Madame Bovary* as tenuous, switching from first- to third-person narration within its initial pages to lead the reader into anticipating familiarity only to find an unsettling critique of bourgeois society. Writing in *American Historical Review*, James Smith Allen noted: "Deconstructive scrutiny of the text reveals this 'ideological crime' committed by Flaubert's implicit stylistic challenge to the social and political values of his day. Just as the text calls into question the literary claims of the narrative subject, it also casts into doubt the bourgeois norms of family and religion." Allen complained, however, that LaCapra is too brief in his analysis of Flaubert's novel, writing that "LaCapra fails to examine fully the historical context of trial and novel, even though such consideration is essential to a proper account of the work's readings." Wallace Fowlie, writing in *Sewanee Review*, was less critical, calling *"Madame Bovary" on Trial* a "closely argued and eloquently composed study." And Ross Chambers wrote in *Modern Language Notes* that LaCapra "has produced a reading of the novel which itself frames the text—situates and 'tries' it—in the light of matters of contemporary concern." Chambers added that *"Madame Bovary" on Trial* "provides a case-study in the writing of intellectual history as an act of interpretation, 'with all the risks and political implications this mode of argument entails.'"

LaCapra told *CA*: "My primary objective has been to reconceptualize the way intellectual history is written, in part by employing approaches developed in recent literary criticism and philosophy. My focus has been upon complex texts and the various contexts that inform them."

BIOGRAPHICAL/CRITICAL SOURCES: Times Literary Supplement, July 28, 1972, December 14, 1979; *New York Times Book Review*, July 15, 1973; *Los Angeles Times Book Review*, February 18, 1979; *Contemporary Review*, June, 1979; *Sewanee Review*, July, 1982; *Modern Language Notes*, December, 1982; *American History Review*, February, 1983.

* * *

La FOLLETTE, Suzanne   1894(?)-1983

OBITUARY NOTICE: Born c. 1894 in Washington; died of a cerebral thrombosis, April 24, 1983, in Stanford, Calif.; cremated and ashes buried in Colfax, Wash. Politician, feminist, editor, and journalist. An early feminist who professed conservative political views, La Follette was active in anti-Communist causes. She worked on several magazines in New York City, including *Nation, Freeman*, and *American Mercury*, and she helped found *National Review* in 1955. La Follette also was the author of two books, *Concerning Women* and *Art in America*. Obituaries and other sources: *Washington Post*, April 27, 1983; *New York Times*, April 27, 1983; *Chicago Tribune*, April 29, 1983; *Newsweek*, May 9, 1983; *Time*, May 9, 1983.

* * *

LAIDLAW, W(illiam) A(llison)   1898-1983

OBITUARY NOTICE: Born July 15, 1898; died February 3, 1983. Educator and author. Educated in classics and philosophy, Laidlaw accepted his first academic post in 1923 at the University of Western Australia. In 1929 he went on to University College, Southampton, where he taught for two years. He then joined the staff of the University of St. Andrews, serving there until 1946. Laidlaw's final academic post was at Queen Mary College, London, where he was professor of classics from 1949 until his retirement in 1964. The educator wrote a number of scholarly works, including *A History of Delos, The Prosody of Terence*, and *Latin Literature*. Obituaries and other sources: *International Authors and Writers Who's Who*, 8th edition, Melrose, 1977; *Who's Who*, 133rd edition, St. Martin's, 1981; *London Times*, February 18, 1983.

* * *

LALONDE, Robert   1947-

PERSONAL: Born July 22, 1947, in Oka, Quebec, Canada;

son of Paul (a painter) and Lucienne (Lavigne) Lalonde; married France Capistran (a film distributor), December 2, 1978; children: Stephanie. *Education:* Attended College Sainte-Therese, 1960-68, and Conservatoire national d'art dramatique, 1968-71; received baccalaureate es arts and licence en arts. *Home:* 4300 Fabre, Montreal, Quebec, Canada H2J 3T6.

CAREER: Actor and scriptwriter for Canadian Broadcasting Corporation, 1971—. Teacher at National Theater School. *Awards, honors:* Prix Robert Cliche for best first novel, 1981, for *Sweet Madness.*

WRITINGS: Sweet Madness, Beaufort Books, 1981; *Le Dernier Ete des indiens* (title means "The Last Indian Summer"), Le Seuil (Paris, France), 1982; *Au beau mitan du lit* (title means "In the Middle of the Bed"), Le Seuil, 1983.

Plays: "Comme chien et chat" (two-act; title means "The Child and the Kitten"), first produced in Montreal, Quebec, at Centre d'essai Theatre, September, 1980; "Comme du Tchekhov" (one-act; title means "Just Like a Chekhov Play"), first produced in Montreal at Quatre sous Theatre, October, 1982.

SIDELIGHTS: Lalonde told *CA:* "What I'm interested in is love from the male perspective—to show the new man. He is open, soft-spoken, a fighter for peace instead of war—in contrast to the 'prototype.'

"Being an actor, writing for theatre and film, is my greatest interest right now. Currently I am working on a film script and a television series."

*   *   *

LAMBLEY, Peter   1946-

PERSONAL: Born January 15, 1946, in Yorkshire, England; son of Jack (an instrument engineer) and Irene (an accountant; maiden name, Fenton) Lambley; married Peny Barton, December 3, 1966 (divorced); married Dorrian Aiken (a writer), July 4, 1980; children: Catherine, Rupert, Simone. *Education:* University of Cape Town, B.S.S., 1968, B.A. (with honors), 1969, Ph.D., 1971. *Politics:* None. *Religion:* None. *Agent:* Shelley Power, P.O. Box 149A, Surbiton, Surrey, England.

CAREER: University of Cape Town, Cape Town, South Africa, psychologist in university clinic, 1971-73, lecturer in psychology, 1972-73, chairman of departmental teaching program in the diploma in psychological medicine, 1972-73, founding member of the masters degree in clinical psychology course, 1972-73; in private practice in Cape Town, 1973-78; writer and researcher, 1978—. Consultant to Grooteschuur Hospital, Cape Town, 1972-73.

WRITINGS: The Psychology of Apartheid, Secker & Warburg, 1980, University of Georgia Press, 1981; *The Headache Book,* W. H. Allen, 1980; *Insomnia and Other Sleep Disorders,* Sphere, 1982; *How to Survive Anorexia: A Guide to Anorexia Nervosa and Bulimarexia,* Muller, 1983. Contributor of about twenty-two articles to journals in the United States and England, and of a short story to *London Magazine.*

WORK IN PROGRESS: "I am slowly moving out of the realm of abnormal psychology to a study of how abnormality relates to normality."

SIDELIGHTS: In *The Psychology of Apartheid* Lambley draws upon his experiences in South Africa in order to expose the rampant corruption of police, professionals, and government caused by apartheid. Drug-addiction, sexual exploitation, and

other such occurrences led Lambley to conclude that South Africa is a sick, "sociopathic" society, caused to be so by a racist and repressive police state.

Writing in the *Times Literary Supplement,* Meyer Fortes observed that "Lambley insists that his is not an academic treatise; and *The Psychology of Apartheid* is indeed a passionate, personal treatment, presented with a journalistic fluency which often teeters on the edge of sensationalism."

Lambley told *CA:* "Two things really motivate my work. First I try to present what I've seen or discovered as it is; that is, in the context of who I am as much as what the subject is. I like to be independent, not to belong to a university or select school of thought, and I like to be free enough within myself for each new endeavor to be thought of as an object in its own right, irrespective of what I've said or done in the past. You could call this a kind of personal independence.

"My second motivation lies in my belief that quite ordinary people are remarkably intelligent and can understand complex things if encouraged to do so. I write for the ordinary person, trying in a sense to let him look over my shoulder as I work. I don't like to see psychology or psychiatry popularized because this nearly always means that the professional obscures the messy side, the bits he doesn't really understand, the mistakes and the loopholes. In writing, I try to bridge the gap and let the reader see my weaknesses and troubles along with everything else. One reviewer of my *Psychology of Apartheid* (J. J. Westermeyer, *American Journal of Psychiatry*), for example, while saying some nice things about the work, concluded by complaining that the book tells more about 'Lambley, his experiences in South Africa, his own psychology and his limitations as a social scientist than with a clear, well-documented psychosocial picture of apartheid.' But this was precisely what I had intended and sums up, in a sense, what I had tried to do: I would have liked to give a clear picture of apartheid and tried to—the book is about what happened to me as I tried."

BIOGRAPHICAL/CRITICAL SOURCES: Times Literary Supplement, February 13, 1981.

*   *   *

LAMOTTE, Etienne   1904(?)-1983

OBITUARY NOTICE: Born c. 1904; died May 5, 1983, in Brussels, Belgium. Roman Catholic monsignor, educator, translator, and author. Specializing in Oriental studies, Lamotte taught at Louvain University from 1932 until his retirement in 1974. Dedicated particularly to the study and translation of Indian Buddhist texts, the scholar produced *L'Histoire du Bouddhisme Indien,* ranked among his greatest works. Three of his lectures were published in English under the title *The Spirit of Ancient Buddhism.* Lamotte's many translations include the five-volume annotated translation of the Prajnaparamita treatise *Le Traite de la grande vertu de sagesse de Nagarjuna.* Obituaries and other sources: *London Times,* May 18, 1983.

*   *   *

LANDAUER, Jerry Gerd   1932-1981

PERSONAL: Born January 16, 1932, in Rexinger, Germany; came to the United States, 1938; naturalized U.S. citizen, 1944; died of a heart attack, February 27, 1981, in Washington, D.C.; son of Adolph and Meta (Marx) Landauer; married Susan Lois Ecker, June 23, 1963 (divorced). *Education:* Columbia University, A.B., 1953; graduate study at University of Bonn, 1953-54. *Residence:* Washington, D.C.

CAREER/WRITINGS: Worked as copyboy and desk clerk at the *New York Times;* served as local news reporter at *Washington Post,* 1956-60; Capitol Hill reporter for Washington, D.C., bureau of United Press International, 1960-62; reporter for Washington, D.C., bureau of *Wall Street Journal,* 1962-81. *Member:* National Press Club, Sigma Delta Chi, Alumni Association of Columbia College, Tau Epsilon Phi. *Awards, honors:* Raymond Clapper Memorial Award, 1964; Distinguished Service Award from Washington correspondents, 1964; Sigma Delta Chi Award for outstanding journalism, 1964; Drew Pearson Foundation Prize and Worth Bingham Memorial Prize, both for investigative reporting, both 1973.

SIDELIGHTS: Landauer was an award-winning investigative reporter who concentrated on exposing illegal activities in government and business. His 1964 reports on the practice of federal judges accepting appointments within private corporations resulted in judicial reform. In the 1960's he investigated corporate contributions to congressional candidates, and his investigation into bribe taking and tax evasion allegations eventually led to the resignation of vice-president Spiro T. Agnew in 1973.

OBITUARIES: Washington Post, March 1, 1981; *New York Times,* March 1, 1981.*

* * *

LANDEEN, William M. 1891-1982

OBITUARY NOTICE: Born May 7, 1891, in Sundsvall, Sweden; died December 27, 1982, in Riverside, Calif. Historian, educator, and author. A graduate in history, Landeen's first academic post was at Walla Walla College, where he taught from 1921 to 1938, eventually becoming a full professor and college president. He then joined the staff of the State College of Washington (now Washington State University) as professor of history, remaining until 1957. From there Landeen went to La Sierra College, where he taught history and served as president for three short terms during the 1960's. He wrote *E. O. Holland and the State College of Washington* and *Martin Luther's Religious Thought.* Obituaries and other sources: *Directory of American Scholars,* Volume I: *History,* 6th edition, Bowker, 1974; *Chronicle of Higher Education,* January 26, 1983.

* * *

LANDGREN, Marchal E. 1907(?)-1983 .

OBITUARY NOTICE: Born c. 1907 in Woodbury, Conn.; died of cancer, February 13, 1983, in Washington, D.C. Educator, art historian, and author. Landgren taught art history at the University of Maryland and headed the school's museum training program. From 1935 to 1939 he was director of art activities for the New York City Municipal Arts Committee and was also a founder of the Art Barn Association of Washington, D.C. Landgren, who prepared exhibition catalogues for art shows he organized throughout the country, wrote *Years of Art: The Story of the Art Students League of New York.* Obituaries and other sources: *Washington Post,* February 16, 1983; *New York Times,* February 18, 1983.

LANGDON, Philip 1937-

PERSONAL: Born June 15, 1937, in Green Bay, Wis.; son of Harold and Cynthia (Bowers) Langdon; married Florence Budwell (a professor), 1957; children: Harold. *Education:* Attended University of Wisconsin, 1954-56. *Home:* 221 Lewiston Rd., Gross Pointe Farms, Mich. 48236.

CAREER: Worked as automobile assembler in Madison, Wis., 1957-63, Morgan, Tenn., 1963-67, and Pontiac, Mich., 1967-72 and 1977; poet. *Member:* Michigan Poets.

WRITINGS—Poetry: On a Broken Wing, privately printed, 1957; *Raindrops and Sorrow,* O.C. Books, 1974; *First Birth,* O.C. Books/Oakland Arts Press, 1976.

WORK IN PROGRESS: Poems; research for possible book on safety hazards in manufacturing plants.

SIDELIGHTS: Langdon told *CA:* "I wrote my first collection of poems while a sophomore at the University of Wisconsin and had the collection printed the following year. No one seemed much impressed with the poems, so I quit writing them. I moved to Michigan and met an old classmate in 1967. He expressed interest in my work, though I didn't have anything post-1957 to show him. I began writing again, however, and was somewhat astonished to find my work accepted for publication by a local poetry follower. Though no one seemed particularly impressed with my last two collections, I have continued writing anyway."

* * *

LANGER, Sydney 1914-

PERSONAL: Born July 7, 1914, in New York, N.Y.; son of Joseph and Doris Langer; children: Elizabeth, Kenneth. *Education:* Attended Brooklyn College (now of the City University of New York), 1932-35, Dalhousie University, 1935-36, University of Edinburgh, 1936-40, and University of Lausanne, 1940-41. *Politics:* Democrat. *Agent:* James Seligmann Agency, 280 Madison Ave., New York, N.Y. 10016.

CAREER: Member of faculty at New School for Social Reaearch; member of staff at North Shore Hospital, and director of group therapy. *Military service:* U.S. Navy. *Member:* American Academy of Psychoanalysis (fellow), American Psychiatric Association (fellow).

WRITINGS: The Only Security Blanket You Will Ever Need, Beaufort Book Co., 1981.

* * *

LANGLEY, James Maydon 1916-1983

OBITUARY NOTICE—See index for CA sketch: Born March 12, 1916, in Wolverhampton, England; died April 10, 1983. Military officer, businessman, and author. Langley is best remembered for his role in escape and evasion maneuvers during World War II. In 1940 he lost an arm at Dunkirk, was captured, but escaped from a German hospital. Once in France he joined an underground organization, made his way back to England, and then became affiliated with MI9—a secret British escape organization—in 1941. Three years later he was named joint head of IS9, a network to help escapees, those left behind enemy lines, and prisoners of war. His books include *Fight Another Day* and *MI9.* Obituaries and other sources: *London Times,* April 11, 1983.

LANGMAN, Larry 1930-

PERSONAL: Born November 13, 1930, in New York, N.Y.; son of Martin (a laborer) and Eva (Marcus) Langman. *Education:* Long Island University, B.A., 1956; graduate study at St. John's University, Jamaica, N.Y., 1959-60. *Residence:* Flushing, N.Y.

CAREER: Dean of private school in Great Barrington, Mass., 1960-62; worked odd jobs in various U.S. cities, 1962-66; Oceanside High School, Oceanside, N.Y., teacher of English, 1966—.

WRITINGS: (With Milt Fajans) *Cinema and the High School,* Pflaum Press, 1975; *A Guide to American Film Directors: The Sound Era, 1929-1979,* two volumes, Scarecrow, 1981; *The Video Encyclopedia,* Garland Publishing, 1983; *A Guide to American Screenwriters,* Garland Publishing, in press. Contributor to magazines.

WORK IN PROGRESS: American Film Comedy.

SIDELIGHTS: Larry Langman told *CA:* ''I believe there is much material to be mined in American films of the past; we can learn how we lived, where we were, and perhaps where we are headed. I would like to spend the next few years helping to bring these thoughts to light.''

* * *

LANK, Edith H(andleman) 1926-

PERSONAL: Born February 27, 1926, in Boston, Mass.; married Norman Lank (a real estate agent), June 13, 1948; children: Avrum, David, Anna. *Education:* Syracuse University, B.A. (magna cum laude), 1947. *Home:* 240 Hemingway Dr., Rochester, N.Y. 14620. *Office:* Department of Real Estate, St. John Fisher College, 3690 East Ave., Rochester, N.Y. 14618.

CAREER: Westbrook College, Portland, Me., instructor in journalism, 1947-48; licensed real estate broker, 1970—; St. John Fisher College, Rochester, N.Y., special lecturer in real estate, 1976—. Real estate writer for *Democrat and Chronicle,* 1976—. *Member:* National Association of Real Estate Editors, National Association of Realtors, Women in Communications, Inc., Real Estate Educators Association, Jane Austen Society of North America, Phi Beta Kappa. *Awards, honors:* Journalism award from National Association of Realtors, 1979; Media Award from Bar Association of Monroe County, 1982; first place honors from Real Estate Editors Association, 1982.

WRITINGS: Home Buying, Real Estate Education, 1981; *Selling Your Home With an Agent,* Reston, 1982; *Modern Real Estate Practice in New York,* Real Estate Education, 1983. Also author of ''House Calls,'' a syndicated column carried in sixty newspapers, 1976—.

SIDELIGHTS: Lank's career as a real estate broker prompted her to write a syndicated newspaper column, ''House Calls,'' and several books about real estate. In her second book, *Selling Your House With an Agent,* Lank explains real estate financing, sales contracts, income tax assessments associated with the sale of real property and includes many other tips about real estate sales. In his *Los Angeles Times* review, critic David M. Kinchen recommended ''this worthwhile book for anyone considering selling a house—with or without a broker.''

Lank told *CA:* ''A fascinating, expanding career began for me after I turned fifty. My journalism degree gathered dust while I raised three children, although I wouldn't do it differently a second time. In the past six years—teaching, writing, a syn-

dicated column, books, radio, TV, lecturing—I can't wait to see what will happen when I turn sixty!

''I have learned that, for the larger part of the above, one cannot wait for someone to knock on the door and offer a fascinating job. Most of what happened, I made happen.

AVOCATIONAL INTERESTS: Scuba diving.

BIOGRAPHICAL/CRITICAL SOURCES: Los Angeles Times, August 1, 1982.

* * *

LANOUX, Armand 1913-1983

OBITUARY NOTICE: Born October 24, 1913, in Paris, France; died March 23, 1983, in Paris, France. Author. A prolific French writer and recipient of numerous literary awards, Lanoux also served on a number of literary and government committees, including the Fayard Prize jury and the Society of Dramatic Authors and Composers. His first novel, *Le Nef des fous,* won the Populist Prize in 1947. A collection of poems, *Le Colporteur,* won the Apollinaire Prize in 1959. The first two novels of Lanoux's war trilogy, *Le Commandant Watrin* and *Quand la mer se retire,* won Interallie and Goncourt prizes, respectively. He also wrote *Chateaux of the Loire,* a book of description and travel. Other works include novels, short stories, poems, and biographies of Zola and Maupassant. Obituaries and other sources: *International Authors and Writers Who's Who,* 8th edition, Melrose, 1977; *Who's Who in the World,* 5th edition, Marquis, 1980; *International Who's Who,* 46th edition, Europa, 1982; *London Times,* March 30, 1983.

* * *

LANSKY, Bruce 1941-

PERSONAL: Born June 1, 1941, in New York, N.Y.; son of David (a business executive) and Lorretta (a librarian; maiden name, Berkowitz) Lansky; married Vicki Rogosin (an author), May 14, 1967; children: Douglas, Dana. *Education:* Attended St. John's College, 1958-60; New York University, B.A., 1963; graduate study at University of Chicago, 1963-64. *Home:* 16648 Meadowbrook Lane, Wayzata, Minn. 55391. *Office:* Meadowbrook Press, 18318 Minnetonka Blvd., Wayzata, Minn. 55391.

CAREER: Cunningham & Walsh (advertisers), New York, N.Y., account executive, 1965-68; Candy Corp. of America, Brooklyn, N.Y., marketing manager, 1968-70; Pillsbury Co., Minneapolis, Minn., manager of new products, 1970-72; Lansky & Associates (advertising agency), Wayzata, Minn., president, 1973—; Meadowbrook Press, Wayzata, Minn., publisher, 1975—. Director of Rational Life Center, 1982—.

WRITINGS—All Published by Meadowbrook: *The Best Baby Name Book in the Whole Wide World,* 1979; (editor) *Free Stuff for Kids,* 1979; *Successful Dieting Tips,* 1981; *Make Your Own Greeting Cards,* 1981; *Make Your Own Crazy Minerals,* 1982; *Make Your Own Crazy Monsters,* 1982.

SIDELIGHTS: Lansky told *CA:* ''I am the president and publisher at Meadowbrook Press, and therefore am in the lucky position of being able to create books that interest me and get them published. Since Meadowbrook typically does not publish manuscripts from outside authors, I either create or editorally develop (i.e., manage a staff of editors and designers) most of the books the company publishes. I use the word 'create' rather than 'write' because my function is to direct the creative process rather than to write every word in a book. My 'talent' is in coming up with ideas for books that consumers need, determining the contents and format of the books, and seeing them through to completion.''

BIOGRAPHICAL/CRITICAL SOURCES: Washington Post Book World, August 22, 1982.

* * *

LANT, Jeffrey Ladd 1947-

PERSONAL: Born February 16, 1947, in Maywood, Ill.; son of Donald Marshall (a credit manager) and Shirley Mae (Lauing) Lant. *Education:* Attended University of St. Andrew, 1967-68; University of California, Santa Barbara, B.A., 1969 (summa cum laude); Harvard University, M.A., 1970, Ph.D., 1975; Northeastern University, earned certificate, 1976. *Office:* Jeffrey Lant Associates, Inc., 50 Follen St., Suite 507, Cambridge, Mass. 02138.

CAREER: Boston College, Chestnut Hill, Mass., coordinator of student services for evening college, 1976-78; Radcliffe College, Cambridge, Mass., assistant to president, 1978; Jeffrey Lant Associates, Inc. (consultants), Cambridge, founder and president, 1979—. *Awards, honors:* Official citation from Boston City Council, 1977, for work in adult continuing education; official citation from Massachusetts House of Representatives, 1977, and from governor of Massachusetts, 1978, both for work with youth unemployment problem; official citation from governor of Massachusetts, 1982, for services to business; citation from City of Cambridge, 1983, for service to nonprofit organizations.

WRITINGS: Insubstantial Pageant: Ceremony and Confusion at Queen Victoria's Court, Taplinger, 1980; *Development Today: A Guide for Nonprofit Organizations,* JLA Publications, 1980, revised edition, 1982; *The Consultant's Kit: Establishing and Operating Your Successful Consulting Business,* JLA Publications, 1982; (editor) *Our Harvard: Reflections on College Life by Twenty-two Distinguished Graduates,* Taplinger, 1982; *The Unabashed Self-Promoter's Guide: What Every Man, Woman, Child, and Organization in America Needs to Know Abouting Getting Ahead by Exploiting the Media,* JLA Publications, 1983.

SIDELIGHTS: Lant is known for his enterprise and initiative in creating his own consulting firm in 1979. Since 1979, his salary, according to the *Ann Arbor News,* "has multiplied . . . ten times over," and his business has expanded into the publishing world. "We're not real people with real jobs," Lant explained to interviewers. "We're infallible experts people come to." He added: "A consultant has the freedom to do, to say and also to take risks. You take the risk that you're right and can afford to lose a client. That keeps the client in line." Despite his phenomenal success, however, he advises others against simply abandoning their current positions to become consultants. "You'll never succeed as a consultant by just quitting your job," he told the *Pittsburgh Business Times.* "Get so many clients first that you have to quit to handle them all."

Lant told CA: "I'm interested in showing people, in detail, how America works and how to take advantage of circumstances. Each one of my books is an 'insider's' book—a look inside an institution (like Harvard University or the Court of Queen Victoria, going back to my first book), or at a subject which is much misunderstood: like setting up a consulting business or raising money for nonprofit organizations. *The Unabashed Self-Promoter's Guide* strips the media bare and

will tell people and organizations how to exploit it for their own advantage. I've found that people have a hunger for this kind of information, and I shall continue to provide it.''

BIOGRAPHICAL/CRITICAL SOURCES: Christian Science Monitor, December 22, 1980; *Boston Globe, 2,* February 21, 1982, June 26, 1982; *Cambridge Express,* January 30, 1982; *Boardroom Reports,* February 15, 1982; *Boston Business Journal,* February 15, 1982; *Pittsburgh Press,* Mach 4, 1982; *Pittsburgh Business Times,* April 5, 1982; *Ann Arbor News,* April 7, 1982; *Santa Monica Outlook,* April 8, 1982; *Lansing State Journal,* May 6, 1982; *Hartford Advocate,* May 12, 1982; *Cleveland Press,* June 14, 1982; *Business Week,* November 15, 1982; *Washington Post Book World,* November 20, 1982; Geoffrey Bailey, *Maverick,* F. Watts, 1983.

* * *

LAO She
See SHU Ch'ing-ch'un

* * *

LAPOINTE, Paul-Marie 1929-

BRIEF ENTRY: Born September 22, 1929, in Saint-Felicien, Quebec, Canada. Canadian poet. Lapointe has been editor in chief of *Le Magazine Maclean* and a television journalist for Canadian Broadcasting Corporation. He has received a Governor General's Award and the Prix David. Lapointe's books include *The Terror of the Snows: Selected Poems* (University of Pittsburgh Press, 1976). *Biographical/critical sources: Supplement to the Oxford Companion to Canadian History and Literature,* Oxford University Press, 1973.

* * *

LARCO, Isabel Granda 1911(?)-1983
(Chabuca Granda)

OBITUARY NOTICE: Born c. 1911; died following open-heart surgery, March 8, 1983, in Ft. Lauderdale, Fla. Folksinger and songwriter. Known by her professional name, Chabuca Granda, the Peruvian performer was considered one of Latin America's most prominent composers of folk music. Among her many hit songs is "La Flor de la Canela." Obituaries and other sources: *Chicago Tribune,* March 10, 1983.

* * *

LATHAM, Ian 1956-

PERSONAL: Born March 20, 1956, in England. *Education:* Received B.A. (with honors) and diploma in architecture from Oxford Polytechnic. *Home:* 16 Yew Tree Court, Bridge Lane, London N.W.11, England.

CAREER: Architect in London, England.

WRITINGS: (Contributor) Frank Russell, editor, *Art Nouveau Architecture,* Academy Editions, 1979, Rizzoli Interantional, 1981; *Olbrich,* Rizzoli International, 1980; *New Free Style,* Academy Editions, 1980. Contributing technical editor of *Architectural Design,* 1979—.

* * *

LAVELLE, Sheila 1939-

PERSONAL: Born July 12, 1939, in Newcastle-upon-Tyne,

England; daughter of K. A. (a laborer) and M. W. (a cleaning woman; maiden name, Wilson) Edmundson; married Derek James Lavelle (an insurance representative), September 13, 1958; children: Peter John, David Edward. *Education:* Birmingham Teacher Training College, teachers certificate, 1968. *Politics:* Conservative. *Religion:* None. *Home:* 47 Chalklands, Bourne End, Buckinghamshire SL8 5TH, England.

CAREER: Phoenix Assurance Co. Ltd., Newcastle-upon-Tyne, England, junior clerk, 1956-58; teacher at preparatory schools in Birmingham, England, 1968-70, and Ewell, England, 1970-72; High March School, Beaconsfield, England, teacher, 1972-75; writer. *Member:* National Trust, Royal Horticultural Society, Royal Society for the Protection of Birds, Upper Thames Sailing Club, Pentax Camera Club. *Awards, honors:* Silver Pencil Award from De Werkgroep Kinderbock, 1979, for Dutch translation of *Everybody Said No*.

WRITINGS—For children: *Ursula Bear*, Hamish Hamilton, 1977; *Everybody Said No*, A. & C. Black, 1978; *Oliver Ostrich*, A. & C. Black, 1978; *Too Many Husbands*, Hamish Hamilton, 1978; *Ursula Dancing*, Hamish Hamilton, 1979; *My Best Fiend*, Hamish Hamilton, 1979; *Ursula Exploring*, Hamish Hamilton, 1980; *Ursula Flying*, Hamish Hamilton, 1981; *Myrtle Turtle*, A. & C. Black, 1981; *Mr. Ginger's Potato*, A. & C. Black, 1981; *The Fiend Next Door*, Hamish Hamilton, 1982.

WORK IN PROGRESS: Trouble With the Fiend, for children.

AVOCATIONAL INTERESTS: Wildlife conservation, birds and birdwatching, walking, sailing, water color painting, gardening, botany, spinning, dying, and weaving wool.

BIOGRAPHICAL/CRITICAL SOURCES: Times Literary Supplement, July 23, 1982.

*   *   *

La VEY, Anton Szandor 1930-

BRIEF ENTRY: Born April 11, 1930, in Chicago, Ill. American Satanist and author. La Vey, who is best known as the founder of the First Church of Satan in San Francisco, California, became interested in black magic and the supernatural arts while still a teenager. Before he dropped out of high school to become a circus roustabout, La Vey performed with the San Francisco Ballet Orchestra as second oboist. He later became assistant criminologist and photographer for the San Francisco Police Department. By 1960 La Vey was conducting seminars in various occult activities, including cannabalism. During the 1960's he portrayed the devil in Kenneth Anger's motion picture "Inauguration of the Pleasure Dome" and in Roman Polanski's film "Rosemary's Baby." Though La Vey is said to have influenced such bizarre criminal activities as those of Charles Manson and his followers, the Satanist has publicly renounced the more distasteful aspects of the occult arts. La Vey's books include *The Satanic Bible* (University Books, 1969), *The Compleat Witch; or, What to do When Virtue Fails* (Dodd, 1971), and *The Satanic Rituals* (University Books, 1972). *Biographical/critical sources: Western Humanities Review*, summer, 1971; *Newsweek*, August 10, 1971; *Look*, August 24, 1971, *New York Times Book Review*, February 13, 1972; Burton H. Wolfe, *The Devil's Avenger: A Biography of Anton Szandor LaVey*, Pyramid, 1974.

LAWRENCE, Vera Brodsky 1909-
(Vera Brodsky)

BRIEF ENTRY: Born July 1, 1909, in Norfolk, Va. American musician, music historian, educator, and author. A concert pianist for more than thirty-five years, Lawrence also was a member of the music faculties of Curtis Institute of Music and Juilliard School and served on the music staff of Columbia Broadcasting System, Incorporated. Lawrence retired from the concert stage in 1965 to pursue a career as a music historian. Her book *Music for Patriots, Politicians, and Presidents: Harmonies and Discords of the First Hundred Years* (Macmillan, 1975) received a Deems Taylor Award from the American Society of Composers, Authors, and Publishers. Lawrence also edited *Contemporary Music Project for Creativity in Music Education*, 2nd edition (Music Educators' National Conference, 1969), *The Collected Works of Scott Joplin* (New York Public Library, 1970), and Joplin's *Collected Piano Works* (New York Public Library, 1972). *Biographical/critical sources: New York Times*, June 28, 1972, *New York Times Book Review*, December 7, 1975; *Village Voice*, December 15, 1975; *Christian Science Monitor*, February 11, 1976; *Baker's Biographical Dictionary of Musicians*, 6th edition, Schirmer Books, 1978.

*   *   *

LAWSON, Frederick Henry 1897-1983

OBITUARY NOTICE: Born July 14, 1897, in Leeds, England; died May 15, 1983, in Cleveland, England. Lawyer, educator, editor, and author. An Oxford lawyer who frequently lectured in the United States and Europe, Lawson originally trained in constitutional and Roman law, teaching at Merton College, Oxford, from 1930 to 1948. He was then elected to the newly created chair of comparative law at the Oxford University, where he remained until his retirement in 1964. For five years Lawson served as secretary general of the International Association of Legal Sciences. His books include *Negligence in the Civil Law, Introduction to the Law of Property*, and *Remedies of English Law*. Lawson also edited several international law journals. Obituaries and other sources: *The International Who's Who*, 46th edition, Europa, 1982; *Who's Who*, 134th edition, Marquis, 1982; *London Times*, May 17, 1983, May 28, 1983.

*   *   *

LEAPMAN, Michael 1938-

PERSONAL: Born April 24, 1938, in London, England; son of Nathan C. (a shopkeeper) and Leah (Isaacs) Leapman; married Olga Mason (a secretary), June 15, 1965; children: Benjamin. *Education:* Educated in England. *Home:* 13 Aldebert Ter., London SW8 1BH, England. *Agent:* Curtis Brown Ltd., 1 Craven Hill, London W.2, England. *Office: Daily Express*, Fleet St., London EC4, England.

CAREER: Scotsman, Edinburgh, Scotland, reporter, 1961-64; *London Sun*, London, England, reporter, 1964-69; *London Times*, London, New York bureau chief, 1969-72 and 1976-81, editor of *Times Diary*, 1972-76; *Daily Express*, London, columnist, 1981—. *Military service:* Royal Navy, 1956-58. *Member:* National Union of Journalists. *Awards, honors:* Named campaigning journalist of the year by the British Press, 1968.

WRITINGS: One Man and His Plot, J. Murray, 1976; *Yankee Doodles*, Allen Lane, 1982; *Companion Guide to New York*, Prentice-Hall, 1983; *Barefaced Cheek: The Apotheosis of Ru-*

pert Murdoch, Hodder & Stoughton, 1983. Contributor of articles to periodicals, including the *New York Times, New Statesman, Connoisseur,* and *Punch.*

SIDELIGHTS: *Yankee Doodles* is a collection of columns that journalist and humorist Michael Leapman wrote for the *London Times* while working in New York. "He never writes about anything other than the amazing interaction between Leapman and America," wrote Philip Howard in the *London Times.* Howard continued: "In the process he reveals much fun and much insight about both of them and about Brits abroad." In the *Times Literary Supplement* John Lahr wrote: "Leapman has just the right qualities to plumb the joys and absurdities of New York life. A bargain hunter, he is alternately elated and horrified by the American plethora of merchandise and technologies. . . . *Yankee Doodles* . . . is a wry, well-written account of life in the USA, that is, the United States of Advertising."

Leapman told *CA:* "My books have all sprung from my journalism, more or less. I am primarily a journalist and suppose I shall remain so. My first book, *One Man and His Plot,* was about my London vegetable garden, which I had written about in the *Times Diary.* I continue to write about gardening, amongst other things, for the *Daily Express.*"

BIOGRAPHICAL/CRITICAL SOURCES: *Listener,* July 29, 1976, April 15, 1982; *New Statesman,* August 13, 1976; *Punch,* October 20, 1976; *London Times,* April 15, 1982; *Economist,* April 24, 1982; *Times Literary Supplement,* July 30, 1982.

*   *   *

LECKEY, Dolores (Conklin) 1933-

PERSONAL: Born April 12, 1933, in New York, N.Y.; daughter of Joseph Francis Conklin; married Thomas Philip Leckey; children: Mary Kate, Celia Elizabeth Leckey Brace, Thomas Joseph, Colum. *Education:* St. John's University, Jamaica, N.Y., B.A., 1954; graduate study at University of Birmingham; George Washington University, M.A., 1971. *Religion:* Roman Catholic. *Home:* 1802 North Wakefield St., Arlington, Va. 22207. *Office:* U.S. Bishops' Committee on the Laity, National Conference of Catholic Bishops, 1312 Massachusetts Ave. N.W., Washington, D.C. 20005.

CAREER: Worked as a high school English teacher and as a teacher of gifted children; associated with Desales Hall School of Theology, Hyattsville, Md.; National Conference of Catholic Bishops, Washington, D.C., director of U.S. Bishops' Committee on the Laity. Associate member of staff at Shalem Institute for Spiritual Formation. *Awards, honors:* Honorary degree from St. John's University, Jamaica, N.Y., 1978.

WRITINGS: (Contributor) *What in the World Is the Church?,* Diocese of Richmond (Richmond, Va.), 1968; (contributor) *Realities and Visions: The Church's Mission Today,* Seabury, 1976; *The Ordinary Way: A Family Spirituality,* Cross Roads, 1982. Executive editor of "To Build and Be Church: Lay Ministry Resource Packet," U.S. Catholic Conference.

WORK IN PROGRESS: *The Morning Star Is Rising,* on contemporary church issues.

*   *   *

LEE, Barbara 1932-

PERSONAL: Born May 25, 1932, in New York, N.Y.; daughter of Isaac (in business) and Julia (Feldman) Kaplan; married

Robert S. Lee, June 9, 1963 (divorced November, 1980); children: David, Daniel. *Education:* Attended Hunter College (now of the City University of New York), 1949-51, and University of Chicago, 1951-54. *Home:* 4 Washington Square Village, New York, N.Y. 10012. *Office:* Columbia Broadcasting System, Inc., 51 West 52nd St., New York, N.Y. 10019.

CAREER: Newspaper Advertising Bureau, New York City, research project director, 1961-63; Yankelovich, Skelly & White, New York City, research project director, 1963-66; consultant, 1966-75; Columbia Broadcasting System, Inc., New York City, manager of research design and implementation in Office of Social Research, 1975—. Associate of Seminar on Media Mythologies and New York University's Institute for the Humanities; senior research associate at Center for Policy Research. *Member:* American Association for Public Opinion Research.

WRITINGS: (With Masha Kabokow Rudman) *Mind Over Media: New Ways to Improve Your Child's Reading and Writing Skills,* Seaview, 1982. Contributor to magazines, including *Ladies' Home Journal, Parents' Magazine,* and *McCall's.* Editor of newsletter of American Association for Public Opinion Research.

WORK IN PROGRESS: Research on the relationship between video games and computers and children's learning.

SIDELIGHTS: Barbara Lee told *CA:* "My book was stimulated by a study I made of the CBS-TV Reading Program, which made me aware of the ways in which television can be used effectively to encourage children to read. One way is to cause parents to become involved in helping their children learn, and all the media—from comic books to video games—can be a source of learning."

*   *   *

LEE, Fred 1927-

PERSONAL: Born September 8, 1927; married Jean Lavery (an administrator), April 19, 1959; children: Jean, Kara, Thomas, Cristina. *Education:* University of California, Berkeley, B.S.E.E., 1956, M.S.E.E., 1957. *Home and office:* 888 South Mary Ave., Sunnyvale, Calif. 94087.

CAREER: Data Processing Laboratory, Boston, Mass., engineer, 1957-60; Sylvania Electronic Products, Inc., Systems Technology Laboratory, Mountain View, Calif., development engineer, 1960-63; Fairchild Space and Defense Systems Division, Palo Alto, Calif., senior engineer, 1963-64; Melabs, Palo Alto, senior engineer, 1964-66; Varian Associates, Palo Alto, senior engineer, 1966-70; Tri Data, Mountain View, senior engineer, 1971-72; Cal Tex Semiconductors, Santa Clara, Calif., manager of logic design, 1972-74; Tunzi Development Co., Sunnyvale, Calif., associate, 1974-75; consultant, 1975—. *Military service:* U.S. Army, Signal Corps, pilot, 1946-49, 1951-53; became first lieutenant; received Air Medal and Bronze Star. *Member:* Institute of Electrical and Electronics Engineers.

WRITINGS: *The Computer Book,* Artech House, 1978. Contributor to electronics magazines.

WORK IN PROGRESS: Three books that explain the inner workings of computers to young readers.

SIDELIGHTS: Lee told *CA:* "I once had the idea that the best way to convey to a reader what goes on inside a computer would be to let the reader do what the circuits of a computer do when they execute programs. I stored simple instructions in the pages of a book. The reader can then blindly follow the instructions which have him do simple operations and lead him to the pages where subsequent instructions are found—just as actual computer instructions lead the computer's circuits from memory location to memory location and direct them to do simple operations. The instructions stored in the pages are first in plain English and later in code numbers similar to those a computer would use. Since the instructions take only a little space on each page, the rest of the space is devoted to text where I explain in plain and simple language how a computer works and give directions for doing the make-believe programs.

"*The Computer Book* was intended for adults who want to learn how a computer works without having to study technical textbooks. I have written three progressively shorter and easier versions for younger readers.''

*   *   *

LEE, Roy
See HOPKINS, Clark

*   *   *

LEFTWICH, Joseph   1892-1983

OBITUARY NOTICE—See index for *CA* sketch: Born September 20, 1892, in Zutphen, Netherlands; died February 28, 1983. Editor, translator, and author. Leftwich brought Yiddish literature to English audiences. His best-known works are the anthologies *Yisroel* and *The Golden Peacock*. Before devoting himself to free-lance writing and translating, Leftwich worked as an editor for the Jewish Telegraphic Society. His other books include *What Will Happen to the Jews?*, *Herzl, Man and Legend*, *Years Following After*, and *The Way of Their Thoughts*. Obituaries and other sources: *London Times*, March 21, 1983.

*   *   *

LEGGE, Elisabeth Schwarzkopf
See SCHWARZKOPF-LEGGE, Elisabeth

*   *   *

LEHMANN-HAUPT, Christopher (Charles Herbert) 1934-

PERSONAL: Surname is pronounced Lay-mun Howpt; born June 14, 1934, in Edinburgh, Scotland; became U.S. citizen c. 1935; son of Hellmut Lehmann-Haupt (a graphic arts historian and bibliographer) and Letitia L. Grierson (a teacher and editor); married Natalie S. Robins (a writer), October 3, 1965; children: Rachel Louise, Noah Christopher. *Education:* Swarthmore College, B.A., 1956; Yale University, M.F.A., 1959. *Home:* 627 West 247th St., Bronx, N.Y. 10471. *Agent:* Lynn Nesbit, International Creative Management, 40 West 57th St., New York, N.Y. 10019. *Office:* New York Times, 229 West 43rd St., New York, N.Y. 10036.

CAREER/WRITINGS: Book reviewer. A. S. Barnes & Co., New York City, editor, 1961-62; Holt, Rinehart & Winston, New York City, editor, 1962-63; Dial Press, New York City, editor, 1963-65; *New York Times Book Review*, New York City, editor, 1965-69; *New York Times*, New York City, senior daily book reviewer, 1969—. Instructor for Orange County secondary school system and community college, 1959; assistant professor at York College of the City University of New York, 1975-76. Lecturer at U.S. universities and abroad, 1969—. *Military service:* U.S. Army Reserves, 1959-65; became sergeant. *Member:* Century Association.

WORK IN PROGRESS: Innings, a nonfiction book about baseball, completion expected in 1985.

SIDELIGHTS: Christopher Lehmann-Haupt has served as chief daily book reviewer for the *New York Times* since 1969. According to *Esquire*'s D. Keith Mano, the enormity of the critic's influence on book readership is not unlike that of the Catholic Index a few decades ago. "Apparently,'' Lehmann-Haupt related to Mano in an interview, "a bookstore or library will order purely according to whether the book has appeared. Even if I don't like the book. It still becomes *a book* by virtue of the review. I'm told that.''

CA INTERVIEW

CA interviewed Christopher Lehmann-Haupt by phone on July 21, 1982, at his office at the *New York Times*.

CA: You're from a very bookish family. Did you know early that your career would have to do with books?

LEHMANN-HAUPT: Not really. I think it's fair to say that children generally think they're going to go in the opposite direction professionally from their parents. I always did, although my father used to send me copies of *Publishers Weekly* when I was in college, and therefore must have thought I was going to go into a "bookish'' profession. At the end of high school I half-planned to be a doctor. I also toyed with the idea of being an architect. By the time I was finished with college, I thought I wanted to go into the theatre, either as an actor or as a playwright, or to teach something connected with the theatre. I really didn't know until I got out of graduate school that I was going to go in the direction of books. In fact, I kind of backed into it, you might say.

CA: As chief daily book reviewer for the New York Times, *you must work under tremendous pressure. For starters, how do you manage to do the necessary reading?*

LEHMANN-HAUPT: By working long hours and resisting all temptations to play. Seriously, I have the advantage of working at home. In fact, we bought the house we live in specifically with my job in mind. It has a room at one end of the lower floor where I thought I could lock myself away for days on end. The job simply requires long hours. And since I'm not a fast reader (I can read quickly when I'm forced to, but not comfortably), I simply have to put in long hours.

CA: Are you pressured by publishers to review certain books?

LEHMANN-HAUPT: Pressured is putting it too strongly. They don't actually exert too much pressure. I feel pressure because there are always more books to review than I can possibly do—or than *we* can possibly do—in the daily paper. And I know from watching people around me what it takes to write a book, so it hurts every time I have to put one aside, knowing I'm not going to review it, and knowing what the author put into it, even if it's not very good. But—as far as direct pressure from publishers is concerned—they are different from other industries, almost shy about exerting pressure for fear of giving offense. I almost have to encourage publicity people and editors to call me when they feel strongly about something.

CA: How do you decide what books to review?

LEHMANN-HAUPT: We have an elaborate system which begins with the general principle that we work for a newspaper and should cover all those books which in some way constitute news, such as the current example, David McClintick's *Indecent Exposure,* which may have helped cost David Begelman his position as president of Metro-Goldwyn-Mayer. That's a book that has by one means or another managed to create questions in our readers' minds that we're required to answer. What's it like? What does it say? Is it any good? The same would go—and it is unfortunate, from a literary standpoint—for Judith Krantz's next novel. It is incumbent upon us to review it because the money it has already earned has generated enormous publicity and thus made it news. By the same token—and on the more positive note—we will review John Updike's next novel, not necessarily because it's good or bad, but because it's by John Updike. That sort of consideration takes care of anywhere from thirty to fifty percent of the slots we have to fill, depending on the season. For the rest of them, we try to discover first novelists or other new authors. I myself try to do odd subjects, simply as a change of pace in my reading. But in general, our system of selection is so ingrained that it's hard to spell out any more. It happens almost automatically.

CA: Do you get responses from authors who aren't pleased with your reviews?

LEHMANN-HAUPT: Sure. Mostly when I run into them at parties, which I try to avoid doing! Generally, a highly professional author will not respond either way because he or she realizes that when I review a book I am just doing my job, and to say thank you for a good review would imply it was written as a favor, which of course it wasn't. It was done out of respect for the book. Conversely, a very negative review shouldn't be an occasion for retaliation, because it's not a personal matter. Truly professional writers realize this, although I'm sure nobody isn't hurt and angered, deep-down, by a negative review. After all, people don't set out to write bad books.

CA: Do you get much response from general readers?

LEHMANN-HAUPT: A fair amount. I have to say that it's usually inspired by rage or by my having pressed somebody's funny-button, so to speak. I get a fair amount of those letters in which somebody says, "I've been meaning to write you and that review finally pushed me over the edge; I love your style." Or, "I've been muttering to myself for ten years about how awful you are, and this review finally did it." Not many people have the time to write long letters. Lots of people think nice thoughts, I suppose, but relatively few people actually sit down and express them.

CA: Do you have time to read other book reviewers and other book review publications?

LEHMANN-HAUPT: I find the time, and as a general rule, I try to see what other people are doing, simply because it's part of our job as daily newspaper people to be first. So I will pick up *Newsweek* and *Time* to see what they have done, making sure we're reasonably abreast of what *they* regard as current. I certainly look at the Sunday *New York Times Book Review,* usually in advance, again because as a daily paper we want to be first with the kinds of things the Sunday *Book Review* covers, especially on its front page. But I don't like to read other reviewers before I read a book, because no matter how independent one is, it does bias one by a tiny degree. And I don't

like to read them right after I've written a review because I don't like to be contradicted—at least not for a week or two.

CA: In an Esquire *article (March, 1977), D. Keith Mano quoted an unidentified source as saying of you, "Experimental fiction scares him. He's afraid he might get burned." Would you comment on that charge?*

LEHMANN-HAUPT: It certainly wasn't true at the time. It's my impression that, if anything, I was thought of as somebody who was perhaps too open to experimental fiction. Today I would consider it a more valid charge that I am shy of experimentation, not necessarily because I'm less sympathetic to innovation, but because I review it rather less frequently. That is simply because I find it difficult to review experimental fiction in the daily paper; it's very hard to explain in that space what a highly original writer is trying to do. Besides, I sense that if you review too much of it, you risk losing your audience, which tends to be looking for popular entertainment, at least to a large extent. Also, I have to admit that I do find myself getting less and less excited about experimental fiction as time goes by. It isn't a productive time for it or for avant-garde art in general.

Throughout history there have been periods of advance and periods of consolidation in the arts, in alternate cycles, and I think this is a time of consolidation. I suppose it's a cultural reaction to the 1960's and early 1970's, when we all went out on a limb and tried new things maybe more than we really ought to have.

CA: Are there aspects of reviewing that you find troublesome?

LEHMANN-HAUPT: Many people assume that the hardest thing about reviewing is writing negative reviews. I don't find this so. I seem to be known, for some peculiar reason—at least it has been stated in print—as someone whose reviews generally tend to be favorable. I'm not that happy to have this reputation, if in fact I do. People might ask, why *ever* write a negative review? Why bother to review a book you don't like? The answer to that is, the wider your range of reactions as a reviewer the more valid your positive reactions will seem to the reader. If you praised everything, you would devalue the critical currency. So you're almost glad for the opportunity to be negative, if only because it establishes the fact that you're not always positive, and this bolsters your credibility. In short, poor quality in a book does not necessarily create a hateful reviewing situation.

Books containing difficult concepts are hardest to review, I guess. I mean philosophical, economic, and political ideas—whatever—that one has to explain and comment on at the same time in the space of a review. I feel a sense of pressure and woe when I have to do that sort of thing. When I'm dealing with particularly incendiary political or ideological questions in a book, I feel challenged to find a way of reviewing it without having to take a stand, because I don't think it's our function to take stands on such questions. Most regular readers know where I stand politically anyway by now. But it's always difficult to review someone like Norman Podhoretz or Jeane Kirkpatrick; people think they know what you're going to say because you're ideologically hostile to such writers or at least are *thought* to be ideologically hostile.

As it turned out, wherever I stand ideologically, I found I liked Jeane Kirkpatrick's book *Dictatorships and Double Standards* very much. But it's hard to get around the kind of inflammatory reaction that most people have and be able to treat the book for what it is—a book. Just as an illustration: a friend of mine called yesterday and was furious at me for having praised Kirkpatrick's book. When I asked him why, he said he loathed the position she took on Vietnam. Well, she doesn't take that position in the book, so I can't really let it influence my review. It isn't even mentioned in the book.

CA: The New York Times *and the* New York Times Book Review *are considered by many people to have far too much influence on book sales nationwide. Do you think the charge is justified?*

LEHMANN-HAUPT: No review in and of itself is going to have a predictable effect. We can praise to the skies an experimental kind of fiction and not have any effect at all if the readers aren't interested. On the other hand, we can damn Judith Krantz and it won't make the slightest dent in her huge sales. Then again, I recall that *The Day of the Jackal* sold something like twenty-seven thousand copies on the day my favorable review appeared. I don't attribute that to my influence; it was just a happy coincidence. Everybody was looking for that kind of summer book to read at the time. The fact remains, however, that we of the *Times are* unduly powerful, and I think it's unfortunate because I don't think any single medium should be. Moreover, I think it reflects poorly on the state of reviewing in general that one medium should stand so much above others. Given that situation, people are bound to be extraordinarily sensitive to what that medium is doing. And, in a certain sense, I suppose, the more complaints there are the better it is: it means that more people are reading it and reacting. As far as the Sunday *Book Review* is concerned, I don't always agree with what it reviews or how. But then, who does? Except, of course, for the man who's running it, and even *he* possibly has some objections. Selecting the books to be reviewed is just a highly personal and infinitely variable procedure; no two people would do it exactly the same way.

CA: You served as a fiction judge for the 1972 National Book Awards and wrote later about the problems involved in that job. Do you think the selection of book award winners can be appreciably improved?

LEHMANN-HAUPT: My problem with all book prizes is that I don't think literature can be judged by committee. The obvious answer to the problem would be to choose a single judge for a given year and let him or her alone make the selections in each category. That's what they do in some European countries. Then at least we would know that the awards reflected somebody's taste instead of a political process. The American Book Awards system is a catastrophe, and I think in general the selections have reflected that fact, even though a few good books have somehow survived the selection process—which I find so utterly opposed to the notion of creativity and achievement in the arts that I don't even like to think about it anymore.

I do concede that prizes serve the purpose of encouraging writers and also publicizing them. And, after all, a really good book should be brought to the attention of as many readers as possible. But it's laughable when one Pulitzer committee chooses Thomas Pynchon's *Gravity's Rainbow* and then a supervising committee vetoes the decision, as it also did in the selection of Philip Roth's *The Ghost Writer* a few years later. As if questions of literary merit could be settled by one committee squaring off against another.

CA: Are you working on a book now?

LEHMANN-HAUPT: Yes, I'm in the middle of a book that I've been working on for four years now. I scratch away on it at odd hours of the week when I have free time. I hope to have it finished at least in first-draft form by the end of the year. It's a kind of odd book about baseball, tentatively titled *Innings.* It recounts in a sort of novelistic form, although absolutely accurately, the experiences of a character called "the fan" (obviously me) following baseball for a single year. I actually hung around the locker rooms and went to all the major events and tried to be a reporter. I was trying to put myself in the typical fan's shoes and see what it's like to have the fantasy come true of being in the middle of it.

CA: Do you teach now or do any speaking to groups?

LEHMANN-HAUPT: I occasionally can be persuaded to give a speech, but I stopped teaching about four years ago, mostly because the City University system ran out of money. I then spent a year actively seeking speaking engagements because I missed the contact with my students—I like teaching; I liked the chance to be with other people that it gave me. But once I became involved with this book, I've tried to avoid all such commitments and will continue to do so until it's finished. Then maybe I'll look around and see if anything's available in a teaching job, or if any people are interested in hearing me speak.

CA: When you get away from work, do you read, or do you do something completely different?

LEHMANN-HAUPT: I generally do several things completely different. When I'm on vacation, I do try to catch up with what I've missed in the way of books for pleasure, classics I've never gotten around to reading, or books I feel a sense of responsibility to read. But whenever I have a choice, I prefer to do something more physically active, like fishing or sailing or working in the garden.

BIOGRAPHICAL/CRITICAL SOURCES: Esquire, March, 1977.

—*Interview by Jean W. Ross*

*   *   *

LEHNER, Christine (Reine)   1952-

PERSONAL: Born May 15, 1952, in Boston, Mass.; daughter of Philip (a businessman) and Monique (an architectural historian; maiden name, Brancart) Lehner; married Jeffrey Richardson Hewitt (a nurse and writer), September 11, 1976; children: Reine Wing, Tristram Jeffrey Richardson. *Education:* University of California, Santa Barbara, B.A., 1973; Brown University, M.A., 1977. *Home:* 618 Broadway, Hastings-on-Hudson, N.Y. 10706.

CAREER: Pace University, Pleasantville, N.Y., adjunct instructor in literature and communications, 1980—.

WRITINGS: Expecting, New Directions, 1982. Contributor of short stories to *New Directions Anthology, Chelsea, North American Review* and *Agni Review.*

WORK IN PROGRESS: Rivers and Birds and Snow and Ice, or *Climate and the Affections,* tentative titles for a collection of short stories.

SIDELIGHTS: The nine chapters of *Expecting* represent the nine months of pregnancy, beginning with chapter one when C learns that she's pregnant, and ending with the ninth chapter when C gives birth. The chapters between discovery and birth focus on the awe C feels over the new life growing inside her, and the changes she sees in herself. Dreams and fears are explored, as well as C's relations with other women, particularly with her mother and maternal grandmother. Writing in the *Village Voice Literary Supplement*, reviewer M. Mark described Lehner as a "thoroughgoing modernist," and praised her "spare, almost affectless narrative."

Lehner told *CA:* "I write out of a deep sense of inarticulateness. The world is filled with stories and images, but I can only make sense out of them by constructing a story. *Expecting* came out of a desire to connect the imaginative and physical aspects of a pregnancy: the growing of a new life which for nine months (at least) is mysterious even to its creators. We are always in the process of expecting something, but by the time that thing arrives, the situation has changed and expectations are different. The new lives overlap."

BIOGRAPHICAL/CRITICAL SOURCES: *Village Voice Literary Supplement,* November, 1982.

* * *

LEHRER, James (Charles) 1934-

BRIEF ENTRY: Born May 19, 1934, in Wichita, Kan. American broadcast journalist and author. During the 1960's Lehrer worked as a reporter for the *Dallas Morning News* and as a reporter, columnist, and city editor for the *Dallas Times Herald.* He moved to the broadcast industry in 1970 when he joined the staff of KERA-TV, Dallas's public television station, as an executive producer. In 1972 he became the public affairs coordinator of the national Public Broadcasting Service in Washington, D.C. One year later he began co-anchoring the nationally syndicated "MacNeil-Lehrer Report." Lehrer has received George Polk, George Foster Peabody, and Emmy awards for journalism. His books include *Viva Max* (Duell, Sloan & Pearce, 1966) and his memoirs, *We Were Dreamers* (Atheneum, 1975). *Address:* 3356 Macomb, Washington, D.C. 20016. *Biographical/critical sources: National Review,* October 15, 1976; *TV Guide,* October 8, 1977, January 23-29, 1982; *Smithsonian,* May, 1981.

* * *

LEIGH, Mike 1943-

PERSONAL: Born February 20, 1943, in Salford, Lancashire, England; son of Alfred Abraham and Phyllis Pauline (Cousin) Leigh; married Alison Steadman (an actress), September 15, 1973; children: Toby, Leo. *Education:* Attended Royal Academy of Dramatic Art, 1960-62, Camberwell Art School, 1963-64, London School of Film Technique, 1963-64, and Central Art School, 1964-65. *Agent:* A. D. Peters & Co. Ltd, 10 Buckingham St., London WC2 6BU, England.

CAREER: Associate director of Midlands Art Centre, 1965-66; Victoria Theatre, Stoke-on-Trent, England, actor, 1966; assistant director of Royal Shakespeare Co., 1967-68; writer. Director of plays, including "Little Malcolm and His Struggle Against the Eunuchs," 1965, "The Knack," 1967, and "The Life of Galileo," 1970. *Awards, honors:* Golden Hugo Award from Chicago Film Festival and Golden Leopard Award from Locarno Film Festival, both 1972, both for "Bleak Moments"; Best Comedy Award from *Evening Standard* and Best Comedy Award from *Drama,* both 1981, both for "Goose-Pimples."

WRITINGS—Plays: *Abigail's Party* (first produced in London at Hampstead Theatre, 1977), Samuel French, 1979 (also see below); *Goose-Pimples,* Samuel French, 1982 (also see below); *Abigail's Party and Goose-Pimples,* Penguin, 1983.

Unpublished plays: "The Box Play," first produced at Midlands Art Centre Theatre, 1965; "The Last Crusade of the Five Little Nuns," first produced at Midland Arts Centre Theatre, 1966; "Individual Fruit Pies," first produced at East-15 Acting School Theatre, 1968; "Down Here and Up There," first produced in London at Theatre Upstairs, 1968; "Big Basil," first produced at Manchester Youth Theatre, 1968; "Glum Victoria and the Lad With Specs," first produced at Manchester Youth Theatre, 1969; "Bleak Moments," first produced at Open Space Theatre, 1970; "A Rancid Pong," first produced at Basement Theatre, 1971; "Wholesome Glory," first produced in London at Theatre Upstairs, 1973; "The Jaws of Death," first produced at Traverse Theatre, 1973; "The Silent Majority," first produced in London at Bush Theatre, 1974; "Ecstasy," first produced in London at Hampstead Theatre, 1979. Also author of "My Parents Have Gone to Carlisle," 1966, "Nenaa," 1967, "Epilogue," 1969, "Dick Whittington," 1973, and "Babies Grow Old," 1974.

Television plays and screenplays; all broadcast by British Broadcasting Corp. (BBC): "Bleak Moments" (adapted from own play; also see above), 1971; "Hard Labor," 1973; "The Permissive Society," 1975; "Knock for Knock," 1976; "Nuts in May," 1976; "The Kiss of Death," 1977; "Abigail's Party" (adapted from own play; also see above), 1977; "Who's Who," 1978; "Grown-Ups," 1980; "Home Sweet Home," 1982.

SIDELIGHTS: Mike Leigh told *CA:* "All my plays and films have evolved from scratch entirely by rehearsal through improvisation; thus it is inherent in my work that I always combine the jobs of author and director, and I never work with any other writers or directors. I have been pioneering this style of work in England, beginning with the 'Box Play' in 1965."

* * *

L'ENFANT, Julie 1944-

PERSONAL: Born March 16, 1944, in Hodge, La.; daughter of Weldon K. (a music teacher and librarian) and Era Byrd (a music teacher; maiden name, Pullen) Chandler; married Howard W. L'Enfant, Jr. (a professor of law), May 21, 1966; children: Jamie Elizabeth. *Education:* Louisiana State University, B.A., 1965, Ph.D., 1974; University of New Orleans, M.A., 1968. *Home and office:* 10924 Effringham Ave., Baton Rouge, La. 70815. *Agent:* Julie Fallowfield, McIntosh & Otis, Inc., 475 Fifth Ave., New York, N.Y. 10017.

CAREER: University of Kentucky, Lexington, lecturer in English, 1974-75; free-lance writer, 1975—. Publicity writer for Baton Rouge Symphony Orchestra, Baton Rouge, La., 1977-78.

WRITINGS: *The Dancers of Sycamore Street* (novel), St. Martin's, 1983. Contributor to *Southern Review.*

WORK IN PROGRESS: A novel set in London, England.

SIDELIGHTS: L'Enfant told *CA:* "I write about things that haunt me. Place usually comes first, then characters. The novel form is the most natural to me: I like to live with my characters awhile and give them a world. And I always try to show it with clarity and good humor."

* * *

LENNON, Nigey 1954-

PERSONAL: Born July 1, 1954, in Santa Monica, Calif.;

daughter of (stepfather) Duward J. (in business) and Margo (an amateur linguist; maiden name, Demetre) Lennon; married Lionel Rolfe (a writer), November 28, 1975. *Education:* Attended El Camino College, 1971. *Politics:* Social Democrat. *Religion:* None. *Home:* 952 Maltman Ave., No. 201, Los Angeles, Calif. 90026.

CAREER: Writer, 1971—. Band leader and musical composer, 1970—. Founding member of Los Angeles Institute of Quantum 'Pataphysics, 1982—.

WRITINGS: (With husband, Lionel Rolfe) *Nature's Twelve Magic Healers: The Amazing Secrets of Cell Salts,* Parker Publishing, 1978; *Mark Twain in California,* Chronicle Books, 1982; (with Rolfe) *The Heal Yourself Home Handbook of Unusual Remedies,* Parker Publishing, ·1982; (with Bill Griffith) *Alfred Jarry: The Man With the Axe,* Panjandrum, 1983.

Co-author of comic strip, "Suburban Angst," in *Long Beach Free Press,* 1970-71. Contributor of articles and reviews to magazines and newspapers, including *Playboy.* Editor of *Los Angeles Free Press,* 1970-71; West Coast editor of *Off Duty,* 1977.

SIDELIGHTS: In *Mark Twain in California,* Nigey Lennon traces Samuel Clemens's eventful and developing years in the Golden State, from 1861 to 1868. According to Steve Miller of the *Los Angeles Weekly,* the author aptly conveys this "pivotal time in the life of a young Samuel Clemens, during which he first worked as a professional journalist, first used the *nom-de-plume* of Mark Twain, and wrote and published his first short story ('The Notorious Jumping Frog of Calaveras County')." "She also brings to life his poverty, his first attempts on the lecture circuit," wrote Ferol Egan in the *San Francisco Sunday Examiner & Chronicle.* "Within the limitations of a short book, 'Mark Twain in California' gives readers insights into the state of American Letters, Western style."

Lennon proposes in *Mark Twain in California* that these seven Western years transformed Clemens from an irresponsible, awkward youth into a promising literary figure. "All through the book the thesis is proved neatly," Miller asserted, "but with no heavy hand nor pain to the reader. . . . While it's evident that Lennon did a great deal of research both primary and secondary, she has elected not to burden her text with the welter of footnotes and references that would be required to make her statements provable in academia. No, the book's designed as a pleasure-read, and no attempt is made to disguise this." "This is a lighthearted yet well-researched look [at Twain]," concurred Lincoln Haynes in the *Press-Telegraph.* "In a free-wheeling style reminiscent of Twain himself, [Lennon] details the day-to-day adventures with writers, editors, miners, madams and barroom buddies that make up Twain's San Francisco chronicle."

Lennon told *CA:* "I was a product of Southern California suburbia and, because of its de-emphasis of intellectual pursuits, I was considered a freak and a misfit for years. I didn't get much standard education, although my mother insisted on force-feeding me French and Spanish. I went to live in Europe when I was nineteen, came back again, and began writing seriously. I am still at it, though not so seriously.

"My main interests as a writer include humor, satire, surrealism, and absurdity. The nineteenth century fascinates me, probably because the twentieth is so hard to take. Music is another interest, though I suspect that 'writing about music is like dancing about art.' I compose small orchestral and band works, and have done some writing about music. My primary

motivation as a writer is to tackle subjects that may be complex to general readers, and render them readable and exciting to anybody.

"I was inspired to write about Mark Twain and Alfred Jarry because early exposure to their work contributed greatly to my development as a writer, though in very different ways. Twain has been the target of a good many biographers, but nobody ever wrote about the time he spent in California—at least not an entire volume—so, being a native Californian myself, I decided to remedy that grievous omission. As for Jarry, he was the forerunner of too many modern developments to even begin to enumerate—literary and otherwise. His life was also thoroughly fascinating. Since there is no full-length English-language biography of his life, I decided to write one (aided and abetted by illustrator Bill Griffith of San Francisco, the 'Rousseau of the Radiograph')."

BIOGRAPHICAL/CRITICAL SOURCES: Press-Telegraph, August 6, 1982; *Palo Alto Peninsula Times Tribune,* August 7, 1982; *Los Angeles Times,* August 22, 1982; *San Francisco Sunday Examiner & Chronicle,* August 29, 1982; *Los Angeles Weekly,* September 3-9, 1982; *Berkeley Gazette,* September 28, 1982; *Los Angeles Herald Examiner,* October 24, 1982; *San Diego Magazine,* November, 1982.

*   *   *

LE QUEUX, William (Tufnell)   1864-1927

BRIEF ENTRY: Born July 2, 1864, in London, England; died October 13, 1927. British artist, journalist, and author. Le Queux, who claimed to have intimate knowledge of the secret service operations of several European nations, was one of the first contributors to the spy fiction genre. A world traveler and former consul to the Republic of San Marino, Le Queux also worked as foreign editor for the *London Globe* from 1891 to 1893 and as correspondent for the *London Daily Mail* during the Balkan War from 1912 to 1913. His first novel, *Guilty Bonds* (1891), is a fictional account of events observed by the journalist while working in Czarist Russia. The book was subsequently banned in that country. In addition to more than one hundred fifty novels about international intrigue, including *Bolo, the Super Spy* (1918), *Cipher Six* (1919), and *Hidden Hands* (1926), Le Queux produced several volumes of short stories. He also wrote a number of nonfiction books that warned of Britain's vulnerability to European invasion before World War I. *Biographical/critical sources: New Century Handbook of English Literature,* revised edition, Appleton, 1967; *Longman Companion to Twentieth Century Literature,* Longman, 1970; *Encyclopedia of Mystery and Detection,* McGraw, 1976.

*   *   *

LERRIGO, Marion Olive   1898-1968

OBITUARY NOTICE: Born October 27, 1898, in Topeka, Kan.; died September 29, 1968, in North Adams, Mass. Author of books about health education. Lerrigo co-authored a series of sex education books ·for the National Education Association and the American Medical Association. She served on several health education committees, including the White House Conference on Child Health in 1930. Lerrigo's works on health topics include *Caring for Your Disabled Child* (with Benjamin Spock), *Children Can Help Themselves,* and *A Doctor Talks to Nine-to-Twelve Year Olds.* She also wrote a biography, *A Brother Is a Stranger,* with Toru Matsumoto. Obituaries and other sources: *New York Times,* September 30, 1969; *Who Was*

Who in America, With World Notables, Volume V: *1969-1973,* Marquis, 1973.

* * *

LESLIE, Robert B.
See WOOLEY, John (Steven)

* * *

LeSOURD, Catherine
See MARSHALL, (Sarah) Catherine (Wood)

* * *

LESTER, Andrew D(ouglas) 1939-

PERSONAL: Born August 8, 1939, in Coral Gables, Fla.; son of Andrew R. and Dorothy V. (Atkinson) Lester; married Judith A. Laesser (a marriage and family therapist), September 8, 1960; children: Scott, Denise. *Education:* Mississippi College, B.A., 1961; Southern Baptist Theological Seminary, B.D., 1964, Ph.D., 1968. *Religion:* Baptist. *Home:* 1907 Lonlipman Court, Louisville, Ky. 40207. *Office address:* Box 1918, Lexington Rd., Louisville, Ky. 40280.

CAREER: Youth minister at Baptist churches in Memphis, Tenn., 1960, Washington, Miss., 1960-61, Jackson, Miss., 1961-62, and Louisville, Ky., 1966-67; ordained as Southern Baptist minister in 1962; pastor of Baptist church in Bryantsville, Ky., 1962-66; Southern Baptist Theological Seminary, Louisville, Ky., special instructor in psychology and religion, 1967-69; North Carolina Baptist Hospital, Winston-Salem, N.C., assistant director of department of pastoral care, 1969-70, director of counseling services, 1970-71, director of School of Pastoral Care, 1971-77; Southern Baptist Theological Seminary, associate professor, 1977-82, professor of psychology of religion, 1982—. Pastoral counselor at Personal Counseling Service, Jeffersonville, Ind., 1965-69 and 1977—. Visiting professor at Southeastern Baptist Theological Seminary and visiting lecturer at Wake Forest University, both 1972-77. *Member:* Association of Clinical Pastoral Education, American Association of Pastoral counselors, American Protestant Hospital Association (fellow of College of Chaplains), American Association of Marriage and Family Therapists (clinical member).

WRITINGS: (Editor with Wayne E. Oates) *Pastoral Care in Crucial Human Situations,* Judson, 1969; *Sex Is More Than a Word,* Broadman, 1973; *It Hurts So Bad, Lord!: The Christian Encounters Crisis,* Broadman, 1976; (with wife, Judith L. Lester) *Understanding Aging Parents,* Westminster, 1980; *Coping With Your Anger: A Christian Guide,* Westminster, 1983. Contributor to church magazines.

WORK IN PROGRESS: The Pastoral Care of Children in Crisis, publication by Westminster expected in 1985.

SIDELIGHTS: Lester told CA: "I have always been interested in what psychology and theology can teach each other. My basic purpose for writing is to introduce laypersons to some of the insights of psychology of religion and pastoral theology. Popular ideas about the Christian faith are often destructive of personhood. *Coping With Your Anger,* for instance, is an attempt to help Christians understand that the capacity for anger is part of the creation and not the result of sin. *Sex Is More Than a Word* has the same goal, to help Christians recognize that sex is one of God's gifts rather than some demonic aspect

of selfhood. Both anger and sex can help fulfill life and add to love and intimacy if handled ethically."

* * *

LEVENKRON, Steven 1941-

PERSONAL: Born March 25, 1941, in New York, N.Y.; son of Joseph A. (a paperhanger) and Florence (in sales; maiden name, Shader) Levenkron; married Abby Rosen (a therapist), May 25, 1963; children: Rachel, Gabrielle. *Education:* Queens College of the City University of New York, B.A., 1963; Brooklyn College of the City University of New York, M.S., 1969. *Agent:* George Wieser, Wieser & Wieser, Inc., 79 Valley View, Chappaqua, N.Y. 10514. *Office:* 16 East 79th St., New York, N.Y. 10021.

CAREER: Social studies teacher at secondary schools in New York City, 1963-68; guidance counselor at secondary schools in New York City, 1968-74; in part-time private practice of psychotherapy, 1972-74; Montefiore Hospital and Medical Center, Bronx, N.Y., visiting psychotherapist, 1975—; Center for the Study of Anorexia, New York City, clinical consultant, 1981—. *Member:* American Personnel and Guidance Association, American Orthopsychiatric Association, National Association of Anorexia Nervosa and Associated Disorders (member of advisory board). *Awards, honors:* Annual award from the National Association of Anorexia Nervosa and Associated Disorders, 1981, for bringing anorexia nervosa to public attention; *The Best Little Girl in the World* was named best book for young adults by the American Library Association, 1978-79.

WRITINGS: The Best Little Girl in the World (novel), Contemporary Books, 1978; *Treating and Overcoming Anorexia Nervosa,* Scribner, 1982.

WORK IN PROGRESS: A sequel to *The Best Little Girl in the World,* tentatively titled *Kessa: The Best Little Girls in the World, Part II,* publication by Warner Books expected in 1984; *New Emphases in Parenting; Exploitation of Women in the Social Marketplace.*

SIDELIGHTS: Psychotherapist Steven Levenkron blames the prevailing societal attitude that "thin is better" for the dramatic increase in the incidence of anorexia nervosa, a disease described in the *Los Angeles Times* as a "hysterical aversion to food leading to severe weight loss and malnutrition." "As a culture we've become sick on the subject of being thin," Levenkron said. "The message that is given to our young daughters via magazines and the fashion industry that harp on looking skinny, is that females must be thin to be appealing, whereas males can be sturdy."

Levenkron, who works with anorexics, is the author of *The Best Little Girl in the World,* a novel that details the experiences of Francesca, a fictional anorexic. The typical anorexic has an "intense desire to actually be the best little girl in the world," Levenkron explained in the *Los Angeles Times.* "So she feels that if she becomes thinner and thinner, she will become better and better. She doesn't refuse to eat just because she wants to punish her parents as some rebellious kids who run away or turn to drugs do."

Sufferers of anorexia nervosa (92 percent of them are women, and most are under twenty-five years of age) are typically "meek, compliant, perfectionistic overachievers," noted Anne Fadiman in *Life,* echoing Levenkron's assessment of the anorexic personality. "Such generalizations sound sweeping,"

Fadiman continued, "but it is amazing to sit in on a meeting of a parents' self-help group and listen to the mothers: one would think they were all describing the same sweet, tractable daughter, the one who always did well in school and never demanded attention."

Once rare, anorexia now afflicts more than 100,000 people in the United States alone. It can lead to such complications as heart failure, infection, and irreversible hypoglycemia. The mortality rate among anorexics is the highest of any psychiatric disorder. "The remedy for anorexia is simple," Fadiman noted. "All the patient must do is eat. That, unfortunately, is the one thing she will not do, and in order to avoid it, she will use every tool at her disposal, including deceit, manipulation and an intensity of stubbornness that seems incredible in one so frail and weak." Many anorexics who are hospitalized when their weight dips dangerously low will gain weight under supervision—only to return to their self-starvation rituals once they are released from the hospital and the external controls are removed.

Ironically, most anorexics do not have a weight problem when they begin dieting. Such was the case with Jane Daly (a patient of Levenkron's and the subject of Fadiman's *Life* magazine article), who, at 5 feet 8 inches and 135 pounds, could hardly have been considered overweight. What began as a desire to shed a few pounds became an uncontrollable obsession as Jane's weight dropped steadily. By the time she began therapy with Levenkron, Daly weighed 81 pounds and had been hospitalized three times. "She looked," Levenkron recalled, "like a long skinny rag doll from the five-and-ten-cent store."

Treatment of anorexics varies widely. Long-term therapy, particularly psychoanalysis, is less effective than short-term approches, for, as Fadiman pointed out, "a patient might well starve to death before she finished exploring her unconscious." In treating Jane Daly, Levenkron used a method that he calls Nurturant-Authoritative therapy. The method, which he describes in his book *Treating and Overcoming Anorexia Nervosa,* is based on the theory that "anorexics do not know how to accept help, and that in order to teach them how to become adults the therapist must first teach them how to act like children." In order to do this, Levenkron uses such unorthodox techniques as touching the patient to show her that she is not repellent, eating meals with her, and using a mirror to show her each of her protruding bones "in order to persuade her that she cannot see herself correctly." He also encourages his patients to telephone him at home. During her hospitalization, Jane Daly called Levenkron every night. "She would say, 'I'm so scared. The IV is running too fast. They're making me fat.'" Levenkron responded, he said, "in my most soothing, repetitive voice, 'You're not getting too fat. You're very thin. You're not getting fat.' I was like a metronome. I'd talk the way you might talk to a very young child, and after she had heard this iambic pentameter for a while she would lie back in bed and go to sleep."

When her weight reached 92 pounds, Daly was released from the hospital. She began to lose weight again, which is not unusual since "most anorexics gain in the hospital but resume their old eating habits, at least temporarily, as soon as they return home." Eventually, however, she began to gain. "She was beginning to listen when Steve Levenkron told her for the hundredth time that if she gained weight he would be proud of her; that she would be more special, not less; that her thighs were not getting fat; that she could eat a cheeseburger without gaining five pounds; that she was still thinner than every model

in *Seventeen;* that boys were going to like her; and that perhaps the time was coming to say good-bye to some of her magic rituals."

Levenkron also counsels the families of anorexics. He advises them to give attention and emotional support to the anorexic rather than focusing on her reluctance to eat. "Sure, you can force a person to eat by keeping her in her room and taking away her privileges until she relents," he told the *Los Angeles Times.* "But she will eventually slip back into anorexia and you haven't helped that lonely girl as a human being. You have just bludgeoned her out of her symptoms. Just because her bones have disappeared under some flesh for a while does not mean she is healthy. To be healthy, she has to feel integrated with the rest of family and society."

Levenkron told *CA:* "I am interested in shaping psychotherapy for adolescents who have anorexia nervosa by integrating contemporary psychotherapy with feminism. This calls for a rethinking of the kinds of interpretations and meanings attributed to patients' statements in psychotherapy. Such interpretations would take into consideration the effects of role modeling within the family and existential dilemmas of mothers—and women in general—in today's society. This implies less emphasis on traditional Freudian-analytical concepts that were not formulated with an empathic approach to women."

BIOGRAPHICAL/CRITICAL SOURCES: *Los Angeles Times,* August 24, 1979; *Life,* February, 1982; *Discover,* May, 1982.

—*Sketch by Mary Sullivan*

*   *   *

LEVENTHAL, Fred Marc 1938-

BRIEF ENTRY: Born May 17, 1938, in New York, N.Y. American historian, educator, and author. Leventhal began teaching history at Boston University in 1969. He has also taught at University of Edinburgh and Harvard University. Leventhal wrote *Respectable Radical: George Howell and Victorian Working Class Politics* (Harvard University Press, 1971). *Address:* Department of History, Boston University, 226 Bay State Rd., Boston, Mass. 02215. *Biographical/critical sources: New Statesman,* February 12, 1971; *Observer,* March 14, 1971; *Spectator,* April 3, 1971; *American Historical Review,* February, 1972; *Directory of American Scholars,* Volume I: *History,* 7th edition, Bowker, 1978.

*   *   *

LEVIN, Harry 1925-

PERSONAL: Born March 3, 1925, in Baltimore, Md.; son of Morris and Bessie L. (Wolfe) Levin; married Deborah B. Stern, December 25, 1946; children: Diane Lynn (Mrs. William B. Broydrick), David Stern, Rebecca Lee. *Education:* Attended Johns Hopkins University, 1942-43; University of Maryland, B.A., 1948; University of Michigan, M.A., 1949, Ph.D., 1951. *Home:* 1608 Hanshaw Rd., Ithaca, N.Y. 14850. *Office:* Department of Psychology, 206 Uris Hall, Cornell University, Ithaca, N.Y. 14853.

CAREER: Harvard University, Cambridge, Mass., Social Science Research Council fellow, 1950-51, assistant professor of education and research associate in Laboratory of Human Development, 1951-55; Cornell University, Ithaca, N.Y., associate professor, 1955-61, professor of child development and psychology, 1961—, William R. Kenan, Jr., Professor of Psychology, 1967—, chairman of department, 1966—, dean of

College of Arts and Sciences, 1974-78. Visiting associate professor at Stanford University, summer, 1955, 1958; visiting scientist with Harvard-Florence (Italy) project; visiting professor of psychology at Massachusetts Institute of Technology, 1973; visiting professor of psychology and education at Harvard University, 1978-79. Member of resident advising committee of U.S. Office of Education, 1959-61; chairman of psychology panel of Committee on International Exchange of Persons, 1963-66; trustee of Histadrut Israel American Cultural Exchange Institute. *Military service:* U.S. Army, 1944-46. *Member:* American Educational Research Association, American Psychological Association (fellow), Phi Beta Kappa, Sigma Xi. *Awards, honors:* Received fellowships from U.S. Public Health Service, 1961-62, and National Institute of Mental Health.

WRITINGS: (With Robert Richardson Sears) *Patterns of Child Rearing,* Row, Peterson, 1957; (co-author) *A Basic Research Program on Reading,* Cornell University, 1963; *Planning for a Reading Research Program,* Cornell University, 1965; (co-author) *Studies of Oral Reading,* Ithaca, N.Y., 1965; (editor with Eleanor Jack Gibson and James Jerome Gibson) *The Analysis of Reading Skill: A Program of Basic and Applied Research,* Bureau of Research, Office of Education, U.S. Department of Health, Education, and Welfare, 1968; (with Joanne R. Mitchell) *Project Literacy: Continuing Activities,* Bureau of Research, U.S. Office of Education, 1969; (editor with Joanna P. Williams) *Basic Studies on Reading,* Basic Books, 1970; (with Eleanor Jack Gibson) *The Psychology of Reading,* MIT Press, 1975; (with Ann B. Addis) *The Eye-Voice Span,* MIT Press, 1979. Also co-author with A. L. Baldwin of *Pride and Shame in Children,* 1959.

SIDELIGHTS: Harry Levin has published several studies on the subject of reading. In *The Psychology of Reading,* Levin and co-author Eleanor J. Gibson attempt to unify reading processes under cognitive theory. They also examine the processes underlying reading research. According to *Library Quarterly,* "Anyone seriously interested in reading, learning to read, and reading instruction should obtain this book and read it." A second work, *Basic Studies on Reading,* contains fifteen essays selected and edited by Levin and Joanna P. Williams that cover three aspects of the reading process: the relationship of linguistics to reading, the psychological processes involved in reading, and the social variables influencing the reading process. In another collaborative effort, *The Eye-Voice Span,* Levin and Ann B. Addis study the relationship between the eye and the voice in the reading process. The co-authors define this relationship as the eye-voice span, the distance that the eye is ahead of the voice in reading. The book relates philosophical and historical background on the subject, explores text and reader characteristics that influence eye-voice span, and compares oral and silent reading.

BIOGRAPHICAL/CRITICAL SOURCES: Library Quarterly, October, 1976.

* * *

LEVINE, Milton I(sra) 1902-

PERSONAL: Born August 15, 1902, in Syracuse, N.Y.; son of David and Daisy (Baum) Levine; married Jean H. Seligmann (an author and educator), June 14, 1936; children: Carol (Mrs. J. G. Paasche), Ann (Mrs. T. Parker). *Education:* City College of New York (now of the City University of New York), B.S., 1923; Cornell University, M.D., 1927. *Politics:* Democrat. *Religion:* Jewish. *Home:* 302 West 12th St., New York, N.Y.

10014; and Lincolndale, N.Y. 10540. *Office:* 1111 Park Ave., New York, N.Y. 10028.

CAREER: Physician, writer, and editor. New York Nursery and Children's Hospital, New York City, assistant clinical pediatrician, 1929-32; Children's Allergy Clinic, Midtown Hospital, New York City, director, 1929-31; Fifth Avenue Hospital, New York City, assistant clinical pediatrician, 1930-33; Children's Tuberculosis Clinic, Harlem Hospital, New York City, pediatrician, 1932-42; New York Hospital, New York City, assistant attending pediatrician, 1932-52, associate attending pediatrician, 1952-56, attending pediatrician, 1956-71, consulting pediatrician, 1971—; Cornell University Medical College, New York City, instructor, 1933-44, assistant professor, 1944-54, associate professor, 1954-66, professor of clinical pediatrics, 1966-71, professor emeritus, 1971—. Consulting pediatrician to several New York City area schools and agencies, 1930—; director of research, Childhood Tuberculosis Bureau Laboratories, 1931-42; member of executive board, Louise Wise Adoption Agency, 1941-68; consulting pediatrician, Mayor's Committee on Wartime Care of Children, 1942-46; chairman of advisory committee on bacillus Calmette-Guerin, New York State Department of Health, 1947—; member of advisory committee, White House Conference on Children and Youth, 1950, 1960; member of local planning board of City of New York, 1954-64; instructor, New School for Social Research, 1955-60; weekly radio commentator on child care, 1955-56, 1960-61; member of advisory committee, New York Center for Children, 1961-66; daily commentator on child care for Columbia Broadcasting System, Inc., Radio Network, 1968-79; member of advisory boards of American Child Guidance Institute, National Aid to the Visually Handicapped, Playtex Park Research Institute, Parents Without Partners Association, and many other public and private agencies; vice-president and member of board, Foundation for International Child Health; consulting pediatrician, National Psychology Association; lecturer in the field on radio, television, and to educational organizations.

MEMBER: American Academy of Pediatrics (fellow), American Association for the Advancement of Science, American College of Chest Physicians (fellow), American Medical Association (fellow), American Public Health Association (fellow; chairman of committee on camp health standards, 1942—), American Thoracic Society, Association of Maternal and Child Health, National Tuberculosis Association, Royal Society of Health, Society for the Scientific Study of Sex, New York Academy of Scientists, New York Pediatric Society (former president), New York State Medical Society, Cornell Research Society, Phi Delta Epsilon (former president).

WRITINGS—With wife, Jean H. Seligmann, unless otherwise indicated: *The Wonder of Life: How We Are Born and How We Grow Up* (juvenile), Simon & Schuster, 1940, revised edition (illustrated by Judith T. Webster), 1952; *A Baby Is Born: The Story of How Life Begins* (juvenile; illustrated by Eloise Wilkin), Simon & Schuster, 1949, revised edition, Western Publishing, 1978; *Helping Boys and Girls Understand Their Sex Roles* (illustrated by Seymour Fleishman), Science Research Associates, 1953; *Tommy Visits the Doctor* (juvenile; illustrated by Richard Scarry), Golden, 1962; (with Armond W. Mascia) *Pulmonary Diseases and Anomalies of Infancy and Childhood: Their Diagnosis and Treatment,* Harper, 1966; *Your Overweight Child,* World Publishing, 1970; *The Parent's Encyclopedia of Infancy, Childhood, and Adolescence,* Crowell, 1973; (editor) *Pediatric Medicine: Selected*

Papers From the Journal "Pediatric Annals," Publishing Sciences Group, 1975.

Co-author of *Psychology of Physical Illness,* 1952; *Dyspnea in Adults and Children,* 1962; *Pulmonary Pathology in Infants and Children,* 1963; *Human Reproduction,* 1967; *Current Pediatric Therapy,* 1968-72.

Contributor of articles on child care, childhood diseases, child psychology, and sex education to popular magazines and scientific journals.

Author, with wife, of syndicated column on child care; member of usage panel, *American Heritage Dictionary,* 1969; editor, *Pediatric Annals,* 1972—.

BIOGRAPHICAL/CRITICAL SOURCES: New Yorker, March 31, 1975.*

*   *   *

LEVINSON, Henry Samuel 1948-

PERSONAL: Born February 11, 1948, in Cincinnati, Ohio; son of Joseph E. (a physician) and Mimi F. Levinson; married Catherine Kaplan (a research analyst), August 30, 1969; children: Molly, Sarah. *Education:* Stanford University, B.A. (with honors), 1970; Princeton University, Ph.D., 1976. *Residence:* Palo Alto, Calif. *Office:* Department of Religious Studies, Stanford University, Stanford, Calif. 94305.

CAREER: Stanford University, Stanford, Calif., assistant to the provost, 1970-72, assistant professor of religious studies, 1975—. *Member:* American Academy of Religion, American Studies Association, Charles S. Peirce Society, Phi Beta Kappa. *Awards, honors:* Danforth fellowship; National Endowment for the Humanities grant.

WRITINGS: The Religious Investigations of William James, University of North Carolina Press, 1981. Contributor to religious and history journals.

WORK IN PROGRESS: Research on George Santayana.

*   *   *

LEWIS, Alice Hudson 1895(?)-1971

OBITUARY NOTICE: Born c. 1895; died October 24, 1971, in Philadelphia, Pa. Missionary, editor, and author. Following her 1920 marriage to a Presbyterian missionary, Lewis lived in China for eighteen years. When she returned to the United States in 1938, she continued to serve the Presbyterian Board of Foreign Missions, acting as writer and editor for the Board's Office of Interpretation, and she produced children's books for the Friendship Press. Lewis, who was appointed managing editor of the *Y.W.C.A. Magazine* in 1951, served on the Broadcasting and Film Commission of the National Council of the Churches of Christ in the U.S.A. for nine years. *Day After Tomorrow* and *Always an Answer* are among her books for young people. Obituaries and other sources: *Authors of Books for Young People,* Scarecrow, 1964; *New York Times,* October 28, 1971.

*   *   *

LEWIS, Harry 1917-

PERSONAL: Born April 4, 1917, in Newark, N.J.; son of Morris and Rose (Fein) Rubinstein; married Beatrice Jewell Speer, October 9, 1942. *Education:* Montclair State Teachers College (now Montclair State College), B.A., 1937, M.A., 1942; New York University, Ph.D., 1950. *Home:* 48 Brookside Ter., North Caldwell, N.J. 07006.

CAREER: Teacher of mathematics at secondary schools in Newark, N.J., 1939-63; Arts High School, Newark, principal, 1963-70; Jersey City State College, Jersey City, N.J., professor of mathematics education, 1970-77, consultant, 1977—. Instructor at New York University, 1950-52, and New York Actuaries Club, 1959-63. Consultant on general business texts for Gregg Press. *Member:* Newark Council of Teachers of Mathematics (president), Phi Delta Kappa.

WRITINGS: (With R. Robert Rosenberg) *Essentials of Business Mathematics,* 5th revised edition, (Lewis was not associated with earlier editions), Gregg, 1958, 6th revised edition, 1964; (with Rosenberg) *Business Mathematics: Principles and Practice, Complete,* 5th edition (Lewis was not associated with earlier editions), Gregg, 1958, 8th edition, 1975; *Geometry: A Contemporary Course,* D. Van Nostrand, 1964, 3rd edition, McCormick-Mathers, 1973; *Mathematics for Daily Living,* McCormick-Mathers, 1970, teacher's annotated edition, 1980; *College Business Mathematics: A Contemporary Approach,* Delmar, 1976; *Elementary Algebra for College,* D. Van Nostrand, 1978, published as *Elementary Algebra Skills for College,* 1980; *Arithmetic and Algebra for College,* D. Van Nostrand, 1979; *Intermediate Algebra for College,* D. Van Nostrand, 1979. Compiler of *American Business Education*'s "High School Business Mathematics Library," 1960.*

*   *   *

LEWIS, Hunter 1947-

PERSONAL: Born October 13, 1947, in Dayton, Ohio; son of Welbourne Walker and Emily (Spivey) Lewis. *Education:* Harvard University, A.B. (magna cum laude), 1969. *Residence:* Washington, D.C. *Agent:* James Brown, Curtis Brown Ltd., 575 Madison Ave., New York, N.Y. 10022. *Office:* 600 New Hampshire Ave. N.W., Washington, D.C. 20037.

CAREER: Boston Co., Boston, Mass., assistant to the office of the president, 1970-71, vice-president, 1972-73; president of Boston Co. Financial Strategies, Inc., 1971-72; Lewis, Bailey Associates, Inc., Washington, D.C., founding partner, 1973—. Trustee of Groton School, 1979—; trustee and treasurer of American School of Classical Studies at Athens, 1980—. Chairman of the board of Shelburne Farms, Inc.; member of advisory board of Dumbarton Oaks, an affiliate of Harvard University, member of Pension Finance Committee of World Bank. *Military service:* U.S. Marine Corps, 1969-70. *Member:* Knickerbocker Club (New York City), Union Boat Club (Boston), University Club (New York City).

WRITINGS: (With Donald Allison) *The Real World War: The Coming Battle for the New Global Economy and Why We Are in Danger of Losing,* Coward, 1982. Also author of monographs on financial subjects. Contributor of articles to newspapers and magazines, including *Washington Post* and *Atlantic.*

SIDELIGHTS: Financial specialists Hunter Lewis and Donald Allison analyze the current financial crisis in America in their book *The Real World War: The Coming Battle for the New Global Economy and Why We Are in Danger of Losing.* The authors argue that America, like Britain, will face a long phase of economic decline unless American businesses adjust to the new world economy and unless American government provides more support for American industry. "Many of the recommendations are timely and eminently sensible," Daniel Yergin wrote in his *Washington Post Book World* review of *The Real World War*. "For the most part, they are aimed at business decision-makers, who are urged to think globally, to seek larger market shares to lower costs, to take longer time horizons for investments, to avoid letting their investment decisions be governed by Wall Street's fascination with quarterly statements. Government is advised to stop wasting its time on traditional and out-dated antitrust campaigns, and instead to provide long-range support for American industry."

Despite this praise for the authors' suggestions, Yergin admonished Lewis and Allison for "a breezy survey" in which "all the embattled industries blur together, and all the problems seem to be the same." Additionally, Yergin continued, "one might get the impression that American firms have not been competing particularly well in the world, which is not exactly the case." "Deeper focus on a few industries on the part of Lewis and Allison would have left fewer unanswered questions and would have bolstered their argument that the United States is currently going down that same long slide already traveled by Great Britain," Yergin concluded.

BIOGRAPHICAL/CRITICAL SOURCES: Washington Post Book World, August 29, 1982.

*   *   *

LEWSEN, Phyllis 1916-

PERSONAL: Born October 16, 1916, in West Transvaal, South Africa; daughter of Isaac Goldfain (a farmer); married Jack Lewsen (an advocate), March 19, 1939; children: Muriel Lynn Lewsen Rubin, Gwynneth Jill Lewsen Howe-Watson, John. *Education:* B.A. (with honors) and D.Litt. from University of the Witwatersrand. *Politics:* Liberal. *Religion:* Jewish. *Home:* 31 Melrose St., Melrose, Johannesburg 2196, South Africa.

CAREER: Lecturer, associate professor, and reader. *Awards, honors:* Pringle Award, 1974.

WRITINGS: (Editor) *Selections From the Correspondence of J. X. Merriman,* four volumes, Van Riebeeck Society (Capetown, South Africa), 1960; *John X. Merriman: Paradoxical South African Statesman,* Yale University Press, 1982.

WORK IN PROGRESS: Editing *Robert Wilmot: Journey on the Cape Eastern Frontier, 1856; Donald B. Molters as Cape Nature Representative;* essays on Olive Schreiner's political attitudes.

SIDELIGHTS: Reviewing Lewsen's study of former prime minister of South Africa John X. Merriman, Kenneth Ingham wrote in *Times Literary Supplement:* "Lewsen's biography brings out the full flavour of her subject, his brilliance, his arrogance, his impulsiveness, his foresight, his generosity, his obstinacy, his clearsightedness, his prejudices and his remarkable grasp of economic issues, and it places him in a clearly defined historical context. In her preface the author writes that the present book is a shortened version of a fuller work. One wonders, with some admiration, what could possibly have been added which would not detract from so well-rounded an account."

BIOGRAPHICAL/CRITICAL SOURCES: Times Literary Supplement, October 29, 1982.

*   *   *

L'HOMMEDIEU, Dorothy Keasley 1885-1961

OBITUARY NOTICE: Born in 1885; died March 16, 1961.

Dog breeder and author of books for children. L'Hommedieu and her husband owned and operated the Sand Springs Dog Kennels in New Vernon, New York, from 1920 to 1937. After selling the kennels L'Hommedieu began writing canine adventures for children, drawing upon her love for animals and upon her experiences raising cocker spaniels. *Leo, the Little St. Bernard, Togo, the Little Husky,* and *Tyke, the Little Mutt* are among her books about dogs. Obituaries and other sources: *New York Times,* March 17, 1961; *Publishers Weekly,* April 24, 1961; *Authors of Books for Young People,* Scarecrow, 1964.

*   *   *

LIBERMAN, Evsei Grigorevich 1897-1983
(Yevsei Grigorievich Liberman)

OBITUARY NOTICE: Born October 2, 1897, in Slavuta, Ukraine (now U.S.S.R.); died in 1983 in the U.S.S.R. Economist, educator, and author. A Soviet economist whose 1962 *Pravda* article "Plan, Profit, Bonus" caused a stir with its endorsement of the profit-motive as a means of stimulating the Soviet economy, Liberman taught economics at the Kharkov Institute for Engineer-Economists from 1933 to 1963 and at Kharkov State University from 1963 until his death. The author's economic ideas eventually became policy under Leonid I. Brezhnev. His writings include *The Economic Methods to Raise the Efficiency of Socialistic Enterprises, Raising the Efficiency of Social Production,* and the textbook *Organization and Planning on the Industrial Enterprise.* Obituaries and other sources: *Current Biography,* Wilson, 1968, May, 1983; *The International Who's Who,* 46th edition, Europa, 1982; *Washington Post,* March 12, 1983; *New York Times,* March 13, 1983.

*   *   *

LIBERMAN, Yevsei Grigorievich
See LIBERMAN, Evsei Grigorevich

*   *   *

LIBO, Kenneth (Harold) 1937-

BRIEF ENTRY: Born December 4, 1937, in Norwich, Conn. American educator and author. Libo taught English at City College of the City University of New York before becoming editor of the *Jewish Daily Forward* in 1978. He collaborated with Irving Howe on *World of Our Fathers* (Harcourt, 1976), winner of a National Book Award in 1977. Libo and Howe also co-edited *How We Lived: A Documentary History of Immigrant Jews in America, 1880-1930* (Richard Marek, 1979). *Address:* 365 West 20th St., New York, N.Y. 10011. *Biographical/critical sources: New York Times Book Review,* December 2, 1979.

*   *   *

LIEBERMAN, Saul 1898-1983

OBITUARY NOTICE: Born May 28, 1898, in Motol, Poland (now U.S.S.R.); came to United States, 1940, naturalized citizen, 1953; died March 23, 1983, en route to Israel. Rabbi, Talmudist, educator, and author. Lieberman was head of the Rabbinical School of the Jewish Theological Seminary of America in New York and in 1971 became the only non-Israeli to receive the Israeli Prize for literature; especially recognized was his book *Siphre Zutta: The Midrash of Lydda,* considered a definitive edition of this rabbinic commentary. He also received the Harvey Prize in 1976 from the Israel Institute of Technology for two books on Jewish life in Hellenic times and for his research on Palestine during the ages of Greece and Rome. Lieberman was known, too, for discovering one of Maimonides's works on ancient Jewish law. At the time of his death Lieberman had completed twelve books of a planned fourteen-volume commentary on the *Tosefta,* part of the Jewish literature of the first to the third centuries. Obituaries and other sources: *Who's Who in America,* 40th edition, Marquis, 1978; *New York Times,* March 24, 1983; *Chicago Tribune,* March 26, 1983; *Washington Post,* March 31, 1983.

* * *

LIGHTFOOT, Gordon   1938-

BRIEF ENTRY: Born November 17, 1938, in Orillia, Ontario, Canada. Canadian composer, singer, and author. A "compulsive" songwriter, Lightfoot, who has more than four hundred songs to his credit, is able to compose anytime or anywhere. For example, he composed two of his greatest successes while driving to an airport in Arizona and while watching a televised hockey game. Some of his best known songs, recorded by others as well as himself, include "For Lovin' Me," "Early Morning Rain," and the most popular "If You Could Read My Mind," which has been recorded by at least sixty artists. Known for his baritone voice and guitar technique, Lightfoot began singing while still a boy at Kiwanis Club functions, in school productions, and later with barbershop quartets. Upon graduating from high school, the composer studied orchestration and jazz at Westlake College of Music, though he turned to folksinging shortly thereafter when he fell under the influence of Bob Dylan. Lightfoot has received Canada's Juno Award as the nation's top folksinger fifteen times since 1966. In 1967 he was named Canada's foremost male vocalist, and in 1970 he was awarded the Canadian Medal of Service. Lightfoot is credited with at least one platinum and eight gold albums. Several of his albums, including *Old Dan's Records* (1972), *Sundown* (1974), and *Gord's Gold* (1975), have been reproduced as songbooks. In addition, his lyrics for "The Pony Man" were adapted into a children's book for the Harper's Magazine Press in 1972, and poetic selections from Lightfoot's songs are collected in *I Wish You Good Spaces* (Blue Mountain Arts, 1977). *Residence:* Toronto, Ontario, Canada. *Biographical/critical sources:* Milton Okun, *Something to Sing About,* Macmillan, 1968; *Toronto Globe and Mail,* May 4, 1970; *Maclean's Magazine,* December, 1971, May 1, 1978; *Detroit News,* October 20, 1974; *Current Biography,* Wilson, 1978.

* * *

LINDER, Erich   1925(?)-1983

OBITUARY NOTICE: Born c. 1925 in Lemburg, Poland (now U.S.S.R.); died of a heart attack, March 22, 1983, in Milan, Italy. Literary agent, translator, and editor. Linder grew up in Vienna, but when the Nazis invaded Austria he and his family immigrated to Italy. There he began his publishing career, working at Bompiani as a translator and junior editor. He later joined Agenzia Letteraria Internazionale, which under his leadership became one of the largest literary agencies in Europe. Linder was also associated with a German-language agency in Zurich, with Paris's Nouvelle Agence, and with French-American agent Mary Kling. Additionally, he entered into a partnership with Rainer Heumann of Mohrbooks, owned 50 percent of an authors' agency, and was a subagent for American, British, and German copyright holders. Among the Italian authors

he represented were Italo Calvino, Elsa Morante, and Elio Vittorini. Obituaries and other sources: *Publishers Weekly,* April 8, 1983.

* * *

LINDSAY, Rae

PERSONAL: Born July 21 in Garfield, N.J.; daughter of Charles (a residential developer) and Mildred (Cascino) Baldanza; married Alexander M. Lindsay (a writer; deceased); children: Maria Gray, Alexander M., Jr., Robert Charles. *Education:* Received B.A. from Wellesley College. *Office:* R & R Writers/Agents, Inc., 364 Mauro Rd., Englewood Cliffs, N.J. 07632.

CAREER: Seventeen magazine, New York City, assistant publicity director, 1959-61; Lindsay & Gray (public relations agency), New York City, co-owner with husband, Alexander M. Lindsay, 1961-72; Macmillan Publishing Co., New York City, senior publicist, 1978-79; R & R Writers/Agents, Inc. (literary agency), Englewood Cliffs, N.J., president. Director of Writer's Workshop, a seminar on writing, marketing, and publishing. *Member:* American Society of Journalists and Authors, National Press Club, Authors Guild. *Awards, honors:* Grants from Wellesley College Center for Research on Women in Higher Education and the Professions and New Jersey State Council on the Arts, both 1976, both for researching *Alone and Surviving.*

WRITINGS: The International Party Cookbook, Drake, 1974; *The Pursuit of Youth,* Pinnacle, 1976, reissued as *How to Look As Young As You Feel,* 1980; *Alone and Surviving,* Walker, 1977; *Sleep and Dreams,* F. Watts, 1978; (with George Michael) *George Michael's Secrets for Beautiful Hair,* Doubleday, 1981; (with David Outerbridge) *The Hangover Handbook,* Harmony, 1981; (with G. Michael) *George Michael's Hair Care Guide for Men,* Doubleday, 1983; (with Dianne Rowe) *How To Be a Perfect Bitch,* New Century, 1983.

Contributor of twice-weekly syndicated column, "First Person Singular," to twenty newspapers, 1978—. Contributor of articles to periodicals, including *Family Weekly, Runner's World, Woman's Home Companion, Eve, Singles, Woman's World, Travel Day, National Enquirer,* and *Travel World.*

WORK IN PROGRESS: "A nonfiction book with a South African safari guide who hosted Hemingway, Ruark, Gable, Holden, and others on big game hunts"; co-writing a kosher gourmet cookbook; *The Night People; Flying Crooked,* a novel.

SIDELIGHTS: Lindsay's *Alone and Surviving* examines the many problems that plague widows, such as managing finances, raising children, and adjusting to being alone. Based on interviews with one hundred widows, Lindsay's book, which is aimed at women ages thirty-five to fifty-five, offers, according to Alix Nelson in the *New York Times Book Review,* "enough insight, sympathy, practical suggestion and personal honesty . . . to make worthwhile reading for all single women who are heads of households."

Lindsay told *CA:* "I earn most of my income as a writer. What makes that life exciting (aside from the continued uncertainty of whether or not you'll be able to put bread on your table and sneakers on the relentlessly growing feet of three kids) is the opportunity to learn and then pass on that learning to an audience (hopefully) of thousands. I try not to get stuck in one field of expertise, and I therefore take on projects as diverse as hangovers and bitches, and as practical as cookbooks and haircare. I'm also practical enough to collaborate with others, and like most writers of fiction or nonfiction I have a special novel that I'd love to see published some day. I don't see my career as glamorous, in fact, as Tennessee Williams once said, 'writing is the loneliest existence.' I don't see it as an art; for me writing is a craft.''

BIOGRAPHICAL/CRITICAL SOURCES: New York Times Book Review, August 21, 1977.

*   *   *

LIPMAN, Burton E(llis) 1931-

PERSONAL: Born February 19, 1931, in San Francisco, Calif.; son of Paul (a business manager) and Nettie (Greenburg) Lipman; married Diane Goldwasser (a computer programmer), June 21, 1953; children: Michele Lipman Fusillo, Rhonda Lipman Slaff, Joanne. *Education:* Columbia University, B.A., 1953, graduate study, 1953. *Home and office:* Bell Publishing, 15 Surrey Lane, East Brunswick, N.J. 08816.

CAREER: Johnson & Johnson, New Brunswick, N.J., new products manager in plant management, 1953-62; Sun Chemical Co., New York City, manager of planning and control, 1962-64; Mobil Corp., New York City, manager of industrial services, 1964-67; Glamorene Products Corp., Clifton, N.J., vice-president of operations, 1967-78; Lehman Brothers Paint Corp., Jersey City, N.J., president and chief executive officer, 1978-79; American Home Products Corp., Boyle-Midway Division, New York City, vice-president of operations, 1979-82; Bell Publishing, East Brunswick, N.J., founder and president, 1982—. President of Marker Division of Portable X-Ray Service. *Member:* American Management Association, American Production and Inventory Control Society, U.S. Chamber of Commerce, Methods-Time-Measurement Association.

WRITINGS: How to Control and Reduce Inventory, Prentice-Hall, 1974, revised edition, Bell Publishing, 1983; *Successful Cost Reduction and Control,* Prentice-Hall, 1978; *The Executive Job Search Program,* Bell Publishing, 1982; *The Professional Job Search Program: How to Market Yourself,* Wiley, 1983; *How to Become a Vice-President in Two Weeks (More or Less),* Bell Publishing, 1983; *The Seven-day M.B.A.; or, The Business of Life: The Ultimate Business Course,* Bell Publishing, 1983.

SIDELIGHTS: Lipman wrote: ''My books are intended to be a self-contained and comprehensive library for any businessperson, starting with getting the job, through controlling costs and assets, to how to get ahead, plus the moral and economic bases for self-actualization through ethical and just participative management.

''As a successful (big company) businessman, I started writing about 'nuts and bolts'—costs and inventory control. I needed control of my own destiny and formed Bell Publishing to present books that would allow businesspeople to 'do their own thing'—either inside *or* outside the large corporation. I hope to foster the concepts of 'justice in an industrial democracy' for two reasons: to increase our free-world productivity and to help working individuals to be the best they *can* be.''

BIOGRAPHICAL/CRITICAL SOURCES: Chemical Specialties, March, 1974; *Booklist,* April 15, 1983.

*   *   *

LISSIM, Simon 1900-1981

OBITUARY NOTICE: Born October 24, 1900, in Kiev, Russia (now U.S.S.R.); came to the United States, 1941, naturalized citizen, 1946; died of a heart attack, May 10, 1981, in Naples, Fla. Artist, educator, and author. Lissim began his artistic career as an assistant stage designer at the Kiev Repertory Theatre and then worked as stage designer at the Paris Theatre de l'Oeuvre, a position once held by Toulouse-Lautrec. He eventually designed sets for ballet, theatre, and opera in major European capitals, and some of the sets he designed for ''Hamlet'' are displayed in the Shakespeare Memorial Museum at Stratford-Upon-Avon. After immigrating to the United States in 1941, Lissim established the children's art education program at the New York Public Library, teaching there and at the City College of New York. His talents included working in gold, silver, and crystal, and he held 120 porcelain design contracts with such companies as Manufacture Nationale de Sevres, Lenox, and Royal Copenhagen; more than seventy museums in the United States and Europe displayed his work. Lissim received several awards from the International Exhibition Foundation, including the Silver Medal at Paris in 1925 and 1935 and at Barcelona in 1937, and of his more than eighty one-man shows, the last, ''Dreams in the Theater,'' began in 1975 at the Lincoln Center and remained on tour into 1981. Lissim was the author of *How to Become an Artist,* and some of his illustrations for children are included in Fruma Gottschalk's *Runaway Soldier, and Other Tales of Old Russia.* Obituaries and other sources: *New York Times,* May 13, 1981.

*   *   *

LIST, Robert Stuart 1903-1983

OBITUARY NOTICE: Born January 31, 1903, in Wheeling, W.Va.; died May 10, 1983, in Delray Beach, Fla. Publisher and public relations director. Beginning in 1920, List worked in various capacities for the *Washington Times,* the *Rochester Journal-American,* and the *Pittsburgh Sun-Telegraph.* In 1953 he became publisher of the Chicago newspaper *America* and turned it into the city's largest afternoon publication. ''A newspaper must take very seriously its obligations to the people,'' he reflected in a 1966 luncheon address. ''Above all, a newspaper must represent the community honestly and intelligently and never, never sacrifice principle for expediency.'' When Hearst Newspapers sold the publication to the Tribune Company in 1956, List remained on as publisher. In 1969 he retired from the newspaper business and accepted a position as vice-president of public relations for a vending-machine and food-service company. Obituaries and other sources: *Who's Who in Finance and Industry,* 18th edition, Marquis, 1974; *Chicago Tribune,* May 12, 1983.

*   *   *

LITTAUER, Raphael (Max) 1925-

BRIEF ENTRY: Born November 28, 1925, in Leipzig, Germany (now East Germany); came to United States, 1950, naturalized citizen, 1956. American physicist, educator, and author. Littauer was a researcher for General Electric Company before joining the faculty of Cornell University. He became a professor of physics at Cornell in 1965. Littauer co-authored *Accelerators: Machines of Nuclear Physics* (Heinemann, 1962) and was the sole author of *Pulse Electronics* (McGraw, 1965). He co-edited *The Air War in Indochina* (Beacon Press, 1972). *Address:* 1655 Taughannock Blvd., Trumansburg, N.Y. 14886; and Department of Physics, Cornell University, Ithaca, N.Y. 14850. *Biographical/critical sources: New York Times Book Review,* August 13, 1972, December 3, 1972; *American Men* and Women of Science: The Physical and Biological Sciences, 15th edition, Bowker, 1982.

* * *

LITTELL, Robert 1935(?)-

BRIEF ENTRY: Born in 1935 (some sources say 1937 or 1939) in the United States. American editor and author. As a novelist, Littell has been compared to Len Deighton and John Le Carre. Many of the author's novels draw from his personal experiences. For instance, *The Debriefing* (Harper, 1979), about espionage in Washington, D.C., and Moscow, relies on information Littell gathered as *Newsweek*'s general editor in Eastern Europe, the U.S.S.R., and France. Likewise, *Sweet Reason* (Houghton, 1974) is based on Littell's experiences aboard a warship. The novelist received the Crime Writers Association's Gold Dagger Award for *The Defection of A. J. Lewinter* (Hodder & Stoughton, 1973), a Cold War thriller. His other novels include *If Israel Lost the War* (Coward, 1969), which he wrote with Richard Z. Chesnoff and Edward Klein, *The October Circle* (Houghton, 1976), *Mother Russia* (Harcourt, 1978), and *The Amateur* (Simon & Schuster, 1981), which was adapted as a motion picture and released by Twentieth Century-Fox in 1982. *Biographical/critical sources: Newsweek,* January 19, 1976; *Who's Who in Spy Fiction,* Elm Tree Books, 1977; *New York Times,* July 2, 1979, May 13, 1981; *Washington Post Book World,* August 11, 1979; *Los Angeles Times Book Review,* June 5, 1981.

* * *

LITTLE, Geraldine C(linton)

PERSONAL: Born in Portstewart, Ireland; daughter of James Robert (a minister) and Louisa Margaret (a musician; maiden name, Corr) Clinton; married Robert Knox Little (an inventor and company president); children: Rory, Timothy, Rodney. *Education:* Goddard College, B.A., 1971; Trenton State College, M.A.T., 1976. *Home:* 519 Jacksonville Rd., Mount Holly, N.J. 08060. *Office:* Department of English, Burlington County College, Pemberton-Browns Mills Rd., Pemberton, N.J. 08068.

CAREER: Max Levy & Co. (makers of glass screens), Philadelphia, Pa., executive private secretary, 1945-55; Burlington County College, Pemberton, N.J., adjunct professor of English literature and composition, 1977—. Instructor at Cape Cod Writers' Conference, 1979, 1980, and Philadelphia Writers' Conference, 1981; gives readings and lectures; conducts workshops. President of Mount Holly Friends of the Library, 1975, and Mount Holly Community Concert Association, 1977; member of Philadelphia Festival Chorus.

MEMBER: Poetry Society of America, Haiku Society of America (president, 1982), Authors Guild, American Association of University Women, Burlington County Poets (chairman), Mendelssohn Club of Philadelphia. *Awards, honors:* Albert Kreymborg Award from Poetry Society of America, 1977, for "Poem for Murakami Kijo"; Cecil Hemley Award from Poetry Society of America, 1978, for "For Jacqueline du Pre"; First Membership Award from Poetry Society of America, 1978, for "Dying Towards Light"; Gordon Barber Award from Poetry Society of America, 1979, for "Dover: The Present Time, Looking Towards Dunkirk"; Daniel Varoujan Award from New England Poetry Society, 1982.

WRITINGS: Stilled Wind (poems), Bonsai, 1978; *Separation: Seasons in Space* (poetry chapbook), Sparrow, 1979; *Contrasts*

in *Keening: Ireland* (poems), Silver Apples Press, 1982; *Hakugai: Sketches From a Concentration Camp* (book-length poem), Curbstone Publishing, 1983.

Work represented in anthologies, including *Stones and Poets,* Delaware Valley Poets, 1980; *Saturday's Women,* Saturday Press, 1982; *Strong Measures: Recent American Poems in Traditional Forms,* edited by Philip Dacey, 1983. Contributor of poems to newspapers and magazines, including *Nimrod, Prairie Schooner, Jack and Jill, Good Housekeeping, Dance, Commonweal,* and *Poetry Northwest.*

WORK IN PROGRESS: Subjects Oriental, poems, publication expected in 1984.

SIDELIGHTS: Little told *CA:* "I wrote my first poem ever while in my forties and am extremely interested in the dramatic monologue as a form. My poetry has become increasingly attuned to injustice in the world. I like to write long poems like my *Hakugai*—a book-length narrative around one subject—for many values can be probed in this way. I am striving constantly to determine (gulp—a large statement) the meaning of human life—my own and that of the human race.

"Through the writing and publication of much haiku and renga, I became interested in the poets of Japan, and, in particular, women poets of Japan. I found this too narrow a focus for where research and further thinking led me, so I am currently working on a manuscript titled *Subjects Oriental,* which allows a broader selection of material. I have also completed a book for children, *Amergin: Boy Scribe,* about a boy who goes to work in the scriptoriums of eighth-century Ireland to work on illuminated manuscripts. As yet, I have no publisher.

"Writing is hard, hellish work, and the rewards (from the world), as far as poetry goes, are little. Love of the art is the only possible reason to continue in a little-appreciated field. I plead guilty to that love."

* * *

LOEB, Paul Rogat 1952-

PERSONAL: Born July 4, 1952, in Berkeley, Calif.; son of Yosal Rogat (a professor) and Magda (a piano teacher; maiden name, Kosches) Loeb. *Education:* Attended Stanford University, 1970-72; New School for Social Research, B.A., 1973. *Residence:* Seattle, Wash. *Agent:* Harriet Wasserman Agency, 230 East 48th St., New York, N.Y. 10017. *Office:* 1500 Grand, Seattle, Wash. 98122.

CAREER: Liberation, New York City, editor and promotion director, 1974-76; Village Gate Jazz Club, New York City, bartender, 1977-78; free-lance writer. Guest lecturer at universities, including Harvard University, Massachusetts Institute of Technology, University of Missouri, Bucknell University, Catholic University, University of Oregon, and St. Louis University.

WRITINGS: Nuclear Culture: Living and Working in the World's Largest Atomic Complex, Coward, 1982. Contributor to periodicals, including *Village Voice, Humanist, Crawdaddy, Inquiry, Oui, Mother Earth News, New Age, In These Times, Chicago Reader, New West, Seattle Times,* and *Los Angeles Herald-Examiner.*

WORK IN PROGRESS: A book on "the resurgent disarmament movement," tentatively titled *Of Compassion and Hope.*

SIDELIGHTS: Loeb's *Nuclear Culture* documents the evacuation of fifteen hundred farmers from Hanford, Washington, in 1943, and subsequent events occurring in the world's largest nuclear complex there. "Hanford nuclear culture is a place where people have abdicated responsibility on the most important questions," Loeb explained to an interviewer from the *Los Angeles Herald-Examiner.* Loeb discovered that workers in the Hanford complex, which has been producing plutonium since World War II, only vaguely comprehend the personal and public risks the plant involves. "They're not thinking about what the consequences of what they're doing are, immediate or long-term," he observed. For the book, Loeb met with the plant's employees to discuss their own reservations or concerns about working in Hanford. "I wanted to simultaneously give them a voice and then separately make my conclusions," he explained.

Loeb's work was hailed for its informative and provocative substance. John P. Sisk, writing in *Pacific Northwest,* called *Nuclear Culture* "a well-researched, balanced and skillfully organized piece of journalism; the product of an easy, straightforward style, an intelligent curiosity, and a good working knowledge of the atomic industry." Sisk added that Loeb "helps us see that the fear of nuclear energy may be less the fear of some ultimate meltdown than the fear of human nature itself." In the *Dallas Times-Herald,* John Nichols expressed similar views, calling *Nuclear Culture* an "important book," and added that "the book is surprisingly objective, and sympathetic toward its subjects." Nichols concluded, "The questions raised . . . lie at the core of continued human survival."

Loeb told *CA:* "Since the Vietnam War I have been highly concerned about the threats posed by concentrations of unchecked power. The danger of atomic war is only the clearest indication that for all its strengths, our society has also acquiesced in much terrible blindness. *Nuclear Culture* was an attempt to address this blindness by examining the community whose members manufactured the plutonium for Nagasaki and for over half the atomic weapons we now possess. It was an attempt to understand how people of perfectly good will have, step by step, brought us closer to disaster.

"The project I am now working on, tentatively entitled *Of Compassion and Hope,* will explore how ordinary humans are trying to address the unprecedented threats to human life we have helped create. If this resurgent movement succeeds, it will necessarily leave us with a far stronger and healthier society. I would like to document the process by which people are striving for this and, I hope, shed useful light on their efforts."

BIOGRAPHICAL/CRITICAL SOURCES: Los Angeles Times Book Review, April 18, 1982; *Los Angeles Herald-Examiner,* May 19, 1982, July 4, 1982; *Pacific Northwest,* June, 1982; *Progressive,* July, 1982; *Dallas Times-Herald,* July 11, 1982; *Washington Post Book World,* July 25, 1982; *Christian Science Monitor,* August 13, 1982; *In These Times,* September 29, 1982; *Congressional Record,* October 1, 1982; *New Age,* October 5, 1982; *Portland Oregonian,* November 21, 1982.

*   *   *

LOEWENBERG, Peter J(acob)   1933-

PERSONAL: Born August 14, 1933, in Hamburg, Germany; came to the United States in 1937, naturalized citizen, 1943; son of Richard D. (a physician) and Sophie F. (a registered nurse; maiden name, Borowicz) Loewenberg; divorced; children: Samuel, Anna. *Education:* University of California, Santa Barbara, B.A., 1955; graduate study at Free University of

Berlin, 1961-62; University of California, Berkeley, Ph.D., 1965; Southern California Psychoanalytical Institute, Ph.D., 1977. *Home:* 449 Levering Ave., Los Angeles, Calif. 90024. *Office:* Department of History, University of California, Los Angeles, Calif. 90024.

CAREER: California State University, San Jose, instructor in history, 1965; University of California, Los Angeles, assistant professor, 1965-71, associate professor, 1971-77, professor of history, 1977—. Visiting instructor at Southern California Psychoanalytic Institute, 1970-74, instructor, 1974—; visiting lecturer at Piedmont College, 1977; visiting professor at Hebrew University of Jerusalem, 1979 and 1981-82, and University of California, Berkeley, 1982; guest instructor at Los Angeles Psychoanalytic Society and Institute, 1981—; member of faculty at Wright Institute, 1979; Leo Baeck Memorial Lecturer at Leo Baeck Institute, New York, N.Y., 1980; Lionel Trilling Lecturer at Columbia University, 1980.

MEMBER: Conference Group for Central European History, American Historical Association (member of council of Pacific Coast branch, 1973-76), American Psychoanalytical Association (member of executive council of George S. Klein Research Forum in Psychoanalysis, 1970-72), American Academy of Psychoanalysis, California Association of Marriage and Family Counselors, Southern California Psychoanalytic Society (member of executive committee, 1976-78). *Awards, honors:* Fulbright grant for Germany, 1961-62; fellowships from Southern California Psycoanalytic Institute, 1966-71, Social Science Research Council, 1968-69, American Council of Learned Societies, 1970-71, Memorial Foundation for Jewish Culture, 1971-72, Rockefeller Bellagio Study Center, 1979, and National Endowment for the Humanities, 1979-80; Franz Alexander Essay Prize from Southern California Psychoanalytic Institute, 1970, for "The Unsuccessful Adolescence of Heinrich Himmler"; grants from Austrian Institute and Ministry of Education, 1979, and Foundation Pro Helvetia, 1982 and 1983; Guggenheim fellowship, 1981-82.

WRITINGS: Walter Rathenau and Henry Kissinger: The Jew as a Modern Statesman in Two Political Cultures, Leo Baeck Institute (New York), 1980; *Decoding the Past: The Psychohistorical Approach,* Knopf, 1983.

Contributor: Gary Nash and Richard Weiss, editors, *The Great Fear: Race in the Mind of America,* Holt, 1970; Benjamin B. Wolman, editor, *The Psychoanalytic Interpretation of History,* Basic Books, 1971; John L. Snell and Allan Mitchell, editors, *The Nazi Revolution: Hitler's Dictatorship and the German Nation,* second edition, Heath, 1973; *Sosiologi Grunnfag,* Universitets-forlaget (Oslo, Norway), 1973; Anthony Esler, editor, *The Youth Revolution: The Conflict of Generations in Modern History,* Heath, 1974; George Kren and Leon Rappoport, editors, *Varieties of Psychohistory,* Springer Publishing Co., 1976; David Bronsen, editor, *Jews and Germans from 1860 to 1933: The Problematic Symbiosis,* Carl Winter Universitaets-verlag (Heidelberg, West Germany), 1979; Michael Kammen, editor, *The Past Before Us,* Cornell University Press, 1980. Also contributor to *Jahrbuch des Instituts fuer Deutsche Geschichte,* Volume 1, edited by Walter Grab, 1972, and *The Living Past: Western Historiographical Traditions,* 1975.

Contributor to *Race, Change, and Urban Society: Urban Affairs Annual Review,* Volume 5, edited by Peter Orleans and William Russell Ellis, Jr., Sage Publications, 1971, and *International Encyclopedia of Neurology, Psychiatry, Psychoanalysis and Psychology,* Volume 5. Contributor of articles and reviews to journals and periodicals, including *Journal of*

Modern History, Contemporary Psychology, and *Reviews in European History.* Member of board of editors of *Journal of the American Psychoanalytic Association,* 1971-73; contributing editor of *Journal of Psychohistory,* 1973-76; member of editorial board of *Psychohistory Review,* 1979—, and *Historian,* 1980-82.

SIDELIGHTS: Loewenberg told *CA:* "As I received professional training as a historian, it became clear to me that the emotions which move men and women to action or inhibit their behavior were the major neglected factor of historical explanation. As soon as I could, I decided to seek training in the best that the twentieth century had to offer about the determinants of behavior and thought, both rational and irrational. This I did with clinical training in psychoanalysis. For me it provides the important missing elements of conflict, stress, ambivalence, and the ability to make apparently discordant fragments of data fit together to enrich historical explanation and human self-understanding."

* * *

LOFTING, Hugh (John) 1886-1947

BRIEF ENTRY: Born January 14, 1886, in Maidenhead, Berkshire, England; came to the United States in 1912, naturalized citizen; died September 26 (some sources say September 27), 1947, in Santa Monica, Calif. American engineer, illustrator, and children's author. Educated at Massachusetts Institute of Technology and London Polytechnic, Lofting worked as a surveyor and civil engineer in Canada, Africa, and the West Indies before serving with the British Army during World War I. His best-known character, Doctor Dolittle, was created during that war, first appearing in letters the author sent home from the front to entertain his children. *The Story of Doctor Dolittle: Being the History of His Peculiar Life and Astonishing Adventures in Foreign Parts,* the first of Lofting's self-illustrated books about the country physician who preferred treating animals to caring for humans, was published in 1920. The twelve Dolittle books that followed include *The Voyages of Doctor Dolittle,* winner of the 1923 Newbery Medal, *Doctor Dolittle's Zoo* (1925), *Doctor Dolittle in the Moon* (1928), and *Doctor Dolittle's Return* (1933). A movie based on Lofting's character starring Rex Harrison and Anthony Newley was released in 1967. *Biographical/critical sources: New York Times,* September 28, 1947; Edward Blishen, *Hugh Lofting,* Bodley Head, 1968; *Famous Modern Story-Tellers for Young People,* Dodd, 1969; *Longman Companion to Twentieth Century Literature,* Longman, 1970; *Authors of Books for Young People,* 2nd edition, Scarecrow, 1971.

* * *

LOGAN, Sara
See HAYDON, June

* * *

LONG, Laura Mooney 1892-1967

OBITUARY NOTICE: Born August 4, 1892, in Columbus, Ind.; died March 28, 1967, in Indianapolis, Ind. Historian and author of children's books, including *Hannah Courageous, Without Valor, Singing Sisters, Square Sails and Spice Islands,* and several biographies. Long also wrote a weekly newspaper column for the *Columbus Republic,* "Horse and Buggy Days," for ten years. Obituaries and other sources: *Indiana Authors and Their Books: 1917-1966,* Wabash College, 1974.

LONSDALE, Frederick 1881-1954

BRIEF ENTRY: Birth-given name, Lionel Frederick Leonard; born February 5, 1881, in Saint Helier, Jersey, Channel Islands; died April 4, 1954, in England. British playwright. Lonsdale created nearly thirty "drawing room" comedies during his forty-seven years as a playwright. He enjoyed his greatest theatrical success during the 1920's when three of his plays ran simultaneously in London. Providing smart, sophisticated comedy for an urban audience, Lonsdale's *Aren't We All?* (1924; first produced in 1923), *Last of Mrs. Cheney* (1925; first produced in 1925), and *On Approval* (1927; first produced in 1926) are considered to be among the playwright's best efforts. "But for the Grace of God" (1937) and *The Way Things Go* (1951; first produced in 1950) also enjoyed successful West End runs. *Biographical/critical sources: Longman Companion to Twentieth Century Literature,* Longman, 1970; *Who Was Who Among English and European Authors, 1931-1949,* Gale, 1978; *Who Was Who in the Theatre, 1912-1976,* Gale, 1978; *Dictionary of Literary Biography,* Volume 10: *Modern British Dramatists, 1940-1945,* Gale, 1982.

* * *

LORD, Athena V. 1932-

PERSONAL: Born July 21, 1932, in Cohoes, N.Y.; daughter of Athanasius (a restaurateur) and Araluka (a restaurateur; maiden name, Keramari) Vavuras; married Victor Alexander Lord (an attorney), October 3, 1954; children: Sara Matilthe, Christopher James, Victoria Marie, Alexandra Mary. *Education:* Vassar College, B.A., 1953; graduate study at Union College and University, 1975-76. *Residence:* Albany, N.Y.

CAREER: Author of books for children. Albany, N.Y., community ambassador to Spain, 1953; commissioner of Saratoga-Capital District Parks Commission.

WRITINGS—For young readers: *Pilot for Spaceship Earth: R. Buckminster Fuller, Architect, Inventor, and Poet* (biography; Junior Literary Guild selection), Macmillan, 1978; *A Spirit to Ride the Whirlwind* (Junior Literary Guild selection), Macmillan, 1981.

SIDELIGHTS: Lord told *CA:* "I have had a long-standing love of and fascination with words, as I learned to read and write in both English and Greek before starting school at age four. The love affair continued through college, where I majored in creative writing and minored in Russian and Spanish. Writing gives me an excuse to travel, and travel gives me something to write about."

* * *

LOUTHAN, Robert 1951-

PERSONAL: Born June 17, 1951, in Brooklyn, N.Y.; son of Doniphan and Anne (Dannemiller) Louthan. *Education:* Empire State College of State University of New York, B.A., 1976; Goddard College, M.F.A., 1978. *Home:* 33 Lee St., Apt. 2, Cambridge, Mass. 02139.

CAREER: Poet. *Member:* Poets and Writers. *Awards, honors:* Grolier Poetry Prize, 1978; *Transatlantic Review* scholarship to Bread Loaf Writers' Conference, 1978.

WRITINGS: *Shrunken Planets* (poetry), Alice James Books, 1980; *Living in Code* (poetry), University of Pittsburgh Press,

1984. Contributor of poems to magazines, including *American Poetry Review, Hudson Review, New Republic, Paris Review,* and *Partisan Review.*

SIDELIGHTS: A reviewer for the *Boston Globe* wrote of Louthan's work, "Here is a disturbing voice that uses hesitation and sharp editing to create space until space becomes its own rhythm: massive, heavy."

Louthan told *CA:* "The most underrated contemporary poet I know of is Robert Clinton."

BIOGRAPHICAL/CRITICAL SOURCES: Boston Globe, March 30, 1980.

*   *   *

LOWRY, Shirley Park   1933-

PERSONAL; Born June 26, 1933, in San Antonio, Tex.; daughter of Frank Keith (a rainmaker) and Henrietta (Westerhoff) Park; married Ira South Lowry (an economist), September 6, 1955. *Education:* University of California, Berkeley, B.A., 1955, M.A., 1957. *Home:* 535 Radcliffe Ave., Pacific Palisades, Calif. 90272. *Office:* Department of English, Los Angeles Valley College, 5800 Fulton Ave., Van Nuys, Calif. 91401.

CAREER; University of California, Berkeley, teaching assistant, 1955-59; University of Maryland, lecturer for overseas program in Spain and France, 1959-60; Los Angeles Valley College, Van Nuys, Calif., instructor, 1964-66, assistant professor, 1966-80, professor of English, 1980—. *Member:* Society for the Study of Myth and Tradition, Phi Beta Kappa.

WRITINGS; Familiar Mysteries: The Truth in Myth, Oxford University Press, 1982.

WORK IN PROGRESS; "I am considering how a people's world view shapes events."

SIDELIGHTS; In her book, *Familiar Mysteries: The Truth in Myth,* Lowry reviews common themes in myths, legends, folklore, and contemporary stories such as "Star Wars." She explains the symbolism employed in these tales, including in her study an examination of symbols that appear in Jewish and Christian religious traditions. Lowry also discusses the appeal of myths, explaining that they "help people accept life's great mysteries with serenity rather than with horror."

Lowry told *CA:* "What gods in myths do for their people, a civilization helps do for its members: make a world of harmonious order where people can define their purposes and then rationally pursue them. I think of civilization as infinitely precious, and I admire people who guard it, make it spacious, and help other people to climb up into it and dance. I aim, myself, to become civilized.

"My greatest effort is to make sense of the preposterous, make friends with the appalling. That effort, though exhilarating, is strenuous. Thus, during vacations, I like to wander in the mountains because they aren't busy meaning anything at all."

BIOGRAPHICAL/CRITICAL SOURCES; Los Angeles Times Book Review, June 13, 1982; *Classical World,* September-October, 1982.

*   *   *

LUCAS, Henry C(ameron), Jr.   1944-

PERSONAL: Born September 4, 1944, in Omaha, Neb.; son of Henry Cameron (an advertising executive) and Lois (a teacher; maiden name, Himes) Lucas; married Ellen Kuhbach, June 8, 1968; children: Scott Cameron, Jonathan Gerdes. *Education:* Yale University, B.S. (magna cum laude), 1966; Massachusetts Institute of Technology, M.S., 1968, Ph.D., 1970. *Home:* 18 Portland Rd., Summit, N.J. 07901. *Office:* Computer Applications and Information Systems Area, Schools of Business, New York University, New York, N.Y. 10003.

CAREER: Arthur D. Little, Inc., Cambridge, Mass., consultant on information systems, 1966-70; Stanford University, Stanford, Calif., assistant professor of computer and information systems, 1970-74; New York University, New York, N.Y., associate professor, 1974-78, professor of computer applications and information systems and chairman of department, both 1978—. *Member:* Association for Computing Machinery, Institute of Management Sciences, Phi Beta Kappa, Tau Beta Pi.

WRITINGS: Computer-Based Information Systems in Organizations, Science Research Associates, 1973; *Toward Creative Systems Design* (monograph), Columbia University Press, 1974; *Why Information Systems Fail* (monograph), Columbia University Press, 1975; *The Implementation of Computer-Based Models* (monograph), National Association of Accountants, 1976; *The Analysis, Design, and Implementation of Information Systems,* McGraw, 1976, 2nd edition, 1981; (with C. F. Gibson) *Casebook for Management Information Systems,* McGraw, 1976, 2nd edition, 1981; *Information Systems Concepts for Management,* McGraw, 1978, 2nd edition, 1982; (editor with F. Land, T. J. Lincoln, and K. Supper) *The Information Systems Environment,* North-Holland Publishing, 1980; *Implementation: The Key to Successful Information Systems* (monograph), Columbia Universtiy Press, 1981; *Coping With Computers: A Manager's Guide to Controlling Information Processing,* Free Press, 1982.

Contributor: F. Gruenberger, editor, *Efficient Versus Effective Computing,* Prentice-Hall, 1973; R. Schultz and D. Slevin, editors, *Implementing Operations Research/Management Science: Research Findings and Implications,* American Elsevier, 1975; R. Goldberg and H. Lorin, editors, *The Economics of Information Processing,* Volume II, Wiley, 1982; G. Salvendi, editor, *The Handbook of Industrial Engineering,* Wiley, 1982; H. Ansoff, A. Bosman, and P. Storms, editors, *Understanding and Managing Strategies Change,* North-Holland Publishing, 1982.

Contributor of about forty articles and reviews to information systems and management journals. Editor in chief of *Systems, Objectives, Solutions;* associate editor of *MIS Quarterly;* editor of *Industrial Management* (now *Sloan Management Review*), 1967-68, and *Performance Evaluation Review,* 1972-73; member of editorial board of *Sloan Management Review.*

WORK IN PROGRESS: Research on the implementation of information systems; the impact of systems on the organization; and the management of information processing and expert systems.

SIDELIGHTS: Lucas told *CA:* "Information processing is the least well managed part of most organizations. Recent books and research attempt to improve the effectiveness of information processing through better management."

*   *   *

LUEDTKE, Kurt   1939-

BRIEF ENTRY: Born September 28, 1939, in Grand Rapids,

Mich. American journalist, media critic, and screenwriter. Luedtke began his journalism career as a reporter for the *Grand Rapids Press* in 1961, following his graduation from Brown University. In 1963 he joined the staff of the *Miami Herald* and two years later became a reporter for the *Detroit Free Press*, becoming that paper's executive editor in 1973. In 1978 Luedtke left that post and moved to Hollywood to pursue a career as a screenwriter. His first screenplay, "Absence of Malice," which examines the ongoing questions involved in the debate over the right to privacy versus the First Amendment rights of the press, became a highly successful motion picture. The film was nominated for an Academy Award in 1982. *Biographical/critical sources: Who's Who in America*, 42nd edition, Marquis, 1982; *Columbia Journalism Review*, July/August, 1982.

* * *

LUNDSTEEN, Sara W.

PERSONAL: Born in Alexandria, La.; daughter of Harry Wynn (a professor) and Sara (a poet; maiden name, Brandon) Rickey; married Alex Bang (an accountant), November 15, 1951. *Education:* Received B.A. and M.A. from Southern Methodist University; University of California, Berkeley, Ph.D., 1963. *Residence:* Dallas, Tex. *Agent:* Clifford Warren, 400 East Fourth, Edmond, Okla. 73034. *Office:* Department of Education, North Texas State University, Denton, Tex. 76203.

CAREER: University of California, Santa Barbara, assistant professor of education, 1964-67; University of Texas, Austin, associate professor of education, 1967-71; University of California, Irvine, visiting professor of education, 1971-76; North Texas State University, Denton, professor of education, 1977—. President of Creative Studies Institute; member of advisory board of Gooch Early Childhood Center; patron of Dallas Repertory Theatre.

MEMBER: International Reading Association (chairman of studies and research committee; president), American Psychological Association (fellow), National Conference on Research in English (fellow; past president), National Council of Teachers of English (member of executive board; member of board of trustees of Research Foundation), National Association for Gifted Children, American Educational Research Association, National Association for the Education of Young Children. *Awards, honors:* Member of Hall of Fame of International Listening Association, 1981.

WRITINGS: Listening: Its Impact on Reading and the Other Language Arts, National Council of Teachers of English and Educational Resources Information Center, 1971, revised edition published as *Listening: Its Impact at All Levels on Reading and the Other Language Arts*, Educational Resources Information Center, 1979; *Children Learn to Communicate*, Prentice-Hall, 1976; *Ideas Into Practice*, Prentice-Hall, 1976; (editor) *Help for the Teacher of Written Composition: New Directions in Research*, National Council of Teachers of English and Educational Resources Information Center, 1976; *Skapande Samsprak med Barn* (title means "Creative Communication With Children"), Esselte Studium, 1977; (with Goeran Stroemqvist) *Lyssna, Taenka, Tala* (title means "Listen, Think, Speak"), Educational Resources Information Center Clearinghouse on Reading and Communication Skills, 1978; (editor) *Cultural Factors in Learning and Instruction*, Educational Resources Information Center Clearinghouse on Urban Education Institute for Urban and Minority Education, 1978; (with Norma Bernstein-Tarrow) *Guiding Young Children's Learning*, McGraw, 1981; (with Bernstein-Tarrow and others) *Curriculum Ideas for Guiding Young Children's Learning*, McGraw, 1981.

Contributor: William B. Michaels, editor, *Teaching for Creative Endeavor*, Indiana University Press, 1960; Sam Duker, editor, *Listening: Readings*, Scarecrow, 1966; H. A. Robinson and A. T. Burrows, editors, *Teacher Effectiveness in Elementary Language Arts: A Progress Report*, National Council of Teachers of English and Educational Resources Information Center Clearinghouse on Reading and Communication Skills, 1974; Lloyd Ollia, editor, *Handbook: For Administrators on Beginning Reading*, International Reading Association, 1980; Barret J. Mandel, editor, *Three Language-Arts Curriculum Models: Pre-Kindergarten Through College*, National Council of Teachers of English, 1980.

Author of television scripts for "Thinking Improvement Project," 1966. Contributor of articles and reviews to education journals.

WORK IN PROGRESS: A book on persuasive language; a book on creative problem solving; a novel; a television documentary film.

SIDELIGHTS: Sara Lundsteen wrote: "One of my favorite quotations is from *Ulysses*—'Come, my friends,' 'tis not too late to seek a newer world.'" *Avocational interests:* Gardening, singing, travel, dance.

* * *

LUTYENS, (Agnes) Elisabeth   1906-1983

OBITUARY NOTICE: Born in 1906 in London, England; died April 14, 1983, in London, England. Musician, composer, and author. Lutyens composed music in late-romantic and expressionist styles before she found her calling as an atonalist. A pioneering composer in the use of serial techniques, Lutyens helped gain acceptance for the art which was adaptable to various media, including concert, opera, radio play, and film. Among her many works are a cycle of six chamber concertos, the lyric drama *Iris and Osiris*, choral and solo music, and more than two hundred radio scores. She received the City of London Midsummer Prize in 1969 and wrote her autobiography, *A Goldfish Bowl*, in 1972. Obituaries and other sources: *Who's Who*, 126th edition, St. Martin's, 1974; *London Times*, April 15, 1983; *Chicago Tribune*, April 16, 1983; *Washington Post*, April 16, 1983.

* * *

LYFORD-PIKE, Margaret (Prudence)   1911-

HOME: Broomieknowe House, 29 Broomieknowe, Lasswade, Midlothian, Scotland.

CAREER: Roedean School, Brighton, England, staff member, 1933-36; Pate's Grammer School, Cheltenham, England, head of English department, 1939-45; British Broadcasting Corp., Edinburgh, Scotland, radio producer, script writer, broadcaster, 1946-71; author of books for children.

WRITINGS: (Adapter) *Scottish Fairy Tales* (illustrated by Jane Susa Evans), Dent, 1974; (with Rosemary Sutcliff) *We Lived in Drumfyvie*, Blackie & Son, 1975; (reteller) *The King of the Warlocks, and Other Fairy Tales* (illustrated by Shirley Felts), Dent, 1979.

LYNX
  See WEST, Rebecca

*   *   *

LYTTLE, Charles Harold   1885(?)-1980

PERSONAL: Born c. 1885 in Cleveland, Ohio; died of cardiac arrest, May 2, 1980, in Chicago, Ill.; married Marcia Taft Jones; children: Bradford, David. *Education:* Western Reserve University (now Case Western Reserve University), B.A., M.A.; Harvard University, M.A.; Meadville Theological School, B.D., Th.D. *Residence:* Chicago, Ill.

CAREER: Ordained to Unitarian ministry; minister in Brooklyn, N.Y., 1914-24, and Geneva, Ill., 1927-64; Meadville Theological School, Chicago, Ill., teacher of church history, 1924-49; University of Chicago, Chicago, Ill., professor of modern church history, 1943-49.

WRITINGS: (Contributor) *American Society of Church History,* [New York], 1914; *The Pentecost of American Unitarianism: Channing's Baltimore Sermon,* Beacon Press, 1920; *Freedom Moves West: A History of the Western Unitarian Conference, 1852-1952* (bibliography), Beacon Press, 1952. Also editor of *The Liberal Gospel,* an anthology of the writings of William Ellery Channing, 1925, revised edition, c. 1980.

OBITUARIES: New York Times, May 7, 1980.*

M

MACE, Don   1899(?)-1983

OBITUARY NOTICE: Born c. 1899 in Texas; died of a heart attack, March 22, 1983, in Falls Church, Va. Publisher and editor. After serving in the Navy during World War I and working for an oil company and the Civilian Conservation Corps, Mace joined the newly formed military publication *Air Force Times* in 1940. He became editor in 1947 and worked in that capacity until 1967, when he was named publisher of the *Air Force Times* and editorial director of Army Times Publishing, the parent company. Mace served on the board of directors and as a senior publications editor after his retirement in 1973. Obituaries and other sources: *Washington Post*, March 24, 1983.

*   *   *

MACHLUP, Fritz   1902-1983

OBITUARY NOTICE—See index for *CA* sketch: Born December 15, 1902, in Wiener Neustadt, Austria; died after a heart attack, January 30, 1983, in Princeton, N.J. Economist, educator, and author. Machlup was one of the first to consider knowledge an economic resource. He espoused the European liberal tradition and concentrated his attentions on human rights, civil liberties, government intervention in economics, and the power of the marketplace. He also analyzed general and international economic theory, including such subjects as monopolies, oligopolies, cartels, international exchange rates, and gold standards. He taught at several American universities, including Harvard, Princeton, and New York University. His writings include *The Political Economy of Monopoly, The Production and Distribution of Knowledge in the United States*, and *Essays on Economic Semantics*. At the time of his death, Machlup—an American citizen since 1940—was working on a ten-volume series titled *Knowledge: Its Creation, Distribution, and Economic Significance*. He completed only three volumes. Obituaries and other sources: *New York Times*, January 31, 1983.

*   *   *

MACK, Gerstle   1894-1983

OBITUARY NOTICE: Born May 21, 1894, in San Francisco, Calif.; died February 15, 1983, in New York, N.Y. An ar-
chitectural draftsman and author, Mack wrote on a variety of subjects. His works include several books on architecture, biographies on Paul Cezanne and Toulouse-Lautrec, and *The Land Divided*, a history of the Panama Canal. Obituaries and other sources: *American Authors and Books: 1640 to the Present Day*, 3rd revised edition, Crown, 1962; *New York Times*, February 17, 1983; *AB Bookman's Weekly*, March 7, 1983.

*   *   *

MACK, Walter Staunton   1895-

PERSONAL: Born October 19, 1895, in New York, N.Y.; son of Walter Staunton (a president of a textile business) and Alice (Ranger) Mack; married Ruth Juergensen (marriage ended); married Ruth J. Watkins, 1942; children: (first marriage) Anthony Reckford, Florence Ann Mack Kelley; (second marriage) Walter Staunton III, Alice Ruth Mack Sawyer. *Education:* Harvard University, A.B., 1917. *Politics:* Republican. *Religion:* Jewish. *Home:* 530 East 72nd St., New York, N.Y. 10021. *Agent:* Peter Buckley, 160 Bleecker St., New York, N.Y. 10014. *Office:* Compass International, 501 Madison Ave., New York, N.Y. 10022.

CAREER: Bedford Mills, Inc. (textiles), New York City, began as salesman, 1919, became president, 1926; Phoenix Securities Corp., New York City, vice-president, 1934-38, president, 1938-51; Pepsi-Cola Co., Long Island City, N.Y., president and chairman of board, 1951-56; Animex Resources Corp., chairman, beginning in 1970; chairman of board of Compass International, New York, N.Y. Vice-president of William B. Nichols & Co. and Equity Corp.; chairman of board and director of United Cigar-Whelan Stores Corp.; president and chairman of board of Nedicks, Inc.; president of C & C Super Corp.; chairman of board and chief executive officer of Great American Industries, Inc.; president and chairman of Rubatex Corp.; president of Great American Minerals Corp.; chairman of Animex Petroleum Ltd. Director and treasurer of Polls Creek Coal Co., Indian Head Mining Co., and River Coal Co., 1977—. Director of New York board of trade; Republican candidate for New York state senate, 1932; treasurer of Republican company committee for New York state senate, 1932, for New York City, 1934-36; treasurer of Fusion Co. committee for election of Mayor Fiorello La Guardia, 1933; New York state chairman of Volunteers for Eisenhower; chairman of national committee of Republicans and Independents for Johnson, 1964.

Member of mayor's advisory and defense committees; vice-chairman of Greater New York Fund, 1941; director of Queens chamber of commerce and New York World's Fair committee; member of state commission on human rights; director of City Center of Music and Drama; honorary chairman of Queens County cancer committee, 1946, and Queens Greater New York Fund committee, 1946; chairman of Dewey-Warren citizens committee, 1948. Trustee of French and Polyclinic Hospitals. *Military service:* U.S. Navy, 1917-19.

MEMBER: Veterans of Foreign Wars, Litchfield Hunter Breeders Society (treasurer), New York Harvard Club, Boston Harvard Club, Arizona Country Club, Ocean Country Club, Jefferson Island Club, Sky Club. *Awards, honors:* Horatio Alger Award, 1948, for success in the business world; Fiorello La Guardia Award from New York City for "services in arranging free music and dancing in the park"; Thomas Jefferson Award for services in establishing a national scholarship for high school students.

WRITINGS: (With Peter Buckley) *No Time Lost* (autobiography), Atheneum, 1982.

SIDELIGHTS: Mack told *CA:* "Peter Buckley wrote *No Time Lost* after he interviewed me a number of times. In general, the book gives a behind the scenes look into the business world. It also reflects upon the growing discontent of the masses—the poor populations in underdeveloped countries—and the growing pressures at work in their environments. Cuba is such an example."

*   *   *

MacKAYE, William Ross   1934-

BRIEF ENTRY: Born June 1, 1934, in New York, N.Y. American journalist and co-author of *Combat Commander: Autobiography of a Soldier* (Prentice-Hall, 1970). MacKaye has worked for several publications since beginning his journalism career as a reporter for the *Minneapolis Star* in 1958. Ten years later, while serving as religion editor of the *Washington Post,* the newsman won the Supple Award for distinguished religious journalism from the Religion Newswriters Association. In 1975 MacKaye was appointed associate editor of the *Washington Post Magazine. Address:* 3819 Beecher St. N.W., Washington, D.C. 20007; and 1150 15th St. N.W., Washington, D.C. 20071.

*   *   *

MACKENZIE, R. Alec
See MACKENZIE, Richard Alexander

*   *   *

MACKENZIE, Richard Alexander   1923-
(R. Alec Mackenzie)

PERSONAL: Born January 29, 1923, in Genoa, Ill.; son of Harold Mackenzie (a school superintendant); married Gay Wood (a nutritionist), August 16, 1953; children: Melody, Mark. *Education:* U.S. Military Academy, B.S., 1949; University of Iowa, J.D., 1954; graduate studies at University of Chicago and Columbia University. *Office:* Alec Mackenzie & Associates, Inc., P.O. Box 130, 88 Salem St., Greenwich, N.Y. 12834.

CAREER: Legislative assistant to U.S. Senator Alexander Wiley; Young Life Campaign, Inc., Colorado Springs, Colo., executive assistant to director, 1963-64; staff attorney for Health

Insurance Association of America; vice-president of Oscar Mayer & Co., Kartridge Pac Division, Mount Prospect, Ill.; Alec Mackenzie & Associates, Inc., Greenwich, N.Y., president, 1969—. Vice-president of Erickson Foundation; gives seminars on time management, leadership, and the management process in the United States, South America, Europe, and the Far East. *Member:* American Management Association (former vice-president of Presidents' Association).

WRITINGS—Under name R. Alec Mackenzie: *Managing Your Time,* Zondervan, 1969; *The Credibility Gap in Management,* Van Nostrand, 1971; *The Time Trap,* American Management Association, 1972; *New Time Management Methods for You and Your Staff,* Dartnell, 1975; (with Kay Cronkite Waldo) *About Time!: A Woman's Guide to Time Management,* McGraw, 1981.

Films: "The Time Trap," American Media, 1982; also "Communication," American Management Association.

Tape cassette programs: "Managing Time," Advanced Management Reports, 1972; "Time Management for the Secretary," Advanced Management Reports, 1976; "Mackenzie on Time," American Management Association, 1979. Contributor to magazines, including *Fortune, Harvard Business Review, International Management,* and *Management Review.*

WORK IN PROGRESS: Two works on time management—one for managers, the other for secretaries—both for McGraw (Australia); a computerized time management program; a time management notebook/workbook, "Time Tactics," publication by McGraw expected in 1984.

SIDELIGHTS: R. Alec Mackenzie has been actively promoting the management education and professional development of executives and their support staffs for many years through publications, tape cassettes, films, seminars, and lectures throughout North and South America, Europe, and the Far East. His best-known work is "The Management Process in 3-D," an article published by *Harvard Business Review,* considered to be the world's most accepted model of management.

*   *   *

MACKIN, Catherine (Patricia)   1939-1982

PERSONAL: Born August 28, 1939, in Baltimore, Md.; died of cancer, November 20, 1982, in Towson, Md.; daughter of Francis Michael and Catherine (Gillooly) Mackin. *Education:* University of Maryland, B.A. (cum laude), 1960; graduate study at Harvard University, 1967-68.

CAREER/WRITINGS: Free State News, College Park, Md., general assignment reporter and assistant to publisher, 1958-60; *Baltimore News American,* Baltimore, Md., general assignment reporter and city desk rewriter, 1960-63; associated with Washington bureau of Hearst Newspapers, 1963-69, White House correspondent, 1965-67, urban affairs correspondent, 1968-69; National Broadcasting Co. (NBC), New York, N.Y., anchorwoman of news program and investigative reporter for WRC-TV in Washington, D.C., 1969-71, general assignment reporter, 1971-73, correspondent for Los Angeles bureau, 1973-74, and congressional correspondent in Washington, D.C., 1974-77, for NBC-TV; American Broadcasting Co. (ABC), New York, N.Y., Washington correspondent, beginning in 1977. *Member:* White House Correspondents Association, Women's National Press Club (Washington, D.C.), Alpha Omicron Pi. *Awards, honors:* Neiman fellow at Harvard University, 1967-68.

SIDELIGHTS: In 1972 Catherine Mackin made history by becoming the first woman floor reporter at a national political convention. A tenacious newswoman known for her tough-minded interviews and professional calm, the journalist rose through the NBC hierarchy quickly—in fourteen months Mackin went from local newscaster to national correspondent. "It was," she once allowed in a *Grand Rapids Press* interview with Bruce Buursma, "probably luck. There are not as many network correspondents as there are newspaper reporters, and you really do have to be lucky to get a good television job. But to do a good job, I think you have to be trained as a reporter as well as in broadcasting." Mackin believed that her six years as a Washington correspondent with Hearst newspapers held her in good stead.

Covering the news in the nation's capitol for more than a decade, Mackin's Washington years saw a presidential assassination, an impeachment trial, and a presidential resignation. Yet she never ranked her nation-shattering reports. "In the midst of a story," Mackin told Buursma, "you become so involved in the details that you don't consider it part of history. . . . I always hope my best stories are ahead of me." The news correspondent died of cancer on November 20, 1982, at the age of forty-four.

BIOGRAPHICAL/CRITICAL SOURCES: Newsweek, October 16, 1972; *Grand Rapids Press,* January 19, 1975; *Biography News,* March-April, Gale, 1975; *Time,* March 21, 1977.

OBITUARIES: Newsweek, November 29, 1982; *Time,* November 29, 1982.*

*   *   *

MACKLEY, George   1900-1983

OBITUARY NOTICE: Born May 13, 1900, in Tonbridge, Kent, England; died in 1983. Artist, educator, and author. Considered a fine draughtsman and one of the best wood engravers of the twentieth century, Mackley is known particularly for his engravings of canals, boats, and architectural subjects. His book *Wood Engraving,* published in 1948 and reissued in 1981, is among the most detailed texts written on the craft in this century. Mackley's works are displayed in a number of public collections, including those of the Fitswilliam Museum at Cambridge and the Ashmolean Museum at Oxford. As a teacher and headmaster, Mackley is remembered for his work at the Sutton school, where he instituted an art course for talented children. Obituaries and other sources: *Who's Who,* 134th edition, St. Martin's, 1982; *London Times,* February 10, 1983.

*   *   *

MACLEAN, Charles   1946-
(James Konrad)

PERSONAL: Born October 31, 1946, in Yealand Conyers, Lancashire, England; son of Fitzroy Hugh (a writer) and Veronica (a hotelier and cookery writer; maiden name, Fraser) Maclean. *Education:* Oxford University, B.A., 1970. *Agent:* Lynn Nesbit, International Creative Management, 40 West 57th St., New York, N.Y. 10019.

CAREER: Writer. Associate editor for *Ecologist* (magazine), 1972-73; features editor for *Vogue* (magazine), 1973-74. *Member:* Society for Psychic Research, Zoological Society. *Awards, honors:* Scottish Arts Council Award, 1972, for *Island on the Edge of the World.*

WRITINGS: Island on the Edge of the World: The Story of St. Kilda (nonfiction), Stacey, 1972, revised edition, Canongate, 1977; *The Pathetic Phallus* (novel), London Magazine Editions, 1977; *The Wolf Children* (nonfiction), Lane, 1977; (under pseudonym James Konrad) *Target Amin* (fiction), Sphere Books, 1977; *The Watcher* (fiction), Simon & Schuster, 1983.

SIDELIGHTS: Island on the Edge of the World is Maclean's account of the life and death of an island culture. St. Kilda, a group of rocky islands west of the Hebrides, was home to a population completely adapted to its sparse surroundings. St. Kildans had not even heard of money before the late nineteenth century, for until then, the island economy was based almost entirely on its function as a bird-breeding ground. The animals' meat, eggs, oil, feathers, and guano provided food, sustenance, and revenue, supplemented only by limited crops and small herds of cattle and native sheep. Even the body type of the inhabitants revealed perfect adaptation: their muscles and feet were well developed for scaling cliffs to hunt for birds.

Life on the islands began to change during the middle of the nineteenth century. According to Maclean, overactive missionaries, "civilized" diseases, and the introduction of "agricultural improvements" that disrupted the well-established system of communal farming and birding contributed to the eventual disintegration of the St. Kildan culture. "Within 100 years," related Carol Van Sturm in a *Washington Post Book World* review, "the St. Kildans declined from a self-sufficient, healthy culture to a people dependent entirely on mainland charity." The British Government evacuated the island in 1930, after "young people, dissatisfied and hungry for thrills and comforts tasted from afar, abandoned the island en masse, and the remaining, dwindling community no longer knew nor cared how to support themselves."

A *Times Literary Supplement* article deemed Maclean's work "an interesting addition to the already considerable bibliography of Britain's remotest and once more inhabited island," adding that "the writing is sinewy, the assessment of what life was like on St. Kilda is hard, dry, and factual, and, although the book is ostensibly the story of an island community which died because it could not adapt, it is really a tract for the times: an essay on the predicament of modern man." Van Sturm similarly acknowledged that "from the ruins of an extinct island community, Charles Maclean has drawn a profound moral for our time, in a beautiful, well-written book."

In a very different work, *Watcher,* Maclean weaves a psychological thriller that explores the validity of reincarnation. He tells the bizarre tale of a "normal" man, Martin Gregory, who commits a grotesque and violent act with "no catalyst or precedent." The man begins seeing a psychoanalyst who hypnotizes him; Gregory begins "spewing out data on six previous lives he has lived throughout the last thousand years or so," Christopher Lehmann-Haupt described in the *New York Times.* The critic was "mesmerized" by this story of hypnosis and regression. "It is quite remarkable how dexterously Mr. Maclean manipulates us," he concluded.

BIOGRAPHICAL/CRITICAL SOURCES: Times Literary Supplement, September 1, 1972, May 6, 1977; *Spectator,* November, 1977; *Saturday Review,* March 18, 1978; *Atlantic,* June, 1978; *Washington Post Book World,* September 7, 1980; *New Yorker,* October 13, 1980; *New York Times,* February 14, 1983.

MACLEAN, Donald Duart   1913-1983
(Mark Petrovich Frazer)

OBITUARY NOTICE: Born May 25, 1913, in England; died March 6, 1983, in Moscow, U.S.S.R. British diplomat and author who defected to the Soviet Union in 1951 after becoming involved in one of the most famous of the post-World War II spy scandals. Maclean leaked U.S. atomic secrets to the Soviets while serving on a liaison committee dealing with atomic information during his tenure as first secretary at the British Embassy in Washington, D.C., from 1945 to 1948; he then fled from England with accomplice Guy Burgess in 1951. Their disappearance provoked a massive manhunt by Western security services, but they were not heard from again until they appeared in Moscow in 1956. A third man in the spy ring, journalist H.A.R. (Kim) Philby, joined them in Moscow in 1963, but a fourth accomplice, art historian Anthony Blunt, went undiscovered until 1979. Some sources report that an unidentified fifth man obtained asylum in the United States. In Moscow Maclean worked at the Moscow Institute as an analyst of British affairs and wrote under the name Mark Petrovich Frazer. In 1970 he published *British Policy Since Suez: 1956-58.* Obituaries and other sources: *New York Times,* March 12, 1983; *London Times,* March 12, 1983; *Chicago Tribune,* March 12, 1983; *Los Angeles Times,* March 12, 1983; *Newsweek,* March 21, 1983; *Time,* March 21, 1983.

*   *   *

MacSHANE, Denis   1948-

PERSONAL: Born May 21, 1948, in Glasgow, Scotland. *Education:* Merton College, Oxford, M.A., 1969. *Politics:* Labour. *Home:* 2 route de Loex, 1213 Geneva, Switzerland. *Office:* International Metalworkers Federation, 54 bis route des Acadias, Geneva, Switzerland.

CAREER: British Broadcasting Corp., London, England, journalist and producer, 1969-77; National Union of Journalists, London, president, 1978-79; International Metalworkers Federation, Geneva, Switzerland, 1979—.

WRITINGS: Solidarity: Poland's Independent Trade Union, Spokesman Books, 1981; *Francois Mitterrand: A Political Odyssey,* Quartet Books, 1982, Universe Books, 1983. Author of political pamphlets and contributor to *New Statesman* and *Tribune.*

WORK IN PROGRESS: An anthology of socialist poetry; making desultory notes about British foreign policy and international trade unionism.

SIDELIGHTS: MacShane's biography of French president Francois Mitterrand was praised by several critics. Patrick McCarthy, in a *Times Literary Supplement* article, noted that the work "offers a simple, sensible account of Mitterrand's political career. . . . [MacShane's] book will be extremely useful to the general reader who wants to know what to make of the Socialist victory in France in 1981." Francis Wheen of the *New Statesman* and Richard Mayne of the *Observer* concurred, calling *Francois Mitterrand: A Political Odyssey* "an engrossing and well written account" and a "brisk, fluent, *engage* study," respectively.

MacShane told *CA:* "I am a committed, if often skeptical, European socialist who sees writing books as part of the political process. Sitting in comfortable Alpine eeyrie in Switzerland, I have tried to explain foreign political events—Solidarity in Poland and the arrival of Mitterrand in power in

France—to an Anglo-Saxon audience that rarely lifts its head beyond domestic troubles, whether in the United States or the United Kingdom. I dislike jargonized, theory-laden accounts of contemporary politics written by leftists, so I try to explain key developments and people in normal English."

BIOGRAPHICAL/CRITICAL SOURCES: London Times, September 15, 1978; *Guardian Weekly,* September 9, 1981, May 8, 1982; *New Statesman,* May 14, 1982; *Times Literary Supplement,* June 11, 1982, July 16, 1982; *Observer,* June 27, 1982; *Listener,* July 8, 1982.

*   *   *

MAE, Eydie
See HUNSBERGER, Edith Mae

*   *   *

MAENCHEN, Otto John   1894-1969
(Otto J. Maenchen-Helfen)

OBITUARY NOTICE: Born July 26, 1894, in Vienna, Austria; died January 29, 1969, in Berkeley, Calif. Art historian, educator, and author. An authority on Central Asian history and Far Eastern archaeology and ancient art, Maenchen's special interest extended beyond the Far East, from the area of Central Asia through the steppes of South Russia. He began his career doing private research in Vienna, worked as a librarian of the Arbeiterkammer, engaged in independent archaeological work in Russia, taught at the University of Berlin, and wrote for the Social-Democrat paper *Arbeiter-Zeitung.* Maenchen came to the United States in 1938, teaching first at Mills College in Oakland, California, and then at the University of California, Berkeley, where he became a professor and taught the history of Chinese, Japanese, and Indian art. His many books, all published under the name Otto J. Maenchen-Helfen, include *The World of the Huns, China,* and a biography of Karl Marx. Maenchen also wrote more than sixty articles and reviews for such periodicals as the *Journal of the American Oriental Society, American Historical Review, Asia Minor,* and *Byzantion,* coedited the *Central Asiatic Journal* and the *Encyclopedia Dell'Arte* of Rome for many years, and presented papers and gave lectures in the United States, Italy, Japan, Austria, Germany, and England. Obituaries and other sources: *The National Cyclopaedia of American Biography,* Volume 54, James T. White, 1973.

*   *   *

MAENCHEN-HELFEN, Otto J.
See MAENCHEN, Otto John

*   *   *

MAIER, Howard   1906(?)-1983

OBITUARY NOTICE: Born c. 1906; died of cancer, January 28, 1983, in Hallandale, Fla. Television director, political specialist, and author. Maier began working for the Office of War Information in the 1940's, served in the U.S. Army, then returned to the information agency in 1946, eventually becoming an assistant television director and establishing the program "Report From America." He also served as a political specialist for Voice of America and wrote in several genres. His work includes radio scripts for "The Aldrich Family," short stories, and a novel, *Undertow,* based on Army life. Obituaries and other sources: *New York Times,* February 23, 1983.

MAINE, Charles Eric
See McILWAIN, David

*   *   *

MAJOR, Henriette 1933-

PERSONAL: Born January 6, 1933, in Montreal, Quebec, Canada; daughter of Henri (a mechanic) and Yvette Groleau; married Robert Dubuc (a producer), September 12, 1953; children: Suzanne, Patrice. *Education:* Attended Teacher's College and Ecole des Beaux Arts. *Home:* 962 Cherrier, Montreal, Canada H2L 1H7.

CAREER: Author of books for children. Props and script director for Canadian Broadcasting Corp. Has also taught kindergarten, been a puppeteer, and worked on youth newspapers and for women's magazines and programs. *Member:* Union des Ecrivains du Quebec. *Awards, honors:* Canadian Library Association award for children's book of the year, 1971, for *La Surprise de Dame Chenille;* Canada Council children's literature prize, 1978, for *L'Evangile en papier: Texte integral de l'emission de television.*

WRITINGS—All for young people: *Un Drole de petit cheval* (illustrated by Guy Gaucher), Centre de psychologie et de pedagogie (Montreal), 1966; *Le Club des curieux,* Fides, 1967; (with Monic Allard) *Jeux Dramatiques,* Editions heritage, 1969; *A la conquete du temps* (illustrated by Louise Roy-Kerrigan), Editions jeunesse, 1970; *La Surprise de Dame Chenille,* Centre de psychologie et de pedagogie, 1970; *Romulo, enfant de l'Amazonie, sur les Ailes de l'esperance* (photographs by Pierre H. Labelle), Editions du jour, 1973; (with Paul Sainte-Marie) *Bonjour Montreal: Mini guide pour les jeunes avec Bob et Lili/Hello Montreal: The Young People's Mini-Guide With Bob and Lili* (French and English text; illustrated by Robert Henen), Editions heritage, 1975; *Contes de Nulle Part et d'Ailleurs,* l'Ecole des loisirs (Paris), 1975; *Un Homme et sa mission* (photographs by Ken Bell), translation by Jane Springer published as *A Man and His Mission: Cardinal Leger in Africa,* Prentice-Hall, 1976; *L'Evangile en papier,* Fides, 1977; *Elise et l'oncle riche* (illustrated by Michele Devlin), Fides, 1979; *Comment vivent les Quebecois* (text), Hachette (Paris), 1979; (with Claude LaFortune) *La Bible en papier,* Fides, 1979; *Les Premiers pas de l'eglise,* Fides, 1981; *La Ville fabuleuse,* Heritage, 1982; *Ma Soeur Laterre,* Etudes Vivantes, 1982.

WORK IN PROGRESS: La Machine a reves, for Mondia; *Les Mots apprivoises,* for Centre Educatif et Culturel; *L'Ile aux chats.*

SIDELIGHTS: Major told *CA:* "I write for children because I have much respect for them as persons. I try to adopt their point of view on life."

*   *   *

MAKI, John M(cGilvrey) 1909-

PERSONAL: Born November 19, 1909, in Tacoma, Wash.; married in 1936; children: two. *Education:* University of Washington, B.A., 1932, M.A., 1936; Harvard University, Ph.D., 1948. *Office:* Department of Political Science, University of Massachusetts, Amherst, Mass. 01002.

CAREER: University of Washington, Seattle, assistant professor, 1948-51, associate professor, 1951-56, professor of Japanese government and politics, 1956-66; University of Massachusetts, Amherst, professor of government, 1966—, chairman of Asian studies program, 1966-67, vice-dean of arts and sciences, 1967-71. *Member:* American Political Science Association, Association of Asian Studies. *Awards, honors:* Rockefeller fellowship, 1946-48, for study at Harvard University.

WRITINGS: Japanese Militarism: Its Cause and Cure, Knopf, 1945; (compiler) *Selected Documents: Far Eastern International Relations,* University of Washington, 1951; (editor) *Conflict and Tension in the Far East: Key Documents, 1894-1960,* University of Washington Press, 1961; *Government and Politics in Japan: The Road to Democracy,* Praeger, 1962; (editor) *Court and Constitution in Japan: Selected Supreme Court Constitutional Decisions, 1948-60,* University of Washington Press, 1964; (compiler) *We the Japanese: Voices From Japan* (juvenile), Praeger, 1972; (translator and editor) *Japan's Commission on the Constitution: The Final Report,* University of Washington Press, 1981.*

*   *   *

MALEFIJT, Annemarie de Waal
See de WAAL MALEFIJT, Annemarie

*   *   *

MALLONEE, Richard C(arvel) II 1923-

PERSONAL: Surname is pronounced *Mal-lo-nay;* born June 15, 1923, in Fort Sill, Okla.; son of Richard C. (a colonel in the U.S. Army) and Virginia (Givson) Mallonee; married Hester Coffey (an artist), December 28, 1952; children: Hester C., Richard C. III, Arthur G., Eugene C. *Education:* Duke University, B.S.M.E., 1949; University of Washington, Seattle, M.A., 1971, Ph.D., 1979. *Religion:* Protestant. *Home:* 6003 125th Ave. S.E., Bellevue, Wash. 98006.

CAREER: Airesearch Manufacturing Co. of Arizona (manufacturers of pneumatic controls), Phoenix, research engineer, 1956-60; Boeing Co., Seattle, Wash., development engineer, 1961-68; Shoreline Community College, Seattle, professor of engineering, 1968-76; Kenworth Truck Co., Seattle, engineering manager, 1976-82. Consulting engineer; adviser to Bellevue Community College, Cogswell College North, Clover Park Vocational Technical Institute, Oregon Institute of Technology, and Washington State Reformatory. Member of Bellevue Philharmonic League, 1978—. *Military service:* U.S. Army, 1943-46, 1949-53, served in field artillery; became first lieutenant; received Bronze Star. U.S. Army Reserve, 1946-76; became lieutenant colonel. *Member:* American Society for Engineering Education, Pi Mu Epsilon.

WRITINGS: The Naked Flagpole: Battle for Bataan, Presidio Press, 1980.

WORK IN PROGRESS: Kenworth Truck Company: Sixty Years of Innovative Truck Manufacturing.

SIDELIGHTS: Mallonee commented: "My motivation for writing *The Naked Flagpole* was to make available to the public the account of the World War II Battle of Bataan and the subsequent 'death march' and forty-two months in prison camp contained in the diaries of my father, Colonel R. C. Mallonee. His was the only complete and detailed diary of events in that area that survived the war intact. After he returned from prison camp, he allowed the diary to be used for the U.S. Army's official history of the fall of Bataan, but otherwise did not make it available. After his death, I took steps to do that, including a personal visit to the Philippines to verify historical accuracy. My motivation for writing the Kenworth book is in the same category—to preserve great events before it is too late.''

*   *   *

MALONEY, J(oseph) J(ohn)   1940-

PERSONAL: Born October 31, 1940, in St. Louis, Mo.; son of Joseph J. and Bernice (a waitress; maiden name, Wieland) Maloney; married Betty Lou Deford, 1959 (divorced, 1965); married Jean Haley (an editorial writer), 1973 (divorced, 1975); married Christine Poggi, 1976 (divorced, 1982). *Education:* Educated in prison through Hawthorne Institute; attended University of Missouri, 1968-70. *Politics:* Independent. *Religion:* Roman Catholic. *Home and office:* 8506 Titchfield Court #A, St. Louis, Mo. 63123.

CAREER: Prisoner in Missouri State Penitentiary, 1960-72; *Kansas City Star*, Kansas City, Mo., reporter, 1972-78; *Kansas City Magazine*, Kansas City, contributing editor, 1978-80; *Orange County Register*, Santa Ana, Calif., reporter, 1980-81; *Delaware State News*, Dover, Del., news editor, 1982; free-lance writer, 1982—. Paintings exhibited in Missouri and at Galery 79, Paris, 1967. Jefftown Jaycees, first vice-president, 1969, president, 1970. *Military service:* U.S. Army, 1959.

AWARDS, HONORS: Conover Prize for Poetry from St. Louis Poetry Center, 1970; American Bar Association Silver Gavel, 1973, and Kansas Bar/Media Award, 1974, for *Kansas City Star* prison series; American Bar Association Certificate of Merit, 1978, for *Kansas City Star* series on labor racketeering; Best Investigative Story award from American Newspaper Publishers Association, 1978, for series on State Hospital No. 1 in Missouri; Distinguished Service to Journalism award from Penn Valley Community College, 1979; Sigma Delta Chi award from Orange County chapter of Sigma Delta Chi and Orange County Press Club, 1981, for *Orange County Register* stories on the ''freeway killer''; Watchdog Award from Orange County Press Club, 1981, for story ''revealing secret settlement by police to the survivors of a man shot to death by police''; second place awards from Orange County Press Club, 1981, for entertainment writing and crime and justice features.

WRITINGS: Beyond the Wall (poems), Greenfield Review Press, 1973; *I Speak for the Dead* (novel), Andrews & McMeel, 1982. Poetry represented in anthologies, including *Poets A to Z*, edited by David Ray, Swallow Press; and *Light From Another Country*, edited by Joseph Bruchae, Greenfield Review Press, 1983. Contributor of book reviews, poetry, and articles to periodicals, including *Beloit Poetry Journal, Christian Century, Los Angeles Times,* and *Washington Post Book World, New Letters,* and *Focus/Midwest.*

WORK IN PROGRESS: The Chain, a novel; *Man From Topeka*, a book of poems.

SIDELIGHTS: J. J. Maloney fell into a life of crime at an early age. By fourteen he had stolen a car and was sent to a reformatory; by nineteen he had killed a man during an armed robbery and was sentenced to four consecutive life sentences in a state penitentiary. It was during the latter internment that Maloney first began writing poetry, unleashing the literary talent that would eventually turn his life around.

Maloney sent a sample of his poetry to Thorpe Menn, a book review editor for the *Kansas City Star*. The editor printed the works in the newspaper; he encouraged the prisoner to continue writing and to pursue a course of self-education. When Maloney received parole in 1972, the *Star* hired the ex-convict temporarily as a consultant on a prison series. The project went on to win several awards and Maloney was asked to stay on with the newspaper as an investigative reporter.

Maloney's next six years with the *Star* were distinguished by hard-hitting investigations, daring journalistic practices, and a number of newspaper awards. He reported on such controversial subjects as organized crime, labor racketeering, judicial corruption, and charity fraud. Maloney repeated this outstanding performance with the *Orange County Register* in California from 1980 to 1981, breaking the ''freeway killer'' story that led to the apprehension and conviction of the murderer a few months later.

Eschewing investigative reporting for full-time fiction writing in 1982, Maloney produced *I Speak for the Dead*, a novel featuring ex-convict newspaper reporter Nick Riley, ''who investigates mob warfare in a fictional Kansas City riverside development called City Square,'' Arthur S. Brisban described in the *Kansas City Times*. ''The book portrays the mobsters in Kansas City as brutal killers locked in a factional war featuring torture, murder, suicide, betrayal and a host of other despicable actions depicted uncompromisingly by Mr. Maloney.'' Closely resembling the author's own real-life River Quay investigative story, which he broke at the *Kansas City Star*, *I Speak for the Dead* shows Riley fearlessly tapping the criminal and law-enforcement worlds to gather his story. Although the fictionalized reporter appears an idealization of Maloney, the novelist insists that his character is not particularly heroic—just ''a good reporter'' doing his job.

Maloney told *CA:* ''As an ex-convict, I have worked hard to try to escape the stereotype. However, my specialized knowledge in crime seems to doom me to write a great deal on that subject.

''I have deliberately not gone underground, as many successful ex-convicts do. I feel that we are in a time when there is pressure to regress in areas of penology. The number of people in prison has doubled in the last decade, although the crime rate is dropping. A crisis is approaching, and I am beginning to devote more of my writing time to examining the causes of that crisis and some possible solutions.

''As a fiction writer I have tried to examine the role of an investigative reporter in covering organized crime—with the attendant examination of newsroom politics, the limitation of journalism, the fallibility of journalists, and the mercurial nature of 'truth.'

''I have had a unique opportunity—to go directly from prison to the newsroom of a legendary newspaper. Because of those unusual circumstances, my view of journalism will not be the normal one, in some ways. In many ways, however, I was able to overcome the initial liability of being an ex-convict and to subsequently function on my merits as a newspaper reporter. The editors of the *Kansas City Star* nominated me almost every year for the Pulitzer Prize, and by the time I left in 1978, I was considered one of the top reporters at the paper. I went to Orange County and repeated that performance.

''Now I'm trying to choose a different route—journalism by way of book and magazine.

''Each step along the way I've been counseled not to make the change I was preparing to make. In 1966 George McCue, then art editor of the *St. Louis Post-Dispatch*, praised my paintings, saying they were comparable to work being done by outside professionals. I was urged not to give up painting to pursue poetry. In 1967 Thorpe Menn, book editor of the *Star*, wrote in his column that my poems were 'some of the most powerful poetry ever to come out of Mid-America.' Then I became a newspaper reporter, and many bemoaned that I would not be writing poems. Now, after winning many awards as a reporter, I'm being counseled not to turn away from that to write fiction.

"I've always been under considerable pressure to write an autobiography, but so far have chosen not to. Ultimately, though, that may be the medium through which I'm able to express the many things I've been trying to say in so many formats for so long."

BIOGRAPHICAL/CRITICAL SOURCES: Kansas City Times, November 19, 1982; *Kansas City Star*, November 29, 1982; *St. Louis Post-Dispatch*, January 9, 1983.

* * *

MANFREDI, John Francis 1920-

PERSONAL: Born September 28, 1920, in Philadelphia, Pa.; son of Louis (a toolmaker) and Mary (a flower maker; maiden name, Gizzi) Manfredi; married Jean Price (a librarian and securities analyst), 1951; children: Louis Joseph. *Education:* University of Pennsylvania, B.A., 1942; Harvard University, M.A., 1948, Ph.D., 1951. *Office:* Department of Sociology, University of Massachusetts, Amherst, Mass. 01003.

CAREER: University of Massachusetts, Amherst, instructor, 1948-57, assistant professor, 1957-64, associate professor, 1965-80, professor of sociology, 1980—. *Member:* American Sociological Association.

WRITINGS: Fact and Theory in the Social Sciences: Essays in Honor of Douglas G. Haring, Syracuse University Press, 1969; *Periodical Resources in Italian Sociology*, Microfilms International, 1977; *The Social Limits of Art*, University of Massachusetts Press, 1982.

WORK IN PROGRESS: A study of demographic instability and sectarianism, publication expected in 1985.

SIDELIGHTS: Manfredi told *CA:* "I had about ten years' training as a sculptor, but by the time I was eighteen I realized I wasn't really any more than competent. I went to the University of Pennsylvania to study philosophy of the social sciences, then worked at Harvard University under Sorokin and Parsons.

"My work on the social limits of art deals essentially with the kind of constraints that the social system itself places on the artist and the extent to which the conceptions of reality common to a culture determine its art forms."

* * *

MANGO, Cyril (Alexander) 1928-

PERSONAL: Born April 14, 1928, in Istanbul, Turkey; son of Alexander A. and Adelaide (Damonov) Mango; married Mabel Grover, 1953 (marriage ended); married Susan A. Gerstel, 1964 (marriage ended); married Maria C. Mundell, 1976; children: (first marriage) a daughter; (second marriage) a daughter. *Education:* University of St. Andrews, M.A., 1949; University of Paris, Doctor of History, 1953. *Office:* Exeter College, Oxford, England.

CAREER: Harvard University, Dumbarton Oaks Byzantine Center, Washington, D.C., instructor, 1955-58, lecturer, 1958-

61, associate professor of Byzantine archaeology, 1961-63; University of London, King's College, London, England, Koraes Professor of Modern Greek and of Byzantine History, Language, and Literature, 1963-68; Harvard University, Dumbarton Oaks Byzantine Center, professor of Byzantine archaeology, 1968-73; Oxford University, Oxford, England, Bywater and Sotheby Professor of Byzantine and Modern Greek, 1973—. Visiting associate professor of Byzantine history, University of California, Berkeley, 1960-61. *Member:* Society of Antiquaries (fellow), British Academy (fellow).

WRITINGS: (Translator and author of introduction) Photius I, *The Homilies of Photius, Patriarch of Constantinople*, Harvard University Press, 1958; *The Brazen House: A Study of the Vestibule of the Imperial Palace of Constantinople*, I kommission hos Munksgaard (Copenhagen), 1959; *The Mosaics of St. Sophia at Istanbul*, Dumbarton Oaks, 1962; (with Ekrem Akurgal and Richard Ettinghausen) *Treasures of Turkey*, Zwemmer (London), 1967; (with David Jacobs) *Constantinople, City on the Golden Horn* (juvenile nonfiction), American Heritage Publishing Co., 1969; (compiler) *The Art of the Byzantine Empire, 312-1453: Sources and Documents*, Prentice-Hall, 1972; *Byzantine Architecture*, Abrams, 1976; *Byzantium: The Empire of New Rome*, Weidenfeld & Nicolson, 1980, Scribner, 1981.

SIDELIGHTS: According to his critics, Cyril Mango must be recognized as one of the world's leading authorities on the ancient Byzantine Empire. In his books, the noted scholar brings to life the art, architecture, and culture of a world that witnessed the growth of Christianity and that left a rich legacy of artistic tradition. The world that Professor Mango reconstructs is a world neglected by many recent historians. For this reason, Mango's works stand out, as do his insights into a culture which remains, according to critic Peter Brown, "alien." In a *New York Review of Books* discussion of one of Mango's early books, *The Art of the Byzantine Empire*, Brown states: "Professor Cyril Mango's admirable collection . . . encourages us to listen in to the Byzantines themselves talking about their art; but what we hear is an alien language: early Christians insist on saying very different things from what we would when we stand before the same monuments as they had visited and commissioned." By unravelling a seemingly obscure and alien culture, Professor Mango brings the Byzantine Empire forth to take its place in history.

A critic for *Choice* said of *The Art of the Byzantine Empire:* "The student has never been so well served: virtually every important document on Byzantine art is represented at least in part. Others, obscure but revelatory, will be new to most scholars." In Peter Brown's opinion, the great value of this work lies in Professor Mango's ability to present his material in context. The book, notes Brown, "helps to place Christian art firmly in its context at the time when Christianity became the public religion of the empire. . . . In these texts, we seldom find ourselves in front of an isolated artifact; we are immersed in the bustle of an ancient time."

The ancient times referred to in Brown's review were brought to life again in Professor Mango's work, *Byzantium*. The book is divided into three sections. In "Aspects of Byzantine Life," Mango discusses the social and cultural rules that governed daily life. In "The Conceptual World of Byzantium," the author explores then-popular ideas about the universe and its inhabitants, and in "The Legacy," he relates the main features of Byzantine literature and art. In his review of this book, Robert Browning of *Times Literary Supplement* discusses Mango's organization of his work: "As Mango himself disarmingly recognizes, this is a highly eclectic approach. Many topics are left out of [the] account or [are] merely mentioned in passing. . . . Sometimes the problem is the scarcity or obscurity of evidence. But in the main what has shaped the book is the author's own judgment of what is important and what is not. . . . One may occasionally raise an eyebrow at what he deems to be important." Browning also criticizes Professor Mango's view of Byzantine life as static over the course of its thousand-year existence. "In many chapters of the book the thousand years of the Byzantine empire are treated as homogeneous and unchanging. . . . [Consequently] Mango is inclined to use evidence from one period for inferences about another. When he describes the Byzantine ideal of the good life he offers a mosaic of citations from the fourth-century Fathers. . . . Does this really tell us about how men saw the good life in the twelfth century, or the fourteenth?"

These criticisms aside, the majority of *Byzantium*'s reviewers are overwhelmingly favorable in their comments. "Works like this," asserts a writer for *Virginia Quarterly Review*, "if only there were more of them, would undo the mischief done by Gibbon. Because the master ignored Byzantium, . . . because of Edward Gibbons's foolish prejudices and unforgiveable ignorance, we in the West still know next to nothing of the glory that was the Byzantine Empire." Adds Browning, "Let us hope that [Mango] will go on to write another book as elegant as this. . . . Few are so well qualified to do so, both by knowledge of the evidence and by acuity of critical judgment."

BIOGRAPHICAL/CRITICAL SOURCES: Choice, April, 1973, July-August, 1981; *New York Review of Books*, October 3, 1974; *Times Literary Supplement*, September 26, 1980; *Virginia Quarterly Review*, summer, 1981.*

*   *   *

MANIGAULT, Edward   1897(?)-1983

OBITUARY NOTICE: Born c. 1897; died May 26, 1983, in Charleston, S.C. Publisher. After serving in World War I, Manigault joined his family's business, the Evening Post Publishing Company, by starting in the business department of the *Evening Post* newspaper in Charleston, S.C. He worked as a reporter, copy editor, assistant to the editor, and associate to the editor; he then served as secretary and treasurer of the publishing company before becoming president in 1945. Under his leadership Evening Post Publishing, which had already acquired the *Charleston News and Courier* in 1926, grew to include a variety of newspapers: the *Buenos Aires Herald* (Argentina), the *Aiken Standard* (South Carolina), the *Cambridge Banner* (Maryland), and the *Waynesboro News-Virginian;* it also purchased television stations in El Paso, Texas, Pueblo-Colorado Springs, Colorado, Boise, Idaho, and a cable television company in Aiken. Manigault served as the company's chairman of the board from 1959 until his death. Obituaries and other sources: *Chicago Tribune*, May 29, 1983.

*   *   *

MANLEY, Lawrence (Gordon)   1949-

PERSONAL: Born June 9, 1949, in Lebanon, N.H.; son of Gordon (a technician) and Geraldine (Mariotte) Manley; married Ruth Handlin (a scholar), June 11, 1977; children: Jonathan Alfred. *Education:* Dartmouth College, A.B., 1971; Harvard University, A.M., 1973, Ph.D., 1977. *Office:* Department of English, Yale University, New Haven, Conn. 06520.

CAREER: Yale University, New Haven, Conn., assistant professor, 1976-81, associate professor of English, 1981—. Assistant director of studies at Paul Mellon Centre for Studies in British Art, 1981-82. *Awards, honors:* Rene Wellek Prize from American Comparative Literature Association, 1980, for *Convention, 1500-1750;* fellowship from American Council of Learned Societies, 1980.

WRITINGS: Convention, 1500-1750 (nonfiction), Harvard University Press, 1980.

WORK IN PROGRESS: Urban Vision in the Renaïssance; London in the Age of Shakespeare.

SIDELIGHTS: In *Convention, 1500-1750*, Manley surveys historical distinctions made between Nature and Convention, outlining the approaches of Dryden, Spenser, Hobbes, More, Erasmus, Aristotle, Plato, and others to the concepts. "Manley," noted *Times Literary Supplement* reviewer A. D. Nuttall, "argues that the classical conception of a universal, unchanging Nature answered by an almost equally stable world of Convention was gradually replaced, first by a sense of Convention as a historically developing thing and at last by a sense that Nature itself may be fluid."

Michael McCanles, in a *Criticism* review, termed the book "a masterful synthesis of dialectical thesis and widely diverse historical material." Nuttall concurred, judging Manley's work a "masterly study."

BIOGRAPHICAL/CRITICAL SOURCES: Times Literary Supplement, February 13, 1981; *Criticism*, winter, 1981.

*   *   *

MANN, Abby   1927-

PERSONAL: Birth-given name Abraham Goodman; born December 1, 1927, in Philadelphia, Pa.; son of Ben (a jeweler); married Harriet Carr (divorced). *Education:* Attended Temple University and New York University. *Residence:* Beverly Hills, Calif. *Office:* c/o Columbia Pictures Corp., 711 Fifth Ave., New York, N.Y. 10022.

CAREER: Writer and director of motion pictures. Executive producer of motion pictures, including "The Schmid Case" and "After the Fall," both 1969; executive producer of television series, including "Medical Story," 1975-76; executive producer and director of television films, including "King," 1977. *Military service:* U.S. Army, served in World War II. *Awards, honors:* Academy Award for best screenplay from Academy of Motion Picture Arts and Sciences and Writers Guild nomination from Writers Guild of America, both 1961, both for "Judgment at Nuremburg"; Academy Award nomination for best screenplay and Writers Guild nomination, both 1965, both for "Ship of Fools"; co-winner of award from New York Film Critics Association, 1965, for "Ship of Fools"; nominated for more than twenty awards for television films, including "King" and "Skag"; honorary doctorate from Columbia University.

WRITINGS—Published screenplays: *Judgment at Nuremberg* (United Artists, 1961; adapted from own television screenplay [also see below]), Cassell, 1961; *A Child Is Waiting* (United Artists, 1963; adapted from own television screenplay [also see below]), Popular Library, 1963; *Ship of Fools* (Columbia, 1965; adapted from the novel by Katherine Anne Porter), Pressbook, 1965.

Unpublished screenplays: "The Condemned of Altona" (adapted from the play by Jean Paul Sartre), Twentieth Century-Fox,

1963; "Andersonville" (adapted from the novel by MacKinlay Kantor), Columbia Pictures, 1966; "The Detective" (adapted from the novel by Roderick Thorp), Twentieth Century-Fox, 1968; "The Schmid Case," National General, 1969; "After the Fall" (adapted from the play by Arthur Miller), Paramount, 1969; "The Back Room" (adapted from the novel *Justice in the Back Room* by Selwyn Robb), Universal, 1969; "The Marcus-Nelson Murders," Universal, 1973; (with Ernst Tidyman) "Report to the Commissioner" (adapted from the novel by James Mill), United Artists, 1975; (adaptor) "The Children of Sanchez," Lone Star International, 1978. Also author of "What Are We Going to Do Without Skipper?" (adapted from the novel *The Tucson Murders* by John Gilmore), National General Pictures; and "Light in August" (adapted from the novel by William Faulkner).

Television screenplays: "A Child Is Waiting" (also see above), first broadcast by Studio One-TV, 1957; "Judgment at Nuremberg" (also see above), first broadcast by Columbia Broadcasting System (CBS-TV), April 16, 1959; "The Marcus-Nelson Murders" (also see above), first broadcast by Universal MCA-TV in 1973; "King," first broadcast by National Broadcasting Co. (NBC-TV), February 12, 1977.

Novels: *Judgment at Nuremberg* (adapted from own screenplay [also see above]), New American Library, 1961; *Tuesdays and Thursdays*, Doubleday, 1978; *Massacre at Wounded Knee*, Zebra, 1979.

Also author of plays, including "Just Around the Corner" (musical), (with Herbert Cobey) "Sweet Lorraine," "Exodus," (with Cobey) "The Happiest Days" (musical), and "Freud Has a Word for It" (musical).

Also author of scripts for television series, including "Kojak" (adapted from own television screenplay "The Marcus-Nelson Murders" [also see above]), "Skag," "Medical Story," "Studio One," "Alcoa Theatre," "Robert Montgomery Theatre," and "Playhouse 90."

SIDELIGHTS: Abby Mann first gained fame as a television writer, but in 1961 turned to motion pictures with an adaptation of his own television screenplay "Judgment at Nuremberg." The 1961 film was directed by Stanley Kramer, and included Spencer Tracy, Burt Lancaster, Richard Widmark, Maximilian Schell, Montgomery Clift, Judy Garland, and Marlene Dietrich in its all-star cast.

Mann's screenplay chronicles the post-war trial of four German judges accused of sentencing innocent people to concentration camps or death during World War II. Three of the four defendants plead not guilty, but the fourth—Ernst Janning, a renowned scholar and humanitarian before the war—refuses to enter a plea for himself. The trial then centers on the question of Janning's guilt. Halfway through the movie, the prosecution shows actual documentary films taken in the German death camps on the day of liberation. Even these films do not induce Janning to confess; it is not until he hears the moving testimony of a young woman he had falsely convicted of sexual intimacy with a Jew that he admits his guilt.

The plot becomes more complex before the end of the film. The guilt of all the defendants has been established when the Russians suddenly invade Berlin, and Germany becomes an important ally of Western Europe in the emerging Cold War. Consequently, the Nuremberg prosecutor and judge (both Americans) are instructed to "go easy" on the German defendants. The two refuse to compromise their principles, however, and eventually all four defendants are sentenced to life

in prison. But as the 1961 film ends, a chilling epilogue appears on the screen: "On 14 July, 1949, judgment was rendered in the last of the second Nuremberg trials. Of ninety-nine sentenced to prison terms, not one is still serving his sentence."

Reviewers disagreed on the merits of "Judgment at Nuremberg." *Saturday Review* critic Hollis Alpert called it an "entirely absorbing story." Brendan Gill agreed with Alpert in the *New Yorker,* describing it as both "bold and absorbing." And Jason Epstein wrote in *Commentary* that "'Judgment at Nuremberg' is an astonishingly intelligent film which succeeds in raising . . . some of the darkest questions of this dark age." But other critics objected that the film falls short by asking serious questions without providing adequate answers. Harris Dienstfrey charged in *Commentary* that "the film confronts the most difficult moral problems and pretends to meet them head on." "Questions of German responsibility for Nazi action, of Allied legal right to try a conquered nation, of individual guilt in a military state—these worrisome and important matters are all flirted with," Stanley Kauffman agreed in the *New Republic.*

Despite some adverse criticism, Mann received an Academy Award for his "Nuremberg" script. He and Kramer then followed their film success with a second collaboration, a motion picture version of "A Child Is Waiting," again adapted from an Abby Mann television screenplay. The story takes place in an institution for retarded children, and much of the film was shot on location at the Pacific State Hospital in Pamona, California. Mann demanded this sort of authenticity in the film, and according to *Time:* "When Paramount Pictures insisted on using Hollywood kid actors instead of retarded children themselves, Mann emptied his bank account to buy back the option to the script. He wanted real retarded children to show how close to normal they are, or seem." United Artists produced the film.

About the making of "The Condemned of Altona" (another Mann screenplay), *Time* related this story: Displeased with director Vittorio De Sica's film version of his screenplay, Mann "told De Sica to change the film or drop the name of Abby Mann from the screen credits." De Sica complied. *Time* wrote, "Last week, improbable as it may seem, De Sica completed his second week of all-night-every-night revision of the film, while Abby Mann sat on a stool beside him."

Mann was again nominated for an Academy Award in 1965, this time for his adaptation of Katherine Anne Porter's "A Ship of Fools." In 1969 he broke into producing with "The Schmid Case" and "After the Fall," and in 1977 he both produced and directed the television screenplay "King," a project he had begun researching some ten years before.

"King" is a "docudrama" biography of Dr. Martin Luther King, Jr., the black civil rights leader assassinated in 1968. In his drive for authenticity in the film, Mann included newsreels of King's activities, and photographed some scenes in black and white to look like news photos. He also arranged for some of King's most intimate colleagues (including Julian Bond and Ramsey Clark) to make cameo appearances as themselves.

The realistic effects in "King" spurred controversey among critics who thought Mann had blurred the documentary aspects and the dramatic aspects of a docudrama. "It isn't clear where docu ends and drama begins," a *National Review* critic complained. And *Newsweek* similarly objected that "'King' achieves a verisimilitude that often leaves the viewer uncertain of the line between reality and drama." Other reviewers felt that

Mann had shaped the facts to serve his own point of view. Peter Sourian wrote in the *Nation* that the white "barbarism" in the film contrasted with the civilized acts of the blacks until, "if we wished to maintain the pretense of being civilized, we could not help but align ourselves with those blacks." *National Review* agreed: "Mann, like King himself, assumes that everybody, deep in his heart, *agreed* with King, and that the only problem was one of forcing people to face their consciences."

CA INTERVIEW

CA interviewed Abby Mann at his home in Beverly Hills, California, December 5, 1980.

CA: Why do you write? What motivates you?

MANN: I write to change the world. I've never done anything unless I thought I could change the world. Sometimes I do things well, sometimes I do things indifferently, sometimes I don't even do them that well; but, I've always, every time I've been out, I've always wanted to change the world. That's what turns me on. And sometimes I have, I'll tell you immodestly, changed the world. When I think of the breadth of the subjects that I've covered, everything, just to go over the subject matter, it's very broad.

In "Judgment at Nuremberg" I took on the Nuremburg trials, and that in a way was helpful (at least President Kennedy told me that) in extending the statute of limitations in war crimes. In "A Child Is Waiting" I think I was the first one to write about mental retardation. And "The Detective," when it first came out, was one of the first looks at police corruption.

In "The Marcus-Nelson Murders" we were able to get an innocent boy off the electric chair. "King" really had a great deal to do with founding the House Committee on Assassinations; with the head of the police department in Memphis I took my tapes and played them for Andy Young and Coretta King, and then they went to Congress with it, so it's definitely responsible for that. In "Medical Story" I said that one out of every five operations was unneccessary and for profit. And in "Skag," of course, I tried to write about the working man and I also attacked unions for not doing anything about black lung disease and things like that, for which the unions are furious at me, as I knew they would be.

CA: How does recognition that you have changed the world come?

MANN: Well, if you do a good job, you get people angry. I think "King" is the best thing I ever did, and in the black community leaders attacked me because I said that King was the only one to come out against Vietnam at that time, and a lot of them thought that *they* should be more prominent. Fortunately, the King family and Andy Young were supportive.

CA: How do you set out to change the world? Does it start with the story or with the issue?

MANN: There are different things. Sometimes it starts with a thought—being angry at something. I think Bernie Malamud called me the "slasher." I was angry with the fact that every Nazi was released by Truman and because the very reasons we had fought the war seemed to have come to nothing. And as for retarded children, I really cared for them, those that I knew, and I just got to know them by caprice because I was

dating a girl who worked with them. I didn't even know what mental retardation was when I started.

Many times the inspiration will be a social thing; other times it will be a character, or a thought. My ex-wife went through terrible medical problems; doctors were telling her she could have a child, and actually she couldn't. They put her through operation after operation, needlessly, and that gave rise to "Medical Story." So I guess mainly it is things that disturb me that make me do what I do.

CA: And then do you set out to provide a remedy too, or is it enough simply to present the problem?

MANN: I think it's enough. I try to point to a remedy, but it's enough to say what's happened. You take a thing like the "Marcus-Nelson Murders" and socially, in a way, I think that what happened there is so revealing of our society. Here you had George Whitmore, which was the real kid's name. He was accused of killing the Wylie and Hoffard girls. Now, there was a great hue and cry to find that murderer. OK, they found the wrong kid, and then they knew he didn't do it. Eventually, everybody in the Manhattan district attorney's office knew, and the Manhattan police, the Brooklyn D.A.'s office, the Brooklyn police all knew. But here they were ready to let that kid go down the drain . . . and all of them knew he was innocent. And if you ask them, "Why would you do that?," they would look at you as though you were insane.

Now, being a student of Nazism, I don't know if it could ever happen anywhere but Germany, at least not the way that it happened there, but I see echoes of it everywhere, like in the Whitmore kind of thing. There are little murders going on all over, and I think it's getting worse.

CA: How would you characterize yourself as a writer?

MANN: Well, I hope that I'm compassionate about human beings who have no control over their lives, the injustice of our world, and I say that there are really no values.

CA: What made you want to be a writer?

MANN: That's the funniest thing of all. I was a very lonely kid in East Pittsburgh. We were a Jewish family in a town of a lot of Germans and Poles who hated Jews. At first I wanted to be an actor, and then I thought that was a foolish thing for anybody to be, so I started to write because I wanted to be with other people, and laugh and so forth. So I chose, without knowing it, the most lonely profession of all. That shows how life outwits you. That was why at first I had no grandiose ideas about changing the world; I got seduced into that later. I just wanted to get away from my dad's jewelry store and from Pittsburgh. I wanted a life where there would be a lot of laughter and gaiety. And I still haven't found it.

I always read and wrote plays, I had some stuff tried out in summer stock, and then I started to write for television. At that time there was a half-hour series called Cameo Theatre. You wrote a show and turned it in on speculation. I had a small agent, Blanch Gaines, who handled Rod Serling and Frank Gilray at that time.

CA: How do you work?

MANN: I work daily. These days I'm working every day. I'm under a couple of big deadlines and I'm disciplined enough that I work every day. I get up at about six in the morning and work until my two secretaries come at nine. I dictate to them, sometimes I type, but it's very stream of consciousness—no commas, you know.

CA: Don't you have days when you're just not in the mood?

MANN: I find at this particular point that mood is not so important. Music sometimes helps, but other than that, I just work. Now, sometimes it's good to do a draft and then put it away and then go on to something else and come back to it later. I find that's good psychologically because sometimes you get almost too emotionally involved with it and then it's the "forest-for-the-trees department."

CA: How do you feel about reviews?

MANN: Well, naturally, I like good ones, but the ones I remember are bad ones. The kind of reviews that are the best are the ones like: Dalton Trumbo calling me up after he saw the "Marcus-Nelson Murders" on a rerun just to say, "That was good." I said, "Let's talk," and he said, "No, I just wanted to tell you that, good-bye," and he hung up. That review meant far more to me than anything in print.

Or when Spencer Tracy wired me to say he told everybody that "Nuremberg" was his favorite film. Those kind of reviews are reviews that I'll always remember and cherish. Or the kind of review you get from ladies like the neighbor of my folks in Pittsburgh who had a retarded child. The neighbor said that another neighbor had come over and told her that she saw "A Child Is Waiting" and for the first time she was able to understand what the mother of the retarded daughter was going through. That's a kind of review I like to get. Or the review that is the look in the face of a kid that you got off of the electric chair, when he's first released. Those are the reviews that I'll always remember.

You know, art is fragile, and I don't know why people evade saying they want to change the world with their art. Things are fleeting, but if you change somebody's life, that's important, that lasts, that's something tangible.

CA: What do you see for the future of film?

MANN: Right now I think pictures are being made for the wrong reasons. They make a film because the star will do it, or they can get this director, or that producer can get this project. I feel there should be a *reason* for making a picture; it should say something. It's getting to be more of a writers' medium and I think it should be even more so. When you think of Fellini and Bergman, who I think are the two greatest directors today, they both started out as writers. I don't think actors are the best judges of what films should be made. I found "Apocalypse Now" to be a great film; it was a personal statement. He [director Francis Coppola] took chances, he did his homework. You should make films to make a statement, to do something people haven't seen before, or to pen up a new facet of life.

MEDIA ADAPTATIONS: "Judgment at Nuremberg" was adapted into a Broadway play by Ketti Frings, 1970; "King" was adapted into a novel under the same title by William Johnston and published by St. Martin's Press, 1970.

BIOGRAPHICAL/CRITICAL SOURCES: Saturday Review, December 2, 1961, January 26, 1963; *Senior Scholastic,* December 6, 1961, March 20, 1975; *New Republic,* December 11, 1961, January 26, 1963, March 8, 1975; *Commonweal,* December 15, 1961, February 1, 1963; *Time,* December 15, 1961, March 22, 1963, February 24, 1975, February 13, 1978; *New Yorker,* December 23, 1961, February 10, 1975; *Newsweek,* December 25, 1961, February 13, 1978, August 16, 1976; *Commentary,* January, 1962; *Nation,* January 6, 1962, March 11, 1978; *Christian Century,* March 14, 1962; *National Review,* March 31, 1978; *New Times,* May 29, 1978.*

—Sketch by Sketch by Susan M. Finley

—Interview by Judith Spiegelman

*   *   *

MANN, Arthur 1922-

PERSONAL: Born January 3, 1922, in Brooklyn, N.Y.; son of Karl and Mary (Koch) Finkelman; married Sylvia Blut, November 6, 1943; children: Carol Ruth, Emily Betsy. *Education:* Brooklyn College (now of the City University of New York), B.A. (summa cum laude), 1944; Harvard University, M.A., 1947, Ph.D., 1952. *Home:* 4919 South Woodlawn Ave., Chicago, Ill. 60615. *Office:* Department of History, University of Chicago, 1126 East 59th St., Chicago, Ill. 60637.

CAREER: Massachusetts Institute of Technology (MIT), Cambridge, Mass., 1948-55, began as instructor, became assistant professor; Smith College, Northampton, Mass., 1955-66, began as assistant professor, became professor; University of Chicago, Chicago, Ill., professor of American history, 1966—, Preston and Sterling Morton Professor of American History, 1971—. Visiting professor at Columbia University, 1956, at Salzburg Seminar in American Studies, 1958, at University of Massachusetts, 1960, at University of Michigan, 1961, at University of Wyoming, 1962, at Williams College, 1963, and at Harvard University, 1965.

Adviser for "American History" series of McGraw-Hill Films, 1967-73; educational collaborator for "Minorities" series of Coronet Instructional Films, 1969-73; consultant for six filmstrips on "Contemporary America" for Encyclopaedia Britannica Educational Corp., 1982. Co-adviser for Oral History Project of Holocaust Survivors at William E. Weiner Oral History Library, 1974-76. U.S. Department of State lecturer in Venezuela, 1970; U.S. Information Agency lecturer in Australia, Fiji, Indonesia, New Zealand, and Singapore, all 1974, in Portugal, Germany, Yugoslavia, and Romania, all 1976, and in Hong Kong and Japan, both 1979. Panelist for National Endowment for the Humanities, 1972; Fulbright-Hays senior scholar at University of Sydney, 1974. *Military service:* U.S. Army, 1943-46. *Member:* American History Association, American Studies Association, Organization of American Historians, Society of American Historians (fellow). *Awards, honors:* Grant from Social Science Research Council, 1959; fellow of American Council of Learned Societies, 1962-63; Alumni Award of Merit from Brooklyn College, 1968.

WRITINGS: Yankee Reformers in the Urban Age, Belknap Press of Harvard University, 1954, reprinted, Harper Torchbooks, 1966, new edition, University of Chicago Press, 1974; *La Guardia: A Fighter Against His Times, 1882-1933,* Lippincott, 1959, reprinted, University of Chicago Press, 1969; (editor) *The Progressive Era: Liberal Renaissance or Liberal Failure?,* Holt, 1963, 2nd edition published as *The Progressive Era: Major Issues of Interpretation,* Dryden, 1975; *La Guardia Comes to Power: 1933,* Lippincott, 1965, reprinted, University of Chicago Press, 1969, new edition, Greenwood Press, 1981; (compiler) *Immigrants in American Life: Selected Readings* (young adult), Houghton, 1968, revised edition, 1974; (with Neil Harris and Sam Bass Warner, Jr.) *History and the Role of the City in American Life,* Indiana Historical Society, 1972; *The One and the Many: Reflections on the American Identity,* University of Chicago Press, 1979.

Contributor: (And editor) *Growth and Achievement: Temple Israel, 1854-1954,* Riverside Press, 1954; John Higham, editor, *The Reconstruction of History,* Torchbooks, 1962; *Plunkitt of Tammany Hall,* Dutton, 1963; Daniel J. Boorstin, editor, *An American Primer,* University of Chicago Press, 1966, reprinted, Mentor, 1968; Charles U. Daly, editor, *The Quality of Inequality: Urban and Suburban Schools,* University of Chicago Press, 1968; Benjamin Park de Witt, *The Progressive Movement,* University of Washington Press, 1968; Walter J. Reum and Gerald C. Mattran, *Politics From the Inside Up,* Dutton, 1968; Richard Bushman and others, editors, *Uprooted Americans: Essays to Honor Oscar Handlin,* Little, Brown, 1979. Also contributor of articles and book reviews to popular magazines, newspapers, and scholarly journals, including *New York Times, Commentary, Christian Science Monitor, New Leader,* and *Antioch Review.*

Member of editorial board of *Ethnicity;* editorial consultant for *Social Service Review;* editor of "Documents in American History" series, University of Chicago Press; advisory editor in American history for University of Chicago Press, 1969—.

WORK IN PROGRESS: "Trying to see America in comparative context."

SIDELIGHTS: A professor of history at the University of Chicago, Arthur Mann has been exploring, for some thirty years, various aspects of the American past. His book *Growth and Achievement* made "a major contribution to the history of Jewish—and American—religious life," wrote Nathan Glazer in *Commentary.* American liberalism was the subject of Mann's next publication, *Yankee Reformers,* which C. Wright Mills in the *New York Times Book Review* judged "an excellent book in a plain-spoken style only possible to a historian who knows his period and his subject, and also what to do with historical detail in order to reveal its meaning for our own time." Mann's most recent book, *The One and the Many,* impressed Paul Czuchlewski in *America* as making "simple but wise distinctions" in "an important, historically informed contribution to the ongoing debate over American identity, pluralism and ethnicity."

But Mann is most widely known for his two-volume study of Fiorello H. La Guardia, New York City's ninety-ninth mayor. In the first installment, *La Guardia: A Fighter Against His Times,* the author relates the mayor's rise to power and recounts the climax of that ascent during the years of the Great Depression. As an objective historian, Mann attempted to capture the rich character and the political beliefs of a man who lived at a time when both politics and popular attitudes toward it were undergoing great changes. The historian was sustained by the memories of La Guardia's political cronies and by the often-biased documents left by the mayor. "Those old associates of the Mayor who encouraged Mr. Mann to undertake this study, and who helped him in it," Rexford G. Tugwell explained in his *New York Times Book Review* critique of *La Guardia,* "ought to feel well satisfied with the result. They have here something more than an account of the successive days and years of an extra-ordinary, public man. What has been given them is an analysis of one individual's political behavior which has the significance of a general conclusion about all such figures."

A major portion of Mann's book, then, is devoted to a reconstruction of La Guardia's complex personality, an endeavor that critics appreciated. The book's "author . . . is a little more infected with the La Guardia language and excitement," wrote J. D. Hicks in the *American Historical Review.* "Some of his passages might almost have come from La Guardia's own lips." And William German, writing in the *San Francisco Chronicle,* praised the historian's focus on the development of the mayor's character traits, stating: "Mann begins by building a solid foundation of his subject's personality. He never loses this important thread of personality even as he and La Guardia become entangled in the complicated forces of pre-Depression history."

Warmly received by many critics, *La Guardia: A Fighter Against His Times* "is . . . the best book ever written about La Guardia, and a sourcebook for anyone else who attempts the difficult task of doing a better one," noted Warren Moscow in a *Saturday Review* article. Concurring in his *Nation* review, F. J. Cook decided that "Mann has produced a book that has the breadth and scope of an outstanding biographical work."

Mann's second volume on the mayor, *La Guardia Comes to Power: 1933,* also received critical recognition. Oscar Handlin in his *Atlantic* review pronounced it "the best account of an urban election we have ever had." Writing in the *New York Times,* Samuel Kaplan called "the total effect . . . enthralling." J. J. Huthmacher added in the *American Historical Review* that "Mann writes with clarity, cogency, good humor, and a relaxed manner that charms while it convinces the reader. . . . The author's facility in analyzing and using election and census data, moreover, should pass muster with even the most demanding behaviorist."

Mann told *CA:* "The historian is obliged to recreate the dead as they probably were and to present them to the living in ways that the living will understand. Both tasks require one to write in the living language. That is why I am pleased when readers find my work readable. History is one of the oldest forms of literature in Western civilization. That it should also be true to the evidence goes without saying."

BIOGRAPHICAL/CRITICAL SOURCES: New York Times Book Review, October 17, 1954, November 15, 1959, February 15, 1970; *Commentary,* February, 1955; *New Yorker,* November 14, 1959; *Saturday Review,* November 14, 1959; *Christian Science Monitor,* November 17, 1959, November 11, 1965; *Springfield Republican,* November 22, 1959; *San Francisco Chronicle,* November 29, 1959; *New York Herald Tribune,* January 3, 1960; *Nation,* February 13, 1960; *Political Science Quarterly,* June, 1960, September, 1966; *American Historical Review,* July, 1960, April, 1966, October, 1973; *American Academy of Political and Social Science Annals,* July, 1960, March, 1966; *Atlantic,* September, 1965; *Book Week,* October 3, 1965; *New York Times,* November 2, 1965; *Journal of American History,* March, 1966, June, 1980; *Political Science Review,* September, 1966; *Washington Monthly,* September, 1979; *Times Literary Supplement,* February 15, 1980; *America,* March 1, 1980; *Christian Century,* May 12, 1980; *History: Reviews of New Books,* September, 1980; *Reviews in American History,* December, 1980; *Journal of Politics,* May, 1981.

*   *   *

MANN, William S(omervell) 1924-

PERSONAL: Born February 14, 1924; son of Gerald and Joyce Mann; married Erika Charlotte Emilie Sohler in 1948; children:

Domenique, Elizabeth, Madeleine, Mirabelle. *Education:* Attended Winchester College; received B.A. and Mus.B. from Magdalene College, Cambridge. *Home:* 135 Cotherham Park Rd., London S.W.20, England.

CAREER: London Times, London, England, assistant music critic, 1948-60. *Member:* Critics Circle (president, 1963-64).

WRITINGS: Introduction to the Music of J. S. Bach, D. Dobson, 1950; (editor with Louis Leopold Biancolli) *The Analytical Concert Guide: English Edition,* Cassell, 1957; *Richard Strauss: A Critical Study of the Opera,* Cassell, 1964, Oxford University Press (New York), 1966; (translator and author of introduction) Richard Wagner, *Der Ring des Nibelungen,* Friends of Covent Garden, 1964; *The Operas of Mozart,* Oxford University Press, 1977; *Music in Time,* Oxford University Press, 1982. Also author of *Let's Fake an Opera,* with Franz Reizenstein, 1958.*

* * *

MANNING, Beverley J(ane)   1942-

PERSONAL: Born September 20, 1942, in Ticonderoga, N.Y.; daughter of Edward Richard (a steelworker) and Flora (Wallace) Manning. *Education:* State University of New York at Albany, B.A., 1964, M.L.S., 1966. *Politics:* Democrat. *Religion:* Episcopalian. *Home:* 37 Indian Hill Rd., Newington, Conn. 06111. *Office:* Library, University of Connecticut at Hartford, Greater Hartford Campus, West Hartford, Conn. 06117.

CAREER: Elementary school librarian in Wilton, N.Y., 1965-67; high school librarian in Carmel, N.Y., 1967-68; University of Connecticut at Hartford, West Hartford, university librarian, 1968—. *Member:* American Library Association, Connecticut Library Association, Capitol Region Library Council.

WRITINGS: Index to American Women Speakers, 1828-1978, Scarecrow, 1980.

WORK IN PROGRESS: A supplement to *Index to American Women Speakers,* publication expected in 1985; research on women speakers from other countries.

SIDELIGHTS: Beverley Manning told *CA:* "I am doing research in the field of women's speeches, because I feel that it has been a neglected area of women's studies, and of public speaking. Very few women have been included in speech anthologies. Collections of individual women have just begun to be published, and the proceedings of meetings have been lost in obscurity until the last decade. My primary reason for any kind of research is personal satisfaction and excitement."

* * *

MARGOLIS, Julius   1920-

BRIEF ENTRY: Born September 26, 1920, in New York, N.Y. American economist, educator, and author. Margolis taught economics at Tufts College, University of Chicago, and Stanford University. He was a member of the business administration faculty at University of California, Berkeley, from 1954 to 1964 and a professor at University of Pennsylvania from 1969 to 1976. In 1976 he became a professor of economics at University of California, Irvine. Margolis co-authored *Northern California's Water Industry: The Comparative Efficiency of Public Enterprise in Developing a Scarce Natural Resource* (Johns Hopkins Press, 1966). He edited *The Public Economy of Urban Communities* (Resources for the Future, 1965) and *The Analysis of Public Output* (National Bureau of Economic

Research, 1970). Margolis also co-edited *Public Expenditures and Policy Analysis* (Markham, 1970). *Address:* 2337-D, Avenue Sevilla, Laguna Hills, Calif. 92653; and Department of Social Sciences, University of California, Irvine, Calif. 92717. *Biographical/critical sources: Times Literary Supplement,* June 2, 1972; *Who's Who in America,* 42nd edition, Marquis, 1982.

* * *

MARINO, Joseph D.   1912(?)-1983

OBITUARY NOTICE: Born c. 1912; died after a long illness, April 16, 1983, in Clearwater, Fla. Photographic journalist. Marino, who worked for the *Chicago Daily News* for more than fifty years, began as a copy boy when he was fifteen years old. He worked his way up to the position of news photographer and served the newspaper in that capacity until 1977, one year before it went out of business. Marino was the recipient of several Chicago-area prizes for photography. Obituaries and other sources: *Chicago Tribune,* April 19, 1983.

* * *

MARKEVITCH, Igor   1912-1983

OBITUARY NOTICE: Born July 27, 1912, in Kiev, Russia (now U.S.S.R.); died of a heart attack, March 7, 1983, in Antibes, France. Composer, conductor, educator, and author. A musical prodigy who fled to Switzerland with his parents at the outbreak of the Russian Revolution in 1917, Markevitch composed his first symphony when he was eleven years old. A few years later he went to Paris to study composition and piano. By seventeen he had become a protege of Serge Diaghilev, director of the Russian Ballet; at eighteen he made his conducting debut with the Concertgebouw Orchestra in Amsterdam. Esteemed for his professionalism and control, Markevitch was known for his interpretation of Russian, French, and Spanish music. He conducted the Montreal Symphony Orchestra, the Boston Symphony Orchestra, and other leading orchestras in Europe and the Americas, and he taught in Salzburg, Mexico, and at the Moscow Conservatoire. Markevitch's musical compositions include a piano concerto; a cantata, "The Flight of Icarus," with words by Jean Cocteau; and a ballet, "Paradise Lost." In addition to critical essays, his writings include *Organ Point* and *Made in Italy.* Obituaries and other sources: *Who's Who in the World,* 4th edition, Marquis, 1978; *Chicago Tribune,* March 7, 1983; *Los Angeles Times,* March 8, 1983; *London Times,* March 8, 1983; *Washington Post,* May 10, 1983; *Time,* March 21, 1983.

* * *

MARRINER, Ernest (Cummings)   1891-1983

OBITUARY NOTICE—See index for *CA* sketch: Born October 16, 1891, in Bridgton, Me.; died February 8, 1983. Educator and author. Marriner had been associated with Colby College since 1923. He served as the first dean of men and as the first dean of faculty. Since 1957 he acted as the college's historian, producing such works as *The History of Colby College.* His other books include *Man of Mayflower Hill* and *Remembered Maine.* Obituaries and other sources: *New York Times,* February 10, 1983.

* * *

MARSHALL, (Sarah) Catherine (Wood)   1914-1983
(Catherine LeSourd)

OBITUARY NOTICE—See index for *CA* sketch: Born September 27, 1914, in Johnson City, Tenn.; died of heart failure, March 18, 1983, in Boynton Beach, Fla. Author of inspirational books. Marshall's books have sold over eighteen million copies in thirty-five languages. Her most popular books were inspired by her marriage to Peter Marshall, chaplain of the U.S. Senate from 1947 to 1949. She edited a collection of his sermons titled *Mr. Jones, Meet the Master,* and she wrote his biography, *A Man Called Peter,* two years after his death in 1949. *The Best of Peter Marshall* was scheduled to be printed sometime in 1983. Marshall married Leonard Earle LeSourd, executive editor of *Guideposts,* in 1959. She became an editor of the magazine in 1961, and together Marshall and LeSourd established Chosen Books, a publisher of inspirational literature. Marshall's other books include *Christy, God Loves You, The Unwilling Heart, Beyond Ourselves,* and the posthumously published *Watershed.* Obituaries and other sources: *Current Biography,* Wilson, 1955, May, 1983; Catherine Marshall, *Meeting God at Every Turn* (autobiography), Chosen Books, 1981; *New York Times,* March 19, 1983; *Los Angeles Times,* March 19, 1983; *Washington Post,* March 20, 1983; *Chicago Tribune,* March 20, 1983; *Newsweek,* March 28, 1983; *AB Bookman's Weekly,* April 11, 1983; *Publishers Weekly,* April 15, 1983; *School Library Journal,* May, 1983.

* * *

MARSHALL, John Ross 1912-

PERSONAL: Born March 5, 1912, in Wellington, New Zealand; son of Allan and Florence May (Ross) Marshall; married Margaret Livingston (a registered nurse), July 29, 1944; children: John Livingston, Allan Ross, Margaret Anne, Elizabeth Jean (Mrs. Neil Douglas Murley). *Education:* University of New Zealand, LL.M., 1935, B.A., 1947. *Religion:* Presbyterian. *Home:* 22 Fitzroy St., Wellington, New Zealand. *Agent:* Ray Richards, 49 Aberdeen Rd., Milford, Auckland, New Zealand. *Office:* Buddle Findlay, P.O. Box 233, Wellington, New Zealand.

CAREER: Admitted barrister and solicitor of Supreme Court of New Zealand, 1936, named honorary bencher of Gray's Inn, 1973; Parliament, Wellington, New Zealand, National Party member for Mount Victoria, 1946-54, for Karori, 1954-75, minister assistant to prime minister and minister of State Advances Corp., Public Trust Office, and Census and Statistics, 1949-54, minister of health, 1951-54, minister of information and publicity, 1951-57, attorney-general and minister of justice, 1954-57, deputy leader of the opposition, 1957-60, minister of customs, 1960-62, minister of industries and commerce, 1960-69, minister of overseas trade and deputy prime minister, 1960-72, attorney-general, 1969-71, minister of labor and immigration, 1969-72, prime minister of New Zealand, 1972, leader of the opposition, 1973-74; Buddle Findlay (solicitors), Wellington, consultant partner, 1974—. Member of Privy Council, 1966. New Zealand representative to Colombo Plan Conference, 1953, Commonwealth Conference, 1962, Trade Ministries Conference, 1963, 1966, General Agreement of Tariffs and Trade Conference, 1961, 1963, 1966, Economic Commission for Asia and the Far East Conference (ECAFE), 1962, 1964, 1965 (chairman, 1966, 1968, 1970), the United Nations, 1970, and International Labor Organization Conference, 1971; chairman of National Development Conference, 1968-69, National Development Council, 1969-72, New Zealand Commission for Expo 70, and Committee of Inquiry on Registration of Teachers, 1976-77; member of advisory council of World Peace Through Law, 1974—. Chairman of National Bank of New Zealand Ltd., Phillips Electrical Industries of

New Zealand Ltd., Contractors Bonding and Discount Corp. Ltd., Norwich Winterthur Insurance (New Zealand) Ltd., and DRG (New Zealand) Ltd.; member of board of directors of Hallenstein Brothers Ltd. and Norwich Union Life Insurance Society; past member of board of directors of Fletcher Holdings Ltd. *Military service:* New Zealand Army, Infantry, 1940-46; served in Italy and the Pacific; became major.

MEMBER: New Zealand Law Society, United Bible Societies (world vice-president), British Sailors Society (president), Wellington Club, United Services Officers Club. *Awards, honors:* Companion of Honour, 1973; Knight Grand Cross of Order of the British Empire, 1974; LL.D. from Victoria University of Wellington, 1974.

WRITINGS: The Law of Water Courses, Calchment Boards Association, 1955; (editor) *Reform of Parliament,* Institute of Public Administration, 1978; *The Adventures of Dr. Duffer* (juvenile), Collins, 1978; *Dr. Duffer and the Lost City* (juvenile), Collins, 1979; *Dr. Duffer and the Treasure Hunt* (juvenile), Collins, 1980; *Dr. Duffer's Outback Adventures* (juvenile), Collins, 1981; *Memoirs,* Volume 1, Collins, 1983. Contributor to law and political science journals.

WORK IN PROGRESS: Another volume of memoirs; more Dr. Duffer books.

SIDELIGHTS: Sir John told *CA:* "When I was a university student in the 1930's, I wrote many stories for the Children's Hour on the National Radio Station and read them to an unseen and unnumbered audience. Then I put the manuscripts away in a cupboard, where they gathered dust until twenty years later, when they were brought out and read to my own children. They liked them, but in a few years, grew out of them. The stories were again put away, out of sight and out of mind, for another twenty years. Then my daughter Elizabeth, now a teacher, recalled the stories, located them, and read them to her class of six year olds. The children loved them and asked for more. Other teachers read the stories to their classes. They loved them, too, and the teachers told me that the tales should be published.

"I revised the stories and brought them up to date. My first book was a best-seller, and my publisher, Collins, asked for a new book each year. After the original tales were all published I wrote new stories with the same characters: Dr. Duffer, the great scientist and explorer; Hiccup, the Polynesian boy; Peter, the parrot with the very big brain; Patches, the fox terrier. Aeronaut, the machine invented by Dr. Duffer, is also in each; it flies through the air, runs on land, sails on the sea, and dives under the sea as required on the group's voyages of discovery. I have written four Dr. Duffer books and will be writing more, but at the moment I am concentrating on writing my memoirs. The children's books are adventure stories but also pass on much information about the people, flora, fauna, and geography of the countries to which Dr. Duffer and his friends travel."

AVOCATIONAL INTERESTS: Golf, fishing, breeding Connemara ponies.

* * *

MARSHALL, T(homas) H(umphrey) 1893-1981

PERSONAL: Born December 19, 1893, in London, England; died November 29, 1981, in Cambridge, England; son of William C. (an architect) and Margaret (Lloyd) Marshall; married Marjorie Tomson, 1925 (died, 1931); married Nadine Hambourg, 1934; children: Mark. *Education:* Trinity College, Cambridge, M.A.

CAREER: Civilian prisoner of war in Germany, 1914-18; Cambridge University, Cambridge, England, fellow of Trinity College, 1919-25; London School of Economics and Political Science, London, England, lecturer, 1925-30, reader in sociology, 1930-39; British Foreign Office, London, head of German section and deputy director of research department, 1939-44; London School of Economics and Political Science, head of social science department, 1944-50, Martin White Professor of Sociology, 1954-56, professor emeritus, 1956-81. Director of social science department, UNESCO, 1956-60; writer and researcher, 1960-81. Member of Lord Chancellor's Committee on Practice and Procedure of the Supreme Court, 1947-53; educational adviser in British Zone of Germany, 1949-50; member of United Kingdom Committee for UNESCO and United Kingdom delegate to the organization's General Conference, 1952. *Awards, honors:* Companion of Order of St. Michael and St. George, 1947; D.Sc. from University of Southampton, 1969; D.Litt. from University of Leicester, 1970; D.Univ. from University of York, 1971.

WRITINGS: (Editor of revision) George Townsend Warner, *Landmarks in English Industrial History,* Blackie & Son, 1924; *James Watt, 1736-1819,* Small, Maynard & Co., 1925; *The Ethical Factor in Economic Thought,* Ethical Union, 1935; (editor) *Class Conflict and Social Stratification,* Le Play, 1938; (editor) *The Population Problem,* 1938; (with Charlotte Leubuscher) *Training for Social Work,* Oxford University Press, 1946; *Citizenship and Social Class, and Other Essays,* Cambridge University Press, 1950; *Sociology at the Crossroads, and Other Essays,* Heinemann, 1963, published in the United States as *Class, Citizenship, and Social Development: Essays,* Doubleday, 1964; *Social Policy,* Hutchinson, 1965, revised edition published as *Social Policy in the Twentieth Century,* 1967, 4th edition, 1975; (with J. R. Edwards and Eleanor Leigh) *Social Patterns in Birmingham, 1966: A Reference Manual,* Research Publications Services, 1970; *The Right to Welfare, and Other Essays,* Heinemann, 1981. Contributor to economic, history, and sociology journals.

OBITUARIES: London Times, December 3, 1981.*

* * *

MARSHBURN, Joseph Hancock 1890-1975

PERSONAL: Born January 11, 1890, in Josselyn, Ga.; died April 13, 1975; son of M. Thomas and Alice Verina (Hendricks) Marshburn; children: Joseph Hancock. *Education:* University of Georgia, A.B., 1911, A.M., 1912; Harvard University, A.M., 1919. *Politics:* Democrat. *Religion:* Episcopalian.

CAREER: University of Georgia, Athens, instructor in English, 1912-14; Georgia Military College, head of English department, 1914-16, vice-president of college, 1916-17, president, 1917-20; University of Oklahoma, Norman, professor of English, 1920-75, also chairman of department. Reader at Folger Shakespeare Library, 1936, and British Museum, 1948-49; David Ross Boyd Professor of English Literature, 1949. *Member:* American Association of University Professors, Royal Society of Literature, Modern Language Association of America, Lions, Masons, Sigma Chi, Phi Beta Kappa.

WRITINGS: Murder and Witchcraft in England, 1550-1640, as Recounted in Pamphlets, Ballads, Broadsides, and Plays, University of Oklahoma Press, 1972; (editor with Alan R. Velie) *Blood and Knavery: A Collection of English Renaissance*

Pamphlets and Ballads of Crime and Sin, Fairleigh Dickinson University Press, 1973.*

* * *

MARS-JONES, Adam 1954-

PERSONAL: Born October 26, 1954, in London, England; son of William Lloyd (a judge) and Sheila (an attorney; maiden name, Cobon) Mars-Jones. *Education:* Cambridge University, B.A., 1976, M.A., 1978. *Home:* 3 Gray's Inn Square, London WC1R 5AH, England. *Agent:* Aubrey Davis, Hughes Massie Ltd., 31 Southampton Row, London WC1, England.

CAREER: Writer. *Awards, honors:* Benjamin C. Moomaw Prize for Oratory from University of Virginia; Somerset Maugham Award, 1982, for *Lantern Lecture.*

WRITINGS: Fabrications (stories; contains "Hoosh-Mi" and "Bathpool Park"), Knopf, 1981 (published in England as *Lantern Lecture* [contains "Lantern Lecture," "Hoosh-Mi," and "Bathpool Park"], Faber, 1981).

SIDELIGHTS: Adams Mars-Jones's *Fabrications* contains two novella-length satirical stories. "Hoosh-Mi" is an irreverent glimpse into the life of the queen of England, here named Elizabeth Regina. The monarch dies of rabies transmitted to her by an affectionate dog. The pet, in turn, had been infected by a transcontinental bat of American origin. Elizabeth's final days are marked by behavior that doesn't seem to stretch beyond the boundaries of royal decorum until she takes a disoriented romp through downtown London shortly before her death.

"Bathpool Park," a chronicle of the trial of burglar Donald Nielson, "The Black Panther," focuses on the British system of justice. Mars-Jones examines the physical and conceptual nature of the courtroom, detailing the roles of judge, policemen, and witnesses, and at the same time speculates on Neilson's motivation for kidnapping and his reaction to the accidental death of his hostage.

Reviewers Patricia C. Mager of the *Washington Post Book World* and Galen Strawson of the *Times Literary Supplement* were impressed by Mars-Jones's first effort. Mager commented, "In each of the two stories in this self-conscious, clever volume the role dictated by society becomes 'the person,'" and when the individual cast in the role does not quite fit the prescribed pattern trouble results." Mager added, Mars-Jones "has in good measure the qualities that one attributes to a brilliant young writer." Strawson, in a *Times Literary Supplement* review of *Lantern Lecture,* the English edition, which contains a title story in addition to "Hoosh-Mi" and "Bathpool Park," noted that "there is something punk, in the modern sense of the word, about this extremely clever and original collection of stories. It's to do with the emotionally deadpanned style of delivery, the technical impassivity of the allusive, *cloisonne* construction."

BIOGRAPHICAL/CRITICAL SOURCES: Times Literary Supplement, October 9, 1981; *Washington Post Book World,* November 1, 1981; *Los Angeles Times Book Review,* November 1, 1981; *London Times,* February 28, 1983.

* * *

MARTIN, John Hanbury 1892-1983

OBITUARY NOTICE: Born April 4, 1892, in Worcestershire, England; died February 3, 1983, in Menton, France. Politician and author. Best known as the Labour party member of Parliament for Central Southwark from 1939 to 1948, Martin gradually moved to the right wing of the party and in 1951 informed Labour leader Clement Attlee that he could not back a Labour government that included Ernest Bevin and Harold Wilson. Noted for his sensitivity to the plight of the underprivileged, Martin helped found and direct the Southwark Housing Association, beginning in 1930. He also wrote *Corner of England,* which documented post World War I poverty in Southwark. Though not a pacifist, Martin believed in the cause of lasting peace, and he addressed the difficulties that plague peace movements in his 1937 book *Peace Adventure.* Obituaries and other sources: *Who Was Who Among English and European Authors, 1931-1949,* Gale, 1978; *Who's Who,* 134th edition, St. Martin's, 1982; *London Times,* February 23, 1983.

* * *

MARTIN, Mario, Jr.
  See MONTELEONE, Thomas F.

* * *

MASON, Ted
  See MASON, Theodore C(harles)

* * *

MASON, Theodore C(harles)   1921-
  (Ted Mason)

PERSONAL: Surname originally Bowman; name legally changed; born July 27, 1921, in Berkeley, Calif.; son of Bayard B. (an engineer) and Lilah (Dale) Bowman; married Betty Jane Baker, March 25, 1945 (divorced, c.1960); married Rita Jeannette Bolduc, April 28, 1978; children: (first marriage) Shelley Lynn. *Education:* University of Southern California, A.B., 1949; graduate study at Sacramento State College, 1955-56. *Home and office:* 38253 Via Del Largo, Murrieta Hot Springs, Calif. 92362.

CAREER: Los Angeles Times, Los Angeles, Calif., proofreader, 1950-51; *Arizona Republic,* Phoenix, reporter, 1951-52; *Arizona Free Press,* Phoenix, reporter, editor, and columnist, 1952-53; Advertising Counselors of Arizona, Phoenix, copywriter, 1953, television director, 1954; Louis Landau Advertising, Sacramento, Calif., copy chief and director of radio and television advertising, 1954-58; Batten, Barton, Durstine & Osborn (advertising agency), San Francisco, Calif., copywriter, 1958-59; Ramsey Advertising, Los Angeles, copy chief, 1959-66, vice-president and creative director, 1966-69; freelance technical and industrial writer in Redondo Beach and Murrieta Hot Springs, Calif., 1969—. Consultant in corporate communications to Borg-Warner Corp., Chicago, Ill., and Los Angeles, 1969—. *Military service:* U.S. Navy, 1939-45; served in Pacific theater; became radioman first class; received Silver Star, Bronze Star, Philippine Liberation Medal, Philippine Republic Presidential Unit Citation. *Member:* American Battleship Association, U.S. Naval Institute, Society of Wireless Pioneers, Veterans of Foreign Wars, Pearl Harbor Survivors Association, Old Timers Communicators of Southern California, U.S.S. *California* Reunion Association, U.S.S. *Houston* Association, Phi Kappa Phi. *Awards, honors:* Ancient Order of the Deep, 1943; Order of the Golden Dragon, 1943; Golden Shellback Award, 1944; *Battleship Sailor* was named a notable naval book of 1982 by U.S. Naval Institute.

WRITINGS: Applied Engineered Cementing, privately printed, 1969; *Applied Engineered Stimulation,* privately printed, 1970; (contributor) Paul Stillwell, editor, *Air Raid: Pearl Harbor!; Recollections of a Day of Infamy,* Naval Institute Press, 1981; *Battleship Sailor* (Military Book Club selection), Naval Institute Press, 1982. Author of articles for newspapers under name Ted Mason. Contributor to journals.

WORK IN PROGRESS: South Pacific Sailor (tentative title), memoirs, 1942-45, publication expected in 1985; a biography of Audie Murphy; *The Crowded Hours,* a novel; two collections of poems, *A Twentieth Century Bestiary* and *Songs of a Sentimentalist* (tentative title).

SIDELIGHTS: In *Battleship Sailor* Theodore Mason recalls the 1941 bombing of Pearl Harbor by the Japanese and the tense months that preceded the devastation. A radio operator on the U.S.S. *California,* Mason witnessed the bombing from the mainmast of the ship. "This is no airy 'Mr. Roberts' reminiscence," wrote Gladwin Hill in the *Los Angeles Times.* "Mason, a Californian, has been through the newspaper and advertising career mills, and has an extraordinary eye for detail, near-total recall, and a zest for bloodhound-like research." A *West Coast Review of Books* critic opined: "Mason's accounting of those days and his personal involvement is a page-turner that delights the reader. Anybody who wants to know about how things were need only open this book and read it through. . . . There's nary a dull spot throughout."

Mason told *CA:* "*West Coast Review of Books* liked everything about *Battleship Sailor* except its 'hokey title.' The reviewer's quibble about the title illuminates a central problem facing the author of a rather specialized historical memoir. The question is whether to orient the book toward its natural, if limited, audience, or to broaden its appeal for the casual reader and thereby risk alienating one's peers through the resulting (and inevitable) inaccuracies and distortions. Rightly or wrongly, I chose the first course. Interestingly, a good number of civilians, including women, have enjoyed the book, despite its title. But since I was unsparing in my criticism of certain captains and admirals, and of the rigid caste system that separated officers and enlisted men (modeled after the Royal Navy), I anticipated some resentment and hostility from alumni of the U.S. Naval Academy.

"Most of the Navy memoirs and autobiographies to date have been written by long-term, high-ranking, career officers. That is what is wrong with them, and that is what I set out to rectify in *Battleship Sailor.* My battle cry is 'Thank God for the rebels!'

"My sequel, *South Pacific Sailor,* focuses on my wartime experiences in the South and Central Pacific. I have also invested a good deal of time in research for a biography of the late Audie Murphy. He was the most-decorated soldier of World War II, and a one-time acquaintance. The biography will explore the nature of valor in combat and the often tragic consequences for heroes in peacetime.

"I have also written a novel, *The Crowded Hours.* It has aged rather gracefully into a period novel of the early 1960's. Despite the parlous state of the novel today—the lower the quality, it seems, the greater the sales potential—I am considering refurbishing the book and sending it out into the world.

"The many poems I have written over the years, in both traditional and free-verse forms, were put away. I considered them exercises in creativity and style: reminders to myself that there is a great deal more to a writer's life than the production of ephemeral articles or glossy corporate facilities reports—or even books.''

BIOGRAPHICAL/CRITICAL SOURCES: Annapolis Publick Enterprise, August, 1982; Library Journal, September 1, 1982; San Diego Union, October 10, 1982; West Coast Review of Books, October 25, 1982; Mountain Democrat-Times, November 3, 1982; Sacramento Bee, November 28, 1982; Retired Officer, December, 1982; Los Angeles Times Book Review, December 26, 1982.

* * *

MASUDA, Yoneji 1909-

PERSONAL: Born March 4, 1909, in Tokyo, Japan; son of Toyosaku (an artist) and Mume (Aikawa) Masuda; married Fujie Asada, October 27, 1940; children: Shigeru. Education: Attended Towa Dobun University, 1941-43. Home: 4-14-11 Jingumae Shibuya-Ku, Tokyo, Japan 150. Office: Institute for Information Society, 2-15-29 Shinjuku, Shinjuku-Ku, Tokyo, Japan.

CAREER: Aich Institute of Technology, Nagoya, Japan, chief professor, 1963-67; Japan Computer Usage Development Institute, Tokyo, Japan, executive director, 1967-76; Institute for Information Society, Tokyo, president, 1978—; New York Institute of Technology, New York, N.Y., professor emeritus of information science, 1982—. Founded Japan Computer Usage Development Institute, c. 1963. Member: Japan Future Society, Japan Creativity Society, Computer Aided Instruction Society.

WRITINGS: Konpyutopia, Daiyamondo Sha, 1970, published as The Computopia, Diamond Publishing, 1970; MIS Nyumon, Nippon Keizai Shinbun Sha, 1974, published as Introduction to MIS, Nipon Kezai Press, 1974; Jyoho Keizai Gaku, Sangyo Nortisu Daigaku, 1974, published as The Information Economics, Sangyo Noritsu University, 1974; The Information Society as Post Industrial Society, World Future Society, 1981; Sentan Shakai, TBS Buritanika, 1982, published as The High Technology Society, TBS Britannica, 1982. Also author of Jyoho Shakaika Keikaku (title means ''Plan for an Information Society: Japan's National Goal Toward the Year 2000''), 1971.

WORK IN PROGRESS: Life of the Future Information Society, a report to the Government Social Policy Council.

SIDELIGHTS: Masuda is considered by many observers to be one of Japan's foremost theoretic technologists. Robert Arnold Russel, writing in Executive, described Masuda as ''arguably the most influential thinker of the information age.'' Russel added: ''Perhaps more than anyone else, he is responsible for the currently potent political idea that the Third World is susceptible to economic develoment through the introduction of inexpensive information technology such as teaching pocket computers . . . and cheap ground stations for educational and resource satellite information systems which the Americans advocate.''

Masuda told CA: ''When I look back on the latter half of my life, I almost worked at pioneering new social subjects, for example labor economics, productivity, and modern management. This work fascinated me, but after about five years I lost my interest in these subjects because I felt that I perfectly understood the origin of them. However, after my encounter with computers, in spite of more than seventeen years with my career, my passion for computers grew stronger as years went by. The reason is the unlimited progress of technology and its

epochal impact on the human society. During these years, I poured all my efforts into constructing a framework of the emerging Information Society. My intellectual and philsophical travel with computers will continue until the end of my life.''

BIOGRAPHICAL/CRITICAL SOURCES: Executive, November, 1982.

* * *

MATHEWS, Denise
See MATHEWS, Patricia J.

* * *

MATHEWS, Patricia J. 1929(?)-1983
(Denise Mathews, a joint pseudonym)

OBITUARY NOTICE: Born c. 1929 in Pennsylvania; died of cancer, May 17, 1983, in Dale City, Va. Apartment manager and author. Mathews worked as resident manager of apartments in Virginia and the District of Columbia and became president of the Washington, D.C., chapter of the National Society of Professional Resident Managers in 1976. She wrote the novel Intimate Strangers with her daughter Denise Hrivnak under the pen name Denise Mathews. Obituaries and other sources: Washington Post, May 19, 1983.

* * *

MATHEWS, Russell Lloyd 1921-

PERSONAL: Born January 5, 1921, in Geelong, Australia; son of Percival Samuel and Rose Florabell Alveria (Goslin) Mathews; married Joan Marie Tingate, December 13, 1947; children: Susan Joan, Peter Lawrence. Education: University of Melbourne, B.Com. (with first class honors), 1949. Home: 22 Cobby St., Campbell, Australian Capital Territory 2601, Australia. Office: Centre for Research on Federal Financial Relations, Australian National University, P.O. Box 4, Canberra, Australian Capital Territory 2600, Australia.

CAREER: Australian National University, Canberra, assistant to vice-chancellor, 1949-53; University of Adelaide, Adelaide, Australia, reader, 1953-57, professor of commerce, 1958-64; Australian National University, professor of accounting and public finance, 1965-74, director of Centre for Research on Federal Financial Relations, 1972—. Member of interim council and council of Canberra College of Advanced Education, 1967-72; member of interim board and board of management of Australian Graduate School of Management, 1973-78; member of Commonwealth Grants Commission, 1972—, and Royal Commission of Inquiry Into Land Tenures, 1973-75; chairman of Committee of Inquiry Into Inflation and Taxation, 1975, and Advisory Council for Intergovernment Relations, 1977-79. Military service: Australian Army, Infantry, 1941-46; became captain; mentioned in dispatches. Member: Academy of the Social Sciences in Australia (fellow), Australian Society of Accountants (fellow). Awards, honors: Commander of the Order of the British Empire, 1978.

WRITINGS: (With J. M. Grant) Inflation and Company Finance, Law Book Co., 1958, 2nd edition, 1962; Militia Battalion at War, 58/59th Battalion Association, 1961; Accounting for Economists, F. W. Cheshire, 1962, 2nd edition, 1965; (with R. I. Downing, H. W. Arndt, and A. H. Boxer) Taxation in Australia: Agenda for Reform, Melbourne University Press, 1964; Public Investment in Australia, F. W. Cheshire, 1967.

The Accounting Framework, F. W. Cheshire, 1971, revised edition (with Ronald Ma), Longman Cheshire, 1979; (with W.R.C. Jay) *Federal Finance: Intergovernmental Financial Relations in Australia Since Federation*, Nelson, 1972; (with Jay) *Measures of Fiscal Effort and Fiscal Capacity in Relation to Australian State Road Finance*, Centre for Research on Federal Financial Relations, Australian National University, 1974; *Revenue Sharing in Federal Systems*, Centre for Research on Federal Financial Relations, Australian National University, 1980; *Fiscal Equalisation in Education*, Centre for Research on Federal Financial Relations, Australian National University Press, 1983.

"Australian Federalism" series; published by Australian National University Press, except as noted: *Australian Federalism 1977*, 1978; . . . *1978*, 1979; . . . *1979*, 1980; . . . *1980*, 1980; . . . *1981*, Centre for Research on Federal Financial Relations, Australian National University, 1983.

Editor; published by Australian National University Press, except as noted: (With R. J. Chambers and Louis Goldberg) *The Accounting Frontier*, F. W. Cheshire, 1965; (with Jay) *Government Accounting in Australia*, F. W. Cheshire, 1968; *Intergovernmental Relations in Australia*, Angus & Robertson, 1974; *State and Local Taxation*, 1977; *Federalism in Australia and the Federal Republic of Germany: A Comparative Study*, 1980; (with Wilfred Prest) *The Development of Australian Fiscal Federalism*, 1980; (with B. S. Grewal and H. G. Brennan) *The Economics of Federalism*, 1981.

Published by Centre for Research on Federal Financial Relations, Australian National University: *Fiscal Equalisation in a Federal System*, 1974; *Fiscal Federalism: Retrospect and Prospect*, 1974; *Responsibility Sharing in a Federal System*, 1975; *Making Federalism Work: Towards a More Efficient, Equitable, and Responsive Federal System*, 1976; *Local Government in Transition: Responsibilities, Finances, Management*, 1978; *Urban Federalism: Urban Studies in a Federal Context*, 1981; *State Taxation in Theory and Practice*, 1981; *Regional Disparities and Economic Development*, 1981; *Public Policies in Two Federal Countries: Canada and Australia*, 1982; *Public Sector Borrowing in Australia*, 1982.

* * *

MATHIESEN, Egon 1907-1976

OBITUARY NOTICE: Born November 25, 1907, in Esbjerg, Denmark; died in 1976. Artist and author. A self-taught artist, Mathiesen wrote and illustrated children's books, including *Blue-Eyed Pussy, Oswald the Monkey*, and *Jungle in the Wheat Field*, which won a prize in the *New York Herald Tribune* Children's Spring Book Festival in 1960. He also received the Danish government prize for children's books and the Eckersberg Medal from the Royal Academy of Denmark for his painting "Children's Play." Mathiesen's murals adorn several public buildings, including the Tivoli Concert Hall in Copenhagen and the City Hall of Varde. Obituaries and other sources: *Illustrators of Children's Books, 1957-1966*, Horn Book, 1968; *Illustrators of Books for Young People*, 2nd edition, Scarecrow, 1975.

* * *

MATTHEWS, Roy T(homas) 1932-

PERSONAL: Born February 14, 1932, in Franklin, Va.; son of Roy Thomas and Maria (Holland) Matthews; married LeeAnn

Goodrich (an academic administrator), March 20, 1959; children: Randolph Pretlow, Elizabeth Lee. *Education:* Washington and Lee University, B.A., 1954; Duke University, M.A., 1956; University of North Carolina at Chapel Hill, Ph.D., 1966. *Politics:* Democrat. *Home:* 4207 Woodcraft, Okemos, Mich. 48864. *Agent:* Michael Larsen/Elizabeth Pomada, 1029 Jones St., San Francisco, Calif. 94109. *Office:* Department of Humanities, Michigan State University, East Lansing, Mich. 48824.

CAREER: Georgia State College for Women (now Georgia College at Milledgeville), Milledgeville, instructor in social studies, 1958-60; University of North Carolina at Chapel Hill, instructor in modern civilization, 1961-64; University of Houston, Houston, Tex., instructor in European history, 1964-65; Michigan State University, East Lansing, instructor, 1965-66, assistant professor, 1966-71, associate professor, 1971-76, professor of humanities, 1976—. Member of Michigan Department of Education's Council on Post-Secondary Education, 1975-78. *Member:* North American Conference on British Studies, Victorian Society in America (vice-president of Michigan chapter, 1980—), American Association of University Professors (president of Michigan State University chapter, 1973-75; president of the Michigan conference, 1975), Phi Beta Kappa.

WRITINGS: (With Peter Mellini) *In "Vanity Fair,"* University of California Press, 1982. Contributor to *British History Illustrated, Educational Technology, The Shaw Review*, and *University College Quarterly*.

WORK IN PROGRESS: The English Art: British Cartoons and Caricature Since 1841, with Mellini, publication expected in 1985.

SIDELIGHTS: In their book *In "Vanity Fair,"* Matthews and Mellini duplicate caricatures from the late-nineteenth-century British magazine *Vanity Fair*, annotating the reproductions with biographical information. The result, observed critic Edward Sorel in the *New York Times Book Review*, is "a wonderfully entertaining documentary of the period." Sorel remarked that the authors "seem to enjoy debunking the magazine's upper-class bias but wisely offer enough of the original text to give the reader a sense of the prose style."

Matthews told *CA:* "My advice to all aspiring authors is: never, never give up in pursuit of a publisher; write on what interests you; be willing to accept criticism but do not compromise your own standards; keep up your contacts and friendships regardless of how lonely you become in writing. To academic authors: combine your teaching and scholarly interests in your writing; write as if you were writing for your students, not for other scholars. Do not underestimate the intelligence of your readers. Only research and write on topics that you find stimulating and fun.

"Seeing your name in print and reading favorable reviews of your work is one of the most gratifying experiences in life. But you must remember that there are many disappointments along the way, that you must make sacrifices in your time and efforts and forsake other interests and pleasures, and that family will have to pay a certain price for your pursuits.

"Writing in the area of popular art forms, cartoons, and caricatures has sharpened my eye and broadened my interest. I now collect prints and cartoons and even have a cottage industry, along with a friend, of buying and selling prints, in particular *Vanity Fair* caricatures. I have also mounted art exhibits of those caricatures, an experience that has helped me better understand displaying and presenting visual art to the public. Since *Vanity Fair* was published until 1914, my co-author and I were able to interview people whose lives were directly affected by the magazine. Thus we bridged the gap between the written record from the past and the personal experiences of those still alive today. Our search for materials and sources introduced us to worlds far beyond academia, and this was very important for our own education. Also, researching the origins and evolution of cartooning and caricaturing from the Italian and French sources has been a most rewarding and exciting experience. To work with a co-author, who is also a close friend, and to work with editors and publishers reinforces your faith in the basic goodness and potential of all of us.''

BIOGRAPHICAL/CRITICAL SOURCES: New York Times Book Review, September 26, 1982.

*   *   *

MAXWELL, Margaret F(inlayson)   1927-

PERSONAL: Born September 9, 1927, in Schenectady, N.Y.; daughter of Frank E. (an electrical engineer) and Harriett (a teacher; maiden name, Rallison) Finlayson; married W. LeGrand Maxwell, April 7, 1954; children: Robert LeGrand, Brian James, Bruce Allan. *Education:* Pomona College, B.A. (magna cum laude), 1948; University of California, Berkeley, B.L.S., 1950; George Washington University, M.A., 1953; University of Michigan, Ph.D., 1971. *Politics:* Democrat. *Religion:* Church of Jesus Christ of Latter-day Saints (Mormons). *Home:* 2733 East Elm St., Tucson, Ariz. 85716. *Office:* Graduate Library School, University of Arizona, Tucson, Ariz. 85719.

CAREER: Library of Congress, Washington, D.C., intern, 1950-51, cataloger, 1951-56; Upper Iowa University, Fayette, associate librarian, 1956-66, instructor in English and library science, 1966-68; University of Michigan, Ann Arbor, lecturer in library science, 1968-71; University of Arizona, Tucson, assistant professor, 1971-72, associate professor, 1972-79, professor of library science, 1979—. *Member:* American Library Association (past chairperson of Library History Round Table), Association of American Library Schools, Southwest Library Association, Arizona State Library Association, Arizona Historical Society, Phi Beta Kappa. *Awards, honors:* Prize from American Library Association, 1978, for article, ''The Lion and the Lady: The Firing of Miss Mary Jones.''

WRITINGS: Shaping a Library: William L. Clements and the Clements Library of Americana, N. Israel, 1973; (with Donal D. Dickinson and W. David Laird) *Voices From the Southwest,* Northland Press, 1976; *Handbook for the Anglo-American Cataloguing Rules* (AACR2), American Library Association, 1980; *A Passion for Freedom: The Life of Sharlot Hall,* University of Arizona Press, 1982. Contributor of articles and reviews to library and history journals.

WORK IN PROGRESS: Research on women in Arizona history.

SIDELIGHTS: Maxwell wrote that her work ''reflects the dual thrust of my interests: library cataloging and history. My present teaching assignment includes courses in cataloging, the history of the book, and the history of children's literature.

''Through my research on Sharlot Hall, I have come to recognize that half of Arizona's history—the part played by Arizona's women—remains largely ignored and unchronicled. Some of Arizona's women were pioneer feminists; others led

more conventional lives. But Arizona's history is colored by the efforts of all kinds of women: those who quietly brought order and civilization to the raw frontier as they worked beside their husbands and those whose lives reflect their anguished need to be recognized as fully contributing and independent humans rather than as auxiliaries to husbands and fathers. Sharlot took the latter role; her life says much to women today.''

*   *   *

MAYER, Albert Ignatius, Jr.   1906-1960

OBITUARY NOTICE: Born May 25 (some sources say June 9), 1906, in Cincinnati, Ohio; died June 4, 1960; buried at Cemetery of Spring Grove, Cincinnati, Ohio. Realtor, political volunteer, public servant, and author. Mayer joined his uncle's real estate firm, Theodore Mayer & Brothers, during the 1920's and became a senior member in 1947. He retained that position until his death, also serving as a partner from 1950, in the firm of Edgemon, Fast & Mayer Brothers, acting land acquisition agents for the Ohio turnpike. Mayer was involved in a variety of community and political organizations as well and was an active member of the Republican party. He was minority whip in the Ohio House of Representatives in 1936, worked on Robert A. Taft's campaign during the Republican presidential election in 1940, served as Republican campaign chairman of Cincinnati in 1941, and represented Ohio as a delegate to the Republican National Convention in 1956. His books, which were written for young people, include *Falconer's Son, Olympiad,* and a story about Germany in the tenth century titled *Defense of the Castle.* Obituaries and other sources: *Ohio Authors and Their Books: Biographical Data and Selective Bibliographies for Ohio Authors, Native and Resident, 1796-1950,* World Publishing, 1962; *The National Cyclopaedia of American Biography,* Volume 47, James T. White, 1965; *Who's Who in Library and Information Services,* American Library Association, 1982.

*   *   *

MAYER, Debby
See MAYER, Deborah Anne

*   *   *

MAYER, Deborah Anne   1946-
(Debby Mayer; Anna Christensen, a pseudonym)

PERSONAL: Born May 2, 1946, in Schenectady, N.Y.; daughter of Byrne W. Mayer (a physician) and Anne (an administrative assistant; maiden name, Christensen) Clark. *Education:* Skidmore College, B.A., 1968; City College of the City University of New York, M.A., 1982. *Politics:* Independent. *Religion:* Christian. *Residence:* New York, N.Y. *Agent:* Gloria Loomis, Watkins/Loomis, Inc., 150 East 35th St., New York, N.Y. 10016.

CAREER: Ingenue (magazine), New York City, assistant to fiction editor, 1968-69; assistant to managing editor of Pegasus Publishing Co., 1969-70; free-lance writer and editor, 1970-71; Poets & Writers, Inc., New York City, coordinator in readings/workshop program, 1972-74, editor of *Coda* (magazine), 1974-82. *Member:* Authors Guild. *Awards, honors:* Creative Artists Public Service grant from New York state, 1979, for short stories manuscript; MacDowell Colony and Millay Colony fellowships, both 1980; Jerome Lowell DeJur Award of the City College Fund, 1981, for *Sisters.*

WRITINGS—Under name Debby Mayer: *Literary Agents: A Complete Guide,* Poets & Writers, 1978, revised edition, 1983; *Sisters* (novel), Putnam, 1982. Contributor of articles to newspapers and magazines, including *The Villager, Outside,* and *Coda,* and of short stories, one under the pseudonym Anna Christensen, to magazines, including *Zone, Gallimaufry, Redbook, Ingenue,* and *fiction international.*

WORK IN PROGRESS: A novel, tentatively titled *Carolina,* completion expected in 1984.

SIDELIGHTS: Mayer told *CA:* "*Sisters* is a 'what if' story: what if a single working woman in New York suddenly became the guardian of her eight-year-old half sister who'd been growing up in rural Vermont? I put off writing it for a year because I still believed that old saw, 'write about what you know,' and I have never raised children in New York City or anywhere else. But I liked the idea so much I made the leap, and wrote the book by observing children, thinking about them a lot, and using my imagination. The first chapter of *Sisters* is based on my own experience; the rest is fiction.

"For *Carolina* I'm observing dancers, learning Spanish, traveling to Mexico and Central America, and following the political situations in those countries more carefully than I might otherwise. So far there's one scene in the book based on my experience; the rest I'm making up.

"I couldn't have written *Sisters* without the support—financial, professional, and psychic—of Poets & Writers, Inc. There I had a fascinating part-time job that paid decently and brought me in touch with people who both read books and thought up good practical jokes. I couldn't have started *Carolina* without the option money CBS paid me for *Sisters*."

*   *   *

MAYFIELD, John S.   1904-1983

OBITUARY NOTICE: Born in 1904 in Meridian, Tex.; died of a respiratory ailment, April 26, 1983, in Bethesda, Md. Bibliophile, librarian, and author. Mayfield spent more than sixty years involved in bibliographical research and librarianship, working as a librarian with the Montgomery County public library system and as curator of manuscripts and rare books at Syracuse University. Over the years he amassed the greatest private collection of books and manuscripts by and about poet Algernon Charles Swinburne. However, he opposed the idea of collecting for investment and donated books and manuscripts to institutions in both England and the United States. Mayfield also published numerous articles on Swinburne and was considered an authority on the poet's life and works as well as an expert in nineteenth- and twentieth-century English and American literature. He was noted for his helpfulness to scholars, whether professionals or young students, and was in demand as a guest lecturer at American, British, and Japanese universities. He became a founding member of the Manuscript Society in 1948. Obituaries and other sources: *Washington Post,* April 30, 1983; *London Times,* May 21, 1983; *AB Bookman's Weekly,* May 23, 1983.

*   *   *

MAYO, James
    See COULTER, Stephen

McALPIN, Heller   1955-

PERSONAL: Born May 10, 1955, in Newark, N.J.; daughter of Norman (a business executive) and Rosalyn (Breg) Heller; married David Mark McAlpin (an architect), June 10, 1978. *Education:* Princeton University, B.A., 1977; Columbia University, M.F.A., 1979. *Residence:* New York, N.Y. *Agent:* Robert Cornfield Literary Agency, 145 West 79th St., New York, N.Y. 10024.

CAREER: Free-lance writer, 1979—. *Member:* Princeton Club of New York. *Awards, honors:* Princeton-in-Asia/Osawa fellowship, 1976.

WRITINGS: Nostalgia (novel), Scribner, 1982. Contributor to magazines and newspapers, including *Prime Time, Savvy, Country Journal, Backpacker,* and *New Jersey Monthly.* Contributing editor of *Princeton Town Topics,* 1978—.

WORK IN PROGRESS: High Hopes, "a novel set in a corporate town on Connecticut's Gold Coast, about the children of corporate executives as they reach adulthood."

SIDELIGHTS: McAlpin told *CA:* "It seems to me that the first goal of fiction is to engage the reader's interest and imagination—the writer being the first reader. The single most important piece of writing advice I have picked up was in J. D. Salinger's *Seymour: An Introduction,* in which the narrator urges the writer to 'remember before ever you sit down to write that you've been a reader long before you were ever a writer.' Then, he says, ask yourself what you would most like to read in the whole world. If you are a writer, chances are that precise book won't exist, so the next step is to 'just sit down shamelessly and write the thing yourself.' (Easier said than done.)

"*Nostalgia* is a book that, simply put, I wanted to be able to read. I am also looking forward to being able to read *High Hopes.* Both, while fiction, are set in a social milieu with which I am quite familiar. In Volume V of his series *Children of Crisis: Privileged Ones,* Robert Coles notes that there is much less literature—particularly nonfiction—about the well-to-do and rich than about the underprivileged because the wealthy 'have the means to obtain privacy.' He also notes, 'Since it is the well-to-do, by and large, who buy books, and who don't lack an interest in themselves, one wonders why they have been so forsaken by field workers of various kinds.' The upper middle class is perhaps better represented in fiction than in sociological studies, but I have read surprisingly few novels—good, non-glamorized tales, that is—about the particular pressures peculiar to the maturing offspring of wealthy parents, and it is this subject that particularly interests me in my novel in progress, *High Hopes.*"

*   *   *

McCABE, Charles Raymond   1915-1983

OBITUARY NOTICE: Born January 24, 1915, in New York, N.Y.; died of a stroke, April 30, 1983, in Telegraph Hill, Calif. Journalist. Known for his wit, originality, and irascible style, McCabe worked as a syndicated columnist for the *San Francisco Chronicle* and other papers from 1958. According to the *Chronicle*'s executive director William German, McCabe's "column was a sharp intellectual exercise that helped set the unique tone of the newspaper." McCabe began his career reporting for the *New York American* from 1937 to 1938, then worked in public relations, served in the Navy, and worked for the United Press (now United Press International) in Washington, D.C. He was the recipient of the Munoz-Marin Journalism Award in 1940 and wrote several books, including *Damned Old Crank, The Fearless Spectator, Tall Girls Are More Grateful,* and *The Good Man's Weakness.* Obituaries and other sources: *Who's Who in America,* 42nd edition, Marquis, 1982; *Chicago Tribune,* May 4, 1983.

* * *

McCALL, Dorothy Lawson   1889(?)-1982

PERSONAL: Born c. 1889 in Boston, Mass.; died April 2, 1982, in Portland, Ore.; daughter of Thomas W. Lawson (in copper business); widowed, c. 1938; children: Tom, Henry, Dorothy McCall Chamberlain, Jean McCall Babson.

CAREER: Writer. *Awards, honors:* Named outstanding mother of America, 1976.

WRITINGS: Ranch Under the Rimrock, Binford & Mort, 1968; *The Copper King's Daughter: From Cape Cod to Crooked River,* Binford & Mort, 1972.

OBITUARIES: Chicago Tribune, April 5, 1982.*

* * *

McCARR, Ken(neth George)   1903-1977

PERSONAL: Born September 25, 1903, in Neillsville, Wis.; died May 6, 1977; son of Edward and Amelia (Weisner) McCarr; married Esther Hyde, April 20, 1939. *Education:* Attended school in Stevens Point, Wis. *Politics:* Republican. *Religion:* Roman Catholic.

CAREER: Worked as registrar of United Trotting Horse Association, Columbus, Ohio, and as editor of *Horseman* and *Fair World,* Indianapolis, Ind.

WRITINGS: The Kentucky Harness Horse, University Press of Kentucky, 1978.*

(Date of death provided by wife, Mrs. Kenneth McCarr.)

* * *

McCARTER, Neely Dixon   1929-

PERSONAL: Born October 4, 1929, in Gastonia, N.C.; son of Robert William and Nell (Dixon) McCarter; married Jean Maxwell, May 28, 1954; children: Robert Sidney, Robin, Jeanette, Shirley Jean. *Education:* Presbyterian College, A.B., 1950; Columbia Theological Seminary, B.D., 1953, postdoctoral study, 1968; Union Theological Seminary, Th.M., 1958; Yale University, M.A., 1959, Ph.D., 1961. *Home:* 1307 Whitby Rd., Richmond, Va. 23227. *Office:* Office of the Dean, Union Theological Seminary, Richmond, Va. 23227.

CAREER: Ordained minister of the Presbyterian Church in the United States, 1953; University of Florida, Gainesville, Presbyterian university pastor, 1953-58; Columbia Theological Seminary, Decatur, Ga., professor of Christian education, 1961-66; Union Theological Seminary, Richmond, Va., Robert and Lucy Reynolds Critz Professor of Christian Education, 1966—, dean, 1973—. Guest professor of Christian education at Graduate Theological Union, 1969. *Member:* American Educational Studies Association, Association of Professors and Researchers of Religious Education.

WRITINGS: A Basis for Study: A Theological Prospectus for the Campus Ministry, Richmond, Va., 1959; (with Charles S. McCoy) *The Gospel on Campus: Rediscovering Evangelism in the Academic Community,* John Knox, 1959; *Hear the Word*

of the Lord (young adult; illustrations by Dudley Cook and Richard Loader), CLC Press, 1964; *Help Me Understand, Lord: Prayer Responses to the Gospel of Mark,* Westminster, 1978.

* * *

McCARTNEY, Mike
See McCARTNEY, Peter Michael

* * *

McCARTNEY, Peter Michael   1944-
(Mike McCartney, Mike McGear)

PERSONAL: Born January 7, 1944, in Liverpool, England; son of James and Mary (Mohin) McCartney; married Rowena Horne, May 29, 1982; children: Benna, Theran, Abbi, Josh. *Education:* Attended Liverpool Institute. *Politics:* "Democratically Republic." *Religion:* "Latter Day School of Tomorrow." *Home:* Sunset Heswall, Liverpool, England.

CAREER: Worked as salesman and barber's apprentice, 1962; musician, under pseudonym Mike McGear, in Scaffold during 1970's.

WRITINGS: (Under name Mike McCartney) *The Macs: Mike McCartney's Family Album,* Delilah Books, 1981.

Also author of songs, under pseudonym Mike McGear, featured on solo recordings and on recordings by Scaffold.

SIDELIGHTS: McCartney's *The Macs* includes photographs of his brother Paul during his years with The Beatles and humorous asides on both the pictures and events throughout Mike's life. Kenneth Funsten, writing in the *Los Angeles Times,* described *The Macs* as "a folksy, well-intentioned autobiography." Funsten noted that the book contains "letters of hope from promoters, telegrams, even post cards from Hamburg."

BIOGRAPHICAL/CRITICAL SOURCES: Los Angeles Times, January 14, 1982.

* * *

McCAW, Kenneth Malcolm   1907-

PERSONAL: Born October 8, 1907, in Chatswood, New South Wales, Australia; son of Mark and Jessie (Hempton) McCaw; married Valma Marjorie Stackpool, July 13, 1968; children: Margaret, Owen. *Home:* Woodrow House, 1 Charlish Lane, Lane Cove, New South Wales 2066, Australia.

CAREER: Solicitor in New South Wales, Australia, 1933-65; Government of New South Wales, Sydney, Australia, attorney-general, 1965-75; writer, 1975—. Appointed Queen's Counsel, 1972. Liberal member for Lane Cove of New South Wales Legislative Assembly, 1947-75. Convocation member of Macquarie University; honorary life governor of Royal Prince Alfred Hospital; past member of board of trustees of New South Wales College of Law, Sydney Grammar School, Australian Museum, Food for New South Wales Babies, and Good Samaritans. *Member:* Royal Blind Society of New South Wales, Lane Cove Businessmen's Club (founding member), Lane Cove Lions Club (charter member), Retinal Dystrophy Society (patron and life member). *Awards, honors:* Knight Bachelor, 1975.

WRITINGS: People Versus Power, Holt, 1978.

SIDELIGHTS: Kenneth McCaw told *CA:* "*People Versus Power* is about the machinery of institutions of democracy and how they protect individual freedom. The book was prompted by lengthy practical experience of the working of these institutions and the ways in which they differ from dictatorship, communism, and socialism.'' *Avocational interests:* Reading and writing Braille.

*   *   *

McCOMAS, Annette Peltz   1911-

PERSONAL: Born June 26, 1911, in San Francisco, Calif.; daughter of Alfred I. (a merchant) and Jennifer (Miller) Peltz; married Jesse Francis McComas (a publisher, literary agent, writer, and editor), November 23, 1938 (divorced, 1961); children: Anthony Francis (deceased). *Education:* University of California, Berkeley, A.B., 1933; Columbia University, M.A., 1937. *Home:* 1275 Drury Rd., Berkeley, Calif. 94705.

CAREER: Merritt College, Oakland, Calif., professor of English, speech, drama, and humanities, 1956-77; writer, 1977—. Theatrical director, 1937—.

WRITINGS: (Editor) *The Eureka Years: Boucher and McComas' Magazine of Fantasy and Science Fiction, 1949-54,* Bantam, 1982.

WORK IN PROGRESS: Editing *Eureka II; The Listening Hill,* a novel; *The Wistful Wyvern,* a children's book.

SIDELIGHTS: Annette McComas told *CA:* "I have written all my life, but my interest in pursuing a professional career has come at age seventy, when my involvement in directing for the theater is dwindling to occasional commitments. I am also deeply into learning photography, especially design and abstractions, and I hope to develop a book with text. So I am in essence a novice as a writer and editor—so far."

*   *   *

McCORD, Anne   1942-

PERSONAL—Office: School of Education, University of Reading, London Rd., Reading RG1 5AQ, England.

CAREER: Teacher, 1964-71; British Museum of Natural History, London, England, higher scientific officer, 1971-78; University of Reading, Reading, assistant registrar, 1978—; writer of children's nonfiction.

WRITINGS—All for children: *All About Early Man,* W. H. Allen, 1974; *The Children's Picture Prehistory of Early Man,* illustrations by Bob Hersey, Usborne, 1977; *The Children's Picture Prehistory of Prehistoric Mammals,* illustrations by Hersey, Usborne, 1977; *Dinosaurs,* Usborne, 1977; *Children's Encyclopedia of Prehistoric Life,* illustrations by Hersey, Usborne, 1977.

*   *   *

McCORMICK, Claire
See LABUS, Marta Haake

*   *   *

McCRACKEN, Kenneth David   1901-1983

OBITUARY NOTICE: Born November 12, 1901, in Paxton, Ill.; died February 23, 1983, in La Grange, Ill. Attorney and author. McCracken began practicing law in 1930 with the Chicago firm now known as Bell, Boyd & Lloyd. He was made a partner in 1940, but his career was interrupted by World War II. Called to active duty in the Naval Reserve in 1940,

McCracken's first assignment was as an instructor at the Midshipmen's School at Northwestern University's Chicago campus. He later served as navigation officer on carriers stationed in the Pacific, including the U.S.S. *Nassau* and the U.S.S. *Independence,* and in 1944 published *Baby Flat-Top,* a book based on his wartime experiences. McCracken returned to practicing law after the war and specialized in trust and estate law until his retirement in 1973. Obituaries and other sources: *Who's Who in America,* 40th edition, Marquis, 1978; *Chicago Tribune,* February 26, 1983.

*   *   *

McCRAE, John   1872-1918

BRIEF ENTRY: Born November 30, 1872, in Guelph, Ontario, Canada; died of pneumonia and cerebral infection, January 28, 1918, in Wimereux, Boulogne, France. Canadian physician, poet, and author of *A Textbook of Pathology* (1914). A medical officer during the Boer War and World War I, McCrae is best remembered for his poem "In Flanders Fields," which was first published in *Punch* on December 8, 1915, and used as a military recruiting incentive in the United States. The poem was subsequently published, along with other poems by McCrae, in a volume entitled *In Flanders Fields* (1919). *Biographical/ critical sources: The Oxford Companion to Canadian History and Literature,* Oxford University Press, 1967; *Longman Companion to English Literature,* Longman, 1977; *Twentieth-Century Literary Criticism,* Volume 11, Gale, 1983.

*   *   *

McCULLOCH, Derek (Ivor Breashur)   1897-1967
(Uncle Mac)

OBITUARY NOTICE: Born November 18, 1897, in Plymouth, Devonshire, England; died June 1, 1967. Broadcaster, editor, and author. McCulloch joined the British Army at age seventeen but was discharged after active service in World War I cost him an eye, a leg, and a lung. He became a London announcer for the British Broadcasting Corporation (BBC) in 1926, organizer of the "Children's Hour" program in 1933, and served as program director from 1938 to 1950. Although he was best known for his role as the friendly Uncle Mac on the "Children's Hour," McCulloch also produced thousands of other broadcasts. Especially popular was the "Toytown" series which he narrated and played in as Larry the Lamb. In addition, McCulloch edited numerous editions of the BBC "Children's Hour Annual," served as children's editor of the *News Chronicle* from 1950 to 1953, and wrote and edited a variety of children's books under the name Uncle Mac. Among them are *Cornish Adventure, Cornish Mystery, Every Child's Pilgrim's Progress, Travellers Three, The Son of the Ruler,* and *Uncle Mac's Children's Hour Story Book.* He was awarded the Order of the British Empire in 1939. Obituaries and other sources: *The Who's Who of Children's Literature,* Schoken, 1968; *Who Was Who Among English and European Authors, 1931-1949,* Gale, 1978.

*   *   *

McCULLY, Emily Arnold
See ARNOLD, Emily

*   *   *

McDANIEL, C. Yates   1907(?)-1983

OBITUARY NOTICE: Born c. 1907 in Suzhou, China; died

March 14, 1983, in Florida. A journalist with the Associated Press (AP) for thirty-six years, McDaniel is best remembered as the last correspondent to leave Singapore before it was overrun by the Japanese in 1942. He escaped via lifeboat and junk, then journeyed through the interior of northern Sumatra. McDaniel began his AP career as a foreign correspondent in the South Pacific, became bureau chief in Detroit, and then spent twenty-two years working in Washington, D.C. He retired in 1971. Obituaries and other sources: *New York Times*, March 18, 1983.

* * *

McDERMOTT, Alice 1953-

PERSONAL: Born June 27, 1953, in Brooklyn, N.Y.; daughter of William J. and Mildred (Lynch) McDermott; married David M. Armstrong (a research neuroscientist), June 16, 1979. *Education:* State University of New York, B.A., 1975; University of New Hampshire, M.A., 1978. *Home:* 2 Midland Gardens, Bronxville, N.Y. 10708. *Agent:* Harriet Wasserman, 230 East 48th St., New York, N.Y. 10017.

CAREER: Writer. University of New Hampshire, Durham, N.H., lecturer in English, 1978-79. Worked as fiction reader for *Redbook* and *Esquire*, 1979-80. Consulting editor of *Redbook*'s Young Writers Contest. *Member:* Associated Writing Programs, Poets and Writers, International Women's Writing Guild.

WRITINGS: A Bigamist's Daughter (novel), Random House, 1982. Contributor of short stories to *Redbook, Mademoiselle, Seventeen,* and *Ms.*

WORK IN PROGRESS: A novel.

SIDELIGHTS: McDermott's *A Bigamist's Daughter* concerns Elizabeth Connelly, a twenty-six-year-old editor at a vanity publisher. Cynical yet compassionate, Connelly indulges her writer-customers as they reveal their secrets to her. Her clients actually believe that they have suffered so that they can chronicle their anguish in writing, and Connelly isn't about to tell them that their expression ceases after the book is written and that, as LeAnne Schreiber noted in the *New York Times*, "Vista books never get further than the company stockroom." Connelly eventually becomes involved with a Southern client still in search of an ending for his novel about a bigamist. Consequently, Connelly ponders her own father's frequent absence from home as she was growing up. Schreiber praised the humor in *A Bigamist's Daughter*. "The laughter is wicked but not cruel," she wrote. A reviewer for the *Los Angeles Times* wrote that "McDermott has a brisk, no-nonsense approach to romance: While the characters are shallow, they're typical enough of their generation to seem authentic."

McDermott told *CA:* "The writing program at the University of New Hampshire has been vital to my career. The two years I spent there helped me to establish my goals as a writer, my work habits and my commitment to the craft. The writers I studied with (primarily Mark Smith) at UNH and the other student/writers I met there provided, and continue to provide, the support and encouragement and criticism every writer needs."

BIOGRAPHICAL/CRITICAL SOURCES: New York Times, February 1, 1982; *Los Angeles Times,* February 18, 1982; *Newsweek,* March 22, 1982; *Chicago Tribune Book World,* January 2, 1983.

McDONAGH, John Michael 1944-

PERSONAL: Born March 15, 1944, in Huntington, N.Y.; son of John Thomas and Catherine (McMahon) McDonagh; married Martha Frances Dickmann (a dietitian), June 28, 1969; children: Catherine, Brian, John C. *Education:* Fordham University, B.A., 1965; Duquesne University, M.A., 1969; University of Oklahoma, Ph.D., 1971. *Politics:* Democrat. *Religion:* Roman Catholic. *Home and office:* 2 Carnegie Ave., Huntington, N.Y. 11743.

CAREER: St. Mary's College, South Bend, Ind., assistant professor of psychology and chairman of department, 1971-73; Catholic Charities, Rockville Center, N.Y., staff psychologist, 1974—. Assistant professor at New York Institute of Technology, 1976-77, adjunct assistant professor, 1977—. Director of Biofeedback and Counseling Services of Huntington. Soccer coach of Cold Spring Harbor League. *Military service:* U.S. Public Health Service, staff psychologist at Hospital Unit in Milan, Mich., 1969-71; became senior scientist. *Member:* International Association for Near Death Studies, American Psychological Association, Biofeedback Society of America, Association of Christian Therapists, Suffolk County Psychological Association, Phi Beta Kappa. *Awards, honors:* Scholar of French Government at University of Strasbourg, 1963-64.

WRITINGS: Christian Psychology: Toward a New Synthesis, Cross Roads, 1982. Contributor to professional journals.

WORK IN PROGRESS: Research toward a better integration of modern psychology with ancient religious insights.

SIDELIGHTS: McDonagh wrote: "The interpretation of ancient religious wisdom into a modern idiom continues to be a challenge. Twentieth-century Westerners tend to dismiss much if not most of their own religious heritage, and I believe this is very unfortunate. Modern psychology has become a religion for many, and people need to see how this new 'religion' relates to the traditional ones, since both the old and the new spring from the human quest for the meaning of life, and from that inevitably follows a series of questions about how one ought to live life."

* * *

McDONALD, Dianna
See SHOMAKER, Dianna

* * *

McDONOUGH, Jerome 1946-
(Jerry McDonough)

PERSONAL: Surname is pronounced Mick-*dunn*-a; born November 26, 1946, in Seguin, Tex.; son of Jerome Charles (a professor) and Dorothy (a draftsperson; maiden name, Munson) McDonough; married Raenell Roberts (a musician), December 21, 1978; children: Brian Christopher. *Education:* West Texas State University, B.S., 1968, M.A., 1972. *Politics:* Democrat. *Religion:* Catholic. *Home:* 6106 Dartmouth, Amarillo, Tex. 79109. *Agent:* Jay Garon, 415 Central Park West, New York, N.Y. 10025.

CAREER: Pioneer Corp., Amarillo, Tex., editor and writer for corporate magazine *The Jet,* 1969-70; Caprock School, Amarillo, Tex., theatre director, 1970—; playwright. Part-time instructor in creative writing at Amarillo College, 1970-81. *Military service:* U.S. Army Reserve, 1968-74. *Member:* Dramatists Guild. *Awards, honors:* Second place for Curtain Playwrighting Award from Kansas Theatre Association, 1974, for "Fables"; first place awards from Texas Educational Theatre Association Playwriting Contest, 1975, for "Asylum," and 1978, for "Eden."

WRITINGS—Plays: *The Betrothed* (one-act), Samuel French, 1972; *Transceiver* (one-act), Samuel French, 1974; *A Short Stretch at the Galluses* (one-act; adapted from the musical by McDonough and John Gibson, "A Stretch at the Galluses"; also see below), Eldridge Publishing, 1974; *Dirge* (one-act), Baker's Plays, 1975; *The Noble's Reward* (one-act), Eldridge Publishing, 1975.

Plays; published by I. E. Clark: *Filiation* (one-act), 1973; *Fables* (five scenes; first produced at West Texas State University, fall, 1973), 1974; *Asylum* (five scenes), 1975; *A Christmas Carol* (one-act; adapted from the novella by Charles Dickens), 1976; *Requiem* (one-act), 1977; *Eden* (one-act), 1978; *O, Little Town* (one-act), 1978; *Stages* (one-act), 1979; *It's Sad, So Sad When an Elf Goes Bad* (one-act), 1979; *Plots* (five scenes), 1981; *The Nearest Star* (one-act), 1981; *Juvie* (one-act), 1982; *Limbo* (one-act), 1983.

"The Old Oak Encounter" (one-act), anthologized in *A Pocketful of Wry*, edited by I. E. Clark, I. E. Clark, 1974.

Also co-author, with John Gibson, of "A Stretch at the Galluses" (two-act musical; book and lyrics by McDonough, music by Gibson), first produced in Amarillo, Texas, at Theatre 66, summer, 1970.

Contributor to periodicals, sometimes under name Jerry McDonough, including *Writer's Digest, Dramatists Guild Quarterly, Texas Poetry,* and *Prolog.*

WORK IN PROGRESS: The Least of These, Christmas play; *Sweet Smoking Pipe,* nonfiction; *Sneakers, George Elias Whiffledown,* and *I Heard Mama Say,* children's books; contemporary and religious songs; a play "on the possibilities of some impossible relationships"; a musical.

SIDELIGHTS: McDonough told *CA:* "I was driven to write because I had always been awed by people who were called by the title of 'writer.' I assumed, of course, that such people never ventured from their penthouses to visit Earth.

"Even earlier than such assumptions came the appeal of concrete rewards. My fourth-grade year, the local Catholic newspaper sponsored an essay contest on the topic 'What Christmas Means to Me.' First prize was twenty-five dollars. Second prize was fifteen. My mother recalled a story from her childhood which I immediately plagiarized, wrote up, and shipped off. God didn't award me first prize, but he encouraged me with second. I gave five dollars to the Catholic missions and squandered the rest on a nine-year-old's best imitation of loose living.

"My next brush with print came in the ninth grade when my epic play, 'It Happened in White Dove' (twelve scenes, twelve locations, eight minutes in length), appeared in the mimeographed school newspaper. I suppose my awe of writers hit about this time. I was convinced that my eighth grade English teacher, Mrs. Lauch, had written most of our stories under a variety of pen names.

"During high school and most of college I ignored writing. The final semester of undergraduate school, though, I enrolled in creative writing and met that evil mistress, the Desire for Publication. Publication eluded me, though, during six months of Army Reserve training and my first year employment at Pioneer Corporation as editor of *The Jet.* But fame was ap-

proaching. First came an acceptance letter and then, six months later, the moment of a lifetime—my name in print (national print)—in that revered literary monthly, *Mini-Bike Guide.*

I published under the name Jerry for short features and articles during this period, but opted for Jerome as I moved into longer things. My theory was that Shakespeare's friends probably called him Bill, but it just didn't have enough class for posterity. Who was I to do less?

"My by-line appeared in publications as disparate as *Texas AAA Motorist* and *Authorship* (National Writer's Club). I tried formula short fiction and even confessions and humorous adventure stories, but nothing clicked. A poem, 'Sylvia Came Around,' appeared in the premiere issue of *Texas Poetry.* Several attempts were made to create panel comic-strips with a variety of artists. Not even one panel was ever completed.

"During these other forays, however, my playwriting had started meeting with success. It became obvious that energies wasted on other projects could be more profitably directed toward the stage. So, for the period of roughly 1974 through 1980, playwriting became the sole thrust of my work. As always, directing and teaching kept food in my mouth and the mouths of my wife, Raenell, and our supreme joy, Brian.

"An early personal influence was the writer Loula Grace Erdman. Her graduate creative writing class made me feel a part of the writer's world for the first time. Her criticism and that of the class was unrelenting and unwelcome, but after I cooled down I invariably discovered that they had been right. I would fix my piece, return to the class, read again and resent the new comments as much as I had the first ones. Strange—heaven in a hell disguise. Lou was magic. For years she was the first person I called when I appeared in print or received an acceptance. Lou is gone now but we can share a small bit of her through her work, particularly *A Time to Write.*

"Other personal influences included Dr. A. K. Knott, a renaissance man of enormous personal charm who alleged that one day he would open a teacher's college called Knott Normal; vivacious, exciting creative writing teacher Kathleen (Collins) Cook; pragmatist Carol Finch; public relations professional Robert O. Mills; theatre director William A. Moore, and scores of actors and actresses and students who were always my teachers. My very, very earliest touching by the theatre came through the work of my father, Jerome Charles McDonough. The compassion in my work I owe to my mother, Dorothy.

"A wonderful Yankee named William Talbot was my first contact with the world of theatre publishing. Above his 'Senior Editor, Samuel French, Inc.,' signature block, the letter read, 'We'd like to publish "The Betrothed" and will send you a contract covering it shortly.' Just like that. Great moments are sometimes the humblest. Samuel French published 'Transceiver' two years later, but then a problem developed. My work had taken a rather experimental turn and French was unable to support yet another experimenter in a catalog which already contained much such material. I reluctantly sought publication elsewhere while retaining a most enjoyable professional relationship with Talbot.

"Between 'The Betrothed' and 'Transceiver' I had cajoled I. E. Clark into publishing 'Filiation.' I was not too pleased with the experience, though, as Clark had demanded exhaustive re-writes. When the experimental phase arrived, Clark was included in the submission rotation. I was astonished when the letter came accepting 'Fables' and aggravated when I noted that he wanted revision again. Initially, I didn't like the revision ideas. But I considered the suggestions for a week and it turned out that they were valid and strengthened the play. Somewhere in my brain a little bell rang—the pattern was familiar. What my dear Lou could no longer provide, I. E. Clark could.

"My name and Clark's must always be linked. His then tiny company had no business venturing off into the nether reaches of contemporary theatrical style, but Clark felt that pieces with what he considered literary merit would find a stage. Thankfully, his instincts proved correct. Since that time, I. E. Clark has been the unseen force behind most of my work.

"My writings have mostly attacked mindlessness, whatever its form. Personal freedom, a humanely responsible personal freedom, has been a dominant theme of mine. My fondest hope is that my son, Brian, may always be happy, and my writings have tried to point the way in a world in which such happiness is possible—or away from worlds where it is not. My principal vocational interest is the theatre, particularly in the area of developing new works for the stage. Within this context, I try to stay open to new possibilities and to always define theatre in the broadest terms."

AVOCATIONAL INTERESTS: Composing music, travel.

*   *   *

McDONOUGH, Jerry
See McDONOUGH, Jerome

*   *   *

McGEAR, Mike
See McCARTNEY, Peter Michael

*   *   *

McHENRY, Dean E(ugene)   1910-

PERSONAL: Born in 1910 near Lompoc, Calif.; son of William Thomas (a farmer) and Virgie (Hilton) McHenry; married Jane Snyder (a researcher), February 23, 1935; children: Sally McHenry Mackenzie, Dean, Nancy McHenry Fletcher, Henry. *Education:* University of California, Los Angeles, B.A., 1932; Stanford University, M.A., 1933; University of California, Berkeley, Ph.D., 1936. *Home:* 6821 Bonny Doon Rd., Santa Cruz, Calif. 95060.

CAREER: Williams College, Williamstown, Mass., instructor in government, 1936-37; Pennsylvania State College (now University), University Park, assistant professor of political science, 1937-39; University of California, Los Angeles, assistant professor, 1939-45, associate professor, 1945-50, professor of political science, 1950-63, chairman of department, 1950-52, dean of Division of Social Sciences, 1947-50, academic assistant to president of university system, 1958-60, university dean of academic planning, 1960-63; University of California, Santa Cruz, professor of comparative government, 1963-74, chancellor, 1961-74, professor emeritus and chancellor emeritus, 1974—. Fulbright lecturer in Australia, 1954; member of board of advisers of U.S. Naval Postgraduate School, 1970-74. Member of board of trustees of College Entrance Examination Board, 1964-67. Member of board of directors of Longs Drug Stores, Inc., 1974—. *Military service:* U.S. Marine Corps Reserve, 1948-60; became captain.

MEMBER: Western Association of Schools and Colleges (member of Senior Commission, 1968-70, 1972-74), Western College Association (president, 1972-74), California Academy

of Sciences (fellow), Phi Beta Kappa. *Awards, honors:* Social Science Research Council grant, 1941-43; Carnegie fellowship for New Zealand, 1946-47; Litt.D. from University of Western Australia, 1963; LL.D. from University of Nevada, 1966, and Grinnell College, 1967; Danforth Foundation grant for England and the South Pacific, 1969.

WRITINGS: The Labour Party in Transition, Routledge, 1938; *A New Legislature for Modern California,* Haynes Foundation, 1940; *His Majesty's Opposition: Structures and Problems of the British Labour Party, 1931-1938,* University of California Press, 1940; (with John Henry Ferguson) *The American Federal Government,* McGraw, 1947, 14th edition, 1981; (with Ferguson) *The American System of Government,* McGraw, 1947, 14th edition, 1981, (with Winston Winford Crouch) *California Government: Politics and Administration,* University of California Press, 1949.

The Third Force in Canada: The Cooperative Commonwealth Federation, 1932-1948, University of California Press, 1950, reprinted, Greenwood Press, 1976; (with Ferguson) *Elements of American Government,* McGraw, 1950, 9th edition, 1970; (with Ferguson and E. B. Finscher) *American Government Today,* McGraw, 1951; (with Crouch, J. C. Bollens, and S. Scott) *State and Local Government in California,* University of California Press, 1952; *The University of Nevada: An Appraisal,* [Carson City, Nevada], 1956; *Survey of Higher Education in the Kansas City Area: Higher Education in Kansas City,* [Kansas City, Missouri], 1957.

(With Richard P. Ditton) *Self-Guiding Auto Tours in Yosemite National Park,* [Yosemite National Park, California], 1965; *Policy Implementation in Rural Africa: The Case of Ujamaa Villages in Tanzania,* African Studies Association, 1973; (with others) *Academic Departments: Problems, Variations, and Alternatives,* Jossey-Bass, 1977. Editor of *Arboretum Associates Bulletin,* 1976—.

*   *   *

McHUGH, Vincent   1904-1983

OBITUARY NOTICE: Born December 23, 1904, in Providence, R.I.; died of respiratory complications, January 23, 1983, in Sacramento, Calif. Educator, editor, and author. McHugh worked variously as editor in chief of the New York office of the Federal Writer's Project during the Depression, as a staff writer for the *New Yorker,* as writer-director of the Office of War Information Films, as a contract writer for Paramount Pictures, and as a merchant marine correspondent. He also lectured at Claremont College, taught at the Writers' Conference at Boulder and in the Rocky Mountains, and taught at the universities of Kansas City, Missouri, and New Hampshire. McHugh is best remembered, however, as a poet and novelist. His novels, which mix fantasy with realism, include *Caleb Catlum's America,* a satire on American history, and *I Am Thinking of My Darling,* a 1943 publication that became a best-seller and the basis for a film. His last volume of poems, a collaborative effort with K. C. Kwock in 1980, is an English translation of one hundred fifty classical Mandarin poems, titled *Old Friends From Far Away.* McHugh was also the author of book reviews, magazine articles, and a collection of short stories. Obituaries and other sources: *Twentieth-Century Authors: A Biographical Dictionary of Modern Literature,* H. W. Wilson, 1942, 1st supplement, 1955; *Concise Dictionary of American Literature,* Greenwood Press, 1969; *New York Times,* January 27, 1983.

McILWAIN, David 1921-
(Charles Eric Maine, Richard Rayner, Robert Wade)

PERSONAL: Born January 21, 1921, in Liverpool, England; son of David (an engineer) and Carolyn (Jones) McIlwain; married Joan Lilian Hardy, 1947 (divorced, 1960); married Clare Mary Came, 1961; children: four daughters, two sons. *Address:* c/o Ace Books, Charter Communications, Inc., 360 Park Ave. S., New York, N.Y. 10010.

Career: Journalist, 1948—. Free-lance writer and consultant. *Member:* Crime Writers Association, National Union of Journalists.

WRITINGS—Science fiction novels, except as noted; under pseudonym Charles Eric Maine: *Spaceways: A Story of the Very Near Future*, Hodder & Stoughton, 1953, published as *Spaceways Satellite*, Avalon, 1958; *Timeliner: A Story of Time and Space*, Rinehart, 1955; *Crisis 2000*, Hodder & Stoughton, 1955; *Escapement*, Hodder & Stoughton, 1956, published as *The Man Who Couldn't Sleep*, Lippincott, 1958; *High Vacuum*, Ballantine, 1957; *Isotope Man*, Lippincott, 1957; *The Tide Went Out*, Hodder & Stoughton, 1958; *World Without Men*, Ace Books, 1958; *Fire Past the Future*, Ballantine, 1959 (published in England as *Count-Down*, Hodder & Stoughton, 1959); *Subterfuge*, Hodder & Stoughton, 1959.

Calculated Risk, Hodder & Stoughton, 1960; *He Owned the World*, Avalon, 1960 (published in England as *The Man Who Owned the World*, Hodder & Stoughton, 1961); *The Mind of Mr. Soames*, Hodder & Stoughton, 1961; *The Darkest of Nights*, Hodder & Stoughton, 1962, published as *Survival Margin*, Fawcett, 1968; *Never Let Up*, Hodder & Stoughton, 1964; *B.E.A.S.T.: Biological Evolutionary Animal Simulation Test*, Hodder & Stoughton, 1966; *The World's Strangest Crimes* (nonfiction), Hart Publishing, 1967, reprinted as *The Bizarre and the Bloody: A Clutch of Weird Crimes—Each Shockingly True!*, 1972; *World Famous Mistresses* (nonfiction), Odhams, 1970; *The Random Factor*, Hodder & Stoughton, 1971; *Alph*, Doubleday, 1972; *Thirst*, Ace Books, 1978.

Author of general fiction under pseudonym Robert Wade and crime novels under pseudonym Richard Rayner. Author of radio play "Spaceways," first broadcast by British Broadcasting Corp., 1952.

AVOCATIONAL INTERESTS: Physics, photography, music.*

* * *

McINNES, Edward 1935-

PERSONAL: Born in 1935, in Ayr, Scotland; son of William (a minister) and Sophia (O'Hara) McInnes; married Jean Kilgour (a dental surgeon), 1964; children: Katharine, Alison, Fiona, Iain. *Education:* University of London, B.A., 1958, M.A., 1961; University of Edinburgh, Ph.D., 1974. *Office:* Department of German, University of Hull, Hull HU6 7RX, England.

CAREER: Freie Universitaet, Berlin, East Germany, instructor, 1961-62; University of Edinburgh, Edinburgh, Scotland, lecturer, 1962-73, reader in German, 1973-74; University of Strathclyde, Glasgow, Scotland, professor of German studies, 1974-78; University of Hull, Hull, England, professor of German, 1978—.

WRITINGS: German Social Drama, 1840-1900: From Hebbel to Hauptmann, Akademischer Verlag Heinz, 1976; *J.M.R. Lenz: "Die Soldaten"* (title means "J.M.R. Lenz: 'The Soldier'"), Hanser Verlag, 1977; *Morality of Doubt: Brecht and the German Dramatic Tradition*, University of Hull, 1980; *Das deutsche Drama des Neunzehnte Jahrhunderts* (title means "German Drama of the Nineteenth Century"), Schmidt Verlag, 1982; *Max Halbe: "Jugend,"* University of Hull, 1983. Also author of *Hauptmann Centenary Lecture*, 1964, and (with Anthony Harher) *German Today*, 1967.

Contributor of more than thirty articles to German and British journals. Member of editorial board of *New German Studies*.

WORK IN PROGRESS: The Drama of the Sturm und Drang.

SIDELIGHTS: McInnes told *CA:* "German drama in the eighteenth and nineteenth centuries offers, in my view, the most interesting attempts in European literature to experiment with traditional tragic structures and themes and to make them responsive to modern empirical modes of thought. The vitality of central dramatic traditions in German literature separates it from all the other literatures of Europe."

* * *

McKENNA, Terry 1949-

PERSONAL: Born November 24, 1949, in London, England; son of John and Edna McKenna; married Miranda Jaquarello (an actress); children: Dante, Reuben. *Education:* Central School of Speech and Drama, London, England, Diploma in Dramatic Art, 1971. *Home:* Manor Farm Cottage, Thurning, Melton Constable, Norfolk NR24 2LP, England. *Agent:* Murray Pollinger, 4 Garrick St., London WC2E 9BH, England.

CAREER: Worked as singer and trucker; artist and illustrator, 1976—. Work exhibited at National Theatre, 1982.

WRITINGS—Self-illustrated, juvenile: *The Fox and the Circus Bear*, Gollancz, 1982; *Tomboy*, Dinosaur, 1982.

Illustrator; all by Martin Waddell; "The Mystery Squad" series; published by Blackie & Son: *The Mystery Squad and the Deadman's Message*, 1984; . . . *and the Artful Dodger*, 1984; . . . *and the Whistling Teeth*, 1984; . . . *and Mr. Midnight*, 1984.

WORK IN PROGRESS: A picture book using a theatrical approach to the comic strip; an adventure comic strip, self-illustrated.

SIDELIGHTS: Terry McKenna has worked on illustration projects to be used in Third World countries, including a work on green deserts for the Sudan.

He wrote: "Working in comic strip form is, although highly demanding, a very exciting method of combining writing with illustrating. Perhaps the motivation for this approach comes from my background in drama: a comic strip gives you the opportunity to express the visual impact at all stages. The personalitites of the characters involved are, for me, the starting point and the major influence on the story; I feel that working them through a comic strip satisfies the need to present all sides of them. Visual comedy plays an important part in my work and, here again, the comic strip is a particularly suitable medium."

* * *

McLEAN, George 1905(?)-1983

OBITUARY NOTICE: Born c. 1905; died of a stroke, March

1, 1983, in Tupelo, Miss. Publisher. McLean was the owner and chief executive officer of the *Northeast Mississippi Daily Journal* for almost fifty years. He salvaged the bankrupt bi-weekly *Tupelo Journal* in 1934, increasing the paper's paid circulation until it was the largest in the country for a city of Tupelo's size. In what was to become a model program for Mississippi, the paper, beginning in 1977 and covering a ten year period, granted the Lee County elementary schools more than one million dollars for reading aides. McLean served on Governor William Winter's Quality Education Committee, was active in organizations to help the poor in northeastern Mississippi, and was the recipient of local, state, and national honors. Obituaries and other sources: *New York Times*, February 2, 1983.

*   *   *

McMAHON, Charles P. 1916(?)-1983

OBITUARY NOTICE: Born c. 1916; died of a heart attack, March 29, 1983, in New Smyrna Beach, Fla. Business executive and newsman. McMahon, whose journalism career was twice interrupted by military service, began working for Associated Press in 1934. During the late 1930's he served as a volunteer with the Republican forces during the Spanish Civil War. The newsman was next employed by United Press (now United Press International), for whom he worked from 1940 to 1956, except for a short stint with the U.S. Army during World War II. When McMahon retired from the news business in 1956, he became a vice-president of the National Association of Home Builders. Obituaries and other sources: *Washington Post*, April 1, 1983.

*   *   *

McMAHON, Jeremiah 1919-

PERSONAL: Born January 27, 1919, in New York, N.Y.; son of Denis and Anna Louise (Casey) McMahon. *Education:* Attended Carnegie Institute of Technology (now Carnegie-Mellon University). *Politics:* Liberal. *Home:* 6655 Los Leones Dr., Tucson, Ariz. 85718.

CAREER: Professional dancer in New York, N.Y.; writer, 1962—; painter, 1970—.

WRITINGS: Devil's Channel (novel), Pyramid Publications, 1972; *Marmozi*, Harcourt, 1974.

WORK IN PROGRESS: A biography of Marcus Blechman; a travel book.

AVOCATIONAL INTERESTS: Travel (including China).

*   *   *

McMAHON, Robert J. 1949-

PERSONAL: Born May 13, 1949, in Flushing, N.Y.; son of William J. and Mary (Sullivan) McMahon; married Elinor Alison April (an occupational therapist), August 14, 1976. *Education:* Fairfield University, B.A., 1971; University of Connecticut, M.A., 1972, Ph.D., 1977. *Home:* 615 Northwest 11th Ave., Gainesville, Fla. 32607. *Office:* Department of History, 4131 GPA, University of Florida, Gainesville, Fla. 32611.

CAREER: U.S. Department of State, Washington, D.C., historian, 1977-82; University of Florida, Gainesville, assistant professor of history, 1982—. *Member:* Organization of American Historians, Society for Historians of American Foreign Relations.

WRITINGS: Colonialism and the Cold War: The United States and the Struggle for Indonesian Independence, 1945-49, Cornell University Press, 1981. Contributor to history journals.

WORK IN PROGRESS: An analysis of U.S. relations with India and Pakistan since 1947.

*   *   *

McMILLAN, Roddy 1923-1979

OBITUARY NOTICE: Born March 23, 1923, in Glasgow, Scotland; died July 9, 1979. Actor and author. McMillan studied for a stage career at the Glasgow Unity Theatre, making his acting debut as James Flay in a 1944 production of "Song of Tomorrow" at Queen's Theatre, Glasgow. McMillan later acted in films and held the lead in the television series "The Vital Spark" and "Daniel Pike." A playwright, he also appeared in his own plays, including "All in Good Faith" in Glasgow and "The Bevellers" in Edinburgh and London. Obituaries and other sources: *Who's Who in the Theatre: A Biographical Record of the Contemporary Stage*, 16th edition, Pitman, 1977.

*   *   *

McVEY, Ruth T(homas) 1930-

PERSONAL: Born October 22, 1930, in Allentown, Pa. *Education:* Bryn Mawr College, B.A., 1952; Harvard University, M.A., 1954; Cornell University, Ph.D., 1961. *Office:* Department of Economics and Politics, School of Oriental and African Studies, University of London, London W.C.1, England.

CAREER: Yale University, New Haven, Conn., research associate in Southeast Asian studies, 1961-63; Massachusetts Institute of Technology, Center for International Studies, Cambridge, research associate in Southeast Asian studies, 1963-65; Cornell University, Center for International Studies, Ithaca, N.Y., research fellow, 1965-66, visiting lecturer, 1966-67, research associate of Modern Indonesia Project, 1967-68; University of London, School of Oriental and African Studies, lecturer in economics and politics, 1969—, reader in politics, 1976—. *Member:* American Siam Society, Association of Asian Studies, Royal Ethnographic Society.

WRITINGS: The Development of the Indonesian Communist Party and Its Relations With the Soviet Union and the Chinese Peoples' Republic, Center for International Studies, Massachusetts Institute of Technology, 1954; *The Soviet View of the Indonesian Revolution: A Study in the Russian Attitude Towards Asian Nationalism*, Cornell Modern Indonesia Project, 1957; *Bibliography of Soviet Publications on Southeast Asia*, Department of Far Eastern Studies, Cornell University, 1959; (editor with Harry J. Benda) *The Communist Uprisings of 1926-1927 in Indonesia: Key Documents*, Cornell Modern Indonesia Project, 1960; *The Rise of Indonesian Communism*, Cornell University Press, 1965; (editor with Herbert Feith and others) *Indonesia* (young adult), Human Relations Area File Press, 1963, revised edition, 1967; (author of introduction) Achmed Sukarno, *Nationalism, Islam, and Marxism*, Cornell Modern Indonesia Project, 1970; (with Benedict R. Anderson) *A Preliminary Analysis of the October 1, 1965, Coup in Indonesia*, Cornell Modern Indonesia Project, 1971; (editor with Adrienne Suddard) *Southeast Asian Transitions: Approaches Through Social History*, Yale University Press, 1978.

MEACHER, Michael Hugh   1939-

PERSONAL: Born November 4, 1939, in Hemel Hempstead, Hertfordshire, England; son of George Hubert (a farmer) and Doris (a secretary; maiden name, May) Meacher; married Molly Christine Reid (a social worker), 1962; children: David, Nigel, Sally, Roslyn. *Education:* Received diploma (with first-class honors) from New College, Oxford, 1962; London School of Economics and Political Science, London, Diploma in Social Administration, 1963. *Politics:* Labour. *Religion:* Church of England. *Home:* 45 Cholmeley Park, London N6, England. *Office:* House of Commons, London S.W.1, England.

CAREER: Secretary for Danilo Dolci Trust, 1963-64; University of Essex, Essex, England, research fellow in social gerontology, 1964-66; University of York, Yorkshire, England, lecturer in social administration, 1966-69; University of London, London School of Economics and Political Science, London, England, lecturer in social administration, 1970; member of English Parliament for Oldham West District, 1970—, parliamentary undersecretary of state in Department of Industry, 1974-75, in Department of Health and Social Security, 1975-76, and in Department of Trade, 1976—. *Member:* Fabian Society.

WRITINGS: (With John N. Agate) *The Care of the Old,* Fabian Society, 1969; *Taken for a Ride: Special Residential Homes for Confused Old People,* Longman, 1972; *New Methods of Mental Health Care,* Pergamon, 1979; *Socialism With A Human Face: The Political Economy of Britain in the 1980's,* Allen & Unwin, 1982; *The Struggle for Full Employment: Labour's Alternative Economic Strategy,* Penguin, 1983. Contributor of articles on economic and social policy to magazines and newspapers.

SIDELIGHTS: In his *Times Literary Supplement* review of Meacher's fourth book, *Socialism With a Human Face: The Political Economy of Britain in the 1980's,* critic Christopher Hitchens noted that Meacher wrote with ''energy and conviction'' in his argument for a defensible definition of socialism. In his chapter ''Does a Socialist Society Already Exist?'' Meacher reaches ''a humane and reasonable conclusion,'' Hitchens wrote, and his chapters on the power of the state and the permanent bureaucracy are ''well researched and presented.'' Despite his objections that Meacher's tone is one of ''agonized reappraisal'' and that ''*Socialism With a Human Face* suffers . . . from being poorly written,'' Hitchens recommended it as ''a thoughtful and useful book.''

Meacher told *CA:* ''My interest is in radical political innovation (socialist), and I have a strong interest in humanitarian issues, poverty, civil rights, and democratic issues.''

BIOGRAPHICAL/CRITICAL SOURCES: Times Literary Supplement, June 25, 1982.

*   *   *

MEADOWS, Eddie S(pencer)   1939-

PERSONAL: Born June 24, 1939, in LaGrange, Tenn. *Education:* Michigan State University, Ph.D., 1970; postdoctoral study at University of California, Los Angeles. *Office:* Department of Music, San Diego State University, 5300 Campanile Dr., San Diego, Calif. 92182.

CAREER: Affiliated with department of music, San Diego State University, San Diego, Calif., 1972—.

WRITINGS: Jazz Reference and Research Materials: A Bibliography, Garland Publishing, 1981.

WORK IN PROGRESS: Reference and research material on black American music.

*   *   *

MECHIN, Jacques Benoist
See BENOIST-MECHIN, Jacques

*   *   *

MEHER BABA
See BABA, Meher

*   *   *

MEIER, Joel F(rancis)   1940-

PERSONAL: Born January 18, 1940, in Minden, Neb.; son of William Henery (an attorney) and Mabel (Utter) Meier; married Patricia Dee Schmadeke, August 22, 1965. *Education:* University of Nebraska, B.S., 1962, M.S., 1965; Indiana University, Re.D., 1973; postdoctoral study at University of Colorado, 1974. *Home:* 9615 Old Mill Trail, Missoula, Mont. 59802. *Office:* School of Forestry, Science Complex 465, University of Montana, Missoula, Mont. 59812.

CAREER: University of Nebraska, Lincoln, instructor in physical education and recreation, 1962-63; U.S. Peace Corps, Washington, D.C., Outward Bound training officer in Puerto Rico, 1963-64; University of Nebraska, instructor, 1964-67, assistant professor of physical education and recreation and director of campus recreation and intramural activities, 1967-70; University of Montana, Missoula, assistant professor, 1970-74, associate professor, 1974-79, professor of recreation management, 1979—, director of studies in recreation, 1970-77, chairman of department of health, physical education, and recreation, 1975-77, director of studies in recreation at School of Forestry, 1977-79. Senior Fulbright lecturer at University of Otago, 1980; guest lecturer at Dunedin Teachers College, Victoria University of Wellington, and Lincoln College, Canterbury, New Zealand, all 1980; guest on radio programs in New Zealand; participant in conferences and workshops all over the United States and New Zealand. Member of Recreation, Leisure Services, and Resource Education National Council on Accreditation, 1979-82; member of National Council on Outdoor Education and Camping, 1970—; member of National Joint Continuing Steering Committee for Community Schools/Community Education, 1978-79. Member of Montana Community Education Task Force for the Office of Public Instruction, 1977-81; member of Montana Community Education Talent Bank, 1981—. Member of Missoula Community Council and chairman of its recreation committee, 1971-72; member of Missoula County Land Planning Committee, 1974-75; president of board of directors of Bikecentennial ''76,'' 1973-78; member of board of directors of Missoula Young Men's Christian Association, 1974-77. Consultant to New Zealand Mountain Safety Council, Community Coordinated Child Care, Inc., and Swan River Boys Camp.

MEMBER: American Alliance for Health, Physical Education, Recreation, and Dance (life member; member of Northwest District executive board, 1974-77; member of national alliance assembly, 1975—; Northwest District vice-president for recreation, 1975-76; member of board of governors, 1977-79), American Association for Leisure and Recreation (member of national executive council, 1973-79; president, 1978-79), Society of Park and Recreation Educators (chairperson of communications committee, 1973-75; chairperson of committee on community educators, 1977-78), American Camping Association, National Intramural-Recreational Sports Association (life member), New Zealand Association for Health, Physical Education, and Recreation (honorary member), Montana Association for Health, Physical Education, Recreation, and Dance, Montana Recreation and Park Association (western regional chairperson, 1981), Five Valleys Park Association (member of board of directors, 1976-78; president of board of directors, 1979-80), Phi Epsilon Kappa (past president), Mu Epsilon Nu, Phi Delta Theta, Phi Delta Kappa.

AWARDS, HONORS: Distinguished service award from Phi Epsilon Kappa, 1969; fellowship from Lilly Endowment Fund, 1974; certificates of appreciation from National Recreation and Park Association, 1976, and American Association for Leisure and Recreation, 1976, 1977, 1978, 1980, 1981; grants from Montana Arts Council, 1975, State of Montana Social and Rehabilitation Services, 1975, U.S. Department of Health, Education, and Welfare, 1975, Tennessee Valley Authority, 1977, National Joint Continuing Steering Committee on Community Education, 1979, Charles Stewart Mott Foundation, 1979, and Arkwright Wilderness Studies Endowment, 1979-80.

WRITINGS: (Contributor) Charles W. Pozoldt, editor, *Innovations in Teaching,* National Recreation and Park Association, 1973; (contributor) Alan N. Hale, editor, *Directory of Programs in Outdoor Adventure Activities,* Outdoor Experiences, 1975; (with A. Viola Mitchell) *Camp Counseling: Leadership and Programming for the Organized Camp,* 6th edition (Meier was not associated with earlier editions), Saunders, 1983; (with Talmage W. Morash and George E. Welton) *High Adventure Outdoor Pursuits: Organization and Leadership,* Brighton, 1980; *Backpacking,* W. C. Brown, 1980; (contributor) Fred Martin, editor, *Leisure Today: Selected Readings,* Volume II, American Alliance of Health, Physical Education, Recreation, and Dance, 1980; (editor with Alan Trist) *Outdoor Training Guide,* New Zealand Outdoor Training Advisory Board, 1980; (contributor) Robert Lucas, editor, *Forestry Handbook,* revised edition, Society of American Foresters, in press. Contributor to academic journals. Editor of *MRPA Teller,* 1975-77; guest editor of *Journal of Physical Education and Recreation,* April, 1978.

WORK IN PROGRESS: Outdoor Leadership, publication expected in 1985.

SIDELIGHTS: Meier told *CA:* "My books and other publications deal with the subject of outdoor recreation, including the role of the leader in activities such as backpacking, mountaineering, camping, and other outdoor and wilderness pursuits. The texts focus on academic and experimental aspects of outdoor leadership. The intent is to present those components needed by anyone seriously interested in working in the field of outdoor recreation. My motivation for writing on these subjects is to share ideas so others might enjoy the same outdoor experiences that have brought me so much personal satisfaction and enjoyment. Frankly, I would rather do these things than write about them."

AVOCATIONAL INTERESTS: Backpacking, winter mountaineering, whitewater kayaking, alpine and nordic skiing, hiking, camping, flying small aircraft (with private pilot's license).

* * *

MEILAENDER, Gilbert 1946-

PERSONAL: Born January 31, 1946. *Education:* Received Ph.D.

from Princeton University. *Religion:* Lutheran. *Agent:* Harold Moldenhauer, 16401 Nine Mile Rd., East Detroit, Mich. 48021. *Office:* Department of Religion, Oberlin College, Oberlin, Ohio 44074.

CAREER: Associated with Oberlin College, Oberlin, Ohio.

WRITINGS: The Taste for the Other: The Social and Ethical Thought of C. S. Lewis, Eerdmans, 1978; *Friendship: A Study in Theological Ethics,* University of Notre Dame Press, 1981.

SIDELIGHTS: Meilander told *CA:* "Having learned at the age of seventeen that I was unable to hit the curve ball, I was moved to do the next best thing: study theology."

BIOGRAPHICAL/CRITICAL SOURCES: Commonweal, February 1, 1980, February 26, 1982.

* * *

MELONE, Albert P(hilip) 1942-

PERSONAL: Born April 25, 1942, in Chicago, Ill.; son of Dominic A. (an electronics technician) and Catherine (Bongeorno) Melone; married Peggy Harles, August 26, 1971; children: Dominic, Ann, Peter. *Education:* Mount San Antonio College, A.A., 1962; California State University, Los Angeles, B.A., 1964, M.A., 1967; attended Loyola Marymount University, 1964-65; University of Iowa, Ph.D., 1972. *Home:* 109 North Rod Lane, Carbondale, Ill. 62901. *Office:* Department of Political Science, Southern Illinois University, Carbondale, Ill. 62901.

CAREER: Idaho State University, Pocatello, lecturer, 1966, instructor in government, 1967; California State University, Los Angeles, instructor in political science, 1968; North Dakota State University, Fargo, assistant professor, 1970-75, associate professor of political science, 1975-80, chairperson of department, 1973-76; Southern Illinois University, Carbondale, visiting associate professor, 1979-80, associate professor of political science, 1980—. *Member:* American Political Science Association, Law and Society Association, American Judicature Society, Midwest Political Science Association, Western Political Science Association, Pi Sigma Alpha.

WRITINGS: Lawyers, Public Policy, and Interest Group Politics, University Press of America, 1977; (with Carl Kalvelage) *Primer on Constitutional Law,* Palisades, 1982; (contributor) Stuart S. Nagel, Erika Fairchild, and Anthony Champagne, editors, *The Political Science of Criminal Justice,* C. C Thomas, 1982; *Administrative Law Primer,* Palisades, 1983; *Primer in Political Science,* Palisades, 1983; *Foundations of Criminal Justice Research,* Palisades, 1983; (with H. B. Jacobini and Kalvelage) *Research Essentials of Administrative Law,* Palisades, 1983; (with Morley Segal and Kalvelage) *Political Science: Thinking, Researching, and Writing About the Discipline,* Palisades, in press. Contributor of articles and reviews to law and political science journals.

SIDELIGHTS: Melone told *CA:* "My writing entails an attempt to explain the puzzle which is American politics. While others find the study of the poor and powerless a significant avenue for investigation, I prefer to focus upon the rich and the powerful. My earliest and recurrent writings reflect that commitment. The greatest problem I face is deciding what not to research and publish. It is important to press forward with the original idea, tolerating occasional diversions but returning to those themes which remain truly important."

MELUCH, R(ebecca) M. 1956-

PERSONAL: Born October 24, 1956, in Ohio; daughter of Andrew D. (a psychologist) and Emma (Klemstein) Meluch. *Education:* University of North Carolina, Greensboro, B.A., 1978; University of Pennsylvania, M.A., 1981. *Home:* 29520 Schwartz Rd., Westlake, Ohio 44145. *Agent:* Frances Collin, 110 West 40th St., New York, N.Y. 10018.

CAREER: Writer. *Member:* Science Fiction Writers of America.

WRITINGS—Science fiction novels: *Sovereign*, New American Library, 1979; *Wind Dancers*, New American Library, 1981; *Wind Child*, New American Library, 1982.

WORK IN PROGRESS: A novel, tentatively titled *Jerusalem Fire;* a screenplay based on *Wind Dancers*, for George Addison Productions.

SIDELIGHTS: Meluch commented: "To become a writer it is useful to learn anything and everything besides English. My undergraduate degree is in theater, my graduate degree in ancient history. I have worked on an archaeological excavation in Israel, and hold a black belt in *tai kwon do*. All of these show up in different guises within my science fiction novels."

* * *

MENDEL, Sydney 1925-

BRIEF ENTRY: Born July 9, 1925, in London, England. Educator and author. Mendel has taught English at University of British Columbia and Western Washington State College. He joined the faculty of Dalhousie University in 1962 and became associate professor of English in 1966. Mendel wrote *Roads to Consciousness* (Allen & Unwin, 1974). *Address:* Department of English, Dalhousie University, Halifax, Nova Scotia, Canada B3H 3J5.

* * *

MENDONSA, Eugene L(ouis) 1942-

PERSONAL: Born October 17, 1942, in Vallejo, Calif.; son of Eugene L. (in business) and Dora (a nurse; maiden name, Middleton) Mendonsa; married Martha Iolani Chavez, September 16, 1962 (divorced, 1977); married Luzia Martins Vaz, December 28, 1980; children: Matthew, Melissa, Thomas. *Education:* Received B.S. (cum laude) and M.Sc. from Brigham Young University; Cambridge University, Ph.D., 1975. *Home:* 12617 B Caswell Ave., Los Angeles, Calif. 90066. *Office:* Department of Anthropology, University of California, Los Angeles, Los Angeles, Calif. 90024.

CAREER: University of California, Los Angeles, assistant professor of anthropology, 1976—. President of Centro Cultural Cabrillo, 1980-82. *Military service:* U.S. Army, 1960-64, served in medical corps. *Member:* American Anthropological Association (fellow), Royal Anthropological Institute of Great Britain and Ireland (fellow).

WRITINGS: The Politics of Divination, University of California Press, 1982. Contributor to anthropology journals.

WORK IN PROGRESS: The Politics of Reproduction, completion expected in 1984.

* * *

MENNEL, Robert McKisson 1938-

BRIEF ENTRY: Born October 18, 1938, in Toledo, Ohio.

American historian, educator, and author. Mennel began teaching American history at University of New Hampshire in 1973. He wrote *Thorns and Thistles: Juvenile Delinquents in the United States, 1825-1940* (University Press of New England, 1973), and he was among the editors of *Children and Youth in America: A Documentary History* (Harvard University Press, 1970-74). *Address:* Department of History, University of New Hampshire, Durham, N.H. 03824. *Biographical/critical sources: American Historical Review*, February, 1974.

* * *

MERKIN, Robert (Bruce) 1947-

PERSONAL: Born February 5, 1947, in Washington, D.C.; son of Harry (an insurance broker) and Helen (Rosenthal) Merkin; married Cynthia Marie Wald (a manufacturing executive), April 18, 1977. *Education:* Attended New York University, 1965-68, and Montgomery College, 1973. *Residence:* Northampton, Mass. *Agent:* Wendy Weil, Julian Bach Literary Agency, Inc., 747 Third Ave., New York, N.Y. 10017.

CAREER: Copyboy and reporter for *Washington Daily News*, Washington, D.C.; *Montgomery County and Prince Georges County Sentinel*, feature writer, reporter, and makeup editor, 1975-76; *Miami News*, Miami, Fla., reporter, rapid transit correspondent, feature writer, and author of column, 1976-78; *Amherst Record*, Amherst, Mass., editor, 1980; manager of bookstore in Washington, D.C. *Military service:* U.S. Army, 1969-71. *Member:* Planet Mongo Rocket Forces (amateur rocket club; emperor for life, 1980—). *Awards, honors:* Feature writing and news awards from Maryland Newspaper Association, both 1976.

WRITINGS: The South Florida Book of the Dead (novel), Morrow, 1982.

WORK IN PROGRESS: A novel for Morrow.

SIDELIGHTS: Merkin told *CA:* "I've wanted to write fiction since my early teens, and the first subject to overwhelm me enough to disrupt my life was the illicit drug industry in south Florida, on which I reported for the *Miami News*. The resulting manuscript, from which two novels are being carved, required two-and-a-half years to complete (including time out for newspaper work).

"I find the stasis and paralysis of contemporary American fiction vile and reprehensible (just as I'm sure some find the action of my work vile and reprehensible). I was determined that *something* had to happen in any first novel of mine. The box score: ten dead, two wounded."

BIOGRAPHICAL/CRITICAL SOURCES: Library Journal, June 15, 1982.

* * *

MEYER, Lillian Nicholson 1917(?)-1983

OBITUARY NOTICE: Born c. 1917 in St. Louis, Mo.; died of a heart attack, May 12, 1983, near Washington, D.C. Educator, artist, and author. Meyer taught in the St. Louis public schools, at Washington University, and in the Montgomery County schools but is best remembered for her botanical drawings which appeared in scientific journals. She is also the author of a book, *A Pinch of Herbs*. Obituaries and other sources: *Washington Post*, May 14, 1983.

MICHAUD, Stephen G(age)   1948-

PERSONAL: Born March 7, 1948, in Burlington, Vt.; son of Clayton Napoleon and Marion (Gage) Michaud; married Susan Denise Harper, June 11, 1983. *Education:* Menlo College, A.A., 1968; Stanford University, A.B., 1970. *Residence:* New York, N.Y. *Agent:* Kathy Robbins, 866 Second Ave., Suite 403, New York, N.Y. 10017.

CAREER: Newsweek, New York City, writer and reporter in New York City, 1970-77, Houston, Texas, 1973; *Business Week,* New York City, research editor, 1977-79; writer, 1979—. *Member:* National Association of Science Writers, Authors Guild.

WRITINGS: (With Hugh Aynesworth) *The Only Living Witness* (nonfiction), Simon & Schuster, 1983. Contributor to magazines, including *Smithsonian, Esquire,* and *Venture.*

WORK IN PROGRESS: A book on toxic substances in the environment.

SIDELIGHTS: Michaud told *CA:* "From 1979 to 1983 my full-time preoccupation was Theodore Robert Bundy, serial murderer, who is The Only Living Witness. The book is based upon extensive investigative work done by my partner, Hugh Aynesworth, as well as hundreds of hours of taped interviews we conducted with Bundy on Death Row at the Florida State Prison near Starke.

"The writer's life would be wonderful if one didn't have to write. Unfortunately, I cannot earn a living doing anything else. For the nonfiction writer, there is no adequate compensation for the endless hours of interviewing and research, or the long, lonely days at the typewriter. The only reliable sustenance comes from the heat of obsessive devotion to the craft. On the other hand, I do recommend a career in letters to anyone with a large and fragile ego, the obsessive and compulsive, gossips, snoops, misanthropes, loners, and those of independent means. Just don't ever *call* yourself a writer without blushing."

*   *   *

MICUNOVIC, Veljko   1916-1982

PERSONAL: Born January 16, 1916, in Velestovo, Montenegro (now part of Yugoslavia); died after a long illness, August 2, 1982, in Yugoslavia; son of Jovan and Marica Micunovic; married Budislava Dapcevic in 1950; children: one son, one daughter. *Education:* Attended University of Belgrade.

CAREER: Diplomat and government official. Helped organize national uprising in Montenegro; political leader in Montenegro, Bosnia, and Serbia territories (now part of Yugoslavia); associated with government of Yugoslavia, Belgrade, 1949-51, assistant minister of the interior, 1952, assistant minister of foreign affairs, 1952, ambassador to Soviet Union and Mongolia, 1956-58, undersecretary of state for foreign affairs, 1958-61, deputy secretary of state, 1961-62, ambassador to United States, 1962-67, president of Foreign Affairs and International Relations Committee of Federal Assembly, 1967-69, ambassador to the Soviet Union, 1969-71. Member of Presidium of Yugoslavia, 1971-74; member of Council of the Federation of Yugoslavia, 1974-82; member of central committee of Yugoslavia League of Communists, 1934-82. *Military service:* People's Liberation Army, 1941; received Partisan Memorial Badge. *Awards, honors:* Order of National Hero of Yugoslavia; first class award for meritorious services to the people.

WRITINGS: Moskovske godine: 1956-58, Liber, 1977, translation by David Floyd published as *Moscow Diary,* introduction by George Kennan, Doubleday, 1980.

SIDELIGHTS: Moscow Diary is a memoir of Micunovic's experiences while serving as Yugoslav ambassador to the Soviet Union from 1956 to 1958. The book was warmly received by many critics who welcomed the author's insights into Soviet foreign policy under the direction of then Soviet Premier Nikita Khrushchev. As Adam B. Ulam explained in *American Spectator,* Micunovic talks "a good deal about Soviet politics during the period of transition between Stalin's despotism and what eventually emerged as the oliogarcho-bureaucratic leadership with which we have been familiar for the past 15 years." Writing in the *Times Literary Supplement,* Duncan Wilson similarly noted that "Micunovic's diary of 1956-8 is a document vital for the understanding of relations between the countries of the communist world from the mid-1950s onwards."

Wilson continued: "Micunovic took up his appointment at a critical time. In June 1955, there had been a spectacular Soviet-Yugoslav reconciliation . . . [which] was, in Micunovic's view, the necessary prelude to a new style of Soviet foreign policy and to a major effort by the Soviet leaders to court 'progressive forces' on a world-wide scale, especially in Asia." "The times were certainly interesting," Peter S. Prescott agreed in *Newsweek,* adding, "The record that Micunovic kept of these events is important, and not only because candid revelations from Communist officials are a rarity," but also because, "as a communist, Micunovic was made privy to what was happening to a degree that no Western ambassador was."

Prescott further noted that Micunovic "is a perceptive observer with a knowledge of history, a frosty wit and an eye for irony and detail. Adept with anecdotes and the kind of quotation that fixes character, he offers devastating portraits of the Kremlin leadership in his time." And Wilson described *Moscow Diary* "as a work of considerable historical importance . . . accessible and digestible to the general reader, not only to the specialist . . . it is also full of good incidental stories which vividly evoke the Moscow scene," and concluded that "it can be thoroughly recommended as a classic of modern history and as an excellent read."

BIOGRAPHICAL/CRITICAL SOURCES: New York Times Book Review, February 17, 1980; *Newsweek,* February 25, 1980; *New Republic,* April 5, 1980; *Times Literary Supplement,* April 25, 1980; *Spectator,* April 26, 1980; *London Times,* May 22, 1980; *American Spectator,* July, 1980.

OBITUARIES: New York Times, August 3, 1982.*

*   *   *

MIDDELDORF, Ulrich Alexander   1901-1983

OBITUARY NOTICE: Born June 23, 1901, in Stassfurt, Germany (now East Germany); naturalized U.S. citizen; died February 20, 1983, in Florence, Italy. Art historian and author. An expert in Italian Renaissance sculpture and decorative arts, Middeldorf received his training in Europe, then came to the United States, where he spent nearly twenty years teaching at the University of Chicago. He became chairman of the art history department, honorary keeper of drawings at the Art Institute, and nurtured a generation of scholars, many of whom went on to hold influential positions in American museums and universities. In 1953 he accepted a position as director of the German Institute in Florence. Under his guidance the library quadrupled in size and became world famous among students of Italian art. During his career Middeldorf was awarded the Order of Merit from both Germany and Italy. He also wrote numerous articles and published several books, including *Raphael's Drawings* and *Sculpture From the Samuel H. Kress Collection*. Obituaries and other sources: *Who's Who in the World*, 3rd edition, Marquis, 1976; *Directory of American Scholars*, Volume 1: *History*, 7th edition, Bowker, 1978; *New York Times*, March 1, 1983; *London Times*, March 1, 1983; *Time*, March 14, 1983.

* * *

MIDDLETON, Richard 1945-

PERSONAL: Born February 4, 1945, in Great Britain. *Education:* Clare College, Cambridge, B.A., 1966; University of York, D.Phil., 1970. *Office:* Open University, Milton Keynes, Buckinghamshire MK7 6AA, England.

CAREER: Open University, Milton Keynes, England, senior lecturer in music, 1972—.

WRITINGS: Pop Music and the Blues, Gollancz, 1972; (editor with David Horn) *Popular Music*, Cambridge University Press, Volume I, 1982, Volume II, 1983.

BIOGRAPHICAL/CRITICAL SOURCES: New Statesman, December 15, 1972; *Times Literary Supplement*, February 23, 1973.

* * *

MILBERG, Warren H(oward) 1941-

PERSONAL: Born January 10, 1941, in New York, N.Y.; son of Louis and Winifred (Lesser) Milberg; married Jacqueline Hess (a writer and editor), May 4, 1980. *Education:* Washington College, Chestertown, Md., B.S., 1962; Auburn University, M.P.A., 1974; U.S. Air Command and Staff College, Honor Graduate, 1974; Naval War College, Honor Graduate, 1980. *Home:* 7229 Evanston Rd., Springfield, Va. 22150. *Office:* Office of the Secretary of Defense/Net Assessment, Pentagon, Washington, D.C. 20301.

CAREER: U.S. Air Force, career officer, 1962—, strategic policy and intelligence officer at headquarters, 1969-74, Defense Intelligence Agency, 1974-76, and Central Intelligence Agency, 1976-78; present rank, colonel. Affiliated with Secretary of Defense. Senior research associate at Fletcher School of Law and Diplomacy, 1978-79. *Awards, honors*—Military: Bronze Star; Vietnamese Cross of Gallantry; Vietnamese Cross of Honor.

WRITINGS: (Editor with Uri Ra'anen and Robert Pfaltzgraff, and contributor) *Intelligence Policy and National Security*, Shoe String, 1981. Contributor to military journals.

WORK IN PROGRESS: The Cuban Missile Crisis: A Turning Point in Cold War Politics.

SIDELIGHTS: Milberg wrote: "Foreign policy is developed and implemented on the basis of an infinite variety of inputs—some rational, some not. Understanding and describing these inputs, as well as the vagaries of people, bureaucracies, and nations, is *the* major challenge facing the contemporary author of books and articles on foreign affairs." Milberg has traveled extensively throughout Asia and the Pacific.

AVOCATIONAL INTERESTS: Reading, sailing, jogging, tennis.

MILBURN, George 1906-1966

OBITUARY NOTICE: Born April 27, 1906, in Coweta, Indian Territory (now Oklahoma); died September 22, 1966. Author best known for his short stories. Milburn spent most of his life traveling and free-lance writing. He spent two years in Chicago writing joke collections and editing "classics" for a paperback book publisher; he lived and wrote in an attic in the French Quarter of New Orleans for a year; he was a screenwriter in Hollywood; and he contributed articles and fiction to a variety of magazines, including *Harper's*, the *New Yorker, Vanity Fair, New Republic,* and other American and European periodicals. Milburn's short stories were collected into two volumes, *Oklahoma Town* and *No More Trumpets and Other Stories*. He also wrote two novels, *Catalogue* and *Flanigan's Folly*, received a Guggenheim fellowship for travel in England and Spain in 1934, and was a MacDowell fellow in 1948. Obituaries and other sources: *American Authors and Books: 1640 to the Present Day*, 3rd revised edition, Crown, 1962; *New York Times*, September 23, 1966; *Publishers Weekly*, October 17, 1966; *Who Was Who in America, With World Notables*, Volume IV: *1961-1968*, Marquis, 1968; *Contemporary American Authors: A Critical Survey and 219 Bio-Bibliographies*, AMS Press, 1970; *Who Was Who Among North American Authors, 1921-1939*, Gale, 1976.

* * *

MILLER, Alden Holmes 1906-1965

OBITUARY NOTICE: Born February 4, 1906, in Los Angeles, Calif.; died October 9, 1965; buried in Lower Lake Cemetery, Calif. Scientist, educator, and author. Miller was a professor of zoology at the University of California, where he also served as curator of birds at the Museum of Vertebrate Zoology and the Museum of Paleontology. In 1943 the American Ornithologists' Union honored him with the Brewster Medal. An active member of a variety of professional organizations, Miller served on the editorial boards of *Pacific Coast Avifauna* and *Evolution*. He also edited *Condor*. His many publications include *Ecological Factors Influencing Speed of Evolution* and *Lives of Desert Animals*. Obituaries and other sources: *Who Was Who in America, With World Notables*, Volume IV: *1961-1968*, Marquis, 1968.

* * *

MILLER, Ann
See COLLIER, Lucille Ann

* * *

MILLER, Frank 1925-1983

OBITUARY NOTICE: Born in 1925 in Kansas City, Mo.; died of a heart attack, February 17, 1983, in Des Moines, Iowa. Cartoonist. Miller worked as a staff artist for the *Kansas City Star* before moving to the *Des Moines Register*, where he gained acclaim in 1963 for his Pulitzer Prize-winning cartoon portraying the aftermath of a nuclear war. His style was described in *Newsweek* as "an affecting mix of homespun humor and populist outrage." Obituaries and other sources: *World Encyclopedia of Cartoons*, Chelsea House, 1980; *Washington Post*, February 20, 1983; *Newsweek*, February 28, 1983.

MILLER, Helen Topping   1884-1960

OBITUARY NOTICE: Born December 8, 1884, in Fenton, Mich.; died February 4, 1960; buried in Morristown, Tenn. An author who began writing for children's magazines when she was ten years old, Miller published four hundred short stories and eleven magazine serials in periodicals such as the *Saturday Evening Post, Good Housekeeping,* and *McCall's.* She was a prolific novelist as well, with most of her fifty books focusing on the Reconstruction period of the South. Her works for children include a series of stories about Christmas in the lives of prominent Americans, such as *Christmas at Monticello, With Thomas Jefferson; Christmas at Mount Vernon, With George and Martha Washington;* and *Christmas With Robert E. Lee.* Two of her books, *Nightshade* and *Christmas at Sagamore Hill,* were published posthumously. Obituaries and other sources: *New York Times,* February 5, 1960; *Publishers Weekly,* February 15, 1960; *Time,* February 15, 1960; *Who Was Who in America, With World Notables,* Volume IV: *1961-1968,* Marquis, 1968; *Authors of Books for Young People,* 2nd edition, Scarecrow, 1971; *American Novelists of Today,* Greenwood Press, 1976; *Michigan Authors,* 2nd edition, Michigan Association for Media in Education, 1980.

* * *

MILLER, Kent S(amuel)   1927-

BRIEF ENTRY: Born November 19, 1927, in Fremont, N.C. American psychologist, educator, and author. Miller, who began teaching at Florida State University in 1956, became a professor of psychology in 1967 and a research associate at the university's Institute for Social Research in 1971. He wrote *Managing Madness: The Case Against Civil Commitment* (Free Press, 1976) and *The Criminal Justice and Mental Health Systems: Conflict and Collusion* (Oelgeschlager, Gunn & Hain, 1980). Miller also co-edited *Mental Health and the Lower Social Classes* (Florida State University, 1966) and *Comparative Studies of Blacks and Whites in the United States* (Seminar Press, 1973). *Address:* Department of Psychology, Florida State University, Tallahassee, Fla. 32306.

* * *

MILLER, Lynn F(ieldman)   1938-

PERSONAL: Born October 9, 1938, in Newark, N.J.; daughter of George M. (a lawyer) and Helene G. Fieldman; married Arthur H. Miller (a lawyer), August 24, 1958; children: Jennifer Lyn, Jonathan Daniel. *Education:* Barnard College, B.A., 1959; Rutgers University, M.L.S., 1971, M.A., 1977. *Home:* 934B Village Dr. W., North Brunswick, N.J. 08902. *Office:* Media Services, Rutgers University Libraries, College Ave., New Brunswick, N.J. 08903.

CAREER: Alma White College, Zarepheth, N.J., head librarian, 1971; Rutgers University, New Brunswick, N.J., 1971—, began as instructor, became associate professor and reference librarian at Douglass College, 1971-79, media services librarian, 1979—, founding member of Women Studies Institute. Member of New Jersey State Librarian's Task Force on a New Library Network for New Jersey, 1979-81, and Statewide Planning Group, 1982-83; member of board of directors of Women Helping Women and Printmaking Council of New Jersey, 1976-78. Founding member of West Side Community Cooperative Nursery School, 1963-65; vice-president of Metuchen Community Council for Theater Six, 1967-68, president, 1968-69;

coordinator of sidewalk arts program, Metuchen Arts Council, 1969-70. Director of plays; gives readings; curates art shows.

MEMBER: American Library Association, Association of College and Research Libraries (member of state chapter board of directors, 1977-78; state president, 1982-83), American Association of University Professors, Women's Caucus for Art (member of New Jersey advisory board, 1982-83), LITA (Library and Information Technology Association), League of Women Voters (member of board of directors, 1965-69), New Jersey Library Association (member of executive board, 1978-81), Beta Phi Mu. *Awards, honors:* Award from New Jersey Committee for the Humanities, 1982, for Artists Books Program.

WRITINGS: (Editor) *Directory of New Jersey Women Artists,* Divison on Women, New Jersey Department of Community Affairs, 1977, 3rd edition, 1981; (editor with M. E. Comtois) *Contemporary American Theater Critics: A Biographical Directory and Anthology of Their Works,* Scarecrow, 1977; (editor) *Directory of Library Instruction Programs in New Jersey,* New Jersey Library Association, 1979; (with Sally S. Swenson) *Lives and Works: Talks With Women Artists,* Scarecrow, 1981. Contributor to library and education journals. Also project director of *Artists Books: From Me Traditional to Me Avantgarde* (catalog of exhibitions held at Rutgers' libraries).

WORK IN PROGRESS: Research (including interviews) on women film and video directors.

SIDELIGHTS: Miller told *CA:* "Since I am not an artist myself but intrigued with creativity, my work on women in the arts stems from a need to explore the roots of creativity. I tell myself that curating shows and administration can be art forms, but I know that is a rationalization. I am constantly inspired, piqued, and spurred on by the varied accomplishments of women in the arts who serve for me as role models of the synthesizing imagination I'd like to unleash in myself."

BIOGRAPHICAL/CRITICAL SOURCES: Art in America, May, 1976; Lucy Lippard, *From the Center,* Dutton, 1976; *Feminist Art Journal,* summer, 1976; *Womanart,* spring, 1977; *Newsletter* of Women's Caucus for Art/New Jersey, March, 1980; *Choice,* March, 1982; *Fiberarts,* March/April, 1982.

* * *

MILLER, Martha Porter   1897(?)-1983

OBITUARY NOTICE: Born c. 1897 in New Haven, Ky.; died of a heart ailment, April 19, 1983, in Washington, D.C. Genealogist and publisher. Between 1940 and 1960 Miller worked first for the Civil Service Commission, then for a farm equipment manufacturer, and finally for the Federal Trade Commission. She was best known, however, for her work with the Daughters of the American Revolution and as head genealogist for the Children of the American Revolution. She published a quarterly, *The Kentucky Genealogist,* from 1950 until 1978. Obituaries and other sources: *Washington Post,* April 21, 1983.

* * *

MILLER, Merton Howard   1923-

BRIEF ENTRY: Born May 16, 1923, in Boston, Mass. American economist, educator, and author. After working as an economist for the U.S. Treasury Department and the Federal Reserve Board, Miller began teaching. In 1961 he became a professor of banking and finance at University of Chicago, and later was named E. E. Brown Professor. Miller has also taught at London School of Economics and Political Science, London, and at Carnegie Institute of Technology (now Carnegie-Mellon University). He co-authored *The Theory of Finance* (Holt, 1972) and *Macroeconomics: A Neoclassical Introduction* (Irwin, 1974). Miller also co-edited *Essays in Applied Price Theory* (University of Chicago Press, 1980). *Address:* Graduate School of Business, University of Chicago, 5836 South Greenwood Ave., Chicago, Ill. 60637. *Biographical/critical sources: Who's Who in America,* 40th edition, Marquis, 1978.

*   *   *

MILLS, Claudia   1954-

PERSONAL: Born August 21, 1954, in New York, N.Y.; daughter of Charles Howard (a safety engineer) and Helen (a teacher; maiden name, Lederleitner) Mills. *Education:* Wellesley College, B.A., 1976; Princeton University, M.A., 1979. *Home:* 7009 Poplar Ave., Takoma Park, Md. 20912. *Office:* Center for Philosophy and Public Policy, University of Maryland, College Park, Md. 20742.

CAREER: Four Winds Press, New York, N.Y., editorial secretary and production assistant, 1979-80; University of Maryland, College Park, editor of *QQ: Report From the Center for Philosophy and Public Policy,* 1980—. *Member:* Society of Children's Book Writers, Phi Beta Kappa.

WRITINGS: Luisa's American Dream (juvenile), Four Winds, 1981; *At the Back of the Woods* (juvenile), Four Winds, 1982; *The Secret Carousel* (juvenile), Four Winds, 1983; (editor with Douglas MacLean) *Liberalism Reconsidered,* Rowman & Littlefield, 1983; *The Living Know* (juvenile), Macmillan, in press.

SIDELIGHTS: Mills told *CA:* "I have been writing books for children and teenagers since I was a child and a teenager. My autobiographical manuscript, *T Is for Tarzan,* written when I was fourteen, was widely circulated through my junior high school, as adolescent friends and foes waited turns to see how they were slandered.

"I didn't begin serious professional writing, however, until I left graduate school impulsively in mid-year to take a secretarial job at Four Winds Press. I occupied myself during the four-hour round-trip commute from Princeton by writing picture-book and novel manuscripts, which I submitted to four Winds Press under various pseudonyms. It was very easy—but so disheartening—to slip a rejected manuscript unobtrusively into my book bag.

"Finally a manuscript proved promising enough on a first skim for the editor to hand it over to me, her secretary, for a reader's report. I took the challenge and wrote an objective, candid report on my own manuscript, including suggestions for needed revisions. The editor forwarded to the author (me) her 'excellent reader's report' and then I dutifully took my own suggestions in rewriting. I finally confessed my duplicity when the manuscript was completed. Fortunately, the editor had a keen sense of humor, and the manuscript was published as *At the Back of the Woods.*"

*   *   *

MILNE, Edward James   1915-1983

OBITUARY NOTICE: Born October 18, 1915; died March 23, 1983. Politician and author. A Labour party member of Parliament for fourteen years, Milne was best known for his cru-

sade against corruption in the Labour movement in northeast England. Because of his activities, Milne was dismissed from his party post just prior to the February, 1974, election. He nevertheless ran in the upcoming election as an Independent Labour candidate and was victorious over the official Labour candidate. He subsequently lost elections in October, 1974, and in 1979. Milne's controversial 1976 autobiography, *No Shining Armour,* involved the politician in several libel suits. In some of the cases prominent figures received public apologies and substantial compensation for damages resulting from accusations of wrongdoing in the book. Milne, however, brought successful legal action against two members of Parliament, John Ryman and William Hamilton. *Obituaries and other sources: The International Year Book and Statesmen's Who's Who,* Kelley's Directories, 1982; *Who's Who,* 134th edition, St. Martin's, 1982; *London Times,* March 26, 1983.

*   *   *

MILTON, Arthur   1922-

PERSONAL: Born June 7, 1922, in New York, N.Y.; children: Donna Eve Conte, Robert V. Conte, Claudia Marie, Robert Laurence, Linda Sue, Patricia Ann. *Home:* 425 East 58th St., New York, N.Y. 10022. *Office:* 301 East 57th St., New York, N.Y. 10022.

CAREER: Feature writer for *Financial World;* associated with Arthur Milton & Co., Inc. (brokers of life insurance company stock); registered broker for Securities and Exchange Commission. Broadcaster for Armed Forces Radio; guest on television and radio programs; public speaker. Sponsor of New York State's College of Insurance; insurance and finance consultant. *Member:* General Insurance Brokers Association (past member of board of directors), Atlantic Alumni of the Life Insurance Agency Management Association (past member of board of directors).

WRITINGS: Life Insurance Stocks: The Modern Gold Rush, Citadel, 1963; *How to Get a Dollar's Value for a Dollar Spent,* Citadel, 1964; *Life Insurance Stocks: An Investment Appraisal,* Timely Publications Corp., 1965; *Inflation: Everyone's Problem,* Citadel, 1968; *Insurance Stocks: A Fortune to Share,* Information, Inc., 1969; *You Are Worth a Fortune,* Citadel, 1977; *Will Inflation Destroy America?,* Citadel, 1977; *How Your Insurance Policies Rob You,* Citadel, 1981. Also author of *Something More Can Be Done!* (public safety pamphlet). Contributor to business magazines.

SIDELIGHTS: Milton has combined his background in insurance and his work as a registered broker of the Securities and Exchange Commission to become a successful author. He was active in the insurance industry as an agent, general agent, and general insurance broker. He came into contact with top management executives, and became convinced that management is one of the keys to proper appraisal of an insurance company. Another of his concerns is consumer protection legislation, and his views on this subject have been published in the *Congressional Record.*

*   *   *

MINK, Louis Otto, Jr.   1921-1983

OBITUARY NOTICE—See index for CA sketch: Born September 3, 1921, in Ada, Ohio; died January 19, 1983, in Hartford, Conn. Educator and author. Mink began his career at Yale University in 1950. Two years later he became a faculty member of Wesleyan University's philosophy department. His writings include *Mind, History, and Dialectic: The Philosophy of R. G. Collingwood* and *Finnegan's Wake Gazetteer*. Obituaries and other sources: *Chronicle of Higher Education,* February 2, 1983.

* * *

MISIUNAS, Romuald John 1945-

PERSONAL: Born February 9, 1945, in Vetlanda, Sweden; came to the United States in 1954, naturalized citizen, 1959; son of Walter Vladas (a teacher) and Elizabeth (a teacher) Misiunas; married Audrone Kubilius (a banker), May 1, 1971. *Education:* Loyola University, Chicago, Ill., B.S., 1965; Yale University, M.A., 1967, Ph.D., 1971. *Office:* Concilium on International and Area Studies, Yale University, New Haven, Conn. 06520.

CAREER: University of Nebraska, Lincoln, visiting assistant professor of history, 1970-72; Williams College, Williamstown, Mass., assistant professor of history, 1972-79; Yale University, New Haven, Conn., research associate of Concilium on International and Area Studies, 1980—. Visiting research associate at University of Warsaw, 1975-76. *Member:* American Historical Association, Association for the Advancement of Baltic Studies (vice-president, 1973-74), Society for the Advancement of Scandinavian Studies, American Association for the Advancement of Slavic Studies.

WRITINGS: (Editor with V. Stanley Vardys) *The Baltic States in Peace and War, 1917-1945*, Pennsylvania State University Press, 1978; (with Rein Taagepera) *The Baltic States: Years of Dependence, 1940-1980*, University of California Press, 1983. Contributor to scholarly journals.

* * *

MISKIMIN, Harry A(lvin, Jr.) 1932-

BRIEF ENTRY: Born September 8, 1932, in East Orange, N.J. American historian, educator, and author. Miskimin joined the faculty of Yale University in 1960, becoming a professor of history in 1971. His books include *Money, Prices, and Foreign Exchange in Fourteenth-Century France* (Yale University Press, 1963), *The Economy of Early Renaissance Europe, 1300-1460* (Prentice-Hall, 1969), *The Medieval City* (Yale University Press, 1977), and *The Economy of Later Renaissance Europe, 1460-1600* (Cambridge University Press, 1977). *Address:* Department of History, Yale University, New Haven, Conn. 06520. *Biographical/critical sources: Times Literary Supplement,* March 24, 1978; *American Historical Review,* October, 1978, February, 1979.

* * *

MITCHELL, Harold P(aton) 1900-1983

OBITUARY NOTICE—See index for *CA* sketch: Born May 21, 1900, in Carnock, Scotland; died April 8, 1983, on Marshall's Island, Bermuda. Businessman, politician, and author. A successful businessman, Mitchell inherited and revived his family's glassworks operation as a young man. His business concerns eventually branched out into mining and farming enterprises overseas, particularly coal mining in Canada and growing sugar, bananas, and citrus fruits in the West Indies. He also maintained farming interests in Brazil, Guatemala, Honduras, and Fiji. Mitchell served as a Conservative member of Parliament from 1931 to 1945. He was an authority on the Caribbean,

producing such works as *Cooperation in the Caribbean, Caribbean Patterns: A Political and Economic Study of the Contemporary Caribbean,* and *The Caribbean in Relation to the Integration of Latin America.* His other books include *Downhill Ski-Racing* and *In My Stride.* Obituaries and other sources: *London Times,* April 12, 1983.

* * *

MITCHELL, Margaret (Munnerlyn) 1900-1949 (Peggy Mitchell)

BRIEF ENTRY: Born November 8, 1900, in Atlanta, Ga.; died from injuries sustained after being struck by an automobile, August 16, 1949, in Atlanta, Ga.; buried in Oakland Cemetery, Atlanta, Ga. American journalist and author. Margaret Mitchell worked on the staff of the *Atlanta Journal,* writing as Peggy Mitchell, from 1922 until an ankle injury forced her resignation. Beginning in 1926, Mitchell worked for nearly ten years on her only novel, the overwhelmingly successful *Gone With the Wind* (1936). A story of survival in the Civil War South, *Gone With the Wind* won the 1937 Pulitzer Prize for literature, set a record for most sales in one day (50,000 copies), became the longest work of fiction printed in Braille (thirty volumes), and inspired the motion picture of the same name, which, since its 1939 premiere, has ranked among the top money-making films. *Biographical/critical sources: Twentieth-Century Authors: A Biographical Dictionary of Modern Literature,* 1st supplement, H. W. Wilson, 1955; *Cyclopedia of World Authors,* Harper, 1958; *Longman Companion to Twentieth Century Literature,* Longman, 1970; *Dictionary of Literary Biography,* Volume 9: *American Novelists, 1910-1945,* Gale, 1981; *Twentieth-Century Literary Criticism,* Volume 11, Gale, 1983.

* * *

MITCHELL, Peggy See MITCHELL, Margaret (Munnerlyn)

* * *

MOCKLER, Mike 1945-

PERSONAL: Born April 5, 1945, in Reading, England; son of Reginald and Gwen (Lloyd) Mockler; married Patricia Bates (a teacher), September 2, 1967. *Education:* University of Sheffield, B.A. (with honors), 1967; University of Bristol, Certificate of Education, 1968. *Politics:* Liberal. *Religion:* Church of England. *Home:* Gulliver's Cottage, Chapel Rise, Avon Castle, Ringwood, Hampshire, England.

CAREER: Teacher of English at a grammar school in Eastleigh, Hampshire, England, 1968-72; Ferndown Upper School, Ferndown, Wimborne, Dorset, England, head of English department, 1972-83; Highcliffe Comprehensive School, Highcliffe, Christchurch, Dorset, senior master, 1983—.

WRITINGS: Birds in the Garden, Blandford, 1982; (editor and contributor) *Flights of Imagination* (poems), Blandford, 1982; (contributor of photographs) Ron Freethy, *How Birds Work,* Blandford, 1982.

Contributor of articles and photographs to magazines and newspapers, including *Observer Colour Supplement, Amateur Photographer,* and *Wildlife.*

SIDELIGHTS: Mockler told *CA:* "My interest in birds stretches back a long ways—the best part of fifteen years. My delight in photographing them came a little later. When I realized the joy of capturing on film the detailing of birds, which often tends to be overlooked as 'ordinary' or 'common,' I was soon hooked! I became well known in the part of England where I live for my talks and the high standards of my slide shows. The idea of writing a book grew naturally out of the popularity of these talks and my desire to communicate my enthusiasm to others.

"*Birds in the Garden* was written for the average householder who wants more information about the birds he sees every day, without having to read reams of scientific data and graphs. More than half of the photographs are my own, taken over a number of years while I was studying birds.

"*Flights of Imagination* is a completely different kind of book, though it is also inspired by my love of birds and literature. It is an anthology of poems about birds, with specially commissioned paintings to illustrate them. Most of the poetry is modern, including a poem of my own, but the English nineteenth-century poet, John Clare, is also included. The book was launched with an exhibition of the original paintings used in it. The original of the cover painting was, in fact, bought by an American on holiday in England."

*   *   *

MODEL, Lisette   1906-1983

OBITUARY NOTICE: Born November 10, 1906, in Vienna, Austria; died of heart and respiratory disease, March 30, 1983, in New York, N.Y. Photographer, educator, and author of *Lisette Model: An Aperture Monograph.* Recognized as a major photographer, Model is best known for her pictures of overweight people. Among her most noted works are "Woman on a Doorstep" and "Bather at Coney Island." Model became a photographer for *Harper's Bazaar* after coming to the United States with her husband in 1938. Obituaries and other sources: *Who's Who in America,* 42nd edition, Marquis, 1982; *Contemporary Photographers,* St. Martin's, 1982; *New York Times,* March 31, 1983; *Chicago Tribune,* April 1, 1983; *Washington Post,* April 1, 1983; *Time,* April 11, 1983.

*   *   *

MODESITT, L(eland) E(xton), Jr.   1943-

PERSONAL: Born October 19, 1943, in Denver, Colo.; son of Leland Exton (an attorney) and Nancy Lila (in real estate; maiden name, Evans) Modesitt; married Christina Alma Gribben (an educator), October 22, 1977; children: Leland Exton III, Susan Carnall, Catherine Grant, Nancy Mayo, Elizabeth Leanore, Kristen Linnea. *Education:* Williams College, B.A., 1965; graduate study at University of Denver, 1970-71. *Politics:* Republican. *Religion:* United Methodist. *Home:* 3213 Latigo Ct., Oakton, Va. 22124. *Office:* Office of Legislation, U.S. Environmental Protection Agency, 401 M St., S.W., Washington, D.C. 20460.

CAREER: C. A. Norgren Co. (industrial pneumatics company), Littleton, Colo., market research analyst, 1969-70; Koebel & Co. (real estate and construction firm), Denver, Colo., sales associate, 1971-72; legislative assistant to U.S. Representative Bill Armstrong, 1973-79; administrative assistant to U.S. Representative Ken Kramer, 1979-81; U.S. Environmental Protection Agency, Washington, D.C., director of Office of Legislation, 1981—. Lecturer in science fiction writing at Georgetown University, 1980-81. *Military service:* U.S.

Navy, 1965-69; became lieutenant. *Member:* Delta Kappa Epsilon.

WRITINGS: The Fires of Paratime, Timescape, 1982. Contributor to science fiction magazines, including *Analog Science Fiction-Science Fact, Galaxy,* and *Isaac Asimov's Science Fiction Magazine.*

WORK IN PROGRESS: A science fiction novel tentatively titled *The Hammer of Darkness,* publication by Timescape expected in 1984.

SIDELIGHTS: Modesitt told *CA:* "Writers write. They have to, or they would not be writers. I am a writer who worked at it long enough to become an author. Virtually all of my early and formal training in writing was devoted to poetry—where I had a choice! I did not write my first science fiction story for publication until I was twenty-nine, and my first novel was published just before my thirty-ninth birthday.

"Although the various aspects of power and how it changes people and how government systems work and how they don't are themes underlying what I write, I try to concentrate on people—on heroes in the true sense of the word. A man who has no fear is not a hero. He's a damned fool. A hero is a man or woman who is shivering with fear and who conquers that fear to do what is right.

"I also believe that a writer simultaneously has to entertain, educate, and inspire. If he or she fails in any of these goals, the book will somehow fall flat."

BIOGRAPHICAL/CRITICAL SOURCES: Environmental Forum, October, 1982, April, 1983; *Los Angeles Times Book Review,* December 19, 1982.

*   *   *

MOLNAR, Ferenc   1878-1952

BRIEF ENTRY: Born January 12, 1878, in Budapest, Hungary; died after a long illness, April 1, 1952, in New York, N.Y.; buried in Linden Hill Cemetery, New York, N.Y. Hungarian playwright and author. Although Molnar was graduated from law school, he chose to become a newspaper reporter, a career he followed until the end of World War I. Molnar achieved a level of success with his early plays, most notably the light comedies *Liliom* (1921), *The Swan* (1922), and *The Guardsman* (1924), that he failed to equal with his later works, partly because of his desire to devote much of his time to developing his celebrityhood. In 1940 he came to the United States to escape the Nazis. Molnar did some screenwriting for Hollywood, and he was also the author of several novels and many humorous articles for magazines. *Address:* Hotel Plaza, New York, N.Y. 10019. *Biographical/critical sources: Twentieth-Century Authors: A Biographical Dictionary of Modern Literature,* 1st supplement, H. W. Wilson, 1955; *Who Was Who in America,* Volume III: *1951-1960,* Marquis, 1966; *Longman Companion to Twentieth Century Literature,* Longman, 1970.

*   *   *

MONAGAN, Charles A(ndrew)   1950-

PERSONAL: Born March 8, 1950, in Waterbury, Conn.; son of John Stephen (a lawyer and member of U.S. House of Representatives) and Rosemary (Brady) Monagan. *Education:* Dartmouth College, B.A., 1972. *Residence:* Wolcott, Conn.

Agent: Robert Cornfield Literary Agency, 145 West 79th St., New York, N.Y. 10024.

CAREER: Meriden Journal, Meriden, Conn., reporter, 1972-75; free-lance writer, 1975-77; *Connecticut,* Fairfield, staff writer, 1977-78, associate editor, 1978-79, editor, 1979-80; free-lance writer, 1980——.

WRITINGS—Humor books: *The Neurotic's Handbook,* Atheneum, 1982; (with Mick Stevens) *Poodles From Hell,* Avon, 1983; *The Whole Shebang,* Atheneum, in press.

Contributor to magazines, including *Playboy, Oui, Glamour,* and *Northeast.*

SIDELIGHTS: In *The Neurotic's Handbook,* Charles Monagan explores the "Era of the Neurotic," humorously chronicling the modern-day occurrences that prompt and reflect neurosis. Such nerve-fraying sources are empty ice cube trays, wrong lines in banks and supermarkets, and drivers who have their turn signals on but don't turn. He wrote the book as "a guide and a comfort," Monagan explained to Joy Horowitz in a *Los Angeles Times* interview, and added that "the main idea here is that we're all in this thing together." In *The Neurotic's Handbook* Monagan "offers sympathetic and sometimes gut-busting insight into the normal-to-neurotic passages in life," Horowitz concluded.

Monagan told *CA:* "*The Neurotic's Handbook* is a very nervous person's guide to life in the modern world, including blind dates, shallow breathing, alien cultures, New Year's Eve, touching the bottom of the lake with your feet, appendix operations, true love, and just about anything else you can think of. *Poodles From Hell* presents the work of Howard Inkley, a would-be cartoonist who dies in a tragic laundromat accident before he has a chance to publish his work. He comes back to earth, however, and, using a living cartoonist as a medium, depicts the true story of death, life after death, and the history of the world, including evolution, the rise of civilization, and life in the future. *The Whole Shebang* is an unnatural field guide to the natural world."

BIOGRAPHICAL/CRITICAL SOURCES: Providence Journal, January 2, 1983; *Los Angeles Times,* January 25, 1983.

*   *   *

MONFALCONE, Wesley R.   1942-

PERSONAL: Surname is pronounced Mon-*fal*-cun; born October 24, 1942, in Newport News, Va.; son of Frank (a draftsman) and Pauline Monfalcone; married Rebecca Holt (a registered nurse), August 14, 1965; children: Mark, Alisa, Todd. *Education:* Bluefield Junior College, A.A., 1962; University of Richmond, B.A., 1964; Southern Baptist Theological Seminary, M.Div., 1968, M.Th., 1972, D.M., 1973. *Home:* 1396 Waveland Ave., Jensen Beach, Fla. 33457. *Office:* Martin Memorial Hospital, P.O. Bin 2396, Stuart, Fla. 33495.

CAREER: Associate pastor of Baptist church in Annandale, Va., 1968-71; University of Louisville, Louisville, Ky., chaplain director at university hospital, 1972-81; Martin Memorial Hospital, Stuart, Fla., chaplain director, 1981——. Clinical instructor at University of Louisville, 1975-81; adjunct professor at Southern Baptist Theological Seminary, 1977-81. *Member:* College of Chaplains (fellow), Association for Clinical Pastoral Education, Phi Beta Kappa, Phi Theta Kappa.

WRITINGS: Coping With Abuse in the Family, Westminster, 1980. Contributor to theology journals and *Home Life.*

MONMONIER, Mark Stephen   1943-

PERSONAL: Surname is pronounced Mon-mon-ear; born February 2, 1943, in Baltimore, Md.; son of John Carroll (a railway accountant) and Martha (an elementary school teacher; maiden name, Mason) Monmonier; married Margaret Janet Kollner, September 4, 1965; children: Jo Young-Joo (adopted). *Education:* Johns Hopkins University, B.A., 1964; Pennsylvania State University, M.S., 1967, Ph.D., 1969. *Politics:* Independent. *Religion:* Roman Catholic. *Home:* 302 Waldorf Parkway, Syracuse, N.Y. 13224. *Office:* Department of Geography, Syracuse University, Syracuse, N.Y. 13210.

CAREER: University of Rhode Island, Kingston, assistant professor of geography, 1969-70; State University of New York at Albany, assistant professor of geography, 1970-73; Syracuse University, Syracuse, N.Y., associate professor, 1973-79, professor of geography, 1979——. Consultant to U.S. Geological Survey. *Member:* American Congress on Surveying and Mapping, Association of American Geographers (chairman of cartography specialty group, 1980-81), American Cartographic Association (vice-president, 1982-83; president, 1983-84), Pi Tau Sigma, Tau Beta Pi.

WRITINGS: Maps, Distortion, and Meaning, Association of American Geographers, 1977; *Computer-Assisted Cartography,* Prentice-Hall, 1982; (with George A. Schnell) *The Study of Population: Elements, Patterns, and Processes,* Charles A. Merrill, 1983. Contributor of more than eighty articles to scientific journals. Associate editor of *American Cartographer,* 1977-82, editor, 1982——.

WORK IN PROGRESS: A book "on the likely future effects on the form and use of maps because of advances in computers and telecommunications," publication expected in 1984; a sampler atlas illustrating a wide variety of interesting maps.

SIDELIGHTS: Monmonier told *CA:* "I am bothered by the strong but false dichotomy between scholarly writing and good journalism. Too many geographers have lost sight of the need for good geography—good writing about the earth—and have channeled all of their efforts toward writing for perhaps one or two dozen academics. At a time when we seem to be getting away from methodologies that isolate us from our data, academics that can (and there are many) should address a larger audience from time to time. Universities and graduate schools, moreover, should actively promote popularization, and academic journals should demand for their readers lucid review articles as well as clear, concise technical reports. I plan to maintain a strong foothold in pure research on digital cartography, but I also want to share my enthusiasm and insight with a wide audience, on different levels."

*   *   *

MONROE, Harriet   1860-1936

BRIEF ENTRY: Born December 23, 1860, in Chicago, Ill.; died September 26, 1936, in Arequipa, Peru. American editor, playwright, and poet. Monroe was the founding editor of *Poetry: A Magazine of Verse,* which introduced the poetry of such figures as Ezra Pound, T. S. Eliot, W. B. Yeats, Wallace Stevens, and Carl Sandburg. Monroe issued *The Passing Show: Five Modern Plays in Verse* (1903), several volumes of verse, including *You and I* (1914) and *The Difference* (1924), and a book of essays titled *Poets and Their Art* (1926). She also edited *The New Poetry: An Anthology of Twentieth-Century Verse in English* (1917) with Alice Corbin Henderson. *Biographical/critical sources:* Harriet Monroe, *A Poet's Life: Seventy Years in a Changing World*, Macmillan, 1938; *Twentieth-Century Authors: A Biographical Dictionary of Modern Literature*, H. W. Wilson, 1942; *The Oxford Companion to American Literature*, 4th edition, Oxford University Press, 1965; *Notable American Women, 1607-1950: A Biographical Dictionary*, Belknap, 1971; *Twentieth-Century Literary Criticism*, Volume 11, Gale, 1983.

* * *

MONTELEONE, Thomas F.   1946-
(Mario Martin, Jr.)

BRIEF ENTRY: Born April 14, 1946, in Baltimore, Md. American psychotherapist and author. Involved in science fiction since 1972, Monteleone has nine novels and more than thirty-five short stories to his credit. Many of his works, including the short story "Chicago" (1973) and the novels *Seeds of Change* (Laser Books, 1975) and *The Time-Swept City* (Popular Library, 1977), show the effects of technology in an extreme form. Monteleone's short stories and novelettes, first serialized in magazines, have been anthologized in *The Arts and Beyond: Visions of Man's Aesthetic Future* (Doubleday, 1977) and *Dark Stars and Other Illuminations* (Doubleday, 1981). In 1973 his short story "Agony in the Garden" was nominated for a Nebula Award, as were "Breath's a Ware That Will Not Keep" (1975), nominated in 1976, and "Camera Obscura" and *The Time-Swept City*, both nominated in 1977. Monteleone was a finalist in the 1973 John W. Campbell Memorial Award competition and in the 1978 Maryland Theatrical Association's one-act play tournament. His novels include *The Time Connection* (Popular Library, 1976), *The Secret Sea* (Popular Library, 1979), *Night Things* (Fawcett Books, 1980), *Ozymandias* (Doubleday, 1981), and *Day of the Dragonstar* (Berkeley Books, 1983). Monteleone also writes juvenile fiction under the pseudonym Mario Martin, Jr. *Address:* 605 Upland Rd., Baltimore, Md. 21208. *Biographical/critical sources: Commonweal*, March 17, 1978; *Analog*, June, 1978, September, 1979; *Encyclopedia of Science Fiction: An Illustrated A to Z*, Grenada, 1979; *Twentieth-Century Science Fiction Writers*, St. Martin's, 1981; *VOYA*, June, 1981.

* * *

MOORE, Geoffrey Herbert   1920-

PERSONAL: Born June 10, 1920; son of Herbert Jonathan Moore; married Pamela Marguerite Munn, 1947 (marriage ended, 1962); children: one son, one daughter. *Education:* Attended Emmanuel College, Cambridge, 1946, M.A., 1951; attended University of Paris. *Office:* Department of American Studies, University of Hull, Hull HU6 7RX, England.

CAREER: Instructor in English at University of Wisconsin, 1948-49; Tulane University, New Orleans, La., assistant professor of English, 1949-51; British Broadcasting Corp., England, editor and producer of "Television talkS," 1952-54; University of Kansas, Lawrence, Rose Morgan Professor, 1954-55; Victoria University of Manchester, Manchester, England, lecturer, 1955-59, senior lecturer in American literature, 1960-62; University of Hull, Hull, England, professor of American literature and head of department of American studies, 1962—, dean of faculty of arts, 1967-69. Visiting professor at University of Kansas City and University of New Mexico, 1948,

1949, University of Southern California and Claremont College, 1950, York University, 1969-70, University of Tunis, 1970-71, Harvard University, 1971, University of Duesseldorf, University of Heidelberg, University of Freiburg, and University of Mainz, all 1972.

Extramural lecturer at University of London and Cambridge University, both 1951-52; visiting lecturer at University of Mainz, University of Goettingen, and University of Frankfurt, 1959, University of Montpellier, University of Aix-en-Provence, and University of Nice, 1967, 1971, University of Frankfurt, University of Heidelberg, University of Mainz, University of Saarbruecken, and University of Tuebingen, 1967, 1968, and University of Perpignan, University of Turin, University of Florence, University of Pisa, University of Rome, University of New Delhi, University of Hyderabad, University of Madras, University of Bombay, and University of Calcutta, 1971. Fellow at Indiana University, summer, 1970, and University of California, San Diego, 1974. *Member:* British Association for American Studies, Savile Club. *Awards, honors:* Rockefeller Foundation fellow at Harvard University, 1959-60; senior scholar of American Council of Learned Societies, 1965.

WRITINGS: Poetry From Cambridge in Wartime, Fortune Press, 1946; *The Penguin Book of Modern American Verse*, Penguin, 1954; (editor) *Fifty-Eight Short Stories by O. Henry*, Collins, 1960; *American Literature and the American Imagination*, University of Hull, 1964; *Poetry Today*, Longmans, Green, 1958, Folcroft, 1969; (editor) *American Literature: A Representative Anthology of American Writing From Colonial Times to the Present*, Faber, 1964; (editor) *The Penguin Book of American Verse*, Penguin, 1977. Also author (under a pseudonym) of *Voyage to Chivalry*, 1947. Contributor to magazines, including *American Mercury* and *Kenyon Review*, and newspapers. Founder and editor of *Bridge*, 1946.

AVOCATIONAL INTERESTS: Swimming, driving.

* * *

MOORE, Roger George   1927-

PERSONAL: Born October 14, 1927, in London, England; son of George and Lily (Pope) Moore; married Doorn Van Steyn, c. 1945 (divorced, 1953); married Dorothy Squires (a singer), (divorced); married Luisa Mattioli, April 11, 1968; children: Deborah, Geoffrey, Christian. *Education:* Attended Royal Academy of Dramatic Arts, 1944-45. *Agent:* c/o International Creative Management, Inc., 8899 Beverly Blvd., Los Angeles, Calif. 90048; and c/o London Management, 235/241 Regent St., London W1, England.

CAREER: Actor in motion pictures, including "Rachel Cade," 1961, "No Man's Land," 1961, "Live and Let Die," 1973, "Gold," 1974, "The Man With the Golden Gun," 1974, "Shout at the Devil," 1975, "The Spy Who Loved Me," 1977, "Moonraker," 1979, "For Your Eyes Only," 1981, and "Octopussy," 1983; and television series, including "Ivanhoe," 1957-58, "The Alaskans," 1959, "Maverick," 1960, "The Saint," 1962-68, and "The Persuaders," 1972-73; and stage productions. Director of television episodes. Chairman of Stars Organization for Spastics, 1973-75, vice-president, 1976-77. *Military service:* British Army, 1945-48; became captain. *Member:* Garrick Club.

WRITINGS: Roger Moore as James Bond: Roger Moore's Own Account of Filming "Live and Let Die," Pan Books, 1973, published as *Roger Moore's James Bond Diary*, Fawcett, 1973.

SIDELIGHTS: Moore is best known for his characterizations of the suave, unruffled, and dapper protagonist of the popular television series "The Saint" and as the equally sophisticated and witty, if immeasurably more dangerous, secret agent James Bond of the renowned film series. As Simon Templar in "The Saint," Moore played a debonair adventure lover who casually rescued beautiful women from evil when he wasn't savoring bourbon or testing one of his sleek sports cars. After six years as Templar, Moore switched from bourbon to martinis, "shaken, not stirred," and from Ferraris to speedboats and satellites as he dropped the television series only to accept, within five years, the role of James Bond in the series made popular with actor Sean Connery in the 1960's.

Moore's six appearances as James Bond have resulted in phenomenal box-office results, with most of the films finishing among their year's most successful movies. In "Live and Let Die," Moore introduced audiences to a more humorous interpretation of the famed spy. Ever resourceful, Moore's Bond evades captors by hopping across the backs of alligators or converting an automobile into an underwater ship to evade attackers. The films have also become known for their spectacular openings. For example, in one film Moore's Bond escapes enemies by stealing a steely-dentured foe's (named Jaws) parachute and in another avenges an attack by spearing his assailant's wheelchair with a helicopter. The tongue-in-cheek wit and unflappable self-control Moore accentuates in his performances as Bond have assured that character's popularity with international movie audiences throughout the 1970's and into the '80's.

AVOCATIONAL INTERESTS: Swimming, painting, skiing, tennis, sketching.

BIOGRAPHICAL/CRITICAL SOURCES: New York Times, August 8, 1965; Time, January 8, 1973; John Williams, The Films of Roger Moore, BCW Publications, 1977; People, August 13, 1979.

*   *   *

MOORE, Susanna 1948-

PERSONAL: Born December 9, 1948, in Bryn Mawr, Pa.; daughter of Richard Dixon (a physician) and Anne (Shields) Moore; children: Lulu Linnane Sylbert. Education: Attended a private preparatory school in Honolulu, Hawaii. Agent: Wallace & Sheil Agency, Inc., 177 East 70th St., New York, N.Y. 10021.

CAREER: Home script reader for actors and motion picture studios, 1967-80; motion picture art director, 1980-82. Writer. Awards, honors: American Book Award nomination for best first novel of 1982 and Sue Kaufman Prize for first fiction from American Academy-Institute of Arts and Letters, both 1983, both for My Old Sweetheart.

WRITINGS: My Old Sweetheart (novel), Houghton, 1982.

SIDELIGHTS: Susanna Moore's My Old Sweetheart is the tale of a young woman growing up in Hawaii in the 1950's. Despite a deeply disturbed family, heroine Lily Shields manages the journey to independence and maturity. "'My Old Sweetheart' is one of those rare books that really does show us how people grow and change," Bruce Allen commended in the Chicago Tribune Book World. "Moore's prose is modestly lyrical, yet it succeeds admirably in casting her troubled characters in vivid relief: They loom larger than life, seem, somehow, emblems of the age that weighs so heavily on them."

Moore told CA: "I designed the sets for two motion pictures—one in New York, the other in New Zealand."

BIOGRAPHICAL/CRITICAL SOURCES: Chicago Tribune Book World, February 13, 1983.

*   *   *

MORA, Carl J(ose) 1936-

PERSONAL: Born June 17, 1936, in New York, N.Y.; son of Eduardo and Angelica (Mena) Mora; married Jeehoon Lee (a medical transcriptionist), September 7, 1963; children: Vincent, Valerie. Education: City College of the City University of New York, B.A., 1967; New York University, M.A., 1969; University of Alabama, Ph.D., 1978. Home: 9709 Avenida de la Luna N.E., Albuquerque, N.M. 87111. Office: Sandia National Laboratories, Albuquerque, N.M. 87185.

CAREER: Western Electric, New York City, technical editor, 1960-65; Kollsman Instrument Corp., New York City, technical editor, 1965-69; University of Alabama Press, University, associate editor, 1969-72; University of New Mexico Press, Albuquerque, managing editor, 1972-78; Sandia National Laboratories, Albuquerque, science writer, 1978—. Military service: U.S. Army, 1956-58; served in Korea. Member: New Mexico Commodore Users Group, South Eastern Conference of Latin American Scholars, New Mexicans for Space Exploration, Albuquerque Astronomers.

WRITINGS: (Translator with Elizabeth Gard) Beatriz Reyes Nevares, The Mexican Cinema: Interviews With Thirteen Directors, University of New Mexico Press, 1976; Mexican Cinema: Reflections of a Society, 1896-1980, University of California Press, 1982. Contributor of articles and reviews to magazines, including Mankind, Nuestro, and Journal of Popular Culture.

WORK IN PROGRESS: Continuing research in Latin American cinema, especially Mexican.

SIDELIGHTS: Carl J. Mora told CA: "I lived in Mexico in my youth, and became familiar with the country's cinema. I continued to see Mexican films in New York. A few years ago, I noticed that, among the plethora of books about U.S. and foreign cinema, there were none on Latin American film. Therefore, I decided to draw on my strong background in the subject, and wrote Mexican Cinema.

"Latin America has a rich cinematic tradition dating back to the mid-1890's. The three principal film-producing countries in the region are Mexico, Brazil, and Argentina. Of these, Mexico by far has had the most important film industry in terms of quantity and popularity throughout Latin America. Although highly commercialized and bureaucratized, Mexican cinema has had its share of quality filmmaking, especially from the mid-1930's through the 1950's, and from 1970 until 1976. The 'New Latin American Cinema,' a leftist-oriented, independent film movement, gained international recognition beginning in the 1950's. Most of the cineasts who form part of this movement are from Argentina, Bolivia, Brazil, Chile, and Cuba.

"The almost total absence of Latin American films from U.S. screens is unfortunate since it cuts Americans off from a window on an increasingly important part of the world. Political and social ferment throughout Latin America more and more is going to be reflected in its films. It would behoove American critics and distributors to pay closer attention to the motion pictures being made by our southern neighbors."

BIOGRAPHICAL/CRITICAL SOURCES: Los Angeles Times Book Review, July 11, 1982.

*   *   *

MORGAN, M(argaret) Ruth   1942(?)-1983

OBITUARY NOTICE: Born c. 1942; died March 31, 1983. Medieval historian, lecturer, and author of *The Chronicle of Ernoul and the Continuations of William of Tyre* and *La Continuation de Guillaume de Tyr.* Morgan, whose works were noted for their clarity and wit, was a prominent teacher in England. She was a fellow of Girton College, Cambridge, where she lectured in French and directed studies in modern and medieval languages. Obituaries and other sources: *London Times,* April 19, 1983.

*   *   *

MORGAN, William   1944-

PERSONAL: Born June 13, 1944, in Princeton, N.J.; son of Minot Canfield (an education administer) and Kate (Davis) Morgan; married Carolyn Johnson (a potter), 1978; children: Lindsay. *Education:* Dartmouth College, A.B., 1966; Columbia University, M.A. and Certificate in Architecture, both 1968; University of Delaware, Ph.D., 1971. *Office:* Department of Fine Arts, University of Louisville, Louisville, Ky. 40292.

CAREER: Princeton University, Princeton, N.J., lecturer in art and archaeology, 1971-74; University of Louisville, Louisville, Ky., assistant professor, 1974-76, associate professor, 1976-81, professor of fine arts, 1981—. Visiting fellow at National Collection of Fine Arts, Smithsonian Institution, 1971. Trustee of Louisville Preservation Alliance, 1974-81; chairman of Kentucky Historic Preservation Review Board, 1975—; member of Kentucky Heritage Council, 1982—.

MEMBER: Society of Architectural Historians, British National Trust, National Trust for Scotland. *Awards, honors:* Fellow of American Friends of Attingham at British National Trust, 1966; fellow of English-Speaking Union at Jesus College, Oxford, 1971; nominated for Pulitzer Prize for criticism, 1980, for architectural criticism in *Louisville Courier-Journal;* grant from National Endowment for the Humanities, 1982.

WRITINGS: (With Aaron Siskind) *Bucks County: Photographs of Early Architecture,* Horizon Press, 1974; (with Samuel Thomas) *Old Louisville: The Victorian Era,* Louisville Courier-Journal and Times, 1975; *Louisville: Architecture and the Urban Environment,* William L. Bauhan, 1979; *Portals: Photographs by William Morgan,* William L. Bauhan, 1981; *The Almighty Wall: The Architecture of Henry Vaughan,* Architectural History Foundation, 1983.

Author of introduction: Asher Benjamin, *The American Builder's Companion,* Dover, 1968; Marianna Van Rensselaer, *H. H. Richardson and His Works,* Dover, 1969; Grant Holcomb III, *Frisco Funk,* Castleroom Press, 1971; Marian Sweeney, *Maxfield Parrish Prints: A Collector's Guide,* William L. Bauhan, 1974.

Architecture critic for *Louisville Courier-Journal,* 1975-80; book review editor of *Landscape Architecture,* 1976-78.

WORK IN PROGRESS: An Architectural and Cultural History of Dublin, New Hampshire, completion expected in 1985.

MORGHEN, Raffaello   1896-1983

OBITUARY NOTICE: Born September 19, 1896, in Rome, Italy; died May 26, 1983. Educator, medieval historian, and author of books in his field. Morghen taught history at universities in Rome and was a professor emeritus at the University of Rome from 1971. His books include *Christian Medieval Era, Medieval Civilization on Decline,* and *Dante the Prophet.* Obituaries and other sources: *International Authors and Writers Who's Who,* 8th edition, Melrose, 1977; *The International Who's Who,* 46th edition, Europa, 1982; *Chicago Tribune,* May 26, 1983.

*   *   *

MORICE, Dave   1946-
(Dr. Alphabet, Joyce Holland)

PERSONAL: Born September 10, 1946, in St. Louis, Mo.; son of Gilbert J. (in real estate sales) and Lillian (a secretary; maiden name, Murray) Morice. *Education:* St. Louis University, B.A., 1969; University of Iowa, M.F.A., 1972. *Politics:* "Apolitical." *Religion:* "Areligious." *Residence:* Iowa City, Iowa. *Agent:* Gail Hochman, Brandt & Brandt, Inc., 1501 Broadway, New York, N.Y. 10036. *Office:* Poetry Comics, P.O. Box 585, Iowa City, Iowa 52244.

CAREER: Presenter of poetry performances, as Dr. Alphabet, 1973—, including "Poetry Marathon Number One" (1000 poems in twelve hours), 1973, "Poetry Marathon Number Two" (mile-wide Haiku), 1974, "Poem on Joyce Holland's Dress" (written on the *Tomorrow* television program), 1974, "Poem Across a One-Thousand-Foot-Long Suspension Bridge," New Hope, Pa., 1976, "Ten-Hour Blindfold Marathon," New Hope, 1977, "Poem Wrapping a City Block," Iowa City, Iowa, 1977, and "Poem Off the Top of the Eight-Story Jefferson Building," Iowa City, 1979; Iowa Arts Council, Des Moines, teacher of creative writing and art, 1975-80; University of Iowa, Iowa City, computer typesetter, 1980-83; affiliated with *Poetry Comics,* Iowa City. Member of sales staff at Iowa Book & Supply, 1977-80. *Member:* Coordinating Council of Literary Magazines, Poets and Writers.

WRITINGS: (Under pseudonym Joyce Holland) *The Tenth J,* Toothpaste Press, 1972; (under pseudonym Dr. Alphabet) *Poetry City, U.S.A.,* Happy Press, 1977; *Quicksand Through the Hourglass,* Toothpaste Press, 1978; (under pseudonym Joyce Holland) *The Final E,* Happy Press, 1979; *A Visit From St. Alphabet,* Toothpaste Press, 1980; *Dot Town,* Toothpaste Press, 1981; *The Happy Birthday Handbook,* Toothpaste Press, 1982; *How to Make Poetry Comics* (monograph), Poets & Writers, 1983. Editor of *Gum,* 1970-73. Editor, under pseudonym Joyce Holland, of *Matchbook,* a magazine of one-word poetry, 1970-75.

Stageplays: "The Umbrella That Predicted the Future" (three-act), first produced in Iowa City, Iowa, at Wesley House Auditorium, 1974; "A Light Draw" (one-act puppet play), first produced in Iowa City at the Mill, 1975; "Stargazers" (one-act), first produced in Iowa City at the Wheel Room, 1977; "The Naked Stage" (one-act), first produced in Iowa City at the Mill, 1982.

WORK IN PROGRESS: Illustrating a cartoon introduction to computers by Henry Mullish, publication by Simon & Schuster expected in 1984; *Computerverse,* "games for generating poetry"; "The Idiot and the Odyssey," an epic fantasy poem for children; an animated poetry cartoon; a poetry video game.

SIDELIGHTS: Dave Morice told *CA:* "Most of my poems are written on paper with a typewriter or pencil. Some have been written on other surfaces, including bridges, streets, and buildings, using other writing implements, like spray-paint, whitewash and mop, and felt-tipped cane. I've written rhymed and unrhymed poems, realistic and surrealistic, sense and nonsense, traditional and nontraditional. It all involves words in space, time, and imagination.

"I usually write when I want to write, no matter what the circumstances. I enjoy sitting down at a typewriter and letting the poems happen—sometimes for page after page. Back in the early seventies, during the Actualist poetry movement, we had great parties with a typewriter in the middle of the living room. Amidst wine and smoke, someone would inevitably slip a page into the machine and say, 'Wanna do a collab?' The circumstances were there prompting our poems."

* * *

MORLEY, (John) Geoffrey (Nicholson) 1905-1983

OBITUARY NOTICE: Born April 17, 1905, in Retford, Nottinghamshire, England; died in 1983. Journalist. Best known for his work as parliamentary correspondent for the *London Times* from 1947 to 1961, Morley wrote sketches for the *Times* that captured the turbulence of the political climate of the Commons and the Lords. The newsman was chosen chairman of the press gallery by his colleagues in 1955. Obituaries and other sources: *London Times*, April 16, 1983.

* * *

MORRIS, Max 1913-

PERSONAL: Born August 15, 1913, in Glasgow, Scotland; son of Nathan (a teacher) and Annie Morris; married Margaret Howard (a historian), February 18, 1961. *Education:* University of London, B.A. (with first-class honors), 1934. *Politics:* Labour. *Home:* 44 Coolhurst Rd., London N8 8EU, England.

CAREER: Willesden Secondary Technical School, London, England, teacher, beginning in 1939; Down Lane Central School, Tottenham, England, deputy head, 1960-62; Chamberlayne Wood Secondary School, London, headmaster, 1962-67; Willesden High School, London, headmaster, 1967-78. Chairman of London Regional Examining Board. *Military service:* British Army, Royal Army Service Corps, 1941-46; became captain. *Member:* National Union of Teachers (executive member and former president).

WRITINGS: The People's Schools, Gollancz, 1939; *From Cobbett to the Chartists*, Lawrence & Wishart, 1948; *Your Children's Future*, Lawrence & Wishart, 1953; *An A to Z of Trade Unionism and Industrial Relations*, Heinemann, 1982. Contributor to education journals and newspapers.

WORK IN PROGRESS: An autobiographical history of education and teachers, beginning in 1939.

SIDELIGHTS: Morris told *CA:* "I am writing the autobiography because, as an executive member and former president of the National Union of Teachers, I was involved in most major educational developments in Britain over a long period of time and shared many interesting experiences with education ministers."

AVOCATIONAL INTERESTS: Travel (Europe, Asia, the United States).

MORRISON, Bruce 1904(?)-1983

OBITUARY NOTICE: Born c. 1904 in Onawa, Iowa; died April 11, 1983, in St. Petersburg, Fla. Sportswriter. Morrison, who wrote for the *Chicago Sun-Times* from 1943 to 1970, was noted for his coverage of the Chicago Bears football team. He was also a nationally known turf handicapper. Obituaries and other sources: *Chicago Tribune*, April 15, 1983.

* * *

MORSE, Thomas S(purr) 1925-

PERSONAL: Born May 25, 1925, in Santa Barbara, Calif.; son of Darwin S. (a farmer) and Kate (Winthrop) Morse; married Patricia Birt (a writer), June 26, 1948; children: Jeffrey, Kate Morse Erwin, Amy Morse Harding, Peter. *Education:* Cornell University, B.S., 1949, M.D., 1953. *Home and office:* Green Meads Farm, Richmond, Mass. 01254.

CAREER: Bellevue Hospital, New York, N.Y., intern, 1953-54; Boston Children's Hospital and Boston City Hospital, Boston, Mass., resident, 1954-60; Children's Medical Center, Columbus, Ohio, attending surgeon, 1960-79. Professor at Ohio State University, 1960-79, and Albany Medical College, 1979-80. *Military service:* U.S. Marine Corps, 1943-46; became sergeant. *Member:* American Trauma Society (president, 1976-78), American Medical Association, American Academy of Pediatrics, American Pediatric Surgical Association, American Association for Surgery on Trauma, American Burn Association.

WRITINGS: A Gift of Courage (nonfiction), Doubleday, 1982. Contributor of nearly seventy articles to medical journals.

WORK IN PROGRESS: A book for lay readers, *How Children Get Hurt, and What to Do About It*, publication by Doubleday expected in 1984.

SIDELIGHTS: Morse wrote: "*A Gift of Courage* is an account of my life as a children's surgeon. All the children in the book are real and every word is true. The title comes from an episode in which I had concluded that it was futile to continue efforts to save the life of a desperately ill little boy. A laboratory technician convinced me (gave me the courage) to try once more. He is alive and well.

"In addition to providing an account of how one becomes a children's surgeon, the book describes many of the conditions that bring children to a surgeon and what he tries to do for them. It traces the giant strides that have been made during the past thirty years and describes some of the problems for which solutions remain obscure. It is filled with information, the validity of which is confirmed by the president of the American Medical Association, that should be helpful and reassuring to parents whose children face the prospect of undergoing surgery."

* * *

MORTIMER, Mary H.
See COURY, Louise Andree

* * *

MOSKOWITZ, Robert 1946-

PERSONAL: Born October 27, 1946, in Newark, N.J.; son of

George (a certified public accountant) and Carolyn (Handler) Moskowitz; married Francine Levy (a hospital administrator), June 30, 1968; children: Jake, Alex. *Education:* University of Pennsylvania, B.A., 1968; graduate study at New School for Social Research, 1969-71. *Home:* 4741 Larkwood, Woodland Hills, Calif. 91364. *Agent:* Peter Miller Agency, 1021 Avenue of the Americas, New York, N.Y. 10018. *Office:* Personal Productivity Center, P.O. Box 6375, Woodland Hills, Calif. 91365.

CAREER: Prentice-Hall, Inc., Englewood Cliffs, N.J., management editor, 1968-70; consultant in private practice, 1970—. *Member:* Mensa. *Awards, honors:* Silver medal from New York Television and Film Festival, 1979, for film "Time Management for Supervisors."

WRITINGS: How to Organize Your Work and Your Life, Doubleday, 1981.

Film scripts: "Time Management for Supervisors," released by Education for Management in 1979.

Audio tape scripts; for American Management Association: "Personal Selling," 1974; "Total Time Management," 1975; "Basic Business Psychology," 1977; "How to Avoid Personal Obsolescence," 1977; "Assertiveness for Career and Personal Success," 1977; "Creative Problem Solving," 1978; "How to Evaluate Performance and Assess Potential," 1979. Contributor to magazines.

WORK IN PROGRESS: Divorce Experiences; "The Treasure," a film on treasure hunting on land and underwater.

SIDELIGHTS: Moskowitz told *CA:* "I write to share what I learn. My titles reflect my personal odyssey. I try to set myself up for experiences that I can translate into published works. For instance, I restored a one-hundred-year-old home and wrote about it in a magazine series.

"My personal struggle is to write deeper and deeper experiences—to move away from simple behavior and add more sense of feeling, motivation, and meaning to my material."

*   *   *

MOSLEY, Leonard O(swald)   1913-

PERSONAL: Born February 11, 1913 (some sources say 1916), in Manchester, England; son of Leonard Cyril (an engineer) and Anna Althea (Glaiser) Mosley; married Isabel Allen (died, 1943); married Gwendolen Muriel Fraser-Smith (marriage ended); married Deirdre Hamblen. *Education:* Attended Sorbonne, University of Paris, and University of Berlin. *Home address:* P.O. Box 94, Captiva Island, Fla. 33924. *Agent:* JCA Literary Agency, 242 West 27th St., New York, N.Y. 10001; and John Farquharson Ltd., Bell House, Bell Yard, London WC2, England.

CAREER: Western Telegraph, Urmston, Lancashire, England, reporter, 1930-31; *Montreal Star,* Montreal, Quebec, reporter, 1931; Minsky's Burlesque Theatre, New York City, assistant stage manager, 1931-32; *Daily Mirror,* New York City, reporter, 1932; United Press International, Los Angeles, Calif., reporter, 1932; Universal Pictures, Hollywood, Calif., scriptwriter, 1933-35; Kemsley Newspapers (now Thomson Newspapers), Manchester and London, England, columnist and foreign correspondent, 1936-39, chief war correspondent in Europe, Ethiopia, North Africa, and the Far East, 1939-45; *Daily Express,* London, chief of Mediterranean and African bureaus, 1945-48, drama critic, 1948-53, film critic, 1953-66; full-time

writer, 1966—. *Member:* Authors Guild of America, Writers Guild of Great Britain. *Awards, honors:* Officer of Order of British Empire, 1946; Officer of Order of St. John of Jerusalem, 1973.

WRITINGS: So I Killed Her (novel), M. Joseph, 1936, Doubleday, 1937; *So Far So Good* (autobiography), M. Joseph, 1937; *No More Remains* (novel), Doubleday, 1937; *War Lord* (novel), M. Joseph, 1938; *Downstream,* M. Joseph, 1939, published as *Europe Downstream,* Doubleday, 1940; *Parachutes Over Holland,* Withy Grove, 1940; *Report From Germany,* Gollancz, 1945; *Gideon Goes to War,* Arthur Barker, 1955, Scribner, 1956; *Castlerosse,* Arthur Barker, 1956; *The Cat and the Mice,* Arthur Barker, 1957, Harper, 1958, published as *Foxhole in Cairo,* Hamilton & Co., 1960; *The Seductive Mirror* (novel), Arthur Barker, 1958; *The Glorious Fault: The Life of Lord Curzon,* Harcourt, 1960, published in England as *Curzon: The End of an Epoch,* Longmans, Green, 1960; *The Last Days of the British Raj,* Weidenfeld & Nicolson, 1961, Harcourt, 1962; *Faces From the Fire: The Biography of Sir Archibald McIndoe,* Weidenfeld & Nicolson, 1961, Prentice-Hall, 1962; *Duel for Kilimanjaro,* Weidenfeld & Nicolson, 1963; *Haile Selassie: The Conquering Lion,* Weidenfeld & Nicolson, 1964, Prentice-Hall, 1965; *Hirohito: Emperor of Japan* (Book-of-the-Month Club selection), Prentice-Hall, 1966; (with Robert Haswell) *The Royals,* Frewin, 1966; *The Battle of Britain,* Stein & Day, 1969; *On Borrowed Time: How World War II Began* (Book-of-the-Month Club selection), Random House, 1969.

Backs to the Wall: The Heroic Story of the People of London During World War II, Random House, 1971, published in England as *London Under Fire, 1939-1945,* Pan, 1972; *Power Play: Oil in the Middle East,* Random House, 1973, published in England as *Power Play: The Tumultuous World of Middle East Oil, 1890-1973,* Weidenfeld & Nicolson, 1973; *The Reich Marshal: A Biography of Hermann Goering,* Doubleday, 1974; *Lindbergh: A Biography* (Literary Guild selection), Doubleday, 1976; *Dulles: A Biography of Eleanor, Allen, and John Foster Dulles and Their Family Network* (Book-of-the-Month Club selection), Dial, 1978; *Blood Relations: The Rise and Fall of the du Ponts of Delaware,* Atheneum, 1980; *The Druid,* Atheneum, 1981; *Marshall: Hero For Our Times,* Hearst, 1982; *Zanuck: The Rise and Fall of Hollywood's Last Tycoon,* Little, Brown, in press.

SIDELIGHTS: Formerly a journalist, critic, and novelist, Leonard Mosley is perhaps best known for his biographies of figures such as Charles Lindbergh, one of Mosley's boyhood heroes. *Lindbergh: A Biography* is a comprehensive look at the aviator's life that, despite the author's admitted "family interest" in the subject, contains, according to Kenneth S. Davis in the *New York Times Book Review,* "no philosophical and few analytically psychological interpretations. What he does do is tell the Lindbergh story from birth to death in plain but lively style, assessing with a humanely balanced judgement and presenting through a sympathetic yet by no means uncritical understanding new information on several portions of this story." Davis concluded: "[Mosley's] work is a valuable service to historical truth and popular understanding."

Mosley's subsequent book, *Dulles,* is a portrait of America's Dulles family: Eleanor, an economist with the State Department, Allen, former director of the Central Intelligence Agency, and John Foster, once Secretary of State. Based on Mosley's many interviews with Eleanor Dulles and associates of the siblings, the book was attacked by Ms. Dulles, who claimed that Mosley implied that she and her brother manipulated foreign policy during the Eisenhower administration. Eleanor called Mosley's depiction a ''school-boy approach'' to history for its insinuation that ''three people could connive to produce foreign policy.'' *New York Times* critic Christopher Lehmann-Haupt, however, felt Mosley ''built his thesis in order to tell a story or two. . . . His purpose in developing such theses is to lay tracks on which his narrative will run smoothly. . . . We don't take Mr. Mosley's 'Dulles' that seriously. We take it as fun and diverting gossip and a chance for Leonard Mosley to bring together the many good stories he has mined from the published record and his talks and correspondence with the great and near-great of that period.'' A *New Yorker* reviewer deemed the book ''an engrossing group portrait,'' and Richard H. Ullman of the *New York Times Book Review* opined: ''Even if Mosley does not sufficiently illuminate the web that bound the three Dulleses, the fact that he does so at all is a contribution. . . . He does not tell us as much as we would wish to know, but no one else tells us anything.''

Mosley highlighted another family, the du Ponts of Delaware, in his book *Blood Relations*. Gathering information from previously unpublished interviews with and letters by the clan, Mosley details some of the steamy scandals centered around the family and also relates how the du Ponts' business deals made them one of the wealthiest families in the United States. ''There is . . . plenty of family gossip here, most of it tasteless little tidbits about the family's marriage woes . . . all cheaply designed to titillate rather than reveal,'' wrote G. C. Zilg in a *Nation* review. Noting ''the saga of the du Ponts in America is one long litany of power plays, petty squabbles, intrafamily lawsuits, wholesale hypocrisy, adultery, and suicide,'' Dan Rottenberg said in a *Chicago Tribune Book World* review that '''Blood Relations' is . . . almost *too* interesting: With all the feuds and fornications Mosley has chosen to dwell on, you might get the impression that money-making is something the du Ponts did in their spare time.'' Nevertheless Rottenburg concluded: ''The du Pont saga is an important story that has largely been ignored because it seemed confusing and full. Without sensationalizing that story, Mosley has made it clear and exciting. For that he deserves our gratitude.''

Mosley's next book offers a fictionalized biography of Gwyn Evans, the World War II Nazi spy in England who used the moniker ''the Druid.'' Frances Taliaferro, writing in the *New York Times Book Review*, found the book ''thoroughly entertaining'' and said it ''reads like one of the richer inventions of classic espionage fiction.''

According to Joseph E. Persico, Mosley ''faced a challenge'' as a biographer of General George Marshall in that ''Marshall was a general who commanded no great armies, a soldier whose name is linked to no famous battle.'' In his *Washington Post* review, however, Persico applauded Mosley's *Marshall*. ''Mosley stirs in the spices to bring a rather resistant subject to more pulsating life. . . . The spirit and flavor of George C. Marshall, his essential greatness, rise from these pages.'' In the *New York Times* critic Herbert Mitgang concurred, writing: ''Leonard Mosley has unearthed the details of his public *and* private life, and written a readable and solid biography. . . . It isn't a simple valentine. By pointing out some of Marshall's mistakes in judgement along the road to greatness, the author shows Marshall to be a public servant who continued to grow in stature when he took on his heaviest tasks well into his 60's. . . . Mosley, a wartime correspondent, military historian and biographer . . . is well-equipped to tell the story of General Marshall's career.''

MEDIA ADAPTATIONS: The Cat and the Mice was adapted for the motion picture ''Foxhole in Cairo'' by Paramount in 1960 and starred James Robertson Justice and Adrian Hoven.

CA INTERVIEW

CA interviewed Leonard Mosley by phone January 15, 1981, at his home on Sanibel Island, Fla.

CA: You came by cattle boat from your native Manchester, England, to Canada, worked on the Montreal Star, *then went to work in New York at Minsky's burlesque theater and later at the* New York Daily Mirror. *What began this sequence of moves and jobs?*

MOSLEY: It was youthful experience, trying to get experience and to see something of the world. They had a marvelous arrangement in Britain in those days that travel and other expenses one incurred as a free-lance writer—I was writing articles the whole time—could be charged against income tax, in the same way one could charge for educational expenses. We had very understanding income tax authorities in Britain; they still are, in fact.

CA: Had you gotten bored with school?

MOSLEY: Yes, indeed.

CA: You had some idea of being a professional writer when you were quite young?

MOSLEY: Yes, I was always writing. I won a prize in the *Manchester Guardian* ghost-story competition when I was very young, twelve or thirteen. That stimulated me into going on. I had always been interested in being a foreign correspondent.

CA: Was working on the Daily Mirror *something of a shock to you?*

MOSLEY: Yes. It was highly stimulating. As a matter of fact, I got that job through Lord Castlerosse, who was a well-known gossip writer and Irish peer. He was a friend of Walter Winchell, who at that time was a well-known gossip columnist in the United States. It was Lord Castlerosse who introduced me to Walter Winchell, who then introduced me to a man who turned out to be a private enemy of his, Emile Gauvreau, who was then editing the *Daily Mirror*. And Gauvreau offered me the job. They also had another English correspondent on the staff at that time, Lady Rena Terrington, who was also an Anglo-Irish peeress. They rather specialized, I think, in getting the English point of view. I was working as a sort of dogsbody, a ''go-fer,'' and that's how I got first insight into Charles Lindbergh. During the Hauptmann trial in Flemington, New Jersey, I was running copy across from the courtroom to the hotel, and I saw something of Lindbergh. That really nagged me to write his biography later, so I did.

CA: You went from the Daily Mirror *to a job on* Fortune?

MOSLEY: Yes. I was a sort of researcher at *Fortune*. They had whole teams of researchers who moved around on various stories. I remember I worked on one called ''Women in Business,'' and they also did a large issue on burlesque theaters. That was the first time they started flexing their muscles beyond normal orthodox business. I was very useful, because I knew a little about it. Gypsy Rose Lee and Ann Corio, both quite well known striptease artists in those days, were practically my mentors. I think *Fortune* either coined or ferreted out that word *ecdysiast* for *stripteaser,* to make it sound better.

CA: How did you become a Hollywood screenwriter?

MOSLEY: I had always been interested in films. Later on I became a film critic. It so happened that I knew Eleanor Holm. My sister was a champion swimmer for Britain, and she had met Eleanor Holm, the great swimming champion from the United States who was banned from the American team in the 1936 Olympic Games for having imbibed champagne aboard ship, which was against the rules of training. Undoubtedly she would have been as much the heroine as Jesse Owens was the hero that year if she had been allowed to swim; she could beat everybody. She knew Carl Laemmle, Jr., in Hollywood and got me an introduction to him, which got me a job. I worked in Hollywood for about a year.

CA: Did you find it exciting?

MOSLEY: Very much so, yes.

CA: As a newspaper columnist you covered the Spanish Civil War and were expelled by both sides. Could you elaborate on your expulsion?

MOSLEY: I was trying to tell too much of the truth about the militant Communist activities on the Republican side, and trying to tell too much of the German and Italian activities on the Franco side. There was a lot going on there, and I was trying to get it out.

CA: You've been a journalist, historian, biographer, film critic, and fiction writer. Have you enjoyed all of those roles?

MOSLEY: Very much, yes. I think I most enjoy my present job of being a biographer. It enables one to take characters who may have been written about before and research them and go back to their former colleagues and acquaintances and adversaries and find out something new about them.

CA: When you set out to write Lindbergh, *there were already Charles A. Lindbergh's autobiographies and at least two other biographies. For your book, you had access to source material not previously available to writers, including Harold Nicolson's* Diaries and Letters, 1930-39. *What do you think your book added of most significance?*

MOSLEY: I think it showed the great authentic American hero as more human because he had warts, and what I think I did illuminate was that he was possibly the most straightforward and honest man ever produced in the United States, in which there have been a lot of straightforward and honest men produced, and that was the cause of his downfall—or temporary downfall, anyway—in the period of World War II. He was a very truthful man, and therefore he never believed that people would lie to him. The Germans lied to him and he repeated those lies. The German Luftwaffe, or air force, was not as strong in those days as he was being told. The German officials flew him from airfield to airfield, often displaying planes that he had already seen in other airfields. He reported back to Joseph Kennedy, the American ambassador in London, and to the American envoy to France, and they both reported it to prime ministers Neville Chamberlain in London and Daladier in France, who were panicked into appeasing the Germans at

a fatal moment when they might have gotten away with standing up to them.

CA: Are there any comments you'd like to make on Anne Morrow Lindbergh's book The Flower and the Nettle, *which was published about the same time as your biography?*

MOSLEY: I was in touch with her and she was extremely nice. There were some intensely personal letters which I came into possession of but did not use in my biography, and she was very grateful for that. She said, ''I only wish that I could turn over all of Charles's papers to you, but I made a deathbed promise to him that nothing of the papers would be shown to anybody until his own full diaries appeared.'' Of course they hadn't been published by the time my book came out. But in a quiet and not official way she was very helpful.

CA: You were on the scene during several crucial movements and battles of World War II, including the invasion of Normandy in 1944. What was the most exciting, most dangerous of those times for you personally?

MOSLEY: I suppose the dropping on D-Day on the Caen bridges. I dropped as a correspondent with the Sixth British Airborne Division, and it was very exciting; we expected to be overrun at any moment. There were two parachute divisions dropped— the Americans were dropped on the Cherbourg Peninsula and we were dropped on the Caen bridges. Both ends of the invasion were very vulnerable because we didn't have very heavy weapons. Both sides expected to get the brunt of the attack, and we particularly because we were nearer to the German divisions. What we did not know was that the deception program carried out by the British and the Americans was successful: the Germans were persuaded that it was not the real invasion. One owes one's life to that, really; Rommel held his forces in the Pas de Calais for a fatal three weeks believing that Patton and another army would be coming in there and that saved the invasion.

It was a very exciting time. We did get attacked quite a bit, and it was a bad night. The weather had been poor on June 5, 1944, when the original invasion was supposed to have taken place. It was postponed for a day, but the weather didn't particularly improve; it was blowing badly and we were all blown about five miles off course and landed in swamps and other such places. Our particular plane landed on a machine-gun post, and about sixteen out of twenty-five were shot. So it was quite a night, and a rather bizarre night, because the British, being British, had various calls for the rallying of their paratroopers in the middle of the night. Some were blowing boy scout whistles, others were doing rattles, and some were doing birdcalls, so the night air was filled with the most extraordinary cries. It was rather like some exotic Malayan jungle.

CA: How did you happen to become a film critic?

MOSLEY: When I was in Berlin I used to write about the continental cinema, and I'd always been interested in films and had written a lot about it, so when I got back to London and joined the *Daily Express* I was asked to become their film critic. I enjoyed it very much.

Of course being a film critic in England, as I think also in America, is very convenient if you want to write books, because you see the films in comparative privacy at the beginning of the week, and then write the film notices, and then have three or four days at the end of the week to write or do the research for books.

CA: Does British film criticism differ in any way from film criticism in the United States?

MOSLEY: British film criticism used to contemplate much, much more on personality than American criticism did, but I think they're both pretty much the same right now, or rather the personality reporting has been transferred to television reviewing. But British film critics were always much more personal than the older American film critics were. Not so much nowadays.

CA: Are there particular critics that you read regularly?

MOSLEY: I read John Simon very much for the theater; I think he's an extraordinarily brilliant critic. And Clive Barnes, who used to be my assistant when I was away researching—I used to take three months off as a film critic and Clive Barnes would take my column over. This was before he came to the *New York Times* and the *New York Post*. He's a brilliant critic, there's no doubt about it. He's fantastic on both the theater and ballet, and he's very good on films too.

CA: In Power Play: Oil in the Middle East, *you wrote, "What most worries Western strategists when they contemplate the part the Middle East is destined to play in the world fuel situation is neither the expense nor the shortage of oil, but the increasing tendency of Arab militants to attempt to use oil as a political weapon." How directly do you think the oil problem relates to the tension between the United States and Iran?*

MOSLEY: I think the Americans have always felt a little guilty about Iran because they were persuaded by the British to intervene in the crisis that occurred in the 1950's, under Mosaddegh, which began a purely British-Iranian crisis. At the request of the British, America intervened and restored the shah to the throne. They got as a reward for that a large share of Iranian oil, and I think they have always felt guilty about it. The American government and politicians, the more idealistic ones, feel rather more guilty about bringing off coups than the older European colonial powers. I don't believe the British worry at all about what they did in Iran in 1954, but the Americans still do. It seems to be forgotten by the rest of the world, including Iran, that the British and the Americans were partners in that particular enterprise.

CA: Are there contemporary historians that you especially respect and enjoy reading?

MOSLEY: Yes, very much so. I think it would be invidious to mention any because they belong to both spectrums. I think nonfiction, and particularly history, is being brilliantly written today in the United States.

CA: You haven't written fiction since 1952. Did you make a conscious decision to stop writing fiction?

MOSLEY: I think, quite honestly, that was purely economic. Unless one has blockbusting best-sellers, one cannot live on one's fiction books. Thanks to the first big biographical blockbuster I had, *Hirohito*, I was able to write nonfiction books, and all of them—touch wood—have been very great successes.

CA: Did most of your nonfiction books originally come out of your contacts as a correspondent?

MOSLEY: To a certain extent, yes. Also, I like searching for new facets of famous people who have not been shown as they really were. General George Marshall is a particular example of that. He turned down a million dollars to write his own autobiography, because he honestly believed that reviewers would write about the bitchy things he'd said about some of his wartime colleagues and the statesmen he knew. That would revive old controversies and start new ones. So he never wrote it. There have been books about George Marshall, but his story and the sort of person he was and what he was really involved in have never completely been told. It will be quite a revelation to the American public, I think, when they find out the true story about him.

CA: You do a great deal of research on your books. Is there any one book that you've most enjoyed doing the research for?

MOSLEY: I particularly enjoyed the one on Marshall. We researched at the George Marshall Foundation in Virginia for a long time. We went to California and the Far East. My wife researches with me, and we went to see Abba Eban. When Marshall was secretary of state he was closely involved with the controversy over the 1948 Arab-Israeli War and whether the United Nations should admit Israel; it's a fascinating story which had never been told. I found the documents in the Marshall Foundation on the American side, so we went over to Israel to get Abba Eban's side, and it was quite a riveting story.

CA: Do you enjoy the traveling you do in researching your books?

MOSLEY: Very much indeed.

CA: Are you making a permanent home now in Florida?

MOSLEY: Yes.

CA: How did you happen to choose Florida?

MOSLEY: While I was doing the du Pont book, I had come down to Jacksonville and northern Florida to research with one of the du Pont brothers-in-law about the Florida side of the du Pont family's operations. When I was ready to start writing and collating all the research, we wanted to look for a place in Florida for the winter to get the materials together, and an acquaintance said, "Have you ever tried Sanibel Island?" We flew down to Miami and drove across the Tamiami Trail from Miami to the Gulf of Mexico. As soon as we crossed the causeway onto Sanibel Island, we knew it was for us. It's one of the barrier islands. Two-thirds of it is a federal game reserve, and it is a remarkable place. [Mosley now resides on Captiva Island, Florida.]

CA: Your second book, published in 1937, was the autobiography So Far So Good. *Could that title serve now as a description of your life?*

MOSLEY: Yes, I suppose it could—so far so good, and so far so bad.

CA: Are you planning another autobiography?

MOSLEY: There have been approaches from publishers for another autobiography.

CA: If you had it to do over, is there anything you'd change about your life or your career?

MOSLEY: I would like to have done without World War II and the Vietnamese War. I'm fascinated with the ifs of history. What if, in 1938, Neville Chamberlain had not gone to see Hitler and Mussolini and signed the Munich Pact? World War II might still have been avoided.

BIOGRAPHICAL/CRITICAL SOURCES: Best Sellers, June 1, 1969; *Christian Science Monitor,* June 24, 1969, March 28, 1978; *Time,* June 27, 1969, February 27, 1978; *Esquire,* September, 1969; *Virginia Quarterly Review,* autumn, 1969, autumn, 1978; *Detroit News,* December 12, 1971, November 13, 1980; *New York Times,* July 10, 1973, March 5, 1976, March 9, 1978, March 14, 1978, March 25, 1980, October 1, 1982; *New York Times Book Review,* April 11, 1976, February 26, 1978, April 13, 1980, March 29, 1981; *Listener,* July 20, 1976, April 15, 1982; *New Statesman,* August 13, 1976; *Newsweek,* February 27, 1978; *New Republic,* March 18, 1978; *New Yorker,* April 10, 1978; *Saturday Review,* April 29, 1978; *New York Review of Books,* May 4, 1978; *Economist,* July 8, 1978, April 24, 1982; *Chicago Tribune Book World,* April 13, 1980; *Nation,* May 3, 1980; *Washington Post Book World,* June 15, 1980; *Washington Post,* October 5, 1982.

—Sketch by Nancy S. Gearhart

—Interview by Jean W. Ross

*   *   *

MOUNTAIN, Marian
See WISBERG, Marian Aline

*   *   *

MOWSHOWITZ, Abbe 1939-

PERSONAL: Surname is pronounced *Moe*-sho-wits; born November 13, 1939, in Liberty, N.Y.; son of Jacob (in business) and Minnie (Rosenbloom) Mowshowitz; married Harriet Hobson (a scholar), February 1, 1964; children: Jed, Seth. *Education:* University of Chicago, S.B., 1961; University of Michigan, M.A., 1965, M.S., 1966, Ph.D., 1967. *Office:* Division of Science and Technology Studies, Rensselaer Polytechnic Institute, Troy, N.Y. 12181.

CAREER: Human Science Research, Inc., McLean, Va., research associate, 1962-63; University of Michigan, Ann Arbor, research assistant in applied mathematics at Mental Health Research Institute, 1963-67, assistant research mathematician, 1967-68; University of Toronto, Toronto, Ontario, assistant professor of computer science and industrial engineering, 1968-69; University of British Columbia, Vancouver, assistant professor, 1969-74, associate professor of computer science, 1974-79; Graduate School of Management, Delft, Netherlands, visiting professor of computer science, 1979-80; Croton Research Group, Inc., Croton-on-Hudson, N.Y., director, 1980-82; Rensselaer Polytechnic Institute, Troy, N.Y., professor and research director of Division of Science and Technology Studies, 1982—. *Member:* International Federation of Information Processors, Association for Computing Machinery (member of advisory board of Special Interest Group on Computers and Society), Sigma Xi.

WRITINGS: Conquest of Will: Information Processing in Human Affairs, Addison-Wesley, 1976; *Inside Information: Computers in Fiction,* Addison-Wesley, 1976; *Human Choice and Computers,* North-Holland Publishing, 1980; *The Machinery of Power: Computers and Social Stability,* W. H. Freeman, in press.

SIDELIGHTS: Mowshowitz wrote: "As an undergraduate at the University of Chicago, I studied mathematics and the philosophy of science. The work in mathematics shaped my early career choice, but my interest in philosophy, especially social philosophy, reasserted itself after a period of quiescence during which I studied, taught, and conducted research in mathematics and computer science. For the past dozen years, I have been thinking and writing about the social impact of science and technology. A major theme in my recent work is the influence of computer technology on the balance between organizational mechanisms of social control and the exercise of individual responsibility."

*   *   *

MULLIKEN, Robert Sanderson 1896-

PERSONAL: Born June 7, 1896, in Newburyport, Mass.; son of Samuel Parsons and Katherine Mulliken; married Mary Helen von Noe, December 24, 1929 (died March 15, 1975); children: Lucia Maria (Mrs. John P. Heard), Valerie Noe. *Education:* Massachusetts Institute of Technology, B.S., 1917; University of Chicago, Ph.D., 1921. *Politics:* Independent. *Home:* 5825 Dorchester Ave., Chicago, Ill. 60637. *Agent:* Marvin Yelles, 111 Fifth Ave., New York, N.Y. 10003. *Office:* 320 Jones Chemistry Building, University of Chicago, 5735 University Ave., Chicago, Ill. 60637.

CAREER: Researcher on war gases in Washington, D.C., 1917-18; technical researcher with New Jersey Zinc Co., 1919; conducted research on separation isotopes, 1920-22; University of Chicago, Chicago, Ill., national research fellow, 1921-23; Harvard University, Cambridge, Mass., national research fellow, 1923-25; New York University, Washington Square College, New York, N.Y., assistant professor of physics, 1926-28; University of Chicago, associate professor, 1928-31, professor of physics, 1931-61, Ernest DeWitt Burton Distinguished Service Professor, 1956-61, Distinguished Service Professor of Physics and Chemistry, 1961—. Researcher on molecular spectra and molecular structure, 1923—. Visiting fellow of St. John's College, Oxford, 1952-53; distinguished research professor at Florida State University, 1965-71; Baker Lecturer at Cornell University, 1960; visiting professor in Bombay, India, 1962, and at Indian Institute of Technology, 1962; Silliman Lecturer at Yale University, 1965; Jan Van Geuns Visiting Professor at University of Amsterdam, 1965. Director of Information Division of Plutonium Project, Chicago, 1943-44. Scientific attache at American embassy in London, England, 1955. *Military service:* U.S. Army, Chemical Warfare Service, 1918.

MEMBER: International Academy of Quantum Molecular Science, American Physical Society (fellow; chairman of Division of Chemical Physics, 1951-52), American Association for the Advancement of Science (fellow), American Philosophical Society, American Chemical Society, American Academy of Arts and Sciences, National Academy of Sciences, Indian National Academy of Science (fellow), Royal Irish Academy (fellow), Royal Society (foreign member), Royal Society of Science of Liege (corresponding member), London Chemical Society (fellow), Societe de Chimie Physique (honorary member), Gamma Alpha, Quadrangle Club, Cosmos Club.

AWARDS, HONORS: Guggenheim fellowship for Europe, 1930, 1932; Sc.D. from Columbia University, 1939, Marquette University and Cambridge University, 1967, and Gustavus Adolphus College, 1975; medal from University of Liege, 1948; Fulbright fellowship for England, 1952-53; Ph.D. from University of Stockholm, 1960; Gilbert N. Lewis Medal from

American Chemical Society, 1960, Theodore W. Richards Medal, 1960, Peter Debye Award, 1961, J. G. Kirkwood Award, 1964, Willard Gibbs Medal, 1965; Nobel Prize for Chemistry, 1966.

WRITINGS: Selected Papers of Robert S. Mulliken, edited by D. A. Ramsay and Jurgen Hinze, University of Chicago Press, 1975.

WORK IN PROGRESS: A scientific autobiography.

* * *

MUSE, Beatriz de Regil 1901(?)-1983

OBITUARY NOTICE: Born c. 1901 in Biarritz, France; died of a heart attack, April 5, 1983. Publisher. Muse and her husband founded *Manassas Messenger,* a weekly newspaper. Muse was also active in civic affairs in the communities of Reston and Manassas, Virginia. Obituaries and other sources: *Washington Post,* April 9, 1983.

* * *

MUSIL, Robert (Elder von) 1880-1942

BRIEF ENTRY: Born November 6, 1880, in Klagenfurt, Carinthia, Austria; died April 15, 1942, in Geneva, Switzerland. Austrian playwright and novelist. Musil gained recognition as a writer with his first novel, *Die Verwirrungen des Zoeglings Toerless* (1906; translated as *Young Toerless,* 1955). Among the works he subsequently issued are a collection of short stories, *Die Vereinigungen* (1911; translated as *Unions,* 1965), and two plays, *Die Schwaemer* (title means ''The Visionaries''; 1921) and *Vinzenz und die Freundin bedeutender Maenner* (title means ''Vincent and the Girl Friend of Important Men''; 1923). Musil supplemented his income from his early writings with various jobs in the Austrian Government, but pursued writing full time from 1922 until his death. In 1938 the author and his Jewish wife fled Austria for Switzerland, where Musil later died, destitute and forgotten. He achieved his greatest fame with the three-volume novel *Der Mann ohne Eigenschaften* (1930-1942; translated as *The Man Without Qualities,* 1953, 1954, and 1960), which he began writing in the early 1920's and left unfinished at his death. *Biographical/critical sources:* Burton Pike, *Robert Musil: An Introduction to His Work,* Cornell University Press, 1961; *Encyclopedia of World Literature in the Twentieth Century,* updated edition, Ungar, 1967; *The McGraw-Hill Encyclopedia of World Biography,* McGraw, 1973; Frederick G. Peters, *Robert Musil: Master of the Hovering Life,* Columbia University Press, 1978; *Twentieth-Century Literary Criticism,* Volume 12, Gale, 1983.

* * *

MYERS, Samuel 1897(?)-1983

OBITUARY NOTICE: Born c. 1897; died April 20, 1983, in Homestead, Fla.; buried in Miami, Fla. News photographer best known for his picture of the tragic explosion of the German dirigible *Hindenburg.* Myers, who also photographed such notable people as Orville and Wilbur Wright, Ty Cobb, Amelia Earhart, Albert Einstein, and Babe Ruth, worked for twenty years with the Associated Press. For many years Myers was the official photographer of the Miss America pageant, and, according to his grandson Scott Segal, he had taken pictures of every U.S. president from Theodore Roosevelt to Richard Nixon. Much of Myers's work appeared on the front pages of

newspapers throughout the world. Obituaries and other sources: *Chicago Tribune,* April 23, 1983.

* * *

MYRSIADES, Kostas J. 1940-

PERSONAL: Born May 21, 1940, in Vourliotes, Samos, Greece; came to the United States in 1948, naturalized citizen, 1957; son of John (a vintner) and Mary (Laghos) Myrsiades; married Linda Suny (an assistant professor of management), 1965; children: Yani, Leni. *Education:* University of Iowa, B.A., 1963; Indiana University, M.A., 1965, Ph.D., 1972; University of Athens, Certificate in Classical and Modern Greek, 1966. *Home:* 370 North Malin Rd., Newtown Square, Pa. 19073. *Office:* Department of English, West Chester State College, Main Hall, West Chester, Pa. 19380.

CAREER: Greek-American Cultural Institute, Athens, Greece, instructor in English, 1965-66, 1969; West Chester State College, West Chester, Pa., assistant professor of English, 1969-73; Deree College, Athens, assistant professor of Greek and director of modern Greek program and Center for Hellenic Studies, 1973-74; West Chester State College, associate professor, 1974-77, professor of English, 1977—, member of executive committee of Institute of Ethnic Studies, 1976—. Member of Hellenic-American League of Philadelphia, 1969—; chairman of Modern Greek Studies Group of Philadelphia, 1969-73.

MEMBER: Modern Language Association of America, Modern Greek Studies Association, American Literary Translators Association, National Association of Self-Instructional Programs, Parnassos Greek Cultural Organization of New York, Association of Pennsylvania State College and University Faculty. *Awards, honors:* Lilly fellow at University of Pennsylvania, 1981.

WRITINGS: Takis Papatsonis, G. K. Hall, 1974; (contributor) Kostas E. Tsiropoulos, editor, *Timi ston T. K. Papatsoni* (title means ''In Honor of Takis K. Papatsonis''), Tetradhia Eythinis, 1976; (editor and translator, with Kimon Friar) Yannis Ritsos, *Scripture of the Blind,* Ohio State University Press, 1979; (contributor) Athina Kallianesi, editor, *Afieroma ston Yanni Ritso* (title means ''Festschrift for Yannis Ritsos''), Kedhros, 1981; *I piisi tou Yanni Ritsou ke i ethniki antistasis ke alla dhokimia* (title means ''The Poetry of Yannis Ritsos and the Greek Resistance and Other Essays''), Kedhros, in press; (editor and author of introduction) *Approaches to Teaching Homer's Iliad and Odyssey,* Modern Language Association of America, in press.

Contributor to *Encyclopedia of World Literature in the Twentieth Century* and *Dictionary of Literary Biography.* Contributor of more than one hundred articles, poems, translations, and reviews to language and literature journals in the United States and Greece. Guest editor of *College Literature,* 1976, 1978, *Falcon,* 1978, *Grove: Contemporary Poetry and Translation,* 1979, and *Durak: An International Magazine of Poetry,* 1980.

WORK IN PROGRESS: Editing, translating, and writing introductions to *Selected Poems: Yannis Ritsos* and *Takis Papatsonis: The Ursa Minor and Other Poems,* with Kimon Friar; translating and writing introductions to *Karaghiozis, the Laic Theatre of Modern Greece: Three Classic Plays,* with wife, Linda S. Myrsiades, and *Yannis Ritsos: Monemvasia and Women of Monemvasia,* with Friar; studying and translating for *Translating From the Modern Greek Oral Tradition.*

SIDELIGHTS: Myrsiades told *CA:* "My interest lies in the poetry of the world's longest continuous literary tradition, that is, in Homer and the poetry of contemporary Greece. I am especially interested in modern Greek poets who, like Papatsonis and Ritsos, use Homeric myths to speak of man and the human condition in new and contemporary ways. Moving from Homer to the contemporary poets of Greece allows me to study both the Alpha and the Omega of Greek culture. Translating these works provides me with an opportunity to explode both the richness and the Greekness (*romiosini*) of these works into an equally rich language—English. Moreover, dealing with Greek literature as an entity without dividing it into several separate languages (classical, Byzantine, modern) permits me to emphasize the Hellenic (that which is universally Greek without regard to specific locality) rather than the Greek (the purely local)."

N

NADER, George   1921-

BRIEF ENTRY: Born in 1921 in Pasadena, Calif. American actor and author. Nader began his film career with Universal Pictures during the 1950's. He has appeared as a leading man or, more recently, as a character actor in more than forty screenplays and television films. These include "Four Guns to the Border," "Unguarded Moment," "Nowhere to Go," "Murder at Midnight," and "Beyond Atlantis." He has also written a science fiction novel, *Chrome* (Putnam, 1978). *Biographical/critical sources: International Motion Picture Almanac*, Quigley, 1982.

*   *   *

NAGENDA, Musa
See HOWARD, Moses L(eon)

*   *   *

NAHA, Ed   1950-

PERSONAL: Born June 10, 1950, in Elizabeth, N.J.; son of George Harry and Christina Agnes (McGann) Naha. *Education:* Newark State College, B.A., 1972. *Politics:* "Ranting liberal." *Residence:* Santa Monica, Calif. 90405. *Agent:* Frommer Price Literary Agency, 185 East 85th St., New York, N.Y. 10028.

CAREER: CBS Records, New York City, manager of East Coast publicity, 1972-75, associate producer of East Coast artists and repertory, 1975-77; *Future Life*, New York City, co-editor, 1977-80; writer.

WRITINGS: Horrors: From Screen to Scream, Avon, 1975; *The Rock Encyclopedia*, Grosset, 1978; *The Science Fictionary*, Seaview, 1980; *Wanted* (short fiction), Bantam, 1980; *The Paradise Plot* (futuristic mystery), Bantam, 1980; *The Films of Roger Corman: Brilliance on a Budget*, Arco, 1982; *The Suicide Plague* (futuristic mystery), Bantam, 1982.

Screenplays: "Camp Bottomout," New World Pictures, 1984; "The Wizard Wars," New World Pictures, 1984. Also author of screenplay "Thanksgiving."

Author of columns "Screen Scoops," *New York Post*, 1980—, "Nahallywood," *Heavy Metal*, 1983—, and "L.A. Offbeat," *Starlog*, 1983—. Contributor to magazines and newspapers,

including *Oui, Playboy, Rolling Stone, Swank, Genesis,* and *Gallery*.

WORK IN PROGRESS: A historical novel set in Los Angeles in 1939; a medieval fantasy set in Japan in 1984.

SIDELIGHTS: Naha wrote: "I have always suspected my mother of taking strange drugs prior to my birth. This would explain my wanting to work long hours and spew out many words for very little money. It is a gratifying existence, in a sado-masochistic sense. I would recommend writing full time to all those interested in designer hair shirts.

"On a slightly more serious note—a somber F-sharp—I think I have always tried, in both my fiction and nonfiction, to entertain and enlighten readers in an accessible manner. I've never felt that a 'fun' read necessarily meant a lightweight one.

"I've also always enjoyed being sneaky and flaunting trends whenever possible without people ever noticing it.

"Since science fiction and mystery tomes often boast determined, two-fisted and goal-oriented heroes, I made my futuristic sleuth an ordinary guy who gets stuck in extraordinary circumstances and who dearly desires to extricate himself from said circumstances with all his limbs intact. So much for goals.

"In terms of film, since the current trend seems to lean towards 'R'-rated sex and/or violence flicks, I decided to try to fashion my scripts in the 'PG' territory. I managed to write and sell three in a year, two comedies and a fantasy-adventure.

"I'm not sure what all of this proves except, perhaps, it serves as an illustration that you don't have to be a convicted murderer-friend of Norman Mailer to pay your rent via writing . . . although, let's face it, it probably helps.

"Any well-known authors out there willing to sponsor a down 'n' dirty double-parker who has many unpaid parking tickets, feel free to drop me a line."

AVOCATIONAL INTERESTS: Reading, drinking, "rowdy behavior in general."

BIOGRAPHICAL/CRITICAL SOURCES: Village Voice, December 15, 1975; *Washington Post Book World*, December 28, 1980; *New York Daily News*, June 14, 1981, November 21, 1982; *Creem*, May, 1982; *Seattle Post-Intelligencer*, May 18, 1982; *Baltimore News American*, June 6, 1982; *Los Angeles Herald Examiner*, December 5, 1982.

NASBY, A(sher Gordon) 1909-1983

OBITUARY NOTICE: Born January 17, 1909, in Jackson, Minn.; died March 23, 1983, in Minneapolis, Minn. Clergyman and author of *Sunrise in the West.* Following his ordination in 1935, Nasby served in Milwaukee and Madison, Wisconsin. After moving to Chicago, he became pastor of Edison Park Lutheran Church in 1938 and remained there until his retirement in 1978. Nasby was also president of the Tri-State Pastoral Conference for nine years and was chairman of the Ecumenical Conference of the Evangelical Lutheran Church. Obituaries and other sources: *Who's Who in Religion,* Marquis, 1977; *Chicago Tribune,* March 26, 1983.

* * *

NASSIVERA, John 1950-

PERSONAL: Born July 28, 1950, in Glens Falls, N.Y. *Education:* Boston University, B.A., 1972; McGill University, Ph.D., 1977. *Residence:* Dorset, Vt. *Agent:* Susan F. Schulman, 165 West End Ave., New York, N.Y. 10023.

CAREER: Teacher at McGill University, Montreal, Quebec, 1973-77, and Columbia University, New York City, 1977-79; New Dramatists, New York City, literary manager, 1979-80. Producing director of Dorset Theatre Festival, Dorset, Vt., 1976—. *Member:* Dramatists Guild, New Dramatists. *Awards, honors:* National Endowment for the Arts fellowship, 1982.

WRITINGS—Plays: The Penultimate Problem of Sherlock Holmes (first produced in Dorset, Vt., at Dorset Theatre Festival, 1978, produced Off-Broadway at Hudson Theatre, 1980), Samuel French, 1980; "Sweeney Todd or the String of Pearls," first produced at Dorset Theatre Festival, 1980; "Phallacies," first produced at Dorset Theatre Festival, 1980, produced in Washington, D.C., at New Playwrights Theatre, 1982; "Four of a Kind," first produced at Dorset Theatre Festival, 1981. Also author of television documentary, "Electra."

SIDELIGHTS: John Nassivera's "Phallacies," a satire of psychiatry, concerns the plight of a little-known writer named Zeno Costini who wants to quit smoking. He seeks the assistance of Carl Jung and Sigmund Freud and is caught in the middle when the warring psychiatrists offer differing explanations for his habit. Freud relates neuroses to infantile sexuality, Jung formulates ideas about the collective unconscious, and a chain-smoking Costini is left to find his own cure.

David Richards of the *Washington Post* criticized the play for imitation, noting its close relation to Tom Stoppard's "Travesties," but allowed, "even in these acts of imitation, Nassivera reveals some real gifts." "'Phallacies,'" observed Richards, "is a meritorious comedy of ideas."

BIOGRAPHICAL/CRITICAL SOURCES: Washington Post, January 15, 1982.

* * *

NAUMBURG, Margaret 1890-1983

OBITUARY NOTICE: Born May 14, 1890, in New York, N.Y.; died February 26, 1983, in Needham, Mass. Educator, psychologist, art therapist, and author of works in her field. Naumburg founded Manhattan's Walden School, which, opening in 1915 with ten pupils and two teachers, advocated an educational philosophy centered around developing the skills and interests of children naturally, without the aid of a formal curriculum. In the 1930's Naumburg began working at the New York Psychiatric Institute, where she used artistic expression as a means of diagnosing and treating disturbed adults and children. Her works include *The Child and the World* and four books on art therapy, including *Schizophrenic Art* and *Psychoneurotic Art.* Obituaries and other sources: *Who's Who of American Women,* 2nd edition, Marquis, 1961; *New York Times,* March 6, 1983.

* * *

NEAL, Nelson 1921(?)-1983

OBITUARY NOTICE: Born c. 1921; died of abdominal cancer, February 13, 1983, in Chicago, Ill. Reporter and editor for United Press (now United Press International) for thirty-eight years. Neal, who was also a founding member of the Wire Service Guild, received a Bronze Star for heroism during World War II. Obituaries and other sources: *Chicago Tribune,* February 15, 1983, February 20, 1983.

* * *

NEBENZAHL, Kenneth 1927-

BRIEF ENTRY: Born September 16, 1927, in Far Rockaway, N.Y. American rare book dealer and author. Nebenzahl, president of Kenneth Nebenzahl, Incorporated, for more than twenty years, became a trustee of Adler Planetarium in 1969 (and chairman in 1977) and a member of Lloyd's of London in 1978. He has also been an active supporter of public and university libraries and has served on the faculty of Chicago's Newberry Library. His books include *Atlas of the American Revolution* (Rand McNally, 1974) and *A Bibliography of Printed Battle Plans of the American Revolution, 1775-1795* (University of Chicago Press, 1975). *Address:* 135 Crescent Dr., Glencoe, Ill. 60022; and 333 North Michigan Ave., Chicago, Ill. 60611.

* * *

NEELY, James C. 1926-

PERSONAL: Born October 26, 1926, in Harrisburg, Pa.; son of William Hardin (a judge) and Jean (Chamberlain) Neely; married first wife, Pamela, April 19, 1963 (divorced, 1975); married Patricia McKrone (a nurse), March 17, 1977; children: (first marriage) Christopher, Heather; (second marriage) Stephen, Robert. *Education:* Princeton University, A.B., 1948; Columbia University, M.D., 1953. *Politics:* Republican. *Home:* 1915 Pierce St., San Francisco, Calif. 94115. *Office:* 3838 California St., Suite 516, San Francisco, Calif. 94118.

CAREER: Private practice of surgery, 1960—. Associate clinical professor at University of California; director of medical education at San Francisco Children's Hospital; medical director of U.S. Mint, San Francisco, Schlage Lock Co., and Ingersol Rand Co. *Military service:* U.S. Navy, pharmacist's mate. *Member:* American Board of Surgery.

WRITINGS: Gender: The Myth of Quality, Simon & Schuster, 1981. Contributor to magazines, including *Esquire, Yale Quarterly Review,* and *Columbia.*

WORK IN PROGRESS: A book on medicine; a book on life in the medical profession.

AVOCATIONAL INTERESTS: Reading, travel, tennis, skiing, sailing.

NEFF, Emery E. 1892-1983

OBITUARY NOTICE—See index for *CA* sketch: Born March 23, 1892, in Delaware, Ohio; died April 24, 1983, in Keene, N.H. Educator and author. Neff began his long association with Columbia University in 1919. He had been a professor emeritus of comparative literature there from 1955. His books include *Carlyle and Mill, The Poetry of History,* and *Edwin Arlington Robinson.* Obituaries and other sources: *New York Times,* April 18, 1983.

* * *

NEHER, Andre 1914-

PERSONAL: Born October 22, 1914, in Obernai, France; son of Albert and Rosette (Strauss) Neher; married Renee Bernheim, December 25, 1947. *Education:* University of Strasbourg, Dr. es Lettres, 1947. *Home:* 14 Rehov Ussishkin, Jerusalem, Israel.

CAREER: Ordained rabbi, 1947; University of Strasbourg, Strasbourg, France, professor of Hebrew language and literature, 1948—, head of department, 1955-70. Visiting professor at University of Tel Aviv, 1968-74, member of board of governors, 1968—; member of board of governors of Haifa University, 1972—. Vice-president of ZF of France, 1949; member of central committee of Alliance Israelite Universelle, 1962—; chairman of Jewish Intellectuals in France, 1965-71. *Member:* International Union for Jewish Studies (member of executive committee, 1957), World Jewish Congress (chairman of French section and International Cultural Commission, 1965-71). *Awards, honors:* Named Sage of Israel by Prime Minister Ben Gurion, 1957; chevalier of French Legion of Honor.

WRITINGS: Moise et la vocation juive, Editions du Seuil, 1956, translation by Irene Marinoff published as *Moses and the Jewish Vocation,* Harper, 1959; *L'Essence du prophetisme,* Presses Universitaires de France, 1955, translation by William Wolf published as *The Prophetic Existence,* A. S. Barnes, 1969; *L'Exil de la parole: Du silence biblique au silence d'Auschwitz,* Editions du Seuil, 1970, translation by David Maisel published as *The Exile of the Word: From the Silence of the Bible to the Silence of Auschwitz,* Jewish Publication Society, 1981.

Not in English: *Amos: Contribution a l'etude du prophetisme,* J. Vrin, 1950; *Notes sur Qohelet,* Editions de Minuit, 1951; *Jeremie,* Librairie Plon, 1960; *L'Existence juive: Solitude et affrontoments,* Editions du Seuil, 1962; (with wife, Renee Neher) *Histoire du peuple d'Israel,* Librairie d'Amerique et d'Orient Adrien-Maisonneuve, three volumes, Klincksieck, 1966-74; *Le Puits de l'exil: La Theologie dialectique du Maharal de Prague,* A. Michel, 1966; *De l'hebreu au francais,* Klincksieck, 1969; *Dans tes portes, Jerusalem,* A. Michel, 1972; *David Gans, 1541-1613: Disciple du Maharal, assistant de Tycho Brahe et Jean Kepler,* Klincksieck, 1975.

Author of teleplay, "To Be a Jew." Contributor to *Encyclopedie francaise* and *Hebrew Encyclopedia.* Contributor of about three hundred articles to magazines.

BIOGRAPHICAL/CRITICAL SOURCES: Times Literary Supplement, December 25, 1981.

NEIL, Hugh Michael 1930-

BRIEF ENTRY: Born November 16, 1930, in Amsterdam, N.Y. American artist, educator, and author. Neil began teaching art education at State University of New York College at Buffalo in 1964. He founded the Youth Art Gallery in New York and has won state and local awards for his work as an artist. Neil wrote *Identity and Teacher Learning* (International Textbook, 1968). *Address:* 8645 Sunset Dr., Clarence, N.Y. 14221; and Cassety Hall, State University of New York College at Buffalo, 1300 Elmwood Ave., Buffalo, N.Y. 14222. *Biographical/critical sources: Leaders in Education,* 5th edition, Bowker, 1974.

* * *

NEIPRIS, Janet
See WILLE, Janet Neipris

* * *

NELSON, Jean Erichsen
See ERICHSEN-NELSON, Jean

* * *

NERVO, Amado (Ruiz de) 1870-1919

BRIEF ENTRY: Born August 27, 1870, in Tepic, Mexico; died May 24, 1919, in Montevideo, Uruguay. Mexican journalist, novelist, and poet. Considered one of Mexico's foremost modernist poets, Nervo began his literary career as a journalist in Mazatlan, Mexico, before moving in 1894 to Mexico City, where he issued a novel, *El Bachiller* (1895), and his first volume of poetry, *Perlas negras* (1898). Many of Nervo's poems, which reflect his religious training and morality, were written from 1905 to 1918 while he served as secretary to the Mexican legation in Madrid, Spain. They were published in the volumes *Los jardines interiores* (1905), *Serenidad* (1914), *Elevacion* (1917), and *Plenitud* (1918; translated as *Plenitude,* 1928). *Biographical/critical sources:* Esther Turner Wellman, *Amado Nervo: Mexico's Religious Poet,* Instituto de las Espanas en los Estados Unidos, 1936; *The Penguin Companion to American Literature,* McGraw, 1971; *Cassell's Encyclopaedia of World Literature,* revised edition, Morrow, 1973; *Twentieth-Century Literary Criticism,* Volume 11, Gale, 1983.

* * *

NESTOR, William P(rodromos) 1947-

PERSONAL: Born July 29, 1947, in Atlantic City, N.J.; son of George Peter and Sophie (Prodromos) Nestor; married Florence Karis (a teacher), November 1, 1970; children: W. Ryan. *Education:* Glassboro State College, B.A., 1970; Antioch Graduate School, Keene, N.H., M.S.T., 1975. *Religion:* Greek Orthodox. *Home address:* Jacksonville Stage, Green River Village, Vt. 05301. *Office:* New England Solar Energy Association, P.O. Box 541, Brattleboro, Vt. 05301.

CAREER: Elementary school teacher in Attleboro, Mass., 1970-72, and Millburn, N.J., 1972-74; New Hampshire Environmental Education Center, Hillsboro, director, 1974-75; New England College, Henniken, N.H., assistant professor of environmental studies, natural history, and education, 1975-80; Hitchcock Center for the Environment, Amherst, Mass., executive director, 1980-82; New England Solar Energy Association, Brattleboro, Vt., editor of *Northeast Sun,* 1982—.

Member: National Science Teachers Association. *Awards, honors: Into Winter* was named an outstanding science book for children by Children's Book Council of National Science Teachers Association, 1982.

WRITINGS: Into Winter (juvenile), illustrations by Susan Banta, Houghton, 1982. Contributor to newsletters.

WORK IN PROGRESS: A novel, based on his sailing trip from Key West, Fla., to Honduras in 1981.

SIDELIGHTS: Nestor wrote: "Understanding the natural environment—its systems and cycles—fosters in each of us a reverence for our life support system.

"My experience with elementary-age students emphasized the wealth of opportunity for enhancing education through the natural curiosity inherent in human interaction with the natural environment. *Into Winter* provides natural history information about the winter season while fostering exploration and discovery through a variety of activities for experiencing the natural world in winter."

AVOCATIONAL INTERESTS: Bicycling, canoeing, snowshoeing, cross-country skiing, racquetball, wilderness travel.

* * *

NGARA, Emmanuel 1947-

PERSONAL: Born December 24, 1947, in Chegutu, Rhodesia (now Zimbabwe); son of Patrick (a teacher) and Ottilia Ngara; married Teboho Motanyane (a teacher), December 14, 1974; children: Rutendo, Shingai, Tapiwa. *Education:* University College of Rhodesia (now University of Zimbabwe), B.A. (with honors), 1970; University of London, M.Phil., 1974, Ph.D., 1977. *Residence:* Harare, Zimbabwe. *Office:* Department of English, University of Zimbabwe, Box MP167, Mount Pleasant, Harare, Zimbabwe.

CAREER: University of Botswana, Lesotho, and Swaziland, Roma, Lesotho, lecturer in English, 1973-75; National University of Lesotho, Roma, lecturer in English, 1975-78; University College of Swaziland, Kwaluseni, senior lecturer in English, 1978-80; Zimbabwe Ministry of Foreign Affairs, Harare, deputy ambassador in Addis Ababa, Ethiopia, 1980-82; University of Zimbabwe, Harare, senior lecturer in English, 1982—, chairman of department of English, 1983—. *Awards, honors:* History award from Mambo Press, 1966, for family history competition; prize from British Broadcasting Corp. Arts and Africa Poetry Competition, 1982, for "A Time to Dance."

WRITINGS: Stylistic Criticism and the African Novel, Heinemann, 1982; *Bilingualism, Language Contact, and Language Planning,* Mambo Press, 1982; *Art and Ideology in the African Novel,* Heinemann, 1983; *Teaching Literature in Africa,* College Press, 1983; *Songs From the Temple,* College Press, 1983. Contributor to *African Book Publishing Record.*

SIDELIGHTS: Ngara told *CA:* "African writers are constantly searching for a new social vision and new aesthetic standards. The best of these writers are committed writers who are concerned with both artistic forms and ideological problems.

"It is my view that if the critic is to perform his duties adequately, he should in turn be sensitive to the concerns of the artist and develop critical norms which give a satisfactory account of the content and form of the art of his day. It is for this reason that in *Stylistic Criticism and the African Novel* I tried to develop a theory of criticism which takes full account of the artist's concern with language and form in relation to

ideological content. In other words, a full appreciation of the language and aesthetic stances of African writers is only possible if the critic understands the conditions under which African authors write and the problems they are trying to grapple with.

"The burden of *Art and Ideology in the African Novel* is to search for critical norms which adequately handle the problem of the relationship between art and ideology and enable the critic and student of literature to examine systematically the influence of Marxism on African writers. In this connection it is necessary to point out that the influence of Marxism in Africa is now too important to be ignored.

"In *Bilingualism, Language Contact, and Language Planning* I have examined the problem of the relationship between African languages and former colonial languages. If both groups of languages are to be used to the benefit of African countries, proper planning is needed so that the role of each language in the state is clearly defined."

* * *

NICHOLS, Paul D(yer) 1938-

PERSONAL: Born February 26, 1938, in Teaneck, N.J.; son of Charles Henry (an engineer) and Viola F. (a secretary; maiden name, Peters) Nichols. *Education:* Attended Norwich University, 1956-60. *Residence:* South Woodstock, Conn.

CAREER: Plumber in Woodstock, Conn., 1975-76; school bus driver in Woodstock, 1977—. Driver at Amherst College, 1978-80; foreman at Schilberg Iron and Metal Co., 1981—; in real estate.

WRITINGS: Big Paul's School Bus (juvenile), illustrations by William Marshall, Prentice-Hall, 1981.

SIDELIGHTS: Paul D. Nichols told *CA:* "As I was driving my school bus I noticed kindergarteners were quite confused on how to enter and leave the bus. I wrote *Big Paul's School Bus* to give pre-school children an idea of what to expect during the first year of school."

* * *

NICHOLSON, Dorothy Nelis 1923-

BRIEF ENTRY: Born March 26, 1923, in Piqua, Ohio. American educator and author. Nicholson, who has been deeply involved in church work since 1950, became director of Park Place Church of God Nursery School in 1968. She wrote *So You Work With Kindergartners* (Warner Press, 1960), *Toward Effective Teaching: Young Children* (Warner Press, 1970), and *I Can Choose—Leader's Guide: A Cooperative Vacation Ventures Series Course for Use in Nursery* (United Church Press, 1974). Nicholson also adapted Elsie Egermeier's *Favorite Bible Stories: Selected Stories for Young Children* (Warner Press, 1970) for contemporary readers.

* * *

NIDDITCH, Peter (Harold) 1928-1983

OBITUARY NOTICE: Born September 15, 1928; died after a short illness, February 12, 1983. Educator, philosopher, and author of works in his field. Professor of philosophy at the University of Sheffield from 1969, Nidditch was known for his expertise in the areas of logic and the philosophy of science. His books include *Introductory Formal Logic of Mathematics,*

Propositional Calculus, The Development of Mathematical Logic, and *The Philosophy of Science.* Before his death Nidditch was general editor of a multi-volume edition of the works of John Locke. Obituaries and other sources: *Who's Who,* 132nd edition, St. Martin's, 1980; *The Writer's Directory: 1982-1984,* Gale, 1981; *London Times,* February 21, 1983.

* * *

NIESEWAND, Peter 1944-1983

OBITUARY NOTICE—See index for *CA* sketch: Born in 1944 in South Africa; died of cancer, February 4, 1983, in London, England. Journalist and author. Niesewand worked as a free-lance reporter in Rhodesia during the 1970's. His articles so angered the white majority there that he was imprisoned and held in solitary confinement for seventy-two days. He was expelled from the country in 1973, took up residence in London, and joined the *Guardian*'s staff as a reporter. *In Camera: Secret Justice in Rhodesia* recounts his prison experiences. He was named international reporter of the year in 1973 and again in 1976. Niesewand began a series of thrillers in 1981. Only *Fallback* and *Scimitar* were completed at the time of his death. His other writings include *A Member of the Club* and *The Underground Connection.* Obituaries and other sources: *London Times,* February 8, 1983; *Chicago Tribune,* February 10, 1983; *Washington Post,* February 12, 1983.

* * *

NIMMO, Derek (Robert) 1933-

PERSONAL: Born September 19, 1933, in Liverpool, England; son of Harry and Marjorie (Sudbury-Hardy) Nimmo; married Patricia Sybil Anne Browne, April 9, 1955; children: Timothy, Amanda, Piers. *Education:* Attended school in Liverpool, England. *Politics:* Liberal. *Religion:* Church of England. *Home:* 110 Lexham Gardens, London W.8, England.

CAREER: Professional actor, 1955—, including roles in plays "Waltz of the Toreadors" and "Same Time Next Year," films "Casino Royale" and "A Talent for Loving," and television series "If It's Saturday Night It Must Be Nimmo," "Just a Nimmo," "Sorry I'm Single," and "Life Begins at Forty." Producer. *Member:* Garrick Club, Athenaeum Club. *Awards, honors:* Award from Variety Club; silver medal from Royal Television Society.

WRITINGS: (Editor and author of introduction) *Nimmo's Choice: A Collection of Cartoons,* Mowbray, 1974; *Derek Nimmo's Drinker's Companion,* Hamlyn, 1979.

* * *

NIOCHE, Brigitte

PERSONAL: Born in Offenbach, West Germany; came to the United States in 1969; daughter of Bruno and Friedel (Missislian) Haltner; married Jacques Nioche, December 27, 1962 (separated); children: Marc. *Education:* Attended Haute Couture Academy, Sydney, Australia, 1959-61, Fleuri Delaporte Ecole de Dessin, Paris, France, 1962, and New School for Social Research, 1975. *Home and office:* 201 West 70th St., New York, N.Y. 10023. *Agent:* Henry Morrison, Inc., 58 West 10th St., New York, N.Y. 10011.

CAREER: Fashion coordinator in Paris, France, 1963-64; Foster Agency, Montreal, Quebec, fashion model, 1965-67; TMI, New York City, fashion model, 1967-71; Hovel (sportwear boutique), New York City, owner and manager, 1970-76; Hearst Magazines, New York City, office manager, 1977-78; Your Image Plus (fashion consultants), New York City, owner, 1978—.

WRITINGS: The Sensual Dresser, Perigee Books, 1981.

WORK IN PROGRESS: Two books on fashion.

SIDELIGHTS: In her book, *The Sensual Dresser,* and through her fashion consulting firm, Nioche stresses that women can achieve the "right image" without sacrificing sensuality, which Nioche deems "a major feminine asset." Suggesting women incorporate V-necklines, soft, shimmering fabrics, and glittering jewels into their wardrobes, Nioche says: "It is subtle changes in dressing that create the sensual image. Looking sensual does not exclude being elegant, stylish, and appropriately dressed. . . . Regardless of what else you do in life, you will always be a woman, and you must combine this fact with all other aspects of your life."

* * *

NIXON, Howard Millar 1909-1983

OBITUARY NOTICE: Born September 3, 1909, in London, England; died February 18, 1983. Librarian and author of works about bookbinding. As a young man, Nixon worked in the library of Westminster Abbey, where he developed an interest in the history of bookbinding. He later became an assistant cataloger on the staff of the British Museum. During his thirty-eight years of service with the British Museum, Nixon helped establish its library as the world center for the study of bookbinding. Nixon's publications include *Twelve Books in Fine Bindings, English Restoration Bookbindings,* and *Five Centuries of English Bookbinding.* Obituaries and other sources: *Who's Who in Librarianship,* Bowes & Bowes, 1954; *Who's Who,* 134th edition, 1982; *London Times,* February 28, 1983.

* * *

NOONE, John 1936-

BRIEF ENTRY: Born February 7, 1936, in Darlington, England. British educator and author. Noone has lectured at University of Alexandria, University of Libya (now University of Benghazi), and Kyoto University. He received the Geoffrey Faber Memorial Prize for his novel *The Man With the Chocolate Egg* (Hamish Hamilton, 1966) and an Arts Council award for his novel *The Night of Accomplishment* (Hamish Hamilton, 1974). *Address:* 45 Avenue Lancaster, Brussels 1180, Belgium. *Biographical/critical sources: Observer,* October 20, 1974; *New Statesman,* October 25, 1974.

* * *

NORBU, Thubten Jigme
See THUBTEN Sigme Norbu

* * *

NORRIS, Christopher Neil Foxley
See FOXLEY-NORRIS, Christopher Neil

* * *

NORTON, Charles A(lbert) 1920-

PERSONAL: Born October 18, 1920, in Cincinnati, Ohio; son

of Charles Clifford and Elsie (Grosse) Norton; married Harriet Schetter (an insurance specialist), April 18, 1942; children: Charles T., Clifford, Phillip, Sylvia Norton Litschgi, LaVerne Norton Bergland. *Education:* Attended Southern Ohio Business College, 1930-40, and University of Cincinnati, 1942-65. *Religion:* United Methodist. *Home and office:* 9882 Prechtel Rd., Cincinnati, Ohio 45247.

CAREER: Baldwin Piano Co., Cincinnati, Ohio, in engineering and administration, 1944-60; self-employed sales represenative and manufacturers' agent in Cincinnati, 1960-62; Lloyd Library, Cincinnati, member of library staff, 1962-65; Miami University, Oxford, Ohio, member of library staff, 1965-74; free-lance writer, 1974—. *Member:* Queen City Writers (vice-president, 1981; president, 1982-83).

WRITINGS: Melville Davisson Post: Man of Many Mysteries (self-illustrated with photographs), Bowling Green University, 1973; (contributor) Matthew J. Bruccoli and C. E. Frazer Clark, editors, *Fitzgerald/Hemingway Annual 1973,* Microcard Edition Books, 1974; (contributor) Melville Davisson Post, *The Complete Uncle Abner,* University Extension, University of California, San Diego, 1977; *Writing Tom Sawyer: The Adventures of a Classic* (self-illustrated with photographs), McFarland & Co., 1983; *A Look Back, a Look Ahead: Celebrating One Hundred Fifty Years of Faith, 1832-1982* (self-illustrated with photographs), Groesbeck United Methodist Church, 1982. Contributor to *Mark Twain Society Bulletin.*

WORK IN PROGRESS: Sam Clemens, a novel based on the life of Mark Twain; *Creator and Creation,* poems.

SIDELIGHTS: Charles A. Norton commented: "My writing interests span forty years or more. First I published essays and poems in newspapers and small serial publications. About 1961 I developed an interest in books, and after 1967 concentrated on literary criticism and biography. My current objectives are to publish a novel and a collection of poems.

"As a member of the Queen City Writers, I enjoy working with beginners and taking part in organizing annual seminars for writers. My most important discovery is that successful writing requires discipline, research, and a daily work schedule."

AVOCATIONAL INTERESTS: Collecting books (especially works of significant American authors), photography (including nature photography and photographs for his own books), gardening.

*   *   *

NORTON, (William) Elliot   1903-

BRIEF ENTRY: Born May 17, 1903, in Boston, Mass. American drama critic. Norton was a newspaper reporter from 1926 to 1934. He then became a drama critic for such newspapers as the *Boston Post, Boston Daily Record,* and *Boston Sunday Advertiser,* and in 1973 for the *Boston Herald American.* He also has taught dramatic literature at Emerson College, Boston College, and Boston University. In 1958 Norton made his television debut in "Elliot Norton Reviews," for which he won a George Foster Peabody Broadcasting Award from the University of Georgia. His other honors include an Antoinette Perry Award and a gold medal from the American College Theatre Festival. Norton wrote *Broadway Down East: An Informal Account of the Plays, Players, and Playhouses of Boston From Puritan Times to the Present* (Trustees of the Public Library of the City of Boston, 1978). *Address:* 126 Church

St., Watertown, Mass. 02172; and 300 Harrison Ave., Boston, Mass. 02106.

*   *   *

NORTON, Victor   1906-1983

OBITUARY NOTICE: Born in 1906 in South Africa; died May 4, 1983, in Cape Town, South Africa. Editor of the *Cape Times* for twenty-seven years. Known for his pointed editorial commentary, Norton became involved in the political controversy that ensued after a nationalistic government emerged in South Africa in 1948. He led the *Times* in its attack upon those policies of the new government that the news staff regarded as unjust. Rhodes University bestowed an honorary doctorate of literature upon Norton. Obituaries and other sources: *Who Was Who Among English and European Authors, 1931-1949,* Gale, 1978; *London Times,* May 6, 1983.

*   *   *

NORWAK, Mary   1929-

PERSONAL: Born January 20, 1929, in London, England; daughter of John William Chamberlain and Laura (Duffin) Stock; married John Michael Norwak, September 8, 1955 (died August 7, 1965); children: Sophia, Matthew, Unity. *Education:* Attended private secondary school in Elstree, England. *Politics:* Conservative. *Religion:* Church of England. *Home:* Cley Old Hall, Cley Next the Sea, Holt, Norfolk, England. *Agent:* Barbara Hargreaves, Daviot, Inverness, Scotland.

CAREER: National Trade Press, London, England, journalist and editor beginning in 1948; United Trade Press, London, journalist and editor ending in 1952; Conde Nast Publications, New York, N.Y., promotions editor of *Vogue* and *House and Garden,* 1952-55; free-lance writer, 1955—. Chairman of North Norfolk Conservative Women's advisory committee; member of executive committee of Norfolk's Worker's Institute; member of Cley Parochial Church Council; consultant to Graham Kemp Associates. *Member:* Norfolk Society (member of executive committee).

WRITINGS: Cooking With Fruit, Transatlantic Arts, 1960; *The Five O'Clock Cookbook,* Transatlantic Arts, 1960; (editor with Maureen Owen) *The A to Z Party Book,* Daily Mirror, 1964; *Farm House Cakes and Home Baked Bread,* Farmers Weekly, 1966, published as *Home Baked Bread and Cakes,* Hamlyn, 1973.

A to Z of Home Freezing, Sphere, 1971, revised edition, 1978; *Freezer and Fridge Cookery,* Ward, Lock, 1971; *Mixer and Blender Cookery,* International Publications Service, 1971; *A Calendar of Home Freezing,* Sphere, 1972, revised edition, 1978; *Cooking Into Europe,* Ward, Lock, 1973; *Beginner's Guide to Home Freezing,* Merrimack Book Service, 1973; *The Complete Farmhouse Cookbook,* Compton Russell Ltd., 1973; *Mary Norwak's Book on Jams, Marmalades, and Sweet Preserves,* Sphere, 1973; *The Complete Book of Barbecues,* Pelham Books, 1974; *The Complete Home Freezer,* Ward, Lock, 1974; *Deep Freezing,* Sphere, 1974; (with Keith Mossman) *Growing, Freezing, and Cooking,* Elm Tree, 1974; *Preparing Food for Your Freezer,* Ward, Lock, 1974; *Mary Norwak's Save Money Cookbook,* Luscombe, 1975; *The English Farmhouse Kitchen,* Follett, 1975; *Kitchen Antiques,* Praeger, 1975; *The Pie Book,* illustrations by Chris Evans, M. Joseph, 1975; *Cooking for Your Freezer,* Ward, Lock, 1975.

The Fruit Book, Merrimack Book Service, 1976; *Deep Freezing Menus and Recipes,* Sphere, 1976; *Breads, Buns, and*

Yeastcakes, Futura Publishing, 1976; *Country Cookbook,* Hamlyn, 1976; *Something to Collect,* Pelham Books, 1976; *Preparing Food for Your Freezer,* Bobbs-Merrill, 1977; *From Garden to Table,* Elm Tree, 1977; *Toffees, Fudges, Chocolates, and Sweets,* Pelham Books, 1977; (with Violet W. Stevenson) *All About Growing For Your Freezer,* Hamlyn, 1977; (with K. Mossman) *Home Grown,* Spectator Publications, 1977; *Complete Freezer Recipes,* Ward, Lock, 1977; *The Complete Mixer and Blender,* Ward, Lock, 1977.

The Complete Vegetable Cookbook, Harbor House, 1978; (with Peggy Hutchinson) *Grandma's Preserving Secrets,* Foulsham, 1978; (with Hutchinson) *Farmhouse Cooking,* Foulsham, 1978; *East Anglian Recipes,* East Anglian Magazine, 1978; *The Complete Book of Home Preserving,* Ward, Lock, 1978; *Pressure Cooking and Other Methods of Fuel-Saving Cookery,* Pelham Books, 1978; *Five Hundred Recipes for Breads, Cakes, and Biscuits,* Hamlyn, 1978; *Budget With Your Freezer,* Sphere, 1978; *The Best of Country Cooking,* Dent, 1979; (with Bill Crabtree) *The Best Wine Recipes,* Foulsham, 1979; *The Complete Book of Home Baking,* Ward, Lock, 1979; (with Sheila Macrae) *The Scottish Cookbook,* Foulsham, 1979; *Creative Meat Cooking,* Everest House, 1979; *The Poultry Cookbook,* Elm Tree, 1979.

East Anglian Ragbag, East Anglian Magazine, 1980; *Crockpot Cooking,* Futura Publications, 1980; *Self-Sufficiency for Children,* Pelham Books, 1980, Merrimack Book Service, 1981; *Moulinex: The Food Processor Cookbook,* Ward, Lock, 1980; (editor) Annette Yates, *The Baby Food and Family Cookbook,* Foulsham, 1981; *Buying and Cooking Vegetables,* Woodhead-Faulkner, 1981; *A Feast of Vegetables,* Foulsham, 1981; *The Foolproof Cookbook,* David & Charles, 1982; *English Puddings,* Batsford, 1982; (with Jackie Burrow) *Health Food Cookbook,* Octopus, 1982; *Mary Norwak's Guide to Home Freezing,* Ward, Lock, 1982.

Contributor to magazines, including *Farmers Weekly, Lady,* and *Freezer Family.* Editor of *Freezer World,* 1978-80.

WORK IN PROGRESS: British Cakes; Twentieth-Century Food.

* * *

NOSSAL, Gustav Joseph Victor 1931-

PERSONAL: Born April 6, 1931, in Bad Ischl, Austria; son of Rudolf Immanuel and Irene Maria Nossal; married Lyn Dunnicliff (a speech therapist), November 19, 1955; children: Katrina Anne, Michael Peter, Brigid Suzanne, Stephen Mark. *Education:* University of Sydney, B.Med.Sci., 1952, B.Med. & Surg., 1954; University of Melbourne, Ph.D., 1960. *Home:* 46 Fellows St., Kew, Victoria 3101, Australia. *Office:* Walter and Eliza Hall Institute, Royal Melbourne Hospital, Victoria 3050, Australia.

CAREER: Royal Prince Alfred Hospital, Sydney, Australia, senior resident officer, 1955-56; Walter and Eliza Hall Institute of Medical Research, Melbourne, Australia, research fellow, 1957-59, deputy director, 1961-65, director, 1965—; Stanford University, Palo Alto, Calif., assistant professor of genetics, 1959-61. Professor of medical biology at University of Melbourne, 1965—; visiting scientist at Pasteur Institute, 1968-69; visiting professor at University of Oregon, 1970, and University of California, Berkeley, 1973. Member of advisory committee on medical research for World Health Organization, 1973—; chairman of Western Pacific Regional Advisory Committee on Medical Research, 1977; member of Australian Science and Technology Council; member of board of directors

of C.R.A. Ltd.; member of awards assembly of General Motors Cancer Research Foundation (chairman, 1977—). *Member:* International Transplantation Society (vice-president, 1971-73), Australian Academy of Science (fellow; member of council, 1970-76), Australian and New Zealand Association for the Advancement of Science (president, 1970), Australian Academy of Technological Sciences (fellow), National Academy of Science (United States; foreign associate member), Royal Society (England; fellow), American Academy of Arts and Sciences (foreign honorary member), American Association of Immunologists (honorary member), Royal College of Physicians of London (fellow), Indian National Science Academy (fellow), French Society of Immunology (honorary member), American Heart Association (fellow), New York Academy of Sciences (fellow).

AWARDS, HONORS: Research Medal from Royal Society of Victoria, 1964; Science Award from Phi Beta Kappa, 1969; Commander of Order of the British Empire, 1970; Emil von Behring Prize from Philipps University, 1971; Rabbi Shai Shacknai Memorial Prize from University of Jerusalem, 1973; created Knight Bachelor, 1977; gold medal from Ciba Foundation, 1978; Burnet Medal from Australian Academy of Science, 1979; M.D. from University of Mainz, 1981.

WRITINGS: Antibodies and Immunity, Basic Books, 1968, 2nd edition, 1978; (with G. L. Ada) *Antigens, Lymphoid Cells, and the Immune Response,* Academic Press, 1981; *Medical Science and Human Goals,* Edward Arnold, 1975; *Nature's Defences: New Frontiers in Vaccine Research,* Australian Broadcasting Commission, 1978.

Contributor: *Radiation Biology,* Butterworth, 1958; M. Holub and L. Jaroskova, editors, *Mechanisms of Antibody Formation,* Publishing House of the Czechoslovak Academy of Sciences, 1960; Heidelberger and Plescia, editors, *Immunochemical Approaches to Problems in Microbiology,* Rutgers University Press, 1961; W. H. Taliaferro and J. Humphrey, editors, *Advances in Immunology,* Volume II, Academic Press, 1962; M. Hasek and A. Lengerova, editors, *Mechanisms of Immunological Tolerance,* Academic Press, 1962; G. W. Richter and M. A. Epstein, editors, *International Review of Experimental Pathology,* Volume I, Academic Press, 1962; A. Bussard, editor, *Acquired or Natural Immune Tolerance Towards Defined Antigens,* Academic Press, 1963; D. O. White, editor, *A Post-Graduate Course in Cell Culture,* Cell Culture Society of Victoria, 1963; R. A. Good and A. E. Gabrielson, editors, *International Conference on the Thymus,* Harper, 1964; *Symposium of the Czechoslovak Academy of Sciences on Mechanisms of Antibody Formation,* Academic Press, 1965; E. N. Willmer, editor, *Cells and Tissues in Culture,* Academic Press, 1966; G.E.W. Wolstenholme and R. Porter, editors, *The Thymus: Experimental and Clinical Studies,* Churchill, 1966; J. Killander, editor, *Nobel Symposium Three: Gamma Globulins,* Interscience, 1967; F. T. Rapaport and J. Dausset, editors, *Human Transplantation,* Grune, 1968; C. A. Williams and M. Chase, editors, *Methods in Cell Immunology,* Academic Press, 1969; *The Harvey Lectures,* Academic Press, 1969; M. Landy and W. Braun, editors, *Immunological Tolerance: A Reassessment of Mechanisms of the Immune Response,* Academic Press, 1969.

Contributor: J. Sterzl and M. Riha, editors, *Developmental Aspects of Antibody Formation and Structure,* Volume II, Academic Press, 1970; H. Messel and S. T. Butler, editors, *Molecules to Man,* Shakespeare Head Press, 1971; A. Maekelae, Anne Cross, and T. U. Kosunen, editors, *Cell Interactions and Receptor Antibodies in Immune Responses*, Academic Press, 1971; B. D. Kahan and R. A. Reisfield, editors, *Transplantation Antigens*, Academic Press, 1972; M. Marois, editor, *Theoretical Physics to Biology*, Karger, 1973; J. K. Pollak and J. Wilson Lee, editors, *The Biochemistry of Gene Expression in High Organisms*, A.N.Z. Co., 1973; Ivan Roitt, editor, *Essays in Fundamental Immunology*, Basil Blackwell, 1973; R. Doll and I. Vodopija, editors, *Host Environment Interactions in the Etiology of Cancer in Man*, International Agency for Research Against Cancer, 1973; E. H. Kone and H. J. Jordan, editors, *The Greatest Adventure: Basic Research That Shapes Our Lives*, Rockefeller University Press, 1974; D. H. Katz and B. Benacerraf, editors, *Immunological Tolerance: Mechanisms and Potential Therapeutic Applications*, Academic Press, 1974; E. Diczfalusy, editor, *Immunological Approaches to Fertility*, Karolinska Institute, 1974; E. M. Hersh and M. Schlamowitz, editors, *Immunological Aspects of Neoplasia*, Williams & Wilkins, 1975; F. O. Schmitt, D. M. Schneider, and D. M. Crothers, editors, *Functional Linkage in Biomolecular Systems*, Raven Press, 1975; G. P. Talwar, editor, *Regulation of Growth and Differential Function in Eukaryote Cells*, Raven Press, 1975; *Australia 2025*, Electrolux, 1975; J. J. Marchalonis, editor, *Comparative Immunology*, Blackwell Scientific Publications, 1976; Max Samter, editor, *Immunological Diseases*, Volume I, Little, Brown, 3rd edition, 1978; S. T. Waddell, editor, *Prospect 2000: A Conference on the Future*, Australian and New Zealand Association for the Advancement of Science, 1979.

Contributor: M. Fougereau and J. Dausset, editors, *Immunology Eighty*, Academic Press, 1980; H. Waters, editor, *The Handbook of Cancer Immunology*, Volume VIII: *Tumor Antigens: Structure and Function*, Garland Publishing, 1981; J. T. Woodcock, editor, *Manufacturing Resources of Australia*, Australian Academy of Technological Sciences, 1981; H. Fudenberg, editor, *Biomedical Institutions, Biomedical Funding, and Public Policies*, Plenum, 1982.

Contributor of nearly three hundred articles to medical and scientific journals, including *Scientific American*.

WORK IN PROGRESS: Research on cellular immunology, with special reference to immunological tolerance and mechanisms of antibody synthesis.

NOTESTEIN, Frank Wallace   1902-1983

OBITUARY NOTICE: Born August 16, 1902, in Alma, Mich.; died of emphysema, February 19, 1983, in Langhorne, Pa. Research demographer and co-author of *Controlled Fertility* and *The Future Population of Europe and the Soviet Union*. Notestein is best known as founder of the Office of Population Research, which was devoted to family planning and population control. Based at Princeton University, where Notestein served as professor of demography from 1945 to 1959, the research center was the first of its kind in the nation. Notestein was also director of the population division of the United Nations from 1946 to 1948 and was adviser to India on matters of population control in 1955. Obituaries and other sources: *Blue Book: Leaders of the English-Speaking World*, St. Martin's, 1976; *Who's Who in America*, 41st edition, Marquis, 1980; *Chicago Tribune*, February 22, 1983; *New York Times*, February 22, 1983.

*   *   *

NUTINI, Hugo G(ino)   1928-

BRIEF ENTRY: Born June 26, 1928, in Puemo, Chile. Anthropologist, educator, and author. Nutini taught at Los Angeles State College, University of Puerto Rico, and George Washington University before he began teaching anthropology at University of Pittsburgh in 1970. He wrote *San Bernardino Contla: Marriage and Family Structure in a Tlaxcalan Municipio* (University of Pittsburgh Press, 1968) and co-authored *Ritual Kinship: The Structure and Historical Document of the Compadrazgo System in Rural Tlaxcala* (Princeton University Press, 1980). Nutini also co-edited *Game Theory in the Behavioral Sciences* (University of Pittsburgh Press, 1969) and *Essays on Mexican Kinship* (University of Pittsburgh Press, 1976). *Address:* Department of Anthropology, University of Pittsburgh, 4200 Fifth Ave., Pittsburgh, Pa. 15260. *Biographical/critical sources: American Men and Women of Science*, 13th edition, Bowker, 1976.

O

O'CONNOR, Anthony ?-1983(?)

OBITUARY NOTICE: Author of the novel *He's Somewhere in There* and *Clubland: The Wrong Side of the Right People.* O'Connor was secretary of the Cavalry (now Cavalry and Guards Club) for many years and, during World War II, served in the Royal Air Force. Obituaries and other sources: *London Times,* February 10, 1983.

*   *   *

O'CONNOR, John E. 1943-

BRIEF ENTRY: Born August 13, 1943, in New York, N.Y. American historian, educator, and author. O'Connor began teaching American history at New Jersey Institute of Technology in 1969. He is also coordinator of the institute's man and technology program and co-editor of *Film and History Journal.* O'Connor's publications include *Teaching History With Film* (American Historical Association, 1974), *Film and the Humanities* (Rockefeller Foundation, 1977), *American History/American Film: Interpreting the Hollywood Image* (Ungar, 1979), *William Paterson: Lawyer and Statesman, 1746-1806* (Rutgers University Press, 1979), and *The Hollywood Indian: Stereotypes of Native Americans in Films* (New Jersey State Museum, 1980). He also edited *I Am a Fugitive From a Chain Gang* (University of Wisconsin Press, 1981), a title from the "Warner Brothers Screenplay" series. *Address:* Department of Humanities, New Jersey Institute of Technology, 323 High St., Newark, N.J. 07102.

*   *   *

O'CONNOR, Rory 1951-

PERSONAL: Born November 20, 1951, in New York. *Education:* Attended Boston College, 1968-72. *Politics:* "Anarchy." *Religion:* Zen Buddhist. *Office:* WCVB-TV, 5 TV Pl., Needham, Mass. 02192.

CAREER: Producer at WCVB-TV, Needham, Mass.

WRITINGS: (With Stephen Hilgartner and Richard C. Bell) *Nukespeak: Nuclear Language, Visions, and Mindset,* Sierra Books, 1982.

O'DONOGHUE, Gregory 1951-

BRIEF ENTRY: Irish educator and poet. O'Donoghue has worked at University College in Cork and at Queen's University in Kingston, Ontario. He wrote a book of poems, *Kicking* (Gallery Press, 1975). *Address:* Beaufort, Dunmore Lawn, Ballinlough, County Cork, Ireland.

*   *   *

O'HARA, Kenneth

PERSONAL: Born in Wateringbury, Kent, England. *Address:* c/o Ian Henry Publications Ltd., 38 Parkstone Ave., Hornchurch, Essex RM11 3LW, England.

CAREER: Writer.

WRITINGS:—Novels: *A View to a Death,* Cassell, 1958; *Sleeping Dogs Lying,* Cassell, 1960, Macmillan, 1962; *Underhandover,* Cassell, 1961; *Double Cross Purposes,* Cassell, 1962; *Unknown Man, Seen in Profile,* Gollancz, 1967; *The Birdcage,* Gollancz, 1968, Random House, 1969; *The Company of St. George,* Gollancz, 1972; *The Delta Knife,* Gollancz, 1976; *The Ghost of Thomas Penry,* Gollancz, 1978; *The Searchers of the Dead,* Gollancz, 1979. Also author of *Nightmare's Nest,* 1982.

SIDELIGHTS: O'Hara is the author of numerous murder/mystery novels, most of which have received little notice. Those that have been reviewed, however, have met with approval. *Unknown Man, Seen in Profile,* for example, inspired a *Times Literary Supplement* critic to write: "The telling is sophisticated and urbane, sometimes almost to the point of classy copywriting." Of O'Hara's next book, *The Birdcage,* Allen J. Hubin of the *New York Times* wrote: "*The Birdcage* plumbs the crevices of a psychosis with delicate skill. This is a novel cinematic in expression." And T. J. Binyon, in the *Times Literary Supplement,* called *The Ghost of Thomas Penry* "a well-told, neatly enigmatic story, which, while invoking the supernatural, does not depend on it."

BIOGRAPHICAL/CRITICAL SOURCES: Times Literary Supplement, May 4, 1967, April 7, 1978; *New York Times Book Review,* November 2, 1969.*

OLAN, Levi Arthur 1903-

PERSONAL: Born March 22, 1903, in Cherkassy, Russia (now Ukrainian S.S.R.); came to the United States in 1906, naturalized citizen, 1912; son of Max and Bessie (Leshinsky) Olan; married Sarita Messer, June 9, 1931; children: Elizabeth Olan Hirsch, Frances, David. *Education:* Attended University of Rochester, 1921-24; University of Cincinnati, B.A., 1925; Hebrew Union College, Rabbi, 1929. *Home:* 3131 Maple Ave., Dallas, Tex. 75201. *Office:* 8500 Hillcrest St., Dallas, Tex. 75225.

CAREER: Rabbi of Jewish congregation in Worcester, Mass., 1929-49; Temple Emanu-El, Dallas, Tex., rabbi, 1949-70, rabbi emeritus, 1970—. Visiting lecturer at Southern Methodist University; visiting professor at Texas Christian University, University of Texas, Austin, Emory University, University of Texas, Arlington, Houston Institute of Religion and Human Development, Southern Methodist University, and Leo Baeck College, London, England. President of Jewish Family Service, 1932-40; member of Central Conference of American Rabbis (president, 1967-69). Member of board of regents of University of Texas. *Member:* Dallas United Nations Association (president, 1960). *Awards, honors:* D.D. from Hebrew Union College, 1955; D.H.L. from Austin College, 1967, and Southern Methodist University.

WRITINGS: Judaism and Modern Theology (monograph), Central Conference of American Rabbis, 1956; *Freedom and Responsibility* (monograph), Central Conference of American Rabbis, 1965; *Judaism and Immortality,* Union of American Hebrew Congregations, 1971; *Prophetic Faith and the Secular Age,* Ktav, 1982.

*   *   *

O'LAOGHAIRE, Liam
See O'LEARY, Liam

*   *   *

OLDHAM, Mary 1944-

PERSONAL: Born June 7, 1944, in Nottinghamshire, England; daughter of Alec (a milkman) and Marjorie (Pickford) Oldham. *Education:* Attended College of Librarianship, Wales, 1965-66; London School of Economics and Political Science, London, B.Sc., 1977. *Politics:* "Left of center." *Religion:* Anglican. *Home:* 5 Milford Cottages, Newtown, Powys, Wales. *Agent:* Hughes Massie Ltd., 31 Southampton Row, London WC1B 4HL, England.

CAREER: Schools librarian at Montgomeryshire County Library, 1969-72; Clwyd Library Service, Clwyd, Wales, organizer of school libraries, 1972-74; information officer for British Steel Corp., 1978-81.

WRITINGS: A Horse for Her, Hastings House, 1969 (published in England as *A Dream of Horses,* Harrap, 1969); *The White Pony,* Hastings House, 1981.

WORK IN PROGRESS: The Hafod on the Hill, a novel for teenagers, comparing rural and urban life.

*   *   *

O'LEARY, Liam 1910-
(Liam O'Laoghaire)

PERSONAL: Born September 25, 1910, in Youghal, Ireland; son of Denis and Alice (Burke) O'Leary. *Education:* Attended National University of Ireland, University College, Dublin, 1928-33. *Politics:* "Liberal (but that's a long story)." *Religion:* "Humanist." *Home:* Garden Flat, 74 Ranelagh Rd., Dublin 6, Ireland. *Office:* Film Department, Radio Telefis Eireann, Donnybrook, Dublin 4, Ireland.

CAREER: Department of Industry and Commerce, Dublin, Ireland, civil servant, 1934-44; Abbey Theatre, Dublin, Ireland, producer, 1944-46; free-lance broadcaster, film director, actor, and journalist, 1947-53; National Film Archive, London, England, acquisitions officer, 1953-66; Radio Telefis Eireann, Dublin, film acceptance officer, 1966—. Director of "Cinema Ireland," exhibition at Trinity College, Dublin, 1976.

MEMBER: Society of Authors, British Film Institute, Irish Film Society (founder; member of board of directors, 1936-43), Cinema Theatre Association, Royal Dublin Society, Dublin Little Theatre Guild (founder, 1934). *Awards, honors:* Medals from Brussels International Exhibition, 1958, and National Film Studios of Ireland, 1978.

WRITINGS: (Under name Liam O'Laoghaire) *Invitation to the Film,* Kerryman, 1945; *The Silent Cinema,* Vista Books, 1965; *Rex Ingram: Master of the Silent Cinema,* Barnes & Noble, 1980. Contributor to magazines and newspapers, including *Ireland Today, Bell, Leader, Irish Monthly,* and *Silent Cinema.*

WORK IN PROGRESS: The Cinema in Ireland, 1896-1982, publication expected in 1984; an autobiography, *Indifferent Honest,* publication expected in 1985.

SIDELIGHTS: O'Leary told *CA* that cinema is his main interest, followed by theatre. As a film director, his credits include "Mr. Careless" and "Portrait of Dublin" and he has appeared in the films "Stranger at My Door" and "Men Against the Sun." His acting roles include King Lear, Hamlet, Mio in "Winterset," The Captain in Strindberg's "The Father," and Everyman.

O'Leary commented: "My interest in the theatre was stimulated largely by the presentation of Shakespearean plays by Anew McMaster and Michael MacLiammoir at my local Wexford theatre. From my early days I was fascinated by all the films from every country that appeared at the local theatre. These were films now recognized as classics, such as 'The Atonement of Gosta Berling,' 'Metropolis,' the films of Chaplin, Mary Pickford, and Douglas Fairbanks. My books on the cinema derived from these early experiences and from reading the books of Paul Rotha, Bardeche, and Brassillach, and the highbrow magazine *Close Up.* My youthful recollections of the films of Rex Ingram stimulated me to write his biography. His eminence in the world of films and his Irish origins combined to produce *Rex Ingram: Master of the Silent Cinema.* There is now a growing appreciation of his work endorsed by many filmmakers whom he inspired.

"The events of Irish film history have never been charted and this research engaged my attention. As to my autobiography, which I am now preparing, this will, I hope, clarify my ideas about life and the practice of my art—which has nearly always been outside the establishment. I work better in freedom."

AVOCATIONAL INTERESTS: Gardening, education, travel (Kenya, Czechoslovakia, the United States, France, Germany, Belgium, Finland).

BIOGRAPHICAL/CRITICAL SOURCES: Times Literary Supplement, July 18, 1980; *Observer,* August 17, 1980.

OLIVER, Andrew 1906-1981

PERSONAL: Born March 14, 1906, in Morristown, N.J.; died October 20, 1981, in Boston, Mass.; son of William H. P. and Lydia (Seabury) Oliver; married Ruth Blake, February 21, 1936; children: Andrew, Jr., Daniel, Ruth Oliver Morley. *Education:* Harvard University, A.B., 1928, LL.B., 1931.

CAREER: Practiced law in New York City, 1934-44; Alexander & Green (law firm), New York City, partner, 1944-70; historian and writer, 1970-81. Member of board of trustees of General Theological Seminary, 1948-68, and Boston Athenaeum; president of Charlotte Palmer Phillips Foundation, 1961-72, and Essex Institute, 1973-74; member of council of Institute for Early American History and Culture, 1967-70; commissioner of National Portrait Gallery. Chancellor of Episcopal Diocese of New York, 1961-71. *Awards, honors:* D.Canon Law from General Theological Seminary, 1970.

WRITINGS: Portraits of John and Abigail Adams, Balknap Press, 1967; (editor with David Evans and John Kerslake, and contributor of notes) *The Notebook of John Smibert,* Massachusetts Historical Society, 1969; *Benjamin Constant: Ecriture et conquete du moi,* Lettres modernes, 1970; *Portraits of John Quincy Adams and His Wife,* Belknap Press, 1970; (editor) *The Journal of Samuel Curwen, Loyalist,* two volumes, Harvard University Press, 1972; *The Portraits of John Marshall,* University Press of Virginia, 1977; *Auguste Edouart's Silhouettes of Eminent Americans, 1839-1844,* University Press of Virginia, 1977; (editor with James Bishop Peabody) *The Records of Trinity Church, Boston, 1728-1830,* Colonial Society of Massachusetts, 1980, Volume II, 1982; (with Bryant F. Tolles, Jr.) *Windows on the Past: Portraits at the Essex Institute,* Essex Institute, 1981.

BIOGRAPHICAL/CRITICAL SOURCES: Virginia Quarterly Review, spring, 1971.

OBITUARIES: New York Times, October 22, 1981; *AB Bookman's Weekly,* December 7, 1981.*

* * *

OLIVER, Raymond (Davies) 1936-

PERSONAL: Born January 28, 1936, in Arlington, Mass.; son of Raymond Joseph and Bernice (Davis) Oliver; married Mary Anne McPherson (a professor and writer), August 28, 1959; children: Kathryn, Nathan. *Education:* Oberlin College, B.A., 1957; University of Wisconsin—Madison, M.A., 1958; Stanford University, Ph.D., 1967. *Religion:* Anglican. *Office:* 322 Wheeler Hall, University of California, Berkeley, Calif. 94720.

CAREER: University of California, Berkeley, assistant professor, 1965-71, associate professor of English, 1971—, director of Education Abroad Program at University of Bordeaux, 1982-84. *Member:* American Association of University Professors, Phi Beta Kappa.

WRITINGS: Poems Without Names (criticism), University of California Press, 1970; *To Be Plain* (verse translations), Robert L. Barth, 1981; *Entries* (poems), David R. Godine, 1982; *Private Stock* (poems), Robert L. Barth, 1982.

WORK IN PROGRESS: A technical study of the short poem; a work in prose and verse on *Beowulf* and Anglo-Saxon culture; a book of poems on historical themes.

SIDELIGHTS: Oliver told *CA:* "I write poetry to make sense of experience, to celebrate it, and to fix it in memorable form. 'Form' is a key word. Everything I write is in strict metrical form—iambics, usually rhymed—because that, and that only, gives a sense of definitiveness, like the sense of things fitting exactly into position when you turn the right key in the lock. And strict form is easy to remember, therefore lends itself to being memorable; we still remember about Humpty Dumpty, even though he goes back to Indo-European times, because his career was preserved in rhyme and meter—a consideration not lost on song-writers even now.

"Every object (a road, a tree, a meal), every piece of bric-a-brac from my own daily life, any fragment of U.S. or European history, is potentially a window that opens up on human experience. I am not a poetic specialist; my theme is miscellany, on principle. Anything goes. A 'philosophy of life' will emerge as it emerges, over the years, inductively. Above all, I want the world, piece by piece, to enter into my poetry with a minimum of distortion.

"Because variety of experience is important, and because I am obsessed with language, especially in its aural aspect, I have learned French and German very thoroughly, and have lived for years in Germany, France, and England. I have also learned, with varying degrees of competence and for the same reasons, Latin, Portuguese, Russian, and Greek."

AVOCATIONAL INTERESTS: "My principal hobby is food, which goes well with poetry and languages and travel. All in all I think that life, like God, is meant to be enjoyed, precisely and in depth."

BIOGRAPHICAL/CRITICAL SOURCES: Chicago Tribune Book World, September 26, 1982.

* * *

OLSON, Alison Gilbert 1931-

BRIEF ENTRY: Born October 10, 1931, in Oakland, Calif. American historian, educator, and author. Olson taught at Smith College, Rutgers University, Colorado College, and American University before becoming a professor of history at University of Maryland. Her books include *The Radical Duke: Career and Correspondence of Charles Lennox, Third Duke of Richmond* (Oxford University Press, 1961), *Anglo-American Political Relations, 1675-1775* (Rutgers University Press, 1970), and *Anglo-American Politics, 1660-1775: The Relationship Between Parties in England and Colonial America* (Oxford University Press, 1973). *Address:* Department of History, University of Maryland, College Park, Md. 20740. *Biographical/critical sources: American Historical Review,* December, 1971, December, 1974; *Times Literary Supplement,* May 3, 1974.

* * *

O'MALLEY, Charles Donald 1907-1970

OBITUARY NOTICE: Born in 1907 in Alameda, Calif.; died in 1970. Historian, educator, and author. Educated at Stanford University, O'Malley became a professor of the history of medicine at the University of California Medical School in Los Angeles in 1959. He wrote *The History of Medical Education* and translated *The Controversy on the Comets of 1618* and Thomas Bartholin's *On the Burning of His Library* [*and*] *On Medical Travel.* Obituaries and other sources: *Isis,* fall, 1970; *The Author's and Writer's Who's Who,* 6th edition, Burke's Peerage, 1971.

O'NEILL, Frank F.   1926(?)-1983

OBITUARY NOTICE: Born c. 1926; died of a heart attack and kidney failure, February 13, 1983, in Salisbury, N.C. Newspaper editor and reporter in Idaho and North Carolina and for the *Baltimore News Post.* O'Neill lived at the Salisbury Veterans Administration Hospital after suffering an injury in a traffic accident in 1964. Obituaries and other sources: *Washington Post,* February 19, 1983.

* * *

O'NEILL, Judith (Beatrice)   1930-

PERSONAL: Born June 30, 1930, in Melbourne, Australia; daughter of John Ramsden (a school inspector) and Beatrice (a teacher; maiden name, McDonald) Lyall; married John Cochrane O'Neill (a lecturer in theology), April 17, 1954; children: Rachel, Catherine, Philippa. *Education:* University of Melbourne, B.A. (with honors), 1950, M.A., 1952; Institute of Education, London, P.G.C.E., 1953. *Home:* 2 Westminster College Bounds, Cambridge CB3 0BJ, England. *Agent:* A. P. Watt Ltd., 26/28 Bedford Row, London WC1R 4HL, England.

CAREER: University of Melbourne, Victoria, Australia, tutor in English, 1954-55; Open University, Buckinghamshire, England, tutor and counselor, 1971-73; St. Mary's Convent, Cambridge, England, English teacher, 1974-82; free-lance writer, 1982—. *Awards, honors:* Third prize, Rigby Anniversary Literary Contest (Australia), 1982, for *Jess and the River Kids.*

WRITINGS: Martin Luther (juvenile), Cambridge University Press, 1975; *Transported to Van Diemen's Land* (juvenile), Cambridge University Press, 1977.

Editor of criticism series published by Allen & Unwin: *Critics on Keats,* 1967; *Critics on Charlotte and Emily Bronte,* 1967; *Critics on Pope,* 1968; *Critics on Marlowe,* 1969; *Critics on Blake,* 1970; *Critics on Jane Austen,* 1970.

WORK IN PROGRESS: Jess and the River Kids, fiction for young adults; *The Summer at Ironbark Mill,* a children's novel set in early twentieth-century Australia, completion expected in 1984.

SIDELIGHTS: O'Neill told *CA:* "The discovery that my own great-grandparents were transported to Australia for petty theft in the nineteenth century led me to research their lives in detail and to make it the basis for my schools topic book, *Transported to Van Diemen's Land. Jess and the River Kids* draws on my own childhood in a town on the Murray River in Australia in 1943. Although I have lived in England for more than twenty years and intend to stay here, I like to write about Australia, where I was born and grew up, and where my parents and grandparents were born."

* * *

ORDE, Lewis   1943-

PERSONAL: Born January 23, 1943, in Reading, Berkshire, England; son of Coleman (a builder) and Berthe (Glinert) Orde. *Education:* Educated in London, England. *Politics:* "A confusing mixture." *Home and office:* 130 South Estes Dr., Apt. H8, Chapel Hill, N.C. 27514. *Agent:* Harvey Klinger, 301 West 53rd St., New York, N.Y. 10019.

CAREER: Leicester Mercury, Leicester, England, reporter, 1967-68; *Men's Wear* (textile trade publication), London, England,

reporter, 1968-70; United Trade Press, London, editor of clothing publications, 1970-75; Tip Top Tailors, Toronto, Ontario, communications manager and editor of house magazine, 1975-77. *Military service:* U.S. Army, 1964-67; became specialist fifth class. *Member:* Authors Guild.

WRITINGS—Novels: *The Difficult Days Ahead,* Paperjacks, 1977; *Rag Trade,* St. Martin's, 1978; (with Bill Michaels) *The Night They Stole Manhattan,* Putnam, 1980; *The Lion's Way,* Arbor House, 1981; *Heritage,* Arbor House, 1981; *Munich Ten,* Arbor House, 1982.

SIDELIGHTS: Orde told *CA:* "I like to take the summer off. No other job allows me to work just seven to eight months of the year. That's a terrible reason for being an author, but in my case it's the most truthful one. About twice a year I get the urge to look for a job, if only to have people to talk to. But I'm happy to say that I have not succumbed to that urge yet! It's also the only way I'm ever likely to strike it rich—much like buying a ticket on the Irish Sweepstakes, but you never know your luck. Basically I am a storyteller, capable of spinning a yarn. I'm certainly not a grammarian—but I believe that the ability to tell a story well, using credible characters, is more important than an extended formal education. My own education certainly was not extended—I left school at fifteen; much to the relief of my headmaster who wrote on one of my report cards, 'This boy is inclined to leave his brains on the soccer field or the cricket pitch, depending upon the season.' In retrospect, it was the only nice thing he said about me!"

AVOCATIONAL INTERESTS: Opera, sports, reading, "people, lazing around."

BIOGRAPHICAL/CRITICAL SOURCES: Time, April 14, 1980; *New York Times Book Review,* April 27, 1980.

* * *

OSBORN, David (D.)   1923-

BRIEF ENTRY: Born in 1923 in New York, N.Y. American playwright, screenwriter, and novelist. Osborn has worked as a test pilot, television director and camera operator, and public relations representative. He is best known, however, for his writings, which have been nominated for awards by the Motion Picture Academy of Arts and Sciences, the British Academy of Television Arts and Sciences, and the Writers Guild. Screenplays by Osborn include "Malaga" (Warner Brothers, 1962), "Maroc Seven" (Paramount, 1967), and "Deadlier Than the Male" (Continental, 1967); Osborn also collaborated with Liz Charles-Williams on the screen adaptation of his novel *Open Season* (Dial, 1974). He also wrote *The Glass Tower* (Hodder & Stoughton, 1971) and *The French Decision* (Doubleday, 1980). *Address:* c/o Henry Morrison, Inc., 58 West 10th St., New York, N.Y. 10011. *Biographical/critical sources: Times Literary Supplement,* March 19, 1971; *New York Times Book Review,* April 28, 1974; *Washington Post Book World,* August 11, 1974.

* * *

OSBORNE, Adam   1939-

PERSONAL: Born March 6, 1939, in Bangkok, Thailand; came to the United States in 1961, naturalized citizen, 1967; son of Arthur and Lucia (Lipsziczudna) Osborne; married Barbara Ann Burdick; children: (first marriage) Ian, Paul, Alexandra. *Education:* University of Birmingham, B.Sc., 1961; University of Delaware, M.Ch.E., 1966, Ph.D., 1967. *Office:* Osborne Computer Corp., 26538 Danti Court, Hayward, Calif. 94545.

CAREER: Adam Osborne & Associates, Inc. (publisher), Berkeley, Calif., founder and president, 1970-81; Osborne Computer Corp., Hayward, Calif., chairman of board of directors, 1980—. *Member:* Institute of Electrical and Electronics Engineers.

WRITINGS: Introduction to Microcomputers, Osborne & Associates, 1975, Volume I, 1976, Volume II, 1976, Volume 0, 1977, 3rd edition, McGraw, 1982, Volume III, 1978; *8080 Programming for Logic Design,* Osborne & Associates, 1976; *6800 Programming for Logic Design,* Osborne & Associates, 1977; *Z80 Programming for Logic Design,* Osborne & Associates, 1978; *Running Wild: The Next Industrial Revolution,* Osborne & Associates, 1979; *8089 I/O Processor Handbook,* Osborne & Associates, 1980; (with Carroll S. Donahue) *PET/CBM Personal Computer Guide,* Osborne & Associates, 1980; *CBASIC User Guide,* Osborne & Associates, 1981; *Business Systems Buyers Guide,* Osborne & Associates, 1981; *4&8 Bit Microprocessor Handbook,* Osborne & Associates, 1981; *16 Bit Microprocessor Handbook,* Osborne & Associates, 1981.

WORK IN PROGRESS: Neworld, a "science fiction satire dealing with the day when high technology no longer automatically promises people a better life."

SIDELIGHTS: Osborne told *CA:* "*Running Wild: The Next Industrial Revolution* was probably the first of the 'what will electronics do to society?' books of the current crop. I wrote it in 1977 because at that time I was concerned that high technology would generate many of the problems that are indeed being encountered today."

* * *

OSBORNE, Maureen 1924-

PERSONAL: Born in 1924 in London, England; daughter of Cecil and Dora Gunning; married Maurice C. Osborne, 1955; children: Julian Paul, Colette Virginia, Christopher Mark. *Education:* Attended University of London. *Home:* 15 Oakhill Rd., Hare Hill, Addlestone, Surrey, England.

CAREER: Worked as a secretary early in career; writer of children's plays for British Broadcasting Corp. Teacher at Adult Literacy Centre. *Wartime service:* Auxiliary Territorial Service, World War II.

WRITINGS—For children: Twice Upon a Time (illustrated by Eileen Browne), Heinemann, 1977; *The Castle of the Winds* (mystery), Heinemann, 1978; *Here Comes the Horrobilly* (illustrated by Browne), Heinemann, 1979; *The Horrobilly Goes to School* (illustrated by Browne), Heinemann, 1979; *The Kettlewitch,* Heinemenn, 1981.

WORK IN PROGRESS: A book about gypsies for children age ten and older.

SIDELIGHTS: Maureen Osborne told *CA* about the sources of her material: "Fortunately I have a good memory and can draw from my own childhood and from family stories told to me by my mother. I also use snippets I overhear, fragments of pop songs, classical music, my own fears, and family jokes for inspiration. Everything is grist to my mill! From a very early age I have loved words; as soon as I could write I copied out my favorite ones in a huge old ledger. As a teenager I read incessantly.

"I enjoy reading both prose and poetry. The latter I like to learn by heart when possible. I get many invitations to read excerpts from my books to groups of children all over the country. I have worked up a program lasting an hour, which includes reading, singing, and dancing with the children.

"I learned to play the clarinet when I was over forty, and started horse-riding at the same time. I love walking in Surrey, where I live, and talking to friends. My current ambition is to write a full-length play and have it put on in London's West End."

* * *

OSENENKO, John 1918-1983

OBITUARY NOTICE: Born October 4, 1918, in Bayonne, N.J.; died of a heart attack, February 22, 1983, in Ocala, Fla. News executive and journalist. After working twenty years with the North American Newspaper Alliance and the Bell McClure Syndicate, Osenenko was employed by the *New York Times,* where he acted as manager of special features from 1971 to 1978. In 1979 Osenenko started his own company, Editors, News and Features International, Incorporated, which he formed in association with Hollywood syndicated columnist Marilyn Beck. Obituaries and other sources: *Who's Who in the East,* 14th edition, Marquis, 1974; *Who's Who in America,* 41st edition, 1980; *New York Times,* February 26, 1983.

* * *

OSGOOD, Charles
See WOOD, Charles Osgood III

* * *

OTAKE, Sadao 1913(?)-1983

OBITUARY NOTICE: Born c. 1913; died of a heart ailment, March 25, 1983, in Tokyo, Japan. Journalist. Otake was head of news bureaus in Washington, D.C., and Bonn, West Germany. He also edited the *Reader's Digest* for publication in Japan. Obituaries and other sources: *Washington Post,* March 31, 1983.

* * *

OWEN, (Benjamin) Evan 1918-

PERSONAL: Born January 5, 1918, in London, England; son of Evan William and Agnes Ellen Owen; married Beatrice Mary Morris, November 30, 1940; children: Laurence Evan, Gillian Margaret. *Education:* Attended Birmingham Training College. *Home:* 35 High St., Watlington, Oxford OX9 5PZ, England.

CAREER: Writer and educator. Teacher of and adviser in remedial education, Oxfordshire Education Committee, 1955—. Part-time staff tutor at Oxford University Department of Education, 1960-74; part-time course tutor at Open University, 1975—; served on literature panel of Southern Arts Association, 1979-82. *Member:* United Kingdom Reading Association.

WRITINGS—All for children: Adventures of Bill and Betty, illustrations by Margery Gill, six books, Oxford University Press, 1954; (editor) *Blackwell's Junior Poetry Books,* illustrations by Kathleen Gell, four books, Basil Blackwell, 1960; (with Ian Gemmell) *The Night Sky,* illustrations by F.T.W.

Cook, Basil Blackwell, 1965; *What Happened Today?: An Almanack of History,* illustrations by Jack Townend, three volumes, Basil Blackwell, 1967; (compiler) *Pergamon Poets,* Pergamon, Volume I: *Roy Fuller and R. S. Thomas,* 1968, Volume III: *Robert Browning and Alfred Lord Tennyson,* 1968, Volume IV: *Kathleen Raine and Vernon Watkins,* 1968, Volume V: *Gerard Manley Hopkins and John Keats,* 1969, Volume X: *Charles Causley and Laurie Lee,* 1970 (Owen was not associated with other volumes in the series); *Carford Readers,* illustrations by Jill Bennett, Pergamon, 1971, Book 1: *Carford Is a Big Town,* Book 2: *The Five Friends,* Book 3: *At School,* Book 4: *At Work,* Book 5: *The Halls and Martins,* Book 6: *The New Car,* Book 7: *After the Match,* Book 8: *Fire!; Not Like Johnny,* illustrations by Dan Pearce, Evans Brothers, 1973; *Football's for Schoolkids,* illustrations by Pearce, Evans Brothers, 1973; *You're On Your Own,* illustrations by Pearce, Evans Brothers, 1973, Harvey House, 1978; *Freestyle Champ,* illustrations by Pearce, Evans Brothers, 1974; *Saturday Afternoon,* illustrations by Robin Laurie, Blackie & Son, 1976; *Fire Is a Killer,* Blackie & Son, 1976; *On Patrol,* Blackie & Son, 1976; *People Who Care,* Blackie & Son, 1976; *Lower End Farm,* illustrations by Anna Dzierzek, Blackie & Son, 1978; *Ways to Reading,* Visual Publications, 1978; *Getting There,* illustrations by Douglas Phillips, Blackie & Son, 1978; *Sport,* Evans Brothers, 1981; *Inner City Books* (fiction series), Evans Brothers, 1983.

Series editor, Athena Books, 1968, and Pergamon Poets, 1968-70. Contributor of articles to periodicals, including *Contemporary Review, Teacher, Fortnightly, Teacher's World,* and to *Birmingham Post.* Reviewer of fiction, poetry, and criticism for *Oxford Mail,* 1955-69.

*   *   *

OWENS, Carolyn 1946-

PERSONAL: Born April 27, 1946, in Monticello, Minn.; daughter of Roland Lloyd (in sales) and Pearl (Pool) Starry; married William Owens (a pipefitter foreman), August 20, 1966; children: Kim, Christy. *Education:* Attended high school in St. Louis Park, Minn. *Religion:* "Born-again Christian." *Home:* 5243 Brookside Court, Edina, Minn. 55436.

CAREER: Writer, 1977—. *Member:* National League of American Pen Women (first vice-president, 1982-83), Minnesota Christian Writers Guild. *Awards, honors:* Sherwood E. Wirt Award from Decision School of Christian Writing, 1981, for *A Promise of Sanity.*

WRITINGS: Gateway to the Gospel, Bergee Corp., 1979; *Glimpse Into Genesis,* Bergee Corp., 1979; *Be-Attitudes for Children and Parents,* Bethany House, 1982; (with Melody Beattie) *A Promise of Sanity,* Tyndale, 1982; *Color Me Cuddly* (juvenile), Bethany House, 1982; *Color Me Loved* (juvenile), Bethany House, 1982; *More Be-Attitudes for Children and Parents,* Bethany House, 1983.

WORK IN PROGRESS: Help for Pregnant Teens, with Linda Roggow, publication by Zondervan expected in 1985; *Happy Mind/Healthy Spirit* (tentative title); a short book of meditations for mental patients.

SIDELIGHTS: Carolyn Owens told *CA:* "My faith in the Lord Jesus Christ urges me to work on books that will further his kingdom. I am interested in researching many aspects of mental illness, as well as areas of health, exercise, and nutrition.

"I began writing professionally in 1977. After attending the Decision School of Christian Writing, I believed God had called me to this profession. My choice of subject matter is prompted by the fact that God has healed me from paranoid schizophrenia. There have been many miracles in my life, and by sharing them, I hope to give readers inspiration and encouragement. My personal view is that our Creator has answers to everyday living and wants us to know those answers too. They are found in God's love letter to us—the Bible.

"My activity books and coloring books were all suggested to me by other people. I just took those suggestions and 'ran with them.' The best advice I can give to any writer is: 'Find a gap and fill it.'"

BIOGRAPHICAL/CRITICAL SOURCES: Home Life, November, 1980, December, 1982; *Solo,* July-August, 1982.

P

PACKER, Rod Earle 1931-

PERSONAL: Born November 9, 1931, in Dallas, Tex.; son of N. S. and Jessie M. (Jay) Packer; married Suzanne Lillian McKendrick (a real estate broker), June 21, 1959; children: Bruce P., Brent C. *Education:* Yale University, B.A., 1953; graduate study at University of Southern California; Southern Methodist University, M.A., 1957; University of Minnesota, Ph.D., 1960. *Home and office:* 29-29A Estancia Dr., Marana, Ariz. 85238.

CAREER: WFAA-TV, Dallas, Tex., producer and director, 1953-56; KTCA-TV, St. Paul, Minn., producer and director, 1957-59; General Dynamics Corp., Groton, Conn., electronic display and training systems analyst, 1959-61; Bunker-Ramo Corp., Los Angeles, Calif., and Sierra Vista, Ariz., human factors coordinator, 1961-65; Dunlap & Associates, Darien, Conn., and Santa Monica, Calif., senior scientist in training systems, 1965-68; Cochise College, Douglas, Ariz., associate professor of speech and psychology, 1968-69; director of personnel development at Circle K Corp., 1969-72. Assistant professor at University of Arizona, 1969-70, and Pima Community College.

WRITINGS: The Computing Investor, MicroComputing Research, 1981; *The Investor's Computer Handbook,* Hayden, 1982; *Computer-Based Investment Analysis,* Prentice-Hall, in press. Contributor to scientific and computer journals. Editor and publisher of *Tomorrow's Convenience Stores Newsletter.*

WORK IN PROGRESS: "A complex desktop microcomputer software program, with explanatory textbook, to automate technical analysis of common stock trading to the point that the program will literally compete with its own user/investor, to sharpen his own portfolio strategies and trading profits."

SIDELIGHTS: Packer wrote: "With a liberal arts education in the Yale tradition, and advanced research on the psychology of mass persuasion and the electronic media at the University of Minnesota, I emphasize in my writing the popularization of technical advances in a much broader, informative, and entertaining style than that of pure 'tech writers' in electronics and professional free-lancers on the future of technology. As a full-time stock market investor for many years, I am clear about details and advantages of computer enhancement of analysis. I do this both for the individual investor and for society's evolution into a computerized environment."

PAGEL, Walter T. U. 1898-1983

OBITUARY NOTICE: Born November 12, 1898, in Berlin, Germany; died March 25, 1983, in London, England. Pathologist, scientist, medical historian, and author noted for placing the discoveries of important medical figures within their religious and philosophical contexts. Pagel, who co-authored a textbook titled *Pulmonary Tuberculosis,* spent much of his career studying that subject. He worked at the Berlin Municipal Tuberculosis Hospital and was a lecturer in pathology and the history of medicine at the University of Heidelberg before immigrating to Paris during Hitler's rule. After becoming a British citizen in 1939 Pagel was appointed assistant pathologist at Central Middlesex Hospital, and in 1956 he became a part-time consultant pathologist at Clare Hall Sanatorium in Barnet, a position he held until his retirement in 1967. Pagel's books include *Religious Motives in the Medical Biology of the Seventeenth Century, The Religious and Philosophical Aspects of van Helmont's Science and Medicine,* and *William Harvey's Biological Ideas.* Obituaries and other sources: *Who's Who in the World,* 3rd edition, Marquis, 1976; *London Times,* April 4, 1983.

* * *

PAIN, Barry (Eric Odell) 1864-1928

BRIEF ENTRY: Born September 28, 1864, in Cambridge, England; died May 5, 1928, in Watford, England. British humorist, journalist, and author. Pain, who was graduated from Cambridge University as a classical scholar, spent four years working as an army coach before embarking on a career in journalism. His short stories and novels examine working-class life in a dry, satirical way, as exemplified by *Eliza* (1900), *Robinson Crusoe's Return* (1907), and *Marge Askinforit* (1920). Pain also wrote serious tales about the supernatural, including *The Shadow of the Unseen* (1907) and *Going Home* (1921). *Biographical/critical sources: Twentieth-Century Authors: A Biographical Dictionary of Modern Literature,* H. W. Wilson, 1942; *Longman Companion to Twentieth Century Literature,* Longman, 1970; *Encyclopedia of Mystery and Detection,* McGraw, 1976; *Who's Who in Horror and Fantasy Fiction,* Elm Tree Books, 1977.

PAIS, Abraham 1918-

PERSONAL: Born May 19, 1918, in Amsterdam, Netherlands; came to the United States in 1946, naturalized citizen, 1954; son of Jesaya (a schoolteacher) and Kaatje Paisvan (a schoolteacher; maiden name, Kleef) Pais; married, 1956 (marriage ended); married Sara Ector (a television executive), 1978; children: (first marriage) Joshua; (second marriage) Daniel (stepson). *Education:* University of Amsterdam, B.Sc., 1938; University of Utrecht, M.S., 1940, Ph.D., 1941. *Religion:* Jewish. *Home:* 1161 York Ave., New York, N.Y. 10021. *Office:* Department of Theoretical Physics, Rockefeller University, 1230 York Ave., New York, N.Y. 10021.

CAREER: Niels Bohr Institute, Copenhagen, Denmark, Rask Oersted fellow, 1946; Institute of Advanced Study, Princeton, N.J., member, 1947-50, professor of physics, 1950-63; Rockefeller University, New York, N.Y., professor of physics, 1963—. *Member:* National Academy of Sciences, American Academy of Arts and Sciences, American Physical Society (fellow), Royal Netherlands Academy of Science. *Awards, honors:* R. Oppenheimer Memorial Prize from Center for Theoretical Physics, 1979, for contributions to fundamental particle physics; *Subtle is the Lord* was nominated as best science book of 1982 by American Book Awards, 1983.

WRITINGS: Subtle Is the Lord: The Science and the Life of Albert Einstein, Oxford University Press, 1982.

WORK IN PROGRESS: Further books on the history of science.

SIDELIGHTS: Pais told *CA:* "I chose 'Subtle is the Lord' as the title of my book since Einstein once said: 'Subtle is the Lord but malicious He is not.'"

*   *   *

PAKENHAM, Francis Aungier 1905-
(Frank Pakenham, Seventh Earl of Longford)

PERSONAL: Born December 5, 1905, in London, England; son of Thomas (Fifth Earl of Longford and professional soldier) and Mary (Villiers) Pakenham; married Elizabeth Harman (a writer), 1931; children: Thomas, Patrick, Michael, Kevin, Antonia Pakenham Fraser, Judith Kazantzis, Rachel Billington, Catherine (died, 1969). *Education:* New College, Oxford, M.A., 1927; studied politics at Christ Church, Oxford, 1934-36 and 1952-64. *Politics:* Labour. *Rligion:* Roman Catholic. *Home:* Bernhurst, Hurst Green, East Sussex, England; and 18 Chesil Court, Chelsea Manor Street, London S.W. 3, England.

CAREER: University Tutorial Courses, Stoke-on-Trent, England, tutor, 1929-31; Christ Church, Oxford, England, lecturer in politics, 1932-34; prospective parliamentary Labor candidate, 1938; served as personal assistant to William Beveridge, 1941-44; served as lord-in-waiting to the king, 1945-46; British Parliament, London, England, parliamentary undersecretary of state in War Office, 1946-47; Duchy of Lancaster, England, chancellor, 1947-48; British Government, England, minister of civil aviation, 1948-51, first lord of admiralty, 1951; chairman of National Bank Ltd., 1955-63; British Parliament, leader of House of Lords, 1964-68; National Youth Employment Council, London, chairman, 1968-71; Sidgwick & Jackson (publisher), London, England, chairman, beginning in 1970, currently director; writer, 1935—.

Associated with Conservative Party Economic Research Department, 1930-31; served as Lord Privy Seal, 1964-65 and 1966-68, and as secretary of state for colonies, 1965-66. Co-founder of New Bridge for Ex-Prisoners, 1956, and of New Horizon Youth Center, 1964. Chairman of Angio-German Association. Public speaker; guest on television programs. *Military service:* Oxford and Bucks Light Infantry, 1939-40. *Member:* Garrick Club. *Awards, honors:* Privy councillor, 1948; knight of the Order of the Garter, 1971; knight commander of the Order of St. Gregory.

WRITINGS: Problems of the Ex-Prisoner: Report of the Pakenham/Thompson Committee, National Conference of Social Services (London), 1961.

Under name Frank Pakenham, Seventh Earl of Longford; nonfiction: *Peace by Ordeal: An Account, From First-Hand Sources, of the Negotiation and Signature of the Anglo-Irish Treaty, 1921,* J. Cape, 1935, new edition, Sidgwick & Jackson, 1972; (with Roger Opie) *Causes of Crime,* C. C Thomas, 1958; *The Idea of Punishment,* Herder Book Center, 1961; *Humility,* Collins, 1969; *Pornography: The Longford Report,* Coronet Books, 1972; (with Anne McHardy) *Ulster,* Weidenfeld & Nicolson, 1981.

All biographies, except as noted: *Born to Believe: An Autobiography,* J. Cape, 1953; *Five Lives* (autobiography), Hutchinson, 1964; (with Thomas P. O'Neill) *Eamon de Valera,* Hutchinson, 1970, Houghton, 1971; (editor with John Wheeler-Bennet and Christine Nicholls, and contributor), *The History Makers: Leaders and Statesmen of the Twentieth Century,* St. Martin's, 1973; *The Life of Christ,* Sidgwick & Jackson, 1974, published as *Jesus: A Life of Christ,* illustrated by Richard Guffari, Doubleday, 1975; *The Grain of Wheat* (autobiography), Collins, 1974; *Abraham Lincoln,* introduction by wife, Elizabeth Longford, Weidenfeld & Nicolson, 1974, Putnam, 1975; *Kennedy,* Weidenfeld & Nicolson, 1976; *Francis of Assisi: A Life for all Seasons,* Weidenfeld & Nicolson, 1978; *Nixon: A Study in Extremes,* Weidenfeld & Nicolson, 1981; *Pope John Paul II,* M. Joseph, 1982.

WORK IN PROGRESS: A book about Christianity.

SIDELIGHTS: "I started my professional life at Oxford you know," Frank Pakenham told the *New York Times.* "Once you've done that, you are intimidated by nothing"—not even personal criticism. The *Sunday Times*'s most caricatured figure of 1972, Pakenham is often portrayed by an unflattering press as Britain's most unusual moral crusader or "a Wodehousian English eccentric, apparently unaware of his own oddness," commented John Calder in the *Spectator.* More accurately, he is, said Lord Kinros in *Books and Bookmen,* "a good, kind, endearing, high-principled Christian" who embarked on a career as a Conservative politician in 1931. Four years later, Pakenham moved to the Labour party, spurred by his wife's influence, by his belief in human equality, and, most significantly, by his study of the gospels. These explorations of the Word prompted his conversion to Catholicism in 1940 and intensified his campaign to uplift the dignity and morality of humans.

Feeling that he was wasting away in the Cabinet, that he could accomplish more in his career, Pakenham left politics on a decision of conscience. When a mandate lowering the age of compulsory school attendance was passed by his peers, a law the politician felt was unfair to and not in the best interests of the youth of his country, he resigned from government service, though he still maintained his interest in social reform.

While a member of the House of Lords, Lord Longford secured many gains for the underprivileged members of society, especially convicts and battered wives. "I am strongly attracted to outcasts," he once remarked, "people who are despised by society." This empathy for the disadvantaged comes from his military experience when he was invalided from the army with a nervous breakdown in 1940. Lord Longford explained: "With prisoners, ex-prisoners, outcasts generally and all those who hesitate to show their faces abroad, I have one unfailing and unforeseen point of contact. I can say and mean and be believed—'I also have been humiliated.' The gulf is bridged as if by magic. If my sense of compassion has been strengthened and activated from any human experience, it is from my own infirmities and the indignities I have myself undergone."

With an attitude of fundamental decency, the Earl of Longford views all people as basically good, no matter what situation they find themselves in, no matter the crimes they have committed. Espousing the theory of loving the sinner but hating the sin, he channeled much of his effort into reforming the British penal system. He lobbied to make prisons more humane, more rehabilitative institutions. In the course of his investigation of the prison system, Lord Longford managed to befriend "spectacularly wicked" criminals such as Ian Brady, Myra Hindley, and the Kray twins. Lord Longford, according to a writer in the *Times Literary Supplement,* "has a real talent for kindness and a perfectly clear perception of what is needed."

Of greater magnitude than his prison reforms was Pakenham's campaign against pornography, on even an aesthetic level. For example, during the trial of *Lady Chatterley's Lover* the solicitor for the defense asked Pakenham to testify on behalf of the work, but the earl refused, saying: "I am a Puritan." "But D H Lawrence was a Puritan," the solicitor replied. "But not my kind of Puritan," was Pakenham's response. His investigations into pornography earned the author the euphemisms of Lord Porn and Pornford as well as provided him with, in his own words, "an experience of inquiries which no one in politics could equal." His crusade began when Pakenham's son-in-law took the earl to a production of "Oh! Calcutta." Appalled, Pakenham walked out of the performance and endeavored to revive "the old restraints on indecency" that he thought "were in danger of total extinction." He began a committee to look into the evils of pornography. The group visited porn shows throughout the world, many of which Pakenham left, to produce *Pornography: The Longford Report.* The gist of this study generated a new definition of pornography: "That which exploits and dehumanises sex, so that human beings are treated as things and women in particular as sex objects." According to Kinross's review of *Grain of Wheat,* Pakenham emerged from these investigations and his social reform campaigns "as a man of many causes, the Crusader Extraordinary for right against wrong." He "stems from the sprouts of his *Grain of Wheat* with ears of porn," said the reviewer, "as one of our more commendable and loveable eccentrics."

Pakenham continued his efforts of social reform in his writings. As Gore Vidal suggested in the *New Statesman,* "Frank is, simply, good. There is no other word. Best of all, he wants us to share with him through his many testaments his many good actions. That's why he writes books and gets on television programmes." *The Life of Christ,* for example, was written out of the author's need to share his faith with others. It is the product of years of meditation. In the eyes of many critics, biographies of Christ are usually just projections of the writer's image of himself, but "mercifully," Peter Hubblethwaite noted in the *Times Literary Supplement,* "Lord Longford does not try to mould Christ into his own image, but rather submits to him as the model of 'humility, forgiveness and a spiritual view

of suffering.'" Likewise, Lord Longford's biography of St. Francis of Assisi illustrates that helping the underprivileged is an expression of God's love. In total, *Francis of Assisi,* wrote Cecil Northcott in the *Contemporary Review,* is a "most readable and attractive study of St. Francis."

Generally, Lord Longford writes on subjects of his personal interest: crime, Ireland, religion, especially individuals he finds fascinating. Many of his biographies have enjoyed critical acclaim; for example, *Pope John Paul II,* which Paul Johnson called "lavish" and "satisfying," and *Eamon de Valera.* The remaining survivor of the 1916 Uprising, de Valera was sentenced to death for his role in the rebellion. The sentence was later commuted, allowing the activist to become the president of Southern Ireland in 1932. Written in collaboration with its subject, the biography includes previously unpublished documents with information on Irish neutrality and secret aid to Britain during World War II. "This is probably the most important book on de Valera yet written," decided L. Bridges in the *National Review.* It is "a valuable work," added *Choice* magazine.

In addition, *Choice* called the author's *History Makers* "a fascinating book" whose "readers will gain a firmer understanding of those men who changed our daily living patterns." This work contains twenty-three profiles of world leaders (such as Mao Tse-Tung, Joseph Stalin, and John F. Kennedy) written by the statesmen's colleagues, observers, historians, or others able to provide stores of anecdotal material. Similarly, one of Pakenham's autobiographies reveals his own adeptness with anecdotes. "Lord Pakenham, to use a Communist 'term of art,'" wrote a *Times Literary Supplement* critic, "is one of the outstanding 'political anecdotists' of our time and . . . [*Born to Believe*] is studded with many conversational gems which must rank as collector's pieces."

Like the earl, Pakenham's wife, his three daughters, two of his sons, and several assorted relatives have all written critically successful books; therefore the family has been dubbed the "literary Longfords." Though he heads the household of authors, Lord Longford does not consider writing his primary occupation. "Writing has only been a subsidiary activity for me," he told the *New York Times.* "It was not my vocation. Deep down I always thought I'd have to go to an office and earn my living. Now that I am elderly, to say the least, writing seems an appropriate activity, but it wouldn't have been when I was a young man."

BIOGRAPHICAL/CRITICAL SOURCES—Books: Bruno Schafer, *They Heard His Voice,* McMullen, 1952; Frank Pakenham, *Born to Believe: An Autobiography,* J. Cape, 1953; Pakenham, *Five Lives* (autobiography), Hutchinson, 1964; Pakenham, *The Grain of Wheat* (autobiography), Collins, 1974; *Authors in the News,* Volume 2, Gale, 1976; Mary Craig, *Longford: A Biographical Portrait,* Hodder & Stoughton, 1978.

Periodicals: *World Republic,* May 20, 1949; *Catholic World,* May, 1950, July, 1953; *Manchester Guardian,* May 26, 1953; *Spectator,* May 29, 1953, November 7, 1970, March 23, 1974, October 26, 1974, June 5, 1982; *Times Literary Supplement,* May 29, 1953, November 30, 1970, November 10, 1972, November 30, 1973, March 8, 1974, October 11, 1974, March 5, 1982; *New Statesman and Nation,* May 30, 1953; *Commonweal,* November 27, 1953; *Books and Bookmen,* August, 1969, February, 1971, December, 1973, April, 1974, January, 1975, January, 1979; *Observer,* October 12, 1969, November 1, 1970, March 3, 1974, September 22, 1974, October 13, 1974, January 23, 1977, November 2, 1980, April 25, 1982.

New York Times Book Review, March 1, 1970, November 19, 1972; *New Statesman*, November 6, 1970, August 31, 1973, March 8, 1974, January 21, 1977, November 3, 1978; *Guardian Weekly*, November 14, 1970, March 16, 1974, January 16, 1977, November 2, 1980, November 22, 1981, April 18, 1982; *Economist*, November 21, 1970, December 29, 1973, March 9, 1974, October 26, 1974, November 20, 1976, December 19, 1981; *Economist Survey*, November 21, 1970; *Christian Science Monitor*, March 11, 1971; *Life*, March 19, 1971, November 3, 1972; *National Review*, June 1, 1971; *Choice*, September, 1971, April, 1973, September, 1974, September, 1975, December, 1978; *America*, September 4, 1971, November 20, 1971; *American Historical Review*, April, 1972; *Atlantic*, October, 1972; *Listener*, March 7, 1974, November 7, 1974, December 9, 1976, October 9, 1980; *Wilson Library Bulletin*, September, 1974.

Contemporary Review, January, 1975, March, 1979, January, 1981; *Christian Century*, June 25, 1975; *Town and Country*, January, 1976; *Review for Religious*, June, 1976; *New York Times*, November 14, 1976; *British Book News*, March, 1981, March, 1982; *Perspective*, November, 1981; *Times Educational Supplement*, December, 1981; *Punch*, May 5, 1982.

—*Sketch by Charity Anne Dorgan*

*   *   *

PAKENHAM, Frank, Seventh Earl of Longford
See PAKENHAM, Francis Aungier

*   *   *

PAKENHAM, Thomas (Frank Dermot) 1933-

PERSONAL: Born August 14, 1933, near Aylesbury, Bucks, England; son of Francis Aungier (Seventh Earl of Longford, politician, and writer) and Elizabeth (a writer; maiden name, Harman) Pakenham; married Valerie Susan McNair Scott (a writer), July 24, 1964; children: two sons, two daughters. *Education:* Magdalen College, Oxford, B.A., 1955. *Home:* Tullymally Castle, County Westmeath, Ireland; and 111 Elgin Crescent, London W. 11, England. *Agent:* Curtis Brown Ltd., 1 Craven Hill, London W2 3EP, England.

CAREER: Free-lance writer, 1956-58; *Times Literary Supplement*, London, England, member of editorial staff, 1959-61; *Sunday Telegraph*, London, England, member of editorial staff, 1961; *Observer*, London, member of editorial staff, 1961-64; writer. Victorian Society, founding member, 1958, and member of committee, 1958-64; Historic Irish Tourist Houses and Gardens Association (HITHA), founding member and member of committee, 1968-72. Treasurer of British-Irish Association, 1972—; Christopher Ewart-Biggs Memorial Trust, secretary and co-founder, 1976—. Research fellow at St. Anthony's College, Oxford, 1979-81. *Member:* Beefsteak, Brooks's, Stephen's Green (Dublin). *Awards, honors:* Cheltenham Prize from Cheltenham Festival of Literature, 1980, for *The Boer War*.

WRITINGS—All nonfiction: *The Mountains of Rasselas: An Ethiopian Adventure*, Reynal, 1959; (with Paul R. Thompson) *Architecture: Art or Social Service*, Fabian Society, 1963; *Universities Explained: An "Observer" Guide to the Universities of England, Scotland, Wales, and Ireland*, [London], 1963; *The Year of Liberty: The Story of the Great Irish Rebellion of 1798*, Hodder & Stoughton, 1969, Prentice-Hall, 1970; *The Boer War*, Random House, 1979.

WORK IN PROGRESS: "My current book is a history of the colonization and decolonization of Africa."

SIDELIGHTS: As a member of the "literary Longfords," Thomas Pakenham is surrounded by writers. His father wrote many books, including a biography of Pope John Paul II; Elizabeth Longford, his mother, is the prolific writer who produced *The Years of the Sword* and *The Pillar of State*. Of Pakenham's sisters, Judith Kazantis is known for her historical folios and poetry while Rachel Billington is a highly-praised novelist, and Antonia Fraser is a renowned biographer. For his part, noted Billington, her brother contributes "exciting historical books, very honest." But in the eyes of Helen Lawrenson, a writer for *Town and Country* magazine, "Tom is probably the most intellectually brilliant of the clan and possibly the most iconoclastic."

Pakenham's first book, *The Mountains of Rasselas: An Ethiopian Adventure*, is based on his travels through Aleppo, Syria, Turkey, Jerusalem, and the Sudan till he arrived in Ethiopia. There the young adventurer (he was just out of Oxford) searched for a legendary prison that housed princes on the top of a mountain until they died or ascended to the throne. Though the subject of a moral allegory and described by sixteenth-century Jesuits, the prison was never found until Pakenham, after many tribulations, located it on a mountaintop 1,000 feet above Ethiopia. "We are the gainers [from this journey],'" said a *Times Literary Supplement* writer, "because he has made an entertaining book of it."

The Year of Liberty, Pakenham's next book, was inspired by his Irish heritage. An heir to an estate in Ireland, the author wrote a book exploring the Irish Rebellion of 1798, a complex historical situation that asserted Ireland's claim of nationhood. The first book on the rebellion in 80 years, *The Year of Liberty* recounts the time when a minority of Irish Protestants ruled a Catholic peasant majority under the threat of a growing third class, the bourgeoisie. This new social group hoped to unify the peasantry, thus overthrowing feudal privileges and British rule with France's aid. On the surface, age-old religious differences dissolved to present a united Irish front. Bloody and sporadic uprisings occurred in counties throughout 1798, leaving 30,000 unburied bodies to litter the countryside or to be eaten by pigs.

Critically-acclaimed, *The Year of Liberty* is considered a detail-oriented work with a military point of view. Reviewers, such as a writer for the *Times Literary Supplement*, noted how effectively Pakenham capitalized on dramatic elements of the Irish Rebellion, including the massacre of Catholics at Dunlavin and the British victory at Ballinamuck. Helen Johnson, writing in *Books*, commented that Pakenham's treatment of the incidents of the rebellion "is scrupulously fair." Concurring, Conor Cruise O'Brien added in the *Observer Review:* "This book is a notable contribution to the history of Ireland, of these islands, and of the revolutionary movement inspired by France. No one before has covered this ground so carefully, or made as full use of the primary sources. It is a solidly based narrative, soberly and lucidly told, with scrupulous fairness." "Thomas Pakenham," a reviewer decided in *Spectator*, "disentangles this fantastically complicated episode of history with immense skill. . . . It is a fine, masterly and absorbing book."

Pakenham's most recent work, *The Boer War*, was eight years in the making, originating from his personal interest in the war in which his grandfathers served. Lauded for his excellent documentation, the author interviewed survivors, visited battle scenes and obtained private letters, secret diaries, and unpublished papers; he even learned Dutch and Afrikaans to translate primary sources on his own. "The grim story has been told before," said Mayo Mohs in *Time*, "but never with such sweep and grieving comprehension."

According to Pakenham, the war began in 1899, due largely to the machinations of Alfred Milner, British high commissioner of South Africa. In his drive for an all-British state, Milner antagonized the Dutch colonists (Boers) in the Transvaal and the Orange Free State who would not give white "Uitlanders" equal rights. Thus in 1899 a long, bloody, and expensive political war ensued. Neither side was prepared for a war that would last three years. Britain particularly anticipated a short, nineteenth-century-style skirmish, but she encountered a lengthy, twentieth-century war instead. Initially Britain expected to suppress the Boers with 10,000 troops, but in the end she sent 450,000 soldiers and spent £200 million. Twenty-two thousand British soldiers died in the war as did 25,000 Boers and 12,000 Africans.

The Boer War studies the psychological and material dimensions of the war. For example, Pakenham looked at the contributions of millionaires, blacks, and Boer women in the historic event. According to Pakenham, the idealism and greed of the "gold bugs," those wealthy industrialists who owned the area's gold mines, escalated the war. Boer women, he found, operated farms in their husbands' absences, supplied troops with food, and were ultimately shoved into the squalor of concentration camps. Blacks, hitherto a little studied group, actively fought under the promise of improved status, an oath the British soon forgot. "In understanding and proclaiming that this was also a black experience—simultaneous with but very different from the experiences of British and Boer soldiers and civilians—Thomas Pakenham has helped to push open a very interesting door indeed," remarked Neal Ascherson in the *New York Review of Books*.

Nevertheless "Pakenham's most original achievement," wrote Ascherson, "is to rescue the reputation of Sir Redvers Buller from its disgrace beneath the billiard table." Maligned by previous histories, Buller proves himself to be a good man in a bad situation, the victim of backbiting British generals. Though Pakenham's evidence restores this general's respectability, it also shows the ineptitude of Frederick Roberts, formerly the lauded British supreme commander. Finally, Pakenham profiles Lord Kitchner, Roberts's successor and the inventor of concentration camps and anti-guerilla tactics that failed.

Critically, *The Boer War* is looked on as quite an accomplishment. As John Gooch explained in the *English Historical Review:* "For an outsider to shoulder his way into the circles of scholarship with a book which demands both recognition and respect is a none too common occurrence. Thomas Pakenham has managed just that with *The Boer War* . . . , a tour-de-force of narrative history which not only tells the story of the war better than it has ever been told, but along the way forces us to revise some of our judgments on the leading military figures of the day."

Piers Brendon agreed in his *Books and Bookmen* critique, saying: "Here at last is a book which has been needed for a generation or more—a radical reappraisal of the Boer War based on the best evidence, a reappraisal which sets straight the record so monumentally biased by (among other things) Leo Amery's seven-volume *Times History of the War in South Africa*. This is something which the professional historians have been too indolent or too obtuse to accomplish (though a 'definitive academic revision' is apparently in preparation) and

it is to his vast credit that the task has been completed by a brilliant amateur, Thomas Pakenham."

Other critics, including Walter Clemons, a writer for *Newsweek*, have noticed the author's "powerful narrative gift," especially suited for fight scenes. "At describing a battle," Gooch submitted, "he has no peer." "Pakenham's book," Clemons continued, "rouses anger at events that took place 80 years ago. This is a hot, impassioned work." "Indeed," Brendon concluded, "no account of this bloody conflict can henceforth be written without reference to his magnificent reinterpretation."

CA INTERVIEW

CA interviewed Thomas Pakenham on October 31, 1980, at work in London.

CA: Your family is known as "the literary Longfords." Coming from that background, did you decide early in your life to become a writer?

PAKENHAM: I wrote my first book, *The Mountains of Rasselas*, in 1959, too soon for anyone to have dreamt of "the literary Longfords." My father was a politician at that time. Before going into politics, he was a university teacher at Oxford and had written one historical book called *Peace by Ordeal*, the history of the Anglo-Irish treaty of 1921. My mother hadn't written anything, and there hadn't been other serious family books. My mother's first book that brought her fame was *Victoria R. I.* (1964), and my sister Antonia Fraser had her first best-seller in 1969. [See *CA* index for individual sketches of the "literary Longfords."]

I went into journalism for about six years after writing my first book, and meanwhile these family best-sellers started to appear. Writing is certainly a common denominator now in our family. But the word "literary" perhaps isn't the right word and certainly wasn't true when I began. I don't know what "literary" means to Americans. To the English, it refers to poetry and creative writing. Professional writers of other kinds, such as journalists and historical writers, aren't necessarily "literary."

CA: You were a Fleet Street journalist. Why did you decide to leave journalism and write books instead?

PAKENHAM: In 1964, when I got my first contract to do a historical book, *The Year of Liberty*, I was working as a Fleet Street journalist. I had inherited my father's family estate in 1961, and I was commuting between Ireland and England. It's not very far, only about four hours travel time. I felt schizophrenic, owning this large estate that employed fifteen people and included a thousand-acre farm. There was forestry and an oversized family house that was falling down. I was supposed to be doing things about that, and I was also supposed to be working as a reporter on Fleet Street. I thought I'd drop out of journalism for a year because I was aware of certain things about Fleet Street which dissatisfied me. I loved the office life: I was exceptionally lucky to work among a very delightful group of people on the *Observer*, and this was my main job. It was sad to leave, but I felt that I should be more independent. I've always been rather a glutton for independence. In fact, *The Mountains of Rasselas* was based on wandering around the world for a year by myself and writing just for myself— not commissioned to do anything. Perhaps I'm a bit of a loner as well as being a very sociable person. I thought I'd leave journalism for a year, do this book, and come back. I enjoyed doing the book so much—even though it took four years—that I eventually left permanently and got my second contract, to do *The Boer War,* which took even longer.

CA: Didn't the research on these two books take about twelve years? You must have an incredible amount of patience.

PAKENHAM: I have always assumed that everyone—except the most impatient people—would like to be a historical writer. Perhaps I'm wrong, but research is such a labor of love for me that I can't imagine anyone else not enjoying it. My father doesn't share this view; he likes quick results. He doesn't enjoy research the way the rest of my family does. We like to put the bits of the jigsaw slowly together, but he doesn't have the patience for that.

CA: The Year of Liberty and The Boer War are not novels, but accounts of historical events. How restricting is that kind of writing to your creative abilities?

PAKENHAM: I have been very flattered when people—and once a novelist—have said that my books read like novels. That's a wonderful idea, but it's probably not true—or they mean my books read like bad novels.

Historians have to deal with motives, and motives are a matter of guesswork. We hardly know our own motives, let alone those of people who have died several hundred years ago. That takes one into the novelist's field: trying to imagine motivation and to reconstruct people.

So there's some overlap between a historical writer like myself and a historical novelist. A historical novelist comes from the other direction. His research is only to fill the gaps in the framework of his fiction. As a historical *writer,* my basic work is factual research, but I'm also trying to extend myself into the world of imagination as far as I can. And how far should I take liberties? It's a very interesting question: How far can the serious historical writer use his imagination?

CA: You once said that you refused to use either of your hereditary titles. Is there any particular reason?

PAKENHAM: I think hereditary titles are, in the worst sense, anachronisms. They've been abolished—at any rate there are no more being created—and a good thing, too.

Our family has this large family house that has been built and rebuilt for over three hundred years—Tullymally Castle. It's got hundreds of feet of second-class battlements appropriate for a poor man's Windsor Castle. I'm all for those battlements, but I know they are anachronisms. I mean, I don't pretend that they're appropriate for modern living. They happen to be a bit of history. I feel rather differently about titles. They're anachronisms, too. But they're not so harmless. What you call yourself is a very personal thing—like the clothes you wear. If I used a title I would feel like someone wearing fancy dress. And, as I'm a writer, I would feel I was flying false colors. You see, a writer or artist or musician wants to be himself. If he's going to succeed, he'll make his name, his identity, for himself without exploiting an inherited title.

CA: The Year of Liberty is about the Irish Rebellion of 1798. How did your interest in that develop?

PAKENHAM: I inherited our house in Ireland in 1961, and it was surrounded by bogs and a good deal of bloody Irish history.

You can't live in Ireland without thinking about the relations between Irish and English and between Catholics and Protestants. When I thought about a subject for my first historical book, the choice seemed obvious. If I'd lived in Lexington, Massachussetts, perhaps I would have written about the American Revolution.

CA: Several critics have noted that you left out what they considered important events—(such as the events in Ulster in 1797)—both before and after 1798, when the rebellion occurred. Was this intentional?

PAKENHAM: I think it's fair criticism. I took rather narrow terms of reference. I was following a journalist's approach, taking a narrow time scale, because that way you get more immediacy and impact. I didn't put in more about Ulster in 1797 because I felt that, as a storyteller, I would be giving away too much of my plot. What happened in Ulster in 1797 was a dress rehearsal for what happened in the whole of Ireland in 1798.

On the other hand, I think I would have brought in more about Ulster if I had been writing in the 1970's and not the 1960's. I finished the book with the phrase, "When shall we lay the ghosts of '98?" That was all too prophetic a phrase! Look at the calendar of events: the Battle of Bogside and the Catholic uprising in Derry. They happened in August, 1969, and my book went to the press in April, 1969. So I later felt a sense of *deja vu,* of a repeating pattern which I had only half anticipated. I would not have guessed that it could all happen so violently again, so cruelly as it did.

CA: One of the reviewers said that the Boer War was "a dress rehearsal for Vietnam." Do you agree?

PAKENHAM: Yes. All guerilla wars have a similarity. Take the Vietnam War, the Algerian War, the Spanish War in Cuba, and the original guerilla war in Spain from which the phrase is coined—"guerilla," meaning "little war." There's a pattern to them all. There were relatively few guerilla wars in the nineteenth century—few that attracted attention—because most of the wars were between the professional soldiers of rival powers and empires. A guerilla war is a people's war, and usually a colonial revolt, a war of ordinary people against an occupying force. The guerilla part of the Boer War came as a great shock to people and to military experts, not only in England but outside England. They assumed that the war would be over when the main battles were over and the capitals were captured. And of course, just as in Vietnam, the experts were wrong. They completely misunderstood the character of the war. They had no idea what tough nuts these simple Boer farmers would be, as tough as the Vietnamese peasants were to prove.

The second feature of guerilla wars is their cruel character. When untrained peasants embark on war, as in 1798, without officers to control them, using homemade weapons, it leads naturally to atrocities and reprisals. The practice of war (as opposed to the theory of war) never gives much room for chivalry, but wars certainly vary in the degree of beastliness. The Vietnam War was high on the scale of beastliness, and the second half of the Boer War not far behind.

Of course, there are important differences between the Boer War and the Vietnam War. The Americans were greatly outnumbered. So, despite their colossal superiority in weapons, they lost the war of attrition. And of course guerilla wars are always wars of attrition. In the Boer War, the British had superiority both in weapons and in numbers. There were five hundred thousand soldiers on the British side as compared to a *maximum* of eighty thousand on the Boer side. So it wasn't surprising that the British won the war. The biggest difference between the Vietnam War and the Boer War is that fact: the British *won* the Boer War. But there are plenty of parallels. The repeating pattern of history is what makes me a history addict.

CA: Could you comment on the effects The Boer War *has had on South Africans?*

PAKENHAM: Can I go back a moment to some lectures I gave about the 1798 rebellion in America promoting *The Year of Liberty?* I had to talk to a group in Boston who were mainly Irish-American Catholics. At the end of the talk, the Catholic priest who had introduced me said, "No one would believe it if we'd said it ourselves!" In other words, there was a clear identification between my narrative and Irish-American folk memory of the Catholic past in the rebellion in 1798. I got the same kind of reaction from people on the opposite side, some Protestants in Ulster. It may sound odd that two Irish communities as sharply divided as Catholics and Protestants can both identify with the same narrative. I regard it as a tremendous compliment to a historian, that people on both sides can approve his work.

I should be delighted if this happens with *The Boer War,* too. I went to South Africa immediately after it came out, and I gave some lectures to Afrikaners and to English-speaking South Africans. I got encouraging reactions from either side. The book is now being translated into Afrikaans. I don't pretend to be objective because no one can be objective. There's no such thing—we all have an inherited point of view. We're born facing one way or the other. But I do lean over backwards to try to be fair.

CA: Both of your grandfathers fought in the Boer War. Were there other interests behind the writing of The Boer War?

PAKENHAM: My grandfather on my mother's side was an English doctor (a nephew, by marriage, of Joseph Chamberlain, the English colonial secretary). He served in the war but didn't fight in it. My grandfather on my father's side was nearly killed in it, leading his Irish tenantry into a death trap. I've always been fascinated by Africa. *The Mountains of Rasselas* is about Ethiopia and its fortresses where I wandered as a young man fresh from the university. I don't have any South African links except the fact that my own grandfathers, like so many other people's, served there. South Africans I met couldn't understand this; they kept saying, "But you must tell us the real reason why you wrote it!" They couldn't get in their heads that anyone was interested in their history who wasn't at least partly South African by birth or adoption. I think most people who study history as a hobby do have that kind of personal link. As a professional historical writer, I don't feel I need a strong link. I do better without one.

CA: Do you ever want to write fiction?

PAKENHAM: Yes. I'd love to write a novel or poetry, but I just don't think I've got it in me. Maybe I'll get drunk one day and try!

CA: Are you working on anything now?

PAKENHAM: Yes, I'm doing a very big book at the moment. I'm not sure what the title will be. The book will be a history of how the European powers colonized Africa and how they were kicked out: colonization and decolonization. It's an enormously ambitious idea. I've got generous help from my American and British publishers. In fact, I'm going back to Africa in ten days for my second trip this year. It'll be my fifth visit to Africa altogether. I don't know whether I will literally visit every single African state, but I will visit all the main ones anyway. The book will consume years of my life, I'm sure.

CA: Is it unusual for a writer to devote that much time to research?

PAKENHAM: I don't know if it is. Maybe I'm very plodding and slow and lazy. It felt a bit odd to vanish under my stone, so to speak, in 1970 and come up again in 1980. Ten years is such a long time. I do hope that this book won't take that long. I wouldn't want to be a Rip Van Winkle when I finish this. I think that if you take research seriously, it can be all-consuming. I *don't* want to write a history of the world, but I do find Africa fascinating.

CA: What are your most difficult research problems?

PAKENHAM: I'm very slow and plodding in reading foreign languages. I had to read Afrikaans and Dutch for this book, and now I've got to learn something of Italian and German. This book on Africa that I'm working on involves six different kinds of empires and imperialism—French, German, Belgian, Italian, Portuguese, and British. I probably won't learn all those languages well enough to read them, but I will have to learn German and perhaps Italian. I love travel, and I travel fast. But I'm a very slow reader in a foreign language.

CA: Do you ever have any film possibilities for your books?

PAKENHAM: There are parallels between my book *The Year of Liberty* and Thomas Flanagan's brilliant novel *The Year of the French.* I don't know how much Flanagan used my book, but I did notice that he found some of his information there. I know that Flanagan's novel is going to be filmed for television. It's a historical novel with a great deal of vivid (and violent) history in it. I've always been attracted to subjects like that, subjects with visual appeal. I hope that one day I will get an offer for either *The Year of Liberty* or *The Boer War.* I'd love to work on the script for either of them, but no one's asked me to yet.

BIOGRAPHICAL/CRITICAL SOURCES: Spectator, February 20, 1959, November 15, 1969, October 13, 1979; *Times Literary Supplement,* February 27, 1959, October 23, 1969, November 23, 1979; *New Statesman,* February 28, 1959, October 24, 1969, August 31, 1979; *Manchester Guardian,* April 3, 1959; *New York Herald Tribune Book Review,* April 26, 1959; *New York Times,* April 26, 1959, November 14, 1976; *New Yorker,* June 13, 1959; *San Francisco Chronicle,* June 28, 1959; *Economist,* October 25, 1969, September 1, 1979; *Observer,* November 9, 1969, September 9, 1979, December 9, 1979, March 21, 1982; *Listener,* November 27, 1969, August 30, 1979; *Guardian Weekly,* December 6, 1969, September 9, 1979.

Books, January, 1970; *Books and Bookmen,* January, 1970, July, 1972, October, 1979; *History Today,* January, 1970, February, 1980; *New York Review of Books,* April 9, 1970, December 6, 1979; *Choice,* September, 1970, December, 1978,

April, 1980; *Authors in the News,* Volume 2, Gale, 1976; *Illustrated London News,* October, 1979; *New Republic,* November 17, 1979; *New York Times Book Review,* November 18, 1979, November 25, 1979, December 30, 1979; *Saturday Review,* November 24, 1979; *Washington Post Book World,* November 25, 1979; *Atlantic,* December, 1979; *Newsweek,* December 3, 1979; *Commonweal,* December 7, 1979.

West Coast Review of Books, January, 1980; *Booklist,* January 1, 1980; *Wall Street Journal,* January 10, 1980; *Chicago Tribune Book World,* February 3, 1980; *Commentary,* June, 1980, May, 1981; *History,* June, 1980; *British Book News,* July, 1980; *Mankind,* February, 1981; *Historian,* February, 1981; *Victorian Studies,* spring, 1981; *English Historical Review,* April, 1982.

—Sketch by Charity Anne Dorgan

—Interview by Mary V. McLeod

* * *

PALMER, Robin 1911-

PERSONAL: Born in 1911 in New York, N.Y.; married Douglas S. Riggs (a medical doctor and professor). *Education:* Attended Vassar College.

CAREER: Writer, 1938—.

WRITINGS—For young people, except as noted: *Furry Ones,* illustrations by Bray Educational Pictures, Whitman Publishing, 1938; *Mickey Never Fails,* illustrations by Walt Disney Studio, Heath, 1939; *Ship's Dog,* illustrations by Rafaello Busoni, Grosset, 1945; *The Barkingtons,* illustrations by Flavia Gag, Harper, 1948; *Wise House,* illustrations by Decie Merwin, Harper, 1951; (with Pelagie Doane) *Fairy Elves: A Dictionary of the Little People With Some Old Tales and Verses About Them,* illustrations by Don Bolognese, Walck, 1964; *Dragons, Unicorns, and Other Magical Beasts: A Dictionary of Fabulous Creatures With Old Tales and Verses About Them,* illustrations by Bolognese, Walck, 1966; (editor) *Wings of the Morning: Verses From the Bible* (adult), illustrations by Tony Palazzo, Walck, 1968; *Centaurs, Sirens, and Other Creatures: A Dictionary, Tales, and Verse From Greek and Roman Mythology,* illustrations by Bolognese, Walck, 1969; *A Dictionary of Mythical Places,* illustrations by Richard Cuffari, Walck, 1975; *Demons, Monsters, and Abodes of the Dead,* Scholastic Book Services, 1978.

Contributor of stories to periodicals, including *Jack and Jill, Child Life,* and *Story Parade.*

BIOGRAPHICAL/CRITICAL SOURCES: New York Herald Tribune Weekly Book Review, May 9, 1948; *New York Times,* June 20, 1948, November 18, 1951; *Saturday Review of Literature,* November 10, 1951; *Times Literary Supplement,* November 30, 1967; *Commonweal,* November 19, 1976.*

* * *

PALMER, Thomas 1955-

PERSONAL: Born March 24, 1955, in White Plains, N.Y.; son of John H. (a computer engineer) and Anne M. (Hulick) Palmer. *Education:* Attended Grinnell College, 1973-74; Wesleyan University, B.A., 1977. *Home:* 29 Morseland Ave., Newton, Mass. 02159.

CAREER: Yale University, New Haven, Conn., researcher, 1979-81; writer, 1981—.

WRITINGS: The Transfer (novel), Ticknor & Fields, 1983.

WORK IN PROGRESS: Danny and Rachel, a novel.

SIDELIGHTS: The Transfer examines the attempts of a small-time hoodlum to break into the Miami cocaine trade and the mob's attempts to have him killed. "Palmer has peered deeper into the heart of a certain darkness," wrote author Thomas Gifford in his *Washington Post Book World* review of *The Transfer,* "he has avoided the cliches which might have tempted others, and he has written a first novel of unusual ambition and achievement in a genre that is so much more rigorously demanding than the usual half-baked reminiscence of the beginner." Ivan Gold, reviewing in *New York Times Book Review,* opined: "At twenty-seven, Thomas Palmer understands how to put a book together, and he understands obsession."

Palmer told *CA:* "My task as a writer is to make something interesting and significant out of events that never happened. My resources are a shared language and common dreams."

BIOGRAPHICAL/CRITICAL SOURCES: Washington Post Book World, January 9, 1983; *New York Times Book Review,* February 20, 1983.

* * *

PANCAKE, Breece D'J 1952(?)-1979

OBITUARY NOTICE: Born c. 1952; died of self-inflicted gunshot wounds to the head in 1979. Author of a book of short stories. *Detroit News* writer Bud Foote, reviewing *The Stories of Breece D'J Pancake,* noted that "in spite of the tragedy of his life . . . the stories deserve to be read standing on their own feet. Pancake was one splendid writer." Foote called Pancake's prose "simple, direct, honest, and so finely crafted that the process of craftsmanship has disappeared." Obituaries and other sources: *Detroit News,* March 13, 1983.

* * *

PARFITT, George (Albert Ekins) 1939-

PERSONAL: Born November 7, 1939, in San Fernando, Trinidad; son of Albert Walter (a priest) and Sara (a nurse; maiden name, Ekins) Parfitt; married Margaret Anne King, April 15, 1962 (divorced, 1979); married Maureen Bell (an information officer), June 27, 1981; children: Stephen, Peter, Elisabeth, Catherine. *Education:* University of Bristol, B.A., 1962, Ph.D., 1966. *Politics:* Socialist. *Religion:* Atheist. *Home:* 4 Elm Ave., Beeston, Nottingham, England. *Office:* School of English Studies, University of Nottingham, Nottingham, England.

CAREER: University of Nottingham, Nottingham, England, assistant lecturer, 1966-68, lecturer in English studies, 1968—. Editor of Byron Press. Member of board of governors of Beeston Girls Secondary School, 1974-77. Member of Beeston Anti-Nuclear Group. *Member:* Association of University Teachers, University of Nottingham Staff Club.

WRITINGS: (Editor with James Kinsley) *John Dryden: Selected Criticism,* Oxford University Press, 1970; (editor) *Silver Poets of the Seventeenth Century,* Dent, 1974; (editor) *Ben Jonson: The Complete Poems,* Penguin, 1975, Yale University Press, 1981; *Ben Jonson: Public Poet and Private Man,* Dent, 1976; (editor) *The Plays of Cyril Tourneur,* Cambridge University Press, 1978; *Poetry of the Seventeenth Century,* Longman, in press. Editor of "Nottingham Drama Texts," University of Nottingham, 1978—. Editor of *Renaissance and Modern Studies.*

WORK IN PROGRESS: *In a Sad Season: Themes in the Literature of the Great War,* publication expected in 1984; editing, with Ralph Houlbrooke, a memoir (with poems) of the seventeenth-century Derbyshire writer Leonard Wheatcroft, tentatively titled *Leonard Wheatcroft,* publication by Whiteknights Press expected "probably" in 1984.

SIDELIGHTS: Parfitt told *CA*: "My writing springs, obviously enough, from my circumstances. Specifically, although I am not primarily a creative writer, my writing relates to creative questions: how have we, as a species, got where we now are, what does our past mean? In England, much of this has to go back to our 'revolution' in the seventeenth century—just as the United States has its revolt against Britain later. The first World War links, for me, with my seventeenth-century interests because that war was another crisis for Britain.

"My writings express my own views insofar as they are my writings. I do not write to please anyone else, although I do try to respond to what seem to me be needs in the people I teach and speak to. But I try to avoid egocentric subjectivism; I listen, as best I can, to the authors I write about and write about them to encourage others to listen to them also. That is what criticism, scholarship, and editing should be about."

BIOGRAPHICAL/CRITICAL SOURCES: *Times Literary Supplement,* February 11, 1977; *Washington Post Book World,* July 11, 1982.

* * *

PARINS, James William 1939-

PERSONAL: Surname is pronounced *Pair*-inz; born November 19, 1939, in Green Bay, Wis.; son of Joseph W. (an electrician) and Marian (Van Beek) Parins; married Marylyn Jackson (a professor), 1977; children: Claire, Craig, James Brady. *Education:* St. Norbert College, B.S., 1964; University of Wisconsin—Madison, M.A., 1970, Ph.D., 1972. *Home:* 223 South Martin St., Little Rock, Ark. 72205. *Office:* Department of English, University of Arkansas, 33rd at University, Little Rock, Ark. 72204.

CAREER: University of Wisconsin—Stevens Point, assistant professor of English, 1971-72; University of Arkansas, Little Rock, assistant professor, 1972-74, associate professor, 1975-80, professor of English, 1980—, chairman of department, 1973-78. Fulbright professor at Leicester Polytechnic School of Humanities, 1982-83. *Military service:* U.S. Marine Corps Reserve, 1957-62. *Member:* Research Society for Victorian Periodicals, Hopkins Society, Midcontinent American Studies Association, South Central Modern Language Association.

WRITINGS: (With Anthony Dube, J. Karl Franson, and Russell E. Murphy) *Structure and Meaning,* Houghton, 1976, 2nd edition, 1983; (editor with Todd K. Bender) *A Concordance to Conrad's "Lord Jim,"* Garland Publishing, 1976; *A Concordance to Pound's "Cantos,"* Garland Publishing, 1978; (with Bender) *A Concordance to Conrad's "Victory,"* Garland Publishing, 1978; *A Concordance to Conrad's "The Nigger of the Narcissus,"* Garland Publishing, 1979; (with Daniel F. Littlefield, Jr.) *A Biobibliography of Native American Writers, 1772-1924,* Scarecrow, 1981; (with Littlefield) *American Indian and Alaska Native Periodicals and Newspapers,* Greenwood Press, Volume I: *1826-1924,* 1983, Volume II: *1925-1960,* in press; *William Barnes,* Twayne, in press.

WORK IN PROGRESS: *The Rise of the Native Press in British and American Colonies in the Nineteenth Century; An Analysis of Early American Indian Writings,* with Daniel F. Littlefield, Jr.; *American Indian and Alaska Native Periodicals and Newspapers,* Volume III: *1961—,* with Littlefield, publication by Greenwood Press expected in 1986; *Coons' Last Poems.*

SIDELIGHTS: Parins wrote: "My vocational interests include the literary and political/historical writings of the English-speaking world, especially the colonial areas in the nineteenth century. The native periodical press in the colonial period is of special interest, for it provides valuable documentation of the process and reaction to imperialism. I first became interested in the subject while collaborating with Daniel F. Littlefield, Jr., on an anthology of American Indian writers from the nineteenth century. It soon became apparent that little biographical, bibliographical, or critical work had been done on American Indians or Alaska natives writing in English from colonial times to the middle of the present century, so we began our present project. As part of the project, we have located and identified some five hundred writers who published, largely in periodicals and newspapers, during the period 1772-1924. In addition, we have identified some 1500 newspapers and periodicals which were published by American Indians or Alaska natives or which focused on affairs and issues important to these people. These publications are the subject of a three-volume work tracing the history of the native press in America from the early part of the last century to the present. Finally, we are analyzing the literary, social, and historical writings by American Indians and Alaska natives to examine their reaction to Euro-American expansion. This analysis is currently underway."

* * *

PARTRIDGE, Jenny (Lilian) 1947-

PERSONAL: Born July 25, 1947, in Romford, England; daughter of Frank Munden and Dorothy (Miles) Partridge; married Nigel Casseldine (a painter and illustrator), April 16, 1971; children: Alice, Nicholas. *Education:* Attended South East Essex Technical College, 1963-68. *Religion:* Church of England. *Home and office:* Westend Cottage, 319 Westward Rd., Ebley, Gloucestershire, England. *Agent:* Christopher Shepheard-Walwyn, 51 Vineyard Hill Rd., London S.W.19, England.

CAREER: Presentation Colour Ltd. (photographic processors), London, England, retoucher, 1967-72; Romany Studio Workshop, Ebley, England, founder and artist, 1972—. *Awards, honors:* Critici in Erba Award from Bologna Children's Book Fair, 1981, for *Mr. Squint.*

WRITINGS—Self-illustrated children's books; all published by World's Work: *Mr. Squint,* 1980; *Colonel Grunt,* 1980; *Peterkin Pollensnuff,* 1980; *Hopfellow,* 1980; *Grandma Snuffles,* 1981; *Dominic Sly,* 1981; *Harriet Plume,* 1981; *Lop-Ear,* 1981; *Oakapple Wood Stories,* 1982; *A Tale of Oakapple Wood,* 1983.

SIDELIGHTS: Partridge told *CA*: "Writing the Oakapple Wood books was a secondary response, as I had been illustrating for some time before it was put to me to try to write stories around my illustrations. At first I found the idea daunting but after several false starts I discovered that the very way I felt about my drawings seemed to add credence to the characters. They existed, and with them the legend of Oakapple Wood, all from the very first pen and ink sketches springing into animated life. I saw the stories take form before me, and in this way the characters almost told their own tales, using me as a willing medium. Oakapple Wood is a real place to me, and there is a warmth of feeling each time I visit it and its many inhabitants, who have become my very good friends since their creation some years ago.''

AVOCATIONAL INTERESTS: Wildlife.

*   *   *

PASTERNAK, Burton 1933-

BRIEF ENTRY: Born March 25, 1933, in New York, N.Y. American anthropologist, educator, and author. Pasternak taught at State University of New York at Buffalo until 1969; he then began teaching anthropology at Hunter College of the City University of New York. He was a Fulbright lecturer in Taipei, Taiwan, in 1966. Pasternak wrote *Kinship and Community in Two Chinese Villages* (Stanford University Press, 1972) and *Introduction to Kinship and Social Organization* (Prentice-Hall, 1976). *Address:* Department of Anthropology, Hunter College of the City University of New York, 695 Park Ave., New York, N.Y. 10021.

*   *   *

PATMAN, (John William) Wright 1893-1976

PERSONAL: Born August 6, 1893, in Patman's Switch, Tex.; died of pneumonia, March 7, 1976, in Bethesda, Md.; son of John N. (a cotton farmer) and Emma (Spurlin) Patman; married Merle Connor, February 14, 1919 (died, July, 1967); married Pauline Tucker, October 9, 1968; children (first marriage) Connor Wright, James Harold, William Neff, a fourth son (deceased). *Education:* Cumberland University, LL.B., 1916.

CAREER: Cotton farmer, 1913-14; assistant to prosecuting attorney of Cass County, Tex., 1916-17; Texas House of Representatives, representative, 1921-24; district attorney for Fifth Judicial District in Cass County and Bowie County, Tex., 1924-29; U.S. House of Representatives, Washington, D.C., Democratic representative from Texas, 1929-76, chairman of Committee on Banking and Currency and Small Business Committee, vice-chairman of Joint House and Senate Defense Production Committee. Practiced law in Hughes Springs, Tex. *Military service:* U.S. Army, 1917-1919; served as machine gunner; became first lieutenant.

WRITINGS: Patman's Appeal to Veterans, Peerless Printing, 1934; *Bankerteering, Bonuseering, Melloneering,* Peerless Printing, 1934; *The Robinson-Patman Act: What You Can and Cannot Do Under This Law,* Ronald, 1938, reprinted as *Complete Guide to the Robinson-Patman Act,* Prentice-Hall, 1963; *Veterans' Benefits,* U.S. Government Printing Office, 1940, revised edition, 1941; (compiler) *Our American Government— What Is It? How Does It Function?: Two Hundred Fifty-Two Questions and Answers,* U.S. Government Printing Office, 1941; *Our American Government— What Is It? How Does It Function?: Two Hundred Eighty-Three Questions and Answers,* U.S. Government Printing Office, 1942; *Our American Government and How It Works: One Thousand One Questions Answered,* Bantam, 1968, new revised edition published as *Our American Government and How It Works: One Thousand One Questions and Answers,* 1968, 7th edition published as *Our American Government and How It Works: Six Hundred Ninety-Seven Questions and Answers,* Barnes & Noble, 1974; *The Federal Reserve System,* U.S. Government Printing Office, 1976.

SIDELIGHTS: Patman's dedication to the "little man" remained constant throughout his long political career. In the 1930's he led and won a fight to secure cash bonuses for veterans of World War I. That struggle placed him in bitter conflict with financier and U.S. Secretary of State Andrew Mellon, and eventually led to Mellon's replacement. In 1936 Patman was able to implement the Robinson-Patman Act, or Fair Trade Practices Act, to control price discrimination by chain stores.

In the 1940's, Patman began a persistent attack against America's banks, particularly the powerful Federal Reserve banks. Though he never won his major objective, to link the economic policies of the Federal Reserve with those of the administration in power, he was able to claim several smaller victories, including the establishment of federal credit unions and an increase in customer services at banks and savings and loan associations.

Later in his career, the populist representative from Texas won for President Richard Nixon the authority to impose wage and price controls in times of economic stress. After the Watergate break-in, Patman was one of the first legislators to press for stringent congressional investigation of the incident, which led to Nixon's resignation from the presidency.

Though Patman was often criticized for his relentless and domineering attitude toward banks and "big money," it appeared that his underlying motivation was a genuine concern for the welfare of the voters he represented for nearly fifty years.

BIOGRAPHICAL/CRITICAL SOURCES: Biography News, May, 1974.

OBITUARIES: New York Times, March 7, 1976.*

*   *   *

PATRICK, Martha 1956-

PERSONAL: Born November 22, 1956, in Kent, England; daughter of William Pitt (an antique dealer) and Rosemary (a farmer; maiden name, Pulvertaft) Patrick. *Education:* Courtauld Institute of Art, London, B.A. (with honors), 1979; Institute of Education, London, P.G.C.E., 1982. *Politics:* Liberal. *Home:* Ladwood Farm Acrise, Folkestone, Kent, England.

CAREER: Victoria and Albert Museum, London, England, art research assistant and lecturer, 1979-81; Sedgehill School, London, teacher of English and French, 1981—. Member of British archaeological expedition to Iraq, 1975. Volunteer social worker in young people's hostels and educational programs. *Member:* Buddhist Society (council member, 1979—).

WRITINGS: Buddhists and Buddhism (juvenile), Wayland, 1982.

WORK IN PROGRESS: Researching creation myths.

SIDELIGHTS: Patrick's *Buddhists and Buddhism* is one of a series of books designed to explain the principles and traditions of a variety of religions. According to a *Times Literary Supplement* review by Richard Lannoy, "priority is given to clear exposition of principal doctrines and practices as they affect everyday life in the modern context, including that of people who have settled in the West." Lannoy reserved special praise for Patrick's description of the Buddhist community at Chithurst, Hampshire, lauding it as "perhaps the most valuable chapter for English readers."

Patrick told *CA:* "My main interests are art history and world religions. I also enjoy teaching, sailing, and other leisure time activities.''

BIOGRAPHICAL/CRITICAL SOURCES: Times Literary Supplement, July 23, 1982.

*   *   *

PATTEE, Howard Hunt, Jr. 1926-

BRIEF ENTRY: Born October 5, 1926, in Pasadena, Calif. American biologist, educator, and author. Pattee has been a professor of theoretical biology and systems theory at State University of Binghamton since 1975. He has also taught at Stanford University and State University of New York at Buffalo, and he was a National Science Foundation fellow at Sweden's Karolinska Institute in 1959. Pattee edited *Hierarchy Theory: The Challenge of Complex Systems* (Braziller, 1973). *Address:* School of Advanced Technology, State University of New York at Binghamton, Binghamton, N.Y. 13901.

*   *   *

PATTEN, Robert L(owry) 1939-

PERSONAL: Born April 26, 1939, in Oklahoma City, Okla.; son of Charles H. (a banker) and Helen (Lowry) Patten; divorced; children: Jocelyn S., Christina S. *Education:* Swarthmore College, B.A. (with high honors), 1960; Princeton University, M.A., 1962, Ph.D., 1965; also attended Bedford College, London, 1963-64. *Home:* 1400 Hermann Dr., No. 17G, Houston, Tex. 77004. *Office:* Department of English, Rice University, P.O. Box 1892, Houston, Tex. 77251.

CAREER: Bryn Mawr College, Bryn Mawr, Pa., lecturer, 1964-66, assistant professor of English, 1966-69; Rice University, Houston, Tex., assistant professor, 1969-71, associate professor, 1971-76, professor of English, 1976—, director of Friends of the Fondren Library, 1971-77. Visiting fellow at Victorian Studies Centre, University of Leicester, 1980-81, and Princeton University, 1981-82; member of alumni council at Swarthmore College, 1976-79. President of Houston Committee for the Humanities and Public Policy, 1976-77; director of Texas Committee for the Humanities, 1979-80; member of board of directors of Security National Bank, Norman, Okla., 1977-80 and 1983—, and Cultural Arts Council of Houston, 1979-80. Lecturer at colleges and universities; public speaker. American coordinator of Julian Huxley Memorial Fund, 1980—.

MEMBER: International P.E.N., Modern Language Association of America, American Association of University Professors, Victorian Society in America, National Council of Teachers of English, College English Association, Dickens Fellowship, Dickens Society (chairman of executive committee and board of trustees, 1972, 1974; vice-president, 1975; president, 1976), Society of Authors, South Central Modern Language Association, Phi Beta Kappa, Grolier Club. *Awards, honors:* Woodrow Wilson fellowship, 1960-61; Fulbright scholarship for University of London, 1963-64; younger humanist fellowship from National Endowment for the Humanities, 1968-69, senior fellowship, 1977-78; grant from American Philosophical Society, 1972; Guggenheim fellowship, 1980-81.

WRITINGS: (Editor and author of introduction) Charles Dickens, *The Pickwick Papers*, Penguin, 1972; (editor) *George Cruikshank: A Revaluation*, Princeton University Library, 1974; *Charles Dickens and His Publishers*, Clarendon Press, 1978.

Contributor: Robert B. Partlow, Jr., editor, *Dickens the Craftsman: Strategies of Presentation*, Southern Illinois University Press, 1970; Partlow, editor, *Dickens Studies Annual*, Volume II, Southern Illinois Press, 1972; U. C. Knoepflmacher and G. B. Tennyson, editors, *Nature and the Victorian Imagination*, University of California Press, 1977; Partlow, editor, *Dickens Studies Annual*, Volume VII, Southern Illinois Press, 1978; George P. Landow, editor, *Approaches to Victorian Autobiography*, Ohio University Press, 1979.

Contributor of more than fifty articles and reviews to literature journals and newspapers. Editor of *Dickens Studies Newsletter*, 1969-72, *Flyleaf*, 1971-73, and *SEL: Studies in English Literature, 1500-1900*, 1978-84; guest editor of *Princeton University Library Chronicle*, 1973-74; subeditor of *Dickens Studies Annual*, 1970-79.

WORK IN PROGRESS: George Cruikshank: His Life, Work, and Times, for Clarendon Press; a Dickens companion to *The Christmas Books*, for Allen & Unwin, completion expected in 1987.

SIDELIGHTS: Robert L. Patten told *CA:* "My interest in Dickens grew out of my general interest in literature, which is at once popular, mimetic, and extravagantly imaginative. At first I concentrated on his art, convinced that he was a more careful and responsible craftsman than many of his critics would allow. Eventually I became involved in understanding how external constraints—in particular the format of serial fiction—shaped his imagination. *Charles Dickens and His Publishers* was an attempt to explain how an author's relations to his format, his publishers, and his audience affected his art. Those same issues are raised by the career of George Cruikshank, though in more complicated ways because Cruikshank lived through several eras and mastered more than one genre. Cruikshank's life is instructive also because he outlived his fame, bringing to a Victorian culture an imperfectly-tamed Georgian sensibility that seemed to his late contemporaries exaggerated and unbalanced. Hence, he was not accurately memorialized after his death, and in the succeeding century his immense—but often richly innovative and acute—art has been neglected."

BIOGRAPHICAL/CRITICAL SOURCES: Times Literary Supplement, August 11, 1972, July 26, 1974; *Dickens Studies Newsletter*, December, 1972, September, 1976, December, 1981; *Dickensian*, May, 1973, January, 1975, autumn, 1980; *Victorian Studies*, December, 1974, spring, 1980; *Nineteenth-Century Fiction*, March, 1975, March, 1980; *Library*, September, 1975; *Burlington*, June, 1976; *Victorian Periodicals Newsletter*, March, 1977; *Guardian*, November 30, 1978; *Financial Times*, December 2, 1978; *Listener*, December 14, 1978; *Sunday Telegraph*, December 24, 1978; *Economist*, December 30, 1978; *Country Life*, January 11, 1979; *Books and Bookmen*, February, 1979; *Houston Post*, March 25, 1979; *Author*, spring, 1979; *British Book News*, April, 1979; *Choice*, June, 1979; *SEL: Studies in English Literature, 1500-1900*, autumn, 1979; *Times Higher Education Supplement*, November 23, 1979; *Journal of English and German Philology*, January, 1980; *American Book Collector*, March-April, 1980; *Notes and Queries*, October, 1980; *Review of English Studies*, November, 1980; *Atlantic Quarterly*, winter, 1980; *Studies in the Novel*, spring, 1982.

*   *   *

PATTERSON, Frank Harmon 1912-

BRIEF ENTRY: Born July 5, 1912, in New Britain, Conn. American educator and author. Patterson joined the faculty of Boston University in 1949 and became a professor in 1950. He served as chairman of the department of humanities from 1950 to 1967, and he was named professor emeritus in 1973.

Patterson wrote *Words in Action* (American Book Co., 1968). *Address:* Beacon 21, Apt. A-16, 1111 Old Dixie Highway, Jensen Beach, Fla. 33457. *Biographical/critical sources: Directory of American Scholars,* Volume II: *English, Speech, and Drama,* 6th edition, Bowker, 1974.

*   *   *

PATTERSON, John McCready   1913-1983

OBITUARY NOTICE: Born December 18, 1913, in Richmond, Va.; died of cancer, April 24, 1983, in Washington, D.C. Government official and author of the mystery novel *Doubly Dead.* Patterson was a reporter for newspapers in Richmond, Virginia, and New York City before moving to Washington, D.C., in the early 1940's. There he worked for the Office of War Information, the Justice Department, and the State Department. From 1952 to 1954, he was an attache at the U.S. Embassy in London. Patterson was also a member of the Mystery Writers of America. Obituaries and other sources: *Who's Who in America,* 42nd edition, Marquis, 1982; *Washington Post,* April 26, 1983.

*   *   *

PAWLICKI, T(homas) B(ert)   1930-

PERSONAL: Born December 28, 1930, in St. Catherines, Ontario, Canada; son of Anthony (in shoe repair) and Anne (Baczenski) Pawlicki. *Education:* Attended public school in Vancouver, British Columbia. *Home:* 843 Fort St., Victoria, British Columbia, Canada V8W 1H6.

CAREER: Sign writer in Victoria, British Columbia, 1955—. Speaker at University of Toronto, 1981. Publicity executive for local bicycle clubs, 1949-55; bicycle racer (international), 1949-59; judo instructor for Young Men's Christian Association (YMCA), 1962. *Member:* Planetary Association for Clean Energy, American Association of Meta-Science, Society for the Investigation of the Unexplained.

WRITINGS: How to Build a Flying Saucer, Prentice-Hall, 1981; *Dimension of Consciousness: A Unified Field Geometry,* Prentice-Hall, in press. Contributor to magazines, including *Pursuit.*

WORK IN PROGRESS: The Secret of Spiritual Power in Judo, Karate, Aikido, Kung-fu, and Other Martial Arts.

SIDELIGHTS: Pawlicki wrote: "*How to Build a Flying Saucer* is a sergeant's revolution in the politics of science. It is a social satire revealing that knowledge is manufactured like automobiles for sale to markets. The customers are conditioned by advertising to believe in (buy) certain brand names and discredit products that threaten to upset the economic stability of the knowledge industry.

"The UFO phenomenon is a case to illustrate the point. The public has been sold the belief that antigravity is utterly beyond human comprehension. As a consequence, the moral majority denies UFO testimony as delusion. The immoral minority endorses the prevailing belief by the proposition that, *if* antigravity is beyond human ken, *then* UFOs must be extraterrestrial. No one questions the premise.

"In *How to Build a Flying Saucer,* I question the premise. As soon as antigravity is examined free of taboo, it is immediately apparent that antigravity is no more superhuman than aerial flight. Since my book was published, readers have sent me *patents* for antigravity machines. So far as I can read engi-

neering specifications, none of them will work. But the Wright brothers had a lot of ideas that wouldn't work, too, before they got them refined enough to take off.

"Mark you well! The purpose of my book and inventions is not to prove that UFOs exist, but only to demonstrate that the technology is within human ken—like flight, atomic power, and interplanetary exploration. That is *all* that my inventiveness is intended to prove.

"The case of pyramid engineering is an unequivocal attack on the knowledge industry for deliberate suppression of information in order to secure the economic advantage of the professional class to the disadvantage of the working class. Engineering technology sufficient to construct megalithic monuments with hand-operated, stone age machinery has been part of the lore of the construction trades since the Stone Age. The suppression that delayed the publication of these facts for ten years of my life made an exciting object lesson in itself.

"The same investigative attitude that establishes the factual base for the fantasy, *How to Build a Flying Saucer,* is applied to formulate a serious unified field theory in *Dimensions of Consciousness.* The unquestioned premise of established science is that the theories of relativity and quantum field mechanics are pure abstractions of highest mathematics, utterly beyond any human intellect to visualize. Models described in *Dimensions of Consciousness,* which *any* reader can build with kitchen materials to prove for himself, expose the big lie. The belief structure separating mind from matter is demolished. A new science, a new psychology, and a new religion is the result. Naturally, it will be Romans and Christians all over again.

"Although *Dimensions of Consciousness* relates my own studies, the thesis is typical of radical research being done by heretics all around the world. Because my work is conceived and proven with no mathematics above the junior high school level, making it a vulgate version of advanced physics within everyone's comprehension, exclusive possession of scientific truth is no longer the prerogative of a privileged class.

"The organizers of the PACE (Planetary Association for Clean Energy) symposium described my unified field equation as the most radical, revolutionary, and lucid theory ever to come to their attention. I was invited to deliver it to an international audience and panel of the most creative physicists alive. The forum was unanimous in condemning the school system for suppressing knowledge to the advantage of the social power structure. Ironically, we expressed these views under the prestigious auspices of the power establishment. Economics compels stranger bedfellows than politics."

*   *   *

PAXTON, Mary Jean Wallace   1930-
(Sister M. Jean Wallace)

PERSONAL: Born November 10, 1930, in Gary, Ind.; daughter of John James (an attorney) and Ruth (Johnson) Wallace; married Robert G. Haagens, December 28, 1972 (died February 14, 1976); married David E. Paxton (a sales agent), December 27, 1978; children: (first marriage) Jan Gerard. *Education:* St. Mary's College, Notre Dame, Ind., B.S., 1957; University of Notre Dame, Ph.D., 1964. *Address:* Route 1, Box 637B, Jacksonville, Ala. 36265. *Office:* Department of Biology, Jacksonville State University, Jacksonville, Ala. 36265.

CAREER: Entered Congregation of the Sisters of Holy Cross, 1949, took vows, 1952, released from vows, 1970; St. Mary's

College, Notre Dame, Ind., assistant professor, 1964-66, associate professor of biology, 1965-68; Harvard University, School of Public Health, Boston, Mass., research associate, 1968-71; Massachusetts General Hospital, Boston, research associate, 1971-73; Rhode Island College, Providence, assistant professor of biology, 1973-78; part-time teacher and writer, 1978-81; Jacksonville State University, Jacksonville, Ala., assistant professor of biology, 1981—. *Member:* American Association for the Advancement of Science, American Association of University Women, Endocrine Society, Society for Research in Reproduction, Sigma Xi.

WRITINGS: The Female Body in Control, Prentice-Hall, 1981; *Endocrinology*, Willard Grant Press, 1983.

Under name Sister M. Jean Wallace: (With Benedict J. Duffy) *Biological and Medical Aspects of Contraception,* University of Notre Dame Press, 1969.

SIDELIGHTS: Mary Paxton told *CA:* "*The Female Body in Control* was written in order to give women a framework or point of reference for understanding what happens to their bodies under various physiological circumstances. I have combined several facets of my research and teaching to produce this book.

"While working in research at the Harvard School of Public Health and the Massachusetts General Hospital, I became interested in the endocrinology of reproduction. Later, I taught this subject (general endocrinology). My interest in the subject, and my editor at Willard Grant Press, led me to write a textbook, *Endocrinology.*"

* * *

PAYNE, Emmy
See WEST, Emily Govan

* * *

PAYNE, (Pierre Stephen) Robert 1911-1983
(Richard Cargoe, John Anthony Devon, Howard Horne, Valentin Tikhonov, Robert Young)

*OBITUARY NOTICE—*See index for *CA* sketch: Born December 4, 1911, in Saltash, Cornwall, England; died of complications following a heart attack and stroke, February 18, 1983, in Hamilton, Bermuda. Linguist and author. Payne was a prolific writer who produced more than one hundred books, averaging two books per year. Though he began as a poet, the writer established himself as a biographer with his "highly readable" chronicles of Karl Marx, Charlie Chaplin, Greta Garbo, Adolf Hitler, Shakespeare, and many others. As a novelist, he concentrated on merging the East with the West, notably in works such as *Forever China* and *The Palace in Peking.* He also discovered and completed an unfinished novel by Leonardo Da Vinci, which he titled *The Deluge.* In addition to his writing talents, Payne was a skilled interpreter known for his translations of Boris Pasternak's short stories. He was the founder and director of the translation center at Columbia University as well as the chairman of P.E.N.'s translation center. He had just completed a book on the Crusades and was researching Indian art and the life of William Blake at the time of his death. Payne's books—many of which were written under pseudonyms—include *The Tormentors, Gershwin, Chaing Kai-shek,* and *Report on America.* Obituaries and other sources: *Current Biography,* Wilson, 1947, April, 1983; *New York Times,* February 22, 1983; *London Times,* February 23, 1983; *Los Angeles*

Times, February 24, 1983; *Washington Post,* February 26, 1983; *AB Bookman's Weekly,* March 7, 1983; *Newsweek,* March 7, 1983; *Time,* March 7, 1983; *Publishers Weekly,* March 11, 1983.

* * *

PAZ, Carlos F(ernando) 1937-

PERSONAL: Born April 4, 1937, in Guatemala City, Guatemala; came to the United States in 1952, naturalized citizen, 1973; son of Carlos O. and Raquel Zoe (Ramirez) Paz; married Chun Ok, November 21, 1973; children: Lesley Ann, Anne Marie. *Education:* Attended Los Angeles City College, 1974-75, and San Antonio College, 1978-81. *Home:* 6933 Ashbrook, San Antonio, Tex. 78239.

CAREER: U.S. Army, career officer, 1955-75, instructor in electronics at Fort Gordon, 1967-68, and Fort Sill, 1969, served in Vietnam, 1968-72, and Korea, 1972-75; University of Texas, Health Science Center, San Antonio, police officer, 1979—. *Member:* International Platform Association.

WRITINGS: Practice for U.S. Citizenship: Everything You Need to Know About the Test, Arco, 1982, 2nd edition, 1983.

WORK IN PROGRESS: Another book, publication by Arco expected in 1983.

SIDELIGHTS: Paz wrote: "The greatest satisfaction received from the publication of my book is that several persons, who had waited many years to become naturalized because they were afraid to take the test, will soon become citizens."

BIOGRAPHICAL/CRITICAL SOURCES: San Antonio Express News, April 11, 1982; *Southside Sun,* April 15, 1982.

* * *

PEAKER, G(ilbert) F. 1903(?)-1983(?)

OBITUARY NOTICE: Born c. 1903, in Yorkshire, England; died c. April 4, 1983. Educational researcher and author of *Plowden Children Four Years Later.* A self-taught statistician, Peaker did not begin his work in educational research until he was forty-six years of age. Peaker's publications set the standard for works in their field. A writer in the *London Times* noted that it was the statistician's "ability to combine perspicacity, testimony and memory from his early experiences of schooling that made him such an outstanding researcher." Obituaries and other sources: *London Times,* April 4, 1983.

* * *

PEARCE, Frank 1909-

PERSONAL: Born October 3, 1909, in Plymouth, England; son of Charles Cecil (in Royal Navy) and Blanche (Medland) Pearce; married Vera Alice Hodder, April 15, 1933; children: Derek Francis. *Education:* Attended private grammar school in Plymouth, England. *Religion:* Protestant. *Home:* Greentrees, 11 Bickland Hill, Falmouth, Cornwall TR11 4JH, England. *Agent:* Julian Friedmann Literary Agency Ltd., 15 Catherine St., Covent Garden, London WC2B 5JZ, England.

CAREER: Devon County Swimming Association, Torquay, England, coach, 1934-41; teacher at private boarding school in Dartmouth, England, 1946-54; hotelier in Turbay, England, 1954-73; writer, 1973—. *Military service:* Royal Navy, 1940-45. *Member:* Hotels Association (chairman, 1964-65), Torquay Leander Swimming and Life Saving Society (chairman, 1956-61).

WRITINGS—Nonfiction: *The Ship That Torpedoed Itself,* Baron Jay, 1975; *Along the Fal,* Century Lithograph, 1976; *St. Agnes: Portrait of a Cornwall Village,* Tester Bantam, 1977; *Brandy for the Parson,* Century Lithograph, 1977; *Mayday, Mayday, Mayday,* Tester Bantam, 1977; *Last Call for H.M.S. Edinburgh,* Atheneum, 1982.

WORK IN PROGRESS: The Rebels and *Bochym,* novels based on Cornish history.

SIDELIGHTS: During World War II, Pearce served on the cruiser H.M.S. *Trinidad,* which escorted Russian convoys from Iceland to Murmansk. It was the only ship in British naval history to be hit by its own torpedo, and was the subject of Pearce's first book. The book was later made into a television documentary.

Pearce told *CA:* "The trauma of the World War II years (blitzes in British cities, Atlantic convoy sinkings, Russian convoy survival) served to influence a compulsion to write about my own experiences. The details were printed indelibly on my mind, and I now have a sense of satisfaction that I may have left a record for posterity of the ordeals and sacrifices that were made in those days to maintain freedom.

"My research on Cornish history has produced a wealth of fascinating detail. It has given me great pleasure to reproduce it as documentary and as fiction."

*   *   *

PEARY, Dannis 1949-
(Danny Peary)

PERSONAL: Born August 8, 1949, in Philippi, W.Va.; son of Joseph Y. (a professor) and Laura (Chaitan) Peary; married Suzanne Rafer (an editor), June 21, 1980; children: Zoe. *Education:* University of Wisconsin-Madison, B.A., 1971; University of Southern California, M.A. (with honors), 1975. *Residence:* New York, N.Y. *Agent:* Christine Tomasino, Robert L. Rosen Associates, 7 West 51st St., New York, N.Y. 10019. *Office:* 17 Stuyvesant Oval 2C, New York, N.Y. 10009.

CAREER: Writer, 1971—; script reader for Brut Productions, 1975; sports editor for *Los Angeles Panorama,* 1976; photo researcher for Workman Publishing, 1977.

WRITINGS—Under name Danny Peary: *Close-Ups: The Movie Star Book,* Workman, 1978; (editor with brother, Gerald Peary) *The American Animated Cartoon: A Critical Anthology,* Dutton, 1980; *Cult Movies,* Delta, 1981; *Cult Movies 2,* Dell, 1983. Contributor of articles to newspapers and magazines, including *Philadelphia Bulletin, TV Guide-Canada, Boston Globe, Newsday,* and *Films and Filming.*

SIDELIGHTS: The American Animated Cartoon is a collection of articles by animators and others involved in the animation industry. Selections include Art Babbit's explanation of the drawing techniques used in Goofy cartoons and Richard Thompson's comments on his Road Runner-versus-Coyote film shorts and Buggs Bunny and Daffy Duck cartoons. Winsor McCay, R. Bray, and Vlad Tytla are among other animators represented. Walt Disney's testimony before the House Un-American Activities Committee is reproduced in *The American Animated Cartoon,* as are John Canemaker's articles about several of the early developers of animation.

According to *Los Angeles Times Book Review* critic Charles Solomon, the book is "valuable for the amount of information compressed in readily accessible form." "The fact that enough serious criticism exists to fill a book like 'The American Animated Cartoon' is indeed a hopeful sign," he added. "This medium is finally receiving its due respect and attention."

Peary told *CA:* "I treat film as a pop culture: part art, part mass entertainment. I write for no specific audience, but my intention is to make the serious film student more of a fan and the fan more of a student. I choose projects that require research because I am very enthusiastic about film and want to learn as much as I want to enlighten the reader."

BIOGRAPHICAL/CRITICAL SOURCES: Los Angeles Times Book Review, October 12, 1980.

*   *   *

PEARY, Danny
See PEARY, Dannis

*   *   *

PEAVY, Linda 1943-

PERSONAL: Born November 5, 1943, in Hattiesburg, Miss.; daughter of Wyatt Gaines (a forest products dealer) and Claribel (a teacher; maiden name, Hickman) Sellers; married Howard Sidney Peavy (a professor of environmental engineering), December 21, 1962; children: Erica, Don. *Education:* Mississippi College, B.A., 1964; University of North Carolina, M.A., 1970. *Home:* 521 South Sixth, Bozeman, Mont. 59715. *Office:* P.S., A Partnership, 1104 South Fifth, Bozeman, Mont. 59715.

CAREER: High school teacher of English and journalism in Jackson, Miss., 1964-66, and Baton Rouge, La., 1966-69; Oklahoma Baptist University, Shawnee, instructor in English, 1970-74; P.S., A Partnership, Bozeman, Mont., partner and writer, 1974—. Poet/writer with Montana Arts Council, 1982—. Gives readings (sometimes on radio programs) and workshops. *Member:* Society of Children's Book Writers, Montana Institute of the Arts.

WRITINGS: (With Jere Day) *The Complete Book of Rockcrafting,* Drake, 1976; *Have a Healthy Baby: A Guide to Prenatal Nutrition and Nutrition for Nursing Mothers,* Drake, 1977; *Canyon Cookery: A Gathering of Recipes and Recollections From Montana's Scenic Bridger Canyon,* Artcraft, 1978; (with Andrea Pagenkopf) *Grow Healthy Kids!: A Parents' Guide to Sound Nutrition,* Grosset, 1980.

Children's books: *Allison's Grandfather* (picture storybook), illustrations by Ron Himler, Scribner, 1981; (with Ursula Smith) *Food, Nutrition, and You,* Scribner, 1982; (with Smith) *Women Who Changed Things,* Scribner, 1983.

Work represented in anthologies, including *With Joy: Poems for Children,* edited by T. E. Wade, Jr., Gazelle, 1976; *The Poetry of Horses,* edited by William Cole, Scribner, 1979; *Rapunzel, Rapunzel,* edited by Katharyn Machan Aal, McBooks Press, 1980; *Cracks in the Ark,* edited by Richard Morgan and Phyllis Fischer, Writers for Animal Rights, 1982. Contributor of poems and stories to magazines, including *Texas Review, Cottonwood Review, South Dakota Review, Pierian Spring, Southern Exposure, Antigonish Review,* and *Old Hickory Review.*

WORK IN PROGRESS: All Our Conflicts Into Harmony: Humans and the Environment, for young adults, with Ursula Smith, publication expected in 1984; *A Tangle of Kudzu,* stories for adults; *More Than Muse,* a book on friendships between women writers.

SIDELIGHTS: Linda Peavy commented: "Poetry and fiction allow me to express the feelings that are mine during one small moment in time. The poem or story that results from this expression of feeling about a single event, person, or place represents my own personal perspective on this one aspect of life. It is simply that—a single person's view on a single aspect of life. Only when it is shared with others does the intensely personal expression take on another dimension.

"Different kinds of sharing bring different rewards. Since readers seldom correspond with authors, I have only the reactions of editors, critics, and friends by which to judge whether my published work has spoken to others. Conversely, readings, workshops, and work in schools and communities all allow for a more direct sharing. It is in that sharing that I realize my poems have value for these fellow travelers who seem to need to have their private perceptions expressed by a writer. It is as if such an expression somehow validates the worth of the inward journey for us all.

"For two of my nonfiction books, I was the writer and another woman was the expert, and I thoroughly enjoyed both projects. But I've found my greatest satisfaction in working with another writer whose love of research, writing, and editing are equal to my own. Though my writing partner and I have worked together (as well as separately) on many nonfiction projects, working on women's biographies has become our obsession. We're fierce admirers of those women whose accomplishments show that they never regarded overwhelming odds against success as insurmountable obstacles.

"Though many beginning writers seem to see writing for children as an 'easy' way to break into print, I consider writing for children and young adults as one of the greatest challenges a serious writer can accept."

AVOCATIONAL INTERESTS: Hiking, birdwatching, backpacking, cross-country skiing.

*   *   *

PECKINPAH, (David) Sam(uel)   1925-

PERSONAL: Born February 21, 1925, in Fresno, Calif.; son of David E. (a judge) and Fern (Church) Peckinpah; married second wife, Begonia Palacias (an actress), 1962 (marriage ended); married Joey Gould; children: one son, three daughters. *Education:* Received B.A. from Fresno State College; received M.A. from University of Southern California. *Agent:* Chasin-Park-Citron Agency, 10889 Wilshire Blvd., Los Angeles, Calif. 90024.

CAREER: Screenwriter and/or director of television productions, including the series "Gunsmoke," "Broken Arrow," "The Westerner," and "The Rifleman," and the teleplay "Noon Wine," 1967; and motion pictures, including "The Deadly Companions," Pathe-American, 1961, "Ride the High Country" (also released as "Guns in the Afternoon"), Metro-Goldwyn-Mayer, 1962, "The Ballad of Cable Hogue," Warner Bros., 1970, "Junior Bonner," Cinerama, 1972, "The Getaway," National General, 1972, "Pat Garrett and Billy the Kid," Metro-Goldwyn-Mayer, 1973, "The Killer Elite," United Artists, 1975, "Cross of Iron," Avco-Embassy, 1977, and "Convoy," United Artists, 1978 (also see WRITINGS). Actor in motion pictures, including "Invasion of the Body Snatch-

ers," 1956. *Military service:* U.S. Marines, c. 1943-45. *Member:* Academy of Motion Picture Arts and Sciences, Directors Guild of America, Writers Guild of America. *Awards, honors:* Award from Writers Guild, 1967, for "Noon Wine"; best foreign film award from Association of Spanish Critics, 1970, for "The Ballad of Cable Hogue"; and other film awards.

WRITINGS—Screenplays; and director, unless otherwise noted: (With Harry Julian Fink and Oscar Saul) "Major Dundee," Columbia, 1965; (screenwriter only; with Robert Towne) "Villa Rides!," Paramount, 1968; (with Walon Green) "The Wild Bunch," Warner Bros., 1969; (with David Zelag Goodman) "Straw Dogs" (adapted from the novel *Siege at Trencher's Farm,* by Gordon Williams), Cinerama, 1971; (with Gordon Dawson) "Bring Me the Head of Alfredo Garcia," United Artists, 1974.

Also writer for television series, including "Gunsmoke," "Broken Arrow," and "The Rifleman."

SIDELIGHTS: Peckinpah's career as director of graphically violent, yet curiously romantic films has been one of extremes. During the early 1960's he was hailed as director John Ford's successor for his mastery of the western genre as exemplified in "The Deadly Companions" and "Ride the High Country." Then word of his eccentric and often costly technique resulted in his forfeiture of "Major Dundee" and his dismissal from "The Cincinnati Kid." As the decade ended, however, Peckinpah's career was revived when his neo-western, "The Wild Bunch," was hailed as a masterpiece. Another turn-of-the-century work, "The Ballad of Cable Hogue," was greeted with similar enthusiasm by viewers. But his career plummeted once again when his contemporary drama of vengeance, "Straw Dogs," was deemed a fascist and misogynist work, and subsequent films, notably "Pat Garrett and Billy the Kid" and "Cross of Iron," were marred by studio tampering. Peckinpah consequently holds few illusions about filmmaking. "I'm just a dummy," he told Dan Yergin during filming of "Straw Dogs." "I get a script and try to make a picture, that's all."

Peckinpah broke into the film industry as an actor in "The Invasion of the Body Snatchers." He also wrote an early draft of the screenplay for that film as well as dialogue for other projects for Allied Artists. In the late 1950's he began writing for the television series "Gunsmoke" and "Broken Arrow." He then directed segments for another series, "The Westerner," which he created with Bruce Geller. When that series ended, Peckinpah resumed writing screenplays, notably "One-Eyed Jacks," which director and principal actor Marlon Brando had re-written. "Marlon screwed it up," Peckinpah later contended. He noted that the original script portrayed the main character as a vicious outlaw, and that Brando had the script altered because "in those days he had to end up as a hero."

After "The Westerner" was cancelled, actor Brian Keith agreed to act in an adaptation of A. S. Fleischman's *Yellowleg,* a novel of the Old West, and he convinced the film's producer to hire Peckinpah as director. Working with a miniscule budget, Peckinpah managed to fashion a compelling and suspenseful version of Fleischman's tale of men transporting a coffin through Apache territory. Although the film, entitled "The Deadly Companions," drew few viewers, it proved sufficiently crafted to ensure Peckinpah further opportunities as a director.

In 1962 Peckinpah directed his second film, "Ride the High Country." This western detailed the slowly consuming greed of two aging marshals guarding a shipment of gold. Unceremoniously released by its distributor—it was shown as the bottom half of drive-in double-features—the film nevertheless managed to develop an audience, thanks largely to the enthusiasm of critics such as the *New York Herald-Tribune*'s Joseph Morgenstern, who called it "a consummate work of art." It later received prizes from film festivals in Mexico and Belgium.

Peckinpah's third film, the western "Major Dundee," fared less favorably with viewers, many of whom found the film confusing and incoherent. The work, which Peckinpah wrote and directed, concerns an obsessive, guilt-ridden officer's efforts to lead an army of prisoners and criminals into Mexico to rescue three youths kidnapped by Apaches. Dundee's eventual triumph is a hollow one, for the rescue proves costly to his troops, and he seems ignorant of the conflict's lesson that war is a hellish action. Much of Peckinpah's depiction of war's gruesome nature was ruined, according to the director, by his producers, who removed fifty-five minutes of footage, including most of the final conflict. "You could have driven a freight train sideways through the holes left in that picture," Peckinpah complained. "It still makes me cry when I see it."

His troubles continued as filming commenced on "The Cincinnati Kid," a chronicling of the gambling milieu which was anticipated as Peckinpah's first contemporary work. The film's producers, worried by reports from Columbia that Peckinpah was incapable of finishing a film on schedule or within budget, dismissed him after only four days of work. For the next four years Peckinpah was unable to secure work as a director. He returned once again to screenwriting, though he was appalled by the film industry's rendering of his work.

Finally, in 1967, one of Peckinpah's followers in television hired him to direct an adaptation of Katherine Anne Porter's *Noon Wine* for the network. The result proved an enormous success with critics and helped revive interest in his work. The following year, another executive impressed with Peckinpah's work hired him to direct "The Wild Bunch," the story of an outlaw gang that flees to Mexico only to be destroyed by the Mexican army. Upon release, the film was greeted with wild enthusiasm from critics such as Richard Schickel, who called it "the first masterpiece in the new tradition of 'the dirty western,'" and *New York Times*'s Vincent Canby, who was particularly impressed with Peckinpah's use of slow motion during the graphic and violent action sequences. Canby declared that Peckinpah's technique "at first heightens the horror of the mindless slaughter, and then—and this is what really carries horror—makes it beautiful, almost abstract, and finally into terrible parody." He added: "Although the movie's conventional and poetic action sequences are extraordinarily good and its landscapes beautifully photographed . . . , it is most interesting in its almost jolly account of chaos, corruption and defeat. All personal relationships in the movie seem somehow perverted into odd mixtures of noble sentimentality, greed and lust."

Like its predecessors, however, "The Wild Bunch" was poorly treated by its producers, who authorized the deletion of four scenes after the film was released. Canby protested that "three of the four 'lifts' definitely reduce the humanity that runs through the movie in ironic counterpoint to the vividly overstated violence." He added: "It's still an important work of movie literature, but some chapters have been torn out."

Peckinpah's following work, "The Ballad of Cable Hogue," was also poorly handled by Warner Brothers. The film, which concerns an aging entrepreneur's peculiar struggles after establishing a waterhole in the desert, was scarcely promoted and distributed by the company and was left, like "Ride the High Country" eight years earlier, in drive-ins as the bottom half of double-features. But like its predecessor, "The Ballad of Cable Hogue" proved a sufficiently worthy work to overcome its poor handling and develop a following. Canby, who noted that "this fine film wasn't as much released by Warner Brothers as dismissed by them," deemed it one of the year's ten best films. He praised the fine performances Peckinpah elicited from Jason Robards and Stella Stevens, and added that the film was his "gentlest, boldest, and perhaps most likable film to date." Late in 1970, "The Ballad of Cable Hogue" was declared the best foreign film by the Association of Spanish Critics.

In 1971 Peckinpah completed his most controversial film, "Straw Dogs." The work, in which he attempted to illustrate ethnologist Robert Ardrey's concept of man as an animal which represses its violent tendencies, documents the frightening force of suddenly unleashed violence. It centers on the confrontation between a meek mathematics professor who shelters a retarded man and a band of vicious villagers who pursue him. The thugs, who accuse the idiot of murdering a young girl, incur the professor's wrath after breaking into his home and raping his wife. He retaliates by shooting off one man's foot, hurling boiling liquid in the faces of two other assailants, thwarting a fourth intruder with a claw-like device, and convincing his wife to blast the final attacker through the chest with a shotgun.

Critics disagreed on the merits of "Straw Dogs." *National Observer*'s Bruce Cook called it Peckinpah's "best movie," and *New Yorker*'s Pauline Kael acknowledged it as "a fascist work of art." Canby was less impressed. "It is an intelligent movie," he conceded, "but interesting only in the context of [Peckinpah's] other works." Also writing in the *New York Times,* Peter Schjeldahl found the film's message "less than intoxicating" and reacted "with astonishment to the idea that the brutal, atrocious mess . . . is supposed to be some sort of happy ending."

Peckinpah claimed that many viewers missed the point of "Straw Dogs." He called the professor the antagonist of the work, contending that he "was maneuvering himself into a situation where he'd be forced to let the violence . . . out." Peckinpah added that the professor "found out he had all those instincts and it made him sick, sick unto death, and yet at the same time he had guts enough and sense enough to stand up and do what he had to do." In another interview, he goodnaturedly characterized "Straw Dogs" as an opportunity "to work with something other than horses and saddles as means of transportation."

Peckinpah followed "Straw Dogs" with "Junior Bonner," an admiring and often funny portrait of rodeo life which he deemed his best work to date. The film focuses on Bonner's struggle with his declining skills on the rodeo circuit where, at forty, he is no longer certain of his abilities with the animals, particularly a large bull named Sunshine. For Peckinpah, Bonner's awkward brushes with contemporary Western society are also a source of humor. He portrays Bonner's brother, Curly, as a down-home but frantic real-estate agent whose Reato Rancheros is described as "home on the range retirement," and Curly's wife, Ruth, as an equally peculiar Bonner who declares, "There never was a horse that couldn't be rode and there never was a cowboy that couldn't be throwed." Canby was quite impressed with "Junior Bonner," which he called "a superior family comedy" disguised as a rodeo film. He much preferred Peckinpah's "benignly comic mood" to the "gross, intellectual mayhem" of "Straw Dogs." Despite the generally favorable critical reception—Canby named it among the year's twenty finest films—"Junior Bonner" was a box-office disappointment.

Perhaps Peckinpah's next effort, "The Getaway," was an overt attempt to recoup the large audiences he had enjoyed with films such as "The Wild Bunch" and "Straw Dogs." With its extreme violence, including spurting blood and slow-motion gunplay, and minimal characterization, "The Getaway" was able to capitalize somewhat on the popular action films of actors such as Charles Bronson, Clint Eastwood, and "The Getaway"'s own Steve McQueen. Reviewers, however, were in general agreement that plot implausibilities and random violence rendered the film an inferior work.

Peckinpah's subsequent work has been marred by either poor, excessive editing, weak distribution, or minimal financing. His return to the western genre, "Pat Garrett and Billy the Kid," boasted an intriguing cast, including James Coburn, singer/songwriters Kris Kristofferson and Bob Dylan, and eminent staples of the genre such as Jack Elam, Chill Wills, and Slim Pickens, as well as an appropriately sombre screenplay by novelist Rudolf Wurlitzer, but received mostly unfavorable notices upon release in 1973. Peckinpah claimed that extensive revising by several editors severely marred the film. "The heart of the film is missing," he insisted. He revealed that an entire character was deleted from his version, and that Bob Dylan's soundtrack was altered to feature his singing throughout the work. "I only had Dylan sing twice," Peckinpah contended, "but obviously [producer] Gordon Carroll wants to sell a Bobby Dylan album." He was extremely disappointed with the producer's tampering and called his own version "the best film I ever made."

A few years after the release of "Pat Garrett and Billy the Kid," some critics revised their initial objections. Elements that had been deemed pretentious, especially several cryptic exchanges between Garrett and "the Kid," were later acknowledged to be remorseful laments for a west that was no longer wild, and some of the shootouts, which had seemed graphic and pointlessly violent—especially those involving characters played by Pickens and Elam—were reappraised as solemn, mutually respectful showdowns between men who neither requested nor accorded quarter. "In the confrontation between a man who will compromise and a man who can not," wrote Aljean Harmetz in the *New York Times,* "at a time when adaptation offers the only chance of survival, lies the film's enormous and disturbing power."

In 1974 Peckinpah completed his most pessimistic work, "Bring Me the Head of Alfredo Garcia." The title character has foolishly impregnated the daughter of a Mexican aristocrat, and the film centers on the efforts of a down-and-out pianist, Benny, to locate Garcia's head—he had previously died and been decapitated by others interested in the aristocrat's reward—and present it in return for the prize money. Throughout the film, Benny kills others attempting to steal the head—which has rapidly decomposed within a blood-caked and pungent burlap sack—while striving to reach Mexico. When he finally arrives at the aristocrat's villa, Benny is so disgusted by the landowner's superior indifference to the carnage caused by the demand that he shoots him and attempts to escape with the reward. Upon reaching the gates, however, Benny finally collapses amid a seemingly endless round of gunfire from the guards. Several reviewers found the film morbid and self indulgent. Canby suggested that Benny's physical resemblance

to Peckinpah "may allow the film to be read as some kind of crazy comment by Peckinpah on Peckinpah's adventures as an innocent among the wolves of Hollywood." Like "Pat Garrett and Billy the Kid," however, "Bring Me the Head of Alfredo Garcia," enjoyed a re-evaluation during the late 1970's, and some critics, while conceding that the film was technically flawed—due to miniscule funds, Peckinpah was forced to film evening scenes during daylight with falsifying lenses—acclaimed it an eccentric but powerful work by a major director.

Most reviewers were disappointed with Peckinpah's next film, "The Killer Elite." The movie, which documents the moral malaise of a CIA agent who is betrayed by his employers as part of a plot involving Japanese terrorists and Chinese anticommunists, was considered incoherent and needlessly drawn out by Canby. "Mr. Peckinpah is mannered and inventive," Canby declared, "and these qualities both give the film its strengths and undermine it horrendously." He also objected to the film's climactic battle on warships as "absurd." "This director thinks he can do anything he wants," Canby charged, "and he is nearly right: But he is a long way from his audience."

Canby's dissatisfaction with Peckinpah continued in 1977 when he called "Cross of Iron" Peckinpah's "least interesting, least personal film in years." The work, which was rumored to have been as altered by editors as were "Major Dundee" and "Pat Garrett and Billy the Kid," awkwardly depicts a group of German soldiers struggling on the Russian front in 1943. Scenes featuring dramatic exchanges among the officers are flawed by haphazard accents from the English-speaking cast, and battle scenes are rendered absurd by seemingly repetitious depictions of bodies hurtling through the air from the impact of explosions. Canby, who had been an enthusiastic patron of Peckinpah's "The Wild Bunch" and "The Ballad of Cable Hogue," regretted the director's association with the film. "I can't believe that the director ever had his heart in this project," Canby complained, adding that the film "looks to have been prepared for the benefit of the people who set off explosives."

In 1978 Peckinpah completed "Convoy," a film romanticizing a group of truckers united in their defiance of southwestern America's speed limits. While many critics denounced "Convoy" as Peckinpah's most shallow work, Pauline Kael defended it as "a sunny, enjoyable picture." She acknowledged the technical inadequacy of the post-synchronized soundtrack, but added, "The visual music of the moving trucks is enough to carry the film for the first hour." Kael was especially impressed with Peckinpah's iconic rendering of the trucks. "Seeing this picture," she contended, "you recover the feelings you had as a child about the power and size and noise of trucks, and their bright distinctive colors and alarming individuality."

In the early 1980's, rumors circulated that Peckinpah would return to filmmaking despite the critical and commercial shortcomings of his previous works. Although it was reported that he had become disenchanted with directing while filming "Convoy"—he even allowed James Coburn to direct certain scenes during the actor's visit to the filming site—producers were attempting to procure his services for an adaptation of one of Robert Ludlum's bestsellers. For Peckinpah, who was considered one of America's finest filmmakers in the early 1970's, the opportunity may mark his return to the directorial pantheon. And though he harbors little sentiment for the cutthroat world of Hollywood, he maintains equal indifference to his own fluctuating stock in the film world. "I'm like a good whore," he once commented. "I go where I'm kicked."

AVOCATIONAL INTERESTS: Scuba diving, surfing.

BIOGRAPHICAL/CRITICAL SOURCES, New York Times, April 12, 1962, June 26, 1969, July 6, 1969, July 20, 1969, May 14, 1970, January 20, 1972, February 20, 1972, May 21, 1972, August 3, 1972, December 20, 1972, May 24, 1973, June 3, 1973, June 17, 1973, July 8, 1973, September 30, 1973, August 15, 1974, September 15, 1974, December 18, 1975, May 12, 1977, June 28, 1978, July 2, 1978, December 7, 1980; *New York Herald Tribune,* June 21, 1962; *Sight & Sound,* summer, 1962, summer, 1965, spring, 1973; *Life,* July 25, 1969, August 11, 1972; *Guardian,* October 27, 1969; *Film Quarterly,* fall, 1969, spring, 1975; *Film Heritage,* fall, 1970, winter, 1973-74; *New York Times Magazine,* October 31, 1971; *New Yorker,* January 29, 1972, December 23, 1972, January 12, 1976, September 24, 1978; *Toronto Globe and Mail,* May 13, 1972; *Playboy,* August, 1972; Max Evans, *Sam Peckinpah: Master of Violence, Being the Account of the Making of a Movie and Other Sundry Things,* Dakota Press, 1972; *Rolling Stone,* July 5, 1973; *Western Humanities Review,* spring, 1975; *Take One,* March, 1977; *Time,* July 4, 1977; Paul Seydor, *Peckinpah: The Western Films,* University of Illinois Press, 1980; *Film Comment,* January-February, 1981; *Contemporary Literary Criticism,* Volume 20, Gale, 1982.*

—*Sketch by Les Stone*

* * *

PELL, Walden II   1902-1983

OBITUARY NOTICE: Born July 3, 1902, in Quogue, Long Island, N.Y.; died of cancer, March 23, 1983, in Elkton, Md. Clergyman, educator, and author. Ordained a deacon of the Protestant Episcopal Church in 1927 and a priest in 1928, Pell served as headmaster of St. Andrew's School in Middletown, Delaware, from 1930 to 1957. He was the author with Powel Dawley of *The Religion of the Prayer Book* and compiler of *A History of St. Andrew's School.* Obituaries and other sources: *Who's Who in America,* 42nd edition, Marquis, 1982; *New York Times,* March 25, 1983.

* * *

PELLEW, Jill (Hosford)   1942-

PERSONAL: Born April 4, 1942, in Burnley, England; daughter of Frank (a historian and university administrator) and Jane (Hosford) Thistlethwaite; married Mark Edward Pellew (a diplomat), December 11, 1965; children: Adam Lee, Dominic Stephen. *Education:* St. Hilda's College, Oxford, B.A., 1964, M.A., 1966; Queen Mary College, London, M.A., 1970, Ph.D., 1976. *Politics:* Social Democrat. *Religion:* Church of England. *Home and office:* 27 Alderney St., London SW1V 4ES, England.

CAREER: Worked as civil servant in Ministry of Defence, 1964-65; part-time teacher of history at universities, including University of Sussex, 1981 and 1982, and overseas programs of Hollins College, 1981—, and Central University of Iowa, 1983—. Free-lance historian. *Member:* Diplomatic Service Wives Association (England), University of London Women's Club. *Awards, honors:* Award from Social Science Research Council, 1977-80, for study of the Home Office, 1848-1914.

WRITINGS: The Home Office, 1848-1914: From Clerks to Bureaucrats, Heinemann Educational Books, 1982. Contributor of articles to *Victorian Studies* and *International Review of Administrative Sciences.*

WORK IN PROGRESS: A book about the administration of aliens legislation in Britain; research on the development of various British institutions.

SIDELIGHTS: Writing in the *Times Literary Supplement,* book reviewer R. T. Shannon noted that Pellew had "cunningly selected the seventy best years to write about" in her history of English bureaucratic government. *The Home Office, 1848-1914* covers a period when there was dramatic change in the structure of British Government, Shannon noted. It was a time when "gentlemen who had to be clerks were transformed into bureaucrats who needed to be gentlemen. . . . The self-contained departmental structures of the old unreformed service, with its systems of recruitment by patronage, promotion by seniority and emoluments by fees and perquisites, were transformed into a liberal profession geared to an ethic of merit and trained expertise dedicated to an ideal of the public interest," wrote Shannon in explanation of Pellew's topic.

Pellew told *CA:* "For the past ten years, my interest has lain in the nineteenth-century British Civil Service in the context of wider social and economic developments arising out of the 'industrial revolution.' My particular field has been the Home Office and its wide remit of responsibilities. One of its particular responsibilities has been aliens control; it has also inspired me to look at other institutions, hence my recent and future interests for research and writing."

BIOGRAPHICAL/CRITICAL SOURCES: Times Literary Supplement, July 30, 1982.

* * *

PELSHE, Arvid Yanovich   1899-1983

OBITUARY NOTICE: Born February 7, 1899, near Riga, Kurland, Russia (now U.S.S.R.); died of lung cancer, May 29, 1983. Soviet government official, politician, and author of works on the history of the Communist party in the Soviet Union and the history of the revolutionary movement in Latvia. The oldest member of the ruling Soviet Politburo, which he joined in 1966, Pelshe played a major role in the Russian Revolution of 1917. He was also the only man in leadership who had served in the Communist party before the revolution and who knew Vladimir Ilich Lenin. Before acquiring his position on the Politburo, Pelshe worked as a secret policeman and political commissar. His books include *The Task of the Intelligentsia in the Struggle Against Latvian Nationalism* and *The Triumph of Leninist-Stalinist National Policy.* Obituaries and other sources: *Who's Who in the Socialist Countries,* K. G. Saur, 1978; *Who's Who in the World,* 5th edition, Marquis, 1980; *The International Who's Who,* 46th edition, Europa, 1982; *Washington Post,* May 31, 1983; *London Times,* May 31, 1983; *Chicago Tribune,* June 1, 1983; *Newsweek,* June 13, 1983; *Time,* June 13, 1983.

* * *

PEPITONE, Joe   1940-
(Joseph Anthony Pepitone)

BRIEF ENTRY: Born October 9, 1940, in Brooklyn, N.Y. American professional baseball player and author. During the 1960's Pepitone played at first base and in the outfield for the New York Yankees. Known for his prowess at the plate, the athlete hit more than two hundred home runs during the first ten years of his career. Personal problems began to affect Pepitone's performance, and in 1969 he was traded to the Houston

Astros. The next year he joined the Chicago Cubs, where his hitting became more consistent. Pepitone also ventured into business, opening a men's fashion salon in Brooklyn and a bar in Chicago. He wrote *Joe, You Coulda Made Us Proud* (Playboy Press, 1975). *Biographical/critical sources: Current Biography*, Wilson, 1973; *New York Times Book Review*, November 9, 1975.

* * *

PEPITONE, Joseph Anthony
  See PEPITONE, Joe

* * *

PERETZ, Isaac Loeb   1851(?)-1915
  (Yitzkhok Leibush Peretz)

BRIEF ENTRY: Born in 1851 (some sources say 1852) in Zamosc, Poland; died of a heart attack, April 3, 1915. Polish lawyer, poet, playwright, and author of fiction. Peretz, a Polish Jew, practiced law for ten years until his interest in Jewish social problems prompted authorities to revoke his license. He then turned his attention to pursuing a literary career, at first writing in Hebrew and later, to serve the masses of uneducated Jews, in Yiddish. Peretz contributed greatly to the growing Yiddish literary movement with his poetry and short stories, a selection of which comprises his first published book, *Familiar Pictures* (1890). He was also a major force in the development of the Jewish theatre, infusing mysticism and symbolism into his plays, *Die goldene Kaite* (title means "The Golden Chain" 1907), *Klezmer* (title means "The Band"; 1907), *Bonche Shveig* (title means "Bonche the Silent"; 1907), and *Der Hoiker* (title means "The Hunchback"; 1914). *Biographical/critical sources:* Maurice Samuel, *Prince of the Ghetto*, McClelland, 1948; *McGraw-Hill Encyclopedia of World Biography*, McGraw, 1973.

* * *

PERETZ, Yitzkhok Leibush
  See PERETZ, Isaac Loeb

* * *

PERINBANAYAGAM, Robert S(idharthan)   1934-

PERSONAL: Born February 14, 1934, in Rangoon, Burma; came to the United States in 1962; son of Saravanamuttu H. (a professor) and Amirtha (Singham) Perinbanayagam. *Education:* University of Ceylon, B.A., 1959; University of Minnesota, M.A., 1964, Ph.D., 1967. *Politics:* "Humanist." *Religion:* "Humanist." *Home:* 321 East 66th St., New York, N.Y. 10021. *Office:* Department of Sociology, Hunter College of the City University of New York, 695 Park Ave., New York, N.Y. 10021.

CAREER: University of Missouri, Columbia, instructor, 1966-67, assistant professor of sociological theory and collective behavior, 1967-70; New School for Social Research, New York City, assistant professor of sociology, 1970-72; Hunter College of the City University of New York, New York City, assistant professor, 1972-76, associate professor of social theory and social psychology, 1977—. *Member:* American Sociological Association, American Association for Asian Studies, Society for the Study of Symbolic Interaction.

WRITINGS: (Contributor) G. P. Stone and Harvey A. Farberman, editors, *Social Psychology Through Symbolic Interaction*,

Wiley, 1981; (contributor) Adrian Furnham and Michael Argyle, editors, *The Psychology of the Social Situation*, Pergamon, 1981; *The Karmic Theater: Self, Society, and Astrology in Jaffna*, University of Massachusetts Press, 1982; *Language, Self, and Action*, Southern Illinois University Press, in press.

WORK IN PROGRESS: Everyday Therapeutics, publication expected in 1984.

SIDELIGHTS: Perinbanayagam reported that his goal is to "discover and report the sources of meaning and significance in everyday life."

* * *

PERLMUTTER, Ruth Ann   1924-

PERSONAL: Born February 9, 1924, in New York, N.Y.; daughter of Harry (a merchant) and Sarah (a merchant; maiden name, Altman) Osofsky; married Nathan Perlmutter (national director of Anti-Defamation League), April 2, 1943; children: Dean, Nina. *Education:* University of Denver, B.A., 1952; also attended Brooklyn College of the City University of New York, Wayne State University, and New School for Social Research. *Politics:* "Eclectic." *Religion:* Jewish. *Home:* 1 Gracie Ter., New York, N.Y. 10028. *Agent:* Toni Mendez, Inc., 140 East 56th St., New York, N.Y. 10022.

CAREER: Director of Women's Division of Florida Bonds for Israel, 1958-59; University of Miami, Coral Gables, Fla., lecturer in sociology, 1959-60; director of New York City Personal Aides to Home-Bound (P.A.T.H.) Program, 1964; Model Cities Elderly Services Program, Cambridge, Mass., director, 1971-72; Workmen's Circle Social Services Department, New York, N.Y., director, 1974-76; writer. Owner and breeder of horses. Public speaker; community consultant.

WRITINGS: (With husband, Nathan Perlmutter) *The Real Anti-Semitism in America*, Arbor House, 1982. Contributor to magazines and newspapers, including *Call* and *New Leader*.

SIDELIGHTS: The Real Anti-Semitism in America is an examination by Perlmutter and her husband Nathan, national director of B'nai B'rith's Anti-Defamation League, into what they felt to be a growing trend during the 1970's and into the 1980's toward a re-emergence of anti-Semitism, veiled in the guise of anti-Zionism. They cite as the beginning of this latest round of anti-Semitism the Arab-Israeli Six-Day War of 1967. The Soviets, they claim, began instigating anti-Jewish feelings among their Third World allies to gain favor with Arab nations in an attempt to extend their sphere of influence to the Middle East.

The results of this Soviet-backed ploy, the authors contend, resulted in the revival of prejudices that had lain dormant since World War II in many countries outside of the Arab world, including the United States. The authors compared a 1981 public opinion poll on feelings towards Jews with one conducted in 1964 and noted that among former Jewish allies in the civil rights days of 1964, most notably blacks, white liberals, and liberal Protestant churches, anti-Semitism had grown. By contrast, Jews in 1981 discovered new support from white conservatives and Christian fundamentalists.

According to *Commentary* reviewer Lucy S. Dawidowicz, the American news media, whose views are considerably to the left of the general public according to public opinion polls, and the United Nations, which in 1975 passed a resolution equating Zionism with racism, have also contributed to the rise of anti-Semitism in the United States through their repeated and biased attacks on Israel. The resultant anti-Israeli sentiment, the Perlmutters conclude, then easily spills over onto all Jews regardless of their nationality. The authors expressed little concern over the activities of such hate groups as the Ku Klux Klan and the neo-Nazis, whose appeal is small and generally rejected. They also dismissed the increase of vandalism against Jews by suburban, middle-class teenagers, noting that these cases almost never involve organized political motivation.

Dawidowicz termed *The Real Anti-Semitism in America* "an indispensable work for anyone who cares not only about the security of Jews but also about the many faces that America shows to the world." (She also noted that the book is not an official policy statement of the Anti-Defamation League.) Ellen Willis, in a *New York Times Book Review* critique, opined that the Perlmutters were pointing fingers at the wrong culprits, choosing instead to blame "oil-thirsty capitalists" for the rise in anti-Semitism. *New Leader* reviewer Stephen J. Whitfield disagreed with Willis's assessment, and expressed the opinion that "Nathan and Ruth Ann Perlmutter have addressed the antinomy facing American Jews realistically, and with little recourse to sentimental liberal pieties."

Ruth Ann Perlmutter told *CA:* "The thesis of our book is that in the hardball game of anti-Semitism in the 1980's, anti-Zionism has become the handy tool of the more lethal, less obvious anti-Semites of both the Right and the Left. Diplomats who would never burn a cross on the lawn of a Jewish home repeat lies daily in their United Nations palace on the East River about Jews and Israel. Their 'inspiration' to anti-Semitic violence is the lethal poison to be fought and feared."

AVOCATIONAL INTERESTS: Art, singing, travel.

BIOGRAPHICAL/CRITICAL SOURCES: Sports Illustrated, May, 1977; *Commentary,* October, 1982; *New York Times Book Review,* October 3, 1982; *New Leader,* October 4, 1982.

* * *

PERRY, Troy D(eroy) 1940-

BRIEF ENTRY: Born July 27, 1940, in Tallahassee, Fla. American minister and author. An ordained minister of the Metropolitan Community Church, Perry founded the Universal Fellowship of Metropolitan Community Churches in 1969. He became a member of the board of directors of the National Gay Task Force in 1977 and the Gay Rights National Lobby in 1981. Perry wrote *The Lord Is My Shepherd and He Knows I'm Gay: The Autobiography of the Reverend Troy D. Perry* (Nash Publishing, 1972) with Charles L. Lucas. He also was contributing editor of *Is Gay Good?: Ethics, Theology, and Homosexuality* (Westminster, 1971). *Address:* 5300 Santa Monica Blvd., No. 304, Los Angeles, Calif. 90029. *Biographical/critical sources: Washington Post Book World,* October 7, 1973; *Who's Who in the West,* 18th edition, Marquis, 1982.

* * *

PERTSCHUK, Michael 1933-

PERSONAL: Born January 12, 1933, in London, England; American citizen born abroad; son of David and Sarah (Baumander) Pertschuk; married Carleen Joyce Dooley, September, 1954 (divorced December, 1976); married Anna Phillips Sofaer (an artist), April, 1977; children: (first marriage) Mark, Amy. *Education:* Yale University, B.A., 1954, J.D., 1959. *Politics:* "Progressive Democrat." *Religion:* Jewish. *Home:* 3411 Rodman St. N.W., Washington, D.C. 20008. *Office:* Federal Trade

Commission, Pennsylvania Ave. at Sixth St. N.W., Washington, D.C. 20580.

CAREER: Law clerk to U.S. District Court Judge Gus O. Solomon, Portland, Ore., 1959; Hart, Rockwood, Davies, Biggs & Strayer (law firm), Portland, associate, 1960-62; legislative assistant to Senator Maurine B. Neuberger of Oregon, 1962-64; U.S. Senate Commerce Committee, Washington, D.C., trade relations counsel, 1964-68, chief counsel and staff director, 1968-77; Federal Trade Commission, Washington, D.C., chairman, 1977-81. Professorial lecturer at American University; adjunct professor at Georgetown University; lecturer at Brookings Institution. Public member of National Interagency Council on Smoking and Health, 1973-76; member of National Commission on Product Safety, 1967-70, and National Commission for Review of Antitrust Laws and Procedures; member of council of Administrative Conference of the United States. *Military service:* U.S. Army, 1954-56. *Member:* National Academy of Public Administration. *Awards, honors:* LL.D. from Yale University, 1959.

WRITINGS: Revolt Against Revolution: The Rise and Pause of the Consumer Movement, University of California Press, 1982.

SIDELIGHTS: In *Revolt Against Revolution,* former Federal Trade Commission (FTC) chairman Michael Pertschuk recounts some of the history of the U.S. consumer movement and discusses the movement's possible future. Prior to his affiliation with the FTC, Pertschuk served as chief counsel of the Senate Commerce Committee, where he worked "hand in glove with [Ralph] Nader creating much of the important regulatory legislation of the 1960s and '70s," noted Peter H. Schuck in the *Washington Post Book World.* In his laudatory review of *Revolt Against Revolution,* Schuck applauded Pertschuk for "writing with grace, humor and scrupulous honesty." According to Schuck, Pertschuk draws upon "his own experiences as a Washington insider and . . . maintains that corporate dominance of the social agenda is virtually inevitable." Schuck concludes by praising Pertschuk's "candid, moving epilogue," in which he "acknowledges, and then seeks to reconcile, the dogged contradictions between populism and politics, possibility and pessimism, that he has so engagingly laid bare."

BIOGRAPHICAL/CRITICAL SOURCES: Washington Post Book World, December 12, 1982.

* * *

PESKIN, Allan 1933-

BRIEF ENTRY: Born March 16, 1933, in Cumberland, Md. American historian, educator, and author. Peskin joined the faculty of Cleveland State University in 1964; he was appointed professor of American history in 1981. Peskin edited *North Into Freedom: The Autobiography of John Malvin, Free Negro, 1795-1880* (Press of Case Western Reserve University, 1966). His book *Garfield: A Biography* (Kent State University Press, 1978) won a Ohioana Book Award for biography in 1979. *Address:* Department of History, Cleveland State University, Cleveland, Ohio 44115. *Biographical/critical sources: New Republic,* May 27, 1978; *Virginia Quarterly Review,* autumn, 1978; *Times Literary Supplement,* November 24, 1978; *American Historical Review,* April, 1979.

* * *

PETERSON, Dale 1944-

PERSONAL: Born November 20, 1944, in Corning, N.Y.; son

of Paul G. (an engineer) and Hazel (a registered nurse; maiden name, Peterson) Peterson; married Wyn Kelley, June 26, 1979; children: Britt Kelley. *Education:* University of Rochester, B.A., 1967; Stanford University, M.A., 1969, Ph.D., 1977. *Residence:* Stanford, Calif. *Office:* 261 Hamilton, No. 211, Palo Alto, Calif. 94301.

CAREER: Veterans Administration Hospital, Menlo Park, Calif., psychiatric nursing attendant, 1969-71; Stanford University, Stanford, Calif., instructor in writing, 1977-78; ARS Construction, Palo Alto, Calif., carpenter, 1978-79; Rainbow Designs, Palo Alto, carpenter, 1979-80; full-time writer, 1980—.

WRITINGS: (Editor) *A Mad People's History of Madness,* University of Pittsburgh Press, 1982; *Big Things From Little Computers: A Layperson's Guide to Personal Computing,* Prentice-Hall, 1982; *Genesis II: Creation and Recreation With Computers,* Reston, 1983; (editor) *Intelligent Schoolhouse: Readings on Computers and Learning,* Reston; 1983; (with Bill Lucas, John MacMillan, and Richard Tabor) *The C Programming Handbook,* Prentice-Hall, in press; (with Don Inman and Ramon Zamora) *Color Computer LOGO,* Wiley, in press. Contributing editor, and author of monthly column "Greetings From Uncle Bert," in *Rainbow* magazine.

WORK IN PROGRESS: The Dolphins's Pearl, "a piece of written fiction embedded in a video game for the Apple and Atari home computers"; *The Secret Cat and Other Stories: Introductions to Computer Fun* (tentative title), five children's stories to introduce concepts in programming for microcomputers; a philosophical book about computers, completion expected in 1984.

SIDELIGHTS: Dale Peterson told *CA:* "I think of myself as a frustrated fiction writer. I wrote some short stories that I thought were pretty good, got tired of receiving rejection slips, then wrote a novel, thinking the publication of that would get stories published. I got tired of receiving rejection slips, so I put together *A Mad People's History of Madness,* thinking that the publication of a nonfiction work would help get the novel published. Meanwhile I supported myself by being a graduate student and then (having graduated) a carpenter.

"*A Mad People's History of Madness* is unique; it is the only history of psychiatry as told by mental patients. It covers five and a half centuries of psychiatry, from 1436 to 1976, is based upon selections from twenty-six mental patient autobiographies, but includes extensive background material on psychiatric history, which I wrote.

"I became interested in mental patient autobiographies during the two years that I worked as a psychiatric nursing assistant. In gathering material for the book, I went through indexes in most major libraries here and in England. I then read the material and selected the pieces I thought were most interesting and representative.

"The leap from a doctorate in literature to psychiatry, thence to carpentry and computers, may seem a little strange, but I believe there is a common thread (excepting carpentry, which was soup-in-the-pot activity). My psychiatry book was really the work of a literature person and humanist looking at psychiatry. Similarly with my book on computers. Generally I write about computers from a 'humanist' perspective—being less concerned about the nuts and bolts and more about the philosophical and human aspects of this technology.

"During the period of carpentry I had been writing children's stories (which I couldn't get published). Then one day I called up Prentice-Hall and told them they needed a book about computers written by someone (me) who knew nothing about the subject. That was my first computer book, *Big Things From Little Computers.* My second computer book, *Genesis II,* is about computers in the visual arts, music, writing, and games. It is a coffee-table book with lots of illustrations, including a color section containing computer-generated art.

"My plan is to earn enough money so that I can afford to take some time off and write fiction."

* * *

PETERSON, Levi S(avage) 1933-

PERSONAL: Born December 13, 1933, in Snowflake, Ariz.; son of Joseph (a teacher of English) and Lydia Jane (an elementary school teacher; maiden name, Savage) Peterson; married Althea Sand (a teacher of Spanish), August 31, 1958; children: Karrin. *Education:* Brigham Young University, B.A., 1958, M.A., 1960; University of Utah, Ph.D., 1965. *Politics:* Democrat. *Religion:* Church of Jesus Christ of Latter-day Saints (Mormons). *Home:* 1561 25th St., Ogden, Utah 84401. *Office:* Department of English, Weber State College, 3750 Harrison Blvd., Ogden, Utah 84408.

CAREER: Weber State College, Ogden, Utah, assistant professor, 1965-68, associate professor, 1968-72, professor of English, 1972—, chairman of department, 1970-73, director of honors program, 1973-82. President of Utah Trails Council, 1977-79. *Member:* Association for Mormon Letters (member of board of directors, 1978-82; president, 1981), Western Literature Association (member of executive council, 1973-75), Rocky Mountain Modern Language Association, Utah Academy of Sciences, Arts, and Letters (member of board of directors, 1973-81), Phi Kappa Phi, Kiwanis International. *Awards, honors:* First prize from Utah Art Council, 1978, for collection of stories "The Confessions of Augustine," published as *The Canyons of Grace;* first prize from Association for Mormon Letters, 1978, for stories "The Confessions of Augustine" and "Road to Damascus"; first prize from Center for the Study of Christian Values in Literature, 1981, for story "The Gift."

WRITINGS: The Canyons of Grace (stories), University of Illinois Press, 1982. Contributor to history and western American literature journals. Editor of *Encyclia: Journal of the Utah Academy of Sciences, Arts, and Letters,* 1977-81.

WORK IN PROGRESS: A novel set in the 1950's in the remote ranch country of south central Utah.

SIDELIGHTS: Peterson told *CA:* "I grew up in a Mormon village in northern Arizona. I was a Mormon missionary in Switzerland and Belgium from 1954 to 1957; as a result, I speak French. Intellectually I believe I am a humanist and a citizen of the world; emotionally I still live in the stern ambiance of a frontier Mormon town.

"One of my fictional purposes is to explore the penitential impulse in human beings. Although my characters, as Mormons with rural roots, are fundamental Christians, I hope to reveal universal preoccupations and themes through them. I hope, through a carefully modulated narrative voice, to avoid moralizing or preachment. I am not personally interested in doctrinal or ideological issues; rather I am interested in the tensions which arise among characters who rationalize their lives in doctrinal terms."

BIOGRAPHICAL/CRITICAL SOURCES: Chicago Tribune, February 6, 1983.

PETRIE, Catherine 1947-

PERSONAL: Born October 22, 1947, in Elkhorn, Wis.; daughter of Landon Ellery (in truck and car rentals) and Mary (Neuman) Petrie; married Keith Yurica (an accountant), June 24, 1982. *Education:* Attended Wheaton College, Wheaton, Ill., 1965-68; University of Wisconsin—Whitewater, B.S., 1969, M.S.E., 1972; graduate study at University of California, Los Angeles, 1981—. *Politics:* Republican. *Religion:* Christian. *Home:* Route 2, Petrie Rd., Lake Geneva, Wis. 53147.

CAREER: Reading Consultant in Pine Ridge, S.D., 1970-72, Edgewater, Colo., 1972-78, San Dimas, Calif., 1978-80, and Lake Geneva, Wis., 1980-81; Professional Tour Consultants, Inc., Lake Geneva, owner and director, 1981—. Co-sponsor of Food Day in Denver, Colo., 1978. *Member:* American Association of University Women (representative to the United Nations).

WRITINGS—For children; published by Childrens Press: *Hot Rod Harry*, 1982; *Sand Box Betty*, 1982; *Joshua James Likes Trucks*, 1982; *Seed*, 1983; *Night*, 1983; *Rain*, 1983.

SIDELIGHTS: In *Joshua James Likes Trucks* Petrie uses an eighteen-word vocabulary in summing up young Joshua's taste in trucks. *Hot Rod Harry* also has a limited vocabulary, at twenty-nine words, and *Sandbox Betty* relies on rhyme and repetition, telling its story in three-to-five-word sentences.

Petrie told *CA:* "I wrote beginning-to-read books for my nephew and niece who, at four and five years old, were ready to read but lacked appropriate reading materials for those initial efforts."

* * *

PFEFFER, Jeffrey 1946-

PERSONAL: Born July 23, 1946, in St. Louis, Mo.; son of Newton S. (a jeweler) and Shirlee (Krisman) Pfeffer. *Education:* Carnegie-Mellon University, B.S. (with distinction) and M.S. (with distinction), both 1968; Stanford University, Ph.D., 1972. *Home:* 2151 Greenways, Woodside, Calif. 94061. *Office:* Graduate School of Business, Stanford University, Stanford, Calif. 94305.

CAREER: Research Analysis Corp., McLean, Va., member of technical staff, 1968-69; University of Illinois, Urbana-Champaign, instructor, 1971-72, assistant professor of business administration, 1972-73; University of California, Berkeley, assistant professor, 1973-75, associate professor of business administration, 1975-79; Stanford University, Stanford, Calif., professor of business, 1979—. Thomas Henry Carroll-Ford Foundation Visiting Professor of Business Administration at Harvard University, 1981-82. *Member:* Academy of Management (chairperson of Organization and Management Theory Division, 1980-81), American Sociological Association (member of council, 1975-78), Phi Kappa Phi.

WRITINGS: Organizational Design, AHM Publishing, 1978; (with G. R. Salancik) *The External Control of Organizations: A Resource Dependence Perspective*, Harper, 1978; *Power in Organizations*, Pitman, 1981; *Organizations and Organization Theory*, Pitman, 1982.

Contributor: Patrick E. Connor, editor, *Dimensions in Modern Management*, Houghton, 1974; *Energy Industry Investigation*, Part I: *Joint Ventures*, U.S. Government Printing Office, 1976;

Barry M. Staw, editor, *Psychological Foundations of Organizational Behavior*, Goodyear Publishing, 1977; Paul S. Goodman, Johannes M. Pennings, and other editors, *New Perspectives on Organizational Effectiveness*, Jossey-Bass, 1977; M. W. Meyer and other editors, *Environments and Organizations*, Jossey-Bass, 1978; Morgan McCall and Michael Lombardo, editors, *Leadership: Where Else Can We Go?*, Duke University Press, 1978; Mary Zey-Farrell, editor, *Readings on Dimensions of Organizations*, Goodyear Publishing, 1979; Richard M. Steers and Lyman W. Porter, editors, *Motivation and Work Behavior*, 2nd edition, McGraw, 1979.

Contributor: Daniel Katz, R. L. Kahn, and J. S. Adams, editors, *The Study of Organizations*, Jossey-Bass, 1980; A. D. Szilagyi and M. J. Wallace, editors, *Readings in Organizational Behavior and Performance*, 2nd edition, Goodyear Publishing, 1980; L. L. Cummings and R. B. Dunham, editors, *Introduction to Organizational Behavior*, Irwin, 1980; G. T. Martin and M. N. Zald, editors, *Social Welfare in Society*, Columbia University Press, 1981; Cummings and B. M. Staw, editors, *Research in Organizational Behavior*, Jai Press, Volume III, 1981, Volume V, 1983; S. B. Kiesler, J. N. Morgan, and V. K. Oppenheimer, editors, *Aging: Social Change*, Academic Press, 1981; Gardner Lindzey and Elliot Aronson, editors, *Handbook of Social Psychology*, Volume I, 3rd edition, Addison-Wesley, 1983.

Contributor of more than sixty articles and reviews to business journals. Associate editor of *American Sociological Review*, 1980-83; member of editorial board of *Administrative Science Quarterly*, 1975-77, 1980—, and *Academy of Management Journal*, 1976-78; member of board of editors of *Industrial Relations*, 1975—; advisory editor of *Sociological Quarterly*, 1976-78.

* * *

PHELPS, Ashton 1913-1983

OBITUARY NOTICE: Born December 30, 1913, in New Orleans, La.; died March 21, 1983. Publisher. Phelps was a lawyer for thirty years before starting a career as a newspaper publisher. From 1967 to 1979 Phelps served as president and publisher of the Times-Picayune Publishing Corporation. He was also a member of the board of directors of the American Newspaper Publishers Association. Obituaries and other sources: *Who's Who in the South and Southwest*, 18th edition, Marquis, 1982; *New York Times*, March 22, 1983.

* * *

PHILLIPS-JONES, Linda 1943-

PERSONAL: Born March 3, 1943, in South Bend, Ind.; daughter of Robert M. (a civil servant and chemical analyst) and Priscilla (an executive secretary; maiden name, Tancy) Phillips; married G. Brian Jones (a psychologist and researcher), February 16, 1980; children: (stepdaughters) Laurie, Tracy. *Education:* University of Nevada, B.S., 1964; Stanford University, A.M., 1965; University of California, Los Angeles, Ph.D., 1977. *Religion:* Christian. *Residence:* Los Gatos, Calif. *Office:* American Institutes for Research, P.O. Box 1113, Palo Alto, Calif. 94302.

CAREER: International Training Consultants, Saigon, Vietnam, trainer and curriculum specialist, 1966-71; private career and personal development consultant, 1972—. Research scientist for American Institutes for Research, 1979—; personal counselor at Coalition of Counseling Centers (Christian organization), 1981—. Member of National Speakers Team, Palo Alto; member of board of directors of San Jose's Indochinese Resettlement and Cultural Center. *Member:* American Psychological Association, American Society for Training and Development, American Personnel and Guidance Association, National Vocational Guidance Association, Association for Religious and Values Issues in Counseling.

WRITINGS: (With husband, G. Brian Jones, and H. N. Drier) *Developing Competencies for Training Career Guidance Personnel* (monograph), American Vocational Association and National Vocational Guidance Association, 1981; *Mentors and Proteges: How to Establish, Strengthen, and Get the Most From a Mentor-Protege Relationship,* Arbor House, 1982. Contributor to magazines, including *Glamour, New Woman, Woman,* and *Business WOMAN.* Editor of *Christian Counselor.*

WORK IN PROGRESS: Continuing research on mentoring relationships, structured mentoring programs, "negative mentoring," stress management, building of self-esteem, marriage improvement, and effective counseling strategies.

SIDELIGHTS: Linda Phillips-Jones wrote: "Unlike many of my colleagues in research and psychology, I prefer to write for the layperson. I like to translate what experts find into everyday strategies that will help my readers face Monday morning at the office or Friday night dinner with a new friend.

"A *Library Journal* review of *Mentors and Proteges* recommended the book for public libraries, stating that 'the case examples and step-by-step approach appear to make what is often an important factor in career success a more rational and accessible pursuit.'

"That is exactly what I intended. I approached this book from the point of view of the prospective protege, who is very much like the client I see in counseling. What does he or she need to feel and know to tackle the somewhat mysterious task of finding the right mentor—not only for a career, but for any important area of life? What do mentors know that proteges don't? Assuming that proteges are in a somewhat vulnerable position to start with, what can I give them that will provide a detour around some errors and pain and save time in the process?

"Not everyone has favored my approach. One reviewer called the book 'misleading' and took me to task for thinking that 'programming' of mentor-protege relationships is possible.

"In the personal counseling I do, mostly with women who range in age from fifteen through their fifties, I find that once feelings are explored and shared, I am asked to be more specific in offering how-to's, and my clients do better. They appreciate steps, examples, demonstrations, even sample 'scripts' to use in their interpersonal problem solving. Of course, they modify these to fit their own language, personalitites, and situations, but the specifics give them a concrete 'rough draft' with which to begin. We 'program' together. I attempt to carry this philosophy over into my writing.

"As I write this, I am about to celebrate my fortieth birthday, a major milestone for me. My forty years have been rich with travel and change (the years in Vietnam, numerous vacation journeys, thirty-seven residences since I was a child), unusual work, some successes, and intriguing, loving friends. The glue that has held this together has been my Christian faith. The next fifty years promise to be just as exciting and full of change.

I intend to be a better mentor to many—through my personal contacts and through the words I write."

BIOGRAPHICAL/CRITICAL SOURCES: Calgary Herald, September 9, 1982; *Kansas City Times,* September 14, 1982; *Los Angeles Times,* December 17, 1982; *Executive Educator,* April, 1983.

* * *

PICKFORD, Cedric Edward   1926-1983

OBITUARY NOTICE—See index for *CA* sketch: Born June 23, 1926, in Stockport, Cheshire, England; died suddenly on May 3, 1983. Educator and author. Pickford was a scholar in the fields of Arthurian studies and medieval drama. He had been a professor of medieval French literature at the University of Hull. He had served the university in various capacities since 1950, assuming his professorial duties in 1965. Pickford's books include *Alixandre l'Orphelin: A Prose Tale of the Fifteenth Century, Arthurian Literature in the Middle Ages, The Song of Songs: A Twelfth-Century French Version,* and *The Arthurian Bibliography,* which he compiled with R. W. Last. Obituaries and other sources: *London Times,* May 12, 1983.

* * *

PIKE, Margaret (Prudence) Lyford
    See LYFORD-PIKE, Margaret (Prudence)

* * *

PILKINGTON, Walter   ?-1983

OBITUARY NOTICE: Died January 2, 1983. Librarian and author of *Hamilton College, 1812-1962.* A friend of Ezra Pound and trustee of the Pound literary estate, Pilkington helped assemble the Ezra Pound Collection at Hamilton College. Pilkington was also a librarian emeritus at the school. Obituaries and other sources: *Library Journal,* March 1, 1983.

* * *

PINCHOT, David   1914(?)-1983

OBITUARY NOTICE: Born c. 1914; died April 25, 1983, in Park Ridge, Ill. Publisher. Pinchot, who owned and operated Davco Publishers, Incorporated, edited and helped develop history textbooks and filmstrips for children who are slow to learn. The texts, which include *History of Your America, History of Your World,* and *People Who Made America,* were distributed to schools in almost every state. Pinchot was also associated with the U.S. History Society. Obituaries and other sources: *Chicago Tribune,* April 27, 1983.

* * *

PISOR, Robert (Louis)   1939-

PERSONAL: Surname rhymes with "wiser"; born December 7, 1939, in Bellefontaine, Ohio; son of Charles Trudeau (in business) and Violet (an elementary school teacher; maiden name, Peoples) Pisor; married Ellen Waters (a dance company manager), June 16, 1962; children: David Charles, Karl Trudeau. *Education:* College of Wooster, B.A., 1961; Columbia University, M.S., 1963. *Home:* 17555 Parkside, Detroit, Mich. 48221. *Agent:* Philip G. Spitzer, 111-25 76th Ave., Forest Hills, N.Y. 11375. *Office:* WDIV-TV, 550 West Lafayette, Detroit, Mich. 48231.

CAREER: WILE-AM, Cambridge, Ohio, announcer, 1960; WWST-AM-FM, Wooster, Ohio, announcer, 1961; WNBC-TV, New York City, news writer, 1962; WNDT-TV, New York City, news writer, 1962; *Detroit News,* Detroit, Mich., politics writer, 1963-74; press secretary to Detroit Mayor Coleman A. Young, 1975-77; *Monthly Detroit* (magazine), Detroit, editor, 1980; WDIV-TV, Detroit, newspaper critic and political analyst, 1981—. *Member:* Detroit Press Club, Sigma Delta Chi. *Awards, honors:* David Sarnoff Fellowship from RCA Corp., 1962; Pulitzer Traveling Fellowship from Columbia University, 1963; O'Leary Award from University of Michigan, 1973, for excellence in political writing; Emmy Award from Detroit chapter of Academy of Television Arts and Sciences, 1981, for writing series on Detroit newspaper wars; prize for nonfiction from Society of Midland Authors, 1982, for *The End of the Line.*

WRITINGS: The End of the Line: The Siege of Khe Sanh (nonfiction), Norton, 1982.

SIDELIGHTS: Robert Pisor spent two years in Vietnam, reporting on the war for the *Detroit News.* His book, *The End of the Line,* centers on the 1968 siege of Khe Sanh, a three-month-long battle in South Vietnam that transfixed the U.S. military command on the eve of the historic Tet Offensive. Pisor explores the strategies, politics, and misdirections that led up to the siege, profiles the opposing military commanders, and details the actions of American General William Westmoreland, who, the author declares, "wanted this battle."

Pisor's book received generally favorable reviews from critics, several of whom found that his chronicle of Khe Sanh had much to say about the Vietnam War in its entirety. "Pisor has done more than unravel and describe the complexities of the siege of Khe Sanh," declared Otto J. Scott in the *Los Angeles Times.* "He has . . . managed to clarify the overall pattern of the war in Vietnam." "To make this clear is a marvelous achievement for a historian," concluded Scott, "but Pisor has exceeded even that." Gene Lyons echoed this opinion in *Newsweek,* where he claimed that *The End of the Line* demonstrates how the siege of Khe Sanh "symbolizes the entire war in miniature." "Anybody attracted to the again fashionable delusion that the United States might have 'won' in Vietnam," Lyons added, "ought to read and meditate upon 'The End of the Line.'" He reiterated that, in Pisor's work, "all the lessons are here in concise and readable form." Harry G. Summers, Jr., found occasional fault with Pisor's handling of dialogue in what he deemed "an otherwise excellent book." "For those who have not yet begun . . . a reexamination of the Vietnam conflict," the critic suggested in the *New Republic,* "Robert Pisor's *The End of the Line* is a good place to start."

Writing in *Best Sellers,* Gregory F. Pierce hailed *The End of the Line,* noting that in his examination of Khe Sanh "Pisor writes a beautiful mix of personal, political, and military history." William J. Teague, in the *Dallas Morning News,* lauded the book as "a tightly written, penetrating analysis . . . of what was the greatest battle of wits and strategy in the war."

Pisor told *CA:* "If this study of a single battle in a larger war can help Americans—especially that generation that fought in World War II—begin to understand some of the strange truths of Vietnam, I will be pleased indeed. Only by looking back at this sad chapter in our history can we hope to discern the path and avoid the pitfalls that lie ahead."

BIOGRAPHICAL/CRITICAL SOURCES: New Republic, July 12, 1982; *Best Sellers,* August, 1982; *Washington Post Book World,* August 22, 1982; *Los Angeles Times,* August 25, 1982; *Newsweek,* August 30, 1982; *Dallas Morning News,* October 31, 1982.

*   *   *

PLATT, D(esmond) C(hristopher St.) M(artin)   1934-

BRIEF ENTRY: Born in 1934 in Canton, China. British educator and author. Platt was a fellow of Queens' College, Cambridge, and St. Antony's College, Oxford. He also served as chairman of the Society for Latin American Studies from 1973 to 1975. Platt wrote *Finance, Trade, and Politics in British Foreign Policy, 1815-1914* (Clarendon Press, 1968), *The Cinderella Service: British Consuls Since 1825* (Archon Books, 1971), and *Latin America and British Trade, 1806-1914* (A. & C. Black, 1972). He edited *Business Imperialism, 1840-1930: An Inquiry Based on British Experience in Latin America* (Clarendon Press, 1977). *Address:* Brill House, Brill, Aylesbury, Buckinghamshire, England. *Biographical/critical sources: American Historical Review,* June, 1972, October, 1978; *Times Literary Supplement,* January 21, 1972, December 22, 1972.

*   *   *

PLOMMER, (William) Hugh   ?-1983

OBITUARY NOTICE: Died March 1, 1983. Lecturer and author of various scholarly works. Plommer became a lecturer on Greek and Roman architecture at Cambridge University in 1954 and wrote books on architecture, including *The Line of Duty* and a revision of the first volume of *Simpson's History of Architectural Development.* He also published a collection of poems and a verse satire of university life. Obituaries and other sources: *London Times,* March 12, 1983.

*   *   *

PLUMPTRE, Arthur Fitzwalter Wynne   1907-1977

PERSONAL: Born June 5, 1907, in Montreal, Quebec, Canada; died June, 1977; son of Henry Pemberton and Adelaide Mary Wynne (Willson) Plumptre; married Beryl Alyce Rouch, May 21, 1938; children: Judith, Timothy. *Education:* University of Toronto, B.A., 1928; King's College, Cambridge, M.A., 1936.

CAREER: University of Toronto, Toronto, Ontario, began as lecturer, became assistant professor of political economy, 1930-41; Canadian Legation, Washington, D.C., financial attache, 1942-45; Wartime Prices and Trade Board, Ottawa, Ontario, secretary, 1945-47; *Saturday Night,* Toronto, associate editor, 1947-49; Department of External Affairs, Ottawa, head of Economic Division, 1949-52, minister and deputy head of Canadian delegation to North Atlantic Treaty Organization Conference and Organization for European Economic Cooperation in Paris, France, 1952-54; Department of Finance, Ottawa, director of International Economic Relations Division, 1954, assistant deputy minister of finance, 1955-65; International Bank for Reconstruction and Development, executive director for Canada, Ireland, and Jamaica, 1962-65; University of Toronto, professor of political economy and principal of Scarborough College, 1965-72. Visiting professor at Carleton University. Assistant secretary of Royal Commission on Banking and Currency in Canada, 1933; Washington representative of Canada's Wartime Prices and Trade Board, 1942-45; executive director of International Monetary Fund for Canada, Ireland, and Jamaica, 1962-65. Member of board of governors of International Development Research Centre, 1970, and special adviser to president. *Awards, honors:* Commander of Order of the British Empire.

WRITINGS: Central Banking in the British Dominions, University of Toronto Press, 1940; *Mobilizing Canada's Resources for War,* Macmillan of Canada, 1941; *The Socio-Economic Environment of Scarborough College: The Sixties,* [West Hill, Ontario, Canada], 1972; *Three Decades of Decision: Canada and the World Monetary System, 1944-75,* McClelland & Stewart, 1977.*

(Date of death provided by wife, Beryl Plumptre.)

* * *

POKROVSKY, Boris Aleksandrovich 1912-

BRIEF ENTRY: Born January 23, 1912, in Moscow, Russia (now U.S.S.R.). Soviet producer of operas and ballets and author. Pokrovsky was in charge of productions at Moscow's Gorki Theatre from 1934 to 1943 and at the Bolshoi Theatre, where he was named chief producer in 1952. He organized the Moscow Chamber Theatre and is a professor at Lunacharsky Institute. Pokrovsky's awards include an Order of Lenin, Bulgaria's Order of Kirill and Mifodiy, and at least four state prizes from the U.S.S.R. He co-authored *The Bolshoi: Opera and Ballet at the Greatest Theater in Russia* (Morrow, 1979). *Address:* Flat 34, Gorki St., 15 Moscow, U.S.S.R.; and Bolshoi Theatre, 1 Ploshchad Sverlova, Moscow, U.S.S.R. *Biographical/critical sources: New York Times Book Review,* January 27, 1980.

* * *

POLKINGHARN, Anne T(oogood) 1937-

PERSONAL: Born July 9, 1937, in Ottawa, Ill.; daughter of Loren S. and Mildred B. Toogood; married Donald L. Polkingharn; children: Julie, Karen. *Education:* University of Iowa, B.A., 1959; University of Hawaii, M.A., 1968. *Home:* 339 St. Ann's Dr., Laguna Beach, Calif. 92651. *Office:* Harbor Day School, 3443 Pacific View Dr., Corona del Mar, Calif. 92625.

CAREER: University of California, Irvine, subject cataloger at library, 1968; Harbor Day School, Corona del Mar, Calif., librarian, 1969—. Conducts workshops. *Member:* International Reading Association, California Reading Association, California Media and Library Educators. *Awards, honors:* Grant from National Association of Independent Schools, 1980.

WRITINGS: (With Catherine Toohey) *Creative Ideas From Library Shelves,* Libraries Unlimited, 1983.

SIDELIGHTS: Polkingharn told *CA:* "I have given children's literature workshops and ideas to teachers' in-service groups for the past eight years. Our ideas bring teachers and librarians together in a cooperative effort, using children's literature to extend children's thinking, comprehension, and imagination. The activities we provide are original and allow children to respond to the books presented.

"In schools we often analyze, dissect, examine, and divide material. In our activities we try to connect, unite, and integrate the experiences of literature with the child's experiences, using reading skills, writing skills, comprehension skills, and imagination."

POLSKY, Abe 1935-

PERSONAL: Born August 13, 1935, in Philadelphia, Pa.; son of Max (a yard goods retailer) and Helen (Matkes) Polsky; married Merrily Dixon (a researcher), May 5, 1974; children: Matthew. *Education:* University of California, Los Angeles, B.A., 1957. *Residence:* Santa Barbara, Calif. *Agent:* Lettie Lee, Ann Elmo Agency, 60 East 42nd St., New York, N.Y. 10017.

CAREER: Worked as a social worker in Los Angeles, Calif., 1965-68; scriptwriter for television and films, 1968-77; playwright, 1979—. Teacher of dramatic writing, University of California, Santa Barbara, 1980-81, and Santa Barbara City College, 1981-83. *Member:* Writers Guild of America, Dramatists Guild, Ensemble Repertory Theatre (Santa Barbara).

WRITINGS: Devour the Snow (two-act play; first staged reading in Hollywood at Anta West Theatre, November, 1974; produced off-Broadway at Hudson Guild Theatre, May 2, 1979; produced on Broadway at Golden Theatre, November 7, 1979), Dramatists Play Service, 1980; "The Baby" (screenplay), first produced November, 1971. Also author of screenplays "The Firebrand"/"Mother Jones," 1980, "Hocus Pocus," 1981, and "G-MAN," 1982, as yet neither published nor produced. Author of scripts for television series, including "Kung Fu" and "Bonanza."

WORK IN PROGRESS: "Shenanigans," a comedy in seven scenes; several screenplays "as yet untitled and in various stages of development."

SIDELIGHTS: Polsky's courtroom drama, "Devour the Snow," is based on the true story of the Donner Party, a pioneer band that became snowbound in California's Sierra Nevada mountains during the winter of 1846-47. The survivors of the group resorted to cannibalism, but, as Walter Kerr noted in the *New York Times,* "it is very, very clear that the real victims are the survivors." One of the victimized survivors of that winter was Lewis Keseberg, a German immigrant and outsider to the group. Once back in civilization rumors spread that Keseberg had not only engaged in cannibalism, but that he had deliberately murdered children for food, plundered graves, and raped and slaughtered Tamsen Donner, wife of leader George Donner. Infuriated by these attacks on his honor, Keseberg brought a suit for slander against his accusers.

"Devour the Snow" recreates the slander trial as it may have occurred, using the actual verdict and the names of some of the participants. The trial "is a serious attempt to deal not only with cannibalism but also with prejudice, . . . collaborative guilt and heroism under pressure," Mel Gussow observed in a *New York Times* review. He added: "From the author's point of view, the truth of the episode remains buried under the snow in the mountains. What we see are strands of conscience, greed and madness, as revealed by an unusual roster of characters who demonstrate the anguish of their horrible experience."

Also writing in the *New York Times,* Nan Robertson described how the testimony Polsky created for the play "underscores the horror." "Relentlessly and with relish, [a witness] describes the sawed-off limbs and broken skulls of the corpses left in the snow; goes on to even gorier details, and all the while, gnaws on a beef bone that is his courtroom lunch." "For some reviewers," Robertson observed, "the sheer rawness of the material was almost too much." But, according to Kerr, "raw emotion is the play's natural element, and it continues to assert a power that bodes well for the playwright's future." "There's a gift at work here," Kerr concluded, and

Time reviewer T. E. Kalem agreed, writing that Polsky "is a welcome addition to the select company of playwriting naturals."

Polsky told *CA:* "The stimulation of travel abroad has been of much value. The experience of teaching has enriched me as a writer and human being. I very much enjoy living and working in Santa Barbara. Being essentially a private sort of individual, I prefer to leave it at that."

BIOGRAPHICAL/CRITICAL SOURCES: New York Times, May 14, 1979, October 31, 1979, November 8, 1979, June 20, 1980; *Time,* May 21, 1979; *New Yorker,* May 28, 1979, November 19, 1979.

* * *

POND, L. W.
   See CHUTE, Robert M.

* * *

PONTING, Kenneth   1913-1983

OBITUARY NOTICE: Born January, 1913, in Trowbridge, England; died May 12, 1983, in Spain. Historian and author of works about the textile industry. Ponting worked in the mill of Samuel Salter Limited as a dyer, designer, and managing director before becoming director of the Pasold Research Fund, which had been set up to promote work on the history of textiles. Ponting ran the Fund for fifteen years, also lecturing and traveling widely. His books include *Leonardo Da Vinci's Drawings of Textile Machines, History of the West of England Cloth Industry,* and *The Wool Trade Past and Present.* Obituaries and other sources: *London Times,* May 21, 1983.

* * *

POOLE, Ernest   1880-1950

BRIEF ENTRY: Born January 23, 1880, in Chicago, Ill.; died of pneumonia, January 10, 1950, in Franconia, N.H. American journalist, playwright, and novelist. In 1902 Poole moved to New York City, where he lived in the University Settlement House and tried his hand at writing short stories. After a number of unsuccessful attempts, the author turned to journalism. Poole's muckraking articles brought him recognition, prompted reforms in tenement conditions and child labor laws, and spurred an antituberculosis campaign. The journalist's subsequent projects included reporting on the Chicago stockyard strike of 1904 and on the Russian rebellion of 1905. In 1906 Poole turned to fiction again, this time writing plays and novels. Though the author's works for the stage proved unsuccessful, his novels pleased both critics and the public. Poole's works include *The Harbor* (1915), the Pulitzer Prize-winning *His Family* (1917), *The Village: Russian Impressions* (1918), and *The Dark People: Russia's Crisis* (1918). In 1940 the author produced *The Bridge: My Own Story,* an autobiography. *Biographical/critical sources: Twentieth-Century Authors: A Biographical Dictionary of Modern Literature,* H. W. Wilson, 1942, 1st supplement, 1955; *Who Was Who in America,* Volume II: *1943-1950,* Marquis, 1963; *American Novelists of Today,* Greenwood Press, 1976; *Dictionary of Literary Biography,* Volume 9: *American Novelists, 1910-1945,* Gale, 1981.

* * *

POPKIN, Zelda F.   1898-1983

OBITUARY NOTICE—See index for *CA* sketch: Born July 5,

1898, in Brooklyn, N.Y.; died of a heart attack, May 25, 1983, in Silver Spring, Md. Journalist, public relations executive, and author. Popkin was the *Wilkes-Barre Times Leader's* first female general assignment reporter. She left her position to return to school. She then became her husband's partner in a public relations firm, working with him from 1919 until his death in 1943. Popkin later joined various organizations in an administrative capacity. Her early novels were detective thrillers such as *Death Wears a White Gardenia* and *Murder in the Midst,* while her later works concern Judaism. Two of her novels, *Quiet Street* and *Death of Innocence,* were adapted into television productions. Her other books include *Open Every Door, Herman Had Two Daughters,* and *Dear Once.* Obituaries and other sources: *New York Times,* May 27, 1983; *London Times,* May 31, 1983.

* * *

POWERS, Francis Gary   1929-1977

OBITUARY NOTICE: Born August 17, 1929, in Jenkins, Ky.; died in a helicopter crash, August 1, 1977, in Encino, Calif. Aviator and author. Powers is best remembered as the U.S. pilot whose military reconnaisance plane was shot down over the Soviet Union in 1960, whereupon he was captured and exchanged in 1962 for the Russian spy Rudolf Abel. Powers was piloting a helicopter as a Los Angeles television reporter when the vehicle apparently ran out of fuel and crashed. He was the co-author with Curt Gentry of *Operation Overflight: The U-2 Pilot Tells His Story for the First Time.* Obituaries and other sources: *New York Times,* June 16, 1970, August 2, 1977; *Who Did What,* Crown, 1974; *Political Profiles: The Kennedy Years,* Facts on File, 1976; *Newsweek,* August 15, 1977; *World Almanac Book of Who,* World Almanac Publications, 1980.

* * *

PRAIN, Ronald (Lindsay)   1907-

PERSONAL: Born September 3, 1907, in Iquiqui, Chile; son of Arthur Lindsay and Amy Gertrude (Watson) Prain; married Esther Pansy Brownrigg, April 23, 1938; children: Graham Lindsay, Angus Lindsay. *Education:* Attended Cheltenham College. *Home:* Waverley, Granville Rd., St. George's Hill, Weybridge, Surrey KT13 0QJ, England; and 43 Cadogan Sq., London SW1X 0HX, England.

CAREER: Anglo Metal Co., London, England, director, 1926-40; Roan Selection Trust International Group of Copper Mining Companies, London, began as director in 1930's, chief executive, 1943-68, chairman, 1950-72; writer, 1972—. Controller of Diamond Die and Tool Control for British Ministry of Supply, 1940-45, controller of Quartz Crystal Control, 1943-45. First chairman of Merchant Bank of Central Africa Ltd., 1956-66, Agricultural Research Council of Rhodesia and Nyasaland, 1959-63, and Merchant Bank (Zambia) Ltd., 1966-72; chairman of Botswana RST Group, 1959-72, and Council of Commonwealth Mining and Metallurgical Institutions, 1961-74; president of Cheltenham College Council, 1972-80. Member of board of directors of Australian Selection (Pty.) Ltd., Monks Investment Trust Ltd., Pan-Holding South Africa, Climax Molybdenum Co. of Europe, Metal Market and Exchange Co. Ltd., 1943-65, San Francisco Mines of Mexico Ltd., 1944-68, International Nickel Co. of Canada Ltd., 1951-72, Wankie Colliery Co. Ltd., 1953-63, Selection Trust Ltd., 1955-78 (chief executive, 1943-68), Minerals Separation Ltd., 1962-

78, Foseco Minsep Ltd., 1969-80, and Barclays Bank International, 1971-77; past member of board of directors of Bamangwato Concessions Ltd.; honorary member of BNF Metals Technology Centre.

MEMBER: British Overseas Mining Association (president, 1952), Institute of Metals (president, 1960-61), Overseas Development Institute (member of council, 1960-80), Copper Development Association (honorary president), Overseas Mining Association (member of council), Institution of Mining and Metallurgy (fellow), Metals Society (honorary member), Institute for Archaeo-Metallurgical Studies (member of board of trustees), Brooks's Club, White's Club, Marylebone Cricket Club.

AWARDS, HONORS: Officer of Order of the British Empire, 1946; Knighted, 1956; ANKH Award from Copper Club of New York, 1964, for most outstanding contribution to copper industry; gold medal from Institution of Mining and Metallurgy, 1968, for services to the mining industry, particularly in Zambia; platinum medal from Institute of Metals, 1969, for services to metallurgical industry.

WRITINGS: Copper: The Anatomy of an Industry, Mining Journal, 1975; *Reflections on an Era,* Metal Bulletin, 1981. Also author of *Selected Papers,* four volumes, Roan Selection Trust.

SIDELIGHTS: In *Reflections on an Era,* Ronald Prain recalls his thirty-five years as head of Roan Selection Trust, the copper mining conglomerate of Zambia (Northern Rhodesia). During his tenure as chairman and chief executive, from 1943 to 1978, Zambia became an independent state and the third largest producer of copper in the world. "It was a period of continuous crisis," Philip Mason noted in a *Times Literary Supplement.* The problems Prain encountered in his post ranged from transportation snags and labor disputes to race-wars and the eventual transfer of power from colonial to native hands. "This is the autobiography of a man who played a big part in the practical business of producing wealth," Mason concluded, "but also used his unusual political and social foresight for peaceful development in the revolutionary circumstances which everywhere accompanied the liquidation of the Empire. There is much here of importance to the historian."

Sir Ronald told *CA:* "All the writing I have done relates to some part of the mining industry and results really from my having to fulfill a great many speaking engagements. My involvement in the mining industry is due principally to the fact that I was born in Chile, which is a mining country, and that my father knew people in that industry in London. All this is described in *Reflections on an Era.*

"The era I describe in my book is really two eras. The first is the era of fifty years of private enterprise in mining, much of which has now come to an end. The other era saw the end of British colonialism in Africa."

AVOCATIONAL INTERESTS: Cricket, tennis, travel.

BIOGRAPHICAL/CRITICAL SOURCES: Times Literary Supplement, October 2, 1981.

*   *   *

PRCHAL, Mildred   1895-1983

OBITUARY NOTICE: Born August 24, 1895, in Chicago, Ill.; died February 26, 1983, in Berwyn, Ill. Gymnastics and dance instructor and author. During the late 1960's Prchal became known for her innovative work in modern gymnastics, which served as the basis of popular aerobic exercises. A member of the Gymnastic Hall of Fame, Prchal wrote and illustrated *Artistic Gymnastics.* Obituaries and other sources: *Who's Who of American Women,* 10th edition, Marquis, 1977; *Chicago Tribune,* March 2, 1983.

*   *   *

PRESTON, James J(ohn)   1941-

PERSONAL: Born January 12, 1941, in Hollywood, Calif.; son of Louis (a painter) and Hazel (Lathrop) Preston; married Carolyn Pastore (a teacher), February 11, 1967; children: Christina Marie, Thomas Carey, Jeremy Winslow. *Education:* San Francisco State University, B.A., 1967; University of Vermont, M.Ed., 1970; Hartford Seminary Foundation, Ph.D., 1974. *Politics:* Democrat. *Religion:* Episcopalian. *Home address:* R.D. 3, Box 414, Glenn Dr., Oneonta, N.Y. 13820. *Office:* Department of Anthropology, State University of New York College at Oneonta, Oneonta, N.Y. 13820.

CAREER: Principal of school for children with learning disabilities in Burlington, Vt., 1967-70; Utkal University, Orissa, India, research affiliate, 1972-73; Northwestern Connecticut Community College, Winsted, instructor in anthropology, 1973-74; State University of New York College at Oneonta, assistant professor, 1974-79, associate professor of anthropology, 1979—, chairman of department, 1975-78. Visiting scholar at University of North Carolina, 1977; visiting lecturer at State University of New York College at Plattsburgh, 1979; public speaker. Director of local Community Program on Coping With Death, 1978; life member of N.K. Bose Foundation. *Military service:* U.S. Army, 1962-63.

MEMBER: American Anthropological Association, Association for Asian Studies, Society for the Scientific Study of Religion. *Awards, honors:* National Endowment for the Humanities fellowship, 1977; grants from American Council of Learned Societies for India, 1978, and New York State Office for the Aging, 1978; Walter B. Ford professional development grant from State University of New York College at Oneonta, 1982.

WRITINGS: (Editor with Bhahagrahi Misra, and contributor) *Community, Self, and Identity: Styles of Communal Living in World Cultures,* Mouton, 1978; *Cult of the Goddess: Religious Change in a Hindu Temple,* Vikas Publishers, 1980; (editor and contributor) *Mother Worship,* University of North Carolina Press, 1982.

Contributor: John Morgan, editor, *Critical Essays in Religion and Culture,* University Press of America, 1979; Susan Seymour, editor, *Transformation of a Sacred City: Bhubaneswar, India,* Westview, 1980; J. S. Yadava and Vinayshil Gautam, editors, *The Communication of Ideas,* Concept Publishing, 1980; Giri Raj Gupta, editor, *Religion in Modern India,* Vikas Publishers, 1983.

Contributor of articles and reviews to anthropology journals. Anthropology editor of *Intellect,* 1977; book review editor of *Mentalities,* 1982-83.

WORK IN PROGRESS: The Anthropology of Imaginative Experience, completion expected in 1985; research on religious experience and the creative imagination.

SIDELIGHTS: Preston wrote: "All of my work is devoted to a deeper understanding of the role of the human imagination in the development of our concepts of the universe. This is particularly true of my writings on religion. My forthcoming book on imaginative experience is an attempt to probe into the fundamental principles operative in the human imagination. Unfortunately, the social and behavioral sciences have neglected this vital aspect of human nature. Religion represents a powerful exercise of imagination in order to understand the many invisible forces believed to impinge upon our lives.

"My interest in Indian religions (particularly Hinduism) has included studies of temples as cultural institutions, the elaborate use of iconography, and the great variety of sacred imagery available for Indians to express their conception of the sacred."

* * *

PRESTON, Thomas R(onald) 1936-

BRIEF ENTRY: Born October 31, 1936, in Detroit, Mich. American educator and author. Preston became a professor of English at University of Wyoming in 1973. He has also taught at Duquesne University, University of Florida, Loyola University in New Orleans, and University of Tennessee at Chattanooga. He wrote *Not in Timon's Manner: Feeling, Misanthropy, and Satire in Eighteenth-Century England* (University of Alabama Press, 1975). *Address:* Department of English, University of Wyoming, Box 3294, Laramie, Wyo. 82071. *Biographical/critical sources: Times Literary Supplement,* November 21, 1975.

* * *

PRICE, Margaret (Evans) 1888-1973

OBITUARY NOTICE: Born March 20, 1888, in Chicago, Ill.; died November 20, 1973. Artist, illustrator, toy designer, and author of novels and children's books. Price was founder with her husband, Irving Price, and Herman G. Fisher of the Fisher-Price toy company during the 1930's. Her paintings have been exhibited at the Albright Art Gallery in Buffalo, New York, and at the Museum of the New York Historical Society, which houses a permanent collection of her works. Price's children's books include *Legends of the Seven Seas* and *Animals Marooned,* and her novels for adults include *Mirage* and *Night Must End.* Obituaries and other sources: *American Authors and Books: 1640 to the Present Day,* 3rd revised edition, Crown, 1962; *Who's Who of American Women,* 4th edition, Marquis, 1967; *New York Times,* November 24, 1973; *Who Was Who Among North American Authors, 1921-1939,* Gale, 1976; *Who Was Who Among English and European Authors,* Gale, 1978.

* * *

PRINGLE, Mia (Lilly) Kellmer 1920(?)-1983

OBITUARY NOTICE—See index for *CA* sketch: Born c. 1920 in Vienna, Austria; died February 21, 1983. Authority on child development and education and author. Pringle was the first director of the National Children's Bureau in 1963. Under her direction, the bureau developed an impressive publication series and conducted applied research projects. Pringle—before accepting her appointment with the bureau—lectured in educational psychology and served as the deputy head of the Department of Child Study at the University of Birmingham. She was also active on national and international committees. Her books include *The Needs of Children, National Child Development Study, The Emotional and Social Adjustment of Blind Children,* and *Deprivation and Education.* Obituaries and other sources: *London Times,* February 25, 1983.

PROSE, Francine 1947-

BRIEF ENTRY: American author. Prose's literary creations are based on legends and myths. *Stories From Our Living Past* (Behrman House, 1974) retells Jewish morality tales, including "Daniel in the Lion's Den" and "The Goat That Made the Stars Sing." Similarly, her first novel, *Judah and Pious* (Atheneum, 1973), is written in the tradition of a European folktale, and *Mary Laveau* is based on myths surrounding the nineteenth-century New Orleans mystic and politician. Prose's other books include *The Glorious Ones* (Atheneum, 1974), *Animal Magnetism* (Putnam, 1978), *Household Saints* (St. Martin's, 1981), and *Hungry Hearts* (Pantheon, 1983). *Biographical/critical sources: New York Times,* February 17, 1973, September 15, 1977; *New York Times Book Review,* February 25, 1973, July 12, 1981; *Newsweek,* March 12, 1973, February 18, 1974, August 3, 1981; *Mademoiselle,* February, 1975.

* * *

PRUNTY, Merle C(harles) 1917-1983

OBITUARY NOTICE—See index for *CA* sketch: Born March 2, 1917, in St. Joseph, Mo.; died November 6, 1982, in Athens, Ga. Educator and author. Prunty had been associated with the University of Georgia since 1946. He began there as a professor of geography and went on to become the acting vice-president for academic affairs as well as the faculty adviser to the president. His books include *The Central Gulf South, This Favored Land,* and *Lands of Promise,* which he wrote with E. B. Fincher. Obituaries and other sources: *Chronicle of Higher Education,* January 5, 1983.

* * *

PUSEY, Nathan Marsh 1907-

PERSONAL: Born April 4, 1907, in Council Bluffs, Iowa; son of John Marsh and Rosa (Drake) Pusey; married Anne Woodward, June 10, 1936; children: Nathan, James, Rosemary Pusey Hopkins. *Education:* Harvard, A.B., 1928, Ph.D., 1937. *Home:* 200 East 66th St., A-501, New York, N.Y. 10021.

CAREER: Lawrence College, Appleton, Wis., sophomore tutor, 1935-38; Scripps College, Claremont, Calif., assistant professor of history and literature, 1938-40; Wesleyan University, Middletown, Conn., assistant professor, 1940-43, associate professor of classics, 1943-44; Lawrence College, Appleton, president, 1944-53; Harvard University, Cambridge, Mass., president, 1953-71, president emeritus, 1971—. President of the Andrew W. Mellon Foundation, 1971-75, and United Board for Christian Higher Education in Asia, 1979-83. *Member:* American Academy of Arts and Sciences, Council on Foreign Relations, Century Association.

WRITINGS: The Age of the Scholar: Observations on Education in a Troubled Decade, Harvard University Press, 1963; *American Higher Education, 1945-1970: A Personal Report,* Harvard University Press, 1978; *Lawrence Lowell and His Revolution,* Harvard University Press, 1980.

SIDELIGHTS: In *American Higher Education,* Nathan Pusey records developments in college education that he witnessed during his years as president of Harvard University. He notes progress in the areas of international studies and graduate education, and addresses the problems of campus unrest in the 1960's and shortages of funds for colleges. Writing in the *New York Times Book Review,* Doris Grumbach criticized his survey for being "limited in most of its referential matter to what happened at Harvard,'' though she conceded that Pusey had intended to write a "personal history" of post-World War II education in America.

Pusey told *CA:* "Over the years most of my writing has been confined to scores, if not hundreds, of more or less topical, ephemeral speeches. Though greatly reduced in volume now, it still is."

BIOGRAPHICAL/CRITICAL SOURCES: New York Times Book Review, June 11, 1978.

* * *

PUTNAM, George Palmer   1887-1950

BRIEF ENTRY: Born September 7, 1887, in Rye, N.Y.; died of uremic poisoning, January 4, 1950, in Trona, Calif. American publisher, explorer, and author. Putnam joined his family's publishing company, G. P. Putnam's Sons, in 1919, after first serving in the field artillery during World War I. He remained with the firm until 1930, when he left to become vice-president of Brewer & Warren, another publishing company. An interest in exploration and adventure led Putnam to participate in two Arctic expeditions, one to Greenland in 1926 and one to Baffin Land (now Baffin Island) in 1927. He also directed the experimental flight that first brought his future wife, aviatrix Amelia Earhart, to public attention. Putnam wrote nearly one dozen books, including *Soaring Wings: A Biography of Amelia Earhart* (1939), *Duration* (1943), *Death Valley and Its Country* (1946), *Mariner of the North: The Life of Captain Bob Bartlett* (1947), *Hickory Shirt: A Novel of Death Valley in 1850* (1949), and *Up in Our Country* (1950). *Biographical/critical sources:* George Palmer Putnam, *Wide Margins: A Publisher's Autobiography,* Harcourt, 1942; *New York Times,* January 5, 1950; *Illustrated London News,* January 14, 1950; *Publishers Weekly,* January 14, 1950; *Time,* January 15, 1950; *Who Was Who in America,* Volume II: *1943-1950,* Marquis, 1963.

* * *

PYE, Norman   1913-

PERSONAL: Born February 11, 1913, in Wigan, England; son of John Whittaker and Hilda Constance (Platt) Pye; married Isabella Jane Currie, December 5, 1940; children: Alistair Grierson, Michael Richard. *Education:* Victoria University of Manchester, B.A. (with first class honors), 1935; attended Cambridge University, 1937-38. *Religion:* United Reformed. *Home:* 127 Spencefield Lane, Evington, Leicestershire LE5 6GG, England.

CAREER: Victoria University of Manchester, Manchester, England, assistant lecturer, 1938-46, lecturer, 1946-53, senior lecturer in geography, 1953-54; University of Leicester, Leicester, England, professor of geography and head of department, 1954-79, professor emeritus, 1979—, dean of faculty of science, 1957-60, pro-vice-chancellor, 1963-66. Cartographer with Hydrographic Department of British Admiralty, 1940-46. Member of Cambridge University's expedition to Spitzbergen, 1938. Member of Northamptonshire Education Committee, 1956-74, Schools Council, 1970-78, and Heritage Education Group, Department of the Environment. Member

of Corby Development Corp., 1965-80, and board of directors of Jones & Park Ltd. *Member:* Royal Geographical Society (past member of council), Royal Meteorological Society (past member of council), Institute of British Geographers (past member of council), Geographical Association (honorary vice-president, 1979-83).

WRITINGS: (Editor and contributor) *Leicester and Its Region,* Leicester University Press, 1972. Editor of *Geography,* 1965-80.

WORK IN PROGRESS: An article, "Athabaska Tar Sands Oil Development," publication expected in 1984; *Corby: The Physical and Economic Planning of a New Town,* completion expected in 1985.

AVOCATIONAL INTERESTS: Travel (United States, Canada, eastern and western Africa).

* * *

PYLE, Howard   1853-1911

BRIEF ENTRY: Born March 5, 1853, in Wilmington, Del.; died November 9, 1911, in Florence, Italy. American artist, illustrator, novelist, and children's author. Pyle attended art schools in Philadelphia and New York City and worked as an illustrator for *St. Nicholas, Harper's,* and *Scribner's Monthly* before embarking on a writing career. In 1883 his *Merry Adventures of Robin Hood of Great Renown in Nottinghamshire* was published. Over the next twenty-five years, Pyle wrote and illustrated fifteen children's books, including *Pepper and Salt; or, Seasoning for Young Folk* (1886), *The Story of Jack Ballister's Fortunes* (1895), *The Garden Behind the Moon: A Real Story of the Moon Angel* (1895), and *The Story of the Champions of the Round Table* (1905). In addition, Pyle produced six novels for adults and illustrated the works of several well-known authors, including Alfred Lord Tennyson, Oliver Wendell Holmes, and John Greenleaf Whittier. He taught illustration at Drexel Institute in Philadelphia from 1894 to 1900 and later established his own art school in Wilmington, Delaware. *Biographical/critical sources:* Elizabeth Nesbitt, *Howard Pyle,* Walck, 1966; H. C. Pitz, *Howard Pyle: Writer, Illustrator, Founder of the Brandywine School,* Potter, 1975; *Illustrators of Books for Young People,* 2nd edition, Scarecrow, 1975; *The Lincoln Library of Language Arts,* 3rd edition, Frontier Press (Columbus, Ohio), 1978; *Twentieth-Century Children's Writers,* St. Martin's, 1978.

* * *

PYM, Michael   1890(?)-1983

OBITUARY NOTICE: Born c. 1890 in London, England; died of cancer, March 16, 1983, in Fairfax, Va. Dog breeder and journalist. Pym, who was one of the original members of the Women's National Press Club (now Washington Press Club), worked as a reporter for the *Milwaukee Journal* and as a correspondent in India for the *New York Herald Tribune.* In later years she began raising Japanese chin dogs and served as honorary life president of the Japanese Chin Club of America. Obituaries and other sources: *Who's Who of American Women,* 3rd edition, Marquis, 1964; *Washington Post,* March 22, 1983.

R

RABINS, Peter V(incent) 1947-

PERSONAL: Surname is pronounced *Ray*-bins; born September 8, 1947, in Everett, Mass.; son of Alexander S. (an importer) and Sylvia (a nurse; maiden name, Goldberg) Rabins; married Karen Briefer, August 17, 1969; children: Alicia, Stephanie, Nora. *Education:* University of Florida, B.A., 1969; Tulane University, M.D. and M.P.H., both 1973. *Office:* Department of Psychiatry, Johns Hopkins University, 600 North Wolfe St., Baltimore, Md. 21205.

CAREER: Charity Hospital, New Orleans, La., intern, 1973-74; University of Oregon Health Sciences Center, Portland, resident in psychiatry, 1974-77; Johns Hopkins University, Baltimore, Md., assistant professor of psychiatry, 1977—. Director of T. Rowe and Eleanor Price Teaching Service.

WRITINGS: (With Nancy L. Mace) *The Thirty-Six Hour Day: A Family Guide to Caring for Persons With Alzheimer's Disease, Related Dementing Illnesses, and Memory Loss in Later Life,* Johns Hopkins University Press, 1982.

WORK IN PROGRESS: Research on psychiatric problems of older people.

SIDELIGHTS: Rabins commented: "Our book is an extended version of a family handbook we wrote at our patients' request. The title *Thirty-Six Hour Day* reflects the experiences of some family members caring for a person suffering from dementia, for the physical and emotional impact often more than fills a twenty-four hour day. The book is structured around our belief that families need both concrete information and emotional support; thus, it provides current information about the disorders which cause thinking impairment in later life, suggests solutions to specific problems which may arise, and discusses the psychological and social impact on family care-givers."

BIOGRAPHICAL/CRITICAL SOURCES: Johns Hopkins, December, 1982.

*   *   *

RADLEY, Eric John 1917-

PERSONAL: Born June 12, 1917, in Ratnapura, Ceylon (now Sri Lanka); son of John Benjamin (a minister) and Florence Sophia (Roberts) Radley; married Margaret Elisabeth Cobb (a secretary), August 28, 1948; children: Peter, Helen Radley Penfold, Mary, Rosemary. *Education:* University of London, B.A., 1938, Diploma in Education, 1939. *Politics:* Liberal. *Religion:* United Reformed. *Home:* Elton Farm, Newnham on Severn, Gloucestershire, England.

CAREER: Farmer in Newnham on Severn, England, 1940—. Lecturer in literature and economic history at West Gloucestershire College of Further Education, 1961-79, and Workers' Educational Association, 1981—. Member of Gloucestershire County Council.

WRITINGS: Notes on British Economic History From 1700 to the Present Day, Basil Blackwell, 1967; *Country Diary,* Forest of Dean Newspapers, 1976; *Objective Tests in Economic and Social History From 1700 to the Present Day,* Hodder & Stoughton, 1979. Author of "Country Diary," a weekly column appearing in Forest of Dean newspapers, 1954—. Contributor to local newspapers.

WORK IN PROGRESS: A collection of stories "with farmhouse settings," publication expected in 1983; another *Country Diary* collection, publication expected in 1983.

SIDELIGHTS: Radley told *CA:* "For me the problem of writing is to prevent it from becoming submerged by everyday activities that appear unavoidable and worthwhile, but which consume time, energy, and thought. I have many ideas in my mind, but am not sure whether or not I should allow my public work (on the county council) to come first. The countryside around me is richly evocative of history and nature, subjects for musing, thought, and description.

"'Country Diary' began because I had seen brief articles in newspapers about the countryside and thought I would like to try myself. It has continued with only a week missed here and there ever since February, 1954. A writer about the countryside has an infinite number of objects spread out before him. These include every type of bird or animal, any and every thing that happens on a farm, whether technical, historical, important, or trivial, and people, incidents, activities, and occupations. Colors, tastes, sounds, and smells are included in the subject matter as well.

"Beauty and rich variety of life are important to me. Although I am a farmer, I want to conserve nature, and I believe, too, that in spite of the bewildering complexities and the terrible contradictions, life is good, especially human life."

RADO, Alexander
   See RADO, Sandor

*   *   *

RADO, Sandor   1900-1981
   (Alexander Rado)

PERSONAL: Born in 1900 in Hungary; died August 19, 1981, in Budapest, Hungary. Education: Studied law in Budapest, Hungary, and geography in Germany.

CAREER: Rosta (Soviet news agency), Vienna, Austria, correspondent and director, 1920-22; worked in Germany, 1922-24, and Moscow, 1924-26; Geopress (map news service), founder and director in Germany, Paris, France, and Switzerland, 1927-43; National Institute of Cartography, Budapest, Hungary, department head. Head of Soviet intelligence in Geneva, Switzerland, 1938. Professor at Karl Marx University of Economics, Budapest, 1958-66. Founder of international news service for map makers, Cartactual, 1965. Military service: Soviet Army, 1942-45; became colonel. Member: Hungarian Communist Party. Awards, honors: Kossuth Prize, 1963.

WRITINGS: (Editor) Hungarian Cartographical Studies, Cartographia, 1968; Direktornak Doratol (memoirs), [Hungary], 1970, German translation by J. A. Underwood published as Dora jelenti, Kossuth Konyvkiado (Budapest, Hungary), 1971, English translation from the German edition published as Code Name Dora, Abelard, 1977. Editor in chief of National Atlas of Hungary, 1967.

Under name Alexander Rado: Guide to the Soviet Union, State Publishing Department, Russian Soviet Federated Socialist Republic, 1925, reprinted as Guide-Book to the Soviet Union, Neuer Deutscher-Verlag, 1928; The Atlas of To-day and To-morrow, Gollancz, 1938.

Author of more than one dozen atlases and cartographic reference books in Hungarian.

SIDELIGHTS: Rado worked in Germany and Moscow in the 1920's. He was recruited by Russian military intelligence as early as 1935, and was a colonel in the army of the Soviet Union in 1942. He worked as a spy during World War II, and returned to the Soviet Union in 1945, where he was arrested. He spent ten years at hard labor, but was released in 1955, after the death of Stalin. Rado spent the rest of his life in Hungary, working as a cartographer.

BIOGRAPHICAL/CRITICAL SOURCES: Economist, May 7, 1977.

OBITUARIES: New York Times, August 21, 1981.*

*   *   *

RAE, Daphne   1933-

PERSONAL: Born August 15, 1933, in Ceylon (now Sri Lanka); daughter of John Phimester and Ray (Thomson) Simpson; married John Malcolm Rae (a headmaster and writer), December 31, 1955; children: Siobham Rae Tinker, Penelope Rae Hickmore, Alyce, Emily, Shamus, Jonathan. Education: Received diploma in psychology. Politics: "Floating voter." Home and office: 17 Dean's Yard, Westminster School, London SW1P 3PB, England. Agent: Curtis Brown Ltd., 1 Craven Hill, London W2 3EP, England.

CAREER: Writer. Justice of the peace. Volunteer social worker in India. Member: RAC.

WRITINGS: Love Until It Hurts, Hodder & Stoughton, 1981; A World Apart (nonfiction), Lutterworth, 1983. Writer for television and radio. Contributor to magazines.

BIOGRAPHICAL/CRITICAL SOURCES: Best Sellers, November, 1981.

*   *   *

RAHNER, Karl   1904-

PERSONAL: Born March 5, 1904, in Freiburg im Breisgau, Germany (now West Germany); son of Karl R. (a teacher) and Luise (Trescher) Rahner. Education: Studium der Philosophie, Pullach, Germany (now West Germany), licentiat d. philosophie, 1927; Studium der Theologie, Valkenburg, Holland, Lic. Theol., 1933; postgraduate study at University of Freiburg, 1934-36; University of Innsbruck, Dr. Theol., 1936. Religion: Roman Catholic. Residence: Innsbruck, Austria.

CAREER: Entered Society of Jesus (Jesuits), 1922, ordained Roman Catholic priest, 1932; University of Innsbruck, Austria, teacher, 1936-39; Diocese of Vienna, Austria, instructor in pastoral theology, c. 1939-45; College of St. John Berchman, Pullach, West Germany, teacher of theology, c. 1945-48; University of Innsbruck, teacher, 1948, professor of dogmatic theology, 1949-64; University of Munich, West Germany, professor of philosophy of religion, 1964-67; University of Muenster, West Germany, professor of dogmatic theology, beginning 1967, currently emeritus professor. Peritus at Vatican Council II; member of commission appointed by Pope Paul VI to evaluate theological trends, 1969.

WRITINGS—In German: Gefahren in heutigen Katholizismus, Johannes Verlag, 1950 (also see below); Von der Not und dem Segen des Gebetes, F. Rauch, 1956, 3rd edition, Herder, 1964; Die Gnade wird es vollenden, Verlag Ars Sacra, 1957; Glaubend und Lieband, Verlag Ars Sacra, 1957; Gott liebt dieses Kind: Zu einer Taufe, Verlag Ars Sacra, 1957; Das Geheimnis unseres Christus: Die heilige Euchariste, Verlag Ars Sacra, 1959.

Vom Glauben inmitten der Welt, Herder, 1961, 2nd edition, 1962; Auferstenung des Fleisches: Koennen wir noche daran glauben?, Butzon & Bercker, 1962; Vortage analasslich der internationalen Herbsttagung des Wirtschaftsring e.V., [Germany], 1962; Gegenwart des Christentums, Herder, 1963, 2nd edition, 1966; Kirche im Wandel: Nach dem Zweiten Vatikanischen Konzil, Butzon & Bercker, 1965; Ueber den Dialogue in der pluralistischen Gelleschaft, Stadt Pforzheim, 1965; Bergend un Heiland: Ueber das Sakrament der Kranken, Verlag Ars Sacra, 1965; (with Uta Ranke-Heinemann) Der Protestantismus: Wesen und Werden, Driewer, 1965; (with Max Horkheimer and Carl Friedrich Weizsacker) Ueber die Freiheit, Kreuz Verlag, 1965.

(With Edward Schillebeeckx and J.G.M. Willebrands) Christendom en Wereld, J. J. Romen, 1966; Intellektuelle Redlichkeit und christlicher Glaube, Herder, 1966; (with Oscar Cullman and Heinrich Fries) Sind die Erwartungen erfuelet?: Ueberlegungen nach dem Konzil, Hueber, 1966; Vom Sinn des kirchlichen Amtes, Herder, 1966; (with Albert Goerres) Der Leib und das Heil, Matthais-Gruenewald-Verlag, 1967; Dir eine Mittler und die Vielfalt der Vermittlungen, Steiner, 1967; Ich glaube an Jesus Christus, Benziger, 1968; (with others, and author of foreword) Die Antwort der Theologen, Patmos-

Verlag, 1968, 2nd edition, 1969; (with Eberhard Juengel and Manfred Seitz) *Die praktische Theologie zwischen Wissenschaft und Praxis*, Kaiser, 1968.

(With Karl-Heinz Weger) *Theologie der Erbsuende*, Herder, 1970; *Kritisches Wort: Aktuelle Probleme in Kirche und Welt*, Herder, 1970; *Freiheit und Manipulation in Gesellschaft und Kirche*, Koesel-Verlag, 1970; (with Adolph Exeler and Johannes B. Metz) *Helfe zum Glauben: Adventsmeditationen* (contains "Fregender Glaube" by Exeler, "Glaube als gefaehrliche Erinnerung" by Metz, and "Mitte des Glaubens" by Rahner), Benziger, 1971; (with Anita Roeper) *Objektive und subjektive Moral*, Herder, 1971; (with Juengel) *Was ist ein Sakrament?: Vorstoeese zur Verstaerdigg*, Herder, 1971; *Experiment Mensch: Vom umgang zwischen Gott und Mensch*, Siebenstern Taschenbuch Verlag, 1973; *Was sollen wir jetzt tun?: Vier Meditationen*, Herder, 1974 (also see below); *Vorfragen zu einem oekumenischen Amtsvertaendris*, Herder, 1974; *Pater Karl Rahner, S.J., zum 70*, Herder, 1974; (author of afterword) Sigmund Gripp, *Abschied von Morgan: Aus dem Leben in einem Jugendzentrum*, Patmos-Verlag, 1974.

Herdusforderrerung des Christen: Meditationen, Reflexionen, Herder, 1975; (contributor) Eszter Gabriella Banffy, *Marxistische Ethik in der ungarischen Lituratur*, Ungarishes Kirchensoziolog Institute, 1976; *Glaube als Mut*, Benziger, 1976; (with Herbert Vorgrimler and Kuro Fuessel) *Kleines theologisches Woerterbuch*, Herder, 1976, new edition, 1978; *Toleranz im Kirche: Freiheit und Manipulation in Gesellschaft und Kirche*, Herder, 1977; (contributor) *Ermutigung zum Gebet* (contains "Gebet zu den Heiligen"), Herder, 1977; (with Christian Modehn and Hans Zwietetholer) *Befreiende Theologie*, Kohlhammer, 1977; (with Modehn and Michael Goepfert) *Volkreligion: Religion des Volkes*, Kohlhammer, 1979; (with Weger) *Was sollen wir noche Glauben?: Theologen stellen sich der Glaubensfragen eine neuen Generation*, Herder, 1979.

In English translation: *Geist in Welt: Zur Metaphysik der endlichen Erkenntnis bei Thomas von Aquin*, Koesel-Verlag, 1939, 3rd edition, 1964, translation by William Dych published as *Spirit in the World*, Herder & Herder, 1968; *Hoerer des Wortes: Zur Grundlegung einer Religionsphilosophie*, Koesel-Pustet, 1941, new edition (edited by Metz), 1969, translation by Michael Richards published as *Hearers of the Word*, Herder & Herder, 1969; "Nature und Gnade," published in *Gefahren in heutegen Katholizismus*, Johannes Verlag, 1950, translation by Dinah Wharton published as *Nature and Grace and Other Essays*, Sheed & Ward, 1963, published as *Nature and Grace: Dilemmas in the Modern Church*, 1964; *Das freie Wort in der Kirche: Die Chancen des Christendums*, Johannes Verlag, 1953, translation by G. R. Lamb published as *Free Speech in the Church*, Sheed & Ward, 1959; *Maria Mutter das Herrn: Theologische Betrachtungen*, Herder, 1956, translation by W. J. O'Hara published as *Mary, Mother of the Lord: Theological Meditations*, Herder, 1963, new edition, Anthony Clarke, 1974; *Ewiges ja*, Verlag Ars Sacra, 1957, translation by Salvator Attanasio published as *The Eternal Yes*, Dimension, 1970.

(With Vorgrimler) *Kleines theologisches Woerterbuch*, Herder, 1961, 11th edition, 1978, translation by Richard Strachan published as *Theological Dictionary*, edited by Cornelius Ernst, Herder, 1965 (published in England as *Concise Theological Dictionary*, Burnes & Oates, 1966); *Worte ins Schweigan*, F. Rauch, 1963, published with *Gebets der Einkehr* as *Worte ins Schweigan [und] Gebetes der Einkehr*, Herder, 1973, translation of former by James M. Demske published as *Encounters*

With Silence, Newman Press, 1960; (contributor) Ludwig Klein, editor, *Deskussion ueber die Bibel*, Matthias-Gruenewald-Verlag, 1963, Mainz, 1964, translation by Richard Kavanagh published as *The Bible in a New Age*, Sheed & Ward, 1965; *Kleines Kirchenjahr*, Verlag Ars Sacra, c. 1964, translation by John Shae published as *The Eternal Year*, Helicon, 1964; (contributor) *The Word: Readings in Theology* (translated articles), foreword by R.A.F. MacKenzie, P. J. Kennedy, 1964; *Ueber der Episkopat*, [Germany], c. 1965, translation by Edward Quinn published as *Bishops: Their Status and Function*, Burnes & Oates, 1964, Helicon, 1965; *Alltaegliche Dinge*, Benziger, 1964, translation by M. H. Hellan published as *Everyday Things*, Sheed & Ward, 1965.

Im heute Glauben, Benziger, 1965, translation by Ray Ockenden and Rosaleen Ockenden published as *Faith Today*, Sheed & Ward, 1967; *Heilige Strund un Passionsandacht*, Herder, 1965, translation by Dych published as *Watch and Pray With Me*, Herder, 1966, later published as *Watch and Pray With Me: The Seven Last Words*, Seabury Press, 1966; *Betrachtungen zum ignatianischen Exerzitienbuch*, Koesel-Verlag, 1965, translation by Kenneth Barker published as *Spiritual Exercises*, Herder, 1965; (with Roeper) *Die vierzehn Stationen in Leben des N. N.*, Butzon & Bercker, 1965, translation by Dolores Sablone published as *The Fifteenth Station*, Burnes & Oates, 1968; (with Karl Lehmann) "Kerygma und dogma," published in *Die grundiagen heilsgeschichteicher Dogmatik*, edited by H. U. von Balthasar, [Germany], 1965, translation published as *Kerygma and Dogma*, Herder & Herder, 1969; (with Roger Garaudy and Metz) *Der Dialogue oder aerdert sich das Verhaeltris zwischen Katholizismus und Marxismus?*, Rowohltz, 1966, translation published as *Can a Christian Be a Marxist?: A Dialogue Among a Marxist Philosopher and Two Christian Theologians*, Argus Communications, 1969; *Das Konzil: Ein neuer Beginn*, Herder, 1966, translation by D. C. Herron and R. Albrecht published as *The Church After the Council*, Herder & Herder, 1966; *Biblische Predigten*, Herder, 1966, translation by Desmond Forristal and Strachan published as *Biblical Homilies*, Herder, 1966.

(With brother, Hugo Rahner) *Gebete der Einkehr*, O. Mueller, 1967, translation published as *Prayers for Meditation*, Herder & Herder, 1962 (also see above); *Glaube der die Erde liebt*, Herder, 1967, translation by O'Hara published as *Everyday Faith*, Herder & Herder, 1968; *Glaubst du an Gott?* (selections from volumes III-VII of Rahner's *Schriften zur Theologie* [see below]), Verlag Ars Sacra, 1967, translation by Strachan published as *Do You Believe in God?*, Newman Press, 1969; *Belief Today* (contains "Everyday Things," "Faith Today," and "Intellectual Integrity and Christian Faith"), translated by M. H. Heelan, preface by Hans Kueng, Sheed & Ward, 1967, later published as *Belief Today: Three Theological Meditations*, 1973 (also see above); "Der dreifaltige Gott als tranazendenter Urgrund der Heilsgeschichte," published in *Mysterium salutis*, Benziger, 1967, translation by Joseph Donaclel published as *The Trinity*, Burnes & Oates, 1970, Seabury Press, 1974; *Knechte Christe: Meditationen zum Priestertum*, Herder, 1967, translation published as *Servants of the Lord*, Herder & Herder, 1968; *The Christian of the Future* (partial translation by O'Hara of Volume VI of Rahner's *Schriften zur Theologie*), Herder & Herder, 1967 (also see below); *Grundlegung der Pastoraltheologie als praktische Theologie*, [Germany], c. 1968, translation by O'Hara published as *Theology of Pastoral Action*, adapted by Daniel Morrissey, Herder & Herder, 1968; *Gnade als Freiheit: Kleine theologische Bienaege*, Herder, 1968, translation by Hilda Graef published as *Grace in Freedom*, Herder & Herder, 1969.

Einuburg priesterlicher Existenz, Herder, 1970, translation by Quinn published as *The Priesthood*, Herder & Herder, 1973; *Chancen des Glaubens: Fragmente eine modernen Spiritualitat*, Herder, 1971, translation by Quinn published as *Opportunities for Faith: Elements of a Modern Spirituality*, Society for Promoting Christian Knowledge, 1974, Seabury Press, 1975; *Strukturwandel der Kirche als Dufgahe und Chance*, Herder, 1972, translation by Quinn published as *The Shape of the Church to Come*, Seabury Press, 1974; *Auch Heute weht der Geist: Ueber der Sakrament der Firmung*, Verlag Ars Sacra, 1974, translation published as *A New Baptism in the Spirit: Confirmation Today*, Dimension Books, 1975; *Wagnis des Christen: Geistl*, Herder, 1974, translation published as *Christian at the Crossroads*, Seabury Press, 1975 (translation by V. Green published in England as *The Religious Life Today*, Burnes & Oates, 1976); *Die siebenfaeltige Gabe: Ueber der Sakrament der Kirche*, Verlag Ars Sacra, 1974, translation published as *Mediations on the Sacraments*, Seabury Press, 1977.

Man darf sich vergiben lassen, Verlag Ars Sacra, c. 1975, translation published as *Allow Yourself to Be Forgiven: Penance Today*, Dimension Books, 1975; *Meditations on Hope and Love* (selections from *Was sollen wir jetzt tun?* and *Gott ist Mensch geworden*), translated by Green, Burnes & Oates, 1976; *Grundkurs des Glaubens: Einf. in der Begriff der Christentums*, Herder, 1976, translation by Dych published as *Foundations of Christian Faith: An Introduction to the Idea of Christianity*, Seabury Press, 1978; *Erfahrung des Geistes: Meditationen auf Pfingsten*, Herder, 1977, translation published as *The Spirit in the Church*, Seabury Press, 1979; (with Paul Imhof and Helmuth Nils Loose) *Ignatius von Loyola* (biography), photographs by Loose, Herder, 1978, translation by R. Ockenden published as *Ignatius of Loyola*, Collins, 1979; (with Weger) *Our Christian Faith: Answers for the Future*, translated from original German manuscript by Francis McDonagh, Crossroads, 1981.

Multivolume works: *Schriften zur Theologie*, twenty volumes, Benziger, 1954-82, translation published as *Theological Investigations*, Volume I: *God, Christ, Mary, and Grace*, translated by Cornelius Ernst, Helicon, 1961; Volume II: *Man in the Church*, translated by Karl-H. Kruger, Darton, Longman & Todd, 1963, Helicon, 1964; Volume III: *The Theology of the Spiritual Life*, translated by K.-H. Kruger and Boniface Kruger, Helicon, 1967; Volume IV: *More Recent Writings*, translated by Kevin Smith, Helicon, 1966; Volume V: *Later Writings*, translated by K.-H. Kruger, 1966; Volume VI: *Concerning Vatican Council II*, translated by K.-H. Kruger and B. Kruger, Helicon, 1969; Volume VII: *Further Theology of the Spiritual Life: Part One*, translated by David Bourke, Herder & Herder, 1971; Volume VIII: *Further Theology of the Spiritual Life: Part Two*, translated by Bourke, Herder & Herder, 1971; Volume IX: *Writings of 1965-1967: Part One*, translated by Graham Harrison, Herder & Herder, 1972; Volume X: *Writings of 1965-1967: Part Two*, translated by Bourke, Herder & Herder, 1973; Volume XI: *Confrontations: Part One*, translated by Bourke, Darton, Longman & Todd, 1974; Volume XII: *Confrontations: Part Two*, translated by Bourke, Darton, Longman & Todd, 1974; Volume XIII: *Theology, Anthropology, Christology*, translation published by Darton, Longman & Todd, 1975; Volume XIV: *Ecclesiology, Questions in the Church, the Church in the World*, translation published by Darton, Longman & Todd, 1975; Volume XV: *Penance in the Early Church*, translation published by Seabury Press, 1980; Volume XVI: *Experience of the Spirit: Source of Theology*, translation published by Seabury Press, 1979; Volume XVII: *Jesus, Man, and the Church*, translation published by Darton, Longman & Todd, 1982; Volume XX: *Concern for the Church*, translation published by Crossroads, 1982.

Sendung und Gnade: Bietrage zur Pastoraltheologie, Tyrolia-Verlag, 1959, 4th edition, 1966, translation by Cecily Hastings published as *Mission and Grace: Essays in Pastoral Theology*, Sheed & Ward, Volume I: *The Christian Commitment: Essays in Pastoral Theology*, 1963, Volume II: *Theology for Renewal: Bishops, Priests, Layity*, translated with Strachan, 1964, Volume III: *Christian in the Marketplace*, 1966.

"Quaestiones disputatae" series; German manuscripts published by Herder, except as noted; translations published by Herder & Herder, except as noted: *Visionen und Prophezeiungen*, Tyrolis, 1952, revised edition published as *Visionen und Prophezeiungen: Zweite unter Mitarbeit von P. Th. Baumann*, Herder, 1958, translation by Charles Henky and Strachan published as *Visions and Prophesies*, 1964 (also see below); *Ueber die Schriftinspiration*, 1958, 2nd edition, 1965, translation by Henky published as *Inspiration in the Bible*, 1961, 2nd edition (revised by Morton Palmer), 1964 (also see below); *Zur Theologie des Todes: Mit einem Exkurs ueber das Martyrium*, 1958, translation by Henky published as *On the Theology of Death*, 1961, 2nd edition (revised by O'Hara), 1965, new edition, Seabury Press, 1973; *Das Dynamische in der Kirche*, 1958, 3rd edition, 1965, translation by O'Hara published as *The Dynamic Element in the Church*, 1964.

Kirche und Sakrament, 1960, translation by O'Hara published as *The Church and the Sacraments*, 1963 (also see below); (with Joseph Ratzinger) *Episkopat und Primat*, 1961, translation by Kenneth Barker and others published as *The Episcopate and the Primacy*, 1962 (also see below); (with Paul Overhage) *Das Problem der Hominisation: Ueber den biologischen Ursprung des Menschen*, 1961, 3rd edition, 1965, translation by O'Hara published as *Hominisation: The Evolutionary Origin of Man as a Theological Problem*, 1965; *Was ist Haeresle?*, [Germany], c. 1964, translation by O'Hara published as *On Heresy*, 1964 (also see below); *Inquiries* (contains "Inspiration in the Bible," "Visions and Prophesies," "The Church and the Sacraments," "The Episcopate and the Primacy," and "On Heresy"), 1964, later edition published as *Studies in Modern Theology*, 1965.

(With Ratzinger) *Offenbarung und Ueberlieferung*, 1965, translation by O'Hara published as *Revelation and Tradition*, 1966; (with Angleus Haeussling) *Die vielen Messen und das eine Opfer: Eine Untersuchung ueber die Rechte vorm der Messhaeufigkeit*, 1966, translation by O'Hara published as *The Celebration of the Eucharist*, 1968; (with Johannes Neumann and Wilhelm Steinmueller) *Zur Reform des Theologiestudiums*, 1969; (with Hans Kueng) *Zum Problem unfehlbarkeit: Antworten auf die Anfrage*, 1971; (with Wilhelm Thuesing) *Christiologie, Systematisch und Exegisch: Arbeitsgrundlagen fuer eine interdisziplinaere Vorlesung*, 1972, translation by David Smith and Green published as *A New Christology*, Seabury Press, 1980.

Editor: (With Josef Neurer) *Der Glaube der Kirche in der Urkunden der Lehrverkuendegung*, F. Pustet, 1951, 8th edition (edited with Weger), 1971, translation published as *The Teaching of the Catholic Church as Contained in Her Documents by Joseph Neuner, S.J., and Heinrich Roos, S.J.*, Mercier Press, 1966; Heinrich Josef Dominik, *Enchiridon symbolorum: Definitionum et declarationum de rebus fidei et morum quod*

Ioannem B. Umberg denuo editit Carolus Rahner, 31st edition (Rahner was not associated with earlier editions), Herder, 1957; (with Heinrich Suso Brechter and Josef Hoefer) *Lexikon fuer Theologie und Kirche: Begruendet von Michael Buchberger*, Herder, 1957-65; (with Anton Boehm and others) *Haeresien der Ziet: Ein Buch zur Unterscheidung der Geister*, Herder, 1961; (with Vorgrimler) *Diaconia in Christo: Ueber die Erneuerung des Diakonates*, Herder, 1962; (with Otto Semmelroth) *Theologische Akademie*, Volumes I-X (Rahner was not associated with Volumes XI-XIII), J. Knecht, 1965-76.

Religionsfreitheit: Ein Problem fuer Staat und Kirche, Hueber, 1966; (with Mario von Galli and Otto Baumhauer) *Reformation au Rom: Die Katholische nach dem Konzil*, Wunderlich, 1967; (with Vorgimler) *Kleines Konzilskompendium: Alle Konstitutionen, Dekrete und Erklaerungen des 2. Vaticanums in der bischoeflich genehmigten Uebersetzung*, Herder, 1971, 4th edition, 1968; *The Pastoral Approach to Atheism*, translated by Theodore L. Westow and others, Paulist Press, 1967; (with others) *Sakramentum mundi: An Encyclopedia of Theology*, six volumes, 1968-70, later published as *Encyclopedia of Theology: The Concise Sacramentum mundi*, Seabury Press, 1975; *The Renewal of Preaching: Theory and Practice*, Paulist Press, 1968; (with Bernhard Haering) *Wort in Welt: Studien zur Theologie der Verkuendigung*, G. Kaffke, 1968; (with Herman Volk, Rudolf Haubst, and Semmelroth) *Martyria, Leiturgia, Diakonia*, Matthias-Gruenewald-Verlag, 1968; (with Morrissey) *Studies in Pastoral Theology*, Herder, 1968; *The Identity of the Priest*, Paulist Press, 1969.

(With Heinrich Schlier and Guenther Bornkamm) *Die Ziet Jesu*, Herder, 1970; (with Josef Schreiner, and contributor) *Die Kirche im Wandel der Gesellschaft*, Echter-Verlag, 1970; *Herders theologisches Taschenlexikon*, eight volumes, Herder, 1972-73; (with Karl Lehman) *Marsch ins Getto?: Der Weg der Katholiken in der Bundesrepublik*, Koesel-Verlag, 1973; (with Bernhard Grom) *Ist Gott noch gefragt?: Zur Funktionslosigkeit des Gottesglauben*, Patmos-Verlag, 1973; (with Bernhard Welte) *Mut zur Tugend: Ueber die Faehegheit, Menschlicher zu Leben*, Herder, 1979.

In English: *Happiness Through Prayer*, Newman Press, 1958, later edition published as *On Prayer*, Paulist Press, 1968; (with others) *The Future of Man and Christianity*, Argus Communications, 1969; *Meditations on Priestly Life*, Sheed & Ward, 1973; *The Courage to Pray*, Seabury Press, 1980.

In other languages: (Contributor) Dolcino Favi, *Vaticn Secondo*, La Locusta, 1963; *Studi sull'obedienza*, [Italy], c. 1968, translation published as *Obedience and the Church*, Corpus Books, 1968; *Le Message de Jesus et l'interpretation moderne* (selections from *Gott in Welt*), edited by R. Schrackenburg, A. Voetle, H. Schuermann, F. Muessner, and others, Editions du Cerf, 1969 (also see below). Also author, with Henri di Riedmatter, Marie-Dominique Chenu, Edward Schillebeeckx, and others, of *De Kirk in de wereld van deze tijd*, c. 1967.

Compilations: Vorgrimler and Metz, editors, *Gott in Welt: Festgabe fuer Karl Rahner*, two volumes, Herder, 1964; Martin Redfern, compiler, *Karl Rahner, S.J.*, Sheed & Ward, 1972; A. Vargas Machuca, editor, *Teologia y mundo contemporaneo: Homenaje a K. Rahner en su setenta cumpleanos*, Ediciones Cristinidad, 1975; Gerald A. McCool, *A Rahner Reader*, Seabury Press, 1975; Lehmann and Alberto Raffelt, editors, *Rechenschaft des Glaubens: Karl-Rahner-Lesebuch*, Benziger, 1979; John Griffiths, editor, *Prayers and Meditations: An Anthology of the Spiritual Writings of Karl Rahner*, Seabury Press, 1980; William Kelly, editor, *Theology and Discovery: Essays in Honor of Karl Rahner, S.J.*, Marquette University Press, 1980.

Contributor of articles to periodicals, including *Theological Studies* and *Woodstock Letters*.

SIDELIGHTS: "Compared to Karl Rahner," Martin E. Marty of the University of Chicago once remarked, "most other contemporary Christian theologians are scrub oak." Even when paralleled with notable twentieth-century thinkers such as Karl Barth and Paul Tillich, the Jesuit "in terms of balance is perhaps the greatest of the three," determined George A. Lindbeck, a prominent Protestant scholar. Though he shuns his celebrity status, Rahner, held by many to be the most influential teacher of the modern Catholic Church, is considered, at least in Thomas Sheehan's view, "the most brilliant Catholic theologian since Thomas Aquinas."

Entering the Society of Jesus at the age of eighteen, Rahner led a rather constant spiritual life, which sprang from his traditional Catholic background and was relatively unaffected by external happenings, including experiences in Nazi Germany when a school he was attending was closed by the regime. As Rahner noted in an *America* interview, "The remarkable, unusual, but obvious thing about my spiritual life was that all the new situations somehow revealed and brought home the one same ancient and genuine feature—by pointing ever and again toward God and His life." Influenced predominantly by his family and by the spirituality of St. Ignatius Loyola—gained through prayer and religious formation more than by studying philosophy and theology—Rahner is the disciple of no contemporary thinker, though he has been taught by Martin Heidegger and greatly influenced by Joseph Marechal. The author of over 3,500 books and articles, the Jesuit writes with a primarily pastoral, not theoretical, end in mind. He stated: "I have never or at least very seldom done theology for theology's sake, like 'art for art's sake.'"

With an optimistic bent in his teachings, the theologian asserts that all humanity naturally moves toward God, who is the final and absolute future reached only through death. The center of this theology, as Rahner revealed to Leo J. O'Donovan in *America*, "can't be anything else but God as mystery and Jesus Christ, the crucified and risen One, as the historical event in which this God turns irreversably toward us in self-communication."

For Rahner, God is a primary, essential, and incomprehensible mystery for which there is no adequate representation, so when God reveals himself as in a vision, he reveals only his mystery. A believer, then, must submit totally to the mystery, surrendering to that which he does not understand yet longs for. "If people are hungry for meaning," the Jesuit disclosed, "that is a result of the existence of God. If God does not exist, the hunger is absurd. The hunger is a longing that cannot be satisfied. A desire for God presumes the existence of God. If you have a longing for a mountain of gold, that may or may not be satisfied. But a longing for God cannot be taken away. Man is a being who does not live absurdly because he loves, because he hopes, and because God, the holy mystery, is infinitely receptive and acceptant of him."

Hence, the believer attains a knowledge, achieved because that knowledge transcended itself through love. "One should never stop thinking too early," Rahner explained. "The true system of thought really is the knowledge that humanity is finally directed precisely not toward what it can control in knowledge but toward the absolute mystery as such; that mystery is not just an unfortunate remainder of what is not yet known, but rather the blessed goal of knowledge which comes to itself when it is with the Incomprehensible One, and not in any other way.''

A believer must make a personal decision, accepting the obligations and responsibilities of faith, which brings about his change of heart. Some inherit belief, accepting and growing in the faith of their families; others search and struggle before they are able to assert their faith. Either way, as Rahner pointed out, the greatest stumbling block to faith today is life itself, the everyday as well as the catastrophic frustrations and misfortunes that overwhelm the spirit. Current times, he said, make believing all the more difficult since one individual cannot conquer all the disciplines, such as science and technology, necessary to prove the reasonableness of faith. Thus the priest wrote in volume five of the *Theological Investigations:* ''The real argument against Christianity is the experience of life, this experience of darkness.''

In Rahner's words, the emptiness of life is filled by God, and ''God is God—incomprehensible mystery to which man must give himself without understanding, but in faith and hope and love.'' To experience the nearness of God in the turmoil of living, man must confront this insolvable mystery and accept it in an act of self-surrendering love.

Anyone who accepts life, despite its shortcomings, accepts God, since God exists in the individual as the center of man. Therefore, in accepting himself, a man accepts God, ''for anyone who really accepts *himself,* accepts a mystery in the sense of the infinite emptiness which is man,'' revealed the Jesuit. ''He accepts himself in the immensity of his unpredictable destiny and—silently, and without premeditation—he accepts the One who has decided to fill this emptiness (which is the mystery of man) with his own infinite fullness (which is the mystery called God).''

Anything man says about himself, then, is a statement about God, and conversely anything man says about God is a statement about himself. Man finds God in love, for that is what God is. ''In love,'' wrote Rahner in *Encounters With Silence,* ''the gates of my soul spring open, allowing me to breathe a new air of freedom and forget my own petty self. In love my whole being streams forth out of the rigid confines of narrowness and anxious self-assertion, which make me a prisoner of my own poverty and emptiness. In love all the powers of my soul flow out toward You, wanting never more to return, but to lose themselves completely in You, since by Your love You are the inmost center of my heart, closer to me than I am to myself.''

To God, everything is ever present, which puzzles man because it is more than he can comprehend. A human must take all the forces in his life (such as goodness, strength, and courage) and ''order'' them so that one does not overcome the others, bringing chaos; for example, strength becoming brutish and violent or courage becoming foolhardy. God, on the other hand, is all as he is infinite: the boundless abode of all forces in compatability. Only man's love for God escapes tempering, for here order and moderation are needless. In loving God totally, man finds all he searches for because God is all, thus satisfying man's longing for the limitless.

Man's accepting the mystery of God in faith and hope is manifested in the human heart of Jesus. As a man, Christ is the self-expression of God, the ''Word of God among us.'' God's revelation, the essence of Christianity, comes through Jesus,

the Godman. ''The whole of the history of salvation and the history of revelation,'' Rahner advised in the *Woodstock Letters,* ''is the divinely ordered history of man's coming-to-himself, which is a reception of the divine self-communication, having its unsurpassible high priest (subjectively and objectively) in the person of Jesus Christ.''

Regardless of the ways the world may change, man stays a question without an answer just as God will remain incomprehensible, man's transcendent goal. To attain this goal, man must surrender totally and unconditionally to the mystery, accepting God's unexplainable nature by accepting human life and death. However the world evolves, said Rahner, it ''will [still] be a world overshadowed by that wordless mystery we call God; a world in which we come into existence without being consulted and in which death is an entering into mystery.''

In his theology, Rahner endeavors to express traditional dogma so that modern culture will understand and embrace it as contemporary and relevant. ''Christian Faith,'' he wrote, ''has by its very nature a new historical form in any given age. God Himself is changeless, but His call to men has a history. Therefore, it makes sense to speak of and ask about the Faith *today*. Each age and each individual must realize the Faith anew, and in many respects differently than it was done in previous ages. Likewise, within a given age, there are many different situations in which men live—the European and the African realize the same Faith in a different form, as do the peasant and the scientist.''

By hoping to make the church intellectually respectable, the theologian becomes a ''double agent.'' ''On the one hand,'' Eugene Kennedy maintained in the *New York Times Magazine,* ''he has been a loyal son for the Church who has never believed in throwing out even the driest husks of traditional Catholic teaching and practice; instead Rahner re-examines them to see if living cells still exist that can be scraped free and replanted in the soil of the modern world. On the other hand, once Rahner has established this continuity between the past and the present, he is a philosophical Burbank of mutations and permutations, giving birth to blooms of thought that appear radically transformed.''

The Jesuit sees a transformation of the Church into a world organization that respects the cultural identity of individual churches as well as non-Christians. Though unaware that they are called by God, many of these ''anonymous Christians'' still find salvation in a loving, but incomprehensible, God. ''An orthodox theologian is forbidden to teach that everybody will be saved,'' Rahner explained. ''But we are allowed to *hope* that all will be saved. If I hope to be saved, it is necessary to hope that for all men as well. If you have reason to love one another, you can hope that all will be saved.''

A transcendental Thomist, Rahner bases his theology in human historical experience. This involves every aspect of individual human experience. For instance, the Jesuit once wrote an essay on the Beatles, suggesting that scholars who hope to understand the modern world study pop music. Rather than investigating Church-related topics only, the theologian deals with issues that affect all of humanity, a relatively new approach.

Earlier this century, the Church opposed such modernism ardently, with Pope Pius X requiring priests to take oaths against the movement and with Catholic theologians studying the writings of St. Thomas Aquinas exclusively. Though Aquinas argued for the marriage of faith and reason, the Church's interpretation yielded a closed system of thought. In fact, although Rahner is not a modernist in the sense rejected by the Church, a dissertation adviser rejected the Jesuit's first thesis, later published as *Spirit in the World*, because he believed it did not accurately reflect St. Thomas's thinking.

In contrast to the Church's dogmatic positivism and formal theories, including Aquinas's five proofs for the existence of God, Rahner, without disagreeing with all of the Church's principles, offers God as the incomprehensible mystery. Shifting from rigid dogma to the ambiguity of the unexplainable, the priest submits that faith is accepting the mystery which is indispensable to man. He contended: "You shouldn't explain, but show that you cannot explain everything. The theologian reduces everything to God and explains God as unexplainable. Christianity intensifies our experience of mystery; it makes us more aware of it; it makes the mysterious more absolute. Christianity makes demands on mankind and prepares us for the acceptance of mystery." "The mystery of the universe," he went on to say, "the mystery that cannot be explained, that is what attracts me."

For the future, Rahner sees a changing church with the possibilities of ending the celibacy of the priesthood or ordaining women in response to the shortage of priests. Perhaps the pope will be moved from Italy to a more geographically sensible location, but with any alteration, the theologian maintained, "you have to make a distinction between dogmatic teaching and ecclesiastical discipline." No matter how radical the changes appear, Rahner is not a revolutionary. He has defended the Church when other theologians attacked, and according to Eugene Kennedy, he "is not a man to incite rebellion in the Catholic Church, but he has certainly provided the theological underpinnings for transformations that he feels are inevitable."

BIOGRAPHICAL/CRITICAL SOURCES—Books: Karl Barth and others, *Theologians of Our Time*, edited by Leonhard Keinisch, University of Notre Dame Press, 1964; Herbert Vorgrimler and Charles Muller, *Karl Rahner*, [Paris], 1965; Donald L. Gelpi, *Life and Light: A Guide to the Theory of Karl Rahner*, Sheed & Ward, 1966; Vorgrimler, *Karl Rahner: His Life, Thought and Works*, translated by Edward Quinn, Burnes & Oates, 1966; Florent Gaboriau, *Interview sur la Mort avec Karl Rahner*, [France], 1967; Patrick Granfield, *Theologians at Work*, Macmillan, 1967; Louis Roberts, *The Achievement of Karl Rahner*, Herder & Herder, 1967; Josef Speck, *Karl Rahners theologische anthropologie*, Koesel-Verlag, 1967; Martin Redfern, *Karl Rahner*, Sheed & Ward, 1972; William J. Kelly, editor, *Theology of Discovery: Essays in Honor of Karl Rahner, S.J.*, Marquette University Press, 1980; Leo J. O'Donovan, editor, *A World of Grace*, Seabury Press, 1980.

Periodicals: *Catholic World*, July, 1960, March, 1969, April, 1969, May, 1970, August, 1970; *Christian Century*, November 2, 1960, November 27, 1963, February 24, 1965, November 10, 1965, November 16, 1966, January 11, 1967, February 15, 1967, September 4, 1968, August 20, 1969, August 27, 1969, October 15, 1969, December 31, 1969, November 22, 1972, March 12, 1975, June 2, 1976, March 9, 1977, April 20, 1977, November 16, 1977, October 25, 1978, August 29, 1979, August 13-20, 1980, November 18, 1981, April 7, 1982; *Time*, December 14, 1962; *Woodstock Letters*, February, 1964; *Critic*, February, 1964, December, 1964-January, 1965, April, 1965, February, 1966, October, 1968, November, 1969, May-June, 1975, December, 1979, October, 1980; *Commonweal*, February 28, 1964, October 30, 1964, February 26, 1965, February 25, 1966, February 28, 1969, June 20, 1969, October

24, 1969, February 26, 1971, August 10, 1973, February 22, 1974, February 28, 1975, December 5, 1975, April 29, 1977, December 23, 1977, October 27, 1978, March 2, 1979, February 29, 1980, January 30, 1981, May 21, 1982.

Theology Digest, spring, 1964, summer, 1965, summer, 1967, February, 1968; *America*, May 9, 1964, November 7, 1964, February 6, 1965, September 25, 1965, January 1, 1966, October 22, 1966, November 12, 1966, May 6, 1967, February 10, 1968, November 16, 1968, December 21, 1968, March 15, 1969, May 3, 1969, July 5, 1969, October 11, 1969, November 29, 1969, February 14, 1970, August 8, 1970, November 28, 1970, November 18, 1972, July 23, 1973, December 15, 1973, June 7, 1975, November 15, 1975, May 29, 1976, November 13, 1976, March 19, 1977, August 13-20, 1977, February 25, 1978, May 6, 1978, March 10, 1979, January 26, 1980, March 21, 1981, March 14, 1982.

New York Times Book Review, January 3, 1965, March 16, 1969, March 12, 1978; *Christianity and Crisis*, October 18, 1965; *Choice*, February, 1966, February, 1967, October, 1967, November, 1968, March, 1969, May, 1973, November, 1973, July-August, 1975, November, 1975, February, 1976, September, 1978, April, 1979, September, 1980, July, 1982; *Times Literary Supplement*, May 12, 1966, May 4, 1967, October 26, 1967, July 31, 1970, September 25, 1970, May 12, 1972, November 24, 1972, September 6, 1974, May 30, 1975, September 3, 1982; *Books and Bookmen*, March, 1968, September, 1979; *Encounter*, summer, 1968; *Review for Religious*, January, 1969, March, 1969, May, 1969, September, 1969, January, 1970, May, 1970, July, 1970, November, 1970, November, 1973, May, 1974, July, 1975, January, 1976, July, 1979; *Review of Metaphysics*, September, 1969.

Theology Today, April, 1970, October, 1979, April, 1980, October, 1980, January, 1982; *Catholic Library Association*, May, 1970, December, 1975, December, 1976, May, 1979, May, 1980; *Ecumenical Review*, July, 1975; *Best Sellers*, October, 1976, September, 1979, November, 1979, May, 1980, April, 1981, April, 1982; *New Catholic World*, September, 1978, November, 1980; *Interpretation*, January, 1979; *The Catholic Mind*, March, 1979; *Journal of Religion*, July, 1979; *New York Times Magazine*, September 23, 1979; *Religious Studies Review*, January, 1981, April, 1982; *Modern Age*, spring, 1982; *New York Review of Books*, February 4, 1982; *U.S. Catholic*, November, 1982.

—*Sketch by Charity Anne Dorgan*

*   *   *

RAJANEN, Aini

PERSONAL: Surname is pronounced *Rah*-yah-nen. *Education:* University of Minnesota, B.S., 1970.

CAREER: Elementary school teacher in Minnesota, 1964-68; writer.

WRITINGS: Of Finnish Ways, Dillon, 1981; *A Tale for St. Urho's Tay*, Dillon, 1981.

WORK IN PROGRESS: A retelling of the Kalevala, the Finnish national epic, for children.

SIDELIGHTS: Rajanen told *CA:* "The main reason I prefer to remain anonymous is, I think, the feeling that I wish I'd done better. All the flaws I didn't see before publishing rise up to smite me, and I'm distressed to think that everyone who reads my work sees how far short it falls of what I meant it to be."

RAJEC, Elizabeth M(olnar) 1931-

PERSONAL: Born July 23, 1931, in Bratislava, Czechoslovakia; came to the United States in 1957, naturalized citizen, 1962; daughter of Lorinc and Tereza (Hinterschuster) Molnar; married Stephen L. Rajec, August 5, 1961. *Education:* Columbia University, B.S., 1963; Rutgers University, M.L.S., 1964; City University of New York, Ph.D., 1975. *Home:* 500 East 77th St., New York, N.Y. 10021. *Office:* City College of the City University of New York, 135th St. and Convent Ave., New York, N.Y. 10031.

CAREER: Institute of Cultural Relations, Budapest, Hungary, interpreter, 1951-54; Institute of Czechoslovak Culture, Budapest, librarian, 1954-56; Frankfurter-Graf (dress studio), New York City, fashion assistant, 1957-64; City College of the City University of New York, New York City, librarian and associate professor, 1964—. *Member:* American Library Association, Modern Language Association of America, Kafka Society of America, American Name Society, American Federation of Teachers, New York Library Association, Rutgers University Alumni Association, Delta Phi Alpha (Epsilon Beta chapter). *Awards, honors:* Fulbright grant, 1982-83.

WRITINGS: Namen und ihre Bedeutungen im Werke Franz Kafkas: Ein interpretatorischer Versuch (title means "Names and Their Meanings in the Works of Franz Kafka"), Lang, 1977; (editor) *The Study of Names in Literature: A Bibliography*, K. G. Saur, 1978, *Supplement*, 1981; (contributor) *International Kafka Bibliography*, Francke, 1982. Contributor to scholarly journals.

WORK IN PROGRESS: Research on playwright Ferenc Molnar.

SIDELIGHTS: Elizabeth Rajec has worked as a translator. Her languages include German, Hungarian, Slovak, and her native Czech. *Avocational interests:* Travel (Europe, the Orient).

*　　*　　*

RAMBO, Lewis Ray 1943-

PERSONAL: Born December 29, 1943, in Stephenville, Tex.; son of Harold J. (in business) and Gwendolyn (in business; maiden name, Gibson) Rambo; married Pamela Moser, August 24, 1967 (divorced February 5, 1980); children: Anna Catherine. *Education:* Abilene Christian University, B.A., 1967; Yale University, M.Div., 1971; University of Chicago, M.A., 1973, Ph.D., 1975. *Religion:* Church of Christ. *Home:* 35 Woodland Ave., Apt. 8, San Anselmo, Calif. 94960. *Office:* Department of Religion and Personality Sciences, San Francisco Theological Seminary, San Anselmo, Calif. 94960.

CAREER: Trinity College, Deerfield, Ill., assistant professor of psychology, 1975-78; San Francisco Theological Seminary, San Anselmo, Calif., assistant professor, 1978-81, associate professor of religion and personality sciences, 1981—. Assistant professor at Graduate Theological Union, Berkeley, Calif., 1978-81, associate professor, 1981—. *Member:* American Psychological Association, American Academy of Religion, Society for the Scientific Study of Religion, Religious Research Association, Association for the Sociology of Religion. *Awards, honors:* Fellow of National Endowment for the Humanities, 1978.

WRITINGS: (Editor with Donald Capps and Paul Ransohoff) *Psychology of Religion: A Guide to Information Sources*, Gale,

1976; *The Divorcing Christian*, Abingdon, 1983; *Conversion: Tradition, Transformation, and Transcendence*, Oxford University Press, in press.

SIDELIGHTS: Rambo told *CA:* "The interface between religion and psychology provides the domain of my academic and personal life. Psychology, and the other human sciences of sociology and anthropology, give us methods and theories to explore human consciousness, social processes, and cultural dynamics. Religion is a vast human enterprise in which meaning, purpose, transcendence, and mystery are manifested in dramatic forms. In addition to religion, I find the theatre and cinema to be what I call 'escapes to reality.' Human experience, with all its struggles, perversity, and promise, is distilled in vivid form in movies and plays, and in religious myths, rituals, and symbols.

"The two focuses of my current work are divorce and conversion. Because of personal experience, divorce is important to me, and I hope that my skills as a counselor, minister, and scholar can assist others who are experiencing that particular trauma. Conversion fascinates me because it demands cross-disciplinary research and theory and requires the understanding of a powerful and sometimes perplexing mode of personal and social change."

*　　*　　*

RANDELL, John Bulmer 1918-1982

PERSONAL: Born August 25, 1918; died April 30, 1982; son of Percy G. and Katie E. (Bulmer) Randell; married Margaret Davies, 1944; children: one daughter. *Education:* Welsh National School of Medicine, B.Sc., 1938, M.B., B.Ch., 1941, D.P. M., 1945, M.D., 1960.

CAREER: St. Ebba's Hospital, Epsom, England, psychiatric registrar; medical officer at Cefn Coed Hospital, 1941; medical officer at Sully Hospital, 1941-42; Guy's Hospital, London, England, first assistant medical officer at York Clinic, 1946-48; physician of psychological medicine at Charing Cross Hospital, 1949-82. Psychotherapist at St. George's Hospital, 1948-51; assistant psychiatrist at St. Thomas' Hospital, 1949-59; neuropsychiatric specialist at Ministry of Pensions. *Military service:* Royal Naval Volunteer Reserve, 1942-46; became temporary surgeon lieutenant. *Member:* Savile Club.

WRITINGS: Sexual Variations, foreward by Desmond Curran, Priory Press, 1973, Technomic Publishing, 1976.

AVOCATIONAL INTERESTS: Photography, cooking, gardening.

OBITUARIES: London Times, May 11, 1982.*

*　　*　　*

RANK, Benjamin (Keith) 1911-

PERSONAL: Born January 14, 1911, in Heidelberg, Australia; son of Wreghitt and Bessie Rank; married Barbara Lyle Facey, October 26, 1938; children: Helen Rank Willett, Andrew, Juliet Rank Phillips, Mary Rank Gray. *Education:* University of Melbourne, M.B., B.S., 1934, M.S., 1937; Royal College of Physicians, L.R.C.P., 1937. *Religion:* Anglican. *Home:* 12 Jerula Ave., Mount Eliza, Victoria 3930, Australia. *Office:* 29 Royal Parade, Parkville, Melbourne, Victoria 3052, Australia.

CAREER: Royal Melbourne Hospital, Melbourne, Australia, honorary plastic surgeon, 1946-66, consulting plastic surgeon,

1966—, chairman of board of postgraduate education, 1968-75, member of board of management, 1971-82, vice-president of hospital, 1979-82. Consulting plastic surgeon to Department of Repatriation, Queen Victoria Hospital, and Royal Victorian Eye and Ear Hospital; chief reparative surgeon at Peter MacCallum Clinic, 1964-79; chairman of committee of managemet at Victorian Plastic Surgery Unit, Preston, and Northcote Community Hospital, 1966—. Member of Victoria Motor Accident Board; chairman of Consultative Council Casualty Service, Victoria Health Commission; chairman of Victoria Council of St. John's Ambulance. Colombo Plan international aid professor in the 1950's; Commonwealth Traveling Professor of Surgery in Canada, 1958; visiting professor at Harvard University, 1976; lecturer in Australia, England, the United States, Canada, and India. *Military service:* Australian Army, Medical Corps, 1941-46; became lieutenant colonel.

MEMBER: Royal Australasian College of Surgeons (fellow; president, 1966-68), Australian College of Speech Therapy (fellow; foundation chairman), Royal College of Surgeons (fellow), British Association of Plastic Surgeons (president, 1965), Royal College of Surgeons (Canada; honorary fellow), Royal College of Surgeons (Edinburgh; honorary fellow). *Awards, honors:* Companion of Order of St. Michael and St. George, 1955; knighted, 1972; Companion of Order of St. John, 1983.

WRITINGS: (With A. R. Wakefield and J. T. Hueston) *Surgery of Repair as Applied to Hand Injuries,* 1953, 4th edition, Williams & Wilkins, 1973; *Jerry Moore and Some of His Contemporaries,* Hawthorn, 1975. Contributor of about seventy articles to medical journals in Australia, England, and the United States.

WORK IN PROGRESS: Head and Hands, "a personal biography" (which details the founding and development of the specialty of plastic surgery in Australia).

SIDELIGHTS: Sir Benjamin told *CA:* "History has so much to teach—for change is not always synonymous with progress. I wrote about Jerry Moore because he was a man whose contributions to our system did not get the recognition they deserved. As so often happens, the names of figureheads of the time tend to obliterate the real achievers. . . . My own philosophies and standards, I hope, will come through in the book I have just completed, *Head and Hands.*"

* * *

RANKINE, Paul Scott   1909(?)-1983

OBITUARY NOTICE: Born c. 1909 in England; died of congestive heart failure, February 11, 1983, in Washington, D.C. Political official and journalist. Rankine worked as an official of the British Ministry of Health in Washington, D.C., in the late 1930's and, during World War II, worked for the British Information Service. From 1944 to 1956 he was employed as chief of the Reuter news bureau. Rankine then became an adviser to British ambassadors until his retirement in 1970. Obituaries and other sources: *Washington Post,* February 14, 1983.

* * *

RANNIT, Aleksis   1914-

BRIEF ENTRY: Born October 14, 1914, in Kallaste, Estonia (now U.S.S.R.). Art historian and author. Rannit was chief curator of prints and rare books at the Lithuanian National Library from 1941 to 1944. He has also been a professor of art history at University of Freiburg and Yale University. Rannit wrote *Donum Estonicum: Poems in Translation* (Elizabeth Press, 1976), *Cantus Firmus* (Elizabeth Press, 1978), and a book of poems, *Kaljud* (Eesti Kirjanike Kooperativ, 1969). He co-edited *Estonian Poetry and Language: Studies in Honor of Ants Oras* (Kirjastus Vaba Eesti, 1965). *Address:* Yale University, Box 1603A, New Haven, Conn. 06520. *Biographical/critical sources: World Literature Today,* autumn, 1977; *Saturday Review,* July 8, 1978.

* * *

RASPONI, Lanfranco   1914-1983

*OBITUARY NOTICE—*See index for *CA* sketch: Born December 11, 1914, in Florence, Italy; died April 9, 1983, in Rio de Janeiro, Brazil. Agent and author. Rasponi was a prominent figure in New York society during the 1940's and 1950's. He acted as a publicity agent for Italian opera singers, including Renatta Tebaldi and Franco Corelli, and for the Quo Vadis and the Colony, two New York restaurants. He wrote on society and the performing arts. Rasponi's books include *The International Nomads, The Golden Oases,* and *The Last of the Prima Donnas.* Obituaries and other sources: *New York Times,* April 12, 1983, June 2, 1983.

* * *

RAUSCHNING, Hermann   1887-1982

OBITUARY NOTICE: Born July 8 (some sources say August 7), 1887, in Thorn, West Prussia (now Torun, Poland); died in 1982 in Portland, Ore. Politician and author. In 1933 Rauschning was appointed president of the German senate by Adolf Hitler. Within two years he found himself disillusioned and alienated from the goals of Hitler's National Socialist party. After resigning his post, Rauschning was forced to flee to Switzerland, and he later immigrated to the United States. The former Nazi's critical analyses of Hitler and his rule were published in *The Revolution of Nihilism, The Voice of Destruction,* and *Time of Delirium.* Obituaries and other sources: *Twentieth-Century Authors: A Biographical Dictionary of Modern Literature,* 1st supplement, H. W. Wilson, 1955; *Encyclopedia of the Third Reich,* McGraw, 1976; *Aufbau,* February 26, 1982.

* * *

RAWLYK, George Alexander   1935-

PERSONAL: Born May 19, 1935, in Thorold, Ontario, Canada; son of Samuel and Mary (Kautesk) Rawlyk; married, August 18, 1959; children: two. *Education:* McMaster University, B.A., 1957; University of Rochester, M.A., 1962, Ph.D., 1966. *Office:* Department of History, Queen's University, Kingston, Ontario, Canada K7L 3N6.

CAREER: Mount Allison University, Sackville, New Brunswick, Canada, lecturer in history, 1959-61; Dalhousie University, Halifax, Nova Scotia, Canada, assistant professor of history, 1963-66; Queen's University, Kingston, Ontario, Canada, associate professor, 1966-69, professor of history, 1969—. Researcher for Royal Commission on Bilingualism and Biculturalism, 1965-67. *Member:* Canadian Historical Association, Canadian Political Science Association, Organization of Canadian Historians, American Historical Association, Champlain Society. *Awards, honors:* Canada Council fellowship, 1967, senior fellowships, 1971-72, 1981-82.

WRITINGS: (Editor and author of introduction) *Historical Essays on the Atlantic Provinces*, McClelland & Stewart, 1967; (editor) *Joseph Howe: Opportunist? Man of Vision? Frustrated Politician?*, Copp Clark, 1967; *Yankees at Louisbourg*, University of Maine Press, 1967; *Revolution Rejected, 1775-1776*, Prentice-Hall, 1968; (with Ruth Hafter) *Acadian Education in Nova Scotia: An Historical Survey to 1965*, Information Canada, 1970; (Contributor) *Colonists and Canadians*, Macmillan, 1971; (contributor) *Essays on the Left*, McClelland & Stewart, 1971; (with Gordon Stewart) *A People Highly Favored of God*, Archon Books, 1972; *Nova Scotia's Massachusetts: A Study of Massachusetts-Nova Scotia Relations, 1630-1784*, McGill-Queen's University Press, 1973; (editor) *The Atlantic Provinces and the Problems of Confederation*, Breakwater Press, 1979; (with Bruce W. Hodgins and Richard P. Bowles) *Regionalism in Canada: Flexible Federalism or Fractured Nation?*, Prentice-Hall, 1979; *Streets of Gold*, Peter Martin Associates, 1981; (with Kevin Quinn) *The Redeemed of the Lord Say So*, QTC (Kingston, Ontario, Canada), 1981; (with M. A. Downie) *Acadian pour de bon* (title means "A Proper Acadian"), Kids Can Press, 1982; *The New Light Letters and Spiritual Songs*, Hantsport, 1983; *Henry Alline and the Evangelical Tradition*, Lancelot Press, in press. Contributor to magazines, including *Queen's Quarterly*.

SIDELIGHTS: Rawlyk told *CA:* "I am now particularly interested in the ways in which Evangelical religion influences English-Canadian culture, especially during the period 1776 to 1843."

BIOGRAPHICAL/CRITICAL SOURCES: American Historical Review, June, 1975.

* * *

RAY, N(ancy) L(ouise)   1918-
(Nan Hunt)

PERSONAL: Born September 16, 1918, in Bathurst, New South Wales, Australia; daughter of Edwin (an orchardist) and Katie (a stenographer; maiden name, Hazlewood) Ray; married Walter Gibbs Hunt (a grazier), November 18, 1967 (died December 8, 1975); children: three (stepchildren). *Education:* Educated in Australia. *Religion:* Christian. *Home and office:* 219 Peel St., Bathurst, New South Wales 2795, Australia. *Agent:* A. B. Ingram, 10/6 Boronia St., Wollstonecraft, New South Wales 2065, Australia.

CAREER: Western Stores & Edgleys Ltd., Bathurst, New South Wales, Australia, stenographer, 1935-43; Aeronautical Supply Co. Pty Ltd., Mascot, Australia, secretary, 1947-48; Briginshow Brothers Pty Ltd., Milsons Pointe, Australia, secretary, 1948-50; Bowes & Craig (chartered accountants), Sydney, Australia, secretary, 1950-67; writer. *Military service:* Women's Australian Auxiliary Air Force, 1943-46; became sergeant. *Member:* Australian Society of Authors, Children's Book Council of Australia. *Awards, honors:* Premier's Literary Award for best children's book from the state of New South Wales, 1982, for *Whistle Up the Chimney.*

WRITINGS—Juvenile novels: *Roma Mercedes and Fred*, Collins (Sydney, Australia), 1978; *The Everywhere Dog*, Collins, 1978; *The Pow Toe*, Collins, 1979; *There Was This Man Running*, Collins, 1979, Macmillan, 1981; *Nightmare to Nowhere*, Collins, 1980.

Juvenile picture books; under pseudonym Nan Hunt: *Whistle Up the Chimney*, illustrations by Craig Smith, Collins, 1981; *An Eye Full of Soot and an Ear Full of Steam*, illustrations by

Smith, Collins, 1983; *Wild and Wooly*, illustrations by Noela Hills, Lothian, 1983.

Short stories and poetry represented in anthologies, including *Beneath the Sun*, edited by Patricia Wrightson, Collins, 1972; *Too True*, compiled by Anne Bower Ingram, Collins, 1974; and *Emu Stew*, edited by Wrightson, Kestrel Books, 1976.

WORK IN PROGRESS: Two juvenile novels, *A Fist Full of Wind*, and *Stubbies, Thongs and Hairy Legs.*

SIDELIGHTS: Ray told *CA:* "I try to give children 'a good read' with dashes of humor. I make no apology for trying to stretch their imaginations, challenge them with the feelings and limitations of adults, or open their eyes to situations of fear and grief, which all come suddenly to many children. I try to be honest.

"Picture-book texts are a difficult discipline. To leave all the adjectives to the artist is the hardest thing I know in writing. Each work must be right."

* * *

RAYNER, Richard
See McILWAIN, David

* * *

READ, Leonard Edward   1898-1983

OBITUARY NOTICE—See index for *CA* sketch: Born September 26, 1898, in Hubbardston, Mich.; died of a heart attack, May 14, 1983, in Irvington-on-Hudson, N.Y.; cremated. Educator and author. Read served as the president of the Foundation for Economic Education, an organization he established in 1946 to promote his free-market philosophy and his thoughts on minimal government intervention. He also founded the Mont Pelerin Society to discuss free-market theories. Read's books include *Romance of Reality, The Free Market and Its Enemy, To Free or Freeze,* and *The Path of Duty.* Obituaries and other sources: *New York Times,* May 16, 1983; *Chicago Tribune,* May 17, 1983.

* * *

RECK, Franklin Mering   1896-1965

OBITUARY NOTICE: Born November 29, 1896, in Chicago, Ill.; died October 14, 1965, in Manchester, Mich.; buried at Oak Grove Cemetery, Manchester, Mich. Editor and author of books for children. Reck was managing editor of *American Boy* magazine from 1934 to 1941. His books include *Radio From Start to Finish, Stories Boys Like,* and *The Romance of American Transportation.* Obituaries and other sources: *New York Times,* October 16, 1965; *Publishers Weekly,* November 8, 1965; *Who Was Who in America, With World Notables,* Volume IV, *1961-1968,* Marquis, 1968.

* * *

REDFIELD, Alfred Clarence   1890-1983

OBITUARY NOTICE: Born November 15, 1890, in Philadelphia, Pa.; died March 17, 1983, in Falmouth, Mass. Oceanographer and author of works on physiology, biochemistry, and oceanography. Redfield's last book was *The Tides of the Waters of New England and New York,* published on the internationally known oceanographer's ninetieth birthday. Obituaries and other sources: *Blue Book: Leaders of the English-*

Speaking World, St. Martin's, 1976; *Who's Who in America,* 41st edition, Marquis, 1980; *The International Who's Who,* 46th edition, Europa, 1982; *American Men and Women of Science: The Physical and Biological Sciences,* 15th edition, Bowker, 1982; *Washington Post,* March 25, 1983.

*   *   *

REESE, (John) Terence   1913-

PERSONAL: Born August 28, 1913, in Epsom, England; son of John (a confectioner and hotelier) and Anne (a hotelier; maiden name, Hutchings) Reese; married Alwyn Sherrington (in business), 1970. *Education:* Attended Bradfield College and New College, Oxford. *Home:* 18a Woods Mews, Park Lane, London W.1, England.

CAREER: Writer and bridge expert. Bridge correspondent for *Evening News,* London, England, 1948-80, *Observer,* London, 1950—, *The Lady,* 1954—, and *The Standard,* 1980—. *Member:* St. James Bridge Club, Clermont Golf Club, Sunningdale Golf Club, Berkshire Golf Club. *Awards, honors:* Winner of numerous British, European, and world bridge championships.

WRITINGS: (With Hubert Phillips) *The Elements of Contract,* British Bridge World, 1937, 2nd edition, revised, Eyre & Spottiswoode, 1948; *Reese on Play: An Introduction to Good Bridge,* Edward Arnold, 1947, 2nd edition, R. Hale, 1975; (with Phillips) *How to Play Bridge,* Penguin Books, 1945, revised edition, Parrish, 1958; (with Phillips) *Bridge With Mr. Playbetter,* Batchworth Press, 1952; *The Expert Game,* Edward Arnold, 1958, new edition, R. Hale, 1973; *Master Play, the Expert Game: Contract Bridge,* Coffin, 1960, reprinted as *Master Play in Contract Bridge,* Dover, 1974; *Play Bridge With Reese,* Sterling, 1960; *Modern Bidding and the Acol System,* Nicholson & Watson, 1960; *Bridge,* Penguin Books, 1961, new edition, Hodder & Stoughton, 1980; *Develop Your Bidding Judgment,* Sterling, 1962, reprinted as *Bidding a Bridge Hand,* Dover, 1972; *The Game of Bridge,* Constable, 1962; (with Anthony Watkins) *Poker, Game of Skill,* Faber, 1962, Merrimack Book Service, 1964; *Learn Bridge With Reese,* Faber, 1962, revised edition, Hamlyn/American, 1978; (with Watkins) *Secrets of Modern Poker,* Sterling, 1964; *Bridge for Bright Beginners,* Sterling, 1964; *Your Book of Contract Bridge,* Faber, 1965, Transatlantic, 1971; *Story of an Accusation,* Heinemann, 1966, Simon & Schuster, 1967; (with Boris Schapiro) *Bridge Card by Card,* Hamlyn/American, 1969; (adapter from the French) Benito Garozzo and Leon Yallouze, *The Blue Club* (with foreword by Omar Sharif), Faber, 1969.

Precision Bidding and Precision Play, W. H. Allen, 1972, Sterling, 1973, 2nd edition, R. Hale, 1980; *Advanced Bridge* (adapted from *Play Bridge With Reese* and *Develop Your Bidding Judgment*), Sterling, 1973; (with Robert Brinig) *Backgammon: The Modern Game,* W. H. Allen, 1975, Sterling, 1976; *Play These Hands With Me,* W. H. Allen, 1976; *Bridge by Question and Answer,* Arthur Barker, 1976; *Bridge at the Top* (autobiography), Merrimack Book Service, 1977; *Begin Bridge With Reese,* Sterling, 1977; *Winning at Casino Gambling: An International Guide,* Sterling, 1978; *The Most Puzzling Situations in Bridge Play,* Sterling, 1978; (with Jeremy Flint) *Trick Thirteen* (novel), Weidenfeld & Nicolson, 1979; (with Patrick Jourdain) *Squeeze Play Made Easy: Techniques for Advanced Bridge Players,* Sterling, 1980 (published in England as *Squeeze Play Is Easy,* Allen & Unwin, 1980); *Bridge Tips by World Masters,* R. Hale, 1980, Crown, 1981; (with Eddie Kantar) *Defend With Your Life,* Merrimack Book Ser-

vice, 1981; (with David Bird) *Miracles of Card Play,* David & Charles, 1982.

With Albert Dormer: *Bridge Player's Dictionary,* Sterling, 1959, revised and enlarged edition, 1963, adaptation published as *Bridge Conventions, Finesses and Coups,* Sterling, 1965; *Blueprint for Bidding: The Acol System Applied to American Bridge,* Sterling, 1961; *The Acol System Today,* Edward Arnold, 1961, revised edition published as *Bridge, the Acol System of Bidding: A Modern Version of the Acol System Today,* Pan Books, 1978; *The Play of the Cards,* Penguin Books, 1967, new edition, R. Hale, 1977; *Bridge for Tournament Players,* R. Hale, 1968; *How to Play a Good Game of Bridge,* Heinemann, 1969; *How to Play a Better Game of Bridge,* Stein & Day, 1969; *Practical Bidding and Practical Play,* Sterling, 1973; *The Complete Book of Bridge,* Faber, 1973, Saturday Review Press, 1974; *The Bridge Player's Alphabetical Handbook,* Merrimack Book Service, 1981.

With Roger Trezel; all published by Fell, except as noted: *Safety Plays in Bridge,* 1976; *Elimination Play in Bridge,* 1976; *Blocking and Unblocking Plays in Bridge,* 1976; *Snares and Swindles in Bridge,* 1976; *When to Duck, When to Win in Bridge,* 1978; *Those Extra Chances in Bridge,* 1978; *The Art of Defence in Bridge,* Gollancz, 1979; *Master the Odds in Bridge,* Gollancz, 1979.

Editor: Ely Culbertson, *Contract Bridge Self-Teacher,* revised edition, Faber, 1965; Culbertson, *Contract Bridge Complete,* 7th edition, revised, Faber, 1965; Alfred Sheinwold, *Improve Your Bridge,* Jenkins, 1965; Josephine Murphy Culbertson, *Contract Bridge Made Easy the New Point Count Way,* Faber, 1966. Former editor of *British Bridge World* magazine.

WORK IN PROGRESS: Bridge: The Modern Game, for Faber; an adaptation from the French of *Omar Sharif's Life in Bridge,* for Faber.

SIDELIGHTS: Reese told *CA:* "Since 1976 I have played very little bridge and prefer to lose my money at backgammon. Tournament bridge is being ruined by the World Bridge Federation with its ghastly regulations, screens, and so forth."

BIOGRAPHICAL/CRITICAL SOURCES: Life, June 4, 1965; *Time,* June 4, 1965; *McCall's,* September, 1965; *New Statesman,* December 30, 1966; *Times Literary Supplement,* April 13, 1967; *Nation,* September 18, 1967.

*   *   *

REGOSIN, Richard L(loyd)   1937-

BRIEF ENTRY: Born September 3, 1937, in Brooklyn, N.Y. American educator and author. Regosin taught at Dartmouth College before he joined the faculty of University of California, Irvine, where he became a professor of French in 1978. He wrote *The Poetry of Inspiration: Agrippa d'Aubigne's "Les Tragiques"* (University of North Carolina Press, 1970) and *The Matter of My Book: Montaigne's "Essais" as the Book of the Self* (University of California Press, 1977). *Address:* 18241 Yellowwood, Irvine, Calif. 92715; and Department of French, University of California, Irvine, Calif. 92664. *Biographical/critical sources: Times Literary Supplement,* December 25, 1970, July 28, 1978; *Modern Language Journal,* February, 1972, January, 1979, July, 1980; *Virginia Quarterly Review,* spring, 1979.

REICH, Edward   1903(?)-1983

OBITUARY NOTICE: Born c. 1903; died May 31, 1983, in Mount Kisco, N.Y. Consumer advocate and author of articles and books. Reich, founder of the Consumer Education Association, was a member of the Consumers Union board of directors for thirty years and also served as the organization's vice-president and treasurer. He wrote *Consumer Goods: How to Know and Use Them* with Carlton John Siegler. Obituaries and other sources: *New York Times,* June 2, 1983.

*   *   *

REID, Dorothy M(arion)   ?-1974

OBITUARY NOTICE: Born in Edinburgh, Scotland; died March, 1974, in Victoria, New Brunswick, Canada. Librarian, educator, folklorist, and author. Reid became nationally recognized in Canada when her book *Tales of Nanabozho* was selected book of the year for 1965 by the Canadian Library Association. Reid gathered much of her knowledge of Indian legends and folklore while living in small towns throughout Canada. A librarian from 1956 to 1967 in Fort William, Ontario, Reid was also the host of a weekly children's story hour on radio called "The Magic Carpet." Reid received Canada's Centennial Medal in 1967. Obituaries and other sources: *Profiles,* Canadian Library Association, 1975.

*   *   *

REISCH, Walter   1903-1983

OBITUARY NOTICE: Born May 23, 1903, in Vienna, Austria; died of pancreatic cancer, March 28, 1983, in Los Angeles, Calif. Motion picture director and screenwriter. Reisch began his career as a journalist in Berlin before an interest in entertainment led him to writing screenplays for more than thirty German and Austrian silent movies. When Hitler came to power in 1933, Reisch returned to Austria from Germany and shortly thereafter fled to England, where he wrote and directed "Men Are Not Gods." In 1937 he arrived in the United States and began a successful career writing screenplays in Hollywood (sometimes in collaboration with Billy Wilder and Charles Brackett), notably for such films as "Ninotchka," a satire on communism touted by studio press agents as the film in which Greta Garbo laughed; "Gaslight," which earned an Academy Award for Ingrid Bergman; and "Titanic," for which Reisch, along with Brackett and Richard Breen, won an Oscar in 1953. He also wrote the screenplays for "The Girl in the Red Velvet Swing," "The Remarkable Mr. Pennypacker," and "Journey to the Center of the Earth." Obituaries and other sources: *Los Angeles Times,* March 30, 1983; *Chicago Tribune,* April 1, 1983; *Washington Post,* April 1, 1983; *London Times,* April 4, 1983; *Time,* April 11, 1983.

*   *   *

REITCI, John G(eorge)   1922-1983
(Jack Ritchie)

OBITUARY NOTICE: Born February 26, 1922; died of a heart attack, April 23, 1983, in Milwaukee, Wis. Author of more than five hundred short stories in the crime and mystery genre. Reitci's work was featured in the "Best Detective Stories of the Year" series seventeen times between 1961 and 1979 and appeared in nearly all of the Alfred Hitchcock anthologies. The mystery writer's offbeat sense of humor increasingly crept into his fiction during the course of his career and by the 1970's

had become his trademark. Reitci won an Edgar Award in 1981 for "The Absence of Emily." One of his short stories, "A New Leaf," was made into a motion picture, and several others have been adapted for television. Only one collection of Reitci's short stories has been published, *A New Leaf and Other Stories.* He also wrote a novelette, *Next in Line.* Obituaries and other sources: *Twentieth-Century Crime and Mystery Writers,* St. Martin's, 1980; *New York Times,* April 26, 1983; *Washington Post,* April 26, 1983; *Chicago Tribune,* April 27, 1983.

*   *   *

REITERMAN, Tim   1947-

PERSONAL: Born August 20, 1947, in San Francisco, Calif.; son of Milton Francis (a labor negotiator) and LaVerne Marie (a school administrator; maiden name, Martinotti) Reiterman; married Susan M. Gallison (a reference librarian), September 11, 1976; children: Amanda. *Education:* University of California, Berkeley, B.A., 1969, M.A., 1971. *Agent:* Michael Larsen/Elizabeth Pomada, 1029 Jones St., San Francisco, Calif. 94109. *Office:* San Francisco Examiner, 110 Fifth St., San Francisco, Calif. 94103.

CAREER: Associated Press, San Francisco, Calif., reporter, 1969-77; *San Francisco Examiner,* San Francisco, Calif., reporter, 1977—. *Awards, honors:* McQuade Award from Association of Catholic Journalists, 1978, for expose on chlorine hazards; top news story and photo awards from Hearst Newspapers, 1978, and award from San Francisco Bar Association, 1978, all for Guyana People's Temple coverage; award from International Association of Firefighters, 1981, for series on San Francisco Fire Department.

WRITINGS: (With John Jacobs) *Raven: The Untold Story of the Rev. Jim Jones and His People* (nonfiction), Dutton, 1982.

SIDELIGHTS: Raven: The Untold Story of the Rev. Jim Jones and His People, the effort of Reiterman and collaborator John Jacobs, was judged "the most valuable book on Jonestown to date" by David Evanier in a *National Review* critique. Evanier praised the work for its "illuminating and memorable" vignettes and found that "despite its length, there is little fat— no spuriously invented dialogue, no irrelevant information or unnecessary analysis."

Reiterman, a member of the press corps that accompanied Congressman Leo Ryan on an investigative trip to Guyana in 1978, was wounded in the attack at Kaituma Airport in which Ryan and four others were killed while Jones and 900 of his followers perished in the suicides and murders in Jonestown. Evanier related the effectiveness of *Raven* to "its massive research and wealth of extraordinary details coupled with an objective and largely non-ideological point of view." According to the reviewer, "Reiterman talked to everyone connected with Jones," tracing his beginnings as a small-town loner "attracted to religion as a source of warmth and community" and detailing his corruption of the powerful role of religious leader.

A particularly revealing early episode, noted Evanier, came after the ten-year-old Jones established his first church in a barn loft. Jones "sat on the only chair, and his classmates were allowed to sit on the floor before him. . . . When his friend refused to take his orders one day, Jones shot a .22 caliber rifle at him, barely missing him." In his final years, a drug-addicted and paranoid Jones established a church based on spying and subterfuge, practiced "healing tricks" on cancer victims, and subjected his zealots to degradation, sadism, and his own perversions before leading 900 of them to death.

"*Raven* does not explain Jones," concluded Evanier. "But through its accumulation of excellent details, he is understood by the book's end, without apology, exaggeration, superfluous information, or psychoanalysis." Peter Renner also praised the biography in a *Dallas Times Herald* review, noting, "Tim Reiterman and John Jacobs . . . have written a straightforward biography of Jones. 'Raven' . . . begins at the beginning and moves, deftly and with great drama, to its ineluctable, tragic, finale. . . . Jones' biography is told in a direct, reportorial manner, allowing the story to unfold itself." In a *New York Times Book Review* critique, Barbara Bright found fault with the work's introductory chapters, but conceded, "for the rest of the book Mr. Reiterman succeeds like a master." Bright termed Reiterman's descriptions of Jones's madness "strong" and "sensitive," and declared *Raven* a "powerfully written and well-researched book, documenting a peculiarly American tragedy."

BIOGRAPHICAL/CRITICAL SOURCES: Newsweek, December 4, 1978; *Time,* December 4, 1978; *National Review,* April 16, 1982; *Kirkus Reviews,* September 3, 1982; *Los Angeles Times Book Review,* December 12, 1982; *New York Times Book Review,* December 26, 1982; *Dallas Times Herald,* January 2, 1983.

*   *   *

REITHER, Joseph   1903-

PERSONAL: Born September 27, 1903, in Brooklyn, N.Y.; son of Joseph O. (a broker) and Emma (a teacher and musician; maiden name, Twitchell) Reither. *Education:* University of Virginia, B.A., 1934, M.A., 1935; further graduate study at University of Rome and University of Florence, both 1935-36, and University of Pennsylvania, 1936-38. *Politics:* Independent. *Home:* 102 West 183rd St., Bronx, N.Y. 10453.

CAREER: University of Virginia, Charlottesville, instructor in history and history of music, 1934-35; New York University, New York, N.Y., instructor, 1938-43, assistant professor, 1945-63, associate professor, 1963-68, professor of history, 1968-72, professor emeritus, 1972—. Lecturer at Manhattan School of Music, 1949-54, and Hunter College (now of the City University of New York); guest on television and radio programs; public speaker. Adviser to Office of War Information, 1942-43. *Military service:* U.S. Army Air Forces, Intelligence, chief of Logistical Services Branch and Technical Services Branch, 1943-45. *Member:* American Historical Association, American Academy of Political and Social Science, Rachmaninoff Society (member of board of advisers, 1950—), Phi Gamma Delta.

WRITINGS: World History: At a Glance, New Home Library, 1943, revised edition, Dolphin Books, 1965, published as *World History: A Brief Introduction,* McGraw, 1973; (editor) *Masterworks of History: Digests of 11 Great Classics,* Volume I: *Herodotus, Thucydides, Caesar, Tacitus,* Volume II: *Bede, Macaulay, Bancroft, Beard,* Volume III: *Gibbon, Symonds, Carlyle,* Doubleday, 1948, reprinted, McGraw, 1973; (with Stringfellow Barr) *The Pilgrimage of Western Man,* Harcourt, 1949. Also contributor to *A Pictorial History of the Army Air Force,* edited by Bayrd Still. Contributor to history and music journals.

REMI, Georges   1907-1983
(Herge)

*OBITUARY NOTICE—*See index for *CA* sketch: Born May 5, 1907, in Brussels, Belgium; died of leukemia, March 3, 1983, in Brussels, Belgium. Cartoonist best known as the creator of the comic-book hero Tintin, a boy reporter-adventurer who traveled throughout the world, even to the moon, fighting drugs, gunrunners, and corrupt politicians. Remi began the Tintin comics in 1929 and produced twenty-three books that sold seventy million copies in thirty-two languages. Some of his titles include *Tintin au Pays des Soviets, Tintin au Congo, Tintin in Tibet,* and *Tintin in the Picaros.* Obituaries and other sources: *New York Times,* March 5, 1983; *London Times,* March 5, 1983; *Washington Post,* March 5, 1983; *Chicago Tribune,* March 6, 1983; *Time,* March 14, 1983.

*   *   *

RENDELL, Ruth   1930-

PERSONAL: Born February 17, 1930, in London, England; married Donald Rendell, 1950 (divorced); children: one son. *Education:* Educated in Essex, England. *Address:* 3 Shepherds Close, London N.6, England.

CAREER: Reporter and subeditor for express and independent newspapers in West Essex, England, 1948-52; writer. *Awards, honors:* Edgar Allan Poe Award from Mystery Writers of America, 1975; Gold Dagger from Crime Writers Association, 1977.

WRITINGS—All novels: From Doon With Death, John Long, 1964, Doubleday, 1965; *To Fear a Painted Devil,* Doubleday, 1965; *In Sickness and in Health,* Doubleday, 1966 (published in England as *Vanity Dies Hard,* John Long, 1966); *A New Lease of Death,* Doubleday, 1967; *Wolf to the Slaughter,* John Long, 1967, Doubleday, 1968; *The Secret House of Death,* John Long, 1968, Doubleday, 1969; *The Best Man to Die,* John Long, 1969, Doubleday, 1970; *A Guilty Thing Surprised,* Doubleday, 1970; *No More Dying Then,* Hutchinson, 1971, Doubleday, 1972; *One Across, Two Down,* Doubleday, 1971; *Murder Being Once Done,* Doubleday, 1972; *Some Lie and Some Die,* Doubleday, 1973; *The Face of Trespass,* Doubleday, 1974; *Shake Hands Forever,* Doubleday, 1975; *A Demon in My View,* Hutchinson, 1976, Doubleday, 1977; *A Judgement in Stone,* Hutchinson, 1977, Doubleday, 1978; *A Sleeping Life,* Doubleday, 1978; *Make Death Love Me,* Doubleday, 1979; *The Lake of Darkness,* Doubleday, 1980; *Put on by Cunning,* Hutchinson, 1981; *Death Notes,* Pantheon, 1981; *Master of the Moor,* Pantheon, 1982.

Short story collections: *The Fallen Curtain: Eleven Mystery Stories by an Edgar Award-Winning Writer* (contains "The Fallen Curtain," "People Don't Do Such Things," "A Bad Heart," "You Can't Be Too Careful," "The Double," "Venus' Fly-trap," "His Worst Enemy," "The Vinegar Mother," "The Fall of a Coin," "Almost Human," and "Divided We Stand"), Doubleday, 1976 (published in England as *The Fallen Curtain and Other Stories,* Hutchinson, 1976); *Means of Evil and Other Stories* (contains "Means of Evil," "Old Wives' Tales," "Ginger and the Kingsmarkham Chalk Circle," "Archilles Heel," and "When the Weeding Was Over"), Hutchinson, 1979, published as *Five Mystery Stories by an Edgar Award-Winning Writer,* Doubleday, 1980.

SIDELIGHTS: "It's infuriating to see Ruth Rendell consistently referred to as the new Agatha Christie," wrote Cryptus in the *Detroit News.* "The fact is that Rendell . . . is incomparably better, attempting more and achieving more." Indeed, since issuing her first novel, *From Doon With Death,* in which she introduced her recurring sleuth, Chief Inspector Wexford of murder-prone Kingsmarkham, Sussex, England, Rendell has been applauded by critics for her deftness of characterization, ingenious plots, and surprising conclusions. Francis Wyndham of the *Times Literary Supplement* recognized Rendell's combining of a "masterly grasp of plot construction with a highly developed faculty for social observation." Wyndham added: "Ruth Rendell's remarkable talent has been able to accommodate the rigid rules of the reassuring mystery story (where a superficial logic conceals a basic fantasy) as well as the wider range of the disturbing psychological thriller (where an appearance of nightmare overlays a scrupulous realism)."

Rendell's adroitness at building suspense is also admired by reviewers. In a *New York Times Book Review* critique of *A Demon in My View,* Newgate Callendar wrote: "Nothing much seems to happen, but a bit here, a bit there, a telling thrust, and suddenly we are in a sustained mood of horror. Rendell is awfully good at this kind of psycho-suspense." Writing in the *Los Angeles Times Book Review* about *Lake of Darkness,* Charles Champlin noted: "[It] is . . . a cleverly plotted story whose several strands, seemingly only tentatively connected at the start, move toward a last, violent knotting (the sort of construction Alfred Hitchcock, who preferred suspense to the classic timetable mystery, might well have enjoyed)." Also reviewing *The Lake of Darkness* was *New York Times Book Review's* Callendar, who opined: "Her writing style is muted, purposely so, and that makes the extraordinary situations all the more biting. She has worked out a special field for herself, and she continues to pursue it with ingenuity." And commenting on *Master of the Moor,* T. J. Binyon of the *Times Literary Supplement* said, "Immaculately written and constructed, this is another of Ruth Rendell's skilful studies in abnormal psychology; a powerful, intriguing, if ultimately depressing novel."

BIOGRAPHICAL/CRITICAL SOURCES: Times Literary Supplement, February 23, 1967, December 21, 1967, April 23, 1970, October 1, 1976, June 5, 1981, July 23, 1982; *New York Times Book Review,* June 25, 1967, June 23, 1968, August 24, 1969, February 26, 1974, June 2, 1974, December 1, 1974, April 27, 1975, November 23, 1975, February 27, 1977, January 23, 1979, October 14, 1979, February 24, 1980, November 9, 1980; *Saturday Review,* January 30, 1971; *Detroit News,* August 12, 1979; *Los Angeles Times Book Review,* August 3, 1980, May 8, 1983; *Washington Post Book World,* September 20, 1981; *Chicago Tribune Book World,* December 19, 1982.*

*   *   *

RENSHON, Stanley Allen   1943-

BRIEF ENTRY: Born July 1, 1943, in Philadelphia, Pa. American political scientist, educator, and author. Renshon began teaching political science at Herbert H. Lehman College of the City University of New York in 1972. He also served as consultant to the National Commission on Marihuana and Drug Abuse. Renshon wrote *Psychological Needs and Political Behavior: A Theory of Personality and Political Efficacy* (Free Press, 1974). He edited *Handbook of Political Socialization: Theory and Research* (Free Press, 1977). *Address:* Department of Political Science, Herbert H. Lehman College of the City University of New York, Bronx, N.Y. 10468.

REVEL, Jean-Francois
See RICARD, Jean-Francois

*   *   *

REYNOLDS, Frank   1923-1983

OBITUARY NOTICE: Born November 29, 1923, in East Chicago, Ill.; died of viral hepatitis complicated by bone cancer, July 20, 1983, in Washington, D.C. Television journalist and author. Reynolds, one of the pioneers in television journalism, began his broadcasting career as a sports reporter for a Hammond, Indiana, radio station in 1947. He became a television news reporter on station WBKB-TV in Chicago in 1950 and in 1951 began a twelve-year stint as a reporter for the Columbia Broadcasting System's (CBS) Chicago affiliate, WBBM-TV. Reynolds spent two years with the American Broadcasting Companies (ABC) affiliate in Chicago before receiving an assignment to the ABC network news Washington bureau in 1965. He was teamed with Howard K. Smith in 1968 as co-anchor of the "ABC World News Tonight," but low ratings resulted in Reynolds's being replaced by Harry Reasoner in 1970. Reynolds continued to report for ABC News, covering political conventions and NASA's manned space flight launchings and providing commentary on and analyses of presidential speeches and press conferences. He returned to the "ABC World News Tonight" anchor desk in 1978 and, with co-anchors Max Robinson and Peter Jennings, brought the program's ratings to parity with those of its competitors. Aside from his political analysis and the writing of televised documentaries on Vietnam and Third World strife, Reynolds is also remembered for his on-the-air anger when he was provided information that led him to erroneously announce the death of White House Press Secretary James Brady following the 1981 assassination attempt on President Ronald Reagan. In 1969 he received the George Foster Peabody Award for excellence in the broadcasting medium. Reynolds was the co-author of *Somebody Please Love Me,* a study of narcotics and youth. Obituaries and other sources: *Times,* November 21, 1969; *TV Guide,* September 1, 1979; *Who's Who in America,* 42nd edition, Marquis, 1982; *Detroit Free Press,* July 20, 1983, July 21, 1983; *Chicago Tribune,* July 21, 1983; *New York Times,* July 21, 1983; *Los Angeles Times,* July 21, 1983; *Newsweek,* August 1, 1983; *Time,* August 1, 1983.

*   *   *

REYNOLDS, Jack
See JONES, Jack

*   *   *

REYNOLDS, Mary Trackett   1914-

PERSONAL: Born January 11, 1914, in Milwaukee, Wis.; daughter of James P. and Mary (Nachtwey) Trackett; married Lloyd George Reynolds (an economist), June 12, 1937; children: Anne Frances (Mrs. James F. Skinner), Priscilla (Mrs. Kermit Roosevelt, Jr.), Bruce Lloyd. *Education:* University of Wisconsin—Madison, B.A., 1935, M.A., 1935; further graduate study at Radcliffe College, 1935-36; Columbia University, Ph.D., 1939. *Home:* 75 Old Hartford Turnpike, Hamden, Conn. 06517. *Office:* 604 Yale Station, New Haven, Conn. 06520.

CAREER: Queens College (now of the City University of New York), Flushing, N.Y., instructor, 1939-40; Hunter College (now of the City University of New York), New York, N.Y., instructor, 1941-42; Johns Hopkins University, Baltimore, Md., associate in political science, 1942-43; Hunter College, lecturer, 1945-47; Connecticut College, New London, Conn., lecturer, 1947-48, assistant professor of political science, 1948-50; University of Bridgeport, Bridgeport, Conn., assistant professor of political science, 1950-51; Yale University, New Haven, Conn., research associate in economics, 1959-67; freelance writer, 1967-73; Yale University, visiting lecturer in English, 1973—. Research assistant for President's Committee on Administrative Management, 1936; senior economist for National Economic Committee, 1940; administrative assistant at Glenn L. Martin Aircraft Co., 1942-43; editorial assistant for public administration committee of Social Science Research Council, 1944-45; consultant to National Defense Advisory Commission, 1949, National Municipal Association, 1956, Organization for Economic Cooperation and Development (Paris), 1964, and U.S. State Department, Agency for International Development (USAID), 1965; member of board of directors of New Haven Hospital Auxiliary.

MEMBER: American Political Science Association, Dante Society of America, American Association of University Professors, American Society for Public Administration, League of Women Voters (former local president), Women's Civic League, Phi Beta Kappa, Lawn Club, Appalachian Mountain Club.

WRITINGS: Interdepartmental Committees in the National Administration, Columbia University Press, 1939, AMS Press, 1968; *Joyce and Dante: The Shaping Imagination,* Princeton University Press, 1981. Also contributor of articles to professional journals.

WORK IN PROGRESS: A Guide to "Finnegans Wake"; The Irish Literary Revival.

SIDELIGHTS: In *Joyce and Dante: The Shaping Imagination* Reynolds demonstrates the influence of the Italian poet Dante Alighieri on the writings of James Joyce. *Times Literary Supplement* critic Richard Brown pointed out that Reynolds "researched in detail the history of Joyce's reading of Dante, from unearthing his college curriculum to acquiring the actual copies of Dante's works which he possessed."

BIOGRAPHICAL/CRITICAL SOURCES: Times Literary Supplement, January 15, 1982.

*　　*　　*

RICARD, Jean-Francois   1924-
(Jean-Francois Revel)

BRIEF ENTRY: Born January 19, 1924, in Marseilles, France. French philosopher, critic, and author. Ricard, who has been a teacher of philosophy in Algeria, Mexico, Italy, and France, wrote a three-volume history of philosophy. He became literary editor and columnist for *L'Express* in 1966 and was appointed director of the publication in 1978. Ricard is best known for his social criticism, which has attracted attention on both sides of the Atlantic. In *As for Italy* (Dial, 1959) the author denounced Italian life, people, and sensibilities. Ricard's vehement criticism of the French political system in *The French* (Braziller, 1966) has been credited by some observers with prompting the resignation of President Charles De Gaulle in 1969. *Without Marx or Jesus: The New American Revolution Has Begun* (Doubleday) was issued by Ricard in 1971. The book, which argued that the last hope for preserving the world lay with the United States, shocked and outraged European readers. Additional works by Ricard include *On Proust* (Li-

brary Press, 1972) and *The Totalitarian Temptation* (Doubleday, 1977). *Address:* 55 quai de Bourbon, 75004 Paris, France; and *L'Express,* 25 rue de Berri, Paris 4e, France. *Biographical/critical sources: Current Biography,* Wilson, 1975; *Esquire,* November 1977; *Virginia Quarterly Review,* winter, 1978.

*　　*　　*

RICCI, Larry J.   1948-

PERSONAL: Born February 19, 1948, in New Jersey; son of Loreto A. and Helen (Ardizzone) Ricci; married Annette V. Lauria (a registered nurse), December 6, 1969; children: Judith Anne, Christian Michael. *Education:* Newark College of Engineering (now New Jersey Institute of Technology), B.S., 1969. *Religion:* Roman Catholic. *Home:* 314 Cindy St., Old Bridge, N.J. 08857. *Agent:* Denise Marcil Literary Agency, 316 West 82nd St., New York, N.Y. 10024. *Office:* McGraw-Hill, Inc., 1221 Avenue of the Americas, New York, N.Y. 10020.

CAREER: Diamond Shamrock Corp., Castle Hayne, N.C., chemical engineer, 1969-74; McGraw-Hill, Inc., New York, N.Y., managing editor of news, 1974—. *Member:* American Institute of Chemical Engineers, New York Business Press Editors.

WRITINGS: Separations Techniques, McGraw, Volume I, 1980, Volume II, 1981; *High-Paying Blue-Collar Jobs for Women,* Ballantine, 1981; (editor) *Synfuels Engineering,* McGraw, 1981. Contributor to popular magazines, including *Glamour* and *Redbook,* and engineering journals.

SIDELIGHTS: Ricci told *CA:* "I got into writing by the back door, I guess. For five years I worked for a chemicals manufacturer. Then I took a job with McGraw-Hill's technical magazine, *Chemical Engineering.* They needed someone with a technical degree to work as an editor of technical news. After some publishing experience, I started free-lance writing on the side. I wrote magazine articles concentrating on careers, which led to my first book."

*　　*　　*

RICCIARDI, Lorenzo   1930-

PERSONAL: Born May 11, 1930, in Milan, Italy; son of Giulio Cesare and Maria Gambarotta Ricciardi; married Mirella (a photographer; maiden name, Rocco), March 2, 1957; children: Marina, Amina. *Education:* Attended University of Milan, 1948-50. *Politics:* "I love freedom." *Religion:* "Catholic from my waist up." *Home:* 1502 San Ysidro Dr., Beverly Hills, Calif. 90210. *Agent:* Peter Miller, 1021 Avenue of the Americas, New York, N.Y. 10018.

CAREER: Writer and director of film "Venere Creola," 1965; Safari Company, Kilifi, Kenya, producer of films and documentaries, 1973-79; writer and director of television special "Voyage of Mir-El-Lah," 1979. Director of Sea-Safari (Kenya), 1970-79.

WRITINGS: The Voyage of the Mir-El-Lah, photographs by Mirella Ricciardi, Viking, 1981; *The Property of the Third Reich,* W. H. Allen, 1982.

WORK IN PROGRESS: Love Shock, a novel; *Once Upon a Time in America,* a book based on the film by Sergio Leone.

SIDELIGHTS: In *The Voyage of the Mir-El-Lah,* Lorenzo Ricciardi recounts his five-year journey on a traditional Arabian dhow around the Arabian Gulf and down the African coast. Fired with the romantic dream of traveling as sailors of old, the author and his photographer wife began their voyage at the port of Dubai and encountered numerous adventures along the way, including falconing with a sheik, false imprisonment, storms and landslides, and extraordinary diving and fishing. Although Ricciardi began his trek not knowing port from starboard, the adventurer became, in the end, as seasoned and as seaworthy as any ancient mariner.

Ricciardi told *CA:* "Writing about one's own adventures or experiences is re-living them. To feel once more the best moments of your life and enjoy them for what they have given you, adds to your life and self."

*   *   *

RICE, Keith A(lan)   1954-

PERSONAL: Born April 3, 1954, in Evansville, Ind.; son of Robert W. and Gladys I. (McGregor) Rice. *Education:* Indiana State University, B.S., 1976. *Home:* 1917 B Lincoln Ave., Evansville, Ind. 47714. *Office:* New-Kro Oil Co., 2521 Lynch Rd., Evansville, Ind. 47711.

CAREER: New-Kro Oil Co., Evansville, Ind., accountant, 1977—.

WRITINGS: Out of Canaan (novel), Scribner, 1983.

WORK IN PROGRESS: War Ration Book Four (tentative title), a novel about the home front during World War II; research for a sequel to *Out of Canaan,* beginning about fifteen years after the first novel ended.

SIDELIGHTS: Rice's *Out of Canaan* is the story of sixteen-year-old Samuel Mead's investigation into the life of his great-grandmother, Daliah, an exhausted wife and mother who had left her family and eventually befriended a millionaire. She faces another crisis when she becomes pregnant and tries to determine which man, her husband or the millionaire, has impregnated her. Susan Isaacs, writing in the *New York Times Book Review,* declared: "One of the author's accomplishments is to make Daliah real, relevant in her need to be someone but true to her time and place. The year is 1892 and she is a poor, young, uneducated country woman who has chosen to live by her wits." Isaacs added, "In his debut as a novelist, Keith A. Rice has created a credible character and a memorable landscape."

Rice told *CA:* "*Out of Canaan* was written more from mood than circumstance. I hoped to achieve texture as much as story. *Out of Canaan* as a title signifies the search, and loss of something promised, the belief in hope above all else, and the promise which is just beyond the character's grasp.

"I have been a painter for years, and my writing captures a visual sense, the creation of place to which I add characters to populate and play against that visual background. I began seriously writing when I was no longer able, as a painter, to translate what I saw in my head to the canvas. I have been intrigued by light, its texture and quality. I was not ambitious or dedicated (or good) enough to take light and move it through the static embrace of hue and pigment. By writing I was capable of changing light, like collapsing hundreds of paintings and the change of light across them, one on top of another. I approach my writing as such.

"I have enjoyed southern writers because they too have a defined attachment to place before theme. Writers such as Welty, O'Connor, Capote, McCullers, Faulkner, Agee, and Caldwell satisfy my eye for the textures I recognized already.

"I have little advice for aspiring writers: I am but an aspiring writer myself! My World War II novel, in three parts (two completed—the third killing me) will detail the lives of two brothers, and one brother's girlfriend, who, though they spent much of their story on the homefront, were truly casualties as if they had seen battle. I am trying to distill the stories of my parents, relatives, and working associates for whom that war was the one great event of memory. I have heard the stories. Through fiction I hope to tell that ardor that even forty years later still creates reverence and myth."

BIOGRAPHICAL/CRITICAL SOURCES: Louisville Courier-Journal, May 1, 1983; *New York Times Book Review,* May 15, 1983; *Chattanooga Times,* May 18, 1983.

*   *   *

RICHARDSON, R(alph) Daniel   1931-

PERSONAL: Born November 23, 1931, in Wadesboro, N.C.; son of Ralph D. and Louise (Teal) Richardson; married Mary Alyce Barber (a registered nurse), June 9, 1962; children: Daniel, Kathleen, Matthew. *Education:* George Washington University, B.A., 1957; University of Maryland, M.A., 1960, Ph.D., 1969. *Office:* Department of History, Roanoke College, Salem, Va. 24153.

CAREER: Roanoke College, Salem, Va., instructor, 1967-69, assistant professor, 1970-75, associate professor, 1976-81, professor of modern European history, 1982—. *Military service:* U.S. Navy, 1950-52. *Member:* American Military Institute, Phi Alpha Theta, Sigma Delta Pi, Pi Gamma Mu.

WRITINGS: Comintern Army: The International Brigades and the Spanish Civil War, University Press of Kentucky, 1982. Contributor to *Virginia Social Science Journal, Canadian Journal of History, Military Affairs,* and *Red River Valley Journal of World History.*

WORK IN PROGRESS: Research on naval operations during the Spanish Civil War.

SIDELIGHTS: Richardson told *CA:* "Perhaps it was reading Hemingway's *For Whom The Bell Tolls* that first sparked my interest in the Spanish Civil War and the International Brigades. At any rate, as a graduate student I did a seminar paper on the subject and have been with it ever since. At first I accepted the widely held and highly romanticized view of that war as a clear-cut struggle between 'democracy' and 'fascism,' with the International Brigades standing foresquare in the democratic corner. This greatly oversimplified view has exhibited amazing staying power despite the work of many historians pointing out the complexities of that struggle. The widespread sympathy for the Loyalist side and the identification of that side with 'democracy' have made it difficult for many to accept or acknowledge the key role played by the Comintern on the Loyalist side. These same emotional atttchments have made it difficult for many to accept a sharp focus on the International Brigades as a Comintern-controlled military and political entity. And yet that is what the record shows.

"My book is the first in-depth study of the politics of the Brigades. I place them in the larger context of the complex political-military alignments of Loyalist Spain and in the broader Soviet-Comintern strategy of the popular front era. The fame of the Brigades has stemmed primarily from their military exploits, exploits certainly deserving of the recognition that they have received. But the Brigades were much more than simply a military force. No realistic understanding of the significance of the Brigades is possible without an appreciation of their intrinsically political nature and role. Using a wide array of sources in English, Spanish, French, Italian, and German, and a thorough analysis of the Brigades' own voluminous literary output, my book shows that the Brigades were a significant political, ideological, and propagandistic instrument which was used effectively by the Comintern for its own purposes, not only in Spain but on the larger world stage and that they were, from beginning to end, an integral part of that interlocking directorate which was the Soviet-Comintern apparatus in Spain.

"My current research interest is the naval side of the Spanish Civil War. In my previous work on that war I became aware of the almost complete lack of published work on that entire area of operations. Although I am still in the preliminary stages of this project, I find it a fascinating story. I hope to eventually write a book on it, filling the vacuum which now exists."

AVOCATIONAL INTERESTS: Sailing, travel (Europe, Latin America).

*   *   *

RIDGWAY, Judith   1939-
(Judy Ridgway)

PERSONAL: Born November 10, 1939, in Stalybridge, Cheshire, England; daughter of Leslie Randal (a company director) and Lavinia (Bottomley) Ridgway. *Education:* University of Keele, B.A., 1962. *Home and office:* 124 Queens Court, Queensway, London W2 4QS, England. *Agent:* Gloria Mosesson, 290 West End Ave., New York, N.Y. 10023.

CAREER: Northwestern Gas Board, Manchester, England, public relations executive, 1963-68; Thompson Yellow Pages Ltd., London, England, public relations manager, 1969-73; Welbeck Public Relations, London, associate director, 1973-79. Director of London Cooks (caterers). Cooking demonstrator at Ludlow festival, 1981. *Member:* Society of Authors.

WRITINGS—Under name Judy Ridgway; all cookbooks, except as noted: *The Vegetarian Gourmet*, Ward, Lock, 1979, Prentice-Hall, 1981; *Salad Days*, Foulsham, 1979; *Home Preserving*, Teach Yourself Books, 1980; *The Seafood Kitchen*, Ward, Lock, 1980; (editor) *The Colour Book of Chocolate Cookery*, Hamlyn, 1981; *Mixer, Blender, and Processor Cookery*, Teach Yourself Books, 1981; *The Breville Book of Toasted Sandwiches*, Martin Books, 1982; *101 Fun Foods to Make*, Hamlyn Children's Books, 1982; *Waitrose Book of Pasta, Rice and Pulses*, Hamlyn, 1982; *Home Cooking for Money* (on selling and marketing home-grown produce), Piatkus Books, 1983; *The Little Lemon Book*, Piatkus Books, 1983; "Making the Most of" series; publication by David & Charles, all 1983: *Making the Most of Rice, . . . Pasta, . . . Potatoes, . . . Bread, . . . Eggs, . . . Cheese; Cooking 'Round the World*, Macmillan Educational, 1983; *The Barbecue Cookbook*, Ward, Lock, 1983; *The Little Bean Book*, Piatkus Books, 1983; *The German Food Cookbook*, Martin Books, 1983; *Frying Tonight*, Piatkus Books, in press. Contributor to magazines, including *Woman and Home, Living*, and *Winepress*.

WORK IN PROGRESS: A book on consumer press relations, publication by Gower Press expected in 1984; a book on how to run small businesses such as wine bars and caterers, publication by Kogan Page expected in 1984; researching material for a biography of Lady Mary Wortley Montague.

SIDELIGHTS: Ridgway's career as a culinary writer and caterer grew out of her hobby of cooking and experimenting with recipes. Her cookbooks now number more than a dozen, and, according to *Daily Telegraph* writer Avril Groom, her "success is all the more remarkable because she had no cookery training." "One of her great strengths as a cookery writer is that, as a working woman, she understands working women's culinary problems very well," Groom opined, adding that Ridgway's recipes often call for inexpensive and easy-to-find ingredients.

Ridgway told *CA:* "I have specialized in food and cooking, but am now looking to expand my writing into other fields."

AVOCATIONAL INTERESTS: Classical music, opera, reading, and visiting the countryside.

BIOGRAPHICAL/CRITICAL SOURCES: Daily Telegraph, May 15, 1980.

*   *   *

RIDGWAY, Judy
See RIDGWAY, Judith

*   *   *

RIESER, Dolf   1898-1983

OBITUARY NOTICE: Born in 1898 in South Africa; died April 4, 1983. Painter, engraver, and author. After earning a doctorate in plant genetics Rieser became interested in painting during the 1920's. He later studied etching and engraving under Joseph Hecht. Rieser, who had been living in Paris, fled that city for England the day the Nazis entered Paris. He then offered his services to the British Special Operations Executive. Following the war the artist developed new techniques for color printing and for printing on translucent plastic and laminates. Rieser illustrated Joseph Conrad's *Heart of Darkness* with copper plate engravings and was the author of *Art and Science*. Obituaries and other sources: *London Times*, April 13, 1983.

*   *   *

RIFKIND, Simon H(irsch)   1901-

PERSONAL: Born June 5, 1901, in Meretz, Russia; came to the United States in 1910, naturalized citizen, 1924; son of Jacob and Celia (Bluestone) Rifkind; married Adele Singer, June 12, 1927; children: Richard Allen, Robert Singer. *Education:* City College (now of the City University of New York), B.S., 1922; Columbia University, LL.B., 1925. *Politics:* Democrat. *Religion:* Jewish. *Home:* 936 Fifth Ave., New York, N.Y. 10021. *Office:* 345 Park Ave., New York, N.Y. 10154.

CAREER: Legislative secretary to U.S. Senator Robert F. Wagner, 1927-33; Wagner, Quillinan & Rifkind, New York City, partner, 1930-41; U.S. District Court, Southern New York District, New York City, federal judge, 1941-50; Paul, Weiss, Rifkind, Wharton & Garrison, New York City, partner, 1950—. Herman Phleger Visiting Professor of Law at Stanford University, 1975. Partner of Stevenson, Rifkind & Wirtz, 1957-61. Chairman of Presidential Railroad Commission, 1961-62; co-chairman of President's Commission on the Patent System, 1965-66. Deputy police commissioner of New York City, 1951-52; member of New York City Board of Higher Education, 1954-66, and New York State Commission of Governmental Operations of the City of New York, 1959-61; member of board of directors of Beth Israel Medical Center, 1972—; chairman of board of directors of Charles Revson Foundation and Tudor Foundation; member of board of directors of Norman and Rosita Winston Foundation; director of Municipal Assistance Corp., 1975. Member of board of directors of Emerson Radio and Phonograph Corp., 1955-66, Sterling National Bank & Trust Co. of New York, 1955—, Revlon, Inc., 1956—, Loews Corp., 1959-77, S. Klein's Department Stores, Inc., 1963-67, and McAndrews & Forbes Group, Inc.

MEMBER: American Bar Association, American College of Trial Lawyers (regent, 1967-71; president, 1976-77), New York State Bar Association, New York County Lawyers Association (past member of board of directors), Association of the Bar of the City of New York, Phi Beta Kappa, Zeta Beta Tau, Harmonie Club.

AWARDS, HONORS: Honorary degrees include Litt.D. from Jewish Theological Seminary, 1950, LL.D. from Hofstra College (now University), 1962, Brandeis University, 1977, and City College of the City University of New York, 1978, and J.D. from Hebrew University of Jerusalem, 1980; Medal of Freedom from U.S. Army, 1946; Townsend Harris Medal from City College of the City University of New York, 1948; Louis Marshall Memorial Medal from Jewish Theological Seminary, 1962; medal of excellence from Columbia University, 1973.

WRITINGS: (With Jerome N. Frank, Stanley H. Fuld, and others) *The Basic Equities of the Palestine Problem,* edited by Moshe Davis, privately printed, 1947, reprinted, Arno, 1977. Author of government reports. Contributor to journals.

SIDELIGHTS: Rifkind told *CA:* "In the fall of 1945, I was requested by Secretary of War Robert Patterson and General Dwight D. Eisenhower, commanding general of the European theater of operations, to proceed to the occupied zone in Germany, and there to advise General Eisenhower on Jewish affairs. This invitation was prompted by the fact that a large number of Jews had been rescued from the German concentration camps and crematoria and were now in the care of the U.S. Army in Germany.

"During my stay in that post, General Eisenhower requested me to proceed to Palestine and to report to him concerning conditions there, in view of the fact that there was a pervasive desire on the part of the Jews in the displaced persons centers to immigrate to that country. At the time Great Britain was the mandatory power in Palestine and was opposed to such a movement.

"The United Nations undertook consideration of the subject of Palestine in 1947. *Basic Equities* was written as a brief to be considered by the United Nations in connection with the resolution of that concern."

*   *   *

RIGGIO, Thomas P(asquale) 1943-

PERSONAL: Born January 28, 1943, in New York, N.Y.; son of Anthony and Anna R. (Cappola) Riggio; married Milla Cozart (a professor of English), June 21, 1969; children: Anna Maria, Thomas Pasquale II. *Education:* Fordham University, B.A., 1964; Harvard University, M.A., 1967, Ph.D., 1972. *Home:* 20 Dearborn Dr., Manchester, Conn. 06040. *Office:* Department of English, University of Connecticut, U-25, Storrs, Conn. 06268.

CAREER: University of Connecticut, Storrs, assistant professor, 1972-80, associate professor of English, 1980—. *Member:* Modern Language Association, American Studies Association,

Phi Beta Kappa. *Awards, honors:* Woodrow Wilson fellowship, 1964-65; grant from American Council of Learned Societies, 1977.

WRITINGS: Theodore Dreiser: American Diaries, 1902-26, University of Pennsylvania Press, 1982. Contributor to journals, including *American Quarterly, American Literature,* and *Modern Fiction Studies.*

WORK IN PROGRESS: An edition of Dreiser/Mencken correspondence, 1907-1945, publication by University of Pennsylvania Press expected in 1985.

SIDELIGHTS: Theodore Dreiser began keeping a diary on the advice of his physician when he sank into a state of near physical and mental collapse following the failure of his first novel, *Sister Carrie.* Riggio's edition of Dreiser's *American Diaries* pulls together intermittent notes from three periods in the author's life: the early, illness-inspired entries of 1902 and 1903; those written from 1917 to 1919 after Dreiser moved to Greenwich Village; and a third set composed in California from 1919 to 1926, the period when Dreiser finally achieved success with the novel *An American Tragedy.*

Unlike the diaries of other literary figures, Dreiser's daily accounts include little or no direct reflection on his art. They concentrate almost totally on Dreiser's moment-to-moment activities, revealing his overwhelming sexual appetite and concern with the cost of living. Critic Kenneth S. Lynn noted in *American Scholar* that "to every bedroom, . . . Dreiser carried a manuscript. A workaholic as well as a womanizer, Dreiser saw no reason not to kill two birds with one stone by combining copulation with composition." "On the evidence of the diary," Lynn related, "one might add that Dreiser's mood swings were manic-depressive, that he was a compulsive worker who could not keep anxiety at bay without the anodyne of virtually nonstop writing, and that he had remarkably little aptitude for self-analysis." "All that the diarist was able to say about himself," assessed Lynn, "was that he was frightened of poverty and failure."

Lynn deemed Riggio's introduction to the diaries "exceptionally able," an opinion shared by Richard Lingeman, who, in a *Nation* article, termed Riggio's remarks "a model of biographical criticism." Lingeman praised Riggio for a "scholarly salvage operation" that "has brought up some buried treasure and a lot of useful factual ballast. . . . The material provides the most intimate autobiographical account we have of certain periods of Dreiser's life." Lingeman concluded that in *American Diaries* "the portrait of Dreiser that emerges . . . is not a radically new one, but now it has acquired the cumulative power of fact that a Dreiser novel has."

Alfred Kazin, in his *New York Times Book Review* critique, conceded that "these diaries by one of the most powerful novelists of the century have no intrinsic literary interest," but added, "What [Dreiser] generally put down . . . is an unrelievedly crass but oddly fascinating account . . . of his daily activities." "A novelist's diary," Kazin continued, "is usually not so much a confession as an unwitting display—and practice—of narrative method. . . . Diaries, even when they leave out much we would like to know, reproduce the writer's professional habit of mind and gift of observation." "Dreiser's," Kazin declared, "is no exception."

Riggio told *CA:* "My writing is moving more and more in the direction of biography, which seems to combine history and criticism in a narrative form not unlike a work of art. My present work I see as a stage on the way to the writing of full-scale biography.''

BIOGRAPHICAL/CRITICAL SOURCES: *New York Times Book Review*, August 22, 1982; *Nation*, September 18, 1982; *American Scholar*, autumn, 1982; *Times Literary Supplement*, September 24, 1982.

* * *

RIPA, Karol 1895-1983

OBITUARY NOTICE: Born March 21, 1895, in Lisko, Poland; died March 17, 1983, in Silver Spring, Md. Diplomat, humanitarian, and journalist. Ripa was exiled to Siberia in 1915 for his part in the struggle for Polish independence from Russia (now U.S.S.R.). He was active in government during Poland's brief period of autonomous rule between the two world wars, serving in the Congress of Poles, as vice-consul of the Republic of Poland, as director of immigration, and as commissioner for the Convention of the World League of Poles in Warsaw. In 1935 he became consul general of Poland in Pittsburgh, Pennsylvania, and in 1939 became consul general of Poland in Chicago, Illinois. Ripa left Polish government service following World War II and worked in the World Catholic Youth Organization as an international radio news commentator and host of the radio program "From My Viewpoint." During this period he also served as director of the American Press Services and as president of the Polish-Hungarian World Federation, of which he was a founder. Obituaries and other sources: *Who's Who in Polish America*, reprinted, Arno, 1970; *Chicago Tribune*, March 21, 1983.

* * *

RITCHIE, Jack
See REITCI, John G(eorge)

* * *

RIZZOLI, Andrea 1914-1983

OBITUARY NOTICE: Born September 15 (one source says September 16), 1914, in Milan, Italy; died of heart failure, May 31, 1983, in Nice, France. Publisher. In 1970 Rizzoli inherited his father's publishing empire and served as the firm's chairman until he retired in 1978. During his tenure as head of the company, Rizzoli arranged for the purchase of the well-known Italian newspaper *Corriere della Sera*. The paper's financial losses, along with an embezzlement scandal involving the publisher's sons, has left the future of the Rizzoli empire in doubt. Obituaries and other sources: *Chicago Tribune*, June 1, 1983; *New York Times*, June 2, 1983; *London Times*, June 4, 1983; *Publishers Weekly*, June 24, 1983.

* * *

ROACH, Jack L. 1925-

BRIEF ENTRY: Born September 25, 1925, in Buffalo, N.Y. American sociologist, educator, and author. Roach taught sociology at State University of New York at Buffalo for five years before joining the faculty of University of Connecticut in 1965. He received the Helen DeRoy Award from the Society for the Study of Social Problems in 1960. Roach co-edited *Social Stratification in the United States* (Prentice-Hall, 1969), *Radical Sociology* (Basic Books, 1971), and *Poverty: Selected Readings* (Penguin, 1972). *Address:* Department of Sociology, University of Connecticut, Storrs, Conn. 06268.

ROBBINS, Frank 1917-

PERSONAL: Born September 9, 1917, in Boston, Mass. *Education:* Studied at the Boston Museum of Fine Arts School and the National Academy of Design. *Address:* c/o National Cartoonists Society, 9 Ebony Ct., Brooklyn, N.Y. 11229.

OFFICE: Cartoonist and illustrator of books. Author and illustrator of comic strips, Associated Press, 1939-44, King Features Syndicate, 1944—. Writer and contributor of artwork to National Comics. Work represented in exhibitions, including Whitney Museum of American Art, 1956, Corcoran Gallery of Art, 1957, 1958, Toledo Museum of Art, 1957, 1958, National Academy of Design, 1957, 1958, and Audubon Artists, 1957, 1958. *Member:* National Cartoonists Society. *Awards, honors:* Rockefeller grant, 1932; National Academy of Design prize, 1935.

WRITINGS—Comic strips: "Scorch Smith," Associated Press, 1939-44; "Johnny Hazard," King Features Syndicate, 1944—. Writer for National Comics, including such titles as "Batman," "The Flash," and "The Unknown Soldier."

Illustrator; written by Howard Liss; published by Messner: *Football Talk for Beginners*, 1970; *Basketball Talk for Beginners*, 1970; *Hockey Talk for Beginners*, 1973; *Bowling Talk for Beginners*, 1973; *Auto Racing for Beginners*, 1975; *Skiing Talk for Beginners*, 1977.

Contributor of artwork for "The Shadow," National Comics. Also contributor of illustrations to magazines, including *Look*, *Life*, *Saturday Evening Post*, and *Cosmopolitan*.

* * *

ROBERTS, Dennis W(ayne) 1947-

PERSONAL: Born October 15, 1947, in Sacramento, Calif.; son of Harold Franklin and Velma Roberts; married Linda Elliott (a word processor), November 15, 1969. *Education:* California Polytechnic State University, B.S., 1969; also attended Bethany Bible College, Santa Cruz, Calif., 1974-75. *Religion:* Assemblies of God. *Home:* 1205 Bennington Court, Roseville, Calif. 95678. *Agent:* Don Tanner Literary Associates, 428 South Brea Blvd., Brea, Calif. 92621. *Office:* 115 Washington St., Roseville, Calif. 95678.

CAREER: Grass Valley Union, Grass Valley, Calif., advertising representative, 1969-70; C. O. Boggess Advertising, Sacramento, Calif., account executive, 1971-73; Bethany Bible College, Santa Cruz, Calif., director of college relations, 1975-78; free-lance writer and advertising copywriter, 1978-80; Prison Ministries, Sacramento, assistant to director, 1980-81; free-lance writer, 1981—. Member of board of directors of Prison Ministries Center, Inc., 1981—. *Military service:* California National Guard, 1970-75. *Awards, honors:* Higher Goals in Christian Journalism Award from Evangelical Press Association, 1980, for humor article "Bring on the Bromide Seltzer."

WRITINGS: (Contributor) Doug Wead, editor, *People's Temple, People's Tomb*, Logos International, 1979; *Well, Excu-u-use Me!* (evangelism), Harvest House, 1980; *God Made Him to Prosper* (Christian growth), Restoration Fellowship, 1980. Contributor to magazines, including *Moody Monthly, Christian Life, Youth Alive!, Charisma, Voice, Quiet Hour*, and *Logos Journal*. Editor of *Pardoned*; past editor of *Reflections of Bethany Bible College*.

WORK IN PROGRESS: A book on Bobby Novak, an ex-convict who became director of Prison Ministries in Sacramento.

SIDELIGHTS: Roberts commented: *"Writer's Indigestion* recently called me 'the least known writer in the history of the English language, with the possible exception of C. Frederick Dobson,' who taught me everything I know about obscurity. (Don't bother trying to look Fred up in any anthology. We unknown authors pay millions each year to insure that our names remain out of the public eye. So far, I have gotten my money's worth, as did Fred.)

"I wish I could show press reviews to authenticate my anonymity, but I have already paid out thousands of dollars this year to keep my name out of their columns. Sorry.

"Right now you're probably saying, 'Gee, remaining a literary unknown sounds like a full-time job.' Well, you're right, it is. but don't be discouraged. Sure it's hard work, and the hours are bad, but the field is wide open and the rewards priceless. Imagine the thrill—and relief—of watching Norman Mailer or Jimmy Breslin sweating through another tedious interview on the Carson show, realizing that there, but for the grace of God, go thee and me. I'll tell you, there's no feeling quite like it.

"'Golly, What's-your-name,' you're saying now, 'I'm convinced! How can I, So-and-So, become a literary unknown?' If you're reading this, which apparently you are, you've probably generated a best-seller or two, and you've had it with the degenerating, debilitating, creativity-quashing life of a millionaire celebrity author. You yearn for the days when you were a struggling young (or struggling old) writer who couldn't get his byline in a church bulletin; the days before sun-tanned agents called you 'Baby'; those wonderful years before idolatrous English majors clamored for your autograph after sampling your awesome spoken wit in a packed-out auditorium. Well, I'd like to help you, Bub, but you made your bed, and now you're going to have to, etc.

"If, by chance, you are still one of the few remaining unknown authors, however, there is hope for you. The key is in the words of Jesus: Don't let your right hand know what your left is doing. It's hard to type (or word-process) that way, but no editor in his right mind will accept a manuscript that says things like 'Oh, Fawn, you foolish little minx, you half-tablespoon of margarine melted slowly in a large bowl.'

"One final word of caution: lest you be tempted to throw away your hard-won obscurity, remember that celebrities are often the targets of drug-crazed loonies. And what are those loonies seeking? Recognition, of course. Now, do you want to be in the same class as a bunch of loonies?

"I rest my case."

*   *   *

ROBERTS, Howard R(adclyffe)   1906-

PERSONAL: Born March 26, 1906, in Villanova, Pa.; son of Howard Radclyffe and Eleanor Page (Butcher) Roberts; married Enid Hazel Warden, August 23, 1933; children: Pauline Stella, Radclyffe Burnand, Eleanor Page. *Education:* Princeton University, B.S., 1929; University of Pennsylvania, Ph.D., 1941. *Home:* 651 Darby-Paoli Rd., Villanova, Pa. 19085. *Office:* Academy of Natural Sciences, 19th St. and Parkway, Philadelphia, Pa. 19103.

CAREER: University of Pennsylvania, Philadelphia, instructor in zoology, 1935-41, honorary lecturer, 1956—; Academy of

Natural Sciences, Philadelphia, Pa., research associate in entomology, 1936-46, director and chief executive officer, 1947-72, research fellow in department of entomology, 1971—. Wistar Institute of Anatomy and Biology, trustee and secretary; Children's Seashore House, Atlantic City, N.J., secretary, 1956-65, treasurer, 1970-75, president, 1975—. *Military service:* U.S. Army, 1942-45, served with malaria survey unit in Pacific Theatre; became captain. *Member:* American Association for the Advancement of Science, Entomological Society of America, Society for the Study of Evolution, Society for Systematic Zoology, Academy of Natural Sciences (trustee), Fairmount Park Art Association (trustee), Sigma Xi.

WRITINGS: The Beginner's Guide to Underwater Photography (juvenile), McKay, 1978; *Food Safety,* Wiley, 1981.

*   *   *

ROBERTS, Kenneth (Lewis)   1885-1957

BRIEF ENTRY: Born December 8, 1885, in Kennebunk, Me.; died July 21, 1957, in Kennebunkport, Me.; buried in Arlington National Cemetery, Arlington, Va. American journalist and author of historical novels. Roberts began his literary career as editor of Cornell University's humor magazine, *Widow,* during his college years. He went on to edit the *Boston Sunday Post*'s humor page and to contribute verse, plays, and editorials to popular humor magazines. After World War I Roberts served for ten years as a roving reporter for the *Saturday Evening Post,* covering a vast range of topics; his early books were collections of these articles. By 1928 Roberts had begun work on his first historical novel, *Arundel* (1930), the story of Benedict Arnold's heroic march to Quebec. A meticulous researcher, the author sought out firsthand accounts of historical events rather than relying upon secondary reports by other historians. This quest for truth and accuracy in research characterized all of Roberts's historical works, including *Northwest Passage* (1937), *Oliver Wiswell* (1940), and *Boon Island* (1956). In 1957 Roberts received a special Pulitzer Prize for having "long contributed to the creation of greater interest in our early American history." *Biographical/critical sources:* Kenneth Roberts, *I Wanted to Write,* Doubleday, 1949; *Who Was Who in America,* Volume III: *1951-1960,* Marquis, 1966; *Longman Companion to Twentieth Century Literature,* Longman, 1970; *American Novelists of Today,* Greenwood Press, 1976; *Dictionary of Literary Biography,* Volume 9: *American Novelists, 1910-1945,* Gale, 1981.

*   *   *

ROBERTS, Philip Davies   1938-

PERSONAL: Born October 9, 1938, in Sherbrooke, Quebec, Canada; son of Geoffrey Davies and Mary (Williams) Roberts; married Carol Lynn Berney, December 1, 1978; children: Rachael Ann, Megan Leah. *Education:* Acadia University, B.A., 1959; Oxford University, B.A. (with honors), 1962, M.A., 1966; University of Sydney, B.Mus., 1979. *Home:* 1201 North Fess, Bloomington, Ind. 47401; also residences in Canada and Costa Rica. *Agent:* Katherine Kidde, Kidde, Hoyt & Picard, 335 East 51st St., New York, N.Y. 10022.

CAREER: British Institute, Madrid, Spain, English teacher, 1962; Reuters News Agency, London, England, sub-editor, 1963-66; Peters/Bishop & Partners, London, public relations consultant, 1966-67; University of Sydney, Sydney, Australia, lecturer, 1967-74, senior lecturer in English, 1974-79; freelance writer, 1980—; *Tico Times,* San Jose, Costa Rica, staff writer, 1982—. Founder and editor of Island Press, 1970-79. *Awards, honors:* Rhodes scholar at Oxford University, 1959; Chapman Memorial Prize for poetry from Oxford University, 1962.

WRITINGS: Just Passing Through (poems), Ladysmith Press, 1969; (with Geoff Page) *Two Poets,* University of Queensland Press, 1971; (editor with J. C. Bright and P. M. Bright) *Models of English Style,* Science Press, 1971; *Crux* (poems), Island Press, 1973; *Will's Dream* (poems), University of Queensland Press, 1975; *Selected Poems,* Island Press, 1978. Contributor to *English Studies* and *Semiotica.* Poetry editor of *Sydney Morning Herald,* 1970-74.

WORK IN PROGRESS: The Reader's Guide to English Poetry, a technical manual for newcomers.

SIDELIGHTS: Roberts told *CA:* "I write to communicate at least one possible way of looking at things. My writing habits are irregular—I am at the opposite end of the spectrum from those who write regularly every day a painstaking couple of pages. Apart from my poetry, the books I have written have so far been quite didactic, a step away from school books, though I hope not altogether humorless.

"I was much influenced at the start of my writing career by Robert Graves, who gave enthusiastic advice and criticism for a number of years. Since then, I have been most influenced by foreign poets: the Greeks Safevis and Kavafis, the Czech Holub, the Russian Pasternak, the French St. John Perse, to mention a few. English poets I particularly admire are Skelton, Donne, Herbert, Blake, and Whitman. I react to poetry as being closer to music than to 'meaningful' speech.

"In the near future I hope to write books dealing with traditional ballads (words and music), nursery rhymes (ditto), and being a landlord (words only)."

*   *   *

ROBERTSON, Durant Waite, Jr.   1914-

PERSONAL: Born in 1914; son of Durant Waite Robertson; married Betty Hansen; children: Durant, Douglas, Susanna. *Education:* University of North Carolina, B.A., 1935, M.A., 1937, Ph.D., 1945. *Home:* 421 Whitehead Circle, Chapel Hill, N.C. 27514.

CAREER: Princeton University, Princeton, N.J., currently Murray Professor of English Literature Emeritus. *Member:* Mediaeval Academy of America (fellow), Renaissance Society of America, American Association for the Advancement of Science. *Awards, honors:* American Council of Learned Societies fellowship, 1945-46; Guggenheim fellowship, 1957; D.Litt., 1973; fellowship from National Humanities Center, 1980-81.

WRITINGS: (With Bernard F. Huppe) *Piers Plowman and Scriptural Tradition,* Princeton University Press, 1951; (translator) *St. Augustine's On Christian Doctrine,* Liberal Arts Press, 1958; *A Preface to Chaucer: Studies in Medieval Perspectives,* Princeton University Press, 1962; (with Huppe) *Fruyt and Chaf,* Princeton University Press, 1963; *Chaucer's London,* Wiley, 1968; *The Literature of Medieval England,* McGraw, 1970; *Abelard and Heloise,* Dial, 1972; *Essays in Medieval Culture,* Princeton University Press, 1980. Contributor to scholarly journals.

WORK IN PROGRESS: Research on Chaucer's *Canterbury Tales,* in the context of fourteenth-century English society, developments in that society, and contemporary attitudes toward them.

ROBERTSON, James Wilson   1899-

PERSONAL: Born October 27, 1899, in Broughty Ferry, Scotland; son of James and Margaret Eva (Wilson) Robertson; married Nancy Walker, July 21, 1926; children: James, Caroline (Mrs. D.G.T. Alexander). *Education:* Balliol College, Oxford, B.A., 1922, M.A., 1930. *Religion:* Church of Scotland. *Home:* Old Bakehouse, Cholsey, Oxfordshire OX10 9NU, England.

CAREER: Sudan Political Service, assistant district commissioner, 1922-33, district commissioner, 1933-36, compensation commissioner of Jebel Aulia Dam, 1936, sub-governor of White Nile Province, 1937-39, deputy governor of Gezira Province, 1939, acting governor, 1940-41, assistant civil secretary, 1941-42, deputy civil secretary, 1942-45, civil secretary, 1945-53; Uganda Co. Ltd., director, 1954-55; Government of Nigeria, governor general and commander-in-chief, 1955-60; Uganda Co. Ltd., director, 1961-69; Barclays Bank, director, 1961-71. Chairman of British Guiana Constitutional Committee, 1954; commissioner of Kenya Coastal Strip Inquiry, 1961; governor of Queen Mary College, University of London, 1961-72; member of executive council of Royal Commonwealth Society for the Blind, 1961—; chairman of Royal Overseas League, 1962-68; deputy chairman of National Committee for Commonwealth Immigrants, 1965-68. *Member:* Athenaeum Club, London. *Awards, honors:* Member of Order of the British Empire, 1931, knight commander, 1948; companion of Order of St. Michael and St. George, 1953; Knight Grand Cross of the Royal Victorian Order, 1956; LL.D. from University of Leeds, 1961; knight of the Thistle, 1965.

WRITINGS: Transition in Africa From Direct Rule to Independence (memoirs), C. Hurst & Co., 1974.

*   *   *

ROBERTSON, Wally
See ROBERTSON, Walter

*   *   *

ROBERTSON, Walter   1892-1983
(Wally Robertson)

OBITUARY NOTICE: Born May 16, 1892, in Glasgow, Scotland; died February 10, 1983. Cartoonist. Robertson's career began in 1914 with an assignment to produce sixteen drawings per week for *Merry and Bright.* During World War I the cartoonist served in France, where he produced a sketchbook of drawings capturing the horrific reality of war. It was Robertson's unfulfilled wish to have the collection published. He joined the staff of Amalgamated Press in 1918 and remained there for thirty years, drawing such characters as Waddles, Marmy and His Ma, and Luke and Len the Odd Job Men. Robertson was also regarded as the "prime duplicator," reproducing the style of other cartoonists so well that he would fill in for them when they were ill or on vacation. As a result, however, of the British tradition of maintaining the anonymity of cartoonists, Robertson's name was unknown to his readers. In 1980 he received the Ally Sloper Award for service to British comics. Obituaries and other sources: *London Times,* February 16, 1983.

ROBESON, Paul (Leroy Bustill) 1898-1976

OBITUARY NOTICE: Born April 9, 1898, in Princeton, N.J.; died January 23, 1976, in Philadelphia, Pa. Singer, actor, civil rights activist, and author. Robeson was one of the first prominent black Americans to publicly and forcefully speak out against racial inequality. The son of a runaway slave, Robeson distinguished himself at Rutgers College (now Rutgers University) both academically and athletically. Following his graduation from Rutgers, Robeson attended Columbia Law School, supporting himself by playing professional football. He was disappointed with the opportunities available to him as a black man in the legal profession so he turned to a career in the theatre. Robeson's work with the Provincetown Players caught the attention of playwright Eugene O'Neill, who cast Robeson as the lead in two O'Neill plays, "Emperor Jones" and "All God's Chillun Got Wings." Robeson appeared in numerous other plays, including "Black Boy," "Show Boat," and "Othello," and in eleven motion pictures. In addition to his acting roles, Robeson was an accomplished vocalist who made many concert appearances and recordings. He and his wife spent a great deal of time in Europe, where the racial climate was more tolerant and where he became associated with members of left-wing political causes. After World War II Robeson's political views and his outspoken praise of the Soviet Union led the House Committee on Un-American Activities to label the actor a Communist sympathizer. Despite government investigations and the loss of public support, Robeson continued to make speeches supporting the "scientific socialism" of the Soviet Union, which led to the revocation of his U.S. passport in 1950 and his being awarded the Stalin Peace Prize by the Soviets in 1952. He regained his passport in 1958 and left the United States until 1963, when he returned in ill health and, it was rumored, disillusioned with communism. Robeson underwent a resurgence of popularity among the American liberal community during the early 1970's. In 1958 Robeson wrote an autobiography, *Here I Stand.* Obituaries and other sources: *New York Times,* January 24, 1976; *Newsweek,* February 2, 1976; *Time,* February 2, 1976; *Who Was Who in America, With World Notables,* Volume VI: *1974-1976,* Marquis, 1976; *Current Biography,* Wilson, 1977.

*   *   *

ROBEY, Edward George (Haydon) 1900-1983

OBITUARY NOTICE: Born in 1900; died March 5, 1983. Jurist and author. Robey, the son of famous British music hall comedian Sir George Robey, was called to the Bar by the Inner Temple in 1925. He began an eighteen-year career as a public prosecutor in 1932. In 1945 Robey was appointed to the Attorney General's Executive for Prosecution of the Major War Criminals at Nuremberg, and from 1954 to 1972 served as a magistrate in London, England. He was the author of an autobiography, *The Jester and the Court.* Obituaries and other sources: *Who's Who,* 134th edition, St. Martin's, 1982; *London Times,* March 11, 1983.

*   *   *

ROBINS, Eli 1921-

PERSONAL: Born February 22, 1921, in Houston, Tex.; married Lee Nelken (a professor of sociology), February 22, 1946; children: Paul, James, Thomas, Nicholas. *Education:* Rice University, B. A., 1940; Harvard University, M. D., 1943. *Office:* Department of Psychiatry, School of Medicine, Washington University, 4940 Audubon Ave., St. Louis, Mo. 63110.

CAREER: Mount Sinai Hospital, New York, N. Y., rotating intern, 1944; Massachusetts General Hospital, Boston, assistant resident in psychiatry, 1944-45; McLean Hospital, Waverly, Mass., resident in psychiatry, 1945-46; Pratt Diagnostic Hospital, Boston, fellow in psychiatry, 1948, resident in neurology, 1948-49; Barnes Hospital, St. Louis, Mo., fellow in psychiatry, 1949-51; Washington University, St. Louis, instructor, 1951-53, assistant professor, 1953-56, associate professor, 1956-58, professor of psychiatry, 1958-66, Wallace Renard Professor of Psychiatry, 1966-, head of department, 1963-75. Attending psychiatrist at St. Louis City Hospital, 1951—; assistant psychiatrist at Barnes and Allied Hospitals, 1951-63, psychiatrist-in-chief, 1963-75, psychiatrist, 1975-; visiting psychiatrist at St. Louis State Hospital, 1958-. Heinrich Waelsch Lecturer at Columbia University, 1976. Member of advisory board of World Federation of Neurology's Commission of Neurochemistry, 1960—; chairman of National Institute of Mental Health's subcommittee on biological sciences, 1961. *Military service:* U. S. Army, chief of neurologic and psychiatric services at Murphy General Hospital, Waltham, Mass., 1947-48.

MEMBER: International Brain Research Organization, International Psychiatric Association for Advancement of Electrotherapy, International Society of Neurochemistry, International Society of Psychoneuroendocrinology, American Academy of Neurology, American Association for the Advancement of Science (fellow), American College of Neuropsychopharmacology (fellow), American Federation for Clinical Research, American Psychiatric Association (fellow), American Psychopathological Association, American Society of Biological Chemists, American Society for Clinical Investigation, American Society for Neurochemistry, Association for Research in Nervous and Mental Disease (vice-president, 1960), Society to Conquer Mental Illness (president, 1974—), Histochemical Society, Psychiatric Research Society, Society of Biological Psychiatry, Society for Neuroscience, Classification Society, Royal College of Psychiatrists (fellow), New York Academy of Sciences (fellow), Phi Beta Kappa, Sigma Xi, Alpha Omega Alpha. *Awards, honors:* Fellow of U.S. Public Health Service, 1949-51; gold medal from Society of Biological Psychiatry, 1974; Paul H. Hoch Award from American Psychopathological Association, 1977; award of merit from St. Louis Medical Society, 1978; Salmon Medal from Salmon Committee on Psychiatry and Mental Hygiene, 1981.

WRITINGS: (Editor with S. R. Korey and A. Pope) *Ultrastructure and Metabolism of the Nervous System,* Williams & Wilkins, 1962; (with M. T. Saghir) *Male and Female Homosexuality: A Comprehensive Investigation,* Williams & Wilkins, 1973; (editor) Karl Leonhard, *The Classification of Endogenous Psychoses,* translated by Russell Berman, 5th edition (Robins was not associated with earlier editions), Irvington, 1979; *The Final Months: A Study of the Lives of One-Hundred-Thirty-Four Persons Who Committed Suicide,* Oxford University Press, 1981.

Contributor: E. Podoldky, editor, *The Neuroses and Their Treatment,* Philosophical Library, 1957; H. A. Abramson, editor, *Neuropharmacology,* Josiah Macy, Jr., Foundation, 1959; R. Cancro, editor, *The Schizophrenic Syndrome: An Annual Review,* Brunner, 1971; Thomas A. Williams, Martin M. Katz, and James A. Shield, Jr., editors, *Recent Advances in the Psychobiology of the Depressive Illnesses,* U. S. Government Printing Office, 1972; J. Zubin and F. A. Freyhan, editors, *Disorders of Mood,* Johns Hopkins University Press, 1972; R. W. Albers, B. Agranoff, and other editors, *Basic Neuro-*

chemistry, Little, Brown, 1972; M. Rolf, L. N. Robins, and M. Pollack, editors, *Life History Research in Psychopathology*, Volume XI, University of Minnesota Press, 1972; A. Sudilvosky, S. Gershon, and B. Beer, editors, *Predictability in Psychopharmacology: Preclinical and Clinical Correlations*, Raven Press, 1975; S. Hagop, Akiskal, and William L. Webb, editors, *Psychiatric Diagnosis: Exploration of Biological Predictors*, Spectrum, 1978; H. M. Van Praag, M. H. Lader, and other editors, *Handbook of Biological Psychiatry*, Part I: *Disciplines Relevant to Biological Psychiatry*, Dekker, 1979; Judd Marmor, editor, *Homosexual Behavior: A Modern Appraisal*, Basic Books, 1980.

Contributor to *International Encyclopedia of Psychiatry, Psychology, Psychoanalysis, and Neurology*. Contributor of about one hundred fifty articles to medical journals. Member of editorial board of *Journal of Neurochemistry*, 1968-74, *Medical World News*, 1970-79, and *Communications in Psychopharmacology*, 1975—; member of advisory editorial board of *Biological Psychiatry*, 1970-75, member of editorial board, 1975-77, member of editorial committee, 1977—; member of editorial advisory board of *Neurochemistry International*, 1980—.

WORK IN PROGRESS: Research on the effects of probenecid on tricyclic therapy of depression; research on positron emission tomography (PET) of anxiety attacks in anxiety neurosis; psychological studies of Emmanuel Kant.

SIDELIGHTS: Robins told *CA:* "The motivation for a good deal of my work in psychiatry stems from being taught by Mandel E. Cohen and Raymond D. Adams at Harvard Medical School and by Edwin F. Gildea and Oliver H. Lowery at Washington University. I have worked in the areas of experimental neurochemistry, clinical psychiatric study, and biochemical studies of psychiatric topics (mainly neurotransmitters)."

* * *

ROBINSON, Alice M(erritt)   1920-1983

OBITUARY NOTICE—See index for *CA* sketch: Born December 4, 1920, in Islip, N.Y.; died of a heart attack, March 18, 1983, in New York, N.Y. Educator, administrator, and author. Robinson served as the director of Specialized Consultants in Nursing since 1975. She also edited *RN* magazine and *Nursing Outlook*. Prior to 1963, she concentrated on hospital work at George Washington University Hospital, the Veterans Administration Hospital in Little Rock, Arkansas, Boston State Hospital, and Vermont State Hospital. Her books include *The Psychiatric Aide: His Post in Patient Care*, *The Unbelonging*, and *Clinical Writing for Health Professionals*, which she wrote with Lucille Netter. Obituaries and other sources: *New York Times*, March 23, 1983.

* * *

ROBINSON, Betsy Julia   1951-

PERSONAL: Born February 7, 1951, in New York, N. Y.; daughter of Richard I. (a salesman) and Edna (a writer; maiden name, Randall) Robinson. *Education:* Attended National Theatre Institute, 1971; Bennington College, B. A., 1973. *Home:* 57 West 70th St., New York, N. Y. 10023. *Agent:* Helen Merrill, 337 West 22nd St., New York, N. Y. 10011.

CAREER: Francis Thompson, Inc., New York City, apprentice film editor and projectionist, 1969; Cubiculo Theatre, New York City, assistant to program director, box office manager,

and house manager, 1970-71; actress in New York City, 1972—; Educreative Systems, Inc., New York City, manuscript typist, transcriber, and editor, 1974; New York State Council on the Arts, New York City, secretary to the director of public relations, 1975; Poets and Writers, Inc., New York City, circulation manager for *Coda* (magazine), 1976-77; SSC&B Advertising, Inc., New York City, secretary and assistant to television producers, 1979-80; Lisl Cade, New York City, part-time administrative secretary, 1981; New World Records, Recorded Anthology of American Music, Inc., New York City, part-time secretary, 1981-82. *Member:* Dramatists Guild, Ensemble Studio Theatre.

WRITINGS: Plays: "The Shanglers" (two-act; first produced in Waterford, Conn., at Eugene O'Neill Playwrights Conference, July, 1976), published in *New Plays by Women*, edited by Susan LaTempa, Shameless Hussy Press, 1979; "Gladys Mazurky" (two-act), first produced in New York City at Ensemble Studio Theatre, 1978; "The Last Available Burial Ground on Manhattan Island" (one-act; first produced at Ensemble Studio Theatre, 1980), published in *At Rise*, spring, 1980; "Out to Lunch" (one-act), first produced at Ensemble Studio Theatre, 1980; "Inventory" (two-act), first produced in Amherst, Mass, at Theatre in the Works, July, 1982; "The Conquest" (teleplay), first produced at Eugene O'Neill Playwrights Conference, July, 1982; "The Staff Meeting" (one-act), first produced at Ensemble Studio Theatre, October, 1982. Also author of plays "Kin" (three-act), "A Platonic Affair" (three-act), and "WOW" (one-act), as yet unpublished and unproduced. Contributor to magazines, including *Wisdom's Child*.

WORK IN PROGRESS: Third one-act play for a trilogy that includes "The Staff Meeting" and "WOW".

SIDELIGHTS: Robinson told *CA:* "I need to write, If I didn't, I wouldn't. But I do; it fulfills me in a way that nothing else I've ever done has. Sometimes I wish I would find something else more lucrative and as fulfilling, but I haven't. So I write."

* * *

ROCHESTER, Harry A(rthur)   1897(?)-1983

OBITUARY NOTICE: Born c. 1897 in New York, N.Y.; died of a heart ailment, February 8, 1983, in Bethesda, Md. Military officer and author of a book on federal purchasing procedure, *How You Can Sell to the Government: A Clear Comprehensive Guide for Businessmen Large and Small. What to Offer! Where to Go! Whom to See!* Rochester served in the U.S. Navy during both world wars and rose to the rank of captain. Obituaries and other sources: *Washington Post*, February 12, 1983.

* * *

ROCKWELL, Harlow

PERSONAL: Married Anne Foote (a writer and illustrator of books for children), March 16, 1955; children: Hannah, Elizabeth, Oliver Penn. *Home:* 4 Raymond St., Old Greenwich, Conn. 06870.

CAREER: Illustrator and writer of books for children. Art director for an advertising agency. Work has been exhibited at Library of Congress. *Awards, honors: The Toolbox* was selected for the American Institute of Graphic Arts Children's Book Show, 1971-72; *Head to Toe* and *The Awful Mess* were both selected for the American Institute of Graphic Arts Children's Book Show, 1973-74; *Toad* was selected for the Children's Book Showcase, 1973.

WRITINGS—For children; self-illustrated: *ABC Book*, Golden Press, 1961, revised edition, 1967; *Printmaking*, Doubleday, 1973; *My Doctor*, Macmillan, 1973; *The Compost Heap*, Doubleday, 1974; *I Did It*, Macmillan, 1974; *My Dentist*, Greenwillow, 1975; *My Nursery School*, Greenwillow, 1976; *Look at This*, Macmillan, 1978; *My Kitchen*, Greenwillow, 1980; *Our Garage Sale*, Greenwillow, 1981.

Written and illustrated with wife, Anne Rockwell; published by Macmillan, except as noted: *Olly's Polliwogs*, Doubleday, 1970; *Molly's Woodland Garden*, Doubleday, 1971; *The Toolbox*, 1971; *Machines*, 1972; *Thruway*, 1972; *Toad*, Doubleday, 1972; *Head to Toe*, Doubleday, 1973; *The Awful Mess*, Parents' Magazine Press, 1973; *Blackout*, 1979; *The Supermarket*, 1979; *Out to Sea*, 1980; *My Barber*, 1981; *Happy Birthday to Me*, 1981; *I Play in My Room*, 1981.

Illustrator: Eve Witte and Pat Witte, *Touch Me Book*, Golden Press, 1961; A. Rockwell, *Sally's Caterpillar*, Parents' Magazine Press, 1966; Rubie Saunders, *The Calling All Girls Party Book*, Parents' Magazine Press, 1966; Violet Salazar, *Squares Are Not Bad*, Golden Press, 1967; *Little Songs for Little People*, Parents' Magazine Press, 1968.

Contributor of illustrations to periodicals, including *Good Housekeeping*, *McCall's*, and *Parents' Magazine*.

AVOCATIONAL INTERESTS: Sailing, gardening.

*   *   *

ROGERS, Fred B(aker) 1926-

PERSONAL: Born August 25, 1926, in Trenton, N.J.; son of Lawrence H. (a physician) and Eliza C. (an artist; maiden name, Thropp) Rogers. *Education:* Princeton University, A.A., 1947; Temple University, M.D., 1948; University of Pennsylvania, M.S., 1954; Columbia University, M.P.H., 1957; further study, Johns Hopkins University, 1962. *Home:* 301 West State St., Trenton, N.J. 08618. *Office:* Department of Family Practice and Community Health, Temple University School of Medicine, Philadelphia, Pa. 19140.

CAREER: Temple University Hospital, Philadelphia, Pa., intern, 1948-49, chief resident physician, 1953-54; Temple University School of Medicine, Philadelphia, U.S. Public Health Service fellow, 1954-55, assistant professor, 1956-58, associate professor, 1958-60, professor of preventive medicine, 1960—, chairman of department of family practice and community health, 1970-77. Lecturer, Columbia University School of Public Health, 1957-58, University of Pennsylvania School of Nursing, 1964-67; consultant, U.S. Naval Hospital, 1964-73. Diplomate, American Board of Preventive Medicine. *Military service:* U.S. Naval Reserve, active duty, 1950-53; served in Medical Corps in Europe, Japan, and Korea. *Member:* American Public Health Association, American College of Physicians (fellow), American Medical Association (chairman, preventive medicine section, 1963-64), Philadelphia Art Alliance, Sigma Xi, Alpha Omega Alpha, Phi Rho Sigma, Campus Club (Princeton), Franklin Inn Club (Philadelphia), Charaka Club (New York City), Osler Club (London).

WRITINGS: *A Syllabus of Medical History*, Stephenson, 1958, revised and enlarged edition, Little, Brown, 1962; *Help-Bringers: Versatile Physicians of New Jersey*, Vantage, 1960; *Epidemiology and Communicable Disease Control*, Grune, 1963; (editor) Morris Greenberg, *Studies in Epidemiology: Selected Papers*, Putnam, 1965; (with A. Reasoner Sayre) *The Healing Art: A History of the Medical Society of New Jersey*, Medical Society of New Jersey, 1966; *Your Body Is Wonderfully Made* (juvenile; illustrated by Mary E. Cashel), Putnam, 1974.

Author of medical studies; contributor to professional journals. Member of editorial board, *American Journal of Public Health*, 1967-73.

WORK IN PROGRESS: *Doctors and Doctoring on Cape Cod*, a book consisting of reprints of Rogers's articles on the medical history and biography of the region.

SIDELIGHTS: Rogers told *CA:* ''Writing the text of *Your Body Is Wonderfully Made* was stimulated by the fine art work of its illustrator, Mrs. Mary Elizabeth Cashel. Each plate conveyed graphically the function of a body system—circulatory, respiratory, and so forth. The book was designed for young readers, ages eight through twelve, so its message was screened for verbal comprehension by the Fry (Rutgers) Readability Scale. We feel that this work achieved its aim of aiding children in their growth and development.''

*   *   *

ROGERS, Pattiann 1940-

PERSONAL: Born March 23, 1940, in Joplin, Mo.; daughter of William Elmer and Irene (Keiter) Tall; married John Robert Rogers (a geophysicist), September 3, 1960; children: John Ashley, Arthur William. *Education:* University of Missouri, B.A., 1961; University of Houston, M.A., 1981. *Home:* 11502 Brookmeadows, Stafford, Tex. 77477.

CAREER: High school English teacher in Auxvasse, Mo., 1961-62, and St. Charles, Mo., 1962-63; kindergarten teacher in St. James, Mo., 1963-67; School for Little Children, Sugar Land, Tex., teacher, 1978-79; writer. Director of Poetry Readings for Children, 1974-76. *Member:* International P.E.N., Phi Beta Kappa. *Awards, honors:* Young poet's prize from *Poetry Northwest*, 1980, and Roethke Prize, 1981; Tietjens Prize from *Poetry*, 1981, and Hokin Prize, 1982; grant from National Endowment for the Arts, 1982; Voertmann Poetry Award from Texas Institute of Letters, 1982, for *The Expectations of Light*.

WRITINGS: *The Expectations of Light* (poems), Princeton University Press, 1981. Contributor of poems to magazines, including *New Yorker*, *Iowa Review*, *Georgia Review*, *Virginia Quarterly Review*, *Chicago Review*, and *Kenyon Review*.

WORK IN PROGRESS: *Angel of the Field*, poems; *Legendary Performance*, poems.

SIDELIGHTS: Rogers told *CA:* ''Circumstances important to my writing are leisure time and the ability to work within a family environment of economic and emotional security, within a country which permits and supports free expression and intellectual investigation.'' *Avocational interests:* Travel (including England).

*   *   *

ROGERS, Rutherford D(avid) 1915-

BRIEF ENTRY: Born June 22, 1915, in Jesup, Iowa. American librarian and author. Rogers began his library career in 1937 at the New York Public Library. He was chief assistant librarian of the Library of Congress from 1957 to 1962 and deputy librarian from 1962 to 1964. He was director of libraries at Stanford University from 1964 until 1969, when he became university librarian at Yale University. Rogers is also a member of the board of directors of publisher H. W. Wilson and chairman of the board of directors of Research Libraries Group. He wrote *University Library Administration* (H. W. Wilson, 1971). *Address:* 33 Edgehill Ter., New Haven, Conn. 06511; and University Libraries, Yale University, Box 1603A, Yale Station, New Haven, Conn. 06520.

* * *

RONALD, Hugh   1912(?)-1983

OBITUARY NOTICE: Born c. 1912; died March 18, 1983. Publisher. Ronald, who had been in newspaper publishing and the printing businesses in Indiana since the 1940's, published the *Portland Commercial Review* and the *Redkey Times-Journal.* He also served as vice-president of Earlham College from 1968 to 1976. Obituaries and other sources: *Chicago Tribune,* March 22, 1983.

* * *

ROPER, Lanning   1912-1983

OBITUARY NOTICE: Born February 4, 1912, in West Orange, N.J.; died March 22, 1983, in London, England. Horticulturalist, editor, and author. Roper remained in England following service there with the U.S. Navy during World War II. An internationally known horticulturist, Roper worked at the Royal Botanical Gardens in Edinburgh, Scotland, for a number of years and often collaborated with architects in the design of gardens. He became assistant editor of the Royal Horticultural Society's journal in 1951 and served as the gardening correspondent of the Sunday edition of the *London Times* from 1962 to 1975. Roper was also the author of books on garden design and gardening, including *Royal Gardens, Successful Town Gardening, Hardy Herbaceous Plants, The Gardens in the Royal Park at Windsor,* and *The Sunday Times Garden Book.* Obituaries and other sources: *London Times,* March 24, 1983.

* * *

ROSE, Alvin E(manuel)   1903-1983

OBITUARY NOTICE: Born December 13, 1903, in Chicago, Ill.; died May 28, 1983, in Oceanside, Calif. Public housing official, journalist, and author of *The Restless Corpse.* Rose began his journalism career as a reporter for the *Chicago Tribune* in 1927, covering such stories as the St. Valentine's Day massacre in 1929. In 1935 he became city editor of the *Chicago Times.* Three years later he became an official of the Chicago Relief Administration (later known as the Chicago Welfare Administration). Rose held that post until 1957, when he was appointed executive director of the Chicago Housing Authority. He resigned in 1967. Obituaries and other sources: *Who's Who in America,* 38th edition, Marquis, 1974; *Chicago Tribune,* June 5, 1983.

* * *

ROSE, Anna Perrott
See WRIGHT, Anna (Maria Louisa Perrott) Rose

* * *

ROSE, Arnold   1916-1983

OBITUARY NOTICE: Born in 1916 in Manchester, England; died February 13, 1983. Singer, educator, and author. Rose was the founder and principal of the London School of Singing and was the author of two textbooks on vocal technique, *The*

Singer and the Voice and *Contemporary Exercises for Classical and Popular Singers.* Obituaries and other sources: *London Times,* February 21, 1983.

* * *

ROSEN, Sheldon   1943-

PERSONAL: Born August 26, 1943, in New York, N.Y.; son of Manuel (a salesman) and Elizabeth (Heimann) Rosen. *Education:* University of Rochester, B.A., 1965; Syracuse University, M.S., 1966. *Home:* 460 Palmerston Blvd., Toronto, Ontario, Canada M6G 2P1. *Agent:* Susan F. Schulman, 165 West End Ave., New York, N.Y. 10022. *Office:* 110 West 71st St., New York, N.Y. 10023.

CAREER: KVCR-TV, San Bernardino, Calif., assistant to program director, 1966-68; Dayton Co., Minneapolis, Minn., broadcast producer in advertising department, 1968-69; worked at odd jobs and as a day laborer, 1969-71; playwright, 1971—. *Member:* Dramatists Guild, Association of Canadian Television and Radio Artists, Guild of Canadian Playwrights (chairman, 1979-80). *Awards, honors:* Canada Council grants, 1972, 1976-77, and 1978; award from Canadian Authors Association, 1980, for *Ned and Jack.*

WRITINGS—Plays: The Love Mouse (one-act; first produced in Toronto, Ontario, at Learning Resources Centre, 1971), Playwrights Co-op, 1972; *Meyer's Room* (one-act; first produced in Toronto at Poor Alex Theatre, 1971), Playwrights Co-op, 1972; *The Wonderful World of William Bends Who Is Not Quite Himself Today* (two-act; first produced in Toronto at Tarragon Theatre, 1972), Playwrights Co-op, 1972; "The Box" (one-act; first produced in Vancouver, British Columbia, at New Play Centre, 1974), published in *West Coast Plays,* edited by Connie Brissenden, Fineglow Plays, 1975; "Frugal Repast" (one-act; first produced at New Play Centre, 1974), published in *Frugal Repast and the Grand Hysteric,* Playwrights Co-op, 1978; "The Grand Hysteric" (one-act), published in *Frugal Repast and the Grand Hysteric,* Playwrights Co-op, 1978; *Ned and Jack* (two-act; first produced at New Play Centre, 1977), Playwrights Canada, 1979.

Unpublished plays: "Stag King" (three-act), first produced at Tarragon Theatre, 1973; "Alice in Wonderland" (two-act), first produced in Vancouver at PNE Coliseum, 1974; "Molecules" (one-act), first produced in Vancouver at Playhouse Holiday Workshop, 1974; "Like Father, Like Son" (one-act), first produced at New Play Centre, 1975; "Dwelling" (one-act), first produced in Vancouver at Axis Mime, 1977; "Impact" (one-act), first produced at Axis Mime, 1980. Also author of "Waiting to Go," a one-act play as yet unpublished and unproduced.

WORK IN PROGRESS: "Duck and Cover!," a full-length play set in 1953 dealing with the roots of nuclear life in the eighties; "Landmark!," a book musical about the family that built the Brooklyn Bridge.

SIDELIGHTS: Rosen told *CA:* "At this point in my life I'm not sure what my motivations for writing are. I do know that when I'm working well my world feels right and balanced, and when I'm not my life feels pointless and wasteful and all the sleazy, wheeling-dealing aspects of the 'Biz' march to the foreground and trample all the more legitimate and aesthetic reasons for doing what it is I do. Basically, I am a writer. No one is tempting me to be anything else. Right now I'm working well. Today the world is a great and wondrous place."

BIOGRAPHICAL/CRITICAL SOURCES: *London Free Press*, January 29, 1977; *Saturday Night*, July-August, 1979; *Canadian Forum*, May, 1980; *Toronto Globe and Mail*, August 15, 1981.

* * *

ROSENBLOOM, Bert 1944-

PERSONAL: Born February 2, 1944, in Philadelphia, Pa.; son of Max (a merchant) and Dora (Cohen) Rosenbloom; married Pearl Friedman, August 18, 1968; children: Jack Alan, Robyn. *Education:* Temple University, B.S., 1966, M.B.A., 1968, Ph.D., 1974. *Office:* Department of Marketing, College of Business and Administration, Drexel University, 32nd & Chestnut Sts., Philadelphia, Pa. 19104.

CAREER: Rider College, Lawrenceville, N.J., instructor, 1968-72, assistant professor of marketing, 1972-74; Bernard M. Baruch College of the City University of New York, New York, N.Y., assistant professor of marketing, 1974-76; Drexel University, Philadelphia, Pa., associate professor, 1976-79, professor of marketing, 1980—. *Member:* Academy of Marketing Science (member of board of governors), American Marketing Association (vice-president, 1978-79), American Institute of Decision Science, Retail Research Society, Beta Gamma Sigma.

WRITINGS: Marketing Channels: A Management View, Holt, 1978, 2nd edition, 1983; *Retail Marketing*, Random House, 1981. Contributor to marketing journals.

WORK IN PROGRESS: Research on strategic planning in retailing, management of marketing channels, and improving distribution efficiency.

SIDELIGHTS: Rosenbloom told *CA:* "The increased emphasis on strategic planning in marketing in recent years makes a fuller understanding of channel management more important than ever. Great potential exists for improving marketing management through strategically planned marketing channels. The strategic marketing management emphasis of *Marketing Channels: A Management View* and *Retail Marketing* provide the kind of information needed to plan and manage modern marketing channels more effectively."

* * *

ROSENTHAL, Sylvia 1911-

PERSONAL: Born April 24, 1911, in Schenectady, N.Y.; daughter of Abram (a merchant) and Bessie (in business; maiden name, Siegel) Dworsky; married Theodore Rosenthal (a physician), January 29, 1940 (deceased); children: Anne Rosenthal Satin, Michael. *Education:* Attended Emerson College, 1937-39; New York University, B.A., 1943. *Home:* 180 East End Ave., New York, N.Y. 10028.

CAREER: Grolier, Inc. (publisher), New York, N.Y., senior editor, 1961-72, managing editor of *New Book of Knowledge*, 1972-76; free-lance writer, 1976—. Former host of talk show on WHN-Radio; instructor in radio production and scriptwriting for children's programs, Hunter College Extension, producing children's programs for WNYC-Radio and national radio during the early 1940's. *Member:* Authors Guild.

WRITINGS: Live High on Low Fat, Lippincott, 1962, 3rd edition, 1975; *Cosmetic Surgery: A Consumer's Guide*, Lippincott, 1977; (editor) *Fresh Food*, Dutton, 1978; (with Fran Shinagel) *How Cooking Works: An Indispensable Kitchen*

Handbook, Macmillan, 1981. Author of children's radio scripts and records, including "The City Sings for Michael," 1946.

WORK IN PROGRESS: A nonfiction book about a family of five children, three of whom are adopted.

SIDELIGHTS: Sylvia Rosenthal commented: "My first book grew out of my need to follow doctor's orders after my husband had a heart attack. It catapulted me into the subject of food, for which I had always had great enthusiasm and interest. At this point, however, I am experimenting with getting my writing out of the kitchen.

"A low-fat diet can be exciting. People think we have great eats in our home—it's possible to produce fine cream soups, flaming crepes, great meat dishes with fine sauces, lavish-looking desserts, and all manner of goodies without sending your cholesterol soaring. *Live High on Low Fat* has been around since 1962 and mail still comes trickling in from all over the United States and abroad from satisfied customers. Nice. I'm so pleased that its life has now been extended.

"While I've had no personal experience with cosmetic surgery (which doesn't mean I couldn't use it), my research gave me great respect for the process. For *Cosmetic Surgery* I interviewed dozens of plastic surgeons and patients, and I would not discourage anyone with the guts for elective surgery. It's made a lot of people feel better about themselves and, in many cases, brought about great improvement."

BIOGRAPHICAL/CRITICAL SOURCES: *New York Times Book Review*, April 2, 1978; *Christian Science Monitor*, December 3, 1981; *Washington Post Book World*, December 13, 1981.

* * *

ROTBLAT, Joseph 1908-

PERSONAL: Born November 4, 1908, in Warsaw, Poland. *Education:* Received M.A. and Ph.D. from University of Warsaw. *Home:* 8 Asmara Rd., London NW2 3ST, England. *Office:* Medical College, St. Bartholomew's Hospital, University of London, Charterhouse Sq., London E.C.1, England.

CAREER: Scientific Society of Warsaw, Warsaw, Poland, research fellow at radiological laboratory, 1933-39; University of Liverpool, Liverpool, England, Oliver Lodge fellow, 1939-40, lecturer, beginning in 1940, became senior lecturer in physics, to 1949, director of research in nuclear physics, 1945-49; University of London, St. Bartholomew's Hospital, Medical College, London, England, professor of physics, 1950-76, vice-dean of faculty of science. Secretary-general of Pugwash Conferences on Science and World Affairs; assistant director of Atomic Physics Institute, Free University of Poland, 1937-39. President of International Youth Science Fortnight. *Member:* British Institute of Radiology (president), Hospital Physicists Association (president), Polish Academy of Sciences, American Academy of Arts and Sciences. *Awards, honors:* Commander of Order of the British Empire; D.Sc. from University of Bradford, 1973.

WRITINGS: (With Sir James Chadwick) *Radioactivity and Radioactive Substances*, Pitman & Sons, 1953; *Atomic Energy: A Survey*, Taylor & Francis, 1954; (with G. O. Jones and G. J. Whitrow) *Atoms and the Universe*, 1956, third revised edition, Penguin (Harmondsworth, England), 1973; *Science and World Affairs: History of the Pugwash Conferences*, Dawsons of Pall Mall, 1962, published as *History of the Pugwash Conferences*, Taylor & Francis, 1962; (contributor) Charles Henry Dobinson, editor, *The Uses and Effects of Nuclear Energy*, Harrap & Co.,

1964; (editor) *Aspects of Medical Physics*, Taylor & Francis, 1966; *Pugwash: The First Ten Years*, Heinemann, 1967, Humanities, 1968; *Scientists in the Quest for Peace: A History of the Pugwash Conferences*, MIT Press, 1972; (editor) *Nuclear Reactors: To Breed or Not to Breed?*, Taylor & Francis, 1977; *Nuclear Radiation in Warfare*, Taylor & Francis, 1981; *Scientists, the Arms Race, and Disarmament*, Oelgeschlager, 1982. Editor of *Physics in Medicine and Biology*.

*   *   *

ROTHSCHILD, Lincoln   1902-1983

OBITUARY NOTICE—See index for *CA* sketch: Born August 9, 1902, in New York, N.Y.; died March 29, 1983, in Dobbs Ferry, N.Y. Art historian, educator, and author. Rothschild began his career as an art instructor at Columbia University. His later teaching activities included assignments at Adelphi College, Riverdale Country School, and the City College of the City University of New York. Rothschild was a director of the Federal Art Project from 1937 to 1941. During World War II, he worked as a wood patternmaker. His books include *Sculpture Through the Ages*, *Hugo Robus*, and *New Deal Art Projects*. Obituaries and other sources: *New York Times*, April 5, 1983.

*   *   *

ROUGHSEY, Dick   1921(?)-

PERSONAL: Born c. 1921 on Mornington Island, Australia; married; children: six. *Education:* Attended Mornington Island Mission School. *Residence:* Mornington Island, Australia.

CAREER: Author, illustrator, and painter. Has worked as a hunter in the Australian bush, as a stockman on cattle stations, and as a ship's deckhand; began painting in 1960, with work being exhibited throughout Australia. Chairman of Aboriginal Arts Board, 1973. *Awards, honors:* Picture Book of the Year Award commendation, 1974, for *The Giant Devil Dingo*, and Picture Book of the Year Awards, 1976, for *The Rainbow Serpent*, and 1979, for *The Quinkins*, all from Australian Children's Book Council.

WRITINGS: Moon and Rainbow: The Autobiography of an Aboriginal, Reed (Sidney), 1971; *The Giant Devil Dingo* (juvenile), self-illustrated, Collins, 1973, Macmillan, 1975; *The Rainbow Serpent* (juvenile), self-illustrated, Collins, 1975; (with Percy Trezise) *The Quinkins* (juvenile), illustrations by the authors, Collins, 1978.

BIOGRAPHICAL/CRITICAL SOURCES: Books and Bookmen, September, 1972.*

*   *   *

ROUNTREE, Owen
See KRAUZER, Steven M(ark)

*   *   *

ROUSH, Barbara   1940-

PERSONAL: Born October 3, 1940, in New York, N.Y.; daughter of Harold E. (in business) and Dorothy M. (Schweikart) Roush; married Neale Austin (in education), June 21, 1963; children: Glen, Cara. *Education:* Mount Holyoke College, A.B., 1962; Harvard University, A.M.T., 1963. *Home:* 82 boulevard du G. de Gaulle, 92380 Garches, Frances. *Agent:* Elizabeth Pomada, 1029 Jones St., San Francisco, Calif. 94109.

CAREER: High school French teacher in Princeton, N.J., 1963-67; American School of Paris, Paris, France, teacher of English, 1977-78; bartender in San Francisco, Calif., 1980-81. Writer.

WRITINGS: Labor of Love (novel), Avon, 1982.

WORK IN PROGRESS: Mommy, a novel dealing with a daughter's reaction to a mother's suicide; *Garretted*, "a strange novel about a woman who shuts herself up in a garret, then finds that she can't get out."

SIDELIGHTS: Barbara Roush told *CA:* "*Labor of Love* grew out of my desire to convey my feelings for the countryside of the Morvan (where I have a farmhouse), a region not well-known, even among Frenchmen. It started out as a serious poem. It ended up as a hilarious novel (that nevertheless brings a tear or two to the eye). The zany plot, involving the machinations of an expatriate American painter to help a childless couple conceive a baby, includes syzygy, purple cows, and passenger pigeons. Underneath lies the more serious theme that joy and sorrow are inseparable.

"I have lived in France for twelve years. I enjoy living as a foreigner in another country. Somehow I don't have the guilt feelings that arise when I feel foreign among my own countrymen."

AVOCATIONAL INTERESTS: Travel (including Sweden, Spain, the U.S.S.R., Egypt, Morocco, Tunisia, Uganda, and Kenya).

BIOGRAPHICAL/CRITICAL SOURCES: Library Journal, September 15, 1982; *Los Angeles Times Book Review*, September 26, 1982.

*   *   *

ROWE, John Seymour   1936-

PERSONAL: Born in 1936, in Sydney, Australia; son of Dudley S. (a lawyer) and Anne Ellen Rowe; married wife, Marianne, February 17, 1962; children: Luke, Jake. *Education:* Attended Royal Military College, Duntroon, Australia, 1954-57. *Residence:* North Sydney, Australia.

CAREER: Australian Army, career officer, 1954-69, leaving service as major. *Member:* Cabbage Tree Club, Royal Bermuda Yacht Club.

WRITINGS: Count Your Dead: A Novel of Vietnam, Angus & Robertson, 1968; *McCabe, P.M.*, Pan Books, 1972; *Chocolate Crucifix*, Wren Books, 1973; *Warlords*, Holt-Saunders, 1978; *The Aswan Solution*, Doubleday, 1979; *The Jewish Solution*, Holt-Saunders, 1980.

WORK IN PROGRESS: A book of poems.

BIOGRAPHICAL/CRITICAL SOURCES: New York Times Book Review, September 23, 1979.

*   *   *

ROWEN, Betty Jane Rose   1920-

BRIEF ENTRY: Born May 22, 1920, in Brooklyn, N.Y. American educator and author. Rowen began her teaching career in public schools. She has been a member of the education faculty of University of Miami since 1969. Her books include *The Children We See: An Observational Approach to Child Study* (Holt, 1973), *Tuning In to Your Child: Awareness Training for Parents* (Humanics, 1975), and *The Learning Match: A Developmental Guide to Teaching Young Children* (Prentice-

Hall, 1980). *Address:* 5934 Southwest 34th St., Miami, Fla. 33155; and School of Education, University of Miami, Coral Gables, Fla. 33124. *Biographical/critical sources: Who's Who of American Women,* 8th edition, Marquis, 1974.

* * *

ROWLANDS, John Robert 1947-

PERSONAL: Born March 12, 1947, in Oshawa, Ontario, Canada; son of Ross Readman and Gladys Mary (Page) Rowlands; married Jody Johnston (a designer and photographer); children: Jason. *Education:* Attended Ryerson Polytechnical Photographic Arts, 1968-70. *Residence:* Port Perry, Ontario, Canada. *Office:* Access Photography, 424 Birchmount Rd., Scarborough, Ontario, Canada M1K 1M6.

CAREER: Free-lance photographer and writer, 1960—. *Member:* Greenpeace International.

WRITINGS: Spotlight Heroes, McGraw, 1981. Contributor of articles and photographs to magazines, including *RPM, TV Guide,* and *People.*

WORK IN PROGRESS: Researching a book on the Canadian music industry.

SIDELIGHTS: Rowlands commented: "I have been a writer and photographer in the music industry in North America since the early 1960's. I have seen popular music media develop from the beginning. The early days brought small budgets and allowed no creative freedom; now it has reached heights in both these areas and is going in the other direction. The recession has hit the music industry hard, and there is no money to support the original creative art within the industry. I think the party ended in 1978, and that it will never come back, at least not for the black pressed disc we know as a record.

"This industry has allowed me to see a good half of the world. I have worked from Hawaii to London, and seen every major city in between. I toured with the Rolling Stones on their first three North American tours, with the Dave Clark Five in 1964, with the Beatles in 1965 and 1966, and with literally hundreds of other British, Canadian, and American popular music groups.

"At present, I am undertaking research on the Canadian music industry, and sorting through the photographs I have taken and the history that I have taken part in over the last twenty years. I would like to produce a *Spotlight Heroes* type of book (which captures, in stage photographs, twenty years of popular recording artists in America, Canada, and Europe) on the country music industry in the United States and Canada, and a coffee table book that would cover all the entertainers that I have worked with. I have no commitments from any publishers, but I have learned that if you are going to try to do *any* kind of book, you would have to have it produced almost in its entirety before allowing any of the creative people at the publisher's office to get their hands on it. Once a deal is struck on a book, the quality of the original material is at least closely reproduced."

AVOCATIONAL INTERESTS: Photographing landscapes.

* * *

ROYLE, Selena 1904-1983

OBITUARY NOTICE: Born November 6, 1904, in New York, N.Y.; died after breaking a hip, April 23, 1983, in Guadalajara, Mexico. Actress and author. Royle is best remembered for her

screen roles during the 1940's as the doting mother. Her film career came to an end in the early 1950's as a result of accusations by Senator Joseph McCarthy that she was a Communist sympathizer. After several years of unsuccessfully attempting to overcome her blacklisting and find work, Royle and her husband moved to Mexico, where she wrote *A Gringa's Guide to Mexican Cooking* and *Guadalajara, as I Know It, Live It, Love It.* Obituaries and other sources: *International Motion Picture Almanac,* Quigley, 1977; *New York Times,* April 30, 1983; *Los Angeles Times,* May 6, 1983; *Chicago Tribune,* May 8, 1983.

* * *

ROZMAN, Gilbert Friedell 1943-

PERSONAL: Born February 18, 1943, in Minneapolis, Minn.; son of David (an accountant) and Celia (a teacher; maiden name, Friedell) Rozman; married Masha Dwosh (a lawyer), June 25, 1968; children: Thea Dwosh, Noah Dwosh. *Education:* Carleton College, B.A., 1965; Princeton University, Ph.D., 1971. *Home:* 20 Springwood Dr., Lawrenceville, N.J. 08648. *Office:* Princeton University, 2-N-2 Green Hall, Princeton, N.J. 08540.

CAREER: Princeton University, Princeton, N.J., assistant professor, 1970-75, associate professor, 1975-79, professor of sociology, 1979—, bicentennial preceptor, 1972-75. Member of U.S.-U.S.S.R. Binational Commission on Humanities and Social Sciences, 1978—. *Member:* Association for Asian Studies, American Sociological Association, American Association for the Advancement of Slavic Studies, Social Science History Association. *Awards, honors:* Woodrow Wilson fellow, 1965-66; grants from National Science Foundation, 1976-79, National Endowment for the Humanities, 1976-79, Social Science Research Council, 1980—, and National Council on East European and Soviet Research, 1981-83; Guggenheim fellow, 1979-80.

WRITINGS: Urban Networks in Ch'ing China and Tokugawa Japan, Princeton University Press, 1973; (with C. E. Black and others) *The Modernization of Japan and Russia,* Free Press, 1975; *Urban Networks in Russia, 1750-1800, and Premodern Periodization,* Princeton University Press, 1976; (editor) *The Modernization of China,* Free Press, 1981; *Population and Marketing Settlements in Ch'ing China,* Cambridge University Press, 1982.

WORK IN PROGRESS: Editing *The Transition in Nineteenth-Century Japan: From Tokugawa to Meiji; Soviet Perceptions of Contemporary China;* editing *Soviet Studies of Premodern China: Assessments of Recent Scholarship,* publication by Michigan Publications on East Asia expected in 1984.

SIDELIGHTS: Rozman commented: "I chose to approach international affairs as a sociologist able to use the languages of the major countries, concerned about the histories of their peoples, and eager to apply the comparative method of analysis. I often advise students with an interest in international affairs to concentrate on language skills early and to identify an unconventional specialization that is worth pursuing.

"I became interested in foreign areas in high school, when I was a winner in the *Minneapolis Star*'s world affairs contest. In college and graduate school I chose to study societies that were likely to be of greatest importance during the decades ahead. Because scholarship aid was available, I could attend intensive language courses every summer and accelerate my studies. Increasingly, I realized that my background on three countries gave me unique opportunities to study major aspects of social change, including premodern urbanization, modernization, and the impact of communism.''

*   *   *

RUBINSTEIN, David H(ugh)   1915-

PERSONAL: Born August 6, 1915, in New York, N.Y.; son of Harry (an embroiderer) and Rose Rubinstein; married Hilda Zeitlin, December 22, 1940; children: Barbara Rubinstein Biben, Laurel Rubinstein Gedan. *Education:* Attended Ohio College of Chiropody, 1933-34; First Institute of Podiatry, Pod.G., 1937; Long Island University College of Podiatry, Pod.D. (now D.P.M.), 1948. *Home and office:* 10909 Roundelay Circle, Sun City, Ariz. 85351.

CAREER: Private practice of podiatry in Auburn and Seneca Falls, N.Y., 1937-77; Dr. David H. Rubinstein, Inc., Sun City, Ariz., president, 1978—. President of investment consulting firms in Auburn and Seneca Falls, 1969-77. Lecturer. *Member:* American Podiatry Association (life member), New York State Podiatry Society (life member; president of Central Division, 1955), Masons, B'nai B'rith (president, 1960; member of board of governors, 1966-67; president of Upstate New York council, 1966-67). *Awards, honors:* Mennen Award for Advancement of Podiatry from Mennen Company, 1960.

WRITINGS: Invest for Retirement: A Guide to Financial Independence Through Common Stocks, Macmillan, 1981. Author of ''Let's Discuss Investing,'' a column in *Current Podiatry.*

Contributor of nearly one hundred fifty articles on investing to medical journals and newspapers.

WORK IN PROGRESS: ''Accumulating material for a second book on investing.''

SIDELIGHTS: In *Invest for Retirement: A Guide to Financial Independence Through Common Stocks,* David Rubenstein elaborates on his basic assertion that ''only common stocks have a reasonable chance, through appreciation plus dividend increases, of outpacing inflation over the long term,'' Mark J. Estren described in the *Miami Herald.* The author insists that an investor's best bet lies not in blue-chip stocks, but rather in those certain stock issues that the market overlooks because of emotional factors, disguising their true value. ''Direct, candid, reasonable, and to the point,'' Estren concluded, ''Rubinstein's advice is well worth considering not only by those aged 48 and over (at whom the book is nominally aimed) but also by anyone who would rather plan for retirement than hope against hope for it somehow to take care of itself. . . . [His] modest claims and no-nonsense approach to investment, coupled with his strong warnings against all fixed-income investments, should provide anyone willing and able to invest the time with an effective way to build toward retirement.''

Rubinstein told *CA:* ''For many years I was engaged in the private practice of podiatry in a small town in Upstate New York. In 1945, with the passage of the Full Employment Act by Congress, I recognized that we would be entering a period of inflation. From that moment on, all my spare time was devoted to studying investments and financial matters and the effect of inflation in France and Germany. In the first few years I made the usual mistakes and took my losses as part of my education. I profited from my mistakes and eventually became successful in the stock market on a continuous basis.

''In 1969, with the advent of the six-year bear market, wherever I went I heard the usual lamentations from dentists, podiatrists, physicians, lawyers, accountants, personal friends, and acquaintances on how much money they had lost in the stock market. Recognizing my success in the market, several professional friends asked me to manage their portfolios and I became registered with the Securities and Exchange Commission as an investment adviser.

''In 1971 I commenced writing my column for *Current Podiatry,* a national journal going to every podiatrist in the United States, in an effort to educate them to avoid the mistakes that I had made earlier. I believe that although most people learn from experience, the wise person learns from someone else's experience. I lectured at podiatry seminars and investment clubs. I used my column to discuss questions of general interest from readers across the country.

''Having achieved financial independence through intelligent investing and taken early retirement from podiatry, I'm devoting my time to helping others achieve financial freedom. Recently I have taken on several additional portfolios for personal portfolio management and have been invited to guest lecture at a local community college in Arizona, speaking to classes on 'investing for retirees.'

''My writing is straightforward, sincere, and direct. I call a spade a spade and write exactly the same way I would speak to an individual sitting in my office. I derive great satisfaction when an apt description or metaphor comes to mind. Anything that helps better explain an idea or thought gives me a 'high.' I feel education, information, or experience are nothing without the ability to communicate them to others.

''Having had life-long investing success, I am disturbed to find most people with their lives and futures adversely affected by unintelligent, haphazard investing—especially when I can show them the way. Why keep stumbling in the darkness when someone is offering to guide you?

''I'm fortunate that I do not have a mental block when it comes to writing. I love my subject and never resent the time necessary for research. Every time I'm at a party someone can be expected to bring up the subject of investing to either 'pick my brain' or brag about the one stock they bought that finally 'went up.' As a result of the topsy-turvy approach to investing followed by most people, each of these conversations results in an article written simply to explain the fallaciousness of popular beliefs.

''The contemporary attitude on the part of young people to 'live for today, for tomorrow we may all be incinerated' can result in an entire generation eventually reaching their sixties without being financially able to enjoy the best and freest years of their lives. Though it is true that we may all be incinerated by nuclear war, what if we are *not* incinerated? To look forward to living on county welfare in retirement is hardly an attractive prospect. Not planning for the future *assures* no future. Not planning for retirement results in no retirement.

''The pre-inflation thinking of retirees today is causing great insecurity among them as inflation ravages their plans. I believe that the only difference between a rut and a grave is depth and I'm trying to get retirees out of their ruts before they are deep enough to become graves.

''Inflation is guaranteed by acts of Congress. As long as we have inflation, I feel that *intelligent* investing in *undervalued* common stocks is the best way to combat it. The term 'undervalued' is misused by analysts and brokers; too often a corkscrew is used as a yardstick, resulting in repeated losses. In *Invest for Retirement* I devote many pages to the determination of value of common stocks.''

BIOGRAPHICAL/CRITICAL SOURCES: *Sun City Citizen,* September 10, 1980; *Arizona Republic,* December 2, 1981; *Arizona News Sun,* January 11, 1982, January 12, 1982, March 31, 1982; *Miami Herald,* March 8, 1982; *Phoenix Gazette,* May 26, 1982.

* * *

RUFFIN, C(avlbert) Bernard III 1947-

PERSONAL: Born November 22, 1947, in Washington, D.C.; son of C. Bernard, Jr. (a police officer) and Lillian (a personnel officer; maiden name, Jones) Ruffin. *Education:* Bowdoin College, A.B., 1969; Yale University, M.Div., 1972. *Politics:* Independent Conservative. *Home and office:* 767 North Van Dorn St., Alexandria, Va. 22304.

CAREER: Ordained Lutheran minister, 1974; intern pastor of Lutheran church in Loganton, Pa., 1972-73; pastor of Lutheran church in Alexandria, Va., 1974-76; Holy Comforter Lutheran Church, Washington, D.C., assistant pastor, 1976—; South Lakes High School, Reston, Va., social studies teacher, 1982—. Substitute teacher at public schools in Fairfax County, Va., 1976-82; member of board of directors of Capital Lutheran High School, 1979-82. *Member:* Hymn Society of America (member of executive committee, 1980-82), Afro-American Historical and Genealogical Society, Phi Beta Kappa.

WRITINGS: *Fanny Crosby,* United Church Press, 1976; (with Stella M. Fries and Janet Z. Gabler) *Some Chambersburg Roots: A Black Perspective,* privately printed, 1980; *Padre Pio: The True Story,* Our Sunday Visitor, 1982.

WORK IN PROGRESS: A collection of the ''last words'' of famous people; *Twelve Apostles,* publication by Our Sunday Visitor expected in 1984; research on religion, history, and genealogy.

SIDELIGHTS: Ruffin told *CA:* ''I am a Christian traditionalist who believes in the inerrancy of the Scriptures and am interested in writing serious works to advocate that point of view. I am also interested in American history and the history of Western civilization.

''*Padre Pio* is about an Italian Capuchin priest who lived from 1887 to 1968 and who, for fifty years, displayed on his hands, feet, and side the *stigmata,* or 'wounds of Christ.' He allegedly worked many miracles.''

AVOCATIONAL INTERESTS: Classical music (especially opera).

* * *

RUITENBEEK, Hendrik M(arinus) 1928-1983

OBITUARY NOTICE—See index for *CA* sketch: Born February 26, 1928, in Leiden, Netherlands; died of a rare infection, May 25, 1983, in New York; buried in the Protestant Cemetery in Rome. Psychoanalyst, educator, and author. Hendrik Ruitenbeek was an expert on Sigmund Freud. He wrote *Freud and America* and edited *Freud as We Knew Him.* Ruitenbeek gained prominence as a psychoanalyst by advocating equal rights for homosexuals. He taught at New York University, the Institute of Practicing Psychotherapists, Brooklyn College, and Principia College. His books include *The Male Myth, New Group*

Therapies, The New Sexuality, and *Psychotherapy: What's It All About.* Obituaries and other sources: *Washington Post,* May 27, 1983; *New York Times,* May 27, 1983.

* * *

RUMBERGER, Russell W(illiam) 1949-

PERSONAL: Born September 16, 1949, in Kansas City, Mo.; son of Allen B. and Ellen Rumberger. *Education:* Carnegie-Mellon University, B.S., 1971; Stanford University, M.S., 1978, Ph.D., 1978. *Office:* Institute for Research on Educational Finance and Governance Building, Stanford University, Stanford, Calif. 94305.

CAREER: Ohio State University, Columbus, research associate, 1979-80; Stanford University, Stanford, Calif., research associate, 1981—.

WRITINGS: *Overeducation in the Labor Market,* Praeger, 1981; (with Martin Carney and Derek Sheaver) *The New Social Contract,* Harper, 1983. Contributor to scholarly journals.

WORK IN PROGRESS: Research on social mobility and public sector employment, education and productivity, and technology, work, and education.

SIDELIGHTS: Rumberger told *CA:* ''My interest in overeducation was spurred by my own observations of the relationship between education and jobs. During the 1970's, I increasingly witnessed cases of college graduates taking jobs incommensurate with their education. The more obvious cases were persons with bachelor degrees taking jobs as secretaries and waiters, or Ph.D.s taking jobs driving cabs and working in bars. The less obvious were graduates taking jobs that appeared commensurate, but were not. My own experiences as an engineer illustrated this. Students learn much more in school than they ever have the opportunity to apply in their work. It makes work unrewarding, workers often perform poorly, and there are a variety of adverse social consequences. I've become increasingly interested in the organization of work and the barriers to making work more demanding and stimulating.''

* * *

RUNYON, A(lfred) Milton 1905-1983

OBITUARY NOTICE: Born December 22, 1905, in Plainfield, N.J.; died of a heart attack, May 3, 1983, in Roslyn, Long Island, N.Y. Publishing executive. Runyon was credited with playing a major role in the financial success of Doubleday & Company through his successful management of the firm's Literary Guild and Dollar Book Club. Runyon joined the company in 1937 and retired in 1971. Obituaries and other sources: *Who's Who in America,* 38th edition, Marquis, 1974; *New York Times,* May 5, 1983; *Publishers Weekly,* May 20, 1983.

* * *

RUSSELL, Mariann Barbara 1935-

PERSONAL: Born May 23, 1935, in New York, N.Y.; daughter of Theodore and Cecilia Ann Russell. *Education:* St. John's University, Jamaica, N.Y., B.A., 1955; Columbia University, M.A., 1957, Ph.D., 1965. *Home:* 334 South Seventh Ave., Mount Vernon, N.Y. 10550. *Office:* Department of English, Sacred Heart University, Bridgeport, Conn. 06606.

CAREER: English teacher at public schools in New York, N.Y., 1955-57; Morgan State University, Baltimore, Md., instructor in English, 1961-62; Cheyney State College, Cheyney, Pa., instructor, 1964, assistant professor, 1965, associate professor of English, 1966-69; Sacred Heart University, Bridgeport, Conn., professor of English, 1969—. *Member:* Modern Language Association of America, National Council of Teachers of English, College Language Association, National Council of Negro Women. *Awards, honors:* John Hay Whitney fellowship, 1955-56; National Endowment for the Humanities fellowship, 1974-75.

WRITINGS: Melvin B. Tolson's Harlem Gallery: A Literary Analysis, University of Missouri Press, 1981. Contributor to language journals, *Mythlore,* and *Obsidian.*

WORK IN PROGRESS: Research on ritual drama.

SIDELIGHTS: Russell commented: "An interest in New York City and Harlem, as well as poetry, led to my book. My interest in ritual drama was sparked by conversation with an African professor at the University of Ibadan." *Avocational interests:* Travel, photography.

*   *   *

RUST, Claude 1916-

PERSONAL: Born October 4, 1916, in Bronx, N.Y.; son of Henry Dietrich (an electrician) and Anna May Rust; married Rosemarie Brooks, November 14, 1948; children: Bruce, Diane. *Education:* Attended Alviene Academy of Dramatic Arts, 1947-48, New York City Radio-Television Institute, 1949, School of Radio Technique, 1950, and New York City Magazine Institute, 1958-59. *Home:* 60 First St., East Rockaway, N.Y. 11518. *Agent:* Lois de la Haba Associates, 142 Bank St., New York, N.Y. 10014.

CAREER: Telegraph messenger, grocery clerk, and professional dancer, 1929-42; artists' and photographers' model, 1947-49; WMGM-FM Radio, New York City, announcer, 1949; WDAD-Radio, Indiana, Pa., announcer, 1950; Voice of America, New York City, radio studio technician, 1951-53; United Nations, New York City, radio studio technician, 1953-83. *Military service:* U.S. Army, Infantry, 1942-45; served in Italy, France, Germany, and Austria. *Member:* Steamship Historical Society, Authors Guild, Authors League of America, American Legion, Society of the Third Infantry Division, New York Historical Society, Bronx Historical Society.

WRITINGS: The Burning of the General Slocum (nonfiction), Elsevier/Nelson, 1981. Contributor to *Military Engineer.*

WORK IN PROGRESS: A novel, tentatively titled *The Last Bottle,* about the two minds of the alcoholic (the struggle between the thinking and primal minds) and the world as seen through the alcoholic haze.

SIDELIGHTS: Rust told *CA:* "Upon the death of my mother in 1953, in going over her papers, I came across a program of a memorial service for the victims of the *General Slocum* disaster of 1904 and discovered that my grandmother had been one of them. This set me wondering: How could over a thousand people perish on a burning ship in the middle of New York City's East River while hundreds looked on? To find the answer, I interviewed survivors, pored over papers, periodicals, books, pictures, maps, and charts, and reconstructed the deck plans of the ill-fated excursion boat. All the while I was learning to write and develop a style with which to present a

taut and dramatic account of the disaster. While doing research in another field at the same time, I drifted into the weird realm of the alcoholic, the subject of my latest effort.

"Being a 'problem drinker,' I wish to tell what it is like to be an alcoholic. I want to tell how he thinks and why he thinks that way. Since *The Lost Weekend,* no book has probed deeply enough for me. I would like to take up where Charles Jackson left off and go deeper into the alcoholic mind: the phenomenon of craving, the horrors of the D.T.'s, and the alcoholic's struggle to relate to the 'real' world. In doing so, perhaps I can educate the apathetic by shock."

*   *   *

RUTTENBERG, Joseph 1889-1983

OBITUARY NOTICE: Born July 4, 1889, in St. Petersburg, Russia (now Leningrad, U.S.S.R.); came to the United States in 1893, naturalized citizen, 1910; died May 1, 1983, in Los Angeles, Calif. Cinematographer, photographer, film innovator, and photojournalist. Ruttenberg began his career as a photojournalist with the *Boston Globe* and as a producer of newsreels before going to work for the original Fox Studios (now Twentieth Century-Fox) as a cinematographer. During the course of his career, Ruttenberg won four Academy Awards and was nominated for six others. He was noted for his ability to make black-and-white film appear to have three-dimensional qualities and for contributing to the development of sound on film and color film. After working for Fox, Ruttenberg spent three decades with Metro-Goldwyn-Mayer, where he was cinematographer for such films as "A Day at the Races," "The Philadelphia Story," "Mrs. Miniver," "Gaslight," and "Gigi." Obituaries and other sources: *Who's Who in America,* 41st edition, Marquis, 1980; *New York Times,* May 5, 1983; *Chicago Tribune,* May 7, 1983; *Washington Post,* May 7, 1983; *London Times,* May 12, 1983.

*   *   *

RUTTER, Michael (Llewellyn) 1933-

PERSONAL: Born August 15, 1933, in Brummanna, Lebanon; son of Llewellyn Charles (a medical practitioner) and Winifred (Barber) Rutter; married Majorie Heys (a nurse practitioner and psychosexual counselor), December 27, 1958; children: Sheila Carol Rutter Mellish, Stephen Michael, Christine Ann. *Education:* University of Birmingham, M.B., Ch.B. (with distinction), 1955, M.D. (with honors), 1963; University of London, D.P.M. (with distinction), 1961. *Residence:* London, England. *Office:* Department of Child and Adolescent Psychiatry, Institute of Psychiatry, University of London, De Crespigny Park, London SE5 8AF, England.

CAREER: Held various training positions in pediatrics, neurology, and internal medicine, 1955-58; Maudsley Hospital, London, England, registrar, 1958-61, senior registrar, 1961, member of scientific staff of Medical Research Council Social Psychiatry Research Unit, 1962-65, honorary consultant child psychiatrist, 1966—. Fellow of Center for Advanced Study in the Behavioral Sciences, Pala Alto, Calif., 1979-80. Senior lecturer at Institute of Psychiatry, London, 1965-68, reader, 1968-73, professor, 1973—.

MEMBER: Association for Child Psychology and Psychiatry (chairman, 1973-74), British Paediatric Association, Royal

College of Physicians (fellow), Royal College of Psychiatrists (fellow), Royal Society of Medicine (fellow), British Psychological Society (honorary fellow), American Academy of Pediatrics (honorary fellow), American Academy of Child Psychiatry (honorary member).

AWARDS, HONORS: Nuffield medical traveling fellow at Yeshiva University, 1961-62; Belding traveling scholar in United States, 1963; Goulstonian Lecturer, Royal College of Physicians, 1973; research award from American Association on Mental Deficiency, 1975; Rock Carling fellow of Nuffield Provincial Hospitals Trust, 1979; C. Anderson Aldrich Award from American Academy of Pediatrics, 1981.

WRITINGS: Children of Sick Parents: An Environmental and Psychiatric Study, Oxford University Press, 1966; (with Philip Graham and William Yule) A Neuropsychiatric Study in Childhood, Heinemann, 1970; (editor with Jack Tizard and Kingsley Whitmore) Education, Health, and Behaviour, Longmans, Green, 1970, Robert E. Krieger, 1981; (editor) Infantile Autism: Concepts, Characteristics, and Treatment, Churchill Livingstone, 1970; Maternal Deprivation Reassessed, Penguin (Harmondsworth, Middlesex, England), 1972, 2nd edition, 1981, published as The Qualities of Mothering: Maternal Deprivation Reassessed, Jason Aronson, 1974; (editor with J.A.M. Martin) The Child With Delayed Speech, Heinemann, 1972; (with David Shaffer and Michael Shepherd) A Multi-Axial Classification of Child Psychiatric Disorders, World Health Organization, 1975; Helping Troubled Children, Penguin, 1975, Plenum, 1976; (with Nicola Madge) Cycles of Disadvantage, Heinemann Educational Books, 1976; (editor with Lionel Hershov) Child Psychiatry: Modern Approaches, Blackwell Scientific Publications, 1977; (editor with Eric Schopler) Autism: A Reappraisal of Concepts and Treatment, Plenum, 1978; (with Barbara Maughan, Peter Mortimore, and others) Fifteen Thousand Hours: Secondary Schools and Their Effects on Children, Harvard University Press, 1979; Changing Youth in a Changing Society: Patterns of Adolescent Development and Disorder, Nuffield Provincial Hospital Trust, 1979, Harvard University Press, 1980.

(Editor) Scientific Foundations of Developmental Psychiatry, Heinemann Medical Books, 1980; (with Henri Giller) Juvenile Delinquency: Trends and Perspectives, Penguin, 1983; (editor with Norman Garmezy) Stress, Coping, and Development in Children, McGraw, 1983; (editor) Developmental Neuropsychiatry, Guilford Press, 1983; (editor with R. Russell Jones) Lead Versus Health: Sources and Effects of Low Level Lead Exposure, Wiley, 1983; (contributor) E. M. Hetherington, editor, Carmichael's Manual of Child Psychology, Volume IV: Social and Personality Development, Wiley, 1983; A Measure of Our Values: Goals and Dilemmas in the Upbringing of Children, Quaker Home Service Committee, 1983; (editor with Carroll Izard and Peter Read) Depression in Childhood: Developmental Perspectives, Guilford Press, in press.

European editor of Journal of Autism and Developmental Disorders, 1974—; member of editorial board of Journal of Child Psychology and Psychiatry, Psychological Medicine, Journal of Special Education, Child Psychiatry and Human Development, Journal of Abnormal Child Psychology, Applied Psycholinguistics, and Applied Research in Mental Retardation.

WORK IN PROGRESS: Conducting a study of "normal and abnormal child development, with particular focus on the links between experiences in childhood and functioning in adult life, factors in the child and in his environment leading to resilience in the face of adversity, the characteristics that make for effective schooling, the skills involved in interviewing, the characteristics of good parenting and the factors that facilitate it, and the study of autistic, depressed, and hyperkinetic children."

BIOGRAPHICAL/CRITICAL SOURCES: APA Monitor, June, 1980; New Society, Volume 62, number 1049/50, 1982.

*　　*　　*

RYAN, Peter Allen 1923-

PERSONAL: Born September 4, 1923, in Melbourne, Australia; son of Emmett Francis and Alice Doreen (Allen) Ryan; married Gladys Aylward Davidson, May 23, 1947; children: Andrew Peter, Sally Nina. Education: University of Melbourne, B.A. (with honors), 1948. Religion: None. Home and office: 932 Swanston St., Carlton, Victoria 3053, Australia.

CAREER: United Service Publicity Proprietary Ltd., Melbourne, Australia, director, 1953-57; Imperial Chemical Industries of Australia and New Zealand Ltd., Melbourne, manager of public relations, 1957-61; University of Melbourne, Parkville, Australia, assistant to vice-chancellor, 1962; Melbourne University Press, Melbourne, director, 1962—. Military service: Australian Army, 1942-45; served in Pacific theater. Member: Association of Australian University Presses (president, 1966, 1967, 1974, 1975, 1976), Australian Society of Authors, Australian Journalists Association.

WRITINGS: Fear Drive My Feet, Ryerson Press, 1959; Redmond Barry, Melbourne University Press, 1972; (general editor) Encyclopaedia of Papua and New Guinea, University of Papua and New Guinea, 1972. Also author of The Preparation of Manuscripts, 1966. Contributor to magazines, including Age and Australian, and newspapers.

*　　*　　*

RYLSKI, Aleksander Scibor
See SCIBOR-RYLSKI, Aleksander

*　　*　　*

RYSKIND, Morrie 1895-
(John P. Wintergreen)

BRIEF ENTRY: Born October 20, 1895, in New York, N.Y. American playwright, screenwriter, and syndicated columnist. Ryskind's Of Thee I Sing (Knopf, 1932; first produced in 1931) which he wrote with George S. Kaufman, holds the distinction of being the first musical comedy to be published in text form. A satirical view of politics during the 1920's and 1930's, the musical highlights the presidential campaign of John P. Wintergreen. A rousing success, "Of Thee I Sing" enjoyed 441 Broadway performances and won the Pulitzer Prize for drama in 1932, becoming the first musical to receive the award. The play's sequel, Let 'Em Eat Cake (Knopf, 1933; first produced in 1933), describes Wintergreen's unsuccessful campaign for reelection and its consequences. That same year, Ryskind published The Diary of an Ex-President (Minton, 1932) under the name John P. Wintergreen. Supposedly the former president's journal, found during the construction of a new subway, Diary continues the Wintergreen satire. "It's absurdity is amusing," wrote a New York Times reviewer, "sometimes by its very antic quality, sometimes because underneath its clowning there

is a real bullseye hit of sarcastic humor.'' Ryskind's other plays
include ''Animal Crackers'' (1928) and ''Strike Up the Band''
(1930), both written with Kaufman. He also wrote the screenplays for ''Animal Crackers'' (Paramount, 1933), ''A Night
at the Opera'' (Metro-Goldwyn-Mayer, 1935), and ''Where
Do We Go From Here?'' (Twentieth Century-Fox, 1945). *Address:* 605 North Hillcrest Rd., Beverly Hills, Calif. 90210.

Biographical/critical sources: New York Times, July 31, 1932;
Nation, August 17, 1932; David Ewen, *New Complete Book
of the American Musical Theatre,* Holt, 1970; *Who's Who in
World Jewry: A Biographical Dictionary of Outstanding Jews,*
Olive Press, 1978.

S

SABOM, Michael Bruce 1944-

PERSONAL: Born September 28, 1944, in Houston, Tex.; son of William Oscar (a businessman) and Felicia (Slataper) Sabom; married Claire Diane Bowers, July 29, 1972; children: Michael Shay. *Education:* Colorado College, B.A., 1966; University of Texas, M.D., 1970. *Religion:* Christian. *Home and office:* 1707 Coventry Rd., Decatur, Ga. 30030.

CAREER: Cardiologist. Licensed to practice medicine in Texas, Florida, Tennessee, and Georgia. University of Florida, Gainesville, intern, 1970-71, resident in medicine, 1973-75, fellow in cardiology, 1975-77, instructor in medicine at Shands Teaching Hospital, 1977-78; Baylor University, Waco, Tex., instructor in health sciences, 1971-73; School of Medicine, Emory University, Atlanta, Ga., assistant professor of medicine, 1978-83; private practice of cardiology in Atlanta, Ga., 1983—. *Military service:* U.S. Army, Medical Corps, 1971-73; served as instructor in health sciences; became captain. *Member:* American Heart Association (fellow), American College of Cardiology, American Federation for Clinical Research, Phi Beta Kappa, Alpha Omega Alpha.

WRITINGS: Recollections of Death: A Medical Investigation, Harper, 1981.

WORK IN PROGRESS: Further research into Near-Death Experiences (NDEs).

SIDELIGHTS: Recent medical advances in the resuscitation of patients near or at the point of clinical death have brought forth from survivors strikingly similar descriptions of phenomena experienced at the threshold of death. Accounts of these Near-Death Experiences, first popularized by Dr. Raymond Moody with the 1975 publication of *Life After Life* [see *CA* 93-96], have sparked a growing scientific interest in the subject.

In *Recollections of Death* Sabom approaches the subject on a more scientific level, using systematic methodology, statistical techniques, and data tables in addition to personal interviews with 116 subjects. Sabom divides Near-Death Experiences into two classifications: the "autoscopic experience," in which the patient, in an out-of-body state, is aware of his physical surroundings and is often able to describe minute details of his resuscitation; and the second type, the "transcendental experience," in which the patient leaves the earthly plane, often through a long tunnel, and is transported to a place of light and beauty populated by dead friends and relatives.

The implication drawn by Moody and others, most notably those who have had Near-Death Experiences, is that ego consciousness or "soul" survives death and continues to function in some altered, nonmaterial form. Sabom shares this belief, but has not been content to allow explanations of the nature of the experience to remain in the purview of philosophy and religion. In his attempt to provide scientifically-oriented answers to the inevitable questions that arise from such ethereal phenomena, Sabom has examined the physio-chemical and medical explanations of the Near-Death Experience based on survivors' reports. He concludes that such experiences do occur, that they are usually pleasant, and that an adequate medical or scientific explanation for the Near-Death Experience is presently not available. The possibility of a splitting apart of a nonphysical "mind" from the physical brain at the point of near death to account for the verified accuracy of many of the out-of-body Near-Death Experiences is entertained.

Sabom told *CA:* "Although the interpretation and meaning of the NDE is presently being debated in the medical community, the occurrence of the NDE in a sizable proportion of near-death survivors is without dispute. These experiences should be taken seriously by physicians and paramedical personnel since the NDE often has a powerful impact on the physical and spiritual lives of survivors of critical illness.

"For me personally, this research into the NDE has strengthened my faith in the Christian religion and has convinced me of the importance of a spiritual reality which is occurring in many of my patients while physically unconscious and near death."

Recollections of Death: A Medical Investigation has been published in French, German, Dutch, Italian, Norwegian, and Finnish in addition to British and Canadian editions.

BIOGRAPHICAL/CRITICAL SOURCES: Time, February 8, 1982; *Times Literary Supplement,* March 26, 1982; *New England Journal of Medicine,* July 29, 1982.

*   *   *

SACKS, Karen 1941-

PERSONAL: Born November 21, 1941, in New York, N.Y.; daughter of Jacob (a teacher) and Sylvia (a teacher; maiden name, Schechter) Brodkin; married William Sacks; children:

Benjamin, Daniel. *Education:* Brandeis University, A.B., 1963; Harvard University, M.A., 1964; University of Michigan, Ph.D., 1971. *Home:* 8718 Geren Rd., Silver Spring, Md. 20901. *Office:* Business and Professional Women's Foundation, 2012 Massachusetts Ave. N.W., Washington, D.C. 20036.

CAREER: Wayne State University, Detroit, Mich., part-time instructor in anthropology, 1968; Oakland University, Rochester, Mich., instructor, 1968-70; assistant professor of sociology and anthropology, 1970-75; Fordham University at Lincoln Center, New York, N.Y., visiting assistant professor of social sciences, 1975-76; University of Minnesota, Minneapolis, visiting assistant professor of anthropology, 1976; Clark University, Worcester, Mass., assistant professor of sociology and anthropology, 1976-80; American University, Washington, D.C., lecturer in anthropology, 1981; Business and Professional Women's Foundation, Washington, D.C., director of research and information services, 1981—. Fellow at Center for the Study of the Family and the State, Institute for Public Policy, Duke University, 1978-80, visiting scholar, 1980-82, research associate in anthropology, 1982-84. Conducted field work in Puerto Rico, 1965; public speaker; organizer of conferences on women and work.

MEMBER: American Anthropological Association, National Women's Studies Association, Northeast Anthropological Association, Women in Foundations/Corporate Philanthropy, Capital Area Sociologists for Women in Society. *Awards, honors:* Grant from National Science Foundation, 1982-84.

WRITINGS: Sisters and Wives: The Past and Future of Sexual Equality, Greenwood Press, 1979; (editor with Dorothy Remy) *My Troubles Are Going to Have Trouble With Me,* Rutgers University Press, in press.

Contributor: Robin Morgan, editor, *Sisterhood Is Powerful,* Random House, 1970; Michelle Rosaldo and Louise Lamphere, editors, *Women, Culture, and Society,* Stanford University Press, 1974; Larry Reynolds and James Henselin, editors, *Social Problems in American Society,* 3rd edition, Allyn & Bacon, 1978; Jean O'Barr, editor, *Perspectives on Power: Women in Asia, Africa, and Latin America,* Center for International Studies, Duke University, 1982. Contributor of articles and reviews to anthropology journals and popular magazines, including *Ms., Monthly Review, Radical Teacher,* and *Jewish Currents.*

WORK IN PROGRESS: TLC (tentative title), a book on women hospital workers.

SIDELIGHTS: Sacks told *CA:* "I'm interested in women workers, both their family and work lives. The average woman today is doing two jobs and getting paid for less than one. I write about (and conduct research on) the ways women cope creatively with and prevail against the odds against them. As an activist and an academic, I want my writing to help women organize for equity and change."

* * *

SAFIR, Leonard 1921-

PERSONAL: Surname is pronounced Safire; born June 5, 1921, in New York, N.Y.; son of Oliver Crouse (a manufacturer) and Ida (Panish) Safir. *Education:* Attended University of California, Los Angeles, 1938-41. *Home:* 500 East 77th St., New York, N.Y. 10162. *Agent:* Morton L. Janklow & Associates, Inc., 598 Madison Ave., New York, N.Y. 10022. *Office:* Norton Simon, Inc., 230 Park Ave., New York, N.Y. 10017.

CAREER: New York Daily Mirror, New York City, feature writer, 1941-42; WNBC-Radio, New York City, chief writer for the "Tex and Jinx" show, 1946-48; Young & Rubicam, Inc., New York City, editor and chief writer for radio program, "We, the People," 1948-50; WNBC-Radio and WNBC-TV, New York City, manager in advertising and promotion, 1950-52; National Broadcasting Co. (NBC-TV), New York City, associate producer of the "Today" show, 1952-55, staff associate of the "Tonight" show, 1956-57; independent program planner in New York City, 1957-58; American Broadcasting Co. (ABC-TV), New York City, director of research for "Crossroads" program, 1959-60; NBC-TV, New York City, associate producer of "1-2-3-Go!" program, 1961; ABC-TV, New York City, staff producer of "Wide World of Sports," 1962-63; Safire Public Relations, Inc., New York City, senior account executive, 1963-70; Norton Simon, Inc., New York City, editor in corporate communications, 1971—. *Military service:* U.S. Army, Medical Administrative Corps, 1942-46; became first lieutenant. *Member:* National Academy of Television Arts and Sciences.

WRITINGS: (With brother, William Safire) *Good Advice,* Times Books, 1982.

WORK IN PROGRESS: Continuing work on a possible *Good Advice II.*

SIDELIGHTS: Safir told *CA:* "*Good Advice* is a collection of more than two thousand quotations from ancient and modern sources, offering instruction on the best ways to live the good life. This personal treasury was created in a labor of love by me and my brother, William Safire (the Pulitzer-Prize winner and *New York Times* columnist who added an 'e' to the family name because that is how the name is pronounced).

"Quotation books contain mostly observations ('He who hesitates is lost'), but *Good Advice* actually tells you what to do ('Look before you leap'). Imperatives in business, money, oratory, politics, love, marriage, sex, life, and death are abundant in the book. Sources include Homer, Shakespeare, Dickens, Emerson, Freud, Einstein, Damon Runyon, Dale Carnegie, Norman Vincent Peale, Golda Meir, Noel Coward, and Barbara Walters.

"My brother and I share a favorite quotation from the book, attributed to Napoleon Bonaparte: 'If you start to take Vienna—take Vienna.'"

* * *

SAINT-GALL, Auguste Amedee de
See STRICH, Christian

* * *

St. JOHN, Leonie
See JENKINS, Nancy (Harmon)

* * *

SALMON, Nathan Ucuzoglu 1951-

PERSONAL: Original name, Nathan Salmon Ucuzoglu; name legally changed in 1978; born January 2, 1951, in Los Angeles, Calif.; son of Mair (a factory worker) and Rebecca (a medical clerk; maiden name, Sene) Ucuzoglu; married Eileen Conrad (a public information officer), August 28, 1980. *Education:* University of California, Los Angeles, B.A., 1973, M.A., 1974, C.Phil., 1977, Ph.D., 1979. *Religion:* Atheist. *Home:*

16514 Casimir Ave., Torrance, Calif. 90504. *Office:* Department of Philosophy, University of California, Riverside, Calif. 92521.

CAREER: Princeton University, Princeton, N.J., assistant professor, 1978-82; University of California, Riverside, associate professor of philosophy, 1982—. *Member:* American Philosophical Association, Royal Institute of Philosophy.

WRITINGS: Reference and Essence, Princeton University Press, 1981; *Frege's Puzzle,* Bradford Books/MIT Press, in press. Contributor of articles to *Journal of Philosophy* and *Philosophical Studies.*

SIDELIGHTS: Reference and Essence is a study of linguistic and philosophical questions advancing the author's argument that current theories of reference are distinctly independent of theories about the essence of objects. According to Christopher Peacocke, who reviewed the book in the *Times Literary Supplement,* "this is a valuable and reliable critical survey of the American literature [on the subject of the theory of reference] of the past ten years, one that should be of much help to students." "Salmon's arguments are clear and decisive," Peacocke praised, and his book "leaves one eager to learn the results of Salmon's future development . . . of these themes."

Salmon told *CA:* "I write on analytical metaphysics and the philosophy of language."

BIOGRAPHICAL/CRITICAL SOURCES: Times Literary Supplement, October 8, 1982.

* * *

SALVATORE, Nicholas 1943-
(Nick Salvatore)

PERSONAL: Born November 14, 1943, in Brooklyn, N.Y.; son of Nicholas Anthony (a lawyer) and Katherine (a secretary; maiden name, McManus) Salvatore; married Ann H. Sullivan (a librarian), September 20, 1974; children: Gabriella, Nora. *Education:* Hunter College of the City University of New York, B.A., 1968; University of California, Berkeley, M.A., 1969, Ph.D., 1977. *Home:* 235 Elm St., Ithaca, N.Y. 14850. *Office:* School of Industrial and Labor Relations, Cornell University, Ithaca, N.Y. 14850.

CAREER: College of the Holy Cross, Worcester, Mass., assistant professor of U.S. history, 1976-81; Cornell University, Ithaca, N.Y., assistant professor of U.S. history, 1981—. *Member:* American Historical Association, Organization of American Historians. *Awards, honors:* Bancroft Prize from Columbia University, 1983, for *Eugene V. Debs: Citizen and Socialist.*

WRITINGS: (Under name Nick Salvatore) *Eugene V. Debs: Citizen and Socialist,* University of Illinois Press, 1982. Contributor to history and labor journals.

WORK IN PROGRESS: A social history of late nineteenth-century American unionism.

SIDELIGHTS: In a *Washington Post Book World* review of Salvatore's *Eugene V. Debs: Citizen and Socialist,* Reid Beddow wrote that "this sober, well-researched life of Debs . . . will be the standard biography for many years to come."

BIOGRAPHICAL/CRITICAL SOURCES: Washington Post Book World, February 13, 1983; *New York Times Book Review,* May 22, 1983.

SALVATORE, Nick
See SALVATORE, Nicholas

* * *

SALZER, Felix 1904-

PERSONAL: Born June 13, 1904, in Vienna, Austria; came to the United States in 1939, naturalized citizen, 1945; son of Max and Helene (Wittgenstein) Salzer; married Hedi Lemberger-Lindtberg, September 16, 1939. *Education:* University of Vienna, Ph.D., 1926. *Home:* 179 East 70th St., New York, N.Y. 10021.

CAREER: Mannes College of Music, New York, N.Y., professor of music, 1940-56, director, 1948-55; professor, 1962-64; Queens College of the City University of New York, Flushing, N.Y., professor of music, 1963-74; Mannes College of Music, professor of music, 1974—. Visiting lecturer at University of California, Los Angeles, 1960, Peabody Conservatory of Music, 1962, New School for Social Research, 1962-63, and University of Oregon, summer, 1965. *Member:* American Musicological Society (chairman, 1963-65).

WRITINGS: Structural Hearing: Tonal Coherence in Music, two volumes, Dover, 1952, 2nd edition, 1962; (with Carl Schachter) *Counterpoint in Composition: The Study of Voice Leading,* McGraw, 1969; (author of introduction and glossary) Heinrich Schenker, *Five Graphic Music Analyses,* Dover, 1969; (editor) *The Music Forum,* Columbia University Press, Volume I, 1967, Volume II, 1970, Volume III, 1973, Volume IV, 1976, Volume V, 1980, Volume VI, 1983.

* * *

SAMPFORD, Michael 1924(?)-1983

OBITUARY NOTICE: Born c. 1924; died after a short illness, February 7, 1983. Mathematician, educator, editor, and author. Sampford became associated with D. J. Finney's research group of biometric statisticians at Oxford University during the 1940's. In 1967 he joined the staff of the University of Liverpool, where he was responsible for the creation and development of the department of computational and statistical science. Sampford edited *Biometrics* from 1962 to 1967 and was the author of *An Introduction to Sampling Theory.* Obituaries and other sources: *London Times,* February 15, 1983.

* * *

SAMSON, Jack
See SAMSON, John Gadsden

* * *

SAMSON, John Gadsden 1936-
(Jack Samson)

BRIEF ENTRY: Born March 19, 1922, in Providence, R.I. American magazine editor and author of books about the outdoors. Samson, who was appointed editor of *Field and Stream* in 1970, has worked as a foreign correspondent in Japan and Korea for United Press International, as a staff writer in New York City for Associated Press, and as a radio and television news director in Albuquerque, New Mexico. He also owned a public relations agency from 1965 to 1970. Samson's books include *Line Down!: The Special World of Big-Game Fishing* (Winchester Press, 1973), *Falconry Today* (Walck, 1976), *The Sportsman's World* (Holt, 1976), *Successful Outdoor Writing*

(Writer's Digest, 1979), and *The Pond: The Life of the Aquatic Plants, Insects, Fish, Amphibians, Reptiles, Mammals, and Birds That Inhabit the Pond and Its Surrounding Hillside and Swamp* (Knopf, 1979). *Address:* 27 West 44th St., New York, N.Y. 10036; and *Field and Stream,* 383 Madison Ave., New York, N.Y. 10017.

*　　*　　*

SANDERS, Buck
See FRENTZEN, Jeffrey

*　　*　　*

SANDFORD, Christopher　1902-1983

OBITUARY NOTICE: Born December 5, 1902, in Cork, Ireland; died February 27, 1983. Book designer and publisher. Sandford specialized in producing fine illustrated editions of books for both collectors and the general public. He headed Golden Hours Press and Golden Cockerel Press from the 1930's until 1959, when the market for such books no longer supported the cost of their publication. Obituaries and other sources: *Who's Who in Art,* 20th edition, Art Trade Press, 1982; *London Times,* March 21, 1983.

*　　*　　*

SANDS, Melissa　1949-

PERSONAL: Born July 27, 1949, in Mt. Vernon, N.Y.; daughter of Frederick Otto and Grace (a teacher; maiden name, Griffith) Scharr; married Michael Sands (a musician and teacher), February 14, 1979. *Education:* State University of New York at Albany, B.A., 1971; graduate study at Long Island University, C. W. Post Center, 1976-77. *Politics:* "Democrat Feminist." *Residence:* Islip, N.Y. *Agent:* Roslyn Targ, 250 West 57th St., Suite 1932, New York, N.Y. 10107. *Office:* Mistresses Anonymous, P.O. Box 151, Islip, N.Y. 11751.

CAREER: Lowell and Lynwood Ltd. and Barnell Loft, Baldwin, N.Y., writer of educational materials, 1975-77; Center for Media Development, Great Neck, N.Y., editor of educational materials, 1977; Santillana Publishing Co., New York, N.Y., writer of educational materials, 1978; writer, 1978—. Substitute teacher for junior and senior high schools in New York, 1975-77. *Member:* Mistresses Anonymous (founder, president, and research director).

WRITINGS: The Mistress' Survival Manual, Berkley Publishing Group, 1978; *The Making of the American Mistress,* Berkley Publishing Group, 1981; *The Second Wife's Survival Manual,* Berkley Publishing Group, 1982; *The Passion Factor,* Berkley Publishing Group, 1983; *How to Be a Winner in Love,* St. Martin's Press, in press. Editor of newsletter *Triangle Tabloid,* 1981-82. Contributor to periodicals, including *Ms., Women Who Work,* and *Cosmopolitan.*

WORK IN PROGRESS: Researching the question, "Do women play?"

SIDELIGHTS: In the first issue of Mistresses Anonymous' national newsletter, *Triangle Tabloid,* Melissa Sands explained: "In 1976, I found myself desperately in love with a married man. I never thought this kind of thing would happen to me. . . . Then, through work, I met a mistress here, through hobbies and socially I met another mistress there. It was almost instinctive how we mistresses sense each other. I began a consciousness-raising group at my home on Monday nights. Of course we talked of nothing but our married men and so we called our group Mistresses Anonymous. . . . Our common ground held us together as we listened and talked to each other. Our communication was our lifeline. It destroyed one of the mistress' greatest problems, isolation."

A local newspaper story appeared about the group, sparking a great deal of curiosity. National television programs, like the "Phil Donahue Show" and "Good Morning America," sought to feature Sands and the members of Mistresses Anonymous. Magazines and newspapers pursued the story as well. The once clandestine self-help group became part of the public consciousness, and Sands received thousands of sympathetic and supportive letters from mistresses all over the country. Requests for chapters of Mistresses Anonymous became frequent.

In answer to this national demand for help, Sands wrote *The Mistress' Survival Manual,* relating the consciousness-raising program she used in her group; she published a follow-up book, *The Making of the American Mistress,* a few years later. In 1981 Mistresses Anonymous became a national organization with a bimonthly newsletter, and in 1982 the author produced *The Second Wife's Survival Manual,* a primer for the woman who marries the man whose mistress she once was. "In her own case, [Sands] makes clear, it worked," Clarence Peterson observed in the *Chicago Tribune Book World.* "[*The Second Wife's Survival Manual*] may at least help the mistress to look before she leaps."

Sands told *CA:* "My personal life has always been the initial seed of motivation for my research and writing. I had wanted to be a writer since age twenty-one and found that a 'literary addiction' was a tough road to hoe. It is still, and I think probably always will be.

"My success began with *The Mistress' Survival Manual.* In a way, I turned around a painful experience—loving a married man—into a quest to save others from the experience, to help others get out. I wrote of affairs, second marriages, affairs at the office—and read thousands and thousands of letters, personal testimonies of romantic mistakes and broken hearts.

"Now, after nearly a decade, I realize that I seem destined to seize upon the scandalous subject that lies close to the hearts of millions of people and eludes public confession—like an affair. It seems my role to write about romantic behavior and to try to illuminate the pitfalls and trapdoors—in a culture that only recommends condemnation, blame, or therapy. Most of us can survive romantically and psychologically with a little help from consciousness-raising and conscience.

"My work is private and public, time-consuming and rewarding. I have always been more work-oriented than leisure-oriented. And therefore, at middle-age, I've begun to question this with investigative zeal, which has led to a new area of research: do women play, or is romance women's play?

"My aspirations are: to be read, to help people help themselves; to be able to travel and do cross-cultural research; to get a Ph.D. and learn the scientific method now that I know the 'mass market' method.

"My main interests have always been concerned with the heart and with the mind."

BIOGRAPHICAL/CRITICAL SOURCES: Triangle Tabloid, summer, 1981; *Chicago Tribune Book World,* May 23, 1982; *Los Angeles Times Book Review,* June 20, 1982.

SAPIETS, Janis   1921-1983(?)

OBITUARY NOTICE: Born in 1921 in Latvia (now U.S.S.R.); died c. 1983. Clergyman and news broadcaster. An ordained Lutheran minister, Sapiets spent time in displaced persons camps in Europe following World War II. In 1947 he arrived in England, and in 1962 he joined the British Broadcasting Corporation's Russian Service, where he became head of the BBC's research and information department and editor of religious programming to the Soviet Union. Obituaries and other sources: London Times, April 20, 1983.

*   *   *

SARKAR, Asoke   1911(?)-1983

OBITUARY NOTICE: Born c. 1911; died February 17, 1983, in Calcutta, India. Editor and publisher of Ananda Bazar Patrika, the leading newspaper in Bengal, India. Obituaries and other sources: London Times, March 11, 1983.

*   *   *

SARLOS, Robert Karoly   1931-

PERSONAL: Born June 6, 1931, in Budapest, Hungary; came to the United States in 1957, naturalized citizen, 1962; son of Miklos (in sales) and Erzsebet (a clerk) Sarlos; married Charlotte Harris (an instructor in English as a second language), April 21, 1962; children: Lilian, Tibor. Education: Attended Eotvos Lorand University, 1955-56; Occidental College, B.A., 1959; Yale University, Ph.D., 1965. Residence: Davis, Calif. Office: Department of Dramatic Art, University of California, Davis, Calif. 95616.

CAREER: Lathe operator in Budapest, Hungary, 1950-51, and Long Beach, Calif., 1957; Mitchell College, New London, Conn., instructor in English, 1962-63; University of California, Davis, lecturer, 1963-64, acting assistant professor, 1964-65, assistant professor, 1966-70, associate professor, 1970-79, professor of dramatic art, 1979—. Member of board of trustees of Woodland Opera House, 1979—, vice-president, 1980-82. Member: International Federation for Theatre Research, American Society for Theatre Research.

WRITINGS: (Contributor) C. T. Prouty, editor, Studies in the Elizabethan Theatre, Shoe String, 1961; Jig Cook and the Provincetown Players: Theatre in Ferment, University of Massachusetts Press, 1982; (contributor) L. W. Connolly, editor, Touring and Founding in the North American Theatre, Greenwood Press, 1982. Contributor to theatre and history journals.

WORK IN PROGRESS: Editing an anthology of previously unpublished Provincetown plays; Miklos Gabor on the Actor's Internal Technique.

SIDELIGHTS: Sarlos wrote: "I believe firmly in live theatre as an essential element of a lively culture. Theatre scholars profit from practical theatre experience, and theatre scholarship should pay dividends to the living theatre.

"I became interested in the Provincetown Players as the theatrical environment of O'Neill. By the time I wrote my dissertation on the group, I had become more fascinated with the process of production of all the disparate plays by a variety of people than by the O'Neill plays themselves."

*   *   *

SARNA, Jonathan D(aniel)   1955-

PERSONAL: Born January 10, 1955, in Philadelphia, Pa.; son of Nahum Matthias (a professor) and Helen Horowitz (an assistant librarian) Sarna. Education: Hebrew College, Boston, Mass., B.H.A. (with honors), 1974; Brandeis University, B.A. (summa cum laude), 1975, M.A. (Judaic studies), 1975; Yale University, M.A. (history), 1976, M.Phil., 1978, Ph.D., 1979. Home: 2649 Losantiville Ave., Apt. 1, Cincinnati, Ohio 45237. Office: Department of History, Hebrew Union College-Jewish Institute of Religion, 3101 Clifton Ave., Cincinnati, Ohio 45220.

CAREER: American Jewish Historical Society, Waltham, Mass., archivist, 1973-75, acting assistant librarian, 1976; America-Holy Land Project of American Jewish Historical Society and Institute for Contemporary Jewry, Waltham, researcher, 1975-77; Hebrew Union College-Jewish Institute of Religion, Cincinnati, Ohio, visiting lecturer, 1979-80, assistant professor of American Jewish history, 1980—, academic adviser at Center for the Study of the American Jewish Experience, 1981—. Lecturer at universities. Director of applied research for Survivors of Hitler's Germany in Cincinnati Oral History Project, sponsored by American Jewish Archives and National Council of Jewish Women, 1980; director of American Jewish Experience Curriculum Project, 1982—. Member of leadership council and Jewish education committee of Cincinnati Jewish Federation; member of board of directors of American Jewish Committee and University of Cincinnati Hillel Foundation; co-director of Kehilla: A Jewish Community Think Tank.

MEMBER: American Historical Association, Organization of American Historians, American Jewish Historical Society (member of academic council), Immigration History Society, Association for Jewish Studies, Society for Historians of the Early American Republic, Canadian Jewish Historical Society, Phi Beta Kappa. Awards, honors: Seltzer-Brodsky Essay Prize from YIVO Institute, 1977, for "The American Jewish Response to Nineteenth-Century Christian Missions"; Bernard and Audre Rapoport fellow at American Jewish Archives, 1979-80; National Jewish Book Award nomination, 1981, for Jacksonian Jew; fellow of Memorial Foundation for Jewish Culture, 1982-83, and American Council of Learned Societies, 1982.

WRITINGS: (Editor) Jews in New Haven, Jewish Historical Society of New Haven, 1978; Jacksonian Jew: The Two Worlds of Mordecai Noah, Holmes & Meier, 1981; (editor and translator) "People Walk on Their Heads": Moses Weinberger's Jews and Judaism in New York, Holmes & Meier, 1982.

Contributor: Nathan W. Kaganoff, editor, Guide to America-Holy Land Studies, Volume I, Arno, 1980, Volume II, Praeger, 1982; David Gerber, editor, The Encounter of Jew and Gentile in America: New Historical Perspectives, University of Illinois Press, 1984. Contributor of about eighty articles and reviews to journals, including Journal of American History, Spectator, Commentary, Midstream, Nation, Jewish Digest, Ethnicity, and Tradition, and newspapers.

WORK IN PROGRESS: A Reader in American Jewish History, publication by Holmes & Meier expected in 1985; The Jewish Publication Society and American Jewish Culture, 1888-1988, publication by Jewish Publication Society expected in 1988; Jewish-Christian Relations in the United States, publication expected in 1990.

SIDELIGHTS: Sarna told CA: "My interest in American Jewish history dates back to high school. Before then, I had already become fascinated by America's past (not surprising, considering that I am the first in my family to be born here), and I had been introduced to Jewish history which I learned from my father beginning when I was old enough to listen to stories.

American Jewish history, which I discovered on my own as a teenager, synthesized these two interests and promised to explain something of the world which I was struggling to understand. Later, I realized that the field was still in its formative stages of development: filled with searching questions waiting to be asked and answered. Here was a frontier worth conquering, and I plunged in head first. As a high school senior I tried to write the history of American anti-Semitism.

"Being at Brandeis University as an undergraduate permitted me to work at the American Jewish Historical Society, located on the Brandeis campus. There I discovered the endless joys of grappling with primary sources, the raw materials of history, and I began to get a grasp of the history field as a whole. By the time I entered Yale, I had learned enough to know that I wanted to explore what seemed to me to be a central theme in American Jewish history: the effort to be American and Jewish at the same time. My study of Mordecai Noah, one of the first American Jews to be prominent in both the secular and Jewish communities, followed naturally, and the title summarizes the thesis: 'Jacksonian Jew' shows attempted synthesis, 'the *two* worlds of Mordecai Noah' demonstrates that tensions remained.

"My work on Mordecai Noah brought me into contact with early nineteenth-century sources of American Jewish history (by contrast, most recent work in the field dates to the post-1881 period), and this remains one important focus of my research. But I also discovered, while working on Noah, that no serious study of the interactions between Jews and non-Jews in this country had ever been written. This seemed to me to be a great challenge, and I have consequently been gathering material and formulating a conceptual scheme, which I hope one day will result in my writing a full-scale historical analysis of Jewish-Christian relations in the United States. In the meantime, I am focusing more narrowly on three issues: the relationship between Christian missionaries and American Jews, the nature of American anti-Semitism, and the culture of American Jews in its non-Jewish context.

"My approach to American Jewish history generally and to Jewish-Christian relations in particular has been heavily influenced by contemporary writings in history, religion, and social science, particularly those dealing with structural tensions, ambivalences, and historical complexity. American Jewish history must, in my opinion, be informed by the latest findings in American history and Jewish history. At the same time, the field must also be making creative strides of its own, from which others should be able to learn. Too often, American Jews have viewed themselves—and been viewed—only narrowly and in the present. One of my challenges as an American Jewish historian is to change this: to forge a field that speaks to current concerns while putting them in broader historical perspective, thereby shedding light on past and present at once."

*   *   *

SASULY, Richard   1913-
(Alex Furth)

PERSONAL: Surname is pronounced Sa-*soo*-lee; born December 14, 1913, in Washington, D.C.; son of Max (a statistician) and Sonia (Kasner) Sasuly; married Elizabeth Lazareff, August, 1940 (divorced September, 1963); married Lucille Daneri (a teacher), June 19, 1968; children: Angela. *Education:* University of Arizona, B.A., 1935; Columbia University, M.A., 1936; attended Stanford University, 1950-51. *Home and office:* 724 Laurel Ave., Burlingame, Calif. 94010. *Agent:* Jacques

de Spoelberch, J de S Associates, Inc., Shagbark Rd., Wilson Point, South Norwalk, Conn. 06854.

CAREER: Washington Post, Washington, D.C., copy boy, 1931; *Washington Herald,* Washington, D.C., reporter, 1934; U.S. Resettlement Administration, Washington, D.C., speech writer, 1936-37; California State Relief Administration, San Francisco and Los Angeles, statistician and economist, 1938-41; U.S. Farm Security Administration, Washington, D.C., statistician and economist, 1941-43; *Federated Press,* Washington, D.C., manager of Washington bureau and columnist, 1947-55; *World Wide Medical News,* feature writer in New York, N.Y., 1956-60, head of West Coast bureau in San Francisco, 1960-63; University of California, Los Angeles, senior statistician and research associate at School of Public Health, 1963-67; California Regional Medical Programs, San Francisco, associate director, 1967-73. Member of board of trustees of Lattman Foundation of Washington, D.C., 1971—; consultant to Foundations for Medical Care and Council on Health Plan Alternatives. *Military service:* U.S. Army, 1943-45. *Member:* American Public Health Association, Authors League of America, National Association of Science Writers.

WRITINGS: I. G. Farben, Boni & Gaer, 1947; (editor) *Comprehensive Health Care,* Public Affairs Press, 1969; *The Search for the Winning Horse,* Holt, 1979; *Bookies and Bettors,* Holt, 1982.

Author of scripts for television plays, under pseudonym Alex Furth, including episodes for "You Are There" and "Danger."

Contributor to magazines and to labor newspapers.

WORK IN PROGRESS: Ailments of a Health Care System, publication by Holt expected in 1985.

SIDELIGHTS: Sasuly told *CA:* "I hope to write only that which I am strongly convinced needs to be said. I was prompted to do science writing because of my interest in probabilism, while gambling and bookmaking fascinate me because understanding of odds is the basis of both. I am also intrigued by unexpected endings from clear beginnings: reform that produced abolition of child labor (absolutely needed) also led to prohibitions of drinking and betting (awful mistakes). And, in health care, success against *acute* sickness (pneumonia, for example) led in thirty-five years to increases in *chronic* disease—far harder and more expensive to manage."

*   *   *

SAUNDERS, Ernest   1901(?)-1983

OBITUARY NOTICE: Born c. 1901 in Hamden, Conn.; died May 24, 1983, in New Haven, Conn. Engineer and author. Saunders founded the Connecticut Afro-American Historical Society in 1971 and was the author of *Blacks in the Connecticut National Guard* and *The Autobiography of a Dual American.* Obituaries and other sources: *New York Times,* May 29, 1983.

*   *   *

SAVAGE, Robert L(ynn)   1939-

PERSONAL: Born February 26, 1939, in Fort Worth, Tex.; son of Henry Carroll and Helen Marie (Donahue) Savage; married Barbara Grace Brown, January 4, 1980; children: Georgia Faye, Naomi Lynne. *Education:* Tarleton State College, A.S., 1961, B.A., 1963; University of Houston, M.A., 1966; University of Missouri, Ph.D., 1971. *Home:* 109 North School,

No. 3, Fayetteville, Ark. 72701. *Office:* Department of Political Science, University of Arkansas, CC619, Fayetteville, Ark. 72701.

CAREER: Auburn University, Montgomery, Ala., assistant professor of government, 1971-74; University of Arkansas, Fayetteville, assistant professor, 1974-77, associate professor, 1977-82, professor of political science, 1982—. Visiting adjunct assistant professor at University of Houston, summer, 1979; research associate at Bureau of Public Administration, University of Tennessee, 1981. Chairperson of professional panels; member of Comparative State Politics Network. Member of Fayetteville Community Development Committee, 1976-78, chairperson, 1977-78; member of board of advisers of Ozark Institute, 1977-81; member of board of directors of Arkansas Household Research Panel, 1980—; consultant to Arkansas Endowment for the Humanities and Alabama Energy Management Office. *Military service:* U.S. Air Force, 1956-59.

MEMBER: International Communication Association, American Political Science Association, Association for Politics and the Life Sciences, Speech Communication Association, Conference for Federal Studies, Policy Studies Organization, Classification Society, Southern Political Science Association, Southwestern Political Science Association (member of executive council, 1981-83), Midwestern Political Science Association, Arkansas Political Science Association (vice-president, 1977-78; president, 1978-79; member of executive board, 1979-80), Georgia Political Science Association, Pi Sigma Alpha. *Awards, honors:* Grants from U.S. Department of Housing and Urban Development, 1975, FABCO Research Fund, 1979, and Arkansas Endowment for the Humanities, 1980.

WRITINGS: (With Dan D. Nimmo) *Candidates and Their Images: Concepts, Methods, and Findings,* Goodyear Publishing, 1976; *The Literature of Systematic Quantitative Comparison in American State Politics: An Assessment,* Center for the Study of Federalism, Temple University, 1976, revised edition, 1979; (with Charles R. Britton) *Popular Perceptions of Banks Among Arkansans: Explorations in Institutional Imagery,* Bureau of Business and Economic Research, University of Arkansas, 1981.

Contributor: Daniel J. Elazar and Joseph Zikmund II, editors, *The Ecology of American Political Culture: Readings,* Crowell, 1975; Dan D. Nimmo and Keith R. Sanders, editors, *Handbook of Political Communication,* Sage Publications, 1981; John Kincaid, editor, *Political Culture, Public Policy, and the American States,* Institute for the Study of Human Issues (Philadelphia, Pa.), 1982.

Correspondent for *Comparative State Politics Newsletter,* 1979. Arkansas reporter for *Midwest Review of Public Administration,* 1980-81. Contributor of about thirty articles and reviews to political science journals. Editor of newsletter of Arkansas Political Science Association, 1978-80; guest editor of *Political Communication Review,* 1981, and *Publius;* review editor of *Human Communication Research,* 1977-78; member of editorial board of *American Journal of Political Science,* 1983—.

WORK IN PROGRESS: The Diffusion of Political Information, publication by Sage Publications expected in 1985; *Women's Policies in the American States: Studies in Comparative Analysis,* with Diane Blair; *Regionalism in Tennessee Politics: A Study in the Development of Political Subcultures and Political Myths.*

SIDELIGHTS: Savage told *CA:* "I began writing poetry when I was thirteen for my own amusement. Those early forays in writing were largely sublimated as I later developed a strong professional interest in understanding human behavior in the political arena. Very early in that professional development I came to recognize politics as largely symbolic behavior with the central purpose of resolving value conflicts within societies. As a consequence my work has tended to emphasize culture as the context and communication as the means of political actions."

*   *   *

SAWYER, Diane   1946(?)-

BRIEF ENTRY: Born c. 1946 near Glasgow, Ky. American broadcast journalist. Formerly America's 1963 Junior Miss, Sawyer began her career as a weather forecaster and correspondent with a television station in Louisville, Kentucky. Beginning in 1970, she worked in the White House press office during President Richard Nixon's second term. When Nixon resigned because of the Watergate scandal, Sawyer accompanied him to his San Clemente, California, retreat out of loyalty and friendship. She later explained, "It was something that honor demanded." While in California, Sawyer assisted Nixon in the writing of his memoirs. In 1978 she joined the staff of Columbia Broadcasting System (CBS) as a general assignment reporter, eventually serving as State Department correspondent. By 1981 the journalist co-anchored "Morning With Charles Kuralt and Diane Sawyer," held to be the most sober, sophisticated morning show on television. *Address:* Columbia Broadcasting System, Inc., 51 West 52nd St., New York, N.Y. 10019. *Biographical/critical sources: Vogue,* February 15, 1972, January, 1982; *TV Guide,* February 28/March 6, 1981; *New York Times,* September 30, 1981; *People,* November 9, 1981; *Glamour,* March, 1982; *Esquire,* July, 1982.

*   *   *

SAWYER, Mark
See GREENHOOD, (Clarence) David

*   *   *

SCACCO, Anthony M., Jr.   1939-

PERSONAL: Born July 23, 1939, in Waterbury, Conn.; son of Anthony (a machinist) and Nancy (Cipsiano) Scacco. *Education:* Fairfield University, B.S.S., 1962; Northeast Missouri State University, Bs.Ed., 1963; University of New Hampshire, M.A., 1963; University of Massachusetts, Ed.D., 1975; Florida Institute of Technology, Ph.D., 1980. *Home and office:* 110 Wilkenda Ave., Waterbury, Conn. 06708.

CAREER: Case worker for state of Missouri, 1963-64; social director of Head Start program for state of Maine, 1964-68; psychological counselor and education director for State of Connecticut Department of Corrections, 1968-72; private practice in psychology and psychotherapy, 1980—. Ombudsman for juvenile division of State of Connecticut Department of Corrections, 1969; lecturer and adjunct professor of criminology and police science at University of New Haven, 1970; senior teacher at Meriden School for Boys and Cheshire Reformatory, 1972. Expert witness in court cases relating to sexual phenomena. Has addressed subjects in his field in workshops and lectures, and on radio and television shows. *Member:* American Psychological Association (affiliate), American Society of Political and Social Sciences, American Society of Criminology, Academy of Religion and Psychical Research,

New York Transit Police Benevolent Association (honorary member).

WRITINGS: Rape in Prison, C. C Thomas, 1975; (editor) *Male Rape,* AMS, 1982. Contributor to journals and periodicals, including *Angolite, Nursing Care, Sexual Medicine Today, Behavior Today, Sexuality Today, Funeral Service Insider, Law Enforcement,* and *Law and Order.*

WORK IN PROGRESS: The Psychology of Buckminster Fuller.

SIDELIGHTS: Scacco told *CA* that his goal is "to continue to study the most dynamic and now the most threatened unit of our civilization—that of the family." In his effort to aid in the preservation of the family, Scacco has worked with families on such problems as alcohol and drug addiction, child abuse, infidelity, and incest. And in his work in correctional facilities, Scacco has helped families to adjust when a member returns home following a stay in a detention center. "This requires not only family work," Scacco said, "but also integrating alienated family members with the rest of the community, the latter being often suspicious of receiving a youngster who has served jail time back into their midst. I might state that this involvement encompasses the larger 'family'—that of the community itself." A unique program that Scacco initiated to ease offenders back into society involved placing the adjudicated offenders in the homes of police officers, "sharing in a kind of family life not known to the offender prior to this unique study."

Scacco continued: "I have the pleasure of combining, with my academic qualifications in criminology, police science, and psychology, pragmatic, on-the-job experience in several areas of criminal justice. In the field of corrections I have served alongside the correctional officers in the state of Connecticut and other states for several years. I have walked the tiers with these men and been on the inside on a regular eight-to-five working schedule. My job as education director and psychological counselor has required that I spend time inside the cell blocks of the institutions where I have been employed, and this on a consistent basis.

"I had the unique experience of seeing a jail 'gear up' for a possible major assault during the Panther demonstration in the seventies, while at the New Haven Jail. I was in the streets with the correctional staff, the police, and even the National Guard. I know the smell of tension and of probable and horrendous violence. I know also the sweet odor of settlement—settlement among police, the military, and the citizens.

"As senior teacher at the Meriden School for Boys I know what it is to chase a runaway through plowed fields, through running brooks, only to lose him in the dense growth of High Mountain; to sit with the other officers and personnel and ask why, why did he run when this was the only home he knew—the only place that cared.

"At the Cheshire Reformatory I personally felt the caged feeling of the young inmates each day I served as education coordinator. I know the feeling of being a bird in a three-tiered cage, suspended again inside yet another all-encompassing prison. I know what it is to be locked in a room with fifteen young men, ages eighteen to twenty-two, teaching them while being aware that their convictions ranged from arson to assault to first-degree murder.

"The men and women who protect the streets of New York are no strangers to me. In order to understand the threats they face I affiliated with many precincts. My concern for the pro-

tection of the officers on the job is evidenced by my being instrumental in the movement to make bulletproof vests available for each officer in New York and its boroughs.

"The underground caverns of the New York subway system are also familiar to me as are the officers (and now their four-legged protectors, which I encouraged be adopted) that protect the millions that use this means of transportation each day. I studied the needs of the New York Transit Police, walked these catacombs with them, and successfully completed my doctorate with their protection in mind because the study involved body image and the psychology of wearing bulletproof vests—a study intent on keeping these men alive, alive to do their jobs well and to continue to bring up their families. As a ballistics consultant to local, state, federal, and military personnel, I know firsthand the threats faced by these officers. I know the grief of attending the funeral of an officer who unfortunately left his vest home one tragic day.

"As an expert witness in several federal court cases I have experienced the frustrations and dejection of police who know of the guilt of many a criminal but who see them released because of an infraction in evidentiary procedure. As an instructor of many officers, I feel their eagerness to learn the ramifications of ever-changing judicial procedures with the hope of being not only able to apprehend criminals but to see justice done.

"I have taught courses on juvenile delinquency and policy science and have seen many an officer, after an eight to ten hour day on the streets, attend evening classes to attain higher education. I have witnessed 'hardened cops' become part of a unique educational program, instituted at my prompting, whereby they take juveniles serving active time into their homes to interact with their own families in a unique attempt to reach young men and women long since turned off to law-abiding society.

"To all I say, I am not a pure academic, for my experience in criminal justice is both *in vitro* and *in vivo.* And for this I am proud. I am tainted, and proudly so, with the seal of criminal justice as it exists on a daily basis, with its frustrations, its aggravations, but more so, its hope. Through all of the aforementioned message, one virtue remains mine—hope. Hope for the men and women—our police, our correctional officers, our wardens, and our judges. Hope to uphold the law, to interpret the law, to be humane in our task, to inform and instruct and to help salvage the lives of both aggressor and victim. I am proud to be instrumental in the effort to make these goals possible as a dedicated professional in the field of criminal justice."

BIOGRAPHICAL/CRITICAL SOURCES: Los Angeles Times Book Review, April 11, 1982.

*   *   *

SCANLAN, Patrick F. 1895(?)-1983

OBITUARY NOTICE: Born c. 1895 in New York, N.Y.; died March 27, 1983, in North Bellmore, Long Island, N.Y. Editor. Scanlan served as editor of the *Tablet,* the official publication of the Roman Catholic Diocese of Brooklyn, New York, from 1917 to 1968. Obituaries and other sources: *New York Times,* March 29, 1983.

*   *   *

SCHABERT, Kyrill S. 1909(?)-1983

OBITUARY NOTICE: Born c. 1909; died following heart surgery, April 7, 1983, in New York, N.Y. Publishing executive. Schabert was best known as one of the founders, with Helen and Kurt Wolff, of Pantheon Books. He was president of the firm from 1943 to 1962 and later served as associate managing director of the American Book Publishers Council (now the Association of American Publishers) and as director of the central exhibit of U.S. books at the Frankfurt (West Germany) Book Fair. Obituaries and other sources: *New York Times,* April 11, 1983; *Publishers Weekly,* April 29, 1983.

*   *   *

SCHAEPER, Thomas J(erome) 1948-

PERSONAL: Born January 17, 1948, in Covington, Ky.; son of Jerome Joseph and Ruth (Kohmescher) Schaeper; married Kathleen Cooney (a high school teacher), August 7, 1977. *Education:* Thomas More College, A.B. (summa cum laude), 1970; Ohio State University, M.A., 1971, Ph.D., 1977. *Home:* 603 Putnam St., Olean, N.Y. 14760. *Office:* Department of History, St. Bonaventure University, St. Bonaventure, N.Y. 14778.

CAREER: International Telephone & Telegraph Service Industries Corp., Columbus, Ohio, security manager, 1977-78; Bradley University, Peoria, Ill., visiting assistant professor of history, 1978-79; St. Bonaventure University, St. Bonaventure, N.Y., assistant professor, 1979-82, associate professor of history, 1982—. Lecturer at Ohio State University, Newark, summer, 1977. President of Olean Friends of the Library, 1981-82, member of board of directors, 1981—; public speaker on historical topics.

MEMBER: American Historial Association, Society for French Historical Studies, Social Science History Association, American Society for Eighteenth-Century Studies, Societe d'Etude du Dix-Septieme Siecle, Centre Interuniversitaire d'Etudes Europeennes, Societe Francaise d'Etude du Dix-Huitieme Siecle, New York State Association of European Historians (secretary, 1981—), Allegany Area Historical Association (program chairman), Phi Alpha Theta. *Awards, honors:* Travel grant from Canadian Historical Association, 1978; grants from Centre Interuniversitaire d'Etudes Europeennes, summer, 1980, and American Philosophical Society, summer, 1981; Gilbert Chinard scholar of Institut francais de Washington, 1981.

WRITINGS: The Economy of France in the Second Half of the Reign of Louis XIV, Centre Interuniversitaire d'Etudes Europeennes, 1980; (editor with Islay Nicholson Bergreen) *Our Allegany Heritage, 1831-1981: A Sesquicentennial Review,* Citizen Publishing House, 1981; *The French Council of Commerce, 1700-1715: A Study of Mercantilism After Colbert,* Ohio State University Press, 1983.

Contributor of more than twenty articles and reviews to library, history, and French studies journals. Assistant editor of annual, *The Eighteenth-Century: A Current Bibliography,* 1981—; guest editor of *Cithara,* 1982, book review editor, 1982—.

WORK IN PROGRESS: Research on Jacques-Donatien Leray de Chaumont and the American Revolution; studying the administration of trade and industry in eighteenth-century France.

SIDELIGHTS: Schaeper told *CA:* "I began to specialize in seventeenth- and eighteenth-century French history because I was fascinated by such persons as Louis XIV and Voltaire and topics such as the French Revolution. Up to this point most of my publications have been intended for professional historians rather than for the general public. But I believe that my research will contribute to major revisions in the interpretation of the reign of Louis XIV. On a broader level, my work challenges standard views on the growth of government regulation of business in the modern world.

"My next long-range project excites me because it will be attractive to a wider audience. It concerns a little-known Frenchman who played a huge role in the American revolution. The story concerns such persons as Benjamin Franklin, John Paul Jones, and the Marquis de Lafayette. The story of Jacques Donatien Leray de Chaumont is both important and dramatic."

*   *   *

SCHIAPPA, Barbara D(ublin) 1943-

PERSONAL: Born December 3, 1943, in Murray, Ky.; daughter of Orville O. (an automobile dealer) and Cordie Maie (Faust) Dublin; married Charles F. Schiappa (in computer system design and management), September 28, 1974. *Education:* Attended Murray State University, 1967-69. *Home and office:* 135 Stearns St., Carlisle, Mass. 01741.

CAREER: Accredited medical record technician, 1971; Murray-Calloway County Hospital, Murray, Ky., director of medical records department, 1965-70; Emerson Hospital, Concord, Mass., supervisor of medical record department, 1970; Massachusetts Hospital Association, Burlington, manager of statewide health record data system, 1970-76; free-lance writer, 1977—. *Member:* Authors Guild.

WRITINGS: Mixing: Catholic-Protestant Marriages in the 1980s, Paulist/Newman, 1982. Contributor to magazines, including *Sports Illustrated, Boston, Parents' Choice, Miniature Collector,* and *Yankee,* and newspapers.

WORK IN PROGRESS: A novel set in western Kentucky, tentatively titled *Home Runs,* about a young man who wants to play major league baseball.

SIDELIGHTS: Schiappa told *CA:* "When Paulist Press editors proposed that I write a contemporary book on Catholic-Protestant marriages, I initially questioned the need for such a book. My husband, a Catholic of Italian descent, and I, a Protestant and native Kentuckian, had had no problems as a result of our different Christian heritages and beliefs. With the spirit of ecumenism today, the thousands of interfaith couples who marry each year can find acceptance and guidance in their churches. I wondered, then, if there were enough issues and areas of potential conflict to justify the book.

"As I began to research the subject, I discovered that the few available books were severely outdated and negative, and that most were written from a biased viewpoint, painting a grim future for Christian-mixed couples and advising readers to avoid such marriages. I imagined a young couple considering marriage today and going to the library or a bookstore to seek a book that might help them understand and resolve their differences. I knew then that something *had* to be written to help couples in the 1980's, and as I thought about my own marriage and why it was working so well, I realized that I had to write this book. I wrote *Mixing* because I truly believe that Christian-mixed marriages in which the partners love, understand, and respect each other can be an experience in spiritual growth and unity.

"Not a book of rights and wrongs, formulas, or easy answers, *Mixing* is a practical, how-to book that recognizes the rights of married persons to their own beliefs. It guides readers on an ecumenical journey in search of solutions that will help them develop a lasting, growing relationship and raise their children without either partner forfeiting his or her faith identity. Through interviews with Catholic and Protestant clergy and couples whose married lives range from six months to over twenty years, as well as my personal experience, *Mixing* examines real-life situations that couples may encounter.

"The book emphasizes open, honest communication and raises the important questions that couples should consider before marriage: What do the modern churches really teach about Christian-mixed marriages? How will your parents react? What will your pastors say? Where will you worship? How will you raise your children? What if you have equally strong commitments to your church communitites? What if you disagree on the importance of religion in your daily lives? What if one or both of you have been away from your churches and want to return?

"Summarized in a single sentence, the theme of *Mixing* is this: It is not similar backgrounds that make a marriage work but similar dedication of the partners to their faith, mutual respect, and a willingness to work together toward mutual understanding and growth.

"*Mixing* attempts to fill the gap between outdated, pre-ecumenical books and clergy-authored books that tend to be biased toward the church of the author. The book has special value, I believe, because it is solution-oriented—not just another study—and because it transcends my own viewpoint and employs the tools of journalism to examine the issue from all sides."

*   *   *

SCHMIDT, Arno (Otto) 1914-1979

OBITUARY NOTICE: Born January 18, 1914, in Hamburg, Germany; died June 3, 1979. Author. Following his release from a prisoner-of-war camp at the end of World War II, Schmidt became a prize-winning novelist with such books as *Leviathan, Brans Haide, Kaff, Koehe in Halbtrauer, Die Ritter vom Geist,* and *The Egghead Republic.* Obituaries and other sources: *Encyclopedia of World Literature in the Twentieth Century,* supplement, Ungar, 1975; *International Authors and Writers Who's Who,* 8th edition, Melrose, 1977; *Who's Who in the World,* 4th edition, Marquis, 1978; *World Authors: 1970-1975,* H. W. Wilson, 1980; *The International Who's Who,* 44th edition, Europa, 1980.

*   *   *

SCHMIDT, Claire Harman 1957-
(Claire Harman)

PERSONAL: Born September 21, 1957, in Guildford, England; daughter of John Edward (a teacher) and Patricia (a teacher; maiden name, Mullins) Harman; married Michael N. Schmidt (a publisher), August 25, 1979; children: Charles, Isabel. *Education:* Victoria University of Manchester, B.A. (with first class honors), 1979. *Home:* Thornleigh, Park Road, Chapel-en-le-Frith, Derbyshire, England.

CAREER: Poetry Nation Review, Manchester, England, coordinating editor, 1979—, editor of supplement, "Sylvia Townsend Warner: A Celebration," 1981.

WRITINGS—Under name Claire Harman: (Editor) *Collected Poems of Sylvia Townsend Warner,* Viking, 1982; (editor) *Selected Poems of Sylvia Townsend Warner,* Chatto & Windus, in press.

WORK IN PROGRESS: The Life of Sylvia Townsend Warner, publication expected in 1987 or 1988.

SIDELIGHTS: Schmidt told *CA:* "I became involved with Sylvia Townsend Warner when I found her hiding under a desk in my husband's publishing office. That is to say, I found an enormous package of Sylvia's poems there, awaiting an editor. Such good poems, too, and such an arresting and intriguing author behind them. Then there were the novels to discover, and the stories, and the other fascinating miscellaneous writings. Her peculiarly English wit and her highly literate (and totally nonacademic) intelligence have endeared her whole body of work to me. Her ghost, with gleeful malice, is refusing to let any of it be put through the Ph.D. machine without a fight. My two small children are her willing corporeal accomplices."

*   *   *

SCHMIDT, Peggy Jeanne 1951-

PERSONAL: Born August 10, 1951, in Lorain, Ohio; daughter of Eddie M. and Phyllis A. Schmidt; married Joseph Tabacco (a lawyer), September 6, 1981. *Education:* Bowling Green State University, B.A. (cum laude), 1972; graduate study at Columbia University. *Residence:* New York, N.Y. *Office:* c/o Walker & Co., 720 Fifth Ave., New York, N.Y. 10019.

CAREER: Glamour, New York, N.Y., assistant college editor, 1972-73, education and career editor, 1974-80; free-lance writer and lecturer, 1980—. *Member:* Road Runners of New York, Women Ink, The Writers' Room.

WRITINGS: Making It on Your First Job When You're Young, Inexperienced, and Ambitious, Avon, 1981; *Making It in the Big City: A Woman's Guide to Living, Loving and Working There,* Coward, 1983. Contributor of articles to *New York Times, Family Weekly,* and *Working Woman.*

WORK IN PROGRESS: A series of career books for college students, publication by Walker & Co. expected in 1984.

SIDELIGHTS: Making It On Your First Job includes discussions about college curriculum and career choices, tips on securing salary increases, and guidance on how to recognize when the time has come to move on to another position. According to *Ms.* reviewer Susan McHenry, *Making It On Your First Job* is "an especially helpful guide, both for preparing yourself to be a successful candidate in today's competitive job market, and for realistically planning your transition from campus life to the working world."

BIOGRAPHICAL/CRITICAL SOURCES: Ms., October, 1981; *Esquire,* August, 1982.

*   *   *

SCHMUCKE, Anne
See STRICH, Christian

*   *   *

SCHNEIDER, Anna
See SEQUOIA, Anna

*   *   *

SCHOENBERG, Arnold 1874-1951

BRIEF ENTRY: Born September 13, 1874, in Vienna, Austria; came to United States in 1933; naturalized U.S. citizen, April

11, 1941; died July 13, 1951, in Los Angeles, Calif. American musical composer, artist, educator, and author. Schoenberg is best known for developing a revolutionary method of musical composition that involves the use of all twelve notes in the chromatic scale. A controversial technique, the twelve-tone system was slow to gain acceptance, but it subsequently became a major influence on twentieth-century music. Schoenberg, who was associated with expressionist artists Oskar Kokoschka and Egon Schiele, was also a painter. His art generated much controversy when it appeared in exhibitions during the early 1900's. Schoenberg lived in his native Austria until he fled the impending Holocaust in 1933. He then came to the United States, where he became a professor of music at University of Southern California and University of California, Los Angeles. The Schoenberg Institute at University of Southern California was named in Schoenberg's honor following the composer's death. His writings include *Style and Idea* (1950), *Structural Functions of Harmony* (1954), *Preliminary Exercises in Counterpoint* (1963), *Letters* (1964), and *Fundamentals of Musical Composition* (1967). *Address:* 116 North Rockingham Ave., Los Angeles, Calif. *Biographical/critical sources: Spectator,* February 23, 1974, April 26, 1975; *Observer,* February 24, 1974; *New York Review of Books,* September 18, 1975; *Times Literary Supplement,* November 7, 1975; *Christian Science Monitor,* March 24, 1976; *Baker's Biographical Dictionary of Musicians,* 6th edition, Schirmer Books, 1978.

* * *

SCHONBERG, Arnold
See SCHOENBERG, Arnold

* * *

SCHOWALTER, John E(rwin)   1936-

PERSONAL: Born March 15, 1936, in Milwaukee, Wis.; son of Raymond P. (a physician) and Martha (Kowalke) Schowalter; married Ellen Lefferts (a mutual fund adviser), June 11, 1960; children: Jay, Bethany. *Education:* University of Wisconsin—Madison, B.S., 1957, M.D., 1960. *Residence:* New Haven, Conn. *Office:* Child Study Center, Yale University, New Haven, Conn. 06510.

CAREER: Yale-New Haven Hospital, New Haven, Conn., intern in pediatrics, 1960-61; Cincinnati General Hospital, Cincinnati, Ohio, resident in psychiatry, 1961-63; Yale University, New Haven, resident in child psychiatry at Child Study Center, 1963-65, assistant professor, 1967-70, associate professor, 1970-75, professor of pediatrics and psychiatry, 1975—, chief of psychiatry at Child Study Center, 1975—. *Military service:* U.S. Army, 1965-67. *Member:* American Academy of Child Psychiatry (member of council, 1979-82), Society of Professors of Child Psychiatry (president, 1982-84), Association for the Care of Children's Health (president, 1983-85).

WRITINGS: (With Walter Anyan) *Family Handbook of Adolescence,* Knopf, 1979; (senior editor, with Paul Patterson, Austin Kutscher, Stephen Gullo, and David Peretz) *The Child and Death,* Columbia University Press, 1983.

* * *

SCHREIBER, Georges   1904-1977

OBITUARY NOTICE: Born April 25, 1904, in Brussels, Belgium; died in 1977. Painter, cartoonist, illustrator, and author of *Bambino the Clown.* Schreiber contributed illustrations to periodicals, including *Fortune, Nation,* and *Saturday Review.* Obituaries and other sources: *Who's Who in American Art,* Bowker, 1980.

* * *

SCHULTZ, George J(oseph)   1932-

BRIEF ENTRY: Born April 27, 1932, in Milwaukee, Wis. American advertising and public relations consultant and author. Schultz worked as a news reporter for radio stations and a newspaper in Green Bay, Wisconsin, until 1961. He was a press officer for the U.S. Agency for International Development from 1962 to 1967 and for the U.S. Department of Commerce from 1969 to 1974. He founded Schultz/Princeton Associates in 1974 and AdRep Services in 1977. Schultz edited *Foreign Trade Market Place* (Gale, 1977). *Address:* 325 Oak Lane, Hightstown, N.J. 08520; and Schultz/Princeton Associates, 37 Station Dr., Princeton, N.J. 08550.

* * *

SCHWARTZ, George Leopold   1891-1983

OBITUARY NOTICE: Born February 10, 1891; died April 2, 1983. Economist, journalist, and author. Schwartz was a lecturer at the London School of Economics between the two world wars. He then switched to a career in journalism, becoming economic adviser to the Kemsley Newspapers and deputy city editor of the Sunday edition of the *London Times* from 1944 to 1961. For the next ten years he wrote the newspaper's economic column. Schwartz was the author of *Bread and Circuses* and the co-author of *Insurance Funds and Their Investment.* Obituaries and other sources: *Who's Who,* 134th edition, Marquis, 1982; *London Times,* April 6, 1983.

* * *

SCHWARTZ, Julius   1907-

PERSONAL: Born in 1907. *Residence:* New York City.

CAREER: Science teacher in New York City public schools; instructor in science education at Bank Street College of Education, New York City. Science consultant to Bureau of Curriculum Research for New York City schools and to Midwest Program on Airborn Television Instruction.

WRITINGS—For children, except as noted: *It's Fun to Know Why: Experiments With Things Around Us,* illustrations by Edwin Herron, Whittlesey House, 1952, 2nd edition, illustrations by Herron and Anne Marie Jauss, McGraw, 1973; *Through the Magnifying Glass: Little Things That Make a Big Difference,* illustrations by Jeanne Bendick, Whittlesey House, 1954; *Now I Know,* illustrations by Marc Simont, Whittlesey House, 1955; *I Know a Magic House,* illustrations by Simont, Whittlesey House, 1956; (compiler with Herman Schneider) *Growing Up With Science,* [New York], 1959, 2nd edition, compiled with Susan A. Kailin, Bowker, 1967; *The Earth Is Your Spaceship,* illustrations by Simont, Whittlesey House, 1963; (with Glenn O. Blough) *Elementary School Science and How to Teach It* (adult), revised edition (Schwartz was not associated with original edition), Holt, 1958, 6th edition, 1979; *Uphill and Downhill,* illustrations by William McCaffrey, Whittlesey House, 1965; *Go on Wheels,* illustrations by Arnold Roth, McGraw, 1966; *Magnify and Find Out Why,* illustrations by Richard Cuffari, McGraw, 1972; *Earthwatch: Space-Time Investigations With a Globe,* illustrations by Radu Vero, McGraw, 1977; (with Charles Tanzer) *Biology and Human Prog-*

ress (workbook and teacher's handbook), fifth edition, Prentice-Hall, 1977 (Schwartz was not involved in preparation of the text).

SIDELIGHTS: Julius Schwartz writes to explain basic scientific concepts to children. His books have addressed a wide variety of topics, namely, the earth's orbit, wheels, inventions (including water faucets and phonographs), the sound of the wind, electric shocks, magnifying lenses, and time-space investigations. Critics, notably Alice Dalgliesh in the *Saturday Review,* have commented that Schwartz's works capture the imagination of a child. For example, the author explains the earth's orbit with references to birthdays instead of ordinary, calendar days. Most of Schwartz's books contain experiments for children to try at home or in the classroom.

BIOGRAPHICAL/CRITICAL SOURCES: Saturday Review, May 15, 1954, November 17, 1956, May 11, 1963; *New York Herald Tribune Books,* May 16, 1954, May 12, 1963; *New York Times,* June 6, 1954, November 11, 1956; *Scientific American,* December, 1977.

*   *   *

SCHWARZKOPF-LEGGE, Elisabeth 1915-

PERSONAL: Born December 9, 1915, in Jarotschin, Prussia (now Poland); daughter of Friedrich and Elisabeth (Froehlich) Schwarzkopf; married Walter Legge (died, 1979). *Education:* Attended high school in Berlin, Germany; studied music with Maria Ivoguen. *Office address:* c/o Musical Advisers Establishment, P.O. Box 583, 9490 Vaduz, Lichtenstein.

CAREER: Soprano with Staedtische Opera, Berlin, Germany, beginning in 1946; soprano with Staatsoper, Vienna, Austria; La Scala, Milan, Italy, soprano, 1948-63; Metropolitan Opera, New York, N.Y., soprano, 1964-65; concert singer, 1965-79; writer, 1979—. Performed in London, England, 1948-50, and San Francisco, Calif., 1955; member of faculty of Juilliard School and University of Michigan.

MEMBER: Swedish Academy of Arts and Sciences, Royal Academy of Music (England; honorary member), Societa Nazionale di Santa Cecilia. *Awards, honors:* D.Mus. from Cambridge University and American Academy, Washington, D.C.; Ordre of Danneborg; Grosses Verdienst Kreuz of East Germany; Lilli Lehmann Medal; Orfeo D'Oro Mantova; Golden Star from City of Vienna, Austria.

WRITINGS: (Editor) *On and Off the Record: A Memoir of Walter Legge,* Scribner, 1982.

WORK IN PROGRESS: Memoirs.

*   *   *

SCIBOR-RYLSKI, Aleksander 1927(?)-1983

OBITUARY NOTICE: Born c. 1927; died April 3, 1983. Film director, playwright, screenwriter, and author. Scibor-Rylski was best known for writing Polish screenplays, including "Man of Marble" and "Man of Iron." Obituaries and other sources: *New York Times,* April 7, 1983; *London Times,* April 9, 1983.

*   *   *

SCOTT, David (Aubrey) 1919-

PERSONAL: Born August 3, 1919, in London, England; son of Hugh Sumner (a schoolmaster) and Barbara Easton (Jackson) Scott; married Vera Kathleen Ibbitson, January 21, 1941; chil-

dren: Diana (Mrs. J. B. Unwin), Robert, Andrew. *Education:* Attended University of Birmingham, 1938-39. *Home:* Wayside, Moushill Lane, Milford, Surrey GU8 5BQ, England. *Agent:* Peterborough Literary Agency, 135 Fleet St., London EC4P 4BL, England. *Office:* Ellerman Lines Ltd., Camomile St., London EC3A 7EX, England.

CAREER: British Foreign and Commonwealth Office, London, England, 1948-79, assistant private secretary of secretary of state, 1949, served in Pretoria, Union of South Africa (now Republic of South Africa), 1951-53, seconded to cabinet office, 1954-56, served in Singapore, 1956-58, British deputy high commissioner to Federation of Rhodesia and Nyasaland (now Malawi, Zimbabwe, and Zambia), 1961-63, worked at Imperial Defence College, 1964, deputy high commissioner to India, 1965-67, high commissioner to Uganda and nonresident ambassador to Rwanda, 1967-70, assistant under-secretary of state, 1970-72, high commissioner to New Zealand and nonresident governor of Pitcairn Island, 1973-75, ambassador to Republic of South Africa, 1976-79; Ellerman Lines Ltd., London, England, chairman, 1982—. Director of Barclays Bank International and Mitchell Cotts Group Ltd. Trustee of Southern African Studies Trust and University of York. *Military service:* British Army, 1939-47, served in Royal Artillery; became major.

MEMBER: P.E.N. International, Royal Overseas League, London (chairman, 1981—). *Awards, honors:* Knight Grand Cross of St. Michael and St. George (GCMG), 1974.

WRITINGS: Ambassador in Black and White: Thirty Years of Changing Africa (autobiography), Weidenfeld & Nicolson, 1981. Leader writer for *Egyptian Gazette,* 1946-47.

WORK IN PROGRESS: Second volume of autobiography.

SIDELIGHTS: Scott told CA: "*Ambassador in Black and White* is a personal account based upon my African diplomatic appointments and upon thirty years of political change in Africa."

The book points out, writes Lucy Mair in the *Times Literary Supplement,* "that the diplomat is there first of all to assure the interests of his government, and not to make history in accordance with his own values; also that it is his business to be in touch with those in authority though he may well sympathize with those in opposition."

AVOCATIONAL INTERESTS: Music, opera, bird-watching.

*   *   *

SCOTT, David W(infield) 1916-

PERSONAL: Born July 10, 1916, in Fall River, Mass.; son of Benjamin David and Edith May (Romig) Scott; married Tirsa Lilia Saavedra (an importer), July 10, 1947; children: Tirsa Margaret, Edith Elizabeth. *Education:* Harvard University, A.B., 1938; Claremont Graduate School, M.A., 1940, M.F.A., 1949; University of California, Berkeley, Ph.D., 1960. *Home:* 3016 Cortland Pl. N.W., Washington, D.C. 20008. *Office:* National Gallery of Art, Washington, D.C. 20565.

CAREER: Scripps College, Claremont, Calif., 1947-63, began as lecturer, became professor of art, 1957, chairman of department, 1956-63; Smithsonian Institution, Washington, D.C., assistant director of National Collection of Fine Arts, 1963-64, director, 1964-69; National Gallery of Art, Washington, D.C., planning consultant, 1969—. Professor at Claremont Graduate School, 1957-63; director of Claremont Colleges' Summer Art Institute, 1960-62. *Military service:* U.S. Army

Air Forces, 1942-45; became captain. *Member:* American Association of Museums, College Art Association of America.

WRITINGS: *John Sloan, 1871-1951,* National Gallery of Art, 1971; *John Sloan,* Watson-Guptill, 1975; *Maurice Prendergast,* Artist's Limited Edition, 1980. Advisory editor of *Britannica Encyclopaedia of American Art.**

*   *   *

SCOTT, Lauren
See FRENTZEN, Jeffrey

*   *   *

SCOTT, Ronald Bodley   1906-1982

PERSONAL: Born September 10, 1906, in Bournemouth, England; died in an automobile accident, May 12, 1982, in Italy; son of Maitland Bodley (a physician) and Alice Hilda Durance (George) Scott; married Edith Daphne McCarthy, 1931 (died, 1977); married Jessie Gaston; children: (first marriage) two daughters. *Education:* Brasenose College, Oxford, B.A., 1928, M.A. and B.M., B.Chi., 1931, D.M., 1937.

CAREER: St. Bartholomew's Hospital, chief assistant to medical unit, 1943, physician, 1946-65, senior physician, 1965-71, consulting physician, 1971-82, member of board of governors, 1966-71. Name physician to household of King George VI, 1949; physician to Queen Elizabeth II, 1952-82. Physician at Woolwich Memorial Hospital, 1936-71, Surbiton General Hospital, 1946-64, Florence Nightingale Hospital, 1958-82, King Edward VII Hospital for Officers, 1963-82, and King Edward VII Hospital, Midhurst, 1965-82; principal medical officer for Equity and Law Life Assurance Society, 1952-82; consulting physician to Woolwich Memorial Hospital, 1971—, British Railways, 1957-82, and Royal Navy, 1963-82. Langdon Brown Lecturer at Royal College of Physicians, 1957, Croonian Lecturer, 1970; Lettsomian Lecturer at Medical Society of London, 1957; Thom Bequest Lecturer at Edinburgh's Royal College of Physicians, 1965. Chairman of board of trustees of Migraine Trust, beginning in 1971; member of council of Imperial Cancer Research Fund, beginning in 1968; chairman of research grants committee of British Heart Foundation, beginning in 1970; member of council of Royal College of Physicians, 1963-66, censor, 1970-72, senior censor and vice-president, 1972. *Military service:* British Army, Royal Army Medical Corps, physician, 1941-45; served in the Middle East; became lieutenant colonel. *Awards, honors:* Knight Commander of Royal Victorian Order, 1964, Knight Grand Cross, 1973; Order of the Crown of Brunei, 1970.

WRITINGS: (Editor of revision with Thomas J. Horder) *The Essentials of Medical Diagnosis,* 2nd edition, Cassell, 1952; (editor) Frederick William Price, *Price's Textbook of the Practice of Medicine,* Oxford University Press, 10th edition, 1966, 12th edition, 1978; *Cancer: The Facts,* Oxford University Press, 1979. Contributor to medical journals. Past co-editor of *Medical Annual: A Yearbook of Treatment With a Practitioners' Index.*

OBITUARIES: *London Times,* May 13, 1982.*

*   *   *

SCOTT, Willard H., Jr.   1934-

PERSONAL: Born March 7, 1934, in Alexandria, Va.; son of Herman (in insurance sales) and Thelma (a telephone operator; maiden name, Phillips) Scott; married Mary Dwyer, August 7, 1959; children: Mary, Sally. *Education:* American University, B.A., 1955. *Home:* Route 710, Delaplane, Va. 22025. *Agent:* Bill Adler, 551 Fifth Ave., New York, N.Y. 10020. *Office:* NBC, 30 Rockefeller Plaza, Room 701A, New York, N.Y. 10020.

CAREER: National Broadcasting Co. (NBC), New York, N.Y., page with WRC-TV in Washington, D.C., 1950, broadcaster (with Ed Walker—"The Joy Boys") for WOL-Radio in Washington, D.C., 1950-53, for WRC-AM in Washington, D.C., 1953-72, for Station WWDC in Washington, D.C., 1972-74, weather reporter on "Today" show, 1980—. Weekend disc jockey for Station WINX, 1950. Weather reporter at WRC-AM, 1959-72, and WRC-TV, beginning in 1967. Appeared frequently on television as Ronald MacDonald and Bozo the Clown during the 1960's; announcer on commercials. *Awards, honors:* Named Humanitarian-in-Residence by National Society of Fund Raisers, 1975; named Washingtonian-of-the-Year by *Washingtonian* magazine, 1979.

WRITINGS: *The Joy of Living,* Coward, 1982.

WORK IN PROGRESS: Two cookbooks.

SIDELIGHTS: Willard Scott began reporting the weather on NBC's "Today" show on March 10, 1980. Already renowned as a radio and television personality in Washington, D.C., the broadcaster's zany approach to reporting the weather initially drew negative responses from many "Today" viewers. Clearly, Scott was not adverse to blowing kisses to fans or doffing his wig while on the air. Nor did his appearance fit the "Today" show image; he was "fat, toupeed and gap-toothed . . . sort of a one man *Hee-Haw,*" Dolly Langdon observed in *People.* "I've always had a reputation as a buffoon," admitted Scott.

Yet within the year, Scott was being favorably received by the majority of his viewers. In his autobiography *The Joy of Living,* the broadcaster spoke about his national television success. "I'm a mutation," he wrote. "If you put me on an audience tape, everything is wrong. . . . If you were to look at my resume, you'd see that I'm 48 years old, I'm bald, I'm overweight, I don't make all the smooth moves, and I dress like a slob. . . . I'd never come out of the computer as being a hit . . . yet . . . I take tremendous pride in the fact that I beat the system."

Scott attributes his life-long success to a happy and secure childhood with a loving mother and father. *The Joy of Living* contains many fond anecdotes concerning his parents; Vic Sussman, in the *Washington Post Book World,* noted that "Scott's account of Thelma's long battle with Alzheimer's Disease and Herman's slow wasting away are particularly moving." The critic also remarked that the chapter on the "Joy Boys," the radio comedy team that Scott created with Ed Walker, was one of the best in the volume. "'The Joy of Living' would have been a better book had Scott treated us to more anecdotes about those years," Sussman determined, "and his long career in broadcasting."

"Scott writes the way he talks," Sussman concluded, "gushing boyish ebullience and cornpone, telling stories of his youth, his life-long love of radio, his Virginia farm, and his philosophy. . . . Unfortunately, as do many who achieve national fame, [he] casts himself as a pundit, advising his readers on . . . marriage, divorce, child-rearing, human relations and religion. . . . Still, Scott is a superb performer and many of his fans will welcome this book."

BIOGRAPHICAL/CRITICAL SOURCES: *People,* September 1, 1980; *Washington Post Book World,* September 23, 1982.

*   *   *

SCULLARD, Howard Hayes   1903-1983

OBITUARY NOTICE—See index for *CA* sketch: Born February 9, 1903, in Bedford, England; died March 31, 1983, in London, England. Historian, educator, and author. Scullard was a scholar in the field of ancient history, particularly the history of the Roman Empire. He had been a professor emeritus of ancient history at the University of London since 1970. His writings include *A History of the Roman World From 753 to 146 B.C., Roman Politics, 220 to 150 B.C., The Elephant in the Greek and Roman World,* and *Festivals and Ceremonies of the Roman Republic.* Obituaries and other sources: *London Times,* April 6, 1983; *Chicago Tribune,* April 8, 1983; *Washington Post,* April 9, 1983.

*   *   *

SEASONGOOD, Murray   1878-1983

OBITUARY NOTICE: Born October 27, 1878, in Cincinnati, Ohio; died February 21, 1983. Politician, lawyer, educator, and author. Seasongood first became known during the 1920's, when he successfully led the Charterite movement to establish a new city charter and to clean up the municiple government in Cincinnati. He then served two terms as Cincinnati's mayor. Seasongood was the author of articles on government and law for professional journals, including *Harvard Law Review, American Bar Association Journal,* and *American City.* He also wrote *Selections From Speeches, 1900-1959, of Murray Seasongood.* Obituaries and other sources: *Who's Who in America,* 41st edition, Marquis, 1980; *New York Times,* February 23, 1983; *Chicago Tribune,* February 24, 1983; *Los Angeles Times,* February 24, 1983; *Washington Post,* February 26, 1983.

*   *   *

SEERS, Dudley   1920-1983

OBITUARY NOTICE: Born April 11, 1920; died March 21, 1983, in Washington, D.C. Economist, editor, and author. Seers served as director-general of the economic planning staff of the first Ministry of Overseas Development under British Prime Minister Harold Wilson from 1964 to 1967. He later became director of the Institute of Development Studies. In addition to his many articles about economic development, Seers wrote *Cuba: The Economic and Social Revolution.* Obituaries and other sources: *Who's Who,* 134th edition, St. Martin's, 1982; *London Times,* March 23, 1983.

*   *   *

SEMEIKS, Jonna Gormely   1944-

PERSONAL: Born October 8, 1944, in Tacoma, Wash.; daughter of Edward J. (an electrician) and Alice A. (a teacher; maiden name, Eschenbacher) Gormely; married Juris Semeiks, August 31, 1970 (divorced, 1977); married Harold G. Schechter (a college professor and writer), July 15, 1978; children: (second marriage) Elizabeth Sara, Laura Suzanne. *Education:* Hunter College of the City University of New York, B.A., 1969; Rutgers University, Ph.D., 1981. *Office:* Department of English, Queens College of the City University of New York, Flushing, N.Y. 11367.

CAREER: *Newsweek,* New York, N.Y., assistant to promotion director, 1969-1976; State University of New York, teacher of literature and writing courses at Empire State College branch, 1974-77; Queens College of the City University of New York, Flushing, N.Y., adjunct lecturer, 1975-82, adjunct assistant professor of English, 1983—.

WRITINGS: (Editor with husband, Harold G. Schechter) *Patterns in Popular Culture: A Sourcebook for Writers,* Harper, 1980; (editor with Schechter) *Discoveries: Fifty Stories of the Quest,* Bobbs-Merrill, 1983. Contributor of articles and reviews to scholarly journals.

WORK IN PROGRESS: A collection of stories; a Gothic novel.

SIDELIGHTS: Jonna Semeiks wrote: "In one sense I became a writer when I was very young, by spinning out heroic tales as a child and despairing tales as a post-adolescent. But in another sense I have only recently begun to write, or at least to write fiction, since I spent much of my twenties and part of my thirties first working in the business world, where I tried to become interested in questions of profit, and next attending graduate school. The latter culminated in some published scholarship and textbooks. Although I continue to teach part time in college, I have stopped doing scholarly research and writing. My time is exceedingly limited, but the hours I have left in a week are devoted to writing fiction. I suppose I write because nothing else I have tried to do has given me such deep and keen pleasure: the sense of arriving at some sort of still point where I am, however temporarily, outside the range of all that is noisy and nonessential.

"It is difficult to trace the connections between who one is and what one writes, particularly in my case, because I've come to writing so late. But it strikes me that two things in my history are important. One is that I am a lapsed Roman Catholic, and so I have all kinds of conscious and unconscious feelings about evil and peril lurking everywhere in life, as well as a sometimes highly uncomfortable need for meaning. The other important thing is the fact that, although I live in New York City now, I originally hail from Colorado. I have, as a result, a perennial sense of being an outsider to the Eastern and strictly urban sensibility, a foreignness, in short, that I no longer try to suppress. What has been strengthened by age, if not by geographical proximity, is a love for the Western 'wilderness' and a respect for certain qualitites of mind and character that seem a natural response to that awesome landscape.

"For the last eight months, I have been writing stories, which I hope will become part of a published collection. I have also been blocking out a Gothic novel set in the mountains of Colorado. When I finish that novel, I'd like to begin a more ambitious and serious one about five young people, one of whom kills herself at the end of the 1960's. The novel will show the four remaining friends trying to understand the suicide and to make a world for themselves in the radically different decade of the seventies."

*   *   *

SEQUOIA, Anna
(Anna Schneider)

PERSONAL: Original name, Anna Schneider; named legally changed in 1978; born in New York, N.Y.; daughter of Bernard and Pauline (Rebeck) Schneider. *Education:* Goddard College, B.A., 1979; also attended Bard College, University of Florence, and New York University. *Residence:* New York, N.Y., and Sag Harbor, N.Y. *Agent:* Diane Cleaver, Sanford J. Greenburger Associates, Inc., 825 Third Ave., New York, N.Y. 10022.

CAREER: Editor, book reviewer, direct mail copywriter, and free-lance journalist; co-founder and vice-president of North Country Moutaineering (technical climbing school and wilderness guide service), 1975—. *Member:* Organizing Committee for a National Writers Union, Coalition of New York Women Artists (co-founder).

WRITINGS: (Under name Anna Schneider, with brother, Steve Schneider) *The Climber's Sourcebook*, Doubleday, 1976; (with S. Schneider) *Backpacking on a Budget*, Penguin, 1979; *The Complete Catalogue of Mail Order Kits*, Rawson-Wade, 1981; *The Official J.A.P. Handbook: A Complete Guide to Jewish American Princesses and Princes* (humor), New American Library, 1982; (with Patty Brown) *The Official J.A.P. Paper Doll Book*, New American Library, 1983. Contributor of articles and reviews to *New Times, New York, Climbing.*

WORK IN PROGRESS: Another humor book, publication expected in 1984; a novel, publication expected in 1985.

BIOGRAPHICAL/CRITICAL SOURCES: Times Literary Supplement, December 24, 1982.

* * *

SERENI, Vittorio 1913-1983

OBITUARY NOTICE: Born July 27, 1913, in Luino, Italy; died February 10, 1983, in Milan, Italy. Poet, translator, and author. Sereni translated into Italian the works of Ezra Pound, Paul Valery, Julian Green, and William Carlos Williams. He also published several collections of poetry, including *Frontiere, Diario d'Algeria*, and *Gli strumenti umani.* One collection, *Selected Poems*, was published in English translation. *L'opzione e allegati* and *L'opzione e allegati* are among Sereni's novels. Obituaries and other sources: *Chicago Tribune*, February 13, 1983; *London Times*, February 14, 1983.

* * *

SERT, Josep Lluis 1902-1983

OBITUARY NOTICE: Born July 1, 1902, in Barcelona, Spain; came to the United States, 1939, naturalized citizen, 1951; died of lung cancer, March 15, 1983, in Barcelona, Spain. Architect, educator, and author. Sert studied under the famous French-Swiss modernist LeCorbusier, but is noted for having softened the more austere aspects of traditional modernism. He became dean of the Harvard University School of Design in 1953 and remained in that post until 1969. Sert was a founding member of and partner in an architectual firm, Sert, Jackson & Associates, and worked on the design of cities in Colombia, Peru, and Brazil. His most notable design is the Joan Miro Foundation/Center for the Studies of Contemporary Art, in Barcelona, Spain. Sert wrote *Can Our Cities Survive?: An ABC of Urban Problems, Their Analysis, Their Solutions.* In 1980 he was awarded the Gold Medal of the American Institute of Architects, the profession's highest honor. Obituaries and other sources: *New York Times*, March 17, 1983; *Chicago Tribune*, March 18, 1983; *Los Angeles Times*, March 18, 1983; *Washington Post*, March 19, 1983; *Newsweek*, March 28, 1983.

* * *

SETON, Ernest (Evan) Thompson 1860-1946
(Ernest Seton-Thompson)

BRIEF ENTRY: Birth-given name Ernest Evan Thompson; name

legally changed in 1898; born August 14, 1860, in South Shields, Durham, England; came to United States in 1896, naturalized citizen November 6, 1931; died October 23, 1946, in Santa Fe, N.M.; buried in Seton Village, Santa Fe, N.M. American artist, naturalist, lecturer, illustrator, and author. Seton, who is best known as the founder of the Boy Scouts of America, studied art in Toronto, New York, London, and Paris, and he worked as an illustrator for several publishers and as a naturalist for the government of Manitoba, Canada. After immigrating to the United States, Seton concentrated his efforts on lecturing and free-lance writing. He published his first self-illustrated children's book, *Wild Animals I Have Known*, in 1898. In the twenty-five juvenile books that followed, including *Lives of the Hunted* (1902) and *Johnny Bear, Lobo, and Other Stories* (1935), Seton's intention was to "convey a true notion of the ways of the animals . . . the lives they live and the deaths they die." Seton also published several books on woodcraft, including *The Forester's Manual* (1912), and several volumes on natural history. He won a Camp Fire Gold Medal in 1909 for *Life-Histories of Northern Animals: An Account of the Mammals of Manitoba. Biographical/critical sources: New York Times*, October 24, 1946; Doris Garst and Warren E. Garst, *Ernest Thompson Seton: Naturalist*, Messner, 1959; Julia Seton, *By a Thousand Fires*, Doubleday, 1967; *Longman Companion to Twentieth Century Literature*, Longman, 1970; *The Illustrated Biographical Encyclopedia of Artists of the American West*, Doubleday, 1976.

* * *

SETON-THOMPSON, Ernest
See SETON, Ernest (Evan) Thompson

* * *

SEVERS, Jerome
See WOOLEY, John (Steven)

* * *

SEYLER, Dorothy U(pton) 1938-

PERSONAL: Born May 5, 1938, in Washington, D.C.; daughter of Joseph W. (a retail chain store executive) and Kathryn F. Upton; married David A. Seyler, 1961; children: Ruth Elizabeth. *Education:* College of William and Mary, B.A., 1959; Columbia University, M.A., 1960; State University of New York at Albany, Ph.D., 1969. *Office:* Department of English, Northern Virginia Community College, 8333 Little River Turnpike, Annandale, Va. 22003.

CAREER: Ohio State University, Columbus, instructor in English, 1960-61; University of Kentucky, Lexington, instructor in English, 1961-63; Nassau Community College, Garden City, N.Y., instructor in English, 1969-72; Northern Virginia Community College, Annandale, professor of English, 1972—. Member of Fairfax County Democratic Committee. *Member:* National Council of Teachers of English, South Atlantic Modern Language Association, Southern Conference on Teaching in the Two-Year College, Conference on College Composition and Communication, Phi Beta Kappa.

WRITINGS: (With M. Noel Sipple) *Thinking for Writing*, Science Research Associates, 1978; (with Richard A. Wilan) *Introduction to Literature*, Alfred Publishing, 1981; (with Carol J. Boltz) *Language Power*, Random House, 1982; *Read, Reason, Write*, Random House, 1983. Contributor to literature journals.

WORK IN PROGRESS: Shaping Ideas: A Rhetorical and Thematic Reader.

SIDELIGHTS: Seyler told *CA:* "I am interested in the challenge of teaching persons of all ages and background to write well." *Avocational interests:* Tennis, European travel, attending dramatic productions.

*　　*　　*

SHANDS, Harley Cecil   1916-1981

PERSONAL: Born September 10, 1916, in Jackson, Miss.; died of a ruptured aortic aneurysm, December 4, 1981, in New York, N.Y.; son of Harley Roseborough and Bessie Webb (Nugent) Shands; married Janet Hoffman, March 25, 1943; children: Kathryn N., Betsy Shands Nicolet, Paul H. *Education:* Tulane University, B.S., 1936, M.D., 1939; University of Minnesota, M.S., 1945.

CAREER: Mayo Clinic, resident and fellow in medicine, 1941-45; Massachusetts General Hospital, Boston, research fellow in psychiatry, 1945-48; University of North Carolina, Chapel Hill, associate professor of psychiatry, 1953-61; State University of New York Downstate Medical Center, Brooklyn, professor of psychiatry, 1961-66; St. Luke's-Roosevelt Hospital Center, New York, N.Y., director of department of psychiatry, 1966-81. Clinical professor at Columbia University, 1966-81. *Awards, honors:* Commonwealth Fund fellowship for England, 1958-59.

WRITINGS: Thinking and Psychotherapy: An Inquiry Into the Processes of Communication, Harvard University Press, 1960; *Semiotic Approaches to Psychiatry,* Mouton, 1970; *The War With Words, Structure and Transcendence,* Mouton, 1971; (with James D. Meltzer) *Language and Psychiatry,* Mouton, 1973; *Speech as Instruction: Semiotic Aspects of Human Conflict,* Mouton, 1977.

OBITUARIES: New York Times, December 7, 1981.*

*　　*　　*

SHANE, C(harles) Donald   1895-1983

OBITUARY NOTICE: Born September 6, 1895, in Auburn, Calif.; died after a long illness, March 19, 1983. Astronomer, educator, and author. Shane taught math and astronomy at the University of California from 1920 until 1945, when he became the director of Lick Astronomical Observatory. He served in that post until 1958. During World War II Shane worked on the development of the atomic bomb in the Manhattan Project and was later in charge of personnel at Los Alamos Laboratory, New Mexico, where the first atomic bomb was built. He was the author of *The Distribution of Galaxies.* Obituaries and other sources: *Who's Who in America,* 40th edition, Marquis, 1978; *Chicago Tribune,* March 23, 1983.

*　　*　　*

SHANNON, Monica   1905(?)-1965

OBITUARY NOTICE: Born c. 1905 in Belleville, Ontario, Canada; died August 13, 1965. Author. Shannon wrote children's tales that were included in the anthologies *California Fairy Tales* and *Eyes for the Dark.* She also published a book of poetry, *Goose Grass Rhymes,* and two novels, *Tawnymore* and *Dobry,* for which she won a Newbery Award. Obituaries and other sources: *American Women Writers: A Critical Reference Guide From Colonial Times to the Present,* Ungar, 1979-82.

*　　*　　*

SHAPIRO, David S(idney)   1923-1983

OBITUARY NOTICE—See index for *CA* sketch: Born December 4, 1923, in New York, N.Y.; died of a heart attack, January 26, 1983, in Cambridge, Mass. Psychologist, educator, and author. Shapiro was a clinical psychologist since the 1950's. He held various teaching, consulting, and administrative positions, including associate professor at the Harvard School of Public Health and executive director of Lawrence General Hospital Rehabilitation Center. He is best known for his studies of heart attack victims in Framingham, Massachusetts, and the control and prevention of mental illness in Nova Scotia. Shapiro's books include *The Search for Love and Achievement, Opening Doors for Troubled People,* and *Neurotic Styles.* Obituaries and other sources: *Chicago Tribune,* January 29, 1983.

*　　*　　*

SHAPIRO, Jane P.
See ZACEK, Jane Shapiro

*　　*　　*

SHAPIRO, Sue A.   1947-

PERSONAL: Born May 7, 1947, in New York, N.Y.; daughter of Paul H. (a stockbroker) and Elaine R. Shapiro; married Samuel Clarkson Sugg (a psychiatrist and psychoanalyst), June 10, 1979. *Education:* Brandeis University, B.A., 1968; Yeshiva University, M.A., 1976, Ph.D., 1978; postdoctoral study at New York University, 1978—. *Politics:* Liberal Democrat. *Religion:* Jewish. *Home:* 3 Washington Square Village, New York, N.Y. 10012. *Office:* 80 University Pl., New York, N.Y. 10003.

CAREER: Kingsboro Psychiatric Center, Brooklyn, N.Y., assistant unit head, 1974-77, director of training, 1977-78; private practice of individual psychotherapy, 1978—. Adjunct clinical professor at New York University. *Member:* New York State Psychological Association.

WRITINGS: Contemporary Theories of Schizophrenia, McGraw, 1981; (contributor) J. M. Hunt and N. S. Endler, editors, *Personality and Behavior Disorders,* 2nd edition, Yale University Press, 1983.

WORK IN PROGRESS: A book integrating biological and psychoanalytic concepts on the development of personality; research on the relationship between private experience and public verbalizations.

SIDELIGHTS: Sue Shapiro included among the most important influences on her career "my mother's ambition, productivity, and happiness when she ceased being a housewife and became a musicologist; my study of the piano from the age of seven, which has given me a notion of discipline and patience; my stepfather's encouragement of my mother and his interest in psychology."

AVOCATIONAL INTERESTS: Yoga, the Orient, techniques of body alignment.

*　　*　　*

SHAROT, Stephen   1943-

PERSONAL: Born May 8, 1943, in Windsor, England; son of

David and Pearl (Houtman) Sharot; married Tamar Gut; children: Tali, Dan. *Education:* University of Leicester, B.A., 1965; Oxford University, D.Phil., 1969. *Home:* 76 Erez, Omer, Israel. *Office:* Department of Behavioral Sciences, Ben-Gurion University of the Negev, Beer Sheva, Israel.

CAREER: University of Leicester, Leicester, England, lecturer in sociology, 1970-74; Hebrew University of Jerusalem, Jerusalem, Israel, lecturer, 1974-76; senior lecturer in sociology, 1976-79; Ben-Gurion University of the Negev, Beer Sheva, Israel, senior lecturer in behavioral sciences, 1980—. *Awards, honors:* Harkness Foundation award, 1969-71; Ford Foundation grant, 1981-83.

WRITINGS: Judaism: A Sociology, David & Charles, 1976; *Messianism, Mysticism, and Magic: A Sociological Analysis of Jewish Religious Movements*, University of North Carolina Press, 1982.

WORK IN PROGRESS: Research on ethnic, religious, and socio-economic divisions in Israel.

SIDELIGHTS: Sharot told *CA:* "Most writers on Judaism have confined themselves to the ideas and works of scholars and intellectuals. My focus has been on the religion of the Jewish folk or masses, and I have tried to show the complex links between popular expressions of Judaism and social conditions."

BIOGRAPHICAL/CRITICAL SOURCES: Sociology, May, 1977; *Sociological Analysis*, winter, 1978; *British Journal of Sociology*, September, 1978; *Jewish Journal of Sociology*, December, 1978.

*   *   *

SHATZKIN, Leonard 1919-

PERSONAL: Born July 16, 1919, in Warsaw, Poland; came to the United States in 1920; naturalized U.S. citizen, 1922; son of Isaac and Helen (Feiman) Shatzkin; married Eleanor Oshry, August 4, 1940; children: Michael, Karen, Nancy. *Education:* Attended City College (now of the City University of New York), 1935-38; Carnegie Institute of Technology (now Carnegie-Mellon University), B.A., 1941. *Politics:* Democratic socialist. *Home:* 132 Old Post Rd. N., Croton-on-Hudson, N.Y. 10520. *Office:* 310 East 44th St., New York, N.Y. 10017.

CAREER: House Beautiful, New York City, production manager, 1941-43; associated with Manhattan Project, 1943-46; Viking Press, New York City, production manager, 1946-51; Doubleday & Co., New York City, in production, 1951-56, in sales and marketing, 1956-61; Crowell-Collier Macmillan, New York City, vice-president, 1961-64; McGraw-Hill Book Co., New York City, vice-president for marketing and long-range planning, 1964-70; Planned Production, New York City, founder and president, 1970-78; Two Continents Publishing Group, New York City, founder and president, 1972-78; publishing consultant in New York City, 1978—. Instructor in book production at New York University, 1951-55, and Pratt Institute, 1972.

WRITINGS: (Editor and translator) *The Stars Bear Witness*, Viking, 1947; *In Cold Type: Overcoming the Book Crisis*, Houghton, 1982. Contributor to periodicals, including *Publishers Weekly* and *Daedalus*.

SIDELIGHTS: Shatzkin is an innovator of American publishing. At Doubleday, he helped integrate standardized book specifications, which resulted in lower production costs. He also assisted in the development of a mathematical projection system which yielded reasonably accurate predictions of sales in advance of publication. This innovation allowed Doubleday to save more than $250,000 and eliminated, for the first time in Doubleday's history, the necessity to sell remaining copies as overstock. In the mid-1950's, Shatzkin presided over a sales department at Doubleday that developed a merchandising system, enabling the company to multiply its earnings in some areas by more than 200 percent.

At Crowell-Collier Macmillan, Shatzkin initiated direct distribution of a new paperback line, Collier Books. Although sales of the new line almost realized its projected amount, deficits in other departments within the publishing house resulted in the elimination of several projects, including Collier Books.

Shatzkin joined McGraw-Hill's staff in 1964. There he centralized manufacturing of several divisions, thus lowering costs by more than $2 million. He left McGraw-Hill in 1970 to form Planned Production. Two years later he established Two Continents Publishing. He presided over both companies until 1978, when he left to become a consultant.

Shatzkin told *CA:* "I regret to say that, for the most part, authors are the victims of the failure of book publishing to perform its function in a satisfactory manner. I refer, of course, to that segment of publishing which is called 'trade publishing' and which produces books for sale to the general public through the book trade.

"It is sad that so many deserving manuscripts make the rounds of publishing houses until the author gives up in frustrated discouragement. Frequently, the manuscripts are not read before the form letter of sympathetic rejection is sent. Even when they are read, they rarely get the careful evaluation that would earn them a champion within the publishing house, a champion who is essential to break through the normal timidity that characterizes the authorization to publish.

"Being published does not always represent a victory for the author. The haphazard distribution methods, and the under-staffing and under-management of sales departments guarantees that most published books never see the inside of most bookstores. Sales for the typical trade book are embarrassingly low, not because the public has rejected the book, but rather because the public has never had a chance to even know that the book exists.

"In an industry that is governed more by chance than by plan, inevitably a few deserving authors break through the confusion and purposelessness of publishers' activity to become 'bestsellers' or to sell in respectable quantities despite the inefficiencies of the distribution system.

"Unfortunately, there is no easy solution for the aspiring author. The vanity presses are worse than no publication at all, and self-publication is rarely a practical possibility, except for books which can be effectively sold by mail. Perhaps the best advice to an author in the face of this discouraging prospect for publication and for success after publication is to persist. The odds for successful publication are small, and that is precisely the reason why persistence is essential. Despite the apathy and the routine rejection letters and despite all the discouragement, the author should be determined to keep trying to find a publisher. And when the manuscript is accepted, the author must remember not to leave the fate of the book in the publisher's hands; the author must, if anything, devote even more energy to bringing the book to the attention of the critics, the bookstores, and the general public, than to getting it published in the first place.''

*   *   *

SHAW, Bernard   1940-

BRIEF ENTRY: Born in 1940 in Chicago, Ill. American news correspondent. Shaw began his career as a reporter for the Westinghouse Broadcasting Company's Group W in 1966, becoming a White House correspondent two years later. In 1971 he joined the Washington, D.C., bureau of Columbia Broadcasting System (CBS-News), but moved to Florida in 1977 to serve as the chief of the Miami bureau of American Broadcasting Companies (ABC-News). Since 1982 Shaw has been associated with the Cable News Network (CNN). His major assignments have included coverage of local and national urban affairs, Native Americans in Billings, Montana, and Martin Luther King's assassination. As a special correspondent, Shaw has been affiliated with televised productions for children, including ''What's an Election About?'' and ''What the Oil Crisis Is About.'' *Address:* Cable News Network, Turner Broadcasting System, 1050 Techwood Dr. N.W., Atlanta, Ga. 30318. *Biographical/critical sources: The Negro Almanac,* 3rd edition, Bellwether Publishing, 1976; *Who's Who in America,* 41st edition, Marquis, 1981.

*   *   *

SHAW, Ellen Torgerson
See TORGERSON SHAW, Ellen

*   *   *

SHAW, Lau
See SHU Ch'ing-ch'un

*   *   *

SHERFEY, Mary Jane   1933-1983

OBITUARY NOTICE: Born in 1933 in Brazil, Ind.; died of a heart attack, February 20, 1983, in Rusk, Tex. Psychiatrist and author of *The Nature and Evolution of Female Sexuality.* Obituaries and other sources: *New York Times,* March 12, 1983.

*   *   *

SHERR, Lynn Beth   1942-

BRIEF ENTRY: Born March 4, 1942, in Philadelphia, Pa. American journalist. Sherr was a writer for Conde Nast Publications and for Associated Press during the 1960's and early 1970's; she then became a television correspondent, first for WCBS-TV and later for WNET-TV. In 1976 she became a hostess of television programs for the Public Broadcasting System and in 1977 became a correspondent for American Broadcasting Companies (ABC-TV). Sherr co-authored *The American Woman's Gazetteer* (Bantam, 1976). Her publications also include *The Liberated Woman's Appointment Calendar and Survival Handbook,* which appeared annually from 1971 to 1979. *Address:* ABC-News, American Broadcasting Companies, Inc., 7 West 66th St., New York, N.Y. 10023. *Biographical/critical sources: Washington Post Book World,* July 11, 1976.

SHERROD, Drury   1943-

PERSONAL: Born February 7, 1943, in Dallas, Tex.; son of Drury R. (a business executive) and Mary Nita Sherrod. *Education:* Southern Methodist University, B.A., 1965; Johns Hopkins University, M.A., 1967; Stanford University, M.A., 1969, Ph.D., 1971. *Home:* 427 Cambridge Ave., Claremont, Calif. 91711.

CAREER: Hamilton College, Clinton, N.Y., assistant professor of psychology, 1972-75; University of Oregon, Eugene, visiting assistant professor of psychology, 1975-76; Claremont Colleges, Claremont, Calif., visiting associate professor of psychology, 1977-82; consulting psychologist, 1982—. *Member:* American Psychological Association, Society of Experimental Social Psychologists, Environmental Design Research Association.

WRITINGS: Social Psychology, Random House, 1982.

WORK IN PROGRESS: A book on male friendship, publication expected in 1985; research on the social impact of computers.

SIDELIGHTS: Sherrod commented: ''Random variables exert major influences on decisions and behavior, then we make sense of them. Since alternative meanings are possible, it's important to stay aware that meaning is a temporary construction. We must continually test our theories of our 'self' and our world, to make sure they correspond with the most current 'data' or our experience. My current project on male friendship grew out of the important relationships of my life and a desire to affirm and celebrate them. Why are men less intimate with each other than women are with each other? How does this lack of intimacy affect men's behavior, feelings, work and health? What changes in socialization and circumstances can lead to greater intimacy among males? My work in progress addresses these questions.''

*   *   *

SHERRY, Pearl Andelson   1899-

PERSONAL: Born February 11, 1899, in Chicago, Ill.; daughter of Nathan and Anna (Harris) Andelson; married Edward Sherry, May 12, 1925 (deceased); children: Leonard, Richard. *Education:* Attended University of Chicago. *Home:* 3172 North Sheridan Rd., Apt. 1012, Chicago, Ill. 60657.

CAREER: Writer, c. 1920—. Worked as assistant, reader, and reviewer for *Poetry* (magazine) during the 1920's.

WRITINGS: Fringe (poetry), Will Ransom, 1923; (with Doris Vidaver) *Arch of a Circle* (poetry), Swallow Press, 1980.

Work represented in anthologies, including *The New American Caravan,* 1929; *A Celebration of Cats,* edited by Jean Burden, 1974.

Contributor to numerous literary journals and magazines, including the *Dial, Gyroscope,* and *Southern Review.*

WORK IN PROGRESS: A historical novel.

SIDELIGHTS: Sherry told *CA.* ''The chief influence on my writing career was the Poetry Club at the University of Chicago at a time when some of its carefully selected members were Yvor Winters, Janet Lewis, Elizabeth Madox Roberts, Glenway Wescott, Maurice Lesemann, and Gladys Campbell—my friends for life as well as fellow members of the club.

''My historical novel in progress is based on an actual case during the period of Louis XIV. It includes thorough research on everything, from furniture to education of children, from Saint Simon to the letters of Madame, the king's sister-in-law.

"Like most writers, I write out of a need to express myself in words. In prose I like to write about relationships between and among plausible characters suggested by people I have known, and always in opposition or conformity to the world of their present. In poetry my trend is apt to be toward a more metaphysical aspect."

* * *

SHIELDS, Joyce Farley 1930-

BRIEF ENTRY: Born July 18, 1930, in Leland, Ill. American librarian and author. A librarian since 1954, Shields became reference coordinator of the suburban library system for Oak Park Public Library in 1969. She wrote *Make It: An Index to Projects and Materials* (Scarecrow, 1975). *Address:* 171 North Elmwood, Oak Park, Ill. 60302.

* * *

SHILLING, Dana 1953-

PERSONAL: Born January 22, 1953, in Brooklyn, N.Y.; daughter of Norman Hyman (an attorney) and Janet (a novelist; maiden name, Silverstein) Shilling. *Education:* Goucher College, A.B. (magna cum laude), 1972; Harvard University, J.D., 1975. *Home and office:* Plaintext, 41 Mercer St., Jersey City, N.J. 07302. *Agent:* Peter Ginsburg, Curtis Brown Ltd., 575 Madison Ave., New York, N.Y. 10021.

CAREER: Malcolm A. Hoffmann (antitrust law firm), New York City, associate, 1975; Corporation Counsel of the City of New York, New York City, attorney-trainee, 1976-77; Institute for Business Planning, Port Washington, N.Y., writer and editor of *Pay Planning Ideas* and *Life Insurance Ideas,* 1978-79; New York City Department of Housing Preservation and Development, New York City, attorney, 1979; Plaintext, Jersey City, N.J., president, 1980—. Administrative law judge for New York City Environmental Control Board, 1980. Staff writer for Siegel & Gale, New York City, 1979. *Member:* New York County Lawyers' Association, Phi Beta Kappa.

WRITINGS: (With Howard Hillman) *Howard Hillman's Encyclopedia of World Cuisines,* Penguin, 1979; (with Hillman) *The Cook's Book,* Avon, 1981; *Fighting Back: A Consumer's Guide for Getting Satisfaction,* Morrow, 1982; *Be Your Own Boss,* Morrow, 1983; *Making Wise Decisions,* Morrow, 1983; (editor) William Averill, *Estate Valuation Handbook,* Wiley, 1983. Author of "Rights and Responsibilities," a column in *Current Consumer,* 1981—, and "Women and the Law," a column in *Vogue,* 1983—. Contributing editor of *Business Planning,* 1982—.

WORK IN PROGRESS: How Things Work in the Law, nonfiction, publication expected in 1985; *The Monument,* a novel, publication expected in 1985; *Short Shrift,* a history of male feminists, publication expected in 1986.

SIDELIGHTS: Shilling's book *Fighting Back* tells consumers how to go about seeking restitution when they are dissatisfied with a product or service. In her "relaxed but snappy tone," Shilling gives the reader "the feeling that a problem with a product, a company, the media or government is neither insoluble nor reason for a holy crusade. It's simply something that must be resolved, step by clear-headed step," wrote Stevenson O. Swanson in the *Chicago Tribune.*

To aid the consumer in his or her quest for satisfaction, Shilling provides a series of sample letters that, according to Swanson, "cover just about every situation a consumer is likely to find himself in when he is seeking restitution. One can find blank requests for information under the Freedom of Information Act, letters to elected officials, and even complaints to bar associations, in addition to the more predictable letters to manufacturers."

With her "lawyer's mind for precision and order and a consumer advocate's fervor for the little guy," Shilling has provided disgruntled consumers with an exceptionally complete and helpful guide to "fighting back." "Best of all," Swanson added, "she writes well."

Shilling told *CA:* "I hate obfuscation, and it makes me angry when people are deprived of information and therefore deprived of free exercise of legal and moral rights. Therefore, I spend a fair amount of time designing forms, putting things into plain English, and otherwise explaining things. I suppose I'm a sort of class traitor; I should be making it *harder* for people to understand, which would increase the volume and duration of litigation and enhance the image of lawyers as demiurges rather than tradesmen.

"I have never done any of those writer-y things; I have never been an able-bodied sea-person, forest ranger, or Foreign Legionnaire. I live in a two-story brick house in Jersey City with my two mortgages, Spot and Fido. The kitchen ceiling is declining inexorably, and one of my more modest ambitions is to replace it. The more grandiose ambition is to make my writing sound as good once it reaches the external world as it does inside my head.

"Favorite writers include Iris Murdoch and George Bernard Shaw, and I'm always looking for a way to express thin translucent layers of nuance in good thumping rollicking prose. I'm a fiend for adverbs: surely everyone wants to know not just what was done, but precisely how, and with what perceived and unperceived motives?"

AVOCATIONAL INTERESTS: Reading, ballet dancing, playing the guitar.

BIOGRAPHICAL/CRITICAL SOURCES: Los Angeles Times Book Review, September 5, 1982; *Chicago Tribune,* February 20, 1983; *Washington Post Book World,* March 6, 1983.

* * *

SHINER, Roger A(lfred) 1940-

BRIEF ENTRY: Born May 13, 1940, in Kidderminster, England. Philosopher, educator, and author. Shiner joined the faculty of University of Alberta in 1965 and became a professor of philosophy in 1977. He wrote *Knowledge and Reality in Plato's Philebus* (Van Gorcum, 1974). Shiner also co-edited *New Essays in the Philosophy of Mind* (Canadian Association for Publishing in Philosophy, 1975), *New Essays on Plato and the Pre-Socratics* (Canadian Association for Publishing in Philosophy, 1976), and *New Essays on Contract Theory* (Canadian Association for Publishing in Philosophy, 1977). *Address:* Department of Philosophy, University of Alberta, Edmonton, Alberta, Canada T6G 2E5.

* * *

SHOMAKER, Dianna 1934-
(Dianna McDonald)

PERSONAL: Born April 18, 1934, in Seattle, Wash.; daughter of John David and Mildred Irene (Gagnon) Scheffer; married Keith Rinne, 1956 (died, 1957); married Herbert B. McDonald, 1961 (divorced, 1976); married John Wayne Shomaker (a consulting geologist), December 16, 1978; children: (second marriage) Bradley, Wendy, Kevin, Lynn. *Education:* Los Angeles County General Hospital, Diploma in Nursing, 1957; University of Colorado, B.S.N., 1959; University of Washington, Seattle, M.N., 1962; University of New Mexico, M.A., 1981, doctoral study, 1977—; also attended Central Washington College of Education, 1952, University of Oslo, 1960, University of Michigan, 1978-81, and Wayne State University, 1981. *Politics:* Democrat. *Religion:* Lutheran. *Home:* 7510 Bear Canyon N.E., Albuquerque, N.M. 87109. *Office:* College of Nursing, University of New Mexico, Albuquerque, N.M. 87131.

CAREER: Los Angeles County General Hospital, Los Angeles, Calif., neurology staff nurse, 1957; Taos County Health Department, Taos, N.M., generalized public health nurse, 1958-60; University of Washington, Seattle, premature intensive care staff nurse at university hospital, 1962-63; Washington State Health Department, Seattle, researcher, 1963-64; Hotel Dieu School of Nursing, El Paso, Tex., research coordinator, 1964-70; University of New Mexico, Albuquerque, instructor, 1973-76, assistant professor of nursing, 1976—. Part-time staff nurse at Holy Cross Hospital, Taos, 1958-60; certified American Red Cross Cardio-Pulmonary Resuscitation instructor, 1979—. Public speaker; guest on television programs; presents workshops. Member of advisory board of Southwest Pediatric Pulmonary Institute, 1976-77, Share Your Care Day Center for the Frail Elderly, 1977—, and Albuquerque Visiting Nurse Service, 1982—. Conducted research in Israel and among Indians of the Northwest Coast and the Southwest.

MEMBER: American Nurses Association, Gerontological Society of America, American Public Health Association, American Anthropological Association, Association for Anthropology and Gerontology, Association of Nurse Anthropologists, Western Gerontological Society, New Mexico Nurses Association, New Mexico Senior Coalition on Aging (charter member), University of New Mexico Alumni Association, Sigma Theta Tau (charter member of Gamma Sigma chapter). *Awards, honors:* Second prize and purchase prize from National Small Painting Show, both 1974.

WRITINGS: (Under name Dianna McDonald) *Handbook and Tool With Which to Evaluate Teacher Effectiveness in Diploma Schools of Nursing,* Hotel Dieu School of Nursing, 1968; (under name Dianna Shomaker; with Chiyoko Furukawa) *Community Health Services for the Aged,* Aspen Systems Corp., 1982. Contributor to gerontology, nursing, and anthropology journals (until 1978 under name Dianna McDonald).

SIDELIGHTS: Shomaker told *CA:* "For years I regarded my artwork as a medium for release of tension but I have come to appreciate the application of creativity in teaching and in assessment of client status. In teaching, my artwork has been useful to me in developing lecture outlines, video material, and stimulating demonstrations of nursing skills. I have not used it in art therapy but know of others who have. I can see a wide range of applications of it among older persons and will apply my knowledge in gerontological nursing as the opportunities arise. Time is my major limiting factor now, because I am working on my doctorate and must use the remainder for teaching nursing students. I do volunteer some small amount of time to senior citizen projects, and it is in that area that I have expectations for application of art at some later date. I have taught art courses in the past and think artwork can be

used as therapy to draw clients out of a poor level communication problem, expressing those things that they cannot or will not express in words. I see it as therapeutic for them just as it is for me.

"Anthropology has contributed greatly to my understanding of other cultural values and patterns of behavior, but most importantly it has helped me realize the deeper value of treating people, regardless of their culture, as unique individuals. A trait list of things one might expect from a person who identifies with a specific ethnic group is not a sound basis upon which to develop a plan of nursing care. People must go beyond the label of specific ethnic identification to the processes that they use to adapt to the many situations that confront them in everyday living. Nursing literature sometimes overlooks that major issue or at least minimizes it.

"In regard to anthropology, aging, and nursing care, I have found the theoretical literature and research an invaluable aid in reinterpreting nursing theory. This synthesis can and does provide an exciting challenge to the nurse offering cross-cultural nursing care. Study of other cultures' approaches to care of the elderly broadens the potential that many care facilities have not even begun to think about. It also offers challenges to reanalysis of accepted perspectives about the position of the elderly and their functions in the community. Two of my articles that speak to these issues are 'Navajo Nursing Homes' and 'The Dialectics of Nursing Homes.' I hope to be doing more of this type of research in the very near future.

"Another area where I hope to be doing more research is on the regulations that govern sexual expression by clients who live in nursing homes and the liberation of such regulations that would allow married clients to live together, and in other areas to reexamine the rigidity of rules against sexuality among consenting adults. The rules become so constraining that the clients are treated as though they should have given up such practices when they passed their child-bearing years. I realize there are administrative problems in such areas, but there are many more cultural problems that are the primary source of such constraints, not all of which are valuable."

*   *   *

SHONE, Robert 1906-

PERSONAL: Born May 27, 1906, in Cheshire, England; son of Harold (a steel merchant) and Hannah (Minshull) Shone. *Education:* University of Liverpool, M.Eng., 1930; University of Chicago, M.A., 1934. *Home:* 7 Windmill Hill, London N.W.3, England.

CAREER: London School of Economics and Political Science, London, England, lecturer, 1935-36; director of British Iron & Steel Federation, 1936-53; executive member of Iron and Steel Board, 1953-61; director-general of National Economic Development Council, 1962-66; Oxford University, Oxford, England, research fellow at Nuffield College, 1966-67; City University, London, England, visiting professor of applied economics, 1967—. Special professor at University of Nottingham, 1971-73. Member of board of directors of M & G Group; past member of board of directors of Rank Organisation and APV Holdings. *Member:* Society of Business Economists (president, 1963-68). *Awards, honors:* Commander of Order of the British Empire, 1949, knighthood conferred, 1955; professional achievement award from University of Chicago, 1982; honorary fellow, London School of Economics and Political Science.

WRITINGS: Investment and Economic Growth, Athlone Press, 1966; (editor) *Problems of Investment*, Basil Blackwell, 1971; *Price and Investment Relationships: A Study in Applied Economics*, Elek, 1976.

SIDELIGHTS: Shone told *CA:* "I am concerned with the development of long-term marginal cost-pricing in the steel industry during the 1950's and with the later problems of technical change, investment, and slow economic growth, especially in the United Kingdom. The damaging failure to adopt a 'real,' i.e., non-inflationary, measure of profits has for long been a major concern."

*   *   *

SHU Ch'ing-ch'un   1899-1966
(Lao She, Lau Shaw)

OBITUARY NOTICE: Born February 3, 1899, in Peking, China; committed suicide under duress in October (some sources say September), 1966, in Peking, China. Playwright and author, best known under pseudonym Lao She. Lao She went to London, England, in 1924 to teach Chinese. While in England he was influenced by the works of Charles Dickens and began to write novels in Chinese. He returned to China in 1930, and during the Second Sino-Japanese War (1937-45) wrote political propaganda. He also served as head of the Chinese Writers' Anti-Aggression Association, a group which sought to pull the various Chinese political factions together against the common threat posed by Japan. After the war Lao She lived in the United States for a short time but returned to China after the Communist takeover to hold a series of cultural posts. Lao She became one of the first targets of the Red Guards during the Chinese Cultural Revolution, and, while subject to their harassment, he committed suicide. He was the author of *Rickshaw Boy, The Quest for Love of Lao Lu, The Yellow Storm,* and *Dragon-beard Ditch*. Obituaries and other sources: *Cassell's Encyclopaedia of World Literature*, revised edition, Morrow, 1973; *McGraw-Hill Encyclopedia of World Biography*, McGraw, 1973; *Dictionary of Oriental Literatures*, Volume 1: *East Asia*, Basic Books, 1974; *Encyclopedia of World Literature in the Twentieth Century*, supplement, Ungar, 1975.

*   *   *

SHUMAN, Nicholas R(oman)   1921-

PERSONAL: Born June 30, 1921, in Chicago, Ill.; son of Roman William (a janitor) and Pauline (Stasevich) Shuman; married Marilyn Johnson (a free-lance editor and public relations consultant), February 23, 1952; children: Kristin Mary, Elizabeth Carol, Mark Nicholas. *Education:* University of Illinois, B.A. (with high honors), 1943. *Home:* 1001 West Clarendon Rd., Arlington Heights, Ill. 60004. *Office: Chicago Sun-Times*, 401 North Wabash Ave., Chicago, Ill. 60611.

CAREER/WRITINGS: Chicago Journal of Commerce, Chicago, Ill., began as copyboy, became reporter and copy editor, 1938-46; *Chicago Herald American*, Chicago, copy editor, 1946-47, assistant photo editor, 1947-51; *Chicago Daily News*, Chicago, reporter, copy editor, and financial editor, 1951-65; *World Book Encyclopedia*, Chicago, senior editor, 1965-66; *Chicago Daily News*, Chicago, assistant managing editor, 1966-69, national and foreign editor, 1969-76, chief editorial writer, 1976-78; *Chicago Sun-Times*, Chicago, editorial writer, 1978—. Free-lance magazine writer, 1951—. Instructor in Medill School of Journalism, Northwestern University, Evanston, Ill., 1952-60. Television commentator with WBKB-TV, Chicago, 1958-

61. Founding president of Arlington Heights Human Relations Committee, 1965. *Military service:* U.S. Army Air Forces, 1943-46; liaison pilot, served in European theater; became first lieutenant. *Member:* Chicago Press Club, Sigma Delta Chi, Alpha Kappa Lambda.

SIDELIGHTS: Shuman reads, writes, and speaks Russian, and has some knowledge of French and Spanish as well.

*   *   *

SHWARTZ, Susan Martha   1949-

PERSONAL: Born December 31, 1949, in Youngstown, Ohio; daughter of Ralph Bernard (an attorney) and Lillian (Levine) Shwartz. *Education:* Mount Holyoke College, B.A. (magna cum laude), 1972; attended Trinity College, Oxford, 1970-71; Harvard University, M.A., 1973, Ph.D., 1977. *Politics:* "Idiosyncratic." *Religion:* Jewish. *Home and office:* 409 East 88th St., No. 5A, New York, N.Y. 10028. *Agent:* Russell & Volkening, Inc., 551 Fifth Ave., New York, N.Y. 10017.

CAREER: Ithaca College, Ithaca, N.Y., assistant professor of English, 1977-81; Deutsch, Shea & Evans, New York City, senior writer and researcher, 1981-82; Final Analysis, New York City, junior project director, 1982; BEA Associates, New York City, information coordinator, 1982—. *Member:* Science Fiction Writers of America, Phi Beta Kappa, Harvard Club of New York. *Awards, honors:* Grant from National Endowment for the Humanities, 1978; short story award from *Village Voice*, 1981, for "The Old Man and the C."

WRITINGS: Hecate's Cauldron (fantasy anthology), DAW Books, 1982; *Heritage of Flight* (science fiction novel), Analog, 1983; (contributor) Marion Zimmer Bradley, editor, *Grayhaven*, DAW Books, 1983; *Habitats* (science fiction anthology), DAW Books, in press. Author of "Facts for Fantasy," a column in *Ares*. Contributor to magazines and newspapers, including *Science Fiction Review, Feminine Eye, New York Times, Washington Post,* and *Cleveland Plain Dealer*.

WORK IN PROGRESS: Exiles, a science fiction novel, for Donning; *Marric Unconquered*, a Byzantine fantasy novel.

SIDELIGHTS: Susan Shwartz commented: "For me, the important things are technical mastery, communicating with people, and the joy of a job done as well as I can. Beyond that, I get a thrill out of seeing my work in print; I never dreamed I'd do it.

"I trained as a medievalist in college and graduate school (don't ask me why), and that meant learning languages. What else did it mean? A dangerous fascination for pure research, with rewriting, and with language and background as games and preoccupations. I find my own academic background to be a help—when it comes to finding a setting for a story—and a hindrance, since it keeps me rewriting and slows down my style. I tend to write four and five drafts of a work before I begin to be satisfied, and I plot slowly. On the other hand, coming out of a scholarly tradition's been useful for learning my craft.

"What do my works reflect about me? God only knows: that my characters tend to be faced with the consequences of their actions, that I cannot tolerate sloppy sentiment or thinking, that I'm fascinated by completely realized secondary worlds, my own or other writers'."

AVOCATIONAL INTERESTS: Languages (Latin, French, Greek, German, Middle High German, Old French, Old Norse, Old and Middle English), travel in England and Europe, ballet, opera, parties, clothes, cats, cooking.

* * *

SIDETRACKED HOME EXECUTIVES
See JONES, Peggy
and YOUNG, Pam

* * *

SIFFERT, Robert S(pencer) 1918-

PERSONAL: Born June 16, 1918, in New York, N.Y.; son of Oscar and Sadye (Rusoff) Siffert; married Miriam Sand, June 29, 1941; children: John, Joan Siffert Kochan. *Education:* New York University, A.B. (with honors), 1939, M.D., 1943. *Home:* 45 East 85th St., New York, N.Y. 10028. *Office:* 1010 Fifth Ave., New York, N.Y. 10028.

CAREER: Kings County Hospital, Brooklyn, N.Y., intern, 1943; Mt. Sinai Hospital, New York City, resident in orthopedic surgery, 1946-49, fellow in pathology, 1949-52, member of staff, 1949—, director of orthopedic surgery and orthopedic surgeon in chief, 1960—; in private practice of orthopedics, 1949—; director of department of orthopedics at City Hospital at Elmhurst, 1963—; Mount Sinai School of Medicine, City University of New York, professor of orthopedic medicine and chairman of department, 1966—. Senior orthopedic consultant for New York City Health Department, 1952—; attending orthopedic surgeon at Blythedale Children's Hospital, 1960—. Member of board of directors of National Easter Seal Society, 1975-81; chairman of medical advisory board of Cooperative for American Relief Everywhere (CARE)-Medico, 1982; vice-president and member of board of directors of CARE, 1982. *Military service:* U.S. Army Air Forces, flight surgeon, 1944-46; served in China-Burma-India theater; became captain; received four battle stars.

MEMBER: International Society for Orthopedic Surgery and Traumatology, Orthopedic Research Society, American College of Surgeons (fellow), American Orthopedic Association (fellow), American Academy of Orthopedic Surgery, Association of Bone and Joint Surgeons, New York Academy of Medicine, New York State Medical Society, Phi Beta Kappa, Alpha Omega Alpha, Century Association. *Awards, honors:* Annual award in medicine from New York Public Health Association, 1958, and New York Philanthropic League, 1959.

WRITINGS: How Your Child's Body Grows, Grosset, 1980. Contributor of nearly one hundred articles to medical journals.*

* * *

SILCOX, David Phillips 1937-

PERSONAL: Born January 28, 1937, in Moose Jaw, Saskatchewan, Canada; son of Albert Phillips and Marjorie Emilia Silcox. *Education:* University of Toronto, B.A., 1959, M.A., 1966; attended Courtauld Institute of Art, London, 1962-63. *Home:* 70 Montclair Ave., Apt. 402, Toronto, Ontario, Canada M5P 1P7.

CAREER: Free-lance writer and broadcaster, 1964-65; Canada Council, Toronto, Ontario, senior arts officer, 1965-70; York University, Downsview, Ontario, associate professor of fine arts, 1970-77, associate dean of faculty of fine arts, 1970-77, chairman of department of music, 1971-72, and department of visual arts, 1972-73; Municipality of Metropolitan Toronto,

director of cultural affairs, 1974-82; chairman of Canadian Film Development Corp., 1981—. Visiting lecturer at Carleton University, 1969-70; lecturer at galleries and schools, including Dartmouth College, University of Minnesota, and University of Arizona. Member of board of directors of Canadian Film Development Corp., 1971—, vice-chairman, 1975-78. Assistant director of Canadian Conference of the Arts, 1961, member of board of directors, 1977-81; organizer of First Toronto Outdoor Art Exhibition, 1961; founding member of fine arts committee of Federal Department of Public Works, 1968-70, chairman, 1978-79; member of purchasing committee at Stratford Art Gallery, 1969-73; member of board of directors of Toronto Outdoor Art Exhibition, 1972-81; chairman of Contemporary Acquisitions Committee of Art Gallery of Ontario, 1976-77; chairman of International Sculpture Conference, 1977-78. Founder and member of board of directors of Toronto Theatre Festival, 1979-82, and Toronto International Festival, 1980-82; member of board of directors of Stratford Shakespearean Festival, 1981-82. Vice-chairman of Canadian Post Office task force and design advisory committee on postage stamps, 1969-73; member of board of governors of Massey Hall, 1972-82; vice-chairman of Ontario Arts Council advisory committee on touring, 1972; member of board of directors of Koffler Center, at Jewish Community Center, 1975-82; member of Jack Bush Heritage Trust, 1976-82; arts policy adviser to Laidlaw Foundation, 1978-82. Consultant to Toronto Transit Commission and Canadian Secretary of State.

MEMBER: Royal Society of Art (fellow), Association of Cultural Executives (member of board of directors, 1976-81). *Awards, honors:* Named man of the year by *Toronto Globe and Mail,* 1962; grants from McLean Foundation, 1970, and Canada Council, 1973; fellow of Canada Council, 1974-75; award from Canada Council, 1979.

WRITINGS: (With Harold Town) *Tom Thomson: "The Silence and the Storm,"* McClelland & Stewart, 1977; *Christopher Pratt,* Quintus Press, 1981.

Art critic for *Varsity,* 1960-62, and *Toronto Globe and Mail* and Canadian Broadcasting Corp., both 1964-65. Contributor of articles and reviews to art journals. Guest editor of *Canadian Art,* 1962; member of editorial board of *Studio International,* 1968-76.

WORK IN PROGRESS: A six-volume study of the works of David Milne (1882-1953); a series of monographs on contemporary Canadian artists.

* * *

SILVER, Jody 1942-

PERSONAL: Born May 28, 1942, in New York, N.Y.; daughter of Harry (a chemist) and Reddy (Silvan) Silver; married Wilbur Woods (a city planner), May 9, 1970; children: Leigh. *Education:* Queens College of the City University of New York, B.A., 1964; Hunter College of the City University of New York, M.A., 1969. *Home:* 42 East 12th St., New York, N.Y. 10003.

CAREER: Art teacher at public schools in New York City, 1964-67; New York Institute for Human Development, New York City, coordinator of programs, 1968-69; free-lance illustrator and animator, 1969—; New School for Social Research, New York City, instructor in film animation, 1977—. Animated films include "The Birth of the Big Mamoo," 1973, "A Penny Suite," 1977, work for television program "Sesame Street," Christmas Seals spots for the American Lung Association, and work for Scholastic Productions and American Broadcasting Co. (ABC). *Awards, honors:* Grant from American Film Institute, 1976; awards from the International Society of Animators for "The Birth of the Big Mamoo" and "A Penny Suite."

WRITINGS—For children; self-illustrated: *Rebecca, Margaret, and Nasty Annie,* Grosset, 1978; *Rupert and Polly,* Random House, 1978; *Isadora,* Doubleday, 1981.

Illustrator: Leslie McGuire, *Miss Mopp's Lucky Day,* Parents Magazine Press, 1981.

SIDELIGHTS: Silver told *CA:* "After coming up with several ideas for films for 'Sesame Street' and obtaining a film grant, I began to have the courage to see if I could write a children's book of my own. I must say that I was far more in love with the process of sitting down and illustrating feelings than I was in writing about them.

"Essentially I think my stories are not just for children. They are about how we all interact with one another, but very simply told. My characters are all animals—as I feel more comfortable using them to explore the depths of some very human problems."

* * *

SIMEONE, Diane A. 1953(?)-1983

OBITUARY NOTICE: Born c. 1953; died of skin cancer, April 24, 1983, in Burlington, Mass. Editor. Simeone was the subject of a British Broadcasting Corporation (BBC) documentary on alternative cancer treatments. She was an editor for a textbook publisher, Ginn & Company. Obituaries and other sources: *Chicago Tribune,* April 30, 1983.

* * *

SIMON, Roger David 1943-

PERSONAL: Born July 5, 1943, in Indianapolis, Ind.; son of Sidney and Deborah Simon; married Marna Peres, March 13, 1977; children: Marci, Shira. *Education:* Rutgers University, A.B., 1965; University of Wisconsin—Madison, M.A., 1966, Ph.D., 1971. *Home:* 2241 Montgomery St., Bethlehem, Pa. 18017. *Office:* Department of History, Maginnes 9, Lehigh University, Bethlehem, Pa. 18015.

CAREER: Lehigh University, Bethlehem, Pa., instructor, 1970-71, assistant professor, 1971-77, associate professor of history, 1977—. *Member:* American Historical Association, Organization of American Historians, Society for the History of Technology.

WRITINGS: The City-Building Process, American Philosophical Society, 1978; (with John Bodnar and Michael Weber) *Lives of Their Own: Blacks, Italians, and Poles in Pittsburgh, 1900-1960,* University of Illinois Press, 1982. Contributor to history journals.

WORK IN PROGRESS: Research on the skyscraper and the urban environment.

SIDELIGHTS: Simon told *CA:* "*Lives of Their Own* is a comparison of three ethnic groups. It is intended as a way to contrast black experiences with those of European immigrants. It demonstrates that each group had its own strategies for adjusting to the urban environment, but that blacks clearly were disadvantaged by the discrimination they encountered."

BIOGRAPHICAL/CRITICAL SOURCES: American Historical Review, June, 1979.

* * *

SIMPSON, Helen (De Guerry) 1897-1940

BRIEF ENTRY: Born December 1, 1897, in Sydney, New South Wales, Australia; died October 14 (some sources say October 15), 1940, in London, England. British novelist and playwright. Simpson was educated in France, studied music at Oxford University, and lived in both Australia and England after her marriage in 1927. Her best-known individual works are the historical novels *Boomerang* (1932), which won a James Tait Black Memorial Prize in 1933, and *Under Capricorn* (1937), which was made into a film by Alfred Hitchcock in 1949. In addition to writing several other novels, three short story collections, and eight plays, Simpson collaborated with Clemence Dane on three crime novels featuring actor, theatre manager, and amateur detective Sir John Samaurez: *Enter Sir John* (1928), *Printer's Devil* (1930), and *Re-Enter Sir John* (1932). She also wrote one detective novel, *Vantage Striker* (1931), on her own. Simpson was killed during World War II when German planes bombed the London hospital in which she was recuperating following surgery. *Biographical/critical sources: Saturday Review of Literature,* January 15, 1938; *New York Herald Tribune,* October 16, 1940; *Longman Companion to Twentieth Century Literature,* Longman, 1970; *Encyclopedia of Mystery and Detection,* McGraw, 1976; *Who Was Who Among English and European Authors, 1931-1949,* Gale, 1978.

* * *

SINGH, Ajit 1940-

PERSONAL: Born November 9, 1940, in Lahore, India; son of Durbachan (a lawyer) and Pushpa Singh. *Education:* University of the Punjab, B.A.; Howard University, M.A.; Cambridge University, M.A.; University of California, Berkeley, Ph.D. *Religion:* Sikh. *Office:* Faculty of Economics and Politics, Queen's College, Cambridge University, Sidgwick Ave., Cambridge, England.

CAREER: Cambridge University, Queen's College, Cambridge, England, fellow in economics, 1965—, director of studies in economics. Consultant to United Nations.

WRITINGS: Growth, Profitability and Valuation, Cambridge University Press, 1968; *Takeovers: Their Relevance to the Stock Market and the Theory of the Firm,* Cambridge University Press, 1971; *An Essay on the Political Economy of China's Political Development,* [London], 1975.

WORK IN PROGRESS: Research on de-industrialization of the United Kingdom and other advanced economies, on problems of industrialization in Third World countries, and on the relationship between the two.

* * *

SISLER, Harry Hall 1917-

PERSONAL: Born March 13, 1917, in Ironton, Ohio; son of Harry Chester and Minta Ann (Hall) Sisler; married Helen Elizabeth Shaver, June 29, 1940 (marriage ended, 1978); married Hannelore L. Wass (a professor), April 13, 1978; children: Elizabeth (Mrs. Thomas Rider), David F., Raymond K., Susan (Mrs. Larry Cole). *Education:* Ohio State University, B.Sc., 1936; University of Illinois, M.Sc., 1937, Ph.D., 1939. *Pol-*

itics: Republican. *Religion:* Methodist. *Home:* 6014 Northwest 54th Way, Gainesville, Fla. 32601. *Office:* Department of Chemistry, University of Florida, 201 CRB, Gainesville, Fla. 32611.

CAREER: Chicago City Colleges, Chicago, Ill., instructor in physical science, 1939-41; University of Kansas, Lawrence, instructor, 1941-42, assistant professor, 1942-45, associate professor of chemistry, 1945; Ohio State University, Columbus, assistant professor, 1946-48, associate professor, 1948-55, professor of chemistry, 1955-56; University of Florida, Gainesville, professor of chemistry, 1956—, Distinguished Service Professor of Chemistry, 1979—, chairman of department, 1956-68, director of Division of Physical Sciences and Mathematics, 1964-68, dean of College of Arts and Sciences, 1968-70, executive vice-president, 1970-73, dean of Graduate School, 1973-79. Arthur and Ruth Sloan Visiting Professor at Harvard University, 1962-63. Member of executive committee of chemistry advisory panel of National Science Foundation, 1959-62; member of advisory committee for chemistry of Oak Ridge National Laboratory, 1966-69; member of board of directors of Graduate Record Examinations, 1974-78; consultant to Tennessee Valley Authority, Battelle Memorial Research Foundation, Naval Ordnance Laboratory, and Materials Technology, Inc.

MEMBER: American Chemical Society (national chairman of Division of Chemical Education, 1957-58; chairman of Florida section, 1962), American Association for the Advancement of Science, Florida Academy of Science, Phi Beta Kappa, Sigma Xi, Alpha Chi Sigma, Kappa Phi Kappa, Phi Eta Sigma, Phi Delta Kappa, Phi Lambda Upsilon, Phi Kappa Phi, Kappa Delta Pi, Gamma Sigma Epsilon.

AWARDS, HONORS: American Chemical Society (ACS) outstanding southeastern chemist award, 1960, for chemical research and training; ACS southern chemist award, 1969, for chemical research; ACS James Flack Norris Award, 1979, for contributions to chemical education; Florida Blue Key, 1970, for contributions to the advancement of the University of Florida; Centennial Achievement Award from Ohio State University, 1970; Royal Order of the North Star of Sweden, 1973, for contributions to international understanding through scientific exchange; D.H.C. from University of Poznan, 1977.

WRITINGS: (With C. A. Vander Werf and A. W. Davidson) *General Chemistry: A Systematic Approach,* Macmillan, 1949, 2nd edition, 1959; (with W. T. Lippincott and J. J. Stewart) *A Systematic Laboratory Course in General Chemistry,* Macmillan, 1950, 2nd edition, 1961; (with A. B. Garrett, J. F. Haskins, and Margaret H. Kurbatov) *Essentials of Chemistry,* Ginn, 1951, 2nd edition, 1959; (with Haskins and Kurbatov) *Essentials of Experimental Chemistry,* Ginn, 1951, 2nd edition, 1959; (with Garrett and W. L. Evans) *Semi-Micro Qualitative Analysis,* Ginn, 1951, 3rd edition, 1967; (with Vander Werf and Davidson) *College Chemistry: A Systematic Approach,* Macmillan, 1953, 3rd edition (with Vander Werf, Davidson, and R. D. Dresdner), 1967; *Chemistry in Non-Aqueous Solvents,* Reinhold, 1961; *Electron Structure, Properties, and the Periodic Law,* Reinhold, 1963, 2nd edition, 1973; *Starling* (poems), Storter Press, 1976; (with Dresdner and William T. Mooney) *College Chemistry: A Systematic Approach,* Oxford University Press, 1980; *Of Outer and Inner Space* (poems), Hemisphere Publishing, 1981.

Editor: (With William Jolly) *Metal-Ammonia Solutions,* Dowden, 1972; (with Ralph Pearson) *Hard and Soft Acids and Bases,* Dowden, 1973; (with John Fackler) *Symmetry in Chem-ical Theory,* Dowden, 1973; (with Alan Cowley) *Compounds Containing Phosphorus-Phosphorus Bonds,* Dowden, 1973; (with L. Krannich) *Compounds Containing As-N Bonds,* Dowden, 1976; (with Stephen E. Frazier) *Chloramination Reaction,* Dowden, 1977.

Contributor: M. Cannon Sneed and Robert C. Brasted, editors, *Comprehensive Inorganic Chemistry,* Volume V, D. Van Nostrand, 1956; Charles F. Madden, editor, *Talks With Scientists,* Southern Illinois University Press, 1968.

Editor of chemistry monograph series for Reinhold, 1961-66. Contributor of about two hundred articles to scientific journals. Member of editorial board of *Journal of Chemical Education,* 1955-58.

WORK IN PROGRESS: The Hydronitrogens and Their Derivatives, with Milap A. Mathur and Carol Drum, for Dowden; *Earth, Air, Fire, and Water,* a collection of poems.

SIDELIGHTS: Sisler told *CA:* "There is a tendency on the part of many to cry with alarm concerning the alleged poor quality of today's science students. However, my current undergraduate chemistry classes are among the best I've ever had. Graduate students *do* seem to lack the devotion to getting the job done that was formerly considered necessary for success in graduate school. However, in this it seems to me that they are no different from society generally.

"Science has not been explained to society and is continuously confused with technology and is thus burdened with the blame for technological excesses. This has resulted in a lessened interest in science. Scientists need to give more attention to explaining themselves to the general public.

"To me the English language used with skill and precision is a thing of beauty. Poetry should sing as well as proclaim. The poet should communicate both with the mind and the emotions of the reader. It provides an ideal bridge between the sciences and the humanities when it is used to express scientific ideas. I've tried to do this in many of the poems I've written.

"Much modern poetry lacks both rhythm and rhyme. Such lack can be effective in serving the objectives of the poet. However, it should not be the result of the poet's unwillingness to exercise the mental discipline and professional skill to give meaningful structure to his writing."

*   *   *

SKINNER, Thomas Edward 1909-

PERSONAL: Born April 18, 1909, in Mangaweka, New Zealand; son of Thomas Edward and Alice Skinner; married Mary Ethel Yardley, October 17, 1942. *Home:* 164 Kohimarama Rd., St. Heliers, Auckland 5, New Zealand.

CAREER: New Zealand Shipping Line, Wellington, chairman of board of directors, 1974—. Chairman of New Zealand Shipping Corp. and St. John Ambulance Trust; chairman of board of directors of Container Terminals Ltd.; director of Radio Pacific. Past president of New Zealand Federation of Labour; past chairman of Mount Wellington Trust Board; past deputy chairman of New Zealand Rugby League Football Council and Mount Wellington Borough Council; past member of executive board of International Confederation of Free Trade Unions and governing body of International Labour Organisation and Auckland Grammar School; past member of advisory committee of New Zealand Exports and Shipping Council. Past member of New Zealand Musicians Industrial Union of Workers (secretary), Auckland Theatrical Workers and Places of Amusement Industrial Union of Workers, Auckland Paint and Varnish Manufacturers Employees Industrial Union of Workers, Auckland Fruit and Vegetable Preservers Industrial Union of Workers, Auckland Ship, Yacht, and Boatbuilders Industrial Union of Workers, Auckland Stonemasons Industrial Union of Workers, and Northern Industrial District Glassworkers Union.

MEMBER: National Safety Association of New Zealand (secretary), Actors Equity Association of New Zealand, Auckland Club, Auckland Lions Club, Auckland Rotary Club, Auckland Racing Club, Avondale Jockey Club, Remuera Bowling Club. *Awards, honors:* Knight of Grace of Order of St. John of Jerusalem, 1971; Knight Commander of Order of the British Empire, 1975; Silver Jubilee Medal from Queen Elizabeth II, 1977.

WRITINGS: (With John Berry) *Man to Man: My Own Biography,* Whitman, 1980.

* * *

SKLAREW, Myra 1934-

PERSONAL: Born December 18, 1934, in Baltimore, Md.; daughter of Samuel (a biochemist) and Anne (a librarian; maiden name, Wolpe) Weisberg; married Bruce Sklarew (a psychoanalyst), 1955 (marriage ended, 1976); children: Deborah, Eric. *Education:* Tufts University, B.S., 1956; Johns Hopkins University, M.A., 1970. *Office:* Department of Literature, American University, 215 Gray Hall, Washington, D.C. 20016.

CAREER: Pianist with dance band in Long Island, N.Y., 1949; typist in female admissions of Central Islip State Hospital, lab technician working in chemical assays and cholesterol studies at National Dairy Research Laboratory, bookkeeper for a beer company, all 1952-54; Yale University School of Medicine, New Haven, Conn., research assistant in Department of Physiology, 1955-57; Outdoor Nursery School, Maryland, assistant teacher, 1961-62; president, 1964-65, and adviser to board, 1965-66, of Montgomery County Council of Cooperative Nursery Schools; National Institute of Mental Health and Home Study, Inc., Maryland, tutor with Infant Education Project, 1966-67; American University, Washington, D.C., instructor, 1970-73, professorial lecturer, 1973-76, member of administrative staff, 1976, assistant professor, 1977-81, associate professor of literature, 1981—, director of master of fine arts degree program in creative writing, 1980-82.

Instructor at College of General Studies of George Washington University, 1970-71. Member of board of directors of Green Echo Writer's Center; member of poetry advisory committee of Folger Library; member of literature panel of District of Columbia Commission for the Arts and Humanities. Lecturer or panel member for American Film Institute, Library of Congress, Symposium on Science and Literature, and Folger Seminar. Has given over one hundred poetry readings at colleges, schools, and organizations throughout the United States and in Israel, including Library of Congress, Folger Shakespeare Library, Smithsonian Institution, and Tennessee Poetry Circuit. *Member:* Poetry Society of America, Academy of American Poets, Poets and Writers. *Awards, honors:* Di Castagnola Award from Poetry Society of America, 1972, and poetry award from National Jewish Book Council, 1977, both for *From the Backyard of the Diaspora;* Gordon Barber Award, 1980, for poem "Somnambulist"; National Endowment for the Arts fellowship, 1981.

WRITINGS—Poems: *In the Basket of the Blind,* Cherry Valley, 1975; *From the Backyard of the Diaspora,* Dryad, 1976, new edition, 1981; *The Science of Goodbyes,* University of Georgia Press, 1982; *Blessed Art Thou, No-One,* Chowder Chapbooks, 1982. Poetry recorded for "Contemporary Poet's" series of the Library of Congress.

Contributor of more than three hundred poems, articles, and reviews to magazines and newspapers, including *Quest, New Republic, Moment, New York Times,* and *Carolina Quarterly.*

WORK IN PROGRESS: The Refusal, a novel; *The Difference Between Men and Women,* stories; a book of children's stories; a collection of poems for Jewish holy days.

SIDELIGHTS: Sklarew's *The Science of Goodbyes,* her first major work since the mid-seventies, has met with critical acceptance. Inge Judd commented in a *Library Journal* review that the work is "one of the most appealing, strikingly intelligent books" that she had seen in a while. And Gardner McFall noted in the *Washington Review:* "Though one is first struck by the content of this book and the intellect shaping it, it is important to mention that the poet's clarity and simplicity of style hauntingly support and do justice to her ideas."

Sklarew told *CA:* "*The Refusal,* my novel in progress, wants to be about a girl and her father, a modern retelling of the Electra story, but I don't know how it will turn out in the 1980's. So far there's been no solution, but there is a strange old woman who has a predilection for sleeping in a chicken coop and who eventually goes there to die; some melon men who go around a mountain looking for women; a small boy who spends time under the robes of a priest; a gypsy woman and her son who set up housekeeping on a beach, etc. It's too soon to say more. I've been working on it since 1979. It happens as slowly as making a poem. Only this contains many poems, so it will take many years, if it finally becomes a finished tale. One doesn't know what will happen.

"The stories in *The Difference Between Men and Women* give me a chance to include more: Poetry takes years of experiences and condenses them to a few words; stories open out, letting more of the world in. Mine include my interests in science, music, religion, sex, childhood, separation, memory, cybernetics, language, students, the afterlife, etc. Some of the stories bear the following titles, which might provide a clue to them: 'A Little Sex Goes a Long Way,' 'Saturday Afternoon at the Movies,' 'In the Afterlife Which Is a Library,' 'Certainty,' 'Leaving,' 'Niels Bohr and the Elephant,' 'Cybernetics,' 'The Messenger,' 'August,' 'The Student,' 'Separation,' 'Remember,' and so on. Most of these have not been published.

"My collection of poems for the Jewish holy days is structured around the holy days of the year beginning with Rosh Hashanah, the Jewish New Year, and ending with the Ninth of Av. It includes (or will when it is finished) translations of eight poems into Hebrew, done by the Israeli poet Moshe Dor, and the English originals. Some are liturgical; some have been incorporated into religious services, and others are contemporary expressions of observance or rebellion as the case may be in the latter half of our century.

"My dream is to wake up tomorrow morning and be fluent in Hebrew, Greek, and Arabic so I can read all the contemporary poetry and fiction written by people in these cultures—and the not so contemporary ones later."

BIOGRAPHICAL/CRITICAL SOURCES: Jerusalem Post, August 21, 1970; *Library Journal,* January, 1976, August, 1976,

May 1, 1982; *Small Press Review*, May, 1976; *Chowder Review*, spring-summer, 1976; *Soho Weekly News*, September 23, 1976; *Choice*, November, 1976; *Washington Review of the Arts*, winter, 1976-77; *Sybil-Child*, Volume II, number 2, 1977; *Sewanee Review*, summer, 1977; *Jewish Week*, July 14-20, 1977; *Association of Jewish Libraries Newsletter*, September/October, 1982; *Washington Review*, October/November, 1982; *Washington Post Magazine*, December 5, 1982.

*   *   *

SKOLSKY, Sidney   1905-1983

OBITUARY NOTICE—See index for *CA* sketch: Born May 2, 1905, in New York, N.Y.; died of Parkinson's disease, May 3, 1983, in Los Angeles, Calif. Journalist and author. Skolsky was a well-known gossip columnist who produced films and television programs and wrote screenplays and books. He began writing "Tintypes," his famous Broadway and Hollywood column, in 1929. The column featured biographies of celebrities and included such details as whether or not the star in question wore pajamas. As a gossip columnist, Skolsky was considered modest and never malicious. Supposedly, he coined the name "Oscar" when referring to an Academy Award. Skolsky continued to write his predictions for Academy-Award winners until 1981, five years after his official retirement. In addition to compiling his column, he hosted "Sidney Skolsky's Hollywood," a celebrity interview show broadcast in 1955. Skolsky produced two films, "The Jolson Story" and "The Eddie Cantor Story," as well as two television productions, "Hollywood and the Movies" and "Hollywood: The Golden Era." He co-wrote the 1937 film "The Daring Young Men" and was the sole author of *Times Square Tintypes: Being Typewriter Caricatures of Those Who Made Their Names Along the Not So Straight and Very Narrow Path of Broadway* and *Don't Get Me Wrong—I Love Hollywood*. Obituaries and other sources: *New York Times*, May 5, 1983; *Los Angeles Times*, May 6, 1983; *Washington Post*, May 7, 1983.

*   *   *

SLEZAK, Walter   1902-1983

OBITUARY NOTICE: Born May 3, 1902, in Vienna, Austria; died of a self-inflicted gunshot wound to the head, April 22, 1983, in Port Washington, N.Y. Actor and author. Slezak was in the banking business and appeared in German films and plays before coming to the United States in 1930 to debut in the New York stage production of "Meet My Sister." He gained popularity for his light, musical roles on Broadway during the 1930's, but the roles he played in American movies were more sinister in nature, particularly his portrayal of a Nazi submarine commander in Alfred Hitchcock's 1944 film "Lifeboat." He played an assortment of character roles during his film career, appearing in such motion pictures as "The Fallen Sparrow," "The Spanish Main," and "Bedtime for Bonzo." Slezak, who had been despondent over his ill health for some time before his death, was the author of *My Stomach Goes Traveling* and *What Time's the Next Swan?* Obituaries and other sources: *Chicago Tribune*, April 23, 1983; *Los Angeles Times*, April 23, 1983; *New York Times*, April 23, 1983; *Washington Post*, April 23, 1983; *Newsweek*, May 2, 1983.

*   *   *

SLOAN, Phillip R(eid)   1938-

PERSONAL: Born January 28, 1938, in Salt Lake City, Utah;

son of Reid J. (an accountant) and MaRee (a secretary; maiden name, Scott) Sloan; married Sharon Lee Borg (a bank officer), September 2, 1958; children: Laura T., Mary E., Kathleen M. Sloan Knapp, Sheila A. *Education:* University of Utah, B.S., 1960; Scripps Institution of Oceanography, M.S., 1964; University of California, San Diego, M.A., 1967, Ph.D., 1969. *Politics:* Democrat. *Religion:* Roman Catholic. *Home:* 1844 Kessler Blvd., South Bend, Ind. 46616. *Office:* Program of Liberal Studies, University of Notre Dame, Notre Dame, Ind. 46556.

CAREER: Scripps Institution of Oceanography, La Jolla, Calif., marine research technician, 1964-65; University of Washington, Seattle, assistant professor of history of science, 1969-74; University of Notre Dame, Notre Dame, Ind., assistant professor, 1974-79, associate professor of liberal studies and history of science, 1979—. *Military service:* U.S. Navy Reserve, 1955-63. *Member:* History of Science Society (member of national executive council, 1982—).

WRITINGS: (Editor and translator with John Lyon, and author of introduction) *From Natural History to the History of Nature: Readings From Buffon and His Critics*, University of Notre Dame Press, 1981. Contributor to scientific journals.

WORK IN PROGRESS: Darwin on the Species Problem: The Genesis of Darwin's Species Concept, 1828-1844, completion expected in 1984.

SIDELIGHTS: Sloan commented: "For many years I have been actively interested in the interaction of the natural sciences with the issues of philosophy, religion, and intellectual history. This has particularly meant a concern with the integration of scientific forms of understanding with other ways of understanding."

*   *   *

SLOAN, Raymond Paton   1893-1983

OBITUARY NOTICE—See index for *CA* sketch: Born December 12, 1893, in Brooklyn, N.Y.; died of a stroke, March 20, 1983, in New York, N.Y. Administrator and author. Sloan was an authority on hospital management. He was affiliated with many institutions, including Modern Hospital, Thayer Hospital, and Community Hospital. Since 1953 he had been a vice-president of the Alfred P. Sloan Foundation—named for his brother—and for over twenty years was associated with the Memorial Sloan-Kettering Cancer Center. Sloan wrote *Hospital Color and Decoration*, *This Hospital Business of Ours*, *On a Shoestring and a Prayer*, and *Today's Hospital*. Obituaries and other sources: *New York Times*, March 23, 1983.

*   *   *

SLOTE, Bernice D.   1915(?)-1983

OBITUARY NOTICE: Born c. 1915 in Hickman, Neb.; died February 22, 1983. Educator, scholar, critic, and author. Slote, a professor emeritus at the University of Nebraska-Lincoln, was considered the world's leading scholar on the works of author Willa Cather, as well as an authority on the works of John Keats. She was the author of *Keats and the Dramatic Principle* and the co-author (with James E. Miller, Jr., and Karl Shapiro) of *Start With the Sun: Studies in Cosmic Poetry*. Obituaries and other sources: *Who's Who of American Women*, second edition, Marquis, 1961; *Chicago Tribune*, February 25, 1983.

SMERTENKO, Johan J. 1897(?)-1983

OBITUARY NOTICE: Born c. 1897 in Russia (now U.S.S.R.); died April 29, 1983, in Southbury, Conn. Educator and author. Smertenko was best known for his activities in the establishment of the state of Israel. A graduate of the University of Wisconsin, he served in the U.S. Army during World War I. Smertenko's books include *Alexander Hamilton* and *Palestine in Revolt*. Obituaries and other sources: *New York Times,* May 5, 1983.

* * *

SMITH, Abbot E(merson) 1906-1983

OBITUARY NOTICE: Born June 20, 1906, in Portland, Me.; died of an intestinal disorder, April 2, 1983, in Olympia, Wash. A Central Intelligence Agency official, Smith served in the U.S. Navy during World War II. He graduated from Colby College, attended Harvard University, and, as a Rhodes Scholar, earned his doctorate at Balliol College, Oxford University. Smith's book, *Colonists in Bondage,* is about indentured servitude in America. Obituaries and other sources: *Washington Post,* April 13, 1983.

* * *

SMITH, Arnold Cantwell 1915-

PERSONAL: Born January 18, 1915, in Toronto, Ontario, Canada; son of Victor Arnold and Sarah Cory (Cantwell) Smith; married Evelyn Hardwick Stewart, September 8, 1938; children: Alexandra (Mrs. Harry Gaylord, Jr.), Stewart Cantwell, Matthew Cantwell. *Education:* University of Toronto, B.A., 1935; Christ Church, Oxford, B.A., 1937, B.C.L., 1938, M.A., 1938. *Religion:* Christian (Anglican). *Home:* TH5-300 Queen Elizabeth Driveway, Ottawa, Ontario, Canada K1S 3M6; and Aux Anjeaux, Gavaudun, 47150 Monflanquin, France.

CAREER: Baltic Times, Tallinn, Estonia, editor, 1938-40; University of Tartu, Tartu, Estonia, lecturer in political economics, 1938-40; British Embassy attache in Cairo, Egypt, 1940-41; Office of British Minister of State for the Middle East, Cairo, head of political warfare division, 1941-43; secretary of Canadian legation in Kuibyshev, U.S.S.R., 1943; secretary of Canadian Embassy in Moscow, U.S.S.R., 1943-45; Department of External Affairs, Ottawa, Ontario, served in economic division, 1945-47; National Defense College of Canada, Kingston, Ontario, associate director, 1947-49; counselor with Canadian Embassy in Brussels, Belgium, and head of Canadian delegation to Inter-Allied Preparations Agency, both 1950-53; special assistant to secretary of state for external affairs, 1953-55; Canadian commissioner on International Truce Supervisory Committee for Cambodia, 1955-56; Canadian minister to England, 1956-58; Canadian ambassador to the United Arab Republic, 1958-61; Canadian ambassador to the U.S.S.R., 1961-63; assistant undersecretary of state for external affairs in Ottawa, 1963-65; elected first secretary-general of the Commonwealth of Nations, 1965-75; Carleton University, Ottawa, Lester B. Pearson Professor of International Affairs, 1976-81, adjunct professor, 1981—.

Representative to British Council for Estonia and press attache of British legation, Tallinn, 1939-40; special lecturer in political science and economics at Egyptian State University, Cairo, 1940-42; editor in chief of *Akhbar el Harp, Aera,* and *Cepha,* all Cairo, 1941-43. Canadian representative to United Nations General Assembly, 1947, 1949-51, and 1954; principal adviser to permanent delegation of Canada to the United Nations, 1949; alternate representative of Canada on U.N. Security Council and Atomic Energy Commission, 1949-50. Visiting centennial professor at University of Toronto, 1967; visiting lecturer at Soviet Academy of Science, Moscow, 1977; visiting Cecil and Ada Green Professor at University of British Columbia, 1978; Montague Burton Lecturer in international relations at University of Leeds, 1982; seventy-fifth anniversary lecturer at University of Alberta, 1983. Chairman of board of directors of International Peace Academy, 1976—, North-South Institute, Ottawa, 1976—, and Hudson Institute of Canada, Montreal, 1977—. Member of Duke of Edinburgh's Fifth Commonwealth Study Conference (member of executive committee and council, 1980). Member of board of trustees of Hudson Institute, New York, 1977-81, and Cambridge Commonwealth Trust, 1982—. Member of University College Committee, Toronto University, 1982—.

MEMBER: Newsconcern International Foundation (London; member of board of governors, 1983—), Cambridge University Commonwealth Trust (London; trustee, 1983—), Canadian Bureau of International Education (president, 1976-79), Canadian-Mediterranean Institute (honorary president, 1981—), Royal Commonwealth Society of Canada (honorary president), Royal Commonwealth Society (London; life vice-president, 1975—), Cercle Universitaire (Ottawa), Athenaeum Club.

AWARDS, HONORS: Rhodes Scholar at Christ Church, Oxford, 1935; LL.D. from Ricker College, 1964, Queen's University, Kingston, Ontario, 1966, University of British Columbia and University of Toronto, both 1968, University of New Brunswick, 1969, University of Leeds, 1975, and Trent University, 1979; D.C.L. from University of Michigan, 1966, Oxford University, 1975, and Bishop's University, 1977; Companion of Honor, 1975; R. B. Bennett Commonwealth Prize from Royal Society for the Arts, 1975, for "outstanding services to the Commonwealth"; honorary fellow of Lady Eaton College, Trent University, 1979; Zimbabwe Independence Medal, 1980.

WRITINGS: (Contributor) Norman Penlington, editor, *On Canada: Essays in Honor of Frank H. Underhill,* University of Toronto Press, 1971; (with Clyde Sanger) *Stitches in Time: The Commonwealth in World Politics* (Book-of-the-Month Club alternate selection), General Publishing Co. and Deutsch, 1981, Beaufort Books, 1983; (contributor) Arthur Lall, editor, *International Negotiation and Mediation,* Pergamon, 1983; *The We-They Frontiers—From International Relations to World Politics,* Leeds University Press, 1983. Contributor of numerous articles to learned journals, political reviews, and magazines, including *Geographical Magazine.*

WORK IN PROGRESS: Why North-South Politics?, on relations with developing countries, publication expected in 1984.

SIDELIGHTS: In 1965 Arnold Smith began serving the first of two consecutive five-year terms as first secretary-general of the Commonwealth of Nations. During his ten years in that position, membership in the Commonwealth grew from ten to over forty nations. In *Stitches in Time,* Smith's account of those years, he describes how the Commonwealth secretariat was set up, the process by which he was elected to the position of secretary-general, and the changes that the organization underwent during his term as its leader.

"Smith had to organize an international secretariat from scratch," explained Sidney A. Freifeld in the *Toronto Globe and Mail.* "He scrounged funds, sparked programs of education exchange and technical co-operation, pioneered the use of experts from the new countries and fostered multi-racial attitudes and the shedding of mother-country frames of mind.''

Freifeld praised Smith's candid and frank account of his years as secretary-general. A critic for the *Tanzania Daily News* observed that Smith's account of those years is laced with humor. And J. L. Granatstein, who reviewed *Stitches in Time* for the *Quill & Quire*, found the book ''marvellously undiplomatic in its language; stupidity and pomposity are repeatedly labelled for what they are.'' Granatstein also noted that Smith's book includes ''some new tidbits of information based on hitherto confidential sources,'' and went on to advise: ''Read his book and enjoy it.''

Smith told *CA*: ''My chief interests and activities have always been world politics, motivated by the desire to help mankind develop a decent global community. I see a parallel, at a more mundane level, between my work and that of my brother, Wilfred Cantwell Smith, whose field is the comparative history of world religion.''

AVOCATIONAL INTERESTS: Travel, photography, farming in France, wine making.

BIOGRAPHICAL/CRITICAL SOURCES: George Ronald, *In Search of Canada*, Reader's Digest Association (Canada), 1971; *Quill & Quire*, August, 1981; *Toronto Globe and Mail*, September 5, 1981; *London Standard*, September 29, 1981; *New Statesman*, October 2, 1981; *Tanzania Daily News*, October 24, 1981; *West Africa*, September 27, 1982.

* * *

SMITH, C. Ray   1929-

PERSONAL: Born March 3, 1929, in Birmingham, Ala.; son of Calvin Ray and Sara Amanda (Kelly) Smith; married Leslie Armstrong, December 17, 1971 (divorced, 1978); children: Sinclair Scott. *Education:* Kenyon College, B.A., 1951; Yale University, M.A., 1958. *Home address:* P.O. Box 32, Lenhartsville, Pa. 19534. *Office:* 411 East 50th St., New York, N.Y.. 10022.

CAREER: Interior Design, New York City, assistant editor, 1958-60; *Progressive Architecture*, Stamford, Conn., senior editor, 1961-70; *Theatre Crafts*, New York City, editor, 1969-74; *Interiors*, New York City, editor, 1974-76; Parsons School of Design, New York City, teacher of design history, 1977—. *Military service:* U.S. Army, 1952-54; served in Europe. *Member:* U.S. Institute for Theatre Technology (fellow), American Institute of Architects (fellow), Society of Architectural Historians, Architectural League of New York, Coffee House Club.

WRITINGS: The American Endless Weekend, American Institute of Architects, 1972; *Supermannerism: New Attitudes in Post-Modern Architecture*, Dutton, 1977; *AIGA Graphic Design, U.S.A.: I*, Watson-Guptill, 1980; (with Marian Page) *The Wood Chair in America*, Estelle D. and Stephen B. Brickel, 1982.

Editor: Jo Mielziner, *The Shapes of Our Theatre*, C. N. Potter, 1970; *The Theatre Crafts Book of Costume*, Rodale Press, 1973; *The Theatre Crafts Book of Makeup, Masks, and Wigs*, Rodale Press, 1974; John Margolies, *The End of the Road*, Penguin, 1981.

Contributor to *Encyclopedia of Contemporary Architects, Academic American Encyclopedia*, and *Britannica Encyclopedia of American Art*. Contributor to magazines and newspapers,

including *New York, House Beautiful, Urban Design*, and *Avenue*. Editor of *Oculus*, 1981-83.

WORK IN PROGRESS: Twentieth-Century Interior Design, with Allen Tate, publication by Harper expected in 1984 or 1985; *History of Paul Rudolph's Art and Architecture Building at Yale*.

SIDELIGHTS: Smith told *CA*: ''My work is descriptive, attempting to conjure up a verbal picture and guide to the photographs and plans of the works discussed and illustrated. I am dedicated to telling, foremost, what the designer's intentions have been; my reasoning is that criticism of the applied arts must know the programmatic needs of the client/users in order to form accurate critiques of the final products and, in addition where architecture is concerned, discussion with the designers is essential to an understanding of what is invisible behind or within the walls—air conditioning and structural systems, particularly.

''*The American Endless Weekend* is a short report written for the American Institute of Architects' contribution to an international congress devoted to the subject of recreation and recreation architecture. My report not only investigated the available statistics, to discover that although Americans keep records to convince them that the weekend is variable and overlapping for different segments of the population, overall statistics are seldom kept for yearly attendance but only for peak periods. The report also investigated the status of the arts as spectator recreation for many. In this the report was among the pioneers.

''Mannerism has been perhaps the leading direction of architecture in this country, in Europe and in Japan since around 1960. It corresponds to the architecture mannerism of sixteenth- and seventeenth-century Italy and England. In the 1960's in the United States, as *Supermannerism* describes, this overall mannerist approach was accompanied by a pop-art overtone that made it correspondent also with popular culture—therefore 'supermannerism,' or 'superman-nerism.' ''

AVOCATIONAL INTERESTS: Theater, music, travel.

* * *

SMITH, Cyril   1928-

PERSONAL: Born June 28, 1928, in Rochdale, England. *Education:* Attended boys' grammar school in Rochdale, England. *Religion:* Unitarian-Universalist. *Office:* House of Commons, London SW1A 0AA, England.

CAREER: Civil servant, 1944-45; wages clerk, 1945-48; agent of Liberal party in Stockport, England, 1948-50; agent of Labour party in Ashton-under-Lyne, England, 1950-53, and in Heywood and Royton, England, 1953-55; news agent, 1955-58; production controller with Spring Manufacturing, 1958-63; Smith Springs Ltd., Rochdale, England, director, 1963—. Liberal member of Parliament for Rochdale, 1972—, Liberal spokesperson on employment, 1974—. Member of council of County Borough of Rochdale, 1952—, mayor, 1966-67. *Awards, honors:* Officer of Order of St. John of Jerusalem; member of Order of the British Empire.

WRITINGS: Industrial Participation, W. H. Allen, 1975; *Big Cyril*, W. H. Allen, 1977.

* * *

SMITH, Frank O. M.   ?-1983

OBITUARY NOTICE: Died February 18, 1983, in London,

England. An accountant and author of *This Insubstantial Pageant*, a history of the Tavistock Repertory Company. Smith was involved in nonprofessional theatre for forty-nine years, serving successively as director, chairman, and honorary treasurer of the Tavistock Repertory Company. He was also treasurer of the British Theatre Association (formerly the British Drama League) and was active in the Surrey Playing Field Association. Obituaries and other sources: *London Times*, March 3, 1983.

* * *

SMITH, Fredrika Shumway   1877-1968

OBITUARY NOTICE: Born July 30, 1877 in Chicago, Ill.; died March 7, 1968, in Lake Forest, Ill. Historian and author of children's books. Smith was an active member of several historical organizations, including the Colonial Dames Society, the Illinois Society of Mayflower Descendants, and the Antiquarian Society of the Art Institute of Chicago. She wrote biographies for children as well as other books, such as *The Magic City* (a collection of poems), *Wilderness Adventure*, and *The Fire Dragon*. Obituaries and other sources: *New York Times Book Review*, March 27, 1966, April 2, 1967; *New York Times*, March 8, 1968; *Christian Science Monitor*, May 2, 1968; *The National Cyclopaedia of American Biography*, Volume 55, James T. White, 1974.

* * *

SMITH, Hermon Dunlap   1900-1983

OBITUARY NOTICE: Born May 1, 1900, in Chicago, Ill.; died of injuries sustained in a fall, May 11, 1983, in Lake Forest, Ill. Business executive and author. Smith worked for March & McLennon, an insurance brokerage house, from 1935 to 1971, during which time the firm became the largest of its kind. Smith held several positions with the company, including president, chairman, and chief executive officer. He also served as trustee of the Newberry Library and director of the Orchestral Association of Chicago. Smith, an authority on American history, wrote *The Revolutionary War Journals of Henry Dearborn, 1773-83* and *The Desbarats Country*. Obituaries and other sources: *Who's Who in Insurance*, Underwriter Printing and Publishing, 1976; *Who's Who in America*, 39th edition, Marquis, 1976; *Chicago Tribune*, May 13, 1983.

* * *

SMITH, Johnston
See CRANE, Stephen (Townley)

* * *

SMITH, Margarita G.   1923(?)-1983

OBITUARY NOTICE: Born c. 1923 in Columbus, Ga.; died of heart failure, January 28, 1983, in Manhattan, N.Y. Editor, educator, lecturer, and author. Smith graduated from University of Miami and began her career as a fiction editor of *Mademoiselle* magazine. She is credited with introducing readers to such authors as Flannery O'Connor, Truman Capote, and Tennessee Williams. Sister of the late novelist Carson McCullers, Smith edited a posthumous collection of McCullers's *The Mortgaged Heart*. She also served as editor for other publications, including *Forty Best Short Stories from Mademoiselle* and *Redbook* magazine. She lectured in English at Columbia University and taught at the New School for Social Research.

One of Smith's short stories was featured in *Mademoiselle*, and it won an O. Henry Award in 1943. Obituaries and other sources: *New York Times*, January 31, 1983.

* * *

SMITH, Nigel J(ohn) H(arwood)   1949-

PERSONAL: Born May 4, 1949, in Maracaizo, Venezuela; came to the United States in 1980; son of Cyril Ronald and Molly Patricia (Walden) Smith; married Lisa Williams, October 12, 1975. *Education:* University of California, Berkeley, B.A., 1971, M.A., 1973, Ph.D., 1976. *Religion:* Christian. *Office:* Department of Geography, University of Florida, Gainesville, Fla. 32611.

CAREER: Instituto Nacional de Pesquisas da Amazonia, Manaus, Brazil, researcher, 1976-80; Worldwatch Institute, Washington, D.C., senior researcher, 1980-81; University of Florida, Gainesville, associate professor of geography, 1981—. Consultant to World Bank. *Member:* American Association for the Advancement of Science, Association of American Geographers.

WRITINGS: Man, Fishes, and the Amazon, Columbia University Press, 1981; *Rainforest Corridors: The Transamazon Colonization Scheme*, University of California Press, 1982. Contributor to *Science* and newspapers.

WORK IN PROGRESS: Research on folklore in Amazonia and on agricultural production in developing countries.

SIDELIGHTS: Smith wrote: "Field work has been central to my work on the natural history of man in the tropics. I have done most of my field work in the Brazilian Amazon, along the Transamazon Highway, and along the Amazon River near Manaus. Lately I have further expanded my horizons by examining efforts to improve agricultural productivity in rural areas of highland Peru, and in Mexico, Colombia, and India.

"A command of foreign languages is crucial to opening the window on other cultures; I speak Portuguese, Spanish, and a little French."

* * *

SMOKE, Jim

PERSONAL—Education: Attended Nyack Missionary College and Kings College. *Office:* First Presbyterian Church of Hollywood, 1760 Gower, Hollywood, Calif.

CAREER: Formerly senior staff minister and minister to single adults at Garden Grove Community Church, Calif.; served in Christian ministries in Pennsylvania, Michigan, Florida, and California; currently part-time minister to single adults at First Presbyterian Church of Hollywood, Calif. Workshop and seminar leader.

WRITINGS: Growing Through Divorce, Harvest House, 1976; *Suddenly Single*, Revell, 1982; *Every Single Day*, Revell, 1983. Founder of *Solo*.

SIDELIGHTS: In his ministry Jim Smoke works predominantly as a lecturer and counselor for single adults. He conducts national leadership training seminars for other ministers in the field, and he founded *Solo*, a magazine for adults that have never been married or that have been widowed or divorced. Smoke also conducts divorce recovery workshops. His book, *Growing Through Divorce*, shows individuals how to turn separation into something positive.

SMYTH, John (George) 1893-1983

OBITUARY NOTICE—See index for *CA* sketch: Born October 24, 1893, in Teignmouth, Devonshire, England; died April 26, 1983. Military officer, member of Parliament, broadcaster, journalist, and author. Commissioned in 1912, Smyth was forced to end his distinguished military career in 1942 due to illness. Following retirement from the military, he served as military correspondent and lawn tennis correspondent to the *London Times* and other periodicals. During this period he was also a BBC (British Broadcasting Corporation) commentator. Elected to Parliament in 1950, he became joint parliamentary secretary in 1953 and remained in Parliament until 1966. Many of Smyth's books were written on military subjects or lawn tennis. Among them are *Defence Is Our Business, Lawn Tennis, Behind the Scenes at Wimbledon,* and *Leadership in Battle, 1914-1918.* His autobiography, *The Only Enemy,* appeared in 1959. Obituaries and other sources: John Smyth, *The Only Enemy: An Autobiography,* Hutchinson, 1959; *The Author's and Writer's Who's Who,* 6th edition, Burke's Peerage, 1971; *Blue Book: Leaders of the English-Speaking World,* St. Martin's, 1976; *The Writers Directory: 1982-1984,* Gale, 1981; *Who's Who,* 134th edition, St. Martin's, 1982; *London Times,* April 27, 1983.

* * *

SNOOK, Barbara (Lillian) 1913-

PERSONAL: Born in 1913 in Petworth, England. *Education:* Recieved art teacher's diploma from Brighton College of Art.

CAREER: Writer on embroidery and needlework. Grammar school teacher, 1936-44; Beaverwood School for Girls, Chislehurst, Kent, England, head of art department, 1944-73. *Member:* Association of Assistant Mistresses.

WRITINGS: English Historical Embroidery, Batsford, 1960, new edition published as *English Embroidery,* Mills & Boon, 1974; *Learning to Embroider,* Hearthside, 1960; *Learning to Sew,* Batsford, 1962; *Creative Soft Toys,* Batsford, 1963, Branford, 1964; *Embroidery Stitches,* Batsford, 1963, reprinted, 1978; *Needlework Stitches,* Crown, 1963; *Costumes for School Plays,* Branford, 1965; *Puppets,* Batsford, 1965, Branford, 1966; *Needlework for Juniors* (juvenile), Branford, 1966; *Florentine Embroidery,* Scribner, 1967 (published in England as *Florentine Canvas Embroidery,* Batsford, 1967), abridged edition published as *The Craft of Florentine Embroidery,* Scribner, 1971; *Making Clowns, Witches, and Dragons,* Branford, 1967; *Making Baby Clothes,* Batsford, 1968, Taplinger, 1969.

Costumes for Children (juvenile), Branford, 1970; *Fancy Dress for Children,* Batsford, 1970; *The Creative Art of Embroidery,* Hamlyn, 1972; *Making Masks for School Plays* (juvenile), Plays, 1972 (published in England as *Making Masks,* Batsford, 1972); *Scribble Stitchery,* Branford, 1972; *Making Birds, Beasts, and Insects,* Scribner, 1974; *Embroidery Designs From Pre-Columbian Art,* Scribner, 1975; *The Zoo: Needlecraft for Young Children,* Batsford, 1975; *Embroidery Designs From the Sea,* Taplinger, 1977.

* * *

SNYDER, Tom 1936-

BRIEF ENTRY: Born May 12, 1936, in Milwaukee, Wis. American broadcast journalist. Snyder worked at several net-

work stations and affiliates before joining the staff of National Broadcasting Company (NBC-TV), where he became known for his interviewing style. John Leonard of the *New York Times,* for example, claimed that Snyder "suffers fools rudely, which is what they deserve." In the course of his career, the journalist has interviewed a wide array of individuals, including Jimmy Hoffa, Sybil Leek, Spiro T. Agnew, John Lennon, Jim Jordon, and a transvestite rock groupie. As the host of "Tomorrow," a talk show which debuted in 1973, Snyder addressed controversial topics such as group marriages, male prostitution, suicide, and the Central Intelligence Agency (CIA). From 1974 until 1977, the journalist co-anchored "News Center 4," while simultaneously reporting and writing for the "NBC Sunday News" and reporting for the "NBC News Update." In 1978 he hosted "Prime Time Sunday," which later became "Prime Time Saturday." Snyder also hosted several network specials, notably, "Of Women and Men," with Barbara Walters, "The Legion Disease: What Happened in Philadelphia," and "The National Disaster Survival Test." In 1974 he received an Emmy Award for outstanding program and individual achievement. *Address:* National Broadcasting Co., Inc., 30 Rockefeller Plaza, New York, N.Y. 10020. *Biographical/critical sources: Newsweek,* October 29, 1973, February 4, 1975, July 9, 1979; *Time,* October 29, 1973; *New York Times,* November 4, 1973; *Esquire,* March 28, 1978, July 4, 1978; *New Leader,* September 10, 1979, January 11, 1982; *Current Biography,* Wilson, 1980.

* * *

SOLECKI, Ralph S(tefan) 1917-

BRIEF ENTRY: Born October 15, 1917, in Brooklyn, N.Y. American anthropologist, educator, and author. Solecki began his career in 1948 as an archaeologist for the Smithsonian Institution. He later became a professor of anthropology at Columbia University and was a Fulbright scholar in Iraq and Syria. Solecki has also directed field expeditions to Alaska, Iraq, Sudanese Nubia, Turkey, Syria, Iran, Lebanon, and France. He wrote *Shanidar: The First Flower People* (Knopf, 1971) and *Shanidar: The Humanity of Neanderthal Man* (Allen Lane, 1972). Solecki co-authored *Archaeological Reconnaissances North of the Brooks Range In Northeastern Alaska* (Department of Archaeology, University of Calgary, 1973). *Address:* Department of Anthropology, Columbia University, Schermerhorn Extension, New York, N.Y. 10027. *Biographical/critical sources: American Historical Review,* April, 1975.

* * *

SOLOMON, Joan 1930-

PERSONAL: Born November 26, 1930, in Johannesburg, South Africa; daughter of Philip (a printer) and Rose (a seamstress; maiden name, Isaacs) Mendelsohn; married Louis Solomon (a surgeon), July 1, 1951; children: Caryn, Ryan, Joyce. *Education:* University of Witwatersrand, B.A. (with honors) 1949; University of Cape Town, B.Ed., 1950. *Residence:* London, England.

CAREER: Worked as an English teacher in Johannesburg, South Africa, 1951-52; employed as a child welfare social worker in Cape Town, South Africa, 1952-53; Baragwanath Hospital, Johannesburg, social worker, 1953-54; owner of advertising art studio in Upington, South Africa, 1954-57; free-lance tutor in London, England, 1958-62; University of Witwatersrand, Johannesburg, lecturer in English, 1963-76; taught English as a foreign language in London, 1978-81; Open University, London, lecturer in English, 1981—. Taught creative writing to groups of black students in Soweto, South Africa.

WRITINGS: Kate's Party, Hamish Hamilton, 1978; *Spud Comes to Play,* Hamish Hamilton, 1978; *Berron's Tooth,* Hamish Hamilton, 1978; *A Day by the Sea,* Hamish Hamilton, 1978; *Teaching Children in the Laboratory,* Croom Helm, 1980; *Shabnam's Day Out,* Hamish Hamilton, 1980; *Gifts and Almonds,* Hamish Hamilton, 1980; *Wedding Day,* Hamish Hamilton, 1981; *A Present for Mum,* Hamish Hamilton, 1981. Contributor of articles and photographs to academic journals.

Also author of *Joyce's Day, Joyce Visits Granny, Joyce at the Circus, Sipho's Trumpet, Joyce's ABC, Bobbi's New Year,* and *News for Dad.*

WORK IN PROGRESS: Children's books; research on minority communitites; research on racisim, sexism, and classism in children's literature.

* * *

SOLTOW, James H(arold)   1924-

PERSONAL: Born July 1, 1924, in Chicago, Ill.; son of Lawrence Milton and Gladys Louise (Combs) Soltow; married Martha Jane Stough (a librarian), September 14, 1946. *Education:* Dickinson College, A.B., 1948; University of Pennsylvania, A.M., 1949, Ph.D., 1954. *Politics:* Independent. *Religion:* Episcopal. *Home:* 520 Wildwood Dr., East Lansing, Mich. 48823. *Office:* Department of History, Michigan State University, East Lansing, Mich. 48824.

CAREER: Hunter College (now of the City University of New York), New York, N.Y., lecturer in history, 1952-55; Colonial Williamsburg, Inc., Williamsburg, Va., research fellow, 1955-56; Russell Sage College, Troy, N.Y., instructor in history, 1956-58; Harvard University, Graduate School of Business Administration, Boston, Mass., fellow in business history, 1958-59; Michigan State University, East Lansing, assistant professor, 1959-63, associate professor, 1963-68, professor of history, 1968—, chairman of department, 1970-75. *Military service:* U.S. Army, 1943-46. *Member:* American Historical Association, Organization of American Historians, Economic History Association, Economic and Business Historical Society (president, 1982), Business History Conference. *Awards, honors:* Fulbright fellowship for University of Louvain, 1965-66.

WRITINGS: The Economic Role of Williamsburg, University Press of Virginia, 1965; *Origins of Small Business: Metal Fabricators and Machinery Makers in New England, 1890-1957,* American Philosophical Society, 1965; (editor) *Essays in Economic and Business History 1976, 1977, and 1978,* School of Business Administration, Michigan State University, 1979; (with Sidney Ratner and Richard Sylla) *The Evolution of the American Economy: Growth, Welfare, and Decision Making,* Basic Books, 1979; (editor) *Essays in Economic and Business History, 1979,* School of Business Administration, Michigan State University, 1981.

Contributor to economic journals and *Annals of the American Academy of Political and Social Science.* Member of editorial board of *Business History Review,* 1965-68.

WORK IN PROGRESS: A regional history of the United States— an analysis of differing patterns of economic development.

* * *

SON OF THE SOIL
See FLETCHER, J(oseph) S(mith)

SOPER, Donald Oliver   1903-

PERSONAL: Born January 31, 1903, in London, England; son of Ernest Frankham and Caroline Amelia (Pilcher) Soper; married Marie Gertrude Dean, 1929; children: Anne Soper Horn, Bridget Soper Kemmis, Judith Soper Jenkins, Caroline. *Education:* Attended St. Catharine's College, Cambridge, Wesley House, Cambridge, and University of London. *Office:* West London Mission, Kingsway Hall, Kingsway, London WC2B 6TA, England.

CAREER: Ordained Methodist minister; minister at Methodist missions in London, England, 1926-36; West London Mission, London, superintendent minister, 1936-78. Honorary fellow of St. Catharine's College, Cambridge. President of League Against Cruel Sports; chairman of Shelter, 1974-77; alderman of London County Council and Greater London Council, 1958-65. President of Methodist conference, 1953. *Awards, honors:* Created Baron of Kingsway, 1965.

WRITINGS: Christianity and Its Critics, Hodder & Stoughton, 1937; *The Advocacy of the Gospel,* Abingdon, 1961; *Christian Politics: An Introduction,* Epworth Press, 1977.

Also author of *Popular Fallacies About the Christian Faith, Will Christianity Work?, Practical Christianity Today, Questions and Answers in Ceylon, It Is Hard to Work for God, Tower Hill 12:30, Aflame With Faith, Christ on Tower Hill, Question Time on Tower Hill, Answer Time on Tower Hill, Children's Prayer Time,* and *All His Grace.*

* * *

SOUTHGATE, Vera

PERSONAL: Born in Durham, England; married Douglas Booth, December 14, 1961. *Education:* Attended Neville's Cross College, and University of Birmingham, 1949-56. *Home and office:* 3 Mere Ct., Chester Rd., Mere, Cheshire WA16 6LQ, England.

CAREER: Writer and lecturer on the teaching of reading and author of children's books. School teacher until 1949; Remedial Education Service, Worcester, England, director, 1954-60; University of Manchester, Manchester, England, lecturer in curriculum development, 1960-72, senior lecturer in education, 1972-79. Member of Bullock Committee (Committee of Inquiry Into Reading and the Use of English), 1972-74; director of Schools Council research project, Extending Beginning Reading, 1973-77. *Member:* International Reading Association, United Kingdom Reading Association (founding member; president, 1970-71). *Awards, honors:* Research award from United Kingdom Reading Association, 1982, for best piece of reading research published in the United Kingdom in 1981.

WRITINGS: (With John Havenhand) *Sounds and Words,* six books, University of London Press, 1960; (with Havenhand) *The Fireman* (juvenile; illustrated by John Berry), Ladybird Books, 1962; (with Havenhand) *The Policeman* (juvenile; illustrated by Berry), Ladybird Books, 1962; (with Havenhand) *The Nurse* (juvenile; illustrated by Berry), Ladybird Books, 1963; (with Havenhand) *Penny the Poodle* (juvenile; illustrated by Patricia McGrogan), E. J. Arnold, 1964; *The Story of Cricket* (juvenile; illustrated by Jack Matthew), Ladybird Books, 1964; *The Story of Football* (juvenile; illustrated by Matthew), Ladybird Books, 1964; *The Postman and the Postal Service* (juvenile; illustrated by Berry), Ladybird Books, 1965; (with

Francis W. Warburton) *i.t.a.: An Independent Evaluation*, J. Murray, 1969; *i.t.a.: What Is the Evidence? A Book for Parents and Teachers*, J. Murray, 1970; (with Geoffrey R. Roberts) *Reading: Which Approach?*, University of London Press, 1970; *Beginning Reading*, University of London Press, 1972; (editor) *Literacy at All Levels: Proceedings of the Eighth Annual Study Conference of the United Kingdom Reading Association*, Ward, Lock, 1972; *Extending Beginning Reading*, Heinemann, 1981.

Adaptations; all for children: *Cinderella* (illustrated by Eric Winter), Ladybird Books, 1964; *Pancake Tuesday* (illustrated by A. Saul), E. J. Arnold, 1964; *Jack and the Beanstalk* (illustrated by Winter), Ladybird Books, 1965; *The Elves and the Shoemaker* (illustrated by Robert Lumley), Ladybird Books, 1965; *Sleeping Beauty* (illustrated by Winter), Ladybird Books, 1965; *The Three Little Pigs* (illustrated by Lumley), Ladybird Books, 1965; *Dick Whittington and His Cat*, Ladybird Books, 1966; *The Gingerbread Boy* (illustrated by Lumley), Ladybird Books, 1966; *Little Red Hen*, Ladybird Books, 1966; *Second Book of Nursery Rhymes*, Ladybird Books, 1966; *Puss in Boots*, Ladybird Books, 1967; *Beauty and the Beast* (illustrated by Winter), Ladybird Books, 1968; *Rapunzel*, Merry Thoughts, 1968; *Rumpelstiltskin*, Merry Thoughts, 1968; *Sly Fox and the Little Red Hen*, Merry Thoughts, 1968; *Three Billy Goats Gruff*, Merry Thoughts, 1968; *Chicken Licken*, Ladybird Books, 1969; *The Enormous Turnip* (illustrated by Lumley), Ladybird Books, 1970; *Goldilocks and the Three Bears* (illustrated by Winter), Ladybird Books, 1971; *The Magic Porridge Pot* (illustrated by Lumley), 1971; *The Big Pancake*, Ladybird Books, 1972; *Little Red Riding Hood* (illustrated by Lumley), Ladybird Books, 1972; *The Old Woman and Her Pig* (illustrated by Lumley), Ladybird Books, 1973; *The Princess and the Frog* (illustrated by Capaldi), Ladybird Books, 1973; *The Musicians of Bremen* (illustrated by Lumley and Berry), Ladybird Books, 1974; *The Princess and the Pea*, Ladybird Books, 1979; *Snow White and Rose Red*, Ladybird Books, 1979; *Wolf and the Seven Little Kids*, Ladybird Books, 1979; *Beauty and the Beast* (illustrated by Robert Ayton), Ladybird Books, 1980; *Snow White and the Seven Dwarfs*, Ladybird Books, 1980.

Contributor: J. E. Merritt, editor, *Reading and the Curriculum*, Ward, Lock, 1971; M. Clark and A. Milne, editors, *Reading and Related Skills*, Ward, Lock, 1973; D. Moyle, editor, *Reading: What of the Future?*, Ward, Lock, 1974; A. Cashdan, editor, *The Content of Reading*, Ward, Lock, 1976; (with H. Arnold and S. Johnson) E. Hunter-Grundin and H. U. Grundin, editors, *Reading: Implementing the Bullock Report*, Ward, Lock, 1978; (with Johnson) G. Bray and T. Pugh, editors, *The Reading Connection*, Ward, Lock, 1980; L. O. Ollila, editor, *Beginning Reading Instruction in Different Countries*, International Reading Association, 1981; A. Henry, editor, *Teaching Reading: The Key Issues*, Heinemann.

Author of "Star" series, twenty-five volumes, Macmillan, 1981. Also author of the *Southgate Group Reading Tests*, 1959-62; editorial consultant, *Education Three to Thirteen* (journal), beginning in 1971. Contributor to professional journals, including *British Journal of Educational Psychology*, *Educational Research*, *Educational Review*, and *Reading Research Quarterly*.

*   *   *

SPARKS, James Allen 1933-

PERSONAL: Born May 31, 1933, in Mays Lick, Ky.; son of Shirley Lee (a factory worker) and Lillie Mae (a teacher; maiden name, Snyder) Sparks; married Pauline L. Zahrte, August 13, 1955; children: Elizabeth Carole. *Education:* Transylvania College (now University), B.A., 1955; Pittsburg Theological Seminary, M.Div., 1958; University of Wisconsin—Madison, M.S., 1972. *Politics:* "The party out of office." *Office:* Extension, University of Wisconsin—Madison, 610 Langdon St., Madison, Wis. 53706.

CAREER: Ordained Presbyterian minister, 1958; pastor of Presbyterian churches in Sussex, Wis., 1958-63, and Madison, Wis., 1964-73; University of Wisconsin—Madison, Extension, mental health specialist, 1973-77, assistant professor, 1977-81, associate professor of mental health, 1981—. *Military service:* U.S. Navy, chaplain, 1957. *Member:* Society for the Advancement of Continuing Education for Ministry (member of board of directors, 1971-73, 1979-81). *Awards, honors:* Creativity award from National University Extension Association, 1979, for workshops on handling criticism; certificate of merit from Council for Wisconsin Writers, Inc., 1980, for *Friendship After Forty*.

WRITINGS: *Potshots at the Preacher*, Abingdon, 1977; *Friendship After Forty*, Abington, 1980; *Living the Bad Days: Why They Come and How to Survive*, Abingdon, 1982. Author of "Learning in the 80's," a monthly column in *Church Management: The Clergy Journal*.

SIDELIGHTS: "Writing, teaching, professing, or otherwise fiddling with people's prejudices and entrenched ideas invites criticism," Sparks told *CA*. "Since 1977 I have made a career of learning and teaching how to survive and grow from personal and professional criticism. It's a subject that most of us know intimately, but few handle well and even fewer are willing to admit openly how much it really hurts.

"*Potshots at the Preacher* is about criticism in religious organizations; *Friendship After Forty* includes a chapter on criticism among friends; and *Living the Bad Days* offers a way through the frustration and resentment that can lead to criticism. Learning and growing are painful, but I believe the writer and artist (vulnerable to reviews and rejection) should invite criticism openly. Nevertheless, I brooded for days when one critic of my friendship book advised readers to go to the zoo instead of the bookstore. 'There they can talk about the baboons,' she said, 'and watch the gorilla watching them—that is the stuff friendships are made of.'

"I was hurt and angry at such an insensitive and callous review by an obviously biased and stupid assistant professor. 'Probably trying to make points with her tenure committee,' I thought. Not even a certificate of merit presented to me by the Council for Wisconsin Writers, Inc., can erase from my memory the pain of that one horrible review. The feeling of stopping suddenly in a high-rise elevator still passes through me as I'm reading reviews or rejection slips.

"But somewhere in that 'baboon criticism' is a perspective and some truth about my book or article. Some days I have to lick wounds and then get on with discovering what I can learn from the criticism."

*   *   *

SPECTOR, Debra 1953-

PERSONAL: Born May 12, 1953, in Long Branch, N.J.; daughter of Wallace (in business) and Mary (Bernstein) Spector; married Straw Weisman (a film industry executive), August 4, 1974; children: Erica. *Education:* Ithaca College, B.A., 1974. *Res-*

idence: Northridge, Calif. *Agent:* Stephen M. Blackwelder, J & S Literary Services, 128 Second Pl., Brooklyn, N.Y. 11231.

CAREER: Amalgamated Clothing and Textile Workers Union, New York City, staff writer, 1974-75; Magazine Management Co., New York City, managing editor, 1975-77; Ideal Publishing Co., New York City, editor, 1977-78; *Sassy* (magazine), New York City, managing editor and advice columnist, 1978-79; Macmillan Publishing Co., Inc., New York City, copy editor, researcher, and writer for *Collier's Encyclopedia Yearbook,* 1979-80; Cloverdale Press, New York City, member of editorial staff, 1981-82; free-lance writer, 1982—.

WRITINGS—Novels for young adults: *Night of the Prom,* Bantam, 1982; *Too Close for Comfort,* Bantam, 1983; *First Love,* Bantam, 1983; *Magic Moments,* Bantam, 1983. Contributor to *Worldmark's Encyclopedia of the States.*

WORK IN PROGRESS: A young adult novel.

SIDELIGHTS: Spector told *CA:* "Writing juvenile novels is a natural outgrowth of my years as an editor of teen-oriented publications. Because my books appeal primarily to impressionable teen and pre-teen girls, I feel a responsibility to show them strong role models. Although the stories are purposely on the light side, my heroines are confident, career-minded girls who take responsibility for their own lives. If I've been able to show at least one reader that she doesn't have to be a victim or to find her self-worth only through the eyes of others, then I feel I've done my job well."

*   *   *

SPENCE, Donald P(ond) 1926-

BRIEF ENTRY: Born February 8, 1926, in New York, N.Y. American psychologist, educator, and author. A clinical psychologist since 1952, Spence worked at New York University's Research Center for Mental Health until 1973. At that time he was appointed professor of psychiatry at Rutgers University. He also taught at Stanford University. Spence wrote *Narrative Truth and Historical Truth: Meaning and Interpretation in Psychoanalysis* (Norton, 1982). He edited *The Broad Scope of Psychoanalysis: Selected Papers of Leopold Bellak* (Grune, 1967) and *Psychoanalysis and Contemporary Science* (International Universities Press, 1976). *Address:* Department of Psychiatry, School of Medicine, Rutgers University, Piscataway, N.J. 08854.

*   *   *

SPENCER, James 1932-

PERSONAL: Born December 27, 1932, in Pendleton, Ore.; son of James M. (a civil engineer) and Lona (a teacher; maiden name, Hull) Spencer; married Barbara Glenn (a motion picture and television studio hairstylist), March 30, 1968; children: Mark, Laurie, Danny. *Education:* Attended Los Angeles City College, 1953-55, and Compton Air College, 1952-56. *Politics:* Republican. *Religion:* Protestant. *Home:* 2896 East Appalachian Court, Westlake Village, Calif. 91362.

CAREER: Sales and public relations representative and engineering designer for airlines, aircraft manufacturers, and aircraft dealers, 1954—. Professional artist, 1968—. *Military service:* U.S. Navy, quartermaster, radio operator, and navigator, 1950-53; served in Korea; received Bronze Star. *Member:* Helicopter Association, Oregon Jaycees (vice-president, 1963), Puget Sound Historical Society, Los Angeles Live

Steamers (honorary member). *Awards, honors:* Art awards include first place and judge's award, Esplenade Art Show, 1970; first and second place awards, Ojai Art Association, 1971; second place award, Failart Show, 1974.

WRITINGS: (Assistant editor and contributor) Larry Jensen, *The Movie Railroads,* Darwin Publications, 1981; *The Northwest Loggers,* Volume I: *Rayonier,* Darwin Publications, 1982, Volume II: *Weyerhaueser,* 1983. Contributor to magazines, including *Model Railroader* and *NMRA Bulletin.*

WORK IN PROGRESS: *The Northwest Loggers,* Volume III: *Georgia Pacific,* publication by Darwin Publications expected in 1984, Volume IV: *LongBell Lumber,* publication by Darwin Publications expected in 1984, Volume V: *Simpson,* publication by Darwin Publications expected in 1985, Volume VI: *Donovan Corkery,* publication by Darwin Publications expected in 1986; *The Union Pacific Railroad,* Darwin, 1985; fiction (based on fact) about the Northwest logging industry.

SIDELIGHTS: Spencer wrote: "Since childhood, I have had an avid interest in railroad history, antique aircraft, and stories about the men who made history in these fields. Though many books have been written about them, they were not specific. I elected to learn about the men who did the jobs, to tell their stories, and describe each corporation individually. I wanted to provide, not just dry facts and figures, but human interest stories about the men who actually helped to build the Northwest.

"I have always been involved in painting and drawing, mostly as a result of having been lucky enough to have some talent rub off from my father, who was an illustrator. I began doing art shows of both ink drawings and oil paintings in 1968. I paint mostly in the old Dutch Masters style although I have also done many free form and modern art styles. I am currently concentrating on railroad art and do all my own covers for the railroad book series (the covers are done under the pseudonym James).

"Working on the railroad series has been most rewarding. I've met some grand old-timers and gained many friendships through the course of my research. The deaths of several of these people during the past year have saddened me, but have also given me a sense of urgency to collect as many of the survivors' stories as possible. I am now working closely with several historical societies and archive houses to preserve the photos and artifacts that I've found in my research.

"Much of my interest in the early days of railroading comes from the fact that my family was involved in the building of the West. My father was born in 1883 on the famous Dead Indian Ranch near Ashland, Oregon, which his father homesteaded around 1845. My father taught himself to be a civil engineer and surveyed many of the logging roads in the area. He and his brothers all worked for the Southern Pacific Railroad in California in its early years and when I was researching *Rayonier* I actually met a couple of old-timers who knew my father."

*   *   *

SPERBER, Philip 1944-

PERSONAL: Born February 29, 1944, in New York, N.Y.; son of Sol and Sally (Dolsky) Sperber; married Doreen Strachman, December 27, 1969; children: Shoshana, Ryan, Sara. *Education:* New Jersey Institute of Technology, B.S.E.E., 1965; University of Maryland, J.D., 1969. *Home:* 30 Normandy

Heights Rd., Convent Station, N.J. 07961. *Office:* REFAC International Ltd., 122 East 42nd St., New York, N.Y. 10168.

CAREER: Blair, Olcutt & Sperber, Washington, D.C., partner, 1968-71; Cavitron Corp., New York City, division counsel, 1971-72, manager of legal department, 1972-74, vice-president, 1974-77; International Telephone & Telegraph Corp. (ITT), Harmon Cove, N.J., group executive, 1977-79; REFAC International Ltd., New York City, general manager, 1979-81, vice-president, 1981-82, president, 1982—. Lecturer at universities.

MEMBER: International Executives Association, International Platform Association, Licensing Executives Society (trustee, 1977-79), Ultrasonic Industry Association (vice-president, 1975-77), American Institute of Chemical Engineers, Sales Executives Club, American Bar Association (chairman of Corporation, Banking, and Business Committee, 1976-78), Institute of Electrical and Electronics Engineers (senior member), American Society for Testing and Materials (section chairman, 1976-77), Association for the Advancement of Medical Instrumentation (standards industry co-chairman, 1976-77), New Jersey State Bar Association (councilman, 1976-79), New York State Bar Association (legislation committee chairman, 1975-76), New Jersey Patent Law Association (president), New Jersey Jaycees (director, 1965-66), Maryland Lions International (director, 1970-71).

AWARDS, HONORS: Award from U.S. Jaycees, 1966, for service as outstanding U.S. Jaycee; certificate from American Law Institute, 1976, for contributions to legal education; citations from New Jersey Writers Conference, 1976, for *Intellectual Property Management,* 1979, for *The Science of Business,* and 1981, for *Corporation Law Department Manual;* citation from American Marketing Association, 1977, for contributions to marketing education; award from American Arbitration Association, 1977, for service as a judge; certificate from Graduate School of Business Administration at Rutgers University, 1977, for contributions as an educator; award from American Management Associations, 1978, for contributions to management education; award from New Jersey Institute of Technology, 1981, for contributions to industry and to society in general; named Estrin Alumni Scholar by New Jersey Institute of Technology, 1981, for achievements in journalism.

WRITINGS: Intellectual Property Management: Law-Business-Strategy, two volumes, Boardman, 1974, third edition, 1982; (associate editor) Joseph L. Tramutola, editor, *Patent Manual,* Fairleigh Dickinson University Press, 1974; (contributor) Jack Stuart Ott, editor, *Les Nouvelles* (title means "The Innovations"), Licensing Executives Society, 1976; *Negotiating in Day-to-Day Business,* American Negotiating Institute, 1976; (contributor) J. C. Ross and Kenneth Ross, editors, *Products Liability of Manufacturers: Prevention and Defense,* Practicing Law Institute, 1977; (editor) *The Consumer Clearinghouse,* PDS Industries, 1977; (contributor) Robert Goldscheider, *Licensing in Foreign and Domestic Operations,* Boardman, 1978; *The Science of Business Negotiation,* Pilot Books, 1979; (editor and contributor) *Corporation Law Department Manual,* American Bar Association, 1980; (contributor) Paul D. Rheingold, editor, *Drug Litigation,* Practicing Law Institute, 1981; *Fail-Safe Business Negotiating: Strategies and Tactics for Success,* Prentice-Hall, 1983; *The Negotiating Guide Book for Attorneys,* Callaghan, in press. Editor in chief of *Jaycee News,* 1965-66, *Lion's Den,* 1970-71, *FDCL News,* 1979-80, and *NJPLA News,* 1979-80.

SIDELIGHTS: Sperber told *CA:* "The common thread linking the almost one hundred published papers and books I have written (covering the fields of law, business, technology, medicine, government, and consumerism) is my deep motivation to aid others in the intricacies of their occupations and lives in general.

"There is nothing magical about conducting fail-safe negotiation as long as one is willing to change his thinking, behavior, and actions after learning the fundamentals of prenegotiation planning, bottom-line strategy, prenegotiation maneuvers, positioning, presentation, subconscious suggestion, personality-dependent communication, proxemics, body language, power dressing, ego states, life scripts, communicating styles, negotiation tactics, techniques of obtaining acceptance, breaking deadlocks, closings, and many other considerations.

"Even a 5 percent improvement in company-wide negotiating results can produce massive dollar savings through increased morale and productivity, better advertising messages, decreased purchasing costs, smaller dealer margins, fewer lawsuits, and more sales closings."

*　　　*　　　*

SPINKS, John William Tranter　1908-

PERSONAL: Born January 1, 1908, in Methwold, England; son of John William (in business) and Sarah Jane (Tranter) Spinks; married Mary Strelioff, June 5, 1939. *Education:* King's College, London, B.Sc., 1928, Ph.D., 1930. *Religion:* Anglican. *Home:* 932 University Dr., Saskatoon, Saskatchewan, Canada S7N 0K1.

CAREER: University of Saskatchewan, Saskatoon, assistant professor, 1930-39, professor of physical chemistry, 1939-74, professor emeritus, 1974—, head of department, 1948-59, dean of graduate studies, 1949-59, president of university, 1959-74. Conducted research on spectroscopy at technical secondary school in Darmstadt, Germany, 1933-34. Member of Canadian Atomic Energy Project, 1944-45; member of Saskatchewan Oil and Gas Conservation Board, 1952—; member of Saskatchewan Research Council; past member of National Research Council, Canada Council, and Defense Research Board of Canada. *Military service:* Royal Canadian Air Force, operations research officer, 1943-44.

MEMBER: Royal Society of Canada (fellow), Chemical Institute of Canada (fellow; past president), Institute of International Affairs, American Chemical Society, Faraday Society. *Awards, honors:* Member of Order of the British Empire; D.Sc. from University of London, 1957; LL.D. from Carleton University, 1958, and Assumption College, 1962; Companion of Order of Canada, 1970.

WRITINGS: (Translator) Gerhard Herzberg, *Atomic Spectra and Atomic Structure,* Prentice-Hall, 1937, 2nd edition, Dover, 1944; (translator) Herzberg, *Molecular Spectra and Molecular Structure,* Prentice-Hall, 1939; (with Robert James Woods) *An Introduction to Radiation Chemistry,* Wiley, 1964, 2nd edition, 1976; *A Decade of Change: The University of Saskatchewan, 1959-70,* University of Saskatchewan, 1972; *Two Blades of Grass: An Autobiography of John Spinks,* Western Producer Prairie, 1980. Contributor of more than two hundred articles to scientific journals.

AVOCATIONAL INTERESTS: Archaeology, French and German literature.*

SPITTELER, Carl (Friedrich Georg) 1845-1924
(Felix Tandem)

BRIEF ENTRY: Born April 24, 1845, in Liestal, Switzerland; died December 28 (some sources say December 29), 1924, in Lucerne, Switzerland. Swiss educator, poet, and author. Educated in law and theology in Switzerland, Spitteler was a tutor for a family in Russia (now U.S.S.R.) for eight years. He returned to his Swiss homeland in 1879, and two years later he published his first work, *Prometheus und Epimetheus* (1881; translated as *Prometheus and Epimetheus,* 1931). The epic poem, which Spitteler issued under the pseudonym Felix Tandem, was virtually ignored by critics. A second volume, the prose work *Extramundana* (1883), was also published under the Tandem moniker, but Spitteler abandoned the pen name in his subsequent writings, which include *Gustav* (1892), *Lachende Wahrheiten* (1898; translated as *Laughing Truths,* 1927), and *Conrad der Leutnant* (1898). Spitteler's epic poem *Olympischer Fruehling* (title means "Olympian Spring"; 1900-1910), which was published in five parts, is widely regarded as the poet's finest work. It earned Spitteler the Nobel Prize for literature in 1919. *Biographical/critical sources: Columbia Dictionary of Modern European Literature,* Columbia University Press, 1947; *Encyclopedia of World Literature in the Twentieth Century,* updated edition, Ungar, 1967; *Twentieth-Century Literary Criticism,* Volume 11, Gale, 1983.

* * *

SPIVACK, George 1927-

BRIEF ENTRY: Born May 16, 1927, in New York, N.Y. American psychologist, educator, and author. Spivack worked as a psychologist and research director at Devereux Federation Institute for Research and Training from 1954 to 1967. He then became a professor of mental health at Hahnemann Medical College and Hospital. Spivack has also taught at Villanova University, University of Pennsylvania, Community College of Philadelphia, and Antioch University Without Walls. He co-authored *The Rorschach Index of Repressive Style* (C. C Thomas, 1964), *Social Adjustment of Young Children: A Cognitive Approach to Solving Real-Life Problems* (Jossey-Bass, 1974), *Alternative Teaching Strategies: Helping Behaviorally Troubled Children Achieve; A Guide for Teachers and Psychologists* (Research Press, 1975), *The Problem-Solving Approach to Adjustment* (Jossey-Bass, 1976), and *Problem-Solving Techniques in Childrearing* (Jossey-Bass, 1978). *Address:* Department of Mental Health Sciences, Hahnemann Medical College and Hospital, 230 North Broad St., Philadelphia, Pa. 19102.

* * *

SPOEHR, Alexander 1913-

PERSONAL: Born August 23, 1913, in Tucson, Ariz.; son of Herman Augustus and Florence (Mann) Spoehr; married Anne Harding, August 2, 1941; children: Alexander Harding, Helene Spoehr Clarke. *Education:* University of Chicago, A.B., 1934, Ph.D., 1941. *Religion:* Protestant. *Home:* 2548 Makiki Heights Dr., Honolulu, Hawaii 96822.

CAREER: Field Museum of Natural History, Chicago, Ill., assistant curator, 1940-44, curator, 1944-53; Yale University, New Haven, Conn., professor of anthropology, 1953-62; East-West Center, Honolulu, Hawaii, chancellor, 1962-63; University of Pittsburgh, Pittsburgh, Pa., professor of anthropology, 1964-78, professor emeritus, 1978—. Director of Ber-

nice P. Bishop Museum, 1953-62, member of board of trustees, 1981—; member of Pacific Science Board, 1955-61; U.S. member of South Pacific Commission, 1957-60; member of National Science Foundation advisory committee on the social sciences, 1967-69; member of executive committee of National Research Council's Assembly of Behavioral and Social Sciences, 1972-74. *Military service:* U.S. Naval Reserve, active duty, 1942-45; became lieutenant.

MEMBER: American Anthropological Association (president, 1965), American Association for the Advancement of Science (vice-president of Section H, 1967), National Academy of Sciences, Society for Applied Anthropology, Hawaiian Academy of Science (president, 1961-62), Sigma Xi.

WRITINGS: Majuro: Village in the Marshall Islands, Field Museum of Natural History, 1949; *Saipan: The Ethnology of a War-Devastated Island,* Field Museum of Natural History, 1954; *Marianas Prehistory,* Field Museum of Natural History, 1957; *Zamboanga and Sulu: An Archaeological Approach to Ethnic Diversity,* University of Pittsburgh Press, 1973; *Protein From the Sea: Technological Change in Philippine Fisheries,* University of Pittsburgh Press, 1980. Contributor of about sixty articles to archaeology and ethnology journals. Co-editor of *Ethnology,* 1964-78.

WORK IN PROGRESS: Research on patterns of change in Southeast Asian and Pacific fisheries.

SIDELIGHTS: Spoehr told *CA:* "Anthropological writing is the normal and necessary product of field research. The immersion in the field work experience is for an anthropologist the most powerful influence on both the form and substance of his publications. I am no exception. Most of my career has been concerned with the Pacific, a preoccupation that began with World War II service in Micronesia, and which was followed by field work in the Marshalls, Marianas, and Palau. Thereafter I moved on to the Philippines. My current interest in Southeast Asian and Oceanic fisheries stems from a broader concern with how, over the centuries, the peoples of this part of the world have adapted to a maritime environment and with the changing patterns of their use (and abuse) of the resources of the sea."

* * *

STACHOW, Hasso G(ert) 1924-

PERSONAL: Born March 13, 1924, in Stettin, Germany (now Szczecin, Poland); son of Wilhelm Hermann and Locky Franziska Stachow; married wife, Birgit, June 18, 1974; children: Michael, Beate. *Education:* Educated in Berlin, East Germany. *Home:* Wessobrunner Strasse 19, 8035 Gauting, West Germany. *Agent:* Maria Pelikan, 5500 Fieldston Rd., Riverdale, N.Y. 10471. *Office:* Burda GMBH Arnulfstrasse 197, 8000 Munich 19, West Germany.

CAREER: Gruner and Jahr Publishing Co., Hamburg, West Germany, editor of *Constanze* and editor in chief of *Schoener Wohnen,* 1948-67; Axel Springer Publishing Co., Hamburg and Munich, West Germany, consulting editor in chief, 1967-69; Jahreszeiten Publishing House, Hamburg, editor in chief of *Fuer Sie* (magazine for women), 1970-72; Burda Publishing Co., Munich, editor in chief of *Freundin* (magazine for women), 1972-78, editorial director and editor in chief of *Ambiente* (international architecture and interior decoration magazine), 1979—, and *Das Haus* (house and garden magazine), 1982—. *Military service:* German Army, Infantry, 1942-45.

WRITINGS: Der Kleine Quast, Droemersche Verlagsanstalt, 1979, translated by J. Maxwell Brownjohn as *If This Be Glory,* Doubleday, 1982; *Zeit-Zuender,* Droemersche Verlagsanstalt, 1982.

WORK IN PROGRESS: Historical research on military history since 1900.

SIDELIGHTS: Stachow told *CA:* "I am a descendant of a family of traditional patriots. When in 1933 Hitler seized power my parents were just as pleased as all our friends and neighbors. They all hoped for a change in the miserable economic situation and a revival of the old Prussian virtues such as discipline, reliability, and obedience.

"At the age of nine I became a member of *Deutsches Jungvolk,* a branch of the Hitler Youth Organization, which was the beginning of a rather one-sided, narrow-minded education. I learned that tolerance towards people with different opinions and members of foreign races and religions was something to be contempted. Five years later, in 1939, like most of my compatriots, I was a completely indoctrinated specimen of this dark era in German history.

"It was my grandfather who in my early years had spoken to me about the infamy of the so-called Versailles Peace Treaty, which followed the end of World War I. I was convinced that, above all, my country had to be freed from the obligations of that treaty. The thought that I and other youngsters might one day have to risk our lives to reach this goal did not frighten me.

"At that age, though, I had no idea what this really implied. I was too young to realize how much brightness and color, how many impressing impulses would be lost to me. Undoubtedly, many sources of art, literature, and philosophy were barred to all young Germans due to the rigidness of this education. It is the result of this upbringing that I am trying to show in my book *If This Be Glory.*

"I would not be telling the truth if I did not admit that there was also fun and joyfulness, since I did not know what was really going on. When Hitler declared war I was thoroughly convinced that I was serving a just cause. Later, as a non-commissioned officer of a 'Sturm-Bataillon,' an infantry elite unit in the Eastern theater, I was severely wounded several times. In spite of these painful experiences, I stubbornly stuck to my conviction. Consequently, the breakdown of my country was my own breakdown, too.

"After the war, as a contrast to the narrow-mindedness of my youth, I chose a profession which required perspicacity and the ability to communicate with different people of different opinions and from all walks of life. I became a journalist.

"Destruction is followed by reconstruction, and this was the main concern after World War II was over. During the preceding years we had seen peaceful regions being buried under dust and debris. Often it had been men in German uniforms who had been responsible for the devastation.

"It seemed only natural to me that later on I would develop magazines which deal with creative acts such as planning, building, and decorating a home. Also, as editor in chief of several women's magazines I addressed a readership that since Adam and Eve has been concerned with preserving the human race and society rather than destroying it.

"It was the inquisitive and critical questions of my children, of students, and of young editors that induced me to write down what happened during the decisive years of my life. As an eyewitness in *If This Be Glory,* I refrained from saying what one nowadays expects to read or hear from a former Nazi. I am saying what a then-young Nazi felt, thought, and did. My second book, *Zeit-Zuender,* on the other hand, reflects on the influence of the Third Reich up to the present time.

"I do not have any literary ambitions. I simply want the reader to understand circumstances and implications. Form follows action. Both books are novels and not documentaries because I wanted to stress that I am not only concerned with historically evident details, but also with a subjective truth, thus making both books authentic documents of personal experience."

*   *   *

STAIRS, Gordon
See AUSTIN, Mary (Hunter)

*   *   *

STANGER, Frank Bateman   1914-

PERSONAL: Born August 31, 1914, in Cedarville, N.J.; son of Francis Albert, Jr. (a lawyer and judge) and Sarah Rush (Bateman) Stanger; married M. Mardelle Amstutz, June 2, 1937; children: Marilyn Delle (Mrs. John Woodruff), Frank Bateman, Jr., Jane Louise. *Education:* Asbury College, A.B. (magna cum laude), 1934; Princeton Theological Seminary, Th.B., 1937; Temple University, S.T.M., 1940, S.T.D., 1942. *Politics:* Republican. *Home:* 3367 Ridgecane Rd., Lexington, Ky. 40513. *Office:* Asbury Theological Seminary, Wilmore, Ky. 40390.

CAREER: Ordained United Methodist minister, 1936; pastor of United Methodist churches in Woodruff, N.J., and Rosenhayn, N.J., both 1935-36, Aldine, N.J., 1936-38, Pedricktown, N.J., 1938-41, Woodstown, N.J., 1941-44, Haddon Heights, N.J., 1944-51, and Collingswood, N.J., 1951-59; Asbury Theological Seminary, Wilmore, Ky., professor of pastoral work and preaching, 1959—, executive vice-president of seminary, 1959-62, member of board of trustees, 1959-82, president-elect, 1961-62, president, 1962-82, president emeritus and life trustee, 1982—. Freitas Lecturer at Asbury Theological Seminary, 1956. Dean of Methodist Summer Assembly, 1943-50, president, 1950-59; president of Council of Churches of Greater Camden, N.J., 1945, and Sunday League, 1950-59. Delegate to eight world Methodist conferences; delegate to Methodist general conferences, 1956 and 1972; vice-chairman of curriculum resources committee of United Methodist Church, 1973-80.

MEMBER: Council of Reference OMS International, World Gospel Mission (former director), National Association of Evangelicals, Christian Holiness Association, Association for Professional Education for the Ministry, Wesleyan Theological Society, Evangelical Theological Society, Northeastern Jurisdictional Historical Society of the Methodist Church (president, 1956-60), Theta Phi, Rotary International (president, 1950-51). *Awards, honors:* D.D. from Philathea College, 1953; LL.D. from Houghton College, 1962; member of Kentucky Colonels, 1962; L.H.D. from Asbury College, 1970; D.S.L. from Asbury Theological Seminary, 1982.

WRITINGS: A Workman That Needeth Not to Be Ashamed, Herald Press, 1958; (editor) *The Methodist Trail in New Jersey,* New Jersey Annual Conference, 1961; (contributor) Andrew Blackwood, editor, *Special Day Sermons for Evangelicals,*

Channel Press, 1961; *The Gifts of the Spirit*, Christian Publications, 1974; *God's Healing Community*, Abingdon, 1978. Also associated with the festschrift *A Celebration of Ministry*, 1982.

Contributor to *Encyclopedia of World Methodism* and *Dictionary of Christian Ethics*. Contributing editor, 1961-82, and editor, 1978-82, of *Asbury Theological Seminary Herald*.

WORK IN PROGRESS: "Considering books on the Holy Spirit and spiritual formation."

SIDELIGHTS: Stanger told *CA:* "I have written my books on the field of healing because of the growing interest in the church's ministry of healing and because of the need for practical counsel and instruction in the area of healing. Now that I am retired I want my writing to be a continuation of my spiritual ministries. There is a great need among the rank and file of church members for instruction concerning the Holy Spirit and how to achieve spiritual maturity."

*   *   *

STANLEY, Steven M(itchell)   1941-

PERSONAL: Born November 2, 1941, in Detroit, Mich.; son of William Thomas (in business) and Mildred Elizabeth (Baker) Stanley; married Nell Gilmore (a student), October 11, 1969. *Education:* Princeton University, A.B. (summa cum laude), 1963; Yale University, Ph.D., 1968. *Home:* 1110 Bellemore Rd., Baltimore, Md. 21210. *Office:* Department of Earth and Planetary Sciences, Johns Hopkins University, Baltimore, Md. 21218.

CAREER: University of Rochester, Rochester, N.Y., assistant professor of paleontology, 1967-69; Johns Hopkins University, Baltimore, Md., assistant professor, 1969-71, associate professor, 1971-74, professor of paleobiology, 1974—. *Member:* Geological Society of America, Paleontological Society, Society for the Study of Evolution. *Awards, honors:* Outstanding Paper Award from *Journal of Paleontology*, 1972; named outstanding young scientist of the year in Maryland by Maryland Academy of Sciences, 1973; Charles Schuchert Award from Paleontological Society, 1977; American Book Award nominee in science category for *The New Evolutionary Timetable: Fossils, Genes, and the Origin of Species*, 1982.

WRITINGS: Relation of Shell Form to Life Habits of the Bivalvia (Mollusca), Geological Society of America, 1970; (with David M. Raup) *Principles of Paleontology*, W. H. Freeman, 1971, 2nd edition, 1978; *Macroevolution: Pattern and Process*, illustrations by John Waller and Judy Waller, W. H. Freeman, 1979; *The New Evolutionary Timetable: Fossils, Genes, and the Origin of Species*, Basic Books, 1981. Member of editorial boards of *Evolutionary Theory*, *Paleobiology*, and *American Journal of Science*.

WORK IN PROGRESS: Studying rates and patterns of extinction; an introductory textbook on the history of the earth and its life.

SIDELIGHTS: Steven Stanley's *The New Evolutionary Timetable* provides the general reader with an overview of revisionist evolutionary theory. Unlike the Darwinian "gradualist" view, where change as a result of natural selection is a slow cumulative process, the "punctuational" model proposed by Stanley and other revisionists maintains that species evolve in episodic leaps. According to David M. Raup in the *American Scientist*, Stanley "makes crystal clear that there is no argument within the scientific community over *whether* evolution oc-

curred but only argument about *how* it occurred." Stanley believes "that evolution is not a continuous, gradual process but a process that works in fits and starts."

In *The New Evolutionary Timetable* Stanley reviews the history of traditional Darwinism, using the philosophical and scientific atmosphere of the time in which it arose to explain its original gradualist thrust. He follows with a discussion of the fossil record's importance to paleontology, uses recent fossil evidence to detail the revisionist scheme for the evolution of man, and finally assesses the broad social and philosophical implications of the punctuational theory of evolution.

"The book is mostly about the fossil record and as such will serve also as an excellent introduction to paleontology," Raup explained. "Stanley's principal conclusion is that Darwin's natural selection works and must have played a role in evolution but that the fossil record does not support the Darwinian idea of slow, gradual change."

James Gorman, writing for *Discover*, found *The New Evolutionary Timetable* a "demanding but provocative" work. And in *Nature*, R. D. Martin commented: "This new book attempts to present the case in terms understandable to the non-specialist. Stanley achieves his aim with considerable success, carrying the reader along with a style that is at once lively and informative. Penetrating insights abound as the arguments are presented, and frequent touches of wry humor add a special touch."

Stanley told *CA:* "I have found the writing of prose to be as satisfying an outlet for creative energy as my work in science is. In writing a book for the nonscientist, I have tried to tread the thin line between respectable scholarship and entertaining reading."

BIOGRAPHICAL/CRITICAL SOURCES: Discover, January, 1982; *American Scientist*, January-February, 1982; *Natural History*, February, 1982; *Nature*, April 8, 1982.

*   *   *

STARR, Chauncey   1912-

PERSONAL: Born April 14, 1912, in Newark, N.J.; son of Rubin and Rose (Dropkin) Starr; married Doris Evelyn Diebel; children: Ross, Ariel Starr Wooley. *Education:* Rensselaer Polytechnic Institute, B.A., 1932, Ph.D., 1935; attended Harvard University, 1935-37. *Home:* 95 Stern Lane, Atherton, Calif. 94025. *Office:* Electric Power Research Institute, 3412 Hillview Ave., P.O. Box 10412, Palo Alto, Calif. 94303.

CAREER: Massachusetts Institute of Technology, Cambridge, research associate, 1938-41; Department of the Navy, Bureau of Ships, Washington, D.C., physicist at D. W. Taylor Model Basin, 1941-42; member of radiation lab staff at University of California, 1942-43; Tennessee Eastman Corp., Oak Ridge, member of radiation lab staff, 1943-46; North American Aviation, Inc., Downey, Calif., chief of special research, 1946-49, director of atomic energy research department, 1949-55, vice-president, 1955-66, general manager of Atomics International division, 1955-60, president of division, 1960-66; University of California, Los Angeles, dean of School of Engineering and Applied Science, 1966-73; Electric Power Research Institute, Palo Alto, Calif., president, 1973-78, vice-chairman, 1978—. Adjunct professor at Stanford University, 1974—, and University of California, Los Angeles; member of council of Rockefeller University. Member of energy advisory committee of Office of Technology Assessment; member of energy subcommittee of U.S.-Israel Bi-National Advisory Council for Industrial Research and Development; member of board of advisers for science and technology of Republic of China.

MEMBER: National Academy of Engineering (past vice-president), American Nuclear Society (fellow; founding member; member of board of directors; president), American Association for the Advancement of Science (past member of board of directors), American Physical Society (fellow), American Society of Engineering Research, American Institute of Aeronautics and Astronautics, Society for Risk Analysis, Royal Swedish Academy of Engineering Sciences (foreign member), Sigma Xi, Tau Beta Pi. *Awards, honors:* D.Eng. from Rensselaer Polytechnic Institute, 1964, and Swiss Federal Institute of Technology, 1980; award from Atomic Energy Commission, 1974; Pender Award from University of Pennsylvania, 1975; officer of French Legion of Honor, 1978; Walter H. Zinn Award from American Nuclear Society, 1979; Founders' Award from Electric Power Research Institute, 1980.

WRITINGS: Economic Growth, Employment, and Energy, IPC Science and Technology Press, 1977; *The Growth of Limits,* Pergamon, 1979; *Current Issues in Energy,* Pergamon, 1979. Contributor to scientific journals. Member of editorial board of *Journal of Risk Analysis.**

*   *   *

STARRY, Donn Albert   1925-

PERSONAL: Born May 31, 1925, in New York, N.Y.; son of Don Albert (in business) and Edith (Sortor) Starry; married Leatrice Hope Gibbs, June 15, 1948; children: Michael, Paul, Melissa, Melanie. *Education:* U.S. Military Academy, B.S., 1948; George Washington University, M.S., 1966. *Religion:* Episcopalian. *Office:* Office of the Commander in Chief, U.S. Readiness Command, MacDill Air Force Base, Fla. 33608.

CAREER: U.S. Army, career officer, 1948-83. Commander of 1st Battalion, 32nd Armor in Europe, 1964, commander of 11th Armored Cavalry Regiment in Vietnam and Cambodia, 1969-70, commander of Armor Center at Fort Knox, Ky., 1973-76, commander of U.S. V Corps in Europe, 1976-77, commander of U.S. Army Training and Doctrine Command at Fort Monroe, Va., 1977-81, commander in chief of U.S. Readiness Command at MacDill Air Force Base, Fla., 1981-83; retired as general. *Member:* U.S. Armor Association.

AWARDS, HONORS—Military: Distinguished Service Medal, Distinguished Flying Cross, Air Medal, Legion of Merit, Silver Star, Bronze Star, Purple Heart, Vietnamese Order of Gallantry with palm, French Order of Merit; German Knight Commander's Cross with badge and star; Order of Merit. Other: LL.D. from St. Leo's College; D.M.S. from Norwich University.

WRITINGS: Mounted Combat in Vietnam, U.S. Government Printing Office, 1977; *Armored Combat in Vietnam,* Bobbs-Merrill, 1982. Contributor to magazines, including *Military Review, Army,* and *Armour.*

BIOGRAPHICAL/CRITICAL SOURCES: Parade, November 28, 1982; *New York Times,* November 28, 1982.

*   *   *

STAUFFER, Helen Winter   1922-

PERSONAL: Born January 4, 1922, in Mitchell, S.D.; daughter of Fred Bernhard and Lila (Erie) Winter; married Mitchell H. Stauffer, March 30, 1944; children: Susan, Sally, Robin, Melody. *Education:* Kearney State College, B.A. (magna cum laude), 1964, M.S., 1968; University of Nebraska, Ph.D., 1978. *Office:* Department of English, Kearney State College, 905 West 25th St., Kearney, Neb. 68847.

CAREER: High school English teacher in Grand Island, Neb., 1964-67; Kearney State College, Kearney, Neb., instructor, 1968-72, assistant professor, 1972-74, associate professor, 1974-76, professor of English, 1976—. *Military service:* U.S. Navy, Women Accepted for Volunteer Emergency Service (WAVES), 1942-44. *Member:* Modern Language Association of America, National Council of Teachers of English, National Education Association, Society for the Study of Midwestern Literature, Western Literature Association (president, 1980), Nebraska Council of Teachers of English, Phi Theta Kappa, Pi Delta Phi, Sigma Tau Delta, Delta Tau Kappa, Alpha Delta Kappa, Kappa Delta Pi. *Awards, honors:* Grants from Nebraska State College Research Council, 1972, 1973, 1975-76, and 1982, and from National Endowment for the Humanities, 1976; Mary Major Crawford Award from Kearney State College.

WRITINGS: (Contributor) Merrill Lewis and L. L. Lee, editors, *Women, Women Writers, and the West,* Whitston Publishing, 1980; (contributor) Fred Erisman and Richard W. Etulain, editors, *Fifty Western Writers,* Greenwood Press, 1982; *Mari Sandoz: Story Catcher of the Plains,* University of Nebraska Press, 1982; (editor with Susan J. Rosowski) *Women and Western American Literature,* Whitston Press, 1982. Contributor to journals, including *Great Plains Quarterly, Prairie Schooner,* and *Kansas Heritage.*

WORK IN PROGRESS: A study of women poets of Kearney, Nebraska, and the ways in which their subject matter, attitudes toward their work, and directions of their careers as poets compare with those of male poets.

SIDELIGHTS: Stauffer told *CA:* "My study of Sandoz began with admiration for *Crazy Horse,* her biography of the Oglala Sioux war chief who fought generals Crook and Custer in the Indian wars on the Plains in the 1870's. Her ability to recreate the man and his time was impressive; her understanding of her protagonist and his milieu suggests extensive knowledge of and sympathy for another culture than her own. As I made inquiries into Sandoz's use of sources I discovered that she had access to special information most other researchers overlooked or did not know about. In the process of locating that information and examining Sandoz's use of it, I myself became enthusiastic about Plains history, geography, and sociology. Although I appreciated Sandoz's first book, *Old Jules,* the biography of her father who was important in the settlement of the northwestern Nebraska frontier, it was not until I began the study of *Crazy Horse* and began to read Sandoz's voluminous correspondence that I appreciated the fact that Mari Sandoz had herself led an interesting life: a childhood on a violent frontier; years of frustration and near-starvation in Lincoln, Nebraska, before she published; later years of success, living in New York City, but longing always for the West.

"Although the role of women in the West was not a major issue for Sandoz (with the exception of Gulla Slogum and Miss Morissa, Sandoz's protagonists are usually male), my study of her work led me to an interest in other western women writers and, further, to other experiences of women who helped to develop the country. All too much western literature uses the old mythic plots that tend to treat the female as an adjunct to the male hero. The women's journals and diaries now being published make it clear that female heroes did and do exist, and their stories often refute the idea that there can be little interesting in a female, whether she lives only in fiction or in real life."

* * *

STEAD, Christina (Ellen) 1902-1983

OBITUARY NOTICE—See index for CA sketch: Born July 17, 1902, in Rockdale, Sydney, New South Wales, Australia; died March 31, 1983, in Sydney, Australia. Educator, novelist, and author of short stories. Although she received little recognition throughout most of her career, Stead was hailed at her death as one of the twentieth century's greatest writers. Her 1940 masterpiece, The Man Who Loved Children, was initially ignored, but upon being reissued in 1965, the novel prompted critics to compare Stead to Tolstoi, Dostoevski, and Proust. Among Stead's other novels to receive high praise from critics are House of All Nations and The Dark Places of the Heart; the latter was published in England as Cotter's England. In addition to her fourteen novels, Stead wrote numerous short stories and four novellas. Traveling intermittently, she lived in London, Paris, and the United States before returning to her native Australia in 1974. She was nominated for the Nobel Prize in Literature several times, and received many awards in her later years. Obituaries and other sources: London Times, April 7, 1983; New York Times, April 13, 1983; Newsweek, April 25, 1983; Publishers Weekly, April 29, 1983.

* * *

STEELE, Jack 1914-1980

PERSONAL: Born September 15, 1914, in North Manchester, Ind.; died of cancer, December 31, 1980, in Bennington, Vt.; son of Roscoe and Dessie (Wonderly) Steele; married Barbara Louise Lyons, September 30, 1939; children: Jeffrey L., Peter C. Education: Middlebury College, A.B., 1936; Columbia University, M.S., 1937. Residence: Bennington, Vt.

CAREER/WRITINGS: New York Herald Tribune, New York, N.Y., reporter, 1937-41, midwestern correspondent, 1941-44, served with Washington bureau, 1944-53, became assistant bureau chief; served with Scripps-Howard Newspapers' Washington bureau, 1953, became chief political writer; managing editor of Scripps-Howard Newspaper Alliance, 1967-74; editor of Scripps-Howard News Service, 1974-79. Volunteer worker with the American Heart Association. Member: National Press Club, Gridiron Club (former president and secretary). Awards, honors: Raymond Clapper Award, 1949; Sigma Delta Chi Award, 1949; Heywood Broun Award, 1951; Ernie Pyle Award, 1963.

SIDELIGHTS: Dubbed by Pulitzer Prize-winning reporter Clark R. Mollenhoff as "the father of modern investigative reporting," Jack Steele was an award-winning journalist whose career spanned forty years. President Truman himself presented Steele with the Clapper Award in 1949, commemorating Steele's series of articles exposing influence peddling in the Truman era. Steele's other honors included the 1963 Ernie Pyle Memorial Award for his coverage of the Civil Rights Movement. Racism and civil rights were subjects of major concern to Steele, who also wrote a series of articles about organizations that promoted racism in the United States. These articles were lauded by then Speaker of the House John McCormack as "one of the most constructive pieces of newspaper work I have seen in many years."

OBITUARIES: New York Times, January 2, 1981; Washington Post, January 2, 1981.*

* * *

STEELE, Wilbur Daniel 1886-1970

PERSONAL: Born March 17, 1886, in Greensboro, N.C.; died May 26, 1970, in Essex, Conn.; buried in Pleasantview Cemetery, Hanbury, Conn.; son of Wilbur Fletcher (a minister) and Rose (Wood) Steele; married Margaret Thurston, February 17, 1913 (deceased); married Norma Mitchell Talbot, January 14, 1932; children: (first marriage) Thurston (deceased), Peter. Education: University of Denver, A.B., 1907; studied at Museum of Fine Arts, Boston, Mass., 1907-08, Academie Julian, Paris, France, 1908-09, and Art Students League, 1909-10.

CAREER: Writer, 1921-70. Awards, honors: Second prize from O. Henry Award Committee, 1919, for story "For They Know Not What They Do," special award, 1921, "for maintaining highest level of merit for three years among American short story writers," shared first prize, 1925, for story "The Man Who Saw Through Heaven," first prizes, 1926, for story "Bubbles" and 1931, for story "Can't Cross Jordan"; first prize from short story contest sponsored by Harper's, 1925, for "When Hell Froze"; Litt.D. from University of Denver, 1932.

WRITINGS: Storm, Harper, 1914; Land's End and Other Stories, Harper, 1918; The Shame Dance and Other Stories, Harper, 1923; The Giant's Stair (one-act play), Appleton, 1924, reprinted, Samuel French, 1949; Isles of the Blest, Harper, 1924; The Terrible Woman and Other One-Act Plays, Appleton, 1925; Taboo, Harcourt, 1925; Urkey Island (stories), Harcourt, 1926; The Man Who Saw Through Heaven and Other Stories, Harper, 1927; Meat (novel), Harper, 1928; Tower of Sand and Other Stories, Harper, 1929.

Undertow: A Thrilling Romantic Tale of Love and Sacrifice, Jacobson Publishing, 1930; (with wife, Norma Mitchell) Post Road (two-act play; first produced on Broadway in 1934), Samuel French, 1935; Sounds of Rowlocks, Harper, 1938; That Girl From Memphis, Doubleday, 1945; The Best Stories of Wilbur Daniel Steele, Doubleday, 1946, reprinted, Greenwood Press, 1976; Diamond Wedding, Doubleday, 1950; Full Cargo: More Stories, Doubleday, 1951, reprinted, Greenwood Press, 1976; Their Town, Doubleday, 1952; The Way to the Gold (novel), Doubleday, 1955. Also author of An Arabian Marriage, and "Arab Stuff", Haldeman-Julius Co. Contributor to magazines, including Atlantic Monthly.

OBITUARIES: New York Times, May 27, 1970; Washington Post, May 28, 1970; Publishers Weekly, June 29, 1970; Books Abroad, spring, 1971.*

* * *

STEINBERG, Israel 1903(?)-1983

OBITUARY NOTICE: Born c. 1903 in Lawrence, Mass.; died of a stroke, February 2, 1983, in Phoenix, Ariz. Physician and author. Steinberg is best known for his assistance in the development of angiocardiography, a method used in the diagnosis of heart disease in adults. The widely used technique was devised with Dr. George Porter Robb in 1938 and involves taking X rays of the heart and arteries after a dye has been injected into a blood vessel. Steinberg wrote hundreds of articles on cardiovascular disease, and his book, Angiocardiography, is considered an important contribution to the field of medicine. Obituaries and other sources: *New York Times*, February 17, 1983.

* * *

STEINGOLD, Fred S(aul) 1936-

PERSONAL: Born April 16, 1936, in Highland Park, Mich.; son of Nathaniel and Rosaline Steingold; married Sarah R. Rubenstein (a project manager), January 25, 1959; children: Mark R., David M. *Education:* University of Michigan, A.B., 1957, J.D., 1960. *Home:* 3410 Andover Rd., Ann Arbor, Mich. 48105. *Office:* 320 North Main, No. 102, Ann Arbor, Mich. 48104.

CAREER: Admitted to the Bar of Michigan, 1961; Institute of Continuing Legal Education, Ann Arbor, Mich., publications editor, 1961-65; City of Ann Arbor, assistant city attorney, 1965-67, chief assistant city attorney, 1967-69; Fahrner & Steingold (law firm), Ann Arbor, partner, 1969—. *Member:* American Bar Association, American Trial Lawyers Association, State Bar of Michigan, Washtenaw County Bar Association.

WRITINGS: (Editor with John L. Etter) *Michigan Municipal Law,* Institute of Continuing Legal Education, 1980; (editor) *Michigan Basic Practice Handbook,* Institute of Continuing Legal Education, 1981; *The Practical Guide to Michigan Law,* University of Michigan Press, 1983; *Legal Master Guide for Small Business,* Prentice-Hall, 1983. Contributor to *Inc.*

SIDELIGHTS: Steingold commented: ''I enjoy translating legal topics into plain English. Although I have written both for lawyers and nonlawyers, I find it more challenging to address the latter. I plan to aim most of my future writing at lay audiences. My forte is the practical explanation of the law.

''*The Practical Guide to Michigan Law* grew out of a course I taught for the University of Michigan Center for Adult Education. It covers such topics as making a will, buying a home, obtaining compensation for an injury claim, probating a relative's estate, resolving a landlord-tenant matter, getting divorced, handling a consumer problem, defending against a criminal charge, and setting up a business. These are the subjects about which clients are most likely to consult a lawyer. In addition, there is a discussion of how the legal system works and a step-by-step tour through a typical lawsuit. A glossary defines legal terms in easy-to-understand language.

''*Legal Master Guide for Small Business* is addressed to the owners and managers of small businesses. The five main parts of the book are: Starting Your Business; Acquiring Premises for Your Business; Resolving Your Business Disputes; Handling Your Commercial Relationships; and Protecting Your Business Interests. The book is designed to help the reader understand the legal system, avoid legal pitfalls, and use a lawyer more efficiently.''

* * *

STEPHENS, Henrietta Henkle 1909-1983
(Henrietta Buckmaster)

OBITUARY NOTICE—See index for *CA* sketch: Born in 1909 in Cleveland, Ohio; died after a short illness, April 26, 1983, in Chestnut Hill, Mass. Editor and author. Henrietta Stephens, who wrote under the name Henrietta Buckmaster, is best remembered for her highly acclaimed nonfiction work *Let My People Go: The Story of the Underground Railroad and the*

Growth of the Abolition Movement. Among her numerous other writings are the novels *Deep River* and *Fire in the Heart* and several children's books, including *Flight to Freedom: The Story of the Underground Railroad* and *Women Who Shaped History.* Buckmaster joined the staff of the *Christian Science Monitor* in 1973, where she worked as editor of the paper's fine arts and literary page. Obituaries and other sources: *New York Times,* April 27, 1983.

* * *

STEPHENSON, Richard M(anning) 1918-

PERSONAL: Born December 31, 1918, in Algona, Iowa; son of John Harry (a service station manager) and Lenore (Sheffield) Stephenson; married Phyllis Jean Sullivan (a teacher), June 4, 1949; children: Jill, Robert, David. *Education:* University of California, Los Angeles, B.A. (with honors), 1941; Columbia University, M.A., 1948, Ph.D., 1956. *Home:* 122 Woodland Rd., Piscataway, N.J. 08854. *Office:* Department of Sociology, Rutgers University, New Brunswick, N.J. 08903.

CAREER: Rutgers University, Douglass College, New Brunswick, N.J., instructor, 1948-52, assistant professor, 1952-57, associate professor, 1957-62, professor of sociology, 1962—, chairman of department, 1962-70. *Military service:* U.S. Army, Medical Corps, 1942-45; became technical sergeant. *Member:* American Association of University Professors, American Sociological Association, Danforth Association (chairman of regional selection committee, l967-70), Eastern Sociological Society. *Awards, honors:* Grants from Society for the Investigation of Human Ecology, 1956-57, New York Diabetes Society, 1958, New Jersey Department of Labor and Industry, 1962, Ford Foundation, 1963-66, National Institute of Mental Health, 1965-66, and Dupont Endowment, Crystal Trust, and Delaware Agency to Reduce Crime, all 1968—; Danforth associate, 1960—.

WRITINGS: (With Harry C. Bredemeier) *The Analysis of Social Systems,* Holt, 1962; (contributor) Norman Bruce Johnston, Leonard Savitz, and Marvin E. Wolfgang, editors, *The Sociology of Punishment and Corrections,* 2nd edition, Wiley, 1970; (contributor) Peter Garabedian and Don C. Gibbons, editors, *Becoming Delinquent,* Aldine, 1970; (with Frank R. Scarpitti) *Group Interaction as Therapy: The Use of the Small Group in Corrections,* Greenwood Press, 1974. Contributor to sociology journals and *Annals of the American Academy of Political and Social Science.*

SIDELIGHTS: Stephenson commented: ''My areas of scholarly interest are the sociology of deviant behavior and criminology; I have also worked on social stratification. My research has been directed to the study of delinquency. This has involved an evaluative study of a special correctional facility involving guided group interaction and community studies of delinquency.

''I have also worked in the general area of the analysis of deviance. This is a relatively new field in sociology, and my main interests are in developing conceptual and theoretical dimensions in this area. Since it is new, there is a need for systemization and integration of recent analysis and research directed to testing various hypotheses that have been set forth. I am interested in deviance and the specific deviance of crime because it offers the opportunity to explore more general theory concerning human behavior.

''*The Analysis of Social Systems* was an attempt to set forth for the student a systematic, analytical overview of sociology, which I felt was much needed at the time. I believe there is a continuing need to wed theory to research and to develop, in the process, a more systematic sociology. I have attempted to follow this practice in my own work.''

AVOCATIONAL INTERESTS: Travel (Europe, Japan, the Caribbean), sky diving, scuba diving.

* * *

STEVENS, Edmund William   1910-

PERSONAL: Born July 22, 1910, in Denver, Colo.; son of Edmund William (an oculist) and Florence (Ballance) Stevens; married Nina Andreyevna Bondarenko, May 14, 1935; children: Edmund William, Jr., Anastasia (Marchesa Ferrari d'Collesape). *Education:* Columbia University, B.A., 1932, graduate study, 1932-33; attended Moscow University, 1934. *Religion:* Episcopalian. *Home and office:* 66 Barrow St., New York, N.Y. 10014; and Ulitsa Ryleeva 11, Moscow, U.S.S.R.

CAREER: Translator for publishing house in Moscow, U.S.S.R., 1935-37; correspondent for *Manchester Guardian*, Manchester, England, and *Daily Herald*, London, England, 1937-39; *Christian Science Monitor*, Boston, Mass., war correspondent, 1939-44, Moscow correspondent, 1946-49, chief of Mediterranean News Bureau in Rome, Italy, 1949-55; *Look*, New York City, Moscow correspondent, 1955-58; Time, Inc., New York City, chief of Moscow Bureau, 1958-63; correspondent for Times Newspapers Ltd., 1963—. Writer for Reuters agency, summer, 1938; special correspondent for *Newsday*, 1963, and *Saturday Evening Post*, 1963-68; correspondent for *London Times*, 1964, 1973. Reporter for NBC-Radio, 1971.

MEMBER: Overseas Press Club of America, Associazione della Stampa Estera, Delta Phi. *Awards, honors:* Africa Star; citation from U.S. War Department, 1943; Pulitzer Prize for international reporting, 1950, for work at *Christian Science Monitor;* citation from Overseas Press Club of America, 1956-58; George Polk Memorial Award from Long Island University, 1958.

WRITINGS: Russia Is No Riddle, Greenberg, 1945; *This Is Russia: Uncensored*, Didier, 1950; *North African Powder Keg*, Coward, 1955; (translator from French) Paul Nizan, *Antoine Bloyne*, Monthly Review Press, 1974. Author of syndicated column in *Newsday*, 1963-68.

SIDELIGHTS: As a war correspondent, Stevens reported from Latvia, Romania, and the U.S.S.R. He covered the Finnish war, the invasion of Norway, and the war between Italy and Greece from 1940 to 1941. He was with the Ethiopian campaign in 1941 and with the British Army in the Western Desert from 1942 to 1943. Stevens was a special adviser to General Russell Maxwell in Moscow and traveled throughout the Middle East with Wendell Wilkie in 1942.

* * *

STEVENSON, David   1942-

PERSONAL: Born April 30, 1942, in Largs, Ayrshire, Scotland; son of Alan Carruth and Sheila (Steven) Stevenson; married Wendy B. McLeod; children: Ian McLeod, Neil Alan. *Education:* Trinity College, Dublin, B.A., 1966; University of Glasgow, Ph.D., 1970. *Office:* Department of History, University of Aberdeen, Aberdeen AB9 2UB, Scotland.

CAREER: University of Aberdeen, Aberdeen, Scotland, lecturer, 1970-78, senior lecturer in history, 1978—. *Member:* Royal Historical Society (fellow, 1978), Scottish History So-

ciety (honorary secretary, 1976—). *Awards, honors:* Hume Brown Senior Prize, 1974, for *The Scottish Revolution: 1637-1644*.

WRITINGS: The Scottish Revolution, 1637-1644: The Triumph of the Covenanters, Newton Abbot: David and Charles, 1973; *Revolution and Counter-Revolution in Scotland: 1644-1651*, Royal Historical Society, 1977; *Alasdair MacColla and the Highland Problem in the Seventeenth Century*, John Donald, Ltd., 1980; *Scottish Covenanters and Irish Confederates*, Ulster Historical Foundation, 1981; *The Government of Scotland Under the Covenanters*, Scottish Historical Society, 1982. Editor of *Northern Scotland*, 1980—.

SIDELIGHTS: Stevenson's first book, *The Scottish Revolution, 1637-1644*, covers the political history of Scotland in the years immediately before the Scottish Covenant became involved in the English civil war. It ends with the Scottish troops marching across the English border to aid Parliament in opposition to King Charles I of England. Where *The Scottish Revolution* ends, its sequel, *Revolution and Counter-Revolution*, begins. In the second book Stevenson records the low points in Scottish and English history and the defeats and failures that led to the eventual conquest of Scotland by Cromwell in the second half of the English Civil War.

Edward Playfair, who reviewed both *The Scottish Revolution* and *Revolution and Counter-Revolution* for the *Times Literary Supplement*, lauded Stevenson's attempts to write ''pure political history, with only so much of personalities, battles and religion as is needed to make the events clear.'' An earlier *Times Literary Supplement* review called *The Scottish Revolution* ''an absorbing and excellent book'' and a ''very full account of the rise of the Covenanters.'' And of *Revolution and Counter-Revolution* Playfair wrote, ''this is a remarkably interesting, well-analysed and well-written history.''

BIOGRAPHICAL/CRITICAL SOURCES: Times Literary Supplement, March 8, 1974, September 8, 1978.

* * *

STILGOE, John R.

PERSONAL—Education: Received A.B. from Boston University, M.A. from Purdue University, and Ph.D. from Harvard University. *Office:* Department of Visual and Environmental Studies, Harvard University, 24 Quincy St., Cambridge, Mass. 02138.

CAREER: Professor of visual and environmental studies at Harvard University, Cambridge, Mass.; writer. *Member:* American Society for Environmental History, American Studies Association. *Awards, honors:* Francis Parkman Prize from Society of American Historians, 1982, for *Common Landscape of America: 1580-1845*.

WRITINGS: Common Landscape of America: 1580-1845, Yale University Press, 1982; *Metropolitan Corridor: Railroads and the American Scene*, Yale University Press, 1983.

WORK IN PROGRESS: ''A history of American attitudes toward the ocean edge.''

SIDELIGHTS: In *Common Landscape of Architecture: 1580-1845*, John R. Stilgoe, a professor of landscape architecture, explains the process by which European settlers landscaped the American wilderness with farms, mines, mills, fences, and roads. Employing their medieval European traditions, settlers imitated and adapted the styles of their homelands to produce what Stilgoe termed a landscape that "objectified common sense." Though overwhelmed by the vastness of North America, colonists nevertheless developed four distinct styles of landscapes. Cellular towns dominated New England while the *estencion* was popular in the Spanish Southwest. The tidewater design spread into Virginia, and Pennsylvania and New York established "a uniquely different landscape," the forerunner of space utilization patterns in the West. Around 1790, these traditional approaches yielded to national designs, engineered and promoted by the federal government and to new spatial forms in the western "grid country."

According to Carl Bridenbaugh's *Times Literary Supplement* review, Stilgoe's book is a seminal work on landscape in America. The critic praised the author for his accurate and detailed portrayal of American farm life, noting the importance of often neglected farm lore. "*Common Landscape of America 1580-1845* is a strikingly original book, unusually ambitious in scope," Bridenbaugh claimed. Continuing his applause, the critic concluded his review with the assertion that "*Common Landscape of America* is a massively researched and important introduction to a new view of the development of America." Moreover, a reviewer for the *New Yorker* maintained that the work "will change the way its readers look about them."

Stilgoe told *CA:* "Personal privacy is the foundation stone of American liberty."

BIOGRAPHICAL/CRITICAL SOURCES: New Yorker, August 23, 1982; *Choice*, October, 1982; *Times Literary Supplement*, October 8, 1982; *Landscape Journal*, spring, 1983.

* * *

STOCKANES, Anthony E(dward)   1935-

PERSONAL: Born January 18, 1935, in Chicago, Ill.; son of Edward (a steelworker) and Ann (Mureiko) Stockanes; married Harriet Price (a copyright specialist), January 4, 1966. *Education:* University of Illinois, B.A., 1976. *Home:* 2201 Vermont Ave., Urbana, Ill. 61801.

CAREER: Owner of an apartment building and breeder of dogs. Writer.

WRITINGS: Ladies Who Knit for A Living (short stories), University of Illinois Press, 1981.

SIDELIGHTS: A *Virginia Quarterly Review* critic observed that Stockanes deals with familiar characters and situations in *Ladies Who Knit for A Living*, writing "simply and believably about ordinary emotions and people." A *North American Review* critic, on the other hand, contended that the stories "question and extend the possibilities of the traditional story form." Both reviewers agreed, however, on the quality of Stockanes's writing. "Stockanes is a competent, humane craftsman," the *Virginia Quarterly Review* praised, and the *North American Review* lauded his "meaningful fiction."

BIOGRAPHICAL/CRTITICAL SOURCES: North American Review, June, 1982; *New England Review*, spring, 1982; *Virginia Quarterly Review*, spring, 1982.

* * *

STODDARD, Whitney Snow   1913-

PERSONAL: Born March 25, 1913, in Greenfield, Mass.; son of Charles Nowell and Elizabeth (Snow) Stoddard; married Jean Wilson Read, June 19, 1936; children: Brooks W., Eliz-

abeth Stoddard Phillips, Lawrence. *Education:* Williams College, A.B., 1935; Harvard University, A.M., 1938, Ph.D., 1941. *Office:* Department of Art, Williams College, Williamstown, Mass. 01267.

CAREER: Williams College, Williamstown, Mass., instructor, 1938-42, assistant professor, 1942-48, associate professor, 1948-54, professor of history of art, 1954—, chairman of department of art, 1973—. Mathews Lecturer at Metropolitan Museum of Art, 1967; vice-president of International Center for Medieval Art, 1971-73. *Military service:* U.S. Naval Reserve; became lieutenant. *Member:* College Art Association of America, Mediaeval Academy of America, Society of Architectural Historians. *Awards, honors:* Fulbright grant for France, 1954.

WRITINGS: The West Portals of Saint Denis and Chartres, Harvard University Press, 1952, revised edition, Norton, 1983; *Adventure in Architecture*, Longmans, Green, 1958; *Monastery and Cathedral in France*, Wesleyan University Press, 1962, reprinted as *Art and Architecture in Medieval France*, Harper, 1973; *The Facade of Saint-Gilles-du-Gard*, Wesleyan University Press, 1973; (co-editor) *Macmillan Biography of Architects*, Macmillan, 1982.

* * *

STOETZER, O(tto) Carlos   1921-

PERSONAL: Born June 28, 1921, in Buenos Aires, Argentina; came to United States in 1950; son of Carlos G. (a banker) and Francisca (Hoech) Stoetzer; married Rona Geib, October 29, 1955; children: Anthony, Erik. *Education:* Neuburg-Oberrealschule, B.A., 1938; University of Perugia, certificate, 1942; University of Debrecen, certificate, 1943; University of Freiburg, Dr.jur., 1945; Georgetown University, Ph.D., 1961. *Politics:* Independent. *Religion:* Roman Catholic. *Home:* 1 Rocky Brook Rd., Wilton, Conn. 06897. *Office:* Department of History, Fordham University, Bronx, N.Y. 10458.

CAREER: Pan American Union, Organization of American States (OAS), Washington, D.C., assistant in cultural department, 1950-51, assistant in philatelic division, 1951-53, assistant in travel division, 1953-56, secretary in the Office of the General Assembly, Meeting of Consultation and Permanent Council of the OAS, 1955-61, acting secretary of the Inter-American Institute of Agricultural Sciences, 1958-61; Manhattanville College, Purchase, N.Y., associate professor, 1961-63; Institute for Latin American Studies, Hamburg, Germany, chief of history and law division, 1963-64; Manhattanville College, Purchase, associate professor of political science, 1964-66; Fordham University, Bronx, N.Y., associate professor, 1966-79, professor of history, 1980—. Alliance Francaise du Comte de Fairfield, vice-president, 1969-70, president, 1970-71. Honorary professor at Universidad del Salvador, Buenos Aires, 1982.

MEMBER: Society for Iberian and Latin American Thought (president, 1977-79), Latin American Studies Association, Argentine Association of American Studies, Conference on Latin American History. *Awards, honors:* Knight Commander of Order of Isabella the Catholic from Spanish Government, 1959.

WRITINGS: Panamerika: Idee und Wirklichkeit—Die Organisation der Amerikanischen Staaten (title means "Pan America: Theory and Reality—The Organization of American States"), Uebersee Verlag, 1964, revised edition published as *The Organization of American States: An Introduction*, Praeger, 1965; *El pensamiento politico en la America espanola durante el periodo de la emancipacion, 1789-1825* (title means

''Political Thought in Spanish America During the Period of Emancipation, 1789-1825''), two volumes, Instituto de Estudios Politicos (Madrid), 1966; (contributor) *Idee und Wirklichkeit in Iberoamerika: Beitraege zur Politik und Geistesgeschichte* (title means ''Theory and Reality in Latin America: Studies in the Field of Politics and Intellectual History''), Hoffmann & Campe (Hamburg), 1969; *Grundlagen des Spanischamerikanischen Verfassungsdenkens* (title means ''Foundation of Spanish American Constitutional Thought''), Verfassung & Recht, 1969; *Benjamin Constant and the Doctrinaire Liberal Influence in Latin America,* Verfassung & Recht, 1978; *The Scholastic Roots of the Spanish-American Revolution,* Fordham University Press, 1979; *The Krausean Impact in the Hispanic World,* Fordham University Press, in press.

Contributor of articles to *International Philosophical Quarterly* and *Inter-American Review of Bibliography/Revista Interamericana de Bibliografia,* and to Latin American studies journals in the United States and abroad.

SIDELIGHTS: Stoetzer told *CA:* ''Having been tossed around in my life from one end of the Atlantic to another (Southern Cone, Europe, United States), I developed an early interest in the interaction of the different Western cultures and civilizations, especially that of the Hispanic peoples. This also led to a fairly long association with the Organization of American States and made me aware of the significance of inter-American relations. Over the past three decades I have become increasingly interested in the flow of ideas from the Old World to Latin America and have worked since the 1950's on my main subject: the complex picture of political thought and ideology during the period of independence of Latin America. I am especially interested in the controversial concept of whether the Spanish-American Revolution was an echo of the American and French Revolutions and thus linked to the foreign impact of the Enlightenment, or whether, as I have tried to show, it was a purely Spanish family affair and thus intimately connected with Scholastic philosophy, especially the Late Scholastic version of Spain's Golden Century.

''Finally, in my writings I try to awaken an interest in the Hispanic world and especially a deeper understanding of its culture, thought, and history, so that both North Americans and non-Hispanic Europeans realize that the Hispanic world is a full member of the Western world and wishes to be treated as such.''

*   *   *

STOTT, Douglas W(ayne) 1948-

PERSONAL: Born February 24, 1948, in Atlanta, Ga.; son of Ernest Eugene and Mildred (Schenker) Stott; married Barbara Wojhoski, April 30, 1982. *Education:* Davidson College, A.B., 1970; Northwestern University, M.A., 1971, Ph.D., 1976; Candler School of Theology, M.Th., 1979. *Home:* Hansenhaeuserweg 11, D-3550 Marburg, West Germany.

CAREER: Northwestern University, Evanston, Ill., associate instructor in German, 1973-74; Emory University, Atlanta, Ga., instructor in German, 1979-81; Davidson College, Marburg, West Germany, resident director, 1981—. *Member:* Modern Language Association of America, Stefan George Society, Hoelderlin Society.

WRITINGS—Translator: Hans-Juergen Hermisson and Eduard Lohse, *Faith,* Abingdon, 1981; Klaus Seybold and Ulrich B. Mueller, *Sickness and Healing,* Abingdon, 1981; Erhard Gerstenberger and Wolfgang Schrage, *Woman and Man,* Abing-

don, 1981; Hans van der Geest, *Presence in the Pulpit: The Impact of Personality in Preaching,* John Knox, 1981; Claus Westermann, *Elements of Old Testament Theology,* John Knox, 1982; Walter Zimmerli, *I Am Yahweh,* John Knox, 1982; Adrienne von Speyr, *Confession,* Ignatius Press, 1983.

WORK IN PROGRESS: Hoelderlin, Psalmen, Prophetie (title means ''Hoelderlin, Psalms, Prophecy''), a work applying biblical exegetical methodology (specifically, form criticism) to a nonbiblical, late eighteenth-century German poet, Hoelderlin, who himself had intense religious, even visionary proclivities; research for a popular history of the early German romantic circle (1790-1815: the Schlegel brothers, Novalis, Schelling, Tieck, Schleiermacher, Rahel von Varnhagen and company) with emphasis on the personal relationships, literary salons, and artistic development as revealed not only in the literary works themselves, but above all in their personal correspondence, diaries, and memoirs.

SIDELIGHTS: Stott wrote: ''Although I have been translating only since the late seventies, I have seen quickly the pressures placed on translators in today's literature. The specialized terminology with which one must be familiar poses an ongoing challenge to anyone translating recent material. It is, I suspect, difficult for the lay person to appreciate the time and effort that are often put into finding a single word or phrase. My own favorite experience led me through three cross-references to an obscure passage in the Babylonian Talmud, where I found the terms I needed for a rabbinic potion-formula against hemorrhaging. Now I know what 'fenugreek' is in four languages.

''Since translators in general get very little formal recognition, the value of including them in a publication like *CA* is that a reader can determine what other work a translator has done in a given field; for example, in my own case, in theological studies. How often have I myself—both in my work as a translator and in German and theological studies—wanted that kind of information on a translator!

''As far as my projected works are concerned, the piece on the poet Hoelderlin will be a somewhat esoteric piece of scholarship in the traditional sense. The work on the German romantic circle, however, will present a rather bizarre group of writers, intellectuals, philosophers, para-scientists, eccentrics, and *femmes fatales* to the American reading public at large. I have spent literally years reading and studying the 'works' of these people in the narrower sense, and it has slowly dawned upon me what fascinating, entertaining reading their lives would make.

''My other languages are Latin, French, classical and biblical Greek, and soon classical Hebrew, because of my work on the Psalms.''

*   *   *

STRACZYNSKI, J(oseph) Michael 1954-

PERSONAL: Born July 17, 1954, in Paterson, N.J.; son of Charles (a manual laborer) and Evelyn (Pate) Straczynski; married Kathryn May Drennan (a writer), 1983. *Education:* Attended Kankakee Community College, 1972-73, and Richland College, 1973; Southwestern College, A.A., 1975; San Diego State University, B.A., 1978. *Residence:* Glendale, Calif. *Agent:* Ilse Lahn, Paul Kohner Agency, Inc., 9169 Sunset Blvd., Los Angeles, Calif. 90069; and Valerie Smith, Virginia Kidd Agency, 538 East Harford St., Milford, Pa. 18337.

CAREER: San Diego State University, San Diego, Calif., personal and academic counselor, 1975-77; *Racquetball News,* El

Cajon, Calif., editor in chief, 1978; *Daily Californian*, El Cajon, special correspondent and reviewer, 1978-79; KSDO-AM Radio, San Diego, entertainment editor and theatre and film reviewer, 1979-80; Airstage Radiodrama Productions, San Diego, artistic director and resident writer, producer, director, workshop instructor, and facilitator, 1980-81; *Writer's Digest*, Cincinnati, Ohio, contributing editor and author of column, "Scripts," 1982—. Instructor at Grossmont Junior College, 1978, and San Diego State University, 1979. *Member:* Writers Guild of America West, Psi Chi (life member).

WRITINGS: The Complete Book of Scriptwriting (Book-of-the-Month Club selection), Writer's Digest, 1982.

Plays: "Death in Stasis" (one-act), first produced in Chula Vista, Calif., at Southwestern College, March 7, 1977; "Parting Gesture" (one-act), first produced in San Diego, Calif., at San Diego State University, May 3, 1977; *Snow White* (two-act; first produced in Chula Vista at Southwestern College, June 4, 1977), Performance Publishing, 1978; "Memos From the Other Side" (one-act), first produced in Chula Vista at Southwestern College, December 4, 1977; "The Last Pirate Show" (one-act), first produced in San Diego at San Diego State University, December 9, 1978; "Last Will and Estimate" (one-act), first produced in San Diego at San Diego State University, January 6, 1979; "Movies, Movies" (two-act), first produced in San Diego at Box Office Dinner Theater, April 4, 1979; "The Apprenticeship" (three-act), first produced in San Diego at Marquis Public Theater, March 12, 1980.

Other scripts: "Marty Sprinkle" (television play), first broadcast by KPBS-TV, June 10, 1977; "Love or Money" (film), CrossOver Productions, 1978; (also producer and director) "The Other Side of the Coin" (radio play), first broadcast by KCR-AM/FM Radio, February 9, 1978; "Disasterpiece Theater" (television variety), first broadcast by XETV-TV, January 22, 1980; (also producer and director) "Where No Shadows Fall" (radio play), first broadcast by KPFK-FM Radio, November 18, 1982. Also author of radio play "Encounter at Twilight," 1980.

Work represented in anthologies, including *Shadows Six,* edited by Charles Grant, Doubleday, 1983. Scriptwriter for radio series "Alien Worlds," 1979-80. Contributor of nearly two hundred articles to magazines, including *San Diego, Talent Spotlight,* and *City,* and to newspapers. Editor of *Post Scripps,* 1979, and *Tuned In,* 1980.

WORK IN PROGRESS: Basilisk, a novel; *Shattered Glass,* a novel; "Uncommon Bonds," a screenplay; "Basilisk," a screenplay based on the novel.

SIDELIGHTS: Straczynski told *CA:* "*The Complete Book of Scriptwriting,* my first nonfiction book, is unique in that it is one of the few books to attempt to explore the art, craft, history, and marketing aspects of writing for television, film, radio, and stage, all in the same volume. It is based on my experiences as a writer in these areas and draws on my background as a reporter.

"I always knew I'd be a writer. I used to joke about it, saying I figured I was destined for writing, politics, religion, or some other branch of organized crime. While I was young, I collected and was fascinated by paper clips, blank sheets of paper, pens, pencils, staplers—the basic paraphernalia of writing. I actually began writing poems, short stories, and scripts in high school, where I wrote, directed, and appeared in an assembly-length play in my senior year.

"From there, I went on to college and academic fields that I thought—incorrectly, as it turned out—would aid my work. Along the way, I had my first sitcom produced at age twenty-one, had signed my first contract by the age of twenty-four, and had nearly eighty articles published by the time I finally left school. During this time, I learned that Ray Bradbury's dictum is painfully, perfectly true: In writing, you have to be willing to make the same mistake 999 times so that the thousandth time you don't make that mistake any more.

"I've always been one of those people who wants to do everything at least once. (Add to this a desire not to be pigeon-holed.) So I've written for every field, from nonfiction to fiction, for television, radio, film, and the stage, and in most genres—comedy, science fiction, horror, mainstream drama, and so on. I believe that once a writer has mastered the art of storytelling, he can write in any field. The basic requirements of storytelling are the same, only the mechanics, the window dressings, vary. It's largely just a matter of overcoming one's fear of technology or unknown techniques.

"I write because I was brought up hearing tales of the old country; because it's cheaper than therapy and easier than *real* work; because it pleases me to make little black marks on a sheet of paper and realize that someone is actually going to *pay* me for them; because it's fun; and because I'm an atheist. Though I do not fear death—I've seen it, barely escaped it too many times to let it worry me—I know I'm finite. I know that the gap beside my birthdate will be filled in someday. Like everyone else, I am going to die. But the *words*—the words live on for as long as there are readers to see them, audiences to hear them. It is immortality by proxy. It is not really a bad deal, all things considered."

*   *   *

STRANGE, Philippa
See COURY, Louise Andree

*   *   *

STRASSELS, Paul N.

AGENT: c/o Cheryl Merser, Random House, Inc., 201 East Fiftieth St., New York, N.Y. 10022.

CAREER: Worked as tax-law specialist for U.S. Government, Internal Revenue Service, Washington, D.C.; founder and operator of Money Matters (financial consultants); writer.

WRITINGS: (With Robert Wool) *All You Need to Know About the IRS: A Taxpayer's Guide,* Random House, 1979.

SIDELIGHTS: All You Need to Know About the IRS: A Taxpayer's Guide is an advice and tip book for persons dealing with the Internal Revenue Service (IRS). Its authors provide information about the inner operations of the agency, including explanations of the Taxpayer Compliance Measurement Program for determining who cheats, and how, on their income tax, and how the agency conducts an audit. The book also pinpoints the taxpayer's safest deductions, identifies occupational groups that are targeted for IRS audits, and tells how an individual should prepare for a tax audit.

Paul Strassels and Robert Wool have "made a real effort to compile a practical guide to the way tax returns are handled and what makes the IRS computer flag a return for a possible audit," wrote Anne Chamberlain in the *Washington Post.* But in a *New York Times Book Review* Robert Lamb objected that the book presented "little that's new" in the way of practical information, while neglecting totally "such relevant developments" as inflation, tax resistance, and the balance-the-budget amendment.

BIOGRAPHICAL/CRITICAL SOURCES: New York Times, February 7, 1980; *Washington Post,* February 8, 1980; *New York Times Book Review,* March 23, 1980.*

* * *

STRAUS, Roger A(ustin) 1948-

PERSONAL: Born April 20, 1948, in New York, N.Y.; son of Siegbert (in business) and Trude (Salomon) Straus; married Diane Elizabeth Walker (a registered nurse), May 6, 1967; children: Erica, Amber. *Education:* Attended Antioch College, 1965-67, and New School for Social Research, 1967-68; Humboldt State University, A.B. (magna cum laude), 1973; University of California, Davis, Ph.D., 1977. *Home:* 2 Woodtree Dr., Woodbury, N.Y. 11797. *Agent:* Maryanne Colas, 229 East 79th St., New York, N.Y. 10021.

CAREER: Straus-Artys Corp., Los Angeles, Calif., western regional manager, 1970-72; Center for Clinical Sociology, Davis, Calif., director, 1975-82; Straus-Artys Corp., Great Neck, N.Y., marketing executive, 1982—. Lecturer and workshop instructor at University of California, Davis, 1977-82. Member of Yolo County Mental Health Advisory Board, 1981-82. *Member:* International Society for Professional Hypnosis (regional vice-president, 1976-82; member of board of trustees, 1982—), Clinical Sociology Association (co-founder; member of executive board, 1978-81), Society for the Study of Symbolic Interaction.

WRITINGS: (Contributor) John Lofland, editor, *Doing Social Life: The Qualitative Study of Human Interaction in Natural Settings,* Wiley-Interscience, 1976; *Strategic Self-Hypnosis: How to Overcome Stress, Improve Performance, and Live to Your Fullest Potential,* Prentice-Hall, 1982. Contributor to sociology journals; contributor of poetry to literary magazines. Editor of *Clinical Sociology Newsletter,* 1978-80, and *American Behavioral Scientist.*

WORK IN PROGRESS: Get Off the Roller Coaster: The Easy Way to Lifelong Weight Control; editing *Solving Human Problems: An Introduction to Clinical and Applied Sociology; Mindwork: Unleashing the Power of Creative Imagination;* research on noncoercive persuasion and mindwork.

SIDELIGHTS: Straus told *CA:* "My recent work is predicated upon the ideal of using social and behavioral sciences, both knowledge and perspective, to help people and peer groups attain greater self-directed control over the conditions and circumstances of their lives and upon the idea that humans are active, striving, creative, and competent beings—not merely passive responders to internal or external pressures and forces."

BIOGRAPHICAL/CRITICAL SOURCES: Sociology: An Introduction, Little, Brown, 1983.

* * *

STRICH, Christian 1930-
(Auguste Amedee de Sainte-Gall, Anton Friedrich, Jean Jouvet, Anne Schmucke, Franz Sutter)

PERSONAL: Born October 10, 1930, in Einsiedeln, Switzerland; son of Joseph and Andree (Sutter) Strich; married Anna Diekman (an artist), December, 1962; children: Jakob, Philipp.

Education: Attended high school in Switzerland. *Religion:* Roman Catholic. *Office:* Diogenes Verlag, Sprecherstrasse 8, CH-8032 Zurich, Switzerland.

CAREER: Worked as a bookseller in Zurich, Switzerland, 1950, Frankfurt, West Germany, Paris, France, and London, England, all 1951; Diogenes Verlag, Zurich, part-time assistant editor, 1952—. Art dealer in Zurich, 1965—.

WRITINGS—Editor; in English; under name Christian Strich: (with Anna Keel) Federico Fellini, *Aufsaetze und Notizen,* Diogenes Verlag, 1974, translation by Isabel Quigley published as *Fellini on Fellini,* Delacorte/Seymour Lawrence, 1976; *Fellini's Filme,* Diogenes Verlag, 1976, translation by Anne Elisabeth Suter published as *Fellini's Films,* Putnam, 1977; *Fellini's Faces,* Holt, 1981; *The Most Beautiful European Fairy Tales,* three volumes, Diogenes Verlag, in press.

Editor, except as noted; in German: under name Christian Strich; published by Diogenes Verlag: *Viel Kinder, viel Segen!* (title means "Lots of Kiddies, Lots of Luck"), 1972; Fellini, *Roma,* 1972; (with Remy Charbon and Gerd Haffmans) *Ueber Moliere* (title means "On Moliere"), 1973; Fellini, *Julia und die Geister* (title means "Juliet and the Spirits"), 1974; Fellini, *La Dolce Vita,* 1974; Fellini, *Amarcord,* 1974; Fellini, *8½,* 1974; (with Tobias Inderbitzin) *Liebesgeschichten aus der Schweiz* (title means "Love Stories From Switzerland"), 1976; Fellini, *Fellini's Zeichnungen* (title means "Fellini's Drawings"), 1976; Fellini, *I Vitelloni* (title means "The Lazybones"), 1977; Fellini, *La Strada,* 1977; Fellini, *Die Naechte der Cabiria* (title means "The Nights of the Cabiria"), 1977; Fellini, *Casanova,* 1977; (with Fritz Eicken) *Liebesgeschichten aus Deutschland* (title means "Love Stories From Germany"), 1978; *Das Erich Kaestner Lesebuch* (title means "The Erich Kaester Reader"), 1978; Friedrich Durrenmatt, *Bilder und Zeichnungen* (title means "Paintings and Drawings"), 1978; *Dichteranekdoten* (title means "Poets' Anecdotes"), 1978; (with Claudia Schmoelders) *Ueber Simenon* (title means "On Simenon"), 1978; Fellini, *Orchesterprobe* (title means "Rehearsal of an Orchestra"), 1979; *Das grosse Diogenes Lebenshilfe-Buch* (title means "Popular Aphorisms"), 1979; (with Gerd Haffmans) *Die fuenf Diogenes Lesebuecher klassischer und moderner deutscher* (title means "The Five Diogenes Readers of Classical and Modern Short Stories"), 1980; (translator) Ludwig Bemelmans, *Madeline,* 1980; *Das Diogenes Lesebuch deutscher Balladen* (title means "The Diogenes Reader of German Ballads"), 1981; *Weihnachtsgeschichten* (title means "Christmas Stories"), 1982; Bosc, *Alles, bloss das nicht!* (cartoons; title means "Everything Except This!"), 1982; *Cartoon Classics,* 1982; *Deutsche Liebesgedichte* (title means "German Love Poems"), 1982; (author of text) Chaval, *Autofahren kann jeder!* (title means "Cartoons on How to Drive"), 1982; Bosc, *Du mich auch* (cartoons; title means "Same to You"), 1982.

Editor; in German; under pseudonym Auguste Amedee de Saint-Gall: Fellini, *Casanova,* Diogenes Verlag, 1976.

Editor; in German; under pseudonym Anton Friedrich; published by Diogenes Verlag: *Tomi Ungerer,* 1979; *Felix Vallotton,* 1979; Paul Flora, *Koenigsdramen* (title means "Life at Court"), 1979; Ludwig Richter, *Die Jahreszeiten* (title means "The Four Seasons"), 1979; *Jose Guadalupe Posada,* 1979; *Aubrey Beardsley,* 1980; Honore Daumier, *Mesdames,* 1980; Daumier, *Messieurs,* 1980; *Hildi Hess,* 1981.

Editor; in German; under pseudonym Jean Jouvet; published by Diogenes Verlag: Henri Matisse, *Zeichnungen* (title means "Drawings"), 1982; *Rene Magritte,* 1982; *Giorgio Morandi,*

1982; Pablo Picasso, *Der Zeichner* (title means "Picasso, the Draughtsman"), Volume I: *Picasso, 1893-1929*, Volume II: *Picasso, 1930-1954*, Volume III: *Picasso, 1955-1972*, all 1982.

Editor; in German; under pseudonym Anne Schmucke; published by Diogenes Verlag: *Das grosse Diogenes Kindergeschichtenbuch* (title means "The Big Diogenes Album of Children's Stories"), 1979; *Die lustige Diogenes Schulfibel* (title means "The Amusing Diogenes Spelling Book"), 1980; (with Gerda Lheureux) *Die schoensten Liebesgeschichten aus Frankreich* (title means "The Most Beautiful Love Stories From France"), 1982; *Das Diogenes Lesebuch franzoesischer Erzaehler* (title means "The Diogenes Reader of French Short Stories"), 1982.

Editor of *Tintenfass* (magazine of literature and art), under pseudonym Franz Sutter.

SIDELIGHTS: Strich told *CA:* "I read and love old and new literature, and I try to separate genuine art from monkey art and art officiel."

* * *

STRICK, Philip 1939-

BRIEF ENTRY: British science fiction film critic, educator, and author. Strick, who created an evening science fiction course for adults at University of London in 1969, is director of an important film library. He wrote *Science Fiction Movies* (Octopus Books, 1976). Strick also edited *Antigrav: Cosmic Comedies by SF Masters* (Taplinger, 1975). *Address:* c/o Georges Borchardt, Inc., 136 East 57th St., New York, N.Y. 10022. *Biographical/critical sources: Times Literary Supplement,* May 23, 1975; *New York Times Book Review,* May 23, 1976.

* * *

STRICKLAND, D. A.
    See STRICKLAND, Donald A(llen)

* * *

STRICKLAND, Donald A(llen) 1934-
    (D. A. Strickland)

BRIEF ENTRY: Born August 3, 1934, in Tacoma, Wash. American political scientist, educator, and author. Strickland taught political science at Purdue University and Wayne State University before joining the faculty of Northwestern University in 1969. He wrote *Scientists in Politics: The Atomic Scientists Movement, 1945-46* (Purdue University Studies, 1968) and *The March Upcountry: Deciding to Bomb Hanoi* (Medina University Press International, 1973). Strickland also co-authored *A Primer of Political Analysis* (Markham, 1968). *Address:* Department of Political Science, Northwestern University, Evanston, Ill. 60201.

* * *

STRIKER, Cecil Leopold 1932-

PERSONAL: Born July 15, 1932, in Cincinnati, Ohio; son of Cecil and Delia (Workum) Striker; married Ute Stephan, April 27, 1968. *Education:* Oberlin College, B.A., 1956; New York University, M.A., 1960, Ph.D., 1968. *Office:* Department of History of Art, G-29 Fine Arts Building, University of Pennsylvania, Philadelphia, Pa. 19104.

CAREER: Vassar College, Poughkeepsie, N.Y., instructor, 1962-65, assistant professor of art history, 1965-68; University of

Pennsylvania, Philadelphia, associate professor, 1968-78, professor of history of art, 1978—, chairman of department, 1980—. Fellow at American Research Institute in Turkey, 1965-66, president, 1978—; field archaeologist at Dumbarton Oaks Center for Byzantine Studies, 1966—, fellow, 1972-73; member of U.S. National Committee for Byzantine Studies. *Military service:* U.S. Army, 1954-57. *Member:* Archaeological Institute of America, Association for Field Archaeology, College Art Association of America, Turkish Studies Association, Koldeway Gesellschaft, Oriental Club of Philadelphia. *Awards, honors:* Fulbright grant for Germany, 1960-62; M.A. from University of Pennsylvania, 1972.

WRITINGS: The Myrelaion (Bodrum Camii) in Istanbul, Princeton Unversity Press, 1982.

WORK IN PROGRESS: Editing and writing part of *Kalenderhane in Istanbul: Final Report on Archaeological Explorations, 1966-1978,* with Dogan Kuban and others, publication expected in 1986; *Dendrochronological Investigations in Greece,* with Peter Ian Kuniholm.

* * *

STRONG, Philip Nigel Warrington 1899-

PERSONAL: Born July 11, 1899, in Sutton-on-Hill, Etwall, England; son of John Warrington (a minister) and Rosamond Maria (Wingfield Digby) Strong. *Education:* Selwyn College, Cambridge, B.A., 1921, M.A., 1924; attended Bishops College, 1921-22. *Home:* 11 Cathedral Close, Wangaratta, Victoria 3677, Australia.

CAREER: Ordained priest of Church of England, 1923; curate of churches in South Shields, England, 1922-26, and Leeds, England, 1926-31; vicar of Church of England in Sunderland, England, 1931-36; bishop of New Guinea, 1936-63; archbishop of Brisbane, Australia, and Metropolitan of Queensland, 1963-70. Primate of Church of England for Australia, 1966-70. Proctor of Convocation of York and member of Church Assembly for Archdeaconry of Durham, 1936; sub-prelate of Order of St. John of Jerusalem, 1966—. Member of Legislative Council for Papua and New Guinea, 1955-63. *Military service:* British Army, Royal Engineers, 1918-19; became second lieutenant. Australian Army, honorary senior chaplain, 1943-45; became lieutenant colonel. *Member:* Melbourne Club. *Awards, honors:* Th.D. from Australian College of Theology, 1945; Companion of Order of St. Michael and St. George, 1958; D.D. (Lambeth) from Archbishop of Canterbury, 1968; Knight Commander of Order of the British Empire, 1970.

WRITINGS: The New Guinea Diaries of Philip Strong, 1936-1945, edited by David Wetherell, Macmillan, 1981. Also author of *Out of Great Tribulation,* 1947.

* * *

STUCKY, Steven 1949-

PERSONAL: Born November 7, 1949, in Hutchinson, Kan.; son of Victor E. and Louise (Trautwein) Stucky; married Melissa Jane Whitehead (a musician), August 22, 1970; children: Maura Catharine, Matthew Steven. *Education:* Baylor University, B.Mus., 1971; Cornell University, M.F.A., 1973, D.Mus.A., 1978. *Home:* 622 West Dryden Rd., Freeville, N.Y. 13068. *Office:* Department of Music, Cornell University, Ithaca, N.Y. 14853-0254.

CAREER: Lawrence University, Appleton, Wis., assistant professor of music, 1978-80; Cornell University, Ithaca, N.Y., assistant professor of music, 1980—. *Member:* American Composers Alliance, American Musicological Society, Broadcast Music, Society for New Music (vice-president, 1982—), Music Theory Society of New York State (member of executive board, 1980—). *Awards, honors:* Victor Herbert Prize from American Society of Composers, Authors and Publishers, 1974, and prize from American Society of University Composers, 1975, both for "Piano Quartet"; Deems Taylor Award, 1982, for *Lutoslawski and His Music.*

WRITINGS: Lutoslawski and His Music, Cambridge University Press, 1981.

Compositions: *Movements III,* Shawnee Press, 1976; *Kenningar (Symphony No. 4),* American Composers Edition, 1977-78; *Refrains,* Music for Percussion, Inc., 1979; *Transparent Things: In Memoriam V.N.,* American Composers Edition, 1980; *Sappho Fragments,* American Composers Edition, 1982; *Double Concerto for Oboe, Violin, and Chamber Orchestra,* American Composers Edition, 1982-83.

Contributor to *Musical Times* and Music Library Association's *Notes.*

WORK IN PROGRESS: Composing new works of chamber music and orchestral music; research on Italian composer Luigi Dallapiccola.

SIDELIGHTS: Stucky told *CA:* "Writing and reading good prose is my second love, after music. My own writing has always been and will continue to be a sideline, subordinate to my work as a composer. But I think it is important that composers and other artists express themselves seriously, not only about their own work but about the work of others. To leave such writing entirely to professional scholars and journalists produces a dangerously one-sided view of the arts.

"The working artist cannot, of course, sacrifice either the time or the psychic involvement required to be a thoroughly trained historian or a well-informed critic. I turn to the typewriter only when, so to speak, I can't help it: when I meet a piece of music or a composer I feel compelled to study. That is what happened with Lutoslawski: first encounters with his music were so powerful that I simply *had* to figure out how this music was made. Lutoslawski had solved the same kind of technical problems I was grappling with in my own composing. The more deeply I delved into his work, the more deeply convinced I became that he was one of the great figures of the century—and the more impatient I became with the fragmentary, superficial literature on him which then existed. I saw a chance to contribute something."

*   *   *

STURM, Rudolf 1912-

BRIEF ENTRY: Born April 15, 1912, in Doubravice, Czechoslovakia. American educator and author. Sturm has taught at Boston College, Hershey Junior College, and Skidmore College, where he became professor of Italian and Slavic literature in 1973. His publications include *Czechoslovakia: A Bibliographic Guide* (Library of Congress, 1967) and *Egon Hostovsky: Vzpominky, studie a dokumenty o jiho dile a osudu* (Nakladatelstvi 68, 1974). *Address:* Department of Modern Languages, Skidmore College, Saratoga Springs, N.Y. 12866.

*   *   *

SUCHOCKI, Marjorie Hewitt 1933-

PERSONAL: Surname is pronounced Su-*hock*-y; born August 13, 1933, in Winthrop, Mass.; daughter of Paul and Faith (Nee) Hewitt; children: Catherine Suchocki Orr, Joan, John. *Education:* Pomona College, B.A., 1970; Claremont Graduate School, M.A. and Ph.D., both 1974. *Office:* Pittsburgh Theological Seminary, 616 North Highland Ave., Pittsburgh, Pa. 15206.

CAREER: Pittsburgh Theological Seminary, Pittsburgh, Pa., assistant professor, 1977-80, associate professor of theology, 1980—, director of Doctor of Ministry program, 1981—. *Member:* American Academy of Religion, Society for the Study of Process Philosophy, National Women's Studies Association, College Theology Society, National Organization for Women.

WRITINGS: (Editor with Barry A. Woodbridge and Jay McDaniel) *Alfred North Whitehead: A Primary-Secondary Bibliography,* Philosophical Documentation Center, 1977; (contributor) Florence M. Hetzler and Austin H. Kutscher, editors, *Philosophical Aspects of Thanatology,* Volume II, Arus Press, 1978; (contributor) Jack Rogers, editor, *Introduction to Philosophy: A Case Method Approach,* Harper, 1981; (contributor) Sheila Davaney, editor, *Feminism and Process Thought,* Edwin Mellon, 1981; *God, Christ, Church: A Practical Guide to Process Theology,* Crossroad Publishing, 1982. Contributor to philosophy and theology journals.

WORK IN PROGRESS: Twentieth-Century Eschatology, publication by Crossroad Publishing expected in 1985.

*   *   *

SUGNET, Charles (Joseph) 1944-

PERSONAL: Born June 20, 1944, in Port Huron, Mich.; son of Charles J. (a dentist) and Rose Mary (a librarian; maiden name, Walsh) Sugnet; married R. Regina Strauchon (a compensation specialist), June 25, 1967; children: Charles W., Joshua S. *Education:* Boston College, B.A., 1966; University of Virginia, M.A., 1967, Ph.D., 1970. *Residence:* Minneapolis, Minn. *Agent:* Deborah Rogers Ltd., 5-11 Mortimer St., London W1N 7RH, England. *Office:* Department of English, University of Minnesota, Minneapolis, Minn. 55455.

CAREER: University of Minnesota, Minneapolis, associate professor of English, 1970—. *Member:* Modern Language Association of America, Shakespeare Society of America, Midwest Modern Language Association, Phi Beta Kappa.

WRITINGS: (Editor with Alan Burns) *The Imagination on Trial: British and American Writers Discuss Their Working Methods,* Allison & Busby, 1982. Author of a column in *D'Art.* Contributor of articles to *Change* and *In These Times.*

WORK IN PROGRESS: A book "on metaphors of imperialism."

SIDELIGHTS: Sugnet and Burns's *The Imagination on Trial: British and American Writers Discuss Their Working Methods* is an anthology of interviews with contemporary authors of fiction, including J. G. Ballard, Eva Figes, John Gardner, John Hawkes, Ishmael Reed, and Alan Sillitoe. The collection focuses primarily on these authors' opinions on the role of the imagination and inspiration in the creative process. Writing in the *Times Literary Supplement,* Lachlan Mackinnon noted that "the interviews appear to be offered specifically to young writers, that they may learn some of the secrets of the craft."

Sugnet told *CA:* "How can the marvelous but largely apolitical achievements of post-modern fiction be brought into relation with feminism and leftist politics? If we are to have peace with racial and sexual equality, our whole cultural system will have to be reorganized. *The Imagination on Trial* offered a preliminary survey of this huge project. I hope my next book will approach it more directly.''

BIOGRAPHICAL/CRITICAL SOURCES: *Times Literary Supplement*, June 25, 1982.

*   *   *

SULEIMAN, Susan Rubin

PERSONAL: Born in Budapest, Hungary; came to the United States in 1950, naturalized citizen, 1956; daughter of Michael N. (a rabbi) and Lillian (Stern) Rubin; married Ezra N. Suleiman (a professor of politics), February 27, 1966 (separated); children: Michael, Daniel. *Education:* Barnard College, B.A. (magna cum laude), 1960; University of Paris, Certificat de l'Institut Phonetique, 1961; Harvard University, M.A., 1964, Ph.D., 1969. *Home:* 70 Horace Rd., Belmont, Mass. 02178. *Office:* Department of Romance Languages and Literatures, Harvard University, Cambridge, Mass. 02138.

CAREER: Columbia University, New York, N.Y., instructor, 1966-68, assistant professor of French, 1969-76, director of study program at Reid Hall, Paris, France, 1973; Occidental College, Los Angeles, Calif., assistant professor, 1976-81, associate professor of French, 1981, director of study in France, 1978-79, 1981, coordinator of Interdisciplinary Colloquium on Women and Society, 1979-80; Harvard University, Cambridge, Mass., associate professor of Romance languages and literatures, 1981-83, John L. Loeb Associate Professor of Humanities, 1983—.

MEMBER: Modern Language Association of America, American Comparative Literature Association (member of advisory board), American Association of Teachers of French, Phi Beta Kappa. *Awards, honors:* Woodrow Wilson fellow, 1961-62; traveling fellow of Harvard University, 1965-66; National Endowment for the Humanities grant, 1977, fellowship, 1980; American Council of Learned Societies grant, 1977-78; Guggenheim fellowship, 1983-84; Rockefeller Foundation humanities fellowship, 1984.

WRITINGS: (Editor and author of preface) Paul Nizan, *Pour une nouvelle culture* (title means ''Toward a New Culture''), Grasset, 1971; (translator) Guillaume Apollinaire, *Apollinaire on Art*, edited by Leroy C. Breunig, Viking, 1972; (translator) Saul Friedlander, *History and Psychoanalysis*, Holmes & Meier, 1978; (editor with Inge Crosman, and contributor) *The Reader in the Text: Essays on Audience and Interpretation*, Princeton University Press, 1980; *Authoritarian Fictions: The Ideological Novel as a Literary Genre*, Columbia University Press, 1983; (contributor) Brian Thompson and Carl Viggiani, editors, *Witnessing Andre Malraux: Visions and Revisions*, Wesleyan University Press, 1983.

Contributor of more than thirty articles, translations, and reviews to language and literature journals. Member of editorial boards of the *French Review* and *Style;* member of advisory board of *Camera Obscura: A Journal of Feminism and Film Theory.*

WORK IN PROGRESS: Contributing to *Essays in Feminist Psychoanalytic Literary Criticism*, edited by Shirley Garner, Madelon Gohlke, and Claire Kahane, publication expected in 1984; *Reading the Avant-Garde: Studies on Experimental French Fiction From Surrealism to ''l'Ecriture feminine,''* publication expected in 1986; research on problems of avant-garde writing, women's writing, and feminist theory.

SIDELIGHTS: Suleiman told *CA:* ''The role of the translator in the contemporary literary world is very important, although too rarely recognized. Without competent and dedicated translators there would be no wide-scale cross-cultural communication. Imagine having to learn Russian to read Dostoevsky, Japanese to read Mishima, Spanish to read Borges, Fuentes, Garcia Marquez. All of this is obvious—yet it is a universal fact that translators are (save for a few notable exceptions) underpaid and unappreciated. Reviewers of a book rarely mention the translator, and publishers rarely put the translator's name on the cover.

''This may explain why there are so few full-time literary translators. I myself, like some of my colleagues, translate only occasionally, either because I'm interested in a specific book or because people I can't refuse ask me to do a translation for them. As an occasional occupation, I find translation a highly pleasurable activity: it offers plenty of challenges, but it's still so much easier than writing your own book.

''My own interest in women's writing and feminist theory has evolved gradually over the past ten years. When I first started publishing I was chiefly influenced by the French structuralists, and what most interested me was: *how* do literary works produce certain effects, including the effect of meaning? Today, I am interested not only in that question (I have no intention of renouncing my former allegiances), but also in broader questions relating to the cultural and ideological implications of literary works. Concurrently, I have become more and more involved, both personally and professionally, in questions relating to women.

''I see this kind of evolution among many of my women friends and colleagues. For women of my generation, who went to college in the late 1950's and early 1960's, feminism was not a 'given' from the start: it was something that one *came to,* sooner or later. There were no women's studies programs, no female professors, and above all, there was no body of feminist criticism when I went to graduate school. Today, it is no exaggeration to say that some of the most exciting, most vibrantly new work in literary studies is the work of feminist critics. One does not have to write exclusively about women in order to do feminist criticism. What matters are the questions one asks, not the particular writers or works one is dealing with. And the exciting thing is that many of the questions that seem most interesting today could not even have been formulated, much less explored, twenty years ago.''

*   *   *

SULLIVAN, William M.   1945-

PERSONAL: Born May 2, 1945, in Philadelphia, Pa.; son of James C. and Iretta (Gorman) Sullivan. *Education:* La Salle College, B.A., 1968; Fordham University, Ph.D., 1971. *Home:* 1420 Locust St., Apt. 29Q, Philadelphia, Pa. 19102. *Office:* Department of Philosophy, La Salle College, Philadelphia, Pa. 19141.

CAREER: Allentown College, Center Valley, Pa., associate professor of philosophy, 1971-82; La Salle College, Philadelphia, Pa., associate professor of philosophy, 1982—. *Member:* American Philosophical Association.

WRITINGS: (Editor with Paul Rabinow) *Interpretive Social Science: A Reader*, University of California Press, 1979; *Reconstructing Public Philosophy*, University of California Press, 1982.

WORK IN PROGRESS: *Habits of the Heart;* an analysis of activists and the ''New Politics''; philosophical-sociological research on American commitments to public and private life.

* * *

SUMMERS, Clyde Wilson 1918-

PERSONAL: Born November 21, 1918, in Grass Range, Mont.; son of Carl Douglas and Anna Lois (Yontz) Summers; married Evelyn Marie Wahlgren (a teacher), August 30, 1947; children: Mark, Erica, Craig, Lisa. *Education:* University of Illinois, B.S., J.D., 1942; Columbia University, J.S.D., 1946. *Home:* 753 North 26th St., Philadelphia, Pa. 19130. *Office:* School of Law, University of Pennsylvania, 3400 Chestnut St., Philadelphia, Pa. 19174.

CAREER: University of Toledo, Toledo, Ohio, instructor, 1942-44, assistant professor, 1944-46, associate professor of law, 1946-49; University of Buffalo (now State University of New York at Buffalo), Buffalo, N.Y., associate professor, 1949-54, professor of law, 1954-56; Yale University, New Haven, Conn., visiting professor, 1956-57, professor of law, 1957-65, Garver Professor of Law, 1965-75; University of Pennsylvania, Philadelphia, Fordham Professor of Law, 1975—. Chairman of New York governor's Commission on Improper Union and Management Practices, 1957-59; chairman of Connecticut Advisory Council on Unemployment Insurance, 1961-71; past hearing officer for Connecticut Commission on Human Rights. *Member:* International Society for Comparative Labor Law and Social Legislation (member of executive committee, 1963-70), American Law Institute. *Awards, honors:* LL.D. from University of Louvain, 1966, and University of Stockholm, 1978.

WRITINGS: (Co-editor) *Labor Relations and the Law,* Little, Brown, 1952; (co-editor) *Employment Relations and the Law,* Little, Brown, 1957; (editor with Benjamin Aaron and Joseph Shister) *Public Policy and Collective Bargaining,* Harper, 1962; (with Harry H. Wellington) *Cases and Materials on Labor Law,* Foundation Press, 1968, 2nd edition (with Wellington and Alan Hyde), 1982, *Statutory Supplement,* 1968, *1974 Case Supplement,* 1974; (with Aaron, Thomas Christensen, David Feller, Robert Koretz, Robert I. Rabin, and Charles Morris) *The Future of Labor Arbitration,* American Arbitration Association, 1976; (with Rabin) *The Rights of Union Members: An American Civil Liberties Union Handbook,* Avon, 1979. Contributor to law journals.

WORK IN PROGRESS: Research on comparative labor law, worker participation, rights of union members, and rights of non-union workers.

SIDELIGHTS: Summers told *CA:* ''In all of my research and writing, I seem unable to escape for long from preoccupation or distracting concern with the problem of the rights of the individual in a collective society and the need for participation and democratic processes in the individual's working life. Whether dealing with the internal political structures of unions, the processes of collective bargaining, the responsibilities of arbitrators, or the rights of non-union workers, this ultimately becomes a recurrent if not dominating theme. Some might say, with only some overstatement, that if you have read three things I have written, you have read them all. But I have no apologies; the importance of the problem is, for me, worthy of the effort. Every man is entitled to two grand passions—love of a loving wife and commitment to a worthy idea. And one of each is enough.

''Although I study and write as a lawyer, my concern is less with the law than with life. Beyond the legal rules I want to understand how institutions function and social processes work. Most of my time and effort is spent studying the structure and political processes of unions, the role and functioning of our collective bargaining system, and the operational problems of governmental agencies. In my view, all of this is necessary if one is to be even a passable legal scholar in labor law. My regret is that there is not time to be more than a rank amateur in the surrounding disciplines. Because of this, even tentative conclusions are reached with trepidation, which is compensated for and concealed by positiveness of assertions.''

* * *

SUMMERS, Hal
See SUMMERS, Henry Forbes

* * *

SUMMERS, Henry Forbes 1911-
(Hal Summers)

PERSONAL: Born August 18, 1911, in Bradford, England; son of Herbert Henry and Sarah (Forbes) Summers; married Rosemary Roberts, March 31, 1937; children: Nicholas, Richard, Lucy (Mrs. Russell V. Jones). *Education:* Trinity College, Oxford, B.A., 1934. *Home:* Linden Gardens, Tunbridge Wells TN2 5QU, England.

CAREER: Associated with Ministry of Health, London, England, 1934-56; Department of the Environment, London, under secretary, 1956-71. Chairman of Quaker Southern Housing Association. *Awards, honors:* Companion of the Bath, 1961.

WRITINGS—Books of poems; under name Hal Summers: *Smoke After Flame,* Dent, 1944; *Hinterland,* Dent, 1947; *Visions of Time,* Hand and Flower Press, 1951; *Tomorrow Is My Love,* Oxford University Press, 1978; *The Burning Book,* Book League, 1983.

* * *

SUNDERMAN, Lloyd Frederick 1905-1983

OBITUARY NOTICE: Born in 1905; died January 11, 1983, in Toledo, Ohio. Educator and author. Sunderman was chairman of music at University of Toledo. His books include *Historical Foundations of Music Education in the United States,* *New Dimensions in Music Education,* and *School Music Teaching: Its Theory and Practice.* Obituaries and other sources: *Chronicle of Higher Education,* January 26, 1983.

* * *

SUN Yefang 1908-1983

OBITUARY NOTICE: Born October 24, 1908, in Jiangsu Province, China; died of cancer, February 22, 1983, in Peking, China. Economist, reformist, and author. As a senior economic adviser to Premier Zhao Ziyang, Sun helped formulate theories advocating China's economic liberalization. Sun was educated in the Soviet Union, worked as a Chinese Nationalist party organizer through World War II, and began work as an economist when the Communists came to power in 1949. He wrote twenty-three major papers during the three years prior to his death, and was featured in seven articles appearing in the journal *Economic Research.* Sun also wrote *Some Theoretical Problems of Socialist Economy.* Obituaries and other sources:

New York Times, February 24, 1983; *Chicago Tribune,* February 25, 1983; *Los Angeles Times,* February 27, 1983; *London Times,* March 2, 1983.

*   *   *

SUTHERLAND, Daniel E(llyson)   1946-

PERSONAL: Born March 5, 1946, in Detroit, Mich.; son of Monte Henry Milliron (stepfather; a carpenter) and Dorothy Nell Parrish; married Diane Kim Bowman (a linguist), September 1, 1978; children: Christopher Michael. *Education:* Wayne State University, B.A., 1968, M.A., 1973, Ph.D., 1976. *Office:* Department of History, McNeese State University, Lake Charles, La. 70609.

CAREER: McNeese State University, Lake Charles, La., assistant professor, 1977-82, associate professor of American history, 1982—. *Military service:* U.S. Naval Reserve, 1964-72; active duty, 1968-70; became petty officer second class. *Member:* Organization of American Historians, Southern Historical Association, Louisiana Historical Association. *Awards, honors:* Research grants from Society of Colonial Dames, 1975, and National Endowment for the Humanities, 1978.

WRITINGS: Americans and Their Servants: Domestic Service in the United States From 1800 to 1920, Louisiana State University, 1981. Contributor of articles to history and humanities journals. Member of editorial board of *The McNeese Review,* 1981—.

WORK IN PROGRESS: The Southern Carpetbaggers, publication by Louisiana State University Press expected in 1985; editing a collection of excerpts from traveler accounts in the post-Civil War South for inclusion in a two-volume work, publication expected in 1985.

SIDELIGHTS: Americans and Their Servants: Domestic Service in the United States From 1800 to 1920 is an account of how changing economic structures in America affected the status of domestic servants. According to Sutherland, jobs that involved waiting on others came to be regarded as lesser tasks, and the persons who performed these duties were looked down upon by their employers and others as Americans became more affluent. Relations between employers and domestic employees became strained, so people began to perform their own household duties, thus increasing demand for mechanized means of performing such duties and rendering the role of the domestic servant obsolete.

Sutherland told *CA:* "My professional writing career has been conducted under a melancholy cloud. Academic historians, with a few notable exceptions, have long borne the stigma of being dull, plodding, unexciting writers. Current trends toward statistical and quantitative history have tended to solidify this unflattering reputation. The door has been left wide open to the 'popular' historian, i.e., the writer whose training is primarily journalistic. Some popular historians (Bruce Catton and Barbara Tuchman come to mind) are exceptional, both as scholars and writers. However, too many others produce history that is facile, inaccurate, and wrongheaded (academic historians do, too, but not, I fancy, as frequently). Thus the strongest stimulus to my writing has been the belief that academic historians have a responsibility to write for the public rather than for themselves. General readers will not tolerate the inane, esoteric subject matter and style so often found in professional journals, and there is no reason why they should. There is no reason why academic historians cannot produce histories that

are at once scholarly and entertaining, histories that offer something to professionals and laymen alike."

BIOGRAPHICAL/CRITICAL SOURCES: New Yorker, November 30, 1981.

*   *   *

SUTTER, Franz
See STRICH, Christian

*   *   *

SUTTON, George Miksch   1898-1982

OBITUARY NOTICE—See index for *CA* sketch: Born May 16, 1898, in Bethany, Neb.; died December 7, 1982, in Norman, Okla. Zoologist, ornithologist, naturalist, explorer, educator, researcher, illustrator, editor, and author. Before becoming the curator of birds at Cornell University in 1931, Sutton served as state ornithologist for the State of Pennsylvania in the 1920's. He retired as research professor emeritus of zoology and curator emeritus of birds at University of Oklahoma. Also a noted painter of birds, he illustrated his own and other books on birds. Sutton participated in expeditions in Labrador, Hudson Bay, Mexico, Iceland, and the Galapagos. Among his self-illustrated books are *Eskimo Year: A Naturalist's Adventures in the Far North, Mexican Birds: First Impressions, Iceland Summer: Adventures of a Bird Painter,* and *Bird Student: An Autobiography.* Obituaries and other sources: *Chronicle of Higher Education,* January 5, 1983.

*   *   *

SWAINSON, Donald   1938-

PERSONAL: Born November 23, 1938, in Baldur, Manitoba, Canada; son of Ingolfur and Liney (Oleson) Swainson; married Eleanor Garson (a credit counselor), 1963; children: Eirik, Andrew. *Education:* University of Manitoba, B.A., 1960; University of Toronto, M.A., 1961, Ph.D., 1969. *Religion:* Anglican. *Office:* Department of History, Queen's University, Kingston, Ontario, Canada K7L 3N6.

CAREER: Queen's University, Kingston, Ontario, lecturer, 1963-65, assistant professor, 1965-70, associate professor, 1970-79, professor of history, 1979—. Senior officer of Planning and Priorities Committee of cabinet for government of Manitoba, 1972-73. *Member:* Canadian Historical Association, Manitoba Historical Society, Ontario Historical Society.

WRITINGS: Ontario and Conderation, Centennial Commission of Canada, 1967; (with Christopher Ondaatje) *The Prime Ministers of Canada, 1867-1968,* Pagurian, 1968, 2nd edition, 1975; (editor) *Historical Essays on the Prairie Provinces,* McClelland & Stewart, 1970; *J. C. Dent: The Last Forty Years,* McClelland & Stewart, 1971; *John A. Macdonald: The Man and the Politician,* Oxford University Press, 1971; (editor) *Oliver Mowat's Ontario,* Macmillan, 1972; *Macdonald of Kingston,* Thomas Nelson, 1979; *The Buffalo Hunt,* Peter Martin Associates, 1980; (with Brian Osborne) *History of Kingston,* James Lorimer, in press. Contributor to history journals. Member of editorial board of *Whig-Standard.*

WORK IN PROGRESS: The Conservative Tradition in Canada, completion expected in 1985.

SIDELIGHTS: Swainson told *CA:* "My focus is on national politics and the regional societies and political cultures that have evolved in Ontario and the prairie region. *The Conser-*

vative Tradition in Canada is a project that will, I hope, help to explain crucial elements in the political evolution of Canada's national party system.''

*   *   *

SWANSON, Gloria   1899(?)-1983

OBITUARY NOTICE: Birth-given name, Gloria May Josephine Svensson (some sources say Swenson); born March 27 (some sources say March 17), 1899 (some sources say 1897), in Chicago, Ill.; died April 4, 1983, in Manhattan, N.Y. Actress and author. Swanson began her acting career as a teenager and went on to appear in more than sixty motion pictures as well as stage and television productions. Famous for her image as a glamorous star of the silent screen, Swanson played roles from sultry vamps to sophisticated society women in both dramatic films and comedies. She made six pictures for Cecil B. De Mille, including ''Don't Change Your Husband'' and ''Male and Female.'' Her transition from silent films to talkies was made with ''The Trespassers.'' During an interim in which she was not acting, she dabbled in fashion design, marketing her own line of cosmetics, studied sculpture, and hosted a television talk show. The classic film ''Sunset Boulevard'' marked her return to movie stardom in 1950. She appeared on Broadway in the 1971 production of ''Butterflies Are Free'' and starred as herself in the movie ''Airport 1975.'' In 1980 Swanson attracted notoriety with her autobiography, *Swanson on Swanson*, in which she described her affairs and six marriages. Obituaries and other sources: *Current Biography,* Wilson, 1950, May, 1983; *New York Times,* April 5, 1983; *Los Angeles Times,* April 5, 1983; *Washington Post,* April 5, 1983; *Newsweek,* April 18, 1983.

*   *   *

SWANSON, Neil H(armon)   1896-1983

OBITUARY NOTICE: Born June 30, 1896, in Minneapolis, Minnesota; died February 5, 1983, in Baltimore, Md. Editor, journalist, and author. Swanson's career began at the *Minneapolis Journal* when he left the University of Minnesota during his junior year. After serving as company commander for the U.S. Army in France during World War I, he returned to the *Journal* for two more years. Swanson then went on to hold positions with other newspapers, including the *Pittsburgh Press* and the *Baltimore Sun.* During his tenure with the *Sun* the paper won three Pulitzer Prizes. Swanson, who was considered an expert on the War of 1812, wrote nine historical books. One of these, *The Unconquered,* was produced as a movie by Cecil B. De Mille. In 1951 Swanson was awarded a bronze plaque from the Veterans of Foreign Wars for outstanding literary achievement. He was also cited by the National Education Association for his literary works. Obituaries and other sources: *New York Times,* February 7, 1983; *Washington Post,* February 7, 1983; *Chicago Tribune,* February 8, 1983.

*   *   *

SYMONS, Leslie John   1926-

PERSONAL: Born November 8, 1926, in Reading, England; son of Edward John (an organ builder) and Gertrude (Mainwaring) Symons; married Gloria Colville, March 24, 1954; children: Alison Heather, Jennifer Rosalind. *Education:* London School of Economics and Political Science, London, B.Sc., 1953, Ph.D., 1958. *Home:* Squirrels Jump, 17 Wychwood Close, Langland, Swansea SA3 4PH, Wales, United Kingdom.

Office: Department of Geography, University College of Swansea, University of Wales, Swansea SA2 8PP, Wales, United Kingdom.

CAREER: Queen's University, Belfast, Northern Ireland, lecturer in geography, 1953-63; University of Canterbury, Canterbury, New Zealand, senior lecturer in geography, 1963-70; University of Wales, University College of Swansea, Swansea, senior lecturer, 1970-73, reader, 1973-80, professor of geography, 1980—. Simon senior research fellow at University of Manchester, 1967-68. *Military service:* British Army, Royal Engineers, 1944-48. *Member:* Institute of British Geographers, National Association of Soviet and East European Studies, Royal Aeronautical Society.

WRITINGS: (Editor and contributor) *Land Use in Northern Ireland,* University of London Press, 1963; *Agricultural Geography,* G. Bell, 1967, 2nd edition, 1978; (with Lewis Hanna) *Northern Ireland: A Geographical Introduction,* University of London Press, 1967; *Russian Agriculture: A Geographical Survey,* G. Bell, 1972; (editor with Colin White, and contributor) *Russian Transport: An Historical and Geographical Survey,* Bell & Byman, 1975; (editor and contributor) *The Soviet Union: A Systematic Geography,* Hodder & Stoughton, 1982. General editor of ''Geography of the U.S.S.R.,'' a series, Hicks-Smith & Son, 1968-70.

WORK IN PROGRESS: Research on prediction, impact, and effects of snowfall, on Soviet transport, especially air transport, and on applications of aerial work to agriculture.

SIDELIGHTS: Symons told *CA:* ''My interest in the U.S.S.R. evolved from the feeling that this was a country that we in the West knew far too little about and that geographers, especially, had a duty to study objectively—the character of both the people and the country itself, its economy and resources, and its achievements in harnessing these resources. I was especially curious about the collective system of agriculture which was widely studied by economists and political scientists but had been neglected in geographical circles. It appeared that judgments on the virgin lands campaign of the 1950's, advanced by people who were neither agriculturalists nor natural scientists, needed reevaluating—or at least updating—as Soviet thinking became more attuned to the needs of the environment for conservation. I was also anxious to add another language to my capabilities to improve my knowledge of the work of geographers in regions with which most of us were unfamiliar. I traveled as widely as possible in Siberia, Central Asia, and the Caucasus regions as well as European Russia while writing my books on agriculture and, later, transport in the U.S.S.R. Meanwhile I was appointed to the Centre of Russian and East European Studies at Swansea and became involved with wider aspects of the study of the Soviet Union in conjunction with other specialists. The study of Russian transport was a joint undertaking with other geographers and economic historians to fill some gaps in Western knowledge about this facet of the development of Russia and the U.S.S.R.

''My present research project concerning snowfall evolved out of work on agricultural aviation, which is widely used on the Soviet scene. While I was carrying out work on aerial application, severe blizzards in Britain led to a major deployment of helicopters for rescue work. After writing this up with a colleague I began to think in terms of a wider study of the disruption caused by snowfall, and after the severe snowstorms of January, 1982, Dr. A. H. Perry and I were approached by the Welsh Office to study the problem and make recommendations on measures which might be undertaken to reduce the economic and social impact of winter weather in the future. We are now engaged in this work, which will involve international comparisons, and, as in the case of my research into other little-studied fields, I would welcome contacts with persons elsewhere who are interested in sharing ideas on how to make this research more effective.''

AVOCATIONAL INTERESTS: Mountaineering, aviation, railways, philately, music, travel (including the U.S.S.R., Asia, Australia, and New Zealand).

*   *   *

SZIRTES, George   1948-

PERSONAL: Born November 29, 1948, in Budapest, Hungary; son of Laszlo (an engineer) and Magdalena (a photographer; maiden name, Nussbacher) Szirtes; married Clarissa Upchurch (an artist), July 11, 1970; children: Thomas Andrew, Helen Magdalena. *Education:* Leeds College of Art, B.A., 1972; University of London, A.T.C., 1973. *Home:* 20 Old Park Rd., Hitchin, Hertfordshire SG5 2JR, England.

CAREER: Writer. Instructor in writing at schools and colleges in England, 1975-81; St. Christopher School, Letchworth, England, director of art, 1981—. Etchings exhibited at Victoria and Albert Museum. Member of literature panel of Eastern Arts Association, 1981—. *Member:* International P.E.N., Royal Society of Literature. *Awards, honors:* Co-recipient of Geoffrey Faber Memorial Prize from Faber & Faber Ltd. Arts Council, 1980, for *The Slant Door;* fellow of Royal Society of Literature.

WRITINGS: The Iron Clouds (poems), Dodman Press, 1975; *An Illustrated Alphabet* (poems), Mandeville Press, 1978; (with Alistair Elliott, Craig Raine, Alan Hollinghurst, Cal Clothier, and Anne Cluysenaar) *Poetry Introduction 4,* Faber, 1978; *The Slant Door* (poems), Secker & Warburg, 1979; *Homage to Cheval,* Priapus Press, 1981; *November and May* (poems), Secker & Warburg, 1981; *The Kissing Place* (poems), Starwheel Press, 1982.

Work represented in anthologies, including *Writers of East Anglia,* edited by Angus Wilson, Secker & Warburg, 1977; *Poems for Shakespeare,* edited by Patricia Beer, Shakespeare Trust, 1979; and *Poetry Book Society Anthology,* edited by Peter Porter, Poetry Book Society, 1980. Contributor to periodicals, including *Times Literary Supplement, New Statesman, Listener, Encounter,* and *Quarto.*

WORK IN PROGRESS: A collection of poems, for Secker & Warburg; ''a book on the relationship between modern art, provincial art, and art education,'' for Secker & Warburg; a book on art education, for Edward Arnold.

SIDELIGHTS: Szirtes's early work, published along with poems by other writers in *Poetry Introduction 4,* resulted in praise

from Fleur Adcock in *Ambit,* where she called Szirtes ''a dazzlingly visual poet.'' With *The Slant Door,* Szirtes was praised by Anne Stevenson in *Listener* for bringing ''some energetic new blood into English poetry.'' He received more accolades for *November and May.* ''The writing is often darkened by menace,'' noted a reviewer in the *Yorkshire Post,* ''delight is something snatched uneasily in moments of brilliant colour.'' A reviewer for *Observer* was also impressed, noting, ''*November and May* establishes [Szirtes] as one of the very best poets under 40.''

Szirtes told *CA:* ''I arrived in England as a refugee in 1956. My early education was science based, but I began writing and painting at school. I studied fine art and traveled in Europe on a scholarship, the longest stay being in Italy. I was by this time married and had been baptized as a convert to the Baptist Church. My writing at that time probably took its main impetus from those events, and I had in fact begun publishing a few poems. As time has gone on I have had less and less time for painting, though I still produce etchings.

''My first poems appeared in pamphlets and magazines from about 1973 on, slowly to begin with, then more regularly. *An Illustrated Alphabet* consisted of twenty-six etchings and poems based on letters of the alphabet. It was exhibited at the Victoria and Albert Museum.

''It is a difficult and dangerous thing to make general statements about one's poetry. The three areas tentatively defined by various critics seems roughly right to me. Intense visual images combine with a love of order that strives to keep in check certain macabre qualities whose roots probably lie in the violence of the Hungarian uprising of 1956 and in the uprooting and transplantation of my family. I see it as the task of my poetry to preserve as fresh whatever is delightful or miraculous against its wastage or its drastic collapse. I avoid hysteria and confessional writing: my sense of humor would never forgive a total surrender to solemnity or chaos. I like formal writing and admire elegance, but above all I desire an inclusiveness and intensity in poetry which can express itself clearly and colloquially if necessary. I tend to work in a series of reactions against work in hand. I don't like repeating myself, a dislike which leads me to write in an increasing variety of manners and tones. There is, however, I believe, a consistent subsong. The awarding of the fellowship of the Royal Society of Literature was a great honor. I have a young and admirable family and live in a small town between London and Cambridge. My next book will be both quieter and more vulgar.''

BIOGRAPHICAL/CRITICAL SOURCES: Listener, August 17, 1979; *Ambit,* autumn, 1979; *Times Literary Supplement,* January 18, 1980, July 2, 1982; *Observer,* February 7, 1980; *Yorkshire Post,* March 11, 1982.

T

TAAGEPERA, Rein 1933-

PERSONAL: Surname is pronounced *Ta*-ghe-pe-ra; born February 28, 1933, in Tartu, Estonia; naturalized Canadian citizen, 1960; came to the United States in 1961; son of Karl (a professor of veterinary science) and Elfriede Amalie (an economist; maiden name, Erbak) Taagepera; married Mare Ruunk (a lecturer in chemistry), October 14, 1961; children: Tiina-Kai, Salme, Jaan. *Education:* University of Toronto, B.A.Sc., 1959, M.A., 1961; University of Delaware, Ph.D., 1965, M.A., 1969. *Home:* 18191 Mayapple Way, Irvine, Calif. 92715. *Office:* School of Social Sciences, University of California, Irvine, Calif. 92717.

CAREER: E. I. du Pont de Nemours & Co., Wilmington, Del., research physicist, 1964-70; University of California, Irvine, assistant professor, 1970-74, associate professor, 1974-78, professor of social science, 1978—. *Member:* American Political Science Association, Association for the Advancement of Baltic Studies, Peace Science Society, Social Science History Society.

WRITINGS: (Editor with Arvids Ziedonis and Mardi Valgemaae) *Problems of Mini-Nations: Baltic Perspectives,* Association for the Advancement of Baltic Studies, 1973; (with Romauld Misiunas) *The Baltic States: Years of Dependence, 1940-1980,* University of California Press, 1983. Editor of *Baltic Events,* 1967-75.

WORK IN PROGRESS: The Death of Juri Kukk: Softening Without Liberalization in the Soviet Union.

SIDELIGHTS: Taagepera commented: "After earning a Ph.D. in physics, I started taking political science courses in order to figure out the reasons for the Nazi and Soviet occupations of my native Estonia, which resulted in my completing high school in faraway Marrakech, Morocco. Then I began applying the methods of physics to problems like international trade and the arms race, and soon shifted to mathematical social science. However, I still continue to write on the contemporary history of Estonia and other Baltic states. I like reading grammars of exotic languages, and am fluent in Estonian, Finnish, French, and German.

"The major current problem for the Baltic mini-nations in Soviet Russian occupation and a denationalizing inflow of Russian colonists. The longer-term problem is how to contribute to the world's variety by maintaining a full-fledged modern culture based on a language spoken by only one to four million people.

"I was shocked into writing a book on Juuri Kukk when this dissident Estonian chemist died in a Russian prison barely three months after being sentenced to two years. Two years should not be equivalent to a death sentence. I discovered that Kuuk's case illustrated a newly-developing erratic and potentially dangerous pattern in Soviet behavior, oscillating between softness and overreaction."

*   *   *

TAIKEFF, Stanley 1940-

PERSONAL: Born April 27, 1940, in Brooklyn, N.Y.; son of Irving (an attorney) and Lulu (a fashion designer; maiden name, Rosenberg) Taikeff; married Lenore Noval (an administrative assistant), August 4, 1968. *Education:* Hunter College of the City University of New York, B.A., 1963, M.A., 1971. *Home:* 3A Second Place, Brooklyn, N.Y. 11231.

CAREER: Worked as proofreader, free-lance writer, musical instrument repairman, typist-biller, sample clerk in garment district, salesman, and high school English teacher, all prior to 1977; writer, 1977—. Adjunct lecturer in English at La Guardia Community College, 1977—; part-time instructor in dramatic writing at New York University, 1980—. *Military service:* U.S. Army National Guard, 1963-69. *Member:* New Dramatists (member of executive committee, 1978-79). *Awards, honors:* John Golden awards for playwriting, 1970 and 1971; Shubert fellowship, 1971; Office for Advanced Drama Research grant, 1976, for "Don Juan of Flatbush"; Creative Artists Public Service playwriting fellowship, 1981; National Repertory Theatre Play Award finalist, 1981-82.

WRITINGS—Plays: "Denouement" (one-act), first produced in New York City at 13th Street Theatre, March, 1968; "Don Juan of Flatbush" (two-act), first produced in Kansas City, Mo., at Missouri Repertory Theatre, July, 1976; "The Sugar Bowl" (three-act), first produced in New Haven, Conn., at O'Neill National Playwrights Conference, July, 1976; "Ah, Eurydice!" (one-act), first produced Off-Broadway at Vandam Theatre, August, 1977; "In the Modern Style" (one-act), first produced in Minneapolis, Minn., at Cricket Theatre, December, 1979; "Solo Recital" (one-act), first produced in New

York City at New Dramatists, January, 1981; "Last Ferry to Thebes" (two-act; first produced at New Dramatists, January, 1981) in *Best Short Plays, 1978*, edited by Stanley Richards, Chilton, 1978; "The Hermit of Prague" (one-act), first produced at New Dramatists, November, 1981; "Brigitte Berger" (two-act), first produced at New Dramatists, March, 1982; "Aristotle Said" (one-act), first produced at New Dramatists, April, 1982. Also author of "A Cock to Aescelpius" and "The Stamp Family," as yet unpublished and unproduced.

Contributor of poems and plays to magazines, including *Voices of Brooklyn, Manhattan Review, Bitterroot, Dramatics Magazine,* and *Dramatists Guild Quarterly.*

WORK IN PROGRESS: "Civilization and Its Discontents," a one-act play about music, food, civilization, and the dissatisfied; "The Bilateral Varicocele," a one-act play about male infertility as seen through the life of King Longfellow of Longfellowmeadow.

SIDELIGHTS: Taikeff told *CA:* "Although practically everyone wants to be a playwright or to write a play, only a very few actually stick with it. This is because playwriting is the most demanding of the literary arts—and of those who persevere, only a handful are any good. What, in my mind, makes a playwright 'good,' if not 'great,' is the playwright's use of language. The greatest playwrights were verbally gifted. They all heard the 'music' of the language and translated it into unique, artistic theatrical visions.

"I believe very strongly in the written word, in the text of the play, especially in an age when the art of dramatic writing seems like an anachronism. It is important for playwrights to realize that words are all they have when writing a play, that the burden that dialogue carries in a play is enormous: it must tell a story, reveal character, dramatize an event. It must have the power to move people, to seduce them, to manipulate their feelings, and ultimately, to make them feel what it's like to be human at this particular moment of history."

AVOCATIONAL INTERESTS: Clarinet, classical guitar, opera, chamber music, Dixieland jazz, Spanish food, wines, Mexican cigars.

*   *   *

TAMMARO, Thom(as Michael)   1951-

PERSONAL: Born October 18, 1951, in Ellwood City, Pa.; son of Robert (a mill laborer) and Ann (DeTullio) Tammaro; married Sheila R. Coghill (an assistant professor), November 29, 1975. *Education:* Edinboro University, B.S., 1973; Pittsburg State University, M.A., 1974; Ball State University, Ph.D., 1980. *Home:* 5300 West Jackson St., Muncie, Ind. 47304. *Address:* New Center for Multidisciplinary Studies, Moorhead State University, Moorhead, Minn. 56560.

CAREER: Ball State University, Muncie, Ind., instructor, 1977-80, member of Carmichael Residential Instruction Project, 1977-82, assistant professor of English, 1980-83; Moorhead State University, Moorhead, Minn., assistant professor of multidisciplinary studies, 1983—. Gives readings and public lectures; guest on radio programs. *Member:* Modern Language Association of America, Associated Writing Programs, Society for the Study of Midwestern Literature, Indiana Teachers of Writing. *Awards, honors:* Grants from Indiana Arts Commission, 1980, 1981, 1982, and National Endowment for the Arts, 1982.

WRITINGS: Winter Guests: Poems by Grace Butcher, Michael Heffernan, and *Cyril A. Dostal,* Ball State University, 1979;

(editor with Tom Koontz) *The View From the Top of the Mountain: Poems After Sixty,* Barnwood Press, 1982; *Roving Across Fields: A Conversation With William Stafford,* Barnwood Press, 1983; (editor) Robert Bly, *Four Ramages,* Barnwood Press, 1983; (editor) *Translations by Edwin Honig,* Barnwood Press, 1983; (editor) Judson Jerome, *Partita: A Poem in B Flat,* Barnwood Press, 1983; (editor) Jared Carter, *Millenial Harbinger* (poems), Barnwood Press, 1983; (editor) Nick Bozanic, *Tree, Stone, Rock, Water* (poems), Barnwood Press, 1983; (editor) Angela Peckinpaugh and Louise Beebe Hayna, *A Book of Charms,* Barnwood Press, 1983; (contributor) Tetsumuro Hayashi, editor, *Research Opportunities in Arthur Miller and Tennessee Williams,* McFarland Publications, 1984.

Work represented in anthologies, including *It Is the Poem Singing Into Your Eyes,* edited by Arnold Adoff, Harper, 1972. Contributor of poems, articles, and reviews to magazines, including *Bitterroot, Indiana Writes, Midwest Quarterly, Spoon River Quarterly, West Coast Poetry Review, Indiana Review,* and *Debut.*

WORK IN PROGRESS: Sweeping the Rain, a collection of poems.

SIDELIGHTS: Tammaro told *CA:* "I like what Wallace Stevens once said about poetry, 'Poetry is the response to the daily necessity of getting the world right.' For me that's important. It suggests a faith in the possibilities of language. It demands a trust in the sensuous, emotive, and intuitive responses to life. I like the idea of poetry helping us along, nudging us through the day, helping us get things right. If our words and our poems grow from the deepest silences within ourselves, how can we *not* believe in what they speak to us?"

*   *   *

TANDEM, Felix
See SPITTELER, Carl

*   *   *

TARSIS, Valery Yakovlevich   1906-1983

OBITUARY NOTICE: Born September 23, 1906, in Kiev, Russia (now U.S.S.R.); died March 3, 1983, in Bern, Switzerland. Author. Tarsis was a Soviet dissident best known for his autobiographical novel *Ward Seven.* The book is about a writer's experiences in a Moscow mental asylum. Tarsis, whose works were first published in Russia in 1935, was well-received until the author began criticizing the Soviet system. In 1966 he was allowed to leave the Soviet Union, and he never returned. Tarsis's other works include *The Bluebottle* and *The Pleasure Factory,* both in English translation. Obituaries and other sources: *New York Times,* March 4, 1983; *Washington Post,* March 4, 1983; *London Times,* March 5, 1983; *Time,* March 14, 1983.

*   *   *

TASCA, Jules   1938-

PERSONAL: Born December 10, 1938, in Philadelphia, Pa.; son of Edward Michael (an electrician) and Mary (Zaccaria) Tasca; married Beatrice Marie Hartranft (a tennis player), January 29, 1962; children: Edward, Jennifer, Joel. *Education:* Pennsylvania State University, B.A., 1961; Villanova University, M.A., 1963. *Home and office:* 313 Heston Ave., Norristown, Pa. 19401. *Agent:* Lois Berman, 250 West 57th St., New York, N.Y. 10019.

CAREER: Gwynedd Mercy College, Gwynedd Valley, Pa., associate professor of drama, 1963—, chairman of department, 1982—. Visiting professor at Beaver College, Glenside, Pa., 1965, 1982, Villanova University, Villanova, Pa., 1966, and Pennsylvania State University, Abington, Pa., 1966; director of public relations for Philadelphia Playhouse in the Park, 1969. *Member:* Dramatists Guild.

WRITINGS—Plays: *Subject to Change* (three-act; first produced in Chicago at Pheasant Run Theatre, April, 1971), Samuel French, 1970; *The Mind With the Dirty Man* (two-act; first produced in Los Angeles at Mark Taper Forum, March, 1973), Samuel French, 1971; *Tear Along the Dotted Line* (three-act; first produced in Gwynedd Valley, Pa., at Julia Ball Auditorium, 1965), Dramatic Publishing, 1973; *Tadpole* (three-act; first produced in Los Angeles at Mark Taper Forum, 1973), Dramatists Play Service, 1974; *Chop Off Olympus* (three-act; first produced in New York City at Triangle Theatre), Samuel French, 1974; *Five One-Act Plays By Mark Twain* (adaptation; first produced in Gwynedd Valley, Pa., at Julia Ball Auditorium, 1975), Samuel French, 1976; *Susan B!* (one-act; first produced in New York City at Town Hall, 1981), Dramatic, Publishing, 1982.

(Contributor) Howard Teichmann, *George S. Kaufman: An Intimate Portrait,* Atheneum, 1972.

Also author of "Nip 'n Tuck," "Party of the First Part," "One Act by Art Smythe, Full Length Play by Joe Jones," "Romeo and Juliet Are Lovers," "Alive and Kicking," "The Last Damned Witch in Salem," and "Goody One Shoe," as yet unpublished and unproduced.

Co-author of "Hal Linden Special," first broadcast by CBS-TV, April, 1979.

WORK IN PROGRESS: "E = Einstein," a libretto.

SIDELIGHTS: In "The Mind With the Dirty Man," the leader of a small town's censorship board is challenged when his son, an underground filmmaker, plans to show his X-rated work in the local theatre. The plot is complicated by the son's love for the star of his movie and his plan to marry her on opening night in front of the theatre.

In a review of the play's Los Angeles production, a *Variety* critic noted that Tasca "has no particular axe to grind and writes only for entertainment." Tasca verified this estimate in a *Philadelphia Bulletin* article when he stated, "Okay, it's a situation comedy. . . . It's meant to entertain. If people start thinking about it later, and decide that censorship is really kind of silly, so much the better. But there's no sense in satirizing an attitude if you turn off the types that may hold it."

Tasca told *CA:* "I am still writing. Every step is as hard to take as the last. The march is still on. The road is still called Hope. The end of the road is achievement. It is a land of few dwellers. If I get there, perhaps I can hide out until they find me and tell me I can't stay."

BIOGRAPHICAL/CRITICAL SOURCES: Variety, April 4, 1973; *Philadelphia Bulletin,* June 23, 1974; *Authors in the News,* Volume I, Gale, 1976.

* * *

TAYLOR, Alan R(os) 1926-

PERSONAL: Born August 7, 1926, in New York, N.Y.; son of Herbert F. and Madeleine R. Taylor; married Bernedette Ernould. *Education:* Columbia University, B.A., 1950;

Georgetown University, M.S., 1955, Ph.D., 1958. *Religion:* Episcopalian. *Office:* School of International Service, American University, Massachusetts and Nebraska Aves. N.W., Washington, D.C. 20016.

CAREER: Howard University, Washington, D.C., instructor, 1957-60; American University of Beirut, Beirut, Lebanon, assistant professor, 1960-63; researcher at Oxford University, 1963-64; American University, Washington, D.C., began as associate professor, became professor at School of International Service, 1964—.

WRITINGS: Prelude to Israel, Philosophical Library, 1959; (co-editor) *Palestine: A Search for Truth,* Public Affairs Press, 1970; *The Zionist Mind,* Institute for Palestine Studies (Beirut, Lebanon), 1974; *The Arab Balance of Power,* Syracuse University Press, 1982.

* * *

TAYLOR, Anique 1946-

PERSONAL: Given name is pronounced Ah-neek; born May 29, 1946, in Greenwich, Conn.; daughter of Max (a lawyer) and Eva (a guidance counselor; maiden name, Morrison) Taylor; married George Shea (a writer), May 28, 1980 (divorced). *Education:* Sorbonne, University of Paris, Certificat de la Langue Francaise, 1964; attended Antioch College, 1964-66; Silvermine College of Art, A.F.A., 1969; attended Cooper Union, 1969-70; Pratt Institute, B.F.A. (with highest honors), 1973, M.F.A., 1975. *Home:* 322 East 11th St., No. 10, New York, N.Y. 10003.

CAREER: Elementary and junior high school teacher of music, art, and writing in Long Beach, Calif., 1966; preschool teacher in Greenwich, Conn., 1966-67; illustrator for magazines and theatres, fabric and embroidery designer, printmaker, and portrait painter in New York City, 1970-82; East Manhattan School (for gifted children), New York City, kindergarten teacher, 1982-83. Member of Bohemian Arms Unlimited Corp. *Member:* Graphic Artists Guild.

WRITINGS: (With George Shea) *What to Do When You're Bored* (children's book), Simon & Schuster, 1982. Also illustrator of Shea's "Ragamuffins and Redcoats," a children's filmstrip, for Activity Records.

WORK IN PROGRESS: A Book for Lovers, self-illustrated; *Alexander and the Wonderful Dream Door,* a self-illustrated children's book.

SIDELIGHTS: Taylor told *CA:* "I've been collaborating with friends for years—on books, plays, television scripts, comedy routines, and filmstrips. I find that an idea will simmer for months, then I'll sit down and write it all at once. My current children's book, *Alexander and the Wonderful Dream Door,* is a fantasy of a grouchy boy who is fleeing from his nightmares. He is thrown into all sorts of strange situations. In solving his dilemma, he finds the ability to create both the story and the emotional tone of his own dreams. This book is an outgrowth of my work with children—a way to tell them through fantasy the importance of dreaming self-determinedly.

"My stories are in the beginning a feeling, an emotion, or a message that may have been with me for years. When I get a concrete story idea, a situation, an adventure, or a character, I begin to make my lists. I make lists of actions, character changes, situation developments—then words, philosophies, emotions. Then I write down plot developments, ordering each event by number. This is the skeleton of the story. I use the lists to make the story fatten around it.

"After the first draft is written, I put it away and bring it out only when it's distant to me and I can reread it with a stranger's eyes. I do this again and again, each time pulling it tighter so that each word and passage means something to the whole. I hope that in the young there is still a way a thing can be said and known and used—and that maybe from just the telling a life can open and grow.

"Drawing for me is a process of learning to see. Instead of identifying an object for its function, I've learned to see the light, line, tone, and texture of a thing—how it feels and looks, what can be said through it. And so the world has opened itself in a sensual feast for my eyes.

"I do drawing, painting, printmaking, and pen and inks. I work at least five hours a day, having learned that inspiration is an outgrowth of dedication and commitment. The more I work, the more easily ideas come; the more I put into it, the more satisfying it is to me. It's like exercising a muscle.

"I am excited by delicacy of tone and how one color affects another. My work is realistic, though it must also function in the abstract in that all art deals with color, line, tone, composition, texture, and rhythm.

"Lately I have been working on delicately drawn sepia-toned pencil portraits of people from the turn of the century to the present. I am intrigued with how character and emotion can be visible through just the arrangement of feature and expression. I am fascinated by houses, rooms, and neighborhoods where people live—how what people are is reflected in their surroundings and their presentation. How the inside shows on the outside—and how their lives show in their faces."

*　　*　　*

TAYLOR, Charles Alfred 1922-

PERSONAL: Born August 14, 1922, in Hull, England; son of William (a local government officer) and Ethel (Marshall) Taylor; married Nancy Truefitt, April 22, 1944; children: Antony David, Marion Elizabeth Taylor Walker, John Alexander. *Education:* Queen Mary College, London, B.Sc., 1942; Victoria University of Manchester, Ph.D., 1951, D.Sc., 1959. *Home:* 9 Hill Deverill, Warminster, Wiltshire BA12 7EF, England. *Office:* Department of Physics, University College, University of Wales, P.O. Box 78, Cardiff CF1 1XL, Wales, United Kingdom.

CAREER: Admiralty Signals Establishment, Haslemere, England, temporary experimental officer, 1942-45; Metropolitan Vickers Electrical Co., Manchester, England, research physicist, 1945-48; Victoria University of Manchester, Manchester, lecturer, 1948-59, reader in physics, 1959-65; University of Wales, University College, Cardiff, professor of physics and head of department, 1965—. Honorary professor at Royal Institution of Great Britain. Host of Royal Institution Chemistry Lectures, a television series, 1971. Chairman of Welsh Dance Theatre Trust. *Member:* International Council of Scientific Unions (chairman of committee on science teaching, 1978—), Institute of Physics (fellow; vice-president of education), Institute of Acoustics (fellow), Royal Microscopical Society (fellow).

WRITINGS: (With Henry Lipson) *Fourier Transforms and X-Ray Diffraction*, G. Bell, 1958; (with Lipson) *Optical Transforms*, G. Bell, 1964; *The Physics of Musical Sounds*, English

Universities Press, 1965; (with George Harburn and Richard Welberry) *Atlas of Optical Transforms*, G. Bell, 1975; *Sounds of Music*, BBC Publications, 1976; *Images*, Wykeham Publications, 1978. Editor of series, "Penguin Physics Reference Books," Penguin, 1973. Contributor to *New Grove Dictionary of Music and Musicians*.

WORK IN PROGRESS: The Human Element in Science, publication by Wykeham expected in 1985; research on musical instruments from the scientific angle and the popularization of science.

SIDELIGHTS: Taylor commented: "I am increasingly concerned at the poor way in which science is introduced during the early years at school and at the poor image of science presented in the media. When I gave the 1971 Royal Institution Chemistry Lectures (six hours of solo television), I became convinced that something could be done. I now devote an increasing amount of time to public demonstration lectures."

*　　*　　*

TAYLOR, Harold McCarter 1907-

PERSONAL: Born May 13, 1907, in Dunedin, New Zealand; son of James and Louisa Urquhart (McCarter) Taylor; married Joan Sills, April, 1933 (died, 1965); married Judith Samuel, March 21, 1966; children: (first marriage) Michael, Joh, Elizabeth (Mrs. Piers Brim Bowden), Judith (Mrs. H. John M. Bull). *Education:* University of Otago, B.Sc., 1927, M.Sc., 1928; Cambridge University, B.A., 1930, M.A. and Ph.D., both 1933. *Politics:* Conservative. *Religion:* Anglican. *Home:* 192 Huntingdon Rd., Cambridge CB3 0LB, England.

CAREER: Cambridge University, Cambridge, England, fellow of Clare College, 1933-61, lecturer in mathematics, 1933-45, treasurer of university, 1945-63, secretary-general of faculties, 1953-61; University of Keele, Keele, England, vice-chancellor, 1961-67; writer and archaeological researcher, 1967—. Member of Royal Commission on Historical Monuments, 1972-77. *Military service:* British Army, Territorial Army, 1924-45; became lieutenant colonel. *Member:* Society of Antiquaries (vice-president, 1974-78), Royal Archaeological Institute (president, 1972-75). *Awards, honors:* Commander of Order of the British Empire, 1955; LL.D. from Cambridge University, 1967; D.Litt. from University of Keele, 1968, and University of Birmingham, 1983.

WRITINGS: Anglo-Saxon Architecture, Cambridge University Press, Volumes I-II, 1965, Volume III, 1978; *Why Should We Study the Anglo-Saxons?*, Cambridge University Press, 1966; *Deerhurst Studies*, privately printed, 1977; *Repton Studies*, privately printed, Volume I, 1977, Volume II, 1979, Volume III, 1983. Contributor to archaeology journals.

WORK IN PROGRESS: Continuing research on structural archaeology "in order to improve the accuracy with which the surviving churches built before the Norman Conquest in 1066 can be dated."

SIDELIGHTS: Taylor told *CA:* "The art and architecture of England have interested me intensely since I cam here in 1928 from New Zealand—where there are no such treasures of Western civilization that are more than about one hundred years old.

"From the Norman Conquest onward, the history of these treasures can be reliably described in England because of the survival of contemporary written evidence for many of the objects concerned (particularly the buildings). This is *not* so for the Anglo-Saxon era, and experts will differ by well over a century in the dates they claim for buildings and sculptures. These objects therefore present a fascinating challenge to those like myself who wish to unearth their history and to explain how, when, and why they were made and how they were to be used.

"The importance of trying to date such artifacts much more closely than has yet been done lies in the desire to understand the passages of ideas in the development of Western civilization between the Fall of Rome and the rise of the Normans in the second millenium. The uncertainty in dates of buildings and sculptures on *both* sides of the English Channel means that it is impossible to decide with any degree of certainty whether or not all good ideas originated on the Continent and were only later brought to England. In recent years it has been established that some good ideas did have their origin in England, but a great deal still remains to be done in settling the dates of erection of successive stages of major buildings on both sides of the Channel. Only thus can the history of art and architecture of that period be clarified."

AVOCATIONAL INTERESTS: "For many years my first wife and younger son joined me in ski-mountain traversing in the Swiss Alps. Without guides we crossed Switzerland from France to the Austrian frontier."

* * *

TAYLOR, Joan du Plat   ?-1983

OBITUARY NOTICE: Died May 21, 1983. Archaeologist, editor, librarian, and author. Taylor was best known for her accomplishments in nautical archaeology. The first full-time librarian at the London Institute of Archaeology, she conducted excavations in Cyprus and helped launch the famous excavation of the Bronze Age wreck off Turkey's Mediterranean coast. Taylor served on the Council of the Society of National Research and was the first vice-president of the Council for Nautical Archaeology. She also helped found *The International Journal of Nautical Archaeology* and was an editor of the World Underwater Federation's book *Marine Archaeology*. Obituaries and other sources: *London Times*, June 4, 1983.

* * *

TAYLOR, Malcolm Gordon   1915-

PERSONAL: Born August 31, 1915, in Alberta, Canada; son of Charles G. and Ora E. Taylor; children: Deanne Elizabeth, Burke Gordon. *Education:* University of California, Berkeley, B.A., 1942, M.A., 1943, Ph.D., 1949. *Religion:* United Church of Canada. *Home:* 55 Maitland St., Toronto, Ontario, Canada M4Y 1C9. *Office:* School of Public Administration, York University, Toronto, Ontario, Canada M3J 1P3.

CAREER: Worked in industrial relations department at Henry Kaiser Corp., 1941-43; University of Toronto, Toronto, Ontario, associate professor of political economy, 1951-60; University of Alberta, Calgary, principal, 1960-64; University of Victoria, Victoria, British Columbia, president, 1964-68; York University, Toronto, Ontario, professor of public policy, 1969-82. Hannah Lecturer, 1980-81. Chairman of National Manpower Council for Mental Retardation, 1972-76; consultant to Royal Commission on Health Services.

MEMBER: Canadian Political Science Association, Canadian Society for Higher Education (president, 1974-75), Institute of Public Administration of Canada (president, 1959-60), Phi Beta Kappa, Pi Sigma Alpha, Arts and Letters Club. *Awards, honors:* LL.D. from University of Alberta, 1965; J. A. Hannah Book Medal from Royal Society of Canada, 1980; National Health Scientist Award, 1981.

WRITINGS: Administration of Health Insurance in Canada, Oxford University Press, 1956; *Financial Aspects of Health Insurance,* Canadian Tax Foundation, 1958; *Health Insurance and Canadian Public Policy,* McGill-Queen's University Press, 1978. Contributor to scholarly journals. Editor of *Canadian Journal of Public Administration,* 1958-60.

WORK IN PROGRESS: The Canadian Health System in Transition.

* * *

TEAGUE, Michael   1932-

PERSONAL: Born December 25, 1932, in Karachi, Pakistan; son of John (an army officer) and Heather (a writer; maiden name, Fairley) Teague. *Education:* Worcester College, Oxford, M.A. (with honors), 1956. *Home:* 920 South Carolina Ave. S.E., Washington, D.C. 20003. *Office:* 1211 Connecticut Ave. N.W., Washington, D.C. 20036.

CAREER: Downs & Roosevelt, Inc. (public relations firm), Washington, D.C., vice-president, 1964—. Chairman of the Leonard Cheshire Foundation, Inc., 1977-81. *Military service:* British Army, 1951-53; served with Royal Fusiliers and Royal West Africa Frontier Force. *Awards, honors:* University Prize from Royal Asian Society, 1954, for essay "The Sea Route to the Indies."

WRITINGS: Mrs. L.: Conversations With Alice Roosevelt Longworth, Doubleday, 1981.

SIDELIGHTS: Teague's *Mrs. L.* is a profile of Alice Roosevelt Longworth, eldest daughter of President Theodore Roosevelt. Until her death in 1980 at the age of eighty-six, Longworth was well known for her sharp-tongued one-liners about the Washington social set. (She once quipped that Calvin Coolidge looked "as if he had been weaned on a pickle," and mused: "The Kennedys reminded me of all the Irish who came over in the 1840s . . . they were all those marvelous-looking kitchen maids and policemen.") Teague was a good friend of Longworth and was often present at the socialite's daily tea parties, where he recorded many of her conversations, later editing them for his book. "The handsome book that resulted is a delight," wrote critic Charlotte Curtis in the *New York Times Book Review.* Alastair Forbes of the *Times Literary Supplement* commented: "I very much enjoyed Teague's worthwhile exhumation and heartily applaud his excellently produced book and its most captivating illustrations."

BIOGRAPHICAL/CRITICAL SOURCES: Washington Post, July 14, 1981; *New York Times,* August 23, 1981; *Times Literary Supplement,* March 12, 1982.

* * *

TEEGEN, Otto John   1899-1983

OBITUARY NOTICE: Born August 19, 1899, in Davenport, Iowa; died April 8, 1983, in Manhattan, N.Y. Architect and author. A student for two years at the *Ecole des Beaux Arts* in Paris, Teegen was later employed at the firm of Ely Jacques Kahn, and he wrote a book about Kahn for the series *Contemporary American Architects.* Teegen, who helped design major projects in Florida, New York, and Washington, D.C., was

an architect for New York State University from 1949 to 1964, during which time he designed new buildings for twenty-eight of the school's community campuses. His other projects included work on both the Cleveland Exposition in 1936 and the New York World's Fair in 1939, as well as supervision of the color schemes for the 1933 Chicago World's Fair. Teegen was also a fellow of the American Institute of Architects. Obituaries and other sources: *Chicago Tribune*, April 14, 1983.

* * *

TEISER, Ruth 1915-

PERSONAL: Born June 28, 1915, in Portland, Ore.; daughter of Sidney (an attorney) and Betty (Kline) Teiser. *Education:* Attended Mills College, 1932-34; Stanford University, B.A., 1936, M.A., 1938, further graduate study, 1939-41. *Politics:* Democrat. *Home and office:* 932 Vallejo St., San Francisco, Calif. 94133. *Agent:* Frederick Hill, 2237 Union St., San Francisco, Calif. 94123.

CAREER: San Francisco News, San Francisco, Calif., reporter, 1943; free-lance writer and photographer, 1944—. Part-time senior editor and interviewer at Regional Oral History Office, Bancroft Library, University of California, Berkeley, 1965—. *Member:* California Historical Society, Book Club of California, Gleeson Library Associates (fellow), Friends of the Bancroft Library. *Awards, honors:* Award of merit from California Historical Society and silver medal from Commonwealth Club of California, both 1982, both for *Winemaking in California*.

WRITINGS: This Sudden Empire, Society of California Pioneers, 1949; (editor with Catherine Harroun, and contributor) *Printing as a Performing Art*, Book Club of California, 1970; (editor with Harroun, and contributor) Arpad Haraszthy, *Winemaking in California*, Book Club of California, 1978; (with Harroun) *Winemaking in California*, McGraw, 1982; (contributor) Doris Muscatine, Maynard A. Amerine, and Bob Thompson, editors, *Book of California Wine*, University of California Press, in press. Contributor to *World Book Encyclopedia* and *Collier's Encyclopedia*. Contributor of articles and reviews to magazines, including *Westways, Travel, Wine World, Wines and Vines*, and *California Living*, and to newspapers.

WORK IN PROGRESS: A history of winemaking in Monterey County, California, with Catherine Harroun; a biography of printer Lawton Kennedy, publication by Book Club of California expected in 1985.

SIDELIGHTS: Teiser told *CA*: "*Winemaking in California* was the culmination of many years of work on California history and research on California wines; the last three years Catherine Harroun and I worked almost full time on the book. It is a history of winemaking in California, from its beginnings in the late eighteenth century, through the mission period when California was a Spanish colony, through its Mexican years, the Gold Rush, the agricultural and industrial development of the latter nineteenth and early twentieth centuries, Prohibition, and the years since, to the present. It is a span from primitive to highly sophisticated winemaking, and ours is the first book to give a full account of the state's winemaking history."

AVOCATIONAL INTERESTS: Travel (especially Italy).

* * *

ten BOOM, Corrie 1892-1983

OBITUARY NOTICE: Born April 15, 1892, in the Netherlands; died of a heart ailment, April 15, 1983, in Placentia, Calif. Author. Corrie ten Boom was a Dutch Christian who sheltered Jews from the Nazis during World War II. Her experiences in Holland and the concentration camp in Ravensbruck, Germany, became the basis for her best-selling book, *The Hiding Place*, which was adapted as a motion picture and released in 1973. Ten Boom came to the United States after the war, wrote eighteen books, and gave lectures at churches and before Christian groups around the world. Obituaries and other sources: *New York Times*, April 17, 1983, April 21, 1983; *Washington Post*, April 18, 1983; *Detroit Free Press*, April 19, 1983; *Chicago Tribune*, April 20, 1983.

* * *

TERAYAMA, Shuji 1936-1983

OBITUARY NOTICE: Born in 1936 in Japan; died of a kidney ailment, May 4, 1983. Filmmaker, poet, and playwright. Known for the "shock effect" and violent content of his work, Terayama emerged in the late 1950's and early 1960's with numerous stage plays, radio dramas, magazine articles, film scenarios, and a novel. In 1967 he founded a theatre company, and in 1970 the first of his plays, "La Marie Vision," was presented in New York City. The following year his first feature-length film won the grand prize at the San Remo Festival in Italy. Among his more notable plays are "Directions to Servants," "Knock," and "Festival Hide and Seek," which was the official Japanese entry in the festival at Cannes, France. Obituaries and other sources: *New York Times*, May 14, 1983; *London Times*, May 24, 1983.

* * *

THEIS, John William 1911-

BRIEF ENTRY: Born August 21, 1911, in Pittsburgh, Pa. American journalist. In 1933 Theis joined the staff of International News Service (now United Press International [UPI]), working as bureau manager, correspondent in Washington, D.C., and chief of the U.S. Senate staff. He left UPI in 1968 to become Washington, D.C., bureau chief for Hearst Newspapers. In 1976 Theis was appointed senior communications adviser for the American Petroleum Institute. He co-authored *Congress: Power and Purpose on Capitol Hill* (Allyn & Bacon, 1967). *Address:* 705 Winhall Way, Silver Spring, Md. 10904.

* * *

THOMPSON, Alan Eric 1924-

PERSONAL: Born September 16, 1924; son of Eric Joseph and Florence Thompson; married Mary Heather Long, 1960; children: Alice, Matthew, Andrew, Hamish. *Education:* University of Edinburgh, M.A., 1949, M.A. (economic science; with Class I honors), 1951, Ph.D., 1953. *Home:* 11 Upper Gray St., Edinburgh 9, Scotland. *Office:* Department of Economics, Heriot-Watt University, 31-35 Grassmarket, Edinburgh EH1 2HT, Scotland.

CAREER: University of Edinburgh, Edinburgh, Scotland, Carnegie Research Scholar, 1951-52, assistant in political economy, 1952-53, lecturer in political economy, 1953-59; Labour member of Parliament for Dunfermline Burghs, 1959-64; University of Edinburgh, lecturer in political economy, 1964-71; Heriot-Watt University, Edinburgh, A. J. Balfour Professor of Economics of Government and chairman of department of economics, 1972—. Visiting professor at Stanford University's

Graduate School of Business, 1966 and 1968. Parliamentary adviser for Scottish Television, 1966-76; governor of British Broadcasting Corp. (BBC) and chairman of BBC-Scotland, 1976-80. President of Edinburgh Amenity and Transport Association, 1970; chairman of Advisory Board on Economics Education, 1970; commissioner of Royal Fine Art Commission for Scotland, 1976-81; chairman of Newbattle Abbey College, Scotland, 1980—. Economic consultant to Scotch Whisky Association, 1960-70. Member of committee investigating conditions in which young servicemen live, 1969, and of Scottish Committee and Public Schools Commission, 1969-70. Television and radio commentator. *Military service:* British Army, Infantry, 1943-47; served in the Mediterranean. *Member:* Royal Society of Arts (fellow), Association of Nazi War Camp Survivors (honorary vice-president, 1960—), Scottish Arts Club.

WRITINGS: (With others) *Development of Economic Doctrine,* Longman, 1980. Contributor of articles and children's stories and plays to journals.

WORK IN PROGRESS: Research on Parliamentary control of public broadcasting in the United Kingdom and on public responsibility for broadcasting in the United Kingdom.

* * *

THOMPSON, Brian 1935-

PERSONAL: Born May 2, 1935, in London, England; son of A. John (an engineer) and Peggy (Mills) Thompson; children: Peter, Clare, Stephen. *Education:* Trinity College, Cambridge, B.A. (with honors), 1958. *Home:* 7 Spring Mount, Harrogate, North Yorkshire, England. *Agent:* Sheila Lemon, Ltd., 74 Forthbridge Rd., London SW11 5NY, England.

CAREER: Worked as adult education teacher; novelist and playwright, 1973—. *Military service:* King's African Rifles, 1953-55; became lieutenant. *Member:* Theatre Writer's Union, Chelsea Arts Club. *Awards, honors:* Royal Television Society award for documentary film, 1977, 1978, and 1979; fiction award from Yorkshire Arts Association, 1979.

WRITINGS: Portrait of Leeds (history), R. Hale, 1971; *Buddy Boy* (novel), Gollancz, 1977; *Trooper Jackson's Story* (juvenile fiction), Gollancz, 1979. Work has appeared in anthologies, including *Dandelion Clocks,* M. Joseph, 1979, and *Loving Couples,* M. Joseph, 1981.

Also author of plays, including "The Conservatory," "Jones," "Patriotic Bunting," "Ten Mighty Talents," "Tishoo," "Traffic," and "Deccan" (a teleplay).

WORK IN PROGRESS: A play on H. L. Mencken, a novel about expatriate English in Florida, and a children's book set in France.

SIDELIGHTS: "I have been writing for a living since 1973; before this time I was interested in education and the arts. I changed from a secure and reasonably well-rewarded job to one filled with doubt and uncertainty, principally for the doubt and uncertainty. All but a very few of us have it. The ones who don't have doubt are usually the world's enemies. Fiction is a way of expressing doubt and incomprehension with dignity.

"I have always been interested in history. I was a child in Cambridge, where the mighty Eighth United States Air Forces was operational during the Second World War. When I look back on the many things I have written, they have war as their theme. Or perhaps it would be better to say that they are thick with the detail of war, the sound and the fury of it. It is not popular to say it now-a-days, but what personal experience I have had of combat (leaving aside all educated responses to it) has been exciting and very keenly felt. This is the somber side of me. Much of what I do to earn my living is to make people smile, or better, laugh, or best of all, laugh and cry at the same time.

"Novels are especially important to me, and I wish I could concentrate more on that form of fiction. There is something so personal and complete about the resolution of a long prose narrative. The next best thing is sitting in a theater and hearing an audience laugh with pleasure and understanding at a line given by an actor, but springing straight from the heart of you. Having said all this, I could never be a polemical writer. Too much doubt and too great a pleasure in the art of disguise.

"Everything I write has my children in mind, and what books I publish are dedicted to them. I'm quite sure this will make some psychologist I have never met (and never want to meet) tut-tut and blow out his cheeks. But for me, the act of writing is trying to gain the respect of those whom you yourself respect. I respect and admire my children greatly.

"Finally, it is not enough to write books and plays: one must write English. That is a much more demanding occupation, but that's where it's at. If I have a good day at the typewriter, I feel linked, however poorly, to the great practitioners of language, who might be other fictionalists, but might as well be historians, biographers, botanists, or oceanographers."

* * *

THOMPSON, Donald Eugene 1913-

PERSONAL: Born July 10, 1913, in McCallsburg, Iowa; son of Andy and Mabel (Hanson) Thompson; married Jean Beecher (a librarian), June 25, 1938; children: Neil Bruce, Janet Louise. *Education:* Iowa State University, B.S., 1935; University of Illinois, B.S. in L.S., 1937; Temple University, M.A., 1942. *Politics:* Republican. *Religion:* Presbyterian. *Home:* 1103 West Pike St., Crawfordsville, Ind. 47933. *Office:* Library, Wabash College, Crawfordsville, Ind. 47933.

CAREER: Temple University, Philadelphia, Pa., assistant business librarian, 1937-39, business librarian, 1939-40; University of Alabama, University, business librarian, 1940-42, acting director of libraries, 1942-44, assistant director of libraries, 1944-48; Mississippi State College, State College, director of libraries, 1948-55; Wabash College, Crawfordsville, Ind., librarian, 1955-78, archivist, 1982—. *Member:* American Library Association, Indiana Historical Society, Society of Indiana Archivists, Indiana Library Association (president, 1967-68), Montgomery County Historical Society (president, 1981—).

WRITINGS: A Bibliography of Louisiana Books and Pamphlets in the T. P. Thompson Collection of the University of Alabama Library, University of Alabama Press, 1947; (with Peter Hiatt) *Monroe County Library: Planning for the Future,* privately printed, 1966; (with Hiatt) *The Public Library Needs of Delaware County: The Community, the Muncie Public Library, and the Future,* privately printed, 1967; (with J. M. Rothacker) *Directory of Special and Subject Collections in Indiana,* Indiana Library Studies, 1970; *Indiana Authors and Their Books, 1917-1966,* Wabash College, 1974; *Preliminary Checklist of Archives and Manuscripts in Indiana Repositories,* Indiana Historical Society, 1980; *Indiana Authors and Their Books, 1967-1980,* Wabash College, 1981. Author of "The Literary Scene," a monthly column in *Montgomery.* Contributor to library journals and literary magazines.

WORK IN PROGRESS: A literary history of Montgomery, Indiana; subject studies on Indiana authors.

SIDELIGHTS: Thompson told *CA:* "During research for the books on Indiana authors, I became increasingly aware of the great amount of writing done by Indianans and the large number of authors the state has produced. Nearly two dozen people have made remarks about this. Some have said that Indiana has surpassed all other states in both of these categories. This has been documented by a number of statistical studies. On a smaller scale, there are nearly three hundred people currently (as of early 1983) living in Montgomery County, Indiana, who have published articles or poetry in *Montgomery* or in other magazines and newspapers, or who have written books. The literary fertility of Indiana is tremendous.

"In addition to Indiana authors, I am interested in local history. I believe that it is extremely important to collect and record what has happened locally in the form of written stories and oral history. Local repositories should develop a coordinated policy that will allow them to collect and preserve all types of materials that form the basis for local history. Residents should be encouraged to share special knowledge and materials they possess on different subjects. This knowledge should be preserved in the local repositories and methods should be developed to make the information available to those who want to use it."

*   *   *

THOMPSON, James   1902-1983

OBITUARY NOTICE: Born March 24, 1902, in England; died March 31, 1983. Judge and author. Following his education at Edinburgh University, Thompson began a career that took him to various overseas territories. He was called to the English Bar in 1929 and became a resident magistrate in Northern Rhodesia (now Zambia). Thompson's other appointments included judge of Fiji, chief justice of Tonga, and judge, subsequently chief justice, of Malaya (now part of Malaysia). He was the author of *The Laws of the British Solomon Islands* and *The Law of Tonga.* Obituaries and other sources: *London Times,* April 8, 1983.

*   *   *

THOMPSON, Morris Mordecai   1912-

PERSONAL: Born February 6, 1912, in Jersey City, N.J.; son of Barney (a builder) and Rose (Golub) Thompson; married Sophia Shapiro (an editor), February 29, 1936; children: Robert D. *Education:* Princeton University, B.S.Eng., 1934, C.E., 1935. *Home:* 1722 Pine Valley Dr., Vienna, Va. 22180. *Office:* U.S. Geological Survey, MS516 National Center, Reston, Va. 22092.

CAREER: U.S. Geological Survey, Reston, Va., topographic engineer in Reston, Washington, D.C., and Chattanooga, Tenn., 1939-48, research engineer, 1949-60, chief of section for photogrammetry, 1961-62, deputy chief of research in topographic mapping, 1963-65, Atlantic Region engineer, 1966-68, chief of research and technical standards, 1968-75, part-time research engineer, 1975—.

MEMBER: International Cartographic Association (chairman of Commission on Automated Mapping, 1968-72), American Society of Photogrammetry (honorary member), American Congress on Surveying and Mapping (chairman of Cartography

Division, 1968), American Society of Civil Engineers (chairman of Surveying and Mapping Division, 1973-74).

AWARDS, HONORS: American Society of Photogrammetry Abrams Award, 1950, for article "A New Approach to Flight Planning," Fairchild Photogrammetric Award, 1966; distinguished service award from U.S. Department of Interior, 1967; surveying and mapping award from American Society of Civil Engineers, 1977; honor award in cartography from American Congress on Surveying and Mapping, 1980.

WRITINGS: (Editor in chief) *Manual of Photogrammetry,* 3rd edition (Thompson was not associated with earlier editions), American Society of Photogrammetry, 1966; *Maps for America: Cartographic Products of the U.S. Geological Survey and Others,* U.S. Geological Survey, 1979, revised edition, 1982. Contributor to technical journals.

SIDELIGHTS: Thompson told *CA:* "I hold that the development of a technical book can be fully as challenging as the writing of a biography or a novel. The technical writer has to realize that his masterpiece will never reach a mass audience; however, on the other hand, he can be consoled by the knowledge that his work may have value for someone long after today's bestseller has been forgotten.

"In today's world, the role of the cartographer goes far beyond the classical (and still important) function of providing maps that show the location and identity of geographical features and guide the traveler in proceeding from place to place. Modern cartography has taken on the task of providing effective communication in a limitless number of fields by means of a powerful medium: the thematic map. Thematic maps emphasize the geographical distribution of a single phenomenon such as ethnic distribution, movement of oil from source to market, crime statistics, or the prevalence of an epidemic. One sees thematic maps every day in major newspapers and magazines, each map especially prepared to communicate a unique message. The techniques for presenting such maps are constantly being improved with new and imaginative treatments. Thus, the twentieth-century cartographer may be aptly described as a primary communicator and interpreter of the modern world."

*   *   *

THOMPSON, Wayne C(urtis)   1943-

PERSONAL: Born September 11, 1943, in Fort Benning, Ga.; son of W. Claude (in business) and Virginia (a teacher) Thompson; married Susan Leamy (a teacher), September 17, 1966; children: Juliet Suzanne, Catherine Danielle. *Education:* Ohio State University, B.A., 1965; attended University of Goettingen, 1964-65; Sorbonne, University of Paris, Certificat de Langue Francaise, 1965; Claremont Graduate School, M.A., 1971, Ph.D., 1974; University of Freiburg, Diploma of the German Language, 1973. *Home:* 197 Vernon St., Lynchburg, Va. 24501. *Office:* Department of Political Science, Lynchburg College, Lynchburg, Va. 24501.

CAREER: Lynchburg College, Lynchburg, Va., assistant professor, 1973-77, associate professor of political science, 1977—. *Military service:* U.S. Army, 1966-69; became sergeant. *Member:* Association for Canadian Studies in the United States, Council for European Studies, Western Association for German Studies. *Awards, honors:* Earhart fellow in Clarement, California, 1969-71, and East and West Germany, 1975; Woodrow Wilson fellow, 1971-72; Fulbright grant, 1971-72; German Academic Exchange Service fellow in West Germany, 1972-73, 1979; scholar-in-residence of Conference Group on German Politics in Bundestag, Bonn, West Germany, 1976; fellow of National Endowment for the Humanitites, 1977-78; Alexander von Humboldt fellow, 1980-82.

WRITINGS: In the Eye of the Storm (nonfiction), University of Iowa Press, 1980; *Western Europe,* Stryker-Post, 1982; *Canada,* Stryker-Post, in press. Contributor to political science and history journals.

WORK IN PROGRESS: Herbert Wehner: A Political Biography, completion expected in 1985.

SIDELIGHTS: Thompson told *CA:* "I am a specialist on Western Europe and Canada, although I also teach international relations and political philosophy to undergraduate students. I have lived, studied, and taught in Western Europe for many years, and I speak German, French, and bad Spanish. My work straddles the disciplines of political science and history. I try to divide my writing time between scholarly works aimed primarily at my peers, and intelligent, readable works which can be read by interested non-specialists. My greatest objective as a writer is to help Americans open their eyes to the rest of the world."

BIOGRAPHICAL/CRITICAL SOURCES: American Historical Review, June, 1981.

*   *   *

THOMSON, Garry   1925-

PERSONAL: Born September 13, 1925, in Malaysia; son of Robert and Mona (Spence) Thomson; married Saisvasdi Svasti; children: Ben, Neil, Charles, Julian. *Education:* Cambridge University, M.A., 1954. *Religion:* Buddhist. *Office:* National Gallery, Trafalgar Sq., London W.C.2, England.

CAREER: Worked with Imperial Chemical Industries, 1951-55; National Gallery, London, England, research chemist, 1955-60, scientific adviser to board of trustees, 1960—, head of laboratory. President of International Institute for Conservation of Historic and Artistic Works, 1983. *Member:* Buddhist Society (vice-president), Athenaeum Club.

WRITINGS: (Editor) *Recent Advances in Conservation,* Butterworth & Co., 1963; (editor) *Contributions to the London Conference on Museum Climatology,* International Institute for Conservation of Historic and Artistic Works, 1967, revised edition, 1968; *The Museum Environment,* Butterworth & Co., 1978. Also editor of *Conservation of Stone and Wooden Objects,* 1970. Honorary editor of *Studies in Conservation,* 1959-67.

WORK IN PROGRESS: Revising *The Museum Environment.*

SIDELIGHTS: Thomson told *CA:* "My main work is *The Museum Environment,* a textbook for preventing deterioration of museum exhibits of all kinds. With the publisher's compliance I will have revised this book in time for my retirement from the National Gallery in 1985. I am then likely to turn my efforts to helping the West assimilate the messages of Buddhism and the Vedanta without in any way displacing—rather reinforcing—the best of the European religious heritage."

*   *   *

THOMSON, James Miln   1921-

PERSONAL: Born March 14, 1921, in Perth, Australia; son of John and Lillian Maggie Thomson; married Diana May Greagg, February 19, 1944; children: Susan, Rosamund, Mar-

garet (Mrs. Peter Leighton Kesteven), John, Robert. *Education:* University of Western Australia, earned degree, 1943. *Home:* Emmanuel College, Upland Rd., St. Lucia, Brisbane, Queensland 4067, Australia. *Office:* Department of Zoology, University of Queensland, St. Lucia, Brisbane, Queensland 4067, Australia.

CAREER: Commonwealth Scientific and Industrial Research Organization, Division of Fisheries, Cronulla, Australia, research officer, 1945-53, senior research officer, 1953-57, principal research officer, 1957-63; Marineland Oceanarium, Manly, Australia, scientific director, 1963-65; University of Queensland, Brisbane, Australia, senior lecturer, 1965-66, reader, 1967, professor of zoology, 1968—, director of applied ecology, 1973-81; head of department and vice-principal of Emmanuel College and dean of faculty of science. Member of National Committee on Oceanography; Queensland director of Australian Institute of Marine Science, 1981—; member of board of trustees of Queensland Museum, 1971—. Member of Australian delegation to United Nations Law of the Sea Conference, 1960. *Member:* Australian Marine Sciences Association (president, 1965-68), Royal Society of Queensland (president, 1971-72).

WRITINGS: Synopsis of Biological Data on the Grey Mullet "Mugil cephalis" Linnaeus 1758, Commonwealth Scientific and Industrial Research Organization, 1963; *A Bibliography of Systematic References to the Grey Mullets (Mugilidae),* Commonwealth Scientific and Industrial Research Organization, 1964; (with Nancy Taylor and Elizabeth Orr) *Exploration of the Pacific,* School Publications Branch, Department of Education (Wellington, New Zeland), 1968; *Fish of the Ocean and Shore,* Collins, 1974; *A Field Guide to the Common Sea and Estuary Fishes of Non-Tropical Australia,* Collins, 1978. Also author of *The Great Barrier Reef,* 1966, and, with W. Stephenson, M. Blakely, and J. Kikkawa, *Zoology for Senior Forms,* 1967, new edition, 1968. Contributor of about sixty articles to scientific journals. Editor of *Proceedings of the Royal Society of Queensland,* 1966-70.

SIDELIGHTS: Thomson's specialties are marine biology and fishes. He studied fish farming, pearl culture, and oyster farming in Japan in 1948. In 1953, oyster farm and inshore fisheries research took him to India, Italy, France, England, the Netherlands, Denmark, and the United States. He studied fish behavior in Wisconsin and Toronto in 1972. Recently, Thomson has observed museum collections of fish in England, France, Italy, Austria, Germany, and the Netherlands.

*   *   *

THOMSON, John (Edward Palmer)   1936-

PERSONAL: Born January 8, 1936, in Masterton, New Zealand; son of H. Ralph and Elizabeth (Andrews) Thomson; married Jane R.M. Smith, 1960; children: Richard, Roger, Katy, Hamish. *Education:* Victoria University of Wellington, M.A., 1959; Wadham College, Oxford, M.A., 1968; University of Otago, Ph.D., 1975. *Home:* 30 Perth St., Wellington 4, New Zealand. *Office:* Department of English, Victoria University of Wellington, Wellington, New Zealand.

CAREER: University of Otago, Dunedin, New Zealand, junior lecturer, 1962-63, lecturer in English, 1963-69; Victoria University of Wellington, Wellington, New Zealand, senior lecturer in English, 1970—, chairman of department, 1983—.

WRITINGS: Denis Glover, Oxford University Press, 1978; *New Zealand Literature to 1977,* Gale, 1980; *New Zealand Drama,*

Oxford University Press, 1983; Editor of *New Zealand Play-scripts.*

WORK IN PROGRESS: The New Zealand Stage, 1890-1900, for Victoria University Press; research on New Zealand theater in the late nineteenth century.

SIDELIGHTS: Thomson told *CA:* "Katherine Mansfield, one of New Zealand's finest authors, exclaimed in 1915, 'Oh, I want for one moment to make our undiscovered country leap into the eyes of the Old World.' But that has the orientation of a European writer. I prefer the indigenous comment, itself already fifty years old, from an early literary periodical, 'We are hungry for the words that shall show us these islands and ourselves; that shall give us a home in thought.' That for me is the value of New Zealand art and one of the main reasons why I gain special satisfaction from encouraging knowledge and appreciation of the literature of my own country."

*   *   *

THOMSON, Randall J(oseph)   1946-

PERSONAL: Born December 28, 1946, in Seattle, Wash.; son of Robert P. (a professor) and Lois L. (an educator; maiden name, Walker) Thomson; married M. Christine (a writer), 1968; children: Heather Love, Ryan John. *Education:* Attended U.S. Military Academy, 1966-67; University of Texas, B.A., 1972; Indiana University, M.A., 1975, Ph.D., 1978. *Home:* 5217 Kaplan Dr., Raleigh, N.C. 27606. *Office:* Department of Sociology and Anthropology, North Carolina State University, Raleigh, N.C. 27650.

CAREER: U.S. Department of Health, Education and Welfare, Center for Disease Control, West Palm Beach, Fla., public health adviser, 1972-74; University of Texas, Population Research Center, Austin, research associate, 1972; Indiana University, Bloomington, research associate at School of Public and Environmental Affairs, 1976; North Carolina State University, Raleigh, assistant professor of sociology and anthropology, 1977—. Member of Raleigh Park Planning Committee; guest speaker. *Military service:* U.S. Army, 1965-67. *Member:* African Studies Association, American Association of University Professors, American Sociological Association, Association of Voluntary Action Scholars, Society for the Study of Social Problems, Southern Sociological Society, Alpha Kappa Delta. *Awards, honors:* Received grants and fellowships.

WRITINGS: (Editor) *Bringing Sociology Home,* Ginn, 1981; *Principles of Sociology: An Independent Study Course,* University of North Carolina Press, 1982. Contributor to sociology journals.

WORK IN PROGRESS: Sociology: Descriptions, Analyses, and Prescriptions for Goodyear Publishing; research on youth clubs in India, the effects of the Fair Sentencing Act on prison population size, design criteria among architects in North Carolina, and Ronald Reagan's administration policies from 1981 to 1983.

SIDELIGHTS: Thomson told *CA:* "My work in sociology has always taken an applied orientation. While I value theoretical work, my interest is primarily geared to making the literature relevant to students and policy makers alike. *Bringing Sociology Home,* for example, is intended to introduce sociology to college students in North Carolina by utilizing local current events and research. This format encourages the student to apply sociological concepts to increase their understanding of what is happening around them in real-life settings. Likewise, my research in housing alternatives, environmental issues, and

criminology takes an applied approach. My research has sensitized me to the destructive policies of the Reagan administration. I fear that what progress has been made by this country in resolving environmental, criminal justice, inequality, and international relations issues has been set back decades."

*   *   *

THUBTEN Sigme Norbu   1922-
(Thubten Jigme Norbu)

BRIEF ENTRY: Born August 16, 1922, in Tsongon, Tibet. American educator and author. Norbu, brother of the Dalai Lama, was abbot of a monastery in Tibet until 1950. He has taught Uralic and Altaic studies at Indiana University since 1965. Norbu co-authored the critically acclaimed *Tibet: Its History, Religion, and People* (Simon & Schuster, 1968). His other books include *Tibet Is My Country* (Hart-Davis, 1960) and *The Younger Brother, Don Yod: A Tibetan Play—Being the Secret Biography From the Words of the Glorious Lama, the Holy Reverend Blo bZang Ye SHes* (Indiana University Press, 1969). *Address:* Department of Uralic and Altaic Studies, Indiana University, Bloomington, Ind. 47401. *Biographical/critical sources: Saturday Review,* January 25, 1969; *New York Times,* February 6, 1969; *Washington Post Book World,* February 16, 1969; *Atlantic Monthly,* March, 1969; *Times Literary Supplement,* April 9, 1970.

*   *   *

TIGHE, Thomas B.   1907(?)-1983

OBITUARY NOTICE: Born c. 1907; died of a heart attack, May 18, 1983, in Neptune, N.J. Journalist. At the time of his death, Tighe was editor emeritus of the *Asbury Park Press.* During his more than sixty-year association with that newspaper, Tighe moved from a job as a newsboy to the position of general manager. Obituaries and other sources: *New York Times,* May 20, 1983.

*   *   *

TIGNOR, Robert L.   1933-

BRIEF ENTRY: Born November 20, 1933, in Philadelphia, Pa. American historian, educator, and author. Tignor began teaching at Princeton University in 1960 and became a professor of Middle Eastern history in 1976. He wrote *Modernization and British Colonial Rule in Egypt, 1882-1914* (Princeton University Press, 1966), and *The Colonial Transformation of Kenya: The Kamba, Kikuyu, and Maasi From 1900 to 1939* (Princeton University Press, 1976), and co-authored *Egypt and the Sudan* (Prentice-Hall, 1967). He edited *The Political Economy of Income Distribution in Egypt* (Holmes & Meier, 1981). *Address:* Department of History, Princeton University, Princeton, N.J. 08540. *Biographical/critical sources: Times Literary Supplement,* July 20, 1967; *Virginia Quarterly Review,* summer, 1976; *American Historical Review,* October, 1976.

*   *   *

TIKHONOV, Valentin
See PAYNE, (Pierre Stephen) Robert

*   *   *

TIMERMAN, Jacobo   1923-

BRIEF ENTRY: Born Janaury 6, 1923, in Vinnitsa Oblast,

Ukraine, U.S.S.R. Editor, publisher, and author. On April 15, 1977, at 2:00 A.M. Timerman was abducted from his Buenos Aires apartment by twenty armed men representing an extreme right wing faction of Argentina's military. Accused of being a subversive, Timerman, a Zionist, was arrested for publishing *La Opinion*, a newspaper critical of the Argentine Government and its terrorism. He was imprisoned for two years, during which time he endured cruel and bizarre torture, including beatings and electric shocks. Though a military tribunal and the Argentine Supreme Court ordered his release, Timerman remained in prison or under house arrest until his captors succumbed to international pressure exerted by the Vatican, the Carter Administration, and the Inter-American Human Rights Commission, among others. In 1979 the publisher's property was confiscated, his citizenship was revoked, and he was deported to Israel. Timerman recorded his experiences in *Prisoner Without a Name, Cell Without a Number* (Knopf, 1981). He also wrote *The Longest War: Israel in Lebanon* (Knopf, 1982). *Address:* c/o Ma'ariv, Tel Aviv, Israel. *Biographical/critical sources: Washington Post*, September 20, 1979; *New York Times*, September 20, 1979, September 30, 1979, May 7, 1981, December 3, 1982; *Current Biography*, Wilson, 1981; *New York Times Book Review*, May 10, 1981; *Detroit News*, June 14, 1981; *American Poetry Review*, November/December, 1981; *Saturday Review*, December, 1981.

* * *

TIMMS, David 1946-

PERSONAL: Born September 25, 1946, in London, England. *Education:* University of Bristol, B.Ed., 1970; University of Leicester, M.A., 1972. *Home:* 25 Countess Rd., Didsbury, Manchester M13 9PL, England. *Office:* Department of American Studies, Victoria University of Manchester, Manchester M13 9PL, England.

CAREER: Victoria University of Manchester, Manchester, England, lecturer in American literature, 1974—.

WRITINGS: Philip Larkin, Oliver & Boyd, 1973.

* * *

TINTEROW, Gary 1953-

PERSONAL: Born September 26, 1953, in Louisville, Ky.; son of Bernard (a violinist) and Dariese (a fundraiser; maiden name, Warren) Tinterow. *Education:* Brandeis University, A.B., 1976; Harvard University, M.A., 1979, doctoral study, 1979—. *Residence:* Boston, Mass. *Office:* William Hayes Fogg Art Museum, Harvard University, Cambridge, Mass. 02138.

CAREER: Rose Art Museum, Waltham, Mass., acting curator, 1979; affiliated with William Hayes Fogg Art Museum, Cambridge, Mass. *Member:* College Art Association of America. *Awards, honors:* Rousseau fellow at Metropolitan Museum of Art, 1982-83.

WRITINGS: (Editor) *Master Drawings by Picasso*, Braziller/ Fogg Art Museum, 1981.

SIDELIGHTS: Tinterow organized "The Essential Cubism," a retrospective exhibition of Cubist painting and sculpture, at London's Tate Gallery in 1983.

* * *

TIPPETT, Michael (Kemp) 1905-

PERSONAL: Born January 2, 1905, in London, England; son of Henry William and Isabel (Kemp) Tippett. *Education:* Attended Royal College of Music.

CAREER: Writer and composer. Teacher of music; director of music in secondary school, 1940-52; Bath Festival, Bath, England, artistic director, 1969-74; Kent Opera, Kent, England, president, 1978—. *Member:* American Academy of Arts and Letters (honorary member). *Awards, honors:* Commander of Order of the British Empire; D.Mus. from Cambridge University and University of Leeds, 1964, Oxford University, 1967, and University of Bristol, 1970; D.Univ. from University of York, 1966; Companion of Honour, 1970; D.Litt. from University of Warwick, 1974; gold medal from Royal Philharmonic Society, 1976.

WRITINGS: Moving Into Aquarius (essays) Routledge & Kegan Paul, 1959, expanded edition, Paladin, 1975; *The Knot Garden: An Opera in Three Acts*, Schott & Co., 1969; Meirion Bowen, editor, *Music of the Angels: Essays and Sketchbooks of Michael Tippett*, Eulenburg, 1980.

Operas: "The Midsummer Marriage," 1952; "King Priam," 1961; "The Ice Break," 1977.

Orchestral works: "Concerto for Double String Orchestra," 1939; "Fantasia on a Theme of Handel," 1942; "Symphony Number 1," 1945; "Little Music," 1946; "Suite in D," 1948; "Fantasia Concertante on a Theme of Corelli," 1953; "Concerto for Piano and Orchestra," 1955; "Symphony Number 2," 1957; "Praeludium," 1962; "Concerto for Orchestra," 1963; "Symphony Number 3," 1972; "Symphony Number 4," 1977; "Triple Concerto," 1980.

Choral works: "A Child of Our Time," 1941; "Crown of the Year," 1958; "Magnificat and Nunc Dimittis," 1961; "The Vision of St. Augustine," 1966; "The Shires Suite."

Vocal works: "Boyhood's End," 1943; "The Heart's Assurance," 1951; "Songs for Achilles," 1961; "Songs for Ariel," 1962; "Songs for Dov."

Chamber music: "String Quartet Number 1," 1935; "String Quartet Number 2," 1942; "String Quartet Number 3," 1946; "Four Inventions," 1954; "Sonata for Horns," 1959.

Piano and organ works: "Sonata for Piano," 1937; "Fantasia on a Theme of Handel," 1941; "Preludio Al Vespro di Monteverdi," 1945; "Sonata Number 2 for Piano," 1962; "Sonata Number 3 for Piano," 1973.

* * *

TITMUSS, Richard M(orris) 1907-1973

PERSONAL: Born October 16, 1907, in Luton, England; died April 6, 1973, in London, England; son of Morris (a farmer) and Maude Titmuss; married Kathleen Caston Miller; children: one daughter. *Education:* Educated privately.

CAREER: Worked in insurance, industry, and commerce, 1922-42; Cabinet Offices, London, England, historian, 1942-49; Medical Research Council, member of Social Medicine Research Unit, 1949-50; University of London, London School of Economics and Political Science, London, professor of social administration, beginning in 1950. Adviser to Labour party. *Awards, honors:* Commander of Order of the British Empire; D.Tech. from Brunel University; D.Sc. from University of Wales; LL.D. from University of Edinburgh, University of Toronto, and University of Chicago.

WRITINGS: Poverty and Population: A Factual Study of Contemporary Social Waste, Macmillan, 1938; (with Frederick Le

Gros Clark) *Our Food Problem: A Study of National Security*, Penguin, 1939; (with wife, Kathleen Titmuss) *Parents Revolt: A Study of Declining Birth-Rate in Acquisitive Societies*, Secker & Warburg, 1942; *Birth, Poverty and Wealth: A Study of Infant Mortality*, Hamish Hamilton, 1943; (with Fred Grundy and others) *Report on Luton*, Gibbs, Bamforth & Co., 1945; *Problems of Social Policy*, H.M.S.O., 1950, Greenwood Press, 1971, revised edition, Kraus Reprint, 1976; (contributor) *The Family: Report of the British National Conference on Social Work*, National Council of Social Service, 1953; (with Brian Abel-Smith) *The Cost of National Health Service in England and Wales*, Cambridge University Press, 1956; *Essays on "The Welfare State,"* Allen & Unwin, 1958, Yale University Press, 1959, enlarged edition, Unwin University Books, 1963, third edition, introduction by Abel-Smith, Allen & Unwin, 1976.

(With Abel-Smith and Tony Lynes) *Social Policies and Population Growth in Mauritius: Report to the Governor of Mauritius*, Metheun, 1961; *Income Distribution and Social Change: A Study in Criticism*, Allen & Unwin, 1962; (with others) *The Health Services of Tanganyika: A Report to the Government*, Pitman Medical Publishing Co., 1964; *Commitment to Welfare*, Pantheon, 1968, 2nd edition, introduction by Abel-Smith, Allen & Unwin, 1976; *The Gift Relationship: From Human Blood to Social Policy*, Allen & Unwin, 1970, Pantheon, 1971; Abel-Smith and K. Titmuss, editors, *Social Policy: An Introduction*, Allen & Unwin, 1974, Pantheon, 1975; *Welfare and Society*, Heinemann, 1977.

OBITUARIES: New York Times, April 7, 1973.*

* * *

TITTERTON, Ernest William   1916-

PERSONAL: Born March 4, 1916, in Tamworth, England; son of William Alfred (a paper maker) and Elizabeth (Smith) Titterton; married Peggy Eileen (a soil chemist), September 19, 1942; children: Elizabeth Jennifer, Andrew Brian, Ashley Clare Titterton Oates. *Education:* University of Birmingham, B.Sc., 1937, B.Sc. (with honors), 1938, Diploma in Education, 1939, M.Sc., 1940, Ph.D., 1942. *Politics:* "Liberal (Conservative)." *Religion:* Church of England. *Home:* 8 Somers Cres., Forrest, Canberra, Australian Capital Territory 2603, Australia. *Office:* Department of Nuclear Physics, Australian National University, Box 4 G.P.O., Canberra, Australian Capital Territory 2600, Australia.

CAREER: British Admiralty, London, England, member of research team developing radar at University of Birmingham, 1939-43, member of British mission developing nuclear weapons at Los Alamos, N.M., 1943-47; Atomic Energy Research Establishment, Harwell, England, group leader in charge of research team, 1947-50; Australian National University, Canberra, professor of nuclear physics, 1950-81, dean of Research School of Physical Sciences, 1966-68, director of school, 1968-73. Chairman of Australian Atomic Weapons Test Safety Committee, 1957-73; member of National Radiation Advisory Committee, 1957-73, and Defence Research and Development Policy Committee, 1958-71; lecturer at the United Nations.

MEMBER: Australian Institute of Nuclear Science and Engineering (president, 1973-75), Australian Academy of Science (fellow), Australian Academy of Forensic Sciences, Royal Society of Arts and Sciences, Royal Society of Arts (fellow). *Awards, honors:* Elizabeth Cadbury Prize; Companion of Order of St. Michael and St. George, 1957; created Knight Bachelor, 1970.

WRITINGS: Facing the Atomic Future, Macmillan, 1954; *Progress in Nuclear Physics Four*, Pergamon, 1955; *Selected Lectures in Modern Physics*, Conpress Printing, 1958; (with F. P. Robotham) *Inside the Atom*, ABC, 1966; *Uranium: Energy Source of the Future?*, Thomas Nelson, 1979. Writer for television and radio. Contributor of nearly two hundred fifty articles to scientific journals.

WORK IN PROGRESS: Research on nuclear structure physics and energy related problems.

* * *

TODD, Edgeley W(oodman)   1914-

BRIEF ENTRY: Born January 26, 1914, in Deerfield, Ill. American educator and author. Todd was a professor of English at Colorado State University from 1960 until 1980, when he was named professor emeritus. He also taught at Illinois Institute of Technology, Northwestern University, University of Colorado, and Central Washington College of Education. Todd edited *The Adventures of Captain Bonneville, U.S.A., in the Rocky Mountains and the Far West* (University of Oklahoma Press, 1961), *Astoria; or, Anecdotes of an Enterprise Beyond the Rocky Mountains* (University of Oklahoma Press, 1964), and *A Doctor on the California Trail: Diary of Dr. John Hudson Wayman From Indiana to the Gold Fields in 1852* (Old West, 1971). He also co-edited *A Guide to the Charles F. Lummis Collection in the Colorado State University Libraries* (1979). *Address:* 1320 West Oak, Fort Collins, Colo. 80523.

* * *

TOOHEY, Catherine   1949-

PERSONAL: Born April 4, 1949, in Lynwood, Calif.; daughter of Francis R. and Frances M. Toohey. *Education:* Loyola Marymount University, B.A., 1971. *Home:* 17 Bear Paw, No. 20C, Irvine, Calif. 92714. *Office:* Harbor Day School, 3443 Pacific View Dr., Corona del Mar, Calif. 92625.

CAREER: Harbor Day School, Corona del Mar, Calif., primary teacher, 1972—. Conducts workshops. *Member:* International Reading Association, California Reading Association, Orange County Reading Association. *Awards, honors:* Grant from National Association of Independent Schools, 1980.

WRITINGS: (With Anne T. Polkingharn) *Creative Ideas From Library Shelves*, Libraries Unlimited, 1983.

* * *

TORGERSON SHAW, Ellen   1929(?)-1983

OBITUARY NOTICE: Born c. 1929; died of cancer, April 20, 1983, in Los Angeles, Calif. Administrative aid and journalist. Torgerson Shaw worked for United Press International before joining Los Angeles Mayor Tom Bradley's staff as a writer and researcher in 1973. In 1976 she joined the staff of *TV Guide*, for which she wrote a variety of articles. Obituaries and other sources: *Los Angeles Times*, April 21, 1983.

* * *

TORGOFF, Martin   1952-

PERSONAL: Born November 29, 1952, in New York, N.Y.; son of Irving (an athlete; in business) and Bess (in business) Torgoff. *Education:* University of Neuchatel, certificat, 1973; attended Trinity College, Dublin, 1973; State University of

New York College at Cortland, B.A., 1974. *Politics:* Democrat. *Religion:* Jewish. *Agent:* Sterling Lord Agency, Inc., 660 Madison Ave., New York, N.Y. 10021.

CAREER: Instructor in visual and performing arts at elementary school in Bayville, N.Y., 1970-74; Brentano's, Manhasset, N.Y., manager of paperback department, 1974-75; Grosset & Dunlap, Inc., New York City, associate editor in Adult Trade Division, 1975-76; writer, 1976—. Substitute high school teacher in New York City, 1974-75.

WRITINGS: (Editor) Bert Sugar, *The Thrill of Victory,* Hawthorn, 1977; (editor) *Reggie Jackson's Scrapbook,* Dutton, 1978; (editor) Burt Avedon, *Ah, Men,* A & W Pubs., 1978; *Elvis: We Love You Tender,* Delacorte, 1980; (editor and contributor) *The Complete Elvis,* Putnam, 1982. Also contributor to *The Compleat Beatles,* two volumes, Putnam. Contributor to magazines, including *Us.* Contributing editor of *Interview.*

WORK IN PROGRESS: A collection of short stories; a nonfiction book.

SIDELIGHTS: Torgoff wrote: "I intend to establish myself as an important, versatile writer on subjects of personal interest—the arts, politics, sports, pop culture, business, fashion, and the mass media. I also intend to write fiction and screenplays."

*   *   *

TOUW, Kathleen 1949-

PERSONAL: Surname rhymes with "how"; born February 24, 1949, in New Kensington, Pa.; married Rodger W. Touw (a U.S. Treasury employee); children: Steven, Sara. *Education:* Indiana University, B.A., 1971. *Home:* 9110 Bradford Rd., Silver Spring, Md. 20901.

CAREER: Teacher and writer.

WRITINGS: Parent Tricks-of-the-Trade, Acropolis Books, 1981. Contributor to magazines.

SIDELIGHTS: Kathleen Touw wrote: "My children were my inspiration to write a book. Their very presence inspired me to find a more efficient way to parent. While trying to make my job as mother easier, I discovered many time- and money-saving solutions which were collected, categorized, and finally published so all parents could share my ideas and make their job of parenting easier and more enjoyable.

"I have traveled to South America and Spain and have attended school in both these countries."

*   *   *

TRAFZER, Clifford Earl 1949-

PERSONAL: Born March 1, 1949, in Mansfield, Ohio; son of Donald W. (an upholsterer) and Mary Lou (a businesswoman; maiden name, Henry) Trafzer; married Lee Ann Smith (a law student), January 31, 1982. *Education:* Northern Arizona University, B.A., 1970, M.A., 1971; Oklahoma State University, Ph.D., 1973. *Politics:* Democrat. *Home:* 9774 Caminito del Marfil, San Diego, Calif. 92124. *Office:* American Indian Studies, San Diego State University, San Diego, Calif. 92124.

CAREER: Arizona Historical Society, Yuma, museum curator, 1973-76; Navajo Community College, Tsaile, Ariz., instructor in American Indian history, 1976-77; Washington State University, Pullman, assistant professor, 1977-82, associate professor of American Indian history, 1982; San Diego State Uni-

versity, San Diego, Calif., associate professor of American Indian studies, 1982—. Consultant on racism, academics, and Indian history to Colville Confederated Tribe and Shoalwater Bay Indian Tribe. *Member:* American Indian Historical Society, American Historical Association, Organization of American Historians, American Indian Historical Association, Western History Association. *Awards, honors: The Kit Carson Campaign* was nominated for the best nonfiction award from the Western Writers of America and the National Cowboy Hall of Fame, 1982.

WRITINGS: (Contributor) Albert H. Shroeder, editor, *The Changing Ways of Southwestern Indians: A Historical Perspective,* Rio Grande, 1973; *The Judge: The Life of Robert A. Hefner,* University of Oklahoma Press, 1975; *Navajo Raiders and Anglo Expansionists: A Conflict of Interest,* Navajo Community College Press, 1978; *Navajos and Spaniards,* Navajo Community College Press, 1978; (with Richard D. Scheuerman) *The Volga Germans: Pioneers of the Northwest,* University Press of Idaho, 1980; *The Kit Carson Campaign: The Last Great Navajo War,* University of Oklahoma Press, 1982; (editor) *Indians, Superintendents, and Northwest Indian Policy,* University Press of Idaho, 1983; *The Palouse Indians and the Invasion of the Inland Northwest,* University of Oklahoma Press, in press. Contributor to history journals, including *Journal of American History, Pacific Historian, American West, Journal of Arizona History, Chronicles of Oklahoma,* and *Montana.*

WORK IN PROGRESS: White Navajo: The Two Worlds of Son of Tall Paper, a study of Navajo social history as seen through the life of a white Indian trader immersed in Navajo culture.

SIDELIGHTS: Trafzer told *CA:* "I became interested in American Indian history because of my own Indian ancestry, the interest my mother gave me in history, and the need for a new dimension in the historical writings of Indians. American Indian history must be approached through Indian sources as well as white sources and with an understanding of the oral tradition, religious beliefs, language, and other aspects of the specific Indian group one studies."

*   *   *

TREDENNICK, (George) Hugh (Percival Phair) 1899-1981

PERSONAL: Born June 30, 1899, in Birmingham, England; died December 31, 1981; son of G.N.H. Tredennick (a minister); married Louella Margaret Phair, 1924 (died, 1970); children: one son, two daughters. *Education:* Trinity Hall, Cambridge, graduated (with first class honors), 1922.

CAREER: Assistant master at private secondary school in Fleetwood, England, 1923-24; University of Sheffield, Sheffield, England, lecturer in classics, 1924-36; University of London, London, England, reader at Queen Mary College, 1936-46, professor of classics at Royal Holloway College, 1946-66, dean of faculty of arts, 1956-60; writer, 1966-81. *Military service:* British Army, Royal Artillery, served during World War I.

WRITINGS: (Translator with G. Cyril Armstrong) Aristotle, *The Metaphysics,* Heinemann, 1933, Putnam, 1935; (translator) Aristotle, *The Organon,* Harvard University Press, Volume I (with H. P. Cooke), 1938, Volume II (with E. S. Forster), 1960; (translator and author of introduction) Plato, *The Last Days of Socrates; The Apology; Crito; Phaedo,* Penguin, 1954; (translator) Xenophon, *Memoirs of Socrates* [and] *The Symposium (The Dinner Party),* Penguin, 1970; (editor of revision)

The Ethics of Aristotle: The Nichomachean Ethics, translated by J. A. Thomson, revised edition, Penguin, 1977. Contributor to classical journals. Co-editor of *Classical Review,* 1961-67.

OBITUARIES: London Times, January 11, 1982.*

* * *

TREZISE, Philip Harold 1912-

PERSONAL: Born May 27, 1912, in Calument, Mich.; married Ruth Elenor Dorsey, November 28, 1938; children: John, David. *Education:* University of Michigan, A.B., 1936, M.A., 1939; attended National War College, 1949-50. *Home:* 6900 Broxburn Dr., Bethesda, Md. 20817. *Office:* Brookings Institution, 1775 Massachusetts Ave. N.W., Washington, D.C. 20036.

CAREER: Worked as official in Office of Defense Transportation, 1942-43; U.S. Department of State, Washington, D.C., chief research analyst, 1946, chief of Division of Research for the Far East and Near East, 1946-50, adviser to U.S. delegation to the United Nations Commission on the Indonesian Question, 1948, deputy director of Office of Intelligence Research, 1952-55, member of policy planning staff, 1956-57, minister for economic affairs at U.S. embassy in Tokyo, Japan, and director of mission for Agency for International Development, 1957-61, deputy assistant secretary of state for economic affairs, 1961-65, ambassador to Organization for Economic Co-operation and Development in Paris, France, 1966-69, assistant secretary of state for economic affairs, 1969-71, consultant, 1971-77; Brookings Institution, Washington, D.C., senior fellow, 1971—.

Commissioner of Trilateral Commission; director of Atlantic Council, Consumers for World Trade, and Bank of Tokyo Trust Co., 1976—; member of Council on Foreign Relations and advisory boards of Consumer Education Council on World Trade, Inc., and Center for Law and Social Policy; member of advisory council of SAIS U.S.-Japan Study Center; public member of President's Commission on Supplies and Shortages, 1975-76. *Military service:* U.S. Naval Reserve, 1943-46; became lieutenant. *Member:* Council on Foreign Relations, National Economists Club. *Awards, honors:* President's Award for Distinguished Federal Civilian Service, 1965; Distinguished Honor Award from U.S. Department of State, 1971; Distinguished Alumnus Award from University of Michigan Department of Economics, 1980.

WRITINGS: The Atlantic Connection, Brookings Institution, 1975; (co-author) *Asia's New Giant: How the Japanese Economy Works,* Brookings Institution, 1976; (co-author) *Setting National Priorities: The Next Ten Years,* Brookings Institution, 1976; (co-author) *The Politics of Trade,* Columbia University Press, 1978; (editor) *The European Monetary System: Its Promise and Prospects,* Brookings Institution, 1979; (co-author) *Setting National Priorities: Agenda for the 1980s,* Brookings Institution, 1980; (co-author) *Japan and the United States: Economic and Political Adversaries,* Westview, 1980.

* * *

TROUGHTON, Joanna (Margaret) 1947-

PERSONAL: Born September 9, 1947, in London, England; daughter of Patrick (an actor) and Margaret Troughton. *Education:* Received degree with first class honors from Hornsey College of Art, 1969. *Agent:* B. L. Kearley Ltd., 13 Chiltern St., London W1M 1HE, England.

CAREER: Free-lance illustrator for advertising, magazines, and books, 1969—; Harrow School of Art, Middlesex, England, teacher of illustration, 1975—. Part-time teacher of graphics at Barnet College of Art, 1979. *Awards, honors:* Kate Greenaway Medal commendation, 1976, for *How the Birds Changed Their Feathers.*

WRITINGS—All for children; all published by Blackie & Son, except as noted: (Reteller) *Sir Gawain and the Loathly Damsel,* Dutton, 1972; *Soldier, Soldier, Won't You Marry Me?,* 1972; *Spotted Horse,* 1972; (reteller) *Why Flies Buzz: A Nigerian Folk Tale,* 1974; (adapter) *The Story of Rama and Sita,* 1975, British Book Center, 1978; (reteller) *How the Birds Changed Their Feathers,* 1976; (reteller) *What Made Tiddalik Laugh,* 1977; *How Rabbit Stole the Fire,* 1979; *Tortoise's Dream,* 1980; *The Magic Mill,* 1981; (reteller) *The Wizard Punchkin,* 1982; *Blue-Jay and Robin,* 1983.

Illustrator: Greta James, *The Bodhi Tree,* Geoffrey Chapman, 1971; *The Little Mohee: An Appalachian Ballad,* Dutton, 1971; Kevin Crossley-Holland, *The Sea Stranger,* Heinemann, 1972, Seabury, 1974; Barbara S. Briggs, *Cookery Corner Cards,* Mills & Boon, 1973; Geoffrey Trease, *Days to Remember: A Garland of Historic Anniversaries,* Heinemann, 1973; (with Andrew Sier and Barry Wilkinson) Jenny Taylor and Terry Ingleby, *The Scope Storybook,* Longman, 1974; Crossley-Holland, *The Fire-Brother,* Seabury, 1975; Elizabeth Kyle (pseudonym of Agnes Mary Robertson Dunlop) *The Key of the Castle,* Heinemann, 1976; Crossley-Holland, *The Earth-Father,* Heinemann, 1976; Sheila K. McCullagh, *The Kingdom Under the Sea,* Hulton, 1976; James Reeves, reteller, *Quest and Conquest: "Pilgrim's Progress" Retold,* Blackie & Son, 1976; (with Fiona French) Richard Blythe, *Fabulous Beasts,* Macdonald Educational, 1977, published as *Dragons and Other Fabulous Beasts,* Grosset, 1980; Julia Dobson, *The Smallest Man in England,* Heinemann, 1977; John D. Lincoln, *Montezuma,* Cambridge University Press, 1977; Lincoln, *The Fair-Skinned Strangers,* Cambridge University Press, 1977; Robert Nye, *Out of the World and Back Again,* Collins, 1979; Wendy Body, *Clay Horses,* Longman, 1979; Adele Geras, *A Thousand Yards of Sea,* Hodder & Stoughton, 1979; Gillian Wrobel, reteller, *Ali Baba and the Forty Thieves,* Macdonald Educational, 1979; (with Kim Blundell) Michael Pollard, *My World,* Macdonald Educational, 1979; Taylor and Ingleby, *Ganpat's Long Ride* [and] *Shanti and the Snake,* Longman, 1979; Anna Sproule, reteller, *Warriors,* Macdonald Educational, 1980; Sproule, reteller, *Villains,* Macdonald Educational, 1980; Patricia Daniels, reteller, *Ali Baba and the Forty Thieves,* Raintree, 1980; Gail Robinson, *Raven the Trickster,* Chatto & Windus, 1981.

SIDELIGHTS: Troughton told *CA:* "Although I retell myths and legends from all around the world, my favorite areas for stories are North and South America. I'm not sure if this is because the myths were collected in these areas at just the right time, that is before they became too 'civilized,' or whether it is simply that the Indians' stories are so good! They also have the best 'trickster' stories in the world—a group of myths that particularly fascinates me. I suppose that mythology inspires me because it is made up of 'archetypes.' And the study of mythology leads to other areas that interest me—ethnology, ethology, anthropology, etc. I am also very inspired by 'primitive' art.

"The medium I work in is watercolor; I may use other bits and pieces with this (for example, crayon and gouache), but watercolor is my favorite. For line work, I use pen and change the nib size to suit the illustration."

TSHIAMALA, Kabasele   ?-1983(?)
(Kalle Jeef, Joseph Kabasele)

OBITUARY NOTICE: Died after a long illness, c. 1983. Performer and songwriter. Tshiamala helped popularize the highly rhythmic lingala jazz and founded the African Jazz Band in 1949. Among his best-known compositions is "Independence Day Cha Cha," which celebrated the Congo's independence in 1960. Obituaries and other sources: *Chicago Tribune*, February 15, 1983.

*   *   *

TUCKER, Jonathan B(rin)   1954-

PERSONAL: Born August 2, 1954, in Boston, Mass.; son of Leonard W. (a civil engineer) and Deborah Alice (a librarian and English teacher; maiden name, Brin) Tucker; married Karen Fern Fifer, August 24, 1980 (divorced October, 1982). *Education:* Yale University, B.S. (cum laude), 1975; University of Pennsylvania, M.A., 1982. *Home:* 32 Fletcher Rd., Belmont, Mass. 02178.

CAREER: Yale University, New Haven, Conn., research assistant in pharmacology, 1975-76; *Scientific American*, New York, N.Y., associate editor, 1976-79; free-lance medical writer, 1979—. Volunteer worker for Cooperative for American Relief Everywhere (CARE) at refugee camps in Somalia, summer, 1982.

WRITINGS: Ellie: A Child's Fight Against Leukemia, Holt, 1982. Managing editor of *Tufts Diet and Nutrition Newsletter*, 1982—. Contributor to magazines and newspapers, including *Cosmopolitan, Runner, Omni, Harper's Bazaar, Environment, Orbis*, and *New York Times*.

WORK IN PROGRESS: A novel set in East Africa; research on public policy issues with an important scientific or technological component, such as technology transfer to the Third World and the nuclear arms race.

SIDELIGHTS: Tucker wrote: "The fact that my cousin was stricken with leukemia led me to write *Ellie*, although I had been working as a medical writer and editor for some time. Throughout my life I have been torn between interests in the humanities and the sciences, and science/medical writing has provided a way to bridge the gap between Snow's 'two academies.' Now that I have spent a summer working in a refugee relief program in Somalia, I am tempted to try my hand at a work of fiction set in East Africa."

*   *   *

TUDOR, Nancy (Patricia Rice)   1943-

BRIEF ENTRY: Born December 13, 1943, in Ottawa, Ontario, Canada. Canadian librarian and author. Tudor became a cataloger at the Metropolitan Toronto Public Library in 1968. She has also worked at the library at University of Toronto. Tudor and her husband, Dean Tudor, collaborated on *Cooking for Entertaining* (Bowker, 1976), *Jazz* (Libraries Unlimited, 1979), *Grass Roots* (Libraries Unlimited, 1979), *Contemporary Popular Music* (Libraries Unlimited, 1979), and *Black Music* (Libraries Unlimited, 1979).

TUNNER, William H(enry)   1906-1983

OBITUARY NOTICE—See index for *CA* sketch: Born July 14, 1906, in Elizabeth, N.J.; died of heart disease, April 6, 1983, in Gloucester, Va.; buried at Old Chapel, Ft. Myer, Arlington National Cemetery, Arlington, Va. Military officer and author. As expert in military air transport, Tunner began flying in 1929. In World War II, as commander of the ferrying division of the Air Transport Command, Tunner gained international attention with his transport operations across the Himalayas. The 1943 mission, which carried supplies and personnel to China, formed the basis for his 1964 book, *Over the Hump*. Tunner also masterminded the huge airlift operations that supplied thirteen thousand tons of food and coal per day to West Berlin residents during the 1948-49 Soviet blockade. His talents were called into play again in the Korean conflict when supplies were conveyed to U.S. forces trapped in North Korea; this successful operation earned Tunner a Distinguished Service Cross. In May, 1960, he retired from the Air Force as a lieutenant general in command of the joint Military Air Transport Service. Obituaries and other sources: *New York Times*, April 8, 1983; *Chicago Tribune*, April 9, 1983; *Newsweek*, April 18, 1983; *Time*, April 18, 1983.

*   *   *

TURNER, Eric Gardner   1911-1983

OBITUARY NOTICE: Born February 26, 1911, in Sheffield, England; died April 20, 1983, in Inverness, Scotland. Educator and author. Turner, who attended Magdalen College at Oxford University, held teaching positions in humanities and the classics. In 1948 he became a professor of papyrology (the study of papyrus manuscripts) and was the first director of the Institute of Classical Studies. His interests ranged from the Mycenaean Bronze Age to the end of the Roman Empire. His books include *Greek Papyri: An Introduction, Greek Manuscripts of the Ancient World*, and *Typology of the Early Codex*. Turner was a member of the Union Academique Internationale, of which he was president, and the Institute for Advanced Study at Princeton University. Obituaries and other sources: *London Times*, April 22, 1983; *The Author's and Writer's Who's Who*, 6th edition, Burke's Peerage, 1971.

*   *   *

TURNER, Ralph Lilley   1888-1983

OBITUARY NOTICE—See index for *CA* sketch: Born October 5, 1888, in Charlton, England; died April 22, 1983, in Bishop's Stortford, Hertfordshire, England. Linguist, educator, and author. Turner taught in England and India before joining the faculty of the University of London in 1922. Serving as chair of Sanskrit from 1922 and director of the School of Oriental and African Studies from 1936, he retired as professor emeritus of Sanskrit in 1954. He was knighted in 1950. His writings include *A Comparative and Etymological Dictionary of the Nepali Language, Report on a Visit to Nigeria*, and *A Comparative Dictionary of the Indo-Aryan Languages*. Obituaries and other sources: *The International Who's Who*, 46th edition, Europa, 1982; *Who's Who*, 134th edition, St. Martin's, 1982; *London Times*, April 26, 1983.

*   *   *

TURNOCK, David   1938-

PERSONAL: Born August 19, 1938, in Wigan, England; son

of Frederick Stanley (a bank officer) and Dorothy (a teacher; maiden name, Hallows) Turnock; married Edith Marion Bean (a teacher), July 23, 1965; children: Graham, Andrew. *Education:* St. Catharine's College, Cambridge, B.A., 1961, M.A., 1964, Ph.D., 1966. *Home:* 21 Ingarsby Dr., Leicester LE5 6HB, England. *Office:* Department of Geography, University of Leicester, Leicester LE1 7RH, England.

CAREER: University of Aberdeen, Aberdeen, Scotland, assistant lecturer, 1964, lecturer in geography, 1964-69; University of Leicester, Leicester, England, lecturer, 1969-77, reader in geography, 1977—. *Military service:* British Army, 1956-58. *Member:* Institute of British Geographers.

WRITINGS: Patterns of Highland Development, Macmillan, 1970; *Scotland's Highlands and Islands,* Oxford University Press, 1974; *An Economic Geography of Romania,* Bell-Hyman, 1974; *Eastern Europe: Industrial Geography,* Dawson, 1978; *The Lochaber Area, West Highlands of Scotland,* Geographical Field Group, 1978; *The New Scotland,* David & Charles, 1979; *The Human Geography of the Romanian Carpathians,* Geographical Field Group, 1980; *Historical Geography of Scotland Since 1700,* Cambridge University Press, 1982; *Railways of the British Isles,* A. & C. Black, 1982.

WORK IN PROGRESS: Historical Geography of Eastern Europe, publication by Longman expected in 1984.

SIDELIGHTS: Turnock told *CA:* "Much of my writing is concerned with Eastern Europe, arising out of my teaching responsibilities during my first years in university work. Although there is much that is depressing, given the constraints introduced by the Soviet system, it is stimulating to witness rapid development combined with the retention of many traditional cultural manifestations."

*   *   *

TWYMAN, Gib
See TWYMAN, Gilbert Oscar III

*   *   *

TWYMAN, Gilbert Oscar III   1943-
(Gib Twyman)

PERSONAL: Born October 27, 1943, in Independence, Mo.; son of Gilbert Oscar, Jr. (a lithographer) and Clara Anna Amalia (a dance instructor; maiden name, Nolte) Twyman; married Sherry Leigh Stanfield (a teacher), July 16, 1970; children: Matthew Andrew, Emily Elizabeth. *Education:* Attended University of Missouri at Columbia, 1961-63. *Politics:* Independent. *Religion:* Presbyterian. *Home:* 5414 Cherry, Kansas City, Mo. 64110. *Office: Kansas City Star,* 1729 Grand Ave., Kansas City, Mo. 64108.

CAREER: Independence Examiner, Independence, Mo., reporter, 1963-65; *Kansas City Star,* Kansas City, Mo., sportswriter, 1966—. *Military service:* U.S. Air Force Reserve, 1966-71; active duty in 1965-66; became staff sergeant. *Member:* Prison Fellowship. *Awards, honors:* Award for best news story in Missouri from Missouri Press Association, 1965, for coverage of the Denise Clinton kidnapping; named best sportswriter in Kansas City by *Squire* magazine, 1980; nominated for Pulitzer Prize in feature writing, 1983, for three articles.

*WRITINGS—*Under name Gib Twyman: *Born to Hit: The George Brett Story,* Random House, 1982; (contributor) Zander Hollander and Phyllis Hollander, editors, *Ten Greatest Quarter-*

backs of All Time, Random House, 1983. Contributor to magazines, including *Sporting News, Basketball Digest,* and *Sports Illustrated.*

SIDELIGHTS: Twyman told *CA:* "The central thing about me is that I am a Christian. My faith in God is my motivation for life in general, and that includes my professional self."

Twyman elaborated upon the three articles for which he was nominated for a Pulitzer Prize. "The first concerned Filbert Bayi, a Tanzanian former world-record-holding runner who enrolled at the University of Oklahoma. The second explained how in the small town of Gallatin, Missouri, the state-title-contending high school football team helped raise town spirit after a series of murders and a kidnapping. And the third detailed how the Lieweke brothers, who came to Kansas City perceived as disreputable salesmen, established a successful indoor soccer program."

AVOCATIONAL INTERESTS: Bible study, reading, running, canoeing, hiking, cooking, traveling, "the woods and mountains, and working with kids."

*   *   *

TYLER, Ralph Winfred   1902-

PERSONAL: Born April 22, 1902, in Chicago, Ill.; son of William Augustus and Ella Clara (Kimball) Tyler; widower; children: Helen (Mrs. Dominic Parisi), Ralph Winfred, Jr., Ann (Mrs. Aziz Fathy). *Education:* Doane College, A.B., 1921; University of Nebraska, A.M., 1923; University of Chicago, Ph.D., 1927. *Religion:* Congregational. *Home:* 2233 Shiloh Ave., Milpitas, Calif. 95035. *Office:* System Development Foundation, 181 Lytton, Palo Alto, Calif. 94301.

CAREER: University of North Carolina, Chapel Hill, associate professor of education, 1927-29; Ohio State University, Columbus, associate professor, 1929-31, professor of education and research associate in Bureau of Educational Research, 1931-38; University of Chicago, Chicago, Ill., professor of education and university examiner, 1938-53, chairman of department of education, 1938-48, dean of Division of Social Sciences, 1948-53; Center for Advanced Study in the Behavioral Sciences, Palo Alto, Calif., founder and director, 1953-67, director emeritus, 1967—; Systems Development Foundation, Palo Alto, president, 1969—. Member of National Science Board; chairman of National Advisory Council for Research in Vocational Education, Research Advisory Commission of U.S. Office of Education, and National Commission on Resources for Youth; member of Social Science Research Council (president, 1971-72). *Member:* American Educational Research Association, American Statistical Association, National Academy of Education (president, 1965-69).

WRITINGS: Basic Principles of Curriculum and Instruction, University of Chicago Press, 1950; (editor with Richard M. Wolf) *Crucial Issues in Testing,* McCutchan, 1974; *Universal Education in the United States: Milestone Influences on the Past and Future,* School of Education, Indiana University, 1975; (with June Grant Shane) *Ralph Tyler Discusses Behavioral Objectives,* National Education Association of the United States, 1975; *Prospects for Research and Development in Education,* McCutchan, 1976; *Perspectives in American Education: Reflections on the Past, Challenges for the Future,* edited by Dorothy Neubauer, Science Research Associates, 1976.

WORK IN PROGRESS: Revising *Basic Principles of Curriculum and Instruction.*

SIDELIGHTS: Tyler commented: "My major interest is in helping schools and colleges improve their effectiveness. I led a delegation of behavioral scientists to Russia in 1961 and a delegation of state educators to China in 1977. I am also a frequent consultant in Israel."

*   *   *

TYRWHITT, (Mary) Jacqueline   1905-1983(?)

OBITUARY NOTICE: Born in 1905 in Pretoria, South Africa; died c. 1983. Educator, architect, editor, and author. Tyrwhitt's interests were town planning and landscape. Influenced primarily by the modern movement, she was trained at the Architectural Association in London and taught in the United States at the Harvard Graduate School of Design. Tyrwhitt was an editor of several works, including Patrick Geddes's *Cities in Evolution* and Siegfried Giedion's *Mechanization Takes Command*. She also edited *Ekistics* magazine. Obituaries and other sources: *London Times,* March 1, 1983.

U

UHLFELDER, Myra L. 1923-

BRIEF ENTRY: Born September 16, 1923, in Cincinnati, Ohio. American educator and author. Uhlfelder joined the faculty of Bryn Mawr College in 1963 and has been a professor of Latin since 1972. She wrote *De Proprietate Sermonum Vel Rerum* (American Academy in Rome, 1954) and *Nature in Roman Linguistic Texts* (American Philological Association, 1966) and translated *The Dialogues of Gregory the Great*, Book II: *The Life of Saint Benedict* (Bobbs-Merrill, 1967). *Address:* Department of Latin, Bryn Mawr College, Bryn Mawr, Pa. 19010. *Biographical/critical sources: Directory of American Scholars,* Volume III: *Foreign Languages, Linguistics, and Philosophy,* 7th edition, Bowker, 1978.

*   *   *

ULLRICH, Helen D(enning) 1922-

PERSONAL: Born November 28, 1922, in Berkeley, Calif.; daughter of Stephen L. (an executive) and Margaret L. (Woll) Denning; married Robert L. Ullrich (a consultant), September 22, 1962; children: Louise. *Education:* University of California, Berkeley, B.S., 1944; Columbia University, M.A., 1954. *Home:* 1116 Miller Ave., Berkeley, Calif. 94708. *Office:* Society for Nutrition Education, 1736 Franklin St., Oakland, Calif. 94612.

CAREER: University of California Extension Service, Berkeley, nutrition specialist, 1956-63; nutrition consultant in Berkeley, 1963-67; University of California, Berkeley, nutrition specialist, 1968-79; Society for Nutrition Education, Oakland, Calif., executive director, 1973—. *Member:* American Association for the Advancement of Science, American Dietetic Association, American Home Economics Association, American Public Health Association, American Society of Association Executives, Institute of Food Technologists, Society for Nutrition Education.

WRITINGS: (Contributor) Jack Hayes, editor, *Food for Us All: 1969 Yearbook of Agriculture,* U.S. Government Printing Office, 1969; (contributor) Jean Mayer, editor, *U.S. Nutrition Policies in the Seventies,* W. H. Freeman, 1973; (contributor) D. S. McLaren, editor, *Nutrition in the Community,* Wiley, 1976; *Health Maintenance Through Food and Nutrition,* Gale, 1981. Editor of *Journal of Nutrition Education,* 1968-79.

SIDELIGHTS: Ullrich told *CA:* "After working in consumer education with a utility company and a food processor, I spent two years in Hawaii in research on the nutrient content of foods indigenous to the area. From there I went into the field of nutrition education as a nutrition specialist with a state university, presenting programs and training for both the lay public and staff assigned to provide sound nutritional information for the public. After several years, I joined the University of California's Extension Service, again as a nutrition specialist.

"During the years of working with professionals who deal with the public, either in industry or with an educational institution, I realized the need for a specialized journal and, eventually, an organization devoted to all phases of nutrition education. My work in the founding of the *Journal of Nutrition* and the Society for Nutrition Education advanced that goal; however, in addition to helping the professional to be more effective in carrying out nutrition education, I am still concerned that there be effective programs for communicating sound nutritional information to the people, and programs to assess that people have the means to purchase adequate food. I am especially concerned that nutrition education programs—and appropriate food assistance programs—be continued and expanded for schoolchildren and their parents. Food habits are formed early in life, yet our educational process continues throughout life."

*   *   *

ULTEE, (J.) Maarten 1949-

PERSONAL: Born January 13, 1949, in Utrecht, Netherlands; came to the United States in 1953, naturalized citizen, 1959; son of A. J. Ultee (a chemist) and A. L. Wilkinson (a teacher). *Education:* Reed College, B.A., 1969; Johns Hopkins University, M.A., 1971, Ph.D., 1975. *Home:* 20½ Audubon Pl., Tuscaloosa, Ala. 35401. *Office:* Department of History, University of Alabama, Box 1936, University, Ala. 35486.

CAREER: Stanford University, Stanford, Calif., lecturer in undergraduate studies, 1974-75; Hobart and William Smith Colleges, Geneva, N.Y., assistant professor of history, 1975-78; Davidson College, Davidson, N.C., visiting assistant professor of history and humanities, 1979-80; University of Alabama, University, assistant professor of history, 1980—, director of Alabama at Oxford program, 1982 and 1983. Member of Sixteenth-Century Studies Conference. *Member:* American

Catholic Historical Association, Historians of Early Modern Europe. *Awards, honors:* Fellow of National Endowment for the Humanities at University of North Carolina, 1978-79; fellow at Newberry Library, 1980.

WRITINGS: *The Abbey of St. Germain des Pres in the Seventeenth Century,* Yale University Press, 1981; (with C. R. Jensen) *Social Mobility in Early Modern France,* Stanford University Press, in press. Contributor to history journals.

WORK IN PROGRESS: *Letters and the Republic of Letters, 1680-1715,* a long-term study of international scholarly communication.

SIDELIGHTS: Ultee told *CA:* "My European background has been of great value in historical research and writing. I am fluent in Dutch and French, and can read other European languages. I believe that young historians should make every effort to read documents from archives, and to this end I try to visit Europe as often as possible.

"During my graduate studies at Johns Hopkins, I was fortunate to be under the direction of Orest Ranum, a good friend and model for a generation of young French historians. Ranum was able to balance my independent tendencies with the requirements of established historiographical tradition. He encouraged me to do my research in France on less well-known subjects.

"My study of St. Germain des Pres, a powerful Benedictine monastery in Paris, came about when my explorations in archives revealed extensive *series* of documents: accounts, minutes of the chapter, chronicles of memorable events. Monastic life had received little attention from French historians in recent years, but the sources were there for an *Annales*-school history, that is, one emphasizing social and economic trends. I took notes for most of 1971 and 1972, then moved to Leuven, Belgium, where I lived in a Franciscan monastery and enrolled as an independent researcher at the university. Writing and various part-time jobs occupied me from 1973 to 1975. As is the case with many young historians, I have held a series of short-term positions at campuses around the country—and I have fortunately been able to survive. After years of traveling, it is a relief to settle in a larger institution and to see my research efforts appreciated.

"Many historical works are autobiographical, and mine certainly contain autobiographical elements. I have written about monastic scholars and businessmen in my first book and studied the social mobility of eighteenth-century bourgeois in my second. The longer study of international scholarly communication naturally grew out of earlier work, an interest in European culture as a whole, and a faith in the community of scholars. It's a pleasure to know that my students and readers include many people who are *not* professional historians, and that they enjoy my works."

AVOCATIONAL INTERESTS: Collecting old books and maps, listening to string quartets.

*   *   *

UNCLE MAC
See McCULLOCH, Derek (Ivor Breashur)

*   *   *

UNGER, Peter K(enneth)   1942-

BRIEF ENTRY: Born April 25, 1942, in New York, N.Y. American philosopher, educator, and author. Unger, who first

taught at University of Wisconsin—Madison for seven years, joined the faculty of New York University in 1971 and became a professor of philosophy in 1975. He was also a Guggenheim fellow in 1973. Unger wrote *Ignorance: A Case for Scepticism* (Clarendon Press, 1975). He co-edited *Semantics and Philosophy: Essays* (New York University Press, 1974). *Address:* Department of Philosophy, New York University, Washington Sq., New York, N.Y. 10003. *Biographical/critical sources: Times Literary Supplement,* September 5, 1975.

*   *   *

URY, William Langer   1953-

PERSONAL: Born September 12, 1953, in Harvey, Ill.; son of Melvin C. (an attorney and businessman) and Janice (a businesswoman; maiden name, Gray) Ury. *Education:* Yale University, B.A. (magna cum laude), 1975; Harvard University, M.A., 1977, Ph.D., 1982. *Resident:* Cambridge, Mass. *Agent:* Julian Bach Literary Agency, Inc., 747 Third Ave., New York, N.Y. 10017. *Office:* Harvard Law School, Cambridge, Mass. 02138.

CAREER: Harvard University, Cambridge, Mass., executive director of Devising Seminar, Center for International Affairs, 1978-80, associate director of Harvard Nuclear Negotiation Project, 1980—, assistant professor at Harvard Business School, Boston, Mass., 1982—. Lecturer and consultant on negotiation and mediation at Harvard University.

WRITINGS: (With Regina Ziegler, Denis Caillaux, and others) *Energy Use in the Food Sector: An Annotated Bibliography,* Brookhaven National Laboratory, 1978; (with Roger Fisher) *International Mediation: A Working Guide,* International Peace Academy, 1978; (with Fisher) *Getting to Yes: Reaching Agreement Without Giving In,* Houghton, 1981.

Contributor of articles to *Proceedings of the Industrial Relations Research Association, International Journal of the Sociology of Language,* and *Harvard International Review.*

Also author of unpublished manuscripts, (with Annette Hochstein) *The Jerusalem Question: Problems, Procedures, and Options,* 1980, and *Talk Out or Walk Out: Controlling Conflict in a Kentucky Coal-Mine,* 1982.

WORK IN PROGRESS: With Richard Smoke, "a book on negotiating through the nuclear dilemma."

SIDELIGHTS: In *Getting to Yes* co-authors Ury and Fisher advocate a concise, step-by-step method for successful negotiations. They suggest that parties not be dogmatic about their positions, but focus instead on the underlying needs of both sides. Don't allow personality differences to interfere with problem solving, the authors advise, and don't think of each other as adversaries, but as parties working together for mutual gain. *Washington Post* writer Joseph McLellan lauded Fisher and Ury for their common sense approach to negotiations, and noted that *Getting to Yes* "is a joy to read for those who delight in concise, lucid, logical exposition."

BIOGRAPHICAL/CRITICAL SOURCES: *Washington Post,* December 26, 1981; *Times Literary Supplement,* August 27, 1982.

*   *   *

USHER, George   1930-

PERSONAL: Born March 15, 1930, in Swansea, Wales; son

of George (a fitter) and Gwendoline (Hounsell) Usher; married Margaret Helen Dillon, August 29, 1957; children: Christopher George, Jonathan Dillon, Carline Margaret Louise, Elizabeth Mary Gwendoline. *Education:* University of Wales, University College of Swansea, B.Sc., 1951; Emmanuel College, Cambridge, diploma, 1952; Imperial College of Tropical Agriculture, Trinidad, D.T.A., 1953. *Home:* 18 Sutton Grove, Shrewsbury, Shropshire SY2 6DN, England.

CAREER: Ordained priest of Church of England, 1976; British Colonial Overseas Civil Service, Ghana, scientific officer, 1953-57; senior biology master at independent mixed school in Bucknell, England, 1957-80; St. Giles' Church, Shrewsbury, England, curate, 1980—.

WRITINGS: Test Papers in O Level Botany, Allmann, 1964; *Dictionary of Botany,* Constable, 1966; *Introduction to Viruses,* Pergamon, 1970; *Textbook of Practical Biology,* Constable, 1970; *Dictionary of Plants Useful to Man,* Constable, 1974; *Human and Social Biology,* Macdonald & Evans, 1977; *A Level Biology Model Answers,* Artemis Press, 1978; *Chemistry for O Level,* Macdonald & Evans, 1980; *Objective Tests in Certificate Biology,* Macdonald & Evans, 1981. Co-editor of *Chambers Technical Dictionary.*

WORK IN PROGRESS: Further Objective Tests in Sciences, for Macdonald & Evans.

SIDELIGHTS: Usher wrote: "I have changed my vocation from teaching to the full-time ministry, but I am still interested in education. I also hope to write a novel on the Crusades.

"The need for the small public school is receding, and in the United Kingdom their main purpose is changing to that of institutions that give overseas students a grounding in English. They appear to be turning into businesses rather than institutions that have the concern of the pupils at heart.

"The ministry in any church is the most fulfilling vocation that there is. One is constantly being called on to fill a genuine need, both for the community and for the individual. In these days of social change it is becoming increasingly important that the Christian churches display a united front in support of their common ideals.

"My interest in the Crusades generated from my interest in history in general. I am beginning to doubt that the Crusades came about entirely from religious motives and consider that politics and economics played the larger part. I hope to elaborate on this theme in my novel."

*   *   *

USHER-WILSON, Rodney N.   1908(?)-1983

OBITUARY NOTICE: Born c. 1908 in South Africa; died of cancer, February 1, 1983, in Bronxville, N.Y. Clergyman and author. Usher-Wilson, who was a student of theology at St. Augustine's in Canterbury, England, was ordained in the Church of England at Gloucester Cathedral. After serving as a chaplain in India, he came to the United States. Usher-Wilson was active in the Moral Rearmament movement and was the author of *Suicide or Adoration* and *The Mystery of Human Experience.* Obituaries and other sources: *New York Times,* February 7, 1983.

V

VAIL, (Marilyn) Elaine 1948-

PERSONAL: Born February 25, 1948, in Council Bluffs, Iowa; daughter of Jack William (a postal inspector) and Marilyn (an artist; maiden name, Bundy) Ginn; married John Mentzer, September 6, 1969 (divorced March 23, 1973); married Terry Vail (an optometrist), March 26, 1973; children: (second marriage) Brea Terela, Birk Bundy. *Education:* Attended Ohio State University, 1966-68; University of Maryland, B.S.N., 1970; Western Illinois University, M.S., 1975. *Home:* 31 Indian Trail, Macomb, Ill. 61455. *Office:* Department of Health Sciences, Western Illinois University, Macomb, Ill. 61455.

CAREER: Walter Reed General Hospital, Washington, D.C., staff nurse and assistant head nurse, 1970-73, administrative assistant at Walter Reed Army Institute of Nursing, 1972-73; Western Illinois University, Macomb, instructor in health sciences, 1973—. Member of Hastings Center. *Military service:* U.S. Army, Nurse Corps, 1966-73; became captain. *Member:* International Association for Near-Death Studies, American Holistic Nurses Association (founding member), Forum for Death Education and Counseling, Foundation of Thanatology, Mothers Against Drunk Drivers, Illinois Council for the Gifted (vice-president of Macomb chapter, 1982-83), Phi Kappa Phi, Eta Sigma Gamma, Sigma Theta Tau.

WRITINGS: A Personal Guide to Living With Loss, Wiley, 1982. Contributor to nursing journals and local periodicals.

WORK IN PROGRESS: Research on holistic health care practices and healing modalities.

SIDELIGHTS: Elaine Vail wrote: "*A Personal Guide to Living With Loss* is a product of teaching 'Understanding Death and Dying' at Western Illinois University without being able to find a suitably comprehensive text. I finally took my husband's advice to write my own. The book is not a text, though; as the title suggests, it is an effort to help the individual better understand the issues related to dying and living. Many of the anecdotes in it are based on the experiences of the students who have taken the class. I honestly believe that an open confrontation with the idea of death can lead a person to a deeper understanding and appreciation of life.

"One reason I find writing so appealing is that, once done, it stays that way—unlike laundry, dishes, housecleaning, and cooking. Those activities which are so repetitive (and necessary) can be frustratingly undone in virtually no time at all. So, besides forcing me to organize my thoughts and allowing me to share my philosophy with many other people, writing provides a satisfaction and permanence that few other activities offer."

*   *   *

VALE, Malcolm Graham Allan 1942-

BRIEF ENTRY: British historian and author. Vale has been a fellow of St. John's College, Oxford, since 1978. He also has taught at University of Warwick and University of York. Vale wrote *English Gascony, 1399-1453: A Study of War, Government, and Politics During the Later Stages of the Hundred Years' War* (Oxford University Press, 1970) and *Charles VII* (University of California Press, 1974). *Address:* St. John's College, Oxford University, Oxford, England. *Biographical/critical sources: New Yorker,* May 12, 1975; *American Historical Review,* April, 1976.

*   *   *

VAN BROCKLIN, Norm(an Mack) 1926-1983

OBITUARY NOTICE: Born March 15, 1926, in Parade, S.D.; died of a heart attack, May 2, 1983, near Atlanta, Georgia. Athlete, coach, and author. Van Brocklin's career as a professional football player began in 1949 when he was a quarterback for the Los Angeles Rams. In 1957, he was traded to the Philadelphia Eagles and led the team to the National Football League (NFL) championship in 1960. Van Brocklin later coached such teams as the Minnesota Vikings and the Atlanta Falcons, and he was inducted into professional football's Hall of Fame. With Hugh Brown he wrote *Norm Van Brocklin's Football Book: Passing, Punting, Quarterbacking.* Obituaries and other sources: *New York Times,* May 3, 1983; *Newsweek,* May 16, 1983; *Time,* May 16, 1983.

*   *   *

VANCE, Marguerite 1889-1965

OBITUARY NOTICE: Born November 4, 1889, in Chicago, Ill.; died May 22, 1965, in Camden, Me. Editor and author. Vance wrote more than thirty-five books for children, most of which are biographical accounts of historical personages. She created stories with such titles as *Martha, Daughter of Virginia: The Story of Martha Washington; Patsy Jefferson of Monticello; The Story of Nathaniel Hawthorne's Daughter, Rose;* and *Six Queens: The Wives of Henry VIII.* Vance also wrote children's fiction, and she won the Thomas Alva Edison Award in 1960 for *Willie Joe and His Small Change.* Obituaries and other sources: *New York Times,* May 25, 1965; *Publishers Weekly,* May 31, 1965; *Authors of Books for Young People,* 2nd edition, Scarecrow, 1971.

*   *   *

van DAM, Ine   1947-

PERSONAL: Name is pronounced *Ee*-na von Dom; born November 25, 1947, in Eindhoven, Netherlands; came to the United States, 1956, naturalized citizen, 1962; daughter of Hans J. and Ada van Dam. *Education:* University of Washington, Seattle, B.A., 1969; University of Geneva, Interpreter's Diploma, 1972. *Home address:* c/o 6849 34th N.E., Seattle, Wash. 98115.

CAREER: European Economic Communities, Brussels, Belgium, staff interpreter, 1973-74; free-lance translator and conference interpreter in Belgium and California, 1974—. Professor at Monterey Institute of International Studies, 1982—. *Member:* Association Internationale des Interpretes de Conference, Amnesty International (head of Santa Barbara chapter).

WRITINGS: West Coast U.S.A., J. Murray, 1981, Madrona, 1982.

WORK IN PROGRESS: Letters From South America (tentative title), an account of a four-month trip to Latin America; encouraging solo travel.

SIDELIGHTS: Ine van Dam commented: "Language, travel, and people have long been prime interests in my life, and I feel fortunate that my career as a conference interpreter has accommodated all of these. At age thirty-five, I have spent about half my life in the United States and the other half elsewhere, largely in Europe.

"*West Coast U.S.A.* was a logical outgrowth of those interests. It is a cross-cultural guidebook, a look at what makes the West Coast so fascinating to Europeans and what Americans should realize about how Europeans view their neck of the woods.

"Travel is a state of mind, a cleansing of one preconceived world and an acceptance, if not complete understanding, of another such world. Language is the tool which allows us access to other worlds. And, of course, ideally, through exposure to other worlds, we come out with a clearer notion of our own.

"Since I moved back to the United States in 1981, I have continued to travel and work as a conference interpreter, interspersed with teaching duties and time for writing.

"*Letters From South America* is intended less as a guidebook than a travel account for which I have chosen an old-fashioned form: letters written during the trip. It was a trip taken in the face of much opposition: 'You can't travel alone in South America, it's much too dangerous!' Crossing the street can be dangerous, too. Solo travel may not be for everybody, and it may not be the right thing at all times, but only through solo travel does one have even a slight chance of glimpsing what makes another culture tick. If my book encourages even one timid mouse to wag its tail, I shall feel I have accomplished a purpose.

"In the very long run, I would like to tackle a book on language as a reflection of cultural values. As long as we in the United States continue to view other languages as 'foreign,' a purely academic exercise apart from our daily lives, we shall continue to view other people's daily lives as foreign, too. What is needed on this subject is less jargon and more accessibility. I would like to take a stab at that."

*   *   *

VANDERPOOL, James A(lbert)   1916-1983

OBITUARY NOTICE: Born November 4, 1916, in Perryville, Ky.; died of an internal hemorrhage, March 23, 1983, in Frederick, Md. Clergyman, psychologist, and author. Vanderpool graduated from Oklahoma University and received a doctorate from Loyola University in Chicago. Vanderpool, who was a Catholic priest, worked with the District of Columbia Rehabilitation Center for Alcoholics where he was clinical director. He was also a member of the North American Association of Alcoholic Programs and the District of Columbia Public Health Association. His writings include *Person to Person: A Handbook for Pastoral Counseling.* Obituaries and other sources: *Washington Post,* April 2, 1983.

*   *   *

van der VAT, Dan(iel Francis Jeroen)   1939-

PERSONAL: Born October 28, 1939, in Alkmaar, Netherlands; son of Daniel G. (a writer) and Kathleen (Devanney) van der Vat; married Christine Mary Ellis (a teacher), 1962; children: Karen, Sara. *Education:* University of Durham, B.A. (with honors), 1960. *Politics:* "No party, no dogma." *Religion:* None. *Home:* 8 Aquarius, Eel Pie Island, Twickenham TW1 3EA, England. *Agent:* Curtis Brown Ltd., 1 Craven Hill, London W2 3EP, England. *Office: Guardian,* 119 Farringdon Rd., London EC1R 3ER, England.

CAREER: Journal, Newcastle upon Tyne, England, journalist, 1960-63; *Daily Mail,* London, England, reporter, 1963-65; *Sunday Times,* London, reporter, 1965-67; *Times,* London, foreign correspondent, 1967-81; *Guardian,* London, leader writer, 1982—. *Member:* National Union of Journalists, Eel Pie Island Association, Campaign for Nuclear Disarmament.

WRITINGS: The Grand Scuttle: The Sinking of the German Fleet at Scapa Flow in 1919, Hodder & Stoughton, 1982; *The Last Corsair,* Hodder & Stoughton, 1983. Writer for television and radio. Contributor to journals.

WORK IN PROGRESS: Another book of naval history.

SIDELIGHTS: Van der Vat told *CA:* "My work as a journalist took me on special assignments to some twenty countries before I got my wish to be *stationed* abroad. I soon discovered that, far from being glamorous, special assignments to crises in countries hitherto unvisited meant that one learned nothing about them; they were by definition in an abnormal condition—otherwise, I would not have been sent.

"So when I was sent to South Africa by the *Times* to open a new bureau, I at last got my chance to get to know a key country by living in it. I still regard that assignment (from 1969 to the end of 1971) as the best opportunity of my journalistic career. It was followed by more than five years covering Germany, which was no less fascinating if rather more complex. Germany is, after all, somewhat closer to the center of the universe than South Africa, where for some people the earth is still flat and the sun shines for the white man alone.

"My involvement in naval history is the result of a chapter of accidents. I was sent to the Orkney Islands off the northern coast of Scotland in late 1978 to cover one of those highly controversial seal culls. So effective was the protest against the planned slaughter that the cull was eventually cancelled by an embarrassed government. This meant that with the best will in the world I found myself somewhat underemployed in a very special and beautiful part of the world. I began to explore it, and came across a little museum in the town of Stromness which had a special display on the subject of the scuttling of the German fleet after the First World War.

"Like most people, I knew this had happened, but no more than that. Now I was on the shore of the great natural anchorage where it had happened, and I began to realize the scale of the incident. Imagine my astonishment when on going to the local library to discover what books had been written on the subject I was told that there was none. The greatest act of material destruction in all naval or military history did not have a single entire book devoted to it. That is how it began.

"Then the *Times* closed itself down in order to prevent its rebellious print workers from closing it down. This managerial masterstroke led to my being at loose ends on full pay for fifty weeks, time I used to research *The Grand Scuttle* and do all the necessary background reading. My years in Germany had given me the language and the local knowledge to be able to work out where to look. In the course of the research I came across the better-known story of the light cruiser *Emden,* which had given the British so much trouble in the Indian Ocean in the opening months of the First World War with her onslaught on seaborne trade. Even though this story had been told before I felt it deserved retelling, especially as I had discovered that there was some unused material in the German and British archives. Hence *The Last Corsair.*

"There is a third and last episode in the Anglo-German naval history of the First World War which I plan to tackle in book form before I turn my attention to other things in the general field of contemporary history. I shall have to keep these themes to myself for the time being, until I have satisfied myself that they really are worth doing! Suffice it to say for now that my approach is that of a reporter with the chance to give a considered version of an event with all the records available. I have always been in the business of writing stories."

AVOCATIONAL INTERESTS: Travel, photography, modern history, crossword puzzles, linguistics, good food, and wine.

BIOGRAPHICAL/CRITICAL SOURCES: London Times, June 24, 1982; *Daily Telegraph,* June 24, 1982; *Glasgow Herald,* June 28, 1982; *Irish Times,* July 17, 1982; *Economist,* August 14, 1982; *Guardian,* September 23, 1982.

*   *   *

VAN Der ZEE, James (Augustus Joseph) 1886-1983

OBITUARY NOTICE—See index for *CA* sketch: Born June 29, 1886, in Lenox, Mass.; died of cardiac arrest, May 15, 1983, in Washington, D.C. Musician, photographer, and author. For six decades Van Der Zee recorded Harlem life—its events, rituals, and personalities—in thousands of photographs. His life's work was "discovered" in 1969 when his photographs were featured in a Metropolitan Museum exhibition, "Harlem on My Mind." Van Der Zee's book by the same title appeared in 1969 as well, and was revised in 1979. His photographs recorded many aspects of Harlem culture, including weddings, parades, church activities, sporting events, sidewalk scenes,

and funerals. His funeral portraits formed the basis for his 1978 book *The Harlem Book of the Dead.* Van Der Zee also took thousands of portraits during his long career, many of them artistically capturing the images of black leaders in business, sports, religion, entertainment, and the arts. Among those who posed for Van Der Zee are Marcus Garvey, James Weldon Johnson, Adam Clayton Powell, Sr., Countee Cullen, A'Leilia Walker, Muhammad Ali, Eubie Blake, Bill Cosby, and Lou Rawls. Recipient of several honorary doctorates, the distinguished photographer received the Living Legacy Award from President Carter in 1978. Van Der Zee's photographs were collected in books such as *The World of James Van Der Zee.* Obituaries and other sources: *New York Times,* May 16, 1983; *Washington Post,* May 16, 1983; *London Times,* May 17, 1983; *Chicago Tribune,* May 17, 1983; *Newsweek,* May 30, 1983; *Time,* May 30, 1983.

*   *   *

VAN HAAFTEN, Julia 1946-

PERSONAL: Born November 3, 1946, in Lancaster, Pa.; daughter of Egbert (a research engineer) and Dorothy (Gilman) Van Haaften; married Ron Schuck (a magazine editor), May 12, 1973; children: Madeline Dorothy. *Education:* Barnard College, A.B., 1968; Columbia University, M.L.S., 1970. *Home address:* HR1, Box 227, Jersey Ave., Greenwood Lake, N.Y. 10925. *Office:* Art, Prints, & Photographs Division, New York Public Library, Fifth Ave. at 42nd St., New York, N.Y. 10018.

CAREER: New York Public Library, New York, N.Y., librarian, 1970-79, project director, 1979-82, curator in Division of Art, Prints, and Photographs, 1982—. *Member:* American Institute for Conservation.

WRITINGS: (With Jon Manchip White) *Egypt and the Holy Land in Historic Photographs: Seventy-Seven Views by Francis Frith,* Dover, 1980; *From Talbot to Stieglitz: Masterpieces of Early Photography From the New York Public Library,* Thames & Hudson, 1981. Contributor to library journals and photography magazines.

WORK IN PROGRESS: Research on New York city streets, space, scientific photography, and early travel photography.

SIDELIGHTS: Julia Van Haaften commented: "The photography collections in the Central Research Library of the New York Public Library had lain dormant for fifty years. Their discovery has been the motivation for my writing, as well as the principal source of subject matter. I did not intend to be a writer, but a bibliographer. However, the material of my bibliographic discoveries required interpretation and research in order to be communicated adequately. Writing is a natural outgrowth of my interest in the history of photography and visual communication."

BIOGRAPHICAL/CRITICAL SOURCES: New York Times, May 22, 1977, December 20, 1981; *Portfolio,* November-December, 1981; *AB Bookman's Weekly,* January 31, 1982; *Darkroom,* January, 1983; *Washington Post Book World,* May 22, 1983.

*   *   *

VANOCUR, Sander 1928-

BRIEF ENTRY: Born January 8, 1928, in Cleveland, Ohio. American broadcast journalist. One of few Americans to be employed as a journalist by a British newspaper, Vanocur worked as a reporter for both the *Manchester Guardian* and the *London Observer* before joining the staff of the *New York Times*. In 1957 he became a correspondent in Washington, D.C., for National Broadcasting Company (NBC). Vanocur left that position for an assignment in the Midwest the following year, returning to the capital in 1961 to cover the presidential administration of John F. Kennedy. (Vanocur had served as one of the questioners for the Nixon-Kennedy debates in 1960.) He has also taught communications at Duke University and has worked as a columnist for the *Washington Post*. In 1980 the journalist was appointed chief overview correspondent for American Broadcasting Companies (ABC-News). Vanocur contributed to *Memo to JFK From NBC News* (Putnam, 1961). He also edited *A Tribute to John F. Kennedy* (Encyclopaedia Britannica, 1964), with Pierre Salinger. *Address:* American Broadcasting Co. (ABC-News), 1330 Avenue of the Americas, New York, N.Y. 10019. *Biographical/critical sources: New York Times*, December 17, 1961; *Current Biography*, Wilson, 1963; *Harper's Bazaar*, December, 1971; *Newsweek*, December 6, 1971; *Esquire*, January, 1973.

* * *

VEEDAM, Voldemar 1912-1983

OBITUARY NOTICE: Born in 1912 in Estonia; died of cancer, March 2, 1983, in Washington, D.C. Journalist. Veedam's twenty-four-year tenure with Voice of America ended in 1974 when he retired as chief of the Estonian language service. Veedam wrote *Sailing to Freedom*. Obituaries and other sources: *Washington Post*, March 5, 1983.

* * *

VERHAEREN, Emile (Adolphe Gustave) 1855-1916

BRIEF ENTRY: Born May 21, 1855, in Saint-Amand-lez-Puers, Belgium; died November 27 (some sources say November 26), 1916, in Rouen, France; buried in Saint-Amand-lez-Puers, Belgium. Belgian lawyer, poet, and author. Verhaeren was educated in law and joined the firm of Brussels attorney and author Edmond Picard for a time before leaving to devote his life to literature. His first publication was a volume of naturalistic poems, *Les Flamandes* (title means "Flemish Women"; 1883), which portrays peasant life in Flanders. Verhaeren also experimented with a variety of verse forms. *Les Villages illusoires* (1895) is noted for its use of free verse and symbolist techniques, while *Les Rythmes souverains* (1910), which earned the author the title "the Belgian Walt Whitman," has been acclaimed as an epic poem with pantheistic overtones. In addition to poetry, Verhaeren published several unsuccessful plays, including *Les Aubes* (1898; translated as *The Dawn*, 1898) and *Helene de Sparte* (1909; translated as *Helen of Sparta*, 1916). The author fled to France following the German occupation of Belgium during World War I. Verhaeren was en route to Norway when he slipped off a platform at a Rouen railway terminal and was crushed by a train. *Biographical/critical sources: Columbia Dictionary of Modern European Literature*, Columbia University Press, 1947; *Encyclopedia of World Literature in the Twentieth Century*, updated edition, Ungar, 1967; *The Penguin Companion to European Literature*, McGraw, 1969; *Cassell's Encyclopaedia of World Literature*, revised edition, Morrow, 1973; *Twentieth-Century Literary Criticism*, Volume 11, Gale, 1983.

VERHOOGEN, John 1912-

PERSONAL: Born February 1, 1912, in Brussels, Belgium; naturalized U.S. citizen, 1953; son of Rene Louis and Lucy (Vincotte) Verhoogen; married Ilse Goldschmidt, November 28, 1935 (died, 1981); children: Robert, Alexis, Therese, Sylvie Verhoogen Biamonte. *Education:* Received degree in mining engineering from University of Brussels, 1933; received degree in geological engineering from University of Liege, 1934; Stanford University, Ph.D., 1936. *Home:* 2100 Marin Ave., Berkeley, Calif. 94707.

CAREER: University of Brussels, Brussels, Belgium, research assistant in the Belgian Congo, 1936-39; worked in Congo for Fonds National Recherche Scientifique, 1939-40; chief of prospecting service in Congo for Mines d'or de Kilo-Moto, 1940-43; director of production in Congo for Miniere de Guerre, 1943-46; University of California, Berkeley, associate professor, 1947-51, professor of geophysics, 1952-77, professor emeritus, 1977—.

WRITINGS: Mount St. Helens: A Recent Cascade Volcano, University of California Press, 1937; *Thermodynamics of a Magmatic Gas Phase*, University of California Press, 1949; (with Francis J. Turner) *Igneous and Metamorphic Petrology*, McGraw, 1951, 2nd edition, 1960; (with Turner, W. S. Fyfe, and others) *The Earth: An Introduction to Physical Geology*, Holt, 1970; (with Turner and I.S.E. Carmichael) *Igneous Petrology*, McGraw, 1974; *Energetics of the Earth*, National Academy of Sciences, 1980.*

* * *

VERNANT, Jean-Pierre 1914-

PERSONAL: Born January 4, 1914, in Provins, France; son of Jean (a journalist) and Anna (Heilbron) Vernant; married Lida Nahimovitch (a professor), November 30, 1939; children: Claude. *Education:* Sorbonne, University of Paris, agrege de philosophie, 1937. *Home:* 112 Grand-Rue, 92310 Sevres, France. *Office:* Department of Ancient Religions, College de France, 11 Place Marcelin, Berthelot, 75005 Paris, France.

CAREER: In charge of research at Centre National de la Recherche Scientifique, 1948-57; director of studies at Ecole Pratique des Hautes-Etudes, 1957-75; College de France, Paris, professor of the comparative study of ancient religions, 1975—. *Military service:* French Army, 1937-45, served in infantry; became lieutenant colonel; received Croix de Guerre and Croix de la Liberation, was made officer of French Legion of Honor. *Member:* Associe de l'Academie Royale de Belgique. *Awards, honors:* Honorary doctorate from University of Chicago, 1979.

WRITINGS: Les Origines de la pensee greque, Presses Universitaires de France, 1962, revised edition, 1969, 4th edition, 1981, translation published as *The Origins of Greek Thought*, Cornell University Press, 1982; *Mythe et pensee chez les grecs: Etudes de psychologie historique*, Maspero (Paris), 1965, 9th edition, 1982, translation by Janet Lloyd published as *Myth and Thought Among the Greeks*, Routledge & Kegan Paul; (editor) *Problemes de le guerre en Grece ancienne* (title means "Problems of War in Ancient Greece"), La Haye, Mouton & Co., 1968; (author of introduction) Marcel Detienne, *Les Jardins d'Adonis* (title means "The Gardens of Adonis"), Gallimard, 1972; (with Pierre Vidal-Naquet) *Mythe et tragedie en Grece ancienne*, Maspero, 1972, 5th edition, 1981, translation by Janet Lloyd published as *Tragedy and Myth in Ancient Greece*, Harvester Press, 1981; *Mythe et societe en Grece an-*

cienne, Maspero, 1974, 3rd edition, 1981, translation by Janet Lloyd published as *Myth and Society in Ancient Greece,* Harvester Press, 1980, Methuen, 1982; (with Detienne) *Les Ruses de l'intelligence: La Metis des grecs,* Flammarion, 1974, 2nd edition, 1978, translation by Janet Lloyd published as *Cunning Intelligence in Greek Culture and Society,* Humanities, 1978; (contributor) *Divination et rationalite* (title means "Divination and Rationality"), Seuil, 1974; *La Cuisine du sacrifice en pays grec,* Gallimard, 1979; *Religions, histoires, raisons* (title means "Religion, History, Reason"), Maspero, 1979.

SIDELIGHTS: Vernant told *CA:* "My work tries to be a contribution to the foundation of a historical anthropology of ancient Greece."

Myth and Society in Ancient Greece is a collection of essays which illustrates the relationship between myth and societal institutions in ancient Greek culture. According to John Gould, who reviewed the work in a *Times Literary Supplement* article, the essays analyze myth comparatively, "refer[ring] the logic of the myth to a network of related concepts which makes up the 'deep structure' of ancient Greek thinking about the social nature of man." Gould judged Vernant's book "an important work, of rare intelligence, stimulating and discerning."

BIOGRAPHICAL/CRITICAL SOURCES: Times Literary Supplement, August 22, 1980, October 29, 1982, November 12, 1982.

* * *

VINER, George 1913(?)-1983

OBITUARY NOTICE: Born c. 1913; died April 20, 1983, in Bristol, England. Author. Viner co-authored the textbook *The Practice of Journalism.* He was also chairman of the National Council for the Training of Journalists in England. Obituaries and other sources: *London Times,* May 3, 1983.

* * *

VINES, (Henry) Ellsworth (Jr.) 1911-

BRIEF ENTRY: Born September 28, 1911, in Pasadena, Calif. American athlete and author. In 1931 Vines became the youngest player ever to win the U.S. amateur tennis championship; he was nineteen years old. The following year Vines again won the U.S. championship, in addition to taking the singles title at Wimbledon. He became a professional tennis player in 1933, and about ten years later he became a professional golfer as well. Vines wrote *Tennis Simplified for Everybody* (American Sports Publishing, 1933), *How to Play Better Tennis* (McKay, 1938), and *Ellsworth Vines' Quick Way to Better Tennis: A Practical Book on Tennis for Men and Women* (Sun Dial Press, 1939). He is co-author of *Tennis: Myth and Method* (Viking, 1978).

* * *

VINOGRADOV, Ivan M(atveyevich) 1891-1983

OBITUARY NOTICE: Born September 14, 1891, in Tver Region, Russia (now Kalinin, U.S.S.R.); died March 20, 1983, in Moscow, U.S.S.R. Mathematician and author. Vinogradov received awards from more than twenty countries for his influential textbook *Basis of the Theory of Numbers.* He was head of the Steklov Mathematical Institute, as well as an honorary member of the American Philosophical Society of Philadelphia and the American Academy of Arts and Sciences.

Obituaries and other sources: *New York Times,* March 23, 1983; *Chicago Tribune,* March 24, 1983; *London Times,* March 29, 1983; *Time,* April 4, 1983.

* * *

VISHER, Emily B. 1918-

PERSONAL: Born May 21, 1918, in Norwich, Conn.; daughter of Carleton Perkins (a mining engineer) and Mary Rudd (a psychological counselor; maiden name, Gibbs) Browning; married Shirley Seavey Philbrick, August 9, 1941 (divorced, 1959); married John Sargent Visher (a psychiatrist), December 31, 1959; children: (first marriage) Sharon Philbrick Gross, Wendy Philbrick Smith, David, Loren. *Education:* Wellesley College, B.A. (with honors), 1940; University of California, Berkeley, Ph.D., 1958. *Home:* 10475 Albertsworth Lane, Los Altos Hills, Calif. 94022. *Office:* 900 Welch Rd., Suite 400, Palo Alto, Calif. 94304.

CAREER: Nutrition Clinic, Birmingham, Ala., research chemist, 1940-41; Veterans Administration Hospital, San Francisco, Calif., psychology trainee, 1955-59; private practice of clinical psychology in Berkeley, Calif., 1958-66; diagnostic evaluator for California Vocational Rehabilitation Service, Alameda County Welfare Department, and Children's Home Society of California, 1960-66; Veterans Administration Hospital, Menlo Park, Calif., staff psychologist, 1966-68; private practice of clinical psychology in Palo Alto, Calif., 1966—; Kaiser Foundation Hospital, Redwood City, Calif., staff psychologist, 1970-77. Psychology trainee at Berkeley State Mental Hygiene Clinic, 1956-57, and San Francisco's Veterans Administration Clinic and Mental Hygiene Clinic, 1957-59; member of national advisory panel of American Institute for Research, 1979; panelist and public speaker; stepfamily workshop leader; guest on television and radio programs.

MEMBER: Stepfamily Association of America (co-founder; president, 1979—), American Orthopsychiatric Association, American Psychological Association, Stepfamily Association of California (co-founder; vice-president, 1977-78; president, 1979-80), Wellesley College Alumnae Association (president, 1948-49, 1970-71), Phi Beta Kappa, Sigma Xi.

WRITINGS—With husband, John S. Visher: *Stepfamilies: A Guide to Working With Stepparents and Stepchildren,* Brunner, 1979, reprinted as *Stepfamilies: Myths and Realities,* Citadel, 1982; *How to Win as a Stepfamily,* Dembner, 1982.

Contributor: Joseph D. Noshpitz, editor, *Basic Handbook of Child Psychiatry,* Basic Books, 1979; John G. Howells, editor, *Modern Perspectives in the Psychiatry of Middle Age,* Brunner, 1981; Alan S. Gurman, editor, *Questions and Answers in the Practice of Family Therapy,* Brunner, 1981; Froma Walsh, editor, *Normal Family Processes,* Guilford Press, 1982; Robert O. Pasnau, editor, *Psychological Aspects of the Medical Treatment of Adolescents,* Addison-Wesley, 1982; Lillian Messinger, editor, *Therapy With Remarriage Families,* Aspen Systems Corp., 1982. Contributor to journals in the behavioral sciences. Associate editor of *Stepfamily Bulletin,* 1980-82.

WORK IN PROGRESS: Research on programs and services that are helpful to stepfamilies and on concomitants of successful stepfamily functioning.

SIDELIGHTS: When Emily Philbrick and John Visher married in 1959, each brought to the marriage four children from a previous marriage. The strains they encountered as stepparents became a challenge to them, even though Emily is a professional psychologist and John is a psychiatrist. They coped with their problems successfully, and soon friends began seeking out the Vishers for advice on the subject. Since the number of stepfamilies is growing rapidly in the United States, Emily and John Visher have committed themselves, nationally and internationally, to helping stepfamilies cope and prosper.

BIOGRAPHICAL/CRITICAL SOURCES: Contemporary Psychology, Volume 25, number 5, 1980; *Australian Journal of Family Therapy,* October, 1980; *Napa Newspaper,* October 20, 1980; *Arizona Daily Star,* February 12, 1981; *Tucson Citizen,* March 25, 1981; *Houston Chronicle,* April 19, 1981; *San Francisco Examiner,* April 28, 1981; *Amarillo Daily News,* September 18, 1981; *Syracuse Herald-Journal,* October 5, 1981; *Honolulu Star-Bulletin and Advertiser,* October 25, 1981; *Kirkus Review,* March 15, 1982.

*   *   *

VISHER, John Sargent   1921-

PERSONAL: Born March 2, 1921, in Waukesha, Wis.; married Emily B. Philbrick (a psychologist), December 31, 1959; children: (first marriage) four. *Education:* Indiana University, A.B., 1942, M.D., 1944; attended San Francisco Psychoanalytic Institute, 1951-57. *Home:* 10475 Albertsworth Lane, Los Altos Hills, Calif. 94022. *Office:* 900 Welch Rd., Suite 400, Palo Alto, Calif. 94304.

CAREER: Philadelphia General Hospital, Philadelphia, Pa., intern, 1945; University of Minnesota, Minneapolis, resident in psychiatry, 1948-51; Berkeley State Mental Hygiene Clinic, Berkeley, Calif., director of adult services, 1951-56; private practice of psychiatry in Berkeley, 1951-67; Langley Porter Neuropsychiatric Institute, member of faculty, 1966-69, supervising psychiatrist of Community Mental Health Inpatient Service, 1968-69; San Mateo County Mental Health Services, deputy program chief, 1969-72, program chief, 1972-75; North County Mental Health Services, Daly City, Calif., chief of adult outpatient services, 1975—. Associate examiner of American Board of Psychiatry and Neurology, 1955—. Staff psychiatrist at Cowell Hospital and University of California Mental Hygiene Clinic, Berkeley, 1952-57; member of clinical faculty at University of California School of Medicine, San Francisco, 1951-69; lecturer in psychiatry at Stanford University, 1974—. Panelist and public speaker; leader of stepfamily workshops. *Military service:* U.S. Army Air Forces, 1945-47; became captain.

MEMBER: Stepfamily Association of America (co-founder), American College of Psychiatrists (fellow; chairman of finance committee, 1980—), American Psychiatric Association (fellow; member of board of trustees, 1969-71), Northern California Psychiatric Association (chairman, 1978-81), Alpha Omega Alpha.

WRITINGS—With wife, Emily B. Visher: *Stepfamilies: A Guide to Working With Stepparents and Stepchildren,* Brunner, 1979, reprinted as *Stepfamilies: Myths and Realities,* Citadel, 1982; *How to Win as a Stepfamily,* Dembner, 1982.

Contributor: Joseph D. Noshpitz, editor, *Basic Handbook of Child Psychiatry,* Basic Books, 1979; John G. Howells, editor, *Modern Perspectives in the Psychiatry of Middle Age,* Brunner, 1981; Alan S. Gurman, editor, *Questions and Answers in the Practice of Family Therapy,* Brunner, 1981; Froma Walsh, editor, *Normal Family Processes,* Guilford Press, 1982; Robert O. Pasnau, editor, *Psychological Aspects of the Medical Treatment of Adolescents,* Addison-Wesley, 1982; Lillian Mes-

singer, editor, *Therapy With Remarriage Families,* Aspen Publication, 1982. Also contributor to *Medical Aspects of Human Sexuality.*

Contributor to journals in the behavioral sciences. Associate editor of *Stepfamily Bulletin,* 1980-82.

SIDELIGHTS: When Emily Philbrick and John Visher married in 1959, each brought to the marriage four children from a previous marriage. The strains they encountered as stepparents became a challenge to them, even though Emily is a professional psychologist and John is a psychiatrist. They coped with their problems successfully, and soon friends began seeking out the Vishers for advice on the subject. Since the number of stepfamilies is growing rapidly in the United States, Emily and John Visher have committed themselves, nationally and internationally, to helping stepfamilies cope and prosper.

BIOGRAPHICAL/CRITICAL SOURCES: Contemporary Psychology, Volume 25, number 5, 1980; *Australian Journal of Family Therapy,* October, 1980; *Napa Newspaper,* October 20, 1980; *Arizona Daily Star,* February 12, 1981; *Tucson Citizen,* March 25, 1981; *Houston Chronicle,* April 19, 1981; *San Francisco Examiner,* April 28, 1981; *Amarillo Daily News,* September 18, 1981; *Syracuse Herald-Journal,* October 5, 1981; *Honolulu Star-Bulletin and Advertiser,* October 25, 1981; *Kirkus Review,* March 15, 1982.

*   *   *

von EULER, Ulf (Svante)   1905-1983

OBITUARY NOTICE: Born February 7, 1905, in Stockholm, Sweden; died March 10, 1983, in Stockholm, Sweden. Physiologist and author. Von Euler was co-winner of the 1970 Nobel Prize for medicine. His research on the nervous system aided in the treatment of mental illness and Parkinson's disease. Von Euler also discovered hormones now used in birth control pills, and he is the author of *Noradrenaline.* Obituaries and other sources: *Los Angeles Times,* March 12, 1983; *Washington Post,* March 12, 1983; *Chicago Tribune,* March 14, 1983; *Time,* March 21, 1983.

*   *   *

VOSE, Ruth Hurst   1944-

PERSONAL: Born February 10, 1944, in Southport, England; daughter of Thomas (a farmer) and Helena Mary (a teacher; maiden name, Molyneux) Hurst; married James Edward Vose (a farmer), September 19, 1969. *Education:* University of Liverpool, B.A. (with honors), 1966; Blythe College, D.H.P., 1981. *Home and office address:* Moorfield Lane, Scarisbrick, Nr. Ormskirk, Lancashire L40 8JD, England.

CAREER: Pilkington Glass Museum, St. Helens, Merseyside, England, assistant curator, 1966-72; *Ormskirk Advertiser* (group of newspapers), Lancashire, England, senior journalist, 1973-77; free-lance writer, lecturer, and broadcaster, 1978—. Edge Hill College of Higher Education, Ormskirk, Lancashire, publicity consultant, governor, 1978-82, and vice-chairman, 1982. *Member:* L'Association Internationale pour l'Histoire du Verre, National Union of Journalists, Museums Association (associate member), Society for Post-Medieval Archaeology, Association of Hypnotists and Psychotherapists, Historical Society of Lancashire and Cheshire, Glass Circle (London).

WRITINGS: Glass, The Connoisseur, 1975; *Glass,* Collins, 1980; *Agoraphobia,* Faber, 1981; (contributor) Ward Lloyd and Dan Klein, editors, *A History of Glass*, Orbis Publishing Ltd., 1983; *The International Dictionary of Glass*, Country Life, 1984. Also author of scripts for "The Sparkling Stream" and "Old Wives' Remedies and All That," both British Broadcasting Corp. (BBC-Radio) series. Contributor of articles on agriculture and reviews to magazines and newspapers, including *Ormskirk Advertiser* and *Farmers Guardian*. Book reviewer for *Museum Journal*.

WORK IN PROGRESS: Two novels, one with a museum theme, the other with a farming theme; a nonfiction book on psychological transference.

SIDELIGHTS: Initially, Ruth Hurst Vose wrote to fill gaps in the literature of her profession, although she is currently branching out into other literary interests. "All my books," she explained, "have been written with a view to the sort of publications that I needed at various points in my career but that simply did not exist at the time." *Glass*, a volume of "The Connoisseur Illustrated Guides," approaches the problems involved in collecting glass. For the book, Vose developed a cataloguing system whereby the techniques of glassmaking are classified historically. Thus a sample can be identified quickly and easily. According to H. W. Woodward's *Museum Journal* review, "The book is a fine pioneer effort, a useful reference work, full of factual information, neatly abbreviated, assembled and illustrated, to help in the identification of a wide range of glass."

Her second book, also titled *Glass*, investigates the archaeology of four thousand years of glassmaking as well as the origins and evolution of the process. "I was able to write this since I had been professionally studying and excavating glassmaking sites for six years," Vose revealed. "The insight this gave me allowed me to add a genuine enthusiasm and practical understanding of the subject." "It must be said right off," maintained Paul Hollister in the *Glass Club Bulletin*, "that Ruth Hurst Vose nearly always knows precisely what she is writing about, and knows whom to call upon when she is not 100% sure—a tribute to any writer." "Her enthusiasm for the subject," wrote Ada Polak in the *British Book News*, "shines through the soberly professional narrative."

Other critics have noticed the author's competence, calling *Glass* "a good general work" that, in the words of R. J. Hunter's *Times Literary Supplement* review, "provides an excellent background to the subject." Continuing the praise of the book, Philip Whatmoor noted in *Post-Medieval Archaeology* that *Glass* "lives up to the editor's intention to take the reader to the frontiers of knowledge. The general reader will find it readable and stimulating, the specialist will find it indispensable as the first reference book to combine history and archaeology." And Woodward added: "*Glass* is the first book to deal in a comprehensive way with all important aspects of glass history and archaeology."

Since the publication of her first book on glass, Vose has taken up journalism and explored the subject of agoraphobia, from which she suffered. "Using her own experiences and those of other sufferers, she gives great insight into the terrible impact this condition can have on its victims, their families and friends," remarked Pauline A. Stewart in the *Nursing Times*. Producing "a rare and informative book, valuable to therapist and sufferer," Vose, noted Caroline Ridley in *Therapy*, relied on her personal situation to lobby for the understanding of agoraphobia whether the reader is a physician or a patient. As Henry R. Rollin stated in the *British Medical Journal*, "The medical practitioner need not consider it beneath his dignity to read in particular Ruth Hurst Vose's book, which is a most valuable aid to the understanding and treatment of this dreaded complaint."

Despite Vose's past success in the field of nonfiction, her most recent endeavors have been novels. "The desire to write good fiction has always been very strong in me, and I have taken the plunge at last and produced an illustrated novel with a museum theme and a farming novel," Vose remarked. "As a farmer's wife and with seven years as an agricultural correspondent for southwest Lancashire, I feel I am unusually well qualified to write on the latter theme also. If these novels are successful, I intend to remain in fiction writing for some time, since it has been my most enjoyable literary experience to date."

Vose told *CA:* "As one of Britain's leading experts on the history and archaeology of glass, I have had the opportunity of lecturing to specialized university, museum, and society organizations both in the United Kingdom and abroad, including the U.S.A. and Canada. I have appeared on both British and American television in the course of my studies. Professional pressures were finally to take their toll, and after a back-breaking excavation in Manchester and a whistle-stop tour of the U.S.A. and Canada in 1971, I developed the first symptoms of agoraphobia (the phobic fear of public places), which finally led to my having to give up my job.

"In the end I have to be grateful to my agoraphobia, from which I suffered severely for five years, for inadvertently bringing me to a writing career that I now much prefer to my original profession and that has brought me a much greater understanding of humankind. Unable to travel anywhere, at last I had the time to accept commissions to write books on glass, and with a large dictionary of glass and other contributions to publications on the subject in the pipeline, I feel I have made a worthwhile contribution in at least one field of human study. I still keep my hand in by writing reports on excavated glass for archaeologists, which is far less arduous than actually running a dig!

"At the same time I was training to become a journalist. I completed my traineeship in record time, becoming a senior journalist within the Associated Newspaper Group in eighteen months instead of the usual two years. The discipline of journalism, added to my industrial and academic training, made me into a very efficient in-depth researcher for specialized features for newspapers, magazines, and radio series. By this time I had conquered my agoraphobia with the help of a new treatment. With my peculiar talents I decided to write a book on agoraphobia, since I had found much ignorance and even fear of the subject among ordinary people, doctors, and even psychiatrists. I think my two proudest moments were reading good reviews of *Agoraphobia* in the *British Medical Journal*, where it is rare indeed for a lay person's view to be noticed, and one on *Glass* in the Collins series in the *Times Literary Supplement*."

BIOGRAPHICAL/CRITICAL SOURCES: Liverpool Daily Post, November 19, 1966, June 14, 1970, October 2, 1981; *Liverpool Echo*, March 14, 1968, April 23, 1970; *Daily Telegraph*, June 2, 1969; *Catholic Pictorial*, April 19, 1970, May 28, 1972, September 23, 1979; *Museums Journal*, March, 1976, March, 1981; *Weekend Echo*, January 27, 1979, September 6, 1980; *Lancashire Evening Post*, January 27, 1979, October 5, 1981; *Universe*, February 23, 1979; *Farmers Guardian*, March 9, 1979; *Southport Visiter*, September 15, 1979, July 26, 1980, October 9, 1981; *Southport Star*, September 21, 1979; *Glass*

Circle News, September, 1980; *British Book News*, November, 1980; *Times Literary Supplement*, November 7, 1980; *Post-Medieval Archaeology*, volume 15, 1981; *Connoisseur*, February, 1981; *Hobbies*, September, 1981; *Daily Mail*, September 29, 1981; *Choice*, October, 1981; *Evening Post and Chronicle*, October 6, 1981; *Ormskirk Advertiser*, October 8, 1981; *Woman's Realm*, October 17, 1981; *Lancashire Life*, November, 1981; *British Medical Journal*, November 28, 1981; *Glass Club Bulletin*, number 137, 1982; *Association of New Zealand Agoraphobics Newsletter*, 1982; *Archeology*, January, 1982; *Nursing Times*, February 10-16, 1982; *Therapy*, September 30, 1982; *Mediscope*, November 15, 1982.

*   *   *

VROMAN, Mary Elizabeth (Gibson)   1923-1967

OBITUARY NOTICE: Born in 1923 in Buffalo, N.Y.; died in 1967. Educator and author of fiction, nonfiction, and poetry. Vroman is best known for her novel *Harlem Summer*. She was a contributor to *Ladies' Home Journal* and *National Education Association Journal*. Vroman wrote the screenplay and served as technical advisor for the film "Bright Road," which was based on her short story "See How They Run." A member of the Screen Writers Guild, Vroman also won the Christopher Award for inspirational magazine writing. Obituaries and other sources: *New York Times*, April 30, 1967.

*   *   *

VUCINICH, Alexander S.   1914-

BRIEF ENTRY: Born October 23, 1914, in Wilmington, Calif. American sociologist, educator, and author. Vucinich taught at San Jose State College (now University) from 1950 to 1964 and at University of Illinois from 1964 to 1970. He then became a professor of history, sociology, and cultural anthropology at University of Texas. Vucinich has been awarded grants from the American Council of Learned Societies, the Social Science Research Council, and the American Philosophical Society. He wrote *Soviet Economic Institutions: The Social Structure of Production Units* (Stanford University Press, 1952), *The Soviet Academy of Sciences* (Stanford University Press, 1956), *Science in Russian Culture: A History to 1860* (Stanford University Press, 1963), *Science in Russian Culture, 1861-1917* (Stanford University Press, 1970), and *Social Thought in Tsar-*

ist Russia: The Quest for a General Science of Society, 1861-1917 (University of Chicago Press, 1976). *Address:* Department of History, University of Texas, 110 Garrison Hall, Austin, Tex. 78712. *Biographical/critical sources: American Historical Review*, October, 1971, December, 1976; *Times Literary Supplement*, November 26, 1971, January 7, 1977.

*   *   *

VYVERBERG, Henry (Sabin)   1921-

PERSONAL: Born December 31, 1921, in Elbridge, N.Y.; son of Henry John (a Protestant minister) and Bertha (Sabin) Vyverberg. *Education:* University of Rochester, B.A. (with highest distinction), 1942; Harvard University, M.A., 1947, Ph.D., 1950. *Home:* 2106 Woodriver Dr., Apt. 3, Carbondale, Ill. 62901. *Office:* Department of History, Southern Illinois University, Carbondale, Ill. 62901.

CAREER: Alliance College, Cambridge Springs, Pa., associate professor of history, 1950-57; University of Akron, Akron, Ohio, assistant professor, 1957-60, associate professor of history, 1960-68; Southern Illinois University, Carbondale, associate professor, 1968-79, professor of history, 1979—. *Military service:* U.S. Army, Military Intelligence, 1943-46, 1950-51; became master sergeant. *Member:* American Historical Association, Society for French Historical Studies, Renaissance Society of America, Societe d'Histoire Moderne, Phi Beta Kappa.

WRITINGS: Historical Pessimism in the French Enlightenment, Harvard University Press, 1958; *The Living Tradition: Art, Music, and Ideas in the Western World*, Harcourt, 1978. Contributor to *Encyclopedia of Philosophy*. Contributor to history journals.

WORK IN PROGRESS: The Nature and Destiny of Man: Aspects of Diderot's Encyclopedia.

SIDELIGHTS: Vyverberg told *CA:* "My main concern in the past decade has been Western (that is, European and to a lesser extent American) intellectual history, from classical Greece to the present. I also am particularly interested in the French Enlightenment. In response to, and stimulating still further, my broader cultural interests, I have traveled frequently to Europe, and fairly widely in the United States."

W

WADE, Henry William Rawson 1918-

PERSONAL: Born January 16, 1918, in London, England; son of Henry Oswald (a solicitor) and Eileen (Rawson-Ackroyd) Wade; married Marie Osland-Hill, October 15, 1943 (died, 1980); married Marjorie Hope Gill, October 15, 1982; children: (first marriage) John Michael Ackroyd, Edward Henry Rawson. *Education:* Gonville and Caius College, Cambridge, B.A., 1939; Cambridge University, LL.D., 1958. *Home and office:* Master's Lodge, Caius College, Cambridge University, Cambridge, England.

CAREER: Cambridge University, Cambridge, England, fellow of Trinity College, 1946-61, lecturer, 1947-59, reader in English law, 1959-61; Oxford University, Oxford, England, professor of English law, 1961-76; Cambridge University, master of Gonville and Caius College, 1976—, Rouse Ball Professor of English Law, 1978-82. Honorary bencher at Lincoln's Inn, 1964; appointed Queen's Counsel, 1968. *Member:* British Academy (fellow).

WRITINGS: (With Robert Megarry) *The Law of Real Property,* Stevens & Sons, 1957, 5th edition, in press; *Administrative Law,* Clarendon Press, 1961, 5th edition, 1982; *Towards Administrative Justice,* University of Michigan Press, 1963; (with Bernard Schwartz) *Legal Control of Government,* Oxford University Press, 1972; *Constitutional Fundamentals,* Stevens & Sons, 1980. Contributor to law journals.

SIDELIGHTS: Wade's work has taken him to Europe, the United States, Australia and New Zealand, South Africa, Malaysia, China, and Japan. He told *CA:* "*Constitutional Fundamentals* deals with the electoral system, the problem of legislative sovereignty, and the ability of the courts of law to control abuse of governmental power in Britain. Most of my recently published work is in the area of public law."

*　　*　　*

WADE, Ira Owen 1896-1983

OBITUARY NOTICE—See index for *CA* sketch: Born October 4, 1896, in Richmond, Va.; died of pneumonia, March 7, 1983, in Princeton, N.J. Educator and author. An expert on eighteenth-century French literature, Wade began teaching in 1916. He joined the Princeton University faculty in 1927 and retired as John N. Woodhull Professor of Modern Language Emeritus

in 1965. His numerous books include *Voltaire and Candide: A Story in the Fusion of History, Art, and Philosophy, The Intellectual Origins of the French Enlightenment,* and *The Structure and Form of the French Enlightenment.* Obituaries and other sources: *American Authors and Books: 1640 to the Present Day,* 3rd revised edition, Crown, 1962; *Who's Who in America,* 39th edition, Marquis, 1976; *New York Times,* March 9, 1983.

*　　*　　*

WADE, Robert
See McILWAIN, David

*　　*　　*

WAGNER, Jane

PERSONAL: Born February 26 in Morristown, Tenn. *Education:* Attended School of Visual Arts.

CAREER: Writer, actress, and director and producer of motion pictures. Worked as designer with Kimberly-Clark and Fieldcrest; co-writer and producer for comedian Lily Tomlin in various recording, television, and stage performances, including routines for the television series "Laugh-In," 1972—. Textile designs have been exhibited at Brooklyn Museum of Art. *Awards, honors:* Peabody Award, 1969, for television screenplay "J.T."; Child Study Association selection for Children's Books of the Year and Georgia Children's Book Award, 1972, both for *J.T.*; Writer's Guild award, 1975, for "Lily"; Emmy for outstanding writing in a comedy-variety or music special, 1975-76, for "Lily Tomlin."

WRITINGS: J.T. (juvenile; illustrated by Gordon Parks), Van Nostrand, 1969.

For television: "J.T." (teleplay), CBS-TV, 1969; "Earthwatch" (special), PBS-TV, 1975; (with Tomlin and others) "Lily" (television special), 1975; (with Tomlin and others) "Lily Tomlin" (special), ABC-TV, 1975; "People" (special), NBC-TV, 1975.

For stage: (With Tomlin) "Appearing Nightly" (revue), first produced on Broadway at Biltmore Theatre, March, 1977.

Screenplays: "Moment by Moment," Universal Studios, 1978; "The Incredible Shrinking Woman," Universal Studios, 1980.

Recordings; with Lily Tomlin: "And That's the Truth," Polydor 1972; "Lily Tomlin on Stage," Arista, 1977. Also author of material on "Modern Scream."

WORK IN PROGRESS: A screenplay for Metro-Goldwyn-Mayer.

*   *   *

WAGNER, Jon G(regory) 1944-

PERSONAL: Born April 22, 1944, in Wichita, Kan.; son of Joseph M. (a systems operator) and Frances (an artist; maiden name, Finney) Wagner; married Jan Merrill Lundeen, April 1, 1979; children: Nicholas, Joanna. *Education:* Wichita State University, B.A., 1967; Indiana University, M.A., 1972, Ph.D., 1975. *Home:* Route 1, Rio, Ill. 61472. *Office:* Department of Sociology and Anthropology, Knox College, Galesburg, Ill. 61401.

CAREER: Indiana University, Bloomington, lecturer in anthropology, 1971-73; Knox College, Galesburg, Ill., instructor, 1973-75, assistant professor, 1975-81, associate professor of sociology and anthropology, 1981—, chairman of department, 1980—. Member of board of directors of Bishop Hill Heritage Association, Bishop Hill, Ill. *Member:* American Anthropological Association, Society for Human Anthropology.

WRITINGS: (Editor) *Sex Roles in Contemporary American Communes,* Indiana University Press, 1982; (with Roy Anderson and Robert Seibert) *Politics and Change in the Middle East,* Prentice-Hall, 1982. Co-editor of *Anthropology and Humanism Quarterly,* 1975-77, member of editorial board, 1982—.

WORK IN PROGRESS: The anthropological critique of utopian thought.

SIDELIGHTS: Wagner's *Sex Roles in Contemporary American Communes* contains essays on the status of communal living written by six of his fellow anthropologists. These researchers did fieldwork in communes sharing two characteristics: all were religious establishments and were founded by charismatic leaders. In the six communitites both sexes lived within carefully defined, and for the most part, traditional sex roles. Critic Elaine Tyler May called the book "fascinating" in a *Los Angeles Times Book Review* article, adding that in a country moving toward greater equality between the sexes, "the communities described open our eyes to the various ways men and women seek to establish alternatives to the status quo."

Wagner told *CA:* "I consider myself a professional educator above all, and the principal goal of my writings is to elucidate and stimulate. My interests in religion and social change and in humanistic anthropology are closely related to my fascination with a certain paradox of anthropological insight: the (to my mind) undeniable influence of impersonal, deterministic forces in human affairs, and the equally undeniable influence of conscious human aspiration. Most anthropologists today emphasize one side of this dichotomy at the expense of the other, while I prefer to grapple with them as interpenetrating mutual realities."

BIOGRAPHICAL/CRITICAL SOURCES: Los Angeles Times Book Review, July 25, 1982.

*   *   *

WAGNER, Walter 1927(?)-1983(?)

OBITUARY NOTICE: Born c. 1927; died of lung cancer c.

1983. Author of books and of material for television. At one time Wagner wrote for the Art Linkletter television show "House Party." The author of several Los Angeles-based books, Wagner wrote *God Squad, Beverly Hills: Inside the Golden Ghetto,* and *Money Talks.* Obituaries and other sources: *Los Angeles Times,* May 9, 1983.

*   *   *

WAGSTAFF, (John) Malcolm 1940-

PERSONAL: Born May 16, 1940, in Congleton, England; son of Arthur Ronald (a watchmaker and jeweler) and Alice (a secretary; maiden name, Taylor) Wagstaff; married Patricia Ann Thompson (a teacher), September 11, 1962; children: Robert Joseph, Daniel John. *Education:* University of Liverpool, B.A., 1962; graduate study at University of Athens, 1962-63; University of Southampton, Ph.D., 1975. *Agent:* Frances Kelly, 9 King Edward Mansions, 629 Fulham Rd., London SW1, England. *Office:* Department of Geography, University of Southampton, Southampton, Hampshire, England.

CAREER: University of Durham, Durham, England, Centre of Middle Eastern and Islamic Studies, research assistant, 1963-66; University of Southampton, Southampton, Hampshire, England, lecturer, 1966-80, senior lecturer, 1980—. *Member:* Royal Geographical Society, Institute of British Geography, British Society for Middle Eastern Studies, British Institute of Archaeology at Ankara (council member, 1977—). *Awards, honors:* NATO fellowship, 1966-68.

WRITINGS: (With Gerald H. Blake and Peter Beaumont) *The Middle East,* Wiley, 1976; (editor with Colin Renfrew) *An Island Polity: The Archaeology of Exploitation in Melos,* Cambridge University Press, 1982; *The Development of Rural Settlements,* Avebury, 1982. Contributor of articles and reviews to professional journals, including *Balkan Studies, Geographical Review, Journal of Hellenic Studies,* and *Anatolian Studies.*

WORK IN PROGRESS: The Evolution of Middle Eastern Landscapes, for Croom Helm, 1983; Research on the Peloponnese in the eighteenth century and on Lt. Col. William Martin Leake.

SIDELIGHTS: In *An Island Polity: The Archaeology of Exploitation in Melos,* Wagstaff and co-editor Renfrew record the findings of an expedition of archaeologists studying the nature of change. Writing in the *Times Literary Supplement,* A. M. Snodgrass called the book "an admirable presentation of the findings of the expedition's fieldwork." Snodgrass also praised each of the editors, noting that "Malcolm Wagstaff's contributions throughout are conspicuous for their industry, learning and level-headedness."

Wagstaff told *CA:* "Scholars have the duty to communicate the result of their investigations to the public who supports them, and I write partly to fulfill that obligation and partly because writing helps to clarify my own thinking. I find writing both exciting and demanding."

BIOGRAPHICAL/CRITICAL SOURCES: Times Literary Supplement, July 2, 1982.

*   *   *

WAHLER, Robert G(ordon) 1936-

BRIEF ENTRY: Born October 1, 1936, in Bemidji, Minn. American psychologist, educator, and author. Wahler joined the faculty of University of Tennessee in 1964; he became a professor of psychology in 1971. Wahler co-authored *Ecological Assessment of Child Problem Behavior: A Clinical Package for Home, School, and Institutional Settings* (Pergamon, 1976). He co-edited the second edition of *Behavior Disorders: Perspectives and Trends*, (Lippincott, 1969). *Address:* Department of Psychology, University of Tennessee, Knoxville, Tenn. 37916.

*   *   *

WALKER, Everett 1906-1983

OBITUARY NOTICE: Born August 18, 1906, in Brooklyn, N.Y.; died of an apparent heart attack, April 18, 1983, in Montclair, N.J. Journalist. Between 1924 and 1966, Walker held several positions with the *New York Herald Tribune*, including reporter, managing editor, and director. During World War II he helped reestablish the European edition of the *Tribune* and served as a war correspondent. Walker was also managing editor of the *Washington Star* and a consulting editor for the *New York Times*. Obituaries and other sources: *New York Times*, April 20, 1983.

*   *   *

WALKER, Helen M(ary) 1891-1983

OBITUARY NOTICE: Born December 1, 1891, in Keosauqua, Iowa; died January 15, 1983, in Teaneck, N.J. Educator and author. A mathematician, Walker was a member and national president of the American Statistical Association, president of the American Educational Research Association, and Institute of Mathematical Statistics. Her numerous writings include *Algebra, a Way of Thinking, The Measurement of Teaching Efficiency*, and *Elementary Statistical Methods*. Obituaries and other sources: *New York Times*, January 18, 1983; *Chronicle of Higher Education*, February 2, 1983.

*   *   *

WALLACE, Sister M. Jean
See PAXTON, Mary Jean Wallace

*   *   *

WALLANCE, Gregory Joseph 1948-

PERSONAL: Born October 24, 1948, in Washington, D.C.; son of Donald Aaron (an industrial designer) and Shula (a graphics artist; maiden name, Cohen) Wallance; married Elisabeth A. Van Veen (a teacher), January 1, 1981; children: Daniel Isaac. *Education:* Grinnell College, B.A., 1970; Brooklyn Law School, J.D., 1976. *Home:* 821A Union St., Brooklyn, N.Y. 11215.

CAREER: Department of Justice, New York, N.Y., assistant U.S. attorney, 1979—. *Member:* Helsinki Watch Committee, Fund for Free Expression. *Awards, honors:* Nominated for Edgar Award from Mystery Writers of America, 1982, for *Papa's Game.*

WRITINGS: Papa's Game (nonfiction), Rawson, Wade, 1981. Contributor to newspapers.

SIDELIGHTS: Wallance told *CA:* "*Papa's Game* is about one of the worst episodes of police corruption in American history—the theft of the French connection heroin from the headquarters of the New York City Police Department. It demon-

strates, I hope, that without honest public officials, especially those who enforce the laws, you cannot have a stable society, let alone a democratic one."

BIOGRAPHICAL/CRITICAL SOURCES: New York Times Book Review, September 6, 1981.

*   *   *

WALLER, Irene Ellen 1928-

PERSONAL: Born May 8, 1928, in Birmingham, England; daughter of Arthur and Sarah Ann (Dutton) Carter; married Geoffrey Waller (an accountant), 1955; children: Carole Anne, Antony John, Joanne Elizabeth. *Education:* Birmingham College of Art, A.T.D. (Art Teacher's Diploma), 1949. *Home:* 13 Portland Rd., Edgbaston, Birmingham, England.

CAREER: Simpson Godlee, Manchester, England, textile designer, 1948-50; Restall's, Birmingham, England, interior designer, 1950-53; Birmingham Art College, Birmingham, head of School of Woven Textiles, 1953-70; free-lance artist, lecturer, and writer, 1971—. Gives lectures and seminars; guest on television programs, including "Master Craftsman" and "Serendipity." Work exhibited in group and solo shows in England, Canada, and the United States, and in collections, including those in churches and public buildings. *Member:* Royal Society of Arts (fellow), Associate Royal Birmingham Society of Artists (ARBSA). *Awards, honors:* Travel grants from Royal Society of Arts, 1948 and 1969.

WRITINGS: Thread as an Art Form, Studio Vista, 1973, published in the United States as *Designing With Thread,* Viking, 1973; *Tatting: A Contemporary Art Form,* Regnery, 1974; *Knots and Netting,* Taplinger, 1976; *The Craft of Weaving,* Stanley Paul, 1976; *Textile Sculpture,* Taplinger, 1977; *Fine Art Weaving: A Study of the Work of Artist-Weavers in Britain,* Batsford, 1978; *Design Sources for the Fibre Artist,* Davis Publications, 1978.

WORK IN PROGRESS: Art and Reality, "a philosophical and practical study of the visual, artistic, creative process."

SIDELIGHTS: Waller told *CA:* "I have come to the conclusion that my motivation for writing is that I like teaching, and writing is just another form of teaching. I hold sharp views about art education in general and fiber art in particular.

"I believe that art education should be for *everyone*, not for the few—that it should teach us all to *see* and then *do* (in whatever medium is suitable for the individual). I also believe craftsmanship should be well-taught, with attention to basic teaching and with less of the sloppy 'just express yourself' approach.

"My own art work is about the world around me—its landscape, skies, architecture—and how I feel about them."

AVOCATIONAL INTERESTS: Looking at landscape, theater, music, books, gardens, houses.

*   *   *

WALSH, Ernest 1895-1926

BRIEF ENTRY: Born August 10, 1895, in Detroit, Mich.; died of tuberculosis, October 16, 1926, in Monte Carlo, Monaco; buried in Monaco. American editor and poet. Walsh, who contracted tuberculosis at the age of seventeen (a condition that was later aggravated by injuries sustained in a plane crash), was pronounced incurable in 1922. Choosing to spend his remaining years in Europe among the artists and writers he admired, the young man settled in Paris, where he met Ethel Moorhead, a Scottish artist and political activist. Together they created the "little magazine" *This Quarter* in 1925, providing a forum for avant-garde literary expression. Ernest Hemingway, Gertrude Stein, William Carlos Williams, and James Joyce were among the artists the magazine published. After Walsh's death in 1926, Moorhead collected and published a volume of the young man's poetry, *Poems and Sonnets* (1934). *Biographical/critical sources: Dictionary of Literary Biography,* Volume 4: *American Writers in Paris, 1920-1939,* Gale, 1980.

* * *

WALSH, George (Vincent) 1923-

PERSONAL: Born January 21, 1923, in Pittsfield, Mass.; son of George Joseph (an educator) and Delia (a registered nurse; maiden name, Killeen) Walsh; married Eva Suzanne Reis, June 1, 1946 (divorced, 1962); married Catherine Mary Frank, June 8, 1963; children: (first marriage) Michael Francis, Maraed Elsa; (second marriage) Amy Lynn. *Education:* Williams College, A.B. (magna cum laude), 1943; Brown University, M.A., 1945; Princeton University, Ph.D., 1952. *Politics:* "Independent natural-rights, *laissez-faire* capitalist." *Residence:* Geneva, N.Y. *Office:* Department of Philosophy, Salisbury State College, Salisbury, Md. 21801.

CAREER: Hobart and William Smith Colleges, Geneva, N.Y., instructor, 1948-52, assistant professor, 1952-54, associate professor, 1954-56, professor of philosophy and chairman of department, 1956-68; Eisenhower College, Seneca Falls, N.Y., professor of philosophy, beginning in 1968; associated with the Department of Philosophy at Salisbury State College, Salisbury, Md. *Member:* American Philosophical Association, Phi Beta Kappa.

WRITINGS: (Translator with Frederick Lehnert, and editor) Alfred Schutz, *The Phenomenology of the Social World,* Northwestern University Press, 1967. Contributor to *Objectivist.*

WORK IN PROGRESS: A critique of John Rawls's *Theory of Justice,* "considering the book as the one major work that reveals the most basic premises of welfare state-ism and its ultimate aims."

SIDELIGHTS: Walsh told *CA:* "My work has become focused on stating and defending the metaphysical and moral foundations of a truly free society, the kind of society that was only vaguely sketched out by the founding fathers of the United States. By free society, I mean one in which every individual has the right to control his own life, thought, plans, and property without depending on coercive support from others or having to bear the coercive guidance of others. In such a society there would be no duties except to respect the natural and inalienable rights of others. This view, I find, is slowly spreading to an increasing number of people, and I consider it a special calling to share in clarifying its basic concepts, answering objections, and convincing doubters. I have participated in a great many conferences and think tanks devoted to these ideas."

* * *

WALSH, Myles E(ugene) 1937-

PERSONAL: Born June 7, 1937, in New York, N.Y.; son of Myles G. and Dorothy (Warwick) Walsh; married Diana Stro-

ligo (a lecturer), April 28, 1962; children: Robert, James, Marc, Richard. *Education:* St. John's University, Jamaica, N.Y., B.B.A., 1964; Bernard M. Baruch College of the City University of New York, M.B.A., 1970. *Residence:* Kinnelon, N.J. *Office:* CBS Records, Columbia Broadcasting System, Inc., 810 Seventh Ave., New York, N.Y. 10019.

CAREER: Columbia Broadcasting System, Inc., New York, N.Y., member of staff of Data Center, 1967-68, manager of systems and programming for Columbia House Division, 1968-70, director of computer systems for CBS News, 1970-74, general business consultant with Corporate MIS planning staff, 1975-76, director of database systems, 1976-81, director of data library development for CBS Records, 1981—. *Military service:* U.S. Army, Corps of Engineers, 1956-58. *Member:* Association for Systems Management. *Awards, honors:* Elmer Grillo Award from *Journal of Systems Management,* 1979, for *Information Management System/Virtual Storage;* Gellman Hayward from *Journal of Systems Management,* 1981-82, for editorial excellence.

WRITINGS: Information Management Systems/Virtual Storage: A Practical Guide for Managers, Reston, 1980; (contributor) Thomas Rullo, editor, *Advances in Data Base Management,* Heyden, 1980; *Understanding Computers: What Managers and Users Need to Know,* Wiley, 1981; (contributor) M. J. Riley, editor, *Managment Information Systems,* 2nd edition, Holden-Day, 1981; (contributor) Ivan Flores, editor, *Data Processing Handbook,* Van Nostrand, 1982; *Database-Data Communications Systems: A Guide for Managers,* Reston, 1983; *Realizing the Potential of MIS,* Macmillan, in press. Contributor of about twenty-five articles to technical magazines.

WORK IN PROGRESS: Research on electronic data processing, information systems, and the Bible.

SIDELIGHTS: Walsh commented: "I enjoy teaching. This led me to write books in which I attempt to present complex subject matter in a simple form, without making it superficial.

"Individuals need to know the functional aspect of computers in order to put them to use. They need not know 'math.' Many individuals get mired in the technical detail of binary and hexadecimal numbering systems and assembler mnemonics and despair of ever understanding computers. The recent popularity of small microprocessor-based computers shows that all that is unnecessary. *Understanding Computers* helps non-technical individuals to understand computer equipment and software.

"As computers find their way into homes, individuals willing to invest between twenty to forty hours with a primer and a small computer can begin to become proficient in its use. The book *Understanding Computers,* if read prior to the acquisition of the computer, would minimize the time investment required to get familiar with the computer.

"My *Management Information Systems* is an attempt to explain to senior managers and executives the working of systems using computers, and how the potential of computerized information systems can be realized. The database/data communications book describes an extremely complex technology in terms understandable to non-technical managers and executives."

* * *

WALSH, Patricia L(ouise) 1942-

PERSONAL: Born August 23, 1942, in Pine City, Minn.; daughter of Thomas Edward (a farmer) and Bernadine (Gaukel) Maher; married Edward Joseph Walsh (a scientist), June 30,

1973; children: Marnie Lorel. *Education:* St. Mary's School of Nursing, Minneapolis, Minn., R.N., 1963, C.R.N.A., 1965. *Politics:* Independent. *Religion:* Roman Catholic. *Home and office:* 1505 Mapleton Ave., Boulder, Colo. 80302. *Agent:* Virginia Barber, 353 West 21st St., New York, N.Y. 10011.

CAREER: U.S. Foreign Service, Washington, D.C., nurse anesthetist in Vietnam, 1967-68; associated with Hospital Albert Schweitzer in Haiti, 1968-69; worked at hospitals throughout the United States, including Johns Hopkins Hospital in Baltimore, Md.; writer, 1981—. *Member:* American Association of Nurse Anesthetists, Authors Guild. *Awards, honors:* Outstanding service award from U.S. Foreign Service; Jenney Moore fellowship for George Washington University, 1979.

WRITINGS: Forever Sad the Hearts (novel), Avon, 1982. Contributor of book reviews to *Washington Post.*

WORK IN PROGRESS: What So Ever You Do, a novel "about the plight of the medical situation in this country and the hypocrisy of the New Right's religious fervor. The book will include some of the hardships that returnees from Vietnam encountered as well as my feelings on nuclear disarmament, of which I am an avid proponent."

SIDELIGHTS: Patricia Walsh wrote: "I was injured in the Tet offensive in Da Nang in 1968, and required years of surgery and bedrest. That is when I began writing, as a form of occupational therapy. Continued back problems prevent me from practicing medicine.

"I traveled extensively before my injury. I am very conscious of social injustice and reflect that in my writing. I have fourteen siblings and am totally self-educated."

*   *   *

WALZ, Audrey Boyers   1907(?)-1983
(Francis Bonnamy)

OBITUARY NOTICE: Born c. 1907 in Mobile, Ala.; died of cancer, February 14, 1983, in Greenfield, Mass. Author. Under the pseudonym Francis Bonnamy, Walz wrote several mysteries. With her husband, Jay Walz, she also wrote two historical novels, *The Bizarre Sisters* and *The Undiscovered Country,* and *Portrait of Canada.* Obituaries and other sources: *New York Times,* February 17, 1983.

*   *   *

WANG, Chung-shu   1925-

PERSONAL: Born October 15, 1925, in Ningpo, China; son of Xuan-bing (a teacher) and Su-juan (Ling) Wang; married Kai Chen (a teacher), July 15, 1960; children: Jian-zhi. *Education:* Attended Zhejiang University and Peking University, 1946-50. *Politics:* Communist. *Residence:* Beijing, China. *Office:* Number 27, Wangfujing St., Beijing, China 10070.

CAREER: Chinese Academy of Social Sciences, Institute of Archaeology, Beijing, beginning researcher in Han-Tang archaeology, 1950-52, assistant researcher, 1952-78, deputy director, 1978—, research fellow and vice-chairman of scientific committee, 1979—. *Member:* Chinese Society of Archaeology (general secretary, 1979—). *Awards, honors:* Certificate and honorary professorship from National Cuzco University, 1973.

WRITINGS: Han Civilization, Yale University Press, 1982. Contributor to Chinese archaeology journals.

WORK IN PROGRESS: A study of Chinese bronze mirrors of the Three Kingdoms, Western and Eastern Jins, and Southern and Northern Dynasties, with Xu Pingfang.

SIDELIGHTS: Wang told *CA:* "I am interested in archaeology because it studies ancient history not only by documents but mainly by material data. The reason I specialize in the archaeology of the Han Dynasty is because it covers a very important period in Chinese history, and its material data is very rich."

*   *   *

WANG, Zhong-shu
See WANG, Chung-shu

*   *   *

WARD, Donald   1909-

PERSONAL: Born in 1909, in Belmont, Surrey, England; son of Daniel Vincent (a chief inspector of post office telephones) and Ada Amelia (a waitress; maiden name, Sutcliffe) Ward; married Doris Gertrude Kathleen Philpott (a part-time hospital worker), September 25, 1935; children: Brian Edward Sidney, Susan Christine Margaret, Mark Vincent, Lawrence John. *Education:* Attended secondary school in Ramsgate, England. *Politics:* Socialist. *Religion:* Christian. *Home:* 50 Daleside, Orpington, Kent BR6 6EQ, England.

CAREER: British Postal Service, Ramsgate, England, young postman, 1923-29, postman driver in Canterbury, England, 1929-39, postman in London, England, 1939-49, and Mount Pleasant district of London, 1949-72; became postman higher grade. Member of Poets Workshop, National Poetry Centre, London. *Member:* National Federation of Post Office and British Telecom Pensioners. *Awards, honors:* Award from Arts Council of Great Britain, 1972, for *The Dead Snake.*

WRITINGS: The Dead Snake (poems), Allison & Busby, 1971; *A Few Rooks Circling Trees* (poems), Mandeville Press, 1975; *Border Country* (poems), Anvil Press Poetry, 1980.

WORK IN PROGRESS: A poetry pamphlet, publication expected in 1983; a book of poems, publication expected in 1984; a novel.

SIDELIGHTS: Ward told *CA* that life and death are the underlying themes of his poetry. His interest in prose focuses on "relationships of people, one to another; relationships of people to situations; atmosphere; and interior monologue." He also described himself as "intensely romantic." *Avocational interests:* The natural world (especially butterflies), travel, watching football, roaming around cities, walking in the countryside, cycling.

*   *   *

WARD, J(ohn) P(owell)   1937-

PERSONAL: Born November 28, 1937, in Felixstowe, England; son of Ronald Arthur (a theologian) and Evelyn Annie (a teacher and writer; maiden name, Powell) Ward; married Sarah Woodfull Rogers (a farmer), January 31, 1965; children: John Ralph Tristan, Thomas James. *Education:* University of Toronto, B.A., 1959; Peterhouse, Cambridge, B.A., 1961, M.A., 1969; University of Wales, M.Sc., 1969. *Home:* Court Lodge, Horton Kirby, Near Dartford, Kent DA4 9BN, England. *Office:* University College of Swansea, Singleton Park, Swansea SA2 8PP, Wales.

CAREER: University of Wales, University College of Swansea, lecturer in education, 1963—. *Member:* Welsh Academy. *Awards, honors:* Literature award from Welsh Arts Council, 1982, for *Poetry and the Sociological Idea.*

WRITINGS: The Other Man (poems), Christopher Davies, 1969; *The Line of Knowledge* (poems), Christopher Davies, 1972; *From Alphabet to Logos* (experimental poems), Second Aeon, 1973; *Things* (poems), Bran's Head Books, 1981; *To Get Clear* (poems), Poetry Wales Press, 1981; *Poetry and the Sociological Idea,* Harvester Press, 1981; *Raymond Williams* (criticism), University of Wales Press, 1981; *Wordsworth's Language of Men,* Harvester Press, in press. Editor of *Poetry Wales,* 1975-80.

SIDELIGHTS: A noted modern British poet, J. P. Ward has issued several volumes of verse, including *To Get Clear,* a collection of largely metaphysical poems that inspired *Times Literary Supplement* reviewer Anne Stevenson to write: "At his best Ward has a way with narrative which carries a poem through from beginning to end in an irresistible sweep of language. The reader boards a poem as if he were getting on a bus; before he knows it he has arrived at a destination well past anything he expected." Stevenson continued: "Ward . . . manages brilliantly, combining an uncompromising integrity with a contemporary flair for understatement."

Ward also elicited praise from a *Times Literary Supplement* critic for his book *Poetry and the Sociological Idea,* a look at poetry before and after the "sociological idea" which began in the nineteenth century. Charles Madge wrote: "I can say from practical experience that sociology and poetry do not sit easily together. J. P. Ward has written brilliantly about their incompatibility. . . . This is a brilliant and original book."

Ward told *CA:* "By the 'sociological idea' I mean the idea that permeates most contemporary people's minds (including my own) that there is an entity named 'society' within which we live, which has considerable claims on us and considerably forms us. All nations, countries, tribes, and regions are not unique or individual, for they exemplify this overall 'society' notion and can be shown to possess its characteristics. It is the most pervading conception of our era. Because of it, language is seen not as a set of terms matching and evoking realities, but as a means by which we stay in touch with each other—a means by which 'society' exists.

"My book argues that this belief, if dominant, is not compatible with the view and use of language held by poets. I show by close reading of Spenser, Donne, Milton, Pope, and Wordsworth that their use of language is not compatible with even those sociological positions each poet might have been thought most likely to hold. I then show from close readings of Baudelaire, Mallarme, Yeats, Stevens, William Carlos Williams, Eliot, Pound, Hardy, and Berryman, that in the era of the sociological idea (roughly the late nineteenth and twentieth centuries) the poets actually respond to the sociological idea explicitly, finding themselves in enormous tension against it."

BIOGRAPHICAL/CRITICAL SOURCES: Times Literary Supplement, November 27, 1981, May 7, 1982.

*   *   *

WARD, John Stephen Keith   1938-

PERSONAL: Born in 1938, in Northumberland, England; married Marian Trotman; children: Fiona Caroline, Alun James Kendall. *Education:* University of Wales, B.A., 1962; Oxford University, B.Litt., 1964.

CAREER: University of Glasgow, Glasgow, Scotland, lecturer in logic, 1964-66, and moral philosophy, 1966-68; University of St. Andrews, St. Andrews, Scotland, lecturer in moral philosophy, 1969-71; University of London, King's College, London, England, lecturer in philosophy, 1971-74; Cambridge University, Cambridge, England, dean of Trinity Hall, 1974-82; University of London, King's College, F. D. Maurice Professor of Moral and Social Theology, 1982.

WRITINGS: Ethics and Christianity, Allen & Unwin, 1970; *The Development of Kant's View of Ethics,* Basil Blackwell, 1972; *The Concept of God,* Basil Blackwell, 1974; *The Divine Image,* S.P.C.K., 1976; *The Christian Way,* S.P.C.K., 1976; *Rational Theology and the Creativity of God,* Basil Blackwell, 1982.

*   *   *

WARD, John Towers   1930-

PERSONAL: Born July 27, 1930, in Horsforth, England; son of Sidney (a surveyor) and Doris Beatty (a teacher; maiden name, Towers) Ward; married Kay Kidd (a teacher); children: Mark Towers. *Education:* Magdalene College, Cambridge, B.A., 1953, M.A., 1957, Ph.D., 1957. *Politics:* Tory. *Religion:* Anglican. *Home:* 265 Nithsdale Rd., Glasgow G41 5AW, Scotland. *Office:* Department of History, University of Strathclyde, McCance Building, 16 Richmond St., Glasgow G1 1XW, Scotland.

CAREER: Cambridge University, Cambridge, England, Bye fellow at Magdalene College, 1955-56; University of St. Andrews, Dundee, Scotland, lecturer in history, 1956-63; University of Strathclyde, Glasgow, Scotland, senior lecturer, 1963-74, professor of modern history, 1974—. Secretary of Lord Home's Scottish Constitutional Committee, 1968-70; president of Scottish Conservative Trade Unionists, 1962-74, 1975-83. *Military service:* British Army, Intelligence Corps, 1948-50. *Member:* Scottish Conservative Party, Royal Historical Society (fellow), Historical Association, Economic History Society, Social History Society.

WRITINGS: The Factory Movement, 1830-55, Macmillan, 1962; *Sir James Graham,* Macmillan, 1967; *East Yorkshire Landed Estates,* East Yorkshire Historical Society, 1967; (author of introduction) John Fielden, *Curse of the Factory System,* Cass, 1969; *The Factory System,* David & Charles, Volume I, 1970, Volume II, 1973; *Chartism,* Batsford, 1973; *The First Century,* Scottish Conservative Association, 1982.

Editor: *Popular Movements,* Macmillan, 1970, 4th edition, 1980; (with R. G. Wilson) *Land and Industry,* David & Charles, 1971; *The Age of Change,* A. & C. Black, 1975; (with John Butt) *Scottish Themes,* Scottish Academic Press, 1976; (with W. H. Fraser) *Workers and Employers,* Macmillan, 1980. Contributor to journals.

WORK IN PROGRESS: Research on British landed estates, the life of W. B. Ferrand, history of the Scottish Tory party, and history of the trade union National Graphical Association.

SIDELIGHTS: Ward commented: "I find British social and political history fascinating and enjoy writing about it, from a viewpoint that is sometimes novel, as it rests on wide research.

"The landed estates are interesting as the cornerstone of British rural society. They evolved early forms of management, created industries (such as mining) and urban conurbations, and were generally closely involved in politics. And they were highly successful agricultural units.

"My other principal historical interest has been in working class movements and their interaction in nineteenth-century politics. This developed from a long involvement in lecturing to the Workers' Educational Association and various trade union groups."

AVOCATIONAL INTERESTS: Philately, political speaking, collecting books, reading.

* * *

WARD, Theodore 1902-1983

OBITUARY NOTICE: Born September 15, 1902, in Thibodeaux, La.; died May 10, 1983, in Chicago, Ill. Educator and playwright. Early in his career, Ward was involved with the Works Progress Administration (WPA) Playwrights Project, along with such literary figures as Langston Hughes, Richard Wright, and Alain Locke. The playwright, who taught writing seminars in Chicago and New Orleans, wrote twenty-two plays. One, "Our Lan," was produced on Broadway. Ward received many honors, including Negro of the Year in 1947, the Theatre Guild Award, and the 1982 DuSable Writers' Seminar and Poetry Festival Award for Excellence in Drama. Obituaries and other sources: *Chicago Tribune*, May 12, 1983; *Washington Post*, May 13, 1983; *Los Angeles Times*, May 14, 1983; *Newsweek*, May 23, 1983.

* * *

WARDLE, Lynn D(ennis) 1947-

PERSONAL: Born November 15, 1947, in Provo, Utah; son of V. Dennis and Mary (Thompson) Wardle; married Marian Eastwood; children: David, Jonathan. *Education:* Brigham Young University, B.A., 1971; Duke University, J.D., 1974. *Religion:* Church of Jesus Christ of Latter-day Saints (Mormons). *Office:* Department of Law, Brigham Young University, Provo, Utah 84602.

CAREER: Streich, Weeks & Cardon, Phoenix, Ariz., associate lawyer, 1975-78; Brigham Young University, Provo, Utah, assistant professor, 1978-80, associate professor of law, 1980—. Director of National Right to Life Committee, Inc.,and Americans United for Life Legal Defense Fund. *Member:* International Society on Family Law.

WRITINGS: The Abortion Privacy Doctrine, William S. Hein, 1981; (with Mary Anne Q. Wood) *A Lawyer Looks at Abortion*, Brigham Young University Press, 1982.

WORK IN PROGRESS: Family Laws in the United States, publication by Callaghan expected in 1985.

SIDELIGHTS: Wardle wrote: "American law is one of the essential ingredients of the glue that holds our society together and protects our values. Abortion is the most important civil rights issue in our country today. And *Roe* vs. *Wade* is one of the most troubling decisions in modern American law. It is disturbing because the court, with no constitutional precedent and no social mandate, rendered a revolutionary ruling that effectively denied the legitimacy of moral dilemmas and made legally irrelevant the reasons for abortion. *Roe* vs. *Wade* was just the first of many 'abortion privacy' decisions which have taken the notion of 'abortion on demand' to unanticipated extremes. As a result, a constitutional crisis focusing on the court and abortion is developing."

WARKENTIN, Germaine (Therese) 1933-

PERSONAL: Born October 20, 1933, in Toronto, Ontario, Canada; daughter of Gerard Patrick (a clothier) and Therese Mary (a secretary; maiden name, Riley) Clinton; married John H. Warkentin (a professor), December 26, 1956; children: Juliet Mary. *Education:* University of Toronto, B.A., 1955, Ph.D., 1972; University of Manitoba, M.A., 1965. *Home:* 40 Boswell Ave., Toronto, Ontario, Canada M5R 1M4. *Office:* English Section, Victoria College, University of Toronto, Toronto, Ontario, Canada M5S 1K7.

CAREER: United College, Winnipeg, Manitoba, lecturer in English, 1958-59; University of Toronto, Toronto, Ontario, lecturer, 1970-72, assistant professor, 1972-76, associate professor of English, 1976—. *Member:* Modern Language Association of America, Mediaeval Academy of America, Renaissance Society of America, Association of Canadian University Teachers of English, Canadian Society for Renaissance Studies, Association for Canadian and Quebec Literatures. *Awards, honors:* Canada Council fellowship, 1976-77.

WRITINGS: (Editor and contributor) James Reaney, *Poems*, New Press, 1972; (editor) *Stories From Ontario*, Macmillan of Canada, 1974; (editor and author of introduction) W. E. Collin, *The White Savannahs*, University of Toronto Press, 1975; (editor with David Sinclair) *The New World Journal of Alexander Graham Dunlop*, Dundurn Press, 1976.

WORK IN PROGRESS: A monograph on Sir Philip Sidney, *Astrophil and Stella in the Setting of Its Tradition; Il Canzoniere*, verse translation of Francesco Petraria, with James W. Cook.

* * *

WARREN, Kenneth 1931-

PERSONAL: Born September 16, 1931, in Lincoln, England; son of Arthur Robert (an engineer) and Doris May (Blow) Warren; married Jean Elizabeth Elcock, June 29, 1957; children: Peter, John, David. *Education:* Cambridge University, B.A., 1954, Ph.D., 1960; attended University of Wisconsin—Madison, 1954-55. *Religion:* Methodist. *Home:* 12 New Yatt Rd., Witney, Oxfordshire, England. *Office:* School of Geography, Oxford University, Mansfield Rd., Oxford, England.

CAREER: University of Leicester, Leicester, England, lecturer in geography, 1956-66; University of Newcastle-upon-Tyne, Newcastle upon Tyne, England, lecturer in geography, 1966-70; Oxford University, Oxford, England, lecturer in geography and fellow of Jesus College, 1970—. *Member:* Institute of British Geographers.

WRITINGS: The American Steel Industry, 1850-1970: A Geographical Interpretation, Oxford University Press, 1973; *Mineral Resources*, David & Charles, 1973; *The Geography of British Heavy Industry Since 1800*, Oxford University Press, 1976; *World Steel*, David & Charles, 1978; *Chemical Foundations: The Alkali Industry in Britain*, Oxford University Press, 1980.

WORK IN PROGRESS: A study of resource development in Pennsylvania, including lumber, anthracite coal, oil, and coke; a review of developments in the world armaments industry, 1850-1930; research on British steel firms and associated regional economies.

SIDELIGHTS: Warren told *CA:* "Much of the recent work I have undertaken overlaps with the fields of the economist and the economic historian. I believe strongly, however, that the distinctive perspective of the geographer can make a valuable contribution in these fields. Reading about and travel in the northeastern United States encouraged work in the study of resource development in Pennsylvania—a development process stamped on the landscape in population distribution, in depressed area characteristics, and in signs of environmental distress. In the study of world armaments one makes the connection between politics and power on the one hand and with areas of great agglomerations of heavy industry on the other, having the backwardness of the Third World as a key factor.''

*   *   *

WARWICK, Ray   1911(?)-1983

OBITUARY NOTICE: Born c. 1911 in Atlanta, Ga.; died following a stroke, April 15, 1983, in Washington, D.C. Public relations executive and journalist. Warwick worked as a reporter for the *Atlanta Journal* and for the United Press (now United Press International) and Associated Press news services before accepting a public relations position with United Steelworkers of America. Obituaries and other sources: *Washington Post,* April 18, 1983.

*   *   *

WARWICK, Roger   1912-

PERSONAL: Born December 12, 1912, in Birmingham, England; son of Rowland (a company director) and Gertrude Fletcher Jackson (Richards) Warwick; married Carolyn Campbell Rigby (a research pathologist); children: Penelope Warwick Bowers, Antony John Rigby. *Education:* Victoria University of Manchester, M.B., Ch.D., 1937, Ph.D., 1955. *Office address:* c/o Department of Anatomy, Guy's Hospital Medical School, University of London, London S.E.1, England.

CAREER: Manchester Royal Infirmary, Manchester, England, house physician and house surgeon, 1938-39; Cheadle Royal Mental Hospital, Cheadle, England, assistant physician, 1939; Victoria University of Manchester, Manchester, lecturer in anatomy, 1946-55; University of London, Guy's Hospital Medical School, London, England, director of department and professor of anatomy, 1955-80; free-lance writer, 1980—. Examiner in universities in England, the West Indies, Singapore, Hong Kong, Malaya, and Khartoum. *Military service:* Royal Naval Volunteer Reserve, 1939-45; became surgeon lieutenant. *Member:* International Anatomical Nomenclature Committee, Linnean Society, Zoological Society of London, Anatomical Society of Great Britain, Anatomical Society of Ireland. *Awards, honors:* Symington Prize from Anatomical Society of Great Britain, 1953, for research.

WRITINGS: (Editor) *Whillis's Physiology,* 4th edition (Warwick was not associated with earlier editions), Churchill Livingstone, 1957, 5th edition, 1960; (contributor) M. B. Blender, editor, *The Oculomotor System,* Hoeber, 1964; (contributor) L. P. Wenham, editor, *The Roman-British Cemetary at York,* H.M.S.O., 1968; *Introduction to Anatomy,* Newnes, 1965.

(Editor) *Johnson's Synopsis of Whillis's Anatomy,* 19th edition, Churchill Livinstone, 1968; (editor with P. L. Williams) *Gray's Anatomy,* 35th edition (Warwick was not associated with earlier editions), Churchill Livingstone, 1972, 36th edition, 1980, 29th American edition, Saunders, 1973; (editor) Eugene Wolff, *Wolff's Anatomy of the Eye and Orbit,* 7th edition (Warwick was not associated with earlier editions), H. K. Lewis, 1976; (editor) *Nomina Anatomica,* Excerpta Medical Publishing, 1977.

WORK IN PROGRESS: An autobiography; a biography of Henry Gray; new editions of *Wolff's Anatomy of the Eye and Orbit, Gray's Anatomy,* and *Nomina Anatomica.*

SIDELIGHTS: Warwick told *CA:* ''I correspond extensively with friends and scientists all over the world, being completely disillusioned in nationalism and racism. I am waiting a world state and language—about a million years after my death. I am much interested in worldwide radio communication for similar reasons and listen to many countries' external services. I am not very medically inclined—I prefer to be regarded as a human biologist. I have always enjoyed writing, and I found most anatomical texts very dull, so I set out to remedy things. Anyway, writing is the best way to find communion with other minds in distant places.''

*   *   *

WASSERSTEIN, Abraham   1921-

PERSONAL: Born October 5, 1921, in Frankfurt am Main, Germany (now West Germany); son of Bernhard and Cilla Wasserstein; married Margaret Eva Ecker, 1942; children: Bernard, David, Celia (Mrs. Steven Fassberg). *Education:* University of London, B.A., 1949, Ph.D., 1951. *Religion:* Jewish. *Office:* Department of Classics, Hebrew University of Jerusalem, Jerusalem, Israel.

CAREER: University of Glasgow, Glasgow, Scotland, lecturer in Greek, 1951-60; Leicester University, Leicester, England, professor of classics, 1960-69, dean of faculty of arts, 1966-69; Oxford University, Oxford, England, visiting fellow at Centre for Postgraduate Hebrew Studies, 1973-74; Institute for Advanced Study, Princeton, N.J., member of institute, 1975-76; University of Heidelberg, Heidelberg, West Germany, visiting professor, 1980-81; Hebrew University of Jerusalem, Jerusalem, Israel, professor of classical studies. *Member:* Classical Association, Society for the Promotion of Hellenic Studies, Society for the Promotion of Roman Studies, Royal Astronomical Society (fellow).

WRITINGS: Galen's Commentary on the Hippocratic Treatise: Airs, Waters, Places, Israel Academy of Sciences, 1982. Also author of *Josephus,* 1974. Contributor to scholarly journals.

WORK IN PROGRESS: Research on Greek literature, philosophy, and history of science.

*   *   *

WATERMAN, Andrew (John)   1940-

PERSONAL: Born May 28, 1940, in London, England; son of Leonard and Olive (Smith) Waterman; married Angela Marilyn Hannah Eagle, May 21, 1982; children: Rory John Nolan. *Education:* Leicester University, B.A. (first class honors), 1966; graduate study at Oxford University, 1966-68. *Home:* 15 Hazelbank Rd., Coleraine, Londonderry, Northern Ireland, U.K. *Office:* University of Ulster, Coleraine, Londonderry, Northern Ireland, U.K.

CAREER: University of Ulster (formerly New University of Ulster), Coleraine, Northern Ireland, lecturer, 1968-78, senior lecturer in English literature, 1978—. *Member:* Poetry Society, Association of University Teachers. *Awards, honors:* Cholmondeley Award for Poets, 1977; second prize in Arvon Foundation Poetry Competition, 1981, for *Out for the Elements.*

WRITINGS—Poetry: Living Room (Poetry Book Society choice in England), Marvell Press, 1974; *From the Other Country,*

Carcanet Press, 1977; *Over the Wall,* Carcanet Press, 1980; *Out for the Elements* (Poetry Book Society recommendation in England), Carcanet Press, 1981; (editor) *The Poetry of Chess,* Anvil Press Poetry, 1981. Contributor of articles and reviews to journals and newspapers, including *London Magazine, Poetry Wales, P.N. Review,* and *Times Literary Supplement.*

WORK IN PROGRESS: Further poems; a critical book on British poetry since 1910.

SIDELIGHTS: In a *Times Literary Supplement* article, Grevel Lindop characterized Waterman's *Out for the Elements* as "an autobiography framed in a diary: the past recaptured through the preoccupations of the present." The book contains an introductory set of twenty lyrics titled "Given Worlds," which are memories and insights into Waterman's personal experience, follows with another group of "Shorter Poems," and closes with the major works, "Anglo-Irish," a discussion of the situation in Northern Ireland from the author's perspective, and "Out for the Elements," a wide-ranging account of the author's travels in England and Ireland during 1979 and 1980.

Reflecting on the poetic achievement in *Out for the Elements* and some of Waterman's earlier efforts, Lindop declared, "One has the impression of a poet who has found his proper direction, and has begun to produce important work." He continued, "'Out for the Elements' is a rare thing: a long poem which is highly readable, as well as thoroughly contemporary in its techniques and its mode of intelligence. It also goes with sensitivity to the heart of several problems that beset modern Britain."

Waterman told *CA:* "Life provides sufficient motivation for writing poetry; that is, one is nagged to articulate response, to use language to explore and try to clarify various areas of experience. Obviously one could enlarge enormously on this."

AVOCATIONAL INTERESTS: Hill-walking, chess, good conversation.

BIOGRAPHICAL/CRITICAL SOURCES: Listener, April 15, 1976; Michael Schmidt and Peter Jones, editors, *British Poetry Since 1970,* Carcanet Press, 1980; *Encounter,* January, 1982; *London Review of Books,* February 18, 1982; *Times Literary Supplement,* April 16, 1982.

*   *   *

WATKINS, Peter   1934-

PERSONAL: Born February 7, 1934, in London, England; son of Harry Gordon (a publisher) and Gladys (Wood) Watkins; married Angela Berger (a teacher), August 20, 1966; children: Benjamin, Samuel, Jessica. *Education:* St. Peter's College, Oxford, M.A., 1957; attended Wycliffe Hall Theological College, 1957-59. *Politics:* Conservative. *Home:* 7 North Common Rd., Ealing, London W.5., England.

CAREER: Ordained Anglican priest; St. James's Episcopal Church, Birmingham, Mich., assistant minister, 1963-65; vicar in Ealing Common, London, England, 1967—. High school teacher of religion in Ealing, England, 1967—. *Military service:* British Army, 1952-54, served in Korea; became second lieutenant. *Member:* Ealing Cricket Club.

WRITINGS: (With Erica Hughes) *Here's the Church,* illustrations by Gill Tomblin, Julia MacRae, 1980; *David and the Giant* (juvenile), illustrations by Jan Martin, Julia MacRae, 1981; (with Hughes) *Here's the Year,* illustrations by Tomblin, Julia MacRae, 1981; *A Book of Prayer,* Julia MacRae, 1982;

Born to Run, Julia MacRae, 1983. Contributor to magazines, including *Quarterly Review, Theology, Church Times,* and *Harper's.*

WORK IN PROGRESS: A book on religious figures, publication by Julia MacRae expected in 1984; research on the relationship between humour and religion, the history of the church in London, animals in human imagination, symbolism, and language.

SIDELIGHTS: Watkins's book *Here's the Church* provides a guide to the physical structure of a typical church, explaining such features as bells, font, nave, and pulpit. Similarly, *Here's the Year* acquaints the reader with the major Christian festivals by detailing their history and customs. And *David and the Giant* introduces one to the Old Testament tale of the fall of Goliath.

Watkins told *CA:* "I have concentrated on writing books on aspects of religion and Christianity for younger readers because most of the available literature of that kind seems to be either stuffy, shoddy, sentimental, or plain patronizing."

*   *   *

WATNEY, Sanders   ?-1983

OBITUARY NOTICE: Died February 9, 1983. Equestrian and author. Watney founded the British Driving Society, an organization dedicated to the preservation of horse harnessing. With his wife, Brigid, he wrote *Horsepower.* Watney also revised Walter Gilbey's *The Harness Horse.* Obituaries and other sources: *London Times,* February 18, 1983.

*   *   *

WATSON, David Robin   1935-

PERSONAL: Born May 8, 1935, in Bradford, Yorkshire, England; son of Johnson (a company director) and Sarah (Leach) Watson; married Judith Margaret Long (a lecturer), April 4, 1959; children: Mark Stephen, Sarah Nadine, Emma Ruth. *Education:* Oxford University, B.A., 1956, M.A., 1960, B.Phil., 1960. *Home:* 3 West Coates, Edinburgh, Scotland. *Office:* Department of History, University of Dundee, Dundee, Scotland.

CAREER: University of Dundee, Dundee, Scotland, senior lecturer in modern European history, 1961—. Visiting professor at Queen's University, Kingston, Ontario, 1971-72. *Military service:* British Army, 1956-58. *Member:* Royal Historical Society, Societe d'Histoire Moderne.

WRITINGS: The Life and Times of Charles I, Weidenfeld & Nicolson, 1972; *Georges Clemenceau: A Political Biography,* Eyre Methuen, 1974, McKay, 1976.

WORK IN PROGRESS: Research on the policy of the French government towards Russia from 1914 to 1928.

*   *   *

WATSON, Thomas J(oel)   1948-

PERSONAL: Born August 20, 1948, in Logansport, Ind.; son of Donald C. (a merchant) and Edna M. (a secretary; maiden name, Murphey) Watson. *Education:* Ball State University, B.A., 1970. *Home:* 2929 Westwood Blvd., Los Angeles, Calif. 90064. *Agent:* Andrews & Robb, P.O. Box 727, Hollywood, Calif. 90028. *Office address:* P.O. Box 480673, Los Angeles, Calif. 90048.

CAREER: WBST-Radio, Muncie, Ind., program director, 1968-70; CBS-TV, New York, N.Y., manager of national television research, 1971-77; CBS-TV, Los Angeles, Calif., manager of national television research, 1977-83; free-lance writer, 1983—.

WRITINGS: (With Bart Andrews) *Loving Lucy: An Illustrated Tribute to Lucille Ball,* St. Martin's, 1980; (with Betty White) *Pet Love: How Pets Take Care of Us,* Morrow, 1983. Author, editor, and publisher of quarterly newsletter of Lucille Ball fan club organization.

SIDELIGHTS: Watson wrote: "My personal philosophy is to keep moving, keep growing. Change is a very important ingredient to success. When one is in school, change comes relatively easy—it happens every term. In the work world one often has to labor to make things change. I'm constantly attempting to grow.

"*Pet Love: How Pets Take Care of Us* is an overview of the various 'pet therapy' programs in operation around the world today, and a look at what is called 'the human/animal bond.' Included are looks at how dogs are trained for the blind, to assist the deaf, to help quadriplegics, horseback-riding programs for the handicapped, the use of pets in hospitals and nursing homes, pet-facilitated psychotherapy, and the use of animals in prisons—as well as a look at how pets benefit us common, ordinary mortals. Included in the book, also, are autobiographical stories concerning Betty White's own interaction with the animals she has come into contact with all her life.

"My work at CBS Television centered on the Research Department, and included such disparate activities as answering 'trivia' questions for the outside and preparing audience-analysis reports for the inside. Regarding the former, CBS is very good at maintaining adequate records of its own history—the who, what, when, where, and why's of its various radio and television programming. It was my privilege to assist the authors of many books and articles (including biographies of Tallulah Bankhead, Jane Froman, Judy Garland, the Three Stooges, Betty Hutton, and Veronica Lake), as well as to answer the questions of the general public who felt it mandatory that they know the answer to such esoteric questions as 'Who played Teensie and Weensie on an episode of "I Love Lucy?"'

"The latter portion of my CBS job entailed analyzing the television audience (via statistics supplied by the A. C. Nielsen Company), to judge who was watching what when. Our goal, of course, was to provide a schedule of compatible programming that would not be in direct competition with similar shows on one of the other networks. For example, we would not schedule a Doris Day movie directly following a football game. The type of viewer that would watch a football game would probably want to watch, say, a Clint Eastwood picture. At the same time, if there was one Doris Day movie scheduled on network A, we'd try not to schedule a similar show opposite, but provide a clear alternative by scheduling a western or murder mystery.

"Much of the reason and text for *Loving Lucy* was culled directly from a research paper I had completed ten years earlier while a student at Ball State University. Lucille Ball was always a favorite of mine—still is—and there was a need for a photo study of her career. I literally grew up 'loving Lucy,' her various television programs and movies, and this first book assignment was, therefore, the proverbial 'labor of love.'"

WATT, George Steven Harvie
See HARVIE-WATT, George Steven

*   *   *

WAX, Emmanuel   1911-1983
(Jimmy Wax)

OBITUARY NOTICE: Born May 1, 1911, in London, England; died April 23, 1983, in Ramsbury, England. Lawyer, literary agent, and author. As Jimmy Wax, he formed ACTAC Limited, an agency that both commissioned playwrights and represented noted dramatists such as Christopher Fry and Harold Pinter. Wax translated French plays and, with Rudolph Cartier, wrote "Murder in the Studio." Obituaries and other sources: *London Times,* April 29, 1983.

*   *   *

WAX, Jimmy
See WAX, Emmanuel

*   *   *

WEBB, Herschel (F.)   1924-1983

OBITUARY NOTICE—See index for *CA* sketch: Born October 31, 1924, in David City, Neb.; died January 8, 1983, in New York, N.Y. Educator and author. An authority on Japanese history, Webb began teaching at Columbia University in 1957. His *An Introduction to Japan* appeared in 1955. Obituaries and other sources: *Directory of American Scholars,* Volume I: *History,* 8th edition, Bowker, 1982; *Who's Who in America,* 42nd edition, Marquis, 1982; *Chronicle of Higher Education,* January 26, 1983.

*   *   *

WEBB, Igor   1941-

PERSONAL: Born November 8, 1941, in Malacky, Czechoslovakia; son of Michael (a dental technician) and Josephine (a dressmaker; maiden name, Nash) Webb; married Catherine E. Lamb (an editor), July 6, 1968; children: Kelly. *Education:* Tufts University, A.B., 1966; Stanford University, M.A., 1966, Ph.D., 1971. *Home:* 2 Wentworth Mansions, Keats Grove, London N.W.3, England. *Agent:* Charlotte Sheedy Literary Agency, Inc., 145 West 86th St., New York, N.Y. 10024. *Office:* Division of Humanities, Richmond College, Surrey, England.

CAREER: University of Massachusetts, Boston, assistant professor, 1971-77, associate professor of English, 1977-78; Richmond College, Surrey, England, chairman of Division of Humanities, 1979—.

WRITINGS: From Custom to Capital: The English Novel and the Industrial Revolution, Cornell University Press, 1981.

Work represented in anthologies, including *Leaving the Bough: Fifty American Poets of the Eighties,* edited by Roger Gaess, International Publishers, 1982. Contributor of articles and poems to literature journals and literary magazines, including *New Yorker, Southern Review, Poetry, Victorian Studies,* and *Denver Quarterly.* Member of editorial group of *Radical Teacher.*

WORK IN PROGRESS: A novel set in the 1960's; research on post-war world poetry and on Eastern Europe.

SIDELIGHTS: Webb told *CA:* "In my view, the moral and intellectual 'flaw' of our era is the compartmentalization of thought and feeling. Literature is not only taught as if it were autonomous, severed from history and science; it is often written as if it were another specialization. I have tried in my criticism, and in my essays, poems, and fiction, to insist on the connections within art and life—the fundamental connections. In *From Custom to Capital* I argue that the nineteenth century English novel is incomprehensible if dissociated from the wholesale transformation of nineteenth century society. East European writing is especially important in this respect because it treats the whole life of human beings—the person as at once sexual, political, religious. The affluent nihilism of the West is mocked by modest dedication of the East European writers and thinkers. The genuinely original work—in art and politics—is happening *there.*''

BIOGRAPHICAL/CRITICAL SOURCES: Village Voice Literary Supplement, April, 1982; *Times Literary Supplement,* June 18, 1982.

*   *   *

WEBB, Michael Gordon   1940-

PERSONAL: Born March 26, 1940, in Whyteleafe, Surrey, England; son of Herbert Gordon (a civil servant) and Beatrice Mary (Rapley) Webb; married Veronica Willis (an optician), December 27, 1961; children: David, Susan, Paul. *Education:* University of Leicester, B.A., 1962, M.A. (with distinction), 1966. *Home:* 9 Park Rd., Woking, Surrey GU22 7BW, England.

CAREER: United Kingdom Atomic Energy Authority, London, England, economist, 1962-64; University of Leicester, Leicester, England, lecturer in economics, 1964-75; University of York, Heslington, England, senior research fellow at Institute of Social and Economic Research, 1975-80; Kennedy-Donkin (consulting engineers), Woking, England, senior economist, 1980—. Project appraisal expert at United Nations Asian Development Institute, Bangkok, Thailand, 1972-74; consultant to World Bank, Asian Development Bank, and Organization for Economic Cooperation and Development. *Member:* Royal Economic Society, Institute of Fiscal Studies.

WRITINGS: The Economics of Nationalised Industries, Thomas Nelson, 1973; *Pricing Policies for Public Enterprises,* Macmillan, 1976; *Power Sector Planning Manual,* United Kingdom Overseas Development Administration, 1979; *The Economics of Energy,* Macmillan, 1980. Contributor to economic and management journals.

WORK IN PROGRESS: A book on energy and the environment, publication by Allen & Unwin expected in 1984; research on control of nationalized industries.

SIDELIGHTS: Webb told *CA:* ''My career has been concerned with pursuing my belief in the practical importance of microeconomics, at first in public utilities, and now in energy. I have traveled widely, especially in connection with energy projects, in the United States, Mexico, New Zealand, Thailand, the Philippines, India, and Fiji. Much of my work has been concerned with issues of energy pricing and with tariff studies. It has also been concerned with project appraisal in developing countries, where my economics has been employed to promote a more efficient allocation of resources and to help people living in those countries achieve higher standards of living.''

AVOCATIONAL INTERESTS: Photography, classical music, cycling.

WEBER, Max   1864-1920

BRIEF ENTRY: Surname pronounced *Vay-*ber; born in 1864 in Erfurt, Germany (now East Germany); died of pneumonia in 1920 in Munich, Germany (now West Germany). German political economist, sociologist, educator, and author. Weber's early studies of law and legal history convinced him that law, supposedly the ultimate authority in society, was itself dependent upon and determined by a society's economic and technological centext. He became a professor of economics at the University of Heidelberg and also served on the committee that prepared the first draft of the Weimar Constitution. It was Weber's belief that persistent social problems in Germany were unsolvable by means of law, historical economics, or Marxism because of their inherent shortcomings. He therefore proposed a systematic, methodological system for the study of society, a ''science of sociology.'' Deteriorating health forced Weber to curtail his work and resign his professorship. Weber's books, including *General Economic History* (1927), *Protestant Ethic and the Spirit of Capitalism* (1930), *Theory of Social and Economic Organization* (1947), *Methodology of the Social Sciences* (1949), and *On Law in Economy and Society* (1954), are still highly regarded by contemporary sociologists. *Biographical/critical sources: Twentieth-Century Authors: A Biographical Dictionary of Modern Literature,* 1st supplement, H. W. Wilson, 1955.

*   *   *

WECHSBERG, Joseph   1907-1983

OBITUARY NOTICE—See index for *CA* sketch: Born August 29, 1907, in Moravska-Ostrava, Austria (now Ostrava, Czechoslovakia); died April 10, 1983, in Vienna, Austria. Musician, lawyer, journalist, and author. Associated with *New Yorker* magazine for about thirty years, he practiced law and worked as a musician before becoming a free-lance journalist in 1938. Following service in the U.S. Army during World War II, Wechsberg began to write for *New Yorker,* contributing more than one hundred fifty pieces on various topics. He also contributed to periodicals such as *Atlantic, Esquire, Horizon,* and *Town and Country.* His more than thirty books include novels, correspondences, and memoirs as well as writings on history, cuisine, travel, and banking. Among these are *Blue Trout and Black Truffles: The Peregrinations of an Epicure, The Self-Betrayed, The Merchant Bankers, Schubert: His Life, His Work, His Time,* and *The Vienna I Knew: Memories of a European Childhood.* Obituaries and other sources: *New York Times,* April 12, 1983.

*   *   *

WEED, Florence C(ollins)   1897(?)-1983

OBITUARY NOTICE: Born c. 1897 in Tipton, Iowa; died April 15, 1983, in Evanston, Ill. Journalist. For more than twenty years Weed contributed articles about historical sites to the *Chicago Tribune.* She also founded the Hospitalized Veterans Writing Program. Obituaries and other sources: *Who's Who of American Women,* 5th edition, Marquis, 1968; *Chicago Tribune,* April 17, 1983.

*   *   *

WEIDMAN, John   1946-

PERSONAL: Born September 25, 1946, in New York, N.Y.; son of Jerome (a writer) and Elizabeth (a writer; maiden name,

Payne) Weidman; married Lila Coleburn (a therapist), May 27, 1978. *Education:* Harvard University, B.A., 1968; Yale University, J.D., 1974. *Home:* 19 West 76th St., New York, N.Y. 10023. *Agent:* Biff Liff, William Morris Agency, 1350 Avenue of the Americas, New York, N.Y. 10019.

CAREER: Elementary school teacher in New York City, 1968-71; *National Lampoon* (magazine), New York City, contributing editor, 1970-74 and 1976—, editor, 1974-76. *Member:* Writers Guild, Dramatists Guild. *Awards, honors:* Nomination for Antoinette Perry Award (Tony) from American Theatre Wing, 1975-76, for musical play, "Pacific Overtures."

WRITINGS: Pacific Overtures (two-act musical play; first produced on Broadway at Winter Garden Theatre, January, 1976), Dodd, 1976.

WORK IN PROGRESS: "Death and Taxes," a two-act musical about Al Capone and the Internal Revenue Service, with lyrics by Alfred Ultry and music by Robert Waldman.

* * *

WEIGERT, Andrew J(oseph)   1934-

PERSONAL: Born April 8, 1934, in New York, N.Y.; son of Andrew Joseph (an accountant) and Marie Teresa (Kollmer) Weigert; married Kathleen Rose Maas (an administrator), August 31, 1967; children: Karen Rose, Sheila Marie. *Education:* St. Louis University, B.A. (cum laude), 1958, Ph.L., 1959, M.A., 1960; Woodstock College, B.Th., 1964; University of Minnesota, Ph.D., 1968. *Office:* Department of Sociology, University of Notre Dame, Notre Dame, Ind. 46556.

CAREER: High school geometry and sociology teacher and athletic coach at Colegio San Ignacio, P.R., 1960-62; University of Notre Dame, Notre Dame, Ind., assistant professor, 1968-72, associate professor, 1972-77, professor of sociology, 1977—, chairperson of department of sociology, 1980—. Visiting professor at Yale University, 1973-74. *Member:* American Sociological Association, Society for the Scientific Study of Religion, Association for the Sociology of Religion (member of executive council, 1975-77), Society for the Study of Symbolic Interaction. *Awards, honors:* National Science Foundation grant, 1969; grants from O'Brien Fund, 1969-70, 1973-74; Western European Studies Program grant for Germany, 1970; faculty development grant for Spain, 1977.

WRITINGS: (With Darwin Thomas, Viktor Gecas, and Elizabeth Rooney) *Family Socialization and Adolescents: Determinants of Self-Esteem, Religiosity, Conformity, and Counterculture Lifestyles,* Lexington Books, 1974; (with Anthony Blasi and Fabio Dasilva) *Toward an Interpretive Sociology,* University Press of America, 1978; (contributor) W. R. Burr, F. I. Nye, and others, editors, *Contemporary Theories About the Family,* Volume II, Free Press, 1979; *Sociology of Everyday Life,* Longman, 1981; *Social Psychology: An Interpretive Sociology Approach,* University of Notre Dame Press, 1983; *Life and Society: A Meditation on the Social Thought of Jose Ortega y Gasset,* Irvington, 1983.

Contributor of more than forty articles to sociology and religious journals. Associate editor of *Sociological Analysis,* 1971-75, and *Review of Religious Research,* 1978; advisory editor for *Symbolic Interaction,* 1977, 1983.

WORK IN PROGRESS: Society and Identity, with J. Smith Tietge and Dennis Tietge, publication expected in 1984; *Trust as a Social Reality,* with J. David Lewis; *Social Atomism, Realism, and Trust,* with Lewis; *Vital Realism,* with Lewis

and Ray McLain; *Ambivalence and Religion; Metatheoretical Foundations of Human Identity as a Social Production.*

SIDELIGHTS: Weigert told *CA:* "The obvious is difficult to see and more difficult to interpret. The theme of sociology of everyday life focuses our attention on the taken-for-granted arrangements around us and leads us to criticize them in terms of what it means to be human. Indeed, such reflection brings the issue of human identity front and center as a definitive feature of modern life. The social forces such as 'trust-distrust' that shape our self-understanding also threaten the very continuation of the human species. No one claiming to live authentically in today's world can avoid these reflections. Nor can I. My scratchings on paper are aimed at helping me, and hopefully others, to see the obvious and ask the vital questions: How can we survive and do so with dignity?"

* * *

WEINBERG, Sanford Bruce   1950-

PERSONAL: Born June 14, 1950, in Newark, N.J.; son of Harold L. (an engineer) and Florence F. (a librarian) Weinberg; married wife, Janie S. (a psychological counselor), May 20, 1973; children: Amy, Joseph. *Education:* Dickinson College, Carlisle, Pa., B.A., 1972; University of North Carolina, M.A., 1973; University of Michigan, Ph.D., 1975. *Office:* Department of Administrative Sciences, St. Joseph's University, Philadelphia, Pa. 19131.

CAREER: University of Connecticut, Storrs, professor of communication science, 1976-80; St. Joseph's University, Philadelphia, Pa., chairman of department of administrative science, 1980—. Consultant with Weinberg Associates and Executive Technology Associates.

WRITINGS: Synergy, W. C. Brown, 1975; (editor) *Messages: A Reader in Human Communications,* Random House, 1980. Author of "Computer Queries," a column in *Philadelphia Business Journal.*

WORK IN PROGRESS: Cyberphobia.

SIDELIGHTS: Weinberg told *CA* that his work deals with "computer technology—the human interface and the problems of people communicating with computers."

* * *

WEINER, Charles   1931-

BRIEF ENTRY: Born August 11, 1931, in Brooklyn, N.Y. American historian, educator, and author. Weiner has been a professor of the history of science and technology at Massachusetts Institute of Technology since 1974 and director of the school's oral history program since 1975. He was a Guggenheim fellow in Denmark in 1970, and he has served on the editorial staffs of *Tooling and Production* and *Explorer.* Weiner edited *Exploring the History of Nuclear Physics* (American Institute of Physics, 1972) and *History of Twentieth Century Physics* (Academic Press, 1977). He also co-edited *The Legacy of George Ellery Hale: Evolution of Astronomy and Scientific Institutions, in Pictures and Documents* (M.I.T. Press, 1972) and *Robert Oppenheimer: Letters and Recollections* (Harvard University Press, 1980). *Address:* Department of the History of Science, School of Humanities and Social Science, Massachusetts Institute of Technology, Cambridge, Mass. 02139.

WEINTRAUB, Dov 1926-

PERSONAL: Born October 18, 1926, in Warsaw, Poland; son of David (a lawyer) and Bronia (Bychowski) Weintraub; married Shoshana Schmorak (an educationalist), August 14, 1951; children: Ruth, Michael, Dan. *Education:* Hebrew University of Jerusalem, M.A., 1951, Ph.D., 1963. *Religion:* Jewish. *Home:* 9 Ibn Ezra, Jerusalem 92424, Israel. *Office:* Department of Sociology and Social Anthropology, Hebrew University of Jerusalem, Jerusalem, Israel.

CAREER: Ministry of Education, Jerusalem, Israel, deputy director of department of compulsory education, 1950-53; Hebrew University of Jerusalem, instructor, 1959-63, lecturer, 1963-67, senior lecturer, 1967-69, associate professor, 1969-75, professor of sociology, 1975—, Sarah Allen Shaine Professor of Sociology, 1978—, director of Institute for Urban and Regional Studies, 1970-71, chairman of department of sociology and social anthropology, 1972-76. Visiting scholar at London School of Economics and Political Science, London, 1964; visiting professor at Cornell University, 1969-70, University of Wisconsin—Madison, 1971, 1974, Federal University of Rio-Grande-Do-Sul, 1977, and University of California, Davis, 1980-81; academic adviser and senior research fellow at Settlement Study Centre, Rehovot, Israel, 1978—; scientific correspondent for UNESCO, 1980—. *Military service:* British Army, Royal Artillery, 1944-46. Israel Defense Army, Infantry, 1947-49; became lieutenant. *Member:* International Sociological Association, European Society for Rural Sociology (member of executive committee, 1970-74), Israel Sociological Association, Rural Sociological Society, American Association for the Advancement of Science, American Sociological Association.

WRITINGS: (With S. N. Eisenstadt and Nina Toren) *Analysis of Processes of Role Change*, Israel Universities Press, 1968; (with Moshe Lissak and Yael Azmon) *Moshava, Kibbutz, Moshav: Jewish Rural Settlement and Development in Palestine*, Cornell University Press, 1969; *Immigration and Social Change: Agricultural Settlement of New Immigrants in Israel*, Humanities, 1971; (with Miriam Shapiro and Belinda Aquino) *Agrarian Development and Modernization in the Philippines*, Institute of Asian and African Studies, Hebrew University of Jerusalem, 1972; *Social Modernization in the Philippines: The Problem of Change in a Context of Social Stability and Continuity*, Sage Publications, 1973; (editor with Eisenstadt) *Tradition in Modernizing Societies*, Sage Publications, 1975; (with M. Shapiro) *Rural Reconstruction in Greece: Differential Social Prerequisites in the Developmental Process*, Sage Publications, 1975; (with John M. Cohen) *Land and Peasants in Imperial Ethiopia: The Social Background to a Revolution*, Royal Van Gorcum, 1975.

Contributor: Joseph Ben-David, editor, *Agricultural Planning and Village Community in Israel*, UNESCO, 1964; Ovadia Shapiro, editor, *Rural Settlements of New Immigrants in Israel*, Israel Universities Press, 1971; Peter Worsley, editor, *Two Blades of Grass: Rural Cooperatives in Agricultural Modernization*, Manchester University Press, 1971; J. Lin Compton and Ki-Yong Hong, editors, *International Perspectives on Community Development*, Cornell University Press, 1983. Also contributor to *History of Mankind*, 2nd edition, UNESCO.

In Hebrew: (With Rivkoin Bar-Yosef) *Haveka the hevreh shel shvugey the Milhuma* (title means "The Social Background of the Egyptian Prisoners of War"), Israel Defense Army, 1957; *Defusey shinui shel Kevutsot Adatiyot Be moshevey olim* (title means "Patterns of Social Change Among Ethnic Settler Groups in Israel"), Histadruth Yearly, 1965; (contributor) S. N. Eisenstadt and Awraham Zloczower, editors, *Kelitet Aliya*, (title means "Immigrant Absorption"), Magnes Press, 1969; (editor with Arie Shachar, Ilona Shelach, and Eric Cohen) *Arim B'Israel-Mikrea*, (title means "Town and City in Israel: A Reader"), Akademon Press, 1973.

Contributor of about thirty articles to academic journals.

WORK IN PROGRESS: A book on sociological participation in integrated rural regional development and planning, publication expected in 1984.

SIDELIGHTS: Weintraub told *CA:* "It is no mere coincidence that the department of sociology at the Hebrew University came into its own together with the State of Israel. Until then the department had been wholly academic, and it was only in 1949, after the War of Independence and the establishment of the state, that our first empirical research was initiated. Since the state was faced with pressing problems of development, nation-building, and immigrant absorption, it was inevitable that the then-only department of sociology in the country should mobilize itself to help, thereby acquiring an orientation of combining the theoretical and the applied. Naturally, therefore, I too saw the application of sociology to actual social issues as the major challenge. And soon after getting my master's degree I began working on a research project concerned with one of the most crucial problems confronting Israeli society—namely, mass rural settlement and development based on non-selective, heterogeneous, non-agricultural, and mostly 'non-modern' newcomers.

"This challenge has remained with me always. And while I have since then broadened my horizons to include other areas in the disciplinary and the geographical sense, the combination of academic and chiefly theoretical, comparative perspective with a more relevant focus has accompanied me in much of my work. That is to say, I have tried to formulate my research interests as much as possible in a problem-oriented way, and I have approached specific issues in general analytical terms. Similarly, the basic problem which I tackled as a beginner— namely the issue of the relationship of tradition and development—has remained a major concern, and I have followed it up in a variety of settings.

"Indeed, these two points of view continue to exercise a strong influence upon me. Recently I took a leave of absence from my regular pursuits to work as a team sociologist in planning an integrated rural/regional development project in Malawi, certainly with considerable personal satisfaction, and hopefully also with some success."

*   *   *

WEISBORD, Robert G. 1933-

BRIEF ENTRY: Born December 21, 1933, in New York, N.Y. American historian, educator, and author. Weisbord, who lectured at Yeshiva University during the early 1960's, began teaching at University of Rhode Island in 1966 and became a professor of African and Negro history in 1973. His books include *African Zion: The Attempt to Establish a Jewish Colony in the East Africa Protectorate, 1903-1905* (Jewish Publication Society, 1968), *Bittersweet Encounter: The Afro-American and the American Jew* (Negro Universities Press, 1970), *Ebony Kinship: Africa, Africans, and the Afro-American* (Greenwood Press, 1973), and *Genocide?: Birth Control and the Black American* (Greenwood Press, 1975). *Address:* Department of History, University of Rhode Island, Kingston, R.I. 02881.

Biographical/critical sources: American Historical Review, February, 1969, December, 1976; *New York Review of Books*, June 29, 1972.

*   *   *

WEISMAN, Mary-Lou   1937-

PERSONAL: Born November 22, 1937, in New Haven, Conn.; daughter of Herbert Louis (an attorney) and Gertrude (a sculptor; maiden name, Perelmutter) Cohen; married Lawrence Paul Weisman (an attorney), June 4, 1961; children: Adam Paul, Peter Benjamin (deceased). *Education:* Attended Bryn Mawr College, 1955-57; Brandeis University, B.A. (magna cum laude), 1960; studied gestalt therapy techniques at Esalen Institute, 1970-71. *Home and office:* 11 Greenwood Lane, Westport, Conn. 06880. *Agent:* Amanda Urban, International Creative Management (ICM), 40 West 57th St., New York, N.Y. 10019.

CAREER: Oxford University Press, New York City, 1960-63, began as clerk-typist, became assistant editor; Curtis Brown Ltd., New York City, manuscript reader, 1965-68; *Fairpress Newspaper*, Westport, Conn., 1972-76, began as reporter, became humor columnist; *New York Times*, New York City, author of syndicated column "One Woman's Voice," 1978-80; *Connecticut Magazine*, Fairfield, Conn., senior editor, 1980-81; writer, 1982—. Manuscript reader for Sussman & Sugar, New York City, 1961-63; founder and publisher of alternative local newspaper, Westport, Conn., 1968-69. Staff group leader at New Haven Center for Human Relations, 1972-73. Guest on television programs, including "Good Morning, America," 1975-79 and 1982. Instructor at Fairfield University, Fairfield, Conn., 1980-81. Member of Westport Library Advisory Board.

WRITINGS: Intensive Care: A Family Love Story, Random House, 1982. Contributor of articles to periodicals, including *New York Times, Connecticut Weekly, Vogue, Newsweek, Newsday*, and *Woman's Day*.

WORK IN PROGRESS: Writing for magazines and newspapers.

SIDELIGHTS: Weisman's book, *Intensive Care*, chronicles the author's life with a son dying of muscular dystrophy. Though the family's encounters with medicine, psychic healing, and a human potential center are recorded, the book is about Peter—and Weisman's promise that her son's "life must grow steadily and bravely upward, against a declining graph line of utter failure." "While managing to stick to her main purpose, which is to tell the reader a story that wants telling, Weisman lifts Peter like a candle to illuminate so much internal and external territory that 'Intensive Care' exceeds without transgressing the bounds of the book," noted Phyllis Theroux in the *Washington Post Book World*. "And in the end, Weisman gives you Peter, lowering him gently but directly into your lap."

Continuing her praise for the book, Theroux maintained: " 'Intensive Care' is tough, funny, heart-breaking and astute—an astonishing achievement for any writer . . . on her first time out of the gate." Likewise Anatole Broyard, writing in the *New York Times*, remarked: "Mrs. Weisman is a good writer and she manages to bring a desperate humor to 'Intensive Care' without undermining its awful seriousness."

Weisman told *CA:* "The creative engine that drives me is the need to make meaning out of the meaningless—by definition a doomed enterprise. Yet I find the process intriguing, if ambiguous. Still, along the way there are moments of true feeling, soaring instants of inexplicable compassion, and magical syn-

chronicities that befuddle and delight the hard-nosed cynic in me. I work at the ancient art of alchemy, trying to extract gold from baser mettles and hard, slag ironies. Essentially, I suppose, I write to comfort."

BIOGRAPHICAL/CRITICAL SOURCES: New York Times, October 23, 1982; *Washington Post*, October 29, 1982.

*   *   *

WEISS, Allen   1918-

PERSONAL: Born July 11, 1918, in New York, N.Y.; son of Jacob and Lillian (Comick) Weiss; married Florence Golub, July 20, 1941 (died September 5, 1955); married Enid Marks (an antiques dealer), February 21, 1957; children: Susan Louise, Robert Irwin. *Education:* City University of New York, B.S. (cum laude), 1937; New York University, M.B.A., 1939. *Politics:* Democrat. *Religion:* Jewish. *Home:* 8 Tuers Pl., Upper Montclair, N.J. 07043. *Agent:* Ann Elmo Agency, Inc., 60 East 42nd St., New York, N.Y. 10017.

CAREER: Accounting consultant to Social Security Board, 1941-42; certified public accountant, 1946-49; Lever Brothers Co., New York City, member of controller's staff, 1949-58; Knickerbocker Biologicals, Inc., New York City, controller, 1958-61; management consultant in New York City and in West Hartford, Conn., 1961-66; Coopers & Lybrand (certified public accountants), New York City, director of MCS communications, 1966-69; Laventhol & Horwath (certified public accountants), New York City, director of communications, 1970-73. Member of Montclair Housing Advisory Committee, 1976-80. *Military service:* U.S. Coast Guard, 1942-46; became lieutenant senior grade. *Member:* Authors Guild, Authors League of America, Phi Beta Kappa Alumni Association of Northern New Jersey (president, 1970-72).

WRITINGS: (Contributor) *Selected Studies in Modern Accounting*, American Institute, 1965; *The Organization Guerrilla: Playing the Game to Win*, Atheneum, 1975; *Write What You Mean: A Handbook of Business Communication*, American Management Association, 1977.

Author of "Writing Sense," an audio teaching program for American Management Association. Author of "The Communications Clinic," a column in *Supervisory Management*, 1969-71. Editor of "Writing Reports That Work," a programmed instructor course for American Management Association, 1980. Contributor to business and management journals. *CPA Journal*, editor, 1974, managing editor; contributing editor of *Management Adviser*.

WORK IN PROGRESS: Word Guide and *Politics and Economics*.

SIDELIGHTS: Weiss commented: "*The Organization Guerrilla* is an empirical study of management practice and its theoretical base, from the viewpoint of an individual caught up in organized activities. The book explores the impact of structure, systems, and other people on that individual—the 'Spider on a Flywheel'—and his or her options. Included are discussions of the strategies and tactics of politicking, leadership styles, innovation, and communication. The chief purpose of the book is to help newcomers in business, government, or institutional administration adapt to their environments and plan for their survival and progress.

"*Write What You Mean* is a practical guide to business writing and speaking, from brief, informal memos to lengthy reports, and from conversations to formal speeches. The principal objective is to show business writers how to organize their ideas, plan what they are going to say (in detail), and get their messages across in an interesting, readable style. Reader orientation is explained, and the writer is shown how to get started and how to master the mechanics of lean writing.

"In one way or another, each of my books is an attempt to help individuals contend with larger forces that threaten to engulf them. The hope is that, by providing an understanding of 'the system' and an ability to communicate, we can encourage people to do better than merely survive, but rather, to find self-expression and maintain their individuality while working within the existing framework.

"Both books were alternate selections of Macmillan book clubs, and *Write What You Mean* was also a Fortune Book-of-the-Month alternate.

"For the future, I believe it will be useful to me (and illuminating for my readers) to turn my practical background to an examination of political and economic theories, and to study their impact on the real world of affairs."

* * *

WEISS, Bennet A., Jr. 1926(?)-1983

OBITUARY NOTICE: Born c. 1926 in Kenosha, Wis.; died March 5, 1983, in New Orleans, La. Journalist. Weiss was editor of the *Chicago Tribune*'s Indiana edition before retiring in 1972. Obituaries and other sources: *Chicago Tribune,* March 11, 1983.

* * *

WEISS, Bernard J(acob) 1936-

PERSONAL: Born November 21, 1936, in Jerusalem, Palestine (now Israel); came to the United States in 1939, naturalized citizen, 1945; son of Leo and Elka (Greenbaum) Weiss; married, 1965; children: Rachel, Rebecca. *Education:* University of Illinois, B.S., 1958, Ph.D., 1967; University of Chicago, M.A., 1960. *Office:* Department of History, Duquesne University, Pittsburgh, Pa. 15219.

CAREER: Duquesne University, Pittsburgh, Pa., assistant professor, 1966-71, associate professor, 1971-77, professor of history, 1977—, director of History Forum, 1976-79, 1982. *Member:* American Historical Association. *Awards, honors:* Grant from National Endowment for the Humanitites, 1981; Presidential Award for research from Duquesne University, 1982.

WRITINGS: American Education and the European Immigrant, 1840-1940, University of Illinois Press, 1982.

WORK IN PROGRESS: Education and Assimilation in Multi-Ethnic Societies.

SIDELIGHTS: Weiss told *CA:* "As an immigrant myself, I personally identify with the assimilation process that newcomers to America experience. The key to that process, particularly for the young, is the contact with formal educational institutions and practices. From my study of this interrelationship emerges several conclusions that are relevant to the assimilation experience of ethnic minorities on an international scale: that the rate and degree of assimilation is primarily determined by the peculiar cultural traditions of respective ethnic groups; that public policy, particularly regarding education, must take the above into consideration; and that, consequently, ethnic mi-

norities play as great a role in the assimilation process as the larger society they are identified as being part of. I believe that any prolonged exposure to a multi-ethnic milieu, especially in urban American, will substantiate the essential validity of these points."

* * *

WEISS, Louise 1893-1983

OBITUARY NOTICE: Born January 25, 1893, in Arras, France; died May 26, 1983, in Paris, France. Feminist, pacifist, social reformer, lecturer, filmmaker, editor, journalist, playwright, and author of novels, travel books, and memoirs. Distinguished in many fields, Weiss began her literary career by founding and editing, from 1918 to 1934, *L'Europe Nouvelle,* a political weekly dedicated to worldwide disarmament. In the 1930's she was a leader in the French campaign for women's suffrage. During World War II she was active in the French Resistance and edited *La Nouvelle Republique,* an underground newspaper. Weiss founded the Institute for the Science of Peace and was elected to the European Parliament in 1979; she was the latter organization's oldest member. Producer of more than thirty highly acclaimed television documentaries and author of a dozen novels, Weiss received first prize from the Academie Francaise for her 1947 novel of Nazi-occupied France, *La Marseillaise.* Her numerous other awards include Commander of the French Legion of Honor, the Voltaire Prize, and the Henri-Malherbe Prize. She was awarded the Europa Prize for Literature in 1980 for her six-volume autobiography, *Memoirs of a European.* Obituaries and other sources: *Newsweek,* July 15, 1974; *Who's Who in the World,* 6th edition, Marquis, 1982; *New York Times,* May 27, 1983; *Chicago Tribune,* May 28, 1983; *London Times,* May 28, 1983; *Washington Post,* May 30, 1983; *Time,* June 6, 1983.

* * *

WEIXLMANN, Joe
See WEIXLMANN, Joseph Norman

* * *

WEIXLMANN, Joseph Norman 1946-
(Joe Weixlmann)

PERSONAL: Born December 16, 1946, in Buffalo, N.Y.; son of Joseph Norman (in sales) and Mary Catherine (Degenhart) Weixlmann; married Sherilyn Waugh, July 27, 1968 (divorced May 15, 1978); married Sharron Pollack (an artist and teacher), March 14, 1982. *Education:* Canisius College, B.A., 1968; Kansas State University, M.A., 1970, Ph.D., 1973. *Home:* 1601 South Sixth St., Terre Haute, Ind. 47802. *Office:* Department of English, Indiana State University, Terre Haute, Ind. 47809.

CAREER: University of Oklahoma, Norman, instructor in English, 1973-74; Texas Tech University, Lubbock, assistant professor of English, 1974-76; Indiana State University, Terre Haute, assistant professor, 1976-79, associate professor, 1979-83, professor of English, 1983—. *Member:* Modern Language Association of America, College Language Association, Langston Hughes Society. *Awards, honors:* Fellow of National Endowment for the Humanities, 1980-81.

WRITINGS: John Barth: A Descriptive Primary and Annotated Secondary Bibliography, Garland Publishing, 1976; (under name Joe Weixlmann) *American Short-Fiction Criticism and Schol-*

arship, 1959-1977: A Checklist, Swallow Press, 1982; (under name Joe Weixlmann; editor with Chester J. Fontenot) *Black American Prose Theory,* Penkevill Press, 1983. Editor of *Black American Literature Forum,* 1976—.

WORK IN PROGRESS: The Changing Shape of the Contemporary Afro-American Novel.

SIDELIGHTS: Joseph Weixlmann told *CA:* "As a high school student in the early 1960's, I was painfully aware that persons other than white males—'proper,' traditional white males at that—must have consigned their thoughts to paper, but verification of that perception didn't come very quickly. Although drawn politically to the counterculture of the 1960's, I did not, until about 1967, become genuinely familiar with writers like John Barth, and James Joyce before him, and Laurence Sterne before him, who saw writing as a field of (sometimes serious) play; and it was not until my years in graduate school, looking for alternatives to the deadening march of austere men who had come to constitute the inelastic literary pantheon of the West, that I began truly to investigate the writings of American women and blacks.

"Subsequent teaching stints in the Southwest inclined me to familiarize myself with Native American and Chicano literatures. Since coming to understand the term 'American literature' in a pluralistic sense, I have tended to remove myself from the literary mainstream. I may occasionally visit, but I never stay long. My principal interests, as a writer and editor, have, since the early 1970's, focused on interpreting and promoting the writing which I believe in and which fascinates me—writing that blends anti-establishment content with a sense of formal experimentation: works like Toni Morrison's *Song of Solomon,* which challenges the sociopolitical status quo, or like John Barth's *Lost in the Funhouse,* which challenges the literary status quo, or like Ishmael Reed's *Flight to Canada,* which does both."

*   *   *

WELLAND, Colin
See WILLIAMS, Colin

*   *   *

WENDER, Paul H.   1934-

PERSONAL: Born May 12, 1934, in New York, N.Y.; son of Louis (a physician) and Luba (Kibrick) Wender; married Dorothea Schmidt (divorced); children: Leslie and Jocelyn (twins), Melissa. *Education:* Harvard University, A.B., 1955; Columbia University, M.D., 1959. *Office:* Department of Psychiatry, University of Utah, College of Medicine, Salt Lake City, Utah 84132.

CAREER: Barnes Hospital, St. Louis, Mo., intern, 1959-60; Massachusetts Mental Health Center, Boston, resident in adult psychiatry, 1960-62; St. Elizabeth's Hospital, Washington, D.C., resident, 1962-63; Johns Hopkins University, Baltimore, Md., fellow in child psychiatry at Johns Hopkins Hospital, 1962-63, instructor in child psychiatry, 1967-68, assistant professor of pediatrics and psychiatry, 1968-73; University of Utah, Salt Lake City, professor of psychiatry, 1973—. Served as a senior surgeon in the U.S. Public Health Service, 1962-64. Research psychiatrist at National Institutes of Health, 1967-73. *Member:* American Psychiatric Association, American Academy of Child Psychiatry, American Psychopathological Association, American College of Neuropsychopharmacology,

Psychiatric Research Society (president, 1977-78), Utah Psychiatric Association, Phi Beta Kappa, Alpha Omega Alpha. *Awards, honors:* National Institute of Mental Health fellowship, 1964-66; Hofheimer Award from the American Psychiatric Associaton, 1974, for psychiatric research.

WRITINGS: Minimal Brain Dysfunction in Children, Wiley, 1971; *The Hyperactive Child,* Crown, 1973, revised and enlarged edition (with Esther H. Wender) published as *The Hyperactive Child and the Learning Disabled Child: A Handbook for Parents,* 1978; (with Donald F. Klein) *Mind, Mood, and Medicine: A Guide to the New Biopsychiatry,* Farrar, Straus, 1981.

Contributor: D. Rosenthal and Seymour S. Kety, editors, *The Transmission of Schizophrenia,* Pergamon, 1968; S. A. Mednick, F. Schulsinger, J. Higgins, and B. Bell, editors, *Genetics, Environment and Psychopathology,* Elsevier-North Holland, 1974; J. Gordon Millichap, editor, *Learning Disabilities and Related Disorders,* Year Book Medical Publishers, 1974; Rachel Gittelman-Klein, editor, *Recent Advances in Child Psychopharmacology,* Human Sciences, 1975; R. Fieve, H. Brill, and Rosenthal, editors, *Genetics and Psychopathology,* Johns Hopkins University Press, 1976; Robert M. Knights and D. Bakker, editors, *The Neuropsychology of Learning Disorders,* University Park Press, 1976; Lyman C. Wynne, R. L. Cromwell, and Steven Matthysse, editors, *The Nature of Schizophrenia,* Wiley, 1977; Peter Hartocollis, editor, *Borderline Personality Disorders,* International Universities Press, 1977; Vivian M. Rackoff, Harvey C. Stancer, and Henry B. Kedward, editors, *Psychiatric Diagnosis,* Brunner, 1977; Stella Chess and Alexander Thomas, editors, *Annual Progress in Child Psychiatry and Child Development,* Brunner, 1977; Morris A. Lipton, Alberto DiMascio, and Keith F. Killam, editors, *Psychopharmacology: A Generation of Progress,* Raven Press, 1978; Wynne and others, editors, *The Nature of Schizophrenia: New Approaches to Research and Treatment,* Wiley, 1978; Leopold Bellak, editor, *Psychiatric Aspects of Minimal Brain Dysfunction in Adults,* Grune, 1979; M. Schou and E. Stromgren, editors, *Origin, Prevention and Treatment of Affective Disorders,* Academic Press, 1979; James E. Barrett, Robert M. Rose, and Gerald L. Klerman, editors, *Stress and Mental Disorder,* Raven Press, 1979; Lasagna Louis, editor, *Controversies in Therapeutics,* Saunders, 1980; Matthysse, editor, *Psychiatry and the Biology of the Human Brain: A Symposium Dedicated to Seymour S. Kety,* Elsevier-North Holland, 1981.

Contributor of articles to numerous journals, including *American Journal of Psychiatry, American Journal of Orthopsychiatry, Child Development, Medical Opinion, Life Sciences, International Journal of Mental Health,* and *Pediatric News.* Member of editorial board of *Psychiatry* and *Psychiatry Research.*

WORK IN PROGRESS: Research on the role of genetics in the development of psychiatric illnesses and on the mechanism and utilization of drugs for the treatment of psychiatric conditions.

SIDELIGHTS: In *Mind, Mood, and Medicine* Wender and Klein support the contention that many forms of mental illness have a biological base and should therefore be treated with medication rather than relying exclusively on psychotherapy. Among the treatments advocated by the authors is the administration of anti-depressant drugs to people suffering from schizophrenia, depression, separation anxiety, and hysteria. In *New Republic,* British psychoanalyst Anthony Storr observed that Wender and Klein's position "illustrates an approach to mental illness which, though familiar in Great Britain, is less so in the U.S.'' ''In the U.S.,'' explained Storr, ''psychoanalysis has been the dominant force in psychiatry for over 40 years.'' In praise of the authors' balanced presentation, Storr commented: ''It is one of the virtues of this book that the authors recognize that one or other form of psychotherapy may be the treatment of choice in certain types of mental distress. Moreover, even in those conditions that are best treated initially with drugs, the authors recognize that psychotherapy may and should play an important subsidiary role.''

Wender told *CA:* ''Klein and I were prompted to write *Mind, Mood, and Medicine* by a number of motivations, one of which was our awareness of the vast discrepancies between the knowledge of the psychiatric cognoscenti and intelligent laymen regarding the role of biological factors in psychological distress. The well-read layman has been led to believe that most human unhappiness results from wrong attitudes, wrong values, and wrong behavior, which in turn are the derivatives of the manner in which he or she was raised. Not so!

''Current evidence suggests that between 15 and 30 percent of the population has psychological disorders that have a genetic basis and are probably caused through abnormalities in biochemistry. The differences between illnesses so produced and those produced by faulty learning and realistic unhappiness (existential problems) are not widely recognized. As a result, suffering individuals receive inappropriate treatment.

''Our intention in writing the book was to present the intelligent layman with the very powerful evidence that much psychological distress is genetic in origin and biochemically mediated. We wish not only to inform the individual of the status of the field, but, perhaps, to allow him to discriminate between disorder, dislearning, and realistic problems. In addition, we wish him or her to develop a feeling for the way biopsychiatrists think, how their thinking leads to hard scientific experiments, and how this differs from much of the airy philosophical speculation that has beclouded the field.''

AVOCATIONAL INTERESTS: Reading, skiing, flute, piano, chess.

BIOGRAPHICAL/CRITICAL SOURCES: Voice Literary Supplement, October, 1981; *New Republic,* October 21, 1981.

* * *

WENDT, Jo Ann 1935-

PERSONAL: Born May 7, 1935, in Oshkosh, Wis.; daughter of Edgar Richard and Lola (Mowers) Mueller; married Phillip James Wendt (an executive in the computer field), June 11, 1955; children: Paul, Ross. *Education:* University of Maryland, B.A., 1964; Wisconsin State University (now University of Wisconsin—Oshkosh), M.S., 1968. *Home and office:* 1124 Amur Creek Court, San Jose, Calif. 95120. *Agent:* Arthur P. Schwartz, 435 Riverside Dr., New York, N.Y. 10025.

CAREER: Free-lance writer, 1968-79; American Personnel and Guidance Association, Falls Church, Va., staff writer for *Guidepost,* 1979-80; free-lance writer, 1980—. *Member:* Romance Writers of America. *Awards, honors:* Catherine L. O'Brien Award from Stanley Home Products, Inc., 1975, for article, ''What Couples Therapy Can (and Can't) Do for Your Marriage.''

WRITINGS: (Contributor) Lynn Thibodeau, editor, *The Happy Housewife,* Carillon Books, 1977; *Beyond Surrender* (historical romance novel), Avon, 1982; *Beyond the Dawn* (historical romance novel), Warner Books, 1983. Contributor to maga-

zines, including *Army Times, Catholic Digest, Christian Herald, Ladycom,* and *Home Life,* and to newspapers.

WORK IN PROGRESS: A novel set during the period 1757-67, dealing with the last French and Indian war in America and the fall of Fort William Henry.

SIDELIGHTS: Jo Ann Wendt commented: ''I began writing in 1968, while living on Hickam Air Force Base in Honolulu, Hawaii. My youngest child had just started school. The house stood empty most of the day and a typewriter stood ready. It was time to pursue that lifelong dream of 'becoming a writer.'

''I joined a Honolulu writers' group that met monthly. From the members, I began to pick up the 'nuts and bolts' of freelance writing. I plunged in and suffered the usual slew of rejection slips from editors. Discouraged, I turned from short stories and a children's novel to something new. I tried a humor piece. It sold on its first time out. When the second, third, and fourth humor pieces met the same success, I knew I'd found my niche.

''As a military wife, I naturally gravitated to the military market. I began with humor and humorous 'how-to' articles. Then, drawing from my training in the field of mental health, I began to do self-help articles. I became a regular contributor to *Times,* a biweekly magazine supplement to three military newspapers with worldwide circulation: *Army Times, Navy Times,* and *Air Force Times.* For ten years, I wrote for that magazine and others.

''When the historical romance paperback novel, *a la* Rosemary Rogers and Kathleen Woodiwiss, burst upon the publishing scene in the mid-1970's, I began to wonder if I could write one, too. I loved history—I'd minored in it in college. I was determined to try, and said 'no' to free-lance assignments.

''At the end of six months, I had two-thirds of a novel and one very big case of the 'lonesomes.' I'd discovered that fiction writing was a lonely business, so I got a job as a staff writer on a mental health-oriented newsletter in Washington, D.C. The job was the opposite of lonesome. I interviewed people daily and often ran to Capitol Hill to cover hearings.

''I sandwiched in the novel, rising at five in the morning on work days, even earlier on weekends. Appropriately, I finished it on Labor Day, about fourteen months after I'd started it. *Beyond Surrender* was published in 1982.

''I'm now committed to full-time novel writing, despite the long lonely stretches at the typewriter and the self-discipline that fiction writing requires. Research for my historical romances continues to be a joy. I'm strict about accuracy in my novels, and my goal is to provide the reader with not only a rousing good romance, but an accurate picture of the manners and times.

''My husband is now retired from the Air Force, but during our twenty-six years in the military we lived in Hawaii, Japan, New Jersey, Delaware, Florida, Texas, Alabama, and Virginia. While we lived in Japan I climbed Mount Fuji, learned to speak Japanese, and studied the history of Japan. I love to travel. London is my favorite city. When I'm in London, I haunt the British Museum, as would any other writer of historical romance. I dream of visiting Egypt some day and of writing an Egyptian historical romance.''

* * *

WERTIME, Theodore A(llen) 1919-1982

PERSONAL: Born August 31, 1919, in Chambersburg, Pa.;

died of cancer April 8, 1982, in Chambersburg, Pa.; son of Rudolf and Flora (Montgomery) Wertime; married Bernice O. Schultz, June 20, 1940; children: John T., Richard A., Steven F., Charles M. *Education:* Haverford College, B.A., 1939; American University, M.A., 1941; attended Johns Hopkins University, 1942.

CAREER: Foreign Economic Administration, economic analyst, 1942-44; Office of Strategic Services, economic analyst in China, 1944-46; U.S. Department of State, Washington, D.C., economic analyst, 1946-48, political science analyst, 1948-55; U.S. Information Agency, Washington, D.C., manager of communications analysis and deputy director of Office of Research and Analysis, 1955-60; U.S. Department of State, cultural officer at U.S. Embassy in Tehran, Iran, 1960-63; U.S. Information Agency, editor of Voice of America's *Forum,* 1963-68; U.S. Department of State, cultural affairs officer at U.S. Embassy in Athens, Greece, 1968-72; U.S. Information Agency, deputy director of cultural relations at Information Center Service, 1973, program officer for energy, food, and population, 1974-75; University of Pennsylvania, Philadelphia, visiting scientist, beginning in 1975. Research associate in anthropology at Smithsonian Institution's Museum of Natural History, beginning in 1965, and University of Minnesota, Duluth, beginning in 1976; leader of Smithsonian Institution and National Georgraphic Society archaeological expeditions in the Middle East and Far East, 1966-76. *Military service:* U.S. Army, 1944-46. *Awards, honors:* Social Science Research Council grant, 1947-48.

WRITINGS: The Coming of the Age of Steel, University of Chicago Press, 1962; (editor with Alan D. Franklin and Jacqueline S. Olin) *The Search for Ancient Tin: A Seminar,* Smithsonian Institution Press, 1978; (editor with James D. Muhly) *The Coming of the Age of Iron,* Yale University Press, 1980. Contributor to magazines and newspapers.

BIOGRAPHICAL/CRITICAL SOURCES: American Historical Review, Ocrober, 1981.

OBITUARIES: Washington Post, April 16, 1982.*

*   *   *

WEST, Allan M(orrell) 1910-

PERSONAL: Born October 16, 1910, in Portland, Ore.; son of Ray B. (a university dean) and Mary (a teacher; maiden name, Morrell) West; married Ferne Page (a teacher), December 2, 1932; children: Stephen A., Jonathan P. *Education:* Attended University of California, Berkeley, 1928-29; Utah State University, B.S., 1932, graduate study, 1960; also attended University of Chicago, 1952-53, and University of Utah. *Politics:* Democrat. *Religion:* Church of Jesus Christ of Latter-day Saints (Mormon). *Home and office:* 777 East South Temple, Salt Lake City, Utah 84102.

CAREER: Utah State University, Logan, supervisor of tax study, 1937-39; National Resources Planning Board, Salt Lake City, Utah, financial analyst, 1939-42; Utah Education Association, Salt Lake City, director of research, 1942-46, executive secretary, 1946-61; National Education Association, Washington, D.C., associate director of Membership Division, 1961-62, special assistant to executive director, 1962-64, assistant executive director for field operations and urban services, 1964-68, associate executive director, 1968-70, deputy executive director, 1970-72, acting executive director, 1972-73; education consultant, 1973—. Assistant professor of education and executive secretary of Education Communication Service at

University of Chicago, 1952. Member of executive committee of Utah Public School Survey Commission, 1951-53; member of Utah White House conferences on education, 1955, and on children and youth, 1959. Member of board of trustees of Utah Educational Television Foundation, 1956-61, and board of directors of National Foundation for the Improvement of Education, 1972-76, and Utah Symphony, 1976-82.

MEMBER: National Council of State Education Associations (chairman of public relations committee, 1958-61), National Education Association (chairman of rules and bylaws committee, 1956-57), National School Public Relations Association (president-elect, 1960-61), United Nations Association (member of board of directors, 1973-76), Utah Educational Research Council (vice-chairman, 1950-61), Utah Society (president, 1963), Utah Education Association (honorary life member), Phi Delta Kappa. *Awards, honors:* Award from Utah Senate and House of Representatives, 1961; Ed.D. from Utah State University, 1973; special award from National Education Association, 1977.

WRITINGS: The National Education Association: The Power Base for Education, Free Press, 1980. Contributor to education journals. Editor of *Utah Educational Review,* 1946-61.

WORK IN PROGRESS: Continuing research on topics that influence public schools.

BIOGRAPHICAL/CRITICAL SOURCES: Education, March, 1960; *NEA Journal,* December, 1967.

*   *   *

WEST, Emily Govan 1919-
(Emmy Payne, Emmy West)

PERSONAL: Born in 1919; daughter of Gilbert Eaton (an author) and Christine (an author; maiden name, Noble) Govan.

CAREER: Author of books for children.

WRITINGS—All for children; under name Emmy Payne: *Katy No-Pocket,* illustrations by H. A. Rey, Houghton, 1944, reprinted, 1973; *Johnny Groundhog's Shadow,* illustrations by Theo Pascal, Houghton, 1948.

Under name Emmy West, with mother, Christine Noble Govan; published by Sterling, except as noted: *The Mystery at Shingle Rock,* illustrations by Frederick T. Chapman, 1955; *The Mystery at the Mountain Face,* illustrations by Chapman, 1956; *The Mystery at the Shuttered Hotel,* illustrations by Chapman, 1956; *The Mystery at the Indian Hide-out,* illustrations by Chapman, 1957; *The Mystery at Moccasin Bend,* illustrations by Chapman, 1957; *The Mystery of the Vanishing Stamp,* illustrations by Irv Docktor, 1958; *Mystery at the Deserted Mill,* illustrations by Chapman, 1958; *The Mystery at Plum Nelly,* illustrations by Docktor, 1959; *The Mystery at the Haunted House,* illustrations by Docktor, 1959; *Mystery at Rock City,* illustrations by Docktor, 1960; *Mystery at Fearsome Lake,* illustrations by Docktor, 1960; *Mystery at the Snowed-in Cabin,* illustrations by Docktor, 1961; *Mystery of the Dancing Skeleton,* illustrations by Joseph Papin, 1962; *Mystery at Ghost Lodge,* illustrations by Stephen Serrano, 1963; *Mystery at the Weird Ruins,* illustrations by Serrano, 1964; *Mystery at the Echoing Cave,* illustrations by Serrano, 1965; *Mr. Alexander and the Witch,* illustrations by Leonard Shortall, Viking, 1969; *Danger Downriver,* illustrations by Charles Robinson, Viking, 1972.*

WEST, Emmy
See WEST, Emily Govan

*   *   *

WEST, Rebecca   1892-1983
(Lynx)

OBITUARY NOTICE—See index for *CA* sketch: Birth-given name, Cicily Isabel Fairfield; born December 25 (some sources say December 21), 1892, in County Kerry, Ireland; died of pneumonia, March 15, 1983, in London, England. Feminist, historian, political commentator, biographer, journalist, critic, and novelist. Known as one of the twentieth century's finest writers, West, who was universally known by the pen name she borrowed from an Ibsen character, was praised for both her fiction and nonfiction pieces. Her writing is characterized by wit, psychological insight, erudition, compassion, and complexity. West's literary career began in 1911 when she wrote for *Freewoman*, a feminist journal. Her outspoken and brilliant book reviews soon earned West a place among the British literary elite. She published a study of novelist Henry James in 1916 and her first novel, *The Return of the Soldier*, in 1918. *The Strange Necessity*, her first collection of criticism and essays, appeared in 1928. Her 1936 novel of love and marriage in French society, *The Thinking Reed*, is considered by some to be her best novel, although West herself is thought to have preferred her 1966 novel of Russian espionage, *The Birds Fall Down*. Many critics point to two of West's journalistic books as her masterworks. One, *Black Lamb and Grey Falcon: A Journey Through Yugoslavia*, appeared in 1941 and serves as a sort of travelogue-history, described by one critic as "reporting raised to the level of literature." Another of her highly acclaimed journalistic efforts, *The Meaning of Treason*, first appeared in 1947 and was revised and expanded as *The New Meaning of Treason* in 1964. Those two books discuss spies and traitors and examine the relationship between good and evil. West continued to write and publish essays into the 1980's and appeared in the 1981 motion picture "Reds." West's son, Anthony West, himself a celebrated writer, was born during a ten-year relationship between West and author H. G. Wells. Rebecca West was made Dame Commander of the Order of the British Empire in 1959. Obituaries and other sources: *New York Times*, March 16, 1983; *Los Angeles Times*, March 16, 1983; *Chicago Tribune*, March 16, 1983, March 20, 1983; *Time*, March 28, 1983; *Newsweek*, March 28, 1983.

*   *   *

WESTCOTT, Cynthia   1898-1983

OBITUARY NOTICE—See index for *CA* sketch: Born June 29, 1898, in North Attleboro, Mass.; died of a heart ailment, March 22, 1983, in North Tarrytown, N.Y. Plant pathologist, lecturer, and author. From 1921 to 1931 Westcott served as a research assistant in plant pathology at Cornell University. A rose expert, she began in 1933 to maintain an experimental garden as a laboratory for her research on plant diseases and pests. Westcott became known as "the plant doctor" and published a book by that title in 1937. In addition, she lectured extensively, belonged to many professional organizations, and wrote hundreds of articles for periodicals. Among her other books are *The Gardener's Bug Book, Anyone Can Grow Roses*, and *Are You Your Garden's Worst Pest?* Obituaries and other sources: *New York Times*, March 25, 1983; *Chicago Tribune*, March 26, 1983.

WESTERMEYER, Joseph John   1937-

PERSONAL: Born April 8, 1937, in Chicago, Ill.; son of Joseph John and Irene Bridget (McDonagh) Westermeyer; married Rachel Mary Moga, August 4, 1962; children: Michelle Mary, Joseph John. *Education:* Attended College of St. Thomas, 1955-57; University of Minnesota, B.S., 1959, M.D., 1961, M.A., 1969, M.P.H. and Ph.D., both 1970. *Politics:* Independent. *Residence:* St. Paul, Minn. *Office:* Box 393, Mayo University of Minnesota Hospital, 420 Delaware St. S.E., Minneapolis, Minn. 55455.

CAREER: St. Paul-Ramsey Hospital, St. Paul, Minn., rotating intern, 1961-62; Payne Avenue Medical Clinic, St. Paul, general practitioner, 1962-65; U.S. Agency for International Development, Washington, D.C., deputy chief of Division of Public Health in Laos, 1965-67; University of Minnesota, Minneapolis, instructor, 1970-71, assistant professor, 1971-74, associate professor, 1974-78, professor of psychiatry, 1978—, adjunct professor of anthropology and psychology, 1979—, member of psychiatry staff at university hospitals, 1970—, founder and director of acute inpatient service, 1970-72, and day hospital, 1971-73, coordinator of medical student education in psychiatry, 1976—, coordinatory of outpatient clinic for refugees from Southeast Asia, 1977—.

Member of visiting faculty at Bemidji State College, 1974, Brown University, 1976, 1977, University of California, Irvine, and Johns Hopkins University, both 1977, Purdue University, University of South Carolina, and University of Washington, Seattle, all 1978, Mayo Medical School, State University of New York at Buffalo, and Harvard University, all 1980, and Milwaukee Medical College and University of Oklahoma, both 1981; conference director; speaker and workshop leader. Member of Minnesota Department of Public Welfare Medical Policy Committee on Mental Health, 1978-80, and ad hoc Committee on Indochinese Refugees, 1980—; member of board of directors of Indian Guest House, 1969-72, and Juel Fairbanks House (both halfway houses for Indian alcoholics), 1970-73; member of Minneapolis Veterans Administration Hospital Mental Health and Behavioral Sciences Council, 1976-79; consultant to World Health Organization, National Institute on Alcohol Abuse and Alcoholism, and Association of American Indian Affairs.

MEMBER: World Psychiatric Association, American Anthropological Association (fellow), American Association of Family Practice (fellow), American Psychiatric Association (fellow), American Medical Society on Alcoholism (state chairman, 1979—), American Association for the Advancement of Science, American Public Health Association, Society for the Study of Psychiatry and Culture, Society on Medical Anthropology, Research Society on Alcoholism, Association of Behavioral Sciences and Medical Education, Association of Medical Educators and Researchers on Substance Abuse, Association of Academic Psychiatrists, Academy of Medical Research and Education in Substance Abuse (member of board of directors, 1976-78), Career Teachers in the Addictions, Minnesota State Medical Association, Minnesota Psychiatric Society, Alpha Omega Alpha.

AWARDS, HONORS: Meritorious service award from U.S. Agency for International Development, 1967; Ginzburg fellow of Group for the Advancement of Psychiatry, 1969-70; fellow of National Institutes of Health, 1970, 1972, 1978; grants from National Institute of Mental Health, 1971-73, 1973-74, 1973-

75, 1980-81, National Institute of Alcohol Abuse and Alcoholism, 1974-75, 1974-77, 1978-79, Minnesota Medical Foundation, 1974-75, 1977, 1981-82, National Institute of Drug Abuse, 1977-78, State of Minnesota, 1979-80, and Mental Health Services for Indochinese Refugees, 1979-81.

WRITINGS: A Primer on Chemical Dependency, Williams & Wilkins, 1976; (editor) *Anthropology and Mental Health,* Mouton, 1976; (editor with E. Foulks, R. Wintrob, and A. Favazza) *Transcultural Psychiatry,* Spectrum, 1977; *Poppies, Pipes, and People: A Study of Opium and Its Use in Laos,* University of California Press, 1982.

Contributor: *Community Health and Mental Health Care Delivery for North Americans,* MSS Information, 1974; J. O. Waddell, D. B. Heath, and M. W. Everett, editors, *Cross-Cultural Approaches to the Study of Alcoholism,* Mouton, 1976; E. Foulks, R. Wintrob, and others, editors, *Current Perspectives in Cultural Psychiatry,* Spectrum, 1977; A. Schechter and S. J. Mule, editors, *Rehabilitation and Treatment Aspects of Drug Dependence,* CRC Press, 1978; R. Pickens and L. Heston, editors, *Psychiatry and Drug Abuse,* Grune, 1979.

Contributor: (Author of foreword) G. Kane, *Inner City Alcoholism: An Ecological Analysis and Cross Cultural Study,* Human Sciences, 1981; J. Solomon and K. Keely, editors, *Perspectives on Alcohol and Drug Abuse: Similarities and Differences,* PSG Publishing, 1981; C. Nadelson and D. Marcotte, editors, *Treatment Interventions in Human Sexuality,* Plenum, 1982; *Opium in Southeast Asia,* Institute for the Study of Human Issues, 1982; Claude T. Friedmann and Robert A. Faquet, editors, *Extraordinary Symptoms in Psychiatry,* Plenum, 1982; E. M. Pattison and E. Kaufman, editors, *The American Encyclopedic Handbook of Alcoholism,* Gardner Press, 1982; *Alcoholism and Clinical Psychiatry,* Plenum, 1982; A. I. Alterman, editor, *Substance Abuse and Psychopathology,* Plenum, 1983. Also contributor to *Alcoholism and Its Treatment,* edited by C. Whitfield, 1982.

Contributor of more than one hundred articles and reviews to medical journals. Social science editor of *Substance Abuse Newsletter,* 1979—; member of editorial board of *American Journal of Drug and Alcohol Abuse,* 1973—, *Journal of Operational Psychiatry,* 1977—, *American Journal of Public Health,* 1980-84, *Advances in Alcohol and Substance Abuse,* 1980—, *Alcoholism: Clinical and Experimental Research,* 1980—, and *Alcohol and Research World,* 1981—.

WORK IN PROGRESS: Co-editing a book on methadone treatment; co-editing a teaching manual on alcohol and drug abuse; research for the development of a social indicator system for alcoholism and drug abuse; research on social-psychological-health adjustment of refugees from Laos to the United States; research on American Indian patients with alcohol problems.

SIDELIGHTS: Westermeyer's languages include Thai and Lao. *Avocational interests:* Skiing, swimming, running, flying.

*   *   *

WESTMORE, Ann 1953-

PERSONAL: Born June 7, 1953, in Melbourne, Australia; daughter of Gerald Brian (a physician) and Moira (a science teacher; maiden name, Howard) Westmore; married David Hill (a psychologist), January 24, 1978; children: Michael; (stepsons) Stephen, Peter, Mathew. *Education:* University of Melbourne, B.Sc., 1972. *Home and office:* 13 Laver St., Kew, Victoria 3101, Australia.

CAREER: Herald and Weekly Times Ltd., Melbourne, Australia, medical and science reporter, 1973-78; free-lance journalist specializing in science, medicine, and the environment, 1978—. *Member:* Australian Journalists Association, Australian Society of Authors, Australian Society of Women Writers. *Awards, honors:* Awards from Australian Medical Association, 1975 and 1977, both for five best news stories on medical matters in Australia, and 1980, for series of feature articles on *in vitro* fertilization.

WRITINGS: (With Evelyn Billings) *The Billings Method,* Anne O'Donovan, 1980; (with E. Carl Wood) *Test-Tube Conception,* Hill of Content, 1983. Contributor to magazines and newspapers, including *Reader's Digest* and *New Idea.*

WORK IN PROGRESS: "From Hippocrates to Christian Barnard," a play "about the power of the medical scientist and the use to which it is put"; a book about eye health for the lay reader.

SIDELIGHTS: Westmore told *CA:* "My object in writing is to clarify and illuminate issues with a medical and/or scientific component. Issues such as birth control and external fertilization may prove to be time bombs, so a general consideration of such topics is a first step for the interested lay reader.

"Traditionally, the privileged background and training of physicians has promoted a sense of authority, omniscience, and entitlement. Many communities have accepted bossiness and intellectual arrogance as part of the medical manner, and have tacitly condoned the dominant role of physicians in health care decision-making. Now this is changing. Doctors are less inclined to accept absolute responsibility, and recognize that patients should be actively involved in decisions affecting their health care and treatment.

"For their part, many patients can no longer accept that doctors may have the power to make life-or-death decisions on their behalf. Patients are questioning, learning about their bodies, demanding a greater say in treatment, and seeking help from nonorthodox medical practitioners. The turmoil resulting from these changes is surfacing, sometimes with dire consequences for both patients and doctors.

"Examples of practices that encourage increased body self-awareness include breast self-examination and methods of natural birth control involving recognition of the fertile part of the menstrual cycle. The times when women discover breast lumps, or when couples take a chance of conceiving when they know they are fertile, bring home the fact that taking greater control means increased responsibility.

"While many people are seeking a greater degree of control and simplicity in their own health care, this is counterbalanced by the availability of increasingly sophisticated equipment and treatments. These have been introduced into the process of birth and keeping alive those on the point of death, into the treatment of heart disease, cancer, and many other disorders. External fertilization is another example of the lengths to which humankind can and is prepared to go to overcome the potentially devastating problems of infertility.

"Many people, some doctors included, are cautious of these developments. They advocate keeping it simple, and urge us not to be seduced by high technology medicine. The economists also warn of the high cost of such developments.

"Ambivalence about the future directions of health care is understandable. On the one hand, we want good health for as long as possible. On the other, we are uncertain about how to achieve this and do not have bottomless funds to experiment.''

BIOGRAPHICAL/CRITICAL SOURCES: Melbourne Sun, May 26, 1976, June 14, 1978; *Melbourne Herald*, September 4, 1981.

* * *

WETTENHALL, Roger (Llewellyn) 1931-

PERSONAL: Born February 4, 1931, in Hobart, Australia; son of Ralph Henry (a shipping clerk) and Dorothy Mabel (a dental nurse; maiden name, Rumbold) Wettenhall; married, 1955 (divorced, 1975); children: Irene, Lynn, Dean. *Education:* University of Tasmania, Diploma in Public Administration, 1955, M.A., 1959; Australian National University, Ph.D., 1962. *Home:* 12 Carmichael St., Deakin, Australian Capital Territory 2600, Australia. *Office:* Canberra College of Advanced Education, Belconnen, Australian Capital Territory 2616, Australia.

CAREER: Australian Commonwealth Public Service, personnel cadet in Hobart, 1948-51, personnel officer in Adelaide and Hobart, 1952-59; Australian National University, Canberra, research scholar, 1959-61; University of Tasmania, Hobart, lecturer, 1961-65, senior lecturer, 1966-69, reader in political science, 1969-71; Canberra College of Advanced Education, Belconnen, Australia, head of School of Administrative Studies, 1971—. Hallsworth research fellow at University of Manchester, 1964-65; visiting scholar at State University of New York at Albany, autumn, 1978. Consultant to Advisory Council of Intergovernment Relations and Royal Commission on Australian Government Administration. *Member:* International Association of Schools and Institutes of Administration, Royal Institute of Public Administration (president of Australian Capital Territory Group, 1973-75), Tasmanian Historical Research Association (president, 1967-68). *Awards, honors:* Haldane Silver Medal from Royal Institute of Public Administration, 1965, for essay ''The Recoup Concept in Public Enterprise.''

WRITINGS: Railway Management and Politics in Victoria, 1856-1906, Australian Capital Territory Group, Royal Institute of Public Administration, 1961; *A Guide to Tasmanian Government Administration,* Platypus Publications, 1968; *The Iron Road and the State: W. M. Acworth as Scholar, Critic, and Reformer,* University of Tasmania, 1970; *Bushfire Disaster: An Australian Community in Crisis,* Angus & Robertson, 1975; (editor with Martin Painter) *The First Thousand Days of Labor,* Canberra College of Advanced Education, 1975; (editor with G. R. Curnow) *Understanding Public Administration,* Allen & Unwin, 1981; (editor with J. M. Power and J. A. Halligan) *Local Government Systems of Australia,* Australian Government Publishing Service, 1981; *More Opaque Than Clear: The Problem of Ministries and Departments,* University of Queensland Press, 1983. Contributor to political science, public administration, and current affairs journals. Associate editor of *Australian Journal of Public Administration;* member of editorial committee of *International Review of Administrative Sciences.*

SIDELIGHTS: Wettenhall commented: ''As a former public servant with academic preparation mainly in political science, I have been concerned to further the systematic study of public administration, which I believe has too long been relegated to a position of minor importance by the older academic disciplines. I have, of course, been a teacher, too, and in my present position academic administration takes up most of my time.''

WHARTON, George Frederick III 1952-

PERSONAL: born January 28, 1952, in Somerville, N.J.; son of George Frederick, Jr. (a telephone service technician) and Patricia (an office manager; maiden name, Sloan) Wharton. *Education:* University of Connecticut, B.A., 1974; Rutgers University, Ed.M., 1976. *Religion:* Reformed Episcopal. *Home address:* R.D.2, Box 84, Frenchtown, N.J. 08825.

CAREER: Adult Learning Center, Plainfield, N.J., teacher of adult basic education, high school equivalency, and English as a second language, 1975-76; Adult Education Commission, Monmouth County, N.J., director of educational research project, 1976-77; high school biology and chemistry teacher in Basking Ridge, N.J., 1977-78; Rutgers University, New Brunswick, N.J., research assistant and part-time consultant to Institute on Aging, 1978-81; supervisor of education at a small computer company in northern New Jersey, 1981—. Part-time librarian at Somerset County College, Somerville, N.J., 1979-81.

MEMBER: American Association of Adult and Continuing Education (founding member), American Society for Training and Development, American Guild of Organists, U.S. Cycling Federation, Trade and Industrial Education Association of New Jersey, Association for Adult Education of New Jersey, Gerontological Society of New Jersey, New Jersey Association for Community Education, Mountain Plains Adult Education Association, Somerset County Fish and Game Protective Association. *Awards, honors:* Distinguished expert rifleman award from National Rifle Association, 1968.

WRITINGS: (Editor) *A Bibliography on Sexuality and Aging,* Institute on Aging, Rutgers University, 1978; *Sexuality and Aging: An Annotated Bibliography,* Scarecrow, 1981. Contributor to education journals.

WORK IN PROGRESS: Research on computers and education, management and sales training for the computer industry, and informal learning among computer-repair field engineers and technicians.

SIDELIGHTS: George Wharton's *Sexuality and Aging: An Annotated Bibliography* contains over one thousand entries. According to Bill Bytheway in *Ageing and Society,* Wharton's annotations ''are concise and informative. Anyone who wishes to undertake a review of the literature will find the book extremely helpful.'' Augustus E. Stewart, writing in the *Journal of the American Osteopathic Association,* agreed, saying that *Sexuality and Aging* ''should be in every college library, every psychiatric hospital, every hospital and a quick ready reference for anyone who is particularly interested in sexuality, sexual problems and the aging population.''

Wharton told *CA:* ''Education and learning in general interest me. As a result of my recent involvement in corporate education, both technical and non-technical, I have developed a keen interest in management and sales education and technical training on mainframe and microcomputers. My responsibilities have included coordinating hardware and software training for personnel from universities and corporations in the United States, Japan, South America, India, and China. It is important for educators to help rid the corporate and public world of cyberphobia; that is, fear of computers.

''In addition to corporate education and training, I am continually studying gerontology as it relates to the work setting and life in general. My book on sexuality and aging grew out of that interest. The study of aging has become sort of a hobby with me. As the demography of the United States and the world continues to change, people will need to become more aware of and sensitive to the joys and problems of aging.

"My background includes experience in and study of adult literacy and basic education. Adult literacy and basic education are extremely important for the future of the world. Poverty, sickness, unemployment, crime, overpopulation, and misery can be a result of illiteracy. Educators don't seem to realize the magnitude of this problem in the United States and the world, particularly in underdeveloped countries. There doesn't seem to be much financial or political support for programs to eradicate illiteracy."

AVOCATIONAL INTERESTS: "Playing the piano has become a source of relaxation and enjoyment for me. The type of music which interests me most now is Christian music. Two performers I admire are Kurt Kaiser and John Innes."

BIOGRAPHICAL/CRITICAL SOURCES: New Brunswick Daily Home News, October 9, 1965; *Somerset Messenger-Gazette,* October 14, 1965; *RQ,* winter, 1981; *Australian Journal on Ageing,* May, 1982; *Age and Ageing: The Journal of the British Geriatrics Society and the British Society for Research on Ageing,* August, 1982; *Journal of the American Osteopathic Association,* November, 1982; *Ageing and Society,* November, 1982; *Journal of Gerontology,* January, 1983.

*   *   *

WHEELER, Bonnie G(rant)   1943-

PERSONAL: Born July 12, 1943, in Charleston, W.Va.; daughter of Ernest Arlington (a career officer in U.S. Army) and Virginia (Barker) Lindner; married Dennis R. Wheeler (a store manager), June 14, 1961; children: Julie, Timothy, Robert; (adopted children) Rebecca, Benjamin, Melissa. *Education:* Attended high school in Fort Lauderdale, Fla. *Politics:* Republican. *Religion:* Christian and Missionary Alliance. *Home:* 887 10th St., Williams, Calif. 95987. *Office address:* P.O. Box 381, Williams, Calif. 95987.

CAREER: Free-lance writer and public speaker/workshop leader. Co-founder and co-director of Northern California Christian Writers Workshop; member of Colusa County Health Department advisory board, 1980—; member of Williams School Site Council, 1981; chairperson of Colusa County Special Education advisory board, 1981—. Guest on television and radio programs. *Member:* Christian Writers Guild, National Right to Life Committee, Sutter-Buttes Christian Writers Fellowship (co-founder; president). *Awards, honors:* Mount Hermon Inspirational Award from Christian Writers Conference, 1982.

WRITINGS: (Contributor) Muriel B. Dennis, compiler, *Chosen Children,* Good News, 1978; *Of Braces and Blessings,* Christian Herald, 1980; *Challenged Parenting,* Regal Books, 1982; *Time Stewardship for Women,* Vision House, 1983. Contributor to nearly twenty magazines, including *Decision, Moody Monthly, Virtue, Christian Writer, Family Life Today, Looking Ahead, Living With Children, Messenger, Upper Room,* and *Today's Christian Woman.*

WORK IN PROGRESS: The Hurting Spouse; Hey, God?, a series for children.

SIDELIGHTS: Wheeler told *CA:* "Multiple medical problems with our first three children, coupled with a desire for more children, led us to adopt three multiracial children with severe handicaps. Seemingly overnight, we went from the average family with relative anonymity to a much more public image. Our lives have been both enriched and greatly challenged by the addition of these children to our family. As a result of the adoptions and our previous experiences, I share a deep burden with other parents. Through my writing I want to offer these other parents hope and practical help, and I want to encourage people to adopt these special children.

"*Chosen Children* is a book on adoption, written by various adoptive parents. *Of Braces and Blessings* tells the story of our six children. It 'not only proves that the handicapped are God's special children, but makes it abundantly clear that they are innovative, creative, a source of learning, and blessings to those who are considered normal,' said C. Everett Koop, Surgeon General of the United States. 'Bonnie Wheeler's saga will pluck at your heartstrings but you will profit greatly from the experience.' *Challenged Parenting* is a practical handbook for parents of children with handicaps. 'It is indeed a practical handbook for parents,' wrote Harold Wilke, the executive director of the Healing Community, 'with hundreds of suggestions fitting almost any conceivable situation. This is not a "read & toss" book but one to use for reference over and over. Bonnie Wheeler's vision and understanding, clarity of thought and concern for humanity shine forth in these pages.'

"I'm at the research stage for *The Hurting Spouse,* and it will be another practical handbook, but for people with chronically ill spouses. I am also halfway through a series of children's picture books, *Hey, God?,* that will introduce younger readers to children with handicaps.

"As a result of mothering six children, I have a keen—and very necessary—interest in time management. I have developed and direct Bonnie Wheeler's Time Stewardship Workshops, and I am currently under contract for a book on time management. Over my desk I have a quote by Catherine Marshall that is the aim of my practical kind of writing: 'That the printed word reaches through to the emotions of all who read it, that the emotion becomes a touchstone for action.'

"I greatly enjoy teaching at various conferences and workshops, but I believe that my first priorities are God and family. As a result of these priorities I try to limit my out of town engagements to once a month."

BIOGRAPHICAL/CRITICAL SOURCES: Christian Writer, January, 1983.

*   *   *

WHIPPLE, Beverly   1941-

PERSONAL: Born June 30, 1941, in Jersey City, N.J.; daughter of Howard and Beatrice (Bodei) Hoehne; married James W. Whipple (an engineer), September 15, 1962; children: Allen, Susan. *Education:* Wagner College, B.S., 1962; Rutgers University, M.Ed., 1967; further graduate study at University of Pennsylvania, 1974—. *Religion:* Protestant. *Home:* 19 Bartram Rd., Marlton, N.J. 08053. *Agent:* Heide Lang, Sanford J. Greenburger Associates, Inc., 825 Third Ave., New York, N.Y. 10022. *Office:* Department of Psychiatry and Human Behavior, Jefferson Medical College, Philadelphia, Pa. 19107; and Department of Nursing, Gloucester County College, Sewell, N.J. 08080.

CAREER: West Jersey Hospital School of Nursing, Camden, N.J., instructor in nursing, 1962-64; Helene Fuld School of Nursing, Camden, instructor in nursing, 1970-75; Gloucester

County College, Sewell, N.J., assistant professor of nursing, 1975—. Member of faculty at Jefferson Medical College. Vice-president of Burlington County Board of Mental Health, 1976-80. Member of United Presbyterian Church task force on women, 1975-77; director of Woodstream Residents Association, 1967-71. Guest on "The Phil Donahue Show." *Member:* American Nurses Association, American Association of Sex Educators and Counselors, American College of Sexologists, Sex Information and Education Council of the United States, Association of Sexologists, Society for the Scientific Study of Sex, Zeta Tau Alpha, Kappa Delta Pi. *Awards, honors:* Alumnae certificate of merit from Zeta Tau Alpha, 1978; alumnae achievement award from Wagner College, 1983.

WRITINGS: (With Alice K. Ladas and John D. Perry) *The G Spot: And Other Recent Discoveries About Human Sexuality,* Holt, 1982; (contributor) Benjamin Graber, editor, *Circumvaginal Musculature and Sexual Function,* S. Karger, 1982. Contributor to magazines, including *Playboy, Forum,* and *Journal of Sex Research.*

WORK IN PROGRESS: A book on the stress of sex, with George Bach.

SIDELIGHTS: Whipple told *CA:* "I feel that *The G Spot* has helped to validate the experiences of many women, and has helped them to feel better about themselves. It has also stimulated more research in the area of female sexual response.

"Much more research needs to be done on female sexuality, and on the sexual needs of individuals with various kinds of illnesses. I am continuing my work in these areas."

BIOGRAPHICAL/CRITICAL SOURCES: Self, August, 1982, September, 1982; *Playboy,* September, 1982; *Time,* September 13, 1982; *Glamour,* October, 1982.

* * *

WHISLER, John A(lbert) 1951-

PERSONAL: Born January 4, 1951, in Beaverton, Mich.; son of H. Arthur (a teacher) and Betty (a teacher; maiden name, Long) Whisler. *Education:* Manchester College, North Manchester, Ind., B.S., 1973; Memphis State University, M.M., 1975; University of Iowa, M.A., 1977. *Home:* 1536 Third St., No. 6, Charleston, Ill. 61920. *Office:* Booth Library, Eastern Illinois University, Charleston, Ill. 61920.

CAREER: Memphis Public Library, Memphis, Tenn., art and music librarian, 1977-81; Eastern Illinois University, Charleston, assistant professor and coordinator of fine arts services at Booth Library, 1981—. *Member:* Music Library Association, Viola da Gamba Society of America (member of board of directors, 1979-84; executive secretary, 1979—), Illinois Library Association.

WRITINGS: Elvis Presley Reference Guide and Discography, Scarecrow, 1981. Contributor of articles, translations, and reviews to library, art, and music journals. Associate editor of *Journal of the Viola da Gamba Society of America,* 1978—.

SIDELIGHTS: Whisler told *CA:* "The fact that I've written a book about Elvis Presley surprises most people who know me. I was raised in a conservative religious home where Elvis's music was not appreciated, and my musical studies and tastes have been entirely classical. But in the fall of 1977, just three weeks after Presley's death, I found myself employed as a reference librarian in the art and music department of the Memphis Public Library. Here I soon found myself fielding many

questions per day regarding Presley, ranging from the simple to the complex and from the normal to the really weird. (Douglas Marsh, in the religion department, got the best question: a woman wanted to know if Elvis were still dead. She was expecting the resurrection at any moment.) All these questions made me realize that there may be a need for a bibliographic reference tool to aid others in their search for Presley information. This is why I wrote an Elvis book. The time and place in which I found myself seemed to call for it."

AVOCATIONAL INTERESTS: Contemporary ceramic art, especially the works of Robert McGowan; photography, the viola da gamba family of instruments.

* * *

WHITE, Barbara A(nne) 1942-

PERSONAL: Born October 25, 1942, in Norwich, N.Y.; daughter of Frank (an electrician) and Mary (an office nurse; maiden name, Busacker) White; married Harvey Epstein (an engineer); children: Elizabeth. *Education:* Cornell University, A.B., 1964; University of Wisconsin—Madison, M.A., 1965, Ph.D., 1974; Simmons College, M.S., 1976. *Home address:* R.F.D. 1, Mast Rd., Durham, N.H. 03824. *Office:* Department of Special Collections, University of New Hampshire Library, Durham, N.H. 03824.

CAREER: Northwestern University, Evanston, Ill., instructor in English, 1970-72; University of Louisville, Louisville, Ky., assistant professor of English, 1974-75; University of New Hampshire, Durham, associate professor, curator of rare books and manuscripts, 1976—, coordinator of women's studies program, 1980-81. Project humanist for New Hampshire Council of the Humanities, 1980-81. *Member:* National Women's Studies Association, Modern Language Association of America, New England Women's Studies Association, Committee for a New England Bibliography, Northeast Modern Language Association, Phi Beta Kappa, Phi Kappa Phi, Beta Phi Mu.

WRITINGS: American Women Writers: An Annotated Bibliography of Criticism, Garland Publishing, 1977; (contributor) Lina Mainiero, editor, *American Women Writers,* Ungar, Volume I, 1979, Volume II, 1980, Volume III, 1981, Volume IV, 1982; (contributor) Annis Pratt, editor, *Archetypal Patterns in Women's Fiction,* Indiana University Press, 1981; (author of foreword) Jane E. Vallier, *Poet on Demand: The Life, Letters, and Works of Celia Thaxter,* Down East, 1982; (contributor) Susan Koppelman, editor, *Short Stories Written by Women in the United States,* Feminist Press, 1983.

Author of "New Hampshire Writers View the Small Town," script for a film released by University of New Hampshire Media Services in 1981. Contributor to literature journals. Co-editor of *Notes,* Friends of the Library, University of New Hampshire, 1977—; assistant editor of *Perspectives on Contemporary Literature.*

WORK IN PROGRESS: Editing an anthology of fiction by American women, 1790-1870, publication by University of Illinois Press expected in 1983; a book on adolescent heroines in American literature.

SIDELIGHTS: White told *CA:* "I have studied writings by women since 1970 when I taught one of the earliest women's studies courses. A novel we discussed in that course—Carson McCullers's *The Member of the Wedding*—led me to question why girls in coming-of-age novels differ so markedly from the boys we are more familiar with, for example Huck Finn, Stephen Dedalus, Holden Caulfield. I have since found, even in contemporary novels, that adolescent heroines are portrayed as ambivalent about growing up to womanhood, a state they view as powerless and inferior.

"I am also interested in earlier fiction by women, especially the so-called 'sentimental' or 'domestic' fiction written in America before the Civil War. I think some of these much maligned novels were important contributions to the growth of realism and the development of the novel. Feminist critics have thus far been building a critical theory, discovering 'lost' women writers, and reinterpreting works of individual women; now we must begin to write women's literary history."

*   *   *

WHITE, James 1913-

PERSONAL: Born June 16, 1913, in Dublin, Ireland; son of Thomas John and Florence (Coffey) White; married Agnes Bowe, 1941; children: Mary White O'Reilly, Catherine White Smith, Peter, Patrick, Mark. *Education:* Attended Belvedere College, 1924 and 1931. *Home:* 15 Herbert Park, Ballsbridge, Dublin 4, Ireland.

CAREER: Standard, Dublin, Ireland, art critic, 1940-50; *Irish Press,* Dublin, art critic, 1950-59; *Irish Times,* Dublin, art critic, 1959-62; Municipal Gallery of Modern Art, Dublin, curator, 1960-64; National Gallery of Ireland, Dublin, director, 1964-80. Lecturer at University College, 1950—, and Trinity College, Dublin, 1960-63. President of Dublin Regional Tourism and Friends of the National Collections of Ireland; member of advisory council of European Committee on Art Exhibitions; member of Dublin Diocesan Committee on Sacred Art and Architecture (past chairman); trustee of Chester Beatty Library of Oriental Art.

MEMBER: International Council of Museums (chairman for Ireland), Contemporary Irish Art Society, Irish Art Historians Association (chairman), Irish Museums Association, Royal Dublin Society, Kildare Street, University Club. *Awards, honors:* L.L.D. from National University of Ireland, 1970; Chevalier of French Legion of Honor, 1973; Order of Merit of the Italian Republic, 1976.

WRITINGS: Louis Le Brocquy (monograph), La Revue Francaise, 1965; *George Campbell* (monograph), [Dublin], 1962; *Brian Bourke* (monograph), Goldsmith Press, 1963; (with Michael Wynne) *Irish Stained Glass,* Gills, 1963; *The National Gallery of Ireland,* Thames & Hudson, 1968; *Jack B. Yeats,* Secker & Warburg, 1971; *John Butler Yeats and the Irish Renaissance,* Dolmen Press, 1972; (author of introduction) Lady Gregory and Colin Smythe, *Hugh Lane,* Oxford University Press, 1973; *Masterpieces of the National Gallery of Ireland,* Jarrolds, 1977; (author of introduction) Anne Crookshank, *The Painters of Ireland,* Barrie & Jenkins, 1978. Author of museum catalogs.

*   *   *

WHITEFRIAR
. See HISCOCK, Eric

*   *   *

WHITESIDE, Thomas 1918(?)-

BRIEF ENTRY: American journalist and author. Whiteside, who is a staff writer for *New Yorker,* was one of the first

journalists to alert the American public to the dangers of the military's use of chemical defoliants during the Vietnam War in his book *Defoliation* (Ballantine, 1970). Most of Whiteside's books are compiled from investigative articles originally published in *New Yorker,* including *Selling Death: Cigarette Advertising and Public Health* (Liveright, 1971), *Computer Capers: Tales of Electronic Thievery, Embezzlement, and Fraud* (Crowell, 1978), *The Pendulum and the Toxic Cloud: The Course of Dioxin Contamination* (Yale University Press, 1979), and *The Blockbuster Complex: Conglomerates, Show Business, and Book Publishing* (Columbia University Press, 1981). *Biographical/critical sources: New York Times Book Review,* April 30, 1978, April 15, 1979; *New York Times,* May 19, 1978, June 23, 1981; *Washington Post,* May 19, 1978.

*   *   *

WHITFIELD, Raoul 1897(?)-1945
(Ramon Decolta)

BRIEF ENTRY: Born in 1897 (one source says 1898) in New York, N.Y.; died in 1945. American journalist and author. Whitfield, who was raised in the Philippines, served in the Army Air Corps during World War I and later worked as a newspaper reporter. A writer of detective fiction in the vein of Dashiell Hammett and Raymond Chandler, Whitfield contributed more than eighty short stories to the *Black Mask* and other pulp magazines between 1926 and 1934. The most popular of these featured Filipino detective Jo Gar and were written under the pseudonym Ramon Decolta. Whitfield also wrote three crime novels, *Green Ice* (1930), *Death in a Bowl* (1931), and *The Virgin Kills* (1932), and a collection of aviation stories, *Silver Wings* (1932). *Biographical/critical sources: Encyclopedia of Mystery and Detection,* McGraw, 1976.

*   *   *

WHITLAM, (Edward) Gough 1916-

PERSONAL: Born July 11, 1916, in Melbourne, Australia; son of Harry Frederick Ernest (a solicitor) and Martha (Maddocks) Whitlam; married Margaret Elaine Dovey, April 22, 1942; children: Antony Philip, Nicholas Richard, Stephen Charles, Catherine Julia. *Education:* University of Sydney, B.A., 1938, LL.B., 1946. *Home:* 100 William St., Sydney, New South Wales 2011, Australia.

CAREER: Barrister, 1947; associated with New South Wales Bar Council, 1949-53; Australian Parliament, Canberra, Labor member of Parliament for Werriwa, 1952-78, member of Parliamentary committee on constitutional review, 1956-59, leader of Australian Labor party, 1967-77, member of constitutional conventions, 1973-77, leader of the opposition, 1976-78. Prime Minister of Australia, 1972-75; foreign minister, 1972-73. Chifley Memorial Lecturer at University of Melbourne, 1957 and 1975; Roy Milne Lecturer in Armidale and Brisbane, 1963 and 1973; Evatt Memorial Lecturer at University of Sydney, 1966; John Curtin Memorial Lectuer at Australian National University, 1975; T. J. Ryan Memorial Lecturer at Queensland University, 1978. Visiting fellow at Australian National University, 1978-80, and first national fellow, 1980-81; visiting professor at Harvard University, 1979; fellow of Senate of University of Sydney, 1981—. Appointed Queen's Counsel, 1962. *Military service:* Royal Australian Air Force, 1941-45; became flight lieutenant. *Member:* Socialist International (vice-president, 1976). *Awards, honors:* Silver Plate of Honor from Socialist International, 1976; companion of Order of Australia, 1978.

WRITINGS: Socialism Within the Constitution, Victorian Fabian Society, 1961; *Beyond Vietnam: Australia's Regional Responsibility* (pamphlet), Victorian Fabian Society, 1968; *An Urban Nation* (pamphlet), Victorian Fabian Society, 1970; *Labor and the Constitution, 1972-1975*, Heinemann, 1977; *On Australia's Constitution*, Widescofe, 1977; *The Truth of the Matter*, Allen Lane, 1979; *Labor Essays, 1980*, Drummond, 1980; *A Pacific Community*, Harvard University Press, 1981; (contributor) Jeffrey Scott, editor, *Australian Federalism: Future Tense*, Oxford University Press, 1983; (contributor) John Langmore and David Peetz, editors, *Wealth, Poverty and Survival: Australia in the World*, Allen & Unwin, 1983. Also author of *Road to Reform: Labor in Government*, 1975, *Government of the People, for the People, by the People's House*, 1975, and *The New Federalism: Labor's Programs and Policies*, 1976. Contributor to professional journals and magazines, including *Australian Quarterly*.

WORK IN PROGRESS: The Whitlam Governments, publication by Allen Lane expected in 1984; *An Italian Companion*, publication by Queensland University Press expected in 1985.

*   *   *

WHITLOCK, Quentin A(rthur)   1937-

PERSONAL: Born September 3, 1937, in London, England; son of Arthur Edward (a head teacher) and Ethel (Moran) Whitlock; married Elizabeth Margaret W. Potter (a lecturer), February 15, 1964; children: Helen Mary, Emma Louise. *Education:* Queen Mary College, London, B.A. (with honors), 1961. *Home:* 265 Abbeydale Rd. S., Sheffield S17 3LB, England. *Office:* Dean Associates, 45 Canterbury Ave., Sheffield S10 3RU, England.

CAREER: University of Sheffield, Sheffield, England, information officer at Programmed Instruction Centre for Industry, 1967-73; Cegos Italia (management consultants), Milan, Italy, senior consultant, 1973-76; Sheffield City Polytechnic, Sheffield, head of instructional technology unit, 1976-82; Dean Associates (computer-training firm), Sheffield, partner, 1982—. *Military service:* British Army, Royal Army Educational Corps, 1956-58. *Member:* Association of Education and Training Technology (member of council, 1980-84), Network of Practitioners in Education and Training Technology (vice-chairman).

WRITINGS: (Editor with G. T. Page) *Aspects of Educational Technology*, Volume XIII: *Educational Technology Twenty Years On*, Kogan Page, 1979; (with Christopher G. Dean) *A Handbook of Computer-Based Training*, Kogan Page, 1983. Contributor to training technology journals.

SIDELIGHTS: Whitlock told *CA:* "I first became interested in the field of computer-based training (CBT) when I was invited to train a team of authors of CBT lessons for a U.K. bank. As a training specialist with little knowledge of computing, I was struck by the fact that many CBT units were capable of improvement as educational tools. At the same time, I realized that lack of knowledge of what computers can do was a serious handicap to the training design effort.

"Christopher Dean, the co-author of *Handbook of Computer-Based Training*, approached CBT from the opposite direction—as a computing specialist advising ignorant trainers like me what was and was not possible. After running a joint course on CBT, we decided to become partners in a business venture devoted to the CBT domain.

"I retain an active interest in the development of printed learning materials and in author training. It concerns me that many applications of CBT would be more effectively (and cheaply) developed by simple printed texts or guides."

*   *   *

WHITWORTH, Reginald Henry   1910-

PERSONAL: Born August 27, 1910, in Wantage, England; son of Aymer William and Alice Lucy (Hervey) Whitworth; married June Rachel Edwards, June 28, 1946; children: Charles, Patrick, Teresa (Mrs. Roger Palmer). *Education:* Balliol College, Oxford, M.A. (with first class honors), 1938; attended Queen's College, Oxford, 1938-49. *Politics:* Conservative. *Religion:* Church of England. *Home:* Old Manor House, Letcombe Regis, Wantage, Berkshire, England.

CAREER: British Army, career officer, 1940-70, with Grenadier Guards, 1940-57, in SHAPE, 1957-59, instructor at Joint Services Staff College, 1959-61, commander of Berlin Infantry Brigade Group, 1961-63, deputy military secretary at Ministry of Defence in London, 1963-66, general officer commanding Yorkshire District, 1966-67, and Northumbrian District, 1967-68, chief of staff of Southern Command, 1968-70, retiring as major general; Oxford University, Oxford, England, bursar and fellow of Exeter College, 1970-81; writer, 1981—. Chairman of Army Museums Ogilby Trust; member of board of governors of Felsted School, St. Mary's School, and Gordon Boys' School. Chairman of Conservative Party Group of Abingdon Constituency. *Member:* Royal United Services Institute, Society of Army Historical Research. *Awards, honors*—Military: U.S. Bronze Star. Other: Commander of Order of the British Empire; Companion of Order of the Bath.

WRITINGS: Field Marshal Ligonier, Oxford University Press, 1958; *Famous Regiments: The Grenadier Guards*, Leo Cooper, 1974. Contributor to military and history journals. Member of editorial council of *Journal of Army Historical Research*.

WORK IN PROGRESS: William Augustine, Duke of Cumberland, 1721-65; a chapter to be included in *Forts and Fortification in the British Isles*.

*   *   *

WICKES, Kim   1947-

PERSONAL: Born May 27, 1947, in Korea; daughter of George (a powerhouse engineer) and Eva Wickes. *Education:* Attended Wheaton College, Wheaton, Ill., 1965-66; Indiana University, B.Mus., 1969, M.Mus., 1971; attended Vienna Institute of Music and Dramatic Arts, 1973-74. *Home address:* P.O. Box 1370, West Memphis, Ark. 72301.

CAREER: Kim's Ministries, Inc., West Memphis, Ark., director and evangelistic singer, 1976—. Producer and director of radio program "Daybreak With Kim," 1980-81; soloist for Christian Freedom Foundation and Christians Concerned. *Member:* Gospel Music Association, Mu Phi Epsilon, Pi Kappa Lambda. *Awards, honors:* Fulbright fellow in Austria, 1973-74.

WRITINGS: (With Hugh Steven) *Kim: "I Will Make Darkness Light"* (autobiography), Harvest House, 1975. Also author of radio scripts for "Daybreak With Kim," 1980-81. Publisher and contributor to *Christian Love Letter From Kim*.

Producer of and featured artist on record albums, including "The Lord Is My Light," 1978, "Christmas With Kim," 1980, and "Kim Thanks God," 1981.

WORK IN PROGRESS: Treasures of Darkness, nonfiction.

SIDELIGHTS: Sue Ferguson, Kim Wickes's secretary, told *CA* about her employer: "Kim is totally blind from injuries received during the Korean War. Naturally, she has a special interest in the problems of the blind. As a result of Kim's efforts, Senator Vance Hartke introduced a bill to the U.S. Senate in 1973 to provide for paper money to be marked with braille numerals signifying the denomination.

"Kim is a brave and inspiring person who cares for her own business and travels (often alone and often around the world). *Treasures of Darkness* is a collection of stories from her personal experiences, reflecting the peculiar problems of a blind woman with her particular responsibilities. She is also vitally interested in biblical research."

*　　*　　*

WIGHAM, Eric Leonard 1904-

PERSONAL: Born October 8, 1904, in Chungking, China; son of Leonard (a Quaker missionary) and Caroline (a Quaker missionary; maiden name, Southall) Wigham; married Jane Dawson, October 14, 1929; children: Judith Ann Wigham Reeves Field. *Education:* University of Birmingham, M.A. (with honors), 1925. *Politics:* Social Democrat. *Religion:* None. *Home:* Link View, The Avenue, West Wickham, Kent BR4 0DX, England.

CAREER: Newcastle Chronicle, Newcastle upon Tyne, England, reporter and special writer, 1925-29; *Newcastle Evening World,* Newcastle upon Tyne, reporter and special writer, 1929-32; *Manchester Evening News,* Manchester, England, reporter, film critic, literary editor, and leader writer, 1932-40, in London office, 1940-44; *Observer,* London, England, war correspondent from northern Europe, 1944-45; *Manchester Guardian,* Manchester, Labour correspondent, 1945-46; *Times,* London, Labour correspondent, 1946-69; free-lance journalist, 1969-82. Member of Royal Commission on Trade Unions and Employers' Associations, 1965-68. *Member:* National Union of Journalists (life member; chairman of Manchester branch, 1937).

WRITINGS: Trade Unions, Home University Library, 1956, 2nd edition, 1969; *What's Wrong With the Unions,* Penguin, 1961; *The Power to Manage: A History of the Engineering Employers' Federation,* Macmillan, 1973; *Strikes and the Government, 1893-1973,* Macmillan, 1976, revised and enlarged edition published as *Strikes and the Government, 1893-1981,* 1982. Also author of *From Humble Petition to Militant Action: A History of the Civil and Public Services Association,* 1980. Contributor to journals, including *Business News.*

SIDELIGHTS: Wigham told *CA:* "My books arose naturally out of my job as Labour correspondent, which brought me into contact with trade union leaders, employers, and the Ministry of Labour and other government departments over a long period. This association prompted me to reflect on labor relations during a time when they aroused much controversy. *What's Wrong With the Unions* included a long list of faults and suggested remedies, but expressed the conviction that more is right with them than is wrong. The close relations of the unions with the Labour party and of employees with the Conservatives have resulted in regular reversals of labor legislation and policies as governments alternated. This, I have argued, has prevented any stability or steady progress in labor relations."

WILCOX, Donald J(ames) 1938-

PERSONAL: Born August 29, 1938, in Putnam, Conn.; son of Harold A. (an electrician) and Ellen (a bookkeeper; maiden name, Stockton) Wilcox. *Education:* Wesleyan University, Middletown, Conn., B.A., 1961; Harvard University, M.A., 1962, Ph.D., 1967. *Home:* 29 Mill Rd., Durham, N.H. 03824. *Office:* Department of History, University of New Hampshire, HSSC 405, Durham, N.H. 03824.

CAREER: Harvard University, Cambridge, Mass., assistant professor of history, 1967-70; University of New Hampshire, Durham, associate professor, 1970-75, professor of history and chairman of department, 1975—. *Member:* Renaissance Society of America.

WRITINGS: The Development of Florentine Humanist Historiography in the Fifteenth Century, Harvard University Press, 1969; *In Search of God and Self,* Houghton, 1975.

WORK IN PROGRESS: Classical Rhetoric and Medieval Historiography; Sense of Time in Western History, completion expected in 1988.

*　　*　　*

WILENSKI, Peter Stephen 1939-

PERSONAL: Born May 10, 1939, in Lodz, Poland; son of Jan and Halina Wilenski; married Gail Gordon Radford, 1967 (divorced, 1981). *Education:* University of Sydney, M.B., B.S., 1962; Oxford University, B.A., 1966, M.A., 1970; Carlton University, M.A., 1969; Harvard University, M.P.A., 1970. *Politics:* Australian Labour party. *Home:* 7 Springfield Ave., Potts Point, Sydney, New South Wales 2011, Australia. *Office:* Institute of Advanced Studies, Australian National University, P.O. Box 1, Canberra, Australian Capital Territory 2601, Australia.

CAREER: Resident medical officer of Royal North Shore Hospital, 1963-64; Australian Embassy, Saigon, Vietnam, second secretary, 1967-68; Australian High Commission, Ottawa, Ontario, second secretary, 1968-69; member of aid policy section of Department of Foreign Affairs, 1970-71; principal private secretary in Office of the Prime Minister, 1972-74; special adviser to Royal Commission on Australian Government Administration, 1975; secretary of Department of Labour and Immigration, 1975; first division officer of Australian Public Service, 1976—. Fellow of University of Sydney, 1962-64, 1974—; foundation professor at Australian National University, 1977-81, professor, 1981—; visiting professor at University of New South Wales, 1977-81; visiting scholar at National Academy of Public Admiistration, 1980. Member of Australian Development Assistance Advisory Board, 1974-75; chairman of Australian Council for Union Training, 1975; commissioner of Review of New South Wales Government Administration, 1977-82; consultant to Organization for Economic Cooperation and Development and governments of Zimbabwe and Papua New Guinea.

MEMBER: Australian Institute of Political Science (member of board of directors, 1977), Australian Institute of Public Opinion (member of council, 1979-81), Australian Political Science Association, American Political Science Association, American Society for Public Administration, Conference of Socialist Economists, Royal Institute of Public Administration.

WRITINGS: Medical Care Delivery Systems in the People's Republic of China, International Development Research Center, 1976; *Directions for Change,* New South Wales Government Printer, 1977; (with N. Viviani) *The Australian Development* (monograph), Royal Institute of Public Administration, 1978; (editor with S. Encel) *Decisions: Case Studies in Public Policy,* Longman-Cheshire, 1981; *Unfinished Agenda,* New South Wales Government Printer, 1982. Contributor to academic journals.

WORK IN PROGRESS: Democracy, Bureaucracy, and Social Justice (tentative title); research on social justice in Australia and on administrative reform.

* * *

WILHOIT, Francis M(arion) 1920-

BRIEF ENTRY: Born April 24, 1920, in Carthage, N.C. American historian, political scientist, educator, and author. Wilhoit has been a newspaper editorial writer, bank cashier, and language teacher. He also taught history at Mercer University and University of Miami in Coral Gables, Florida, and in 1961 he became a professor of political science at Drake University. In 1973 the educator received the Chastain Award of the Southern Political Science Association. Wilhoit wrote *The Politics of Massive Resistance* (Braziller, 1973) and *The Quest for Equality in Freedom* (Transaction Books, 1979). *Address:* 3103 University Ave., Apt. 6, Des Moines, Iowa 50311; and Department of Political Science, Drake University, 25th St. and University Ave., Des Moines, Iowa 50311. *Biographical/critical sources: American Historical Review,* December, 1975.

* * *

WILKINS, Roger (Wood) 1932-

BRIEF ENTRY: Born March 25, 1932, in Kansas City, Mo. American lawyer, government official, journalist, and author. Wilkins, nephew of late NAACP (National Association for the Advancement of Colored People) head Roy Wilkins, practiced international law in New York City for six years following his graduation from the University of Michigan Law School. In 1962 he became special assistant to the head of the Agency for International Development and two years later went to work in the Justice Department, where he served as assistant attorney general from 1966 to 1969. After leaving government service Wilkins spent three years as program director for the Ford Foundation. From 1972 to 1974 he was an editorial writer for the *Washington Post.* Wilkins then joined the editorial board of the *New York Times,* where he also served as urban affairs columnist. He has since left the *New York Times* and joined the editorial board of *Nation.* Wilkins is the author of *A Man's Life: An Autobiography* (Simon & Schuster, 1982), in which he relates the bittersweet emotions he experienced as a successful black man in the predominantly white ruling class of American society. *Biographical/critical sources: Who's Who Among Black Americans,* 3rd edition, Who's Who Among Black Americans, 1981; *Harper's,* April, 1982; *New York Times,* June 14, 1982; *New York Times Book Review,* June 20, 1982; *Newsweek,* August 2, 1982.

* * *

WILKINSON, Alec 1952-

PERSONAL: Born March 29, 1952, in Mt. Kisco, N.Y.; son of Kirk Cook (an artist) and Carolyn (a magazine writer; maiden name, Gunzer) Wilkinson; married Celia Ownes (an artist), October 7, 1978; children: Benjamin Robertson (stepson). *Education:* Bennington College, B.A., 1974. *Home:* 250 Mul-

berry St., New York, N.Y. 10012. *Agent:* Amanda Urban, International Creative Management, 40 West 57th St., New York, N.Y. 10019. *Office: New Yorker,* 25 West 43rd St., New York, N.Y. 10036.

CAREER: Worked as a police officer in Wellfleet, Mass., 1975; Provincetown Art Association, Provincetown, Mass., researcher, 1978; *New Yorker,* New York, N.Y., reporter, 1981—.

WRITINGS: Midnights: A Year With the Wellfleet Police, Random House, 1982.

SIDELIGHTS: Although Wilkinson had no training in law enforcement, after graduating from college he applied for a job with the nine-man police force of Wellfleet, a small tourist town on Cape Cod. One of only three applicants, he was hired, given a uniform, and assigned to the midnight shift as a rookie officer. Since the area's crime rate was too low to keep a nine-man force busy, especially at midnights, Wilkinson often found himself lonely and bored. So, after serving on midnights for a year, he resigned from the force. His experiences are recorded in *Midnights: A Year With the Wellfleet Police.*

Reviewing the book in *Time,* Paul Gray called *Midnights* "both a comedy of errors and an affectionate portrait of small-town police." *New York Times* reviewer Christopher Lehmann-Haupt agreed, adding that the appeal of Wilkinson's account is in its emphasis on an inexperienced bungler in a quiet little town who brushes up against nothing more serious than unruly drunks, suspicious townspeople, and other things that go bump in the night. Wilkinson's first attempt to make an arrest was "a Keystone Kops affair so badly bungled that it may possibly still be giving the department a hangover," according to Lehmann-Haupt.

In his *New York York Times Book Review* critique author Peter Benchley suggested that "Mr. Wilkinson presents a mundane and apparently uninteresting subject—the days and nights, the trials and tediums, of a policeman's lot in a tiny town—and, by examining it with microscopic attention, fairly enchants the reader into caring about the subject and wanting to read on." "The tedious side of policework rarely figures in TV serials or bestselling novels," Gray concurred. "*Midnights* offers a healthy antidote to all those shoot-em-ups, a reminder that those assigned to protect are often vulnerable and quietly heroic."

BIOGRAPHICAL/CRITICAL SOURCES: New York Times, July 16, 1982; *Time,* July 26, 1982; *Harper's,* August, 1982; *Los Angeles Times,* August 9, 1982; *Washington Post,* August 11, 1982; *New York Times Book Review,* August 22, 1982.

* * *

WILKINSON, C. E. 1948-

PERSONAL: Born June 22, 1948, in Boston, Mass.; daughter of T. L. (a certified public accountant) and Helen (Zubrynska) Wilkinson; married Chris Gianniotis (a systems analyst), May 19, 1981. *Education:* State University of New York College at Old Westbury, B.A., 1971; Sarah Lawrence College, M.F.A., 1973. *Politics:* None. *Religion:* Tibetan Buddhist. *Residence:* New York, N.Y. *Agent:* Howard Morhaim, Howard Morhaim Literary Agency, 501 Fifth Ave., New York, N.Y. 10017.

CAREER: Kuku Ryku Theatre Laboratory, New York, N.Y., associate director, 1971-78, artistic director, 1978—. *Member:* Dramatists Guild. *Awards, honors:* Resident at Millay Colony, 1979.

WRITINGS: For Neruda/For Chile, Beacon Press, 1978.

Plays: (Co-author) "Island" (one-act), first produced in New York, N.Y., at Byrd Hoffman Space, 1973; (co-author) "Going Home" (one-act), first produced in New York, N.Y., at Performing Garage, 1975; "Mr. Cripple Kicks the Bucket" (one-act), first produced in New York, N.Y., at Cloud Chamber, 1977; (co-author) "Briar Rose" (one-act), first produced in New York, N.Y., at Kuku Ryku Theatre Laboratory, 1977; "Ethel and Julius Rosenburg Meet Sacco and Vanzetti; or, Patrick Henry in Hell" (two-act), first produced in New York, N.Y., at Cloud Chamber, 1978; "She Only Beats Her Dogs to Death Because She Is Unhappy" (one-act), as yet unproduced.

Work represented in anthologies, including *An Anthology of Women Poets*, Dremen Press. Contributor of poems to magazines, including *Paris Review, Mississippi Review, Chelsea,* and *Nimrod.*

WORK IN PROGRESS: A novel; "Idi Dada," a musical play about Idi Amin; poems.

SIDELIGHTS: Wilkinson wrote that she is interested in translating arcane Tibetan philosophical tracts.

*   *   *

WILLE, Janet Neipris   1936-
(Janet Neipris)

PERSONAL: Surname is pronounced *Wil*-lee; surname of pen name rhymes with "cypress"; born March 11, 1936, in Boston, Mass.; daughter of Samuel (a salesman) and Dorothy (an administrative assistant; maiden name, Danis) Brown; married Marvin Neipris, September 2, 1957 (divorced, 1979); married Donald J. Wille (an engineer), June 22, 1980; children: Cynthia, Carolyn, Ellen; stepchildren: Christine Wille, Neil Wille. *Education:* Tufts University, B.A. (cum laude), 1957; Simmons College, M.A., 1973; Brandeis University, M.F.A., 1975. *Home:* 4 Washington Square Village, No. 17E, New York, N.Y. 10012. *Agent:* Helen Merrill, 337 West 22nd St., New York, N.Y. 10011. *Office:* Dramatic Writing Department, Tisch School of the Arts, New York University, Washington Square, New York, N.Y. 10003.

CAREER: University of Montana, Missoula, playwright-in-residence, 1975; Drew University, Madison, N.J., instructor in playwriting, 1975-76; Goddard College, Plainfield, Vt., instructor in playwriting in graduate writing program, 1975-79; WCVB-TV (ABC), Boston, Mass., staff writer for comedy series "The Baxters," 1977-80; Harvard University, Cambridge, Mass., instructor in playwriting in continuing education department, 1978-80; Tufts University, Medford, Mass., instructor in creative writing, 1978-81; Smith College, Northampton, Mass., playwright-in-residence and instructor, 1980; New York University, New York, N.Y., associate professor of dramatic writing, 1980— . Member of playwrights unit of Circle Repertory Co., 1980— , and American Place Theatre Women's Project, 1980— . Contributing writer for "Women '77," WBZ-TV, Boston, Mass., 1977, and "Impact," WJZ-TV, Baltimore, Md., 1978. Panelist on "Women in the Media," Harvard University, 1979, "Radio Drama in America and England," WGBH-Radio, Cambridge, Mass., 1979, and "American Drama," Theatre Communications Group of Yale University, 1980. *Member:* Dramatists Guild, Writers Guild of America, East, Authors League of America. *Awards, honors:* Sam S. Shubert playwriting fellowship, 1974-75; National Endowment for the Humanities fellowship in playwriting, 1979-80.

*WRITINGS—*Plays; under name Janet Neipris: "A Time to Remember" (two-act musical), first produced in Boston, Mass., at Statler Hilton, 1967; "Abe Lincoln" (one-act musical), first produced in Winchester, Mass., at Winchester Public Schools, 1969; "The Princess and the Dragon" (one-act musical), first produced in Boston at Boston Arts Festival, 1969; "The Little Bastard" (one-act musical), first produced in Boston at Simmons College, 1971; "Statues" (one-act), first produced in Waltham, Mass., at Brandeis University, 1974, produced in New York at Manhattan Theatre Club, 1977; "Exhibition" (one-act), first produced at Brandeis University, 1975, produced Off-Off Broadway at Cubiculo Theatre, 1975; "The Bridge at Belharbour" (one-act), first produced at Brandeis University, 1975, produced Off-Off Broadway at Cubiculo Theatre, 1975; "Jeremy and the Thinking Machine" (one-act musical), first produced Off-Off Broadway at Thirteenth Street Theatre, 1977; "Flying Horses" (two-act), first produced in Missoula, Mont., at University of Montana, 1977; "Separations" (two-act), first produced in Washington, D.C., at Arena Stage Theatre, 1978; "The Desert" (two-act), first produced in Milwaukee, Wis., at Milwaukee Repertory Theatre, 1979; "Out of Order" (two-act), first produced in New York at Harold Clurman Theatre, 1980; "The Agreement" (one-act), first produced in Westport, Conn., at Town Hall Playwrights Series, 1982. Author of three radio dramas for PBS's "Earplay" series; "The Desert," 1979, "The Agreement," 1980, and "The Piano," 1981.

Also author of "How Does Your Garden Grow," a drama first broadcast by WCVB-TV, Boston, Mass., 1977, and "The President's Assistants," a situation comedy pilot series first broadcast by American Broadcasting Co., 1978. Contributor of articles to newspapers and magazines, including *Washington Star, Sidelines,* and *Writer.*

WORK IN PROGRESS: A play, "The Southernmost Tip."

SIDELIGHTS: Neipris told *CA:* "A recent play, 'Out of Order,' is about a man trying to make order in the universe—that's the playwright's task, too. I'm concerned with moral disconnection. All my plays, though I always think I'm writing a new one, are about the same thing—people looking for connections. I like the play form, particularly, because its major concern is people. Creating a character means making something in the universe that wasn't there before."

*   *   *

WILLEE, Albert William   1916-1982

PERSONAL: Born August 3, 1916, in Brighton, England; died October 18, 1982; married Kathleen Anne Minter (in nursing), September, 1939; children: Paul Andrew, Roger Cedric. *Education:* University of London, B.A. (with honors), 1937, Diploma in Physical Education, 1938; University of Melbourne, B.Ed., 1957; University of Oregon, M.S., 1962, Ph.D., 1964. *Home:* 24 Belgravia Ave., Box Hill North, Victoria 3129, Australia.

CAREER: Assistant master of private boys' secondary school in Nuneaton, England, 1939-40; University of London, Goldsmith's College, London, England, lecturer in physical education, 1947-50; University of Melbourne, Parkville, Australia, 1950-78, began as lecturer, became senior lecturer, reader in human movement studies and chairman of department, 1978-81, director of physical education, 1963-77. *Military service:* Royal Navy, 1940-46. Royal Australian Naval Reserve, 1950-63; became lieutenant commander.

MEMBER: Federation Internationale d'Education Physique (vice-president), International Council for Health, Physical Education and Recreation (past member of executive committee; vice-president, 1977-81), Australian Council for Health, Physical Education and Recreation (life member), Statistical Society of Australia, Ergonomics Society of Australia and New Zealand (chairman of Victorian branch, 1972-76), Australian College of Education, Australian Sports Medicine Federation, Australian Physical Education Association (vice-president, 1964-68), Australian Physical Education Association (vice-president, 1964-68), Australian Universities Physical Education Association (vice-president), Australian Naval Association, Royal Institute of Public Health and Hygiene, Physical Education Association of Great Britain and Ireland (fellow), American Association of Directors of Fitness in Industry, American Academy of Physical Education (corresponding fellow), Victorian State Recreation Council, Victorian Soccer Federation, National Fitness Council of Victoria (member of council and executive committee), United Service Institute of Victoria, Royal Australian Navy Historical Society, Royal Commonwealth Society, Naval and Military Club, Royal Automobile Club of Victoria.

WRITINGS: Small Apparatus for Primary School Physical Education, Melbourne University Press, 1956; *Dynamic Football: A Guide to Fitness,* Lansdowne, 1967; *Have You Ever Seen a Monkey With Back Trouble?,* Unicorn, 1980. Also co-author with L. C. Williams of *Playground Games for Secondary Boys,* 1954. Editor of *Australian Journal of Physical Education,* 1954-60, 1962-75.

[Date of death provided by wife, Kathleen Anne Willee]

* * *

WILLIAMS, Colin   1934-
(Colin Welland)

PERSONAL: Born in July, 1934, in Liverpool, England; son of John Arthur and Norah Williams; married Patricia Sweeney, 1962; children: one son, three daughters. *Education:* Attended Bretton Hall College and Goldsmith's College, London. *Politics:* Labour Party. *Residence:* Barnes, England. *Agent:* c/o Anthony Jones, A.D. Peters Ltd., 10 Buckingham St., London WC2N 6BU, England.

CAREER: Actor and writer. Worked as art teacher, 1958-62; associated with Library Theatre in Manchester, England, 1962-64; actor in stage productions, including "The Birthday Party," and in motion pictures, including "Straw Dogs," 1971, and "Sweeney," 1977. Director of Radio Aire; director of Fulham Rugby League Club. *Awards, honors:* Best television writer and best supporting film actor awards from British Academy of Film and Television Arts, 1970; awards from Writers Guild, 1970, 1973, and 1974; Broadcasting Press Guild Award, 1973; Academy Award for best original screenplay from Academy of Motion Picture Arts and Sciences, 1981, for "Chariots of Fire."

*WRITINGS—*All under pseudonym Colin Welland; published plays: *A Roomful of Holes* (teleplay), Davis-Poynter, 1971; *Say Goodnight to Grandma* (three-act; first produced in Manchester, England, at the Manchester Forum, December 16, 1972; adapted from the teleplay by Welland, "Say Goodnight to Your Grandma"), St. Martin's, 1973; *Roll on Four O'Clock* (teleplay), Palace, 1981.

Screenplays: (With Walter Bernstein) "Yanks," Universal, 1979; "Chariots of Fire," Warner Bros., 1981.

Teleplays: "Bangelstein's Boys," 1968; "Slattery's Mounted Foot," 1970; (with William Gaunt and Janet Key) "Catherine Wheel," 1970; "The Hallelujah Handshake," 1970; "Say Goodnight to Your Grandma," 1970; "Kisses at Fifty," 1973; "Jack Point," 1973; "Leeds—United!" 1974. Also author of "Your Man From Six Counties" and of scripts for "The Wild West Show" series, 1975.

WORK IN PROGRESS: "Chaplin," a screenplay based on the life of Charlie Chaplin.

SIDELIGHTS: Welland is best known for his screenplay "Chariots of Fire." The film earned Academy Awards for best original screenplay and best film of 1981. It tells the true story of runners Harold Abrahams and Eric Liddell and their rivalry in 1924. The film peaks during the 1924 Olympics. Liddell, a devout Christian, refuses to enter a qualifying heat in the 100-meter race because it is to take place on a Sunday. Abrahams, a Jew acutely sensitive to anti-Semitism, is disappointed by Liddell's subsequent absence in this major race. Finding himself pitted against two American runners, however, Abrahams rises to the challenge, and emerges victorious in the 100-meter event. A teammate scheduled to run in the 400-meter race relinquishes his spot so that Liddell can also have his chance at victory. Liddell qualifies, runs, and, like Abrahams, is triumphant. "Chariots of Fire" was praised for both its subtlety and its exciting scenes of competition. "Seeing *Chariots of Fire* is like exploring a wonderful historical restoration," wrote *Time*'s Richard Schickel. He called it "a lovely work" and described it as "strangely evocative and moving." *Saturday Review*'s Judith Crist agreed, deeming "Chariots of Fire" "a stunning film, an inspiring story of aspiration and accomplishment, a fact-based thriller and a perceptive social statement."

Prior to writing "Chariots of Fire," Welland contributed the script to "Yanks," which John Schlesinger directed in 1979. The film features three independent tales of love during World War II. In the *New York Times,* Vincent Canby described it as a film "about the effects of war on people far from the front, making do as best they can under circumstances that are demanding in direct relation to boredom, homesickness, loneliness and inconvenience." Canby only found portions of the film acceptable, however, and complained that "the lovers and their various crises never rise above the perfunctory."

Welland has also gained notoriety in England for his plays. John Lawrence, writing in *The Stage,* noted that both "Bangelstein's Boys" and "Slattery's Mounted Foot" "are concerned about the ways tightly-knit groups of people protect themselves from the hostile attention of outsiders, and specifically, how men create for themselves a kind of mystique which shields them from the realities of life in general, and the emotional demands of their wives in particular." In "Say Goodnight to Your Grandma," Welland also explores the situation of a husband perplexed by the rivalry between his wife and her mother. A reviewer for *The Stage* wrote that "Say Goodnight to Your Grandma" "makes for exciting theatre and reveals considerable powers of observation on the part of its author."

CA INTERVIEW

CA interviewed Colin Welland by telephone on September 12, 1982, at his home in Barnes, near London.

CA: You're highly respected as an actor, playwright, television writer, and screenwriter, having turned to drama after teaching art for four years. Was the move from teaching to acting a complete switch, or had you done some amateur acting before?

WELLAND: I had done some acting at school, but none after that as an amateur. I seem to have an inbuilt resistance to amateur acting. I never felt that it was up to standard, if you know what I mean. I always felt I'd need to demand more of myself than the standards achieved in amateur groups.

CA: How did you decide after teaching art for four years to go into acting?

WELLAND: My wife and I were engaged at the time. She was working at the school just down the road. I was teaching tolerably well, but I was finding that it wasn't making any demands of me. I didn't feel stretched at all. Also I had a resistance to security, knowing exactly what I'd be doing in ten years' time. I missed excitement; I missed uncertainty. I had been regarded as talented in the theatre at school and I'd done some producing at college, so I decided to try that aspect of my abilities, to see if I could break away from the treadmill. I said to Pat, "I want to become an actor," and she said, "Well, I don't want to be married to a teacher for the rest of my life." So I applied around to all the repertory companies in the country and finally got an audition with the Manchester Library Theatre, which was one of the leading reps in the country. The director gave me an audition, and I sang a song from Gilbert and Sullivan that I remembered from school days. Whether he was impressed by my confidence in doing something so banal for an audition I don't know, but he put me in the company, and I was cast in the lead in "The Birthday Party" in the first production of that season. And from then on I never looked back, really.

CA: Then you acted in repertory for a while before you went into television?

WELLAND: I acted for a year in rep. And I regarded it as my university, the best way to learn the craft of the stage and the whole business of being in a profession like that. After a year I was offered a job as a television newscaster in Manchester. I thought it would be a good idea getting out of rep and learning a bit about television, so I did that for about a month. Then I got my first part on television, in an ad-lib show called "The Verdict Is Yours." It presented court cases in which the procedure of law was completely reproduced. I was the accused, and as the accused I had, with the help of actors pretending to be counsels, to prepare a case in my defense, although I wasn't sure whether I was innocent or not. Another group of actors had to prepare a case for the prosecution. The court listened to the case, and viewers were invited in to form a jury to decide whether I was guilty or not. That was my first job on television as an actor, and it was purely ad-lib. From there I went into a long-running series called "Zed Cars," which is "Z Cars" in your terminology. I played a cop, and I was in that series for about three and a half years. That is how my acting career got started.

CA: When did you first get interested in writing?

WELLAND: I'd always been interested in writing. Apart from art, I taught English as well. I had written essays and short pieces on sports for newspapers. I'd always dabbled with the written word. When I became familiar with the television art, I realized that perhaps I had something to say on those terms. So I started to write plays for television, which we have in

this country and you don't seem to have. There are always five or six slots a week in British television where you have single plays which are performed either in the studio or on film, lasting anywhere from fifty minutes to ninety minutes. They're a wonderful opportunity for new writers and young writers to express themselves. It was through this form that I was able to establish myself as a writer. I wrote thirty different plays, varying in length, always contemporary, always commenting on social events and situations, very often involving experiences of my own family or people I knew. Generally the people watching them found them very pertinent to their own experience, and I gained a reputation as a writer who was writing for the common people, the voice of the ordinary person who normally doesn't have a voice.

CA: Do you think your acting experience helped a great deal in writing the plays?

WELLAND: Oh yes. Writers who don't act don't realize the problems. On a very simplistic level, they don't realize that the actors have to breathe; they write mouthfuls that are impossible to speak, tongue twisters. They don't realize the way an actor loves alliteration. They don't give him phrases that he can wrap his tongue around. Equally they don't realize that every actor, regardless of the size of his part, wants to feel that he is making a real contribution to the play or the film, so that the audience are more informed, perhaps more entertained, when he is finished than they were before he came on. So every part I ever write, regardless of its size, I like to make meaty and give the actor something to chew on. I think you'll find that in "Chariots of Fire"; every part has some humor, some pertinence, and certainly you feel that another human being has walked through the screen and not just another cipher.

CA: Are there writers who have directly influenced your own writing?

WELLAND: In the early days Harold Pinter influenced me. I had studied drama at school and at college, but it was always on a very academic level and never got more contemporary than George Bernard Shaw. When I first read Pinter's plays and acted in them, I realized that here was the sort of language I had around me all day and every day, that it was valid and that it did have a place in the creative theatre. That gave me the encouragement to write at the very beginning. It taught me that one didn't have to write in highfalutin, "intellectual" terms and to have a vast vocabulary and to have a keen mind that was able to analyze. One could make a contribution by simply caring, having emotional reactions to situations, listening to and reproducing what one saw around him.

CA: Reviewers have indeed commented on your "considerable powers of observation" and your talent for "seeing the drama of ordinary situations."

WELLAND: Well, the point is that there are stories in abundance in every street, down every alley. I cannot understand why people ask me where I get my stories from. More dramatic power can be generated in a three-room domestic abode than in any palace. This is what I try to build my work on. Pinter did this, you see. Pinter would take a room, put three characters in it, and create a theatrical charge the like of which hadn't been seen for years. You don't need to cover vast panoramas, great canvases, to do this. In fact, that very often diffuses the drama. This is a mistake often made in movies.

CA: Have you done any directing?

WELLAND: I've directed my own work on the stage, but I haven't directed any films.

CA: I think you're best recognized in the United States as the author of the screenplay for "Chariots of Fire." Were you much involved in the production of "Chariots" and your earlier movie, "Yanks"?

WELLAND: Yes. There's a tradition in this country, you see. Most of us have come through television—directors, writers, producers—and here television's values are based on the theatre, in which the writer is paramount. It isn't John Schlesinger's such-and-such a thing on the stage; it's Harold Pinter's "The Birthday Party." And on our television it's Colin Welland's "Kisses at Fifty." However much contribution is made by the director, it is still the author's work. And although we have adopted the film priority to a degree in making the director the kingpin and the autocrat in the valuation of the film, we still feel the writer has a very, very strong contribution to make. Consequently directors and producers who have come up through television are used to using the writer's comments and opinions and expertise and knowledge on the subject which nobody else can have but that the writer has through the creation of the film.

During the filming of "Chariots of Fire," Hugh Hudson would call me from location and say, "We're having difficulty with this line; what do you think it means? What do you think someone's reaction would be? Could you change it for us? Could you rewrite that a little bit?" And I'd probably go to Scotland, if they were filming there, and have a look. In England you are not just a dialogue writer; you are a part of the creative process, and this is something which I would love to see happen in America. I think writers are treated abominably in America. If that changes, it'll be to the benefit of the U.S. film industry as a whole.

CA: Certainly many writers have despaired of writing for American television also, because they feel it's so commercial.

WELLAND: You've got to know your animal. The entertainment business is a big multiringed circus. You've got to know what you're writing for and to accept its rules. I don't think American television has any pretense or any aspirations to be artistic. It's a commercial enterprise, and if you choose to write for it you've got to accept it on those terms. But the film industry, although it is largely a commercial enterprise as well, also aspires to be creative and artistic. And not to recognize the sanctity of the writer's opinion is to play with fire. This business of directors chopping and changing, bringing new writers in, marketing the script out to anybody who'll have a go at it—it's suicide. A script isn't something which has been manufactured by a computer, and you can't treat it like that. It's a living organism. Stick with your writer, I would say; stick with your writer. He's the man who conceived it in the first place. He knows it better than anybody else. Trevor Griffiths, who wrote "Reds" with Warren Beatty, being an Englishman and writing in our tradition, was very upset about the way that script was mauled around. This comes from the days when filmmaking was just a case of taking your camera on your shoulder, going to a location with a few actors, and hiring somebody on hand who could write dialogue. The story came out of improvisation. And that sort of tradition continues in Hollywood.

CA: Have you seen a lot of American theatre?

WELLAND: I haven't seen a lot of it, but what I've seen I've liked. I think British theatre is appalling. It has a tradition that should have died with Noel Coward and Ivor Novello on the light side, and most of its grander productions, like the Royal Shakespeare at the National Theatre (with a few honorable exceptions like "Nicholas Nickleby"), are overblown school productions, which I walk out of. They have no relevance to life as it is lived in 1982. And they play to a captive audience of British snobs and American tourists. The National Theatre is no more national theatre. It is the theatre for the London middle and upper class.

CA: Is there no strong regional theatre either?

WELLAND: There is, but they get nowhere near the United States standard. They are playing to a different audience altogether.

CA: Does writing for television and stage and screen ever present any conflicts for you?

WELLAND: No. Again, you've got to realize the rules and the possibilities of the medium you're working in. Television can offer you intimacy, which can be very precious at times when you're putting over very personal emotions. Somebody whose head is life-size in your living room can tell you things and behave in a manner which is very intimate and not be embarrassing, but when you have a head fifteen feet high doing it in a movie theater, it can be most uncomfortable. Television has the advantage there. But it can't handle the sweeping gesture of the heroic scenes. It could never handle the race in "Chariots of Fire" around the quadrangle or the final four hundred meters.

CA: Do you prefer one to the others?

WELLAND: I prefer writing for film, if I can retain the influence that I now enjoy. I don't want to become an adapter of other people's writing, to be just a fellow they bring in to make something work—and it's very tempting, because they'll offer you lots and lots of money, but I want to retain my original voice if I can. I've only written two films, and they've both been originals. I'd like to keep it that way.

CA: Do you still act?

WELLAND: Yes. I do about three big television roles a year. And they're all contemporary. We have a school of writers in this country. We're all more or less on a par with each other in writing for television. I'm lucky in that I've been able to play a part in the works of every one of them. Dennis Potter, who wrote "Pennies From Heaven," is really our leading television writer, and I've been in his work. So I do enjoy a dual career.

CA: What are you working on right now?

WELLAND: I've just finished the first draft of "Chaplin" for MGM. Bob Chartoff, the producer of "Raging Bull" and one of the most eminent producers in American films, got in touch with me when he had seen "Chariots" and asked me if I was interested in Chaplin. As it happened, I was, so he commissioned me to research and write a movie based on Chaplin's life.

CA: Will it be made there in England?

WELLAND: Part of it will. All the first part of his life, up to the age of twenty, was in England. During the middle part of his life, from twenty to the age of fifty-three, he was in America. From fifty-three to eighty-two he was in England and Switzerland.

CA: Casting that lead could be a real problem, couldn't it?

WELLAND: Oh yes. Casting a star in the part would be appalling, because Chaplin himself was a film star par excellence, and you can't have another star battling with that. You've got to find someone who will *be* Chaplin.

CA: There in England you don't seem to have the star system we have here, and I understand that makes for more economical productions and often better ones.

WELLAND: This is absolutely true. Very often American producers put the cart before the horse, approach a film from completely the wrong end. They say, we've got Robert Redford and we want to make a film about Michael Collins. Collins was the most famous Irish countryman who ever lived, and he looked nothing like Robert Redford. You couldn't have found anybody more removed from Robert Redford. But because they've got Redford and he likes the idea of doing it, I am supposed to sit down and write a film about Michael Collins about Robert Redford. And I can't do it.

I've got a film that's making the rounds now, "Kisses at Fifty." We have had the choice of doing it on a low budget with an unknown cast, which I would prefer, or with a star and an enormous budget. This is the battle one is facing all the time. In this country we have a tradition of casting *right,* regardless of whether that means stars or not. Recently I saw Richard Attenborough's "A Bridge Too Far" on television, and it was almost ridiculous: every scene, in would walk another famous face. The atmosphere and what the film was supposed to be about were completely forgotten because you were so interested in who was going to walk in next. It depends again, though, on whether you're just regarding the film as a commercial enterprise. And there are times when casting a star can be absolutely right; Dustin Hoffman playing Lenny Bruce was marvelous.

CA: How do you get away from writing and acting? Any pastimes, hobbies?

WELLAND: I'm very keen on sports—more nonparticipative than I used to be. I played rugby and cricket until I was around thirty-five. Now I am director of a professional rugby club. I'm very keen on athletics, as you saw in "Chariots of Fire." That's how I divert myself. And I have four kids, which is a diversion in itself.

CA: Do you travel much now?

WELLAND: Yes, we do. That's one of the things I like doing most of all. The kids have been to a lot of places. England is very well positioned for traveling; you can go to all the countries in Europe and you're also within easy reach of the Americas.

CA: Would you like to write something different from what you've done so far?

WELLAND: I'd like to write a really good stage play, a play that goes down as a classic of its sort and is done over and over again, is ageless. I went to see "A Doll's House," by Ibsen, the other night and was inspired. I'd really like to write a play like that.

BIOGRAPHICAL/CRITICAL SOURCES: The Stage, June 25, 1970, December 23, 1970, January 6, 1972, January 25, 1973; *New York Times,* September 19, 1979, September 28, 1979; *Chicago Tribune,* October 26, 1979; *Saturday Review,* September, 1981; *Time,* September 21, 1981.*

—*Interview by Jean W. Ross*

* * *

WILLIAMS, David (Frank) 1909-1983

OBITUARY NOTICE: Born June 26, 1909, in Ruthin, Denbighshire, Wales; died after a long illness, May 5, 1983. Educator, broadcaster, book reviewer, novelist, and biographer. Williams was a teacher and school headmaster who published a comic novel in 1956. Then, in his late fifties, he began devoting himself solely to writing. He wrote literary biographies of such authors as Arthur Hugh Clough, George Meredith, the Benson family, George Borrow, and George Henry Lewes. A broadcaster for the BBC (British Broadcasting Corporation) and a contributor to *Punch* and other periodicals, Williams wrote book reviews for the *London Times* for nearly two decades. Obituaries and other sources: *London Times,* May 7, 1983.

* * *

WILLIAMS, Gertrude 1897-1983
(Lady Williams)

OBITUARY NOTICE: Born January 11, 1897; died February 21, 1983. Educator, economist, and author of books in her field. A professor of social economics, Williams taught at the University of London for nearly fifty years, retiring as professor emeritus of social economics in 1964. She also served on many government and public committees and supported the career of her husband, William Emrys Williams, the first editor of Penguin Books. Two of her books, *The State of the Standard of Living,* published in 1936, and *Women and Work,* published in 1946, were considered innovative. Her other publications include *The Price of Social Security, Apprenticeship in Europe: The Lesson for Britain,* and *The Coming of the Welfare State.* Her 1950 book, *The Economics of Everyday Life,* became popular; it was extensively translated and later appeared in a revised and enlarged edition in 1972. Obituaries and other sources: *Who's Who,* 128th edition, St. Martin's, 1976; *London Times,* March 2, 1983.

* * *

WILLIAMS, Gregory 1952-

PERSONAL: Born November 29, 1952, in Los Angeles, Calif.; son of Dino Alex (an artist) and Barbara (a weaver; maiden name, Turner) Williams. *Education:* University of California, Los Angeles, B.A., 1974. *Politics:* "I vote." *Religion:* "I pray." *Home:* 2677 North Beachwood, Los Angeles, Calif. 90068.

CAREER: Bob Baker Productions, Los Angeles, Calif., puppeteer and writer, 1969-79; Puppet Works, Los Angeles, producer, director, and writer, 1976-80; Krofft Entertainment, Los

Angeles, puppeteer and writer, 1981-82; Willis Bonbon, Jr., and Company, Los Angeles, producer and writer, 1982—. *Member:* Puppeteers of America, Unima International Puppeteers, Phi Beta Kappa.

WRITINGS: The Clarissa Caper (juvenile), San Rio, 1978; *Kermit and Cleopatra* (juvenile), Random House, 1981; *The Case of the Missing Hat* (juvenile), Random House, 1982. Also author of material for stage productions, including "The Nutcracker," 1978 and 1979, and television productions, including "The Barbara Mandrell Show," 1982. Editor of *Conservatory of American Puppeteers,* 1977-79.

WORK IN PROGRESS: Material for television, including a special for "Afterschool," ABC-TV, and a series for the Disney Channel; research for a biography of puppeteer Anthony Urbano tentatively titled *Anthony Urbano: The Forgotten Showman.*

SIDELIGHTS: Williams told *CA:* "I started writing children's books for the Muppets after working as a puppeteer in 'The Muppet Movie.' I find my work schedule bounces from performing with puppets to writing for them. It is a nice combination."

*　*　*

WILLIAMS, Lady
    See WILLIAMS, Gertrude

*　*　*

WILLIAMS, Lovett E(dward), Jr.   1935-

PERSONAL: Born May 10, 1935, in Perry, Fla.; son of Lovett E. and Mary (Jones) Williams; married Pamela Richards (a teacher), July 28, 1967; children: Mary Brooke, Heather Keane. *Education:* Attended Sunflower Junior College, 1953-54; Florida State University, B.S., 1957; Auburn University, M.S., 1959. *Home:* 2201 Southeast 41st Ave., Gainesville, Fla. 32601. *Office:* Florida Game and Fresh Water Fish Commission, 4005 South Main St., Gainesville, Fla.

CAREER: Florida Game and Fresh Water Fish Commission, Gainesville, wildlife research biologist, 1962—. *Military service:* U.S. Coast Guard, 1959-62; became lieutenant junior grade. *Member:* Wildlife Society, American Ornithologists Union, National Wild Turkey Federation, Wilson Society, Florida Audubon Society, Florida Academy of Science, Florida Wildlife Federation. *Awards, honors:* Three National Wild Turkey Awards from Penns Woods Products; outstanding scientific paper award from southeastern section of Wildlife Society Society; named conservationist of the year by Florida Wildlife Federation, 1977.

WRITINGS: The Book of the Wild Turkey, Winchester Press, 1981; (with David H. Austin) *Recent Studies of the Wild Turkey in Florida,* Florida Game and Fresh Water Fish Commission, 1983. Contributor of more than one hundred articles to journals in the natural sciences, and of articles to periodicals.

SIDELIGHTS: Williams told *CA:* "I have been doing research on the wild turkey's ecology and behavior for a long time, all the time reading hogwash in the popular press about turkeys and turkey hunting. Turkey hunters are a rare breed. They don't use bird dogs, boats, fancy guns, or other props in their sport. Their success has a nearly 1.0 correlation with their knowledge and personal skills in turkey hunting. Naturally, they are always searching for ways to improve their knowledge and they want

to know *everything* about the wild turkey. It is pure pleasure to write for such an audience. I like to think that somebody is reading every word very carefully. I think that makes me a better writer. I find it very easy to write factually because nature has done more strange things than anybody can ever make up and he will never find them out. Who needs fiction?"

*　*　*

WILLIAMS, Robert Hugh   1907(?)-1983

OBITUARY NOTICE: Born c. 1907 in Arbor Vitae, Wis.; died of cancer, February 15, 1983, near Wales, Wis. Military officer, consultant, researcher, and author. In World War II Williams led a Marine parachute battalion in the Pacific. He took part in several battles and was decorated with a Navy Cross, a Silver Star, and a Purple Heart. He retired from the Marines as brigadier general in 1956. After earning a master's degree in political science he became a military consultant and researcher. He wrote *The Old Corps: A Portrait of the U.S. Marine Corps Between the Wars* and published numerous journal articles. Obituaries and other sources: *Washington Post,* February 22, 1983.

*　*　*

WILLIAMS, Rosalind H.   1944-

PERSONAL: Born July 24, 1944, in Schenectady, N.Y.; daughter of George L. (an engineer) and Rosalind (a teacher of mathematics; maiden name, Lewis) McFarland; married W. Gary Williams (an environmental chemist), August 14, 1968; children: Laurel P., Owen Guy. *Education:* Attended Wellesley College, 1962-64; Radcliffe College, B.A., 1966; University of California, Berkeley, M.A., 1967; University of Massachusetts, Ph.D., 1978. *Home:* 83 Grasmere St., Newton, Mass. 02158.

CAREER: Abt Associates, Inc., Cambridge, Mass., researcher and writer, 1967-68; NeaRad Corp., Fort Lauderdale, Fla., curriculum developer, 1968-69; high school teacher, 1969-71; Massachusetts Institute of Technology, Cambridge, research fellow of Program in Science, Technology, and Society, 1980-82, lecturer in writing program, 1983—. *Member:* Phi Beta Kappa.

WRITINGS: (With Alice Gordon and others) *The Promise of America,* Science Research Associates, 1969; *Dream Worlds: Mass Consumption in Late Nineteenth-Century France,* University of California Press, 1982; (contributor) Roger Yepsen, editor, *The Durability Factor,* Rodale Press, 1982. Contributor to technical journals and newspapers.

WORK IN PROGRESS: Research for a book on modern technologies and ways in which they have encouraged redefinition of the concept of community, including political implications.

SIDELIGHTS: Rosalind Williams wrote: "*Dream Worlds* had its origin in my dissertation work. While I was looking for a topic I became convinced that most work in the history of technology focuses on artifacts of production, tools, or machinery, while the consumer items that these produce, and the way these items have altered human life, have been slighted.

"In another day and age I probably would have become a college teacher, but because these jobs are scarce today, I've become a writer for a more general audience. There are real dangers in this. It's easy to become sloppy or preachy. But in general I'm quite happy trying to do my bit to look at current problems with the benefit of some historical perspective. Too much scholarship never reaches a wider audience, so I feel that the potential benefits of what I'm trying to do outweigh the dangers."

BIOGRAPHICAL/CRITICAL SOURCES: *New York Times Book Review,* August 15, 1982.

* * *

WILLIAMS, Trevor Illtyd 1921-

PERSONAL: Born July 16, 1921; son of Illtyd and Alma Mathilde (Soehlberg) Williams; married, 1945 (divorced, 1952); married Sylvia Irene Armstead, 1952; children: Darryl, Lloyd, Clare, Adam, Benjamin. *Education:* Queen's College, Oxford, D.Phil., 1945. *Home:* 20 Blenheim Dr., Oxford, England; and Penycwm, Corris Uchaf, Machynlleth, Wales.

CAREER: Deputy editor of *Endeavour,* 1945-54, editor, 1954—. Academic relations adviser to Imperial Chemical Industries, 1962-74. Visiting fellow at Australian National University, 1981. Member of advisory council of Science Museum, London, England. *Member:* Royal Society of Chemistry (fellow), Royal Historical Society (fellow), Society for the History of Alchemy and Early Chemistry (chairman). *Awards, honors:* Dexter Award from American Chemical Society, 1976.

WRITINGS: An Introduction to Chromatography, Blackie & Son, 1946, Chemical Publishing, 1947; *Drugs From Plants,* Sigma, 1947; (editor) *The Soil and the Sea,* Saturn Press, 1949; *The Chemical Industry, Past and Present,* Penguin, 1953; *The Elements of Chromatography,* Philosophical Library, c. 1953; (co-editor) *A History of Technology,* Oxford University Press, Volumes I-V, 1954-58, Volumes VI and VII: *The Twentieth Century,* 1978; (with Thomas Kingston Derry) *A Short History of Technology,* Clarendon Press, 1960; (editor) *A Biographical Dictionary of Scientists,* A. & C. Black, 1969, 3rd edition, 1982; *Alfred Bernhard Nobel: Pioneer of High Explosives,* Priory Press, 1973; *James Cook: Scientist and Explorer,* Priory Press, 1974; *Man the Chemist,* Priory Press, 1976; *A History of the British Gas Industry,* Oxford University Press, 1981; *A Short History of Twentieth-Century Technology,* Oxford University Press, 1982. Editor of *Outlook on Agriculture,* 1982—.

WORK IN PROGRESS: An official biography of Lord Florey, for Oxford University Press.

* * *

WILLIAMSON, Richard 1935-

PERSONAL: Born August 1, 1935, in Barnstaple, England; son of Henry William (a writer) and Ida (Hibbert) Williamson; married Anne Brighton (a researcher), March 9, 1964; children: Brent Calvert, Bryony Georgina. *Education:* Attended a private secondary school in Devonshire, England. *Religion:* Church of England. *Home:* Keepers, West Dean Woods, Chichester, Sussex, England. *Agent:* A. M. Heath & Co. Ltd., 40-42 William IV St., London WC2N 4DD, England. *Office:* Nature Conservancy, 18 Belgrave Sq., London, England.

CAREER: Worked as a forester, 1958-60; in agriculture sales, 1960-62; free-lance journalist, 1962-64; Nature Conservancy, London, England, warden of nature reserve, 1964—. *Military service:* Royal Air Force, 1953-58; served in Cyprus. *Awards, honors:* Civil service writers prize from Civil Service Association, 1977, for *The Great Yew Forest.*

WRITINGS: The Dawn Is My Brother (autobiography), Faber, 1959; *Capreol: The Story of a Roebuck,* Macdonald & Jane,

1974; *The Great Yew Forest,* Macmillan, 1978; (editor) Henry Williamson, *The Otter,* Bodley Head, 1980.

Author of "The Man on the Island," a play broadcast by BBC-TV, 1978. Author of "In the Country," a column in *Daily Mail,* 1959-61, "Nature Diary," in Portsmouth newspapers, 1964-74, and "Nature Trails," in Portsmouth newspapers, 1964—. Contributor to magazines.

WORK IN PROGRESS: The Star Swan, a novel about a girl growing up during World War II, publication expected in 1984; *Jagfalk,* a fourteenth-century tale of an Icelandic girl; a biography of his father, Henry Williamson; a story about a sea eagle.

SIDELIGHTS: Williamson told *CA:* "My father was a very successful writer. I find writing difficult as it is not possible to easily combine writing with a full-time and demanding job.

"*The Star Swan* draws on my own childhood but is written on almost a surrealist level, taking the reader back to the Norse legends. One of the characters from my father's books appears here, which might intrigue the reader. I also plan to write a book about American hunters in Afghanistan, the story of an expedition I undertook in 1972 to the borders of China and Russia.

"I am fascinated by the beauty of birds and animals in beautiful places, and by the fact that man can often equal this beauty if he allows it to occur.

"Obviously my life has been influenced in many ways by my father and by his writings. Also, the writers who greatly influenced him, namely Richard Jeffries and W. H. Hudson, are equally my favorites. But I feel that a writer should somehow reflect more than just the obvious, that he should peel off and reveal layers of thought, and lead the reader into associations of ideas and ideals."

* * *

WILLIS, James 1928-

PERSONAL: Born January 12, 1928, in Dublin, Ireland; son of John Robert (a communications engineer) and Agnes (Fitzpatrick) Willis; married Muriel Loder, October 22, 1955; children: Simon, Emma. *Education:* Guy's Hospital Medical School, London, M.B., B.S., 1954. *Office:* King Faisal Specialist Hospital and Research Center, P.O. Box 3354, Riyadh, Saudi Arabia.

CAREER: Pembury Hospital, Kent, England, house officer in medicine, surgery, and obstetrics, 1954-56; Guys Hospital, London, England, registrar in psychiatry, 1956-58; Warlingham Park Hospital, Croydon, England, senior registrar in psychiatry, 1959-60; senior registrar at Institute of Psychiatry, 1960-62; senior registrar in psychiatry, 1962-64; Stonehouse Hospital, Kent, consultant psychiatrist, 1964-66; Warlingham Park Hospital, consultant psychiatrist, 1967; Guys Hospital, consultant psychiatrist, 1967-76; King Faisal Specialist Hospital and Research Center, Riyadh, Saudi Arabia, psychiatrist, 1976-79, head of Division of Psychiatry, 1979-82, deputy medical director of operations, 1982—. *Military service:* Royal Air Force, 1946-48. *Member:* Royal College of Physicians (fellow), Royal College of Psychiatrists (fellow), Royal Society of Medicine.

WRITINGS: Lecture Notes in Psychiatry, Basil Blackwell, 1964, 6th edition, 1983; *Drug Dependence,* Faber, 1969, 2nd edition, 1974; *Addicts: Drugs and Alcohol Re-Examined,* Pitman, 1973; *Clinical Psychiatry,* Basil Blackwell, 1976.

Contributor: J. Cramer, editor, *Practical Treatment in Psychiatry*, Blackwell Scientific, 1969; *Bibliography of Criminology*, Howard League for Penal Reform, 1976; J. G. Houston, Charles Joiner, and John Trounce, editors, *Short Textbook of Medicine*, Hodder & Stoughton, 1977; *Anorectic Drugs*, Raven Press, 1978; *Current Themes in Psychiatry*, S. P. Publications, 1982. Contributor to *Encyclopedia of Ignorance*. Contributor to medical journals.

WORK IN PROGRESS: A transcultural study of hysteria.

SIDELIGHTS: Willis told *CA:* "Originally my main interest was in general psychiatric practice with a heavy orientation towards biological psychiatry, and this has continued. However, in the early 1960's I began to take an interest in research in drug dependence at a time when drug dependency problems were increasing in England, and I published a number of papers on that topic including a quite interesting early one (the first of its sort) in which I compared demographic, clinical, family and other backgrounds of a matched sample of New York and London heroin addicts. Subsequent to this I was in charge of a drug dependence unit in London, in fact one of the major ones, but with the passage of time I found that working exclusively in one subspeciality didn't suit me. I was appointed to a post in Saudi Arabia, which I found extremely challenging; particularly since when I first came, there were no neurologists in the hospital and for the first two years I was both neurologist and psychiatrist.

"Practicing psychiatry in Saudi Arabia is immensely stimulating for a variety of reasons. One of the chief and most fascinating reasons is that the patients receive enormous support from their families, who will often contain very disturbed and psychotic patients who in ordinary life in the U.K. or U.S.A. would be hospitalized. I find the Saudi patients extremely nice people. On the whole, one can summarize them as a quiet, gentle, well-mannered people, with whom one can very easily relate.

"I came to Saudi Arabia for a change of scenery for two years, but have enjoyed the work and my colleagues so much that I have stayed here. Anorexia Nervosa oddly enough was the subject on which I wrote my first paper in collaboration with my then-chief of staff. Again, it is a subject in which I used to take a great deal of interest, but less now. The enormous increase of this condition in the West is, I am sure, culturally determined by the enthusiasm for slimming. People start slimming and can't stop; and these are usually people with quite severe problems. It is an extremely difficult condition to treat as we all know, with a high mortality (4 percent), and I think the basic approach that one should take to it is one of patience and being prepared to go on readmitting the patient time and time again until he or she goes into remission.

"Regarding my general views on the treatment of drug dependence, I feel that the whole question is rendered impossible by the excessive use of law enforcement which has failed to make any impression at all on the drug problem. I have an extremely liberal view towards the management of drug problems and am in favor of the decriminalization of cannabis. Alcohol of course is the most serious drug problem of the Western world and the only way in my view to do much about that is by education in early adolescence; i.e., teaching people how to drink sensibly and also by making drink fairly expensive. Prohibition in any form has been shown to be a complete waste of time."

WILSON, Carroll L(ouis)   1910-1983

OBITUARY NOTICE—See index for *CA* sketch: Born September 21, 1910, in Rochester, N.Y.; died January 13, 1983, in Providence, R.I. Energy expert, business executive, educator, and author. With a career in both private business and in public service, Wilson served as first general manager of the U.S. Atomic Energy Commission from 1947 to 1951. He joined the Massachusetts Institute of Technology faculty in 1959, retiring as Mitsui Professor Emeritus in 1976. He contributed writings to periodicals and to books such as *Man's Impact on the Global Environment: Assessment and Recommendations for Action*, *Energy Demand Studies: Major Consuming Countries*, and *Energy: Global Prospects, 1985-2000*. Obituaries and other sources: *Current Biography*, Wilson, 1947, March, 1983; *New York Times*, January 13, 1983.

*   *   *

WILSON, John Foster   1919-

PERSONAL: Born January 20, 1919, in Nottingham, England; son of George Henry (a minister) and Leonore Carrick (Foster) Wilson; married Chloe Jean McDermid (a deputy director of the Royal Commonwealth Society for the Blind), July 1, 1944; children: Claire Elizabeth Wilson Hicks, Felicity Jane Wilson Martin. *Education:* Oxford University, B.A., 1939, M.A., 1941, Diploma in Sociology and Social Administration, 1941. *Home:* 22 The Cliff, Roedean, Brighton, Sussex BN2 5RE, England. *Office:* Royal Commonwealth Society for the Blind, Commonwealth House, Haywards Heath, West Sussex RH16 3AZ, England.

CAREER: Royal National Institute for the Blind, London, England, assistant secretary, 1941-49; Royal Commonwealth Society for the Blind, Haywards Heath, England, founder and director, 1950—. Member of faculty at Oxford University, 1941-42. President of International Agency for the Prevention of Blindness, 1975—; member of executive board of World Council for Welfare of the Blind; member of British delegation touring Africa and the Middle East, 1946-47. *Awards, honors:* International humanitarian award from Lions, 1978; World Humanity Award from World Humanity Award Trustees, 1979; Albert Lasker Special Public Service Award from Albert and Mary Lasker Foundation, 1979.

WRITINGS: Blindness in British African and Near East Territories, H.M.S.O., 1947; *Ghana's Handicapped Citizens*, Ghana Government Publication, 1960; *Travelling Blind* (autobiography), Hutchinson, 1962; (editor) *World Blindness and Its Prevention*, Oxford University Press, 1980; (editor) *Disability Prevention: The Global Challenge*, Oxford University Press, 1983. Also author of *The Global Challenge of Avoidable Disability*, 1982. Contributor of stories and poems to various British and American publications.

SIDELIGHTS: Sir John wrote: "As a blind person, traveling some fifty thousand miles a year, mainly through developing countries, I have tried in my writing to express the particular impact of sound, touch, and human contact as giving a distinct and valuable insight into the life and sympathies of people in many countries. Travel literature tends to be so visually oriented that this might be felt to be a useful corrective. I have also tried to relate the strategies of world health and development to the individual predicament of disabled people, who are usually at the bottom of every social and economic heap.

"Doubtless my interest in the prevention of handicap was triggered by annoyance at my own blindness. Overseas travel for a blind person presents some logistical problems but as many compensations in the friendships established with people on airplanes, ships, etc., who enjoy helping me to overcome these difficulties.

"At least half of the disablement that afflicts some 300 million people in the developing countries is due to conditions for which we now have a simple technology of control. The problem is to simplify that technology to the realities of economic life in those countries and to deliver it massively. Our aim, by the end of this century, is to break the link between disablement and population growth in the developing countries and between disablement and aging in the industrialized countries.''

* * *

WILSON, (Daphne) Merna   1930-

PERSONAL: Born May 6, 1930, in Que Que, Rhodesia (now Zimbabwe); daughter of Montague Carey (a miner) and Alice Louisa (in nursing) Hobson; married George Albert Frederick Wilson (an engineer), 1950 (deceased); children: Michael George Carey, Clifford William. *Education:* Attended high school in Umtali, Rhodesia (now Zimbabwe). *Religion:* Anglican. *Home:* 14 Dorchester Rd., Cotswold Hills, Harare, Zimbabwe. *Office address:* P.O. Box 898, Harare, Zimbabwe.

CAREER: Records clerk for Department of Agriculture, 1948-49; worked for North British Insurance Company, 1949, and Johnson & Fletcher (building merchants), 1950-52; in charge of flooring department for Dawson & Dobson Ltd. (engineers), 1952-55; free-lance writer, 1956—; *African World*, London, England, correspondent for Rhodesia, 1965-75; buyer for Farmer's Co-Operative Ltd., 1973-75; Association of Rural Councils, Harare, Zimbabwe, buyers' negotiating officer, 1975—. *Member:* International P.E.N., Poetry Society, Zimbabwe Purchasing Officers Association, Harare Writers Club. *Awards, honors:* Writer of the year (in English) award from International P.E.N. Book Centre, 1977.

WRITINGS: Explosion (novel), R. Hale, 1965; *Turn the Tide Gently* (novel), R. Hale, 1967; *Reap the Whirlwind* (novel), R. Hale, 1969; *A Ring Has No End* (poems), Gazebo Books, 1978; *Python Cave* (juvenile), Modern Press, 1978; *The Country of the Mind* (poems), Kailani Books, 1981; (editor) *The Wilder Shores of Love* (poems), Gemini, 1982. Editor of *Two Tone* (poetry quarterly), 1966 and 1982.

SIDELIGHTS: Wilson told *CA:* "I think it is very important *not* to be influenced by people who don't write poetry, but who, for example, always have plenty to say about it. You must 'do your own thing' as far as poetry is concerned. Other forms of writing have necessarily to follow market patterns. My favorite writing is poetry, for it requires strict discipline.

"I would describe my poems as somewhat emotional and subjective—I can edit clinically but I can't write poetry clinically. Poetry must move my emotions; some of my most successful poems have been written out of deep emotion. People of all classes have come to me and said, 'I understand exactly what you mean. I identify with your work. I can't *understand* a lot of what other poets write.' To me this is higher praise than being admired by other poets for esoteric word usage, etc. I feel that today's poets need to look closely at *what they mean*—and then say it simply and sincerely!

"I would also like to do some television and video scripts—I have written a few and have had fair comment—but my demanding job does not allow much writing time. As a technical

buyer of everything from earth-moving machinery to building, school, and clinic supplies, I often find that people are surprised to discover that I write poetry!''

* * *

WILSON, Paul R(ichard)   1942-

BRIEF ENTRY: Born March 9, 1942, in Christchurch, New Zealand. Australian sociologist and author. Wilson, who was a Fulbright scholar in 1974, wrote *The Other Side of Rape* (University of Queensland Press, 1978) and *Intimacy: A Sex or Love Experience* (Cassell Australia, 1979). He also wrote *Mental Disorder or Madness?: Alternative Theories* (University of Queensland Press, 1979) with Erica M. Bates. Wilson edited *Delinquency in Australia: A Critical Appraisal* (University of Queensland Press, 1977) and *Of Public Concern: Contemporary Australian Social Issues* (University of Queensland Press, 1977), and he co-edited *Two Faces of Deviance: Crimes of the Powerless and the Powerful* (University of Queensland Press, 1978). *Address:* P.O. Box 42, St. Lucia, Queensland, Australia.

* * *

WILSON, Robert McLachlan   1916-

PERSONAL: Born February 13, 1916, in Gourock, Scotland; son of Hugh McLachlan and Janet Nicol (Struthers) Wilson; married Enid Mary Bomford, July 10, 1945; children: Andrew Hugh McLachlan, Peter James McLachlan. *Education:* University of Edinburgh, M.A., 1939, B.D., 1942; Cambridge University, Ph.D., 1945. *Home:* 10 Murrayfield Rd., St. Andrews, Fife, Scotland. *Office:* St. Mary's College, University of St. Andrews, St. Andrews, Fife, Scotland.

CAREER: Ordained minister of Church of Scotland, 1946; minister of Church of Scotland in Strathaven, 1946-54; University of St. Andrews, St. Andrews, Scotland, lecturer, 1954-64, senior lecturer, 1964-69, professor of New Testament, 1969-78, and biblical criticism, 1978—. *Member:* British Academy (fellow), Studiorum Novi Testamenti Societas (president, 1981-82), Society of Biblical Literature (honorary member). *Awards, honors:* D.D. from University of Aberdeen, 1982.

WRITINGS: The Gnostic Problem, Mowbray, 1958; *Studies in the Gospel of Thomas*, Mowbray, 1960; *The Gospel of Philip*, Harper, 1962; *Gnosis and the New Testament*, Basil Blackwell, 1968; (editor) *The Future of Coptology*, E. J. Brill, 1978; (editor) *Nag Hammadi and Gnosis*, E. J. Brill, 1978.

Translation editor: Edgar Hennecke and Wilhelm Schneemelcher, *New Testament Apocrypha*, Westminster, Volume I, 1963, Volume II, 1965; Ernst Haenchen, *The Acts of the Apostles*, Basil Blackwell, 1971; Werner Foerster, *Gnosis*, Clarendon Press, Volume I, 1972, Volume II, 1974; Kurt Rudolph, *Gnosis*, T. & T. Clark, 1982.

Member of editorial board of "Nag Hammadi Studies," a monograph series, published by Leiden Brill, 1971—. Contributor to theology journals in Europe and the United States. Associate editor of *New Testament Studies*, 1967-77, editor, 1977-83.

SIDELIGHTS: Wilson told *CA:* "Gnoticism is for most people a thing of the past, a long-dead heresy now largely forgotten. In fact, it was a serious threat to Christianity at one stage, and it has not even yet entirely disappeared. Some modern 'splinter groups' have at times a distinctly 'gnostic' look! Further, concern with the problems of gnosticism leads one very quickly into the problems of the background and environment of the New Testament and early Christianity. And, finally, a whole collection of ancient gnostic documents was discovered nearly forty years ago—comparable to the discovery of the Dead Sea Scrolls for an earlier period of history. These have not yet been fully evaluated and assessed, so there is still much to be done in this field.

"*Gnosis and the New Testament* was translated into French and German, and two of my articles have been translated for publication in a German encyclopedia."

AVOCATIONAL INTERESTS: Golf.

* * *

WILSON, Rodney N. Usher
See USHER-WILSON, Rodney N.

* * *

WINCHELL, Constance M(abel)   1896-1983

OBITUARY NOTICE—See index for *CA* sketch: Born November 2, 1896, in Northampton, Mass.; died May 23, 1983, in New Paltz, N.Y. Librarian and author. After holding various posts as a librarian, including working for the Merchant Marine Service and for the American Library in Paris, Winchell joined the library staff of Columbia University Libraries in 1925. She served as reference librarian there from 1941 to her retirement in 1962. Winchell participated in the development of what became the Library of Congress National Union Catalog, which serves, among other things, to facilitate interlibrary loans. Her books include *Locating Books for Interlibrary Loan* and the seventh and eight editions of *Guide to Reference Books.* Obituaries and other sources: *American Authors and Books: 1640 to the Present Day,* 3rd revised edition, Crown, 1962; *Current Biography,* Wilson, 1967; *New York Times,* May 25, 1983.

* * *

WINEBERG, Henry J.   1905(?)-1983

OBITUARY NOTICE: Born c. 1905; died March 26, 1983, in Evanston, Ill. Pacifist, civil rights activist, and publisher of *Industrial Market Place,* a trade journal. Wineberg was active in several organizations advocating peace, including the nuclear freeze movement. Obituaries and other sources: *Chicago Tribune,* March 30, 1983.

* * *

WINICK, Charles   1922-

BRIEF ENTRY: Born August 4, 1922, in New York, N.Y. American sociologist, educator, and author. Winick, who became director of the National Advisory Council on Narcotics in 1949, is also a professor of sociology at City College and Graduate Center of the City University of New York. His research and writings, which primarily address social issues, have earned him awards from the Educational Press Association and other organizations. Winick's publications include *The New People: Desexualization in American Life* (Pegasus, 1968), *The Lively Commerce: Prostitution in the United States* (Quadrangle, 1971), *Children's Television Commercials: A Content Analysis* (Praeger, 1973), *Sociological Aspects of Drug Dependence* (CRC Press, 1974), *The Television Experience: What*

Children See (Sage Publications, 1979), and *The Yearbook of Substance Use and Abuse* (Human Sciences, 1980). He also has edited *Yearbook of Drug Dependence* and *Annual Review of Research in Deviance* since 1978. *Address:* Department of Sociology, City College of the City University of New York, Convent and 138th St., New York, N.Y. 10031. *Biographical/critical sources: Motive,* April, 1968; *New York Times,* August 16, 1968, May 5, 1971; *Washington Post Book World,* August 24, 1969, December 7, 1969; *American Men and Women of Science: The Social and Behavioral Sciences,* 13th edition, Bowker, 1978.

* * *

WINSLOW, Gerald A.

PERSONAL: Born in Salem, Ore.; son of Arthur William (a carpenter) and Elsie (Haeder) Winslow; married Betty Jean Wehtje (a school nurse), August 21, 1966; children: Lisa, Angela. *Education:* Walla Walla College, B.A. (cum laude), 1967; Andrews University, M.A. (magna cum laude), 1968; Graduate Theological Union, Ph.D., 1969. *Religion:* Seventh-day Adventist. *Home address:* Route 1, Box 307A, Walla Walla, Wash. 99362. *Office:* Department of Theology, Walla Walla College, College Place, Wash. 99324.

CAREER: Walla Walla College, College Place, Wash., assistant dean of men, 1968-71, instructor, 1971-74, assistant professor, 1974-77, associate professor, 1977-79, professor of religion, 1979—. Visiting professor at Andrews University and Newbold College; adjunct professor at San Francisco Theological Seminary. President of Columbia/Walla Walla Health Systems Council. *Member:* American Philosophical Association, Society of Christian Ethics, Institute of Society, Ethics and the Life Sciences. *Awards, honors:* Danforth associate, 1980.

WRITINGS: Triage and Justice: The Ethics of Rationing and Life-Saving Medical Resources, University of California Press, 1982. Contributor to *Western Journal of Medicine.*

WORK IN PROGRESS: The Ethics of Queuing.

SIDELIGHTS: Winslow commented: "I am moved by the vision of a more just and peaceable society. In this regard I am especially interested in the social institution of medical care. In my spare time I farm (grapes and apples, mostly) with my family."

* * *

WINTER, Keith   1906-1983

OBITUARY NOTICE: Born October 22, 1906, in North Wales; died February 17, 1983, in Englewood, N.J. Educator, novelist, screenwriter, and playwright. Winter worked as a schoolmaster before embarking upon his writing career. Among his novels are *Other Man's Saucer* and *Impassioned Pygmies.* His plays include "The Shining Hour," "Worse Things Happen at Sea," and "The Rats of Norway," which was first produced on Broadway in 1933. Winter also wrote screenplays, including the screenplay for the 1943 film "Above Suspicion." Obituaries and other sources: *The Author's and Writer's Who's Who,* 6th edition, Burke's Peerage, 1971; *International Authors and Writers Who's Who,* 8th edition, Melrose, 1977; *Who Was Who in the Theatre, 1912-1976,* Gale, 1978; *Who's Who,* 134th edition, St. Martin's, 1982; *New York Times,* February 19, 1983.

WINTERGREEN, John P.
See RYSKIND, Morrie

*   *   *

WINTZ, Jack   1936-

PERSONAL: Born February 22, 1936, in Batesville, Ind.; son of Paul J. (a personnel director for a furniture company) and Viola (Thalheimer) Wintz. *Education:* Duns Scotus College, B.A., 1959; attended St. Leonard College, 1959-63; Xavier University, Cincinnati, Ohio, M.A., 1966. *Office: St. Anthony Messenger*, 1615 Republic St., Cincinnati, Ohio 45210.

CAREER: Entered Ordo Fratrum Minorum (Order of Friars Minor; Observant Franciscans; O.F.M.), 1954, ordained Roman Catholic priest, 1963; pastoral assistant of Roman Catholic congregation in Louisville, Ky., 1963-64; high school teacher of English, journalism, and religion in Cincinnati, Ohio, 1964-65; high school teacher of English, drama, and communication arts in Fort Wayne, Ind., 1965-69; teacher and missionary in the Philippines, including teacher of literature at Franciscan Seminary College and Maryknoll College, near Manila, and chaplain for Catholic Family Movement and Cursillo, 1969-72; *St. Anthony Messenger*, Cincinnati, associate editor, staff writer, and photographer, 1972—. Editor of *Catholic Update*, 1973—.

AWARDS, HONORS: Awards from Catholic Press Association, 1975, for "A New Look at Evangelization", 1978 and 1980, for film column, "Screen Testing," 1979, for article, "Fountain Square Fools," 1979, for interview, "Father Bud Kieser," and 1980, for article, "Pope in America"; awards from Cincinnati Editors Association, 1977, for article, "Outreach to Outcasts," 1979, for article, "Fountain Square Fools," 1979, for interview, "Father Bud Kieser," 1980, for article, "Pope in America," and 1982, for column, "Screen Testing"; grant from Hiroshima International Cultural Foundation for journalism project in Japan, 1982.

WRITINGS: (Editor) *Keeping Up With Our Catholic Faith: Explaining Changes in Catholic Thinking Since Vatican II*, St. Anthony Messenger Press, 1975; (editor) *Has Change Shattered Our Faith?: A Hopeful Look at the Church Today*, St. Anthony Messenger Press, 1976; (editor) *Living Our Faith After the Changes*, St. Anthony Messenger Press, 1977; (editor) *Our Journey in Faith*, St. Anthony Messenger Press, 1979. Author of "Screen Testing," a column in *Catholic Telegraph*, 1975—. Contributor of more than seventy-five articles to religious publications, including *St. Anthony Messenger*.

WORK IN PROGRESS: Articles on Hiroshima and Nagasaki.

SIDELIGHTS: Wintz told *CA*: "My work in the Philippines gave me a more international outlook and sensitivity to Third World oppression." As an editor of *St. Anthony Messenger* he hopes to promote "religious education: to keep readers abreast of developments in Catholic teaching and to foster sensitivity to social concerns."

*   *   *

WIPPLER, Migene Gonzalez
See GONZALEZ-WIPPLER, Migene

*   *   *

WISBERG, Marian Aline   1923-
   (Marian Mountain)

PERSONAL: Born March 12, 1923, in Seattle, Wash.; daughter of Charles W. (in wholesale lumber business) and Geraldine (Smithson) Matheus; married Richmond Derby, 1945 (divorced, 1963); married Jack E. Wisberg (a welder), January 9, 1974; children: Richard, Kristin Derby Clarke, Karen Derby Davis, Kataryn, Anne Derby Crosse. *Education:* Attended Mills College, 1942-43. *Religion:* Zen Buddhist. *Home address:* Coastlands, Big Sur, Calif. 93920. *Agent:* Michael Larsen, Michael Larsen/Elizabeth Pomada, 1029 Jones St., San Francisco, Calif. 94109.

CAREER: Window dresser for department store in San Francisco, Calif., 1945-47; puppeteer in San Francisco area, 1953-64; medical receptionist, 1958-62; student director of Zen meditation group in Los Altos, Calif., 1964-69; Zen monk at Zenshinji Monastery, Tassajara, Calif.; caretaker in Big Sur, Calif., 1970-80.

WRITINGS: (Under pseudonym Marian Mountain) *The Zen Environment*, Morrow, 1982.

WORK IN PROGRESS: The Time of the Han, a novel, completion expected in 1986.

SIDELIGHTS: Wisberg told *CA*: "As a close disciple of the late Zen master Shunryn Suzuki, founder of the Zen Center of San Francisco and Tassajara Zen Monastery, I was responsible for collecting and editing talks my Zen master gave in my home in Los Altos, California, in the 1960's. These talks were later published in a book (*Zen Mind, Beginner's Mind*, published by Weatherhill in 1970). After my Zen master's death I felt moved to share with others some of the details of my Zen training. At the time I wrote *The Zen Environment* I was living a secluded life in the mountains of Big Sur, California. Working on the book was a way of encouraging myself to continue my solitary practice of Zen meditation as well as a way of connecting myself with my past and future teachers.

"My life of Zen began after my divorce when I started searching for the unknown source of a nagging dissatisfaction with my life. (I later learned that most of this dissatisfaction came from the habit of living half-heartedly. Zen practice teaches one how to live whole-heartedly.) At a seminar at the Esalen Institute in Big Sur I first learned from Gary Snyder, the Pulitzer Prize-winning Zen Buddhist poet, the practice of zazen (a form of cross-legged meditation that provides the body and mind with the most ideal environment in which to function efficiently and harmoniously under all conditions). The improvement in my mental outlook resulting from the practice of zazen led me to seek out and find my own Zen master.

"*The Zen Environment* is the story of a spiritual adventure that begins in the suburbs of San Francisco and ends in the wilderness of Big Sur. It is not just about a personal experience however. *The Zen Environment* combines Zen life, Zen philosophy, and Zen practices in a more complete and integrated way than can be found in most books on Zen Buddhism. Robert Pirsig, author of *Zen and the Art of Motorcycle Maintenance* who wrote the foreword to *The Zen Environment*, was an inspiration to me. Pirsig, who also is a serious student-practitioner of Zen Buddhism, shows in his writing how the teaching of a philosophy can be integrated into an absorbing personal narrative to add up to more than each would have been if presented separately. *The Zen Environment* may be of particular interest to American writers or students of literature as a means of better understanding what I believe may be the future wave of serious literature in the West—toward a less intellectually compartmentalized form of writing and toward a more interconnected expression of each individual's place in the universe."

WISEMAN, David 1916-

PERSONAL: Born January 13, 1916, in Manchester, England; son of Oscar and Margaret (Hussey) Wiseman; married Cicely Hilda Mary Richards, September 2, 1939; children: Michael, Sally Hilda Wiseman Smith, Patrick, Deborah Margaret Wiseman Rault. Education: Victoria University of Manchester, B.A. (with honors), 1937. Home: 25 Ellers Lane, Auckley, Doncaster, Yorkshire, England. Agent: June Hall, 19 College Cross, London N1 1PT, England.

CAREER: Journal of Adult Education, London, England, editor, 1948-51; high school teacher in Cornwall, England, 1952-59; high school principal in Doncaster, Yorkshire, England, 1959-63, and Cornwall, 1963-75; Cornwall Education Board, Cornwall, adviser on inservice education of teachers, 1975-77; writer, 1977—. Military service: British Army, 1940-46; became major.

WRITINGS—All juvenile novels: Jeremy Visick, Houghton, 1981 (published in England as The Fate of Jeremy Visick, Kestrel, 1982); Thimbles, Houghton, 1982; Blodwen and the Guardians, Houghton, 1983.

WORK IN PROGRESS: Pudding and Pie, a juvenile novel; Ellen Bray, a novel set in England in the 1870's; research for a novel about the Paris Commune in 1871.

SIDELIGHTS: Wiseman wrote: "I regard myself as a storyteller . . . and my background makes me particularly concerned with civil rights, especially the status of women. This becomes a major theme in my adult work. It is present, though not a major theme, in my children's novels.

"Jeremy Visick is the story of a tin miner of nineteenth-century Cornwall who dies with his father and two brothers in an underground accident in Wheal Maid mine. Matthew Clemens, a boy of modern times, is drawn across time to meet Jeremy, to share the horror of the mine, and to bring Jeremy's ghost to rest. At the time of writing Jeremy Visick I lived within a few hundred yards of the old mining area, with its many relics of mining history. I was moved by this to research the social and working conditions of the Cornish miner, with my adult novel, Ellen Bray, in mind. The detail of the background in Jeremy Visick is drawn very precisely from that area, and it is possible to recognize many of the places mentioned.

"Thimbles is another story in which a modern child, Catherine Aitken, is caught up in events of the past, events associated with the struggle for universal suffrage in Britain in the early nineteenth century. It tells, through the eyes of two children of the time, the tale of the Peterloo Massacre, when, in August, 1819, a peaceful demonstration was attacked and dispersed by government troops. Numbers of the demonstrators were killed and many, including women and children, were injured. The event had an important influence on the growth of democracy in Britain. Catherine Aitken, the modern child, is brought, by her involvement in these events, to understand the motives which impel her own father to work for civil rights, in particular the right of labor to organize in unions.

"Blodwen and the Guardians is quite different in tone from my first two juvenile novels, having in it a large element of fantasy. The Guardians of the title are invisible, indefinable, spirits of the stones, set to guard the tombs of warriors of times long past. A construction company plans to drive a road through the center of the tomb, to the horror of the Guardians and the dismay of Blodwen, a girl who lives in a cottage near the tomb. The story tells how Blodwen and the Guardians combine to frustrate the road-builders and save the ancient ways.

"I have a firm personal commitment to civil rights and in particular the rights of women, which necessarily colors my writing. I derive this commitment from my parents and grandparents—my grandmother, for example, was imprisoned as a suffragette in England during the campaign to win votes for women before World War I. Other members of my family have, in different ways, suffered for their beliefs.

"My novel Ellen Bray reflects this commitment. It tells the story of a woman worker in the Cornish mines, who is gradually drawn into the fight for women's rights. A sequel, which I am now researching, deals with another aspect of women and the political struggle, when an English woman becomes caught up in the events of 1870-71 in Paris, France. A third volume is planned to bring the story up to the granting of the vote to women."

*　　*　　*

WISMER, Donald (Richard) 1946-

PERSONAL: Surname is pronounced Whiz-mer; born December 27, 1946, in Chicago, Ill.; son of Donald Minor (a contract administrator) and Katherine (Brandstrader) Wismer; married Leah Rubel, December 17, 1976; children: Sarah Miriam, Asher Zvi. Education: Indiana University, B.A., 1968, M.A., 1973; Southern Connecticut State College, M.S., 1977. Home address: P.O. Box 253, Winthrop, Maine 04364. Agent: Scott Meredith Literary Agency, Inc., 845 Third Ave., New York, N.Y. 10022. Office: Maine State Library, State House Station 64, Augusta, Maine 04333.

CAREER: Indiana University, Bloomington, library assistant, 1967-73; Harvard University, Cambridge, Mass., stack supervisor at Widener Library, 1974-76; Bigelow Laboratory for Ocean Sciences, West Boothbay Harbor, Maine, librarian, 1977; Maine State Library, Augusta, coordinator for Automated Data Services, 1977—. Member: Science Fiction Writers of America, Maine Library Association (president of Special Library Group, 1979-80; member of executive board, 1979—).

WRITINGS: The Islamic Jesus: An Annotated Bibliography of Sources in English and French, Garland Publishing, 1977; Starluck (science fiction novel), Doubleday, 1982. Contributor to library science journals. Editor of Downeast Libraries, 1981—; editor and publisher of Main Home Education, 1981—.

WORK IN PROGRESS: A Roil of Stars, a science fiction novel; Warrior Planet (tentative title), a science fiction novel.

SIDELIGHTS: Wismer commented: "Almost all librarians want to be authors, too, but few take that giant step. The hardest part of writing fiction is sitting down at the word processor and doing it. I've been telling high school classes that two things are essential: first, do it; second, become expert at something, develop a saleable skill. That way, you can always survive if you fail at writing, and few succeed.

"I could write for years about writing style. I believe in simple sentences, linked by adverbs in such a way that the reader is carried bodily from one paragraph to another. Verbosity is sometimes indicated, but rarely. Each genre has its own tradition.

"Write what you like to read, and write what you know. My first novel is science fiction, set on a world not our own, hundreds or thousands of years in the future, but I know the genre from having read science fiction greedily for many years.

"I set the first sixty pages of *Starluck* to paper sometime in 1974. I wrote a sixty-page chase scene on the theory that grabbing the reader's interest is the best way to begin a story. I still think so. I tend to believe that a writer should simply start writing and see where the book leads. Once a framework of ideas is in place (setting, characters, and their backgrounds), a story will proceed logically forward and the plot will twist and turn according to the premises already set forth in earlier pages.

"I propose to write rollicking good stories that can't be put down. They will be science fiction because that's the genre that most excites me, the one I read most, and incidentally the one in which individual titles tend to stay in print. And I also want to inspire, not to any particular religion, but to a vision toward perfection of life. My protagonists in the near future will always tend toward physical exercise, good diet, and the view that life will end, that it's a temporary and valuable thing, something that can't be directed by an effort of will and consequent action. I want my readers to think about that. I want them to distinguish between largely passive activities, such as watching television or listening to music, and active ones, such as learning, doing, and achieving. I want them to take charge of themselves, if only in the long run. Luckily, that sort of attitude makes for good storytelling, and that's what I aim to do."

*   *   *

WISTER, John C(aspar)   1887-1982

OBITUARY NOTICE: Born March 19, 1887; died December 28, 1982, in Swarthmore, Pa. Horticulturist and editor. Wister received many prestigious awards during his lifelong career in horticulture. Founder of several horticultural associations, he was a member of nearly one hundred organizations in his field and in related scientific and recreational fields. In 1930 Wister became the first director of the Arthur Hoyt Scott Horticultural Foundation, which maintains a 240-acre public garden on the campus of Swarthmore College. Swarthmore awarded Wister an honorary doctor of science in 1942. He edited *Woman's Home Companion Garden Book*. Obituaries and other sources: *New York Times*, December 29, 1982.

*   *   *

WITT, Howell Arthur John   1920-

PERSONAL: Born July 12, 1920, in Newport, Wales; son of Thomas Leyshon and Harriet Jane (Ball) Witt; married Gertrude Doreen Edwards, June 18, 1949; children: Elizabeth (Mrs. Robert J. Feigh), David, Helen (Mrs. Peter Krynen), Andrew, Martin. *Education:* University of Leeds, B.A., 1942; attended College of the Resurrection, 1942-44. *Home:* Bishop's House, William St., Bathurst, New South Wales 2795, Australia. *Office:* Diocesan Registry, Bathurst, New South Wales 2795, Australia.

CAREER: Ordained Anglican priest, 1945; assistant curate of Anglican churches in Usk, Wales, 1944-47, and London, England, 1948-49; Woomera Rocket Range, Australia, chaplain, 1949-54; rector of Anglican church in Adelaide, Australia, 1954-57; priest in charge of Anglican church in Elizabeth,

Australia, 1957-65; bishop of Northwest Australia, 1965-81; bishop of Bathurst, 1981—. Missioner of St. Peter's College Mission, 1954-65. *Military service:* Australian Army, chaplain, 1949-65.

WRITINGS: Bush Bishop, Rigby, 1981; *Witt's End*, Western Mount Publications, 1981; *Verily, Verily*, Anglican Information Office, 1983. Also author of *More Witt's End*, 1982.

SIDELIGHTS: Witt told *CA*: "Everything that I've written for publication I've been asked to write. *Bush Bishop* came as a result of after-dinner talks I gave. Someone said they'd make a good book, a publisher heard of it . . . and so it goes on.

"It helps if I have a deadline. 'We want it in the mail tomorrow. . . .'

"*Witt's End* and *More Witt's End* are collections of my weekly articles published in an Australian Sunday newspaper. *Verily, Verily* is a series of Bible studies."

*   *   *

WOLF, Jacqueline   1928-

PERSONAL: Born April 28, 1928, in Epinal, France; came to the United States in 1946; naturalized U.S. citizen, 1960; daughter of Paul (a merchant) and Cyrla (a merchant; maiden name, Baron) Glicenstein; married Jonas Wolf (a sales executive), August 26, 1950; children: Paul, Michele Wolfe Gershon. *Education:* Attended public schools in France. *Religion:* Jewish. *Home:* 10 The Hollows W., Muttontown, N.Y. 11732.

CAREER: Worked in perfume factory, 1946, as salesperson, 1947, and for Air France.

WRITINGS: Take Care of Josette: A Memoir in Defense of Occupied France (autobiography), F. Watts, 1981.

SIDELIGHTS: Take Care of Josette is an autobiographical account of the life of an orphaned Jewess growing up in Nazi-occupied France during World War II. Josette was four years old and Jacqueline fourteen when their parents were taken from the family home by Gestapo agents: "Take care of Josette" was their father's parting plea to the elder daughter. The story of the ensuing struggle for survival as the two girls sought refuge with both Christian and Jewish families before finally leaving for America "emphasizes that even those who escaped death at the hands of the Nazis were not unaffected," a writer opined in the *Ypsilanti Press*. And Arielle North wrote in the *St. Louis Post-Dispatch* that Wolf's memoir "has put the menace of anti-semitism into concrete terms . . . and in the process has recounted a galvanizing story of true grit."

Wolf told *CA*: "*Take Care of Josette* has been extremely well-received by schools and libraries. The story of two very young girls surviving the war on their own proves that people don't have to blame social conditions for their actions and can survive with dignity in spite of the scars.

BIOGRAPHICAL/CRITICAL SOURCES: St. Louis Post-Dispatch, December 6, 1981; *Ypsilanti Press*, June 1, 1982.

*   *   *

WOLF, Robert Charles   1955-

PERSONAL: Born February 27, 1955, in Storm Lake, Iowa; son of Dennis Joseph and Loretta (Mackey) Wolf. *Politics:* Republican. *Religion:* Roman Catholic. *Home:* 3521 Tenth Ave. N., Fort Dodge, Iowa 50501. *Office:* East Lawn Animal Hospital, 2930 Fifth Ave. S., Fort Dodge, Iowa 50501.

CAREER: East Lawn Animal Hospital, Fort Dodge, Iowa, animal caretaker, 1973—. *Member:* National Writers Club, Authors Guild.

WRITINGS: Fossils of Iowa, Iowa State University Press, 1983. Contributor to *Earth Science.*

WORK IN PROGRESS: The Taylorsville Experiment, a science fiction novel; *Brick Walls,* a psychological novel about purgatory; research on Iowa geology, the Antichrist, purgatory, basic human drives, and unidentified flying objects.

SIDELIGHTS: Wolf commented: ''Writing provides excellent therapy. I want my writing to be unique, informative, and helpful, whether it is fiction or nonfiction.

''I enjoy hero stories about ordinary people. Although my two novels may seem to be totally different, they involve ordinary people suddenly faced with extraordinary circumstances. That may come from a notion I have that no person is really completely immoral.

''I believe that writing takes no special talent and that I am proof of that. Anyone can write successfully if he is dedicated and the desire is there, but he should also write what he feels and be a close observer and friend of people.

''*Fossils of Iowa* describes 150 collecting sites in three states for people interested in the fossils and environment of the Paleozoic Era, 230-600 million years ago. *The Taylorville Experiment* involves a typical small Iowa town suddenly faced with a rash of UFO sightings, and pressure is put on the aging town marshal to do something about them. *Brick Walls* involves a man who must suddenly face the fact that he is dead and now must pay for his actions on earth.

''Why did I become a writer? Some people turn to drugs to escape life and its problems. I suppose I did the same thing only my drug is writing. Despite how rough life can get I can always escape through writing.''

AVOCATIONAL INTERESTS: Paleontology, nature, people, philately, drives in the country.

* * *

WOLFE, Ron 1945-

PERSONAL: Born September 14, 1945, in North Platte, Neb.; son of Edward A. (a motel owner) and Marguerite E. (Kinsman) Wolfe; married Janice Leigh Fate (a preschool teacher), June 11, 1972; children: Brandon Edward. *Education:* Hastings College, B.A., 1968. *Home:* 6635 South Rockford, Tulsa, Okla. 74136. *Agent:* William Morris Agency, 1350 Avenue of the Americas, New York, N.Y. 10019. *Office: Tulsa Tribune,* P.O. Box 1770, Tulsa, Okla. 74102.

CAREER: Sherman Democrat, Sherman, Tex., reporter, 1970-72; *Goodland Daily News,* Goodland, Kan., reporter, 1972-74; *Midland Reporter-Telegram,* Midland, Tex., reporter and editor, 1974; *Oklahoma City Times,* Oklahoma City, Okla., feature writer, 1974-80; *Tulsa Tribune,* Tulsa, Okla., feature writer and cartoonist, 1980—.

WRITINGS: Signs of Life (cartoons), Oklahoma Publishing, 1970; (with John Wooley) *Old Fears* (horror stories), F. Watts, 1982. Contributor of stories to *Twilight Zone.*

WORK IN PROGRESS: Full Moon (tentative title), a horror novel, with John Wooley.

SIDELIGHTS: Wolfe told *CA:* ''I think horror stories are fairy tales for grownups. They are a way to go on believing in magic.

There may be no Santa Claus in the real world, but the gleaming-eyed thing in the shadows still seems as likely as ever.

''My first interest in horror stories probably came from watching the old 'Twilight Zone' television series, which made a particular pleasure of my two sales of stories to *Twilight Zone* magazine. I feel like I've joined the club now.

''I've been writing fiction, usually with some sort of fantasy element, for about the past five years. The real start was my involvement with a writers' group called the Robert B. Leslie Foundation (named for the writer of pulp magazine mystery stories, author of the immortal line: 'My roscoe sneezed, ''Kerchow! Kerchow!''').

''John Wooley, the co-writer of *Old Fears,* was pretty much the founder of the group, and that's how we met. Another of the members was Mike McQuay, who wrote the novelization of *Escape From New York.*

''One of my *Twilight Zone* stories, 'Tiger of the Mind,' was somewhat based on my (much hated) experience as a newspaper police reporter. Otherwise, I think of the newspaper writing I do as entirely separate from the fiction—completely different. There is not much place in journalism for turning loose the imagination. It's the difference between telling what is and what might be.

''Another of my interests is cartooning. I may be the world's only combination horror story writer and big-foot gag cartoonist. I suppose I'm attracted to cartoons and horror stories for much the same reason. I like the build-up and surprise elements that are common to both. And the line between laughter and fright is a thin one. Slipping on a banana peel is a horrifying experience for the guy doing the slipping.

''It's been said (by Stephen King, I think) that people read horror stories as a rehearsal for death. But I'm a lot more positive about it than that. I think the fascination is not just to look at Mr. Bones, but to kick him in the shin and get away with it.''

BIOGRAPHICAL/CRITICAL SOURCES: Tulsa Tribune, April 16, 1982.

* * *

WONG, Jade Snow 1922-

PERSONAL: Born January 21, 1922, in San Francisco, Calif.; daughter of Hong (a manufacturer) and Hing Kwai (Tong) Wong; married Woodrow Ong (a travel agent), August 29, 1950; children: Mark Stuart, Tyi Elizabeth, Ellora Louise, Lance Orion. *Education:* San Francisco Junior College, A.A., 1940; Mills College, B.A., 1942. *Politics:* Democrat. *Religion:* Methodist. *Agent:* Curtis Brown Ltd., 575 Madison Ave., New York, N.Y. 10022. *Office:* 2123-2125 Polk St., San Francisco, Calif. 94109.

CAREER: Worked as secretary in San Francisco, Calif., 1943-45; proprietor of ceramics gallery, 1946—; co-owner of travel agency, 1957—; writer. Member of California Council for the Humanities, 1975-81; member of advisory councils for China Institute of New York and Friends of the San Francisco Libraries. Director of Chinese Culture Center, 1978-81. *Member:* International Air Traffic Association, Norcal Pacific Area Travel Association, Museum Society (director, 1976-81). *Awards, honors:* Award for pottery from California State Fair, 1947; Silver Medal for craftsmanship from *Mademoiselle;* award for enamel from California State Fair, 1949; Silver Medal for nonfiction from Commonwealth Club of San Francisco, 1976, for *Fifth Chinese Daughter;* honorary doctorate of humane letters from Mills College, 1976.

WRITINGS: Fifth Chinese Daughter (autobiography), Harper, 1950; *The Immigrant Experience* (nonfiction), Dial, 1971; *No Chinese Stranger* (nonfiction), Harper, 1975. Also author of column in *San Francisco Examiner.* Contributor to periodicals, including *Holiday* and *Horn Book.*

SIDELIGHTS: Wong is best known for her autobiography, *Fifth Chinese Daughter.* In it she documents her assimilation into mainstream America after being raised in a traditional Chinese family. A reviewer for the *New Yorker* called the book "an engrossing story," and Joyce Geary, writing in *New York Times Book Review,* noted that Wong "writes very well, and her writing exudes the delicate femininity only the Asiatic women possess."

Wong told *CA:* "My writing is nonfiction based on personal experiences. So few Chinese Americans have published that I think it is my responsibility to try to create understanding between Chinese and Americans. In my work with ceramics and travel, I follow the same philosophy. Because I am innovative and unconventional, I am often far ahead of my time. Thirty-two years after publication, *Fifth Chinese Daughter* is still in print and used by schools everywhere. I am fluent in English, Cantonese, and have studied Mandarin since beginning my travels in the People's Republic of China. Though I don't think being a woman has been any problem, I give priority to women's responsibility for a good home life; hence, I put my husband and four children before my writing or ceramics. I also believe in serving my community and this work has taken more time than writing a book."

BIOGRAPHICAL/CRITICAL SOURCES: New York Herald Tribune Book Review, September 24, 1950; *New Yorker,* October 7, 1950; *New York Times Book Review,* October 29, 1950; *Commonweal,* November 24, 1950; *Contemporary Literary Criticism,* Volume 17, Gale, 1981.

* * *

WOOD, Charles Osgood III 1933-
(Charles Osgood)

PERSONAL: Professional name, Charles Osgood; born January 8, 1933, in New York, N.Y.; son of Charles and Mary F. (Wilson) Wood; married second wife, Jean Crafton, December 5, 1973; children: Kathleen, Winston, Anne Elizabeth, Emily Jean. *Education:* Fordham University, B.S., 1954. *Office:* CBS News, 524 West 57th St., New York, N.Y. 10019.

CAREER: WGMS-Radio, Bethesda, Md., program director, 1963; WHCT-TV, Hartford, Conn., general manager, 1963-64; American Broadcasting Company (ABC-Radio), news reporter, 1964-67; WCBS-TV, New York City, anchor, 1967-72; CBS News, New York City, radio and television correspondent, 1972—. Host of "Newsbreak" and "The Osgood File," both for CBS-Radio. *Military service:* U.S. Army. *Member:* American Federation of Television and Radio Artists, Radio and Television News Analysts. *Awards, honors:* L.H.D. from St. Bonaventure University, 1977.

WRITINGS—All under professional name Charles Osgood: *Nothing Could Be Finer Than a Crisis That Is Minor in the Morning,* Holt, 1979; *There's Nothing That I Wouldn't Do If You Would Be My POSSLQ,* Holt, 1981.

Lyricist of more than two dozen songs, including "Black Is Beautiful," recorded by Nancy Wilson, and (with John Cacavas) "Gallant Men," recorded by Everett Dirksen.

SIDELIGHTS: "My stuff isn't poetry," Charles Osgood told *People* reporter Gioia Diliberto. "It's just rampant doggerel." Osgood was referring to the rhyming verses that inform and often amuse the nearly 2.5 million Americans who tune in "Newsbreak," Osgood's CBS-Radio spot six mornings each week. Although sometimes covering tragic events and crucial issues, Osgood prefers to share the lighter side of the news (as indicated in the title of his book *Nothing Could Be Finer Than a Crisis That Is Minor in the Morning*) or to reflect on the pressing problems that plague every man (such as socks that vanish in the wash). *Newsweek*'s Betsy Carter quoted Osgood: "Before I choose a piece it has to touch me in some way. It has to be something that either makes me want to laugh or cry, and when I write the piece, I try not to strain out the motions." He also recorded his view in rhyme: "If you're going to talk about sadness and crime, / I say sweetness and light ought to get equal time. / Enough of the clouds and your mourning and whining! / Let's have a bit of the old silver lining! / We've all really had it with trouble and woe. / And if those things exist, why, we don't want to know."

Formerly the station manager of the first U.S. pay television station (WHCT in Hartford, Connecticut), Osgood was a reporter for ABC-Radio news and a television anchorman before joining CBS in 1972. Although primarily a radio correspondent, Osgood headlines the "Sunday Night News," appears regularly on the television program "Universe," and has hosted documentaries for CBS-TV. Still, he maintains that he prefers radio to television. As a child he was an avid radio buff, and during his stint in the army he worked in announcing booths as often as possible and served as the announcer for the U.S. Army Band.

Osgood's "Newsbreak" poems have been collected in two volumes, *Nothing Could Be Finer Than a Crisis That Is Minor in the Morning* and *There's Nothing That I Wouldn't Do If You Would Be My POSSLQ.* Of the former, *New York Times Book Review*'s Jeff Greenfield wrote: "Although his sweet voice may be part of the spell / That he weaves, these pieces do hold up quite well." The latter's title is taken from a verse inspired by the U.S. Census Bureau's acronym for Person of the Opposite Sex Sharing Living Quarters: "You live with me, and I with you / And you will be my POSSLQ. / I'll be your friend and so much more; / That's what a POSSLQ is for."

Despite Osgood's lighthearted slant on the news and his unique reporting style, the correspondent wishes to be thought of as a serious journalist, not as, according to Diliberto, "the Ogden Nash of the airwaves." He told the *People* reporter: "I like to keep my humorous pieces on a high level. If I started wearing hats, acting goofy and doing 'Let's see if I can ride this pony' kind of stuff, I'd really make a fool of myself." Indeed, Osgood takes his work seriously, painstakingly compiling and composing material each day for his two radio segments, the early morning "Newsbreak" and the later broadcast "Osgood File." The task is a challenging one, for as Osgood explains, "I have to express myself much more often than I have something to express."

CA INTERVIEW

CA interviewed Charles Osgood by phone on December 15, 1980, at his office at CBS in New York City.

CA: *Your day begins very early. Would you describe the regular routine you go through in writing the "Newsbreak" show?*

OSGOOD: I get up at four and go to work at five. I write the seven o'clock news for the network, so that really is the first order of business. "Newsbreak" is the second thing that I have to do. While I'm going through the wire services and newspapers to get material for the news, I put to one side those stories that look as if they might be good material for "Newsbreak." I get to work on that after the seven o'clock news.

CA: *Do you always find something to use for that day?*

OSGOOD: I'd better! I don't have a choice; I have to find something. Some days you find something very easily and other days you have to scratch.

CA: *Is there ever a problem in getting additional factual material you might need to build your story for "Newsbreak"?*

OSGOOD: Of course, the problem is that when you find a story, as we often do, on the coast—Seattle or San Diego, for example—the people who are involved in that story are three hours behind us. We sometimes do make phone calls, but if we get to work on the story right after the seven o'clock news goes on the air here, it means it's only slightly after four in the morning there. It's possible to make the connection sometimes, but people are a little sleepy at that hour.

CA: *Do you keep any material on hand just in case you don't get a story together?*

OSGOOD: No, I do not have the so-called "evergreen" to put on the air in case I don't get anything. If I prepared an evergreen, I would use it the next day. You just have to live with a certain amount of panic every day.

CA: *Do you ever get used to the panic?*

OSGOOD: Not exactly, but if you do this every day, you recognize the symptoms when they develop. You can understand how much trouble you're in and react accordingly. Sometimes you start off after a story and discover that you can't really get it together—the information is simply not available. In that case, even though you wish you didn't have to do it, you have to change stories or do something else that day and write fast. The principal requirement for this job is that you have to be able to write fast.

CA: *You turn your news items into verse or prose, some pieces of which you've collected in* Nothing Could Be Finer Than a Crisis That Is Minor in the Morning, *which you dedicated to Dr. Seuss. Was he really an influence?*

OSGOOD: He really has been an influence, especially lately. I've got four little kids—the oldest is six—so there's a fair amount of reading that goes on on that level. Particularly in recent years I've had occasion to read a lot of Dr. Seuss. I think he is very clever. People have asked me who has been my poetic influence, and I have to admit that I'm not the kind of person who does a lot of reading of verse aside from that kind of thing.

CA: *Are you ever put on the spot at a banquet or some such occasion and asked to do an instant verse?*

OSGOOD: I've been asked to do it, but that's really not the way it works. I can't do it unless I'm sitting at a typewriter under a deadline. I almost can't do it any other way. It's not something that you spout off the top of your head. *I* can't anyway.

CA: *Do you get a lot of mail in response to "Newsbreak"?*

OSGOOD: Yes, quite a lot, especially to the verses. A lot of people like to do this as a hobby, so I get letters in verse. And in response to the verse pieces I do, I get a lot of letters asking for copies. A single piece can generate a couple of hundred letters and comments. Most of the mail is nice and very favorable. Usually, it's not that we've kicked up a storm of controversy or anything, although sometimes people do take objection to something and let us know about it.

CA: *Is there a single strangest story that you can recall using on "Newsbreak"?*

OSGOOD: So much of it is strange. We're dealing with fact, and, as the old cliche says, truth is stranger than fiction. Almost every day there's something strange. We did one today about a game that somebody has devised, a board game sort of like Monopoly called Public Assistance. There are two tracks, little rings, and you roll dice and start off with money. I forget all the categories, but one of them is "welfare." And in that one you don't pay taxes and you get money periodically without having to do anything for it. It's obviously a slam at the welfare system, but that's pretty strange as stories go.

CA: *Did you decide early that you wanted to be in radio?*

OSGOOD: Yes, very early. I think from the time I was a kid listening to the radio. There wasn't any television when I was growing up, so radio became my fascination. I always imagined that it would be fun to work with a microphone. It's one of those little self-fulfilling prophecies, to go to where your own fascination leads you.

CA: *Do you still like radio more than television?*

OSGOOD: Yes, I do. I'm doing a lot more television now than I used to. I'm doing regular television anchor work and reporting work, but I still find that radio is easier for me and much more agreeable. I do not hate television at all. I think the possibilities in television are obviously fantastic. But there are some small paradoxes. It seems to me for one thing that radio is much more visual. The problem with television is that since the picture is provided, not very much is left for the audience to provide. I think the pictures that the audience provides in radio are better than the ones we can provide on television.

CA: *How does your difficult schedule affect your family?*

OSGOOD: They'd like to have me home a little more, and I'd like to be home a little more. But it goes with the territory that you have to put in long days; you have to start early and come home late. It involves a certain amount of travel and so on. But it also has some compensations. I try to spend as much time as I can with the kids and my wife. It really isn't terrible. There are jobs that involve a lot more time being away and a lot worse hours than I've got.

CA: *Radio has obviously changed a great deal since you and I were children. Do you have any comments on its functions now and on its future?*

OSGOOD: There was a time back when television first came in when people were predicting the imminent demise of radio. How could it possibly survive when there was now a media that not only produced sound but pictures as well? Since then, radio has done nothing but get bigger and better and stronger and make much more money. There are many more stations, more listeners, a lot more radios than there were in the so-called heyday of radio. I think it has changed in that now it is a primary and almost continuous source of news and information. There used to be just a few newscasts on radio and mostly entertainment. Now there are so many stations, and a lot of them specialize in one thing or another. But news and information stations seem to be the ones that are really doing best—on AM radio especially. I think those stations that do a good job of that will always do well and will get big audiences and attract advertisers and prosper.

Incidentally, because there are so many stations and the field is so big now, there are a lot of jobs to be had in radio. It would be much easier to break into radio than to break into television. It's a good way to start; a lot of very talented people have gotten into radio. If you travel across the country and listen to what people are doing in local stations, particularly the news and information stations, there's just a fantastic amount of talent out there. And people are listening in unprecedented numbers.

CA: Do you think most people who go into radio now do it as a springboard to television?

OSGOOD: It's hard to say. I imagine a lot of them would like to do television. The ideal of course is what I've been able to do, to work in radio and also in television, so you can get the benefit of both. I think they tend to help each other. I'm not known in television very much at all. But people know me from radio, so they seem to accept me better on television than they would otherwise. It works the other way around, too. Once somebody has seen you on a program, they can identify the person behind the voice. It makes you that much more effective on radio.

CA: Music has been more than a hobby for you. You've published at least twenty-five songs.

OSGOOD: Yes, that number has stayed constant for the last few years. My songwriting partner moved to the coast, and we haven't done any songwriting since. John Cacavas is his name, and he lives in Beverly Hills and writes for movies and TV shows. He did the music for "Kojak." He's a very busy composer and arranger for television and movies now. My principal involvement with songwriting was when he was living in New York and we'd get together. He was my former roommate when I was in the army. He and I did "Gallant Men," a song that Senator Dirksen recorded.

CA: Do you still enjoy music as a regular hobby?

OSGOOD: Sure. I've been playing the piano for years. I also play the violin now, and my kids are studying violin. It's a very big part of my life.

BIOGRAPHICAL/CRITICAL SOURCES: Time, December 31, 1973; *New York Times Book Review,* October 14, 1979, September 7, 1980; *Newsweek,* January 7, 1980; *Christian Herald,* July-August, 1980; *Variety,* June 24, 1981; *People,* November 2, 1981.*

—*Interview by Jean W. Ross*

WOOD, David M(ichael) 1934-

BRIEF ENTRY: Born October 16, 1934, in Cleveland, Ohio. American political scientist, educator, and author. Wood joined the faculty of University of Missouri in 1960 and became a professor of political science in 1971. He wrote *Comparing Political Systems: Power and Policy in Three Worlds* (Wiley, 1978) and *Power and Policy in Western European Democracies* (Wiley, 1978). *Address:* Department of Political Science, Middlebush Bldg., University of Missouri, Columbia, Mo. 65211.

*   *   *

WOOD, Harley Weston 1911-

PERSONAL: Born July 31, 1911, in Gulgong, New South Wales, Australia; son of Ernest Lesley (a garage proprietor) and Ruby Evelyn (Oldfield) Wood; married Una Muriel Johnston (a teacher and librarian), January 18, 1936; children: Christopher John, Rosamond Helen (Mrs. Richard Cowley Madden). *Education:* University of Sydney, B.Sc., 1933. *Politics:* "Very little." *Religion:* Methodist. *Home:* 178 Kenthurst Rd., Kenthurst, New South Wales 2154, Australia.

CAREER: Government of New South Wales, Sydney, New South Wales, Australia, assistant astronomer, 1936-37, first assistant astronomer, 1938-43, government astronomer, 1943-74; writer, 1974—. Lecturer at University of Sydney, 1959-71; chairman of Australian National Committee for Astronomy, 1966-74. *Member:* Astronomical Society of Australia (first president, 1966-68), British Astronomical Association (president of New South Wales branch, 1940-42, 1954-55), Royal Astronomical Society, Royal Society of New South Wales (president, 1949-50). *Awards, honors:* Queen Elizabeth II Coronation Medal, 1953; medal from Royal Society of New South Wales, 1962; D.Sc. from University of Sydney, 1965, for contributions to astrometry.

WRITINGS: The Southern Sky, Angus & Robertson, 1965, revised edition, 1967; *Unveiling the Universe,* Angus & Robertson, 1967; *Planets, Suns, and Galaxies,* Angus & Robertson, 1973. Contributor to astronomy journals. Editor of *Astrographic Catalogue, Sydney Section,* thirty-six volumes, 1943-71, and *Melbourne Section,* five volumes, 1955-63. Contributor to *Australian Dictionary of Biography.*

WORK IN PROGRESS: A biography of H. A. Lenehan, Australian Government Astronomer for New South Wales until 1908.

SIDELIGHTS: Wood told *CA:* "My interest in astronomy began with library reading at Mudgee High School about 1925. I resolved then that I would be an astronomer if it became possible. When at university, I had the opportunity to take a course in dynamical astronomy. In 1936 the post of assistant astronomer fell vacant at Sydney Observatory and I got it.

"All of my working life has been devoted to positional astronomy. This field is given fewer resources than it should be. An expenditure in positional astronomy over the whole world of less than half of what is devoted to establishing a large telescope would give a disproportionately great contribution to the advancement of astronomy.

"Positional astronomy is basic to almost all other branches of the science. Since the greater part of the population and wealth is in the Northern Hemisphere, positional astronomy in the south is much behind the north. This is a sad defect that could be righted with resources small in comparison with those sometimes devoted to other purposes in astronomy or allied sciences.

"My writing began with the need to report my work and was extended by a wish to further the cause of education in astronomy.

"In my mind nothing is more firmly fixed than the conviction that the well-established exception, far from proving the rule, actually disproves it."

* * *

WOOD, Maurice Arthur Ponsonby 1916-

PERSONAL: Born August 26, 1916; son of Arthur S. and Jane Elspeth (Piper) Wood; married Marjorie Pennell, 1947 (died, 1954); married M. Margaret Sandford; children: four sons, two daughters. *Education:* Attended Cambridge University. *Home:* Bishop's House, Norwich NR3 1SB, England.

CAREER: Ordained Anglican minister, 1940; curate of Anglican church in London, England, 1940-43; rector of Anglican church in Oxford, England, 1947-52; vicar, rural dean of Islington, and president of Islington Clerical Conference in London, 1952-61; Oak Hill Theological College, London, principal, 1961-71; bishop of Norwich, 1971—. Prebendary of St. Paul's Cathedral, London, 1969-71; chairman of Theological Colleges Principals' Conference, 1970-71. Member of House of Lords, 1975—. *Military service:* Royal Navy, chaplain, 1943-47.

WRITINGS: Christian Stability, Hodder & Stoughton, 1968; *Into the Way of Peace: Blackburn Lent Book,* S.P.C.K., 1982. Also author of *Like a Mighty Army,* 1956, and *You, Suffering,* 1959.

* * *

WOODBURY, Richard B(enjamin) 1917-

BRIEF ENTRY: Born May 16, 1917, in West Lafayette, Ind. American anthropologist, educator, and author. Woodbury taught at University of Kentucky, Columbia University, and University of Arizona. He was a professor of anthropology at University of Massachusetts from 1969 until 1981, when he was named professor emeritus. Woodbury has conducted archaeological field studies in Guatemala and Mexico, has served on the curatorial staff at the U.S. National Museum and Smithsonian Institution, and is active in the Archaeological Conservancy. He was also editor in chief of *American Anthropologist.* His studies have been funded in part by the Wenner-Gren Foundation. Woodbury's books include *The Ruins of Zaculeu, Guatemala* (United Fruit Co., 1953), *Prehistoric Stone Implements of Northeastern Arizona* (Peabody Museum of American Archaeology and Ethnology, Harvard University, 1954), *Civilizations in Desert Lands* (University of Utah Press, 1962), *The Excavation of Hawikuh by Frederick Webb Hodge: Report of the Hendricks-Hodge Expedition, 1917-1923* (Heye Foundation, 1966), and *Alfred V. Kidder* (Columbia University Press, 1973). *Address:* Department of Anthropology, University of Massachusetts, Amherst, Mass. 01002. *Biographical/critical sources: American Men and Women of Science: The Physical and Biological Sciences,* 13th edition, Bowker, 1976.

* * *

WOODEN, Wayne S(tanley) 1943-

PERSONAL: Born November 2, 1943, in San Francisco, Calif.; son of Wesley R. (a rancher) and Katharine (Lilienthal) Wooden. *Education:* Chico State College (now California State University, Chico), B.A., 1965; University of Pennsylvania, M.A., 1970, Ph.D., 1972. *Office:* Department of Behavioral Sciences, California State Polytechnic University, Pomona, Calif. 91768.

CAREER: U.S. Peace Corps, Washington, D.C., volunteer worker in Valencia, Venezuela, 1965-67; University of Hawaii, Hilo, assistant professor of sociology, 1972-77, chairman of department, 1975-77; California State University, Long Beach, lecturer in sociology, 1977-81; California State Polytechnic University, Pomona, assistant professor of behavioral sciences and criminal justice, 1981—. Member of Academy of Criminal Justice Sciences, Hawaii Subarea Health Planning Commission, 1976-77. *Member:* American Sociological Association, American Gerontological Society, Association for Criminal Justice Research, Western Society of Gerontology, Pacific Sociological Association.

WRITINGS: What Price Paradise?: Changing Social Patterns in Hawaii, University Press of America, 1981; (with Jay Parker) *Men Behind Bars: Sexual Exploitation in Prison,* Plenum, 1982; (with Martha Berkey) *Kids Who Torch: Dynamics of Juvenile Firesetters,* Plenum, in press. Associate editor of *Pacific Sociological Review,* 1974-77, and *Journal of Homosexuality,* 1979—.

SIDELIGHTS: Wooden commented: "My early decision to focus on sociology was a result of my service as a Peace Corps volunteer in Venezuela. My graduate training included the topics of stratification, criminology, and socialization, as well as training in family therapy. My research in Hawaii dealt with the impact of tourism and social change upon the island people. I also conducted research on Filipino elders in Hawaii.

"With my employment at California State University, my research interests shifted to areas of gender identity and minority communitites, and I published articles on Japanese American homosexuals and on treatment of sexual minorities in introductory sociology textbooks, and on cultural antecedents and the development of gay communities in South America.

"In terms of some of my research findings, my study on Hawaii focused on the emergence of 'local' as an identity choice for third generation Japanese Americans, in part as a response to their socialization into a multi-cultural environment and in part due to increased conflict with the newcomers to the state. My study on sexual behavior in prison noted the role that the heterosexual jocker plays in using sexual domination as a means of manipulation and control, often selecting as targets vulnerable heterosexual and younger homosexual inmates; our study also documents the range of sexual behavior in this prison. My current research on young fire setters will indicate the developmental stresses which lead to early childhood fire-setting behavior (often physical abuse, recent changes in the home environment) and to adolescent fire-setting behavior (peer rejection and neglect)."

* * *

WOODMAN, John E. 1932(?)-1983

OBITUARY NOTICE: Born c. 1932; died of respiratory failure, January 16, 1983. Editor. Beginning in 1965 he served as a free-lance editor for several Boston publishing concerns. He edited Walter Johnson's multi-volume biography of Adlai Stevenson. Obituaries and other sources: *Publishers Weekly,* February 25, 1983.

WOODS, Richard G(lenn)   1933-

PERSONAL: Born July 22, 1933, in Bartlesville, Okla.; son of George M. (in insurance) and Marian (Hunt) Woods. *Education:* University of Tulsa, B.S., 1955; University of Minnesota, M.A., 1957, further graduate study, 1959-65. *Politics:* Republican. *Religion:* Disciples of Christ. *Home:* 7603 Jervis St., Springfield, Va. 22151. *Office:* Food and Nutrition Service, U.S. Department of Agriculture, 3101 Park Center Dr., Alexandria, Va. 22302.

CAREER: Whirlpool Corp., Benton Harbor, Mich., deferred compensation consultant, 1957-59; Univesity of Minnesota, Minneapolis, co-director of Office for Applied Social Science and the Future, 1968-73; Manitou College, LaMacaza, Quebec, 1973-76; U.S. Senate, Washington, D.C., legislative aide, 1976-81; U.S. Department of Agriculture, Food and Nutrition Service, Alexandria, Va., director of Office of Governmental Affairs, 1981—. *Military service:* U.S. Air Force, 1961-62.

WRITINGS: (With Arthur M. Harkins and Dorothy Speidel) *Indians in Minneapolis* (monograph), League of Women Voters of Minneapolis, 1968; *The Management of Private Enterprise: Progress for the Future* (monograph), University of Minnesota Press, 1971; (contributor) Michael Marien and Warren Ziegler, editors, *The Potential of Educational Futures*, Jones Press, 1972; (with H. S. Becker and G. P. Johnson) *Report of the Delphi Inquiry Into the Future of American Water Resource Utilization and Development* (monograph), University of Minnesota Press, 1973; (editor) *Future Dimensions of World Food and Population*, Westview, 1981. Also co-author of thirty-seven monographs on urban American Indians. Contributor to *Personnel*.

WORK IN PROGRESS: Research on the effectiveness of contemporary domestic U.S. public feeding programs.

SIDELIGHTS: Woods wrote: "The major threat I see to a humane and progressive future is the failure of the political system to make careful and prudent assessments of present and future problems, to make the difficult decisions necessary for remedial action, and to ensure a stable and dependable governmental framework for this society which is neither oppressive nor inefficient."

*   *   *

WOODWORTH, Constance   1911-1983

OBITUARY NOTICE: Born in 1911; died of cancer, March 27, 1983, in Palm Beach, Fla. Executive and editor. She was new products and creative director of Lehn & Fink Products Company. In addition, she served as beauty and fashion editor of *Town and Country* and *Harper's Bazaar* and women's page editor of the *New York Journal-American*. Obituaries and other sources: *New York Times*, March 30, 1983.

*   *   *

WOOLEY, John (Steven)   1949-
(Robert B. Leslie, Jerome Severs)

PERSONAL: Born April 4, 1949, in St. Paul, Minn.; son of John MacFarlane (a high school administrator) and Ruth (a town clerk; maiden name, Seely) Wooley; married Janis Botz (a public school teacher of learning-disabled students), August 16, 1979. *Education:* Oklahoma State University, B.S., 1970;

Central Oklahoma State University, M.A., 1977. *Politics:* "Democrat with Populist leanings." *Religion:* "Nondenominational Christian." *Home address:* Route 1, Box 258, Chelsea, Okla. 74016. *Agent:* Harold Schmidt, William Morris Agency, 1350 Avenue of the Americas, New York, N.Y. 10019. *Office address:* P.O. Box 133, Foyil, Okla. 74031.

CAREER: Ralston-Purina Co., Edmond, Okla., plant sanitarian, 1971; associated with Bruce Webster Films, 1974-77; Oscar Rose Junior College, Midwest City, Okla., teacher of English composition and literature, 1977-79; KWPR-AM Radio, Claremore, Okla., announcer, 1980-82; writer, 1982—. Co-founder of Robert B. Leslie Foundation, 1975-79. *Military service:* U.S. Naval Reserve, 1970-76, active duty, 1971-73; served in the Philippines and Vietnam.

WRITINGS: (With Ron Wolfe) *Old Fears* (novel), F. Watts, 1982; (editor) *Robert Leslie Bellem's Dan Turner, Hollywood Detective*, Popular Press, 1983.

Work represented in anthologies, including *Intro Eight*, edited by George Garrett, Doubleday, 1977. Co-author of *Conservation Comics One*. Author of "The Bookshelf," a column in *Big Reel*, 1979—, and "On the Funk Patrol," a column in *Dream Line*, 1982—. Contributor of poems, short stories, and articles to magazines (sometimes under pseudonyms Robert B. Leslie and Jerome Severs), including *Rolling Stone*, *Dreamweaver*, *Nostalgia Journal*, and *Knave*. Editor of *Dreamtrip*.

WORK IN PROGRESS: *Full Moon*, a novel, with Ron Wolfe, completion expected in 1983; research for a book on films, with Michael Pitts.

SIDELIGHTS: Wooley commented: "My grandmother, Mary M. Wooley, was a poet and writer (and fourth cousin of Lord Byron); she influenced me greatly. I grew up in the small town of Chelsea, Oklahoma, where I read a lot, played baseball, fished, and generally had a swell time. Somewhere along the line, I developed the conviction that cities and masses of people were inherently bad, or at least unfriendly while, conversely, the little map-dot towns and the people who inhabit them were the opposite. This admittedly romantic notion has prevailed with me to this day for better or worse, and much of my writing reflects this attitude.

"Although my published writing to this point is less than insignificant by comparison, I have been influenced by John Steinbeck, Booth Tarkington, Raymond Chandler, James M. Cain, Nathanael West, and a couple of fine, unsung storytellers, William Lindsay Gresham and Robert Leslie Bellem.

"My talent was sharpened and my desire to write fired by the Creative Studies Division of the Central Oklahoma State University English department. There, under novelist Marilyn Harris, I developed my first novel and made the decision, once and for all, to stay with writing and devote my energies to it—even though I had wanted to be a writer, and had written, since childhood."

*   *   *

WORTHINGTON, Edgar Barton   1905-

PERSONAL: Born January 13, 1905, in London, England; son of Edgar (an engineer) and Amy (Beale) Worthington; married Stella Johnson, August 23, 1930 (died November, 1978); married Harriett Stockton (a title examiner and sculptress), June 21, 1980; children: Shelagh Wakeley, Grizelda Hitchcock, Marthe Kiley. *Education:* Gonville and Caius College, Cambridge, B.A., 1927, Ph.D., 1931. *Religion:* Agnostic. *Home:*

Colin Godmans, Furners Green, near Uckfield, Sussex, England.

CAREER: Demonstrator in zoology at Cambridge University, 1933-37; scientist for African Research Survey, 1934-37; director of Freshwater Biological Association of the United Kingdom, 1937-46; scientific secretary of Colonial Research Council, 1946-49; scientific secretary of East Africa High Commission, 1947-51; Secretary-General of Scientific Committee for Africa South of the Sahara, 1951-55; Deputy Director General of Nature Conservancy of the United Kingdom, 1956-65; scientific director of International Biological Programme, 1965-75; environmental consultant in tropical Africa, Asia, and Latin America, 1975—. Scientific adviser for Middle East Supply Council, 1943-45, and development adviser for Uganda, 1946.

MEMBER: Freshwater Biological Association, Nature Conservancy, Royal Geographical Society, Linnean Society (past member of council), Institute of Biology, Zoological Society (fellow). *Awards, honors:* Commander of Order of the British Empire, 1966; Ridder of the Golden Ark (Netherlands), 1970, for services to international conservation; member of Honour International Union for Conservation of Nature and Natural Resources, 1978.

WRITINGS: (With Stella Worthington) *Inland Waters of Africa,* Macmillan, 1933; *Science in Africa,* Oxford University Press, 1938; *Middle East Science,* H.M.S.O., 1946; *Development Plan for Uganda,* Uganda Government, 1946; (with T. T. Macan) *Life in Lakes and Rivers,* Collins, 1951, revised edition, 1972; *Science in the Development of Africa,* Commission de Cooperation Technique en Afrique, 1958; *The Evolution of International Biological Programme,* Cambridge University Press, 1975; *Arid Land Irrigation in Developing Countries,* Pergamon, 1977; *The Nile,* Wayland, 1978; *The Ecological Century,* Oxford University Press, 1983.

WORK IN PROGRESS: Research on ecology, development, and conservation.

SIDELIGHTS: Worthington told *CA:* "As an elderly but still active biologist, who has worked on a variety of subjects in many countries, my message to the rising generations of ecologists is: spend less time learning more and more about less and less, and more time on the practical application of what you already know. Unless proven ecological principles are applied widely during the next few decades, the human species, as well as all other animals and plants, may suffer a gloomy twenty-first century.

"The ecological principles which need following have been related by many authorities. They include limitation of population in balance with renewable resources, control of aggression, and 'small is beautiful.' Human progress will come through diversity, not uniformity, a conclusion I have reached from personal experiences—which I relate in my most recent book."

*   *   *

WOSHINSKY, Oliver Hanson   1939-

BRIEF ENTRY: Born August 6, 1939, in Tientsin, China. American political scientist, educator, and author. Woshinsky has taught political science at Allegheny College, University of Maine, and University of Southern Maine. He wrote *The French Deputy: Incentives and Behavior in the National Assembly* (Lexington Books, 1973). *Address:* Department of Political Science, University of Southern Maine, 96 Falmouth St., Portland, Maine 04103.

WREN, Wilfrid John   1930-

PERSONAL: Born December 22, 1930, in Bromley, England; son of Douglas William (a banker) and V. Norah K. (a teacher; maiden name, Slater) Wren; married June Lucraft-Purser, May 20, 1959 (divorced June, 1979); married Erica Ann Randall (a teacher), October 20, 1979; children: Sarah-Jane, Jonathan William, Piers Christopher Jolyon. *Education:* Peterhouse, Cambridge, B.A., 1952; Middlesex Hospital Medical School, London, L.M.S.S.A., 1956; Cambridge University, M.A., 1975. *Politics:* "Left-wing Conservative, inclining toward Social Democrat." *Religion:* Church of England. *Home:* Rivendell, Waveney Hill, Oulton Broad, Lowestoft, Suffolk NR32 3PR, England. *Office:* 82 Victoria Rd., Oulton Broad, Lowestoft, Suffolk NR33 9LU, England.

CAREER: St. Luke's Hospital, Guildford, England, house surgeon, 1956-58; assistant in general medical practice in Odiham, Hampshire, England, 1961-62; general medical practitioner in Lowestoft, England, 1962—. Member of Lowestoft Town Council, 1968-71; member of Norfolk Health Authority, 1979-82, and Great Yarmouth and Waveney Health Authority, 1982—. *Military service:* Royal Air Force, surgeon and obstetrician, 1958-61; served in Ceylon (now Sri Lanka); became flight lieutenant. *Member:* British Medical Association, Society for the Protection of Rural Wales, Festiniog Railway Society (life member), Suffolk Preservation Society, Waveney and Oulton Broad Yacht Club, Bala Lake Sailing Club.

WRITINGS: The Tanat Valley: Its Railways and Industrial Archaeology, David & Charles, 1968; *Ports of the Eastern Counties,* Terence Dalton, 1976; *The Tanet Valley Light Railway,* Oakwood Press, 1979; *Voices by the Sea: The Story of Choirs at Aldeburgh,* Terence Dalton, 1981. Contributor to medical journals and magazines, including *Shropshire.* Music critic for *Lowestoft Journal.*

WORK IN PROGRESS: Novels; composing a short mass for an unaccompanied four-part choir.

SIDELIGHTS: Wren told *CA:* "I came to the writing of books almost by accident, in my thirties. At that time I wished to record the railway and industrial history of a small valley in mid-Wales where I spent the war years as a boy. To my great surprise, the publisher to whom I submitted the idea at once gave me a contract on the basis of a synopsis and a specimen chapter. Later, I wished to prove to myself that the Welsh book was not just a 'flash in the pan,' and put in for a contract for a book on the East Anglian ports and harbors as one of a series on the British Isles by the same publisher. This series was cancelled, but I signed a contract with another publisher for this book, on which I had done a great deal of work by then. The third book was a revised and more specialized version of part of the first book, fitting in with a railway history series by yet a third publisher. The book on the Aldeburgh Festival arose out of a conversation with a professor of music at the University of East Anglia, who suggested that I combine my writing and my music in one work. As I have sung in the Aldeburgh Festival choir for seventeen years, I was thought to be the ideal person to write the story of the choirs that have performed there since the festival was begun by Benjamin Britten in 1947. This book is, incidentally (as far as we know), the only hardcover ever to have been published in Britain on the history of a choir.

"All my books have been bought by people from the United States and from Holland, but there are not foreign-language versions. All were written *after* having obtained contracts, and so I was spared the usual heartache of amateur authors—that is, hawking completed manuscripts round to publishers and receiving rejection slips.

"My methods of working are perhaps unusual. I research the material on my days 'off-duty' as a doctor; then, when I am ready, my family goes away to stay with friends for a week while I write flat-out for fourteen to sixteen hours a day, existing chiefly on coffee, bowls of cereal, and sleep. I then type two-fingered in triplicate, revising as I go, though in fact the original manuscript (written in longhand using a fountain-pen) usually needs very little revision. I discovered early on that I had a natural style and balance that must be instinctive, and that may have come from the writing of the seventy-two three-hour exams that I had to do in the years of medical training. Perhaps this is the reason why there are so many doctor-authors—or is it that the type of person who goes in for medicine usually has a wide field of interests to start with? I don't know.

"When I travel around, looking at landscapes and towns, I always want to know the history behind what I see, whether it be Iron Age forts, disused railway embankments, or old canals or warehouses. The history of the development of English east coast harbors, for example, is inextricably linked with the rise and fall of relative sea-level over the last two thousand years, with the erosion of headlands and the silting up of estuaries. Consequently, I try to portray the history and geography of an area as one chronological whole. This is how I would like to see these two subjects taught in schools—and, happily, this is indeed now becoming more common in British schools.

"The other creative activity in my life, the composing of music, began in my teens, although I was brought up in a musical family and sang from an early age. While in the sixth form at school, studying sciences for the first medical exams, I was given lessons in composition and organ. I have always written music with performance by specific people in mind—songs for soloist friends, unaccompanied choral works for small choirs (including one that I myself conducted for twelve years), carols for four-part girls' voices of a large Norwich school, and a set of orchestral variations for a youth orchestra. Almost all my pieces—over fifty in all—have been performed, but none as yet published; they have been heard in Guildford and Norwich cathedrals and on Dutch television. A new company in Holland hopes to publish some of my music in the not-too-distant future.

"I live a very full and satisfying life as a traditional family doctor wholly within the framework of the National Health Service, the ethos of which I fully believe in. But my wife and I still find time to sing in three choirs, to sail our dinghy in competitive sailing, and to walk over the Welsh mountains based on our eighteenth-century stone-built cottage in Wales. The best thing is that I find life becomes more and more satisfying the older I get."

*   *   *

WRIGHT, Anna (Maria Louisa Perrott) Rose   1890-1968
(Anna Perrott Rose)

OBITUARY NOTICE: Born October 13, 1890, in New York, N.Y.; died September 4, 1968, in Holmdel, N.J. Educator and author. Wright was a teacher and tutor who added four foster children to her family of five. She chronicled her success with rearing these children in *Room for One More*, a 1950 bestseller.

The book was extensively translated and was also made into a 1952 motion picture starring Cary Grant. Among Wright's numerous books for children are *Offshore Summer, The Laughing Gulls, Barefoot Days,* and *Summer at Buckhorn.* Obituaries and other sources: *Current Biography,* Wilson, 1952; *New York Times,* September 5, 1968; *Publishers Weekly,* November 4, 1968.

*   *   *

WRIGHT, Lafayette Hart   1917-1983

OBITUARY NOTICE—See index for *CA* sketch: Born December 3, 1917, in Chickasha, Okla.; died of radiation pneumonitis while undergoing lung cancer treatment, April 12, 1983, in Baltimore, Md. Educator and author. An expert on taxation procedures and a professor of law, he joined the faculty of the University of Michigan in 1946. Wright served as a consultant to the Internal Revenue Service and received the Civilian Meritorious Service Award from the U.S. Treasury Department in 1957. His books include *Income Tax Law, Corporate Tax Affairs,* and *Needed Changes in IRS Procedures.* Obituaries and other sources: *Who's Who in America,* 42nd edition, Marquis, 1982; *Chicago Tribune,* April 14, 1983; *New York Times,* April 14, 1983.

*   *   *

WRIGHT, Mary Clabaugh   1917-1970

OBITUARY NOTICE: Born September 25, 1917, in Tuscaloosa, Ala.; died June 18, 1970, in Guilford, Conn.; buried in Grove St. Cemetery, New Haven, Conn. Educator and author. An expert in Chinese history, Wright was the first woman to be named full professor at Yale University. While on a research trip to China in late 1941, Wright and her husband, also a scholar of Chinese studies, were interned by the Japanese after the attack on Pearl Harbor and spent the remainder of the war in a prison camp. Her study of Chinese politics and culture in the mid-nineteenth century, *The Last Stand of Chinese Conservatism,* appeared in 1957. Obituaries and other sources: *Who's Who of American Women,* 5th edition, Marquis, 1968; *New York Times,* June 19, 1970; *Notable American Women: The Modern Period,* Belknap, 1980.

*   *   *

WRIGHT, Theon   1904-

BRIEF ENTRY: Born June 24, 1904, in Oroville, Calif. American journalist and author. Wright was a sportswriter for the *Honolulu Advertiser, Oakland Tribune,* and *Newark Ledger.* He has also worked as feature writer, cable correspondent, and aviation editor for United Press International. Wright's nonfiction books include *Rape in Paradise* (Hawthorn, 1966), *World Without Time: The Bedouin* (John Day, 1969), *The Open Door: A Case History of Automatic Writing* (John Day, 1970), *The Big Nail: The Story of the Cook-Peary Feud* (John Day, 1970), *The Disenchanted Isles: The Story of the Second Revolution in Hawaii* (Dial, 1972), and *In Search of the Lindbergh Baby* (Tower, 1981). *Address:* 37-32 80th St., Jackson Heights, New York, N.Y. *Biographical/critical sources: Negro Digest,* May, 1967; *Washington Post Book World,* January 18, 1970; *New Leader,* March 2, 1970; *New York Times Book Review,* September 24, 1972; *American Historical Review,* June, 1973.

WU, William F(ranking) 1951-

PERSONAL: Born March 13, 1951, in Kansas City, Mo.; son of William Quokan (a neurosurgeon) and Cecile (a writer; maiden name, Franking) Wu. *Education:* University of Michigan, A.B., 1973, A.M., 1976, Ph.D., 1979. *Residence:* Prairie Village, Kan. *Agent:* Cherry Weiner Literary Agency, 1734 Church St., Rahway, N.J. 07065.

CAREER: Jackson County Honor Farm, Kansas City, Mo., medical attendant, 1973; City of Los Angeles, Los Angeles, Calif., interview specialist, 1980; writer. *Member:* Science Fiction Writers of America.

WRITINGS: "Psychechain" (one-act play; adapted from the short story "By the Flicker of the One-eyed Flame" by Irvin Paik), first produced in Los Angeles, Calif., at East/West Players Theatre, April 5, 1977; (contributor) Peter Weston, editor, *Andromeda 2*, Futura Books, 1977; Weston, editor, *Andromeda 3*, Futura Books, 1978; *The Yellow Peril: Chinese Americans in American Fiction, 1850-1940*, Archon Books, 1982. Contributor of articles to *Fantasy Newsletter*, and of short stories to *Isaac Asimov's Science Fiction Magazine, Isaac Asimov's Aliens and Outworlders, New Wave Science Fiction*, and *Amazing Science Fiction Stories*.

WORK IN PROGRESS: Science fiction novels and short stories, including *My Chinese Marriage*, with Holly M. Franking, *The Phosphor-Dot Wars*, and *Star*Song*, with Diana G. Gallagher; preparing an article on the children's fantasies of Edward Eager.

SIDELIGHTS: Wu told *CA:* "My principal interest is in Asian Americans and their specific identity as a group that is neither Asian nor white American. My fiction deals primarily with Chinese American characters, often though not always in stories with specifically ethnic topics. I have a limited facility with Mandarin Chinese from college study. Research is secondary to my fiction."

In his book *The Yellow Peril: Chinese Americans in American Fiction, 1850-1940*, Wu argued that the threat of Asian takeover was "the overwhelmingly dominant theme in American fiction about Chinese Americans" from 1850 to 1940. Novels such as Atwell Whitney's *Almond Eyed: The Great Agitator* and Robert Woltor's *A Short and Truthful History of the Taking of Oregon and California by the Chinese in the Year A.D. 1899*, and characters such as Fu Manchu, strengthened the sinister stereotype of Chinese characters. In conclusion, Wu argued that fiction written by Chinese Americans themselves can dispel racist stereotypes, replacing them with realistic images of Chinese Americans.

AVOCATIONAL INTERESTS: Travel and canoeing.

BIOGRAPHICAL/CRITICAL SOURCES: Times Literary Supplement, April 9, 1982.

Y

YAKER, Henri (Marc) 1922-

BRIEF ENTRY: Born October 19, 1922, in Boston, Mass. American psychologist, educator, and author. Yaker has taught at Lincoln University, Hobart College, Seton Hall University, Fairleigh Dickinson University, Rutgers University, and New York Theological Seminary. He has also been a psychologist at state hospitals and at the New Jersey State Prison, and he has worked with retarded children. In 1966 Yaker was appointed director of psychology at Marlboro Psychiatric Hospital. He co-edited *The Future of Time: Man's Temporal Environment* (Doubleday, 1971). *Biographical/critical sources: New York Times Book Review,* September 19, 1971; *Best Sellers,* December 1, 1971; *Times Literary Supplement,* November 10, 1972.

* * *

YARBROUGH, Tinsley E(ugene) 1941-

PERSONAL: Born August 13, 1941, in Decatur, Ala.; son of Herbert Tinsley (a salesman) and Mary Ellen (Cole) Yarbrough; married Mary Alice Thompson (a public school administrator), 1965; children: Sarah Elizabeth, Wesley Cole. *Education:* University of Alabama, B.A., 1963, M.A., 1965, Ph.D., 1967. *Politics:* Democrat. *Home:* 1211 Red Banks Rd., Greenville, N.C. 27834. *Office:* Department of Political Science, East Carolina University, Greenville, N.C. 27834.

CAREER: East Carolina University, Greenville, N.C., assistant professor, 1967-70, associate professor, 1970-75, professor of political science, 1975—, chairman of department, 1979—. *Member:* American Political Science Association, American Society for Public Administration, Southern Political Science Association, Phi Beta Kappa. *Awards, honors:* Woodrow Wilson Fellowship, 1963; fellowship from the National Defense Education Association, 1963-66.

WRITINGS: Judge Frank Johnson and Human Rights in Alabama, University of Alabama Press, 1981. Editor-in-chief of *Politics,* 1971-75. Contributor of journals and periodicals, including *Public Administration Review.*

SIDELIGHTS: Yarbrough's *Judge Frank Johnson and Human Rights in Alabama* chronicles Judge Johnson's support of civil rights in Alabama from 1955 to 1979. *Washington Post Book World*'s David Jonathan Cohen wrote, ''In his carefully and solidly crafted essay, Yarbrough depicts Johnson as a staunch but uncommon Republican: conservative on fiscal, criminal and personal matters, but unflinching in maintaining what he perceives as constitutional protections for human rights.''

BIOGRAPHICAL/CRITICAL SOURCES: Washington Post Book World, July 5, 1981.

* * *

YATES, Madeleine 1937-

PERSONAL: Born April 23, 1937, in Hollywood, Calif.; daughter of Faris (in business) and Olga (an opera singer; maiden name, Abdo) Karma; married Leon Joseph Yates (an import-export superintendent), August 1, 1964; children: Michael John, Elizabeth Adele, Gregory Nicholas. *Education:* Received A.A. from Pasadena City College; also attended California State University, Los Angeles. *Politics:* Republican. *Religion:* Roman Catholic. *Home:* 4264 Commonwealth Ave., Flintridge, Calif. 91011.

CAREER: Merchandising secretary at Young & Rubicam, Los Angeles, Calif.; administrative assistant at Writers Guild of America, West, Los Angeles; interior decorator at Babdaty Studio, Beverly Hills, Calif., and at Flintridge Interiors, Flintridge, Calif. *Member:* International P.E.N., Society of Children's Book Writers, Southern California Council on Literature for Children and Young People.

WRITINGS: Earth Power: The Story of Geothermal Energy (juvenile), Abingdon, 1980; (with Gloria D. Miklowitz) *Young Tycoons: Ten Success Stories* (young adult), Harcourt, 1981; *Sun Power: The Story of Solar Energy* (juvenile), Abingdon, 1982.

SIDELIGHTS: Madeleine Yates told *CA:* ''The glory of man is his power to express thoughts that uplift others to the beauty of life and the nobility of human nature.''

BIOGRAPHICAL/CRITICAL SOURCES: Washington Post Book World, November 9, 1980.

* * *

YONGE, Charlotte (Mary) 1823-1901

BRIEF ENTRY: Surname pronounced Young; born August 11

(some sources say August 13), 1823, in Otterbourne, Hampshire, England; died March 24, 1901, in Elderfield, England. British editor, novelist, and children's author. Yonge, a prolific writer of fiction and history, was editor of the British children's periodical *Monthly Packet* from 1851 to 1900. Of the nearly one hundred juvenile works she produced between 1838 and 1900, most were tales of upper-class family life, written to convey Christian values to an audience of Victorian youngsters. Yonge's popularity reached a peak in the 1850's, when her family sagas *The Heir of Redclyffe* (1853) and *The Daisy Chain; or, Aspirations: A Family Chronicle* (1856) were published. Her later, more didactic works, including *Frank's Debt* (1881) and *The Cross Roads; or, A Choice in Life* (1892), enjoyed less favor with readers. Yonge also wrote the four-volume *Landmarks of History* (1852-57) and *A Parallel History of France and England* (1871). *Biographical/critical sources:* Christabel Rose Coleridge, *Charlotte Mary Yonge: Her Life and Letters,* Macmillan, 1903, reprinted, Gale, 1969; Margaret L. Mare and Alicia C. Percival, *Victorian Best-seller: The World of Charlotte M. Yonge,* Harrap, 1948, reprinted, Kennikat, 1970; *A Dictionary of Literature in the English Language: From Chaucer to 1940,* Pergamon, 1970; *Cassell's Encyclopaedia of World Literature,* revised edition, Morrow, 1973; *Twentieth-Century Children's Writers,* St. Martin's, 1978.

* * *

YOUNG, Agatha
See YOUNG, Agnes Brooks

* * *

YOUNG, Agnes Brooks 1898-1974
(Agatha Young)

OBITUARY NOTICE: Born November 18, 1898, in Cleveland, Ohio; died February 6, 1974, in New York, N.Y. Educator, labor consultant, and author. Young taught at Western Reserve University (now Case Western Reserve University) during the early 1930's and was consultant to both the War Manpower Commission and the Retiring and Reemployment Administration during World War II. Under the pseudonym Agatha Young, she wrote of the medical world in books such as *Scalpel, Men Who Made Surgery,* and *The Hospital.* Obituaries and other sources: *New York Times,* February 8, 1974; *Who Was Who in America, With World Notables,* Volume VI: *1974-76,* Marquis, 1976.

* * *

YOUNG, Harold Chester 1932-

BRIEF ENTRY: Born October 26, 1932, in Cambridge, Mass. American library administrator and author. After almost thirty years as a librarian, Young became assistant director of public services at University of Minnesota in 1975. He wrote *Planning, Programming, Budgeting Systems in Academic Libraries* (Gale, 1976). Young was associate editor of the Library of Congress *National Union Catalog Author List: 1942-62.* He also edited the five-volume *Subject Directory of Special Libraries and Information Centers* (Gale, 1979). *Address:* 313 Farmdale Rd., Hopkins, Minn. 55343; and Wilson Library, University of Minnesota, Minneapolis, Minn. 55455.

* * *

YOUNG, Jim 1930-

PERSONAL: Born August 21, 1930, in Salt Lake City, Utah;

son of Kenneth (a collector) and Alice (Greer) Young; married Jean Hunt (a writer and artist), May 11, 1953; children: Michael Thomas. *Education:* University of California, Berkeley, B.A., 1958. *Home address:* P.O. Box 8, Woodstock, N.Y. 12498.

CAREER: Writer, dealer in art and antiques, and real estate investor, all 1970—. *Military service:* U.S. Army, 1953-55.

WRITINGS: People's Guide to Country Real Estate, Praeger, 1974; *Garage Sale Manual,* Praeger, 1974; *When the Whale Came to My Town* (juvenile; photographs by Dan Bernstein), Knopf, 1975; *Succeed in the World of Music,* Little, Brown, 1977; *Great Trash,* New American Library, 1978; *Buying Right in Country Property,* New American Library, 1979.

SIDELIGHTS: When the Whale Came to My Town is a real-life story about a beached cetacean, waiting to die, and the boy who finds and befriends it. According to Burt Supree's *New York Times Book Review* critique, Jim Young's "writing is simple and direct, unhurried, full of feeling and keen observation. Nothing is overstated."

BIOGRAPHICAL/CRITICAL SOURCES: New York Times Book Review, November 3, 1974.

* * *

YOUNG, Oran R(eed) 1941-

BRIEF ENTRY: Born March 15, 1941, in Yonkers, N.Y. American political scientist, educator, and author. Young worked at Hudson Institute, then taught at Princeton University and University of Texas. In 1976 he became a professor of government and politics at University of Maryland. Young was also a Guggenheim fellow in 1969, and senior editor of *World Politics* from 1968 to 1976. His books include *The Intermediaries: Third Parties in International Crises* (Princeton University Press, 1967), *The Politics of Force: Bargaining During International Crises* (Princeton University Press, 1968), *Systems of Political Science* (Prentice-Hall, 1968), *A Systematic Approach to International Politics* (Center of International Affairs, Woodrow Wilson School of Public and International Affairs, Princeton University, 1968), *Resource Management at the International Level: The Case of the North Pacific* (Nichols Publishing, 1977), and *Compliance and Public Authority: A Theory With International Applications* (Johns Hopkins University Press, 1979). *Address:* East Hill, Wolcott, Vt. 05680.

* * *

YOUNG, Pam 1943-
(Sidetracked Home Executives, a joint pseudonym)

PERSONAL: Born May 8, 1943, in Torrence, Calif.; daughter of William L. (a truck driver) and Dolores (McLaughlin) Young; divorced; children: Michael, Peggy Ann, Joanna. *Education:* Attended Clark College. *Home:* 1401 Northeast 124th St., Vancouver, Wash. 98665. *Agent:* John Boswell Associates, 41 East 51st St., New York, N.Y. 10022. *Office:* 7409 Northeast Hazeldell Ave., Vancouver, Wash. 98665.

CAREER: Homemaker and writer.

WRITINGS—With Peggy Jones, under joint pseudonym Sidetracked Home Executives: *Sidetracked Home Executives: From Pigpen to Paradise,* Warner Books, 1981; *Sidetracked Sisters Catch-Up in the Kitchen,* Warner Books, 1983; *What Miss Cratzberry Never Taught Us,* Warner Books, in press.

SIDELIGHTS: Pam Young and Peggy Jones told *CA:* "In June, 1977, Pam and Peggy hit bottom. They were failing at their chosen profession—homemaking. They were always locked out, left behind, or overdrawn, and their homes were in total chaos and filled with endless clutter. They developed a three-by-five card file system that changed everything. The first book was one positive result of becoming organized.''

*   *   *

YOUNG, Robert
    See PAYNE, (Pierre Stephen) Robert

*   *   *

YOUNG, William J.   1938-

PERSONAL: Born March 2, 1938, in Knoxville, Tenn.; son of James Monroe (a businessman) and Drama Lillian (Weaver) Young; married Edna Carter (a speech therapist). *Education:* University of Tennessee, B.S., 1965, M.S., 1967, Ph.D., 1971. *Home:* 27 Hamilton Circle, Philadelphia, Pa. 19130. *Office:* Department of Geography, Temple University, Broad & Montgomery, Philadelphia, Pa. 19122.

CAREER: Oak Ridge National Laboratory, Oak Ridge, Tenn., engineering aide, 1960-65, consultant, 1967-68; Temple University, Philadelphia, Pa., professor of geography, 1968—. *Military service:* U.S. Army Reserve, 1954-64. *Member:* Association of American Geographers, American Association of University Professors. *Awards, honors:* Award from American Association of Publishers, 1980, for *The United States Energy Atlas.*

WRITINGS: (With David Cuff) *The United States Energy Atlas,* Free Press, 1980. Contributor to geography journals.

WORK IN PROGRESS: Atlas of Disease and Death for the United States; a book ''concerning the best places to live in the United States, based on evaluation of various kinds of health, natural hazard, and socio-economic data.''

SIDELIGHTS: Young told *CA:* ''My interests in epidemiologic studies has led me to the production of *Atlas of Disease and Death for the United States.* I feel that it is a long overdue reference for the epidemiological community.

''To a large degree, the best places to live are based on one's own perception of place. I would like to go beyond perception and literally evaluate each county of the United States on the basis of such things as nearness to hazardous waste sites, dirty air, dirty water, poor health quality, earthquake belts, acid rain, etc. I would imagine the quality environments exist in central Pennsylvania as well as central Alaska or Montana.''

*   *   *

YU, Elena S. H.   1947-

BRIEF ENTRY: Born June 25, 1947, in Fukien, China. Social psychologist, educator, and author. Yu taught sociology at University of St. Thomas, University of Notre Dame, and University of Victoria before she became an adjunct member of the faculty of San Diego State University in 1978. Yu was

also a fellow at University of Notre Dame's Center for the Study of Man in Contemporary Society, and she has worked with refugees from Vietnam. She co-authored *Interviewing Conduct: A Manual for Training Vietnamese* (Vietnamese Refugee Research Project, San Diego, Calif., 1979) and *Fertility and Kinship in the Philippines: An Ethnographic Study* (University of Notre Dame Press, 1980). *Address:* Department of Sociology, San Diego State University, San Diego, Calif. 92182.

*   *   *

YUDOF, Mark G(eorge)   1944-

PERSONAL: Born October 30, 1944, in Philadelphia, Pa.; son of Jack and Eleanor (Parris) Yudof; married Judith Gomel, July 14, 1965; children: Seth Adam, Samara Lisa. *Education:* University of Pennsylvania, B.A., 1965, LL.B., 1968. *Office:* School of Law, University of Texas, 727 East 26th St., Austin, Tex. 78705.

CAREER: Harvard University, Cambridge, Mass., lecturer in education and staff attorney for Harvard Center for Law and Business, 1969-71; University of Texas, Austin, professor of law, 1971—, James R. Dougherty Professor, 1978-79. Chairman of Austin Cable Commission, 1982. Visiting professor of law at University of Michigan, 1983.

WRITINGS: (With David L. Kirp) *Educational Policy and the Law,* McCutchan, 1974, 2nd edition (with Kirp, Tyll van Geel, and Betsy Levin), 1982; *When Government Speaks,* University of California Press, 1982; (with Jefferson B. Fordham) *Local Government Law,* Foundation Press, in press.

WORK IN PROGRESS: Gender Justice Book.

SIDELIGHTS: Yudof told *CA:* ''I am interested in the history of the Fourteenth Amendment and the relationship between liberty and equal protection under the law. The projected book *Gender Justice* deals with these among many questions relating to government policy and sex classifications. I also have a keen interest in local government law, and how local governments raise revenues and distribute services and how they can be made more accountable to citizens.''

AVOCATIONAL INTERESTS: Collecting antique maps.

*   *   *

YURIEFF, Zoya I(osifovna)   1922-

BRIEF ENTRY: Born August 24, 1922, in Siemiatycze, Poland; came to United States, 1947, naturalized citizen, 1952. American educator and author. Yurieff began teaching Russian language and Slavic literature at New York University in 1966. She has also taught at Queens College of the City University of New York, and she has been a member of the editorial board of *Novyj Zhurnal/New Review.* Yurieff wrote *Joseph Wittlin* (Twayne, 1973). *Address:* Department of Slavic Language and Literature, New York University, 19 University Pl., Room 421, New York, N.Y. 10003.

Z

ZACEK, Jane Shapiro 1938-
(Jane P. Shapiro)

PERSONAL: Born November 10, 1938, in New York, N.Y.; daughter of Charles and Dorothy (Gintzler) Perlberg; married Alan M. Shapiro (an architect), June 18, 1961; children: Leslie, Peter. *Education:* Cornell University, B.A. (with honors), 1960; Columbia University, M.A. and Certificate from Russian Institute, both 1962, Ph.D., 1967. *Politics:* Democrat. *Religion:* Jewish. *Home:* 570 Providence St., Albany, N.Y. 12223.

CAREER: University of Cincinnati, Cincinnati, Ohio, instructor in political science, 1963-64; Manhattanville College, Purchase, N.Y., 1965-72, began as instructor, became assistant professor, associate professor of political science and chairman of department, 1972-c. 1980, director of continuing education, 1977. Senior fellow at Russian Institute, Columbia University, 1974-75. Managing editor for international affairs of *Soviet Union. Member:* Amnesty International, American Political Science Association, American Association for the Advancement of Slavic Studies, Phi Beta Kappa.

WRITINGS—All under name Jane P. Shapiro: (Editor with Lenard J. Cohen) *Communist Systems in Comparative Perspective*, Doubleday, 1974; (editor with Peter J. Potichnyj) *Change and Adaptation in Soviet and East European Politics*, Praeger, 1976; (editor with Potichnyj) *From the Cold War to Detente*, Praeger, 1976. Contributor to political science and Slavic studies journals. Member of editorial advisory board of *Soviet Law and Government.*

*   *   *

ZACHARY, Elizabeth 1928-

PERSONAL: Born June 20, 1928, in Monroe, N.C.; daughter of Milton R. (a motorcycle police officer) and Annie Lee (a registered nurse; maiden name, Smoak) Wiggs; married Hugh Zachary (a writer), January 10, 1948; children: Whitney Leigh (Mrs. Allen Walters), Leslie Beth (Mrs. Horace Collier). *Education:* Attended Tampa Art Institute, University of South Florida, and University of North Carolina at Wilmington. *Home:* 7 Pebble Beach Dr., Yaupon Beach, N.C. 28461.

CAREER: Artist, with solo shows in North Carolina and Florida. Works in interior design and business management.

WRITINGS—Novels: *Dynasty of Desire*, Dell, 1978; *The Land Rushers*, Dell, 1979; *The Golden Dynasty*, Dell, 1980; *Blazing Vixen*, Ace Books, 1980; (with husband, Hugh Zachary) *Of Love and Battle*, Ballantine, 1981.

SIDELIGHTS: Elizabeth Zachary wrote: "My life has always been a process of learning and doing, naturally, what comes next. I've lived many varied existences in one lifetime, and have never stopped looking for new experiences.

"Since I live with such a prolific writer as my husband, Hugh, and since I am a voracious reader, it was inevitable that I would become more involved in writing myself. I can't match Hugh's speed in producing a book, but my strength seems to be in plotting, and in those little twists of character which make for excitement in a book.

"I have always been a fan of good historical novels, such as those of Inglis Fletcher—honest books with the history *not* tailored to fit the needs of the writer's plot.

"It was fun to work with Hugh on *Of Love and Battle*. We got into the mood with music from the war era, then pooled our memories of being teenagers during World War II. We don't always agree—sometimes we disagree at the tops of our voices—but through writing we share another experience to be cherished: the ability to share with others that which we are and to touch others in, hopefully, a significant way. I think that's what life is all about."

*   *   *

ZAEHNER, Robert Charles 1913-1974

OBITUARY NOTICE: Born April 8, 1913; died November 24, 1974. Clergyman, educator, and author. After being accepted into the Catholic Church in 1946, Zaehner taught Persian at Oxford University. He later taught at the University of London and Columbia University. His numerous writings on various religions include *Hinduism, The Catholic Church and World Religions, Evolution in Religion*, and *Dialectical Christianity and Christian Materialism*. Obituaries and other sources: *The Author's and Writer's Who's Who*, 6th edition, Burke's Peerage, 1971; *Who Was Who*, Volume VII: *1971-1980*, A. & C. Black, 1981.

ZANGWILL, Israel 1864-1926

BRIEF ENTRY: Born January 21, 1864, in London, England; died August 1, 1926. American social activist, journalist, playwright, and novelist. After growing up in the Whitechapel ghetto of London's East End, Zangwill wrote a series of popular novels depicting the poverty, lifestyles, and values of London's Jewish ghetto population. These included *Ghetto Tragedies* (1893) and *Dreamers of the Ghetto* (1898). Zangwill also wrote several moderately successful plays; *Merely Mary Ann* (1904; first produced in 1903) and *The Melting Pot* (from which the popular term for the assimilation of racial and ethnic groups in America originated; 1909; first produced in 1909) were the best received. A political activist and fervent Zionist, Zangwill helped found the World Zionist Organization in 1897 and used his skills as a writer and orator to further this cause. The author also wrote a number of short stories and a detective novelette, *The Big Bow Mystery* (1892), which is remembered for pioneering the "locked room" mystery technique. *Biographical/critical sources: Encyclopedia of Mystery and Detection,* McGraw, 1976; *Notable Names in the American Theatre,* James T. White, 1976; *Twentieth-Century Crime and Mystery Writers,* St. Martin's, 1980; *Dictionary of Literary Biography,* Volume 10: *Modern British Dramatists, 1940-1945,* Gale, 1982.

* * *

ZANGWILL, Oliver Louis 1913-

PERSONAL: Born October 29, 1913, in East Preston, England; son of Israel and Edith (Ayrton) Zangwill; married Joy Sylvia Moult, 1948 (divorced, 1975); married Shirley Florence Ponter Tribe (a community dentist). *Education:* Attended King's College, Cambridge, B.A., 1939, M.A., 1939. *Home:* 247 Chesterton Rd., Cambridge CB4 1AS, England. *Office:* King's College, Cambridge University, Cambridge CB2 1ST, England.

CAREER: National Hospital for Nervous Diseases, London, England, 1947—, began as psychologist, became emeritus research fellow. Assistant director of Institute of Experimental Psychology, Oxford, England, 1945-51; senior lecturer at Oxford University, 1948-52; professor at Cambridge University, 1952—, professorial fellow of King's College, 1955—. *Member:* British Psychological Society (president, 1974-75), British Association for the Advancement of Science (president of Section J, 1963), Royal Society of London (fellow). *Awards, honors:* D.Sc. from University of St. Andrews.

WRITINGS: An Introduction to Modern Psychology, Philosophical Library, 1950, revised edition, 1963; *Cerebral Dominance and Its Relation to Psychological Function,* C. C Thomas, 1960; (editor with William Homan Thorpe, and contributor) *Current Problems in Animal Behaviour,* University Press, 1961; (editor with C.W.M. Whitty, and contributor) *Amnesia,* Butterworth, 1966, 2nd edition, 1977. Also senior editor and contributor to *Handbook of Psychological Medicine,* Volume I: *General Psychopathology,* 1982. Past senior editor of Thomas Nelson & Sons Ltd. (publisher). Editor of *Quarterly Journal of Experimental Psychology,* 1958-66.

* * *

ZAREFSKY, David (Harris) 1946-

BRIEF ENTRY: Born June 20, 1946, in Washington, D.C. American educator and author. Zarefsky began teaching at Northwestern University in 1968; he became a professor of communication studies and rhetoric in 1982. He was editor of *Journal of the American Forensic Association* from 1977 to 1979. His books include *Complete Handbook on Environmental Control: A Reference Manual for Debaters and Others Interested in the Subject* (National Textbook Co., 1970), *The Comparative Advantage Case* (Championship Debate, 1970), *Complete Handbook on the Administration of Justice: A Reference Manual for Debaters and Others Interested in the Subject* (National Textbook Co., 1971), *Complete Handbook on Financing Education: A Reference Manual for Debaters and Others Interested in the Subject* (National Textbook Co., 1972), *Complete Handbook on Poverty in the United States: A Reference Manual for Debaters and Others Interested in the Subject* (National Textbook Co., 1973), and *Forensic Tournaments: Planning and Administration* (National Textbook Co., 1980). *Address:* Department of Communication Studies, Northwestern University, 1822 Sheridan Rd., Evanston, Ill. 60201.

* * *

ZIEGFELD, Richard E(van) 1948-

PERSONAL: Born October 4, 1948, in Rockford, Ill.; son of Arthur F. (a printer) and Marjorie L. (an apartment manager; maiden name, Day) Ziegfeld; married wife, Paulette, December 12, 1970; children: Adam Weston. *Education:* Luther College, B.A., 1970; University of Texas, M.A. (English), 1973, M.A. (German), 1976, Ph.D., 1976. *Home:* 2965 South Whiting Way, Denver, Colo. 80231. *Office:* McDonnell Douglas Corp., 1390 South Potomac, No. 124, Aurora, Colo. 80012.

CAREER: University of South Carolina, Columbia, assistant professor of comparative literature, 1976-82; McDonnell Douglas Corp., Aurora, Colo., communication specialist and editor, 1982—. Editor for BC Research, 1980—. Section head at Carolina Marathon, 1981 and 1982. *Member:* Modern Language Association of America, American Comparative Literature Association, Columbia Track Club.

WRITINGS: Stanislaw Lem, Ungar, 1983.

Editor of "Dictionary of Literary Biography Yearbook" series; published by Gale: *Dictionary of Literary Biography Yearbook: 1980,* 1981; *... 1981,* 1982; *... 1982,* 1983.

Contributor to *Exilliteratur,* 1982. Contributor to journals, including *Seminar, Modern Fiction Studies, Paris Review,* and *William Carlos Williams Review.*

WORK IN PROGRESS: Trust Is the Measure: Author/Publisher Relationships, 1920-1980.

SIDELIGHTS: Ziegfeld told *CA:* "Much as I would like to write every day year-round, I cannot. I work very hard for concentrated periods, ranging from two to six months. Then I revise and attend to follow-up detail at a desultory pace over several months. When I've finished an article or book, it often takes me months to initiate another new project. For this reason I like to have a number of projects in progress simultaneously so that I have an alternative focus when I set a draft aside to allow it to 'mature.'

"During concentrated writing phases, I work in a highly disciplined manner, using detailed schedules of what I need to write or revise each day. I draw upon overview outlines in which I've organized the main topics and relevant detail. The thesis for each chapter and the detail of my arguments usually emerge during the actual composition activity. In short, for me writing is a process of discovery through which I develop and hone my views.

"I wrote *Stanislaw Lem*, an introductory book on Lem, as advocacy criticism because I wanted to acquaint English-language readers with one of the 'master' writers of the twentieth century. I was drawn to Lem's quixotic world by his brilliant satire, his keen wit, his protean diversity, and his fervent obsession with experimentation.

"Regarding my work in progress, *Trust Is the Measure: Author/Publisher Relationships, 1920-1980,* I became interested in author/publisher relationships while doing research in the Max Frisch-Peter Suhrkamp file, Suhrkamp Verlag Archive, Frankfurt, Germany. I made the trip hoping to uncover more information about Frisch's philosophical concerns. Little material about philosophy showed up, but I became fascinated with the relationship between Frisch and Suhrkamp, and so I wrote about it. After finishing the article, I decided to expand the project into a book, concentrating on American figures. I visited more than a dozen publishing houses and read the files on eighteen different relationships, including William Carlos Williams/James Laughlin, Edmund Wilson/Roger Straus, and Uwe Johnson/Helen Wolff. I also interviewed more than thirty authors, editors, and publishers, including Kurt Vonnegut, William Jovanovich, Samuel Vaughan, and Charles Wright.

"The mode of communication between authors and publishers has changed radically since 1920 because it is so easy to pick up the phone, turn to compatible computers, or hop on a plane. Hence, fewer letters are being written and large gaps are developing in the written, historical record of a relationship.

"Generally the substance of the relationships is the same—how can we improve the book, sales, author reputation, etc.? Deep relationships are less common because there is not as much continuity in the literary market as there once was. Authors are more willing to change publishers if another house will pay the higher auction price, and publishing personnel are busy changing jobs, hoping that if they play 'musical chairs' long enough their careers will someday magically improve. Established writers are not as likely to experience this discontinuity as less well-known writers, but the phenomenon has rendered solid relationships difficult for almost all writers. Despite the obstacles, though, many good relationships still develop. Where the good relationships develop, technological advances have facilitated the maturation and the maintenance of the friendships.

"*Trust Is the Measure* contains three sections: the literary text, the author's career, and an overview of the publishing field. The literary text section uses case studies to indicate the effect the publisher can have on inception, composition, and revision of a book. The career section indicates what services a publisher can offer to influence an author's reception. The evidence presented in the case studies on text and career should prompt procedural changes for textual scholars and biographers who have routinely devoted only scant attention to publishing archive material. The interviews with publishers, editors, and authors have elicited new information from persons seldom questioned about their contribution to the literary product.

"The overview will be useful to literary scholars, to textual scholars, and to publishing personnel because it includes analytical observations about the literary industry. The book will also appeal to a general audience interested in how authors and publishers interact in the literary marketplace."

ZIEGLER, Jack (Denmore) 1942-

PERSONAL: Born July 13, 1942, in New York, N.Y.; son of John Denmore (a sales representative) and Kathleen Miriam (a teacher; maiden name, Clarke) Ziegler; married Jean Ann Rice, April 20, 1968; children: Jessica, Benjamin, Maxwell. *Education:* Fordham University, B.A., 1964. *Residence:* New Milford, Conn.

CAREER: Worked for Columbia Broadcasting System (CBS-TV) in New York, and for KTVU-TV in Oakland, Calif., 1967-69; free-lance writer, 1969-72; free-lance cartoonist, 1972—. Drawings have been exhibited in galleries across the United States, including Bethel Gallery in Connecticut, International Tennis Hall of Fame in Rhode Island, Washington Art Gallery in Connecticut, and Nancy Roth Gallery in New York. *Military service:* U.S. Army, 1966-67. *Member:* Cartoonists Association (founding member; member of board of governors, treasurer, 1981-82), Society of Illustrators.

WRITINGS: Hamburger Madness (cartoon collection), Harcourt, 1978; *Filthy Little Things* (cartoon collection), Doubleday, 1981. Regular contributor of cartoons to *New Yorker.* Contributor of cartoons to *Esquire, New York Times, Cosmopolitan,* and other newspapers and magazines.

WORK IN PROGRESS: The E. F. Project, a collection of cartoon drawings, publication expected in 1984.

SIDELIGHTS: Hamburger Madness is a collection of 150 cartoons poking fun at everything American from hamburgers to old movies. *Newsweek* called the book "a winning first collection," and the *New York Times Book Review* noted that the cartoons are typical examples of "Jack Ziegler's clean draftsmanship and unpredictable, oddball sense of humor." "My favorite book of 1978 is Jack Ziegler's *Hamburger Madness,*" Leonore Fleischer declared in her *Washington Post Book World* review. "If art is purifying and laughter a catharsis, then I'm purer and finer for having spent a few hours with Ziegler," Fleischer explained.

Ziegler's second cartoon collection, *Filthy Little Things,* caused a *New York Times Book Review* critic to announce that "Jack Ziegler's sense of humor defies definition." But other critics still attempted to analyze his work. "Ziegler's drawings reflect the mordant humor of the incongruous and surrealistic," a *Washington Post Book World* reviewer observed. And *Village Voice*'s Eliot Fremont-Smith described Ziegler as "a master of whacky irony."

Ziegler told *CA:* "I'm a cartoonist whose work appears mainly in the *New Yorker.* I've been doing this for about ten years. I try to do cartoons that are hopefully funny, rather than being clever. I would rather have people laugh than say 'Oh yeah, I get it.'"

BIOGRAPHICAL/CRITICAL SOURCES: Washington Post Book World, December 10, 1978, June 28, 1981; *Time,* January 8, 1979; *New York Times Book Review,* February 17, 1980, August 30, 1981; *Village Voice,* December 16, 1981.

*   *   *

ZIMMERMAN, Paul A(lbert) 1918-

BRIEF ENTRY: Born June 25, 1918, in Danville, Ill. American college president, educator, clergyman, and author. Zimmerman was ordained a Lutheran minister in 1944. He taught chemistry and theology at Bethany College and at Concordia Teachers College before he was appointed president of Concordia Lutheran Junior College from 1961 to 1973. In 1973 Zimmerman became president of Concordia College in River Forest, Illinois. He edited *Darwin, Evolution, and Creation* (Concordia, 1959), *Rock Strata and the Bible Record* (Concordia, 1970), and *Creation, Evolution, and God's Word* (Concordia, 1972). *Address:* 946 Clinton Pl., River Forest, Ill. 60305; and Concordia College, 7400 Augusta St., River Forest, Ill. 60305. *Biographical/critical sources: Who's Who in America,* 42nd edition, Marquis, 1982.

*   *   *

ZOLLINGER, Gulielma   1856-1917
(William Zachary Gladwin)

BRIEF ENTRY: Born in 1856 in Illinois; died August 24, 1917, in Newton, Iowa. American author of stories and books for children. Zollinger, who occasionally wrote under the pen name William Zachary Gladwin, began her writing career at the age of fourteen, when she published a short story in *Youth's Companion.* Her first book, *Dan Drummon of the D,* did not appear until 1897, but it was soon followed by *The Widow O'Callaghan's Boys* (1898). The success of this second novel established Zollinger's reputation as a writer. The author's early works often feature a central character who struggles bravely to overcome serious hardships. A visit to England inspired Zollinger to write several books with a British setting, including *A Boy's Ride* (1909) and *Route of the Foreigner* (1910). She had planned to make a second trip to England but was hindered by illness and the onset of World War I. Zollinger died at her home in Newton, Iowa. *Biographical/critical sources: Who Was Who in America,* Volume I: *1897-1942,* Marquis, 1943.

*   *   *

ZUMBO, Jim   1940-

PERSONAL: Born November 9, 1940, in Newburgh, N.Y.; son of Jim, Sr. (in automobile sales) and Mary (Corbo) Zumbo; married Lois Dudley (a teacher), June 8, 1963; children: Janette, Daniel, Judi, Angela. *Education:* Paul Smith's College, A.A.S., 1960; Utah State University, B.S., 1964. *Politics:* Republican. *Religion:* Roman Catholic. *Home and office:* 2795 West 1100 N., Vernal, Utah 84078.

CAREER: Utah Forestry Department, Price, forester, 1964-66; U.S. Military Academy, West Point, N.Y., forester, 1966-74; Bureau of Land Management, Vernal, Utah, wildlife biologist, 1974-78; *Outdoor Life,* New York, N.Y., western editor, 1978-

81, editor-at-large, 1981—. *Member:* Outdoor Writers Association of America (member of board of directors), Wildlife Society, Society of Professional Foresters, Jaycees, Elks.

WRITINGS: Icefishing: East and West, McKay, 1979; *Hunting America's Mule Deer,* Winchester Press, 1981. Contributor of about six hundred articles to outdoor magazines.

WORK IN PROGRESS: All About Deer Hunting in America; Two Hundred Venison Recipes; Hunting Elk in North America.

SIDELIGHTS: Zumbo told *CA:* "My professional training in forestry and wildlife assisted me in my goal of becoming a full-time outdoor writer. My fondness for travel, as well as my hunting and fishing interests, have made outdoor writing a natural career objective."

*   *   *

ZWIRN, Jerrold   1943-

PERSONAL: Born February 28, 1943, in Camden, N.J.; son of Sidney and Pearl (Miller) Zwirn. *Education:* Hunter College of the City University of New York, M.A., 1972; Pratt Institute, M.L.S., 1976. *Home:* 2411 20th St. N.W., Washington, D.C. 20009.

CAREER: Director of research of New York Legislative Service, Inc., 1973-74; archivist and librarian at Printed Archives Branch of National Archives and Records Service, 1976-80; District of Columbia Public Library, Washington, D.C., librarian and readers' adviser, 1981; independent researcher, 1982-83. *Member:* American Library Association, Government Documents Round Table, U.S. Capitol Historical Society.

WRITINGS: Congressional Publications: A Research Guide to Legislation, Budgets, and Treaties, Libraries Unlimited, 1983. Contributor to *Government Publications Review.* Editor of *New York State Legislative Annual,* 1973.

WORK IN PROGRESS: A study of the relationship between legislative decision making and policy choices; further exploration of the value of governmental publications for keeping informed of and understanding public policy.

SIDELIGHTS: Zwirn told *CA:* "*Congressional Publications* was originally intended to be a brief bibliographic guide for personal use, but which unexpectedly expanded beyond anything I envisioned."